New in this edition!!

Cold Fusion
Web Application

Construction Kit,

Second Edition

Ben Forta
with
Michael Dinowitz
Ashley King
Nate Weiss
David E. Crawford
Steven D. Drucker
David Watts
Leon Chalnick
Ronald E. Taylor

Cold Fusion Web Application

Construction Kit,

Second Edition

Cold Fusion Web Application Construction Kit, Second Edition

Library of Congress Catalog No.: 97-80932

ISBN: 0-7897-1414-0

00 99 98   6 5 4 3 2 1

Interpretation of the printing code: the rightmost double-digit number is the year of the book's printing; the rightmost single-digit number, the number of the book's printing. For example, a printing code of 98-1 shows that the first printing of the book occurred in 1998.

Screen reproductions in this book were created using Collage Plus from Inner Media, Inc., Hollis, NH.

Contents at a Glance

V Appendixes

Table of Contents

III Getting Started with Cold Fusion

V Appendixes

Credits

PUBLISHER
Joseph B. Wikert

EXECUTIVE EDITOR
Bryan Gambrel

MANAGING EDITOR
Patrick Kanouse

ACQUISITIONS EDITOR
Angela Kozlowski

DEVELOPMENT EDITOR
Nancy Warner

PROJECT EDITOR
Andrew Cupp

COPY EDITORS
Pat Kinyon
Nancy Albright
Geneil Breeze

TECHNICAL EDITORS
Emily Kim
Josh Dowdell

COORDINATOR OF EDITORIAL SERVICES
Charlotte Clapp

SOFTWARE COORDINATOR
Andrea Duvall

EDITORIAL ASSISTANT
Rhonda Tinch-Mize

TEAM COORDINATOR
Michelle R. Newcomb

BRAND COORDINATOR
Trey Frank

BOOK DESIGNER
Ruth Harvey

COVER DESIGNER
Dan Armstrong

PRODUCTION TEAM
Marcia Deboy
Michael Dietsch
Cynthia Fields
Mike Henry
Linda Knose
Tim Osborne
Staci Somers
Mark Walchle
Maureen West
Trina Wurst

INDEXERS
Erika Millen
Kelly Talbot

Composed in *Century Old Style* and *ITC Franklin Gothic* by Que Corporation.

To Penina, Yisroel, Mendel, and Shmuli, with all my love, always.
—Ben Forta

To my wife for putting up with me during the time it took to put together the book.
—Michael Dinowitz

I'd like to dedicate my contribution to this book to the memory of my grandfather, John Raleigh Harrison. His courage and innovation through persecution and hardship will never be forgotten.
—Ashley King

To my wife Jacki.
—David E. Crawford

For my grandparents, Bess and Lou.
—Steven D. Drucker

To Ernie, Lucas, and Mouse.
—David Watts

About the Authors

Ben Forta is co-founder and Vice President of Development and Technologies for Stoneage Corporation, a company built on much of what is taught in this book. He is also president of EmTek Systems, a consulting firm specializing in database development and data communications. Ben has over 15 years of experience in the computer industry, and spent 6 years as part of the development team responsible for creating OnTime, the industry's most successful calendar and group scheduling product, with over 1,000,000 users worldwide. Ben co-authored the official Allaire Cold Fusion training courses, and now spends a considerable amount of time providing on-site Cold Fusion training for corporate clients. Born in London, England, and educated in London, New York, and Los Angeles, Ben now lives in Oak Park, Michigan with his wife Marcy, and their four children. He welcomes your email at **ben@forta.com**.

Michael Dinowitz is head of House of Fusion, a consulting firm specializing in Cold Fusion, dynamic and database driven apps. His work focuses on merging Cold Fusion with other technologies/languages and using them to their maximum potential. He has been with Cold Fusion almost since its start and hosts the New York Cold Fusion User group. Michael has worked on sites ranging from the Publishers Clearing House commerce engine to the Individual Investor financial site, with many other works in-between. Many of his CFX tags, modules, and apps are available to help Cold Fusion programmers everywhere. As a collector of information, he hosts a site at **http://www.houseoffusion.com** with lots of Cold Fusion-related information.

Ashley E. King is President and founder of Aspx Interactive Media (CreativeAspect, Inc.) where he developed the MrPost! Web Messaging Server for Cold Fusion. Ashley began his fateful foray into the programming world 13 years ago when he developed games and graphics software for Timex Sinclair 1000 and Commodore VIC-20 computers. He continued his programming career at BDM Corporation and as a contractor. Ashley later worked as a graphic artist, radio DJ and touring musician, releasing a CD and founding one of the first web-based music stores with his wife Stephanie. He also founded an ISP and was a principal in a Japanese-American Internet consulting company. Ashley now lives in Salt Lake City, Utah after wandering from his native Albuquerque, New Mexico. When he's not too far behind schedule, Ashley formulates theories on paranormal experiences and writes music. He can be reached via email on the Internet at **ashley@aspx.com**, or via the World Wide Web at **http://www.aspx.com**.

Nate Weiss is the IS Director at International Commerce Exchange Systems, a direct-marketing service for buyers and sellers. Nate used Cold Fusion to design the web, fax, and email services at the core of the company's suite of services, as well as the real-time extranet, which serves as the company's worldwide account management, data-entry, and reporting mechanism. Nate can be contacted at **nweiss@icesinc.com**.

Lieutenant Colonel **David E. Crawford**, CAP, is the Chief of Information Systems for National Headquarters, Civil Air Patrol, Maxwell AFB, Alabama (**http://www.cap.af.mil**) where he manages the day-to-day operations of a seven-person staff providing computer support to the headquarters and 55,000 civilian volunteers of the United States Air Force Auxiliary. He holds an Associate of Arts degree in Computer Programming and a Bachelor of Arts in Computer Information Systems from Northwest Nazarene College, is an Army Reserve officer, a long-time Civil Air Patrol member, and is active in amateur radio (KF4EQM).

Steven D. Drucker is a principal at Fig Leaf Software, his Washington, DC-based software consulting company. Steve started Fig Leaf after being graduated by the University of Maryland at College Park with a B.S. in Computer Science. Steve is the founder of the very first Cold Fusion users group (DC-CFUG), a member of Team Allaire, and an Allaire Agent. As lead programmer for Fig Leaf, he regularly consults for companies in the Fortune 1000 and is currently engaged in developing Cold Fusion–based intranets for Bell Atlantic, GlobalOne, and several DC-based trade associations. He is also lead author of Visual Interdev Database Development for the Web and developed Fig Leaf's courseware "TOP GUN CF Application Development."

David Watts is a web developer at Fig Leaf Software, a company specializing in Cold Fusion–based web application development. He is still amazed that he gets paid for having fun with computers. Prior to his web work, he developed hypertext systems in Windows Help and IBM's IPF. Before he took up computers as a hobby, Dave held a number of interesting occupations, including patent assignment examiner for the U.S. Patent and Trademark Office, and M1A1 Abrams crewman in the U.S. Army. He lives with Ernie, his partner of eight years, and two cats. He can be reached at **dwatts@figleaf.com**, or you can visit his site at **http://www.figleaf.com/**.

Leon Chalnick, upon completing the MBA program at Northwestern's Kellogg Graduate School of Management, went to work for Andersen Consulting in Los Angeles. He left in 1989 and is currently the president of two firms. Professional Information Consulting, Inc. (**http://www.picinc.com**) focuses on custom database application development. Professional Presence Providers, Inc. (**http://www.prprpr.com**) is focused on developing and hosting web sites. Leon's other work for Que includes *Using Paradox 7 for Windows* and *Killer Paradox 5.0 for Windows*. Leon can be reached by email at **leon@prprpr.com**.

Ronald E. Taylor is a programmer analyst for National Headquarters, Civil Air Patrol at Maxwell AFB, Alabama. He is currently developing software using Uniface and Cold Fusion with MS SQL Server as the back end. He holds a Master of Science degree in Computer and Information Science from Troy State University.

Acknowledgments

First and foremost, I'd like to thank the many hundreds of you who took the time to write to me with feedback on the first edition of this book. Your comments, suggestions, and criticisms all helped shape this new edition.

Thanks to everyone at Que and Macmillan for making this book a reality. Very special thanks once again to Angela Kozlowski, my Acquisitions Editor, for all of her time, patience, and advice, and especially for shielding me from unpleasant distractions so that I could concentrate on writing.

Special thanks to Nancy Warner for all of her invaluable feedback and expertise, and for the many design and layout improvements that make this new edition so much more readable and useful.

A very special thank you to my Technical Editor, Emily Kim, for single-handedly raising the overall quality of this book.

Thanks to Ashley King, Dave Crawford, Mike Dinowitz, and Nate Weiss for their outstanding contributions. And an extra thank you for helping out with additional chapters at the last minute. I couldn't have done it without you guys.

Thanks to everyone at Allaire for once again presenting the Internet development community with products that are both powerful and fun to use. Special thanks to Jeremy Allaire for making himself so readily available to the authors throughout the past few months.

The accompanying CD contains a collection of some of the best Cold Fusion add-on tags that I have found. In addition to serving as examples of what Cold Fusion can do, these tags will be of great value to all Cold Fusion developers. A special thank you to all the developers who contributed tags. Unfortunately there are too many of them to name individually here, but full credit is given in the tag documentation on the CD. If you find any of the tags useful, I urge you to email the developers directly to thank them.

And most importantly, thanks once again to my wife Marcy for encouraging me to undertake this project even though she knew that it would mean that she'd see even less of me than before. Without her support, encouragement, understanding, and sacrifices I would not be where I am today. Marcy, with all my heart, I thank you.—Ben Forta

First, I'd like to thank Ben Forta for the opportunity to contribute to such an incredible book. I'd also like to thank Angela Kozlowski for her patience during this project. Thanks to Sumner Swaner for his support, Jeremy Allaire for his inspiration, Angela Stenberg for her advice, and Mike Nimer for keeping things going when I periodically lost touch with planet Earth. Thanks to my family: parents Rodney and Margaret, brothers Kevin and Ulan, and sister Marie, and special thanks to my children Nikki and Dylan and my stepdaughter Courtni Moore for keeping my spirits high and for reminding me that "browsing for cookies on a web" must be the most enjoyable career ever created. Thanks also to Sam Candelaria, Velma Gurule, Brian Jensen, and Gwen Argersinger for the encouragement that still echoes in my mind. Most importantly, thanks to my wife Stephanie for her love and support and for believing that my ideas are more insightful than they are delusional.—Ashley King

I'd like to acknowledge my staff and fellow members at Civil Air Patrol who provided the opportunity to put Cold Fusion to the "real world" test.—David E. Crawford

I'd like to thank my family: grandparents Bess & Louis Storch, parents Rochelle and Lloyd, brother Craig, and wife Mary Ann for their continuing support in what at times has seemed like a quixotic quest for fame and fortune in the software biz. Special thanks to my business partners Rick Stout and Neel Teague who kept the faith, to friends Scott Breach and Ted Karatinos who through their own accomplishments inspire me to achieve, and to David Gallerizzo and Tony Meoni who introduced me to Cold Fusion 1.0.—Steven D. Drucker

Most authors use this section to thank their families, friends and coworkers. Inevitably, someone gets left out, and then there's trouble. So instead, I'd like everyone to consider themselves thanked. You know who you are.—David Watts

We'd Like to Hear from You!

As part of our continuing effort to produce books of the highest possible quality, Que would like to hear your comments. To stay competitive, we *really* want you to let us know what you like or dislike most about this book or other Que products.

Please send your comments, ideas, and suggestions for improvement to:

Que Corporation
201 West 103rd Street
Indianapolis, IN 46290-1097

You can also visit our home page on the World Wide Web at **http://www.mcp.com/**.

Thank you in advance. Your comments will help us to continue publishing the best books available in today's market.

Introduction

Who Should Use This Book

This book is written for anyone who wishes to create cutting-edge, web-based applications.

If you are a webmaster or web page designer and want to create dynamic data-driven web pages, this book is for you. If you are an experienced database administrator who wants to take advantage of the web to publish or collect data, this book is for you too. If you are just starting out creating your web presence, but know that you want to serve more than just static information, this book will help get you there. Even if you are already an experienced Cold Fusion user, this book will provide you with invaluable tips and tricks and will also serve as the definitive Cold Fusion developer's reference.

This book will teach you how to create real-world, web-based applications that solved real-world problems. Along the way you'll acquire all the skills you need to design, implement, test, and roll out world-class applications.

How to Use This Book

This book is designed to serve two different, but complementary, purposes.

First, this book is a complete tutorial of everything you need to know to harness the power of Cold Fusion. As such, the book is divided into four sections, and each section introduces new topics building on what has been discussed in prior sections. Ideally you will work through these sections in order, starting with Cold Fusion basics, and then moving on to advanced topics.

Secondly, this book is an invaluable desktop reference tool. The appendixes contain reference chapters that will be of use to you while developing Cold Fusion applications. Those reference chapters are cross-referenced to the appropriate tutorial sections, so that step-by-step information is always readily available to you.

Part I: Introduction

Part I of this book introduces Cold Fusion and explains what exactly it is that Cold Fusion will let you accomplish. Internet fundamentals are also introduced, as a thorough understanding of these is a prerequisite to Cold Fusion application development.

Chapter 1, "Why Cold Fusion?" explains the concepts of data-driven World Wide Web sites and presents real-world examples of how this technology is being applied on some of the most popular sites on the web. This chapter is not a technical overview of Cold Fusion. Rather, it is a discussion of how Cold Fusion can be used to enhance your Internet or intranet site.

In Chapter 2, "Introduction to Cold Fusion," the core technologies that Cold Fusion is built upon are introduced. The Internet and how it works are explained, as are DNS servers and URLs, web servers and browsers, and web server extensions like CGI and server APIs. A good understanding of these technologies is a vital part of creating web-based applications. This chapter also teaches you how Cold Fusion works and explains the various components that compose it.

Part II: Getting Up and Running

In Part II you'll learn how to install and configure Cold Fusion so that you can begin actual application development.

Chapter 3, "Installing Cold Fusion and Cold Fusion Studio," goes over Cold Fusion's hardware and operating system prerequisites and walks you through the entire process of installing the Cold Fusion Application Server and the Cold Fusion Studio development environment.

Chapter 4, "Administering Cold Fusion," introduces the Cold Fusion Administrator. This web-based program, written in Cold Fusion itself, is used to manage and maintain every aspect of your Cold Fusion Application Server.

Part III: Getting Started with Cold Fusion

Part III teaches the basics of web-based application development, database design, and Cold Fusion development. You'll learn how to create databases and tables, design relational databases, and create ODBC data sources to allow applications to interact with these tables. You'll learn how to use Cold Fusion Studio and you'll also start to create live, web-based applications with Cold Fusion.

Chapter 5, "Designing an Application," introduces fundamental concepts in application design and explains the process by which an application specification is created. Spending time up front on methodical application design pays great dividends later in the development process.

In Chapter 6, "Database Fundamentals," you'll be introduced to databases. Databases are mechanisms for storing and retrieving information, and almost every web-based application you build will sit on top of a databases of some kind. Key database concepts like tables, rows, columns, data types, keys, and indexes are taught, as are the basics of the relational database model. You'll also learn the differences between client/server and shared-file based databases, and the pros and cons of each.

Chapter 7, "Creating Databases and Tables," actually applies the lessons taught in Chapter 6. This chapter walks you through creating databases and tables for the sample application, with detailed step-by-step explanations of the entire process.

In Chapter 8, "Introduction to SQL," you'll learn the basics of the SQL language. SQL is a standard language for interacting with database applications, and all Cold Fusion database manipulation is performed using SQL statements. The link between Cold Fusion and your database itself is via ODBC, so this chapter introduces this technology and walks you through the process of creating ODBC data sources. Chapter 8 will also teach you how to use the SQL SELECT statement, and Chapter 9, "SQL Data Manipulation," introduces three other important SQL statements, INSERT, UPDATE, and DELETE.

Chapter 10, "Introduction to Cold Fusion Studio," introduces Cold Fusion's new development environment. Cold Fusion Studio is a powerful HTML and CFML editor and is chock full of features designed to make web page design and application development a whole lot easier. You'll learn how to use the editor, the tag chooser, the expression builder, the SQL query builder, and how to configure the environment to work the way you do. You'll also learn how to use Studio for remote development.

Chapter 11, "Cold Fusion Basics," is where you'll create your first Cold Fusion application, albeit a very simple one. You'll also learn how to use `<CFQUERY>` to create queries that extract live data from your databases, and how to display query results using `<CFOUTPUT>`. Various formatting techniques will be taught as well, including using tables and lists. One method of displaying data that has become very popular on the web is data drill-down. This approach to data interaction is taught as well.

In Chapter 12, "Cold Fusion Forms," you'll learn how to collect user-supplied data using HTML forms. This data can be used to build dynamic SQL statements providing you with infinite flexibility in creating dynamic database queries. This chapter also teaches you how to create search screens that enable visitors to search on as many different fields as you allow.

Chapter 13, "Using Forms to Add or Change Data," teaches you how to use forms to add, update, and delete data in database tables. The Cold Fusion tags `<CFINSERT>` and `<CFUPDATE>` are introduced, and you'll learn how `<CFQUERY>` can be used to insert, update, and delete data.

In Chapter 14, "Form Data Validation," you'll learn how to perform server-side and client-side validation. Cold Fusion can generate JavaScript client-side validation code automatically, without you even having to learn JavaScript. You'll learn how to use this feature, and how to provide your own validation rules.

Chapter 15, "The Report Writer," teaches the basics of using the bundled Crystal Reports Professional report writer. The report writer allows you to create powerful data-driven reports that can be rendered into HTML on-the-fly using the Cold Fusion `<CFREPORT>` tag.

Chapter 16, "Debugging and Troubleshooting," will teach you the kinds of things that can go wrong in Cold Fusion application development, and what you can do to rectify them. You'll learn how to use Cold Fusion's debugging and logging features, and, most importantly, you'll learn tips and techniques that can help avoid problems in the first place.

Part IV: Advanced Cold Fusion

Part IV teaches you advanced Cold Fusion capabilities and techniques. The chapters in this section have been written with the assumption that you are familiar with basic SQL syntax and are comfortable creating Cold Fusion templates.

Chapter 17, "Advanced SQL," will teach you how to create powerful SQL statements using subqueries and joins. It also explains the advantages and disadvantages of each. You'll also learn how to calculate averages, totals, and counts, and how to use the EXISTS, NOT EXISTS, and DISTINCT keywords.

In Chapter 18, "Advanced Cold Fusion Templates," you'll learn the tips and tricks needed to write powerful, scalable, and manageable applications. You'll learn how to comment your templates so that you, or other developers, will have an easier time maintaining the code in the future. You'll also see how Cold Fusion facilitates code reuse with the `<CFINCLUDE>` tag. And finally, you'll learn how to create "next in records" style interfaces, the same interface used by every major search engine and spider on the Internet!

In Chapter 19, "Enhancing Forms with *CFFORM*," you'll learn how to take advantage of the Cold Fusion supplied Java form controls. These controls include a Windows Explorer style tree control, an editable grid control, a slider control, and a highly configurable text input control. You'll also learn how to embed your own Java applets using the <CFAPPLET> tag.

Chapter 20, "Interacting with Email," introduces Cold Fusion's email capabilities. Cold Fusion allows you to create SMTP-based email messages using its <CFMAIL> tag. You'll learn how to send email messages containing user-submitted form fields, how to email the results of a database query, and how to do mass mailings to addresses derived from database tables. Additionally, you'll learn how to retrieve mail from POP mailboxes using the <CFPOP> tag.

Chapter 21, "Online Commerce," teaches you how to perform real-time electronic commerce, including credit card authorization using CyberCash.

Chapter 22, "Transaction Processing," will teach you the importance of implementing transaction processing to ensure data integrity, and how to use the Cold Fusion transaction processing functions.

In Chapter 23, "Web Application Framework," you'll learn how to take advantage of the Cold Fusion Web Application Framework to add features to your web application like persistent client variables, sophisticated parameter and variable manipulation, and customized error message handling. You'll also learn how to use the application template to establish application-wide settings and options.

Chapter 24, "Session Variables and Cookies," you'll learn how to use client, session, and application variables, and HTTP cookies. These special data types play an important part in creating a complete application that can track a client's state.

Chapter 25, "File Manipulation," introduces the powerful and flexible Cold Fusion <CFFILE> tag. You'll learn how to create, read, write, and append local files. You'll also learn how to add file uploading features to your forms.

Chapter 26, "Full-Text Searching with Verity," introduces the Verity search engine. Verity provides a mechanism to do full-text searches against all sorts of data. The Verity engine is bundled with the Cold Fusion Application Server, and the <CFINDEX> and <CFSEARCH> tags provide full access to Verity indexes from within your applications.

In Chapter 27, "Directory Services," you'll learn all about directory services and the LDAP protocol. You'll also learn how to use the powerful new <CFLDAP> tag, which enables your applications to interact with directory services.

Chapter 28, "MIME Types," will teach you how to serve content, other than HTML, from within your web application.

Chapter 29, "Graphing," introduces the Cold Fusion supplied data graphing Java classes. You'll learn how to display Java-based pie charts, bar graphs, and other graphing formats using these applets; you'll even learn how to write graphing applets of your own.

Chapter 30, "Interfacing with HTTP and FTP Using *CFHTTP* and *CFFTP*," shows you how to use these two important protocols within your applications. The <CFHTTP> and <CFFTP> tags are an important part of creating intelligent agents, which are applications that perform sophisticated data-gathering and manipulation tasks for you.

In Chapter 31, "Version Control," introduces version control and explains why it is such an important application development tool. You'll learn how to use Cold Fusion's built-in version control system and how to interface with existing version control systems of your own.

Chapter 32, "Event Scheduling," teaches you to create tasks that execute automatically and at timed intervals. You'll also learn how to dynamically generate static HTML pages using Cold Fusion's scheduling technology.

Chapter 33, "Custom Tags," teaches you how to extend Cold Fusion by writing tags of your own. Custom tags allow you to encapsulate proven code so that it is reusable and shareable. You'll also learn how to encrypt your code so that others cannot view or modify it.

Chapter 34, "Interfacing with COM and DCOM Objects," introduces COM and DCOM objects. These controls can be written in many languages, including C, C++, Visual Basic, Delphi, and Java. You can plug these objects into your Cold Fusion code using the <CFOBJECT> tag.

In Chapter 35, "CFAPI, The Cold Fusion API," you'll learn how to extend the capabilities of Cold Fusion by writing your own tags. You'll learn how to create DLL's using Microsoft Visual C++, how to write functions that can be called from within Cold Fusion templates, and how to map the tags so that Cold Fusion can interact with them.

Appendixes

Appendix A, "Cold Fusion Tag Reference," is the definitive reference for every Cold Fusion tag, with descriptive explanations, syntax tables, and examples for each. Topics are cross referenced extensively to related topics and appropriate tutorial chapters in the book.

Appendix B, "Cold Fusion Function Reference," is a complete reference of every Cold Fusion function organized by category. Thorough descriptions and examples are given for every function, and extensive cross-references are provided.

Appendix C, "Verity Search Language Reference," is a complete guide to the Verity search language. Using the information provided here, you will be able to perform incredibly complex searches with minimal effort.

The CD-ROM

The accompanying CD-ROM contains everything you need to start writing Cold Fusion applications, including:

- Evaluation version of Cold Fusion 3.1 Professional
- Evaluation version of Cold Fusion Studio
- Source code and databases for many of the examples in this book
- 30 add-on tags designed so you can use them within your own applications
- Additional reference material and resources

So, turn the page and start reading. In no time you'll be creating powerful, web-based applications using the Cold Fusion Application Server.

Introduction

Why Cold Fusion?

by Ben Forta

In this chapter

Introducing Cold Fusion

The fact that you are reading this book suggests that you are interested in publishing information on the World Wide Web and that you are part of a growing number of developers interested in expanding the capabilities of their web sites beyond simple publishing.

What kind of capabilities?

There are now over 1/2 million web sites that attract millions of visitors daily. Most web sites are being used as electronic replacements for newspapers, magazines, brochures, and bulletin boards. The web offers ways to enhance these publications using audio, images, animation, multimedia, and even virtual reality.

No one will dispute that these sites add value to the net because information is knowledge, and knowledge is power. All this information is available at your fingertips (literally). Web sites, however, are capable of being much more than electronic versions of paper publications because of the underlying technology that makes the web tick. Users can interact with you and your company, collect and process mission-critical information in real time, provide new levels of user support, and much more.

The web is not merely the electronic equivalent of a newspaper or magazine—it is a communication medium that is limited only by the lack of innovation and creativity of web site designers.

To help illustrate what Cold Fusion is and where it fits into your web site strategy, look at a few of the more impressive and innovative sites on the World Wide Web:

- Dell Computer Corporation (**http://www.dell.com**)

  Dell is a leading vendor of mail-order computers. Its web site, like many others, enables you to shop for a new computer online. The big difference is that you can customize the computer online. You are presented with a typical configuration with a price tag attached. You may click any of the components or peripherals to add or change them. Click the hard drive line item, for example, and you'll be presented with hard drive options and how they will affect the price. When changes are made to the configuration, the price tag is dynamically recalculated.

- Federal Express (**http://www.fedex.com**)

  The FedEx site hosts a whole array of impressive and innovative features. The most impressive is the online package tracking system. To test the system, I deposited a package (containing chapters that are now part of this book) in a drop box at 9:55 a.m. At 10:05 a.m. I checked the status of the package on the FedEx web site. In less time than it took to click the search button, I was informed that my package was picked up at 10:02 a.m. from the Southfield, MI drop box. FedEx did not design a complete package tracking system for the web but cleverly linked its web site to an already existing application. In doing so, it provides superior customer support and lowers its real-time phone support costs.

- Ticketmaster (**http://www.ticketmaster.com**)

    The Ticketmaster web site is built around a massive database of every major entertainment event in every city at every venue in the United States. The database can be searched by date, artist, event type, state, city, venue, category, and more. The site even contains seating maps of venues hosting events.

These selected sites are truly taking advantage of the World Wide Web.

What Is Cold Fusion?

Until recently, developing sites (like the ones mentioned earlier) was a difficult process. Writing custom web-based applications was a job for experienced programmers only. A good working knowledge of UNIX was a prerequisite, and experience with traditional development or scripting languages was a must.

But all that has changed. Allaire's Cold Fusion enables you to create sites every bit as powerful and capable as the ones listed earlier, without a long and painful learning curve.

So, what is Cold Fusion? Simply put, Cold Fusion is a web application development tool that enables the rapid creation of interactive, dynamic, information-rich web sites.

Cold Fusion does not require coding in traditional programming languages. Instead, you create applications by extending your standard HTML files with high-level formatting functions, conditional operators, and database commands. These commands are instructions to the Cold Fusion processor and form the building blocks on which to build industrial-strength applications.

This method of creating web applications has significant advantages over conventional application development.

- Cold Fusion applications can be developed rapidly because no coding is required other than use of simple HTML style tags.
- Cold Fusion applications are easy to test and roll out.
- The Cold Fusion language contains all the processing and formatting functions you'll need (and the ability to create your own functions if you really run into a dead end).
- Cold Fusion applications are easy to maintain because there is no compilation or linking step, so the files you create are the files used by Cold Fusion.
- Cold Fusion provides all the tools you need to troubleshoot and debug applications.
- Cold Fusion comes with all the hooks needed to link to almost any database application.
- Cold Fusion is fast, thanks to its service-based architecture.

Cold Fusion and Your Intranet or Extranet

Although all the examples mentioned so far have been Internet sites, the benefits of Cold Fusion apply to intranets and extranets too.

Most companies have masses of information stored in different systems. Users often don't know what information is available or how to access it even if they do.

Cold Fusion bridges the gap between existing and legacy applications and your employees. It empowers employees with the tools needed to work more efficiently.

▶ **See** Chapter 2, "Introduction to Cold Fusion," **p. 15**

The Dynamic Page Advantage

Linking your web site to live data is a tremendous advantage, but the benefits of database interaction go beyond extending the capabilities of your web site.

With Cold Fusion you can create dynamic, data-driven web pages. Dynamic web pages are becoming the norm for a good reason. Consider the following:

- Static web pages

  Static web pages are made up of text, images, and HTML formatting tags. These pages are manually created and maintained so that when information changes, so must the page. This usually involves loading the page into an editor, making the changes, reformatting text if needed, and then saving the file. Of course, not everyone in the organization can make these changes. The webmaster or web design team is responsible for maintaining the site and implementing all changes and enhancements. This often means that by the time information finally makes it onto the web site, it's out-of-date.

- Dynamic web pages

  Dynamic web pages contain very little actual text. Instead, they pull needed information from other applications. Dynamic web pages communicate with databases to extract employee directory information, spreadsheets to display accounting figures, client/server database management systems to interact with order-processing applications, and more. If a database already exists, why re-create it for web page publication?

Cold Fusion provides you with a full range of database interaction functions to create complete, dynamic, data-driven web pages. The features include:

- The capability to query existing database applications for data
- The capability to create dynamic queries facilitating more flexible data retrieval
- The capability to execute stored procedures in databases that support them
- The capability to execute conditional code on-the-fly to customize responses for specific situations
- The capability to enhance the standard HTML form capabilities with data validation functions
- The capability to dynamically populate form elements
- The capability to customize the display of dates, times, and currency values with formatting functions

■ The capability to ease the creation of data entry and data drill-down applications with wizards

Powered by Cold Fusion

You are probably planning to use Cold Fusion to solve a particular problem or to fill a specific need. While this book helps you solve that problem, I hope that your mind is now racing and beginning to envision just what else Cold Fusion can do for your web site.

In its relatively short life, Cold Fusion has proven itself to be a solid, stable, reliable, and scalable development platform. It is a remarkable tool that is easy to learn, fun to use, and powerful enough to create real-world web-based applications. With a minimal investment of your time, your web site can be powered by Cold Fusion. ●

Introduction to Cold Fusion

by Ben Forta

In this chapter

Understanding the World Wide Web

The World Wide Web is currently the most talked about publishing medium. Recent statistics indicate that close to 20 million people browse the web (with over 250,000 different web sites) on a regular basis. Hembrecht & Quist, a leading investment firm, forecasts that by the year 2000 the number of regular web users will grow to 200 million.

In August 1981, 213 hosts (computers) were connected to the Internet. By August 1996, that number had grown to over 12 million! The number of web sites on the Internet has grown at the same alarming rate. There were less than 25,000 Internet web sites in June 1995, and exactly one year later there were 230,000.

What has made the World Wide Web so popular? That, of course, depends on whom you ask. Most will agree that these are the two primary reasons:

- Ease of use. Publishing information on the web and browsing for information are relatively easy tasks.
- Quantity of content. With hundreds of thousands of web pages to choose from, and thousands more being created each day, there are sites and pages to cater to almost every surfer's tastes.

A massive potential audience awaits your web site and the services it offers. You could, and should, be offering much more than just static text and images. You need features like:

- Dynamic, data-driven web pages
- Database connectivity
- Intelligent, user-customized pages
- Sophisticated data collection and processing
- Email interaction

Cold Fusion enables you to do all this—and more.

Before starting Cold Fusion development, you need to take a step back. Because Cold Fusion takes advantage of existing Internet technologies, a prerequisite to Cold Fusion development is a good understanding of the Internet, the World Wide Web, web servers and browsers, and how all these pieces fit together.

The Internet

Much ambiguity and confusion surround the Internet, so start with a definition. Simply put, the Internet is the world's largest network.

The networks found in most offices today are Local Area Networks (LANs), which comprise a group of computers in relatively close proximity to each other and linked by special hardware and cabling (see Figure 2.1). Some computers are clients (more commonly known as workstations), others are servers (also known as file servers). All these computers can communicate with each other to share information.

FIG. 2.1
A LAN is a group of computers in close proximity linked by special cabling.

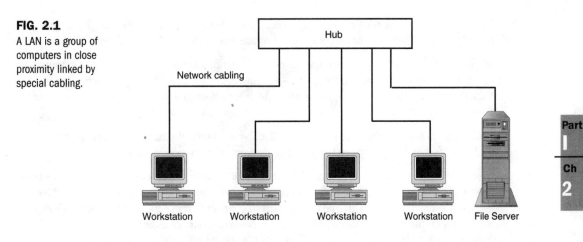

Now imagine a bigger network, one that spans multiple geographical locations. This type of network is typically used by larger companies with offices in multiple locations. Each location has its own LAN that links the local computers together. All these LANs are, in turn, linked to each other via some communications medium. The linking can be anything from a 28.8 baud modem to high-speed T1 connections and fiber-optic links. The complete group of interconnected LANs, as shown in Figure 2.2, is called a WAN, or Wide Area Network.

FIG. 2.2
A WAN is made up of multiple interconnected LANs.

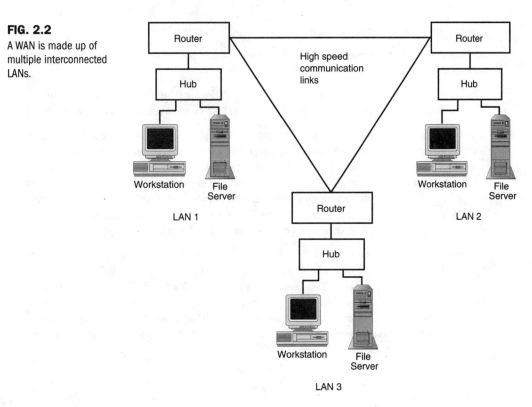

WANs are used to link multiple locations within a single company. Suppose that you need to create a massive network that links every computer everywhere. How would you do this?

You'd start by running high-speed backbones, connections capable of moving large amounts of data at once, between strategic locations—perhaps large cities or different countries. These backbones would be like high-speed, multi-lane, interstate highways connecting various locations.

You'd build in fault tolerance to make these backbones fully redundant so if any connection broke, at least one other way to reach a specific destination would be available.

Next, you'd create thousands of local links that would connect every city to the backbones over slower connections—like state highways or city streets. You'd allow corporate WANs, LANs, and even individual users with dial-up modems to connect to these local access points. Some would stay connected at all times, whereas others would connect as needed.

You'd create a common communications language so every computer connected to this network could communicate with every other computer.

And finally, you'd devise a scheme to uniquely identify every computer connected to the network. This would ensure that information sent to a given computer actually reaches the correct destination.

Congratulations, you've just created the Internet!

Even though this is an over simplification, it is exactly how the Internet works.

The high speed backbones do exist. Many are owned and operated by the large telecommunications companies.

The local access points, more commonly known as POPs, or Points of Presence, are run by phone companies, online services, and local Internet service providers (also known as ISPs).

The common language is IP, the Internet Protocol, except that the term "language" is a misnomer. A protocol is a set of rules governing behavior in certain situations. Foreign diplomats learn local protocol to ensure that they behave correctly in another country. The protocols ensure that there are no communication breakdowns or serious misunderstandings. Computers need protocols, too, to ensure that they can communicate with each other correctly and to be sure that data is exchanged correctly. IP is the protocol used to communicate across the Internet, so every computer connected to the Internet must be running a copy of IP.

The unique identifiers are IP addresses. Every computer, or host, connected to the Internet has a unique IP address. These addresses are made up of four sets of numbers separated by periods, for example 206.246.150.10. Some hosts have fixed (or static) IP addresses; others have dynamically assigned addresses. Regardless of how an IP address is obtained, no two hosts connected to the Internet may be using the same IP address at any given time. That would be like two homes having the same phone number or street address. Information would end up in the wrong place all the time.

A BRIEF HISTORY OF THE INTERNET

The Internet has evolved over the past 25 years to become an incredibly important communications medium. What follows is a brief history of the Internet.

1969—The U.S. Department of Defense starts researching a new networking project. The first node in the network is established at UCLA and, soon after, nodes are set up at Stanford Research Institute, UCSB, and the University of Utah.

1971—The number of connected nodes reaches 15 as additional government and education institutions are brought online. The ability to send email over the Internet is introduced.

1972—Telnet is introduced to permit remote host access over the Internet.

1973—The U.S. Defense Advanced Research Projects Agency begins work on the " Internetting Project" by researching ways to link different kinds of packet networks. File Transfer Protocol (FTP) is introduced.

1977—Email specifications are formalized.

1983—Name server technology is developed at the University of Wisconsin.

1984—Domain Name Service (DNS) is introduced.

1986—The U.S. National Science Foundation starts developing NSFNET, a major Internet backbone. Network News Transfer Protocol (NNTP) is introduced to enhance the performance of Usenet news.

1987—The number of hosts connected to the Internet tops 10,000.

1988—An Internet " worm" cripples the Internet, affecting over 60,000 hosts. Internet Relay Chat (IRC) is introduced.

1989—The number of hosts connected to the Internet tops 100,000.

1991—Gopher is introduced. The World Wide Web is released by CERN, the European Laboratory for Particle Physics, located near Geneva, Switzerland.

1992— The number of hosts connected to the Internet tops one million.

1993—The InterNIC is created to handle directory and domain registration services.

1995—The World Wide Web becomes the service generating the most Internet traffic. InterNIC starts charging an annual fee for domain name registrations.

Internet Applications

The Internet itself is simply a massive communications network and offers very little to most users, which is why it took 20 years for the Internet to become the phenomenon is it today.

The Internet has been dubbed "the Information Superhighway," and that analogy is quite accurate. Highways themselves are not nearly as exciting as the places you can get to by traveling them—and the same is true of the Internet. What make the Internet so exciting are the applications that run over it and what you can accomplish with them.

The most popular application now is the World Wide Web. It is the web that single-handedly transformed the Internet into a household word. In fact, many people mistakenly think that the

World Wide Web is the Internet. This is definitely not the case, and Table 2.1 lists some of the more popular Internet-based applications.

Table 2.1   Some Internet-Based Applications

Application	Description
Email	Simple Mail Transfer Protocol (SMTP) is the most popular email delivery mechanism.
FTP	File Transfer Protocol is used to transfer files between hosts.
Gopher	This menu-driven document retrieval system was very popular before the creation of the World Wide Web.
IRC	Internet Relay Chat allows real-time, text-based conferencing over the Internet.
NFS	Network File System is used to share files among different hosts.
Newsgroups	Newsgroups are threaded discussion lists, of which there are thousands.
Telnet	Telnet is used to log in to a host from a remote location.
WWW	The World Wide Web.

All these different applications, and many others, use IP to communicate across the Internet. The information transmitted by these applications is broken into packets, or small blocks of data, which are sent to a destination IP address. The application at the receiving end processes the received information.

DNS, the Domain Name Service

IP addresses are the only way to uniquely specify a host. When you want to communicate with a host—for example a web server—you need to specify the IP address of the web server you are trying to contact.

As you know from browsing the web, you rarely specify IP addresses directly. You do, however, specify a host name, like **www.mcp.com** (the Macmillan Computer Publishing web site). If hosts are identified by IP address, how does your browser know which web server to contact if you specify a host name?

The answer is the Domain Name Service (DNS). DNS is a mechanism that maps host names to IP addresses. When you specify the destination address of **www.mcp.com**, your browser sends an address resolution request to a DNS server asking for the IP address of that host. The DNS server returns an actual IP address, in this case 206.246.150.10. Your browser can then use this address to communicate with the host directly.

If you've ever mistyped a host name, you've seen error messages telling you that the host could not be found, or no DNS entry was found for the specified host. These error messages mean that the DNS server was unable to resolve the specified host name.

DNS is never needed. Users can always specify the name of a destination host by its IP address to connect to the host. There are, however, some very good reasons not to.

- IP addresses are hard to remember and easy to mistype. Users are more likely to find **www.mcp.com** than they are **206.246.150.10**.

- IP addresses are subject to change. For example, if you switch service providers, you might be forced to use a new set of IP addresses for your hosts. If users only identified your site by its IP address, they'd never be able to reach your host if the IP address changed. Your DNS name stays the same, even if your IP address switches. You only need to change the mapping so the host name maps to the new correct IP address.

- Multiple hosts, each with unique IP addresses, can all have the same DNS name. This allows load balancing between servers, as well as the establishment of redundant servers.

- A single host, with a single IP address, can have multiple DNS names. This enables you to create aliases if needed. For example, **ftp.mcp.com** and **www.mcp.com** might point to the same IP address, and thus the same server.

DNS servers are special software programs. Often your ISP will host your DNS entries so that you don't need to install and maintain your own DNS server software.

You may host your own DNS server and gain more control over the domain mappings, but you inherit the responsibility of maintaining the server. If your DNS server is down, there won't be any way of resolving the host name to an IP address, and no one will be able to find your site.

Intranets and Extranets

Intranets and extranets are currently two of the industry's favorite buzzwords. It was not too long ago that most people thought "intranet" was a typo, but, in a very short period of time, intranets and extranets became recognized as a legitimate and powerful new business tools.

An intranet is nothing more than a private Internet. In other words, it is a private network, usually a LAN or WAN, that enables the use of Internet-based applications in a secure and private environment. As on the public Internet, intranets can host web servers, FTP servers, and any other IP-based services.

Companies have been using private networks for years to share information. Traditionally, office networks have not been information-friendly. Old private networks did not have consistent interfaces, standard ways to publish information, or client applications that were capable of accessing diverse data stores. The popularity of the public Internet has spawned a whole new generation of inexpensive and easy-to-use client applications. These applications are now making their way back into the private networks. The reason that intranets are now gathering so much attention is that they are a new solution to an old problem.

Part
I
Ch
2

Extranets take this new communication mechanism one step further. Extranets are intranet-style networks that link multiple sites or organizations using intranet-related technologies. Many extranets actually use the public Internet as their backbone, and employ encryption techniques to ensure the security of the data being moved over the network.

The two things that distinguish intranets and extranets from the Internet is who can access them and from where they can be accessed. Don't be confused by hype surrounding applications that claim to be " intranet-ready." If an application can be used over the public Internet, it will work on private intranets and extranets too.

Web Servers

As mentioned earlier, the most commonly used Internet-based application is now the World Wide Web. The recent growth of interest in the Internet is the result of the growth of interest in the World Wide Web.

The World Wide Web is built upon a protocol called Hypertext Transport Protocol (HTTP). HTTP is designed to be a small, fast protocol that is well suited for distributed multimedia information systems and hypertext jumps between sites.

The web consists of pages of information on hosts running web-server software. The host is often referred to as the "web server," which is technically inaccurate. The web server is actually software and not the computer itself. There are versions of web server software that can run on almost all computers. There is nothing intrinsically special about a computer that hosts a web server, and there are no rules dictating what hardware is appropriate for running a web server.

The original World Wide Web development was all performed under different flavors of UNIX. The majority of web servers still run on UNIX boxes, but this is changing. There are now web-server versions for almost every major operating system. Web servers hosted on high performance operating systems, like Windows NT, are becoming more and more popular. This is because UNIX is still more expensive to run than Windows NT and is also more difficult to use for the average user. Windows NT has proven itself to be an efficient, reliable, and cost-effective platform for hosting web servers. As a result, NT's slice in the web server operating system pie is growing.

What exactly is a web server? A web server is a program that serves up web pages upon request. Web servers typically don't know or care what they are serving up. When a user at a specific IP address requests a specific file, the web server tries to retrieve that file and send it back to the user. The requested file might be the HTML source code for a web page, a GIF image, VRML worlds, AVI files, and so on. It is the web browser that determines what should be requested, not the web server. All the server does is process that request, as shown in Figure 2.3.

FIG. 2.3
Web servers process requests made by web browsers.

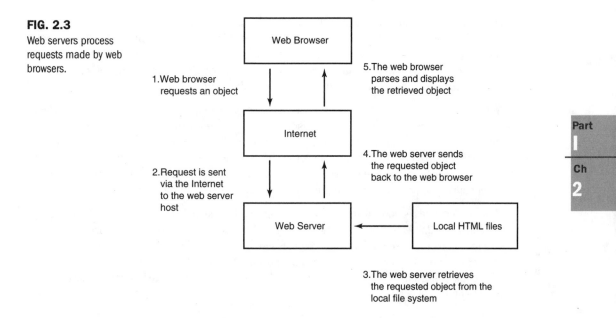

It is important to note that web servers typically do not care about the contents of these files. HTML code in a web page, for example, is markup that the web browser will process, not the web server. The web server returns the requested page as is, regardless of what the page is and what it contains. If there are HTML syntax errors in the file, those errors will be returned along with the rest of the page.

N O T E Some web servers support advanced features so the servers can actually process web pages themselves. For example, Netscape Enterprise server has a feature called "server side includes," which enables you to instruct a web server to include another URL in a specified location within a web page.

You can expect to see more "intelligent" web servers in the future. For now, however, these features are the exception rather than the norm. ▣

Connections to web servers are made on an "as needed" basis. If you request a page from a web server, an IP connection is made over the Internet between your host and the host running the web server. The requested web page is sent over that connection and, as soon as the page is received, the connection is broken. If the received page contained references to additional information to be downloaded, for example GIF or JPG images, each would be retrieved using a new connection. A web page with five pictures in it, therefore, takes at least six requests, or hits, to retrieve it all.

This is why the number of hits is such a misleading measure of web server activity. When you learn of web servers that receive millions of hits in one day, it might not mean that there were millions of visitors. Hits do not equal the number of visitors or pages viewed. In fact, hits are only a useful measure to determine changes in server activity. The number of hits is meaningless in determining how many visitors your web site has had.

Web servers are often not the only IP-based applications running on a single host. In fact, aside from performance issues, there is no reason why a single host cannot run multiple services. For example, a web server, FTP server, DNS server, and a SMTP POP3 mail server can run at the same time. To ensure that each server application only responds to requests and communications from appropriate clients, each server is assigned a port address. If IP addresses are like street addresses, ports can be thought of as apartment or suite numbers.

Most servers use a standard set of port mappings, and some of the more common ports are listed in Table 2.2. Most Web servers use port 80, but you can change that. If desired, web servers can be installed on nonstandard ports to hide web servers. You can also host multiple web servers on a single computer by mapping each one to a different port. Remember that if you do use a nonstandard port mapping, users will need to know the new port number to be able to connect to your server.

Table 2.2   Common IP Port Numbers

Port	Use
20	FTP, File Transfer Protocol
21	FTP, File Transfer Protocol
23	Telnet
25	SMTP, Simple Mail Transfer Protocol
53	DNS, Domain Name Service
70	Gopher
80	HTTP, Hypertext Transfer Protocol (the protocol used by the World Wide Web)
107	Remote Telnet service
109	POP2, Post Office Protocol version 2
110	POP3, Post Office Protocol version 3
119	NNTP, Network News Transfer Protocol
143	IMAP4, Interactive Mail Access Protocol version 4 (used to be used by IMAP2)
194	IRC, Internet Relay Chat
220	IMAP3, Interactive Mail Access Protocol version 3

Port	Use
389	LDAP, Lightweight Directory Access Protocol
443	HTTPS, HTTP running over secure sockets
540	UUCP, UNIX to UNIX Copy

Web Pages

Information on the World Wide Web is stored in pages. A page can contain any of the following:

- Text
- Headers
- Lists
- Menus
- Tables
- Forms
- Graphics
- Multimedia

Web pages are plain text files constructed using HTML, the hypertext markup language. HTML is implemented as a series of easy-to-learn tags, or instructions. Web page authors use these tags to mark up a page of text. Browsers then use these tags to render and display the information for viewing.

HTML is constantly being enhanced with new features and added tags. To ensure backwards compatibility, browsers must ignore tags they do not understand. For example, if you were to use the <MARQUEE> tag to create a scrolling text marquee, browsers that do not support this tag will still display the marquee text, but it will not scroll.

Web pages can also contain hypertext jumps which are links to other pages or web sites. Users can click on links to jump to other pages on the same web site or any page on any site.

The word "Web" in World Wide Web refers to this ability to jump to any web page on any web server, and back again.

Pages on a web server are stored in different directories. When requesting a web page, a user may provide a full path (directory and file name) to specify a particular document.

You can specify a default web page, a page that is sent back to the user when only a directory is specified, with a web server. These default pages are often called index.html or default.htm. If no default web page exists in a particular directory, it will either return an error message or a list of all the available files, depending on how the server is set up.

URLs

Every web page on the World Wide Web has an address. This is what you type into your browser to instruct it to load a particular web page.

These addresses are called Uniform Resource Locators (URLs). URLs are not just used to identify World Wide Web pages or objects. Files on a FTP server, for example, also have URL identifiers.

World Wide Web URLs are made up of up to five parts. These are

- The protocol to use to retrieve the object. This is always "http" for objects on the World Wide Web.
- The web server from which to retrieve the object. This is specified as a DNS name or an IP address.
- The host machine port on which the web server is running. If omitted, the specified protocol's default port is used; for web servers this is port 80.
- The file to retrieve or the script to execute. You'll learn more about the script to execute later in this chapter.
- Optional script parameters, also known as the query string.

Look at a few sample URLs:

- **http://www.mcp.com**

  This URL points to a web page on the host **www.mcp.com**. As no document or path was specified, the default document in the root directory will be served.

- **http://www.mcp.com/343138091147790/que/**

  This URL also points to a web page on the host **www.mcp.com**, but this time the directory **/343138091147790/que/** is specified. As no page name was provided, the default page in the **/343138091147790/que/** directory will be served.

- **http://206.246.150.10/343138091147790/que/**

  This URL points to the same file as the previous example, but this time the IP address is used instead of the DNS name.

- **http://www.mcp.com/343138091147790/que/topten.html**

  Once again, this URL points to a web page on the **www.mcp.com** host. Both a directory and a file name are specified this time. This will retrieve the file **topten.html** from the **/343138091147790/que/** directory, instead of the default file.

- **http://www.a2zbooks.com:81/catalog/internet.html**

  This is an example of an URL that points to a page on a web server assigned to a nonstandard port. As port 81 is not the standard port for web servers, the port number must be provided.

- **http://www.a2zbooks.com/a2z/guestbook.cfm**

    This URL points to a specific page on a web server, but not an HTML page. CFM files are Cold Fusion templates that are discussed later in this chapter.

- **http://www.a2zbooks.com/cgi/cfml.exe?template=/guestbook.cfm**

    This URL points to a script, rather than a web page. **/cgi/** is the directory name (or directory map) to the location where the **cfml.exe** script is located. Anything after the **?** are parameters that are passed to the script. In this example, the web server executes the script CF.EXE, and passes the parameter **template=/guestbook.cfm** to it.

- **http://www.a2zbooks.com/cgi/cf.exe?template=/guestbook.cfm&src=10**

    This URL is the same as the previous example, with one additional parameter. A **?** is always used to separate the URL itself (including the script to execute) from any parameter. Multiple parameters are separated by ampersands (the **&** character).

- **ftp://ftp.a2zbooks.com/pub/catalog.zip**

    This is an example of an URL that points to an object other than a web page or script. The protocol **ftp** indicates that the object referred to is a file to be retrieved from a FTP server using the file transfer protocol. Here the file is **catalog.zip** in the **/pub/** directory.

Links in web pages are references to other URLs. When a user clicks a link, the browser processes whatever URL it references.

Web Browsers

Web browsers are client programs used to access web sites and pages. The web browser has the job of processing received web pages, parsing the HTML code, and displaying the page to the user. The browser will attempt to display graphics, tables, forms, formatted text, or whatever the page contains.

The most popular web browsers now in use are Netscape Navigator, shown in Figure 2.4, and Microsoft Internet Explorer, shown in Figure 2.5. Both browsers are displaying the same Allaire home page, but the pages do not look the same in both browsers.

Web page designers have to pay close attention to the differences between browsers because different web browsers support different HTML tags. Unfortunately there is not one single browser that supports every tag currently in use. Furthermore, the same web page often looks different on two different browsers because every browser renders and displays web page objects differently.

For this reason, most web page designers use multiple web browsers and test their pages in every one to ensure that the final output appears as intended. Without this testing, some web site visitors will not correctly see the pages you published.

FIG. 2.4

Netscape Navigator is the web's most popular browser.

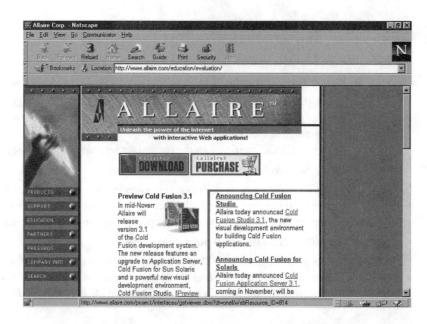

FIG. 2.5

Microsoft Internet Explorer is gaining popularity, particularly among users running Windows 95 or Windows NT.

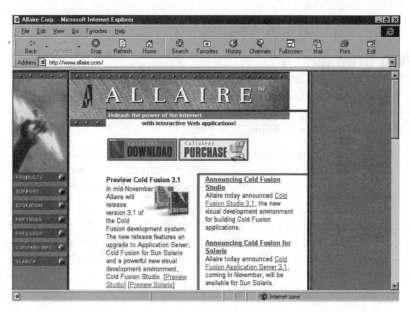

CGI

Web servers can do more than just serve static pages. As mentioned before in the section entitled " URLs," web servers can execute scripts as well. When a web server receives a URL request that references a script, it executes it and returns the script output instead of returning the script.

For example, suppose you had a web site that reported stock quotes. Creating web pages that listed all the stocks by exchange along with their current values would be close to impossible. As fast as you'd update the page and save it, it would be out of date. What you could do, instead, is write a script that takes a stock symbol as a parameter and returns the current value. When a user requests a stock, the web server executes the script referred to in the URL, passes the stock symbol as a parameter, connects the script to your designated system to obtain stock quotes, and generates HTML output containing the quote. This data flow is shown in Figure 2.6.

In order to make it easier to create scripts that work with multiple web servers, a standard script interface was created. Common Gateway Interface (CGI) is a Web server scripting standard. It is important to understand that CGI is not a program or script; it is a mechanism that you can use to connect your script to your web server.

When a CGI script executes, the following occurs:

1. The web server creates a new session in which to execute the script.
2. A set of standard environment variables containing information that the script might need are set. This includes the IP address of the remote host, the URL that was specified, server and browser version information, and so on.
3. The script is then executed within this session, and any parameters are passed to it.
4. The web server captures any output generated by the script.
5. Once the scripts have completed running, the session is terminated and the captured output is sent to the requester's browser.

So, what exactly is a script? That depends on the web server you are running.

In the past, most CGI programs were actually script files often written in scripting languages like Perl, but today scripts can also be executable programs. You can write scripts in C and Visual Basic. Some web servers even enable you to execute batch files as scripts. As long as your program can execute without any user intervention, it can be a script.

 TIP The CGI specification has gone through several revisions. The best place to find up-to-date information on CGI is the W3 Consortium web site, **http://www.w3.org**.

CGI scripts are a very powerful way to extend the capabilities of your web server, and you've probably used them without even realizing it. If you have ever used an Internet search engine, or any intelligent forms, you've probably used CGI scripts. The beauty of CGI is that it is simple to implement, portable, and completely transparent to the end user.

Part
I

Ch
2

FIG. 2.6

You may extend the publishing capabilities of your web server with scripts.

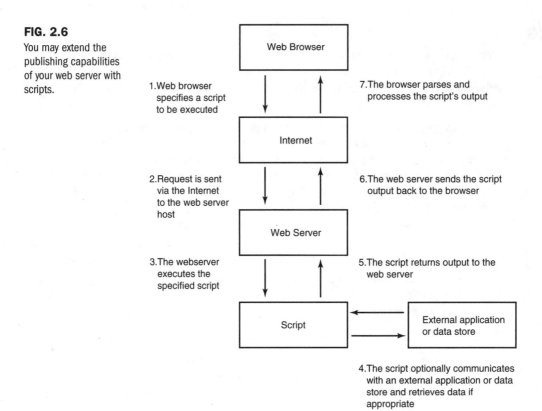

1. Web browser specifies a script to be executed

2. Request is sent via the Internet to the web server host

3. The webserver executes the specified script

7. The browser parses and processes the script's output

6. The web server sends the script output back to the browser

5. The script returns output to the web server

4. The script optionally communicates with an external application or data store and retrieves data if appropriate

Server APIs

As powerful as CGI is, it does have some shortcomings. These are

- The process of creating sessions and executing scripts is time-consuming. Seconds and milliseconds might not sound like a lot of time but, when you have multiple requests running concurrently, these short delays add up.

- CGI applications, by their very nature, must be loaded and unloaded each time they are used. There is no way to load a CGI script and keep it ready for future use.

- CGI applications are entirely separate entities from the web server itself. CGI cannot be used to change the behavior of a web server (perhaps to do URL redirection), or to implement your own security system.

To overcome these shortcomings, web server developers have created interfaces to extend the capabilities of their web servers. These are known as server APIs.

An API is an application programming interface. APIs are used by programmers to write applications that can interact with other applications. A server API is a published interface that enables software developers to write programs that become part of the web server itself. Usually these are Windows Dynamic Load Libraries (DLLs) that are loaded into memory and stay resident at all times. These DLLs hook directly into the guts of the web server to enable you to extend or alter the server's capabilities as needed.

This power and capability does come with a price. Because server APIs are so closely tied to web servers themselves, each is very server-specific. In fact, three different Cold Fusion server APIs are available for three different web servers, as shown in Table 2.3. They are, of course, incompatible with each other.

Part
I
Ch
2

Table 2.3   Server APIs and the Servers They Support

Server API	Supported Servers
ISAPI	Microsoft Internet Information Server
NSAPI	Netscape Commerce, Enterprise, and Fasttrack Servers
WSAPI	O'Reilly Web Site and Web Site Pro

Both CGI and server APIs have a place in the web server arena. CGI is not as powerful or as fast as server APIs, but CGI scripts are simple to implement and can be portable across different computing platforms. Server APIs are not portable, but they are faster and more powerful.

Introducing Cold Fusion

Now look at Cold Fusion to see how it works its magic.

If you're wondering why you went through all this discussion about the Internet, web servers, CGI, and server APIs, here's where it will all fit together.

Cold Fusion Components

Back in the early Cold Fusion days, Cold Fusion was a CGI script. Every time a user would make a Cold Fusion request (displaying data or inserting and updating records), the web server would execute the entire Cold Fusion program. Cold Fusion would process the user's request, perform whatever actions were necessary, and return HTML output back to the user.

As Cold Fusion's feature set grew, so did the application's response time. Because CGI programs are loaded and unloaded as needed, there is no way to maintain variables, settings, database connections, and file handles between each executed session. Performance was a serious problem.

The Allaire development team went back to the drawing board and developed a scalable and elegant new design. They broke Cold Fusion up into multiple parts, as follows:

■ The guts of Cold Fusion, the engine that actually processes the users' requests, became a Windows NT service. As a service, Cold Fusion can remain running at all times, even when no one is logged in to the server. Under Windows 95, which does not support services, this engine is a separate application that remains running at all times. (The new Solaris version of Cold Fusion is modeled on the NT architecture.)

■ Web servers themselves have no idea how to communicate with a Cold Fusion NT service, so server modules were written for the three different server APIs. These server modules are the glue that binds the web server to the Cold Fusion service.

■ For web servers that don't support server APIs, a CGI script, called CFML.EXE, was also created. This CGI script guarantees that any web server that supports the CGI specification can be used with Cold Fusion. Of course, the CGI script interface to Cold Fusion is slower than the server API interfaces, so it should only be used when the server modules cannot be.

The Cold Fusion engine (the service on NT) is the program that actually parses and processes any supplied instructions. Instructions are passed to Cold Fusion using templates.

A template looks much like any HTML file with one big difference. Unlike HTML files, Cold Fusion templates can contain special tags that instruct Cold Fusion to perform specific operations. Listing 2.1 contains a sample Cold Fusion template, one that you'll use later in this book.

Listing 2.1 Sample Cold Fusion Template

```
<CFQUERY
DATASOURCE=" A2Z"
>
INSERT INTO Employees(FirstName, LastName, PhoneExtension)
VALUES('#FirstName#', '#LastName#', '#PhoneExtension#')
</CFQUERY>

<HTML>

<HEAD>
<TITLE>Employee Added</TITLE>
</HEAD>

<BODY>

<H1>Employee Added</H1>

<CFOUTPUT>
Employee <B>#FirstName# #LastName#</B> added.
</CFOUTPUT>

</BODY>

 </HTML>
```

Earlier in this chapter, it was stated that web servers typically passed back the contents of a web page without paying any attention to the file contents.

That's exactly what Cold Fusion does not do. When Cold Fusion receives a request, it parses through the template looking for special Cold Fusion tags (they all begin with the letters CF) or Cold Fusion variables and functions (always surrounded by pound signs). Any HTML or plain text is left alone and is output to the web server untouched. Any Cold Fusion instructions are processed and, if there are results, they are also output to the web server.

The web server can then send the entire output back to the requester's browser.

CFML—The Cold Fusion Markup Language

Cold Fusion's power comes from its capable and flexible language. Cold Fusion Markup Language (CFML) is modeled after HTML which makes it very easy to learn.

CFML extends HTML by adding tags with the following capabilities:

- Read data from, and update data to, databases and tables
- Create dynamic data-driven pages
- Perform conditional processing
- Populate forms with live data
- Process form submissions
- Generate and retrieve email messages
- Interact with local files
- Perform HTTP and FTP operations
- Perform credit card verification and authorization
- Read and write client-side cookies

That's not even the complete list.

The majority of this book discusses Cold Fusion templates and the use of CFML.

URLs

When accessing Cold Fusion templates with your web browser, you need a way to specify which template you want to execute. You do this by specifying the template name in the URL.

Because Cold Fusion is both a CGI application and a server module, two different types of URL syntax are available for you to use. As a general rule, you should always use the server module syntax whenever you can.

Cold Fusion CGI URL Syntax   Look at the CGI syntax first:

```
http://www.a2zbooks.com/cgi/cfml.e XE?template=/a2z/hello1.cfm
```

This example instructs the web server on host `www.a2zbooks.com` to execute `cfml.exe` (the Cold Fusion CGI interface), and specifies that the template to process is `/a2z/hello1.cfm`.

Cold Fusion Server Module URL Syntax   Now see how the same template executes using the server modules URL syntax:

```
http://www.a2zbooks.com/hello1.cfm
```

This URL is both cleaner and simpler because it simply instructs the web server to return the file hello1.cfm.

How does the web server know to execute the template and return the results instead of returning the template itself? The answer is a technology called document type mapping. When Cold Fusion is installed, it configures your web server so that it knows that any file that has an extension of CFM (or CFML) is a Cold Fusion file. Then, whenever a Cold Fusion file is requested, the web server knows to pass the file to Cold Fusion for processing rather than returning it.

Of course, if you ever need to pass parameters to a Cold Fusion template, you still have that option. The example below passes a parameter called src to the template for processing:

```
http://www.a2zbooks.com/hello1.cfm?src=10
```

 If you are using one of the web servers for which Cold Fusion has a server API module available, you should always use it instead of the CGI interface.

Linking to External Applications

One of Cold Fusion's most powerful features is its ability to connect to data created and maintained in other applications. You can use Cold Fusion to retrieve or update data in many applications, including:

- Corporate databases
- Client/server database systems (like Microsoft SQL Server and Oracle)
- Spreadsheets
- Contact management software
- ASCII-delimited files

The way Cold Fusion accesses these applications is via ODBC. ODBC, which is discussed in detail later in this book, is a standard interface that applications can use to interact with a diverse set of external data stores.

The majority of Parts II and III of this book, "Getting Up and Running" and "Getting Started with Cold Fusion," discuss Cold Fusion's database interaction via ODBC. ●

Getting Up and Running

Installing Cold Fusion and Cold Fusion Studio

by Steven D. Drucker, David Watts, and Ben Forta

Preparing to Install Cold Fusion

Before getting started, you need to know that Cold Fusion is extremely easy to install and configure. As long as the basic hardware and software requirements are correctly in place, installing Cold Fusion should take just a few minutes.

N O T E   Cold Fusion comes in two distinct versions, a *workgroup* version and a *professional* version. The biggest difference between them is the types of databases with which they can interact. The workgroup version cannot interact with client-server databases like Microsoft SQL Server, Oracle, and Sybase. The professional version does not have these limitations. The evaluation version on the accompanying CD is the professional version of the Cold Fusion Application Server. ■

Installing Cold Fusion involves the following steps:

1. Verify that you have the correct hardware.
2. Select an operating system, and ensure that it is configured correctly.
3. Select a web server, and ensure that it is installed and is functioning correctly.
4. Perform the actual installation.
5. Test the installation.

The first half of this chapter walks you through each of these steps.

Hardware Requirements

The Cold Fusion Application Server runs on two different types of hardware, Intel-based hardware (capable of running 32-bit Windows) and Sun SPARC hardware running Solaris.

Intel-Based Hardware   Cold Fusion runs under both Windows 95 and Windows NT (on Intel hardware only). The minimum recommended hardware is a Pentium class machine running at 100 MHz.

If you'll be using Windows 95, you should have no less than 32MB of RAM; if you'll be using Windows NT, 64MB of RAM is the minimum. Additional memory will enhance system performance, especially if running Windows NT.

Your computer should have 50MB of disk space available after the web server is installed and configured. Obviously, as you create applications on the server, the amount of disk space needed will increase.

The computer also needs to be connected to a network. Usually this is via a network interface card (or NIC) installed into the computer on an Ethernet or Token Ring network. A modem can also be used to connect the computer to a network.

Sun SPARC Hardware   Cold Fusion requires a minimum of 64MB of RAM, but 128MB is recommended.

Your computer should have 60MB of disk space available after the web server is installed and configured. Obviously, as you create applications on the server, the amount of disk space needed will increase.

The computer also needs to be connected to a network. Usually this is via a network interface card (or NIC) installed into the computer on an Ethernet or Token Ring network. A modem can also be used to connect the computer to a network.

Selecting a Hardware Platform   Cold Fusion runs on two very different hardware platforms, each with its own advantages and disadvantages. So which is right for you? Unfortunately, there is no right or wrong answer, but here are some points to consider when making this decision:

- Almost all of your Cold Fusion code will run seamlessly on either platform. It is therefore possible to change your hardware platform at a later date without having to rewrite all of your code.
- Sun SPARC hardware is considerably more expensive than Intel hardware, and you do not have the selection of vendors and products that you have with Intel-based hardware.
- Intel-based hardware runs 32-bit Windows (Windows 95 or Windows NT), which is easier to install and manage.
- There is far more Intel hardware expertise readily available than Sun SPARC hardware expertise.
- The hardware you have available, and any existing expertise, are primary factors to consider when selecting a hardware platform.
- Sun SPARC hardware generally performs better than Intel-based hardware, and is more scalable.

An evaluation version of the Windows version of the Cold Fusion Application Server is on the accompanying CD. If you would like to obtain a copy of the Solaris version, contact Allaire at 617-761-2000, or at **http://www.allaire.com**.

Selecting an Operating System

Once you have selected the hardware on which you will run your Cold Fusion Application Server, the next step is to select an operating system. The choices available to you are going to be based on the hardware platform you selected.

Operating Systems for Intel-Based Hardware   You have two operating system choices when running Intel-based hardware: Windows 95 (any references to Windows 95 apply to Windows 98 as well) and Windows NT. Windows 95 does not come with a built-in web server, but Windows NT (version 4 or later) does.

Windows 95 is a great testing and development platform, and could also be used for very low volume web sites. Live production web servers should run on Windows NT, not Windows 95. Windows NT was designed to handle greater system loads, and is far more scalable then Windows 95.

N O T E   Cold Fusion will run under both Windows NT Server and Windows NT Workstation. The practical differences between using Server and Workstation are the number of concurrent connections that your web server (and thus Cold Fusion) will be able to handle. Windows NT Workstation limits the number of connections to ten, but Windows NT Server does not have this limitation. ■

To run web services, your operating system must have the TCP/IP protocol installed. You may do this during operating system installation, or once the operating system is already installed. To verify that TCP/IP is installed (and to install it if it is not), do the following:

- Windows 95 users can right-click the Network Neighborhood icon on the Windows 95 desktop and select the Properties option to display the network properties dialog box, shown in Figure 3.1. The TCP/IP protocol should be shown in the Configuration tab. If it is not present, click the Add button to install it.

- Windows NT users can right mouse click the Network Neighborhood icon and select Properties (or select Network from the Control Panel if you are using NT 3.5x) to display the network properties dialog box, shown in Figure 3.2. If it is not present, click the Add button to install it.

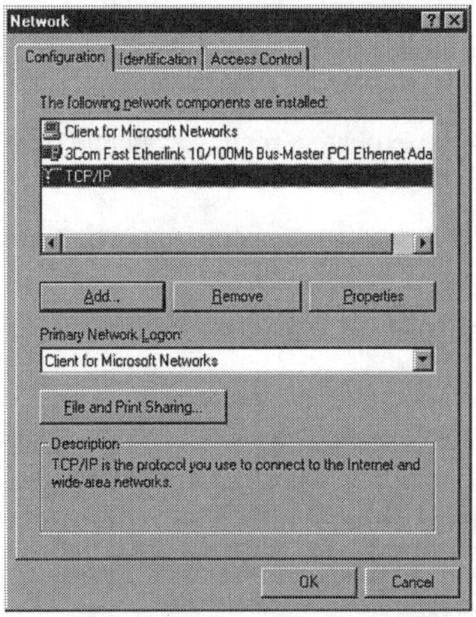

FIG. 3.1

The Windows 95 Control Panel applet shows all installed clients, protocols, and adapters.

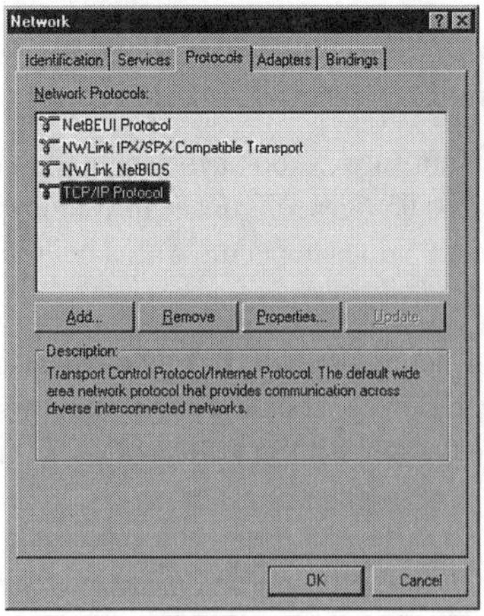

FIG. 3.2

The Windows NT Control Panel applet's Protocols tab displays the installed protocols.

For your web server to function properly, TCP/IP must be installed and configured properly, as must DNS and router settings. Refer to your operating system documentation for details, or contact your network administrator or Internet Services Provider (ISP).

▶ **See** Chapter 2, "Introduction to Cold Fusion," **p. 15**

To verify that TCP/IP is installed and operating properly, do the following:

1. Open an MS-DOS or command prompt window by selecting that option from the Start, Programs menu.

2. Type **PING localhost** or **PING 127.0.0.1** at the DOS prompt. You should see a series of replies echoed onto the screen, as shown in Figure 3.3. If the replies are shown, TCP/IP is installed and working; if not, it is not.

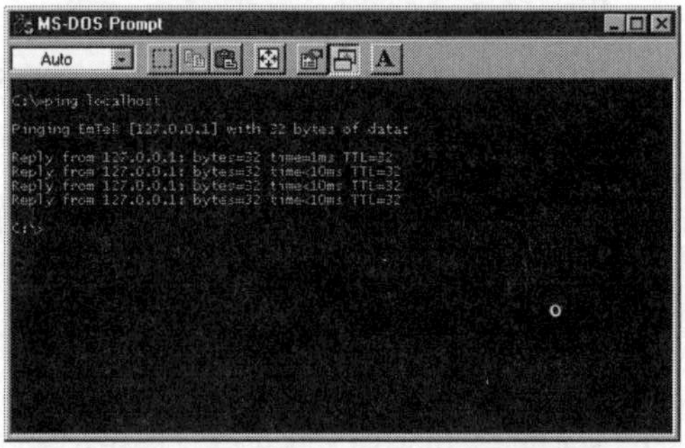

FIG. 3.3
The Ping command may be used to check that the TCP/IP protocol is installed and running.

Part

II

Ch

3

N O T E IP address **127.0.0.1** is a special address that always refers to your own computer, regardless of what the actual IP address is. The host name **localhost** is the host name for this special IP address. ■

Another good way to test that TCP/IP is installed and working is to install a web browser on the server, and try to use it to access other web sites and pages. If you can browse the web, or access other Intranet pages, then TCP/IP is working properly.

N O T E Cold Fusion only supports Windows NT on Intel-based hardware. There is currently no version of Cold Fusion for Windows NT on other hardware, such as DEC Alpha. ■

Operating Systems for Sun SPARC Hardware   If you have opted to use Sun SPARC hardware, the operating system you will use is Sun's Solaris. Cold Fusion requires that you be running Solaris version 2.5.1 or later, and that Solaris Patch 101242-11 or later be installed.

For more information about Sun's SPARC hardware and the Solaris operating system, visit the Sun Internet site at **http://www.sun.com**.

Selecting a Web Server

Your next task is to select a web server. As explained in Chapter 2 web servers are software programs, and you must select a web server that runs on the hardware platform and operating system that you already selected.

Cold Fusion supports several different web servers, allowing you to choose the server that best suits your needs. Table 3.1 lists the supported web servers and the platforms on which they are supported, as well as the URL to visit to obtain additional product information.

Table 3.1 Cold Fusion-Supported Web Servers		
Product	**URL**	**Platforms**
Apache	**http://www.apache.org**	Solaris
Microsoft IIS	**http://www.microsoft.com.iis**	Windows NT, Windows 95
Netscape Enterprise	**http://www.netscape.com**	Windows NT, Solaris Server
O'Reilly WebSite Pro	**http://website.ora.com**	Windows NT, Windows 95

So which web server is right for you? Unfortunately there is no right or wrong answer here, and asking this question of a group of webmasters is likely to elicit strong and differing opinions. Obviously, if you already have a web server installed, or have experience with any particular product, you are best off starting with what you already have or know.

Having said that, here are some points to consider when picking your web server:

- Apache is the most popular web server on the public Internet. It has a solid and proven track record, and is available at no charge from the Apache web site. It is, however, far more difficult to install and configure than any of the other servers listed here. It is supported online by the user community.

- Microsoft IIS (and its Windows 95 counterpart, Microsoft Personal Web Server) are available from Microsoft at no charge. In fact, IIS comes bundled with NT version 4 or later. IIS uses the user lists and security options in NT itself, not requiring you to maintain yet another list of users passwords and rights. This also means that to have a web server login, IIS users must also have a network login.

- Netscape Enterprise Server is the latest addition to a long line of popular commercial web servers. Evaluation versions are available from the Netscape web site. Enterprise Server runs on both Windows NT and Sun Solaris, and the administration is all web-based. Enterprise Server maintains its own user and rights list, and does not integrate its security with the operating system.

- O'Reilly WebSite Pro is extremely popular with ISPs and companies that offer hosting services. It is inexpensive and extremely easy to configure and maintain. An evaluation version is available at the O'Reilly web site.

Cold Fusion supports all of the servers listed above, and the code you write is portable among these servers. This means that you can choose one option now, and then change your mind later on. While this will require you to reconfigure your web server itself, from a Cold Fusion standpoint very little will need to be changed.

TIP The version of Microsoft IIS that is bundled with Windows NT 4 is IIS version 2. If you have decided to use IIS as your web server, it will be well worth your while to upgrade to IIS version 3. You will gain many new features, including the ability to use Cold Fusion pages as default documents. To download the upgrade, visit the IIS page on Microsoft's web site at **http://www.microsoft.com/iis**.

N O T E The list given only has the web servers that Cold Fusion supports using server APIs. Many other web servers are supported via the Cold Fusion CGI interface, but they are not listed here. As explained in Chapter 2, the CGI interface to Cold Fusion should never be used if there is the option of using the server APIs. ■

What's on the CD-ROM

The accompanying CD-ROM contains a 30-day evaluation version of the Professional version of Cold Fusion 3.1 Application Server. This is a complete version of Cold Fusion, and it comes complete with all the documentation and examples. The only restriction is that it will only run for 30 days. This should be enough time for you to evaluate Cold Fusion, and even start writing applications.

Once you have determined that Cold Fusion will work for you, you will need to contact the Allaire Sales Department at 617-761-2000 to order a live copy of Cold Fusion. You can install the live version right over the evaluation version, your applications will be saved, and any settings will still be accessible to you.

On the CD The evaluation version of the Cold Fusion Application Server is saved in the Evaluation directory on the CD-ROM as CF31PROEVAL.EXE.

Installation Checklist

You're about to install Cold Fusion. But before going so, run through this checklist to make sure your server is ready:

- Verify that the hardware you are installing Cold Fusion onto meets the requirements listed above.

- Verify that a supported operating system is installed, and that the TCP/IP protocol is installed and working. (See above for details on how to test this.)

- Check to see if the operating system vendor has published patches or service packs. If any do exist, you might want to consider applying them before proceeding.

- Make sure you have installed a supported web server. See Table 3.1 for a list of servers supported by Cold Fusion.

- Verify that the web server is working. The simplest way to do this is to load a browser on the server and go to **http://localhost**. If the default home page comes up, the web server is working; if not, it is not.
- Make sure that you are logged in with administrative rights (this step does not apply to Windows 95 machines).
- Make sure that there is sufficient disk space *after* the web server is installed.

Once you have checked off the items in this list, you'll be ready to install Cold Fusion.

Installing Cold Fusion

The Cold Fusion installation program walks you through the entire installation process, and usually even detects which web server you have installed and configures Cold Fusion accordingly.

> **NOTE** The installation instructions detailed here are for the Windows versions of Cold Fusion only, as that is the only version bundled with this book. If you have downloaded the Solaris version of Cold Fusion, refer to the documentation that came with it for installation instructions.

Beginning the Installation Process

To start the installation program, run the CF31PRO.EXE found in the Evaluation directory on the accompanying CD-ROM. If you have downloaded Cold Fusion from the Allaire web site, run that executable instead. You should see a welcome screen, similar to the one shown in Figure 3.4.

> **NOTE** All the installation instructions provided here apply to the live version of Cold Fusion, not just to the evaluation version provided on the CD-ROM. The only difference between the two is that when installing the live version you will be prompted for a serial number that you will receive along with the software.

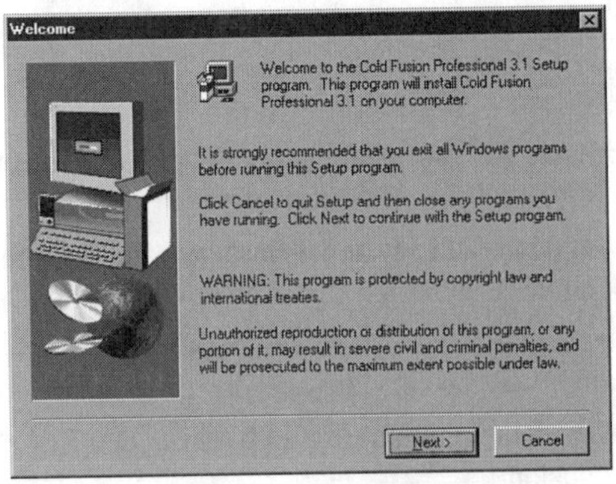

FIG. 3.4
The Cold Fusion installation program walks you through the entire Cold Fusion installation process.

Once you have agreed to the license conditions (and entered your serial number if you are install-ing a live version of Cold Fusion), you will be prompted for the installation directory as shown in Figure 3.5. The default directory is C:\CFUSION, but you may choose another directory if you so desire. It is strongly recommended that you keep the default directory if possible.

FIG. 3.5

To install Cold Fusion into a directory other than the default C:\CFUSION, specify that directory during the installation process.

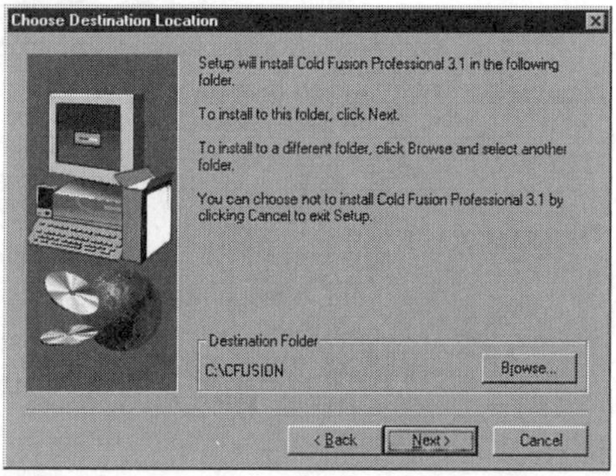

Once you have specified the installation directory, you will be prompted for the components to install. The Select Components dialog box, shown in Figure 3.6, allows you to select any of four components. Table 3.2 lists the components and their descriptions.

FIG. 3.6

You can select any or all Cold Fusion components to be installed.

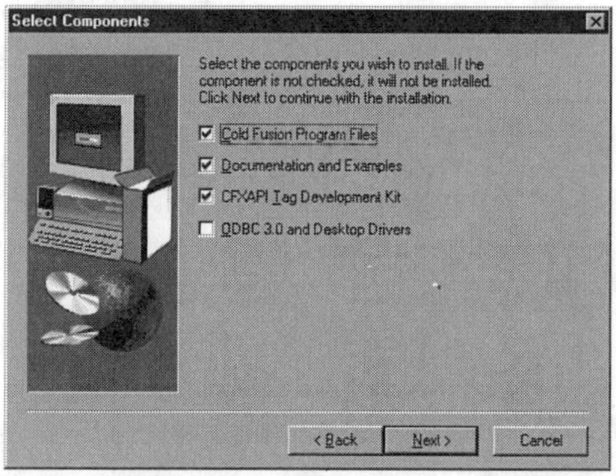

Table 3.2   Cold Fusion Components

Component	Description
Cold Fusion Program Files	Cold Fusion itself. This component is the only one that must be present for Cold Fusion to work.
Documentation and Examples	Complete online documentation and example applica-tions.

continues

Table 3.2   Continued

Component	Description
CFXAPI Tag Development Kit	Everything you need to create your own tags in Microsoft Visual C++ version 4 or later. If you do not have MSVC installed, there is no need to install this component. If the installation program detects that MSVC is present, Cold Fusion tag wizards will automatically be added to it.
ODBC 3.0 and Desktop Drivers	ODBC drivers needed for database interaction. This option is not enabled by default as it is very likely that you already have ODBC drivers installed on your computer. If you want to install the drivers, check this option. To determine whether you have ODBC installed or not, check the Windows Control Panel. If you see an applet called ODBC, ODBC is installed.

T I P   If you omit a component that you want to install at a later date, you can rerun the installation program and just select that component.

The installation program that attempts to automatically detect which web server is installed, and then prompts you to verify the results as shown in Figure 3.7. If you have more than one web server installed, you will be prompted for the server with which Cold Fusion will be used.

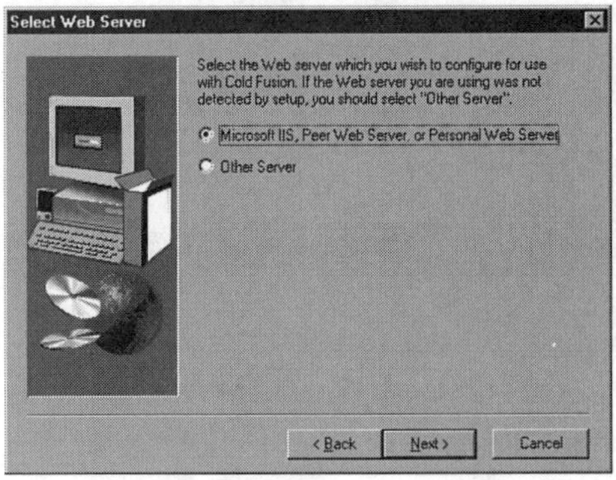

FIG. 3.7
The Cold Fusion installation program attempts to automatically detect which web servers are installed.

T I P   If you are using one of the servers listed in Table 3.1 and the installation program does not automatically detect it, cancel the installation. You might need to reinstall the web server before proceeding.

Once Cold Fusion knows which web server you are using, it will attempt to determine the location of the web server's root directory. The Cold Fusion examples, documentation, and Java applets are installed into subdirectories of this directory. The installation program will display the directory that it wants to use, as shown in Figure 3.8, and you may accept or change it.

FIG. 3.8

Select web server
document directory.

Select Web Server Document Directory

Cold Fusion HTML components, examples and documentation
will be installed into a sub-directory of your Web server's
document directory. Please verify that the directory
selected below is your Web server document directory.

C:\WEBSHARE\WWWROOT

Browse...

< Back   Next >   Cancel

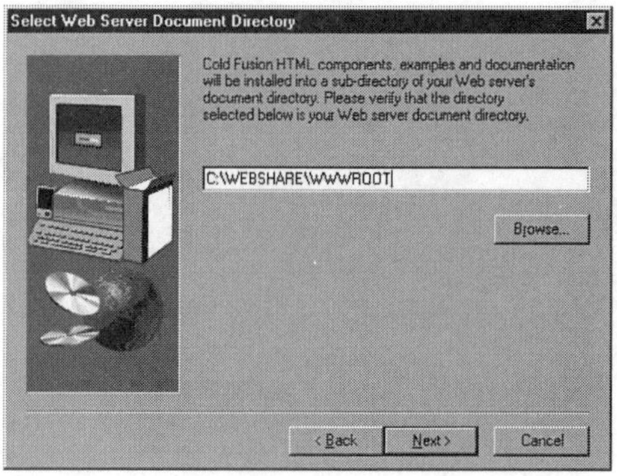

By default, Cold Fusion documentation, examples, and Java applets are installed into directories beneath the web server's root directory. Now you'll be prompted for two passwords, as seen in Figures 3.9 and 3.10. The Administrator password is the password that will be required to administer and configure Cold Fusion using the web-based administration program. The Cold Fusion Studio password is the password that Cold Fusion Studio users will need to be able to access directories, files, and data sources on the server machine.

N O T E If you are reinstalling Cold Fusion, you will not be prompted for the passwords—the existing passwords will be used. ▓

You must provide these passwords, and they can be the same password if you so wish.

▶ **See** Chapter 4, "Administering Cold Fusion," **p. 55**

▶ **See** Chapter 10, "Introduction to Cold Fusion Studio," **p. 169**

FIG. 3.9

The Cold Fusion
Administrator password
is used to configure
and administer the
Cold Fusion Application
Server.

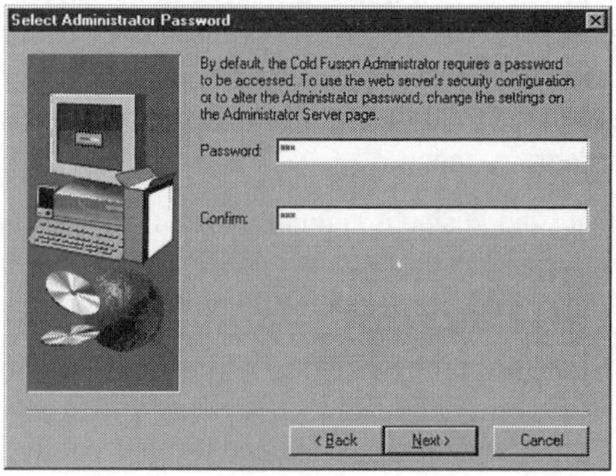

Select Administrator Password

By default, the Cold Fusion Administrator requires a password
to be accessed. To use the web server's security configuration
or to alter the Administrator password, change the settings on
the Administrator Server page.

Password:

Confirm:

< Back   Next >   Cancel

TIP The passwords specified here may be changed at a later time using the Cold Fusion Administrator described in Chapter 4.

FIG. 3.10

The Cold Fusion Studio password is used by Cold Fusion Studio users to access services on the Cold Fusion Application Server.

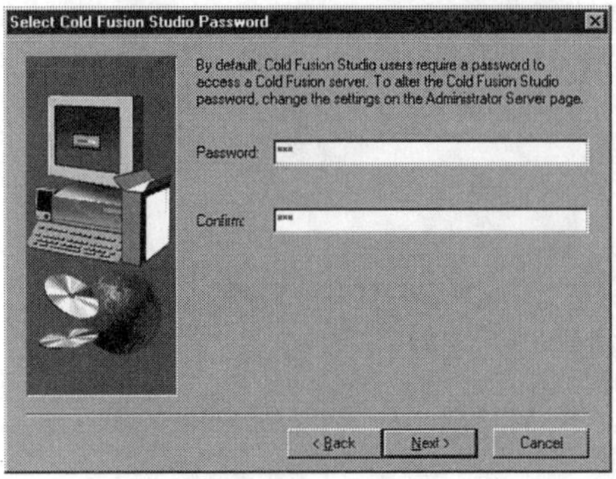

Next the installation program will prompt you for the name of the program group to create, and then you'll be asked to verify all the options selected. Read through the settings and verify that they are correct, and then click the Next button to perform the actual installation.

When you have finished installing Cold Fusion you might be prompted to restart the server.

Testing the Installation

Your next task is to test the installation using the provided test programs. As explained in Chapter 2, in order to process Cold Fusion pages, the Cold Fusion Application Server must be running.

If you are running Windows NT, select the Services applet from the Control Panel. You will see a Cold Fusion service listed, and the status should say "Started." If the service is not started, highlight it and click the Start button.

If you are running Windows 95, an icon will be displayed in the task bar when Cold Fusion is running, as shown in Figure 3.11. You can right-click these icons to stop the server if you so need. To manually start the Cold Fusion Application Server (if it has been stopped, or if it is shown in the task bar), select the Cold Fusion menu option from the Cold Fusion group beneath the Start button's Programs menu.

Once you have verified that Cold Fusion is running, select the Welcome To Cold Fusion option from the Cold Fusion group beneath the Start button's Programs menu. You should see a Getting Started screen similar to the one shown in Figure 3.12.

Select the Installation Test option at the top of the Getting Started column. The Verify Installation and Configuration screen, shown in Figure 3.13, allows you to perform a database lookup and display the results. If this operation succeeds, you'll know that the installation was successful. Select a department from the Department drop-down list, and then click the Verify Query button. If everything is working correctly, you'll see a results page like the one shown in Figure 3.14. If not, a series of suggestions will be made to help you resolve the problem.

FIG. 3.11
The Windows 95 task bar displays the Cold Fusion Application Server icon when Cold Fusion is running.

FIG. 3.12
The Cold Fusion getting started screen provides quick access to documentation, help, testing tools, and links to Allaire.

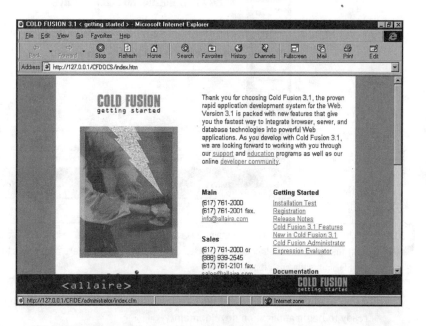

FIG. 3.13
The Verify Installation And Configuration page contains a series of tests that you can run to ensure that Cold Fusion is running properly.

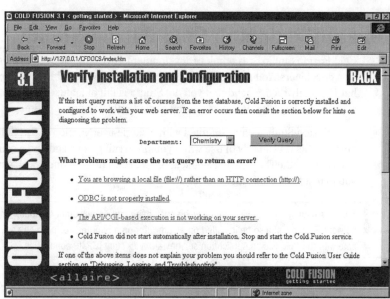

FIG. 3.14
The Test Query Results page will display data retrieved from an Access database if Cold Fusion is functioning properly.

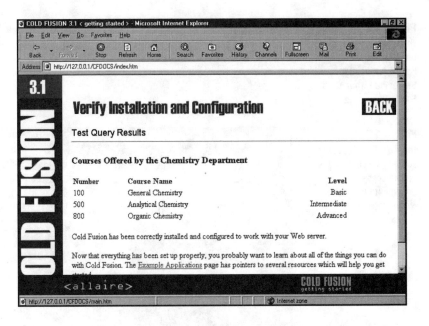

 The Installation Test page also contains links and instructions to other tests that you can perform to verify the operation of other Cold Fusion features. You may use this page at any time to ensure that Cold Fusion is running properly.

If you've made it this far, and I have no reason to assume otherwise, congratulations! You're ready to begin application development.

Preparing to Install Cold Fusion Studio

Cold Fusion Studio is a complete development environment designed especially for Cold Fusion developers. You do not have to use Studio for your Cold Fusion application development, but I strongly recommend that you do. Studio is full of features that will both simplify your application development and save you considerable amounts of time.

Cold Fusion Studio comes bundled with a single-user version of the Cold Fusion Application Server. This is primarily of use when you are writing your code on a computer other than the one running the Cold Fusion Application Server. The separate, local, single-user server allows you to test your applications locally.

T I P Studio is usually *not* installed on the web server itself, but on any other computer on the same network. Studio can also be installed on a computer on a remote site, in which case it will communicate with the Cold Fusion Application server via any existing TCP/IP connection.

N O T E From this point on, when the word "Studio" is used, it is referring to Cold Fusion Studio. ■

Hardware Requirements

Studio runs on Windows 95 and Windows NT only. There is no 16-bit version of Studio, nor is there a UNIX version. However, Studio running on Windows 95 or Windows NT can be used in conjunction with Cold Fusion Application Server running on any platform, including Solaris.

Studio will run on any computer running Windows 95 or Windows NT (Intel only), but a minimum of 32MB of RAM is recommended. 15MB of disk space is also need to install Studio.

What's on the CD-ROM

The accompanying CD-ROM contains a 30-day evaluation version of Cold Fusion Studio. This is a complete version of Studio, and it comes complete with all the documentation and help. The only restriction is that it will only run for 30 days. This should be enough time for you to evaluate the product.

Once you have determined that Studio will work for you, you will need to contact the Allaire Sales Department at 617-761-2000 to order a live copy. You can install the live version right over the evaluation version, and any options and settings will still be accessible to you.

On the CD

The evaluation version of the Cold Fusion Studio is saved in the Evaluation directory on the CD as CFSTUDIO31EVAL.EXE.

Installation Checklist

You're about to install Studio. But before doing so, run through this checklist to make sure your system is ready:

- Verify that the hardware you are installing Cold Fusion Studio onto meets the requirements listed above.
- Make sure that you have sufficient disk space available.
- If you are planning on using Studio's remote access features, make sure that the TCP/IP protocol is installed and working. (See previous details on how to test this.)
- Make sure that you are using the same version of both the Cold Fusion Application Server and Cold Fusion Studio.

Once you have checked off the items in this list, you'll be ready to install Studio.

Installing Cold Fusion Studio

Just like Cold Fusion itself, the Studio installation program makes installing Cold Fusion Studio a very simple task indeed.

> **N O T E** All the installation instructions provided here apply to the live version of Cold Fusion Studio, not just to the evaluation version provided on the CD-ROM. The only difference between the two is that when installing the live version you will be prompted for a serial number, which you will receive along with the software. ■

Beginning the Installation Process

To start the installation program, run the CFSTUDIO31.EXE found in the Evaluation directory on the accompanying CD-ROM. If you downloaded Cold Fusion Studio from the Allaire web site, then run that executable instead. You should see a welcome screen, similar to the one shown in Figure 3.15.

FIG. 3.15
The Cold Fusion Studio installation program walks you through the entire Studio installation process.

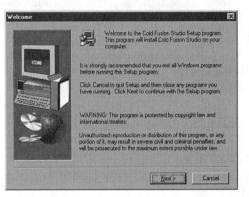

You will then be prompted to agree to the license, enter a serial number (if you are installing a live copy of the software), and enter the destination directory. Once you have provided this information, you will be prompted for the components to install, as shown in Figure 3.16. Unless you are suffering from the lack of disk space, it's recommended that you keep both components selected.

FIG. 3.16
You may select any or all Cold Fusion Studio components to be installed.

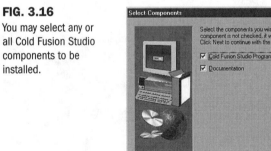

Cold Fusion Studio comes with a selection of spell checkers that you can use to check the spelling of your web and application pages. The USA English dictionary is installed automatically. You may select any of the eight additional dictionaries shown in Figure 3.17.

FIG. 3.17

Cold Fusion Studio comes with eight optional dictionaries that you may use with the built-in spell checker.

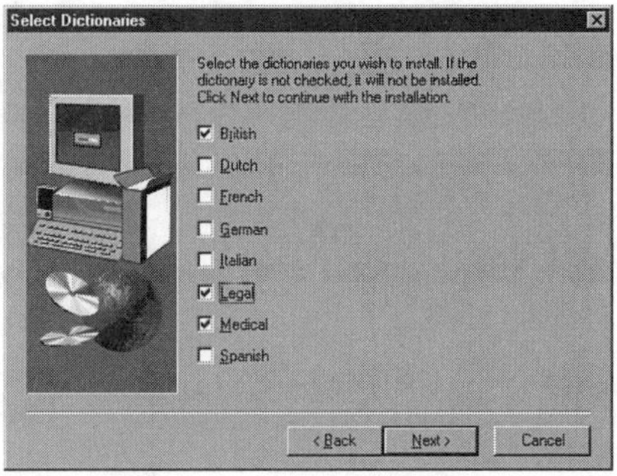

Next the installation program will prompt you for the name of the program group to create, and then you'll be asked to verify all the options selected. Read through the settings and verify that they are correct, and then click the Next button to perform the actual installation.

Testing the Installation

To test Studio, just run the program by selecting it from the Studio program group under the Start button's Programs menu. You are welcome to try it out right now. However, Studio will not be discussed in any detail until Chapter 10. ●

Part

II

Ch

3

Administering Cold Fusion

by David E. Crawford and Ben Forta

In this chapter

Using the Cold Fusion Administrator

The Cold Fusion Administrator is used to manage and configure your Cold Fusion Application Server. The Administrator is a web-based management tool that lets you use your web browser to manage all versions of Cold Fusion, regardless of platform.

To use the Administrator, select the Cold Fusion Administrator from the Cold Fusion program group beneath the Start button's Programs menu. If you have password protection enabled (it is enabled by default when Cold Fusion is installed), you'll be presented with a login screen such as the one shown in Figure 4.1. Enter the password that you specified during the Cold Fusion Application Server installation process to gain access to the Administrator for the first time.

FIG. 4.1

The Cold Fusion Administrator should be protected with a login password.

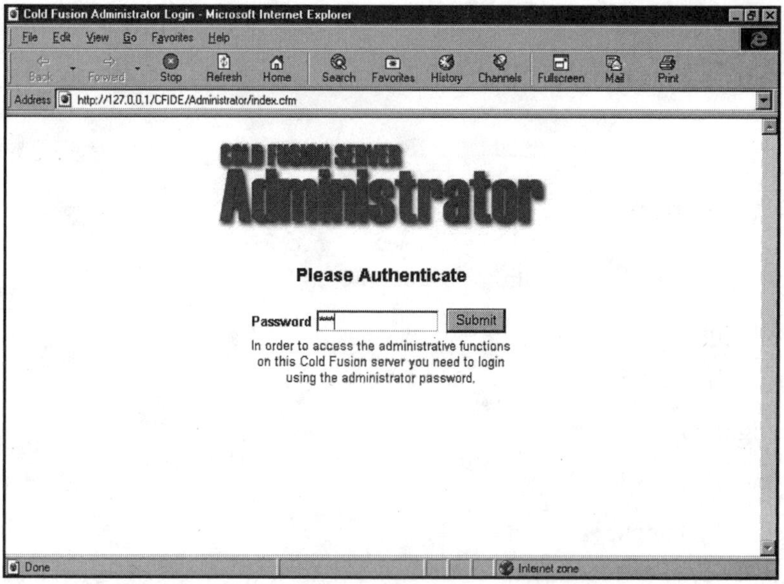

▶ **See** Chapter 3, "Installing Cold Fusion and Cold Fusion Studio," **p. 37**

The Cold Fusion Administrator uses a tab dialog style interface. The left side of the screen contains ten tabs, and clicking any tab displays relevant configuration options.

The rest of this chapter discusses each of these tabs.

TIP
The entire Cold Fusion Administrator program is written in Cold Fusion. The code is encrypted, meaning you can't see the code, but the Administrator demonstrates some powerful Cold Fusion interface techniques that you can adopt for your own applications.

Using the Server Tab

The Server tab, shown in Figure 4.2, is used to configure the behavior of the Cold Fusion Application Server and to obtain server and environment information.

FIG. 4.2
The Server tab is used to configure and manage the Cold Fusion Application Server.

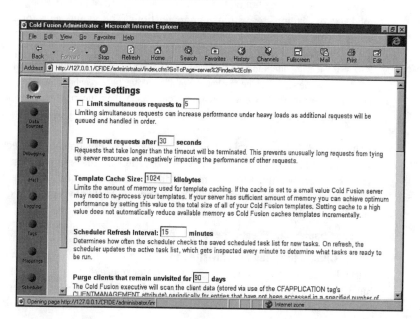

Server Settings

The Server Settings options allow you to configure the Cold Fusion Application Server. When you have made your changes, click the Apply button to save them.

Limit Simultaneous Requests To ?   Cold Fusion can process multiple requests simultaneously. By default there is no limit to the number of requests that can be simultaneously processed. If your applications are extremely load-intensive, or your server cannot handle the load because it is not powerful enough, restricting the number of simultaneous requests can help improve performance.

Of course, the downside of doing this is that additional requests will be queued. So, while those requests that are being processed are processed quicker, those that are queued to be processed will actually take longer to complete.

Timeout Requests After ? Seconds   This is the maximum number of seconds that Cold Fusion should allow for the processing of any particular request. Timing out requests can be disabled altogether, but this is generally not a good idea, as it would allow a badly behaved request (perhaps a slow database connection, or badly written SQL statement) to tie up server resources.

The default value is 30 seconds. If you are working with large complex templates, or complex database operations, you should consider raising this value.

Template Cache Size   This is the maximum amount of memory (in kilobytes) that Cold Fusion may use to cache templates. The ideal number here is something a little bigger than the total size of all templates within your applications. This would allow for all templates to be cached, which will improve system performance.

N O T E   It is important to note that Cold Fusion does not reserve this memory. Rather, it allocates it as needed until the maximum size allowed has been reached. Therefore, there is no real risk in assigning a very high value here. On the other hand, the performance penalty brought about by having too small a cache can be quite severe. ■

Scheduler Refresh Interval   This is how often Cold Fusion should check to see if new events have been added to the scheduled events list. After events are on the list, Cold Fusion checks them once every minute to determine which events need to be run. The default value is every 15 minutes. More information about how to schedule events is presented later in this chapter, in "Using the Scheduler Tab."

▶ **See** Chapter 32. "Event Scheduling," **p. 755**

Purge Clients that Remain Unvisited for ? Days   Cold Fusion client variables are persistent variables stored in the system registry. In order to prevent the registry from becoming filled up, Cold Fusion can automatically purge aged client variables—variables belonging to clients that have not visited your site in a while. The default aged interval is 90 days. You may change this value as needed.

▶ **See** Chapter 24, "Session Variables and Cookies," **p. 557**

Enable Application Variables   Application variables are application wide settings stored in memory on the Cold Fusion server. If you are not using application variables in any of your applications, you can save server memory by disabling them.

Enable Session Variables   Session variables are session-specific settings stored in memory on the Cold Fusion server. If you are not using session variables in any of your applications, you can save server memory by disabling them.

Application and Session Variable Timeouts   Application and session variables are stored in the server's memory until they timeout. This means that if they are not accessed for the specified amount of time, they are deleted. If support for these variables is enabled, you may specify the timeout interval. The default interval for application variables is two days, the default interval for session variables is 20 minutes.

The timeout values specified here are system-wide settings. Application and session variable timeouts may also be specified for specific applications using the <CFAPPLICATION> tag. However, in the event that invalid timeout values are specified at the application level, you may also specify maximum values that should be used instead. In practice, the default and the maximum values should usually be the same.

▶ **See** Chapter 23, "Web Application Framework," **p. 545**

Use a Cold Fusion Administration Password   As you can see from reading this far, the Cold Fusion Administrator is used to manage and configure the Cold Fusion Application Server. Any user with access to the Administrator can completely reconfigure the server and could even render your application inoperable.

By default, the Cold Fusion Administrator is password protected. However, you may opt to remove the password protection. This is not generally an advisable things to do. In fact, there are only two scenarios when you should even consider doing this.

- You are protecting the Administrator at the web-server level (refer to your web server documentation for information on how to do this).
- Your Cold Fusion Server is on an isolated server (a test or demo server, for example) that is not connected to a network or the public Internet.

> **CAUTION**
>
> Your server's Cold Fusion Administrator should *always* be password protected. Without password protection any user can reconfigure the server and even render your applications inoperable.

You can change the Administrator password. To do so enter the new password in the New Password field and then reenter it in the Confirmation field.

Use a Cold Fusion Studio Password   Cold Fusion Studio users can remotely access server directories, files, and data sources. Therefore, Studio access should always be password protected.

By default Cold Fusion Studio is password protected. However, you may opt to remove the password protection. This is not generally an advisable thing to do, as you'd be allowing unauthorized access to your hard disks, files, and databases.

> **CAUTION**
>
> Cold Fusion Server access via Cold Fusion Studio should *always* be password protected. Without password protection any user will have unlimited access to all of your server's hard drives, files, and databases.

You may change the Cold Fusion Studio password. To do so enter the new password in the New Password field and then reenter it in the Confirmation field.

▶ **See** Chapter 10, "Introduction to Cold Studio," **p. 169**

Part

II

Ch

4

Server Information

The Server Information area provides information about your Cold Fusion Server and the environment on which it is running. Make sure you have this information accessible if ever you need to contact Allaire Technical Support.

Using the Data Sources Tab

Cold Fusion uses ODBC data sources to interact with databases. ODBC data sources are typically created and managed using the ODBC applet in the Windows Control Panel. However, because the Windows Control Panel is not accessible from remote computers, the Cold Fusion Administrator has its own interface for creating and configuring ODBC data sources, shown in Figure 4.3.

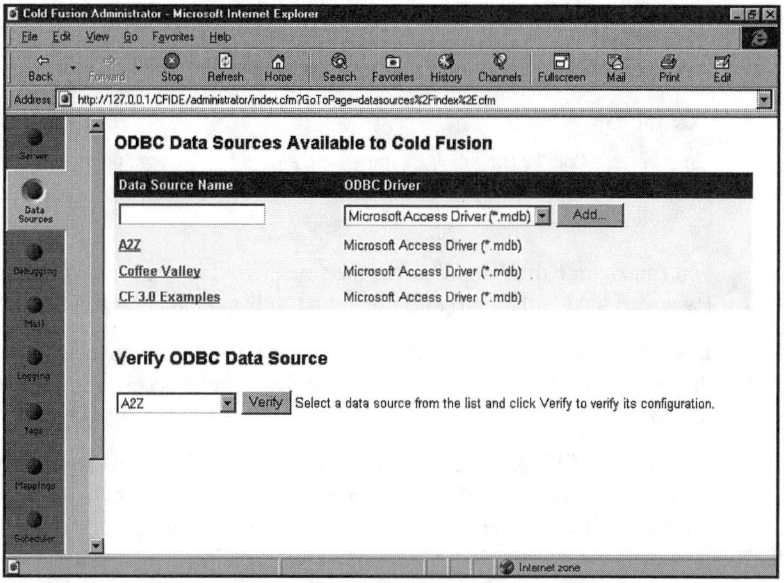

FIG. 4.3
The Data Sources tab is used to create and configure ODBC data sources.

▶ **See** Chapter 8, "Introduction to SQL," **p. 129**

ODBC Data Sources Available to Cold Fusion

The top part of the Data Sources screen displays a list of currently installed data sources. You may click any data source name to view or edit its settings. You may also add new data sources by entering the data source name in the Data Source Name field, selecting the ODBC Driver from the drop-down list, and then clicking the Add button. This will display the Create ODBC Data Source screen shown in Figure 4.4. To add the data source, fill in the appropriate information and click the Create button.

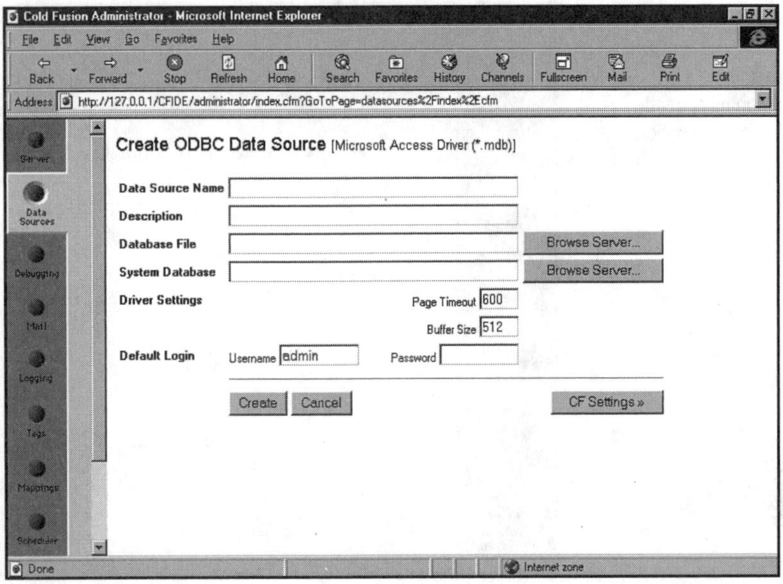

FIG. 4.4

The Data Sources tab can be used to remotely add new ODBC data sources.

N O T E If you are creating a data source to a client-server database such as Microsoft SQL Server, you must click the CF Settings button to expand the create screen so that you may specify the required database login information. ■

Verify ODBC Data Source

After you have created a data source, or whenever you are troubleshooting database interaction problems, it is useful to be able to verify that Cold Fusion can actually communicate with the database using that data source. To verify the configuration of any installed data source, select it from the drop-down list, and click the Verify button. If the data source is working properly, you'll see a screen similar to the one shown in Figure 4.5.

Using the Debugging Tab

The Debugging tab, shown in Figure 4.6, is used to enabled and disable the display of debug information, as well as to specify what debug information should be displayed and to whom. Select as many or as few options as you want, and then click the Apply button to save your changes.

▶ **See** Chapter 16, "Debugging and Troubleshooting," **p. 325**

Part

II

Ch

4

FIG. 4.5

To verify that an ODBC data source is functioning correctly, use the Verify option in the Data Source tab.

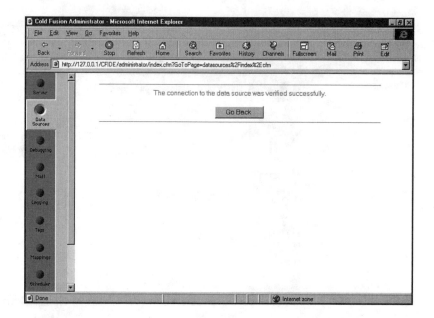

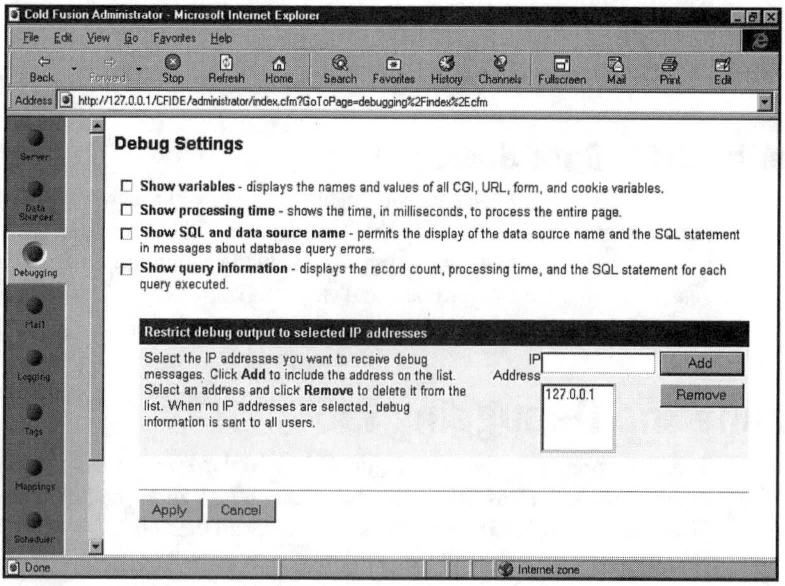

FIG. 4.6

The Debugging tab is used to configure what debug information Cold Fusion should display and to whom.

Show Variables   If the Show Variables option is enabled, Cold Fusion will automatically append a list of CGI variables, URL parameters, form fields, and HTTP cookies to the end of every Cold Fusion page.

Show Processing Time   If the Show Processing Time option is enabled, Cold Fusion will display the total page processing time at the bottom of each and every page.

Show SQL and Data Source Name   If the Show SQL and Data Source Name option is enabled, the data source name and SQL statement will be displayed in any error messages. If you would rather your visitors not know the details of your underlying databases, this option should be disabled. However, during routine debugging sessions, the information provided by enabling this option is extremely useful.

Show Query Information   If the Show Query Information option is enabled, the SQL statement, retrieved record count, and query processing time will be displayed at the end of each template. This option is useful in tracking down badly performing database queries.

> **T I P**   To determine how long Cold Fusion is taking to process, code your page without query processing, and subtract the total amount of time spent processing all queries from the processing time option mentioned above.

Restrict Debug Output to Selected IP Addresses   By default, any and all debugging information is sent to every visitor to your site. To restrict the display of debugging information to specific users, you may enter their IP addresses here. To add an address, enter it into the IP Address field, and click the Add button. The address will be displayed in the list below. To delete an address from the list of addresses to receive debugging information, select the address from the list, and click the Delete button.

> **N O T E**   If debugging is enabled and no IP addresses are specified, then debugging information will be sent to every visitor to your web site. It is therefore a good idea to always have at least one address in the list. You might want to add address **127.0.0.1**, as this refers to the local host (the server itself).

There is an add-on Cold Fusion tag called CFX_Debug on the accompanying CD-ROM. This tag allows you to enable and disable the display of debugging information from within a Cold Fusion template without having to access the Administrator. This is very useful in environments that use dynamic IP addresses.

Using the Mail Tab

Cold Fusion allows developers to programmatically generate email using a tag called <CFMAIL>. The Mail tab, shown in Figure 4.7, is used to configure Cold Fusion so that it may interact with an SMTP mail server in order to deliver your mail. After you have entered the information about your SMTP mail server, click the Apply button. Each of the options is explained in the following section.

▶ **See** Chapter 20, "Interacting with Email," **p. 461**

Part

II

Ch

4

FIG. 4.7

The Mail tab is used to configure an SMTP mail server for use with the Cold Fusion CFMAIL tag.

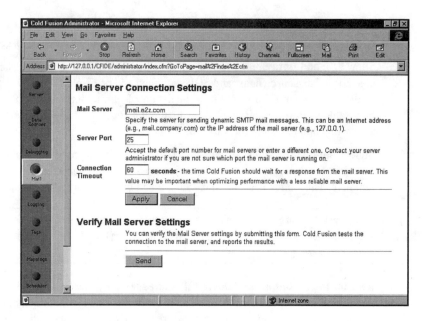

Mail Server Connection Settings

The mail server connection settings include mail server, server port, and connection timeout.

> **CAUTION**
>
> If you try to use the Cold Fusion <CFMAIL> tag without having configured a mail server in the Mail tab, your code will fail and you will generate a Cold Fusion error message.

Mail Server   This setting requires you to enter the DNS name or IP address of your SMTP mail server here. If you do not know this information, contact your mail administrator or ISP.

Server Port   This setting requires you to enter the port number to which your SMTP server is assigned. This should always be left at the default value of 25 unless instructed otherwise by your mail administrator or ISP.

Connection Timeout   This setting requires you to enter the amount of time Cold Fusion should wait for the mail server to respond before timing out. This should only be raised from the default of 60 seconds if you are experiencing problems with an unreliable mail server.

Verify Mail Server Settings

After you have entered the mail server information, or whenever you want to verify that Cold Fusion can communicate with your web server, click the Send button. This instructs the Administrator to simulate sending a mail message. Cold Fusion will let you know if the connection was successful or not, and what the error was if it failed (see shown in Figure 4.8).

FIG. 4.8

Verifying configuration changes can help you find problems like this one, a misspelled mail server name.

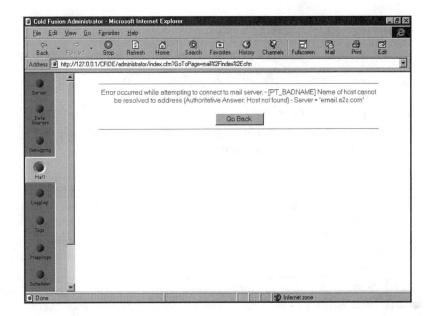

Using the Logging Tab

The Logging tab, shown in Figure 4.9, is used to configure how Cold Fusion logs warnings and errors. Logging and log analyses are important parts of Cold Fusion debugging and trouble-shooting.

FIG. 4.9

The Logging tab is used to configure the Cold Fusion logging functions.

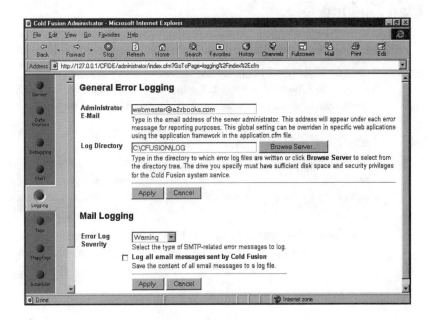

▶ **See** Chapter 16, **p. 325**

N O T E   The Logging tab has two sections, with an Apply button in each. When you make changes to this screen, make sure you click the appropriate Apply button. ■

General Error Logging

You will likely use the default values for all the following options. The only option that you should specify immediately is the Administrator E-Mail.

Administrator E-Mail   If an error occurs, Cold Fusion displays an error message describing the error condition. If you enter an email address here, Cold Fusion will also display it, instructing the visitor to notify that address of the error condition. You can override this address for a specific application by specifying an address in the <CFAPPLICATION> tag in the APPLICATION.CFM file.

▶ **See** Chapter 12, **p. 225**

T I P   Cold Fusion only allows you to specify a single email address for the mail administrator. To have messages sent to multiple recipients, create a mail group on your mail server, and specify that group address in the Administrator E-Mail field.

Log Directory   By default Cold Fusion log files are stored in a directory called LOG beneath the Cold Fusion root directory (usually C:\CFUSION). You may specify an alternate directory if desired.

Mail Logging

The mail logging options, explained in the following sections, are used to debug and troubleshoot problems with outbound mail delivery.

Error Log Severity   By default Cold Fusion logs warnings and errors in the mail server log. You may raise the level to Error to log just error messages, or lower it to Information to log informational messages in addition to all warnings and errors.

CAUTION

Only set the mail error log severity to Information if you absolutely need this information, and then set it back to Warning or Error when you have collected the information you need. Leaving the level at Information for an extended period of time will cause the log file to grow rapidly, consuming lots of disk space.

Log All Email Messages Sent by Cold Fusion   To log the content of all outgoing mail messages, enable this option. This can be useful when debugging mail delivery problems.

CAUTION

Only enable this option when debugging mail delivery problems, and disable it when done. Leaving it enabled for an extended period of time will cause the content of all outgoing messages to be saved, and this can consume large amounts of disk space.

Using the Tags Tab

The Tags tab, shown in Figure 4.10, is used to restrict the use of some potentially dangerous tags, as well as to install CFX tags.

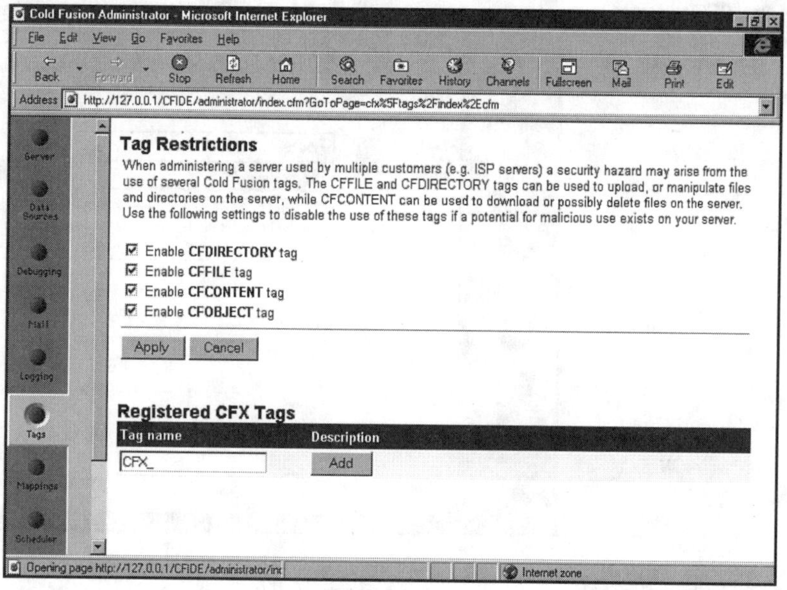

FIG. 4.10

The Tags tab is used to install CFX tags.

Part

II

Ch

4

Tag Restrictions

Several Cold Fusion tags can be misused, compromising system security. This is rarely a problem in typical installations, but in environments where the same Cold Fusion Application Server is shared by multiple organizations (ISP's for example), there might be justification to restrict the use of these tags. The tags are <CFDIRECTORY>, <CFFILE>, <CFCONTENT>, and <CFOBJECT>. By default these tags are all enabled.

▶ **See** Chapter 25, "File Manipulation," **p. 577**

▶ **See** Chapter 28, "MIME Types," **p. 665**

▶ **See** Chapter 34, "Interfacing with COM and DCOM Objects," **p. 789**

> **N O T E** Enabling these tags is not in itself a security risk. These tags can only be abused if users
> have the ability to save Cold Fusion files on the server for execution. As long as users
> cannot save their own files on your server, there is no security risk at all. ∎

Registered CFX Tags

CFX tags (also known as CFAPI tags) are Cold Fusion add-on tags supplied as DLLs. To use
the tag with Cold Fusion it must first be registered. To register your tag you must first copy the
DLL onto your Cold Fusion server, enter its name into the Tag Name field, and click the Add
button to display the New CFX Tag screen, shown in Figure 4.11.

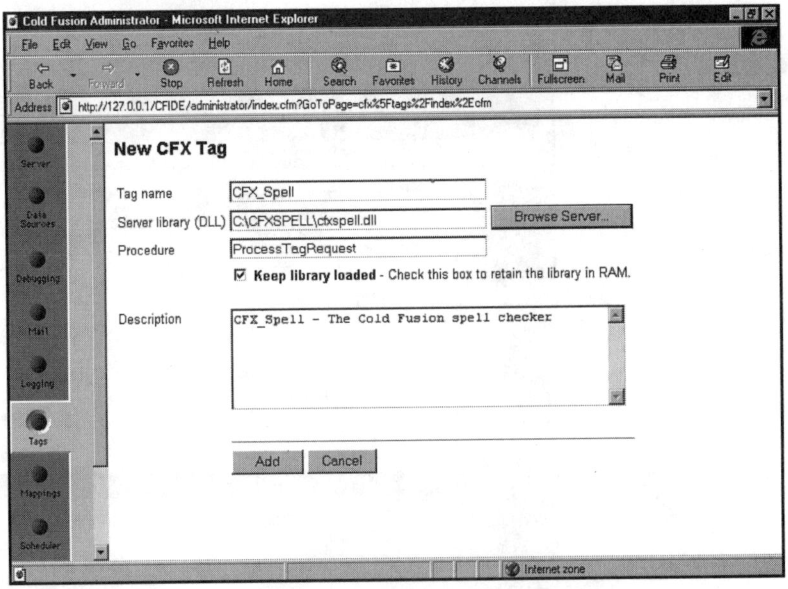

FIG. 4.11
The New CFX Tag screen
is used to add CFX tags
to your Cold Fusion
server.

To register the tag, you must specify the full path to the DLL in the Server Library field, or
click the Browse button to browse the server to find the file. The Procedure field should always
be left with the default value of ProcessTagRequest.

By default, CFX tag DLLs are loaded into memory when they are first used and kept there.
This improves the performance of subsequent calls to the tag. However, resident tags take up
server memory, so if the tag is infrequently used, you might want to disable the Keep Library
Loaded option. The Description is optional.

▶ **See** Chapter 35, "CFAPI, The Cold Fusion API," **p. 807**

A collection of CFX tags are provided on the accompanying CD-ROM.

Using the Mappings Tab

The Mappings tab, shown in Figure 4.12, is used to create Cold Fusion level directory mappings. These allow you to use directory aliases at a Cold Fusion level.

To add a map, enter the alias name in the Logical Path field, and the actual path in the Directory Path field (or click the Browse button to locate the directory).

After the mapping is added, you can use it in all Cold Fusion tags (for example <CFINCLUDE>). However, you will not be able to use it in HTML paths (for example <A HREF> or <IMG> tags).

To edit or delete an existing mapping, click it in the list of currently assigned mappings.

FIG. 4.12

The Mapping tab allows you to configure Cold Fusion level alias mappings.

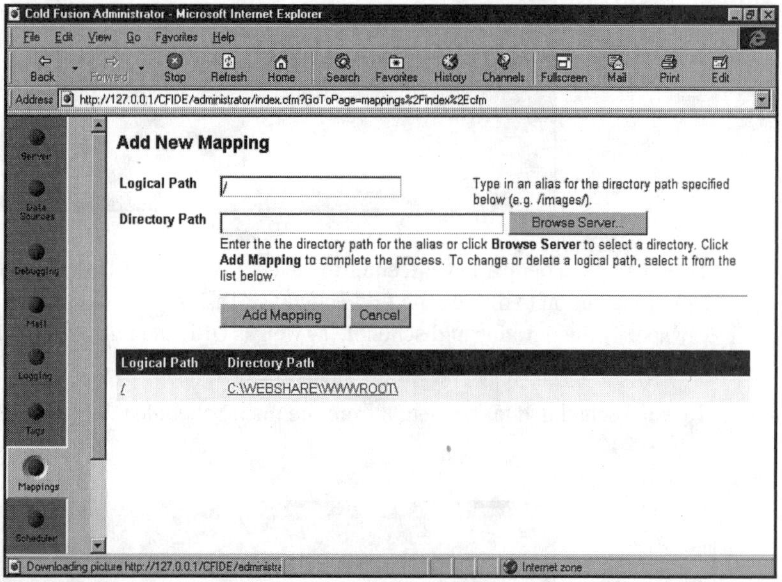

Part

II

Ch

4

N O T E Cold Fusion level mappings are primarily used if using Cold Fusion via its CGI interface. ■

Using the Scheduler Tab

The Cold Fusion Scheduler is used to configure events that Cold Fusion can automatically execute. The Scheduler tab, shown in Figure 4.13, is used to create and configure scheduled events.

FIG. 4.13

The Scheduler tab is used to configure timed events.

To add a new scheduled event, enter the event name in the Task Name field, and click the Add New Task button to display the Add Scheduler Task screen shown in Figure 4.14. Here you can specify the duration and schedule as well as URL and publishing information for the new task.

To edit a scheduled task, select it from the main Schedule tab screen shown previously in Figure 4.13.

FIG. 4.14

The Scheduler screen is used to specify the time, interval, and URL information for the task to be scheduled.

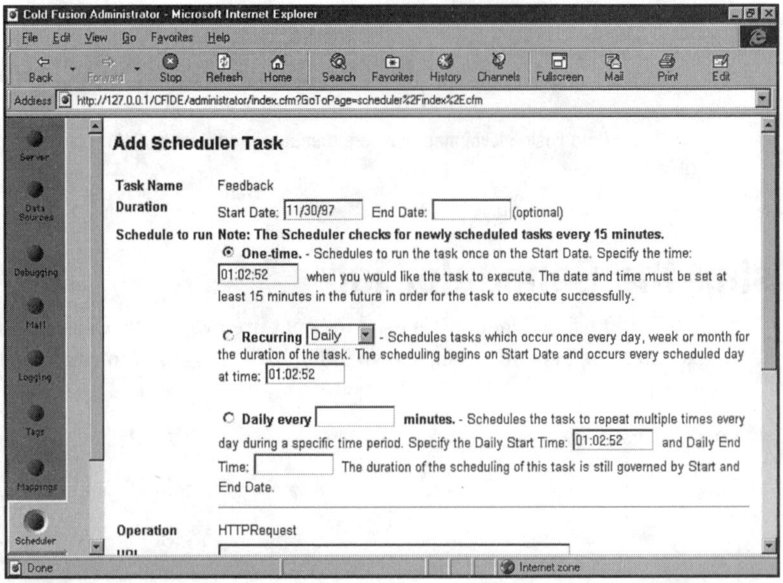

▶ **See** Chapter 32, **p. 755**

Using the Verity Tab

Cold Fusion uses the Verity search engine to facilitate full text searching. Verity stores its index information in *collections*. A collection is a special database used internally by Verity to allow users to perform full text searches. The Verity tab, shown in Figure 4.15, is used to manage these collections.

FIG. 4.15
The Verity tab is used to manage and create Verity collections.

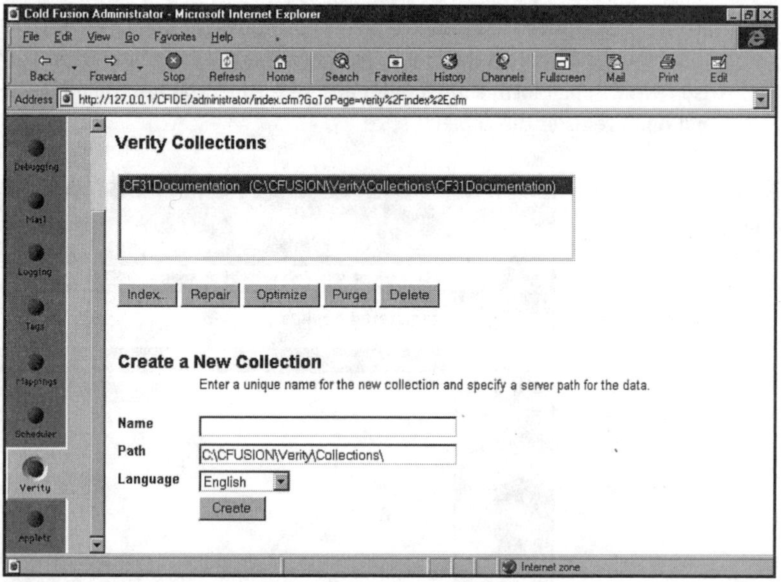

▶ **See** Chapter 26, "Full-Text Searching with Verity," **p. 601**

Verity Collections

To index, repair, optimize, purge, or delete a Verity collection, select it from the list of collections and click the appropriate button.

NOTE The CF31 Documentation collection, shown in Figure 4.15, is automatically created the first time you try to perform a search on the online documentation. ■

Create a New Collection

To create a new Verity collection, enter the unique collection name, specify the path where the collection should be saved (the default path should usually be used), and choose the language of the data being indexed. When the information has been entered, click the Create button.

Part
II

Ch
4

NOTE Verity collections can also be created programmatically using the Cold Fusion <CFINDEX> tag. ■

Using the Applets Tab

Cold Fusion comes with a collection of Java applets you can use to enhance your forms. These are accessed using the Cold Fusion <CFFORM> tag. You can register your own Java applets, and add them to your <CFFORM> forms using the <CFAPPLET> tag.

Registered applets are listed in Applets tab, shown in Figure 4.16. To register a new applet, enter its name in the Applet field, and click the Register New Applet button to display the Register New Applet form shown in Figure 4.17. After you have filled in the form, click the Create button to register the applet.

FIG. 4.16

The Applet tab lists any registered Java applets.

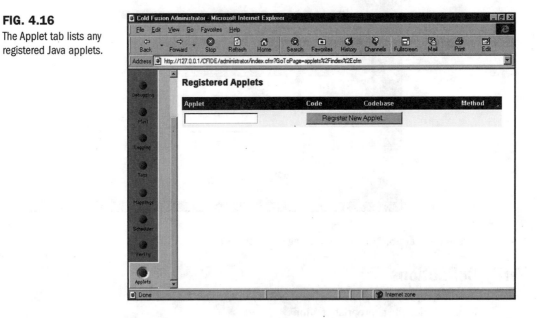

▶ **See** Chapter 20, **p. 461**

FIG. 4.17

Use the Register New Applet form to register your own Java applets for use with the <CFAPPLET> tag.

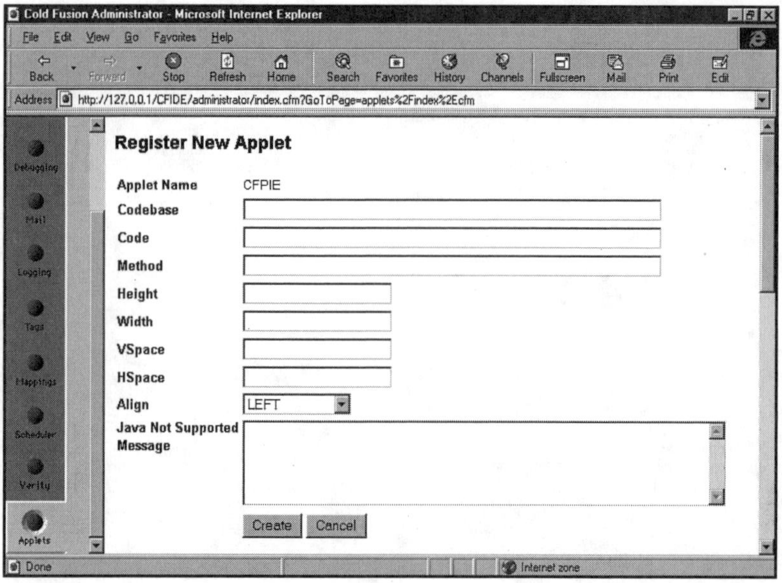

Getting Started with Cold Fusion

Designing an Application

by Ben Forta

In this chapter

Introducing Application Design

The key to successful application development is careful application design. Like anything else, this design requires planning.

The design process has the following four basic steps:

- Educate yourself. Learn the business practices and processes that are currently in place. Find out what works, what doesn't, and what needs fixing.
- Build a high-level goal document based on the knowledge you have acquired, and verify that all goals are included in it.
- Determine what sets of information are needed to attain each of these goals successfully.
- List in detail the data that each of these data sets contains.

Through the rest of this chapter, I explain these steps in detail.

Introducing A2Z Books

A2Z Books is a small bookstore with big ideas. The company prides itself on top-notch customer service and goes out of its way to ensure complete customer satisfaction. A2Z Books is a mail- and phone-order company, and, like many other small companies, A2Z Books is suffering from growing pains.

Just last week you were called into the boss's office and assigned a new project. "Orders are up," the boss said. "Way ahead of year-to-date projections. We've doubled our order-processing staff to handle the load, but we can't seem to keep up. New titles are not being made available to our customers quickly enough, and orders are taking too long to ship out. Our customers have grown to expect better service than we can offer right now. We desperately need to find a way to streamline our operations and eliminate whatever is causing these bottlenecks. I want you to give this some thought and make recommendations. Oh, and I'll need them within the week."

And that is why you're sitting there, amidst piles of pads and sticky notes, trying to work out exactly what is wrong and how you're going to fix it. You know that the manual processes of order taking, shipping, accounting, and billing just cannot work anymore. Computers could, and should, be performing many of these tasks for you. But where do you start?

Educating Yourself

After reading and rereading your notes, you come to the conclusion that you just don't know enough about the individual processes and procedures that make up the day-to-day operations of the company. To design a computer system that will be both usable and useful, you really need to interview personnel around the company to learn just what they do, why they do it, and how the work gets done.

You start to compile a list of questions to ask during the interviews. Starting with the accounting department, you create the following list:

How often are invoices processed?

How is order information provided to you?

How is client information provided to you?

What are the steps you take to create an invoice?

What happens to the invoices after they are printed?

What reports do you run after printing invoices?

Who gets these reports?

You also might want to observe some of these operations being performed. In this way, you can pick up details that you missed during the interview.

TIP When you're conducting these interviews, ask very specific questions and try to obtain very specific answers. Remember, you're talking to someone who does a particular task regularly and who most likely takes many of the details involved for granted. The more explicit your questions are, the more useful the answers will be.

After you have this information in hand, creating a flowchart is often useful. It can depict the steps that make up a complete process, as shown in Figure 5.1. You also can have whoever gave you the information review the flowcharts for accuracy. This way, you can be sure that no steps have been overlooked.

FIG. 5.1
Making flowcharts is an effective way to review and analyze business processes.

This process might sound like a tedious and time-consuming task, but the more preparation you do up front, the more likely your computer program will work the first time and will be accepted. The acceptance, or lack thereof, usually determines the fate of any computer program.

N O T E Often, you might find that people have determined that their business needs computerizing, but they have no idea what they want or what the computer can actually do for them. Bear in mind that computer nonusers usually know only what they want an application to do for them once they have seen the application and then know what they don't like about it.

Too often, programs are designed and implemented by programmers working in a vacuum, without any real knowledge of the problems they are trying to solve. A program like this might be built around great business ideas and work models, but if it requires a change in the way employees go about their business, employees will look for every excuse not to use it. Without mass acceptance, the new program is doomed to fail.

TIP Computers are supposed to make our lives easier, not force us to relearn what we are already familiar with. A computer program that forces people to change the way they work will probably never be used.

The interview process should be conducted thoroughly and should include a diverse set of employees for another important reason. Often, employees view computerization and technology as a threat to their jobs instead of as a boon to their productivity. Although some of this fear might be justified, it is usually the result of computerphobia and horror stories of corporate downsizing. The interview and due-diligence process enables you to reassure employees and to persuade them to buy into your plans and suggestions instead of rejecting them. Making employees feel like they are a part of the application design rather than its victims can go a long way toward boosting mass acceptance.

TIP Never rely on the input of one individual. The more people you interview during the research project, the more likely you are to obtain information that is an accurate reflection of the way business is performed.

Putting It All Together

Armed with all this information, you now might be tempted to actually start application development, knowing that you can make educated suggestions and that you have the data to back them up. But don't run out to buy database applications and development tools just yet. You still have quite a bit more preparation to do.

Before you start actual development, you should document your application goals thoroughly. Include the various components of your application, what each component does, and how the components interact. You can use this document as your roadmap throughout the actual application-development process.

What you should not be documenting, at this point, are databases, tables, and fields. Try not to get caught up in any technical details yet. This document is not a database schema; it is a high-level overview of what your program will do and how it will do it. What data will be stored in which tables and how that data will be stored are not considerations at this stage. You should make sure that the application-design decisions you make are based on business needs and practices, not on features or peculiarities of any particular database system or development tool.

TIP Don't let the features of any database system or development tool influence your high-level application design. You know your business; the designers of the database systems do not. If a particular database system does not have the features you need, you can always pick another one. Switching databases is much easier than switching business practices.

The High-Level Design Document

You now can sift your way through the piles of data sitting in front of you and begin to formulate your application plan. The plan is initially broken down by department, so you can list the needs of each department based on the results of your interviews.

Human Resources Department

You start with the human resources needs and break down the requirements into an organized list, as follows:

- Human resources needs an efficient way to manage employee information, including personal information.
- Some of this information, like lists of current employees and their phone extensions, should be made available to all employees. Other information is highly confidential and should be kept private.
- Human resources wants a way to track employees' days off.

Accounting Department

The human resources list is relatively simple. So next, you try your accounting department, as follows:

- Accounting needs to be able to automate the billing process so they have fewer manual steps between order taking and billing.
- They also have to run reports for upper management on a regular basis. Creating these reports is time consuming, so they need better reporting tools.
- Accounting wants a closer interaction with the shipping and receiving department so they can track when orders ship and, consequently, process returns more quickly.

Marketing Department

The marketing department's chief complaint is that they cannot easily get information they need from other departments. Here's their list of requirements:

- Marketing wants access to the accounting department's customer lists.
- They also want customer histories so they can create targeted marketing programs.
- With the popularity of the Internet and the growing use of email, marketing wants to be able to send email to notify interested customers when specific books become available.
- Marketing also wants to use the World Wide Web to interact with customers. Some of the ideas they want to pursue involve online surveys and communication among employees.

Sales Department

The sales team has the closest interaction with the customers. Therefore, you can safely assume that most requests from the sales department are customer driven. Here's their list of requirements:

- Sales needs a faster way to locate books for customers. Customers might know the title, author's name, publisher, book category, or any other information. The staff needs to locate the correct books no matter what information customers provide.
- Sales also needs a way to check item availability instantly.
- Sales wants to be able to refer to existing customer records when taking orders. This way they won't have to re-enter customer information unnecessarily.
- The sales manager wants to start selling books over the Internet. He wants to allow customers to browse through inventories, search for books, and place orders online.

Shipping and Receiving Department

Shipping and receiving is the place where much of the bottleneck occurs. Their requirements include:

- Receiving needs to be able to make new titles available rapidly.
- They also need to be able to track what books need to be reordered and when.
- To ship orders on the day they are received, shipping wants to be notified automatically of orders waiting for shipment as soon as they are received.
- Shipping wants an easier way to notify accounting when an order is shipped.

N O T E The preceding lists are just examples demonstrating the kind of information to include in a high-level design document. The example lists have been simplified; they are by no means complete. Your own documents will typically be far more detailed than these.

Remember, the more detail you include, the more complete your design will be. Just make sure that it isn't so detailed that it is no longer a high-level document.

You review the design document and refer back to your notes and scribbles to verify that all needs have been included. Just to make sure that you haven't omitted anything, circulate the design document to department heads for their approval.

Determining the Data Requirements

Now that you have your basic application goals documented, the next step is to determine what data sets you need to design the application. The goal-oriented design document implicitly lists all the sets of data you need to build the application. You just need to extract it.

Look through the design goals again and determine the data requirements for each.

- Human resources needs to track employee information. The data needs here are simple.

- Accounting needs two different sets of data: customer data and accounting data.

- Marketing needs customer information and customer histories. Accounting already has both of these data sets.

- Sales needs order-entry data, customer data, and inventory data. Two of these data sets—the order-entry data and the customer data—are already documented as needs of the accounting department.

- Shipping and receiving needs order data and inventory data. Both of these data sets are already listed by other departments.

You can now summarize the data requirements for your entire application in one simple table, as shown in Table 5.1.

Table 5.1   Data Sets Required for A2Z Books

Data Set	Notes
Employee Information	Employee lists, personal information, vacation details
Customer Information	Customer details
Inventory Information	Lists of all book categories, book titles, number in stock, availability
Accounting Information	Invoicing, accounts receivable, financial reporting

There, this list is probably not as intimidating as you thought it would be. In fact, it's rather manageable. Just to make sure that you haven't missed anything, run through the goal list one more time. If you were to have these data sets in place and the tools with which to manipulate them, would you be able to meet all of the desired goals? If yes, you're ready to move on to the final step.

Data Set Details

You're almost there. You have determined the goals for the application and what data sets you need to meet these goals—and all this without thinking about databases and tables. Well, that's not exactly true. Without even realizing it, you have started defining what your database and tables should look like. The data sets listed earlier roughly equate to database tables, and the relationship among these data sets can be translated into relationships among the tables.

Before you can create the tables, however, you need to list the details that make up each data set. Don't worry about how the data is stored and what information will go into which field. They are table-creation concerns, and you're not creating tables yet. Right now, you just want to ensure that you have all the data details you need so you can complete your design documents.

 TIP With most database applications, you can add columns or fields to your database tables after they have been created. However, restrictions that limit you to the types of columns you may add often exist. Therefore, you should make every effort to include all the needed data right now, before you create the application's first table.

The details for the first data set, the one for employee information, are listed in Table 5.2. The Notes column is useful for jotting down details you don't want to forget when you create your tables.

Table 5.2   Data to Be Included in the Employee Information Table

Data	Notes
Name	First name, middle initial, last name
Address	Make sure that space is available for suite or apartment numbers
City	
State	
Zip Code	
Home Phone	Also cellular phone and pager number
Social Security	
Birth Date	
Date of Hire	
Title	
Department	
Phone Extension	
Email Address	

The details for the customer information data set are listed in Table 5.3.

Table 5.3 Data to Be Included in the Customer Information Table

Data	Notes
Name	First name, middle initial, last name
Address	Make sure that space is available for suite or apartment numbers
City	
State	
Zip Code	
Phone	
Email Address	
Customer Since	

The details for the inventory information data set are listed in Table 5.4.

Table 5.4 Data to Be Included in the Inventory Information Table

Data	Notes
Category	Also need a category list.
ISBN	
Title	
Publisher	
Publication Date	
Author	
Pages	
Description	Brief title description.
Number in Stock	
Due Date	This data provides the date more copies are due in, especially if the number in stock is 0.
Location	To help shipping locate the books, tracking where they are stored would be useful.

I'm not going to list all the sample application data sets and their details here. When you're creating your own application, however, make sure that you list every data set and all information details. ●

Part

III

Ch

5

CHAPTER 6

Database Fundamentals

by Ben Forta

In this chapter

Understanding Databases

Say that you have just been assigned a project. You must create and maintain a list of all employees in your company and their phone extensions. The list changes constantly because new employees start working for the company, others leave, and extensions and job titles change.

What do you use to maintain this list? Your first thought might be to use a word processor. You could create the list, one employee per line, and manually insert each employee's name so the list is alphabetical and usable. Your word processor provides you with sophisticated document-editing capabilities, so adding, removing, or updating employees is no more complicated than editing any other document.

Initially, you might think you have found the perfect solution—that is until someone asks you to sort the list by department and then alphabetically within each department. Now you must re-create the entire list, again sorting the names manually and inserting them in the correct sequence. You end up with two lists to maintain. You must add new employees' names to both lists and remove names of employees leaving the company from both lists as well. You also discover that correcting mistakes or simply making changes to your list has become more complicated because you have to make every change twice. Still, the list is manageable. You have only the two word-processed documents to be concerned with, and you can even open them both at the same time and make edits simultaneously.

Okay, the word processor is not the perfect solution, but it is still a manageable solution—that is, until someone else asks for the list sorted by extension. As you fire up your word processor yet again, you review the entire list-management process in your mind. New names must now be added to three lists. Likewise, any deletions must be made to all three lists. If an extension changes, then you need to change just the extension on two lists, and you need to re-sort the third as well.

And then, just as you think you have the entire process worked out, your face pales, and you freeze. What if someone else wants the list sorted by first name? And then what if yet another department needs the list sorted by job title? You panic, break out in a sweat, and tell yourself, "There must be a better way!"

Okay, so this example is a bit extreme, but the truth is that a better way really does exist. You need to use a database.

Databases: A Definition

Start with a definition. A database is simply a structured collection of similar data. The important words here are "structured" and "similar," and the employee list is a perfect example of both.

Imagine the employee list as a two-dimensional grid or table, as shown in Figure 6.1. Each horizontal row in the table contains information about a single employee. The rows are broken up by vertical columns. Each column contains a single part of the employee's record. The First Name column contains only employees' first names, and every employee's first name is listed in this column, one in each row. Similarly, the Last Name column contains only employees' last names.

FIG. 6.1

Databases view data in an imaginary two-dimensional grid.

EMPLOYEES

First Name	Last Name
Adam	Stevens
Adrienne	Green
Dan	Johnson

The employee list contains "similar" data for all employees. Every employee's record, or row, contains the same type of information. Each has a first name, last name, phone extension, department, and job title. The data is also "structured," in that the data can be broken into logical columns, or fields, that contain a single part of the employee record.

Here's the rule of thumb: Any list of information that can be broken into similar records of structured fields should probably be maintained in a database. Product prices, phone directories, invoices, invoice line items, and vacation schedules are all database candidates.

Where Are Databases Used?

You probably use databases all the time, often without even knowing it. If you use a software-based accounting program, you are using a database. All accounts payable, accounts receivable, vendor, and customer information is stored in databases. Scheduling programs use databases to store appointments and to-do lists. Even email programs use databases for directory lists and folders.

These databases are designed to be hidden from you, the end user. You never add accounts receivable invoice records into a database yourself. Rather, you enter information into your accounting program, and it adds records to the database.

Clarification of Database-Related Terms

Now that you understand what a database is, I must clarify some important database terms for you. In the SQL world (you learn about SQL in depth in Chapter 9, "SQL Data Manipulation"), this collection of data is called a table. The individual records in a table are called rows, and the fields that make up the rows are called columns. A collection of tables is called a database.

Picture a filing cabinet. The cabinet houses drawers, each of which contains groups of data. The cabinet is a means of keeping related but dissimilar information in one place. Each cabinet drawer contains a set of records. One drawer may contain employee records, whereas another drawer may contain sales records. The individual records within each drawer are different, but they all contain the same type of data, in fields.

As shown in Figure 6.2, the filing cabinet is the database—a collection of drawers or tables, containing related but dissimilar information. Each drawer contains one or more records, or rows, made up of different fields, or columns.

FIG. 6.2

Databases store information in tables, columns, and rows similarly to how records are filed in a filing cabinet.

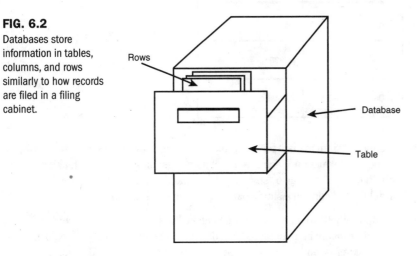

Data Types

Each row in a database table is made up of one or more columns. Each column contains a single piece of data, part of the complete record stored in the row. When a table is created, each of its columns needs to be defined. Defining columns involves specifying the column's name, size, and data type. The data type specifies what data may be stored in a column.

Data types specify the characteristics of a column and instruct the database as to what kind of data may be entered into it. Some data types allow the entry of free-form alphanumeric data. Others restrict data entry to specific data, like numbers, dates, or true or false flags. A list of common data types is shown in Table 6.1.

Table 6.1   Common Database Data Types and How They Are Used

Data Type	Restrictions	Typical Use
Character	Upper- and lowercase text, numbers, symbols	Names, addresses, descriptions
Numeric	Positive and negative numbers, decimal points	Quantities, Numbers
Date	Dates, times	Dates, times
Money	Positive and negative numbers, decimal points	Prices, billing amounts, invoice line items
Boolean	Yes and No, or True and False	On/off flags, switches
Binary	Non-text data	Pictures, sound, and video data

Most database applications provide a graphic interface to database creation, enabling you to select data types from a list. Microsoft Access uses a drop-down list box, as shown in Figure 6.3, and provides a description of each data type.

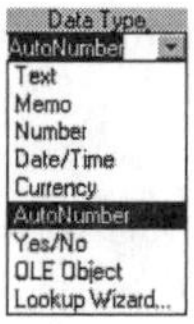

FIG. 6.3
Microsoft Access uses a drop-down list box to enable you to select data types easily.

You use data types for several reasons, in addition to entering all data into simple text fields. One of the main reasons is to control or restrict the data a user can enter into that field. A field that has to contain a person's age, for example, could be specified as a numeric field. This way, the user cannot enter characters into it—only the digits 0 through 9 would be allowed. This restriction helps ensure that no invalid data is entered into your database.

Different data types are also used to control how data is sorted. Data that is entered in a text field is sorted one character at a time, as if it were left justified. The digit 0 comes before 1, which comes before 9, which comes before a, and so on. As each character is evaluated individually, a text field containing the number *10* is listed after *1* but before *2* because *10* is greater than *1* but less than *2*, just as *a0* is greater than *a* but less than *b*. If the value being stored in this column is a person's age, correctly sorting the table by that column would be impossible. Data entered into a numeric field, however, is evaluated by looking at the complete value rather than a character at a time. So *10* is considered greater than *2* instead of less than *2*. Figure 6.4 shows you how data is sorted if numbers are entered into a text field.

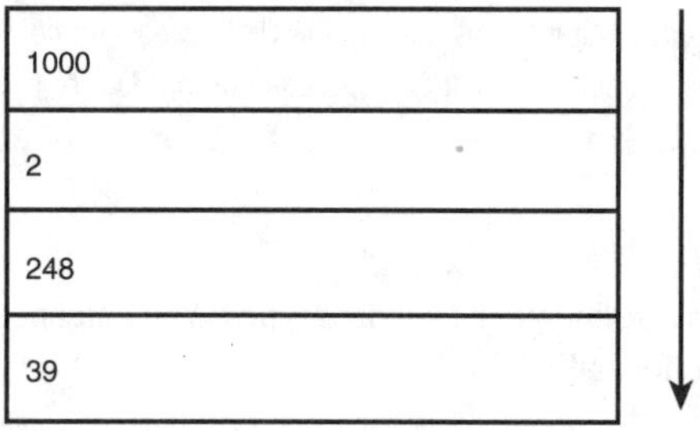

FIG. 6.4
Unless you use the correct data type, data might not be sorted the way you want.

1000
2
248
39

The same is true for date fields. Dates in text fields are evaluated one character at a time, from left to right. The date 02/05/98 is considered less than the date 10/12/97 because the first character of the date 02/05/98—the digit 0—is less than the first character of the date 10/12/97—the digit 1. If the same data is entered in a date field, the database evaluates the date as a complete entity and therefore sorts the dates correctly.

The final reason for using different data types is the storage space that plain-text fields take up. A text field that is large enough to accommodate up to 10 characters takes up 10 bytes of storage. Even if only 2 characters are entered into the field, 10 bytes are still stored. The extra

Part
III

Ch
6

space is reserved for possible future updates to that field. Some types of data can be stored more efficiently when not treated as text. For example, a 4-byte numeric field can store numeric values from 0 to over 4 billion! Saving 4 billion in a text field requires 10 bytes of storage. Similarly, a 4-byte date/time field can store the date and time with accuracy to the minute. Storing that same information in a text field would take a minimum of 14 bytes or as many as 20 bytes, depending on how the data is formatted.

N O T E Different database applications use different terms to describe the same data type. For example, Microsoft Access uses the term `text` to describe a data type that allows the entry of all alpha-numeric data. Microsoft SQL Server calls this same data type `char` and uses `text` to describe variable length text fields. After you determine the type of data you want a column to contain, refer to your database application's manuals to make sure you use the right term when making data type selections.

When you're designing a database, you should give careful consideration to data types. You usually cannot change the type of a field after the table is created. If you do have to change the type, you typically have to create a new table and write routines to convert the data from one table to the new one.

Planning the size of fields is equally important. With most databases, you cannot change the size of a field after the table is created. Getting the size right the first time, and allowing some room for growth, can save you much aggravation later.

CAUTION

When you're determining the size of data fields, always try to anticipate future growth. If you're defining a field for phone numbers, for example, realize that not all phone numbers follow the three-digit area code plus seven-digit phone number convention that is used in the USA. Paris, France, for example, has eight-digit phone numbers, and area codes in small towns in England can contain four or five digits.

Custom Data Types

With some databases, you can define your own data types. You can specify exactly what data is allowed and how it should be formatted.

Take a look at the employee list again. Suppose that you have to track your employees' social security numbers with their records. You can't use a numeric field here because you need to save the social security numbers with the dashes in their correct locations. You could create a text field that stores 11 characters—the length of a social security number with dashes —and require users to enter the data exactly as you want to save it. Doing so, however, requires that you ensure that only numbers are entered and that the dashes are in the correct places. The database does not do this validation automatically for you because, as far as it is concerned, the field is a text field and all text is allowed.

A better solution would be for you to create a data type specifically for social security numbers. Under the hood, this data type actually is an 11-character text field. But unlike a simple text field, this new data type has the dashes exactly where you want them—in positions four and seven—and allowed data would be limited to digits only.

After you define the new data type, you can use it whenever you need to store a social security number in a table. You can simply specify this as the column's data type without having to repeatedly detail the column's characteristics.

N O T E Not all database applications support custom data types, and no fixed set of rules governs those that do. Consult your database's manuals to determine whether custom data types are supported and, if so, how to use them. ■

Using a Database

Now, back to the example. At this point, you have determined that a database will make your job easier and might even help preserve your sanity. You create a table with columns for employee first name, employee last name, Social Security number, department, job title, and extension. You enter your employee list data into the table, one row at a time, and are careful to put the correct data in each column.

Next, you instruct the database application to sort the list by employee last name. In a second or less, the list is sorted, and you print it out. Impressed, you try additional sorts, by first name, and by phone extension. The results of these sorts are shown in Figures 6.5, 6.6, and 6.7.

FIG. 6.5

Data entered once into a Microsoft Access table can be sorted any way you want.

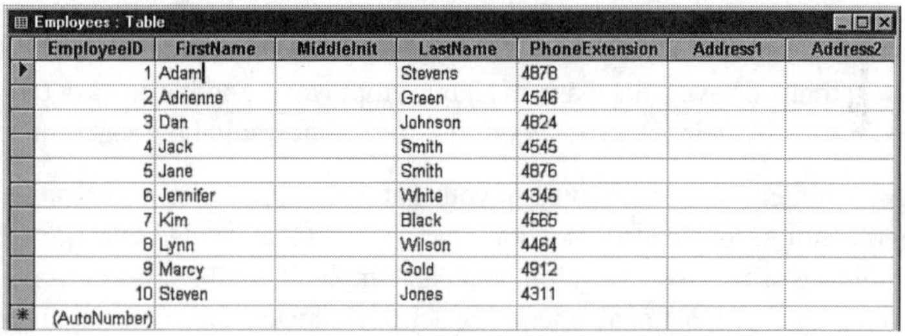

Employees : Table

EmployeeID	FirstName	MiddleInit	LastName	PhoneExtension	Address1	Address2
1	Adam		Stevens	4878		
2	Adrienne		Green	4546		
3	Dan		Johnson	4824		
4	Jack		Smith	4545		
5	Jane		Smith	4876		
6	Jennifer		White	4345		
7	Kim		Black	4565		
8	Lynn		Wilson	4464		
9	Marcy		Gold	4912		
10	Steven		Jones	4311		
* (AutoNumber)						

FIG. 6.6

Data sorted by last name.

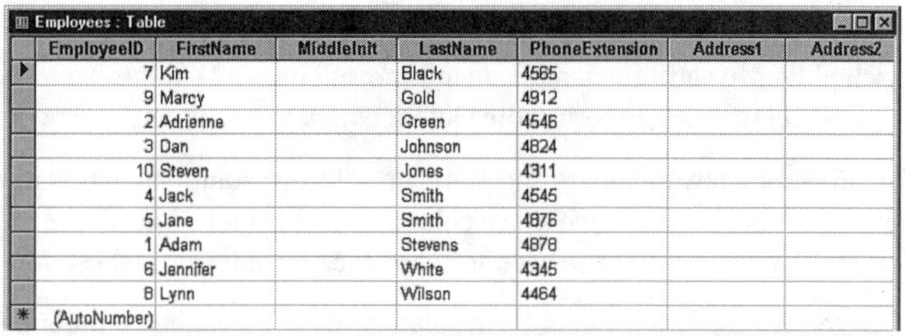

Employees : Table

EmployeeID	FirstName	MiddleInit	LastName	PhoneExtension	Address1	Address2
7	Kim		Black	4565		
9	Marcy		Gold	4912		
2	Adrienne		Green	4546		
3	Dan		Johnson	4824		
10	Steven		Jones	4311		
4	Jack		Smith	4545		
5	Jane		Smith	4876		
1	Adam		Stevens	4878		
6	Jennifer		White	4345		
8	Lynn		Wilson	4464		
* (AutoNumber)						

Part
III

Ch
6

FIG. 6.7

Data sorted by phone extension.

EmployeeID	FirstName	MiddleInit	LastName	PhoneExtension	Address1	Address2
10	Steven		Jones	4311		
6	Jennifer		White	4345		
8	Lynn		Wilson	4464		
4	Jack		Smith	4545		
2	Adrienne		Green	4546		
7	Kim		Black	4565		
3	Dan		Johnson	4624		
5	Jane		Smith	4876		
1	Adam		Stevens	4878		
9	Marcy		Gold	4912		
(AutoNumber)						

You now have two or more lists, but you had to enter the information only once, and, because you were careful to break the employee records into multiple columns, you can sort or search the list in any way needed. Whenever you add or delete employee names or make changes to employees' records, you just need to reprint the lists. The new or changed data is automatically sorted for you.

"Yes," you think to yourself, "this really is a better way."

A Database Primer

You have just seen a practical use for a database. The employee list is a simple database. It involves a single table and a small set of columns. Most well-designed database applications require many tables and ways to link them. To introduce relational databases, you'll revisit the employee list.

Your first table was a hit. You have been able to accommodate any requests for lists, sorted any way anyone could possibly need. But, just as you are beginning to wonder what you're going to do with all your newfound spare time, your human resources department has a brainstorm. "Now that we have a database of all our employees, and it's so easy to manage and maintain, could we add their vacation schedules, too? That would be a real time-saver for us."

"No problem," you say. You open your database application and modify your table. You add two new columns, one called Vacation Start Date and one called Vacation End Date. Now, when an employee schedules a vacation, you can simply fill in the dates in the appropriate columns. You even create a report of all upcoming scheduled vacations. Once again, you and your database have saved the day, and all is well.

Or so you think. Just when things are looking good, you get a call from an employee who wants to schedule two vacation dates, one in June and one in October. Your database has room for only one set of dates. Entering the October vacation dates will overwrite the June dates!

You think for a few moments and come up with two solutions to this new problem. The first solution is simply to add two more columns to your table: Vacation 2 Start Date and Vacation 2 End Date. You can enter the second set of vacation dates into these new columns.

This, you realize, is not a long-term solution at all. Inevitably, someone else will need space for three, four, or even more sets of dates. Adding all these extra columns that will not be used by most records is a tremendous waste of disk space. Furthermore, data manipulation becomes extremely complicated if data is stored in more than one column. If you need to search for who has booked vacation time on a specific date, you have to search multiple columns. This situation greatly increases the chances of getting incorrect results. It also makes sorting data impossible because databases sort data one column at a time, and you have data that must be sorted together spread over multiple columns.

NOTE An important rule in database design is that if columns are seldom used by most rows, they probably don't belong in the table. ■

Your second solution is to create additional rows when an employee wants to book another set of dates. With this solution, you can add as many sets of dates as needed without creating extra columns.

This solution, though, is not workable. Although it does indeed solve the problem of handling more than a predetermined number of vacation dates, doing so introduces a far greater problem. Adding additional rows requires repeating the basic employee information, like name and phone number fields, over and over, for each new row.

Not only does re-entering this information waste storage space, it also greatly increases the likelihood of your being faced with conflicting data. If an employee's extension changes, for example, you have to make sure to change every row that contains that employee's data. Failing to update all rows would result in queries and searches returning conflicting results. If you do a search for an employee and find two rows, both of which have different phone extensions, how do you know which is correct?

This problem is probably not overly serious if the conflicting data is phone extensions. But imagine that the problem is customer billing information. If you re-enter a customer's address with each order and then the customer moves, you could end up shipping orders to an incorrect address.

You should avoid maintaining multiple live copies of the same data whenever possible.

NOTE Another important rule in database design is that data should never be repeated unnecessarily. As you multiply the number of copies you have of the same data, the chances of data entry errors also multiply. ■

One point worth mentioning here is that the "never duplicate data" rule does not apply to backups of your data. Backing up data is incredibly important, and you can never have too many backup plans. The rule of never duplicating data applies only to live data, that is, data to be used in a production environment on an ongoing basis.

Understanding Relational Databases

The solution to your problem is to break the employee list into two separate tables. The first table, the employee list, remains just that—an employee list. To link employees to other records, you add one new column to the list, a column containing a unique identifier for each employee. It might be an employee ID, Social Security number, or just a sequential value that is incremented as each new employee name is added to the list. The important thing is that no two employees have the same ID.

TIP Generally, never reusing record-unique identifiers is a good idea. If an employee with ID number 105 leaves the company, for example, that number should never be reassigned to a new employee. This policy guarantees that there is no chance of the new employee record getting linked to data that belonged to the old employee.

Next, you create a new table with just three columns: an Employee ID column, a Vacation Start Date column, and a Vacation End Date column. As long as no employees have vacations booked, the second table, the vacation table, remains empty. When an employee books vacation dates, you add a row to the vacation table. The row contains the employee ID that uniquely identifies this specific employee and the vacation start and end dates.

The point here is that no employee information is stored in the vacation table except for the employee ID, which is the same employee ID assigned in the employee list table. So how do you know which employee the record is referring to when vacation dates are reported? The employee information is retrieved from the employee list table. When displaying rows from the vacation table, the database relates the row back to the employee list table and grabs the employee information from there. This relationship is shown in Figure 6.8.

This database design is called a *relational database*. Using a relational database, you can store data in different tables and then define links, or relationships, to find associated data stored in other tables in the database. In this example, an employee who booked vacations in both June and October would have two rows in the employee vacation table. Both of these rows contain the same employee ID, and therefore both refer back to the same employee record in the employee list table.

The process of breaking up data into multiple tables to ensure that data is never duplicated is called *normalization*.

Primary and Foreign Keys

The database term for the column or columns that contain values that uniquely identify each row is primary key. A primary key is usually a single column but need not be.

The following are the only two requirements for primary keys:

- Every row must have a value in the primary key. Empty fields, sometimes called null fields, are not allowed.

- Primary key values can never be duplicated. If two employees were to have the same ID, all relationships would fail. In fact, most database applications prevent you from entering duplicate values in primary key fields.

When your human resources department head asks for a list of all upcoming vacations sorted by employee, you can instruct the database to build the relationship and retrieve the required data. The employee list table is scanned in alphabetical order, and, as each employee is retrieved, the database application checks the employee vacation table for any rows that have an employee ID that matches the current primary key. You can even instruct the database to ignore the names of employees who have no vacation time booked at all and retrieve only those who have related rows in the employee vacation table.

N O T E Not all data types can be used as primary keys. You cannot use columns with data types for storing binary data like sounds, images, variable length records, or OLE links as primary keys. ■

The employee ID column in the employee vacation table is not a primary key. The values in that column are not unique if any employee books more than one vacation. All records of a specific employee's vacations contain the same employee's ID. The employee ID is a primary key in a different table—the employee list table. The database term for this kind of key is foreign key. A foreign key is a non-unique key whose values are contained within a primary key in another table.

To see how the foreign key is used, assume that you have been asked to run a report to see who will be out of the office during October. To do so, you instruct the database application to scan the employee vacation table for all rows that have vacation dates in October. The database application uses the value in the employee ID foreign key field in the vacation table to find the name of the employee by using the employee table's primary key. This relationship is shown in Figure 6.8.

FIG. 6.8
The foreign key values in one table are always primary key values in another table, allowing tables to be related to each other.

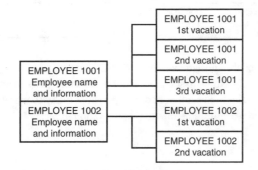

The relational database model helps overcome scalability problems. A database that can handle an ever-increasing amount of data without having to be redesigned is said to "scale well." When you're designing databases, you should always take scalability into consideration.

Now you've made a significant change to your original database, but what you've created is a manageable and scalable solution. Your human resources department is happy once again, and the employee booking two vacations at once (and who obviously has far less work to do than you) is happy, too. Once again, your database management skills save the day.

Different Kinds of Relationships

The type of relationship discussed up to this point is called a *one-to-many* relationship. This kind of relationship allows an association between a single row in one table and multiple rows in another table. In the example, a single row in the employee list table may be associated with many rows in the employee vacation table. The one-to-many relationship is the most common type of relationship in a relational database.

Two other types of relational database relationships also exist: the *one-to-one* relationship and the *many-to-many* relationship.

The one-to-one relationship allows a single row in one table to be associated with no more than one row in another table, as shown in Figure 6.9. This type of relationship is used infrequently. In practice, if you run into a situation in which a one-to-one relationship is called for, you should probably revisit the design. Most tables that are linked with one-to-one relationships can simply be combined into one large table.

FIG. 6.9
One-to-one relation-ships create links between a single row in one table and a single row in another.

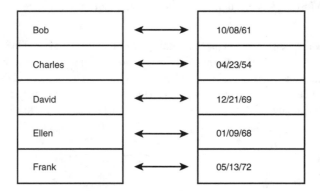

The many-to-many relationship is also used infrequently. The many-to-many relationship allows one or more rows in one table to be associated with one or more rows in another table. This kind of relationship is usually the result of bad design. Most many-to-many relationships can be more efficiently managed with multiple one-to-many relationships.

Indexes

Database applications make extensive use of a table's primary key whenever relationships are used. It is therefore vital that accessing a specific row by primary key value be a fast operation. When data is added to a table, you have no guarantee that the rows are stored in any specific order. A row with a higher primary key value could be stored before a row with a lower value. You should make no assumptions about the actual physical location of any rows within your table.

Now take another look at the relationship between the employee list table and the employee vacation table. To know who has vacation time booked in October, you have the database scan the employee vacation table, and only rows in which October is between the vacation start and end date are selected. This operation, however, returns only the employee ID—the foreign key value. To determine which employee this row is referring to, you have the database check the employee list table, and a single row is selected—the row that has this employee ID as its primary key value.

To find a specific row by primary key value, you could have the database application sequentially read through the entire table. If the first row stored is the one needed, then the sequential read would be terminated. If not, then the next row would be read and then the next, until the desired primary key value is retrieved.

This process might work for small sets of data. Sequentially scanning hundreds, or even thousands, of rows is a relatively fast operation, particularly for a fast computer with plenty of available system memory. But as the number of rows increases, so does the time it takes to find a specific row.

The problem of how to find specific data quickly in an unsorted list is not limited to databases. Suppose that you're reading a book on mammals and are looking for information on cats. You could start on the first page of the book and read everything, looking for the word cat. This approach might work if you have just a few pages to search through. But as the number of pages grows, so does the difficulty of locating specific words and the likelihood that you will make mistakes and miss references.

To solve this problem, books have indexes. The purpose of a book's index is to allow rapid access to specific words or topics spread throughout the book. Although the words or topics referred to in the index are not in any sorted order, the index itself is. Cat is guaranteed to appear in the index somewhere after bison but before cow. To find all references to cat, you would first search the index. Searching the index is a quick process because the list is sorted. You don't have to read as far as dog if the word you're looking for is cat. When you find cat in the index list, you also find the page numbers where cats are discussed.

Databases use indexes in much the same way. Database indexes serve the same purpose as book indexes—allowing rapid access to unsorted data. Just as book indexes list words or topics alphabetically to facilitate the rapid location of data, so do database table indexes list the values indexed in a sorted order. And just as book indexes list page numbers for each index listing, database table indexes list the physical location of the matching rows, as shown in Figure 6.10. After the database application knows the physical location of a specific row, it can retrieve that row without having to scan every row in the table.

FIG. 6.10

Database indexes are lists of rows and where they appear in a table.

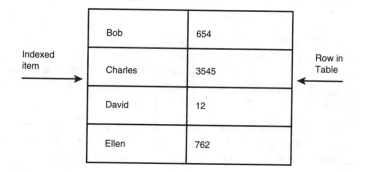

However, two important differences exist between an index at the back of a book and an index to a database table. First, an index to a database table is dynamic. This means that every time a row is added to a table, the indexes are modified automatically to reflect this change. Likewise, if a row is updated or deleted, the index is dynamically updated to reflect this change. As a result, the index is always up-to-date and always useful. Second, unlike a book index, the table index is never explicitly browsed by the end user. Instead, when the database application is instructed to retrieve data, it uses the indexes to determine how to complete the request quickly and efficiently.

The indexes are maintained by the database application and are used only by the database application. You never actually see the index in your database, and, in fact, most modern database applications hide the actual physical storage location of the indexes altogether.

When you create a primary key for a table, it is automatically indexed. The database assumes the primary key will be used constantly for lookups and relationships and therefore does you the favor of creating that first index automatically.

With the employee vacation list, when you run a report to determine who is off during October, the following process occurs. First, the database application scans the employee vacation table to find any rows that have vacation dates that fall anytime in October. This process returns the employee IDs of any employees with vacations booked for that time. Next, the database application retrieves the matching employee name for each vacation table row it has retrieved. To find the matching employee record in the employee list table, it searches the primary key index. The index contains all employee IDs in order and, for each ID, lists the physical location of the required row. After the database application finds the correct index value, it obtains a row location from the index and then directly jumps to that location in the table. Although this process may look overly involved on paper, it actually happens very quickly and in less time than any sequential search would take.

Using Indexes

Now revisit your employee database. Your company has grown dramatically, and the number of employee names in your employee table has grown, too. Lately, you've noticed that operations are taking longer than they used to. The alphabetical employee list report takes considerably longer to run, and as more names are added to the table, the performance drops even more. The database design was supposed to be a scalable solution, so why is the additional data bringing the system to its knees?

The solution here is the introduction of additional indexes. The database application automatically creates an index for the primary key. Any additional indexes have to be explicitly defined. To improve sorting and searching by last name, you just need an index on the Last Name column. With this index, the database application can instantly find the rows it is looking for without having to sequentially read through the entire table.

The maximum number of indexes a table can have varies from one database application to another. Some databases have no limit at all and allow every column to be indexed. This way, all searches or sorts can benefit from the faster response time.

> **CAUTION**
>
> Some database applications limit the number of indexes that any table can have. Before you create dozens of indexes, check to see whether you should be aware of any limitations.

Before you run off and create indexes for every column in your table, you have to realize the trade-off here. As was explained earlier, unlike an index at the end of a book, a database table index is dynamic. As data changes, so do the indexes, and updating indexes takes time. The more indexes a table has, the longer write operations will take. Furthermore, each index takes up additional storage space, so unnecessary indexes waste valuable disk space.

When should you create an index? The answer is entirely up to you. Adding indexes to a table makes read operations faster and write operations slower. You have to decide the number of indexes you create and which columns to index for each application individually. Applications that are used primarily for data entry have less need for indexes. Applications that are used heavily for searching and reporting can definitely benefit from additional indexes.

You should index your employee list table, for example, by last name, as you will often be sorting and searching by your employees' last names. You will seldom need to sort by employees' first names, so you don't have any justification for indexing the First Name column. You still can search or sort by first name if the need arises, but the search takes longer than a last name search. Likewise, the phone extension or department columns might be candidates for indexing. Whether you add indexes is up to you and your determination of how the application will be used.

With some database applications, you can create and drop indexes as needed. You may decide that, before running a batch of infrequently used reports, you want to create additional temporary indexes. They enable you to run your reports faster. After you finish running the reports, you can drop the new indexes, restoring the table to its previous state. The only downside to doing so is that, while the additional indexes are present, write operations are slower. This slowdown might or might not be a problem; again, the decision is entirely up to you.

Indexing on More than One Column

Often you might find yourself sorting data on more than one column. An example could be indexing on last name plus first name. Your employee list table can have more than one employee with the same last name. To correctly display the names, you need to sort on last name plus first name. This way Jack Smith always appears before Jane Smith, who always appears before John Smith, as shown in Figure 6.11.

FIG. 6.11

Indexing data on more than one column is an effective way to achieve the sort order you need.

UNSORTED		SORTED BY LAST NAME		SORT ON FIRST NAME		SORT ON LAST NAME PLUS FIRST NAME	
Steve	Jones	Steve	Jones	Jack	Smith	Steve	Jones
John	Smith	John	Smith	Jane	Smith	Jack	Smith
Jane	Smith	Jane	Smith	John	Smith	Jane	Smith
Jack	Smith	Jack	Smith	Steve	Jones	John	Smith

Part
III

Ch
6

Indexing on two columns, like the last name plus first name, is not the same as creating two separate indexes (one for last name and one for first name). You have not created an index for the First Name column itself. The index is of use only when you're searching or sorting the Last Name column.

As with all indexes, indexing more than one column can often be beneficial, but this benefit comes with a cost, too. Indexes that span multiple columns take longer to maintain and take up more disk space. Here, too, you should be careful only to create indexes that are needed and justifiable.

Understanding the Different Types of Database Applications

All the information described to this point applies to all databases equally. The basic fundamentals of databases, tables, keys, and indexes are supported by all database applications. At some point, however, databases start to differ. They may differ in price, performance, features, security, scalability, and more.

One decision you should make very early in the process is whether to use a *shared-file-based* database, such as Microsoft Access, or a *client/server* database application, such as Microsoft SQL Server. Each has advantages and disadvantages, and the key to determining which will work best for you is understanding the difference between shared-file-based applications and client/server systems.

Shared-File-Based Databases

Databases such as Microsoft Access and Borland dBASE are shared-file-based databases. They store their data in data files that are shared by multiple users. These data files are usually stored on network drives so they are easily accessible to all users who need them, as shown in Figure 6.12.

FIG. 6.12
The data files in a shared-file-based database are accessed by all users directly.

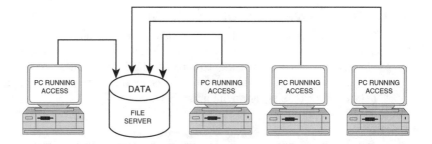

When you access data from a Microsoft Access table, for example, that data file is opened on your computer. Any data you read is read by Microsoft Access running on your computer. Likewise, any data changes are made locally by the copy of Access that is running on your computer.

Considering this point is very important when you're evaluating shared-file-based database applications. The fact that every running copy of Microsoft Access has the data files open locally has serious implications, as you can see in the following list:

- Shared data files are susceptible to data corruption. Each user accessing the tables has the data files open locally. If the user fails to terminate the application correctly, or if the computer hangs, then those files don't close gracefully. Abruptly closing data files like this can corrupt the file or cause garbage data to be written to it.

- Shared data files create a great deal of unnecessary network traffic. If you perform a search for the names of all employees who have vacation time booked in October, the search takes place on your own computer. The database application running on your computer has to make the determination as to which rows it wants and which it does not. For this determination to occur, the application has to know of all the records, including those that it will discard for this particular query. Those discarded records have to travel to your computer over a network connection. Because the data is discarded anyway, unnecessary network traffic is created.

- Shared data files are insecure. Because users have to open the actual data files they intend to work with, they must have full access to these files. This also means that users can delete, either intentionally or accidentally, the entire data file with all its tables.

I'm not saying that you should never use shared-file-based databases. The following are some compelling reasons to use this type of database:

- Shared-file-based databases are inexpensive. The software itself costs far less than client/server database software. Furthermore, unlike client/server software, shared-file-based databases do not require dedicated hardware for database servers.

- Shared-file-based databases are easier to use and easier to learn than client/server-based databases.

Client/Server-Based Databases

Databases such as Microsoft SQL Server and Oracle are client/server-based databases. Client/server applications are split into two distinct parts. The server portion is a piece of software that is responsible for all data access and manipulation. This software runs on a computer that is called the database server. In the case of Microsoft SQL Server, it is a computer running Windows NT and the SQL Server software.

Only the server software interacts with the data files. All requests for data, data additions and deletions, or data updates are funneled through the server software. These requests or changes come from computers running client software. The client is the piece of software with which the user interacts. If you request a list of employees sorted by last name, for example, the client software submits that request over the network to the server software. The server software processes the request; filters, discards, and sorts data as needed; and then sends the results back to your client software. This process is illustrated in Figure 6.13.

Part

III

Ch

6

FIG. 6.13
Client/server databases allow clients to perform database operations that are processed by the server software.

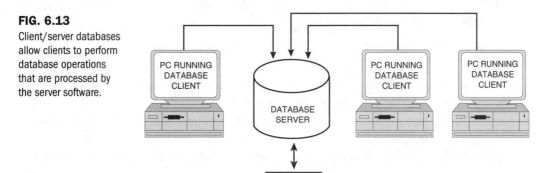

All this action happens transparently to you, the user. The fact that data is stored elsewhere or that a database server is even performing all this processing for you is hidden. You never need to access the data files directly. In fact, most networks are set up so that users have no access to the data, or even the drives on which it is stored.

In the following ways, client/server-based database servers overcome the limitations of shared-file-based database applications:

- Client/server-based data files are less susceptible to data corruption caused by incorrect application termination. If a user fails to exit a program gracefully, or if his or her computer locks up, the data files do not get damaged because the files are never actually open on that user's computer.

- Client/server-based database servers use less network bandwidth. Because all data filtering occurs on the server-side, all unneeded data is discarded before the results are sent back to the client software. Only the needed data is transmitted over the network.

- In a client/server database environment, end users need never have access to the actual physical data files. This lack of access helps ensure that the files are not deleted or tampered with.

As you can see, client/server databases are more secure and more robust than shared-file databases. But all this extra power and security comes with a price.

- Running client/server databases is expensive. The software itself is far more expensive than shared-file database applications. In addition, to run a client/server database, you need a database server. It must be a high-powered computer that is often dedicated for just this purpose.

- Client/server databases are more difficult to set up, configure, and administer. Many companies hire full-time database administrators to do this job.

Which Database Product to Use

Now that you have learned the various types of database systems you can use, how do you determine which is the right one for your application?

Well, unfortunately, this question has no simple answer. To make this decision, you really need to review your application needs, the investment you are willing to make in the system, and what systems you already have in place.

To get started, try to answer as many of the following questions as possible:

Do you have an existing database system in place? If yes, is it current technology that is still supported by the vendor? Do you need to link to data in this system, or are you embarking on a new project that can stand on its own two feet?

Do you have any database expertise or experience? If yes, with what database systems are you familiar?

Do you have database programmers or administrators in-house? If yes, with what systems are they familiar?

How many users do you anticipate will use the system concurrently?

How many records do you anticipate your tables will contain?

How important is database uptime? What is the cost associated with your database being down for any amount of time?

Do you have existing hardware that can be used for a database server?

These questions are not easy to answer, but the effort is well worth your time. The more planning you do up front, the better chance you have of making the right decision. And getting the job done right the first time will save you time, money, and aggravation later.

Of course, there is no way you can anticipate all future needs. At some point you might in fact need to switch databases. If you ever do have to migrate from one database to another, contact the database vendor to determine what migration tools are available. As long as you pick known and established solutions from reputable vendors, you should be safe. ●

Creating Databases and Tables

by Ben Forta

In this chapter

Creating Databases

The moment of truth has arrived. With your copy of the design document you created in Chapter 5, "Designing an Application," you can now create the A2Z Books database.

You can typically create databases and tables in two ways. You can use ODBC and the SQL CREATE TABLE command, or you can use the interactive tools provided with most database systems. Because ODBC and SQL are introduced in the next chapter, you'll create the databases and tables interactively using Microsoft Access.

> **N O T E** All the examples throughout this book use Microsoft Access and Access data files. To try out the examples in this chapter, you need Microsoft Access installed on your computer.

If you don't have Microsoft Access, don't worry. In the next chapter, you begin working with the same Access data files via ODBC. You don't need Microsoft Access installed to access the data files via ODBC, and, instead of creating the data files yourself, you can use the ones provided on the accompanying CD-ROM.

Two sets of data files are included on the CD-ROM. One is fully populated allowing you to proceed directly with the examples in later chapters. The other is empty, and is provided primarily for readers who do not have Microsoft Access installed. ■

Creating the A2Z Database

Each time you run Microsoft Access, you are prompted either to open an existing database or to create a new one, as shown in the dialog box in Figure 7.1. Select the Blank Database option and then click OK.

FIG. 7.1

When Microsoft Access is started, you are prompted either to open an existing database or create a new one.

You then are prompted to name your database. Microsoft Access databases have the .MDB suffix. You don't need to supply this suffix; it is provided for you. Type **A2Z** in the File Name text box and then choose Create. Microsoft Access creates the new database and then displays the Database window, as shown in Figure 7.2.

FIG. 7.2

The Microsoft Access Database window displays all objects in a database and provides tools to manage these objects.

Toolbar —

Objects tabs —

Database window —

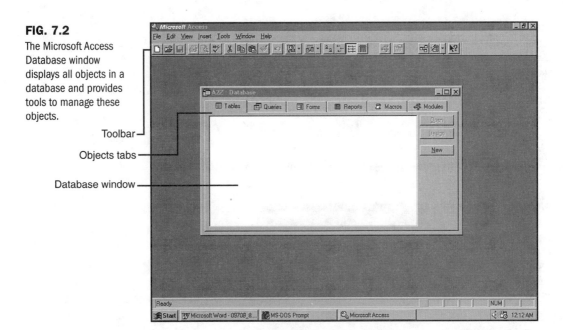

CAUTION

With some operating systems, such as Windows 95, you can create filenames with spaces in them, like A2Z Books.MDB. Although it is a legal operating system filename, it could create problems when you're accessing the database via ODBC, which you'll learn about in the next chapter. As a rule, never use spaces in database filenames.

You have now created a new empty database. The database, you might recall, does not do very much itself. It is like a filing cabinet in which you place new folders to store information.

▶ **See** "Clarification of Database-Related Terms," **p. 89**

Creating Tables

Now that you have created your database, you need to create tables to store your different data sets, as detailed in the design document you created in Chapter 6, " Database Fundamentals." To create a table, select the Tables tab in the Microsoft Access Database window (shown in Figure 7.3) and then choose New.

You are prompted to select a view or wizard to create the new table from the New Table dialog box. Figure 7.4 shows the options from which you can choose. Select Design View and click OK.

Part

III

Ch

7

FIG. 7.3

You must select the Microsoft Access Database window Tables tab to create a new table.

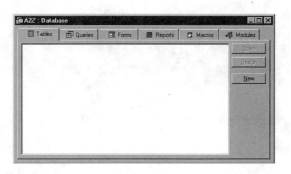

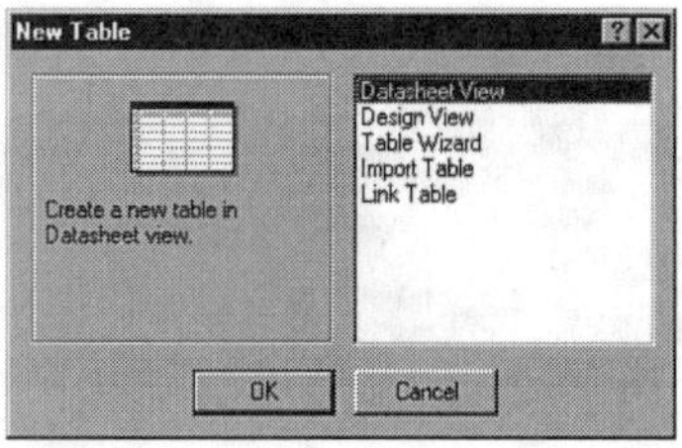

FIG. 7.4

Microsoft Access provides several views and wizards to assist you in creating tables.

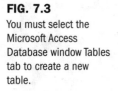

TIP The Microsoft Access Table Wizard is an automated feature for creating tables. If you select the Table Wizard option from the New Table dialog box, Microsoft Access prompts you to specify the type of data you will store in this table, and then it suggests columns that you might need.

The Table Wizard is a useful tool that you will probably use extensively when creating tables. For this present example, however, choose Design View instead so that you can learn more about the table creation process.

You then see the Microsoft Access Table Design View. The view is divided into three columns, as shown in Figure 7.5. In the first column, Field Name, you specify the name of the column. In the second column, Data Type, you select the column's data type. At the bottom of the view window is the Field Properties section, where you can specify field length, default values, index requirements, and more.

N O T E Microsoft Access also provides a third column, Description, where you can save descriptive notes about a particular column. Data you enter into this column appears on the Microsoft Access status bar each time the field is accessed. Because this column is not used when accessing the database via ODBC, you should not use it for these present examples.

CAUTION

Microsoft Access uses the term *field* to describe an SQL table column and *record* to describe a row. Be careful not to confuse these terms.

FIG. 7.5

You use the Microsoft Access Table Design View to define the columns in your table.

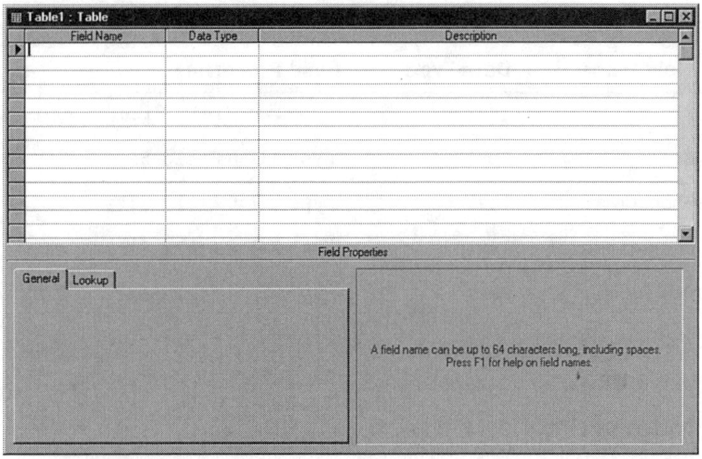

T I P Many database systems, including Microsoft Access and Microsoft SQL Server, allow table names and column names to contain spaces. Although these are valid names, some ODBC drivers have difficulty using names with spaces in them.

As a rule, never use spaces in table or column names.

Creating the Employees Tables

You now can specify all the columns that make up the first table, the employees list table. Fill in the first two columns in the database Design View with the values in the Field Name and Data Type columns in Table 7.1. Field Properties lists any properties you need to set for a specific column. For example, in the EmployeeID column, you should set the New Values option to Increment.

Table 7.1 Employees Table Columns

Field Name	Data Type	Field Properties
EmployeeID	AutoNumber	Select Increment from the drop-down list in New Values.
FirstName	Text	Type 30 in Field Size.
MiddleInit	Text	Type 1 in Field Size.
LastName	Text	Type 30 in Field Size.
Address1	Text	The default size is 50.
Address2	Text	The default size is 50.
City	Text	Type 40 in Field Size.

continues

Part
III

Ch
7

Table 7.1 Continued

Field Name	Data Type	Field Properties
State	Text	Type 5 in Field Size.
Zip	Text	Type 10 in Field Size.
PhoneHome	Text	Type 20 in Field Size.
PhoneCellular	Text	Type 20 in Field Size.
PhonePager	Text	Type 20 in Field Size.
SocialSecurity	Text	Type 11 in Field Size.
DateOfBirth	Date/Time	
DateOfHire	Date/Time	
Title	Text	Type 20 in Field Size.
DepartmentID	Number	Select Long Integer from the drop-down list in Field Size.
PhoneExtension	Text	Type 4 in Field Size.
Email	Text	Type 30 in Field Size.

Before going any further, take a look at some of the data types and properties you defined.

▶ **See** "Data Types," **p. 90**

The EmployeeID column has a data type of AutoNumber. AutoNumber is a special Microsoft Access data type that is automatically filled in each time you add a new row to your table. The value in an AutoNumber column is guaranteed to be unique for every row. By specifying Increment as the New Value option, you instruct that as each new employee is added to the table, the EmployeeID should be set to one higher than the last value used. Because the EmployeeID column is going to be used as a primary key, each employee must have an EmployeeID, and all IDs must be unique. The AutoNumber data type provides a simple way of accomplishing this task.

N O T E AutoNumber is a Microsoft Access–specific feature. Not all database systems have this feature, although many do. Those systems that do, however, might have a different name for it. With Microsoft SQL Server, for example, you can specify a column as an IDENTITY column and specify how the identity value should be generated. ■

Almost all text columns have a specified field size. The default field size in Microsoft Access is 50 characters. This number is more than is needed for name or ZIP code fields, so you can specify a size for each column that makes more sense. If you leave the field size at its default value, you waste lots of storage space.

The two date columns, date of birth and date of hire, are specified as Date/Time columns. You do so to preserve disk space, as well as to ensure correct data sorting, as explained in detail in Chapter 6.

You might wonder why you specify the DepartmentID column as a number instead of text. This is a good example of data normalization. Remember, the rule in data normalization is to never repeat data. If you were to enter the complete department name for every employee into this table, you would have many occurrences of each department name. Every salesperson would have the word Sales in the department column. So you define the department column as a number. Each department is assigned a number, a department ID, and that number is stored in the employee record. If Sales is department 4, then every salesperson has the value 4 instead of the word Sales in the DepartmentID column.

The DepartmentID column has a size of Long Integer specified. With Microsoft Access, like many database systems, you can specify the width of numeric columns. A single-byte column can store 256 values (0–255). A two-byte column can store 65,536 values. As it is unlikely that you'll have 60,000 departments in your company, a single byte is probably sufficient. However, because this column is used to relate this table to the Departments table, it must have the same data type. The Microsoft Access AutoNumber data type is always a Long Integer, so you must use a Long Integer here.

The Employees Table's Primary Key   You have now defined all the columns in your employees list table. Before you save and name the table, however, you need to specify the primary key and any additional indexes you want to use.

▶ **See** "Primary and Foreign Keys," **p. 96**

To specify that the EmployeeID column should be used as the primary key, follow these steps:

1. Select the EmployeeID column by clicking EmployeeID in the Field Name column.

2. From the Edit menu, choose Primary Key to use the selected column as the table's primary key.

Microsoft Access then displays a key symbol in the row selector to the left of the EmployeeID field name, as shown in Figure 7.6. This symbol indicates that the column is the primary key.

As you learned in Chapter 6, a primary key is automatically indexed when it is created. In Figure 7.6 you can see that the Field Properties for the EmployeeID column has been changed to show that this column is now indexed and does not allow duplicates.

The Employees Table's Indexes   Next, you can create the indexes you need to work with this table. One of the sort orders you anticipate using regularly is sorting by phone extensions, so the phone extension column is a good candidate for indexing.

▶ **See** "Indexes," **p. 98**

To create an index for a single column, follow these steps:

1. Select the desired column—in this case, PhoneExtension—by clicking its name in the Field Name column.

2. Select Yes (Duplicates OK) from the drop-down list in the Indexed field.

Part

III

Ch

7

FIG. 7.6

Microsoft Access
indicates the Primary
Key column with a key
symbol.

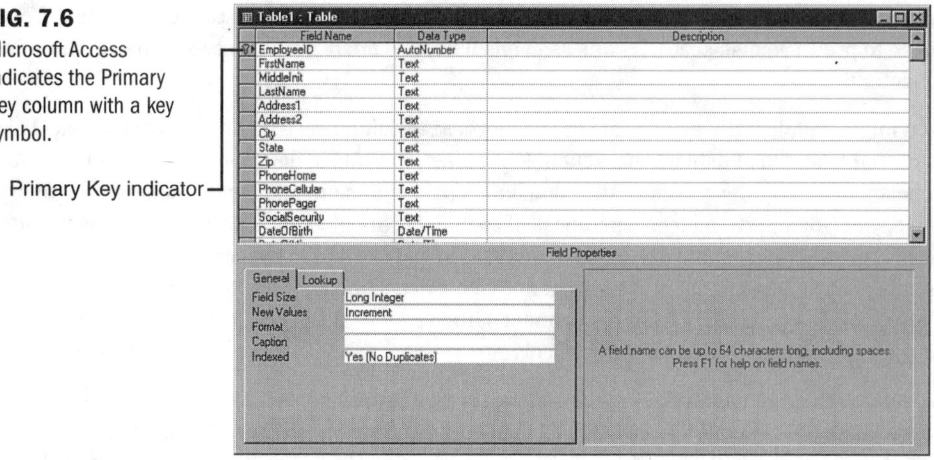

Primary Key indicator ─┘

The other frequently used sort order is last name plus first name. To create an index for multiple columns, follow these steps:

1. From the View menu, choose Indexes to open the Indexes window. Any already defined indexes are listed.

2. In the Index Name column of a new blank row, enter a name for the index you want to create. For the example, type **EmployeeName**.

3. Select the first column you want to index from the drop-down list box in the Field Name column. For the example, select the LastName column.

4. Specify any additional columns to include in the row's index directly beneath the first column of the index. Again, for this example, select FirstName in the row directly beneath LastName, and select MiddleInit in the row beneath that. Your Indexes window should now look like the one shown in Figure 7.7.

5. From the View menu, choose Indexes again to close the Indexes window. (Alternatively, you can click the Indexes window close button to close the dialog box and return to the Design window.)

The last thing left to do is to save the table. From the File menu, choose Save to do so. You are prompted for a table name. Type **Employees** in Table Name and click OK to save the table.

Congratulations, you have successfully created your first table!

The Departments Table   The Department field in the Employees table contains a single value that identifies an employee's department. Your next task then is to create the Departments table.

To create this new table, select the Tables tab in the Microsoft Access Database window, and then choose New. As before, you are prompted to select a wizard or a view. Select Design View and click OK.

The simple Departments table contains only two columns, as listed in Table 7.2. Enter the column information into the Design View window and then select the ID field as the primary key. When it is completed, your window should look like the one shown in Figure 7.8.

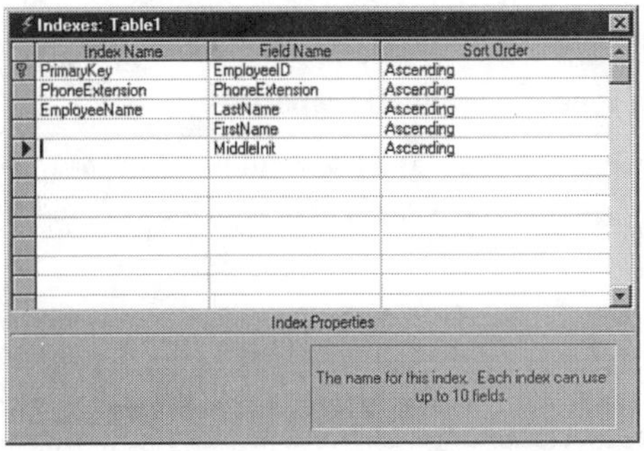

FIG. 7.7

The Microsoft Access Indexes window displays or defines table indexes.

Table 7.2   Departments Table Columns

Field Name	Data Type	Field Properties
ID	AutoNumber	Select Increment from the drop-down list in New Values.
Department	Text	Type 30 in Field Size.

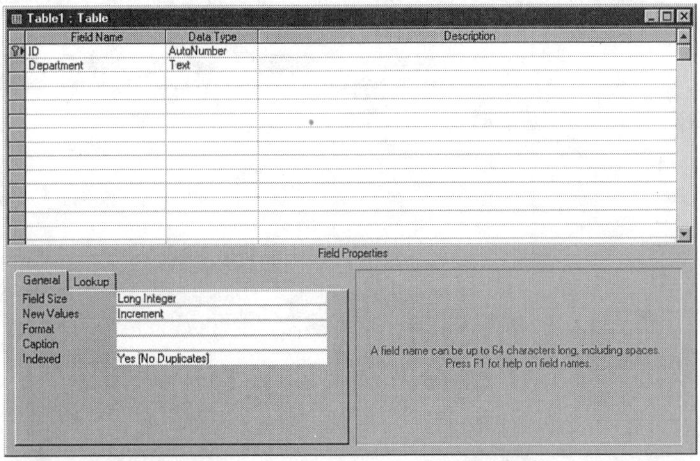

FIG. 7.8

You use the Departments table to map department IDs to department names.

Because the Departments table will never have more than 256 rows, you don't need to create an index to sort by the Description column. Microsoft Access can sort that many rows quickly without having an index, and adding an index creates additional overhead.

Now that your table design is complete, you can save the table with the name Departments.

The Vacations Table   One last table is needed to complete the employee data set as defined in Chapter 5. The Vacations table also is a simple table. Again, you create this new table using the Design View and enter the column information, as shown in Table 7.3.

Part

III

Ch

7

Table 7.3 Vacations Table Columns

Field Name	Data Type	Field Properties
EmployeeID	Number	Field Size must be Long Integer to match the EmployeeID field in the Employees table.
VacationStart	Date/Time	
VacationEnd	Date/Time	

The table does not have an incrementing field for a primary key. Instead, you'll use a combination of the EmployeeID and the VacationStart as the primary key. As no employee can ever have two vacations that start on the same day, this is a safe assumption. So, create a primary key on the EmployeeID field plus the VacationStart field. To do this, select both columns and then click the Primary Key button. The EmployeeID column must relate back to the Employees table and therefore should be indexed too. Set the EmployeeID Indexed property to Yes (Duplicates OK). You must select the Duplicates OK option; otherwise, no one can book more than one vacation. And that prospect is likely to make you very unpopular.

Next, save the table as **Vacations**, which should look like the screen shown in Figure 7.9.

FIG. 7.9
The Vacations table has no primary key.

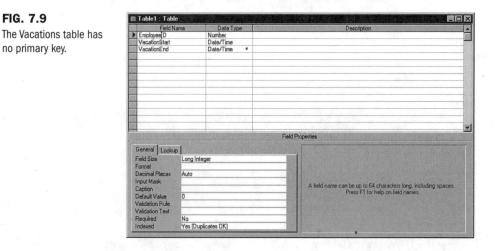

Creating the Inventory Table

The Employees table and all its supporting tables are now ready to use. Next, you need to create the Inventory table. Like the department information in the Employees table, the Inventory table uses a category ID to identify title categories. This way, you can prevent the category information from being duplicated. Create the Inventory table with the information listed in Table 7.4.

Table 7.4 Inventory Table Columns

Field Name	Data Type	Field Properties
BookID	AutoNumber	Select Increment from the drop-down list in New Values.
CategoryID	Number	Select Long Integer from the drop-down list in Field Size.
ISBN	Text	Type 13 in Field Size.
Title	Text	Type 50 in Field Size.
Publisher	Text	Type 50 in Field Size.
PublicationDate	Date/Time	
AuthorFirstName	Text	Type 30 in Field Size.
AuthorLastName	Text	Type 30 in Field Size.
Pages	Number	Select Integer from the drop-down list in Field Size.
Description	Memo	
NumberInStock	Number	Select Integer from the drop-down list in Field Size.
DueDate	Date/Time	
Location	Text	Type 80 in Field Size.

Again, every book needs a way to uniquely identify it, so you create a BookID field with a data type of AutoNumber.

The CategoryID column contains the ID number that identifies a book category. This number relates this book to its appropriate category in the Categories table.

The ISBN column has a data type of Text, even though an ISBN is mostly digits. You make the ISBN value a text field for two reasons. First, an ISBN is usually formatted with hyphens, like 0-7897-1414-0 (this book's ISBN). If you save the ISBN as a number, formatting it correctly for display would be difficult. Second, if you treat it as a real number, an ISBN that starts with 0, as this book's does, loses that 0 when the value is saved. The number 0789714140 is saved as 789714140. Obviously, you don't want this result, so sometimes you need to save numbers as text.

The Pages column is also defined as an Integer. Once again, the range of values of a byte is not enough; many books have more then 256 pages. Therefore, Integer, which can store numbers greater than 60,000, is a more realistic choice.

The Description column uses a data type you have not seen yet. Memo is a variable-length data type. This means that you do not define a field size; instead, space is allocated as needed. If you enter 3K (about 3,000 bytes) of data into the field, then 3K of space is used. If you enter 64K (about 64,000 bytes), then 64K of space is used. Memo is often used for notes that might vary dramatically in size from one row to the next.

> **CAUTION**
>
> Variable-length columns have one very important limitation. They cannot be indexed. Only columns with a fixed, known length can be indexed. If you're going to need indexed access to a column, do not use a Variable-length data type.

N O T E   Different database systems use different terms to refer to variable-length columns. Microsoft Access and Borland dBASE use the term memo, whereas Microsoft SQL Server uses the term text.

In addition, the maximum size of data you can store in a variable-length field varies from one database application to the next. Microsoft Access can store up to 64K (about 64,000 bytes) in a memo field. Microsoft SQL Server can store up to 2G (over 2 billion bytes) in a text field. ▪

The NumberInStock column is also defined as a Number with an Integer for its field size. Again, 256 might not be a large enough range of values.

Your table should now look like the one shown in Figure 7.10.

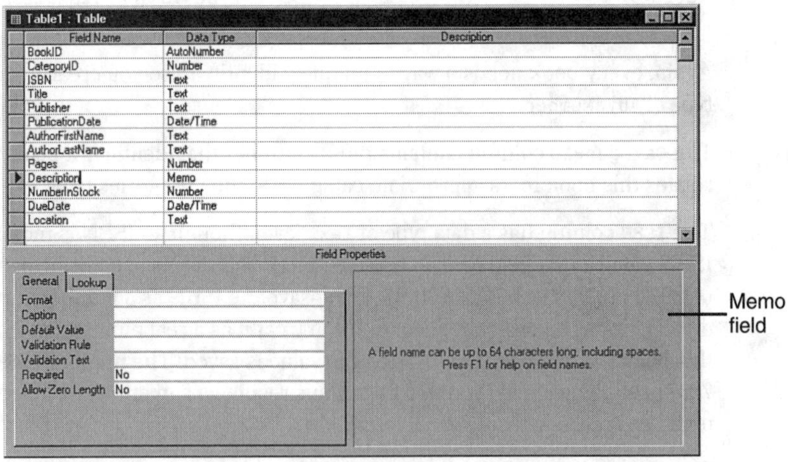

FIG. 7.10
The Inventory table uses a Memo data type to store variable-length data.

Memo field

The Inventory Table's Indexes   The Inventory table has six indexes you should now create:

Create a primary key on the BookID column.

Create a Duplicates OK index on the CategoryID column.

Create a Duplicates OK index on the ISBN column.

Create a Duplicates OK index on the Title column.

Create a Duplicates OK index on the Publisher column.

Create a Duplicates OK index called Author that indexes the AuthorLastName column plus the AuthorFirstName column.

After you define the indexes, your Indexes window should look like the one shown in Figure 7.11.

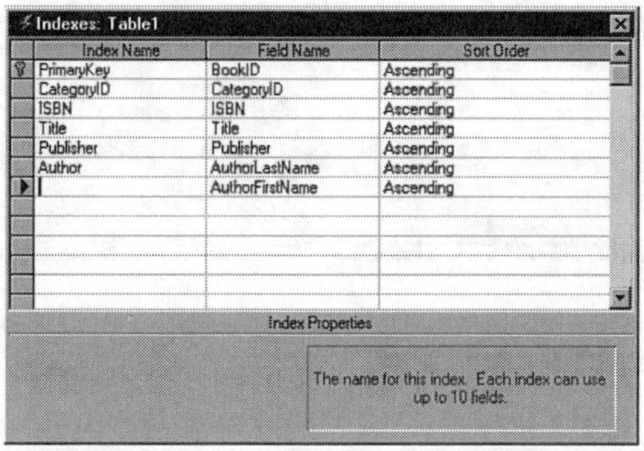

FIG. 7.11

The Inventory table uses both single-column indexes and multiple-column indexes.

Finally, save the table as Inventory.

The Category Table   The Category table stores category IDs instead of categories, just like the department IDs in the Employees table. Now create the Category table as detailed in Table 7.5.

Table 7.5   Category Table Columns

Field Name	Data Type	Field Properties
ID	AutoNumber	Select Increment from the drop-down list in New Values.
Category	Text	Type 30 in Field Size.

Next, create a primary key on the ID column. Your Table Design View window should look like the one shown in Figure 7.12.

Creating the Customer Table

The Customer table is similar to the Employees table. Create this new table using the columns listed in Table 7.6.

FIG. 7.12

You use the Category table to map category IDs into category names.

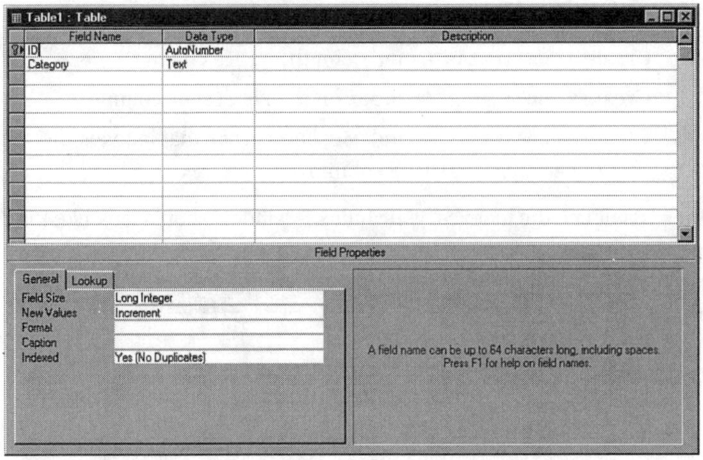

Table 7.6 Customer Table Columns

Field Name	Data Type	Field Properties
CustomerID	AutoNumber	Select Increment from the drop-down list in New Values.
Company	Text	Type 40 in Field Size.
FirstName	Text	Type 30 in Field Size.
MiddleInit	Text	Type 1 in Field Size.
LastName	Text	Type 30 in Field Size.
Address1	Text	Accept the default size of 50.
Address2	Text	Accept the default size of 50.
City	Text	Type 40 in Field Size.
State	Text	Type 5 in Field Size.
Zip	Text	Type 10 in Field Size.
Phone	Text	Type 20 in Field Size.
Email	Text	Type 30 in Field Size.
CustomerSince	Date/Time	

The Customer table will likely be searched in many different ways. And when a customer is waiting on the phone, you want rapid responses to your searches. As you learned in Chapter 6, using indexes creates some trade-offs. More indexes can improve the performance of searches and queries but can also slow down data inserts and updates, so you must make the decision of how many indexes to create for each table individually. Because of your need to respond quickly to the customer on the phone, the Customer table is a prime candidate for extra indexes.

Create the Customer table indexes listed here:

Create a primary key on the CustomerID column.

Create a Duplicates OK index on the Company column.

Create a Duplicates OK index on the Phone column.

Create a Duplicates OK index called Name that indexes the LastName column plus the FirstName column plus the MiddleInit column.

Create a Duplicates OK index called Location that indexes the City column plus State column.

With all these indexes, you and your sales people should have no trouble locating customer information. If a customer's name was misspelled, for example, your staff can search by company name, phone number, or even city and state to locate the required record.

Figure 7.13 shows what your completed Indexes window should look like. After you verify that the indexes are correct, save the table as Customers.

FIG. 7.13

The Customer table is heavily indexed to improve the performance of data retrieval.

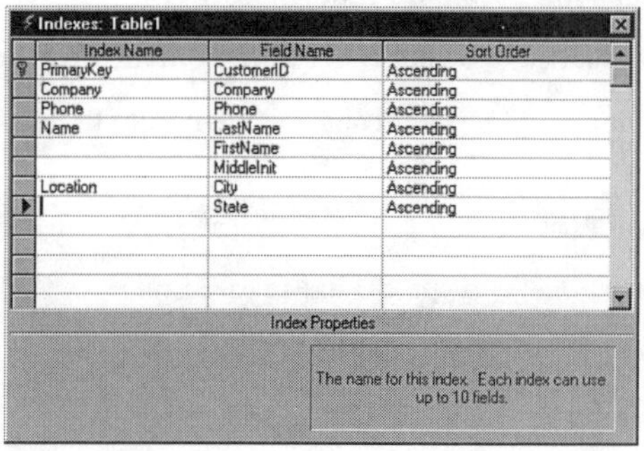

Creating the Order Tables

Order entry is a good example of a type of data that must be normalized. Some order information pertains to the entire order, and other information pertains to individual line items within the order.

To process order entry correctly, you need to create two new tables. The first, the Order table, will store information that is relevant to the entire order. The second, the OrderItems table, will list the individual line items that make up the order. Figure 7.14 shows the relationship between these two tables. As you can see, there is only one entry per order in the Order table. The related OrderItems table, however, contains multiple entries per order, one for each item ordered.

Part
III

Ch
7

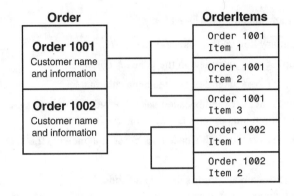

FIG. 7.14

Order entry provides a good example of how data should be normalized.

The Order Table   Create the Order table with the information shown in Table 7.7.

Table 7.7   Order Table Columns

Field Name	Data Type	Field Properties
OrderID	AutoNumber	Select Increment from the drop-down list in New Values.
CustomerID	Number	Select Long Integer from the drop-down list in Field Size.
OrderDate	Date/Time	
PurchaseOrder	Text	Type **30** in Field Size.
ShipTo	Text	Type **50** in Field Size.
ShipCompany	Text	Type **40** in Field Size.
ShipAddress1	Text	
ShipAddress2	Text	
ShipCity	Text	Type **40** in Field Size.
ShipState	Text	Type **5** in Field Size.
ShipZip	Text	Type **10** in Field Size.
ShipMethodID	Number	Select Long Integer from the drop-down list in Field Size.
ShippingCharge	Currency	
Taxable	Yes/No	

The OrderID column stores the unique order ID. You should designate this column as the primary key.

The CustomerID column stores the CustomerID value from the Customer table, linking an order to the appropriate customer. If a customer has more than one order, all those orders have the same CustomerID and are linked to the same Customer row.

ShipMethodID is another column that has been normalized. It contains the ID to relate an order with the ShippingMethod table.

ShippingCharge introduces a new data type, the Currency type. As its name implies, this data type is used to store money amounts.

> **N O T E** Almost all database systems have a currency data type, but they are not all called Currency. Microsoft SQL Server uses the term Money for a similar data type. ■

Taxable is defined as having a Yes/No data type. A column that has a Yes/No data type can accept only two values: Yes and No. This data type is useful for storing flags (a value that indicates if an option is selected or not). Whenever a column can have only one of two responses—Yes or No—then you can use this data type.

> **N O T E** Microsoft Access uses the term Yes/No to describe a data type that has only two states: Yes (On, True) and No (Off, False). Other database systems use different terms to describe this data type. Microsoft SQL Server calls this a Bit data type. ■

The Order Table's Indexes   The Order table has four indexes you should create :

> Create a primary key on the OrderID column.
>
> Create a Duplicates OK index on the CustomerID column.
>
> Create a Duplicates OK index on the OrderDate column.
>
> Create a Duplicates OK index on the ShipMethodID column.

You index the OrderDate column so orders can be sorted by order date, a sort order that you anticipate will be used often. You index the ShipMethodID column so shipping can easily find all orders that need to be shipped via the same method.

After you define the indexes, your Indexes window should look like the one shown in Figure 7.15.

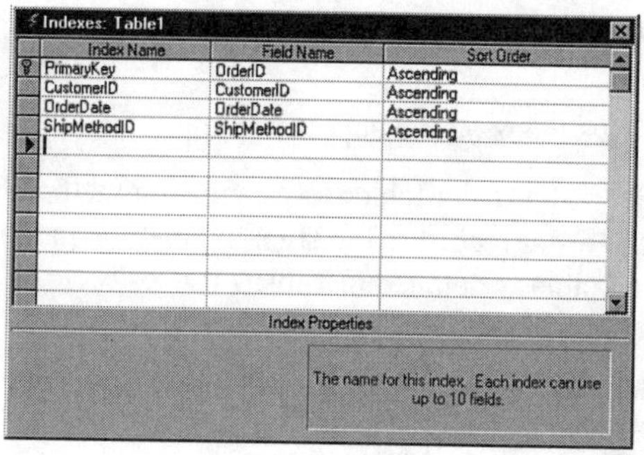

FIG. 7.15
The Order table contains IDs to relate it to three other tables.

Part
III

Ch
7

The OrderItems Table   Create the OrderItems table with the information shown in Table 7.8.

Table 7.8   OrderItems Table Columns

Field Name	Data Type	Field Properties
OrderID	Number	Select Long Integer from the drop-down list in New Values.
OrderLine	Number	Select Byte from the drop-down list in New Values.
BookID	Number	Select Long Integer from the drop-down list in New Values.
Quantity	Number	Select Integer from the drop-down list in New Values.
UnitPrice	Currency	
SalePrice	Currency	

The OrderID column must be a Long Integer because it is the data type of the OrderID in the Order table. The OrderID column in each table is what relates an order to the order items.

OrderLine is the line number within a specific order. You will not have more than 256 line items in each order (your invoices can't even print that many items on a single order), so a byte is adequate.

Create a primary key on OrderID plus OrderLine.

BookID contains the ID of the title ordered and relates back to the Inventory table you created earlier.

The OrderItems Table's Indexes   The OrderItems table has just two indexes you should create:

Create a unique index called Order that indexes the OrderID column plus the OrderLine column. To specify that this index is unique (a Duplicates No index), select Yes from the drop-down list box in the Unique field in the Index Properties area, as shown in Figure 7.16.

Create a Duplicates OK index on the BookID column.

The ShippingMethod Table   The Order table stores shipping method IDs instead of shipping details. These IDs relate the order record to the shipping method in the ShippingMethod table. Create the ShippingMethod table as detailed in Table 7.9.

Table 7.9   ShippingMethod Table Columns

Field Name	Data Type	Field Properties
ID	AutoNumber	Select Increment from the drop-down list in New Values.
ShippingMethod	Text	Type 20 in Field Size.

Create a primary key on the ID column, and save the table as ShippingMethod.

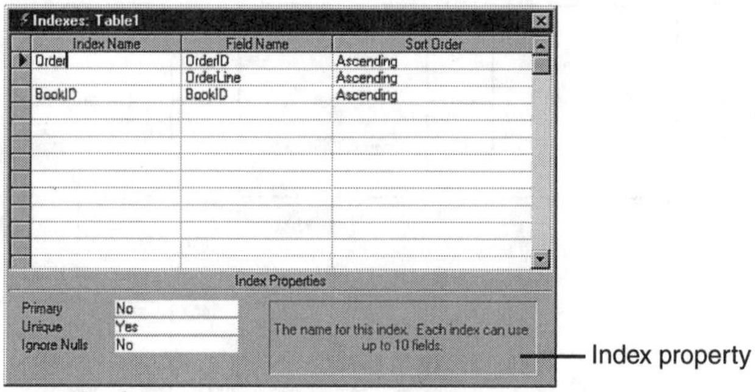

FIG. 7.16

To create a unique index that spans more than one column, you must use the Indexes window.

Index property

Understanding Table Relationships

You have now created nine tables, and almost every one of these tables is related. When an order is placed, for example, the following steps must occur:

1. Every customer must have a record in the Customer table. If it is a new customer, you have to add a new row. If it is an existing customer, you must locate the appropriate row.

2. You create a new order by adding the order information to the Order table. This process generates a new order number.

3. You select the shipping method from the ShippingMethod table, and it is stored in the order record.

4. You enter the items to be ordered. Each item is added to the OrderItems table, one row per item. The rows are related to the order by OrderID.

5. You select the titles from the Inventory table, and the BookID is stored in the OrderItems table. Multiple copies of the same title are entered only once; the Quantity column indicates the number ordered.

If this process sounds rather complex, don't worry about it. As soon as you start building an application that uses these tables, you'll find that it all makes perfect sense. In the meantime, you might find that drawing a flowchart to describe the relationships among tables is worthwhile. The flowchart in Figure 7.17 shows the relationships among some of the tables created in this chapter.

Adding Data with Microsoft Access

In the next chapter, you learn how to create SQL statements to query your tables for data. To do so, you need sample data in your tables. You can use Microsoft Access or whatever front-end application you use to create your tables to add that data.

For your immediate needs, though, you need to add data to the Employees tables. You should add two rows to the Departments table and ten rows to the Employees table.

FIG. 7.17
Almost all the tables created in this chapter are interrelated.

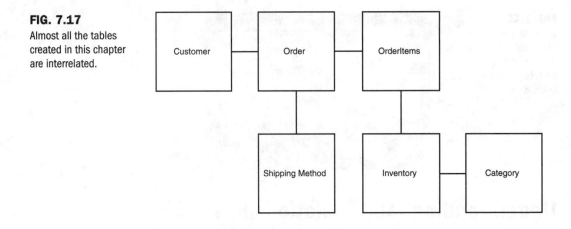

Adding Data to the Departments Table

First, if Access is not currently running, load the program. Then open the A2Z database. You are presented with a list of the available tables. Click the Departments table to select it and choose Open. The table then opens so you can add and edit data, as shown in Figure 7.18.

FIG. 7.18
Microsoft Access opens tables in a grid in which you can add or edit data.

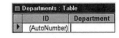

The ID column is an AutoNumber column; you don't enter a value in it because Microsoft Access does that job for you automatically.

In the Department column, type **Sales**. Sales is the first department to create, and Access assigns ID 1 to it. Now click the empty field beneath the Sales field, and type **Accounting**. Access assigns ID 2 to this record. Your completed window should look like the one shown in Figure 7.19.

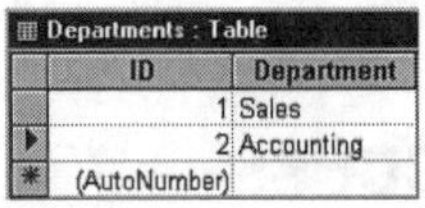

FIG. 7.19
When a table has a column of type AutoNumber, Microsoft Access assigns numbers automatically as new rows are entered.

Adding Data to the Employees Table

Now you're going to add rows to the Employees table. First, save the Departments table by clicking the Save button (the one with the picture of the disk). Then, from the File menu, choose Close to close the table.

Next, open the Employees table by selecting it and double-clicking or by clicking the Open button. You are now going to put values in all the columns. The values you need to enter are listed in Table 7.10. Enter the data for all ten rows. Note that you have to scroll the window to get to the DepartmentID and PhoneExtension columns.

Table 7.10   Sample Data for the Employees Table

FirstName	LastName	DepartmentID	PhoneExtension
Adam	Stevens	1	4878
Adrienne	Green	2	4546
Dan	Johnson	2	4824
Jack	Smith	1	4545
Jane	Smith	2	4876
Jennifer	White	1	4345
Kim	Black	1	4565
Lynn	Wilson	1	4464
Marcy	Gold	1	4912
Steven	Jones	1	4311

After you enter the data, click the Save button and close the window. You're now ready to start learning SQL. ●

Part

III

Ch

7

Introduction to SQL

by Ben Forta

In this chapter

Introducing SQL, the Structured Query Language

SQL, pronounced sequel, is an acronym for Structured Query Language. SQL is a language you use to access and manipulate data in a relational database. It is designed to be both easy to learn and extremely powerful, and its mass acceptance by so many database vendors proves that it has succeeded in both.

In 1970, Dr. E. F. Codd, the man credited with being the father of the relational database, described a universal language for data access. In 1974, engineers at IBM's San Jose Research Center created the Structured English Query Language, or SEQUEL, built on Codd's ideas. This language was incorporated into System R, IBM's pioneering relational database system.

Toward the end of the 1980s, two of the most important standards bodies, the American National Standards Institute (ANSI) and the International Standards Organization (ISO), published SQL standards, opening the door to mass acceptance. With these standards in place, SQL was poised to become the de facto standard used by every major database vendor.

Although SQL has evolved a great deal since its early SEQUEL days, the basic language concepts and its founding premises have remained the same. The beauty of SQL is its simplicity. But don't let that simplicity deceive you. SQL is a powerful language, and it encourages you to be creative in your problem solving. You can almost always find more than one way to perform a complex query or to extract desired data. Each solution has pros and cons, and no solution is explicitly right or wrong.

Before you panic at the thought of learning a new language, let me reassure you that SQL really is easy to learn. In fact, you need to learn only four statements to be able to perform almost all the data manipulation you will need on a regular basis. Table 8.1 lists these statements.

Table 8.1   SQL-Based Data Manipulation Statements

Statement	Description
SELECT	Query a table for specific data.
INSERT	Add new data to a table.
UPDATE	Update existing data in a table.
DELETE	Remove data from a table.

Each of these statements takes one or more keywords as parameters. By combining different statements and keywords, you can manipulate your data in as many different ways as you can imagine.

Cold Fusion provides you with all the tools you need to create web-based interaction to your databases. Cold Fusion itself, though, has no built-in database. Instead, it communicates with whatever database you select, passing updates and requests and returning query results.

Introducing ODBC

The communication between Cold Fusion and the database is via a database interface called Open Database Connectivity, or ODBC. ODBC is a standard Application Programming Interface (API) for accessing information from different database systems and different storage formats.

Working with Database System Differences

The purpose of ODBC is to enable you to access a diverse selection of databases and data formats without having to learn the features and peculiarities of each. ODBC provides a layer of abstraction, accomplished using database drivers, between your client application and the underlying database. The database drivers create a database-independent environment, as illustrated in Figure 8.1. This way, you can write one program and have it work with almost any major database system.

Of course, differences exist between database systems. Microsoft SQL Server, for example, requires you to log in to the database server before you are able to manipulate any data. Based on your login, you are granted or denied access to specific tables or other objects. Microsoft Access, on the other hand, has no concept of login-based security. If you have access to the data file (the MDB file), then you have full access to all data in it.

FIG. 8.1
ODBC creates a database-independent development environment.

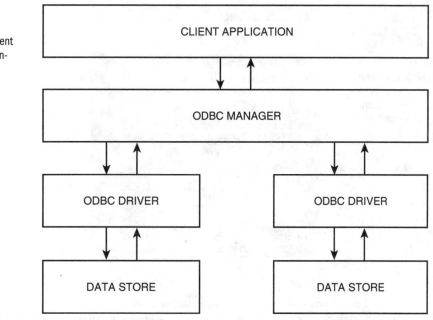

There are other differences, too. To access Microsoft SQL Server, your client application must know the address of the server. This might be an IP address or an NT Server name. To use Microsoft Access data files, you just need to know the drive and path to the data file.

Part of the job of ODBC is to hide these differences from your client application. To accomplish this, each ODBC driver has its own configuration options. When you select the SQL Server ODBC driver, you are asked for a server name, a server login name, and a password, as shown in Figure 8.2. When you select the Access ODBC driver, you are prompted for a file path, as shown in Figure 8.3.

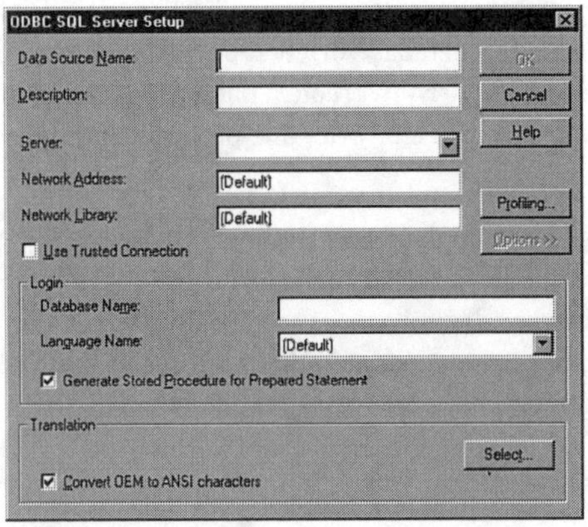

FIG. 8.2

The Microsoft SQL Server ODBC driver prompts you for login information.

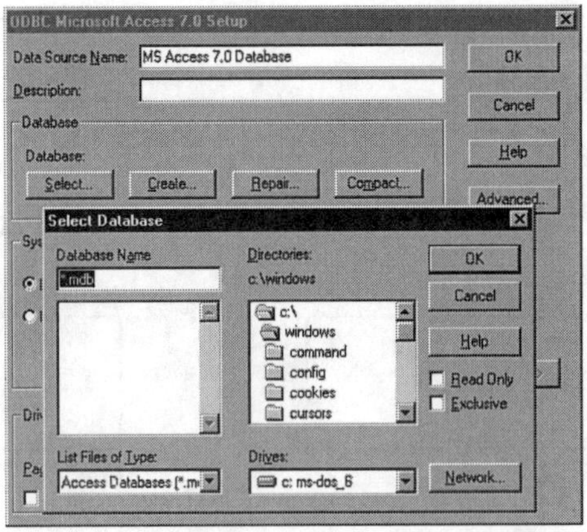

FIG. 8.3

The Microsoft Access ODBC driver prompts you for the file path to the Access data file.

This way, your client software can load any ODBC driver and connect to a database. The ODBC driver you select will handle opening the database, whether it's opening a network file or logging in to a server. All your client software knows is that it must connect to a database; the details of how this process occurs are all hidden.

THE ODBC STORY

ODBC was created in an effort to allow Microsoft Excel, Microsoft's popular spreadsheet program, to access diverse data stores.

In April 1988, Microsoft's Kyle Geiger proposed a model that used database drivers to isolate the native data types of different database applications. This model, in conjunction with a standard application interface, would allow client software to communicate with any message store. To access a particular data store, all that would be required was a driver designed specifically for that data store.

While Geiger worked on his proposal, engineers at DEC, Lotus, and Sybase were working on much the same idea. The four companies joined forces, and between 1988 and 1992 they helped shape the specification.

The original name for this project was Microsoft Data Access API. In early 1989, the effort was renamed Open SQL, and then in the summer of 1989, it was renamed again to SQL Connectivity. Finally, in the winter of 1992, the name was changed one last time to Open Database Connectivity, or ODBC.

The beta version of ODBC 1.0 was released in March 1992, and in September 1992, version 1.0 finally was released. Shortly thereafter, in October 1992, the specification was reviewed and accepted by the ANSI SQL committee.

ODBC itself is not a language; the language used by ODBC is SQL. Part of the magic of the ODBC database driver is that it understands SQL and converts it to whatever is appropriate for any specific database. This way, you can use SQL commands to work with xBASE-based databases, such as Microsoft FoxPro and Borland dBASE, even though they have an entirely different native language.

Herein lies the power of ODBC. The combination of database independence and a common standard language grants ODBC clients a tremendous level of freedom—freedom to use any database they want, freedom to use different databases for different tasks seamlessly and simultaneously, and the freedom to concentrate on application development without having to learn database-specific languages and API's.

Understanding ODBC and Cold Fusion

Cold Fusion is an ODBC client. ODBC enables you to use Cold Fusion with whatever database you choose. If you're using Microsoft Access, Cold Fusion uses the Access driver; if you're using Oracle, the Oracle ODBC driver is used instead. You can even use ODBC to read and write plain-text files. As long as you have the correct ODBC driver, Cold Fusion will support that data store.

Because Cold Fusion is an ODBC client, the database language used by Cold Fusion is SQL. To truly exploit the power of Cold Fusion, you must have a thorough understanding of SQL. Fortunately, by the end of this chapter, you should be enough of a SQL expert to start generating world-class Cold Fusion applications.

Creating an ODBC Data Source

ODBC client applications do not directly load ODBC drivers. In fact, they have no knowledge of what driver to use with any specific database. Rather, the application connects to a data source. A data source appears to your application as a virtual database. Within the data source, all the ODBC settings are configured, including specifying which ODBC driver to use.

Before your application can use an ODBC driver, you must create a data source. Doing so involves the following steps:

1. Select the ODBC driver that is appropriate for the database you plan to use. You have to install the driver if it is not already present on your computer.

2. Name your data source with a unique and descriptive name.

3. Configure the driver-specific settings via the ODBC driver's configuration options.

After you create your data source, any ODBC client application can use it to access or manipulate the database with which it is associated.

N O T E   The ODBC Control Panel applet and basic ODBC drivers are installed by many applications. If you have Microsoft Office installed, then you should have the applet and half dozen drivers installed, too. (If you do not have the drivers installed, run the Office setup again and select "Custom Install," and then select the drivers manually.)

If you need to obtain the applet, new ODBC drivers, or updated versions of existing drivers, the best place to start is the Microsoft FTP server at **ftp.microsoft.com**. ■

Configuring the ODBC Data Source Control Panel Applet

You configure ODBC data sources from within the ODBC applet in the Windows Control Panel. Try bringing up the Windows Control Panel. You should see an applet called ODBC or 32bit ODBC. Double-click the ODBC applet to open the ODBC Data Sources dialog box, as shown in Figure 8.4.

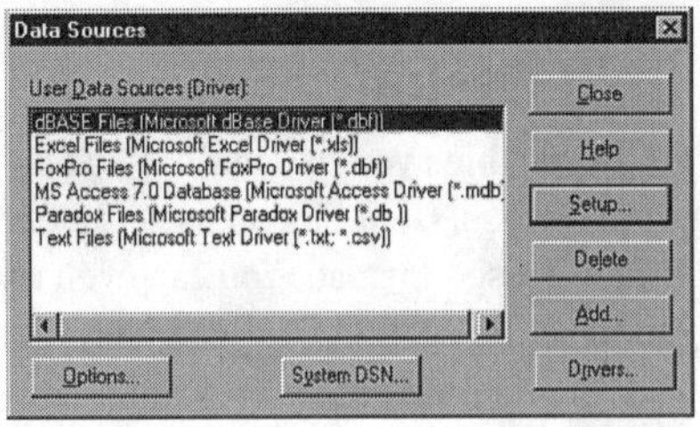

FIG. 8.4
In the ODBC Data Sources dialog box you can create and configure data sources and obtain driver version information.

The User Data Sources box shows the currently installed ODBC data sources, including generic data sources for accessing Microsoft Excel, Microsoft FoxPro, and Text Files. Double-clicking any data source opens the ODBC Setup window for the driver associated with that data source.

N O T E Different versions of the ODBC Manager and the ODBC drivers could have different user interfaces. If the dialog boxes you see on your machine look different from the ones shown here, don't worry. Cold Fusion, and all the code and examples in this book, will still run properly. ▨

Figures 8.5, 8.6, and 8.7 show the Microsoft Excel Setup window, the dBASE Setup window, and the Microsoft SQL Server Setup window, respectively. Each Setup window has a required Data Source Name field and an optional Description field. All other options are driver-specific, and, therefore, vary from one driver to the next.

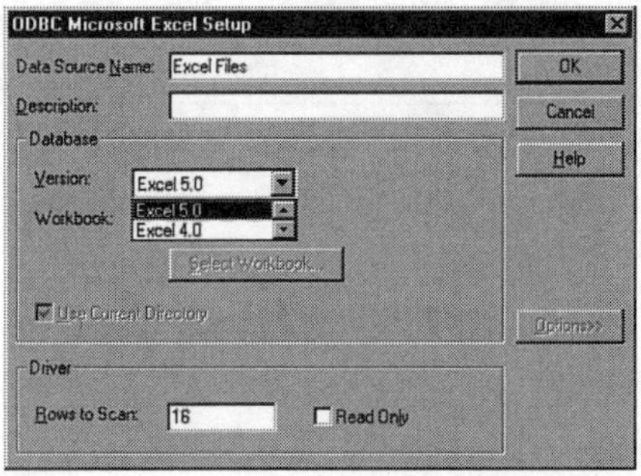

FIG. 8.5

The Microsoft Excel ODBC driver setup prompts for Excel-specific information, including the version of Excel and worksheet-related options.

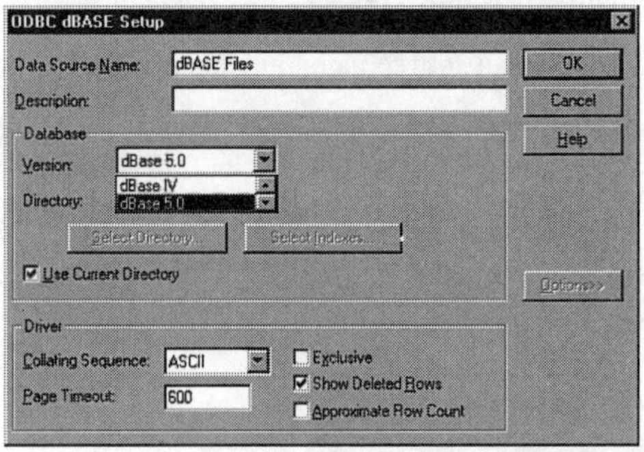

FIG. 8.6

The dBASE ODBC driver setup prompts for dBASE-specific information, including the dBASE version.

The ODBC Data Sources dialog box is also used to configure system-wide ODBC options. These options are all accessed via the buttons listed in Table 8.2.

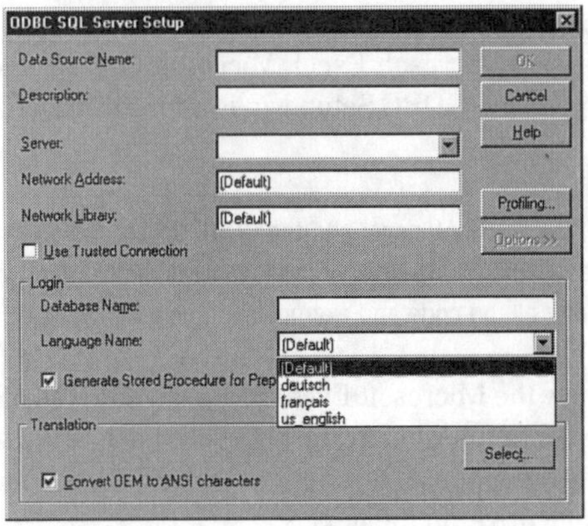

FIG. 8.7

The Microsoft SQL Server ODBC driver setup prompts for network login and address information.

Table 8.2 ODBC Data Source Buttons

Button	Description
Options...	Configure system-wide ODBC options, such as tracing.
System DSN...	Set up data sources that the system, or any user, can use, rather than the local user.
Close	Close the ODBC Data Source dialog box.
Help	Obtain help.
Setup...	Configure the selected data source, which is the same as double-clicking a data source.
Delete	Permanently remove the selected data source.
Add...	Add a new data source using an existing ODBC driver.
Drivers...	Display a list of available ODBC drivers.

Try clicking the Drivers... button now. A Drivers dialog box similar to the one shown in Figure 8.8 should appear. In this dialog box, select any driver by clicking it, and then click the About... button. An About dialog box like the one shown in Figure 8.9 should then appear.

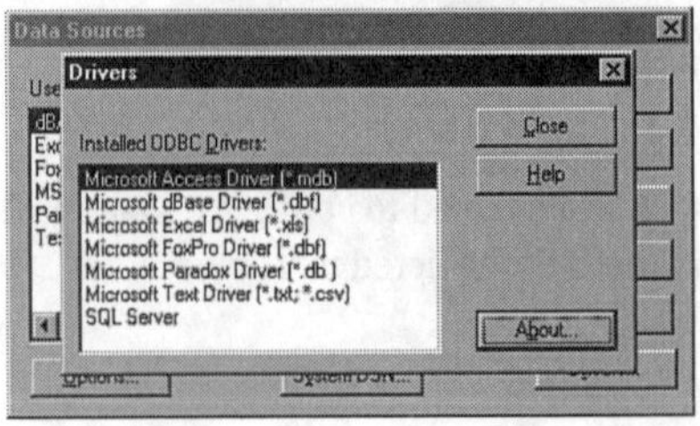

FIG. 8.8

You can check to see what ODBC drivers are installed on your system by clicking the Data Source dialog box's Drivers button.

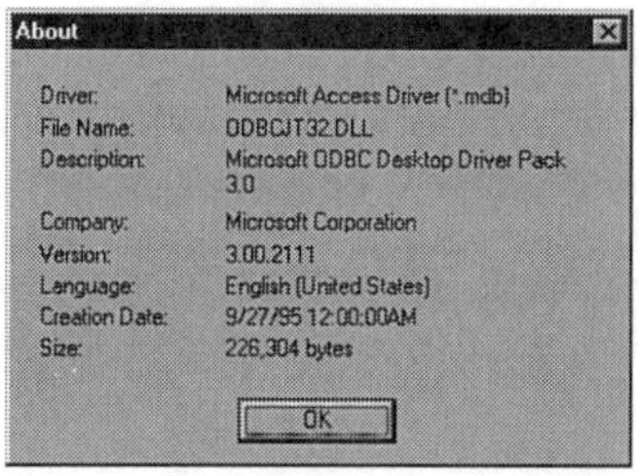

FIG. 8.9

ODBC drivers include descriptions of themselves, vendor information, the release date, and a version number.

Driver:	Microsoft Access Driver (*.mdb)
File Name:	ODBCJT32.DLL
Description:	Microsoft ODBC Desktop Driver Pack 3.0
Company:	Microsoft Corporation
Version:	3.00.2111
Language:	English (United States)
Creation Date:	9/27/95 12:00:00AM
Size:	226,304 bytes

N O T E If you look at the About information for the Access, dBASE, Excel, FoxPro, Paradox, and Text drivers, you may notice that they are all, in fact, the same driver. Microsoft supplies all these drivers as part of its ODBC Desktop Driver Pack, and they are installed automatically with the ODBC applet. ■

Creating a Data Source for the A2Z Books Database

Now that you've learned about data sources, you're ready to put all this newly acquired knowledge to use. In Chapter 7, "Creating Databases and Tables," you created a Microsoft Access database called A2Z. Now you're going to create an ODBC data source for this data file. Here are the steps:

1. Select the ODBC applet from the Windows Control Panel.
2. Click the Add... button to open the Add Data Source dialog box.
3. Select Microsoft Access Driver from the Installed ODBC Drivers list, and click OK to open the ODBC Microsoft Access Setup dialog box.
4. Name the data source by typing A2Z in the Data Source Name field.
5. Click the Select... button to locate the A2Z.MDB file.
6. Click OK to save your new data source.

That's all there is to it. The ODBC Data Sources dialog box now shows the new data source, A2Z, in the list of available User Data Sources, as shown in Figure 8.10.

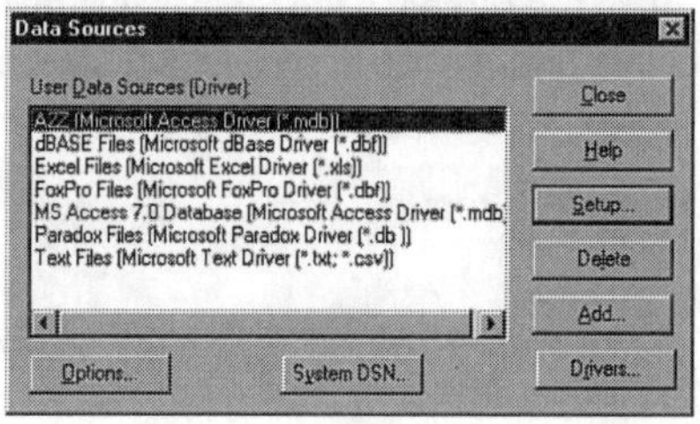

FIG. 8.10

When you add new data sources, they appear in the list of available User Data Sources.

User Data Sources (Driver):

A2Z (Microsoft Access Driver (*.mdb))
dBASE Files (Microsoft dBase Driver (*.dbf))
Excel Files (Microsoft Excel Driver (*.xls))
FoxPro Files (Microsoft FoxPro Driver (*.dbf))
MS Access 7.0 Database (Microsoft Access Driver (*.mdb))
Paradox Files (Microsoft Paradox Driver (*.db))
Text Files (Microsoft Text Driver (*.txt; *.csv))

N O T E Don't confuse ODBC data sources and ODBC drivers. ODBC drivers are dynamic link libraries, or DLLs, that communicate with a specific data store type. A data source is a complete database configuration that uses an ODBC driver to communicate with a specific database.

A data source communicates with only one database. To use an ODBC driver to communicate with two or more of the same types of databases, you need to create multiple data sources that all use the same ODBC driver. ▦

Using Microsoft Query

Now that you have a data source, all you need is a client application with which to access the data. Ultimately, the client you will use is Cold Fusion—after all, that is why you're reading this book. But to start learning SQL without having to learn Cold Fusion, you need to start with Microsoft Query.

Microsoft Query is a SQL query utility. It is a simple ODBC database front end that Microsoft supplies with many of their other applications, including Microsoft Office. With Microsoft Query, you can test ODBC connectivity, interactively build SQL statements, and view the results of SQL queries, all in an easy-to-use environment. Microsoft Query is therefore a useful development and prototyping tool, and one well worth learning.

N O T E If you set up Microsoft Office using the minimum setup, then you might not have Microsoft Query installed. If this is the case, run the Office setup program again and select Microsoft Query from the database tools option. ▦

T I P As you start developing Cold Fusion applications, you will find that most data-retrieval problems are caused by incorrect SQL statements. Microsoft Query is a useful debugging tool because it enables you to test SQL statements interactively. Using Microsoft Query is a powerful way to validate SQL queries and to isolate data-retrieval problems.

Now run Microsoft Query. When the program loads, you should see a screen similar to the one shown in Figure 8.11. Along the top of the screen is the toolbar that gives you quick access to commonly used functions. The toolbar buttons are described in Table 8.3.

Table 8.3 The Microsoft Query Toolbar

Button	Effect
	Create a new query.
	Open a saved query.
	Save the currently selected query.

Button	Effect
SQL	View or edit a query's SQL statement directly.
	Show or hide the available tables pane.
	Show or hide the selection criteria pane.
	Include additional tables in the currently selected query.
Y=	Show only records that match the value of the selection.
Σ	Cycle through totals for the currently selected column.
A↓Z	Sort the table via the currently selected column in ascending order.
Z↓A	Sort the table via the currently selected column in descending order.
!	Execute the query immediately.
(!)	Automatically execute the query as it is created and changed, and show results immediately.
▶?	Display Microsoft Query online help.

FIG. 8.11

Microsoft Query is a multiple document interface (MDI) application. Using it, you can open multiple documents, or in this case queries, at once.

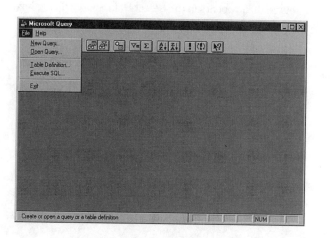

TIP The toolbar buttons in MS-Query have tool-tips assigned to them. Just hold your mouse over any button to display a pop-up title, and a description in the status bar below.

Preparing to Create Queries

You are now ready to create your first query. Click the New Query button to open the Select Data Source dialog box, as shown in Figure 8.12.

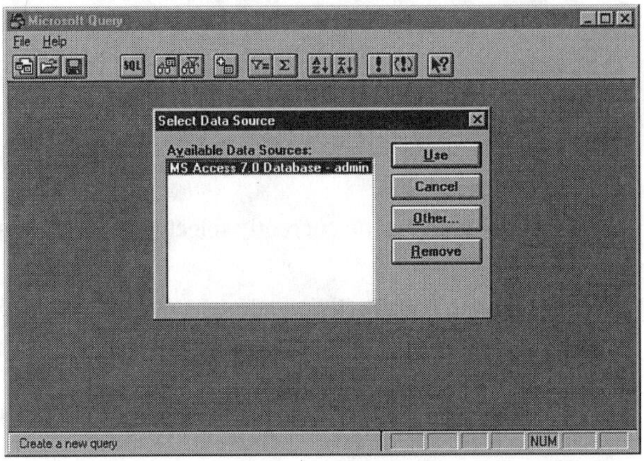

FIG. 8.12
In the Microsoft Query Select Data Source dialog box, you can select the data source for your new query.

The first time Microsoft Query uses a data source you need to add it to the Select Data Source dialog box. To do so, click the Other... button to view the currently available data sources, then select the A2Z data source you just created and click OK.

The A2Z data source then appears in the Select Data Source dialog box, as shown in Figure 8.13. At this point, select the A2Z data source and then click Use.

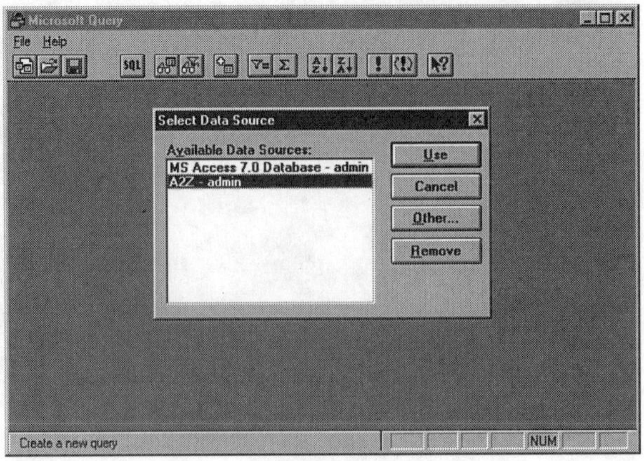

FIG. 8.13
The first time Microsoft Query uses a data source you need to add it to the Select Data Source dialog box.

Creating Queries

With all the preliminaries taken care of, you can roll up your sleeves and start writing SQL. The SQL statement that you will most use is the SELECT statement. You use SELECT, as its name implies, to select data from a table.

Most SELECT statements require at least the following two parameters:

■ What data you want to select, known as the select list. If you specify more than one item, you must separate each with a comma.

■ The table (or tables) to select the data from, specified with the FROM keyword.

When you click Use in the Select Data Source dialog box to open a data source in a new query, Microsoft Query prompts you for the tables to include in this query. This feature is useful for interactively building queries. But, because you're going to learn how to create queries by writing SQL statements yourself, don't select any tables now. Just click the Close button.

Once you have selected your data source, Microsoft Query will display the Query window, shown in Figure 8.14. The top half is used by Microsoft Query to show tables in use and to display their relationships graphically if any are defined. In the bottom half of the screen, the results of your query are displayed.

FIG. 8.14
The Microsoft Query window is split into a table pane and a data pane.

Toolbar —
Table pane —
Data pane —
Current record indicator

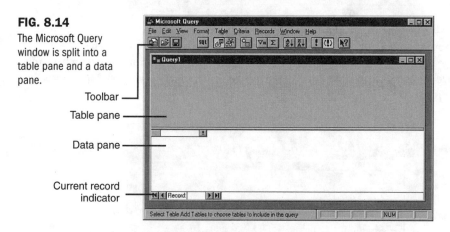

Click the View SQL button (or choose SQL... from the View menu) to open the SQL window. Here, you can view the SQL statement that produced the query results shown, and you also can create and modify SQL statements directly.

The first SQL SELECT you will create is a query for a list of employees' last names and phone extensions. Type the code in Listing 8.1 into the SQL Statement box, shown in Figure 8.15, and then click OK.

Listing 8.1 Simple *SELECT* Statement

```
SELECT
Employees.LastName,
Employees.FirstName,
Employees.PhoneExtension
FROM A2Z.Employees
```

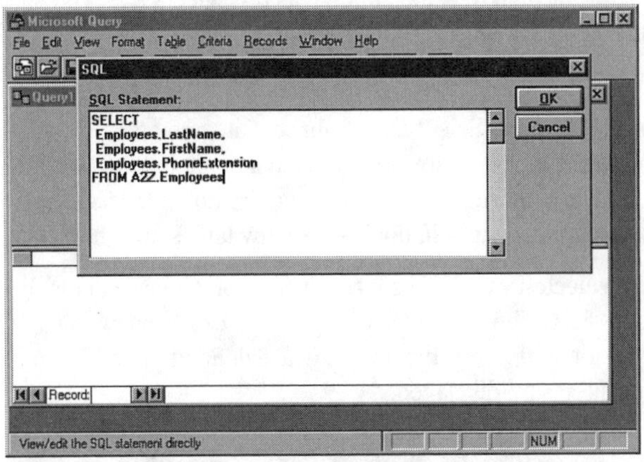

FIG. 8.15

In the SQL window, you can view generated SQL or enter SQL statements directly.

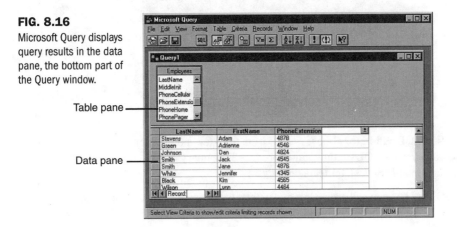

That's it! You've written your first SQL statement. Microsoft Query shows the table you are using in the top half of the screen, and the results of your query appear in the bottom half. You should have 10 records listed, the same 10 records you entered into Microsoft Access directly, shown in Figure 8.16.

FIG. 8.16

Microsoft Query displays query results in the data pane, the bottom part of the Query window.

Table pane

Data pane

N O T E You can enter SQL statements on one long line or break them up over multiple lines. All white-space characters (spaces, tabs, new-line characters) are ignored when the command is processed. If you break a statement into multiple lines and indent parameters, you make the statement easier to read and debug. ■

Before going any further, take a closer look at the SQL code you entered. The first parameter you pass to the SELECT statement is a list of the three columns you want to see. A column is specified as *table.column*, such as Employees.LastName, where Employees is the table name and LastName is the column name.

Because you want to specify three columns, you have to separate them with commas. No comma appears after the last column name, so if you have only one column in your select list, you don't need a comma.

Right after the select list, you specify the table on which you want to perform the query. You always precede the table name with the keyword FROM. The table name itself is fully qualified, meaning it is specified as *database.table*, or in this case A2Z.Employees.

N O T E SQL statements are not case-sensitive; that is, you can specify the SELECT statement as SELECT, select, Select, or however you want. Common practice, however, is to enter all SQL keywords in uppercase and parameters in lowercase or mixed case. This way, you can read the SQL code and spot typos more easily. ■

Now modify the SELECT statement so it looks like the code in Listing 8.2. Click the SQL button to make the code changes and then click OK.

Listing 8.2 *SELECT* All Columns

```
SELECT
Employees.*
FROM A2Z.Employees
```

This time, instead of specifying explicit columns to select, you use an asterisk (*). The asterisk is a special select list option that represents all columns. The data pane now shows every column in the table in the order in which they appear in the table itself.

CAUTION

Generally, you should not use an asterisk in the select list unless you really need every column. Each column you select requires its own processing, and retrieving unnecessary columns can dramatically affect retrieval times as your tables get larger.

Sorting Query Results

When you use the SELECT statement, the results are returned to you in the order in which they appear in the table. This is usually the order in which the rows were added to the table, typically not a sort order that is of much use to you. More often than not, when you retrieve data with a SELECT statement, you want to sort the query results. To sort rows, you need to add the ORDER BY clause. ORDER BY always comes after the table name; if you try to use it before, you generate a SQL error.

Now click the SQL button, and enter the SQL code shown in Listing 8.3., and then click OK.

Listing 8.3 *SELECT* with Sorted Output

```
SELECT
Employees.LastName,
Employees.FirstName,
Employees.PhoneExtension
FROM A2Z.Employees
ORDER BY PhoneExtension
```

Your output is then sorted by the PhoneExtension column, as shown in Figure 8.17.

FIG. 8.17
You use the ORDER BY clause to sort SELECT output.

Sorted by phone extension

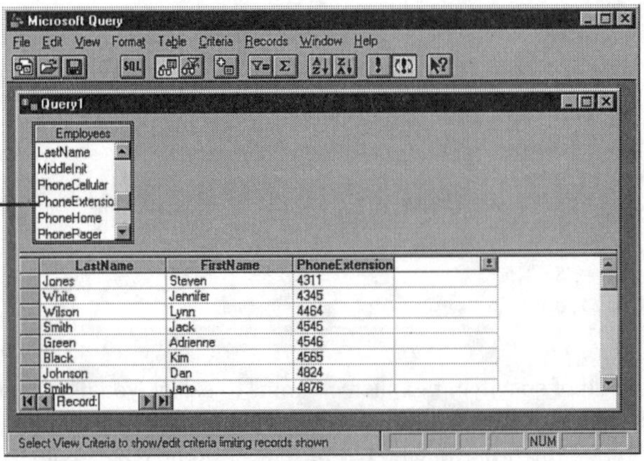

What if you need to sort by more than one column, as you did in the beginning of Chapter 7? No problem. You can pass multiple columns to the ORDER BY clause. And once again, if you have multiple columns listed, you need to separate them with a comma. The SQL code in Listing 8.4 demonstrates how to sort on more than one column by sorting the employee list by last name plus first name. The sorted output is shown in Figure 8.18.

Listing 8.4   *SELECT* with Output Sorted on More Than One Column

```
SELECT
Employees.LastName,
Employees.FirstName,
Employees.PhoneExtension
FROM A2Z.Employees
ORDER BY LastName, FirstName
```

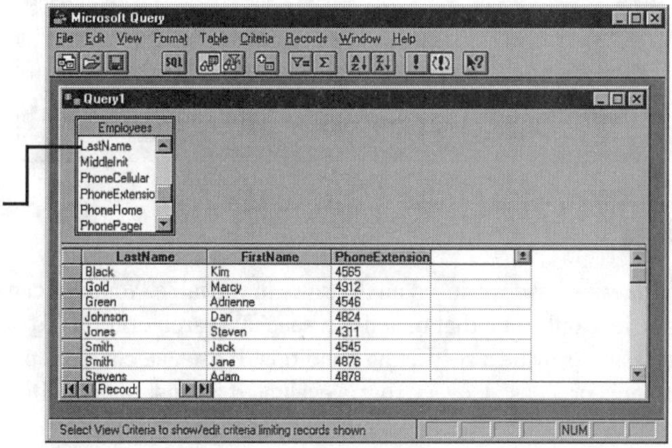

FIG. 8.18

Using the ORDER BY clause, you can sort output by more than one column.

Sorted by last name plus first name

You also can use ORDER BY to sort data in descending order (from Z to A). To sort a column in descending order, just use the DESC (short for descending) parameter. Listing 8.5 retrieves all the employee records and sorts them by extension in reverse order. Figure 8.19 shows the output that this SQL SELECT statement generates.

Listing 8.5   *SELECT* with Output Sorted in Reverse Order

```
SELECT
Employees.LastName,
Employees.FirstName,
Employees.PhoneExtension
FROM A2Z.Employees
ORDER BY PhoneExtension DESC
```

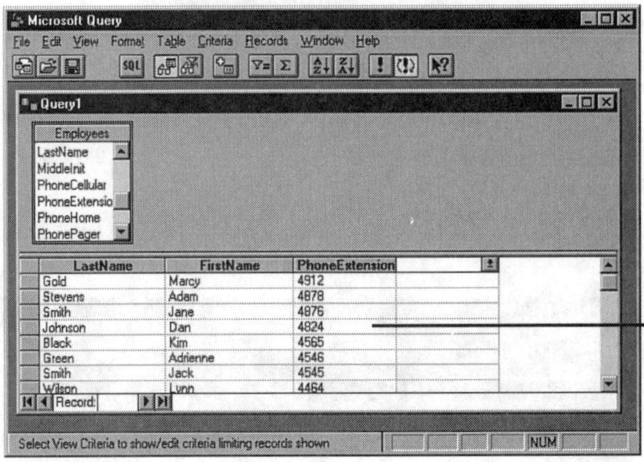

FIG. 8.19

Using the ORDER BY clause, you can sort data in a descending sort sequence.

Sorted in reverse order

Filtering Data

So far, all your queries have retrieved all the rows in the table. You also can use the SELECT statement to retrieve only data that matches a specific search criteria. To do so, you must use the WHERE clause and provide a restricting condition. If a WHERE clause is present, when the SQL SELECT statement is processed, every row is evaluated against the condition. Only rows that pass the restriction are selected.

If you use a WHERE clause, it must appear after the table name. If you use both the ORDER BY and WHERE clauses, the WHERE clause must appear after the table name but before the ORDER BY.

Filtering on a Single Column

To demonstrate filtering, modify the SELECT statement to retrieve only employees whose last name is Smith. Listing 8.6 contains the SELECT statement, and the resulting output is shown in Figure 8.20.

Listing 8.6 *SELECT* with *WHERE* Clause

```
SELECT
Employees.LastName,
Employees.FirstName,
Employees.PhoneExtension
FROM A2Z.Employees
WHERE LastName = 'Smith'
```

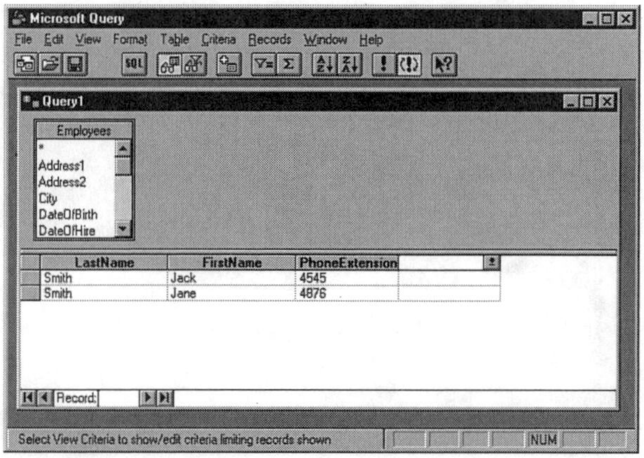

FIG. 8.20
Using the WHERE clause, you can restrict the scope of a SELECT search.

> **N O T E** Text passed to a SQL query must be enclosed within quotes. If you omit the quotes, the SQL parser will think that the text you specified was the name of a column, and you'd receive an error because that column does not exist. Pure SQL allows strings to be enclosed within single quotes ('like this') or within double quotes ("like this"). When passing text in a SQL statement to an ODBC driver, you *must* use single quotes. If you use double quotes, the ODBC parser will treat the first double quote as a statement terminator, ignoring all text after it. ■

Filtering on Multiple Columns

The WHERE clause also can take multiple conditions. To search for Jack Smith, you can specify a search condition in which the last name is Smith and the first name is Jack, as shown in Listing 8.7. As Figure 8.21 shows, only Jack Smith is retrieved.

Listing 8.7   *SELECT* with Multiple *WHERE* Clauses

```
SELECT
Employees.LastName,
Employees.FirstName,
Employees.PhoneExtension
FROM A2Z.Employees
WHERE LastName = 'Smith' AND FirstName = 'Jack'
```

The *AND* and *OR* Operators

Multiple WHERE clauses can be evaluated as AND conditions or OR conditions. The example in Listing 8.7 is an AND condition. Only rows in which both the last name is Smith and the first name is Jack will be retrieved. If you change the clause to the following, other employees with a last name of Smith are retrieved no matter what the first name is:

```
WHERE LastName = "Smith" OR FirstName = "Jack"
```

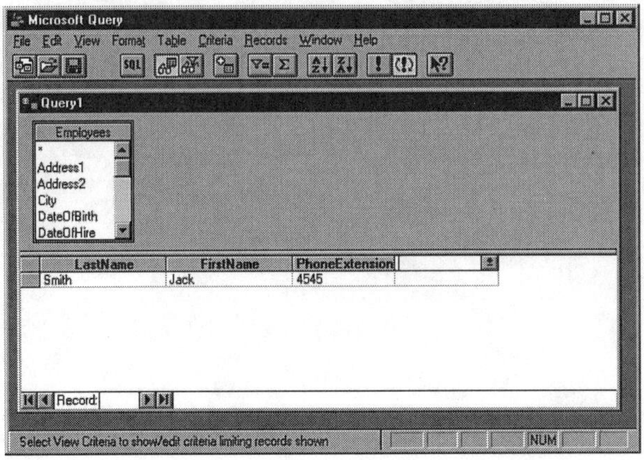

FIG. 8.21

Using multiple WHERE clauses, you can narrow down your search.

Similarly, any employee named Jack is retrieved, regardless of the last name.

You can combine the AND and OR operators to create any search condition you need. Listing 8.8 and 8.9 show two different WHERE clauses that seem to accomplish the exact same thing—specifically, retrieving only Jack Smith and Kim Black.

Listing 8.8   Combining *WHERE* Clauses with *AND* and *OR* Operators

```
SELECT
Employees.LastName,
Employees.FirstName,
Employees.PhoneExtension
FROM A2Z.Employees
WHERE (LastName = 'Smith' AND FirstName = 'Jack')
OR (LastName = 'Black' AND FirstName = 'Kim')
```

Listing 8.9   Combining *WHERE* Clauses with *AND* and *OR* Operators

```
SELECT
Employees.LastName,
Employees.FirstName,
Employees.PhoneExtension
FROM A2Z.Employees
WHERE (LastName = 'Smith' OR LastName = 'Black')
AND (FirstName = 'Jack' OR FirstName = 'Kim')
```

And while both Listings 8.8 and 8.9 would work with our limited data, Listing 8.9 is actually wrong. If there were an employee named "Kim Smith," Listing 8.8 would correctly ignore that record and not retrieve it. Listing 8.9 would retrieve it.

Evaluation Precedence

When a WHERE clause is processed, the operators are evaluated in the following order of precedence:

- Parentheses have the highest precedence.
- The AND operator has the next level of precedence.
- The OR operator has the lowest level of precedence.

What does this mean? Well, look at the WHERE clause in Listing 8.9. (Even though I just said that Listing 8.9 could retrieve invalid data, it's still a good example with which to understand evaluation precedence). The clause reads WHERE (LastName = 'Smith' OR LastName = 'Black') AND (FirstName = 'Jack' OR FirstName = 'Kim'). This clause evaluates to the following:

(LastName = 'Smith' OR LastName = 'Black'). This clause retrieves only people whose last name is Smith or Black.

AND (FirstName = 'Jack' OR FirstName = 'Kim'). Of the names retrieved, this clause keeps only those whose first name is Jack or Kim. The rest are discarded.

The results of this query are shown in Figure 8.22. As you can see, only Jack Smith and Kim Black are retrieved, which is exactly the result you want.

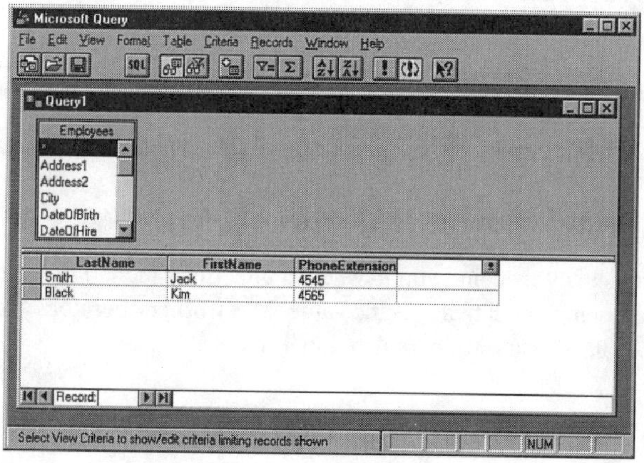

FIG. 8.22
With parentheses, you can control the precedence with which operators are evaluated.

Without the parentheses, the clause would read WHERE LastName = 'Smith' OR LastName = 'Black' AND FirstName = 'Jack' OR FirstName = 'Kim'. Because the AND operator takes precedence over the OR operator, this clause would be evaluated as follows:

WHERE LastName = 'Smith'. This clause retrieves anyone whose last name is Smith, regardless of first name.

OR LastName = 'Black' AND FirstName = 'Jack'. This clause also retrieves anyone whose last name is Black and whose first name is Jack.

OR FirstName = 'Kim'. And finally, this clause also retrieves anyone whose first name is Kim.

The results of this query are shown in Figure 8.23. As you can see, Jane Smith is also retrieved. Because no parentheses bind the Smith restriction with the Jack restriction, the Smith restriction is evaluated by itself. Jane Smith is therefore a valid match.

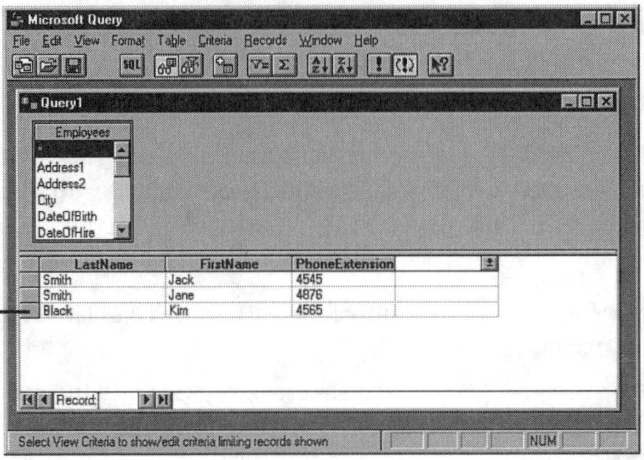

FIG. 8.23
Without parentheses, the default order of precedence is used, and the results might not be what you expect.

This row should not have been — retrieved

Obviously, this result is not what you want. To force the correct evaluation precedence for your operators, you must use parentheses. This way there is no doubt as to what you are trying to retrieve.

TIP Always using parentheses whenever you have more than one WHERE clause is good practice. They make the SQL statement easier to read and easier to debug.

WHERE Conditions

For the examples to this point, you have used only the = (equal) operator. You filtered rows based on their being equal to a specific value. Many other operators and conditions can be used with the WHERE clause; they're listed in Table 8.4.

Table 8.4 *WHERE* Clause Search Conditions

Condition	Description
=	Equal to. Tests for equality.
<>	Not equal to. Tests for nonequality.
<	Less than. Tests that the value on the left is less than the value on the right.
<=	Less than or equal to. Tests that the value on the left is less than or equal to the value on the right.
>	Greater than. Tests that the value on the left is greater than the value on the right.

Condition	Description
>=	Greater than or equal to. Tests that the value on the left is greater than or equal to the value on the right.
BETWEEN	Tests that a value is in the range between two values; the range is inclusive.
EXISTS	Tests for the existence of rows returned by a subquery.
IN	Tests to see whether a value is contained within a list of values.
IS NULL	Tests to see whether a column contains a NULL value.
IS NOT NULL	Tests to see whether a column contains a non-NULL value.
LIKE	Tests to see whether a value matches a specified pattern.
NOT	Negates any test.

= (Testing for Equality)

You use the = operator to test for value equality. The following example retrieves only employees whose last name is Smith:

```
WHERE LastName = 'Smith'
```

< > (Testing for Nonequality)

You use the < > operator to test for value nonequality. The following example retrieves only employees whose first name is not Kim:

```
WHERE FirstName < > 'Kim'
```

< (Testing for Less Than)

By using the < operator, you can test that the value on the left is less than the value on the right. The following example retrieves only employees whose last name is less than C, meaning that their last name begins with an A or a B:

```
WHERE LastName < 'C'
```

<= (Testing for Less Than or Equal To)

By using the <= operator, you can test that the value on the left is less than or equal to the value on the right. The following example retrieves only employees whose phone extension is 4500 or less:

```
WHERE PhoneExtension < '4500'
```

> (Testing for Greater Than)

You use the > operator to test that the value on the left is greater than the value on the right. The following example retrieves only employees whose phone extension is greater than 4800:

```
WHERE PhoneExtension > '4800'
```

>= (Testing for Greater Than or Equal To)

You use the <= operator to test that the value on the left is greater than or equal to the value on the right. The following example retrieves only employees whose first name begins with the letter J or higher:

```
WHERE FirstName >= 'J'
```

BETWEEN

Using the BETWEEN condition you can test whether a value falls into the range between two other values. The following example retrieves only employees whose phone extensions are between 4500 and 4600. Because the test is inclusive, extensions 4500 and 4600 are also retrieved:

```
WHERE PhoneExtension BETWEEN '4500' AND '4600'
```

The BETWEEN condition is actually nothing more than a convenient way of combining >= and <= conditions. You also could specify the preceding example as follows:

```
WHERE PhoneExtension >= '4500' AND PhoneExtension <= '4600'
```

The advantage of using the BETWEEN condition is that it makes the statement easier to read.

EXISTS

Using the EXISTS condition, you can check whether a subquery returns any rows. Subqueries are explained in Chapter 17, "Advanced SQL."

IN

You can use the IN condition to test whether a value is part of a specific set. The set of values must be surrounded by parentheses and separated by commas. The following example retrieves employees whose last names are Black, Jones, or Smith:

```
WHERE LastName IN ('Black', 'Jones', 'Smith')
```

The preceding example is actually the same as the following:

```
WHERE LastName = 'Black' OR LastName = 'Jones' OR LastName = 'Smith'
```

Using the IN condition does provide two advantages. First, it makes the statement easier to read. Second, and more important, you can use the IN condition to test whether a value is within the results of another SELECT statement.

IS NULL and *IS NOT NULL*

A NULL value is the value of a column that is empty. The IS NULL condition tests for rows that have a NULL value; that is, the rows have no value at all in the specified column. IS NOT NULL tests for rows that have a value in a specified column.

The following example retrieves all employees whose PhoneExtension is left empty:

```
WHERE PhoneExtension IS NULL
```

To retrieve only the employees who do have a phone extension, use the following example:

```
WHERE PhoneExtension IS NOT NULL
```

LIKE

Using the LIKE condition, you can test for string pattern matches using wild cards. Two wild-card types are supported. The % character means that anything from that position on is considered a match. You also can use [ ] to create a wild card for a specific character.

The following example retrieves employees whose last name begins with the letter S. To match the pattern, a last name must have an S as the first character, and anything at all after it:

```
WHERE LastName LIKE 'S%'
```

To retrieve employees with an S anywhere in their last names, you can use the following:

```
WHERE LastName LIKE '%S%'
```

You also can retrieve just employees whose last names end with S, as follows:

```
WHERE LastName LIKE '%S'
```

The LIKE condition can be negated with the NOT operator. The following example retrieves only employees whose last name does not begin with S:

```
WHERE LastName NOT LIKE 'S%'
```

Using the LIKE condition, you also can specify a wild card on a single character. If you want to find all employees named Smith but are not sure if the one you want spells his or her name Smyth, you can use the following:

```
WHERE LastName LIKE 'Sm[iy]th'
```

This example retrieves only names that start with Sm, then have an i or y, and then a final th. With this example, as long as the first two characters are Sm and the last two are th, and as long as the middle character is i or y, the name is considered a match.

 TIP Using the powerful LIKE condition, you can retrieve data in many different ways. But everything comes with a price, and the price here is performance. Generally, LIKE conditions take far longer to process than other search conditions, especially if you use wild cards at the beginning of the pattern. As a rule, use LIKE and wild cards only when absolutely necessary.

SQL Data Manipulation

by Ben Forta

In this chapter

Adding Data

All the queries you created in Chapter 8, "Introduction to SQL," were using data that you directly entered into Microsoft Access. Direct data entry is useful in prototyping and testing queries and applications.

In real world applications, however, data must often be added via an ODBC client application. If you're going to collect data via a web-browser form and then have Cold Fusion process the data, Cold Fusion will have to add data to your table.

Using the *INSERT* Statement

To add data to an ODBC table, you'll use the INSERT statement. The INSERT statement is usually made up of three parts:

■ The table in which you want to insert data, specified with the INTO keyword.

■ The column, or columns, in which you want to insert values. If you specify more than one item, each must be separated by a comma.

■ The values to insert, specified with the VALUES keyword.

When you created the Departments table in Chapter 7, "Creating Databases and Tables," you inserted two departments directly into the table using Microsoft Access. The Departments table is made up of just two columns: ID and Department. The ID column is an AutoNumber column, meaning its value is assigned automatically each time a row is added. The Department column, on the other hand, must be specified manually.

Your first task is to add two additional departments to the Departments table: Administration and Shipping & Receiving.

To do this, you'll once again use Microsoft Query, but this time you'll use the Execute SQL feature.

▶ **See** "Creating Tables," **p. 109**

▶ **See** "Using Microsoft Query," **p. 138**

Run Microsoft Query and select File, Execute SQL to display the Execute SQL window shown in Figure 9.1. You'll notice that the Data Sources option is set to <none>, so you need to select the A2Z data source.

▶ **See** "Creating a Data Source for the A2Z Books Database," **p. 137**

Click Data Sources to display the Select Data Source dialog box, shown in Figure 9.2. Select the A2Z data source and then Use. The Execute SQL window now shows the selected data source, shown in Figure 9.3.

FIG. 9.1

The Microsoft Query Execute SQL window is used to directly enter and execute any SQL statement.

FIG. 9.2

To execute a SQL statement, you must first select an ODBC data source.

FIG. 9.3

The Execute SQL window always shows you which data source has been opened.

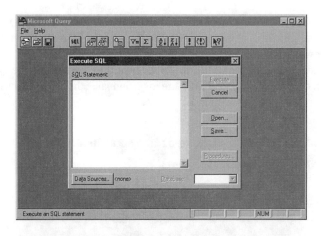

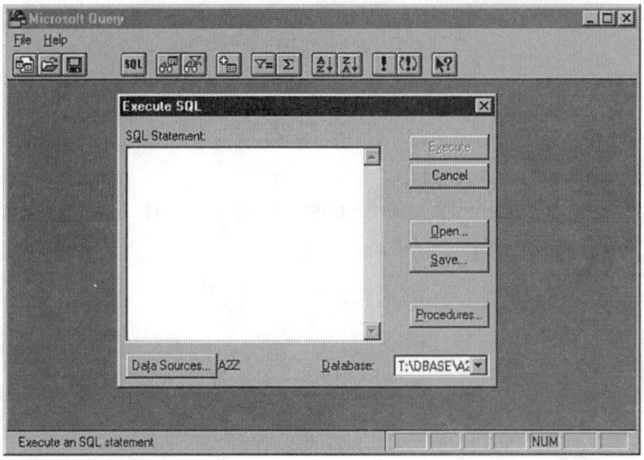

Part

III

Ch

9

Now you're ready to add the department. Listing 9.1 contains the SQL INSERT statement. Enter the statement, exactly as it appears in Listing 9.1, into the SQL Statement box in the Execute SQL Window (shown in Figure 9.4), and then select Execute. Microsoft Query submits your SQL statement to the Access ODBC driver for insertion and then notifies you that the operation was successful (see Figure 9.5). If the insertion fails, the ODBC driver will display an error message describing the reason for the failure.

Listing 9.1 SQL *INSERT* Statement to Add a Department

```
INSERT INTO Departments(Department)
VALUES('Administration')
```

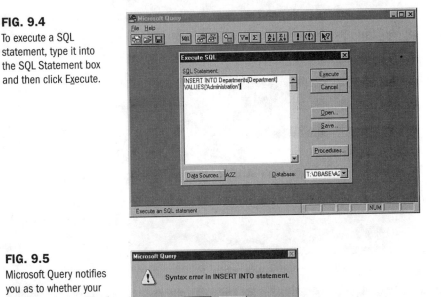

FIG. 9.4
To execute a SQL statement, type it into the SQL Statement box and then click Execute.

FIG. 9.5
Microsoft Query notifies you as to whether your SQL statement executed successfully or not.

Understanding *INSERT*

Now that you've successfully inserted a row using the SQL INSERT statement, take a minute to look at the statement syntax.

The first line of our statement reads:

```
INSERT INTO Departments(Department)
```

The text immediately following the INTO keyword is the name of the table in which the new row is to be inserted. In this case, it is the Departments table.

Next, the columns to add are specified. The columns are listed within parentheses, and if multiple columns are specified, each must be separated by a comma. The Departments table only has one column you need to provide because the ID column is automatically filled in for you. Your INSERT statement specifies only one column—the Department column that contains the department name.

N O T E When you insert a row into a table, you may provide values for as many (or as few) columns as you wish. The only restriction is that any columns that are defined as NOT NULL columns—meaning they may not be left empty—must have values specified. If you do not set a value for a NOT NULL column, the ODBC driver returns an error message and the row is not inserted. ▧

The next line reads:

```
VALUES('Administration')
```

Whenever you INSERT a row, a value must be specified for every column listed. Values are passed to the VALUES keyword, and all values are contained within parentheses, just like their column names. Here you specified a single column, so a single value is passed to the VALUES keyword.

N O T E When inserting rows into a table, columns may be specified in any order. Make sure that the order of the values in the VALUES keyword exactly matches the order of the columns after the table name. ▧

Now add the next department. Modify the SQL statement so that it looks like the one shown in Listing 9.2 and then choose Execute to perform the insertion.

Listing 9.2   SQL *INSERT* Statement to Add a Department

```
INSERT INTO Departments(Department)
VALUES('Shipping & Receiving')
```

You now have four departments in the Departments table. To verify this, use Microsoft Query to select all the rows in the Departments table.

Enter the following SELECT statement in the Execute SQL window, and select Execute.

```
SELECT * FROM Departments
```

As explained in Chapter 8, "Introduction to SQL," the SELECT * means select all columns. As you can see in Figure 9.6, the two new departments were correctly added and Microsoft Access automatically assigned new ID numbers to them.

FIG. 9.6

You can use Microsoft Query to execute SQL statements and verify the results of those statements.

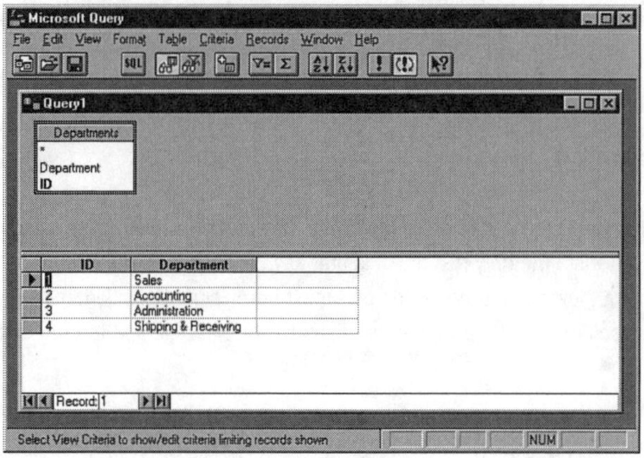

Inserting and Setting Values for Multiple Columns

You've now seen and used the INSERT statement to add a row and specify a value for one column. Setting values for multiple columns is just as simple.

One of your employees, Kim Black, has booked a vacation for two weeks in the summer. You'll need to add that information to the Vacations table. The Vacations table has three columns: the first is the employee ID, which uniquely identifies each employee, and the next two are the vacation start and end dates.

Kim's employee ID is 7, so you enter the SQL statement in Listing 9.3 into the Microsoft Query Execute SQL window, shown in Figure 9.7, and then select Execute. You should receive a confirmation message telling you that the operation was successful and that the row was inserted.

Listing 9.3 Adding a Vacation Record Requires That Three Columns Be Specified

```
INSERT INTO Vacations(EmployeeId, VacationStart, VacationEnd)
VALUES(7, 'Aug 1 1997', 'Aug 15 1997')
```

TIP The exact format of the ODBC date time data type is a little tricky to remember, so most ODBC drivers allow you to specify dates and times as simple strings that they interpret. The parser is not perfect, however, because 'Aug 1st 1997', for example, fails with many ODBC drivers. On the other hand, 'Aug 1 1997' is usually supported. There are no hard and fast rules governing what is and what is not supported, so to minimize incompatibilities, remember to keep the strings as simple as possible.

Verify that the row was correctly added. Use Microsoft Query to select all rows and columns in the Vacations table. Your output should look like the one shown in Figure 9.8.

FIG. 9.7
When multiple columns are passed to SQL INSERT, each must be separated by a comma.

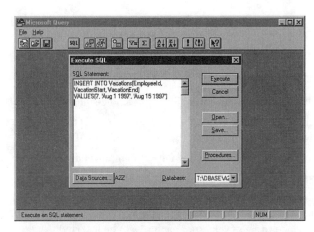

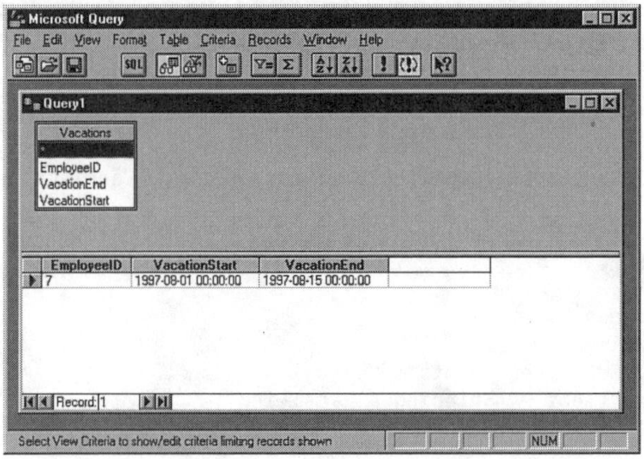

FIG. 9.8
Microsoft Query displays columns in their native format without any special output formatting.

The row is there, but look at the date columns. They contain both a date and a time. The time is 0:00:00 because no time was specified. Why is there a time here at all? The Microsoft Access date/time data type is a date and time data type. If you use just one part of the data type, the other is set to 0. This is perfectly valid and is an acceptable practice.

Adding Multiple Rows

All the INSERT statements you have used so far add single rows to a table. When you need to add multiple rows, you can use an INSERT statement to add them in a single executed statement.

The INSERT statement cannot specify multiple VALUES keywords. To add multiple rows, you must create a SELECT statement that retrieves the values to be inserted and then pass that SELECT statement to the INSERT statement instead of the VALUES keyword.

Don't panic, this is not as confusing as it sounds. To clarify how you could use this functionality, look at an example.

The shipping and receiving department manager has just notified you that his entire department is taking the first week of February off, so you need to add a vacation record to the Vacations table for each employee in that department.

You could do this all manually. The steps would look something like this:

1. Find the department ID for the Shipping & Receiving department.
2. Search for all employees that have a department ID that matches the Shipping & Receiving department ID to retrieve the employee IDs.
3. Add a row to the Vacations table for each employee ID to set the vacation dates.

Although this manual process will work, it is both time-consuming and highly error-prone. A better solution would be to perform the entire operation in one step. To do this, you need to create an INSERT statement that inserts values retrieved by a SELECT statement. The SELECT statement produces a set of values for each row to be inserted.

To try this, enter the SQL statement in Listing 9.4 into the Execute SQL window, shown in Figure 9.9, and Execute the operation.

Listing 9.4   *SELECT* Statement Using *INSERT*

```
INSERT INTO Vacations(EmployeeID, VacationStart, VacationEnd)
SELECT
EmployeeID,
'Feb 1 1997',
'Feb 7 1997'
FROM Employees
WHERE DepartmentID =
(SELECT id FROM Departments
 WHERE Department = 'Shipping & Receiving')
```

FIG. 9.9

A SELECT statement can be passed to an INSERT statement to insert multiple rows in one operation.

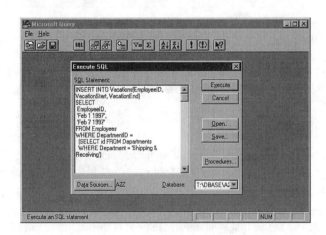

You are not going to cover all the details that make up Listing 9.4 right now. Nested queries (SELECT statements within SELECT statements) are discussed later in Chapter 17, "Advanced SQL." A couple of points are worth noting, though.

As with all INSERT statements, you started by specifying the destination table and the columns that are to be populated. The code INSERT INTO Vacations(EmployeeID, VacationStart, VacationEnd) instructs the ODBC driver that three columns in the Vacations table will be populated with each row added.

Part III

Ch 9

Unlike all of your INSERT statements until now, the INSERT statement in Listing 9.4 does not have a VALUES keyword. Instead, there is a SELECT statement that returns three columns that correspond to the three columns specified after the destination table, as shown in the following code line.

```
SELECT EmployeeID, 'Feb 1 1997', 'Feb 7 1997'
```

The first value returned by the SELECT statement is the EmployeeID that is retrieved from the Employees table. The second and third values are static dates, so the same value returns with every row that was retrieved.

If you SELECT the Vacations table, you'll see that three rows were inserted by this operation with the execution of one SQL statement.

Modifying Data

To update one or more columns, you'll use the SQL UPDATE statement. This usually involves specifying the following:

- The table containing the data you want to update.
- The column or columns you want to update, preceded by the SET keyword. If you specify more than one item, each must be separated by a comma.
- An optional WHERE clause to specify which rows to update. If no WHERE clause is provided, all rows are updated.

Try updating a row. Open the Microsoft Query Execute SQL window and enter the SQL statement shown in Listing 9.5. Your code should look like the example shown in Figure 9.10. Then select Execute to perform the update. Microsoft Query displays a confirmation dialog indicating that the operation completed successfully.

If you now SELECT the contents of the Employees table, you'd see that Kim Black has the title Senior Account Rep.

Listing 9.5 The SQL *UPDATE* Statement Is Used to Update One or More Rows in a Table

```
UPDATE Employees
SET Title='Senior Account Rep'
WHERE EmployeeID = 7
```

Understanding *UPDATE*

Now take a closer look at the SQL statement in Listing 9.5. The first line issued the UPDATE statement and specified the name of the table to update. As with the INSERT and DELETE statements, the table name is required.

Next you specified the column you wanted to change and its new value. The code

```
SET Title='Senior Account Rep'
```

is an instruction to update the Title column with the text 'Senior Account Rep'. The SET keyword is required for an UPDATE operation because it would make little sense to update rows without specifying what to update.

FIG. 9.10
The SQL UPDATE statement is usually used with a WHERE clause.

The SET keyword can only be used once in an UPDATE statement. If you are updating multiple rows, for example, to change "Kim" to "Kimberly" and to set her title to "Senior Account Rep" in one operation, the SET keyword would look like this:

```
SET FirstName='Kimberly', Title='Senior Account Rep'
```

When updating multiple columns, each column must be separated by a comma.

The last line of Listing 9.5 specified a WHERE clause. The WHERE clause is optional in an UPDATE statement. Without it, all rows will be updated. The code

```
WHERE EmployeeID = 7
```

uses the primary key column to ensure that only a single row gets updated.

▶ **See** "Primary and Foreign Keys," **p. 96**

CAUTION
When using the SQL UPDATE statement, be careful to provide a WHERE clause, or all rows will be updated.

Making Global Updates

Occasionally, you will want to update all rows in a table.

For example, in the A2Z Books Employees table, none of the employees have their email address listed. You could update every employee one at a time, but there is a better way. A2Z Books instituted a standard for email addresses to make them easier to remember. All email addresses are made up of the first letter of the first name plus the entire last name. And, of course, all email addresses are @a2zbooks.com.

To perform this update easily, you could update the Email column with a calculated column, a value that is dynamically built for each employee. Look at the code below:

```
LEFT(FirstName, 1)+LastName+'@a2zbooks.com'
```

This is a SQL statement that builds a value based on several other values. The first portion, LEFT(FirstName, 1), extracts the first character from the FirstName column. LEFT() is a function that returns requested left-most characters of a string. LEFT(FirstName, 1) means extract the first character of the FirstName value. LEFT(FirstName, 5) would extract the first five characters of the FirstName value.

Next, you concatenate the entire LastName value and the string @a2zbooks.com to the first character of the FirstName column. Strings are concatenated (added together to make a longer string) with the + operator.

With this statement, you can generate email addresses for every employee in the Employees table. Before you update the table, however, it's a good idea to test the statement. The best way to test this statement, and indeed every SQL statement, is to use it in a SELECT statement first.

To test the statement LEFT(FirstName,1)+LastName+'@a2zbooks.com', enter the code in Listing 9.6 into the Execute SQL window, shown in Figure 9.11. Then select the Execute button to display the statement results.

Listing 9.6 Testing SQL Statements with a *SELECT* Statement

```
SELECT
LEFT(FirstName, 1)+LastName+'@a2zbooks.com'
FROM Employees
```

As shown in Figure 9.12, Microsoft Query displays the calculated column, which contains the correct email address for every employee. As the column has no name, the statement used to build it is shown as the column title instead.

You now know that the statement works correctly and that the calculated value it creates is exactly what you wanted. Now update all the rows in the Employees table. Enter the SQL UPDATE statement shown in Listing 9.7 (see Figure 9.13). Select Execute to update the entire table, and Microsoft Query will display a success notification.

FIG. 9.11

The Microsoft Query Execute SQL window can be used to test SQL statements and WHERE clauses.

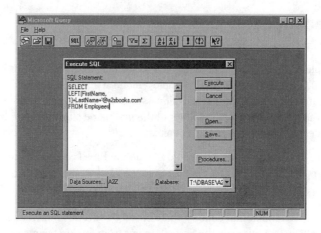

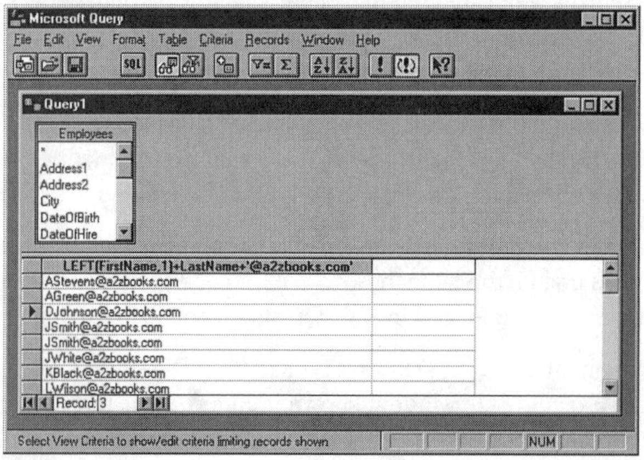

FIG. 9.12

Microsoft Query displays calculated values just as it does any other columns.

TIP   Before executing INSERT, UPDATE, or DELETE operations that contain complex statements or WHERE conditions, you should test the statement or condition by using it in a SELECT statement. If the SELECT returns incorrect statement results, or an incorrect subset of data filtered by the WHERE clause, you'll know that the statement or condition is incorrect too.

The SELECT statement will never change any data, unlike INSERT, UPDATE, and DELETE, so if there is an error in the statement or condition, you'll find out about it before any damage is done.

Listing 9.7   Updating All Rows in a Table with a Calculated Value

```
UPDATE Employees
SET EMail=LEFT(FirstName, 1)+LastName+'@a2zbooks.com'
```

To verify that the operation was successful, try selecting the FirstName, LastName, and Email columns from the Employees table. Your results should look like those shown in Figure 9.14.

FIG. 9.13
Table columns may be updated with calculated values.

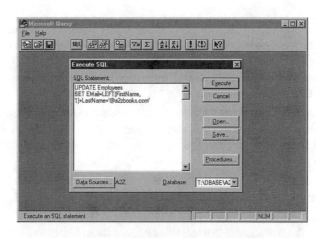

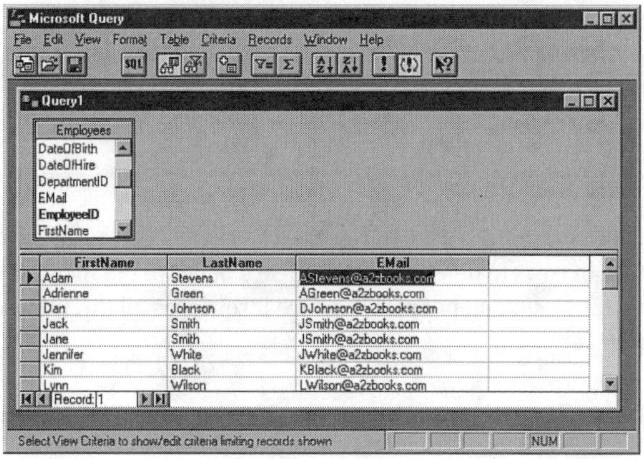

Part

III

Ch

9

FIG. 9.14
Always verify any table-wide changes by displaying the resulting data.

Deleting Data

Deleting data from a table is even easier than adding or updating data—perhaps too easy.

To delete data, you'll use the SQL DELETE statement. DELETE takes only two parameters, one required and one optional. They are

- The name of the table from which to delete the data must be specified immediately following the words DELETE FROM.

- An optional WHERE clause can be used to restrict the scope of the delete process.

The DELETE statement is dangerously easy to use. Look at the following line of code (but don't execute it):

```
DELETE FROM Employees
```

This statement removes all employee records from the Employees table without any warnings or confirmation.

Some databases, in particular client/server databases such as Microsoft SQL Server, offer safeguards against accidental (or malicious) deletions. There are generally two approaches to preventing mass deletion.

One is to create a trigger (a piece of code that runs on the server when specific operations occur) that verifies every DELETE statement and blocks any DELETE without a WHERE clause.

Another popular option is restricting the use of DELETE without a WHERE clause based on login name. Only certain users, usually those with administrative rights, are granted permission to execute DELETE without a WHERE clause. Any other user attempting a mass DELETE will receive an error message, and the operation will abort.

Not all database systems support these techniques. Consult the database administrator's manuals to ascertain what safeguards are available to you.

Usually the DELETE statement is used with a WHERE clause. For example, the following SQL statement deletes a single employee's record from the Employees table.

Listing 9.8   The *DELETE* Statement Is Usually Used with a *WHERE* Clause

```
DELETE FROM Employees
WHERE EmployeeID = 10
```

As with all WHERE clauses, the DELETE statement's WHERE clause can be a SELECT statement that retrieves the list of rows to delete. If you do use a SELECT statement for a WHERE clause, be careful to test the SELECT statement first to ensure it retrieves all the values you want, and only the values you want. ●

CHAPTER 10

Introduction to Cold Fusion Studio

by Ben Forta

In this chapter

Understanding Cold Fusion Studio

It is impossible to cover every aspect of Studio in this single chapter, but I'll attempt to demonstrate some of the most important features to get you up and running. You are encouraged to experiment on your own. There is nothing in Studio that you can break by tinkering. The more you play with Studio, the more you'll discover, and the more useful tool it will be.

To understand what Cold Fusion Studio is, and how it can simplify your application development, you first need to understand what it is not.

Cold Fusion Studio (referred to as "Studio" from this point on) is not a WYSIWYG HTML generator. Nor is it an HTML authoring tool. It will not let you drag and drop page elements onto a page to generate the underlying HTML. In fact, it makes no effort to try to conceal HTML from you.

Quite the opposite in fact, Studio tries very hard to expose all of the underlying code to you, ensuring that you, the developer, have full control over it.

So what exactly is Cold Fusion Studio?

Cold Fusion Studio is an editor, much like Windows Notepad (or DOS's EDIT). With Studio you create and open files, write your code, and save files, just as you would do in any other editor. But that's where the similarity ends. Unlike typical editors, Studio was designed from the ground up as a programmer's editor. It is based on HomeSite, the award winning HTML editor used by over 100,000 web page designers, and boasts a feature set that no other editor can match, including:

- Menus and toolbars provide shortcuts to the most common tags and functions
- Multiple document interface
- Automatic color coding of HTML, CFML, and other languages
- Wizards and templates
- Drag-and-drop editing, and context-sensitive right mouse click options
- Integrated image and thumbnail viewer
- Edit dialog for most HTML and CFML tags (and you can even create your own dialog for your own tags)
- Pop-up help for all HTML and CFML tags
- Automatic tag completion
- Built-in expression builder
- Built-in SQL query builder
- Integrated project management
- Built-in HTML validation
- Open and save files over an Internet connection (using HTTP or FTP)
- Built-in support for version control systems

The bottom line is, if you are serious about web application development, and serious about development with Cold Fusion, then Cold Fusion Studio is a *must*.

Running Cold Fusion Studio

If you haven't already done so, start up Studio by selecting Cold Fusion Studio from your programs menu (usually in a group called Cold Fusion Studio followed by a version number).

N O T E If you have not yet installed Cold Fusion Studio, now would be a good time to do so. Refer to Chapter 3, "Installing Cold Fusion and Cold Fusion Studio," for installation instructions.

If this is your first time running Studio, and you have Microsoft's Internet Explorer installed on your computer, you will see a dialog box like the one shown in Figure 10.1. Studio can use Internet Explorer (or IE) as its internal browser, and selecting Yes from the dialog box in Figure 10.1 enables that option. If you do have IE installed, it is strongly recommend that you select Yes here. (You can always turn this option on or off later if desired.)

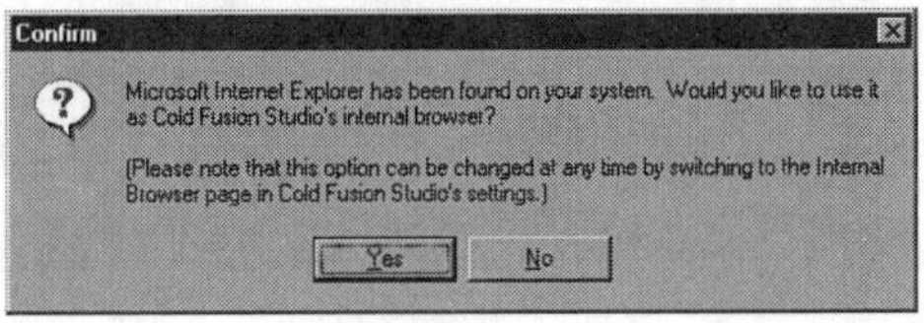

FIG. 10.1
Cold Fusion Studio can use Microsoft Internet Explorer as its internal browser.

Introducing Cold Fusion Studio

Start with a quick guided tour of the Studio environment shown in Figure 10.2.

The top of the screen has two toolbars. The Main Toolbar on the left contains buttons for opening and saving files; performing searches; cut, copy, and paste operations; undo and redo operations; and more. The Tag Toolbar on the right is actually a collection of 10 tabbed toolbars containing over 100 tag shortcuts and wizards. Table 10.1 lists the tabs of the Tag Toolbar, and what each one contains.

Table 10.1   Cold Fusion Studio Tag Toolbars

Tab	Description
QuickTab	Commonly used tags (bold, paragraph and line breaks, links, horizontal rules), and quick start options for creating header and body tags
Fonts	Font face, color, and size control, as well as the heading tags
Tables	Table wizard, all the table tags, and a Quick Table button that creates a basic table for you based on the size you select

continues

Table 10.1   Continued

Tab	Description
Frames	Frame wizard, and all the frame related tags
Lists	Menus, ordered lists, unordered lists, and list items
Forms	Forms and all form field types
Script	Tags for interacting with Java, JavaScript, VBScript, LiveScript, and ActiveX
CFML Basic	Basic Cold Fusion tags, including CFQUERY, CFOUTPUT, CFIF, CFSET, and CFINCLUDE
CFML Advanced	Advanced Cold Fusion tags, including CFCOOKIE, CFMAIL, CFPOP, CFLDAP, CFHTP, CFFTP, and the Verity interface tags
CFFORM	Cold Fusion CFFORM tags, including the Cold Fusion Java controls

FIG. 10.2
The Studio environment is divided into multiple windows and tabs.

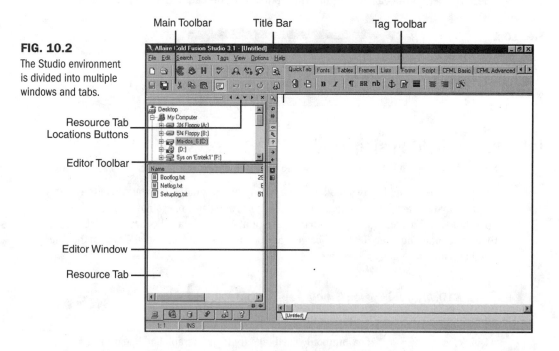

You may select a button from any of these toolbars to automatically insert HTML or CFML tags into the document you are editing. Some buttons insert text, others pop-up dialog boxes, prompting you for additional information, inserting the text after you fill in the fields and click Apply.

You might find it easier to work with the Main Toolbar placed above the Tag Toolbar, instead of to the left of it, as shown in Figure 10.3. This way you won't have to scroll through the Tag Toolbar tabs to see the available tabs. To do this, choose Toolbar Layout from the Options menu, and then select Horizontal.

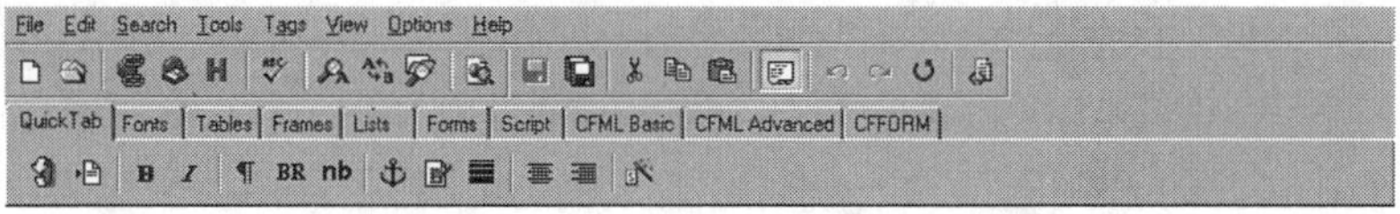

FIG. 10.3
The Main and Tag Toolbars may be aligned horizontally if desired.

To the left of the screen is the Resource Tab. This is a multi-purpose tab that actually contains six different tabs. Table 10.2 lists the tabs and what each is used for. You select the tab you want by clicking the tab selectors at the bottom of the Resource Tab (see Figure 10.4).

Table 10.2   Cold Fusion Studio Resource Tabs

Tab	Description
Local	Local files and directories in a Windows 95 Explorer-style window
Remote	Access for files and directories on a remote server (this is discussed later in this chapter)
Database	Access to ODBC data sources on either a local or remote server (this will be discussed later too)
Projects	Project management, create and work with entire projects rather than one file at a time
Tag Snippets	Create your own code snippets that you can insert into any page
Help	Help library

By default, the tabs on the Resource Tab just show images indicating what each tab does. Studio can display a text description there instead of the graphics, or in addition to them, as shown in Figure 10.4. To display the text, choose Resource Tab Captions from the Options menu, and then select either Text Only or Text and Images.

FIG. 10.4
Cold Fusion Studio can display text description on the Resource Tab tabs.

T I P Hold your mouse over any button to display a pop-up description of what that button does.

The right side of the screen is the Cold Fusion editor itself. This highly customizable editor is where you actually write your web pages. If you click on buttons on any of the Tag Toolbars, the code will be inserted right where the flashing cursor is.

To the left of the editor window is the Editor Toolbar containing ten buttons you can use to control the editor itself. For example, clicking the bottom button displays a color palette selection box that you can use to select colors to use within your HTML tags. Other buttons are used to turn on or off word wrap, the display of line numbers, and pop-up help.

T I P The Resource Tab is a very important part of Cold Fusion Studio, and so you will probably want access to it at all times. However, it does take up a significant amount of screen space. To save space you can hide and display the entire Resource Tab by toggling the F9 key, thus displaying it only when needed. In addition, you can move the entire Resource Tab to the top, bottom, or right side of the screen. To do this, click the Resource Tab Location buttons at the top right of the Resource Tab.

Working with Files

Studio is an editor, and most of your time using Studio will be spent working with files. These will usually be plain HTML web pages or Cold Fusion application pages. Studio gives you several ways to create, open, and manipulate files.

- The File menu contains the standard file manipulation options, like New, Open, Save, and Close.
- The Main Toolbar contains buttons for creating and opening files.
- Double-clicking any file in the local window in the Resource Tab opens that file for editing.

The Studio title bar shows the name of the file currently open and active in the editor window (see Figure 10.9). There is no limit to the number of files that you can open at one time, but more on that when the multiple document interface is discussed later in this chapter.

N O T E If the active file has never been saved, it is named Untitled and that is the name displayed in Studio's title bar. ■

Using the Editor

The heart of Cold Fusion Studio is its editor. This is obviously where you'll do most of your work, and thus, this is where the Studio feature set shines.

This has been said this before, but it bears repeating—Studio is *not* an HTML authoring tool, and it won't write HTML or CFML for you. Studio assumes that you, the developer, want to be in complete control of the application development effort. But at the same time, Studio attempts to simplify the development process, without getting in your way.

To demonstrate the Studio editor, open any HTML or CFML file. Use the File, Open menu option, the Main Toolbar Open button, or just browse through the local files in the Resource Tab and double-click any file to open it.

Using Color Coding

The first thing you'll notice is that the text in the editor window is color-coded. Color coding is used to highlight specific tags or text, and Studio performs all color coding automatically. The following are the two primary reasons to use color coding:

- Color-coded text makes it easy to quickly find specific tags or tag types. For example, all table-related tags are shown in one color, while all Cold Fusion tags are shown in another.

- Color coding makes it easier to find mistakes in your code. If a tag or block of text does not display in the correct color, you'll know right away that you've made a typo there. If you do something as simple as missing the > symbol from the end of the tag, you'll immediately see that the text after the tag is incorrectly color-coded.

Color coding can be turned off by choosing Color Coding from the Options menu, but unless you are working with massive files (so large that Studio takes a significant amount of time to perform the color coding) there is seldom a reason to do so. As a rule, you should always keep Color Coding turned on.

TIP

You can change the colors that Studio uses for color coding by selecting the Tag Colors tab from the Options Settings dialog box (or by pressing F8).

Using Toolbars

As mentioned earlier, the Tag Toolbars provide shortcuts to commonly used HTML and CFML tags. Clicking any button on any Tag Toolbar either inserts tag text or displays a dialog box that prompts you for tag options. To try this out, follow these steps:

1. Close any files you have opened (you can simply right-click the file in the editor window, and select Close).

2. Type the text **My first page written in Studio** in the editor window.

3. Highlight the text you just typed with your mouse.

4. Click the Bold button (the one with the big bold B on it) on the QuickTab toolbar.

Studio automatically applies the HTML bold tags (<B> and </B>) to the highlighted text, as shown in Figure 10.5.

Part

III

Ch

10

FIG. 10.5

Studio allows you to
highlight text and select
a Tag Toolbar button to
apply tags to that text.

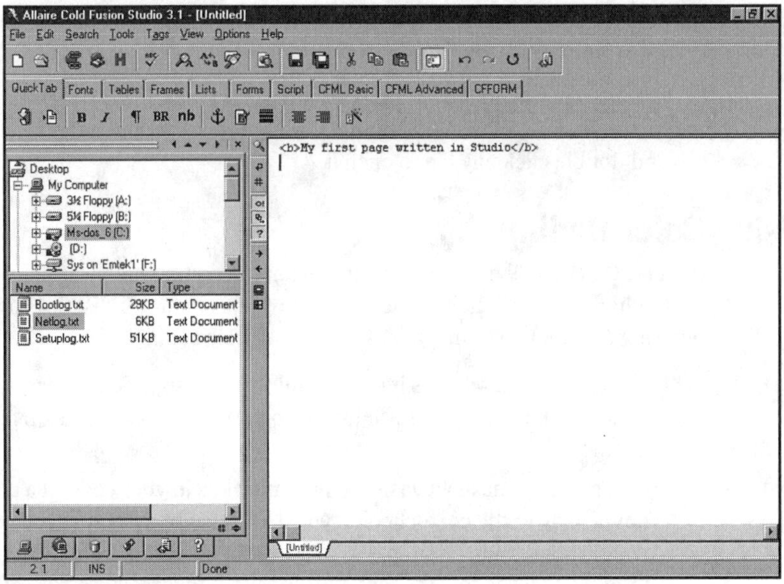

Try another example; this time you'll create an HTML table.

1. Close any files you have opened (you can simply right-click the file in the editor window, and select Close).

2. Select the Tables Toolbar Tag.

3. Click on the Quick Table button (the one on the right) to display a table selection box, as shown in Figure 10.6.

4. Move your mouse down and to the right to select the number of rows and columns you'd like in your HTML table.

5. When you have highlighted the number of desired rows and columns, click your mouse to make the selection.

As shown in Figure 10.7, Studio generated the HTML code for your table, and it even indented the cells to make working with your table easier.

As you can see, the Tag Toolbar buttons are both a tremendous time saver, and a way to help ensure that you don't mistype tags or tag attributes.

CAUTION

When clicking on Tag Toolbar buttons, pay close attention to where you editor cursor is. Studio will insert the selected tag at the current cursor position. If the cursor is in the wrong place (in the middle of another tag for example), that's where Studio will insert the text.

FIG. 10.6
The Quick Table button allows you to quickly generate code to create HTML tables.

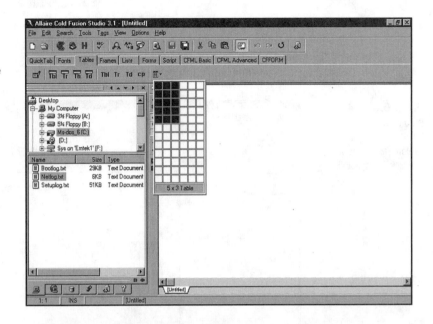

FIG. 10.7
Studio automatically indents generated HTML table code to make working with tables easier.

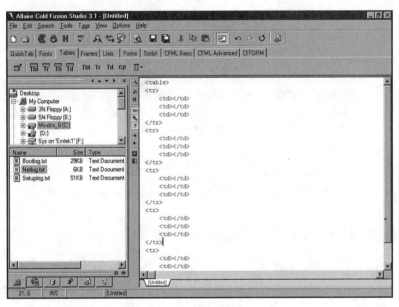

Browsing Your Web Pages

As Studio is not a WYSIWYG authoring tool, what you see in the editor is code, not the generated output. To view the page that your code creates, you need to browse that page.

If you have Microsoft Internet Explorer installed on your computer, Studio can use it internally to display your page, as shown in Figure 10.8. To browse a page this way, just click the Browse button on the Editor Toolbar (it's the top button with a magnifying glass on it). You can also use the F12 key to toggle between edit and browse modes.

FIG. 10.8

Studio can use Microsoft Internet Explorer as its internal browser if it is installed.

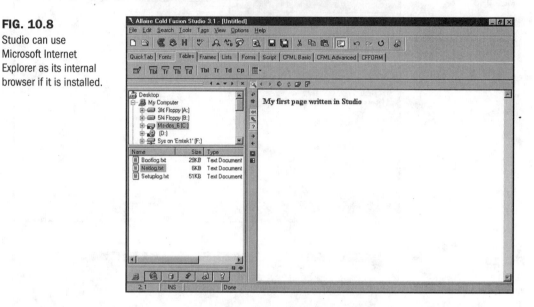

Web developers often need to view their pages in more than one browser. This is generally good practice because of browser incompatibilities and differences. Studio lets you configure external browsers, which can be spawned from within Studio as needed. To set up external browsers, choose External Browsers from the Options menu.

N O T E The internal browser can be used to view HTML files, but not Cold Fusion files because Cold Fusion files need to be preprocessed by the Cold Fusion Application Server. If you attempt to browse a CFM or CFML file, Studio will likely display an error message. ■

Using the Multiple Document Interface

Studio allows you to open multiple files at once. When you open multiple files, each one has a tab at the bottom of the editor window, as shown in Figure 10.9. You may click these tabs to switch between files. The tab belonging to the file that is actually open is shown brighter and in the foreground, so you'll always know which file you are looking at. In addition, the Studio title bar also shows the name of the currently active file.

FIG. 10.9

The Cold Fusion editor window displays a tab for each open document.

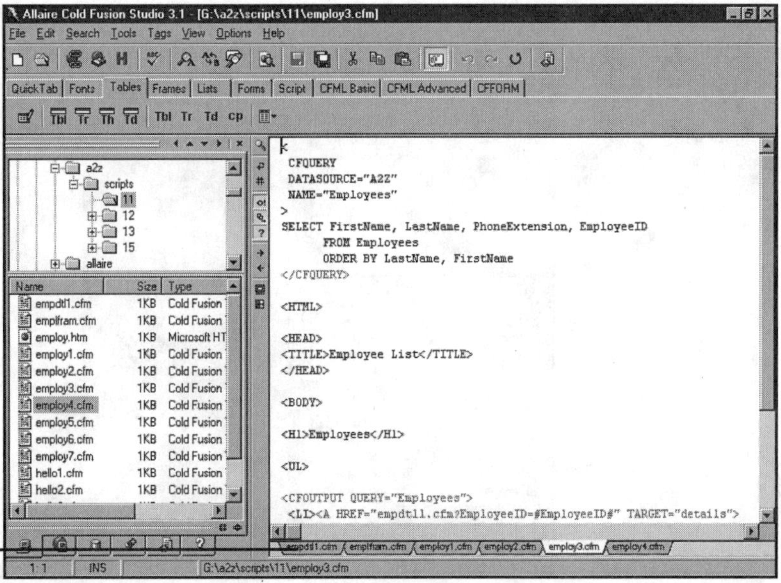

File Name Tabs

The file tabs at the bottom of the editor window have another important use. They indicate which files have been saved and which have not. The text in the tab will change to red as soon as any changes are made to a file, and will remain red until the file is saved. Once the file is saved, the text will be displayed in black. This makes it easy to see which files have not been saved yet.

Using the Right Mouse Button

Probably the most important tip to remember when using Studio is "right-click the mouse." Studio makes extensive use of the right mouse button, particularly in the editor window. Studio's right mouse button support is "context-sensitive." This means that the options displayed will vary, based upon where you right-click. Try right-clicking any tag. You'll see a pop-up menu similar to the one shown in Figure 10.10.

Other right mouse button options include Insert Expression and Insert SQL Statement. These options will be explored later in this chapter.

The right mouse button can also be used in the Resource Tab. Right-click any file or directory to display a pop-up menu of relevant options.

T I P

Use the right mouse button extensively. As it is context-sensitive, you'll always be presented with a list of useful options.

Part

III

Ch

10

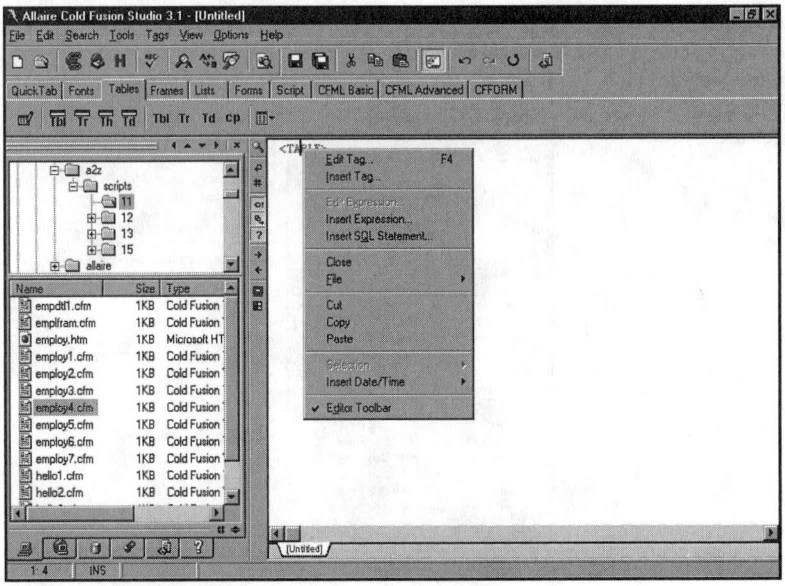

FIG. 10.10
Clicking the right mouse button in Studio displays a pop-up, context-sensitive options menu.

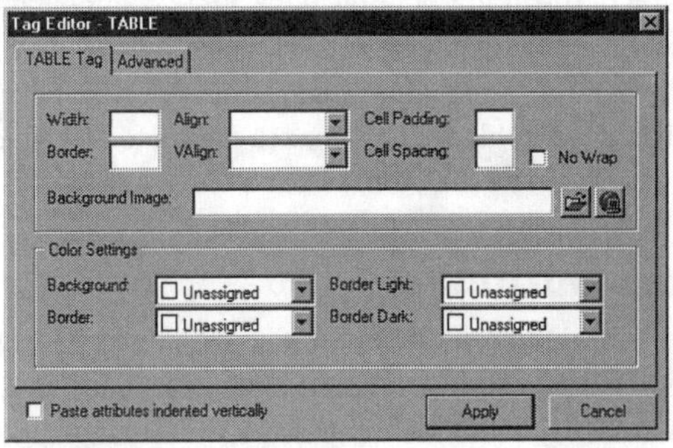

FIG. 10.11
Selecting Edit Tag from the right mouse button menu displays a tag-specific edit dialog box.

Getting Help

Cold Fusion developers have to remember the HTML language, CFML tags and functions, SQL interfaces, and communication with many other protocols and standards. That's a lot of information to remember, and most developers keep a selection of reference books and manuals close by at all times.

Studio greatly simplifies the process of finding the help you need. It boasts an extensive array of help-related features, all designed to give you immediate, useful, and relevant help. The following sections look at some of these features.

Using Tag Completion

Tag Completion is a feature that lets Studio automatically finish writing tags for you. This is an invaluable feature for two reasons.

■ Tag Completion helps ensure that you don't mistakenly miss a tag's required ending tag.

■ Tag Completion writes end tags for you, helping to prevent typos.

To try out Tag Completion, do the following:

1. Close any files you have opened (you can simply right-click the file in the editor window, and select Close).

2. In the editor window, type **<CENTER>**.

As soon as you type the > at the end of <CENTER>, Studio automatically inserts the matching </CENTER> tag, and places your cursor in between them so you can continue typing.

 Tag Completion can be disabled by clicking the Tag Completion button in the Editor Toolbar, or in the Tag Help tab in the Options, Settings dialog box.

 You can add tags to the list of tags to be completed in the Tag Help tab in the Options, Settings dialog box.

Using Tag Tips

Tag Tips are inline, pop-up help dialog boxes, right in your editor window. Tag Tips pop up automatically after your typing cursor (not the mouse cursor) sits for a couple of seconds on a tag. The Tag Tips for the <BODY> tag are shown in Figure 10.12.

 Tag Tips can be disabled by clicking the Tag Tips button in the Editor Toolbar, or in the Tag Help tab in the Options, Settings dialog box. You can also adjust the delay—the number of seconds Studio should wait before displaying the tips.

Using Tag Insight

Tag Insight takes online help to the next level by providing pop-up, interactive, tag-specific help, as shown in Figure 10.13. To try this out, do the following:

1. Close any files you have opened (you can simply right-click the file in the editor window, and select Close).

2. In the editor window, type **<BODY>** and then wait a second or two.

3. Studio will display a pop-up selectable menu of all the attributes appropriate for the tag you are editing, in this case the <BODY> tag.

4. Select any attribute to insert it into your tag.

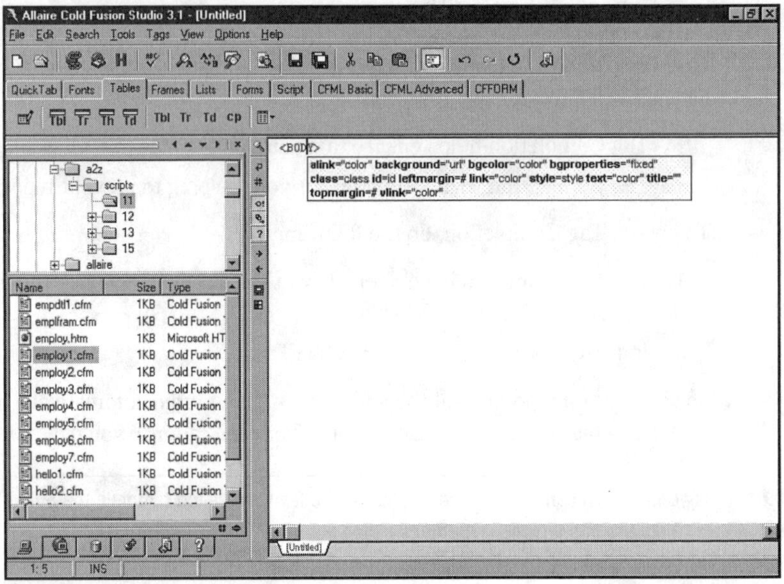

FIG. 10.12
Tag Tips appear right in the editor window to provide tag-specific help.

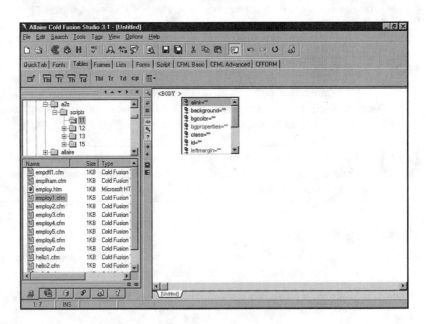

FIG. 10.13
Tag Insights can be used to display interactive, tag-specific help.

 T I P Tag Insight can be disabled by clicking the Tag Insight button in the Editor Toolbar, or in the Tag Help tab in the Options, Settings dialog box. You can also adjust the delay—that is the number of seconds Studio should wait before displaying the menu.

Using Edit Dialog Box Help

Studio can display tag-specific edit dialog boxes to help you create and edit tags. Any options you select or fill in will be added as tag attributes to the tag when you click the Apply button.

Many of these edit dialog boxes, in particular those for Cold Fusion tags, have optional syntax help built right into them. If help is available for a specific tag, two little buttons will be displayed at the bottom right of the dialog box, as shown in Figure 10.14. These buttons toggle on and off the help display, in either the dialog box itself or in a separate window.

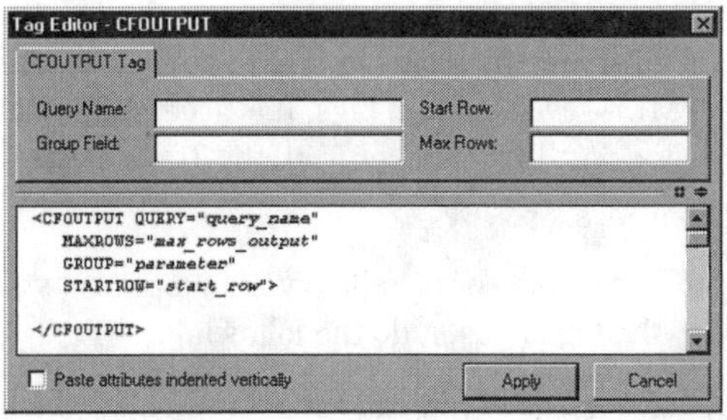

FIG. 10.14

Many tag edit dialog boxes have built-in, embedded syntax help.

```
<CFOUTPUT QUERY="query_name"
    MAXROWS="max_rows_output"
    GROUP="parameter"
    STARTROW="start_row">

</CFOUTPUT>
```

Part

III

Ch

10

Using Online Help

In addition to all the help options just discussed, Studio also has a complete online searchable help library. To access the help, click the Help tab in the Resource Tab (it's the one with the yellow question mark). You'll see a list of Help References that you may browse or search, as shown in Figure 10.15.

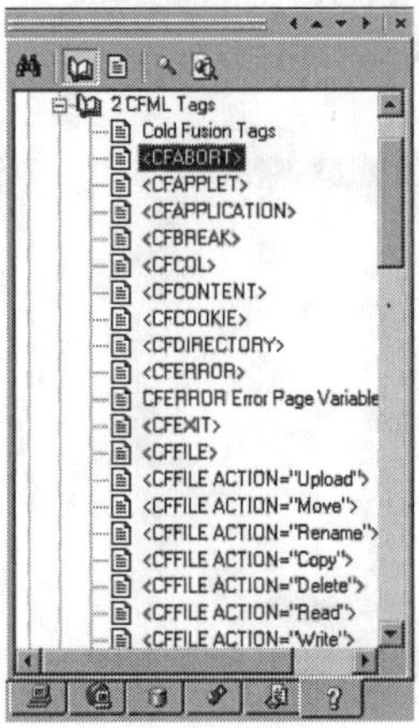

FIG. 10.15

Studio comes with a complete browseable and searchable reference library.

To search for a specific topic, click the Search button (the one with the binoculars on it). This will display a help search dialog box where you can type in any search text.

Using Tags and Expressions

Cold Fusion developers spend much of their time working with tags and expressions, and so Studio provides interactive utilities to make both of these operations easier.

You'll explore two of these interactive utilities: the Tag Chooser and the Expression Builder. Both of these tools, as well as other useful tools, are available as menu selections and as right-click options.

Using the Tag Chooser

The Tag Chooser is a drill down tree interface to HTML and CFML tags, as well as other tag types (like HDML and VTML)—even custom tags. It is accessible via the right-click menu in the editor window, or by choosing Tag Chooser from the Tools menu.

▶ **See** Chapter 33, "Custom Tags," **p. 767**

The primary purpose of the Tag Chooser is to help you find the tag you are looking for by context or category. To try the tag chooser, do the following:

1. Close any files you have opened (you can simply right-click the file in the editor window, and select Close).
2. Right-click in the editor window, and select Insert Tag to display the Tag Chooser dialog box, as shown in Figure 10.16.
3. Expand the HTML tag list by double-clicking HTML tags, or by clicking the + items symbol.
4. Select Tables to display the list of table-related tags.
5. Double-click the TABLE item to display the Table dialog box.
6. Click the Apply button to insert the tag into your document.

FIG. 10.16

The Studio Tag Chooser lets you drill down through a list of tags to find the tag you are looking for.

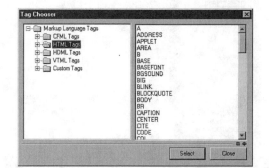

 TIP The Tag Chooser dialog box can also display tag-specific help by clicking either of the help buttons on the bottom right of the dialog box.

Using the Expression Builder

Cold Fusion expressions are collections of references, Cold Fusion functions, variables, and operators. Expressions are an important part of Cold Fusion application development, and so Studio provides an Expression Builder to help you construct and edit expressions. It is accessible via the right-click menu in the editor window, or by choosing Expression Builder from the Tools menu.

N O T E Don't worry if you are unfamiliar with expressions, they are covered extensively throughout this book. For now, you will just be shown how to use the builder so that you can take advantage of it later on. ■

The Expression Builder, shown in Figure 10.17, works much like the Tag Chooser. You select the element type you want (function, constant, operator, or variable), and then drill down to find the specific expression element you are seeking. As you select elements, they are displayed at the top of the Expression Builder dialog box so that you can see and edit the complete expression.

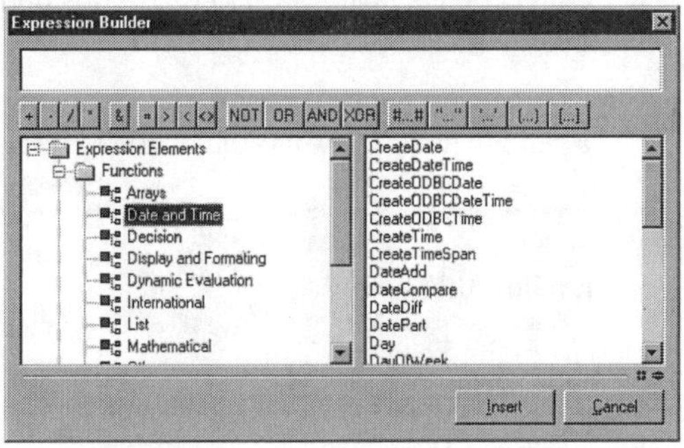

Part

III

Ch

10

FIG. 10.17
The Studio Expression Builder can be used to simplify creating and editing Cold Fusion expressions.

Once you have finished creating or editing an expression, click the Insert button to insert it into your document in the editor window.

T I P The Expression Builder dialog box can also display element-specific help by clicking either of the help buttons on the bottom right of the dialog box.

Accessing Cold Fusion Application Server Services

Unlike web page development, Cold Fusion application development usually involves a high level of integration with services on the Cold Fusion Application Server machine. At a minimum, this integration involves ODBC data sources, as well as files and directories on the server.

Studio can be used to open and work with these services over any Internet connection. This allows developers to work from a computer located anywhere, and still gain full access to the file system as well as the ODBC data sources.

Connecting to a Cold Fusion Server

In order to access these services, you might first tell Studio about your Cold Fusion server, and how to get to it. To do this, select the Remote tab on the Resource Tab (it's the one with the picture of the computer in front of a globe).

Studio supports two forms of remote server connection, direct connection to Cold Fusion servers, and FTP server connections. These are described in Table 10.3.

Table 10.3   Server Types Supported by Cold Fusion Studio

Server	Description
Cold Fusion	Connecting to a Cold Fusion server gives you access to the server's file system and all system ODBC data sources. The connection is made via HTTP. Use this option to connect to a Cold Fusion server.
FTP	Connecting to a FTP server gives you access to the file system on a remote host. Use this connection to transfer files to and from FTP servers.

To add a Cold Fusion Server, follow these steps.

1. Select the Remote tab from the Resource Tab.
2. Right-click in the tab window, and select Add Cold Fusion Server to display the server properties dialog box shown in Figure 10.18.
3. Enter any descriptive name in the description field.
4. Specify the host name or IP address of the server to connect to, use **localhost** or **127.0.0.1** to connect to a local server.
5. Enter the Studio server password in the password field, or leave it blank to be prompted for it each time you access the server. (If you do enter the password, you will not be prompted for it again to gain server access; therefore, anyone who has access to Studio on your computer will also have server access.)
6. Click OK to add the server.

You'll now see the server you added appear in the list of remote servers.

▶ **See** Chapter 3, "Installing Cold Fusion and Cold Fusion Studio," **p. 37**

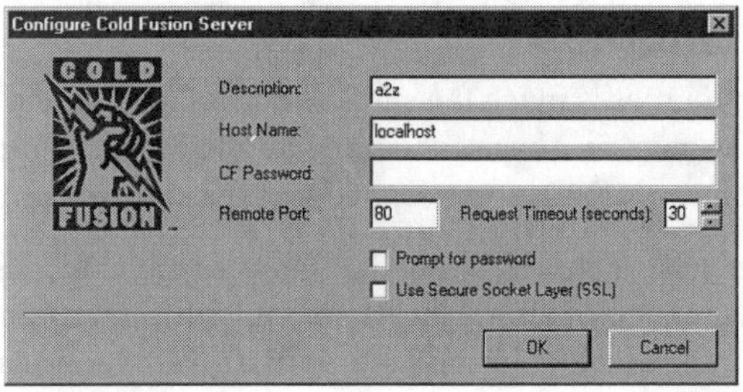

FIG. 10.18
The Configure Cold Fusion Server dialog box is used to add a Cold Fusion Server to the Studio remote server list.

Accessing Server Files

To browse files on a remote server (either a Cold Fusion server or a FTP server), just double-click the server name. You'll be prompted for a password if you did not specify one when setting up the server, and then Studio will attempt to connect to the server. If the connection is successful, you'll see a list of files and directories available on the server, as shown in Figure 10.19.

FIG. 10.19
The Resource Tab Remote tab shows files and directories on the Cold Fusion server machine.

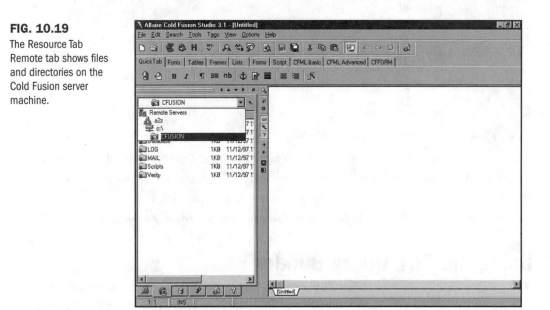

You may double-click any file to open it for editing, just as you would a local file. Studio automatically handles the retrieving of files from the server (using either HTTP or FTP), and saving the files back to the server.

Access Server Data Sources

Accessing server data sources is much the same as accessing files and directories. To access server data sources you must first have configured a Cold Fusion Server for remote access within Studio. You cannot use FTP server connections for data source interaction.

To browse your server's data sources, select the Database tab in the Resource Tab (it's the one with the yellow cylinder on it). You'll see the same Cold Fusion servers that you set up in the Remote tab. Double-click a server to display a list of data sources available on the server, as shown in Figure 10.20.

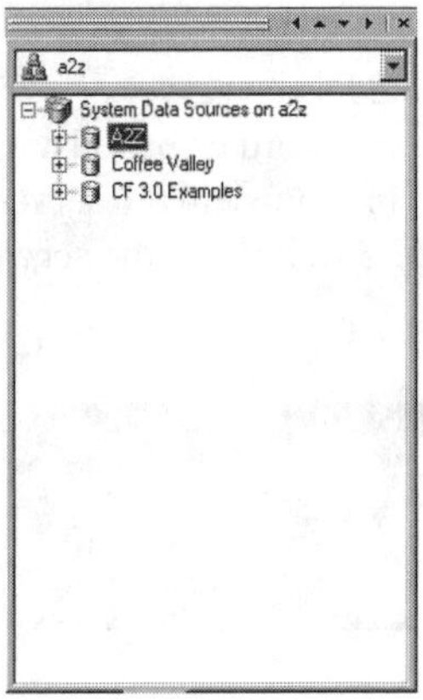

FIG. 10.20
The Resource Tab Database tab gives you remote access to the ODBC data sources on the Cold Fusion Server machine.

Some of the things you can do with this list are

- Expand any data source to view the tables, views, and queries within it.
- Expand any table to see the list of columns within it, and the column data types.
- Double-click a table or view to browse the data contained in it.
- Drag and drop any table, view, or field name into the editor window.

Using the SQL Query Builder

Most Cold Fusion applications interact with databases, and the language used to perform this interaction is SQL. A Cold Fusion tag called <CFQUERY> is used to pass SQL statements to databases to retrieve information from them.

▶ **See** Chapter 8, "Introduction to SQL," **p. 129**

▶ **See** Chapter 11, "Cold Fusion Basics," **p. 193**

To simplify the process of writing SQL statements, Studio has an integrated SQL Query Builder. This interactive tool will actually write SQL code for you; all you do is drag and drop tables and fields, and make simple menu selections.

NOTE The Studio SQL Builder is not a substitute for a working knowledge of SQL. It is designed to get you up and running quickly, and it will help you write much of your SQL code. To fully take advantage of Cold Fusion, you really need to learn SQL as well. ■

Creating Queries

There are several ways to run the SQL Query Builder:

- Right-click any table in the Resource Tab Database tab, and select New Query.
- Select Insert SQL Statement from the right-click menu in the editor window, or from the Tools menu, and then select the database to use.
- Click the database button in the <CFQUERY> tag edit dialog box.

However you invoke the SQL Query Builder, you'll see a screen similar to the one shown in Figure 10.21.

FIG. 10.21
The SQL Query Builder can be used to interactively generate SQL code for your Cold Fusion applications.

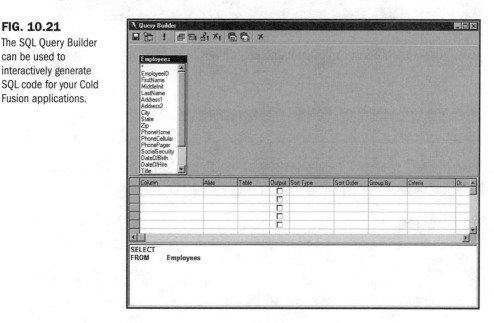

Part
III

Ch
10

The SQL Query Builder screen is divided into three parts. At the top is the list of selected tables. You may select multiple tables here, and even drag and drop them together to create joins or relationships.

▶ **See** Chapter 6, "Database Fundamentals," **p. 87**

The middle pane contains the list of selected columns, and any sort or filter criteria associated with them. The bottom of the screen shows the SQL statement being generated.

As you drag columns from the table list into the selected column list, you'll see the SQL statement change automatically to reflect your selections. Similarly if you select aliases, sort orders, or any other column options, the SQL code will automatically reflect those selections as shown in Figure 10.22.

FIG. 10.22
The SQL Query Builder automatically generates SQL code based on the columns and options you select.

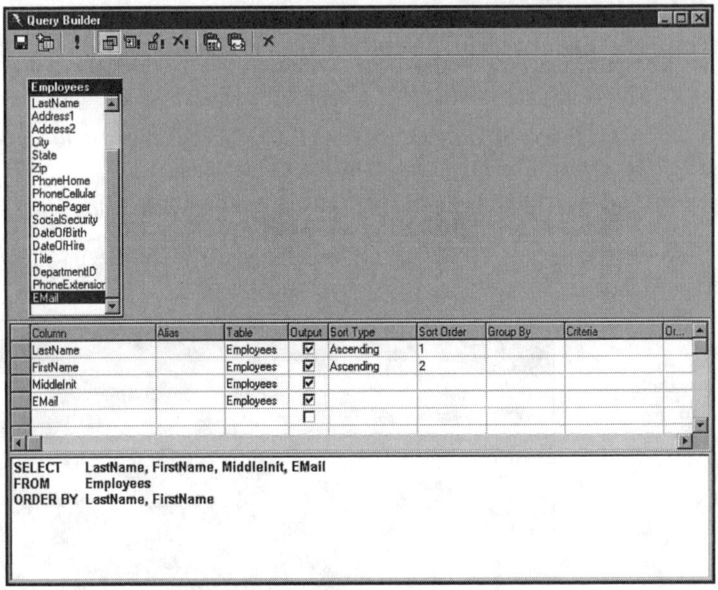

Once you have created the desired SQL statement, you may run the query to see the data that it returns, save the query for future use, or paste the SQL code back into the editor window.

Reusing Queries

Studio allows you to save created queries for future use or modification. Queries may be saved with the SQL Query Builder window.

To open an existing query, select a table from the Database tab, and then expand the list of available queries. Select any saved query to display it in the SQL Query window.

Configuring Studio

Studio is a powerful and flexible editor, and the more you use it, the more you'll want to customize it. Fortunately this is easy to do. The Options menu lists the most frequently used options, several of which you have already used in this chapter.

The Studio Settings dialog box is where you can customize most of Studio's features and options. To display the dialog box shown in Figure 10.23, choose Settings from the Options menu, or press the F8 key. The Settings dialog box has nine tabs, which are described in Table 10.4.

FIG. 10.23

The Settings dialog box is used to configure Studio.

Table 10.4 Settings Dialog Box Tabs

Tab	Description
General	All sorts of editor options, including whether colors are inserted using text or RGB values, and whether or not to lower case all inserted tags
HTML	HTML related options, including whether to match <P> tags with </P>, and whether to insert empty ALT attributes in IMG tags
File Extensions	The list of extensions that Studio should treat as editable files, and the default extension for any new files
Default Template	The HTML (and CFML) code to automatically insert when the New button on the Main Toolbar is clicked
Spelling	Spell checking options, and which dictionaries to use
Editor	Editor font and size, text and background color, and other editor options
Tag Colors	Changes the colors used for the Color Coding
Tag Help	Enables or disables Tag Insight and Tag Tips, and customizes Tag Completion
Internal Browser	Whether or not to use Microsoft Internet Explorer as the built in browser, and mapping options

When you click OK after making any settings changes, Studio automatically saves the changes, ensuring that they are there for future sessions.

Cold Fusion Studio is a powerful and flexible editor designed for Cold Fusion developers in mind. As such, it does much more then edit files. The integrated Tag Chooser, Expression Builder, and SQL Query Builder, all serve to simplify the application development process. With extensive built-in help options and support for remote development, Studio is an invaluable tool. Start using it and you'll wonder how you managed without it. ●

Cold Fusion Basics

by Ben Forta

In this chapter

Using Templates

As you learned in Chapter 2, "Introduction to Cold Fusion," all Cold Fusion interaction is via templates rather than HTML files. Templates can contain HTML, Cold Fusion tags and functions, or both.

Cold Fusion templates are plain-text files, just like HTML files. But, unlike HTML files which are sent to the user's browser, templates are first processed by Cold Fusion. This way, you can embed instructions to Cold Fusion within your templates. If, for example, you want to process user-supplied parameters, retrieve data from a database, or conditionally display certain information, you can instruct Cold Fusion to do so.

But instead of just reading about templates, why don't you create one? The first template you will create just says "Hello" to you. Yes, I know that you can create the same response with any HTML file, but along with saying "Hello," this template also identifies your IP address and the browser you're using. You can't do that with plain HTML.

Create a text file containing the code in Listing 11.1, and save it in your C:\A2Z\SCRIPTS directory as HELLO1.CFM.

On the CD

Listing 11.1   HELLO1.CFM—"Hello" Cold Fusion Templates

```
<HTML>

<HEAD>
<TITLE>Hello!</TITLE>
</HEAD>

<BODY>

<CFOUTPUT>

Hello,<BR>
Your IP address is: <B>#REMOTE_ADDR#</B><BR>
Your browser is: <B>#HTTP_USER_AGENT#</B><P>

</CFOUTPUT>

</BODY>

</HTML>
```

After you create and save the file, load your browser and type **http://yourserver.com/a2z/hello1.cfm** in the URL field (replacing *yourserver.com* with your own server name). Your browser should display a page that looks similar to the one shown in Figure 11.1. Of course, your IP address and browser information will be different.

FIG. 11.1

Using Cold Fusion templates, you can display dynamic data in your web pages.

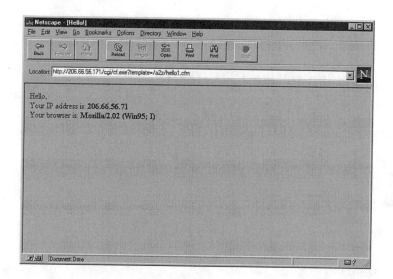

TIP You can use the host name "localhost" to refer to your own machine if you are writing and testing code on the same host that runs Cold Fusion. This is particularly useful if your host does not have a static (fixed) IP address.

Understanding Cold Fusion Templates

Now take a look at the code in Listing 11.1. Most of the code should be familiar to you as standard HTML. The tags for head, title, line breaks, and bold text are all the same HTML you would use in any other web page. What is not standard HTML is the <CFOUTPUT> tag and fields surrounded by pound signs (the # character).

All Cold Fusion-specific tags begin with CF; CFOUTPUT, therefore, is a Cold Fusion-specific tag. You use CFOUTPUT (or Cold Fusion Output) to mark a block of code that Cold Fusion should itself process prior to submitting it to the web server for sending to your browser. When Cold Fusion encounters a <CFOUTPUT> tag, it scans all the text until the next </CFOUTPUT> for Cold Fusion functions or fields delimited by pound signs.

In Listing 11.1, you use two fields, #REMOTE_ADDR# and #HTTP_USER_AGENT#. They are CGI variables that the HTTP server makes available to applications such as Cold Fusion. #REMOTE_ADDR# contains the IP address of your browser, and #HTTP_USER_AGENT# contains the string with which your browser identifies itself. When Cold Fusion encounters the text #REMOTE_ADDR# in the CFOUTPUT block, it replaces the text with the value in the REMOTE_ADDR CGI variable. And when Cold Fusion encounters #HTTP_USER_AGENT# on the next line, it replaces that text with the appropriate CGI variable, too. Instead of sending the text you entered back to your browser, Cold Fusion replaces the file names with the field values and sends those values back to you instead.

▶ **See** "Cold Fusion Basics," **p. 193**

▶ **See** "CGI Environment Variables" on the CD-ROM

Knowing When to Use *CFOUTPUT*

So why do you need the CFOUTPUT block? Well, take a look at what Cold Fusion would have done without it. Listing 11.2 contains a modified version of the code you used earlier; the output appears twice this time, once within a CFOUTPUT block and once not.

On the CD

Listing 11.2 HELLO2.CFM—Demonstration of the Use of *CFOUTPUT*

```
<HTML>

<HEAD>
<TITLE>Hello!</TITLE>
</HEAD>

<BODY>

<I>The next 3 lines <B>are not</B> within a CFOUTPUT block.</I><BR>
Hello,<BR>
Your IP address is: <B>#REMOTE_ADDR#</B><BR>
Your browser is: <B>#HTTP_USER_AGENT#</B><P>

<CFOUTPUT>

<I>The next 3 lines <B>are</B> within a CFOUTPUT block.</I><BR>
Hello,<BR>
Your IP address is: <B>#REMOTE_ADDR#</B><BR>
Your browser is: <B>#HTTP_USER_AGENT#</B><P>


</CFOUTPUT>

</BODY>

</HTML>
```

As you can see from the browser output in Figure 11.2, if you use fields outside a CFOUTPUT block, Cold Fusion displays the field name as you entered it, complete with the delimiting characters. More often than not, this is not the result you want.

TIP Every <CFOUTPUT> must have a corresponding </CFOUTPUT> tag, and vice versa. If you omit either tag, Cold Fusion returns a syntax error.

FIG. 11.2
Fields not contained within a CFOUTPUT block are output as you enter them, not replaced with their values.

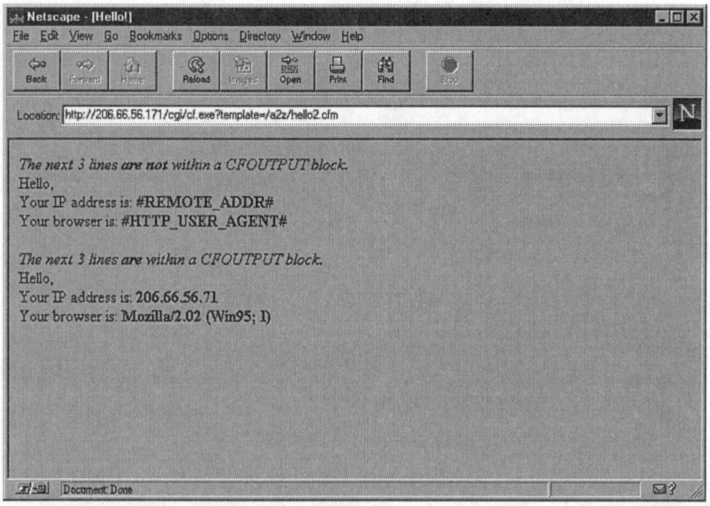
Netscape - [Hello!]
File Edit View Go Bookmarks Options Directory Window Help
Back Forward Home Reload Images Open Print Find Stop
Location: http://206.66.56.171/cgi/cf.exe?template=/a2z/hello2.cfm
The next 3 lines are not within a CFOUTPUT block.
Hello,
Your IP address is: #REMOTE_ADDR#
Your browser is: #HTTP_USER_AGENT#
The next 3 lines are within a CFOUTPUT block.
Hello,
Your IP address is: 206.66.56.71
Your browser is: Mozilla/2.02 (Win95; I)
Document: Done

Passing Parameters to Templates

In the first example, you used Cold Fusion to display dynamic data by specifying the field names for two CGI variables. You also can use Cold Fusion to display process parameters passed to an URL in exactly the same way.

To pass a parameter to a template, you could specify the parameter name and value within the URL. For example, to pass a parameter `NAME` with a value of `BEN`, you add `?NAME=BEN` to the URL. If you specify multiple URL parameters, you must separate each one with an ampersand character (the `&` character).

Try this example yourself. Listing 11.3 contains a template that displays the value of a parameter called `NAME`, if it exists. To display the value, you use the `<CFIF>` tag to create a condition and a Cold Fusion function called `ParameterExists`. If the parameter `NAME` exists, its value is displayed; otherwise, you are notified that the parameter is not passed.

▶ **See** "Using Conditional *INPUT* Fields," **p. 283**

▶ **See** "Processing Form Submissions," **p. 229**

On the CD

Listing 11.3 HELLO3.CFM—Demonstration of URL Parameter Processing

```
<HTML>

<HEAD>
<TITLE>Hello!</TITLE>
</HEAD>
```

continues

Listing 11.3 Continued

```
<BODY>

Hello,<BR>

<CFIF #ParameterExists(name)# IS "yes">
<CFOUTPUT>
The name you entered is <B>#name#</B>
</CFOUTPUT>
<CFELSE>
You did not pass a parameter called NAME
</CFIF>
</BODY>

</HTML>
```

After you create and save the file as **HELLO3.CFM** in the C:\A2Z\SCRIPTS directory, load your browser and type **http://*yourserver.com*/a2z/hello3.cfm?NAME=BEN** (you don't have to use my name; any name will do). Your browser display should look like the one shown in Figure 11.3. Now try the example again, this time without any NAME parameter. You then should see a display like the one shown in Figure 11.4.

So why go to the bother of testing for #ParameterExists(name)#? Well, try removing the <CFIF> statement (you have to remove the <CFELSE> and </CFIF> lines, too) and then type **http://*yourserver.com*/a2z/hello3.cfm** without any NAME parameter. Cold Fusion returns an error message because it has no idea what #name# is. If you instruct Cold Fusion to process a field that does not exist, it complains.

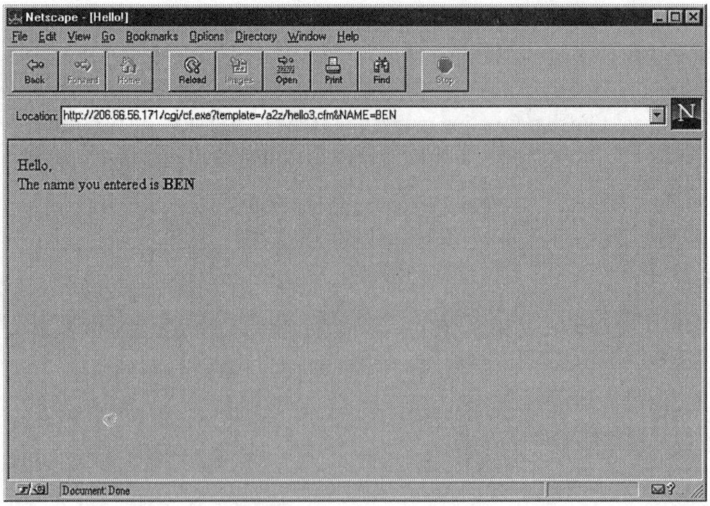

FIG. 11.3

Cold Fusion converts parameters passed to a URL into fields that you can use within your template.

FIG. 11.4

Whenever fields are optional, you should verify that they exist before using them.

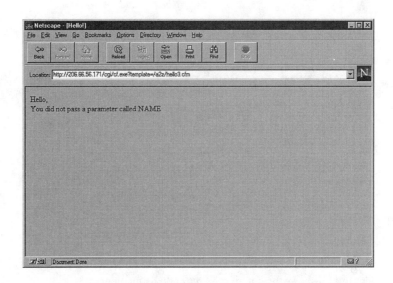

Creating Data-Driven Templates

Now that you've seen what Cold Fusion templates look like and know how to create, save, and test them, return to the A2Z Books example.

Your employee database is set up and populated with data, so your next task is to publish this information on your intranet. This way, your users can access an up-to-date employee list at all times without needing any special software to do so. All they need to access the data is a web browser.

Creating Static Web Pages

Before you create a Cold Fusion template for your database, take a look at how not to create this page. Listing 11.4 contains the HTML code for the employee list web page. The HTML code is relatively simple; it contains header information and then a list of employees in an HTML unordered list.

On the CD

Listing 11.4   EMPLOY.HTM—HTML Code For Employee List

```
<HTML>

<HEAD>
<TITLE>Employee List</TITLE>
</HEAD>

<BODY>

<H1>Employees</H1>
```

continues

Listing 11.4   Continued

```
<UL>
<LI>Black, Kim - Ext. 4565
<LI>Gold, Marcy - Ext. 4912
<LI>Green, Adrienne - Ext. 4546
<LI>Johnson, Dan - Ext. 4824
<LI>Jones, Steven - Ext. 4311
<LI>Smith, Jack - Ext. 4545
<LI>Smith, Jane - Ext. 4876
<LI>Stevens, Adam - Ext. 4878
<LI>White, Jennifer - Ext. 4345
<LI>Wilson, Lynn - Ext. 4464
</UL>

</BODY>

</HTML>
```

Figure 11.5 shows the output that this code listing generates.

FIG. 11.5

You can create the employee web page as a static HTML file.

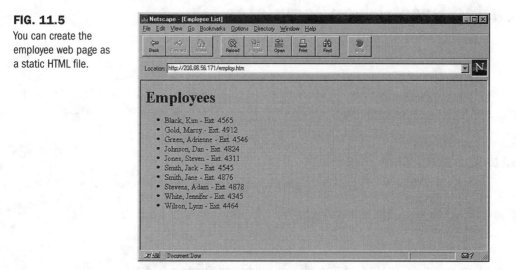

Understanding Dynamic Web Pages

Why, then, is a static HTML file not the way to create the web page? Well, what would you do when a new employee is hired or when an employee leaves the company? What would you do if phone extensions change?

You could directly modify the HTML code to reflect these changes, but you already have all this information in a database. Why would you want to have to enter it all again? You would run the risk of making mistakes, misspelling names, getting entries out of order, and possibly even losing names altogether. As the number of names in the list grows, so will the potential for errors occurring. Plus, during the period between updating the table and updating the web page, employees will be looking at inaccurate information.

An easier and more reliable solution would be to have the web page display the contents of your Employees table. This way, any table changes are immediately available to all employees. You can build the web page dynamically based on the contents of the Employees table.

To create your first Cold Fusion template, enter the code as it appears in Listing 11.5, and save it in the C:\A2Z\SCRIPTS as EMPLOY1.CFM. (Don't worry if the Cold Fusion code does not make much sense yet; I explain it in detail later in this chapter.)

On the CD

Listing 11.5 EMPLOY1.CFM—Sample Cold Fusion Template

```
<
CFQUERY
DATASOURCE="a2Z"
NAME="employees"
>
SELECT FirstName, LastName, PhoneExtension
FROM Employees
ORDER BY LastName, FirstName
</CFQUERY>

<HTML>

<HEAD>
<TITLE>Employee List</TITLE>
</HEAD>

<BODY> .

<H1>Employees</H1>

<UL>

<CFOUTPUT QUERY="employees">
<LI>#LastName#, #FirstName# - Ext. #PhoneExtension#
</CFOUTPUT>

</UL>

</BODY>

</HTML>
```

Part
III

Ch
11

Next, load your browser and type **http://*yourserver.com*/a2z/employ1.cfm** in the URL field (again, replace *yourserver.com* with your own server name). The results are shown in Figure 11.6.

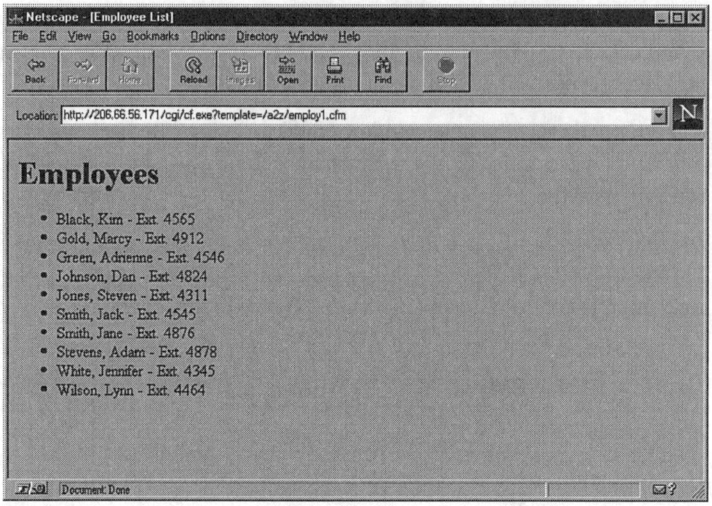

FIG. 11.6

Ideally, the employee web page should be generated dynamically, based on live data.

Understanding Data-Driven Templates

Now, compare Figure 11.5 and Figure 11.6. Can you see the difference between them? Look carefully.

Give up? Well, the truth is that they are not at all different. The screen shots are identical. If you were to look at the HTML source code that generated Figure 11.6, you would see that aside from lots of extra white space, the dynamically generated code is exactly the same as the static code you entered in Listing 11.4, and nothing like the dynamic code you entered in Listing 11.5.

So, how does the code in Listing 11.5 become the HTML source code that generates Figure 11.6? In the following sections, I help you review the code listing carefully.

Using the *CFQUERY* Tag

The first lines in Listing 11.5 are a Cold Fusion tag called CFQUERY. CFQUERY (or Cold Fusion Query) is the tag you use to submit any SQL statement to an ODBC data source. The SQL statement is usually an SQL SELECT statement but also can be INSERT, UPDATE, DELETE, or any other SQL statement.

▶ **See** "Creating an ODBC Data Source," **p. 134**

▶ **See** "Creating Queries," **p. 141**

▶ **See** "*CFQUERY*," **p. 895**

The CFQUERY tag has several attributes, or parameters, that are passed to it when used. The CFQUERY in Listing 11.5 uses the following attributes:

- The NAME attribute is used to name the query and any returned data.
- The DATASOURCE attribute contains the name of the ODBC data source to be used.

Any text that appears between the <CFQUERY> and </CFQUERY> tags is the SQL code that will be passed to the ODBC driver for processing.

> **N O T E** The CFQUERY name passed to the NAME attribute must be unique in each Cold Fusion template. If you try to reuse a query name, Cold Fusion returns an error message. ∎

The query NAME you specify is **Employees**. You will use this name later when you process the results generated by the query.

For the DATASOURCE attribute, you specify **A2Z**, the name of the data source you created in Chapter 9, "SQL Data Manipulation."

The SQL code specified was:

```
SELECT FirstName, LastName, PhoneExtension
FROM Employees
ORDER BY LastName, FirstName
```

This statement selects the columns you need from the Employees table and sorts them by last name plus first name. The SQL statement, like all other passed values, is enclosed within quotation marks.

T I P The SQL statement in Listing 11.5 is broken up over many lines to make the code more readable. Although you can write a long SQL statement that is wider than the width of your browser window, generally you should break up these statements over as many lines as you need.

When Cold Fusion processes the template, the first item it finds is the Cold Fusion tag CFQUERY. Cold Fusion knows which tags it itself must process and which it must pass to the server directly. CFQUERY is a Cold Fusion tag and, therefore, must be processed by Cold Fusion.

When Cold Fusion encounters a CFQUERY tag, it creates an ODBC request and submits it to the specified data source. The results, if any, are stored in a temporary buffer and are identified by the name specified in the NAME attribute. This process happens before Cold Fusion processes the next line in the template.

The CFQUERY code, and indeed all Cold Fusion markup code, never gets sent on to the server for transmission to the browser. Unlike HTML tags that are browser instructions, CFML tags are instructions to Cold Fusion.

The next lines in the template are standard HTML tags: headers, title, and headings. Because they are not Cold Fusion tags, they are sent to the web server and then to the client browser.

Displaying Query Results with the *CFOUTPUT* Tag

Next, in Listing 11.5, you create an HTML unordered list using the <UL> tag. The list is terminated a few lines later with a </UL> tag.

The list of employees itself goes between the <UL> and </UL> tags. Each name is a separate list item and, therefore, begins with an HTML <LI> tag. But, instead of listing the employees as shown in Figure 11.4, you use a CFOUTPUT tag.

CFOUTPUT is the same Cold Fusion output tag you used earlier. But this time you use it to create a code block that outputs the results of a CFQUERY. For Cold Fusion to know which query results to output, the query name is passed to CFOUTPUT in the QUERY attribute. The name you provide is the same name assigned to the NAME attribute of the CFQUERY tag. In this case, the NAME is Employees.

The code between the <CFOUTPUT QUERY="employees"> and </CFOUTPUT> is the output code block. Cold Fusion uses this code once for every row that is retrieved. As 10 rows currently appear in the Employees table, the CFOUPUT code is looped through 10 times. And any HTML or CFML tags within that block are repeated as well, once for each row.

▶ **See** *"CFOUTPUT,"* **p. 891**

Using Database Table Columns

As explained earlier, Cold Fusion uses # to delimit fields. In addition to CGI variables and URL parameters that you used at the beginning of this chapter, Cold Fusion fields can also be columns retrieved by a CFQUERY. Whatever field you use, Cold Fusion replaces the field name with the actual value. So when Cold Fusion processes the output block, it replaces #LastName# with the contents of the LastName column retrieved in the Employee query. Each time the output code block is used, that row's LastName value is inserted into the HTML code.

Cold Fusion fields can be treated as any other text in an HTML document. You can apply any of the HTML formatting tags to them. In the example, the query results need to be displayed in an unordered list. Each employee's name and phone extension is a list item and, therefore, is preceded by the <LI> tag. As the <LI> tag is included within the CFOUTPUT block, Cold Fusion outputs it along with every row.

So, for employee Kim Black at extension 4565, the line

```
<LI> #LastName#, #FirstName# - Ext. #PhoneExtension#
```

becomes

```
<LI> Black, Kim - Ext. 4565
```

Only the <LI> tag is within the CFOUPUT block, and not the <UL> and </UL>, because you want only one list, not many. If the <UL> and </UL> are within the CFOUPUT block, you have a new list created for each employee—definitely not the desired result at all.

Figure 11.6 shows the browser display that this template creates. It is exactly the same result as Figure 11.5, but without any new data entry whatsoever. Welcome to Cold Fusion and the wonderful world of dynamic data-driven web pages.

Using Drill-Down Applications

The nature of the World Wide Web places certain restrictions on data interaction. Every time a web browser makes a request, a connection is made to a web server, and that connection is maintained only for as long as it takes to retrieve the web page. Subsequent selections and web requests create yet another connection—again, just for the specific request.

Simple user interfaces that you may take for granted in most commercial software, such as scrolling through previous or next records with the cursor keys, become quite complex within the constraints of web pages and in how they interact with web servers.

One elegant and popular form of web-based data interaction is the "drill-down" approach. Drill down is designed to break up data so that only what is needed on a single page is displayed. Selecting an item in that page causes details about that item to be displayed. The process is called drilling down because you drill through the data layer-by-layer to find the information you need.

The employee page you just created, for example, displays a simple list of employees and extensions. What if you want to display more information such as title, department, and email address? You can just select more columns in the CFQUERY and display them in the CFOUTPUT code, but doing so would clutter the screen, making it hard to use. A better approach would be to display less information on a page and allow the user to click an employee's name to display more information about that employee. This approach, gradually digging deeper into a data set to find the information you want, is known as drilling down.

Building Dynamic SQL Statements

Creating a drill-down application in Cold Fusion involves creating multiple templates. For example, one template should list the employees, and a second template should display an employee's details.

First, create the detail template. The SQL query in this template has to select detailed user information for a specific user. Obviously, you don't want to create a template for every employee in your database. Doing so would totally defeat the purpose of using templates in the first place. Rather, the template needs to be passed a parameter, a value that uniquely identifies an employee. Fortunately, when you created the Employees table, you created a column called EmployeeID, which contains a unique employee ID for each employee in the table. The code in Listing 11.6 demonstrates how to pass parameters.

On the CD

Listing 11.6   EMPDTL1.CFM—Passing Dynamic Parameters

```
<
CFQUERY
DATASOURCE="a2Z"
NAME="employee"
>
 SELECT LastName,
 FirstName,
 MiddleInit,
 Title,
 PhoneExtension,
 PhoneCellular,
 PhonePager,
 EMail
 FROM Employees
 WHERE EmployeeID = #EmployeeID#
</CFQUERY>

<CFOUTPUT QUERY="employee">

<HTML>

<HEAD>
<TITLE>#LastName#, #FirstName# #MiddleInit#</TITLE>
</HEAD>

<BODY>

<H1>#LastName#, #FirstName#</H1>

<HR>

Title: #Title#
<BR>
Extension: #PhoneExtension#
<BR>
Cellular: #PhoneCellular#
<BR>
Pager: #PhonePager#
<BR>
E-Mail: #EMail#

</BODY>


</CFOUTPUT>
```

Before you look at the web page produced by this code, take a look at the SQL statement in this CFQUERY tag. The SQL SELECT statement selects the columns needed and uses a WHERE clause to specify which row to select. The WHERE clause cannot be hard-coded for any particular employee ID and, therefore, uses a passed field, #EmployeeID#. The #EmployeeID# field is passed to the template as part of the URL.

If an `EmployeeID` of 7 is passed with the URL, the `WHERE` clause `WHERE EmployeeID = #EmployeeID#` becomes `WHERE EmployeeID = 7`—exactly what you need to select the correct row. As you learned earlier, parameters are passed to URLs after the template name, and each parameter is separated by an ampersand character. So, to specify employee ID 7, you add **?EmployeeID=7** to the URL.

Now try this example. Type the URL **http://*yourserver.com*/a2z/ empdtl1.cfm?EmployeeID=7** in the URL field (once again, replace *yourserver.com* with your own server name) in your browser. The resulting output is shown in Figure 11.7.

FIG. 11.7

If you want to create truly dynamic pages, parameters can be passed to Cold Fusion templates and used to create dynamic SQL statements.

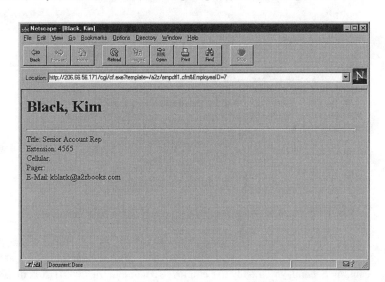

To display the details for another employee, you just need to change the value passed to the URL `EmployeeID` parameter. Try replacing EmployeeID=7 with **EmployeeID=5**. Changing the parameter displays information on a different employee. You can now use the same template to display details for any employee in the database because the web page is data driven.

Implementing Data Drill Down

To complete the drill-down application, you need to modify the employee list page to include links to the employee details page. The code for the updated template is shown in Listing 11.7.

On the CD

Listing 11.7 EMPLOY2.CFM—Building Dynamic SQL Statements

```
<
CFQUERY
DATASOURCE="a2Z"
NAME="employees"
>
SELECT FirstName, LastName, PhoneExtension, EmployeeID
FROM Employees
```

continues

Listing 11.7   Continued

```
ORDER BY LastName, FirstName
</CFQUERY>

<HTML>

<HEAD>
<TITLE>Employee List</TITLE>
</HEAD>

<BODY>

<H1>Employees</H1>

<UL>

<CFOUTPUT QUERY="employees">
<LI><A HREF="empdtl1.cfm?EmployeeID=#EmployeeID#">
#LastName#, #FirstName#</A> - Ext. #PhoneExtension#
</CFOUTPUT>

</UL>

</BODY>

</HTML>
```

Listing 11.7 is the same as Listing 11.5, with two exceptions. First, you now need the EmployeeID value, so you change the SQL SELECT statement in the CFQUERY to also include this column. Second, you modify the employee's name in the CFOUTPUT code block so that it is a hyperlink to the employee detail page.

The new employee name code reads:

```
<LI> <A HREF="empdtl1.cfm?EmployeeID=#EmployeeID#">#LastName#, #FirstName#</A> -
Ext. #PhoneExtension#
```

When Cold Fusion processes employee 7, this line becomes:

```
<LI> <A HREF="empdtl1.cfm?EmployeeID=7">Black, Kim</A> - Ext. 4565
```

This way, the URL needed for the hyperlink is dynamic, too. The URL built for each employee also contains the correct employee ID, which can be passed to the employee detail template.

So now try out this example. Type the URL **http://*yourserver.com*/a2z/employ2.cfm** (again, replace *yourserver.com* with your own server name). Figure 11.8 shows what the output looks like. The only difference between this display and the one in Figure 11.6 is that now the employee names are hyperlinks. You can click any one of these links to display employee details, as shown in Figure 11.9.

FIG. 11.8

You can build hyperlink URLs dynamically to create even more dynamic web pages.

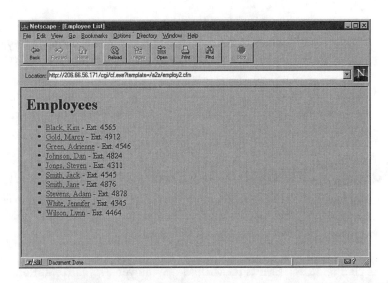

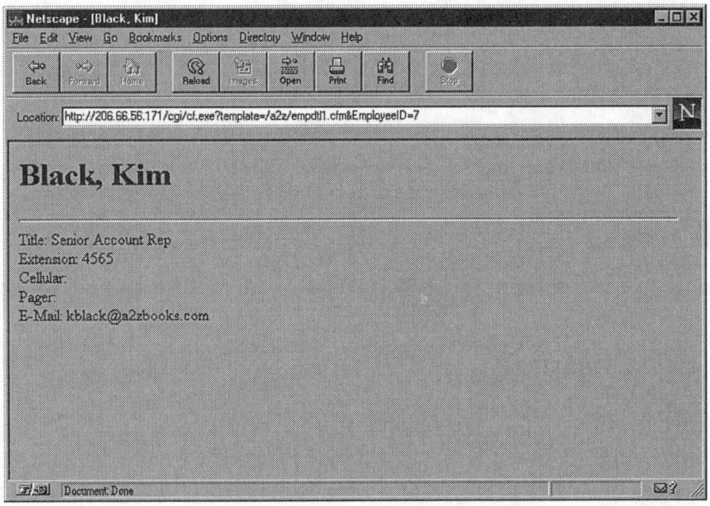

FIG. 11.9

By passing parameters to a Cold Fusion template, you can use the same template to display different records without requiring a different HTML page for each.

Using Frames to Implement Data Drill Down

One problem with the drill-down templates you just created is that every time you view an employee's details you have to click your browser's Back button to return to the employee list page. A more usable approach would be to display the employee list and details at the same time. Fortunately, you can do so easily by using a browser feature called frames. Using frames, you can split your browser window in two or more windows and control what gets displayed within each. Cold Fusion templates are well suited for use within frames.

Creating frames involves creating multiple templates (or HTML pages). Each window in a frame typically displays a different template. If you have two windows, you need two templates. In addition, you always need one more page that is used to lay out and create the frames.

When you create the frames, each window is named with a unique name. In a non-framed window, every time you select a hyperlink, the new page is opened in the same window, replacing whatever contents were there previously. In a framed window, you can use the window name to control the destination for any output.

Creating Frames for Use with Cold Fusion

Now that you have an idea how frames work, the first thing you need to do is create the template to define and create the frames. The code for template EMPLFRAM.CFM is shown in Listing 11.8.

On the CD

Listing 11.8   EMPLFRAM.CFM—Employee Frame Definition and Creation

```
<HTML>

<HEAD>
<TITLE>Employees</TITLE>
</HEAD>

<FRAMESET COLS=" 50%,50%">
<FRAME SRC="employ3.cfm" NAME="employees">
<FRAME SRC="empdtl1.cfm?EmployeeID=0" NAME="details">
</FRAMESET>

</HTML>
```

This template first defines the frames. `<FRAMESET COLS=" 50%,50%">` creates two columns (or windows), each taking up 50% of the width of the browser window.

Then the two columns are defined. The line `<FRAME SRC="employ3.cfm" NAME="employees">` creates the left frame. The NAME attribute names the window, and the SRC attribute specifies the name of the template to initially display within the window when the frame is first displayed.

When the frame is first displayed, no employee is selected yet. Therefore, no information is available for display in the details window, the right frame. The simplest way to display an empty frame is to specify an nonexistent EmployeeID in the URL. You specified an EmployeeID of 0, and so Cold Fusion finds no rows and does not display anything there at all.

The next thing to do is to create the employee list template. Actually, it is the same as the one in Listing 11.7, with one important difference. The URL to display the employee details must include a TARGET attribute to designate in which window to display the URL. If the TARGET is omitted, the new data is displayed in the frame from which it is selected.

The modified code is shown in Listing 11.9. As you can see, the URL has been modified to include the attribute TARGET="details". This attribute specifies that the new URL should be displayed in the frame named details, the right window.

On the CD

Listing 11.9 EMPLOY3.CFM—Using Frames for Data Drill Down

```
<
CFQUERY
DATASOURCE="a2Z"
NAME="employees"
>
SELECT FirstName, LastName, PhoneExtension, EmployeeID
FROM Employees
ORDER BY LastName, FirstName
</CFQUERY>

<HTML>

<HEAD>
<TITLE>Employee List</TITLE>
</HEAD>

<BODY>

<H1>Employees</H1>

<UL>

<CFOUTPUT QUERY="employees">
<LI><A HREF="empdtl1.cfm?EmployeeID=#EmployeeID#"
TARGET="details">#LastName#, #FirstName#</A> - Ext. #PhoneExtension#
</CFOUTPUT>

</UL>

</BODY>

</HTML>
```

Part
III

Ch
11

That's all there is to it. To try out this example, type in the URL **http://yourserver.com/a2z/ emplfram.cfm**. (I am no longer going to remind you to replace *yourserver.com* with your own server name.) Figure 11.10 shows the output as it appears in framed windows. Try clicking any employee's name in the left window, and the right window displays employee details.

FIGURE 11.10

Cold Fusion is well suited for use within HTML frames.

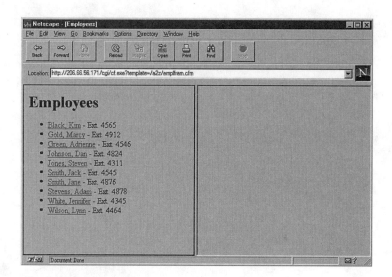

Displaying Results in Tables

Most web browsers now support tables. By using the HTML <TABLE> tag, you can display data in a two-dimensional grid. Tables are useful for presenting lists in a clean, columnar display.

Because HTML tables are used so often to display query results in data-driven pages, and the <TABLE> syntax can be confusing at times, the makers of Cold Fusion created a Cold Fusion tag called CFTABLE. The CFTABLE tag is designed to conceal the details involved in creating HTML tables. All you have to do is tell Cold Fusion what data to put in each column, and Cold Fusion generates the <TABLE> markup code for you.

The CFTABLE tag has another important advantage. It enables you to create tables that can be viewed by all browsers, even those that do not support HTML tables. To do this, Cold Fusion renders the output in a nonproportional font and pads fields with spaces so that they line up in columns. Although the resulting table might not look as good as a true HTML table, it is functional and is supported by all browsers.

▶ See "*CFTABLE*," p. 905

Creating Non-HTML Tables with *CFTABLE*

For an example of the places where you can use CFTABLE, look at the browser output shown in Figure 11.8. Notice how the phone extension is right next to the name and in a different location on the screen depending on how long the employee's name is. If the employees were listed in a table, the data could be presented in a cleaner and more organized fashion.

Listing 11.10 is based on Listing 11.7, but instead of using an unordered list and presenting each employee as a list item, the list is displayed in a table.

Listing 11.10 EMPLOY4.CFM—Using _CFTABLE_ to Display Data in Tables

```
<
CFQUERY
DATASOURCE="a2Z"
NAME="employees"
>
SELECT FirstName, LastName, PhoneExtension, EmployeeID
FROM Employees
ORDER BY LastName, FirstName
</CFQUERY>

<HTML>

<HEAD>
<TITLE>Employee List</TITLE>
</HEAD>

<BODY>

<H1>Employees</H1>

<
CFTABLE
QUERY="employees"
COLHEADERS
>
<
CFCOL
HEADER="employee"
TEXT=" <A HREF=" "empdtl1.cfm?EmployeeID=#EmployeeID#" ">#LastName#, #FirstName#
</A>"
>
<
CFCOL
HEADER="extension"
TEXT="ext. #PhoneExtension#"
>
</CFTABLE>

</BODY>

</HTML>
```

To create the table, you use the tag <CFTABLE QUERY="employees" COLHEADERS>. The CFTABLE tag is a special type of CFOUTPUT and, therefore, requires that you specify a QUERY attribute, just like the one you would provide to CFOUTPUT. You use CFTABLE only to display query results, and the QUERY attribute specifies which result set to process. You use the COLHEADERS attribute to instruct Cold Fusion to create optional column headers for each column in the table.

Next, Cold Fusion needs to know what columns you want to include in your table. You specify each column by using the CFCOL tag. You specify two columns here, one for the employee name and one for the phone extension.

The code for the phone extension column is

```
<CFCOL HEADER="extension" TEXT="ext. #PhoneExtension#">
```

The HEADER attribute specifies the text to use in the column header. This column has a header with the text Extension in it. The TEXT attribute is required; every CFCOL tag must have one. It tells Cold Fusion what you want to display in this column. The TEXT attribute here contains the expression "ext. #PhoneExtension#". As Cold Fusion processes each row, it replaces the #PhoneExtension# field with the value of the retrieved PhoneExtension column.

The employee name column may look more complicated, but it really isn't at all. The source for the column is

```
<CFCOL HEADER="employee" TEXT=
" <A HREF=" "empdtl1.cfm?EmployeeID=#EmployeeID#" ">
#LastName#, #FirstName#</A>">
```

Again, you first specify the text for the optional header in the HEADER attribute. The TEXT attribute contains the text to display, and, because the name has to be a hyperlink, you must specify the A HREF link tag, too.

In fact, the contents of the TEXT attribute are almost the same as the hyperlink tag you used in Listing 11.7 earlier—with one notable exception. Notice that the link tag has double quotation marks around the URL instead of the usual single set of quotation marks. You need the double quotation marks to tell Cold Fusion to treat this as a quote, not as the end of the TEXT attribute. If you were to enter a single quotation mark, Cold Fusion would think that the TEXT attribute ends right after the HREF=. Because it would not know what to do with the text after the quotation mark, Cold Fusion would report a syntax error. This process of using double quotes to indicate an actual quote character is called *escaping*, and the quote character is said to have *been escaped*.

So, now that you understand the code listing, go ahead and run the template. Type in the URL **http://*yourserver.com*/a2z/employ4.cfm**. As you can see in Figure 11.11, the employee names and phone extensions are now displayed in clearly labeled columns

How is this table created without using the HTML <TABLE> tag? Look at the source code generated by Cold Fusion to find out. Select the View Source option in your browser (in Netscape, choose Document Source from the View menu; in Microsoft Internet Explorer, choose Source from the View menu).

As you can see in Figure 11.12, Cold Fusion uses the HTML <PRE> tag, which displays text exactly as it appears in the source code. Usually, web browsers ignore white-space characters, such as spaces and line feeds. The <PRE> tag instructs the browser to maintain all spacing and line feeds, allowing Cold Fusion to lay out the data exactly as it wants the browser to display it.

TIP

Viewing the source code generated by Cold Fusion is useful in debugging template problems. When you view the source, you are looking at the complete output as it was sent to your browser. If you ever need to ascertain why a web page does not look like you intended, a good place to start is comparing your template with the source code it generated.

FIG. 11.11
Cold Fusion can generate non-HTML tables using the CFTABLE tag.

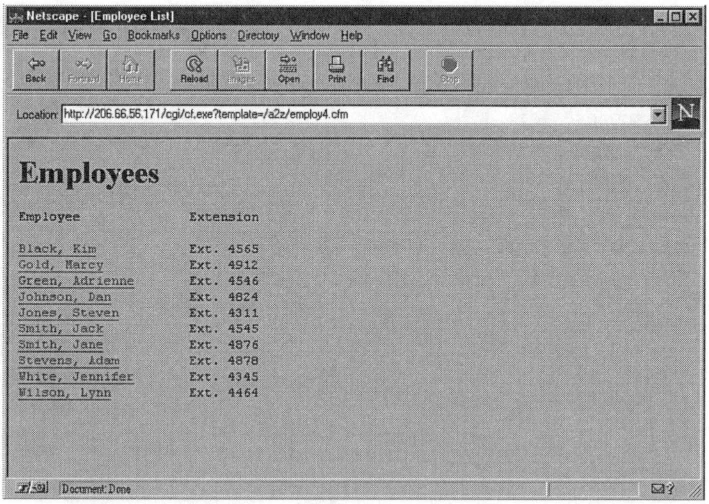

FIG. 11.12
To see how Cold Fusion interprets your template, view the generated markup language code with your browser's View Source option.

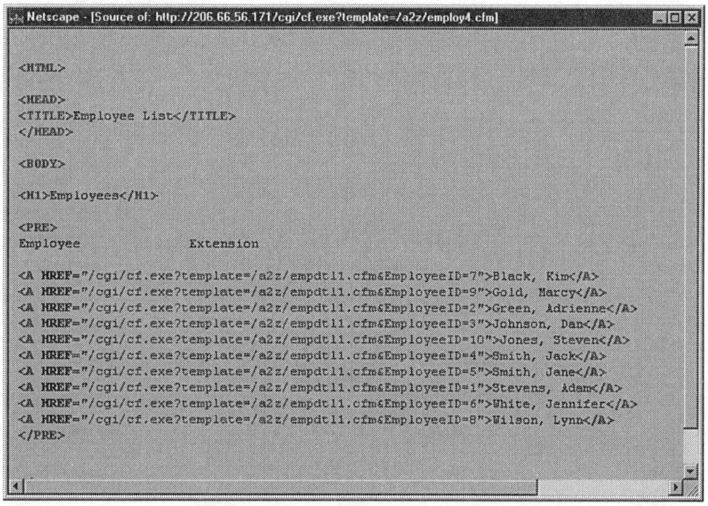

Part
III

Ch
11

Creating HTML Tables with *CFTABLE*

Tables created with the HTML <TABLE> tag, of course, look much better. So Cold Fusion supports HTML tables, too. As you can see in Listing 11.11, to create HTML tables, you just need to specify the HTMLTABLE attribute in the CFTABLE tag.

On the CD

Listing 11.11 EMPLOY5.CFM—Create HTML Tables with *CFTABLE*

```
<
CFQUERY
DATASOURCE="a2Z"
NAME="employees"
>
SELECT FirstName, LastName, PhoneExtension, EmployeeID
FROM Employees
ORDER BY LastName, FirstName
</CFQUERY>

<HTML>

<HEAD>
<TITLE>Employee List</TITLE>
</HEAD>

<BODY>

<H1>Employees</H1>

<
CFTABLE
QUERY="employees"
COLHEADERS
HTMLTABLE
>
<
CFCOL
HEADER="employee"
TEXT=" <A HREF=" "empdtl1.cfm?EmployeeID=#EmployeeID#" ">#LastName#, #FirstName#
</A>"
>
<
CFCOL
HEADER="extension"
TEXT="ext. #PhoneExtension#"
>
</CFTABLE>

</BODY>

</HTML>
```

Figure 11.13 shows the same employee list screen rendered in an HTML table. Note that when you're displaying data in an HTML table, standard fonts are used, not the fixed font used when the <PRE> tag is specified. Therefore, you can safely use any other HTML formatting options in the CFCOL TEXT attribute if required. If you want the name in bold, for example, you can specify

```
TEXT=" <A HREF=" "empdtl1.cfm?EmployeeID=#EmployeeID#" ">
<B>#LastName#, #FirstName#</B></A>"
```

Cold Fusion still can display the table correctly. The <B> and </B> tags are HTML tags, not CFML tags, so Cold Fusion just passes them through to the web server to be sent to your web browser.

FIG. 11.13

You can use the CFTABLE tag to create HTML tables.

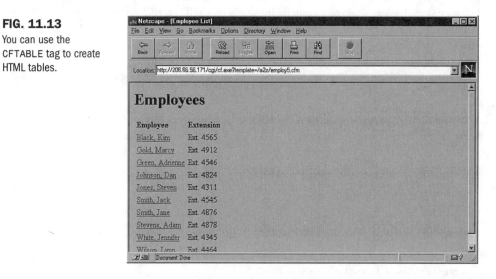

To create this table, Cold Fusion generates HTML table code. This source code, as displayed by the browser's view source function, is shown in Figure 11.14.

FIG. 11.14

Cold Fusion can generate all the required code to create HTML tables.

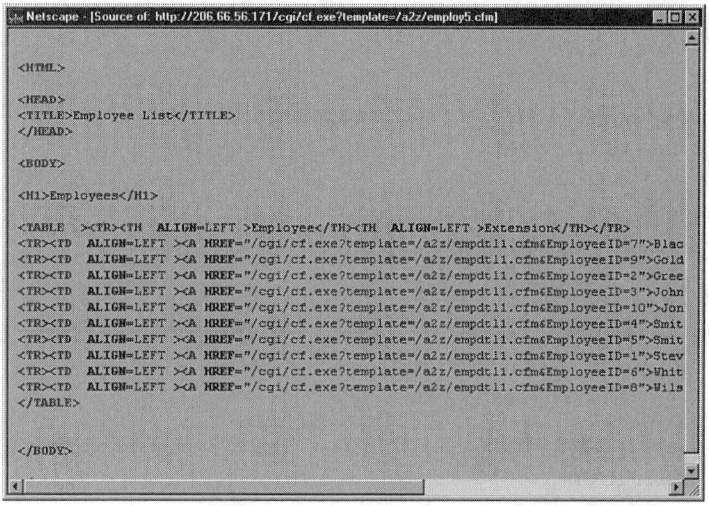

Creating HTML Tables Manually

As good as the Cold Fusion <CFTABLE> tag is, it is very limited. HTML tables support many advanced features such as table headers, cells that span multiple rows or columns, borders and border colors, background colors and images, and more. If you really want to control how your tables are displayed, you must resort to creating your tables manually. Listing 11.12 demonstrates how to create a bordered table manually for the employee list.

On the CD

Listing 11.12   EMPLOY6.CFM—Creating Tables Manually

```
<
CFQUERY
DATASOURCE="a2Z"
NAME="employees"
>
SELECT FirstName, LastName, PhoneExtension, EmployeeID
FROM Employees
ORDER BY LastName, FirstName
</CFQUERY>

<HTML>

<HEAD>
<TITLE>Employee List</TITLE>
</HEAD>

<BODY>

<CENTER>

<TABLE BORDER=5>

<TR>
<TH COLSPAN=2>
<H1>Employees</H1>
</TH>
</TR>

<CFOUTPUT QUERY="employees">
<TR>
<TD>
<A HREF="empdtl1.cfm?EmployeeID=#EmployeeID#">#LastName#, #FirstName#</A>
</TD>
<TD>
Ext. #PhoneExtension#
</TD>
</TR>
</CFOUTPUT>

</TABLE>
```

```
    </CENTER>

    </BODY>

    </HTML>
```

Figure 11.15 shows the output for this listing.

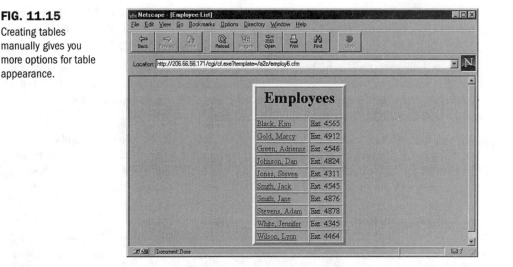

Now look at the code in Listing 11.12. First, you create the table with the <TABLE> tag and specify an optional border. HTML tables can have borders of varying thickness, and the BORDER attribute specifies the border to use. Then you create a table title and place it in a header cell (specified with the tag) that spans two columns.

Next comes the CFOUTPUT. As each query row is output, a new table row is created. For this reason, you include a complete table row (the <TR> tag) and cells (the <TD> tag) within the CFOUTPUT code block. And finally, you close the table with a </TABLE> tag.

As you can see, manually creating tables requires more effort and a better understanding of HTML tables, but the rewards are well worth your time.

N O T E Using HTML tables is a useful way to format data, but a cost is associated with using tables. For a browser to display a table correctly, it cannot display any part of that table until it receives the entire table from the web server. This happens because any row, even one near the end of the table, can have an effect on the width of columns and how the table is formatted. Therefore, if you display data in a table, the user doesn't see any data at all until all the data is present. If you use another type of display—for example, a list—the data is displayed as it is received. The reality is, the page may likely take as long to fully load with or without tables. The downside of using tables is that it takes longer for any data to appear. This, however, does not apply to tables created without the <TABLE> tag. ▪

Grouping Query Results

Before you are introduced to a new level of complexity, review how Cold Fusion processes queries. In Cold Fusion, you create data queries by using the <CFQUERY> tag. CFQUERY performs an SQL operation and retrieves results, if any. Results are stored temporarily by Cold Fusion, and they remain around only for the duration of the processing of the template that contains the query.

To output query results, you use the <CFOUTPUT> tag. CFOUTPUT takes a query name as an attribute and then loops through all the rows that are retrieved by the query. The code block between the <CFOUTPUT> and the </CFOUTPUT> is repeated once for every row retrieved.

All the examples you created to this point displayed results in a single list or a single table. But what do you do if you want to process the results in subsets? For example, suppose you want to list the employees by department. You could just change the SQL statement in the CFQUERY to set the sort order to be department and then, perhaps, by name within each department.

This approach would retrieve the data in the correct order, but how would you display it? If you use CFOUTPUT as you have until now, then every row created by the CFOUTPUT block has to be the same. If one has a department name, then all have to, because every row that is processed is processed with the same block of code. So how do you create the output shown in Figure 11.16?

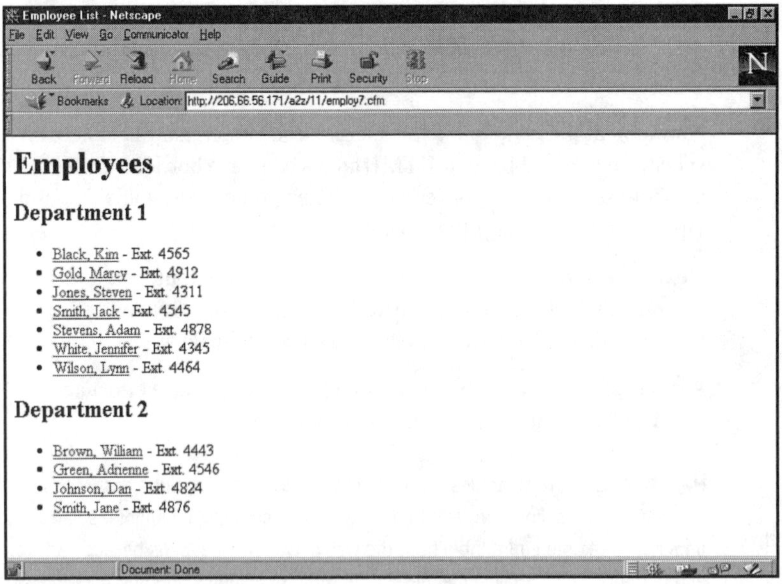
Employee List - Netscape
File Edit View Go Communicator Help
Back Forward Reload Home Search Guide Print Security Stop
Bookmarks Location: http://206.66.56.171/a2z/11/employ7.cfm
Employees
Department 1
Black, Kim - Ext. 4565
Gold, Marcy - Ext. 4912
Jones, Steven - Ext. 4311
Smith, Jack - Ext. 4545
Stevens, Adam - Ext. 4878
White, Jennifer - Ext. 4345
Wilson, Lynn - Ext. 4464
Department 2
Brown, William - Ext. 4443
Green, Adrienne - Ext. 4546
Johnson, Dan - Ext. 4824
Smith, Jane - Ext. 4876
Document: Done

FIG. 11.16 You can use the CFOUTPUT tag to group query results and display them accordingly.

The solution is to group the data results. By grouping, you can have more than one CFOUTPUT loop. To understand how grouping works, look at the template in Listing 11.13.

On the CD

Listing 11.13   EMPLOY7.CFM—Employee List Grouped by Department

```
<
CFQUERY
DATASOURCE="a2Z"
NAME="employees"
>
SELECT DepartmentID, FirstName, LastName, PhoneExtension, EmployeeID
FROM Employees
ORDER BY DepartmentID, LastName, FirstName
</CFQUERY>

<HTML>

<HEAD>
<TITLE>Employee List</TITLE>
</HEAD>

<BODY>

<H1>Employees</H1>

<CFOUTPUT QUERY="employees" GROUP="departmentID">
<H2>Department #DepartmentID#</H2>

<UL>

<CFOUTPUT>
<LI><A HREF="empdtl1.cfm?EmployeeID=#EmployeeID#">#LastName#, #FirstName#
</A> - Ext. #PhoneExtension#
</CFOUTPUT>

</UL>

</CFOUTPUT>

</BODY>

</HTML>
```

The first changes you make are adding the DepartmentID column to the SQL SELECT statement and modifying the sort sequence with ORDER BY DepartmentID, LastName, FirstName. To group results by a column, that column must be the first in the sort sequence. As you want to sort by DepartmentID, that column is now the first in the ORDER BY list.

The big change, however, is the CFOUTPUT block. You now have two of them, one nested inside the other. The outer CFOUTPUT tag also has a new attribute: GROUP="departmentID". A CFOUTPUT tag creates a loop that executes once for each row retrieved by a query. When you add the GROUP attribute, you instruct Cold Fusion to execute the CFOUPUT block only when the group value changes.

If you have seven employees with the same DepartmentID, the GROUP CFOUTPUT block is executed just once. In the list, you have 10 employees who work in two departments. The outer CFOUPUT block gets executed twice, once for each department. The first row processed has a DepartmentID of 1, so the CFOUTPUT block is executed. The next six rows processed also have a DepartmentID of 1, so the CFOUTPUT block is not executed for them. The eighth row has a different DepartmentID, with a value of 2, so the CFOUTPUT block is executed. The next two rows also have a DepartmentID of 2, so no CFOUTPUT block is executed for them. That's just the outer CFOUTPUT block. The inner block gets executed for every row, just like the CFOUTPUT blocks you used earlier.

Now look at the output code in Listing 11.13. The outer CFOUTPUT creates a header for each new group and then starts a new unordered list. The inner CFOUTPUT populates that list until the group is completed. Then the outer CFOUTPUT terminates the list, and the process loops to the next DepartmentID. The results are shown in Figure 11.16.

NOTE Groups can be nested by creating additional CFOUTPUT blocks, one for each group. There is no limit to the number of groups that may be nested as long as the following two conditions are met. First, every group must be part of the sort sequence used to retrieve the data. Second, the order that the columns appear in the ORDER BY clause must match the order of the groupings. ■

Now you can see why the column you want to group on must be the first in the ORDER BY list. For grouping to work, all rows with the same value in the grouping column must be processed as a group. If the group is broken up, as could happen if you do not sort by the grouping column, Cold Fusion executes the outer block at the wrong times, and the resulting groups are fragmented.

Specifying Field Types

You have now used two different types of fields: CGI variables and URL parameters. Cold Fusion supports several field types, as shown in Table 11.1, and fields that are database table columns retrieved with a CFQUERY.

Table 11.1 Cold Fusion Field Types

Field	Description
ATTRIBUTES	Attributes passed to custom tags
CALLER	Caller scope variables
CGI	HTTP CGI variables
CLIENT	Client variables
COOKIE	HTTP client-side cookies
FILE	CFFILE status fields

Field	Description
FORM	HTML form fields
SERVER	Server scope fields
SESSION	Client session fields
URL	Parameters passed to a URL
VARIABLES	Cold Fusion variables

In this chapter, you used two of these field types and CFQUERY results. By the time you finish reading this book, you'll be using them all regularly. Sooner or later, you're going to run into a name collision. For example, you may have a form field with the exact same name as a table column or a variable with the same name as an URL parameter. When this situation occurs, how does Cold Fusion know which one to use? Well, the answer is that Cold Fusion doesn't know. You must specify which to use. And the way you specify is by qualifying the field name with the field type.

Listing 11.14 is the same template you created in Listing 11.3, with one difference. The references to field name are fully qualified as URL.name. The prefix URL states that the variable wanted is a URL variable (as opposed to a FORM variable, or any other variable type). This way, even if you have any other field called name, Cold Fusion still knows to which field you are referring.

On the CD

Listing 11.14   HELLO4.CFM—Avoiding Name Conflicts

```
<HTML>

<HEAD>
<TITLE>Hello!</TITLE>
</HEAD>

<BODY>

Hello,<BR>

<CFIF #ParameterExists(URL.name)# IS "Yes">
<CFOUTPUT>
The name you entered is <B>#URL.name#</B>
</CFOUTPUT>
<CFELSE>
You did not pass a parameter called NAME
</CFIF>
</BODY>

</HTML>
```

Use your browser to view this template. The resulting display should be the same as shown in Figure 11.3.

Cold Fusion Forms

by Ben Forta

In this chapter

Using Forms

In Chapter 11, "Cold Fusion Basics," you learned how to create Cold Fusion templates to dynamically display data retrieved from ODBC data sources. The A2Z Employees table has just 10 rows in it, so the data fits easily within a Web browser window.

But what do you do if you have hundreds or thousands of rows? Displaying all that data in one long list is impractical. Scrolling through lists of names to find the one you want just doesn't work well. The solution is to enable users to search for names by specifying what they are looking for. You can allow them to enter a first name, a last name, or part of a name, and then you can display only the employee records that meet the search criteria.

To accomplish this solution, you need to do two things. First, you need to create your search form using the HTML form tags. Then you need to create a template that builds SQL SELECT statements dynamically based on the data collected and submitted by the form.

▶ See "Creating Queries," **p. 141**

Creating Forms

Before you can create a search form, you need to learn how Cold Fusion interacts with HTML forms. Listing 12.1 contains the code for a sample form that prompts for a first and last name. Create this template, and save it in the C:\A2Z\SCRIPTS directory as FORM1.CFM.

On the CD

Listing 12.1   FORMS1.CFM—HTML Forms Can Be Used to Collect and Submit Data to Cold Fusion for Processing

```
<HTML>

<HEAD>
<TITLE>Learning Cold Fusion Forms 1</TITLE>
</HEAD>

<BODY>

<FORM ACTION="forms2.cfm" METHOD="POST">

Please enter your name and then click <B>Process</B>.
<P>
First name:
<INPUT TYPE="text" NAME="FirstName">
<BR>
Last name:
<INPUT TYPE="text" NAME="LastName">
<BR>
<INPUT TYPE="submit" VALUE="Process">
```

```
</FORM>

</BODY>

</HTML>
```

Next, in your browser, type the URL **http://yourserver.com/ a2z/hello1.cfm** to display the form, as shown in Figure 12.1.

This form is simple, with just two data-entry fields and a submit button, but it clearly demonstrates how forms are used to submit data to Cold Fusion.

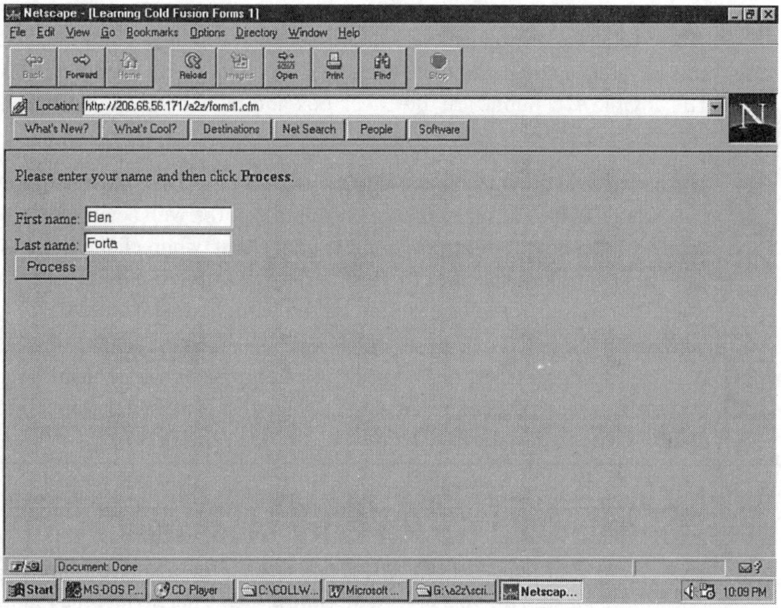

FIG. 12.1
You can use HTML forms to collect data to be submitted to Cold Fusion.

Part
III

Ch
12

Using HTML *FORM* Tags

You create HTML forms by using the <FORM> tag. <FORM> usually takes two parameters passed as tag attributes. The ACTION attribute specifies the name of the script or program that the web server should execute in response to the form's submission. To submit a form to Cold Fusion, you simply specify the name of the Cold Fusion template that will process the form. The following example specifies that the template forms2.cfm should process the submitted form:

```
ACTION="forms2.cfm"
```

The METHOD attribute specifies how data is sent back to the web server. All Cold Fusion forms must be submitted as type POST.

CAUTION

The default submission type is not POST; it is usually GET. If you omit the METHOD="POST" attribute from your form tag, you run the risk of losing form data, particularly in long forms or forms with TEXTAREA controls.

Your form has only two data-entry fields. <INPUT TYPE="text" NAME="FirstName"> and <INPUT TYPE="text" NAME="LastName"> both create simple text fields. The NAME attribute in the INPUT tag specifies the name of the field, and Cold Fusion uses this name to refer to the field when it is processed.

Each form in a field is typically given a unique name. If two fields have the same name, both sets of values are returned to be processed, separated by a comma. Usually, you want to be able to validate and manipulate each field individually, so each field should have its own name. The notable exceptions are the check box and radio button input types, which are described later in this chapter.

The last item in the form is an INPUT type of submit. The submit input type creates a button that, when clicked, submits the form contents to the web server for processing. Almost every form has a submit button (or a graphic image that, when clicked, acts like a submit button). The VALUE attribute specifies the text to display within the button, so <INPUT TYPE="submit" VALUE="Process"> creates a submit button with the text Process in it.

TIP

When you're using an INPUT type of submit, you should always specify button text by using the VALUE attribute. If you don't, the default text Submit Query (or something similar) is displayed, and this text is likely to confuse your users.

Understanding Cold Fusion Error Messages

If you enter your name into the fields and submit the form right now, you receive a Cold Fusion error message like the one shown in Figure 12.2. This error says that template C:\A2Z\SCRIPTS\FORMS2.CFM cannot be found.

This error message, of course, is perfectly valid. You submitted a form to be passed to Cold Fusion and processed with a template, but you have not created that template yet. So, your next task is to create a template to process the form submission.

FIG. 12.2
Cold Fusion returns an
error message when it
cannot process your
request.

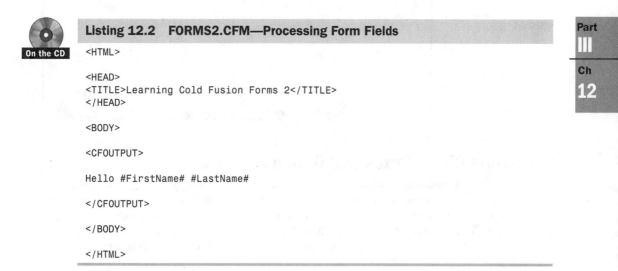

Processing Form Submissions

To demonstrate how to process returned forms, you need to create a simple template that
echoes back the name you enter. The template is shown in Listing 12.2.

Listing 12.2   FORMS2.CFM—Processing Form Fields

On the CD

```
<HTML>

<HEAD>
<TITLE>Learning Cold Fusion Forms 2</TITLE>
</HEAD>

<BODY>

<CFOUTPUT>

Hello #FirstName# #LastName#

</CFOUTPUT>

</BODY>

</HTML>
```

Part
III

Ch

12

Processing Text Submissions

By now the CFOUTPUT tag should be familiar to you; you use it to mark a block of code that Cold Fusion should parse and process. The line Hello #FirstName# #LastName# is processed by Cold Fusion. #FirstName# is replaced with the value you entered into the FirstName field, and #LastName# is replaced with the value in the LastName field in Form 1.

▶ **See** Chapter 11, "Cold Fusion Basics," **p. 193**

Create a template called FORMS2.CFM containing the code in Listing 12.2, and save it in the C:\A2Z\SCRIPTS directory. Then resubmit your name by clicking the form's submit button once again. This time, you should see a browser display similar to the one shown in Figure 12.3. Whatever name you enter into the first and last name fields of Form 1 will be displayed.

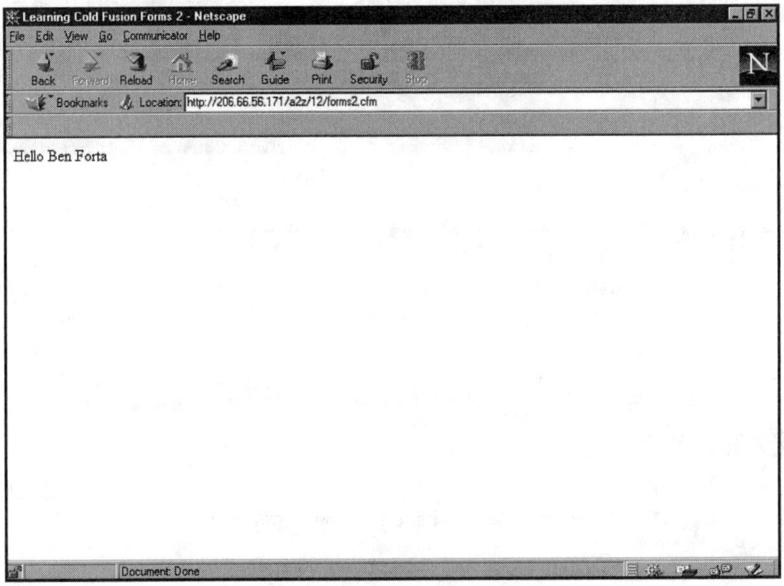

FIG. 12.3

Submitted form fields can be displayed simply by referring to the field name.

Processing Check Boxes and Option Buttons

Other input types that you will frequently use are check boxes and option buttons. Check boxes are used to select options that have just one of two states: on or off, yes or no, and true or false. To ask a user if he or she wants to be notified via email of book availability, for example, you would create a check box field. If the user selects the box, his or her name is added to the mailing list; if the user does not select the box, then his or her name is not added.

Option buttons are used to select one of at least two mutually exclusive options. You can implement a field prompting for payment type with options such as Cash, Check, Credit card, or P.O., for example, as an option button field.

The code example in Listing 12.3 creates a form that uses both option buttons and check box fields.

On the CD

Listing 12.3 FORMS3.CFM—Using Option Buttons and Check Boxes

```
<HTML>

<HEAD>
<TITLE>Learning Cold Fusion Forms 3</TITLE>
</HEAD>

<BODY>

<FORM ACTION="forms4.cfm" METHOD="POST">

Please fill in this form and then click <B>Process</B>.
<P>
Payment type:<BR>
<INPUT TYPE="radio" NAME="PaymentType" VALUE="Cash">Cash<BR>
<INPUT TYPE="radio" NAME="PaymentType" VALUE="Check">Check<BR>
<INPUT TYPE="radio" NAME="PaymentType" VALUE="Credit card">Credit card<BR>
<INPUT TYPE="radio" NAME="PaymentType" VALUE="P.O.">P.O.
<P>
Would you like to be added to our mailing list?
<INPUT TYPE="checkbox" NAME="MailingList" VALUE="Yes">
<P>
<INPUT TYPE="submit" VALUE="Process">

</FORM>

</BODY>

</HTML>
```

Figure 12.4 shows how this form appears in your browser.

Now, before you create FORMS4.CFM to process this form, you should note a couple of important points. First, look at the four lines of code that make up the Payment Type option button selection. Each one contains the exact same NAME attribute, NAME="PaymentType". Clearly, the four input fields have the same name so your browser knows that they are part of the same field. If each option button has a separate name, then the browser does not know that these buttons are mutually exclusive and thus allows the selection of more than one button.

Another important point is that, unlike INPUT type text, option buttons have no associated text or data-entry area. Therefore, for the browser to associate a particular value with each option button, you must use the VALUE attribute. The code VALUE="Cash" instructs the browser to return the value Cash in the PaymentType field if that button is selected.

Now that you can accept option button and check box fields, you're ready to create a template to process them. Create a template called FORMS4.CFM in the C:\A2Z\SCRIPTS directory using the template code in Listing 12.4.

Part
III

Ch
12

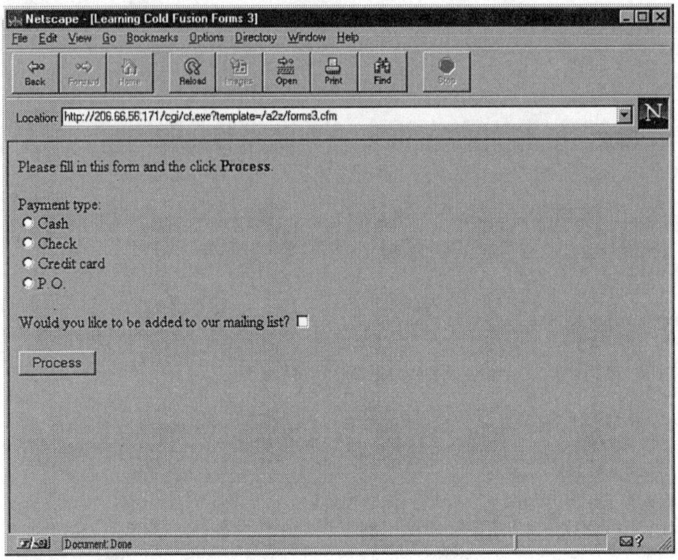

FIG. 12.4

You can use input types of option buttons and check boxes to facilitate the selection of options.

On the CD

Listing 12.4   FORMS4.CFM—Processing Option Buttons and Check Boxes

```
<HTML>

<HEAD>
<TITLE>Learning Cold Fusion Forms 4</TITLE>
</HEAD>

<BODY>

<CFOUTPUT>

Hello,<BR>
You selected <B># PaymentType#</B> as your payment type.<BR>
<CFIF #MailingList# IS "Yes">
You will be added to our mailing list.
<CFELSE>
You will not be added to our mailing list.
</CFIF>
</CFOUTPUT>

</BODY>

</HTML>
```

The form processing code in Listing 12.4 displays the payment type you select. The field PaymentType is fully qualified with the FORM field type to prevent name collisions.

▶ **See** "Specifying Field Types," **p. 222**

When the check box is checked, the value specified in the VALUE attribute is returned; in this case the value is "Yes". If the VALUE attribute is omitted, the default value of "on" will be returned.

▶ **See** "Using CFIF to Create Conditional Code," **p. 294**

Now load form FORMS3.CFM on your browser, select a payment option, and then select the check box. Next, click the Process button. Your browser display should look like the one shown in Figure 12.5.

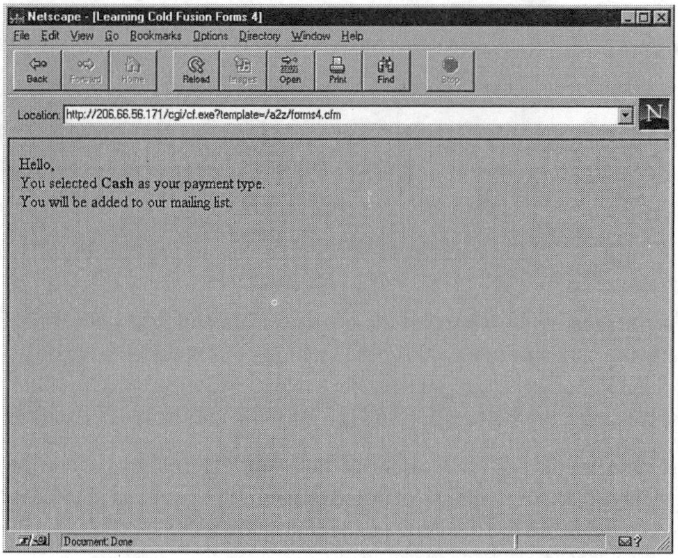

FIG. 12.5

You can use Cold Fusion templates to process user-selected options.

Well, that process worked exactly as intended, so now get ready to complicate things a little. Reload template FORMS3.CFM, and submit it without selecting a payment type or with the MailingList field not selected. As a result, Cold Fusion generates an error message, as shown in Figure 12.6. The field you do not select generates a "Form Field Not Found" error.

Check the code in Listing 12.3 to verify that the form fields do in fact exist. So, why does Cold Fusion report that the form field does not exist? Well, this is one of the quirks of HTML forms. If you select a check box, the on value is submitted; if you do not select the check box, nothing is submitted, not even an empty field. The same is true of option buttons: if you make no selection, the field is not submitted at all. (This behavior is the exact opposite of the text INPUT type, which returns empty fields as opposed to no field.)

So how do you work around this limitation? Well, you can choose from two solutions. You can modify your form processing script to check which fields exist by using the #ParameterExists()# function and, if the field exists, process it.

Part

III

Ch

12

FIG. 12.6

Option buttons or check boxes that are submitted with no value generate a Cold Fusion error.

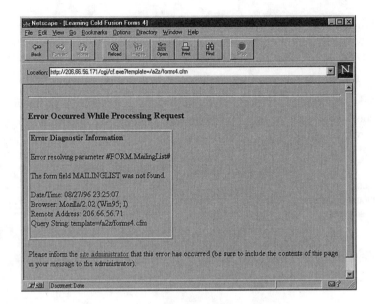

A simpler solution is to prevent the browser from omitting fields that are not selected. You can modify the option button field so that one option is preselected. The users cannot avoid making an option button selection, so they have to make a selection or use the preselected options. To preselect an option button, just add the attribute CHECKED to one of the buttons.

Check boxes are trickier, because by their very nature they have to be able to be turned off. Check boxes are used for on/off states; when the check box is off, there is no value to submit. The solution is to set a default value in the action template. This is done using a Cold Fusion tag called <CFPARAM>. <CFPARAM> allows you to create variables on-the-fly if they do not already exist. Look at this code:

```
<CFPARAM NAME="MailingList" DEFAULT="No">
```

When Cold Fusion encounters this line, it checks to see whether a variable named "MailingList" exists. If it does, processing continues. If, however, it does not exist, Cold Fusion creates the variable, and sets the value to whatever is specified in the DEFAULT attribute. The key here is that either way, whether the variable existed or not, once the <CFPARAM> tag is processed, the variable *does* exist. It is therefore safe to refer to that variable further down the template code.

The updated form is shown in Listing 12.5. The first option button in the PaymentType field is modified to read <INPUT TYPE="radio" NAME="PaymentType" VALUE="Cash" CHECKED>. The CHECKED attribute ensures that a button is checked. The "MailingList" check box has a VALUE of "Yes" when it is checked, and the <CFPARAM> in the action page ensures that if "MailingList" is not checked, the value will automatically be set to "No".

Listing 12.5   FORMS5.CFM—Using Hidden Fields to Set Default Form Values

```
<HTML>

<HEAD>
<TITLE>Learning Cold Fusion Forms 5</TITLE>
</HEAD>

<BODY>

<FORM ACTION="forms4.cfm" METHOD="POST">

Please fill in this form and then click <B>Process</B>.
<P>
Payment type:<BR>
<INPUT TYPE="radio" NAME="PaymentType" VALUE="Cash" CHECKED>Cash<BR>
<INPUT TYPE="radio" NAME="PaymentType" VALUE="Check">Check<BR>
<INPUT TYPE="radio" NAME="PaymentType" VALUE="Credit card">Credit card<BR>
<INPUT TYPE="radio" NAME="PaymentType" VALUE="P.O.">P.O.
<P>
Would you like to be added to our mailing list?
<INPUT TYPE="checkbox" NAME="MailingList" VALUE="Yes">
<P>
<INPUT TYPE="submit" VALUE="Process">

</FORM>

</BODY>

</HTML>
```

Create and save this template as C:\A2Z\SCRIPTS\FORMS5.CFM:

```
<CFPARAM NAME="MailingList" DEFAULT="No">
```

Try using it and experiment with the two fields. You'll find that this form is reliable and robust, and it does not generate Cold Fusion error messages.

Processing List Boxes

Another field type you will frequently use is the list box. Using list boxes is an efficient way to enable users to select one or more options. If a list box is created to accept only a single selection, you can be guaranteed that a value is always returned. If you don't set one of the options to be preselected, the first one in the list is selected. An option always has to be selected.

List boxes that allow multiple selections also allow no selections at all. If you use a multiple selection list box, you once again have to find a way to ensure that Cold Fusion does not generate "Form Field Not Found" errors.

Listing 12.6 contains the same data-entry form you just created but replaces the option buttons with a list box. Save this template as C:\A2Z\SCRIPTS\FORMS6.CFM, and then test it with your browser.

Listing 12.6   FORMS6.CFM—Using a *SELECT* List Box for User Options

On the CD

```
<HTML>

<HEAD>
<TITLE>Learning Cold Fusion Forms 6</TITLE>
</HEAD>

<BODY>

<FORM ACTION="forms4.cfm" METHOD="POST">

Please fill in this form and then click <B>Process</B>.
<P>
Payment type:
<SELECT NAME="PaymentType">
<OPTION>Cash
<OPTION>Check
<OPTION>Credit card
<OPTION>P.O.
</SELECT>
<P>
Would you like to be added to our mailing list?
<INPUT TYPE="checkbox" NAME="MailingList" VALUE="Yes">
<P>
<INPUT TYPE="submit" VALUE="Process">

</FORM>

</BODY>

</HTML>
```

For this particular form, the browser display shown in Figure 12.7 is probably a better user interface. The choice of whether to use option buttons or list boxes is yours, and no hard and fast rules exist as to when to use one versus the other. The following guidelines, however, may help you determine which to use:

- If you need to allow the selection of multiple items or of no items at all, you have to use a list box.
- List boxes take up less screen space. One hundred options take up no more precious real estate than a single option.
- Option buttons present all the options to the users without requiring mouse clicks.

Processing Text Areas

Text area fields are boxes in which the users can enter free-form text. When you create a text area field, you specify the number of rows and columns of screen space it should occupy. This area, however, does not restrict the amount of text that users can enter. The field scrolls both horizontally and vertically to enable the users to enter more text.

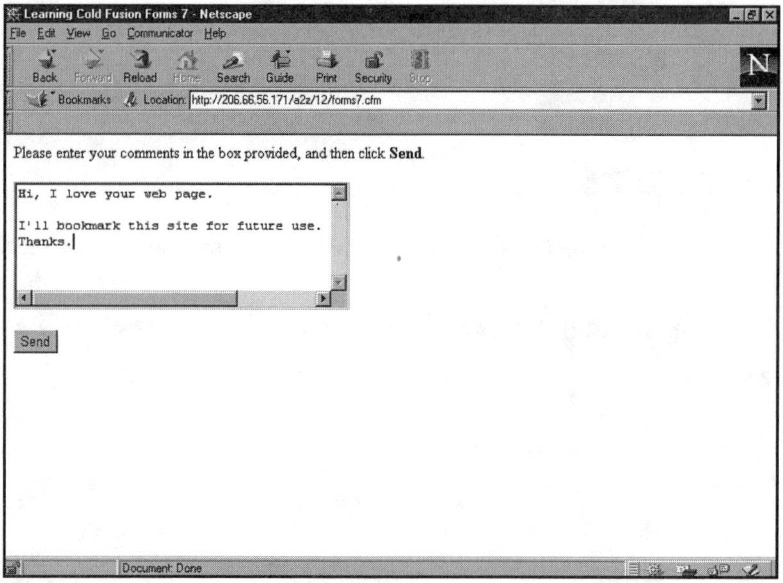

FIG. 12.7
You can use HTML list boxes to select one or more options.

Listing 12.7 creates an HTML form with a text area field for user comments. The field's width is specified as a number of characters that can be typed on a single line; the height is the number of lines that are displayed without scrolling.

TIP

The TEXTAREA COLS attribute is specified as a number of characters that can fit on a single line. This setting is dependent on the font in which the text is displayed, and the font is browser specific. Make sure that you test any TEXTAREA fields in more than one browser because a field that fits nicely in one might not fit at all in another.

Part
III

Ch
12

On the CD

Listing 12.7 FORMS7.CFM—Using a Text Area Field

```html
<HTML>

<HEAD>
<TITLE>Learning Cold Fusion Forms 7</TITLE>
</HEAD>

<BODY>

<FORM ACTION="forms8.cfm" METHOD="POST">

Please enter your comments in the box provided, and then click <B>Send</B>.
<P>
<TEXTAREA NAME="Comments" ROWS="6" COLS="40"></TEXTAREA>
<P>
<INPUT TYPE="submit" VALUE="Send">
```

continues

Listing 12.7 Continued

```
</FORM>

</BODY>

</HTML>
```

Listing 12.8 contains Cold Fusion code to display the contents of a TEXTAREA field.

Listing 12.8 FORMS8.CFM—Processing Free-Form Text Area Fields

```
<HTML>

<HEAD>
<TITLE>Learning Cold Fusion Forms 8</TITLE>
</HEAD>

<BODY>

<CFOUTPUT>

Thank you for your comments. You entered:

<P>

<B>#FORM.Comments#</B>

</CFOUTPUT>

</BODY>

</HTML>
```

Figure 12.8 shows the TEXTAREA field you created, and Figure 12.9 shows how Cold Fusion displays the field.

Try entering line breaks (press the Enter key) in the text field and submit them. What happens to the line breaks? Line break characters are considered white-space characters, just like spaces, by your browser, and all white space is ignored by browsers. "WHITE SPACE IS IGNORED" is displayed no differently than "WHITE   SPACE   IS   IGNORED."

The only way to display line breaks is to replace the line break with an HTML paragraph tag, the <P> tag. You, therefore, have to parse through the entire field text and insert <P> tags wherever needed. Fortunately, Cold Fusion makes this task a simple one. The Cold Fusion #ParagraphFormat()# function automatically replaces every double line break with a <P> tag. (Single line breaks are not replaced because Cold Fusion has no way of knowing if the next line is a new paragraph or part of the previous one.)

FIG. 12.8

The HTML TEXTAREA field is a means by which you can accept free-form text input from users.

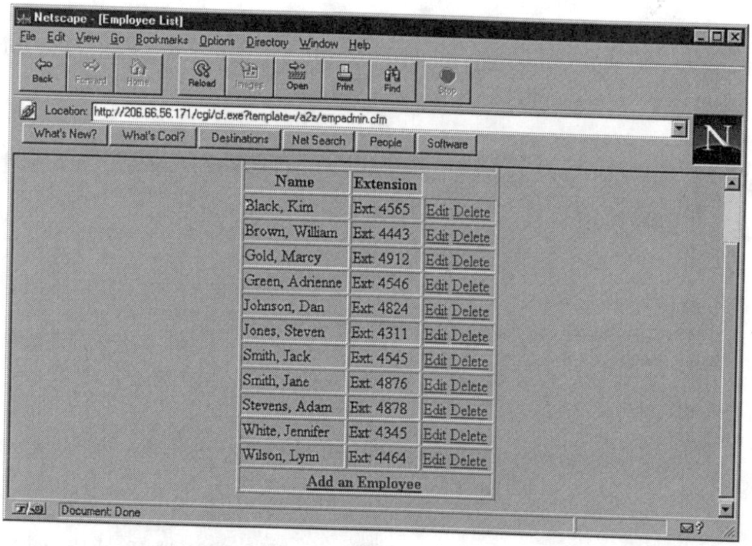

FIG. 12.9

Without Cold Fusion output functions, TEXTAREA fields are not displayed with line breaks preserved.

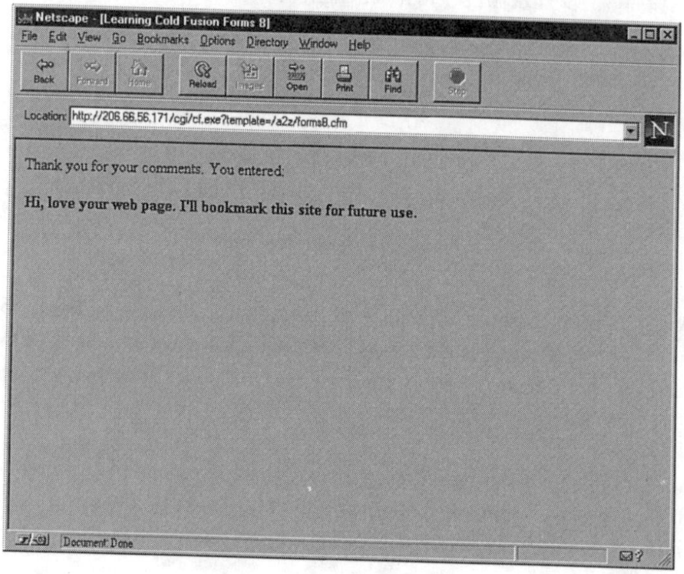

Part
III

Ch
12

TIP The Cold Fusion Replace() and ReplaceList() functions can be used instead of ParagraphFormat() to have greater control over the paragraph formatting. These functions are explained in Appendix A, "Cold Fusion Tag Reference."

The code in Listing 12.9 contains the same comments form as the one in Listing 12.7, with two differences. First, default field text is provided. Unlike other INPUT types, <TEXTAREA> default text is specified between <TEXTAREA> and </TEXTAREA> tags, and not in a VALUE attribute.

Second, you use the WRAP attribute to wrap text entered into the field automatically. WRAP="VIRTUAL" instructs the browser to wrap to the next line automatically, just as most word processors and editors do.

On the CD

Listing 12.9   FORMS9.CFM—The HTML *TEXTAREA* Field with Wrapping Enabled

```
<HTML>

<HEAD>
<TITLE>Learning Cold Fusion Forms 9</TITLE>
</HEAD>

<BODY>

<FORM ACTION="forms10.cfm" METHOD="POST">

Please enter your comments in the box provided, and then click <B>Send</B>.
<P>
<TEXTAREA NAME="Comments" ROWS="6" COLS="40" WRAP="VIRTUAL">
Replace this text with your comments.
</TEXTAREA>
<P>
<INPUT TYPE="submit" VALUE="Send">

</FORM>

</BODY>

</HTML>
```

N O T E   Many browsers do not support the TEXTAREA WRAP attribute. These browsers ignore the attribute and require the users to enter line breaks manually. Because the attribute is ignored when not supported, you can safely use this option when necessary, and your forms do not become incompatible with older browsers. ■

Listing 12.10 shows the template to display the user-supplied comments. The Comments field code is changed to #ParagraphFormat(FORM.Comments)#, ensuring that all line breaks are maintained and displayed correctly, as shown in Figure 12.10.

On the CD

Listing 12.10   FORMS10.CFM—Using the *ParagraphFormat* Function to Preserve Line Breaks

```
<HTML>

<HEAD>
<TITLE>Learning Cold Fusion Forms 10</TITLE>
</HEAD>
```

```
<BODY>

<CFOUTPUT>

Thank you for your comments. You entered:

<P>

<B>#ParagraphFormat(FORM.Comments)#</B>

</CFOUTPUT>

</BODY>

</HTML>
```

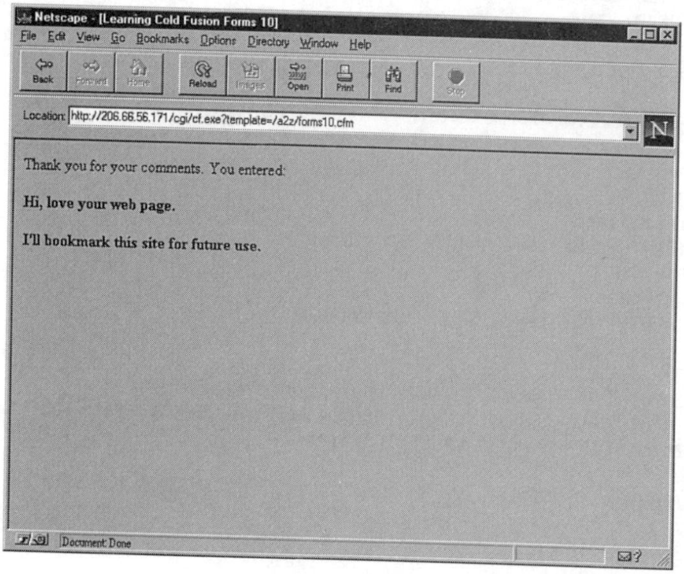

FIG. 12.10

You should use the Cold Fusion `ParagraphFormat()` function to display TEXTAREA fields with their line breaks preserved.

Processing Buttons

The HTML forms specification supports only two types of buttons. Almost all forms, including all the forms that you create in this chapter, have a submit button. Submit, as its name implies, instructs the browser to submit the form fields to a web server.

The second supported button type is reset. Reset clears all form entries, and restores default values if any existed. Any text entered into INPUT TYPE="text" or TEXTAREA fields is cleared, as are any check box, list box, and option button selections. Many forms have reset buttons, but you never need more than one.

Part

III

Ch

12

On the other hand, you may want more than one submit button. For example, if you're using a form to modify a record, you could have two submit buttons: one for Update and one for Delete. (Of course, you also could use two forms to accomplish this task.) If you create multiple submit buttons, you must name the button with the NAME attribute and make sure to assign a different VALUE attribute for each. The code in Listing 12.11 contains a reset button and two submit buttons.

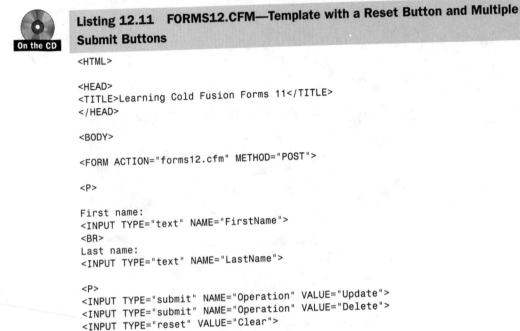

Listing 12.11   FORMS12.CFM—Template with a Reset Button and Multiple Submit Buttons

```
<HTML>

<HEAD>
<TITLE>Learning Cold Fusion Forms 11</TITLE>
</HEAD>

<BODY>

<FORM ACTION="forms12.cfm" METHOD="POST">

<P>

First name:
<INPUT TYPE="text" NAME="FirstName">
<BR>
Last name:
<INPUT TYPE="text" NAME="LastName">

<P>
<INPUT TYPE="submit" NAME="Operation" VALUE="Update">
<INPUT TYPE="submit" NAME="Operation" VALUE="Delete">
<INPUT TYPE="reset" VALUE="Clear">

</FORM>

</BODY>

</HTML>
```

The result of this code is shown in Figure 12.11.

When you name submit buttons, you treat them as any other form field. Listing 12.12 demonstrates how to determine which submit button was clicked. The code <CFIF #FORM.Operation# IS "Update"> checks to see if the Update button was clicked, and <CFELSEIF #FORM.Operation# IS "Delete"> checks to see if Delete was clicked only if Update was not clicked.

FIG. 12.11

When you're using multiple submit buttons, you must assign a different value to each button.

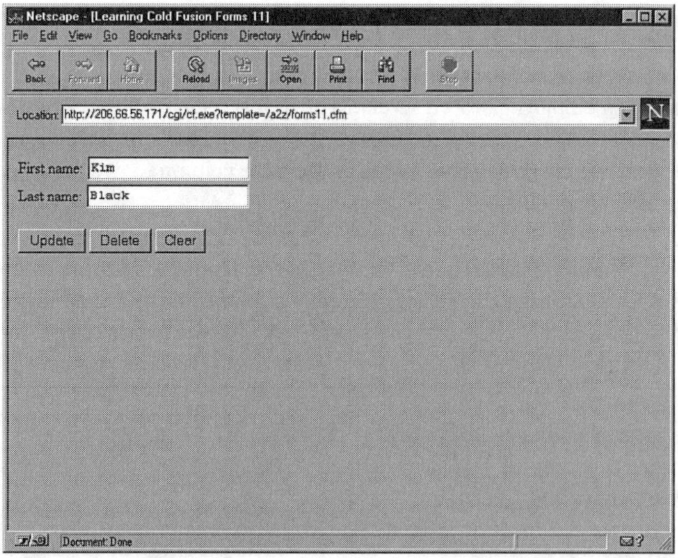

```
Netscape - [Learning Cold Fusion Forms 11]
File  Edit  View  Go  Bookmarks  Options  Directory  Window  Help

 Back  Forward  Home    Reload  Images  Open  Print  Find    Stop

Location: http://206.66.56.171/cgi/cf.exe?template=/a2z/forms11.cfm

First name:  Kim
Last name:   Black

    Update    Delete    Clear


Document: Done
```

On the CD

Listing 12.12   FORMS12.CFM—Cold Fusion Example of Multiple Submit Button Processing

```
<HTML>

<HEAD>
<TITLE>Learning Cold Fusion Forms 12</TITLE>
</HEAD>

<BODY>

<CFOUTPUT>

<CFIF #FORM.Operation# IS "Update">
You opted to <B>update</B> #FirstName# #LastName#
<CFELSEIF #FORM.Operation# IS "Delete">
You opted to <B>delete</B> #FirstName# #LastName#
</CFIF>

</CFOUTPUT>

</BODY>

</HTML>
```

Part

III

Ch

12

Creating Dynamic SQL Statements

Now that you're familiar with forms and how Cold Fusion processes them, you can return to creating an employee search screen. The first screen enables users to search for an employee by last name. To begin, you need an INPUT field of type text. The field name can be anything you want, but using the same name as the table column to which you're comparing the value is generally a good idea.

TIP When you're creating search screens, you can name your form fields with any descriptive name you want. When you're creating insert and update forms, however, the field name must match the table column names so that Cold Fusion knows which field to save with each column. For this reason, you should get into the habit of always naming form fields with the appropriate table column name.

The code in Listing 12.13 contains a simple HTML form, not unlike the test forms you created earlier in this chapter. The form contains a single text field called LastName and a submit button.

On the CD

Listing 12.13 EMPSRCH1.CFM—Code Listing for Employee Search Screen

```
<HTML>

<HEAD>
<TITLE>Employee Search</TITLE>
</HEAD>

<BODY>

<H2>Please enter the last name to search for.</H2>

<FORM ACTION="empsrch2.cfm" METHOD="POST">

Last name: <INPUT TYPE="text" NAME="LastName"><BR>
<P>
<INPUT TYPE="submit" VALUE="Search">

</FORM>

</BODY>

</HTML>
```

Save this form as C:\A2Z\SCRIPTS\EMPSRCH1.CFM, and then go to it with your browser. Your display should look like the one shown in Figure 12.12.

The FORM ACTION attribute specifies which Cold Fusion template should be used to process this search. The code ACTION="empsrch2.cfm" instructs Cold Fusion to use the template EMPSRCH2.CFM, which is shown in Listing 12.14. Create this template, and save it as C:\A2Z\SCRIPTS\EMPSRCH2.CFM.

FIG. 12.12

On the employee search screen, users can search for employees by last name only.

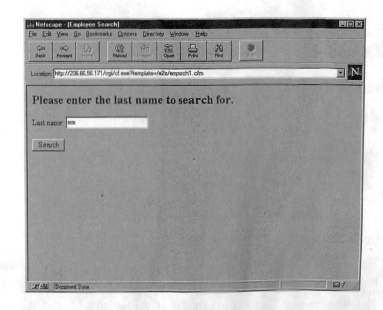

On the CD

Listing 12.14   EMPSRCH2.CFM—Using a Passed Form Field in a SQL WHERE Clause

```
<
CFQUERY
DATASOURCE="A2Z"
NAME="Employees"
>
SELECT FirstName, LastName, PhoneExtension, EmployeeID
FROM Employees
WHERE LastName LIKE '#LastName#%'
ORDER BY LastName, FirstName
</CFQUERY>

<HTML>

<HEAD>
<TITLE>Employee List</TITLE>
</HEAD>

<BODY>

<CENTER>

<TABLE BORDER=5>

<CFOUTPUT QUERY="Employees">
<TR>
<TD>
```

Part

III

Ch

12

continues

Listing 12.14   Continued

```
<A HREF="empdtl2.cfm?EmployeeID=#EmployeeID#">#LastName#, #FirstName#</A>
</TD>
<TD>
Ext. #PhoneExtension#
</TD>
</TR>
</CFOUTPUT>

</TABLE>

</CENTER>

</BODY>

</HTML>
```

The template begins with a CFQUERY tag that specifies the ODBC data source, the SQL statement to execute, and the name Cold Fusion should use to refer to the results set.

The WHERE clause in Listing 12.14 contains a Cold Fusion field rather than a static value. When Cold Fusion parses templates, it replaces field names with the value contained within the field. So, if you search for all last names beginning with Sm, the code WHERE LastName LIKE '#LastName#%' becomes WHERE LastName LIKE 'Sm%'. If no search text is specified at all, the clause becomes WHERE LastName LIKE '%', a wild-card search that finds all records.

▶ See "Creating Queries," **p. 141**
▶ See "Creating an ODBC Data Source," **p. 134**
▶ See "Using the CFQUERY Tag," **p. 202**

You use a LIKE clause to enable users to enter partial names. The clause WHERE LastName = 'Sm' finds only employees whose last names are Sm. Users with a last name of Smith are not retrieved. Using a wild card, as in the clause WHERE LastName LIKE 'Sm%', enables users to search on partial names, too.

Try experimenting with different search strings. The sample output should look like the output shown in Figure 12.13. Of course, depending on the search criteria you specify, you'll see different search results.

Listing 12.15 contains the code for template C:\A2Z\SCRIPTS\EMPDTL2.CFM, which is an updated version of the employee detail template you created in the preceding chapter. The template is changed to enable users to send email directly to employees by clicking their email address. You make this action possible by using the mailto identifier, which instructs the browser to open an email window so that the users can enter mail messages to be sent to the selected address. If employee Kim Black is selected, the code `<A HREF="mailto:#EMail#">` `#EMail#</A>` expands to `<A HREF="mailto:kblack@a2zbooks.com">kblack@a2zbooks.com</A>`, and anyone can click that address to send Kim email. Of course, to prevent errors, the code is conditional, based on an email address being present. `<CFIF #EMail# IS NOT "">` evaluates to `true` only if the `EMail` field is not empty.

FIG. 12.13

By building WHERE clauses dynamically, you can create different search conditions on-the-fly.

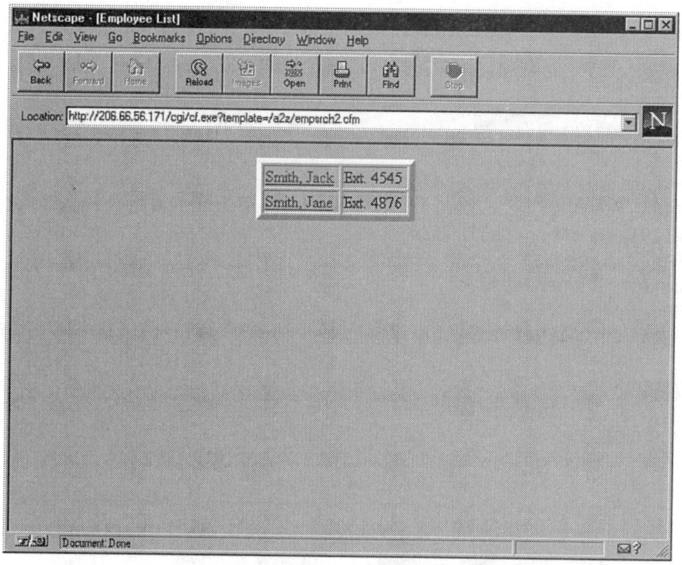

Listing 12.15 EMPDTL2.CFM—Passing Parameters to Templates

Part

III

Ch

12

```
<
CFQUERY
DATASOURCE="A2Z"
NAME="Employee"
>
 SELECT LastName,
 FirstName,
 MiddleInit,
 Title,
 PhoneExtension,
 PhoneCellular,
 PhonePager,
 EMail
 FROM Employees
 WHERE EmployeeID = #EmployeeID#
</CFQUERY>

<HTML>

<CFOUTPUT QUERY="Employee">
```

continues

Listing 12.15 Continued

```
<HEAD>
<TITLE>#LastName#, #FirstName# #MiddleInit#</TITLE>
</HEAD>

<BODY>

<H1>#LastName#, #FirstName#</H1>

<HR>

Title: #Title#
<BR>
Extension: #PhoneExtension#
<BR>
Cellular: #PhoneCellular#
<BR>
Pager: #PhonePager#
<BR>
E-Mail: <CFIF #EMail# IS NOT ""><A HREF="mailto:#EMail#">#EMail#</A></CFIF>

</BODY>

</CFOUTPUT>

</HTML>
```

Building Truly Dynamic Statements

When you roll out your employee search screen, immediately you are inundated with requests. "Searching by last name is great, but what about first name or phone extension?" your users ask. Now that you have introduced the ability to search for data, your users want to be able to search on several different fields, too.

Adding fields to your search screen is simple enough. So, add two fields: one for first name and one for phone extensions. The code for the updated employee search screen is shown in Listing 12.16.

On the CD

Listing 12.16 EMPSRCH3.CFM—Employee Search Screen

```
<HTML>

<HEAD>
<TITLE>Employee Search</TITLE>
</HEAD>

<BODY>

<H2>Please enter your search text below</H2>
```

```
<FORM ACTION="empsrch4.cfm" METHOD="POST">

First name: <INPUT TYPE="text" NAME="FirstName"><BR>
Last name: <INPUT TYPE="text" NAME="LastName"><BR>
Extension: <INPUT TYPE="text" NAME="PhoneExtension">
<P>
<INPUT TYPE="submit" VALUE="Search">
<INPUT TYPE="reset" VALUE="Clear">

</FORM>

</BODY>

</HTML>
```

This form enables the users to specify text in one of three different fields, as shown in Figure 12.14.

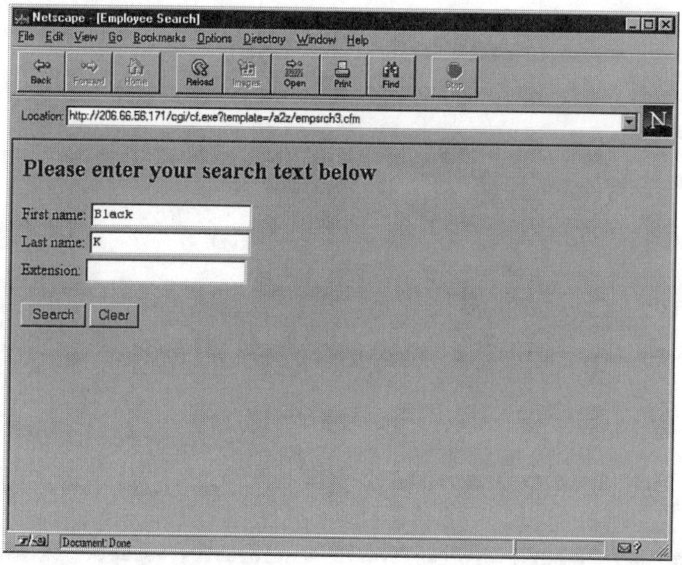

FIG. 12.14

The employee search screen is used to locate employee records by name or part thereof.

Before you can actually perform a search, you need to create the search template. The complete search code is shown in Listing 12.17.

Listing 12.17   EMPSRCH4.CFM—Building SQL Statements Dynamically

On the CD

```
<
CFQUERY
DATASOURCE="A2Z"
NAME="Employees"
```

continues

Part
III

Ch
12

Listing 12.17   Continued

```
>
 SELECT FirstName, LastName, PhoneExtension, EmployeeID
 FROM Employees

 <CFIF #FirstName# IS NOT "">
  WHERE FirstName LIKE '#FirstName#%'
 <CFELSEIF #LastName# IS NOT "">
  WHERE LastName LIKE '#LastName#%'
 <CFELSEIF #PhoneExtension# IS NOT "">
  WHERE PhoneExtension LIKE '#PhoneExtension#%'
 </CFIF>

 ORDER BY LastName, FirstName

</CFQUERY>

<HTML>

<HEAD>
<TITLE>Employee List</TITLE>
</HEAD>

<BODY>

<CENTER>

<TABLE BORDER=5>

<CFOUTPUT>
<TR>
<TH COLSPAN=2>
<H3>Found #Employees.RecordCount# Employees</H3>
</TH>
</TR>
</CFOUTPUT>

<CFOUTPUT QUERY="Employees">
<TR>
<TD>
<A HREF="empdtl2.cfm?EmployeeID=#EmployeeID#">#LastName#, #FirstName#</A>
</TD>
<TD>
Ext. #PhoneExtension#
</TD>
</TR>
</CFOUTPUT>

</TABLE>

</CENTER>

</BODY>

</HTML>
```

Understanding Dynamic SQL

Now, before you actually perform a search, take a closer look at the template in Listing 12.17. The CFQUERY tag is similar to the one you used in the previous search template, but in this one, the SQL SELECT statement in the SQL attribute is incomplete. It does not specify a WHERE clause with which to perform a search, nor does it specify a search order. No WHERE clause is specified because the search screen has to support not one but four search types, as follow:

- If none of the three search fields are specified, no WHERE clause should be used so that all employees can be retrieved.

- If a first name is specified, the WHERE clause needs to filter data to find only employees whose first name starts with the specified text. For example, if John is specified as the search text, the WHERE clause has to be WHERE FirstName LIKE 'John%'.

- If a last name is specified, the WHERE clause needs to filter data to find only employees whose last name starts with the specified search text. So, if you specify Sm as the last name, the WHERE clause must be WHERE LastName LIKE 'Sm%'.

- If you're searching by phone extension and specify 45 as the search text, a WHERE clause of WHERE PhoneExtension LIKE '45%' is needed.

How can a single search template handle all these possible search conditions? The answer is dynamic SQL.

When you're creating dynamic SQL statements, you break up the statement into separate common SQL and specific SQL. The common SQL is the part of the SQL statement that you always want. The sample SQL statement has two: the SELECT FirstName, LastName, PhoneExtension, EmployeeID FROM Employees and the ORDER BY LastName, FirstName.

If no search criteria is provided, then the common text is all the SQL statement you need. If, however, search text is specified, then the number of possible WHERE clauses is endless.

To understand the process of creating dynamic SQL statements, take another look at Listing 12.17. The code <CFIF #FirstName# IS NOT ""> checks to see that the FirstName form field is not blank. If no text is entered into the FirstName field in the search form, this condition fails, and any code until the next <CFELSE> <CFELSEIF> or </CFIF> is ignored.

▶ **See** "Using *CFIF* to Create Conditional Code," **p. 294**

If a value does appear in the FirstName field, the code WHERE FirstName LIKE '#FirstName#%' is processed and appended to the SQL statement. #FirstName# is a field and is replaced with whatever text is entered into the FirstName field. So, if John is specified as the first name to search for, this statement translates to WHERE FirstName LIKE 'John%'. This text is appended to the previous SQL statement, which now becomes the following:

```
SELECT FirstName, LastName, PhoneExtension, EmployeeID
FROM Employees WHERE FirstName LIKE 'John%'
```

All you need now is the ORDER BY clause. Even though the ORDER BY is fixed and does not change with different searches, it must still be built dynamically because the ORDER BY clause must come after the WHERE clause, if one exists. After Cold Fusion processes the code ORDER BY LastName, FirstName, the finished SQL statement reads as follows:

```
SELECT FirstName, LastName, PhoneExtension, EmployeeID
FROM Employees WHERE FirstName LIKE 'John%'
ORDER BY LastName, FirstName
```

▶ **See** *"LIKE,"* **p. 153**

N O T E You cannot use double quotation marks in an SQL statement. When Cold Fusion encounters a double quotation mark, it thinks that it has reached the end of the SQL statement. It then generates an error message because extra text appears where Cold Fusion thinks it should not be. To include text strings with the SQL statement, use only single quotation marks. ▪

Similarly, if a last name of Sm is specified as the search text, the complete SQL statement reads as follows:

```
SELECT FirstName, LastName, PhoneExtension, EmployeeID
FROM Employees WHERE LastName LIKE 'Sm%'
ORDER BY LastName, FirstName
```

The code <CFIF #FirstName# IS NOT ""> evaluates to false because #FirstName# is actually empty, so Cold Fusion checks the next condition, <CFIF #LastName# IS NOT "">. This condition evaluates to true because a last name value is provided. Cold Fusion then processes the next line, the CFSQL statement, and builds the required SELECT statement.

Processing Search Results

Now that the template is complete and all the code to build dynamic SQL is in place, try to perform a search. First, try a search without specifying any search criteria at all. Your browser display should look like the one shown in Figure 12.15.

Notice that the number of employees found is displayed at the top of the table. Cold Fusion stores the number of rows retrieved with a query in a field called RecordCount. To determine how many rows the Employees query retrieves, you use the code Found #Employees. RecordCount# Employees, and, just like any other field, Cold Fusion replaces it with the actual value.

The RecordCount field is also useful for returning messages, or options, if a search returns no data at all. For example, the following code displays an informative message that no records are retrieved:

```
<CFIF #Employees.RecordCount# IS 0>
No employees located, try changing your search criteria.
</CFIF>
```

Try performing different searches using the search form. You can search on any of the fields to retrieve specific records.

FIG. 12.15

With dynamic SQL you can use a single template to perform an infinite number of searches.

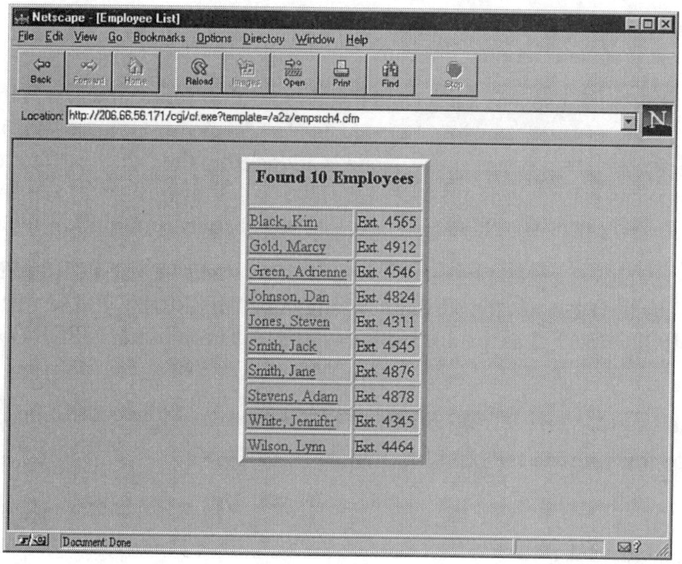

Concatenating SQL Clauses

Now try entering text in both the first name and last name fields. What happens? The answer is not much at all. The dynamic SQL code processes only the first search criteria it encounters. If it finds text in the first name field, it does not even check the last name and phone extension fields. If you follow the flow of the <CFIF> statement, you see that as soon as any condition is true (either a <CFIF> or a <CFELSEIF>) Cold Fusion ceases processing the condition and jumps to the </CFIF> tag.

So how can you search on more than one field? Well, creating a WHERE clause with an unknown number of conditions is more complicated than the WHERE clauses you created earlier. If a particular condition is the first condition in the clause, you need to precede it with WHERE. If it is not the first condition, you need to precede it with an AND. Of course, you have no idea if any fields will be specified. Nor do you know which fields will be specified, if any are. So how do you construct a dynamic SQL statement like this?

One solution is shown in Listing 12.18. The SQL SELECT statement has a dummy WHERE clause, WHERE EmployeeID = EmployeeID. This condition checks to see whether the EmployeeID in a retrieved record matches itself, which, of course, it always does. For example, when the employee with ID 6 is retrieved, the database checks to see whether 6=6. Because only one column is being checked, and the condition involves no complicated arithmetic or subqueries, the check has almost no performance penalty. If no search criteria is specified, then the WHERE clause remains WHERE EmployeeID = EmployeeID, and all records are retrieved.

Right after the CFQUERY are three sets of <CFIF> conditions. Each one checks to see whether a specific search field is provided, and, if so, it is appended to the SQL SELECT statement. So if Kim is entered into the first name field, the new WHERE clause is WHERE EmployeeID =

Part
III

Ch
12

`EmployeeID AND FirstName LIKE 'Kim%'`. This clause correctly filters out only employees whose first name begins with Kim.

Now see what happens if a second field is specified, for example, B in the last name field. The `<CFIF #LastName# IS NOT "">` evaluates to `true` because `LastName` is not empty, and the `AND LastName LIKE '#LastName#%'` code is added from the `LastName` filter to the `WHERE` clause. The new `WHERE` clause reads `WHERE EmployeeID = EmployeeID AND FirstName LIKE 'Kim%' AND LastName LIKE 'B%'`. If you execute this search, only Kim Black is found.

To try this code example, save Listing 12.18 as C:\A2Z\EMPSRCH5.CFM. You also need to modify the `FORM ACTION` attribute in template EMPSRCH3.CFM so that it specifies EMPSRCH5.CFM as the destination template instead of EMPSRCH4.CFM.

On the CD

Listing 12.18   EMPSRCH5.CFM—Employee Search Template That Concatenates *WHERE* Clauses

```
<
CFQUERY
DATASOURCE="A2Z"
NAME="Employees"
>
SELECT FirstName, LastName, PhoneExtension, EmployeeID
FROM Employees
WHERE EmployeeID = EmployeeID

<CFIF #FirstName# IS NOT "">
AND FirstName LIKE '#FirstName#%'
</CFIF>

<CFIF #LastName# IS NOT "">
AND LastName LIKE '#LastName#%'
</CFIF>

<CFIF #PhoneExtension# IS NOT "">
AND PhoneExtension LIKE '#PhoneExtension#%'
</CFIF>

ORDER BY LastName, FirstName

</CFQUERY>

<HTML>

<HEAD>
<TITLE>Employee List</TITLE>
</HEAD>

<BODY>

<CENTER>

<TABLE BORDER=5>
```

```
<CFOUTPUT>
<TR>
<TH COLSPAN=2>
<H3>Found #Employees.RecordCount# Employees</H3>
</TH>
</TR>
</CFOUTPUT>

<CFOUTPUT QUERY="Employees">
<TR>
<TD>
<A HREF="empdtl2.cfm?EmployeeID=#EmployeeID#">#LastName#, #FirstName#</A>
</TD>
<TD>
Ext. #PhoneExtension#
</TD>
</TR>
</CFOUTPUT>

</TABLE>

</CENTER>

</BODY>

</HTML>
```

After you create the template, use your browser to try performing different combinations of searches. You'll find that this new search template is both powerful and flexible. Indeed, this technique for creating truly dynamic SQL SELECT statements will likely be the basis for some sophisticated database interaction in real-world applications.

Part

III

Ch

12

Creating Dynamic Search Screens

The more power and flexibility you give your users, the more they want. Now they want to search by department, too. For example, they may want to display all the Sales department personnel or find a particular employee by specifying a name within a department.

The search screen is simple enough to create. A list of departments is the perfect place to use a list box. You can create a list box with the HTML <SELECT> tag and then list all the departments as <OPTION> tags within it.

Before you modify the search template, however, remember that you're creating data-driven applications. You don't want to have to enter the departments manually in the list box. Rather, you want the list box to be driven by the data in the Departments table. This way, when departments are added or if a department name changes, you can acquire those changes automatically.

The code in Listing 12.19 demonstrates a data-driven form. The CFQUERY at the top of the template should be familiar to you by now. It creates a result set called Departments that contains the ID and name of each department in the database.

The body of the form is essentially the same as the one you created in Listing 12.16, with the exception of the new DepartmentID field. DepartmentID is a list box that displays the names of all the departments. The <SELECT> tag creates the list box and it is terminated with the </SELECT> tag. The individual entries in the list box are specified with the <OPTION> tag, but here that tag is within a CFOUTPUT block. This block is executed once for each row retrieved by the CFQUERY, creating an <OPTION> entry for each one.

The code in Listing 12.19 demonstrates the process of building data-driven forms. The SELECT NAME attribute (don't confuse it with the SQL SELECT statement) contains the name of the field, which is the same as the column in the Employees table that you need to compare against. The CFQUERY block creates the individual options, using the ID field as the VALUE and the department name as the description. When Cold Fusion processes department 2, the Sales department, the code <OPTION VALUE="#id#">#Department# is translated into <OPTION VALUE= "2">Sales.

Also notice that you need to include a blank <OPTION> line in the list box. You need this empty option because you need to be able to not make a selection. Remember that list boxes always must have a selection. Save Listing 12.19 as C:\A2Z\SCRIPTS\EMPSRCH6.CFM.

Listing 12.19   EMPSRCH6.CFM—Data-Driven Employee Search Template

```
<
CFQUERY
DATASOURCE="A2Z"
NAME="Departments"
>
SELECT ID, Department
FROM Departments
ORDER BY Department
</CFQUERY>

<HTML>

<HEAD>
<TITLE>Employee Search</TITLE>
</HEAD>

<BODY>

<H2>Please enter your search text below</H2>

<FORM ACTION="empsrch7.cfm" METHOD="POST">

First name: <INPUT TYPE="text" NAME="FirstName"><BR>

Last name: <INPUT TYPE="text" NAME="LastName"><BR>

Extension: <INPUT TYPE="text" NAME="PhoneExtension"><BR>
```

```
Department:
<SELECT NAME="DepartmentID">
<OPTION>
<CFOUTPUT QUERY="Departments">
<OPTION VALUE="#id#">#Department#
</CFOUTPUT>
</SELECT>

<P>
<INPUT TYPE="submit" VALUE="Search">
<INPUT TYPE="reset" VALUE="Clear">

</FORM>

</BODY>

</HTML>
```

The completed search screen is shown in Figure 12.16.

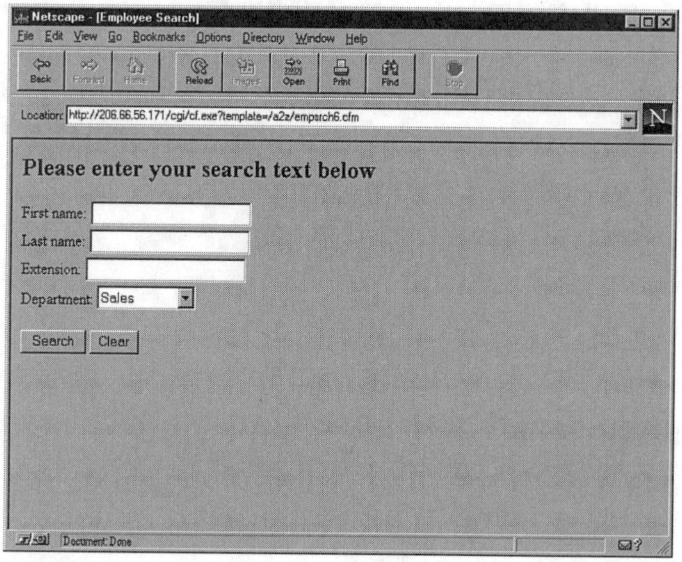

FIG. 12.16

Search forms should use a mixture of input types to create a user-friendly interface.

Part

III

Ch

12

Now you have one last thing left to do: You need to modify the search template to include the new DepartmentID field. The code in Listing 12.20 is updated to include one more possible WHERE condition. The code AND DepartmentID = #DepartmentID# adds the DepartmentID field only if it is specified in the search screen, thereby enabling users to search on as many or as few fields as they want.

Listing 12.20   EMPSRCH7.CFM—Final Employee Search Template

```
<
CFQUERY
DATASOURCE="A2Z"
NAME="Employees"
>
SELECT FirstName, LastName, PhoneExtension, EmployeeID
FROM Employees
WHERE EmployeeID = EmployeeID


<CFIF #FirstName# IS NOT "">
AND FirstName LIKE '#FirstName#%'
</CFIF>

<CFIF #LastName# IS NOT "">
AND LastName LIKE '#LastName#%'
</CFIF>

<CFIF #PhoneExtension# IS NOT "">
AND PhoneExtension LIKE '#PhoneExtension#%'
</CFIF>

<CFIF #DepartmentID# IS NOT "">
AND DepartmentID = #DepartmentID#
</CFIF>

ORDER BY LastName, FirstName

</CFQUERY>

<HTML>

<HEAD>
<TITLE>Employee List</TITLE>
</HEAD>

<BODY>

<CENTER>

<TABLE BORDER=5>

<CFOUTPUT>
<TR>
<TH COLSPAN=2>
<H3>Found #Employees.RecordCount# Employees</H3>
</TH>
</TR>
</CFOUTPUT>
```

```
<CFOUTPUT QUERY="Employees">
<TR>
<TD>
<A HREF="empdtl2.cfm?EmployeeID=#EmployeeID#">#LastName#, #FirstName#</A>
</TD>
<TD>
Ext. #PhoneExtension#
</TD>
</TR>
</CFOUTPUT>

</TABLE>

</CENTER>

</BODY>

</HTML>
```

The final WHERE condition in Listing 12.20 is different from the prior three in two ways. First, the condition checks for equality instead of LIKE. The value you're comparing is an ID value—a number—and numbers either match or don't match. Wild cards don't apply to numbers.

Second, no quotation marks appear around the field identifier. The prior three fields all require quotation marks because they are text values. The DepartmentID is a number, and numbers don't need quotation marks around them. In fact, if you do put quotation marks around the number, you generate an ODBC error because you're comparing a numeric field to a string. ●

Using Forms to Add or Change Data

by Ben Forta

Using a Web Browser as a "Universal Client"

Your online employee list was well received. Everyone now has access to up-to-date employee lists, and they can search for employees by name, department, or phone extension.

You and your users discover that a web browser can be used as a front end to access almost any type of data. Using the same front end, a web browser, makes it easier for people to switch between applications and greatly lowers the learning curve that each new application introduces. Why? Because there is *only* one application to learn: the web browser itself.

The popular term to describe this type of front-end application is *universal client*. This means that the same client application, your web browser, is used as a front end to multiple applications.

Adding Data with Cold Fusion

When you created the employee search forms in Chapter 12, "Cold Fusion Forms," you had to create two templates for each search. One created the user search screen containing the search form, and the other performed the actual search by using the Cold Fusion CFQUERY tag.

Breaking an operation into more than one template is typical of Cold Fusion, and indeed all web-based data interaction. As explained in Chapter 2, "Introduction to Cold Fusion," a browser's connection to a web server is made and broken as needed. Whenever a web page is retrieved, a HTTP connection is made to a web server. That connection is broken as soon as that page is retrieved. Any subsequent pages are retrieved with a new connection that is used just to retrieve that page.

There is no way to keep a connection alive for the duration of a complete process—for example, searching for data. Therefore, the process must be broken up into steps, as you saw in Chapter 12, and each step is a separate template.

Adding data via your web browser is no different. You'll need at least two templates to perform the insertion. One will display the form that you'll use to collect the data, and the other will process the data and insert the record.

Adding data to a table involves the following steps:

1. Display a form to collect the data. The names of any input fields should match the names of the columns in the destination table.
2. Submit the form to Cold Fusion for processing.
3. Cold Fusion adds the row via the ODBC driver by using an SQL statement.

Creating an "Add Record" Form

Forms used to add data are no different from the forms you created to search for data. The form shown in Figure 13.1 is created by using the standard HTML FORM and INPUT tags, as shown in Listing 13.1.

Listing 13.1   C:\A2Z\SCRIPTS\EMPADD1.CFM—Template to Add an Employee

```
<HTML>

<HEAD>
<TITLE>Add an Employee</TITLE>
</HEAD>

<BODY>

<H1>Add an Employee</H1>

<FORM ACTION="empadd2.cfm" METHOD="POST">

<P>

First name:
<INPUT TYPE="text" NAME="FirstName" SIZE="30" MAXLENGTH="30">
<BR>
Last name:
<INPUT TYPE="text" NAME="LastName" SIZE="30" MAXLENGTH="30">
<BR>
Phone Extension:
<INPUT TYPE="text" NAME="PhoneExtension" SIZE="4" MAXLENGTH="4">

<P>
<INPUT TYPE="submit" VALUE="Add Employee">
<INPUT TYPE="reset" VALUE="Clear">

</FORM>

</BODY>

</HTML>
```

The add employee form is shown in Figure 13.1.

The FORM ACTION attribute specifies the name of the template to be used to process the insertion—in this case, EMPADD2.CFM.

Each INPUT field has a field name specified in the NAME attribute. These names correspond to the names of the appropriate columns in the Employees table.

You also specified the SIZE and MAXLENGTH attributes in each of the text fields. SIZE is used to specify the size of the text box within the browser window. Without the SIZE attribute, the browser will use its default size, which varies from one browser to the next.

The SIZE attribute does *not* restrict the number of characters that may be entered into the field. SIZE="30" creates a text field that occupies the space of 30 characters, but if you enter more than 30 characters, the text will scroll within the field. To restrict the number of characters that may be entered, you must use the MAXLENGTH attribute. MAXLENGTH="30" instructs the browser to allow no more than 30 characters in the field.

FIG. 13.1

HTML forms can be used as a front end for data insertion.

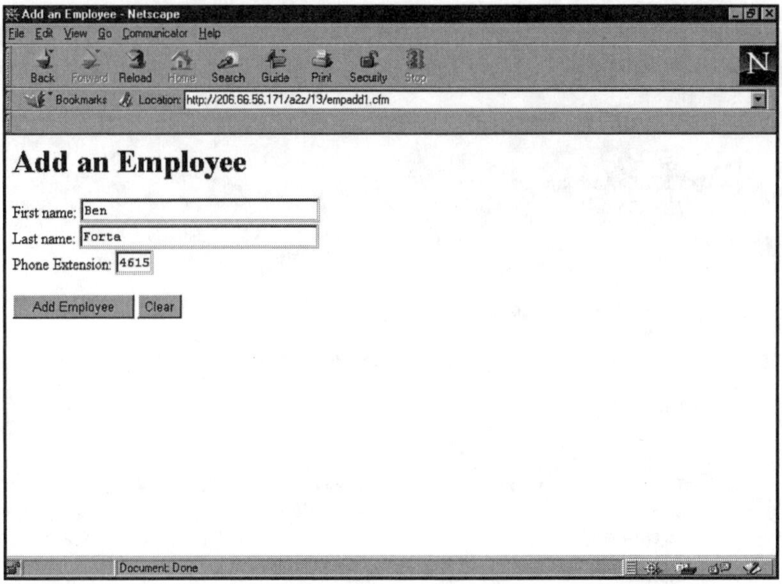

The SIZE attribute is primarily used for aesthetics and the control of screen appearance. MAXLENGTH is used to ensure that only data that can be handled is entered into a field. Without MAXLENGTH, users could enter more data than would fit in a field, and that data would be truncated on insertion.

You do not have to specify the same SIZE and MAXLENGTH values. The following example allocates only 20 characters of screen space for the field but allows 30 characters to be entered. Once 20 characters have been entered into the field, the text will scroll to accommodate the extra characters.

```
<INPUT TYPE="text" NAME="FirstName" SIZE="20" MAXLENGTH="30">
```

TIP For maximum control over form appearance and data-entry, you should *always* use both the SIZE and MAXLENGTH attributes. Without these, the browser will use its own defaults, and there are no rules governing what these defaults should be.

Processing Additions

The next thing you need is a template to process the actual data insertion. To add the row, you'll use the SQL INSERT statement.

▶ **See** "Adding Data," **p. 156**

As shown in Listing 13.2, the CFQUERY tag can be used to pass *any* SQL statement, not just SELECT statements. The SQL statement here is an INSERT statement: it adds a row to the Employees table and sets the FirstName, LastName, and PhoneExtension columns to the form values passed by the browser.

Listing 13.2   C:\A2Z\SCRIPTS\EMPADD2.CFM—Adding Data with the SQL *INSERT* Statement

```
<CFQUERY DATASOURCE="A2Z">
INSERT INTO Employees(FirstName, LastName, PhoneExtension)
VALUES('#FirstName#', '#LastName#', '#PhoneExtension#')
</CFQUERY>

<HTML>

<HEAD>
<TITLE>Employee Added</TITLE>
</HEAD>

<BODY>

<H1>Employee Added</H1>

<CFOUTPUT>
Employee <B>#FirstName# #LastName#</B> added.
</CFOUTPUT>

</BODY>

</HTML>
```

N O T E   The <CFQUERY> in Listing 13.2 has no NAME attribute. NAME is optional and is needed only if you need to manipulate the data returned by <CFQUERY>. As the operation here is an INSERT, no data will be returned, and so the NAME attribute is unnecessary. ■

Save this template as **C:\A2Z\SCRIPTS\EMPADD2.CFM** and then execute the EMPADD1.CFM template with your browser. Then try adding an employee to the table; your browser display should look like the one shown in Figure 13.2.

You can verify that the employee was added by browsing the table with Microsoft Access, Microsoft Query, or any of the employee search templates you created in the last chapter.

Introducing *CFINSERT*

The example in Listing 13.2 demonstrated how to add data to a table by using the standard SQL INSERT command. This works very well if you have to provide data for only a few columns, and if those columns are always provided. If the number of columns can vary, using SQL INSERT gets rather complicated.

For example, suppose that you had two or more data-entry forms for similar data. One might collect a minimal number of fields, while another collects a more complete record. How would you create a SQL INSERT statement to handle both sets of data?

FIG. 13.2

Data can be added via Cold Fusion by using the SQL INSERT statement.

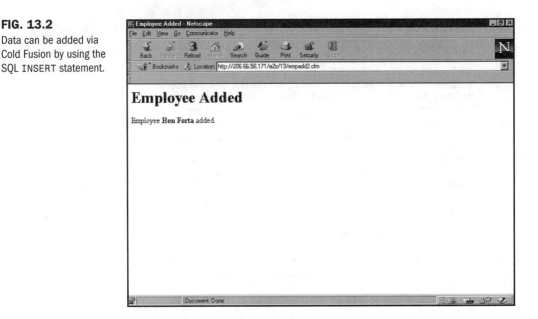

You could create two separate templates with a different SQL INSERT statement in each, but that's a situation you should always try and avoid. As a rule, you should try to never have more than one template perform a given operation. This way, you don't run the risk of future changes and revisions not being applied correctly. If a table name or column name changes, for example, you won't have to worry about forgetting one of the templates that references the changed column.

> **TIP** As a rule, you should never create more than one template to perform a specific operation. This will help prevent introducing errors into your templates in the future when updates or revisions are made. You are almost always better off creating one template with conditional code, rather than creating two separate templates.

Another solution is to use dynamic SQL. You could write a basic INSERT statement, and then gradually construct a complete statement by using a series of CFIF statements.

While this solution might be workable, it is not very efficient. The conditional SQL INSERT code is far more complex than conditional SQL SELECT is. The INSERT statement requires that both the list of columns *and* the values be dynamic. Plus, the INSERT syntax requires that you separate all column names and values by commas. This means that every column name and value must be followed by a comma *except* the last one in the list. Your conditional SQL will have to accommodate these syntactical requirements when the statement is constructed.

A better solution is to use the CFINSERT tag. CFINSERT is a special Cold Fusion tag that hides the complexity of building dynamic SQL INSERT statements. CFINSERT takes the following parameters as attributes:

- DATASOURCE is the name of the ODBC data source containing the table into which the data is to be inserted.
- TABLENAME is the name of the destination table.
- FORMFIELDS is an optional, comma-separated list of fields to be inserted. If this attribute is not provided, all the fields in the submitted form are used.

Look at the following Cold Fusion tag:

```
<CFINSERT DATASOURCE="A2Z" TABLENAME="Employees">
```

This code does *exactly* the same thing as the CFQUERY tag in Listing 13.2. When Cold Fusion processes a CFINSERT tag, it builds a dynamic SQL INSERT statement under the hood. If a FORMFIELDS attribute is provided, the specified field names are used. In this example no FORMFIELDS attribute was specified, so Cold Fusion automatically uses the form fields that were submitted, building the list of columns and the values dynamically.

Try modifying the form in template EMPADD1.CFM so that it submits the form to template EMPADD3.CFM instead of EMPADD2.CFM, and then add a record. You'll see that the code in Listing 13.3 does exactly the same thing as the code in Listing 13.2, but with a much simpler syntax and interface.

On the CD

Listing 13.3   C:\A2Z\SCRIPTS\EMPADD3.CFM—Adding Data with the CFINSERT Tag

```
<CFINSERT DATASOURCE="A2Z" TABLENAME="Employees">

<HTML>

<HEAD>
<TITLE>Employee Added</TITLE>
</HEAD>

<BODY>

<H1>Employee Added</H1>

<CFOUTPUT>
Employee <B>#FirstName# #LastName#</B> added.
</CFOUTPUT>

</BODY>

</HTML>
```

Because CFINSERT builds its SQL statements dynamically, EMPADD3.CFM can be used even if you add fields to the data-entry form. Listing 13.4 contains an updated template that adds several fields to the Add an Employee form. Even so, it still submits data to the same template you just created. Using CFINSERT allows for a cleaner action template, one that will not require changing every time the form itself changes.

Part
III

Ch

13

On the CD

> **Listing 13.4   C:\A2Z\SCRIPTS\EMPADD4.CFM—Template to Add an Employee**

```
<HTML>

<HEAD>
<TITLE>Add an Employee</TITLE>
</HEAD>

<BODY>

<H1>Add an Employee</H1>

<FORM ACTION="empadd3.cfm" METHOD="POST">

First name:
<INPUT TYPE="text" NAME="FirstName" SIZE="30" MAXLENGTH="30">
Middle Initial:
<INPUT TYPE="text" NAME="MiddleInit" SIZE="1" MAXLENGTH="1">
<BR>
Last name:
<INPUT TYPE="text" NAME="LastName" SIZE="30" MAXLENGTH="30">
<BR>
Title:
<INPUT TYPE="text" NAME="Title" SIZE="20" MAXLENGTH="20">
<BR>
Phone Extension:
<INPUT TYPE="text" NAME="PhoneExtension" SIZE="4" MAXLENGTH="4">
<BR>
E-Mail:
<INPUT TYPE="text" NAME="EMail" SIZE="30" MAXLENGTH="30">

<P>
<INPUT TYPE="submit" VALUE="Add Employee">
<INPUT TYPE="reset" VALUE="Clear">

</FORM>

</BODY>

</HTML>
```

Try adding an employee by using this new form; your browser display should look no different than it did before.

Knowing When to Use *CFINSERT FORMFIELDS*

CFINSERT instructs Cold Fusion to build SQL INSERT statements dynamically. Cold Fusion automatically uses *all* submitted form fields when building this statement.

But sometimes you might not want Cold Fusion to include certain fields. For example, you might have hidden fields in your form that are not table columns, like the hidden field shown in

Listing 13.5. That field might be there as part of a security system you have implemented, and it is not a column in the table. If you try to pass this field to CFINSERT, Cold Fusion will pass the hidden Login field as a column. Obviously this will generate a ODBC error, as seen in Figure 13.3.

On the CD

Listing 13.5   C:\A2Z\SCRIPTS\EMPADD5.CFM—Template to Add an Employee

```
<HTML>

<HEAD>
<TITLE>Add an Employee</TITLE>
</HEAD>

<BODY>

<H1>Add an Employee</H1>

<FORM ACTION="empadd3.cfm" METHOD="POST">

<INPUT TYPE="hidden" NAME="Login" VALUE="Bob" >

<P>

First name:
<INPUT TYPE="text" NAME="FirstName" SIZE="30" MAXLENGTH="30">
Middle Initial:
<INPUT TYPE="text" NAME="MiddleInit" SIZE="1" MAXLENGTH="1">
<BR>
Last name:
<INPUT TYPE="text" NAME="LastName" SIZE="30" MAXLENGTH="30">
<BR>
Title:
<INPUT TYPE="text" NAME="Title" SIZE="20" MAXLENGTH="20">
<BR>
Phone Extension:
<INPUT TYPE="text" NAME="PhoneExtension" SIZE="4" MAXLENGTH="4">
<BR>
E-Mail:
<INPUT TYPE="text" NAME="EMail" SIZE="30" MAXLENGTH="30">

<P>
<INPUT TYPE="submit" VALUE="Add Employee">
<INPUT TYPE="reset" VALUE="Clear">

</FORM>

</BODY>

</HTML>
```

Part
III

Ch

13

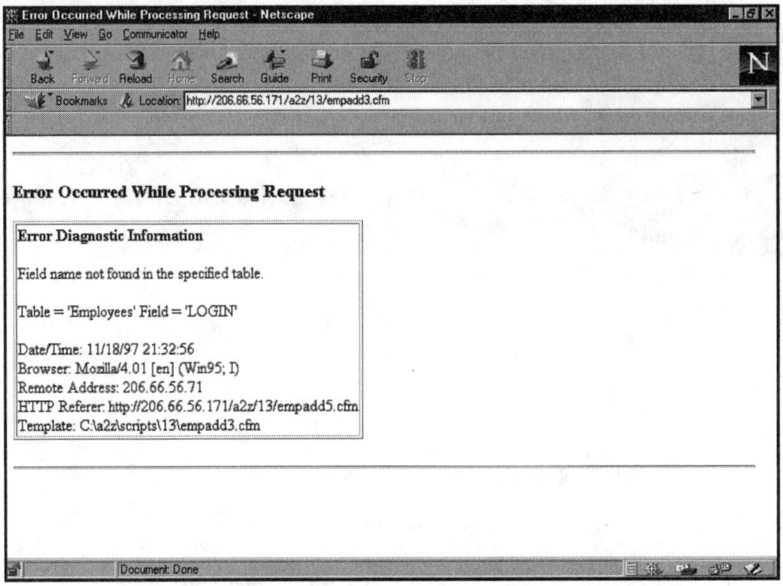

FIG. 13.3
An ODBC error message is generated if Cold Fusion tries to INSERT fields that are not table columns.

To solve this problem, you must use the FORMFIELDS attribute. FORMFIELDS instructs Cold Fusion to process only form fields in the list. Any other fields are ignored.

It is important to note that FORMFIELDS is not used to specify which fields Cold Fusion should process. Rather, it specifies which fields should *not* be processed. The difference is subtle. Not all fields listed in the FORMFIELDS value need be present. If they are, they are processed, and if not, then they're not. Any fields not listed in the FORMFIELDS list are ignored.

Listing 13.6 contains an updated data-insertion template. The CFINSERT tag now has a FORMFIELDS attribute, so now Cold Fusion will know to ignore the hidden Login field in EMPADD5.CFM. The code

```
FORMFIELDS="FirstName, MiddleInit, LastName,
Title, PhoneExtension, EMail"
```

ensures that only these fields are processed, and that any others are ignored.

Listing 13.6   C:\A2Z\SCRIPTS\EMPADD6.CFM—Using the *CFINSERT*
***FORMFIELDS* Attribute to Specify Which Fields Not to Process**

```
<CFINSERT
 DATASOURCE="A2Z"
 TABLENAME="Employees"
 FORMFIELDS="FirstName, MiddleInit, LastName, Title, PhoneExtension, EMail"
>

<HTML>

<HEAD>
```

```
<TITLE>Employee Added</TITLE>
</HEAD>

<BODY>

<H1>Employee Added</H1>

<CFOUTPUT>
Employee <B>#FirstName# #LastName#</B> added.
</CFOUTPUT>

</BODY>

</HTML>
```

Collecting Data for More Than One *INSERT*

Another situation in which CFINSERT FORMFIELDS can be used is when a form collects data that needs to be added to more than one table. By using FORMFIELDS, you can create a template that has two or more CFINSERT statements.

As long as each CFINSERT statement has a FORMFIELDS attribute that specifies which fields are to be used with each INSERT, Cold Fusion will correctly execute each CFINSERT with its appropriate fields.

Comparing *CFINSERT* and SQL *INSERT*

Adding data to tables by using the Cold Fusion CFINSERT tag is simple and helps prevent the creation of multiple similar templates.

So why would you ever *not* want to use CFINSERT? Is there ever a reason to use SQL INSERT instead of CFINSERT?

The truth is, both are needed. CFINSERT can be used only for simple data insertion to a single table. If you wanted to INSERT the results of a SELECT statement, you could not use CFINSERT. Similarly, if you wanted to INSERT values other than FORM fields—perhaps variables or URL parameters—you couldn't use CFINSERT. The following are some guidelines to help you decide when to use each method:

- Whenever possible, use CFINSERT to add data to ODBC tables.
- If you find that you need to add specific form fields, and not all that were submitted, use the CFINSERT tag with the FORMFIELDS attribute.
- If CFINSERT cannot be used because you need a complex INSERT statement or are using fields that are not form fields, use SQL INSERT.

Updating Data with Cold Fusion

Updating data with Cold Fusion is very similar to inserting data. To update a row, you need two templates: a data-entry form template and a data-update template. The big difference between a

Part

III

Ch

13

form used for data addition and one used for data modification is that the latter needs to be populated with existing values, like the screen shown in Figure 13.4.

FIG. 13.4
When using forms to update data, the form fields usually need to be populated with existing values.

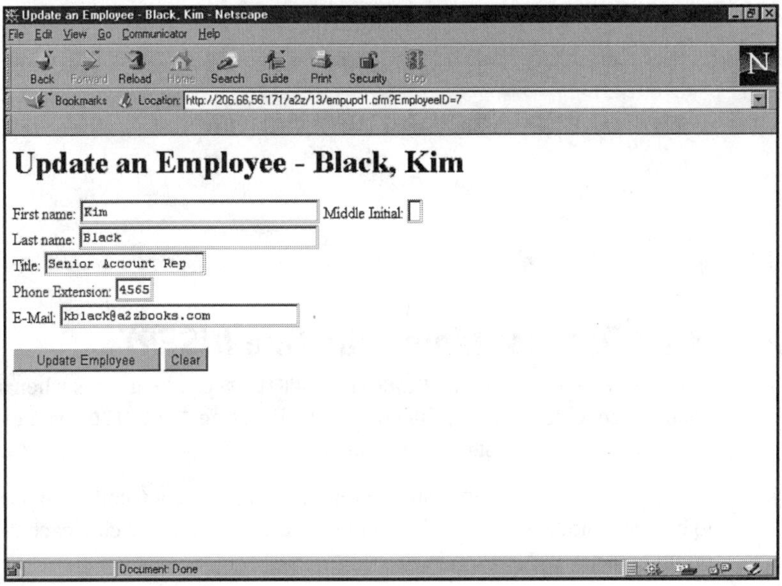

Building a Data-Update Form

Populating a HTML form is a very simple process. First, you need to retrieve the row to be updated from the table. You'll do this with a standard CFQUERY. Then, the retrieved values are passed as attributes to the HTML form.

▶ **See** "The *CFQUERY* Tag," **p. 202**

Listing 13.7 contains the code for EMPUPD1.CFM, a template to update an employee record. To test this template, you must specify an employee ID; without it, Cold Fusion would not know what row to retrieve. To ensure that an employee ID is passed, the first thing you do is check for the existence of the EmployeeID parameter. The code

```
<CFIF ParameterExists(EmployeeID) IS "No">
```

will return TRUE only if EmployeeID was not passed, in which case an error message is sent back to the user, and template processing is halted with the <CFABORT> tag.

Without the <CFABORT> tag, Cold Fusion would continue processing the template. If the CFQUERY statement is processed, an error message would be generated, because the WHERE clause WHERE EmployeeID = #EmployeeID# would be referencing an nonexistent field.

Test the EMPUPD1.CFM template, passing ?EmployeeID=7 as an URL parameter. Your screen should look like the one shown previously in Figure 13.4.

Listing 13.7   C:\A2Z\SCRIPTS\EMPUPD1.CFM—Template to Update an Employee

```
<CFIF ParameterExists(EmployeeID) IS "No">
 Error! No EmployeeID was specified!
 <CFABORT>
</CFIF>

<CFQUERY DATASOURCE="A2Z" NAME="Employee">
 SELECT FirstName,
        MiddleInit,
        LastName,
        Title,
        PhoneExtension,
        EMail
 FROM Employees
 WHERE EmployeeID = #EmployeeID#
</CFQUERY>

<CFOUTPUT QUERY="Employee">

<HTML>

<HEAD>
<TITLE>Update an Employee - #LastName#, #FirstName#</TITLE>
</HEAD>

<BODY>

<H1>Update an Employee - #LastName#, #FirstName#</H1>
<FORM ACTION="empupd2.cfm" METHOD="POST">

<INPUT TYPE="hidden" NAME="EmployeeID" VALUE="#EmployeeID#">

First name:
<INPUT TYPE="text" NAME="FirstName" SIZE="30" MAXLENGTH="30" VALUE=
➥"#Trim(FirstName)#">
Middle Initial:
<INPUT TYPE="text" NAME="MiddleInit" SIZE="1" MAXLENGTH="1" VALUE=
➥"#Trim(MiddleInit)#">
<BR>
Last name:
<INPUT TYPE="text" NAME="LastName" SIZE="30" MAXLENGTH="30" VALUE=
➥"#Trim(LastName)#">
<BR>
Title:
<INPUT TYPE="text" NAME="Title" SIZE="20" MAXLENGTH="20" VALUE=
➥"#Trim(Title)#">
<BR>
Phone Extension:
<INPUT TYPE="text" NAME="PhoneExtension" SIZE="4" MAXLENGTH="4" VALUE=
➥"#Trim(PhoneExtension)#">
<BR>
```

Part
III

Ch
13

continues

Listing 13.7   Continued

```
E-Mail:
<INPUT TYPE="text" NAME="EMail" SIZE="30" MAXLENGTH="30" VALUE=
➥"#Trim(EMail)#">

<P>
<INPUT TYPE="submit" VALUE="Update Employee">
<INPUT TYPE="reset" VALUE="Clear">

</FORM>

</BODY>

</HTML>

</CFOUTPUT>
```

Before you create the data update template, take a closer look at Listing 13.7. The template is similar to the Add an Employee template but has some important differences.

The first thing you do is verify that the primary key, EmployeeID, is present. Then Cold Fusion can retrieve the employee data with the CFQUERY tag. The WHERE clause WHERE EmployeeID = #EmployeeID# selects data by the primary key value, ensuring that no more than one row will ever be retrieved. The rest of the template is contained with a CFOUTPUT tag, allowing you to use any of the retrieved columns within the page body.

▶ **See** "Primary and Foreign Keys," **p. 96**

▶ **See** "Displaying Query Results with the *CFOUTPUT* Tag," **p. 204**

The retrieved data is used throughout the template. Even the page title is dynamically created with the code

```
<TITLE>Update an Employee - #LastName#, #FirstName#</TITLE>
```

To populate the data-entry fields, the current field value is passed to the INPUT VALUE attribute. For employee 7, Kim Black, the code

```
<INPUT TYPE="text" NAME="FirstName" SIZE="30"
MAXLENGTH="30" VALUE="#Trim(FirstName)#">
```

becomes

```
<INPUT TYPE="text" NAME="FirstName" SIZE="30"
MAXLENGTH="30" VALUE="Kim">
```

and so when the FirstName field is displayed, the name Kim will appear in it.

To ensure that there are no blank spaces after the retrieved value, the fields are trimmed with the Cold Fusion Trim() function before they are displayed. Why would you want to do this? Well, some databases, like Microsoft SQL Server, pad text fields with spaces so that they take up the full column width in the table. The FirstName field is a 30-character-wide column, and so the name Kim would be retrieved with 27 spaces after it. The extra space can be very annoying when you try to edit the field. For example, to append text to a field, you'd first have to backspace or delete all those extra characters.

> **TIP**
>
> When populating forms with table column values, it is a good idea to always trim the field first. Unlike in standard browser output, spaces in form fields are *not* ignored. Removing them allows easier editing. The Cold Fusion `Trim()` function removes spaces at the beginning and end of the value. If you wanted to trim only trailing spaces, you could use the `RTrim()` function instead.
>
> ▶ **See** Appendix A, "Cold Fusion Reference," **p. 849**

There is one hidden field in the FORM. The code

```
<INPUT TYPE="hidden" NAME="EmployeeID" VALUE="#EmployeeID#">
```

creates a hidden field called `EmployeeID` that contains the ID of the employee being updated. This hidden field *must* be present. Without it, Cold Fusion would have no idea what row you were updating when the form was actually submitted.

Remember, as explained earlier, HTTP sessions are created and broken as needed, and every session stands on its own two feet. Cold Fusion retrieved a specific row of data for you in one session, but it does not know that in the next session. Therefore, when you update a row, you must specify the primary key so that Cold Fusion knows which row to update.

Processing Updates

Just as with adding data, there are two ways to update rows in a table. The code in Listing 13.8 demonstrates a row update that uses the SQL UPDATE statement.

▶ **See** "Modifying Data," **p. 163**

On the CD

> **Listing 13.8   C:\A2Z\SCRIPTS\EMPUPD2.CFM—Updating Table with the SQL *UPDATE* Statement**

```
<CFQUERY DATASOURCE="A2Z">
 UPDATE Employees
 SET FirstName='#FirstName#',
     MiddleInit='#MiddleInit#',
     LastName='#LastName#',
     Title='#Title#',
     PhoneExtension='#PhoneExtension#',
     EMail='#EMail#'
 WHERE EmployeeID = #EmployeeID#
</CFQUERY>

<CFOUTPUT>

<HTML>

<HEAD>
<TITLE>Employee #LastName#, #FirstName# Updated</TITLE>
</HEAD>
```

Part
III

Ch
13

continues

Listing 13.8 Continued

```
<BODY>

<H1>Employee #LastName#, #FirstName# Updated </H1>
</BODY>

</HTML>

</CFOUTPUT>
```

The SQL statement in Listing 13.8 updates the six specified rows for the employee whose ID is the passed EmployeeID. To test this update template, try executing template EMPUPD1.CFM with different EmployeeID values, and then submit your changes.

Introducing *CFUPDATE*

As you saw earlier with regard to inserting data, hard-coded SQL statements are neither flexible nor easy to maintain. Cold Fusion provides a simpler way to update rows in database tables.

The CFUPDATE tag is very similar to the CFINSERT tag discussed earlier in this chapter. CFUPDATE requires just two attributes: the ODBC data source and the name of the table to update. Also, just like CFINSERT, the following attributes are available to you:

- DATASOURCE is the name of the ODBC data source containing the table to which the data is to be updated.
- TABLENAME is the name of the destination table.
- FORMFIELDS is an optional comma-separated list of fields to be updated. If this attribute is not provided, all the fields in the submitted form are used.

When using CFUPDATE, Cold Fusion automatically locates the row you want to update by looking at the table to ascertain its primary key. All you have to do is ensure that that primary key value is passed, as you did in Listing 13.7 using a hidden field.

The code in Listing 13.9 performs the exact same update as that in Listing 13.8, but uses the CFUPDATE tag rather than the SQL UPDATE tag. Obviously this code is more readable, reusable, and accommodating of form field changes you might make sometime in the future.

On the CD

Listing 13.9 C:\A2Z\SCRIPTS\EMPUPD3.CFM—Updating Data with the *CFUPDATE* Tag

```
<CFUPDATE DATASOURCE="A2Z" TABLENAME="Employees">

<CFOUTPUT>

<HTML>

<HEAD>
```

```
<TITLE>Employee #LastName#, #FirstName# Updated</TITLE>
</HEAD>

<BODY>

<H1>Employee #LastName#, #FirstName# Updated </H1>
</BODY>

</HTML>

</CFOUTPUT>
```

You'll have to change the FORM ACTION attribute in EMPUPD1.CFM to use EMPUP3.CFM to test this form. Make this change and try updating several employee records.

Just as with adding data, the choice to use CFUPDATE or SQL UPDATE is yours. The following are some guidelines to help you decide when to use each method:

- Whenever possible, use CFUPDATE to update data to ODBC tables.
- If you find that you need to update specific form fields, and not all that were submitted, use the CFUPDATE tag with the FORMFIELDS attribute.
- If CFINSERT cannot be used—because you need a complex UPDATE statement or are using fields that are not form fields—use SQL UPDATE.
- If you ever need to update all rows in a table, you must use SQL UPDATE.

Deleting Data with Cold Fusion

Unlike adding and updating data, Cold Fusion provides no efficient way to delete data. Delete is *always* a dangerous operation, and the Cold Fusion developers didn't want to make it too easy to delete the wrong data.

To delete data in a Cold Fusion template, you must use the SQL DELETE statement, shown in Listing 13.10. The code first checks to ensure that an employee ID was passed and terminates if the EmployeeID field is not present. If an employee ID is indeed passed, a CFQUERY is used to pass a SQL DELETE statement to the ODBC data source.

▶ See "Deleting Data," **p. 167**

On the CD

Listing 13.10   C:\A2Z\SCRIPTS\EMPDEL1.CFM—Deleting Table Data with the *SQL DELETE* Statement

```
<CFIF ParameterExists(EmployeeID) IS "No">
 Error! No EmployeeID was specified!
 <CFABORT>
</CFIF>

<CFQUERY DATASOURCE="A2Z">
 DELETE FROM Employees
```

continues

Listing 13.10 Continued

```
 WHERE EmployeeID = #EmployeeID#
</CFQUERY>

<HTML>

<HEAD>
<TITLE>Employee Deleted</TITLE>
</HEAD>

<BODY>

<H1>Employee Deleted</H1>

</BODY>

</HTML>
```

The code

```
DELETE FROM Employees WHERE EmployeeID = #EmployeeID#
```

deletes the record for the employee ID passed. If EmployeeID was 7, the code would translate to

```
DELETE FROM Employees WHERE EmployeeID = 7
```

and the employee with an employee ID of 7 would be deleted from the Employees table.

Reusing Forms

Well, you can now add to, update, and delete from your Employees table. But nothing lasts. Just when you thought you could relax and take a day off, human resources needs you to provide access to additional table columns.

So, you start to modify both the employee add and the employee update forms. You make sure that the additional five fields are added to both templates, and that they are in the same order, spelled the same way, and are the exact same length.

Then you realize that you are doing everything twice. There is really very little difference between the add and update forms, except that one needs existing values prefilled for updating. The form itself is identical.

With all the effort gone to in the past few chapters to prevent any duplication of effort, this seems quite counterproductive—and indeed it is.

The big difference between an add and an update form is whether the fields are prefilled to show current values. By using Cold Fusion conditional expressions, you can, in fact, create a single form that can be used for both adding and updating data.

A new and improved add and update form is shown in Listing 13.11. Listing 13.11 can both add and update records.

Listing 13.11   C:\A2Z\SCRIPTS\EMPAU1.CFM—Template to Display an Employee Add or an Employee Update Form

```
<CFIF ParameterExists(EmployeeID) IS "No">
 <CFSET NewRecord = "Yes">
<CFELSE>
 <CFSET NewRecord = "No">
</CFIF>

<CFIF NewRecord IS "No">
 <CFQUERY DATASOURCE="A2Z" NAME="Employee">
  SELECT FirstName,
         MiddleInit,
         LastName,
         Address1,
         Address2,
         City,
         State,
         Zip,
         Title,
         PhoneExtension,
         EMail
  FROM Employees
  WHERE EmployeeID = #EmployeeID#
 </CFQUERY>
</CFIF>

<HTML>

<HEAD>

<CFIF NewRecord IS "Yes">
 <TITLE>Add an Employee</TITLE>
<CFELSE>
 <CFOUTPUT QUERY="Employee">
  <TITLE>Update an Employee - #LastName#, #FirstName#</TITLE>
 </CFOUTPUT>
</CFIF>

</HEAD>

<BODY>

<H1>
<CFIF NewRecord IS "Yes">
 Add an Employee
<CFELSE>
 <CFOUTPUT QUERY="Employee">
  Update an Employee - #LastName#, #FirstName#
 </CFOUTPUT>
</CFIF>
</H1>
```

continues

Part
III

Ch
13

Listing 13.11   Continued

```
<FORM ACTION="empau2.cfm" METHOD="POST">

<CFIF NewRecord IS "No">
 <CFOUTPUT QUERY="Employee">
  <INPUT TYPE="hidden" NAME="EmployeeID" VALUE="#EmployeeID#">
 </CFOUTPUT>
</CFIF>

First name:
<INPUT TYPE="text" NAME="FirstName" SIZE="30" MAXLENGTH="30"
 <CFIF NewRecord IS "No">
  <CFOUTPUT QUERY="Employee">VALUE="#Trim(FirstName)#"</CFOUTPUT>
 </CFIF>
>
Middle Initial:
<INPUT TYPE="text" NAME="MiddleInit" SIZE="1" MAXLENGTH="1"
 <CFIF NewRecord IS "No">
  <CFOUTPUT QUERY="Employee">VALUE="#Trim(MiddleInit)#"</CFOUTPUT>
 </CFIF>
>
<BR>
Last name:
<INPUT TYPE="text" NAME="LastName" SIZE="30" MAXLENGTH="30"
 <CFIF NewRecord IS "No">
  <CFOUTPUT QUERY="Employee">VALUE="#Trim(LastName)#"</CFOUTPUT>
 </CFIF>
>
<BR>
Address:
<INPUT TYPE="text" NAME="Address1" SIZE="50" MAXLENGTH="50"
 <CFIF NewRecord IS "No">
  <CFOUTPUT QUERY="Employee">VALUE="#Trim(Address1)#"</CFOUTPUT>
 </CFIF>
>
<BR>
<INPUT TYPE="text" NAME="Address2" SIZE="50" MAXLENGTH="50"
 <CFIF NewRecord IS "No">
  <CFOUTPUT QUERY="Employee">VALUE="#Trim(Address2)#"</CFOUTPUT>
 </CFIF>
>
<BR>
City:
<INPUT TYPE="text" NAME="Address1" SIZE="40" MAXLENGTH="40"
 <CFIF NewRecord IS "No">
  <CFOUTPUT QUERY="Employee">VALUE="#Trim(City)#"</CFOUTPUT>
 </CFIF>
>
<BR>
State:
<INPUT TYPE="text" NAME="State" SIZE="5" MAXLENGTH="5"
 <CFIF NewRecord IS "No">
  <CFOUTPUT QUERY="Employee">VALUE="#Trim(State)#"</CFOUTPUT>
 </CFIF>
```

```
>
<BR>
Zip:
<INPUT TYPE="text" NAME="Zip" SIZE="10" MAXLENGTH="10"
 <CFIF NewRecord IS "No">
  <CFOUTPUT QUERY="Employee">VALUE="#Trim(Zip)#"</CFOUTPUT>
 </CFIF>
>
<BR>
Title:
<INPUT TYPE="text" NAME="Title" SIZE="20" MAXLENGTH="20"
 <CFIF NewRecord IS "No">
  <CFOUTPUT QUERY="Employee">VALUE="#Trim(Title)#"</CFOUTPUT>
 </CFIF>
>
<BR>
Phone Extension:
<INPUT TYPE="text" NAME="PhoneExtension" SIZE="4" MAXLENGTH="4"
 <CFIF NewRecord IS "No">
  <CFOUTPUT QUERY="Employee">VALUE="#Trim(PhoneExtension)#"</CFOUTPUT>
 </CFIF>
>
<BR>
E-Mail:
<INPUT TYPE="text" NAME="EMail" SIZE="30" MAXLENGTH="30"
 <CFIF NewRecord IS "No">
  <CFOUTPUT QUERY="Employee">VALUE="#Trim(EMail)#"</CFOUTPUT>
 </CFIF>
>

<P>
<CFIF NewRecord IS "Yes">
 <INPUT TYPE="submit" VALUE="Add Employee">
<CFELSE>
 <INPUT TYPE="submit" VALUE="Update Employee">
</CFIF>
<INPUT TYPE="reset" VALUE="Clear">

</FORM>

</BODY>

</HTML>
```

Understanding Conditional Forms

Now, analyze Listing 13.11. The first thing you do in it is determine if an insert or an update is required. How can you know that? Well, for a record to be updated, an employee ID must be passed; otherwise, Cold Fusion would have no idea which record needs updating. It makes no sense to pass an employee ID when adding a row; the new employee's ID will be assigned when the data is actually inserted into the table.

You can therefore make a safe assumption that if a employee ID is present, this is an update operation, and if not, then it's an addition.

The first line in the template

```
<CFIF ParameterExists(EmployeeID) IS "No">
```

checks to see if `EmployeeID` was specified and sets a variable called `NewRecord` to "Yes" or "No" based on its existence. The code

```
<CFSET NewRecord = "Yes">
```

sets `NewRecord` to "Yes" because the `ParameterExists(EmployeeID)` test returned "No". If `ParameterExists(EmployeeID)` returns "Yes", the code

```
<CFSET NewRecord = "No">
```

sets `NewRecord` to "No".

Either way, once the first five lines of the template have been processed, you'll have a new variable called `NewRecord` that indicates whether a new record is being added. You can then use this variable throughout the template wherever different code is needed for insertions or updates. Of course, you could have named this variable with some other name as well; the actual variable name is not that important, as long as it is descriptive.

N O T E Cold Fusion variables are special fields that you can create at any time, and can contain any values. Once a variable is created during the processing of a template, it is available for use until that processing is complete. Variables are assigned by using the CFSET tag and can be reassigned by using that same tag as needed. ■

The CFQUERY that retrieves the employee record to update is conditional. It would make no sense to try to retrieve a record that does not yet exist in the table, so the entire CFQUERY statement is enclosed in a CFIF statement. The code `<CFIF NewRecord IS "No">` ensures that everything until the matching `</CFIF>` is processed only if this is an update.

The page title is also conditional, so that it accurately reflects the operation being performed. If the operation is an update, the name of the employee being updated is displayed. Of course, displaying the employee name requires displaying dynamic data, so the title is enclosed within a CFOUTPUT block, as shown in the following code, if the operation is an update.

```
<CFOUTPUT QUERY="Employee">
<TITLE>Update an Employee - #LastName#, FirstName#</TITLE>
</CFOUTPUT>
```

The very first field in the form itself is a hidden field. The code

```
<INPUT TYPE="hidden" NAME="EmployeeID" VALUE="#EmployeeID#">
```

creates a hidden field containing the primary key of the record to be updated. This is required for the CFUPDATE tag to work, as explained earlier in this chapter.

But this hidden field is wanted only if the operation is an update. For insert operations, a new employee ID is generated automatically at the time of data insertion. And so the whole INPUT tag is conditional and is processed only if the `<CFIF NewRecord IS "No">` condition returns true. If `NewRecord` is `"Yes"`, all the code until the matching `</CFIF>` tag is ignored.

Using Conditional *INPUT* Fields

Next come all the fields themselves, starting with the `FirstName` field. When adding a new record, the `FirstName` input field needs to look like this:

```
<INPUT TYPE="text" NAME="FirstName" SIZE="30" MAXLENGTH="30">
```

When updating a record, the same field needs one additional attribute, `VALUE`. The parameter passed to the `VALUE` attribute is the FirstName column as retrieved by the `CFQUERY` tag. The complete field for an update operation, therefore, looks like this:

```
<INPUT TYPE="text" NAME="FirstName" SIZE="30"
MAXLENGTH="30" VALUE="#Trim(FirstName)#">
```

As the only difference between the two is the `VALUE` attribute, you can make that conditional too. This will typically involve breaking the `INPUT` field up over multiple lines, but that is allowed and will not break anything. As shown in the following code, the basic `INPUT` tag is first defined, but no terminating > is provided yet. Instead, you test to see if this is an update; if it is, the `VALUE` attribute is included within a `CFOUTPUT` block so that it may be populated with the current value. The terminating > appears after the condition, ensuring that the `VALUE` attribute will be contained within the `INPUT` tag if it is needed.

```
<INPUT TYPE="text" NAME="FirstName" SIZE="30" MAXLENGTH="30"
 <CFIF NewRecord IS "No">
  <CFOUTPUT QUERY="Employee">VALUE="#Trim(FirstName)#"</CFOUTPUT>
 </CFIF>
>
```

And that's all you need to create a conditional `INPUT` tag. The tag is a little more complicated to read, and the generated HTML source code will likely contain multiple lines and blank lines in the middle of the tag. But the benefit here is that if you needed to change any tag attributes, you'd have to make the change only once. Similarly, if you needed to add input fields, you'd have to make changes to only a single template.

The final conditional code in Listing 13.11 is the submit button. Again, you check the value of the `NewRecord` variable so as to be able to specify an appropriate value for the submit button text.

You can now try out this form. If you specify an `EmployeeID` parameter in the URL, like `?EmployeeID=7`, you'll be presented with an update form. Executing the same template without an `EmployeeID` parameter displays an add form. Both forms are shown in Figures 13.5 and 13.6.

But don't submit the form yet. Now you have to create a template that can conditionally perform the actual insert or update.

Part

III

Ch

13

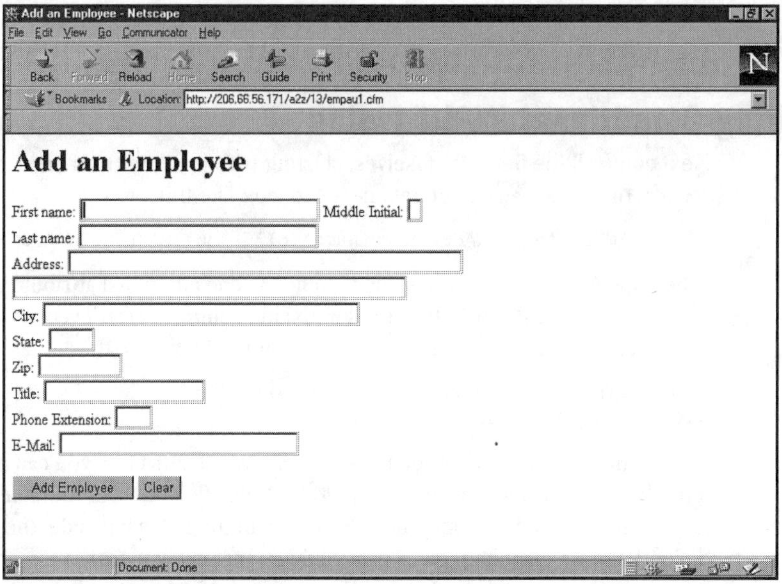

FIG. 13.5
Templates can be reused when using conditional code. This add form is also an update form.

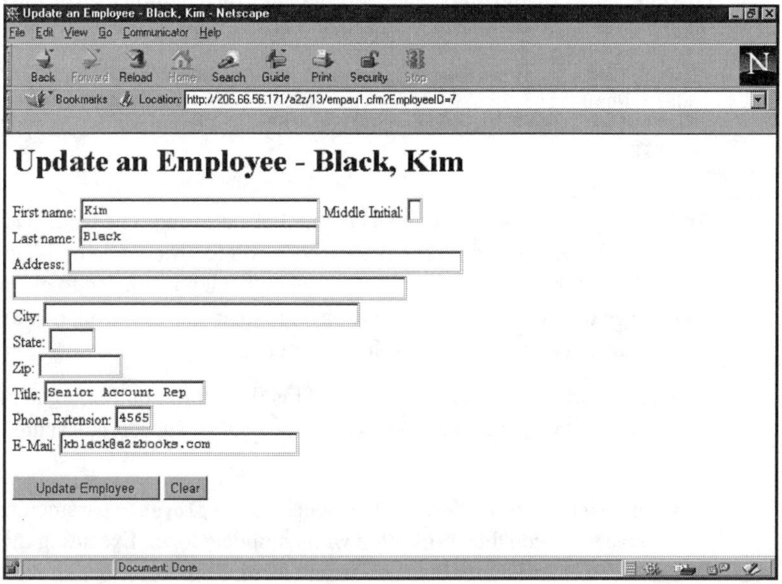

FIG. 13.6
Templates can be reused when using conditional code. This update form is also an add form.

Processing Conditional Forms

Processing a conditional form requires that the destination template ascertain which operation needs to be performed, and there are many ways to do this. These include:

Embedding a hidden field in the form that specifies the operation

Checking for the existence of a specific field, or the lack thereof (similar to what you did in Listing 13.11)

Checking the value of a known entity— for example, the submit button—which could have a different value based on the operation being performed

---

CAUTION

To submit the value of a button, you must name the field with the INPUT NAME attribute. This way, the browser can submit a *name=value* pair for the submit button.

Some older browsers do not support naming submit buttons, and they might ignore the attribute altogether.

For this example, you'll do the same thing you did in the form template itself—that is, checking for the existence of an EmployeeID. The hidden EmployeeID field will be present only if the operation is an update.

The conditional insert and update template is shown in Listing 13.12.

Listing 13.12   C:\A2Z\SCRIPTS\EMPAU2.CFM—Template to Conditionally Insert or Update an Employee Record

```
<CFIF ParameterExists(FORM.EmployeeID) IS "No">
 <CFSET Operation = "Inserted">
 <CFINSERT DATASOURCE="A2Z" TABLENAME="Employees" >
<CFELSE>
 <CFSET Operation = "Updated">
 <CFUPDATE DATASOURCE="A2Z" TABLENAME="Employees">
</CFIF>

<CFOUTPUT>

<HTML>

<HEAD>
<TITLE>Employee #FORM.LastName#, #FORM.FirstName# #Operation#</TITLE>
</HEAD>

<BODY>
<H1>Employee #FORM.LastName#, #FORM.FirstName# #Operation#</H1>
</BODY>

<HTML>

</CFOUTPUT>
```

Just as in the form in Listing 13.11, the first thing you do is check for the presence of the EmployeeID field, but this time you explicitly check for an EmployeeID field within a FORM. For

Part
III

Ch
13

an update to work, the primary key form field must be present. Chances are that no other EmployeeID field would be present, but just to make sure, you preface the field name with the FORM identifier, as follows:

```
<CFIF ParameterExists(FORM.EmployeeID) IS "No">
```

Then, if the EmployeeID does not exist, you execute a CFINSERT; otherwise, you execute a CFUPDATE. It's that simple. You now have a single template that can both insert and update employee records.

Unlike Listing 13.11, here you did not set a variable to indicate which operation to perform. Why not? Well, in Listing 13.11 there were many conditional elements within the code, and so as not to have to repeatedly check for parameter existence, you created a variable that could be checked instead. Here there is only one conditional code block, so you might as well perform the insert or update operations right there within the conditional block.

The other thing you did in the conditional code is set a variable called Operation, which is either set to "Inserted" or "Updated". You then used this variable twice later on, in the title and in the body. In this way, you did not need to create two additional conditional code blocks. The variable contains the appropriate text to be displayed automatically wherever it is used.

N O T E There are an unlimited number of ways to structure your conditional code, and no single approach is right or wrong. The examples in this chapter demonstrate several different techniques, and you will undoubtedly develop several of your own too. The only rule to remember is to make your code readable, manageable, and, wherever possible, reusable. ▪

Using Additional Code Reuse Techniques

While you're on the subject of code reuse, look at another useful way to create reusable forms.

The combination insert and update form you created in Listing 13.11 works very well. The only problem with it is one of manageability. With so many <CFIF> statements, you run the risk of introducing mismatched tags or typos, especially if you were to modify the form at a later date.

As a rule, programmers like to keep all conditional code in one place, creating a simpler program flow. The code in Listing 13.13 shows how to do this.

On the CD

Listing 13.13 C:\A2Z\SCRIPTS\EMPAU3.CFM—Alternate Combination Insert and Update Form

```
<CFIF ParameterExists(EmployeeID) IS "No">
 <CFSET PageTitle = "Add an Employee">
 <CFSET ButtonText = "Add Employee">
 <CFSET FirstName = "">
 <CFSET MiddleInit = "">
 <CFSET LastName = "">
 <CFSET Address1 = "">
 <CFSET Address2 = "">
 <CFSET City = "">
 <CFSET State = "">
```

```
  <CFSET Zip = "">
  <CFSET Title = "">
  <CFSET PhoneExtension = "">
  <CFSET EMail = "">
<CFELSE>
 <CFQUERY DATASOURCE="A2Z" NAME="Employee">
  SELECT FirstName,
         MiddleInit,
         LastName,
         Address1,
         Address2,
         City,
         State,
         Zip,
         Title,
         PhoneExtension,
         EMail
  FROM Employees
  WHERE EmployeeID = #EmployeeID#
 </CFQUERY>
 <CFSET PageTitle = "Update an Employee - " &
Employee.LastName & ", " & Employee.FirstName>
 <CFSET ButtonText = "Update Employee">
 <CFSET FirstName = Trim(Employee.FirstName)>
 <CFSET MiddleInit = Trim(Employee.MiddleInit)>
 <CFSET LastName = Trim(Employee.LastName)>
 <CFSET Address1 = Trim(Employee.Address1)>
 <CFSET Address2 = Trim(Employee.Address2)>
 <CFSET City = Trim(Employee.City)>
 <CFSET State = Trim(Employee.State)>
 <CFSET Zip = Trim(Employee.Zip)>
 <CFSET Title = Trim(Employee.Title)>
 <CFSET PhoneExtension = Trim(Employee.PhoneExtension)>
 <CFSET EMail = Trim(Employee.EMail)>
</CFIF>

<CFOUTPUT>

<HTML>

<HEAD>
<TITLE>#PageTitle#</TITLE>
</HEAD>

<BODY>

<H1>#PageTitle#</H1>

<FORM ACTION="empau2.cfm" METHOD="POST">

<CFIF ParameterExists(EmployeeID)>
 <INPUT TYPE="hidden" NAME="EmployeeID" VALUE="#EmployeeID#">
</CFIF>

<P>
```

continues

Listing 13.13   Continued

```
First name:
<INPUT TYPE="text" NAME="FirstName" SIZE="30"
MAXLENGTH="30" VALUE="#FirstName#">
Middle Initial:
<INPUT TYPE="text" NAME="MiddleInit" SIZE="1"
MAXLENGTH="1" VALUE="#MiddleInit#">
<BR>
Last name:
<INPUT TYPE="text" NAME="LastName" SIZE="30"
MAXLENGTH="30" VALUE="#LastName#">
<BR>
Address:
<INPUT TYPE="text" NAME="Address1" SIZE="50"
MAXLENGTH="50" VALUE="#Address1#">
<BR>
<INPUT TYPE="text" NAME="Address2" SIZE="50"
MAXLENGTH="50" VALUE="#Address2#">
<BR>
City:
<INPUT TYPE="text" NAME="Address1" SIZE="40"
MAXLENGTH="40" VALUE="#City#">
<BR>
State:
<INPUT TYPE="text" NAME="State" SIZE="5"
MAXLENGTH="5" VALUE="#State#">
<BR>
Zip:
<INPUT TYPE="text" NAME="Zip" SIZE="10"
MAXLENGTH="10" VALUE="#Zip#">
<BR>
Title:
<INPUT TYPE="text" NAME="Title" SIZE="20"
MAXLENGTH="20" VALUE="#Title#">
<BR>
Phone Extension:
<INPUT TYPE="text" NAME="PhoneExtension" SIZE="4"
MAXLENGTH="4" VALUE="#PhoneExtension#">
<BR>
E-Mail:
<INPUT TYPE="text" NAME="EMail" SIZE="30"
MAXLENGTH="30" VALUE="#EMail#">

<P>
<INPUT TYPE="submit" VALUE="#ButtonText#">
<INPUT TYPE="reset" VALUE="Clear">

</FORM>

</BODY>

</HTML>

</CFOUTPUT>
```

First, look at the INPUT fields themselves. Notice that there is no conditional code within them as there was before. Instead, every INPUT tag has a VALUE attribute regardless of whether this is an insert or an update. The value in the VALUE attribute is a Cold Fusion variable that is set at the top of the template.

The first thing this template does is determine if this is an insert or an update operation. If it is an update, a <CFQUERY> is used to retrieve the current values. The fields retrieved by that <CFQUERY> are saved into local variables by using multiple <CFSET> tags. If it is an insert operation, obviously no <CFQUERY> is used, but <CFSET> is still used to create empty variables.

Regardless of the operation, once that conditional code has been processed, a set of variables will exist. If the operation is an insert, the variables are empty (although they could contain default values too). If it is an update operation, the variables will contain the current values. Either way, there is a valid set of variables to work with.

The rest of the code in the template just uses these variables, without needing any conditional processing. Even the page title and submit button text can be initialized in variables this way, so <CFIF> tags are not needed for them either.

Obviously, this form is far more elegant and manageable than the one you saw before. You may use either technique, or a combination thereof—whatever suits you and your application.

Creating a Complete Application

Now that you've created add, modify, and delete templates, put it all together and create a finished application.

The templates below are a combination of all you have learned in both this and the previous chapter.

The template shown in Listing 13.14 is the main employee administration page. It displays all the employees in the Employees table and provides links to edit and delete them, as well as to add a new employee. The administration page is shown in Figure 13.7.

On the CD

Listing 13.14   C:\A2Z\SCRIPTS\EMPADMIN.CFM—Employee Administration Template

```
<CFQUERY DATASOURCE="A2Z" NAME="Employees">
 SELECT FirstName, LastName, PhoneExtension, EmployeeID
 FROM Employees
 ORDER BY LastName, FirstName
</CFQUERY>

<HTML>

<HEAD>
<TITLE>Employee List</TITLE>
</HEAD>
```

Part
III

Ch
13

continues

Listing 13.14   Continued

```
<BODY>

<CENTER>

<TABLE BORDER>
<TR>
  <TH COLSPAN=3>
   <H1>Employees</H1>
  </TH>
 </TR>
 <TR>
  <TH>
   Name
  </TH>
  <TH>
   Extension
  </TH>
 </TR>

<CFOUTPUT QUERY="Employees">
 <TR>
  <TD>
   #LastName#, #FirstName#
  </TD>
  <TD>
   Ext: #PhoneExtension#
  </TD>
  <TD>
   <A HREF="empau4.cfm?EmployeeID=#EmployeeID#">Edit</A>
   <A HREF="empdel2.cfm?EmployeeID=#EmployeeID#">Delete</A>
  </TD>
 </TR>
</CFOUTPUT>

 <TR>
  <TH COLSPAN=3>
   <A HREF="empau3.cfm">Add an Employee</A>
  </TH>
 </TR>

</TABLE>

</CENTER>

</BODY>

</HTML>
```

▶ **See** "Displaying Results in Tables," **p. 212**

Listing 13.15 is essentially the same reusable employee add and update form that you created earlier. The only significant change is that the FORM ACTION has been changed so that template EMPAU5.CFM processes the responses.

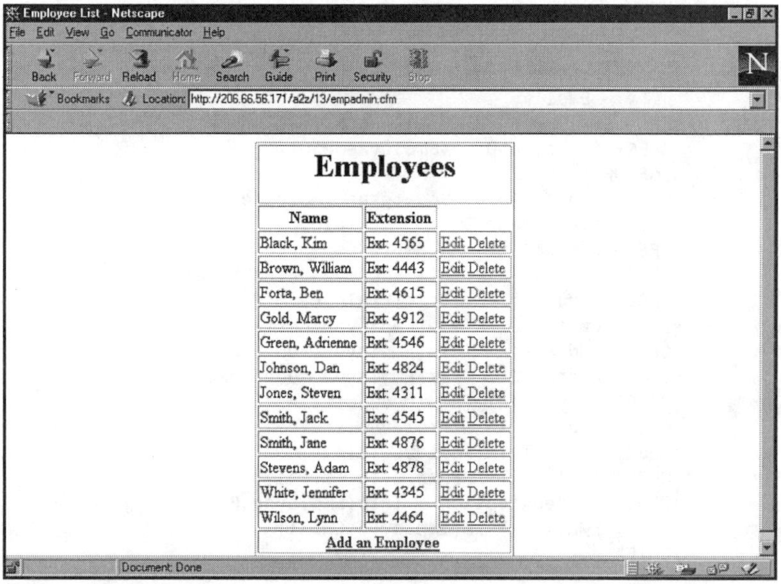

FIG. 13.7

The employee admini-
stration page is used to
add, edit, and delete
employee records.

On the CD

**Listing 13.15   C:\A2Z\SCRIPTS\EMPAU4.CFM—Employee Add and
Update Form**

```
<CFIF ParameterExists(EmployeeID) IS "No">
 <CFSET PageTitle = "Add an Employee">
 <CFSET ButtonText = "Add Employee">
 <CFSET FirstName = "">
 <CFSET MiddleInit = "">
 <CFSET LastName = "">
 <CFSET Address1 = "">
 <CFSET Address2 = "">
 <CFSET City = "">
 <CFSET State = "">
 <CFSET Zip = "">
 <CFSET Title = "">
 <CFSET PhoneExtension = "">
 <CFSET EMail = "">
<CFELSE>
 <CFQUERY DATASOURCE="A2Z" NAME="Employee">
  SELECT FirstName,
         MiddleInit,
         LastName,
         Address1,
         Address2,
         City,
         State,
         Zip,
         Title,
```

Part

III

Ch

13

continues

Listing 13.15   Continued

```
          PhoneExtension,
          EMail
 FROM Employees
 WHERE EmployeeID = #EmployeeID#
</CFQUERY>
<CFSET PageTitle = "Update an Employee - " &
Employee.LastName & ", " & Employee.FirstName>
<CFSET ButtonText = "Update Employee">
<CFSET FirstName = Trim(Employee.FirstName)>
<CFSET MiddleInit = Trim(Employee.MiddleInit)>
<CFSET LastName = Trim(Employee.LastName)>
<CFSET Address1 = Trim(Employee.Address1)>
<CFSET Address2 = Trim(Employee.Address2)>
<CFSET City = Trim(Employee.City)>
<CFSET State = Trim(Employee.State)>
<CFSET Zip = Trim(Employee.Zip)>
<CFSET Title = Trim(Employee.Title)>
<CFSET PhoneExtension = Trim(Employee.PhoneExtension)>
<CFSET EMail = Trim(Employee.EMail)>
</CFIF>

<CFOUTPUT>

<HTML>

<HEAD>
<TITLE>#PageTitle#</TITLE>
</HEAD>

<BODY>

<H1>#PageTitle#</H1>

<FORM ACTION="empau5.cfm" METHOD="POST">

<CFIF ParameterExists(EmployeeID)>
 <INPUT TYPE="hidden" NAME="EmployeeID" VALUE="#EmployeeID#">
</CFIF>

<P>

First name:
<INPUT TYPE="text" NAME="FirstName" SIZE="30"
MAXLENGTH="30" VALUE="#FirstName#">
Middle Initial:
<INPUT TYPE="text" NAME="MiddleInit" SIZE="1"
MAXLENGTH="1" VALUE="#MiddleInit#">
<BR>
Last name:
<INPUT TYPE="text" NAME="LastName" SIZE="30"
MAXLENGTH="30" VALUE="#LastName#">
<BR>
Address:
<INPUT TYPE="text" NAME="Address1" SIZE="50"
```

```
MAXLENGTH="50" VALUE="#Address1#">
<BR>
<INPUT TYPE="text" NAME="Address2" SIZE="50"
MAXLENGTH="50" VALUE="#Address2#">
<BR>
City:
<INPUT TYPE="text" NAME="Address1" SIZE="40"
MAXLENGTH="40" VALUE="#City#">
<BR>
State:
<INPUT TYPE="text" NAME="State" SIZE="5"
MAXLENGTH="5" VALUE="#State#">
<BR>
Zip:
<INPUT TYPE="text" NAME="Zip" SIZE="10" MAXLENGTH="10" VALUE="#Zip#">
<BR>
Title:
<INPUT TYPE="text" NAME="Title" SIZE="20"
MAXLENGTH="20" VALUE="#Title#">
<BR>
Phone Extension:
<INPUT TYPE="text" NAME="PhoneExtension" SIZE="4"
MAXLENGTH="4" VALUE="#PhoneExtension#">
<BR>
E-Mail:
<INPUT TYPE="text" NAME="EMail" SIZE="30"
MAXLENGTH="30" VALUE="#EMail#">

<P>
<INPUT TYPE="submit" VALUE="#ButtonText#">
<INPUT TYPE="reset" VALUE="Clear">

</FORM>

</BODY>

</HTML>

</CFOUTPUT>
```

Listings 13.16 and 13.17 perform the actual data insertions, updates, and deletions. The big change in these templates is that they themselves provide no user feedback at all. Instead, as soon as they finish processing the database changes, they return to the administration screen by using the <CFLOCATION> tag. <CFLOCATION> is used to switch from the current template being processed to any other URL, including another Cold Fusion template. The following sample code instructs Cold Fusion to switch to the empadmin.cfm template:

```
<CFLOCATION URL="empadmin.cfm">
```

In this way, as soon as any change is completed, the updated employee list is displayed, ready for further processing.

Part

III

Ch

13

On the CD

Listing 13.16   C:\A2Z\SCRIPTS\EMPAU5.CFM—Employee Insert and Update Processing

```
<CFIF ParameterExists(FORM.EmployeeID) IS "No">
 <CFINSERT DATASOURCE="A2Z" TABLENAME="Employees">
<CFELSE>
 <CFUPDATE DATASOURCE="A2Z" TABLENAME="Employees">
</CFIF>

<CFLOCATION URL="empadmin.cfm">
```

On the CD

Listing 13.17   C:\A2Z\SCRIPTS\EMPDEL2.CFM—Employee Delete Processing

```
<CFIF ParameterExists(EmployeeID) IS "No">
 Error! No EmployeeID was specified!
 <CFABORT>
</CFIF>

<CFQUERY DATASOURCE="A2Z">
 DELETE FROM Employees
 WHERE EmployeeID = #EmployeeID#
</CFQUERY>

<CFLOCATION URL="empadmin.cfm">
```

Using *CFIF* to Create Conditional Code

The conditions you have created so far have all just test for equality—that is, they have performed a check to determine if a field or value *equals* another value. But you are not limited to testing for equality. Cold Fusion provides a complete set of conditional operators, and you can combine conditions with AND and OR operators too.

The complete list of operators is shown in Table 13.1. Notice that many of the operators have alternate syntax; you may use whichever syntax with which you are comfortable. The syntax GREATER THAN OR EQUAL TO is very descriptive, but is also very wordy and takes up additional screen space, which might force you to have to scroll your screen or wrap text over multiple lines. The abbreviated syntax GTE accomplishes the exact same thing and takes far less space, but is also less intuitive.

Table 13.1   Cold Fusion Conditional Operators

Operator	Alternate	Description
IS	EQUAL, EQ	Check that the right value is equal to the left value
IS NOT	NOT EQUAL, NEQ	Check that the right value is not equal to the left value

Operator	Alternate	Description
CONTAINS		Check that the right value is contained within the left value
DOES NOT CONTAIN		Check that the right value is not contained within the left value
GREATER THAN	GT	Check that the left value is greater than the right value
LESS THAN	LT	Check that the left value is less than the right value
GREATER THAN OR EQUAL	GTE	Check that the left value is greater than or equal to the right value
LESS THAN OR EQUAL	LTE	Check that the left value is less than or equal to the right value

The Boolean operators available to you are shown in Table 13.2.

Table 13.2 Cold Fusion Boolean Operators

Operator	Description
AND	Conjunction, returns TRUE only if both expressions are true
OR	Disjunction, returns TRUE if either expression is true
NOT	Negation

When combining conditions, each condition must be contained within a set of parentheses. The following example checks to see if both the FirstName and LastName fields exist:

```
<CFIF (ParameterExists(FirstName)) AND (ParameterExists(LastName))>
```

To check for either a first name or a last name, you could do the following:

```
<CFIF (ParameterExists(FirstName)) OR (ParameterExists(LastName))>
```

Often you will want to verify that a field is not empty and does not contain blank spaces. The following condition demonstrates how this can be accomplished:

```
<CFIF Trim(LastName) IS NOT "">
```

To check if a value is within a range of values, you can use the CONTAINS operator:

```
<CFIF "KY,MI,MN,OH,WI" CONTAINS State>
```

or

```
<CFIF TaxableStates CONTAINS State>
```

More complex expressions can be created by combining conditions within parentheses. For example, the following condition checks to see if a payment is by check or credit card; if payment is by credit card, it checks to ensure that there is an approval code.

Part
III

Ch
13

```
<CFIF (PaymentType IS "Check") OR ((PaymentType IS "Credit") AND (ApprovalCode IS
NOT ""))>
```

As you can see, the Cold Fusion conditional support is both extensive and powerful. You'll be making much more use of the CFIF tag in upcoming chapters. ●

CHAPTER 14

Form Data Validation

by Leon Chalnick and Ben Forta

Understanding Form Validation

HTML forms are used to collect data from users through several different field types. Forms are used for data entry, as front-end search engines, for filling out orders, signing guest-books, and much more. And while forms have become one of the most important features in HTML, these forms provide almost no data validation tools.

This becomes a real problem when developing web-based applications. You as a developer need to be able to control what data users may enter into what fields. Without that, your programs will constantly be breaking due to mismatched or unanticipated data received from your users.

Thankfully, Cold Fusion provides a complete and robust set of tools with which to implement form data validation, both client-side and server-side.

Since its inception, HTML has always provided web page developers with a variety of ways to format and display data. With each revision to the HTML specification, additional data display mechanisms have been made available. As a result, HTML is a powerful data-publishing tool.

But, while its data presentation options continue to improve, HTML's data collection capabilities leave much to be desired. In fact, they have barely changed at all since the language's very early days.

HTML data collection is performed using forms. HTML forms support the following field types:

- Free-form text fields
- Select box (or drop-down list boxes)
- Radio buttons
- Check boxes
- Multi-line text boxes
- Password (hidden input) boxes

▶ **See** Chapter 12, "Cold Fusion Forms," **p. 225**.

So what's wrong with this list? Actually, there is nothing wrong with the list at all. These field types are all the standard fields you would expect to be available to you in any development language. What is wrong, however, is that these fields have very limited capabilities. The two primary limitations are:

- Inability to mark fields as required
- Inability to define data types or filters—like only accepting digits, a zip code, or a phone number

What this means is that there is no simple way to tell HTML to disallow form submission if certain fields are left empty. Similarly, HTML cannot be instructed to only accept certain values or types of data in specific fields.

HTML itself has exactly one validation option, the MAXLENGTH attribute, which can be used to specify the maximum number of characters that may be entered in a text field. But that's it. There are no other validation options.

To work around these limitations, HTML developers have typically adopted two forms of validation options:

- Server-side validation
- Client-side validation

Comparing Server-Side and Client-Side Validation

Server-side validation involves checking for required fields or invalid values *after* a form has been submitted. The script on the server first validates the form, and then continues processing only if all validation requirements are met. If validation fails, an error message is sent back to the user's browser, the user would then make the corrections, and then resubmit the form. Of course, the form submission has to be validated again upon resubmission, and if the validation fails again, the process has to be repeated.

Client-side scripting allows the developer to embed instructions to the browser within the HTML code. As HTML itself provides no mechanism for doing this, developers have resorted to using scripting languages like JavaScript (supported by both Netscape Navigator and Microsoft Internet Explorer) or VBScript (supported by Microsoft Internet Explorer alone). These interpreted languages support basic data manipulation and user feedback, and are thus well suited for form validation. To validate a form, the page author would create a function to be executed as soon as a Submit button is clicked. This function would perform any necessary validation, and only allow the submission to proceed if the validation checked was successful. The advantage of this approach is that the user does not have to submit a form to find out if there was an error in it. Notification of any errors occurs prior to form submission.

Understanding the Pros and Cons of Each Option

Neither of these options is perfect, and they are thus often used together, complimenting each other. Table 14.1 lists the pros and cons of each option.

Table 14.1 The Pros and Cons of Client and Server Form Validation

Validation Type	Pros	Cons
Server-Side	Most flexible form of validation Validation is browser independent.	User must submit data before validation occurs, any errors require correction and resubmission.
Client-Side	Validation occurs prior to form submission, allowing for a more intuitive and less aggravating user interface.	Not all browsers support scripting languages. Languages have high learning curves.

Part
III

Ch
14

From a user's perspective, client-side validation is preferable. Obviously, users would like to know what is wrong with the data they entered *before* they submit the form for processing. From a developer's perspective, however, server-side validation is simpler to code, and less likely to fall victim to browser incompatibilities.

Using Server-Side Validation

As mentioned earlier, server side validation involves adding code to your application that performs form field validation *after* the form is submitted. In Cold Fusion this is usually achieved with a series of <CFIF> statements that check each field's value and data types. If any validation steps fail, processing can be terminated with the <CFABORT> function.

There are two ways to perform server-side validation in Cold Fusion. You'll look at basic server-side validation first, and then you'll use embedded validation codes to automate the validation where possible.

Using Basic Server-Side Validation

The code shown in Listing 14.1 is a simple login prompt used to gain access to a secure site. The user is prompted for a user id and password. The form itself is shown in Figure 14.1.

Listing 14.1   PROMPT1.CFM—HTML Code for the Simple Login Screen Shown in Figure 14.1

```
<FORM ACTION="login1.cfm" METHOD="POST">

<CENTER>
<TABLE BORDER>
 <TR>
  <TH ALIGN="RIGHT">
   ID:
  </TH>
  <TD>
   <INPUT TYPE="text" NAME="login_id" SIZE="5" MAXLENGTH="5">
  </TD>
 </TR>
 <TR>
  <TH ALIGN="RIGHT">
   Password:
  </TH>
  <TD>
   <INPUT TYPE="password" NAME="login_password" SIZE="20" MAXLENGTH="20">
  </TD>
 </TR>
```

```
<TR>
 <TH COLSPAN="2">
  <INPUT TYPE="submit" VALUE="Login">
 </TH>
</TR>
</TABLE>
</CENTER>

</FORM>
```

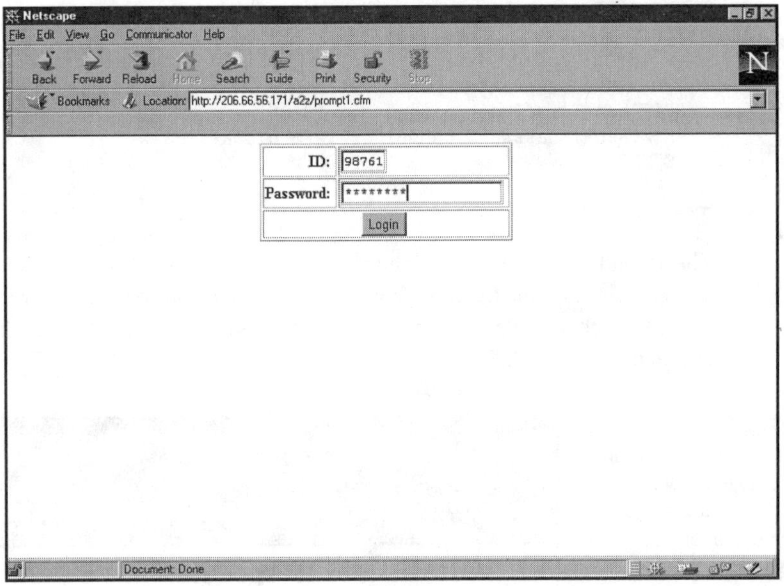

FIG. 14.1

HTML forms support basic field types, such as text and password boxes.

This particular form gets submitted to a template named login1.cfm. That template is responsible for validating the user input, and processing the login only if all the validation rules passed. The validation rules here are

Login id is required

Login must be numeric

Login password is required

To perform this validation, three <CFIF> statements are used, as shown in Listing 14.2. The first <CFIF> checks the length of login_id after trimming it with the Trim() function. The Trim() function is necessary to trap space characters which are technically valid characters in a text field, but are not valid here. If the Len() function returns 0, an error message is displayed, and the <CFABORT> statements halts further processing.

Part

III

Ch

14

Listing 14.2 LOGIN1.CFM—Basic Validation Code

```
<!--- Make sure login_id is not empty --->
<CFIF Len(Trim(login_id)) IS 0>
 <H1>ERROR! ID cannot be left blank!</H1>
 <CFABORT>
</CFIF>

<!--- Make sure login_id is a number --->
<CFIF IsNumeric(login_id) IS "No">
 <H1>ERROR! Invalid ID specified!</H1>
 <CFABORT>
</CFIF>

<!--- Make sure password is not empty --->
<CFIF Len(Trim(login_password)) IS 0>
 <H1>ERROR! Password cannot be left blank!</H1>
 <CFABORT>
</CFIF>
```

The second <CFIF> statement checks the data type. The IsNumeric() function returns Yes if the passed value was numeric (contained only digits, for example), or No"if not. Once again, if the <CFIF> check fails, then an error is displayed and <CFABORT> halts further processing, as shown in Figure 14.2.

FIG. 14.2

<CFIF> statements can be used to perform validation checks and then display error messages if the checks fail.

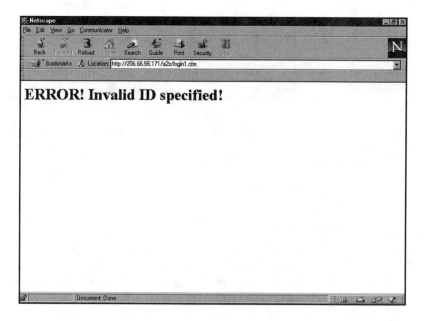

This form of validation is the most powerful and flexible of all the validation options available to you. There is no limit to the number of <CFIF> statements you can use, and there is no limit to the number of functions or tags that you can use within them. You can even perform database operations (perhaps to check that a password matches) and use the results in comparisons.

▶ **See** Appendix B, "Cold Fusion Function Reference," **p. 915**.

TIP

<CFIF> statements can be combined using AND and OR operators if needed. For example, the first two <CFIF> statements shown in Listing 14.1 could be combined to read

```
<CFIF (Len(Trim(login_id)) IS 0) OR (IsNumeric(login_id) IS "No")>
```

The big downside here, however, is that this type of validation code is neither clean nor manageable. If you were to add or rename a field for example, you'd have to remember to update the destination form (the form that the fields get submitted to, as specified in the <FORM> ACTION attribute), as well as the form itself. As your forms grow in complexity, so does the likelihood of your forms and their validation rules getting out of synch.

Using Cold Fusion Embedded Form Validation

To work around this problem, Cold Fusion enables developers to embed basic form validation instructions within a HTML form. These instructions are embedded as hidden form fields. They get sent to the users browser along with the rest of the form fields, but they are not displayed to the user. Nonetheless, when the user submits the form back to the web server, those hidden fields are submitted too. Cold Fusion can then use them to perform automatic field validation.

To add a validation rule, you add a hidden field to the form. The field name must be the name of the field to validate, followed by the validation rule, for example, _required to flag a field as required. The field's VALUE attribute can be used to specify the error message to be displayed if the validation fails. This next line of code tells Cold Fusion that the login_id field is required, and that the error message ID is required! should be displayed if it is not present.

```
<INPUT TYPE="hidden" NAME="login_id_required" VALUE="ID is required!">
```

Cold Fusion supports seven basic validation rules, as listed in Table 14.2. It is important to remember that even though the validation rules are being sent to the browser as hidden form fields, the actual validation still occurs on the server after the form has been submitted.

Table 14.2   HTML Validation Rule Suffixes

Suffix	Description
_date	Date in most common date formats like MM/DD/YY and MM/DD/YYYY (year is optional, and will default to the current year if omitted)
_eurodate	Same as _date, but with day before year (European format)

continues

Table 14.2 Continued

Suffix	Description
_float	Numeric data, decimal point allowed
_integer	Numeric data, decimal point not allowed
_range	Range of values, the minimum and maximum values (or just one of them) must be specified in the VALUE attribute as MIN= and MAX=, for example, "MIN=5 MAX=10"
_required	Field is required and may not be left blank
_time	Time in most common time formats

N O T E There is no limit to the number of validation rules that you can embed in a form. The only restriction is that every validation rule must be embedded as a separate hidden field. So to flag a field as required and numeric, you'd need two embedded rules, as shown in Listing 14.3. ■

To demonstrate using these validation rules, update the login prompt screen you looked at earlier. Listing 14.3 shows the updated form, to which you've added three lines of code.

Listing 14.3 PROMPT2.CFM—Code for Login Prompt Screen with Embedded Field Validation Rules

```
<FORM ACTION="login1.cfm" METHOD="POST">

<CENTER>
<TABLE BORDER>
 <TR>
  <TH ALIGN="RIGHT">
   ID:
  </TH>
  <TD>
   <INPUT TYPE="text" NAME="login_id" SIZE="5" MAXLENGTH="5">
   <INPUT TYPE="hidden" NAME="login_id_required" VALUE="ID is required!">
   <INPUT TYPE="hidden" NAME="login_id_integer"
➡VALUE="Invalid ID specified!">
  </TD>
 </TR>
 <TR>
  <TH ALIGN="RIGHT">
   Password:
  </TH>
  <TD>
   <INPUT TYPE="password" NAME="login_password" SIZE="20" MAXLENGTH="20">
   <INPUT TYPE="hidden" NAME="login_password_required" VALUE="Password is
➡required!">
  </TD>
 </TR>
 <TR>
```

```
  <TH COLSPAN="2">
   <INPUT TYPE="submit" VALUE="Login">
  </TH>
 </TR>
</TABLE>
</CENTER>

</FORM>
```

The first rule you added specified that the "login_id" field is a required field. The second rule further specifies that only numeric data may be entered into the "login_id" field. And finally, the third rule flags the "login_password" field as required too.

So, what happens if the validation rules fail? The screen shown in Figure 14.3 is what gets displayed if non-numeric data was entered into the login field and the password field was left blank.

▶ **See** Chapter 23, "Web Application Framework," **p. 545.**

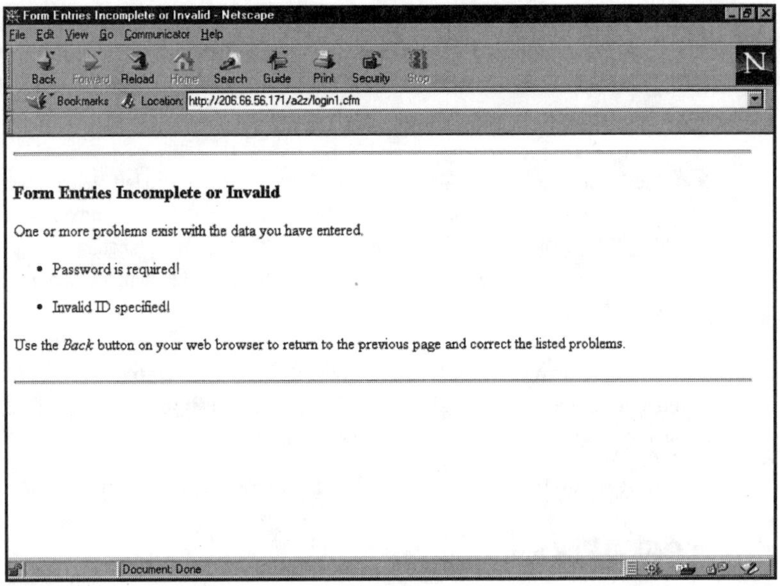

FIG. 14.3

When using embedded form field validation, Cold Fusion automatically displays an error message listing what checks failed.

Form Entries Incomplete or Invalid

One or more problems exist with the data you have entered.

- Password is required!

- Invalid ID specified!

Use the *Back* button on your web browser to return to the previous page and correct the listed problems.

As you can see, the Cold Fusion validation rules are both simple and effective. And best of all, because the validation rules are embedded into the form itself, it is less likely that your forms and their rules will get out of synch.

Part

III

Ch

14

TIP Validation rules can be embedded anywhere in your form, either before or after the field being validated. To make maintaining your code easier, you should establish guidelines governing rule placement. Two popular standards are grouping all the rules together at the very top of the form, or listing validation rules right after the field that they validate.

Using Client-Side Validation

The biggest drawback in using server-side validation is that the validation occurs after form submission. This means that if any validation rules fail, the user will have to go back to the form, make the corrections, and resubmit it again to the server. To make matters worse, many browsers lose the data in the form fields when the back button is pressed, forcing the user to reenter all the data.

Obviously this is not a user-friendly interface. Too many good web sites have lost visitors because their forms were too aggravating to work with.

Fortunately there is an alternative, client-side validation.

Understanding Client-Side Validation

To perform client-side validation, you add a series of browser instructions to your web page. The browser interprets these instructions, and executes them right on the client (the users computer) before the form ever gets submitted to the server.

These instructions are written in scripting languages, like JavaScript (supported by both Netscape Navigator and Microsoft Internet Explorer) or VBScript (based on Visual Basic, and supported by Microsoft Internet Explorer alone). These are interpreted languages that allow you to control browser behavior.

N O T E   Don't confuse JavaScript with Java. Java is a truly compiled object-oriented application development language, one that can be used to write entire programs. JavaScript (including JScript which is a variant of JavaScript) is an interpreted language design to control web browsers. Unlike Java, JavaScript cannot access anything on your computer other than your web browser. ▪

To validate a form you would write a script that would trap the form submission, and only allow it to proceed if a series of validation checks passed. If any checks failed, you would display an error message and prevent the form from being submitted.

Of course, to do this, you'd have to learn JavaScript or VBScript.

Using <CFFORM>

To simplify the process of embedding client side validation scripting code into your forms, Cold Fusion 3 introduced a new tag called <CFFORM>. <CFFORM> is an extremely powerful tag that actually has several distinct functions. The function that you are most interested in here is its support for client-side JavaScript.

▶ **See** Chapter 19, "Enhancing Forms with *CFFORM*," **p. 427**.

So, what can <CFFORM> do for you here? Simply put, <CFFORM> can *automatically* generate JavaScript code to handle most forms of data validation. And the best part of it is that you don't even have to know or learn JavaScript.

To see <CFFORM> in action, once again modify your login screen.

The code in Listing 14.4 is essentially the same code as your original form (Listing 14.1 above). The only thing you've changed is replacing <FORM> with <CFFORM> and </FORM> with </CFFORM>.

On the CD

Listing 14.4   PROMPT3.CFM—Code for *<CFFORM>*-Driven Login Form

```
<CFFORM ACTION="login1.cfm">

<CENTER>
<TABLE BORDER>
 <TR>
  <TH ALIGN="RIGHT">
   ID:
  </TH>
  <TD>
   <INPUT TYPE="text" NAME="login_id" SIZE="5" MAXLENGTH="5">
  </TD>
 </TR>
 <TR>
  <TH ALIGN="RIGHT">
   Password:
  </TH>
  <TD>
   <INPUT TYPE="password" NAME="login_password" SIZE="20" MAXLENGTH="20">
  </TD>
 </TR>
 <TR>
  <TH COLSPAN="2">
   <INPUT TYPE="submit" VALUE="Login">
  </TH>
 </TR>
</TABLE>
</CENTER>

</CFFORM>
```

So what happens when Cold Fusion processes this form? The best way to understand it is to look at the code that this template generated. You can do this by selecting the View Source option in your browser. The code you see should like something like this.

```
<script LANGUAGE=JAVASCRIPT>
<!--
function  _CF_checkCFForm_1(_CF_this)
    {
    return true;
    }
//-->
</script>
<FORM NAME="CFForm_1" ACTION="login1.cfm" METHOD=POST onSubmit=
➥"return _CF_checkCFForm_1(this)">

<CENTER>
<TABLE BORDER>
```

Part

III

Ch

14

```
  <TR>
   <TH ALIGN="RIGHT">
    ID:
   </TH>
   <TD>
    <INPUT TYPE="text" NAME="login_id" SIZE="5" MAXLENGTH="5">
   </TD>
  </TR>
  <TR>
   <TH ALIGN="RIGHT">
    Password:
   </TH>
   <TD>
    <INPUT TYPE="password" NAME="login_password" SIZE="20" MAXLENGTH="20">
   </TD>
  </TR>
  <TR>
   <TH COLSPAN="2">
    <INPUT TYPE="submit" VALUE="Login">
   </TH>
  </TR>
 </TABLE>
 </CENTER>

 </FORM>
```

The first thing you'll notice is that a JavaScript function has been added to the top of the page. The function currently always returns `true`, because no validation rules have been set up yet. As you add validation rules to <CFFORM>, this function will automatically be expanded.

The <CFFORM> and </CFFORM> tags in your code (Listing 14.2) have been replaced with standard HTML <FORM> and </FORM> tags.

The <FORM> tag itself now has a NAME attribute with a unique value that was assigned by Cold Fusion. You could provide a name yourself, in which case Cold Fusion would use your own name instead of generating one for you. If you do specify your own name, make sure that each form on your page is uniquely named.

And finally, an onSubmit attribute was added. This is the JavaScript instruction to your browser that tells it to execute the JavaScript function specified prior to submitting the form to the server. If the specified function returns `true`, the form submission will continue. If the function returns `false`, the submission will be canceled.

Using <CFINPUT>

<CFFORM> creates the foundation on which to build JavaScript validation. To specify the validation rules themselves, you have to use the <CFINPUT> tag. <CFINPUT> does the same thing as the standard HTML <INPUT> tag, and takes the same attributes as parameters. But it also takes additional optional attributes that you can use to specify validation rules.

Look at this code sample:

```
<CFINPUT TYPE="text" NAME="login_id" SIZE="5" MAXLENGTH="5" REQUIRED="Yes">
```

It looks just like a standard <INPUT> tag. The only differences are <CFINPUT> instead of <INPUT>, and the extra REQUIRED attribute which has a value of Yes.

And yet this code does so much more than <INPUT>. This <CFINPUT> tag instructs Cold Fusion to generate the JavaScript code required to flag this field as required.

So, update your login screen once again.

Listing 14.5 is yet another updated version of your login screen. This time you've replaced the "login_id" fields <INPUT> tag with a <CFINPUT> tag.

Listing 14.5   PROMPT4.CFM—Code for Login Prompt Screen with <CFINPUT> Used to Flag Required Field

```
<CFFORM ACTION="login1.cfm">

<CENTER>
<TABLE BORDER>
 <TR>
  <TH ALIGN="RIGHT">
   ID:
  </TH>
  <TD>
   <CFINPUT TYPE="text" NAME="login_id" SIZE="5"
➥MAXLENGTH="5" REQUIRED="Yes">
  </TD>
 </TR>
 <TR>
  <TH ALIGN="RIGHT">
   Password:
  </TH>
  <TD>
   <INPUT TYPE="password" NAME="login_password" SIZE="20" MAXLENGTH="20">
  </TD>
 </TR>
 <TR>
  <TH COLSPAN="2">
   <INPUT TYPE="submit" VALUE="Login">
  </TH>
 </TR>
</TABLE>
</CENTER>

</CFFORM>
```

When Cold Fusion processes this new form, it generates no less than 50 lines of JavaScript code (as shown below), and all automatically.

```
<script LANGUAGE=JAVASCRIPT>
<!--
function _CF_onError(form_object, input_object, object_value,
➥error_message)
   {
```

```
                alert(error_message);
                return false;
        }
    function _CF_hasValue(obj, obj_type)
        {
        if (obj_type == "TEXT" || obj_type == "PASSWORD")
            {
            if (obj.value.length == 0)
                    return false;
            else
                    return true;
            }
        else if (obj_type == "SELECT")
            {
            for (i=0; i < obj.length; i++)
                    {
                    if (obj.options[i].selected)
                            return true;
                    }
            return false;
            }
        else if (obj_type == "RADIO" || obj_type == "CHECKBOX")
            {

            for (i=0; i < obj.length; i++)
                    {
                    if (obj[i].checked)
                            return true;
                    }
            return false;
            }
        }
    function _CF_checkCFForm_1(_CF_this)
        {
        if (!_CF_hasValue(_CF_this.login_id, "TEXT" ))
            {
            if (!_CF_onError(_CF_this, _CF_this.login_id, _CF_this.login
➥_id.value, "Error in login_id text."))
                {
                return false;
                }
            }
        return true;
        }
//-->
</script>

<FORM NAME="CFForm_1" ACTION="login1.cfm" METHOD=POST onSubmit=
➥"return _CF_checkCFForm_1(this)">

<CENTER>
<TABLE BORDER>
 <TR>
  <TH ALIGN="RIGHT">
    ID:
```

```
    </TH>
    <TD>
     <INPUT TYPE="TEXT" NAME="login_id" SIZE=5 MAXLENGTH=5>
    </TD>
   </TR>
   <TR>
    <TH ALIGN="RIGHT">
     Password:
    </TH>
    <TD>
     <INPUT TYPE="password" NAME="login_password" SIZE="20" MAXLENGTH="20">
    </TD>
   </TR>
   <TR>
    <TH COLSPAN="2">
     <INPUT TYPE="submit" VALUE="Login">
    </TH>
   </TR>
  </TABLE>
 </CENTER>

</FORM>
```

As you can see, the <CFINPUT> tag has been replaced by a standard HTML <INPUT> tag. In fact, the generated tag looks exactly the same as the <INPUT> tag looked before you added the <CFINPUT> attributes. Those attributes were used by Cold Fusion to generate the JavaScript code which ensures that a blank "login_id" field cannot be submitted. If the user tries to submit the form, the JavaScript will pop up an error message box as shown in Figure 14.4.

FIG. 14.4
Unless otherwise specified, a default error message is used when JavaScript validation rules fail.

N O T E The pop-up error box is a standard browser dialog box that varies from browser to browser, and there is no way to change what it looks like. The only thing you can change is the actual error message itself. ■

Using *<CFINPUT>* Validation Options

So far you have used <CFINPUT> to flag fields as required. And if you were impressed with that, wait—there's more. <CFINPUT> also lets you specify data type validation rules, as well as customized error messages.

To provide these capabilities, <CFINPUT> supports all the attributes supported by HTML <INPUT>, as well as some additional ones. These are listed in Table 14.3.

Part
III

Ch
14

Table 14.3   *<CFINPUT>* Attributes

Attribute	Description
MESSAGE	Error message text to pop up if this field's validation fails.
ONERROR	The name of a JavaScript function to execute if a validation rule fails, overriding the default error function.
ONVALIDATE	To override the default JavaScript validation code, and to use your own JavaScript, specify the JavaScript function name here.
RANGE	Range of valid values (for numeric data only) specified as "minimum,maximum".
REQUIRED	Set to "Yes" to flag field as required, default is "No".
VALIDATE	One of the nine supported data validation types, as listed in Table 14.4.

The <CFINPUT> VALIDATE attribute takes a data type as a value. The supported data types are listed in Table 14.4.

Table 14.4   *<CFINPUT>* Data Validation Types

Type	Description
Creditcard	Blanks and dashes are stripped and the number is verified using the mod10 algorithm
date	Verifies US date entry in the form mm/dd/yyyy
eurodate	Verifies valid European date entry in the form dd/mm/yyyy
float	Verifies a floating point entry
integer	Verifies an integer entry
social_security_number	Social Security Number in the form ###-##-#### (the hyphen separator can be replaced with a blank)
telephone	Verifies a telephone entry, telephone data must be entered as ###-###-#### (the hyphen separator can be replaced with a blank), the area code and exchange must begin with a digit between 1 and 9
time	Verifies a time entry in the form hh:mm:ss
zipcode	(U.S. formats only) Number can be a 5-digit or 9-digit zip in the form #####-#### (the hyphen separator can be replaced with a blank)

Now that you've seen what <CFINPUT> can do, update your login screen one final time. The code shown in Listing 14.6 uses <CFINPUT> tags for both input fields, and flags both of them as required fields. In addition, the "login_id" has a validation type of "integer" which will prevent the user from entering non-numeric data. And finally, both fields have custom error messages specified using the MESSAGE attribute. If validation fails, then the specified error message will be displayed as shown in Figure 14.5.

Listing 14.6   PROMPT5.CFM—The Completed Prompt Form, with JavaScript Validation

```
<CFFORM ACTION="login1.cfm">

<CENTER>
<TABLE BORDER>
 <TR>
  <TH ALIGN="RIGHT">
   ID:
  </TH>
  <TD>
   <CFINPUT TYPE="text" NAME="login_id" SIZE="5" MAXLENGTH="5"
➥REQUIRED="Yes" VALIDATE="integer" MESSAGE="Numeric ID is required!">
  </TD>
 </TR>
 <TR>
  <TH ALIGN="RIGHT">
   Password:
  </TH>
  <TD>
   <CFINPUT TYPE="password" NAME="login_password" SIZE="20" MAXLENGTH="20"
➥ REQUIRED="Yes" MESSAGE="Password is required!">
  </TD>
 </TR>
 <TR>
  <TH COLSPAN="2">
   <INPUT TYPE="submit" VALUE="Login">
  </TH>
 </TR>
</TABLE>
</CENTER>

</CFFORM>
```

FIG. 14.5
The <CFINPUT> MESSAGE attribute can be used to customize the displayed error message.

Putting It All Together

Before you run off and plug in <CFFORM> and <CFINPUT> into all your templates, there are some other details that you should know.

- Not all browsers support JavaScript, and those that don't will ignore it, allowing your forms to be submitted without being validated.

- It is a good idea to combine the use of JavaScript validation with server-side validation using embedded fields. These will never fail validation if the browser does support JavaScript, and if the browser does not, at least you have some form of validation.

- Older browsers (including some versions of Netscape 3) might have trouble with some of the generated JavaScript, so make sure you test your forms in as many different browsers as possible.

- The JavaScript code can be quite lengthy, and this will increase the size of your web page and thus the time it takes to download it from your web server. ●

CHAPTER 15

The Report Writer

by Ben Forta

In this chapter

Introducing Crystal Reports Professional

Crystal Reports Professional has long been recognized as one of the most powerful and easy-to-use report writers available. This is why so many software vendors, including Allaire, have chosen it as the report writer to be bundled with their applications.

Crystal Reports Professional is popular because:

- It is easy to use and even provides Experts (essentially Wizards with a different name) that step you through the process of creating reports.
- It supports all major databases, including SQL Server, Oracle, and all ODBC drivers.
- It can create reports based on web-server logs and NT system logs.
- It enables you to create reports, charts, graphs, mailing labels, forms, cross-tab reports, and more.
- It provides you with flexible formatting and display options.
- It displays previews of how your report will look using live data.
- It can convert reports into HTML on-the-fly.

It is the last feature in this list that makes Crystal Reports Professional so appealing to Cold Fusion developers.

▶ **See** Chapter 4, "Administering Cold Fusion," **p. 55**

N O T E   Crystal Reports does not have to be installed on the computer running your web server and Cold Fusion. All the files that Cold Fusion uses to interact with Crystal Reports' RPT files are installed during the Cold Fusion installation. ■

A Note from the Author

Crystal Reports Professional version 5 is an extremely powerful and capable report writer. Complete coverage of all of its features is beyond the scope of this book.

This chapter will not teach you everything there is to know about Crystal Reports Professional. Instead, it'll teach you how to create a basic report with the report writer and how to execute that report from within your Cold Fusion templates.

Crystal Reports Professional comes with complete online help and step-by-step tutorials. If you are planning on using the report writer, I strongly urge you to use these tools.

Crystal Reports Professional only reads your data files; it does not write to them. Therefore, there is nothing that you can do within the report writer that will corrupt or damage any data, so don't be afraid to experiment.

Creating Reports with Crystal Reports Professional

To learn how to use the report writer, you'll start by creating a simple report—an employee directory.

You can use Crystal Reports on any computer, not just on the web server machine, but make sure that the ODBC data source you'll use is set up exactly the same way it is on the web server machine. This way, you can be sure that reports created on one computer will work on another.

For starters, load the Crystal Reports program. Click its icon to display the welcome screen shown in Figure 15.1. You'll be presented with two options: to create a new report or to open an existing report. Select the New Report option to display the Report Gallery shown in Figure 15.2. The Report Gallery displays eight popular report types from which you may select but also allows you to create your own type.

FIG. 15.1

The Crystal Reports Professional welcome screen prompts you to either create a new report or open an existing one.

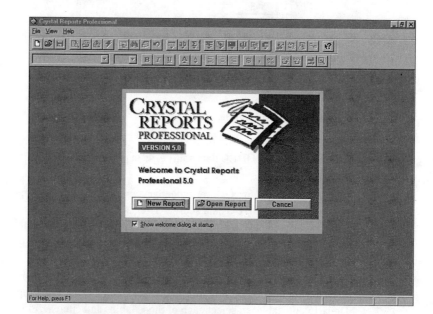

FIG. 15.2

The Report Gallery allows you to pick a report type or create a custom type of your own.

You're going to create a standard report, so select the Standard button to display the Create Report Expert.

The experts are interactive tools that walk you through much of the report design process. Crystal Reports' experts are made up of multiple screens in a tab dialog box, as shown in Figure 15.3. You may jump to any screen by clicking the tab at the top. Alternatively, you may use the << Back and Next >> buttons to walk through the screens while building your report.

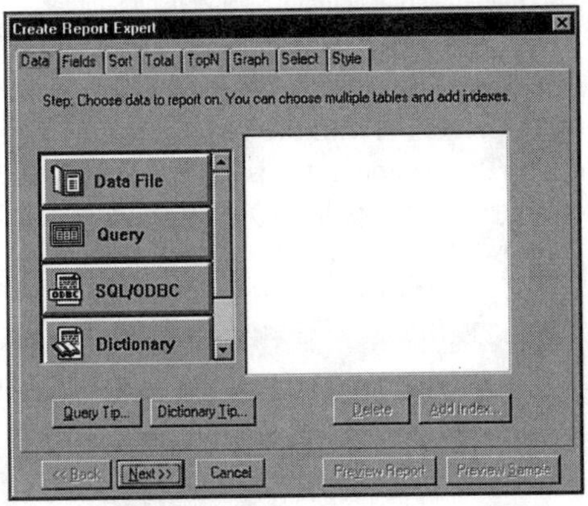

FIG. 15.3

The Create Report Expert walks you through the process of creating a report.

To build your report, follow these steps:

1. The first thing you need to do is specify the tables to be used in this report. You'll be using data from an ODBC data source, so select the SQL/ODBC option from the list of data types.

2. You'll be prompted for a server type. Servers are what Crystal Reports calls any data source, including ODBC data source. The list of servers includes both ODBC data sources (they all have the prefix ODBC) and other sources available to you. You'll be using the A2Z ODBC data source, so select ODBC-A2Z from the list, and then choose OK.

3. Now that you have specified a data source, Crystal Reports can prompt you for the tables to include in the report. For your first report, you'll select the Employees table and the Departments table, so select each of those tables and choose Add. After you have selected both files, choose Done.

4. Because you selected more than one table for your report, the Expert now wants to know how these tables are related. To set relationships between tables, you must locate the related columns in each table and then drag one to the other to link them. The columns that link your two tables are the DepartmentID column in the Employees table and the ID column in the Departments table. Scroll down the list of columns in the Employees table until you find the DepartmentID column and click it. Drag it to the ID column in the Departments table. The Expert draws a white line showing the link between the two tables, as shown in Figure 15.4. (You may choose Arrange to arrange

the tables to clearly see the links.) When you have finished creating the link, choose Next >>.

5. Now the Expert needs to know which fields to include in the report. The left list is the Database Fields list that contains all the available fields sorted by table and fields within a table. The right list is the Report Fields list, which contains any selected fields. To include fields in a report, select them from the left list, and click the Add -> button. Select these fields in this order: `Employees.LastName`, `Employees.FirstName`, `Departments.Department`, `Employees.PhoneExtension`.

6. When displaying your data in the final report, Crystal Reports uses the field name as the column heading, unless you specify alternative text. To specify column heading text, select a field from the Report Fields list and enter the desired text into the Column Heading field. Set the `Employees.LastName` field to `Last Name`, `Employees`, `FirstName` to `First Name`, leave the `Departments.Department` field as is, and set the `Employees.PhoneExtension` field to `Extension`. When you have completed this step, choose Next >>.

7. Now you can specify a sort order. You want the list sorted by last name plus first name. Select `Employees.LastName` from the Report Fields list, and click the Add >> button to select that field. Now do the same for the `Employees.LastName` field. The selected fields are shown in the Group Fields list.

8. Your basic report does not require any of the options in the other Expert screens, so click Preview Report to see what the finished report will look like. As shown in Figure 15.5, the report writer displays a preview of the finished report using live data retrieved from the specified tables.

9. Above the display area in Figure 15.6 are two tabs entitled Design and Preview. The Preview tab, the tab currently selected, allows you to preview the finished report at any time. The Design tab is where you can modify the report layout. Choose the Design tab to show the report Design screen. The Design screen is divided into groups (also called bands). The top group, the Page Header, contains information that will appear at the top of every page in the report. The bottom group, the Page Footer, contains information that will appear at the bottom of each page. The middle group is the Details group that contains the fields that will appear in the body of the report. The Details group is repeated once for every row selected in the final report.

10. To format or change any field or text, you need to right-click it with your mouse. This action displays a context-sensitive menu containing options applicable to the selected field. You'll change the format of the column headers, so select all four column headers at once by clicking your mouse above the first column and then dragging the box outline over all four fields. When you release the mouse button, all four fields will be selected. Now right-click your mouse on any of the selected fields and select the Format Objects_ option. Select the Font page, and set the Font to Arial, the Size to 12, and turn off Underline. Then choose OK. The Design view immediately reflects the changes you just made. (You may also switch to the Preview view at any time to see how the change will effect the final report.)

11. The Page Footer group contains a page number field. This is a useful field for printed reports, but is useless for reports that will display as web pages. When a report is output as a web page, it is formatted as a single page, so you should remove that field. To remove it, click the field to select it and press the Delete key.

12. The last thing you need to do is save and name the report. Crystal Reports saves its reports in RPT files and each RPT file contains a single report. Select the Save option from the File menu and save the report as **EMPLIST.RPT** in the C:\A2Z\SCRIPTS directory.

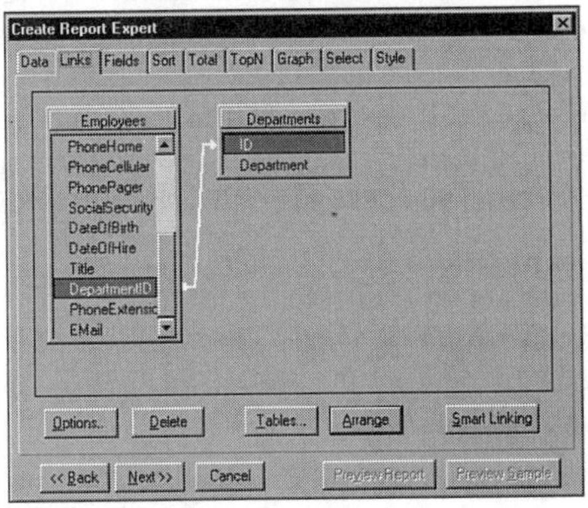

FIG. 15.4
The Expert graphically displays any links established between different tables.

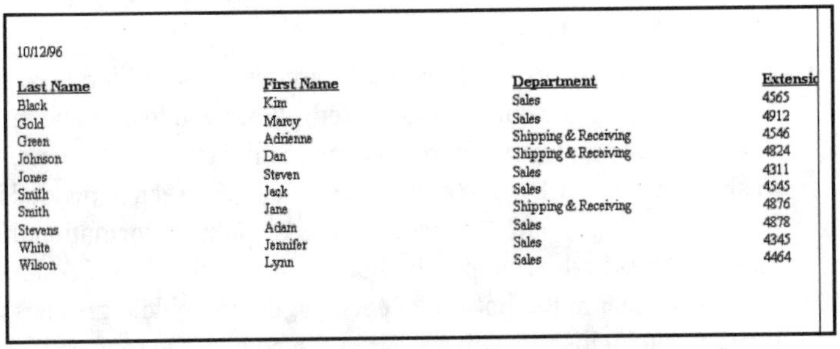
10/12/96

Last Name	First Name	Department	Extensi
Black	Kim	Sales	4565
Gold	Marcy	Sales	4912
Green	Adrienne	Shipping & Receiving	4546
Johnson	Dan	Shipping & Receiving	4824
Jones	Steven	Sales	4311
Smith	Jack	Sales	4545
Smith	Jane	Shipping & Receiving	4876
Stevens	Adam	Sales	4878
White	Jennifer	Sales	4345
Wilson	Lynn	Sales	4464

FIG. 15.5
Crystal Reports Professional previews reports using live data that enables you to see exactly how a finished report will look.

You just created a complete report using the Crystal Reports report writer. You may print this report at any time by selecting Print from the File menu.

NOTE Many of the report writer's formatting features cannot be supported by HTML, so some advanced formatting will be lost when the report output displays in a web page. For example, Crystal Reports allows you to specify single, double, or mixed borders around text, all of which are rendered into HTML as standard TABLE borders. Before rolling out your reports for public use, make sure you test them thoroughly to ensure that the output is acceptable. ■

FIG. 15.6
Use the Design screen to make any changes to a report.

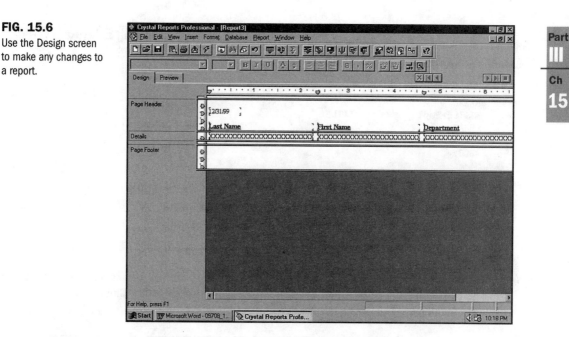

Embedding Reports into Cold Fusion Templates

Reports created with Crystal Reports Professional can easily be printed. Your interest is in its HTML publishing capabilities because Crystal Reports is most often used for printing.

Reports are embedded into Cold Fusion Templates using the <CFREPORT> tag. When Cold Fusion processes a template and encounters a <CFREPORT> tag, it executes a Crystal Reports engine that processes the report and creates an HTML version of the report output.

N O T E Cold Fusion returns an error message if you try to process a report that is already open in Crystal Reports. You must close any reports in the report writer before using them with Cold Fusion. ■

Now create a template to process the report you just created. Listing 15.1 contains the code to process report EMPLIST.RPT. As you can see, the code listing is standard HTML, except for the <CFREPORT> tag. <CFREPORT> requires a single attribute, REPORT, which contains the name (and fully qualified path) of the report to execute. Create a template containing the code in Listing 15.1 and save it as **EMPLIST.CFM** in the C:\A2Z\SCRIPTS directory.

On the CD

Listing 15.1 EMPLIST.CFM—Employee List Displayed Using a Crystal Reports Professional Report

```
<HTML>

<HEAD>
<TITLE>Employee List</TITLE>
<HEAD>

<BODY>

<CFREPORT REPORT=" emplist.rpt" >
</CFREPORT>

</BODY>

</HTML>
```

Now test the report. Load your web browser and go to URL **http://*yourservername*/a2z/ emplist.cfm**. After a few seconds of processing, your browser display should look like the one shown in Figure 15.7.

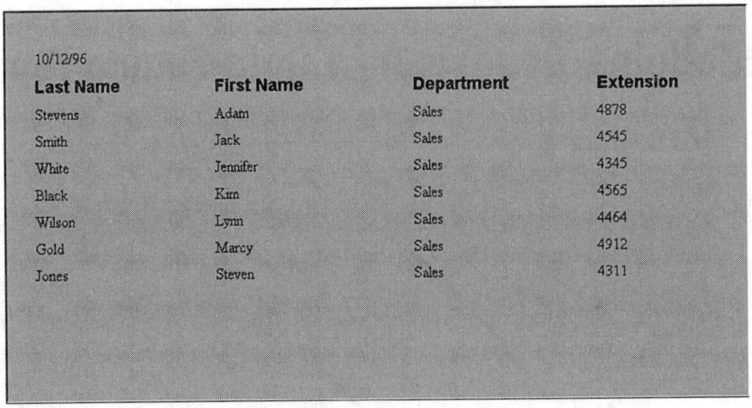

FIG. 15.7
Cold Fusion executes a Crystal Reports Professional engine to process embedded reports.

10/12/96			
Last Name	**First Name**	**Department**	**Extension**
Stevens	Adam	Sales	4878
Smith	Jack	Sales	4545
White	Jennifer	Sales	4345
Black	Kim	Sales	4565
Wilson	Lynn	Sales	4464
Gold	Marcy	Sales	4912
Jones	Steven	Sales	4311

Customizing Reports On-the-Fly

Crystal Reports Professional enables you to interactively create powerful reports that you can easily embed into Cold Fusion.

Cold Fusion also allows you to pass parameters to the Crystal Reports processing engine, enabling you to customize the reports on-the-fly.

For example, the phone list report you created earlier displays all employees in all departments. How could you create a report to display the employees in a single department?

You could create multiple reports and specify a filter condition in each one. One report would filter only the Sales department employees, another would filter just the Shipping & Receiving department employees, and so on.

It can be done, but it is definitely not a scaleable or manageable solution. A better alternative would be to use the same report and modify it on-the-fly by passing additional information to it.

The code in Listing 15.2 shows how this is done. The `<CFREPORT>` tag is the same, but you'll add a line between the `<CFREPORT>` and `</CFREPORT>` tags. The code `{Departments.Department} = "Sales"` is passed to the Crystal Reports engine as a selection filter. In this case, only employees who have a `Departments.Department` value of " Sales" will be included in the report.

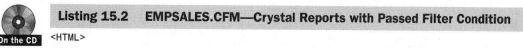

Listing 15.2   EMPSALES.CFM—Crystal Reports with Passed Filter Condition

```
<HTML>

<HEAD>
<TITLE>Employee List</TITLE>
<HEAD>

<BODY>

<CFREPORT REPORT=" emplist.rpt" >
{Departments.Department} = " Sales"
</CFREPORT>

</BODY>

 </HTML>
```

N O T E   Field names passed to Crystal Reports must be fully qualified with the table name and must be enclosed within curly braces. ■

The selection criteria may even be made up of Cold Fusion tags, functions, and fields. For example, instead of hard coding the filter to a department called Sales, you could have compared it to a passed field name. In fact, the entire filter condition could be contained with a `<CFIF>` conditional statement so that the same template could display as many different employee lists as needed.

▶ **See** "*<CFREPORT>*," **p. 897**

CHAPTER 16

Debugging and Troubleshooting

by Ben Forta

In this chapter

Debugging Cold Fusion Applications

As with any development tool, sooner or later you're going to find yourself debugging or troubleshooting a Cold Fusion problem. For a Cold Fusion application to function correctly, many different applications and interfaces have to work seamlessly. The key to quickly isolating and correcting problems is a thorough understanding of Cold Fusion, ODBC data sources, SQL syntax, the CGI interface, URL syntax, and your web server.

If the prospect of debugging an application sounds overly bleak, don't panic. Thankfully, Cold Fusion has powerful built-in debugging and error reporting features. These capabilities, coupled with logical and systematic evaluation of trouble spots, enable you to diagnose and correct all sorts of problems.

This chapter teaches you how to use the Cold Fusion debugging tools, and introduces techniques that will help you quickly locate the source of a problem. But more importantly, because an ounce of prevention is worth a pound of cure, guidelines and techniques will be introduced that will help prevent common errors from occurring in the first place.

Understanding What Can Go Wrong

As an application developer, sooner or later you are going to have to diagnose, or `"debug"`, a Cold Fusion application problem. Because Cold Fusion relies on so many other software components to work its magic, there are a lot of different places where things can go wrong.

As you are reading this chapter, the following assumptions are made:

- You are familiar with basic Cold Fusion concepts.
- You understand how Cold Fusion uses ODBC for all database interaction.
- You are familiar with basic SQL syntax and use.

If you are not familiar with any of these topics, it is strongly recommend that you read the chapters on them before proceeding.

▶ **See** Chapter 2, "Introduction to Cold Fusion," **p. 15**
▶ **See** Chapter 6, "Database Fundamentals," **p. 87**
▶ **See** Chapter 8, "Introduction to SQL," **p. 129**

Almost all Cold Fusion problems fall into one of the following categories:

- Web server configuration problems
- ODBC driver errors
- SQL statement syntax or logic errors
- Cold Fusion syntax errors
- URL and path problems

You'll now look at each of these potential problem areas to learn what can go wrong in each.

Debugging Web Server Configuration Problems

During routine, day-to-day operation of your web server, you should almost never encounter Cold Fusion problems that are caused by web server configuration problems. These kinds of problems almost always occur during the initial Cold Fusion setup, or while testing Cold Fusion for the first time.

When attempting to execute a Cold Fusion script, you receive an error message "Cold Fusion server application not currently running." This error, shown in Figure 16.1, is generated by both the Cold Fusion server modules and the CGI interface when they cannot communicate with the Cold Fusion Application Server.

Part
III

Ch
16

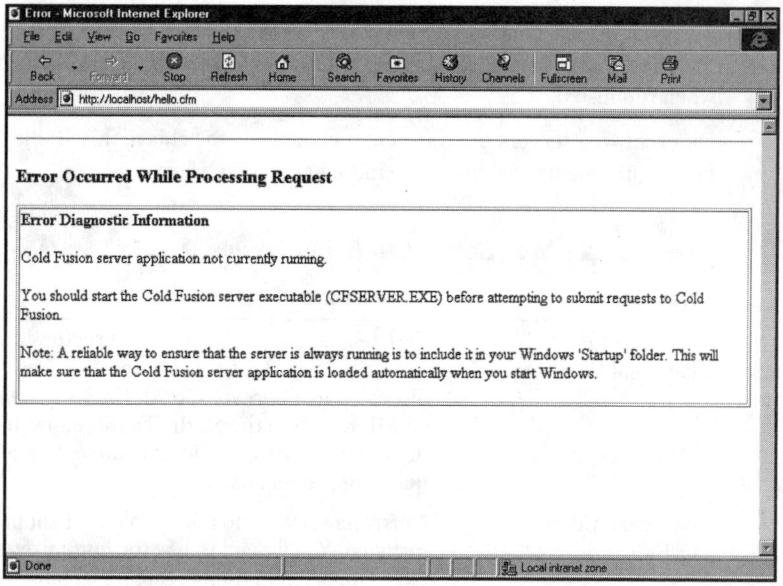

FIG. 16.1

The Cold Fusion Application Server must be running or else all Cold Fusion requests will generate an error message.

The Application Server *must* be running for Cold Fusion to process templates. The steps to verify that the server is running, and to start it if it is not, differ based on your operating system.

If you are running Cold Fusion on a Windows NT machine, you should run the Service applet in the Window NT Control Panel to check whether or not the service is running, and start it if it is not.

If you are running Windows 95, you'll see the Cold Fusion icon on the taskbar (near the clock) when the Application Server is running. If it is not running, select Cold Fusion from the Cold Fusion program groups under your Start button menu.

TIP Windows NT services can be started automatically every time the server is restarted. For a service to start automatically, the service Startup option *must* be set to Automatic. Windows 95 users can automatically start Cold Fusion by ensuring that the Cold Fusion Application Server is in the Programs, Startup group. This setting is turned on by the Cold Fusion installation procedure, and typically should always be left on. However, if the service does not automatically start, check these options.

Every time you try to execute a Cold Fusion script, your browser prompts you to save a file. The most common web server configuration problem in setting up and installing the Cold Fusion CGI is the web server not being able to find the CGI script—the CFML.EXE file. This problem will only effect you if you are using the CGI interface to Cold Fusion. If you are using the web server modules, this is a non-issue.

As explained in Chapter 2, for a web server to execute a CGI script correctly, it has to know that the script is in fact a CGI script that needs to be executed, and not just a file to be served when requested.

Different web servers use different mechanisms to achieve this. Table 16.1 lists the configuration requirements of some of the more popular web servers.

Table 16.1   Web Server CGI Configuration Requirements

Web Server	Configuration
Microsoft IIS and Personal Web Server	The default CGI directory is a directory called SCRIPTS mapped as SCRIPTS in the server properties. You may map another CGI directory to wherever CFML.EXE is installed, or copy CFML.EXE into the SCRIPTS directory. If you do map another directory, make sure the Execute option is enabled in the mapping properties.
Netscape Commerce or Enterprise	Netscape servers do not enable CGI support by default when installed. You'll need to use the administration server to enable CGI support, and then create a mapping to the directory that contains CFML.EXE. You'll then use that mapping in every Cold Fusion URL.
O'Reilly WebSite	The default mapping and directory for CGI scripts is the CGI-SHL directory. Assuming you have not changed this default, just copy the CFML.EXE file into that directory. Of course, you may change the mapped directory, or add another, if you so desire.

If your web server does not know that the CFML.EXE file is a script, it'll try to send you the file every time you make a Cold Fusion request, instead of executing the script and returning the response.

If you are being prompted to save a file, one of the following two things is wrong:

■ You did not set up the script mapping on the web server, and, as a result, the server is trying to serve the script rather than execute it. To fix this make sure the CFML.EXE file is in a CGI or scripts directory (see Table 16.1).

■ Your web server allows you to create multiple maps to the same directory, and you are using the wrong directory mapping.

To verify that the CGI file is being executed and not served, use your browser to go to an URL that specifies the CFML.EXE CGI script, but does *not* specify a Cold Fusion template. If Cold Fusion is installed correctly, and you are using a correct script mapping, you'll receive an error message telling you that no template was specified. If you are prompted to save a file, refer to Table 16.1.

Part

III

Ch

16

N O T E This section only affects users who are using Cold Fusion with its CGI interface. As explained in Chapter 2, this is a practice that should generally be avoided. ■

Debugging ODBC Driver Errors

Cold Fusion relies on ODBC for all it's database interaction. If Cold Fusion cannot communicate with the appropriate ODBC driver, or the driver cannot communicate with the database, then you'll receive ODBC error messages.

ODBC error messages are always generated by an ODBC driver, and *not* by Cold Fusion. Cold Fusion merely displays whatever error message it received from the ODBC driver. However, Cold Fusion often adds its own suggestions to the error screen to help you diagnose the problem, as shown in Figure 16.2.

▶ **See** "Introducing ODBC," **p. 131**

FIG. 16.2

Cold Fusion attempts to display useful information along with ODBC error messages.

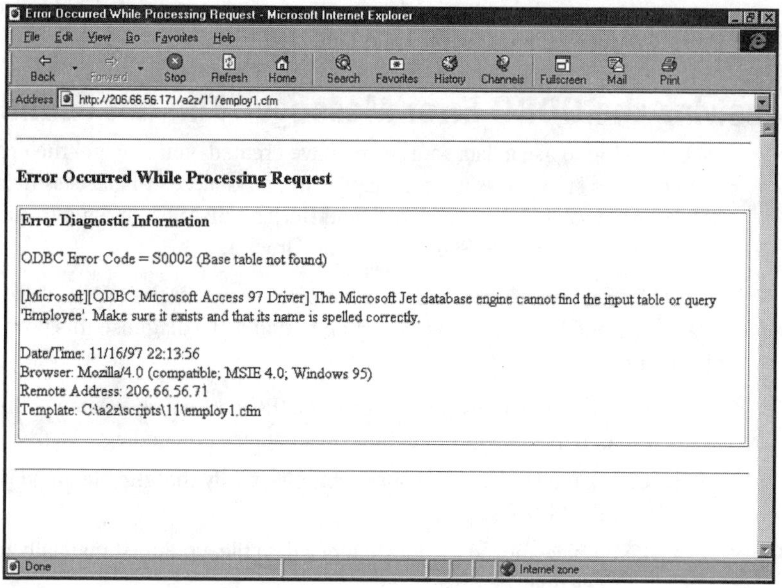

Error Occurred While Processing Request - Microsoft Internet Explorer

File   Edit   View   Go   Favorites   Help

Back   Forward   Stop   Refresh   Home   Search   Favorites   History   Channels   Fullscreen   Mail   Print

Address http://206.66.56.171/a2z/11/employ1.cfm

Error Occurred While Processing Request

Error Diagnostic Information

ODBC Error Code = S0002 (Base table not found)

[Microsoft][ODBC Microsoft Access 97 Driver] The Microsoft Jet database engine cannot find the input table or query 'Employee'. Make sure it exists and that its name is spelled correctly.

Date/Time: 11/16/97 22:13:56
Browser: Mozilla/4.0 (compatible; MSIE 4.0; Windows 95)
Remote Address: 206.66.56.71
Template: C:\a2z\scripts\11\employ1.cfm

Done   Internet zone

ODBC error messages always contain an error number, which, by itself, is usually pretty useless. But following the error number is a text message that describes the problem. The text of these messages varies from driver to driver, and so it would be pointless to list all the possible error messages here. Instead, the more common symptoms are listed, and how to fix the problems that cause them.

> **TIP** You can use the Cold Fusion Administrator to verify that an ODBC data source is correctly set up, and that it is attached to the appropriate data file correctly. To do this run the Cold Fusion Administrator and select the Data Sources tab. Then select the data source from the displayed list, and choose the Verify button. Cold Fusion will attempt to connect to the data source, and will notify you of its success or failure.

Receiving the ODBC Error Message "Data Source not Found"

Cold Fusion communicates with databases via ODBC drivers. These drivers access data sources—external data files. If the ODBC driver reports that the data source could not be found, then check the following:

- Make sure you have created the ODBC data source.
- Verify that the data source name was spelled correctly. ODBC data source names are not case sensitive, so don't worry about that.
- Under Windows NT, ODBC data sources are *user-login specific*. If you create a data source from within the ODBC Control Panel applet while logged in as a user without administrator privileges, then *only* that user will have access to that ODBC data source. To prevent this situation from occurring, always create Cold Fusion's ODBC data sources from within the Cold Fusion Administrator program.

Receiving the ODBC Error Message "File not Found"

When trying to use a data source you have created, you may get the error message "File not found." This error message only applies to data sources that access data files directly (like Microsoft Access, Microsoft Excel, and Borland dBASE), and not to client-server database systems (like Microsoft SQL Server, and Oracle).

The "File not found" error message simply means that the ODBC driver could not locate the data file in the location it was expecting to find it. To diagnose this problem, perform the following steps:

1. Data files must be created before ODBC data sources can use them. If you have not yet created the data file, you must do so before proceeding.
2. Check the ODBC data source settings, verify that the file name is spelled correctly and that the file exists.
3. If you have moved the location of a data file, you must manually update any ODBC data sources that reference it.

Receiving Login or Permission Errors When Trying to Access a Data Store

Some database systems, like Microsoft SQL Server, require that you log in to a database before you may access it. When setting up an ODBC data source to this kind of database, you must specify the login name and password that the driver should use to gain access.

The following steps will help you locate the source of this problem:

1. Verify that the login name and password are spelled correctly, (you will not be able to see the password, only asterisks are displayed in the password field).

2. On some database systems, passwords are case sensitive. Make sure that you have not left the caps-lock key on by mistake.

3. Verify that the name and password you are using does indeed have access to the database to which you are trying to connect. You can do this using a client application that came with your database system. (For example, if you are using Microsoft SQL Server you can use the iSQL/w utility to try and connect to the database with the suspect name and password.)

Receiving the ODBC Error Message "Unknown Table"

After verifying that the data source name and table names are correct, you might still get "unknown table" errors. A very common problem, especially with client/server databases like Microsoft SQL Server, is forgetting to provide a fully qualified table name. There are two ways you can do this:

■ Explicitly provide the fully qualified table name whenever it is passed to a SQL statement. Fully qualified table names are usually made up of three parts, separated by periods. The first is the name of the database containing the table; the second is the owner name (usually specified as dbo); and the third is the actual table name itself.

■ Some ODBC drivers, like the Microsoft SQL Server driver, allow you to specify a default database to be used if none is explicitly provided. If this option is set, then its value will be used whenever a fully qualified name is not provided.

TIP If your ODBC driver allows you to specify a default database name, use that feature. This will allow you to write fewer and simpler hard-coded SQL statements.

Debugging SQL Statement or Logic Errors

Debugging SQL Statements is one of the two types of troubleshooting that you'll spend most of your debugging time doing (the other is debugging Cold Fusion Syntax Errors, which you'll get to next). You will find yourself debugging SQL statements if you run into either of these situations:

- Cold Fusion reports SQL syntax errors. Figure 16.3, for example, is an error caused by misspelling a column name in a SQL statement.
- No syntax errors are reported, but the specified SQL statement did not achieve the expected results.

FIG. 16.3
Cold Fusion displays the SQL error reported by ODBC, and often attempts to provide hints of its own.

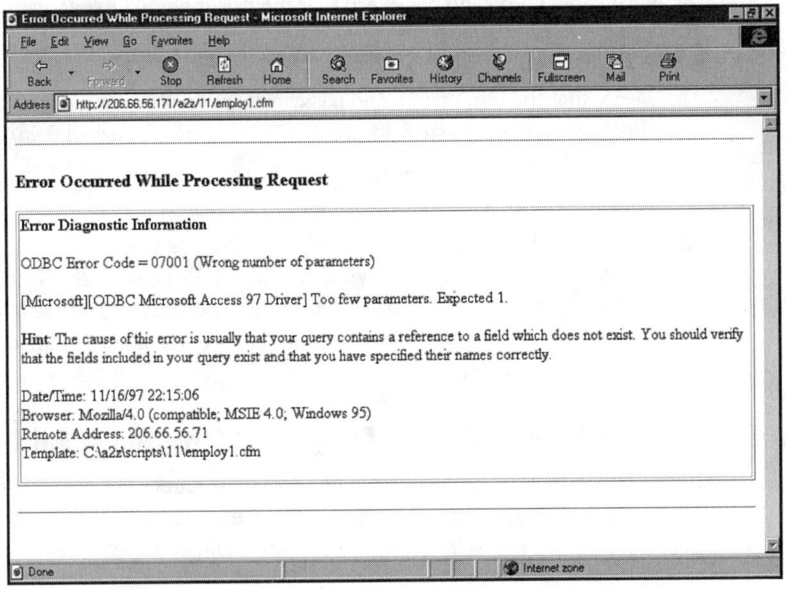

Obviously, a prerequisite to debugging SQL statements is a good working knowledge of the SQL language. So I'm going to assume that you are already familiar with the basic SQL statements—and are comfortable using them.

▶ **See** Chapter 9, "SQL Data Manipulation," **p. 155**

The keys to successfully debugging SQL statements are

1. Isolate the problem. Debugging SQL statements inside of Cold Fusion templates can be tricky, especially when creating dynamic SQL statements. Try executing the same statement from within another ODBC client, like Microsoft Query or Cold Fusion Studio, replacing dynamic parameters with fixed values if appropriate.

2. The big difference between Cold Fusion SQL statements and statements entered into any other ODBC client, is the use of Cold Fusion fields. If you are using Cold Fusion fields within your statement, verify that you are enclosing them within quotation marks when needed. If the value is a string, then it must be enclosed in single quotation marks. If it is a number, then it must not be enclosed in quotation marks.

3. Look at the bigger picture. Dynamic SQL statements are one of Cold Fusion's most powerful features, but this power comes with a price. When you create a dynamic SQL statement, you are effectively relinquishing direct control over the statement itself, and are allowing it to changed based on other conditions. This means that the code for a

single Cold Fusion query can be used to generate an infinite number of queries. Because some of these queries might work, and others might not, debugging dynamic SQL requires that you be able to determine exactly what the dynamically created SQL statement looks like. Thankfully Cold Fusion makes this an easy task, as you will see a little later in the section entitled "Using The Cold Fusion Debugging Options."

4. Break complex SQL statements up into smaller, simpler statements. If you are debugging a query that contains sub-queries, verify that the sub-queries work properly independently of the outer query.

Whenever an SQL syntax error occurs, Cold Fusion displays the SQL statement it submitted. If your SQL statement was constructed dynamically, then the fully constructed statement will be displayed.

If the error occurred during an INSERT or UPDATE operation, then the field names will be displayed as submitted, but the values will be replaced with question marks (except for NULL values which will display as NULL).

▶ **See** "Creating Dynamic SQL Statements," **p. 244**

Debugging Cold Fusion Syntax Errors

The other type of troubleshooting you'll find yourself doing is debugging Cold Fusion syntax errors. Thankfully, and largely as a result of the superb Cold Fusion error reporting and debugging capabilities, these are usually the easiest bugs to find.

Cold Fusion syntax errors are usually one of the following:

- Mismatched pound signs or quotation marks
- Mismatched begin and end tags, for example a <CFIF> without a matching </CFIF>
- A tag with a missing or incorrectly spelled attribute
- Missing quotes around tag attributes
- Using double quotes to delimit strings when building SQL statements instead of single quotes
- Illegal use of tags

If any of these errors occur, Cold Fusion will generate a descriptive error message, as shown in Figure 16.4. The error message lists the problematic code (and a few lines before and after it), and identifies exactly what the problem was.

CAUTION

If your template contains HTML forms, frames, or tables, you might have trouble viewing generated error messages. If an error occurs in the middle of a table, for example, that table will never be terminated, and there is no knowing how the browser will attempt to render the partial table. If the table is not rendered and displayed properly, you'll not see the error message.

FIG. 16.4
Cold Fusion generates descriptive error messages when syntax errors occur.

Error Diagnostic Information

An error has occurred while processing the expression:

    <LI>#LastName#, #FirstName# - Ext. #PhoneExtension

The error occurred on (or near) line 24 of the template file C:\a2z\scripts\11\employ1.cfm.

    19:
    20: <H1>Employees</H1>
    21:
    22: <UL>
    23:
    24: <CFOUTPUT QUERY="Employees">
    25:   <LI>#LastName#, #FirstName# - Ext. #PhoneExtension
    26: </CFOUTPUT>

The expression contains unmatched single quotes, double quotes, or pound signs.

Date/Time: 11/16/97 22:17:20
Browser: Mozilla/4.0 (compatible; MSIE 4.0; Windows 95)
Remote Address: 206.66.56.71

 TIP If you think that an error has occurred but no error message is displayed, you may view the source in the browser. The generated source will contain any error messages that were included in the web page but not displayed.

One of the most common Cold Fusion errors is missing or mismatched tags. Indenting your code, as shown in Listing 16.1, is a good way to ensure that all tags are correctly matched.

Listing 16.1 Nesting Conditional Code Makes Debugging Mismatched Tags Much Easier

```
<CFIF some condition here>
 <CFOUTPUT>
  Output code here
  <CFIF another condition>
   Some other output code here
  </CFIF>
 </CFOUTPUT>
<CFELSE>
 Some action here
</CFIF>
```

TIP You can use the <CFABORT> anywhere in the middle of your template to force Cold Fusion to halt further processing. As you verify that lines of code work, you can move the <CFABORT> tag further down the template.

Cold Fusion Studio users should take advantage of Studio's Tag Insight, Tag Tips, and Tag Completion features to avoid common mismatching problems. Also, the right-click menu's Edit Tag option is useful in helping prevent typos in tags and their attributes.

▶ **See** Chapter 10, "Introduction to Cold Fusion Studio," for more information about Cold Fusion Studio and its tag options.

As Cold Fusion itself processes templates, there is no way to pause processing to inspect variables or logic flow. This type of debugging is commonplace where applications are run on a desktop machine allowing "breakpoints" to be set. A useful workaround to this limitation is writing your own log files while processing a template. Using the <CFFILE> tag you can update a local text file with state information that you can then view with any text editor.

You can use a Custom Tag called CF_Log, which can be found on the accompanying CD-ROM, to simplify the process of writing debugging log files.

Debugging URL and Path Problems

URL and path problems are less of an issue when using server module style URLs than they are with CGI-style URLs. If you are using Cold Fusion's CGI interface, Cold Fusion has to maintain its own mappings and the web server mappings are not used. This is yet another reason why you should always use the server modules if possible.

Referencing Files That Are Not Displayed

Sometimes, when you reference image files—or other files—from within a Cold Fusion template, the files are not displayed. If you are using CGI-style URLs, you may not use relative paths to images or files. Relative paths (paths to files without a full path from the server root) are treated by the browser as being relative to the current page. As the current page is the result of a CGI script, and not an actual file, the relative paths will be incorrect.

As a rule, if you are using CGI-style URLs, any included files (like images) must be somewhere beneath the server root, not in the template directory.

Passing Parameters That Are Not Processed

Parameters that you pass to an URL may not be processed by Cold Fusion, even though you see them present in the URL. URL's are finicky little beasts, and you have to abide by the following rules.

■ URLs may only ever have one question mark character in them. The question mark separates the URL itself from the query.

■ In order to pass multiple parameters in the URL query section, each parameter *must* be separated by an ampersand (the & character).

■ URLs must *not* have spaces in them. If you are generating URLs dynamically based on table column data, you must be sure to trim any spaces from those values. If you must use spaces, replace them with plus signs. Cold Fusion will correctly convert the plus signs back to spaces when used. Use the Cold Fusion URLEncodedFormat() function to convert text to URL-safe text.

Debugging Form Problems

If a form is submitted without data, it can cause an error. There are two ways in which web browsers submit data to web servers. These are called GET and POST, and the submission method to use is specified in the FORM METHOD attribute.

As a rule, forms being submitted to Cold Fusion should always be submitted using the POST method. The default method is GET, and so if you omit (or misspell) the

METHOD = "POST"

Cold Fusion will not be able to process your forms correctly.

When referring to form fields in the action template, you can occasionally get an "Unknown Variable" error message. Radio buttons, checkboxes, and select boxes (list boxes) are not submitted if no option was selected. It is important to remember this when referring to form fields in an action template. If you refer to a checkbox without first checking for its existence, you'll generate an error message if the checkbox was not checked.

The solution is to always check for the existence of any fields or variable before using them. Alternatively, use the <CFPARAM> function to assign default values to fields, thereby ensuring that they always exist.

▶ **See** Chapter 12, "Cold Fusion Forms," **p. 225**

How can you check what form fields were actually submitted, and what their values are? If you have Cold Fusion debugging enabled, any time you submit a form, the form's action page will contain a debugging section describing the submitted form, as shown in Figure 16.5. A field named FORMFIELDS will be present which contains a comma-delimited list of all the submitted fields, as well as a list of the submitted fields and their values.

Using the Cold Fusion Debugging Options

The Cold Fusion debugging options are enabled or disabled via the Cold Fusion Administrator program. To enable debugging you just need to check the debugging options you wish to monitor in the administrators debugging tab, as shown in Figure 16.6. You should also specify the IP addresses you'd like to send debugging information to. At a minimum, the local host IP address (127.0.0.1) should be specified. If no IP address is in the list, debugging information will be sent to anyone who browses any Cold Fusion page.

▶ **See** Chapter 4, "Administering Cold Fusion," **p. 55**

The Cold Fusion debugging options work by appending debugging information to the end of any generated web pages, as shown in Figure 16.7. The exact information that is displayed will vary, based on the options you selected and the contents of your template.

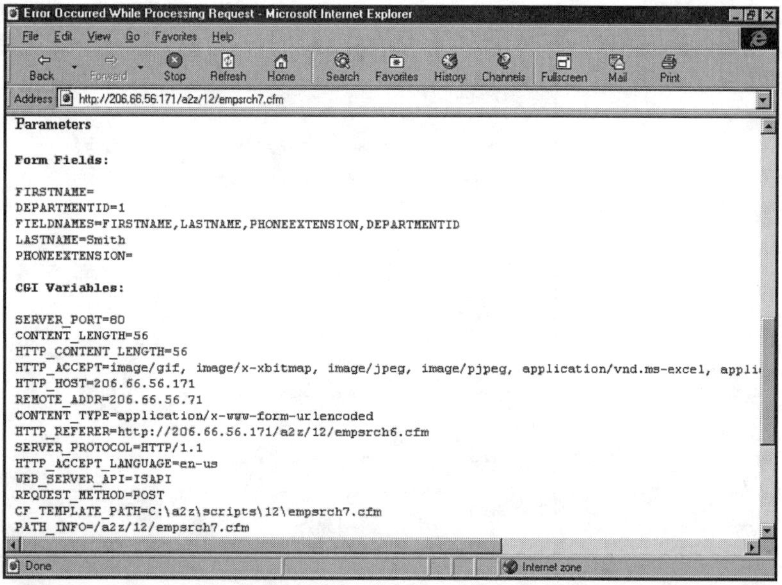

FIG. 16.5

Cold Fusion displays form specific debugging information if debugging is enabled.

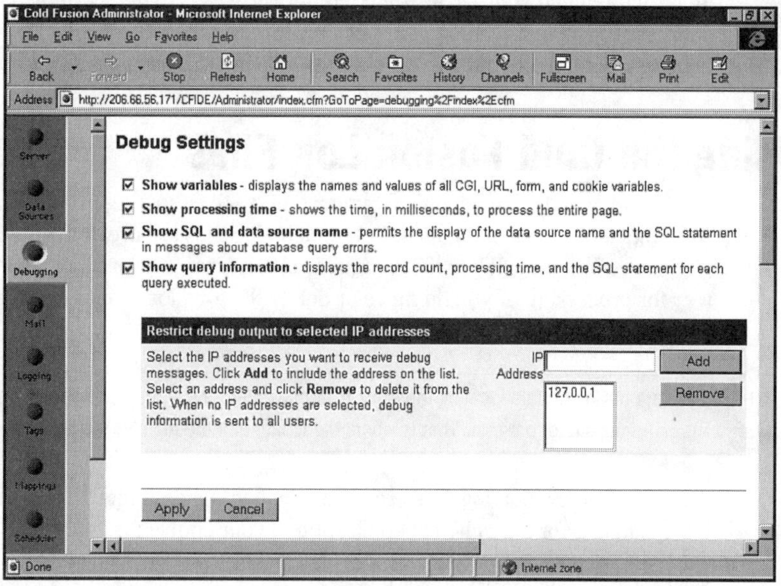

FIG. 16.6

The Cold Fusion Administrator debugging tab allows you to enable debugging options, as well as specifying the IP address where to send debug information.

Part

III

Ch

16

TIP You can restrict the display of debugging information to specific IP addresses. If you enable debugging, you should generally use this feature to prevent debugging screens from being displayed to visitors to your web site.

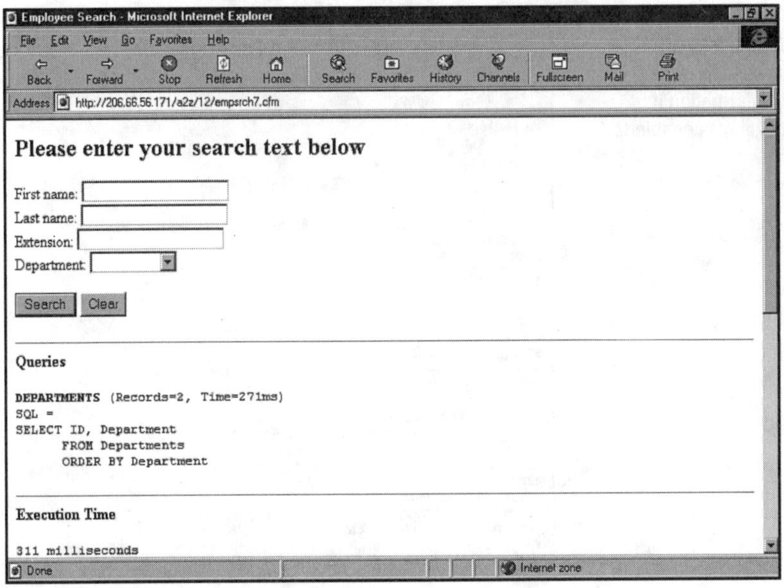

FIG. 16.7

Cold Fusion can append debugging information to any generated web page.

On the CD

You will often find yourself needing temporary access to debug information for specific IP addresses. On the CD-ROM you'll find a CFX tag called CFX_Debug that enables you to simply turn on and off debug information without having to access the Cold Fusion Administrator.

Using the Cold Fusion Log Files

To aid you, and Allaire Technical Support, in troubleshooting problems, Cold Fusion logs all warnings and errors to log files. Cold Fusion log files are created when the Cold Fusion service starts. You may delete these log files if they grow too large, or move them to another directory for processing. If you do move or delete the log files, Cold Fusion will·create new ones automatically.

TIP

If you are having trouble locating the Cold Fusion log files, check the Debugging screen in the Cold Fusion Administrator program. That is where the location of the log files is specified.

All of the Cold Fusion log files are plain-text, comma-delimited files. You may import these files into a database or spreadsheet application of your choice for analysis.

Cold Fusion creates several log files.

- CFIDESERVICE.LOG logs problems with the Cold Fusion IDE service. This log file is primarily of use to Allaire Technical Support.

- CFSERVER.LOG logs every Cold Fusion error reported back to a user. All template errors, including Cold Fusion syntax errors, ODBC errors, and SQL errors, are all written to this log file. This is the log file you will typically want to monitor so that you'll know of any problems that are occurring. Every error message displayed on a visitor's browser is logged here, along with the visitor's IP address and browser information, if possible. The format of this log file is shown in Table 16.2.

■ DBML.LOG logs errors that occurred in the communication between Cold Fusion and your web server. This log file is of very little use to you, and is primarily created to help Allaire Technical Support personnel in the event that you call them for help. The format of this log file is shown in Table 16.3.

■ SERVER.LOG logs system failure messages. If the SMTP mailer cannot be initialized, it will be logged to this file. This log file, too, is of less use to you than to Allaire's Technical Support department. The format of this log file is shown in Table 16.4.

▶ **See** Chapter 32, "Event Scheduling," **p. 755**

Part

III

Ch

16

Table 16.2 CFSERVER.LOG Log File Format

Position	Field	Description
1	Severity	Either "Warning" or "Error."
2	Date	Date that the error occurred.
3	Time	Time that the error occurred.
4	IP Address	IP address of the host that submitted the template that generated the error message.
5	Browser	The name and version number of the browser that submitted the template, and the platform it was running on (this information is usually provided by all browsers whenever a page is requested, some browsers supply more information than others, so there is no guarantee as to what will appear in this field).
6	Error	The error message text exactly as sent to the user.

On the CD

You should definitely get into the habit of inspecting the contents of the CFSERVER.LOG file on a regular basis. To make this easier, you'll find a CFX tag on the CD-ROM called CFX_ViewCFLog. This tag allows you to display and filter the CFSERVER.LOG log file and view it within your web browser.

Table 16.3 DBML.LOG Log File Format

Position	Field	Description
1	Severity	Either "Warning" or "Error."
2	Thread ID	Thread ID, this information will be of use to Allaire Technical Support personnel only.

continues

Table 16.3 Continued

Position	Field	Description
3	Date	Date that the error occurred.
4	Time	Time that the error occurred.
5	Details	Description of the error that occurred (with NT error number if appropriate).

Table 16.4 SERVER.LOG Log File Format

Position	Field	Description
1	Severity	"Information," "Warning," or "Error."
2	Thread ID	Thread ID, this information will be of use to Allaire Technical Support personnel only.
3	Date	Date that the error occurred.
4	Time	Time that the error occurred.
5	Details	Description of the error that occurred.

Some errors are browser-related. If you are having a hard time reproducing reported error messages, try to determine which version of which browser the user was running, and on what platform. You may find that you have run into browser bugs (yes, some versions of popular browsers are very buggy). The CFSERVER.LOG file logs any identification information provided by a browser along with the error message.

End users are notorious for reporting that "an error occurred" *without* specifying what the error message was, what screen they were at, and what they were doing when the error was generated. The log files, and in particular the CFSERVER.LOG file, can help you find an error message if you know roughly when it occurred and who it was sent to.

Preventing Problems

As mentioned earlier, the best approach to troubleshooting Cold Fusion problems (and indeed any development problems), is to prevent them from ever occurring in the first place.

Now, bugs are inevitable. And, as the size of an application grows, so does the likelihood of a bug being introduced. As an application developer you need to have two goals in mind.

1. Develop 100% bug-free code.
2. In the event that your code is not 100% bug-free, make sure that it is at least easy to debug.

As an application developer myself, I know that these are lofty goals. The reality of it is that application development almost always takes longer than planned, and sacrifices have to be made if release dates are to be met. Usually the first thing that gets sacrificed is code quality.

Of course, sooner or later these sacrifices come back to haunt you. Then come the long debugging sessions, rapid code fixes, software upgrades, and possibly even data conversion. Then, as the rapidly patched code often introduces bugs of its own, the whole cycle restarts.

While there is no surefire way of preventing all bugs, there are guidelines and coding practices that can both help prevent many of them, and make finding them easier when they do occur. So, the following are my 10 Commandments of Cold Fusion development.

- I. **Functionality first, then features.** This might seem like an obvious one, but it is one of the most common beginner mistakes. Implementing fancy interface ideas is much more fun than perfecting or optimizing search routines, but the search routines really are more important. And the fancy outputting techniques will clutter the important code and make it even harder to debug.

- II. **Never develop applications on a live server.** Another obvious but often ignored one. That "safe little cosmetic enhancement" might not be as safe or as little as it seems. No enhancement is ever worth bringing an existing working application down to it's knees.

- III. **Test each piece of code individually.** Trying to find a bug amidst a several hundred-line template is like looking for a needle in a haystack. The best way to test code is to isolate it. After you have verified that a SQL statement works properly, plug it into your template—never before.

- IV. **Write code with reuse in mind.** Anything worth doing is worth doing properly, and application development is no exception. When designing a piece of code, it's worth putting in a little extra effort up front to ensure that the code is neither task specific nor hard coded, unless it has to be. Always try to keep the big picture in mind.

- V. **Break long source files into shorter, more manageable ones.** Cold Fusion lets you include templates within other templates. There is a very slight performance penalty in doing this, but the degradation is never enough to warrant long unmanageable templates. Smaller, more focused, templates are easier to maintain, plus they lend themselves very well to code reuse.

- VI. **Comment your code.** You're going to have to revisit it one day, and descriptive template headers and embedded comments will help you remember why you did what you did. This will also help prevent you from making changes without realizing what else they will impact.

- VII. **Use descriptive variable names.** Six months from now you won't remember what `ord` or `var` was used for. A variable name like `order_number` or `OrderNumber` takes a little longer to type, but you *will* remember what it stored.

- VIII. **Don't be scared to waste space.** The "don't kill trees" rule does not apply to software development. Be a little wordier if necessary, space your code properly to make it more readable, and don't cram so much text onto one line that you have to scroll your editor to read it. Yes, the extra white space might make your source files a little bigger, and yes, every character counts when the generated output is transmitted over a slow modem connection. But be a little selfish sometimes; you have to maintain the code, and your time is worth preserving too.

IX. **Set coding standards.** There are no right or wrong ways to present your code. Any coding style is good if it helps make your code easier to read and more maintainable. This becomes even more important if more than one developer is working on a project. If you are part of a team of developers, try to come to some agreement as to what style of variable names to use, when to indent code, what should be capitalized and what should not, and so on.

X. **Implement a version control system.** Cold Fusion applications, by their very nature, are made up of many different source files. And these files change regularly. Version control will let you keep tabs of all changes to each source file and will allow you to restore all files to the state they were in at any prior time. Both of these capabilities will become vital to you as your application grows. Version control applications, like PVCS or Microsoft Source Safe, are inexpensive and are an investment well worth making.

Advanced Cold Fusion

CHAPTER 17

Advanced SQL

by Ronald E. Taylor and Nate Weiss

In this chapter

Using the *DISTINCT* Keyword

In Chapter 8, "Introduction to SQL," you learned how to use the SELECT statement to get information from your database tables. You can add DISTINCT to these SELECT statements in those situations where you don't want to get any duplicate information from your tables.

For instance, if you wanted to find all of the *unique* last names of your employees—that is, without any repeats—you could execute the SQL statement shown in Listing 17.1. The results are shown in Figure 17.1.

On the CD

Listing 17.1 DISTINCT.CFM—Using *DISTINCT* to Eliminate Duplicates

```
<CFQUERY NAME="Report" DATASOURCE="A2Z">
  SELECT DISTINCT LastName
  FROM Employees
</CFQUERY>

<HTML>

<HEAD>
<TITLE>Last Names</TITLE>
</HEAD>

<BODY>

<H1>Last Names</H1>

<CFTABLE QUERY="Report" COLHEADERS HTMLTABLE BORDER>
  <CFCOL HEADER="LastName" TEXT="#LastName#">
</CFTABLE>

</BODY>

</HTML>
```

If you look at the actual data in our Employees table, you see that there are two employees by the name of Smith in there (employee number 4, Jack, and employee number 5, Jane). The inclusion of DISTINCT in the SQL code has kept the "duplicate" last name from appearing. This is a particularly helpful technique when dealing with information like states, area codes, and the like.

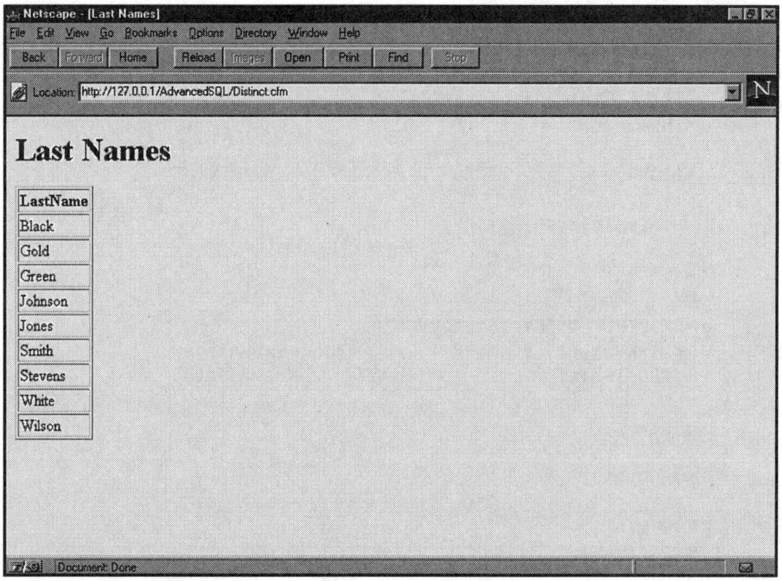

FIG. 17.1
The value "Smith," which appears several times in the database, only shows up once here.

> **Netscape - [Last Names]**
> File Edit View Go Bookmarks Options Directory Window Help
>
> Location: http://127.0.0.1/AdvancedSQL/Distinct.cfm
>
> ## Last Names
>
> | LastName |
> |----------|
> | Black |
> | Gold |
> | Green |
> | Johnson |
> | Jones |
> | Smith |
> | Stevens |
> | White |
> | Wilson |
>
> Document: Done

Part
IV

Ch
17

Using Column Aliases

As you work through the rest of this chapter, you'll need to make use of *Column Aliases* in your code. Providing a Column Alias gives you a way to "rename" a column in the query's results. Nothing about the actual table changes in any way, the column simply appears to have a different name for this one specific query.

For instance, go back to a listing you've already worked with and add column aliases, so that your columns present themselves under different names. Listing 17.2 revises Listing 11.5 (Employ1.cfm template from Chapter 11, "Cold Fusion Basics"). The code is almost exactly the same. All you've done is added column aliases so the FirstName column is presented to Cold Fusion as NameF, and LastName has become NameL.

On the CD

Listing 17.2 EMPLOY1A.CFM—Using *AS* to Create Column Aliases

```
<
CFQUERY
DATASOURCE="A2Z"
NAME="Employees"
>
SELECT FirstName AS NameF, LastName AS NameL, PhoneExtension
FROM Employees
ORDER BY LastName, FirstName
</CFQUERY>

<HTML>
```

continues

Listing 17.2 Continued

```
<HEAD>
<TITLE>Employee List</TITLE>
</HEAD>

<BODY>

<H1>Employees</H1>

<UL>

<CFOUTPUT QUERY="Employees">
 <LI>#NameL#, #NameF# - Ext. #PhoneExtension#
</CFOUTPUT>

</UL>

</BODY>

</HTML>
```

Note that you used NameL and NameF after AS in the SQL statement, and you also used #NameL# and #NameF# to refer to the code in the template itself. If you had left #LastName# in the template code, you would have gotten a "column not found" error from Cold Fusion, because it is now convinced that the only relevant column names are NameL and NameF. This illustrates the important concept that Cold Fusion is not really aware of what your table and column names are—it "believes" whatever your ODBC driver tells it to believe.

N O T E   Even though you provided a Column Alias for the LastName field, you still used the real column name (LastName) in the ORDER BY part of the query. In other words, use column aliases to change the column names that are presented to Cold Fusion. But refer to the columns normally in the WHERE, ORDER BY, and other parts of the query statement itself. ■

You may be asking yourself what the point of all this is. Why would you care whether the column appears under its rightful name of LastName, or masquerades under the "aliased" name of NameL? Well, in reality, of course you probably don't care. But here's a much more useful application of column aliases that allows you to use table columns whose rightful names Cold Fusion considers illegal.

Pretend for a moment that when the Employees table was first created, the designer of the table used the column names "Last-Name" and "First Name" instead of "LastName" and "FirstName." Cold Fusion doesn't allow spaces or dashes in column names, so errors will occur if you try to use the columns in your templates. But all is not lost. You can use column aliases to present Cold Fusion with perfectly respectable column names.

For just as a quick example, look back at Listing 11.5 in Chapter 11. Now look at Listing 17.3. Listing 17.3 is what you would need to use to get the same results as Listing 11.3, if your database had the illegal column names "Last-Name" and "First Name." The AS keyword presents Last-Name to Cold Fusion as LastName, and First Name as FirstName.

On the CD

Listing 17.3   Using Column Aliases to Work Around Illegal Column Names

```
SELECT 'First Name' AS FirstName, 'Last-Name' AS LastName, PhoneExtension
FROM Employees
ORDER BY 'Last-Name', 'First Name'
```

Notice that you used the backtick character around the column names. The backtick character is used by ODBC to indicate that the characters between the backticks are to be treated "literally." For instance, the backticks around First Name make it clear to ODBC that you're talking about a single column named "First Name," rather than two different columns. Different database drivers may or may not have had a problem with the space in the column name, so backticks were used just to be safe.

In short, you had two obstacles to overcome. You had to use AS to prevent an error message from Cold Fusion. You also needed to use backticks to prevent potential error messages from the ODBC driver itself.

You can also use backticks to work around situations where a column name is perfectly legal to Cold Fusion, but is considered illegal to the ODBC driver. For instance, people often make the mistake of creating a column named "Date."

Referring to this "Date" column can cause syntax error messages from the ODBC driver, if the particular ODBC driver considers "Date" to be a reserved word. In such a case, you could use backticks around the column name to avoid the error. It would not be necessary to create a Column Alias with AS in such a case, however, because Cold Fusion has no problem with "Date" being used as a column name.

You can now go ahead and refer to #LastName# and #FirstName# in your CFML without errors, and you didn't have to resort to renaming the actual columns (which presumably could have caused problems if the database was also being used by another application other than Cold Fusion).

Part
IV

Ch
17

Using Aggregate Functions to Report on Your Data

SQL supplies a number of *functions* for your use. There are basically two types of functions in SQL:

- *Scalar functions*—which will be discussed at the end of this chapter—ask questions about individual rows in your database tables. You probably won't use these terribly often, because Cold Fusion's own built-in functions are generally easier-to-use and more flexible.

- *Aggregate functions*, on the other hand, are used to *crunch* information from any number of rows at once into a *summarized* overview of your data. You will find yourself using these functions whenever you want to provide report-style summaries or overviews in your Cold Fusion applications. (Sometimes aggregate functions are referred to as *set functions*.)

There are a total of five aggregate functions in all. Table 17.1 explains what each function does and the types of columns that each function can be used on. Note that Count(*) and Count(Columnname) behave differently, and in some ways can be considered to be two different functions.

Table 17.1 Aggregate Functions

Function	On Numeric Columns	On Date Columns	On Character Columns
COUNT(*)	Counts the number of rows in a table	Same	Same
COUNT(Column)	Counts the actual values found in a column	Same	Same
SUM(Column)	Adds up the total of the values found in a column	n/a	n/a
AVG(Column)	Computes the average of values found in a column	n/a	n/a
MIN(Column)	Finds the smallest value found in a column	Earliest date found in a column	First value (alphabetically) found in a column
MAX	Finds the largest number found in a column	Latest date found in a column	Last value (alphabetically) found in a column

N O T E Note that not every aggregate function can be used with every type of column. For instance, a mathematical concept like "average" makes perfect sense in the context of a column full of numbers, like the Pages column of the Inventory table. However, the mathematical concept of "averaging" doesn't really make sense in the context of a character-type column like the Title column of that same table. While the average of two numbers like 10 and 20 is clearly 15, there's really no way to express an average of *Moby Dick* and *The Hitchhiker's Guide To The Galaxy*. For this reason, the AVG (Column) function is not allowed on character-type columns. ■

The SQL syntax for using the various aggregate functions is identical, and can easily be combined into one SQL statement for a single CFQUERY.

Listing 17.4 demonstrates the functionality of each aggregate function. Note that you can make up any name you want for the computed column that each function returns—I recommend using the column name or part of the column name, then an underscore, then the name of the function you're using. It's easier to keep things straight this way.

On the CD

Listing 17.4   INVRPT1.CFM—Code that Uses All of the Aggregate Functions

```
<CFQUERY NAME="Report" DATASOURCE="A2Z">
  SELECT
    COUNT(*)                  AS Book_Count,
    COUNT(Publisher)          AS Pub_Count,
    MIN(PublicationDate)      AS PubDate_Min,
    MAX(PublicationDate)      AS PubDate_Max,
    SUM(NumberInStock)        AS InStock_Sum,
    AVG(Pages)                AS Pages_Avg
  FROM Inventory
</CFQUERY>

<HTML>

<HEAD>
<TITLE>Inventory Report</TITLE>
</HEAD>

<BODY>

<H1>Inventory Report</H1>

<UL>

<CFOUTPUT>
  <LI>Number of different books:      #Report.Book_Count#
  <LI>Number of publishers:           #Report.Pub_Count#
  <LI>First book published on:        #DateFormat(Report.PubDate_Min)#
  <LI>Last book published on:         #DateFormat(Report.PubDate_Max)#
  <LI>Total number of copies in stock:  #NumberFormat(Report.InStock_Sum)#
  <LI>Average number of pages:        #Report.Pages_Avg#
</CFOUTPUT>

</UL>

</BODY>

</HTML>
```

Take note that in Figure 17.2, `Book_Count` and `Pub_Count` indicate the same value of 6. However, most human beings would probably think that `Pub_Count` would be 4, because there are only four different publishers represented. Unfortunately, with most desktop database drivers such as the Access driver, `Count(Publisher)` doesn't behave in the way that you'd probably expect. It simply counts the number of rows found in the `Publishers` column that have values, not the number of unique Publishers.

Most server-based database systems allow you to use the `DISTINCT` keyword with the `Count` function, which gives the information that you would probably expect intuitively. For instance, Microsoft SQL Server would allow you to use the SQL code in Listing 17.5. Unfortunately, it won't work with the Access, FoxPro, and other file-based database drivers that ship with Cold Fusion 3.1.

Part
IV

Ch
17

FIG. 17.2

Book_Count and Pub_Count appear to be the same.

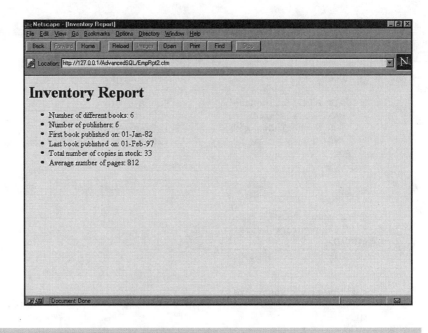

Listing 17.5 Using *DISTINCT* with *Count*

```
SELECT
     COUNT(*)                   AS Book_Count,
     COUNT(DISTINCT Publisher)  AS Pub_Count,
     MIN(PublicationDate)       AS PubDate_Min,
     MAX(PublicationDate)       AS PubDate_Max,
     SUM(NumberInStock)         AS InStock_Sum,
     AVG(Pages)                 AS Pages_Avg
   FROM Inventory
```

The introduction of the DISTINCT keyword would cause Pub_Count to reflect the value of 4 that you'd expect. Book_Count would remain 6, because Count(*) counts the number of physical rows without regard to their contents.

Counting Rows with *COUNT(*)*

The simplest aggregate function is COUNT(*), which simply counts the number of rows found by a query statement. You include the COUNT(*) function in the SELECT part of a query, as if it were a column in your table. Indeed, the value that the function returns is presented to Cold Fusion as if it were a column in a table. This means that you can go ahead and use the value in your Cold Fusion templates in the same ways that you're already familiar with.

The code in Listing 17.6 queries the datasource for the number of rows in the Employees table. The value calculated by Count(*) is returned to the template as a column named Emp_Count. The actual table is not changed in any way.

Listing 17.6 EMPRPT1.CFM—Counting the Number of Rows with *COUNT(*)*

```
<CFQUERY NAME="Report" DATASOURCE="A2Z">
  SELECT COUNT(*) AS Emp_Count
  FROM Employees
</CFQUERY>

<HTML>

<HEAD>
<TITLE>Employee Report</TITLE>
</HEAD>

<BODY>

<H1>Employee Report</H1>

<CFOUTPUT QUERY="Report">
  Total Number Of Employees: #Emp_Count#
</CFOUTPUT>

</BODY>

</HTML>
```

Note that you used your new-found column-aliasing skills to create the column alias of Emp_Count with AS. This is optional as far as SQL is concerned, but it's required for using the value in your Cold Fusion code. People often think that the name of the computed column will be Employees by default, but it's not—the column remains unnamed unless you use AS. That's fine in many environments, but not Cold Fusion, because CFML requires you to refer to columns by name.

The SQL statement generates a new result set that contains just one column, called Emp_Count. There is also just one row in this result set, containing the integer 10, which is the number of rows in the Employees table. When this template is run, it should look like Figure 17.3.

Making Aggregate Functions More Selective with *WHERE*

You can easily make your functions perform their computations only on certain rows by using the WHERE clause, as covered in Chapter 8, "Introduction to SQL." For instance, to have the report in Figure 17.3 computed only for books in Category number 2 (Humor), you could change the SQL statement in Listing 17.5 to the statement in Listing 17.7.

Listing 17.7 Limiting an Aggregate Function's Scope with *WHERE*

```
SELECT
    COUNT(*)                AS Book_Count,
    COUNT(Publisher)        AS Pub_Count,
    MIN(PublicationDate)    AS PubDate_Min,
    MAX(PublicationDate)    AS PubDate_Max,
    SUM(NumberInStock)      AS InStock_Sum,
    AVG(Pages)              AS Pages_Avg
  FROM Inventory
  WHERE CategoryID = 2
```

FIG. 17.3

Using the computed column's alias in your CFML code.

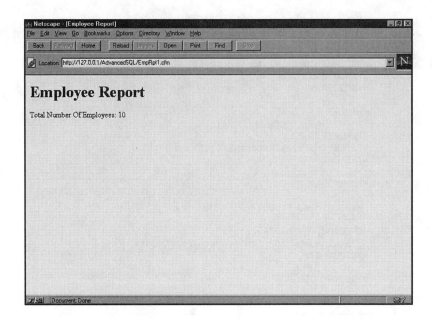

The addition of the WHERE clause tells the database driver that only those rows that meet the criteria specified in the WHERE clause should be considered by the aggregate functions.

You're free to use WHERE in just about any way you would normally. For instance, you could easily make the report operate on more than one category by using OR in the WHERE part of the query, as shown in Listing 17.8. Refer back to Chapter 8, for more information on using WHERE.

Listing 17.8   Using *WHERE, OR*, and Aggregate Functions Together

```
SELECT
    COUNT(*)                 AS Book_Count,
    COUNT(Publisher)         AS Pub_Count,
    MIN(PublicationDate)     AS PubDate_Min,
    MAX(PublicationDate)     AS PubDate_Max,
    SUM(NumberInStock)       AS InStock_Sum,
    AVG(Pages)               AS Pages_Avg
FROM Inventory
WHERE (CategoryID = 2 OR CategoryID = 3)
```

If you're using Cold Fusion Studio (see Figure 17.4), you can create queries that use aggregate functions in Studio's Query Builder. Start by right-clicking the Inventory table from the database tab of the Resource Tab, then selecting New Query... from the pop-up menu.

Now you'll be able to click the column names at the top of the Query Builder. For each column name, select the aggregate function you want from the Group By column at the bottom of the Query Builder—also, provide the alias by typing in the Alias column. A few clicks later, you've built virtually the same query that you came up with in Listing 17.8, without having to concentrate on the SQL syntax involved.

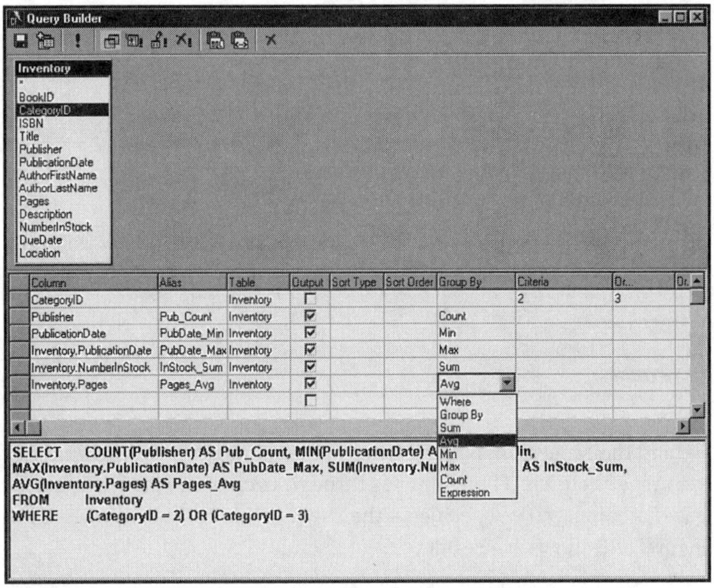

FIG. 17.4
Cold Fusion Studio's query-building facilities support aggregate functions.

Providing "Broken Down" Detail with *GROUP BY*

So far you've used aggregate functions to run simple computations that return only one row of data. Often, you'll want to construct queries that apply the function to every value in a given column. You can get this effect by including a GROUP BY clause in your query.

GROUP BY *column* causes an aggregate function to be computed for each unique value encountered in the column. For instance, say you wanted to find the number of books you had in stock for each category. The query in Listing 17.9 returns a result set with two columns: Category and InStock_Sum. The result set will contain a row for each category, with the corresponding total of copies from each category.

On the CD

Listing 17.9   INVRPT2.CFM—Computing a *SUM* for Each Category

```
<CFQUERY NAME="Report" DATASOURCE="A2Z">
  SELECT Publisher, SUM(NumberInStock) AS InStock_Sum
  FROM Inventory
  GROUP BY Publisher
</CFQUERY>

<HTML>

<HEAD>
<TITLE>Inventory Report</TITLE>
</HEAD>

<BODY>
```

continues

Part IV
Ch
17

Listing 17.9   Continued

```
<H1>Inventory Report</H1>

<UL>

<CFOUTPUT QUERY="Report">
  <LI>#Publisher#:   #NumberFormat(InStock_Sum)#
</CFOUTPUT>

</UL>

</BODY>

</HTML>
```

Behind the scenes, this query causes your database system to find all the unique values in the Publisher column. Then it moves through each of the publishers and applies whatever aggregate functions you've specified—the SUM function in this case—to all of that publisher's rows. Figure 17.5 shows the results.

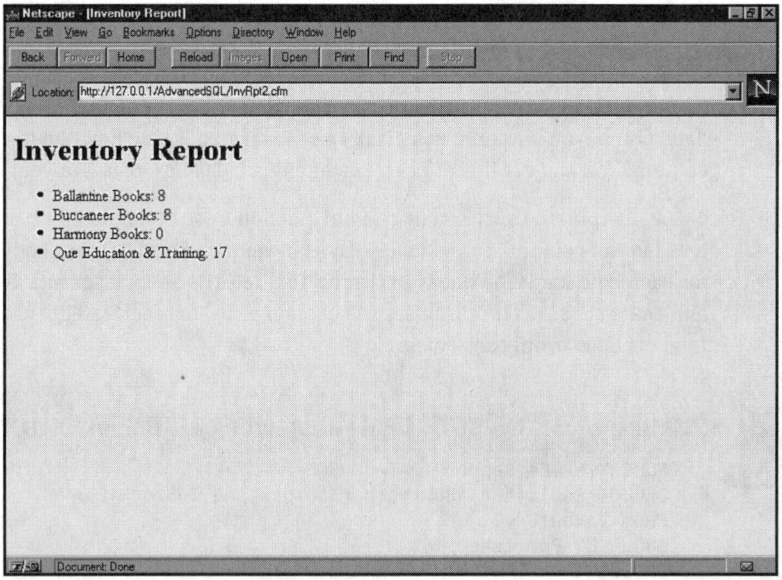

FIG. 17.5

The SUM gets computed for each Publisher.

You can use more than one column in the GROUP BY clause. For instance, you could specify both the Publisher and Category columns. This could be done by replacing the query in Listing 17.9 with the following query:

```
<CFQUERY NAME="Report" DATASOURCE="A2Z">
  SELECT Publisher, AuthorFirstName, AuthorLastName, SUM(NumberInStock)
  AS InStock_Sum
```

```
   FROM Inventory
   GROUP BY Publisher, AuthorFirstName, AuthorLastName
</CFQUERY>
```

Now, instead of merely finding all the unique publishers in the table, your database system will find all the unique combinations of Publisher and Category, and apply the SUM function to all of each publisher's rows for each category. Then all you have to do is refer to AuthorFirstName and AuthorLastName in the CFOUTPUT block, along with Publisher and InStock_Sum. Figure 17.6 shows the results that you might come up with.

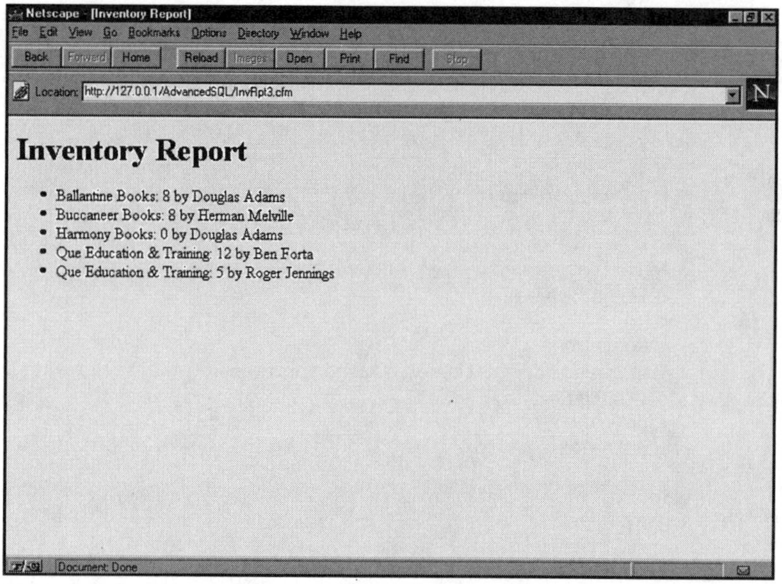

FIG. 17.6

The aggregate function is calculated for every combination of values in the GROUP BY clause.

Part
IV
Ch
17

N O T E If you're using Cold Fusion Studio, you can specify a GROUP BY clause by choosing Group By from the drop-down list in the Group By column for a particular field. ■

Comparing *GROUP BY* in SQL and *GROUP* in *CFOUTPUT*

Don't get confused between GROUP BY in SQL and the GROUP parameter that can be used with the CFOUTPUT tag. As you've just seen, GROUP BY in a query is a standard SQL construct that asks your database about sets of rows. It's usually used along with aggregate functions to get a summarized version of your data.

Using GROUP with CFOUTPUT, on the other hand, is a feature specific to Cold Fusion that has nothing specifically to do with aggregate functions. GROUP asks Cold Fusion to process certain parts of a template—for instance, to display a category heading—only when a new value is encountered in a particular column. It's generally used to avoid a "repeating" effect on your Cold Fusion pages. For instance, you could add a GROUP parameter to your code to eliminate the visual repetition of Que Education & Training on the page. Listing 17.10 shows the code that would accomplish this.

Listing 17.10 INVRPT4.CFM—Adding *GROUP* (as Opposed to *GROUP BY*) to the *CFOUTPUT* Tag

```
<CFQUERY NAME="Report" DATASOURCE="A2Z">
  SELECT Publisher, AuthorFirstName, AuthorLastName, SUM(NumberInStock)
  AS InStock_Sum
  FROM Inventory
  GROUP BY Publisher, AuthorFirstName, AuthorLastName
</CFQUERY>

<HTML>

<HEAD>
<TITLE>Inventory Report</TITLE>
</HEAD>

<BODY>

<H1>Inventory Report</H1>


<CFOUTPUT QUERY="Report" GROUP="Publisher">
  <P>#Publisher#:
  <UL>
  <CFOUTPUT>
    <LI>#AuthorFirstName# #AuthorLastName#: #NumberFormat(InStock_Sum)#
  </CFOUTPUT>
  </UL>
</CFOUTPUT>


</BODY>

</HTML>
```

Figure 17.7 shows the results of Listing 17.10. See "Grouping Query Results" in Chapter 11 for more information on CFOUTPUT's GROUP parameter.

Displaying the "Top n" Records Sooner or later, nearly every company president will put a request in to her tech people for a report that shows the top 10 clients, the top 100 products, or what have you.

In most cases, you take care of this quite easily by grabbing an existing template and adding an ORDER BY clause to the SQL statement and a MAXROWS parameter to the CFQUERY tag. As you learned in Chapter 8 using ORDER BY with DESC sorts a query's results—largest values first—according to the column you specify. The MAXROWS parameter causes the query to only return a certain number of rows. Therefore, by adding a MAXROWS=2 parameter to a query that's been sorted with DESC, you end up with the 2 top values.

For instance, the Listing 17.11 is a "Top 2" version of the report you put together in Listing 17.9. Figure 17.8 shows the results of Listing 17.11.

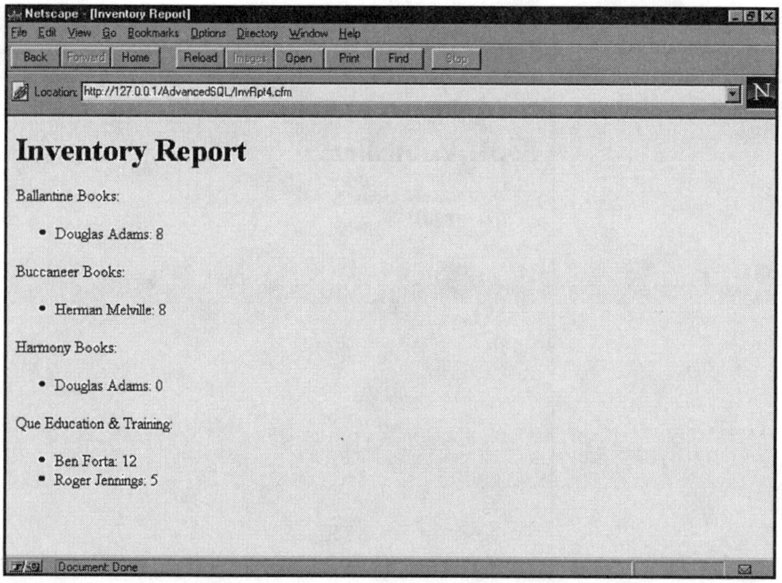

FIG. 17.7
SQL's GROUP BY and
CFOUTPUT's GROUP
can be used together.

Part
IV

Ch
17

Listing 17.11   INVRPT2A.CFM—Adding *MAXROWS* and Reversing the Sort Order

On the CD

```
<CFQUERY NAME="Report" DATASOURCE="A2Z" MAXROWS=2>
  SELECT Publisher, SUM(NumberInStock) AS InStock_Sum
  FROM Inventory
  GROUP BY Publisher
  ORDER BY SUM(NumberInStock) DESC
</CFQUERY>

<HTML>

<HEAD>
<TITLE>Inventory Report</TITLE>
</HEAD>

<BODY>

<H1>Top 2 Publishers</H1>

<UL>

<CFOUTPUT QUERY="Report">
  <LI>#Publisher#:   #NumberFormat(InStock_Sum)#
</CFOUTPUT>

</UL>

</BODY>

</HTML>
```

FIG. 17.8
You can use MAXROWS and ORDER BY to create "Top n" types of reports.

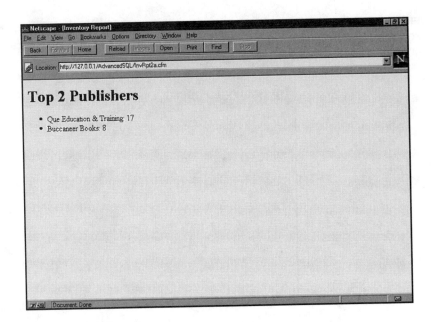

Note that you are able to use aggregate functions in the ORDER BY part of the query. In general, just about any function or expression that is allowed in the SELECT part can also be used in the other parts of a query, such as the WHERE or ORDER BY parts.

Selecting Only Certain Aggregated Values with *HAVING*

You've seen how you can use WHERE to cause the aggregate functions to run their computations only on certain rows. The aggregate functions are calculated on only those rows that pass the tests called for in the WHERE clause. So what if you wanted to choose which rows are returned in a different way—based not on what the values are *before* the aggregate functions do their work, but *after*?

You guessed it, you use the HAVING keyword for this purpose. Compared to everything else you're learning in this chapter, HAVING is relatively obscure, and you probably won't use it much. But it is important to know that it's there if you need it.

For instance, what if you wanted to adapt the SQL in Listing 17.10 so that it only showed the counts for the authors for which there are more than five copies in stock? By adding a HAVING clause to the SQL in Listing 17.10, you tell your database system to do all the same computations as before—but then to only return the computed rows that pass the tests in the HAVING clause. Listing 17.12 shows the modified SQL statement.

Listing 17.12 Adding *HAVING* to Choose Which *GROUP BY* Rows You Want

```
SELECT Publisher, AuthorFirstName, AuthorLastName,
➥SUM(NumberInStock) AS InStock_Sum
  FROM Inventory
  GROUP BY Publisher, AuthorFirstName, AuthorLastName
  HAVING SUM(NumberInStock) > 5
```

Figure 17.9 shows the result of replacing the SQL statement in Listing 17.10 with the SQL statement in Listing 17.12.

FIG. 17.9

This template uses SUM, GROUP BY, HAVING, and GROUP together.

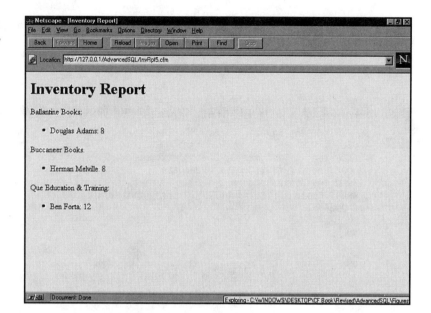

Selecting Data From Two Tables Using Joins

The design of the tables in your A2Z database calls for a number of relationships between the various tables. Concentrate for a little while on the Customer, Order, and OrderItems tables. You'll recall from Chapter 7, "Creating Databases and Tables," that when you created these tables, you were also implicitly creating the following conceptual relationships between them:

- There is a one-to-many relationship between the Customer and Orders tables. In other words, any one customer can make any number of orders.

- There is also a one-to-many relationship between the Orders and OrderItems tables. In other words, any one order can consist of any number of items.

Refer to Chapter 6, "Database Fundamentals," to refresh your memory about one-to-many and other types of table relationships.

Obviously, in order for this three-table design to be useful, you need to be able to use the SELECT statement to get data from more than one table. SQL makes this simple, relying on a simple concept called a *join*.

You specify a join by using special SQL syntax that "links" two tables together to get the desired results. Of course, you already know in your head what the relationship between the two tables is. Join syntax is what you use to describe the relationship between the tables that you're using in a particular query.

Part
IV

Ch
17

Take a look at Listing 17.13. In some ways, it looks like the simple SELECT queries you've already explored. But there are three big differences:

- There are two tables listed in the FROM part.
- The = sign is used to "join" the two tables in the WHERE part.
- Because there is more than one table involved, simple "dot notation" in the form *Tablename.Columnname* is used to refer to the columns.

Listing 17.13 ORDERRPT1—Joining Tables Together with *WHERE*

```
<CFQUERY NAME="Report" DATASOURCE="A2Z">
  SELECT
    Customers.CustomerID, Customers.Company,
    Orders.OrderID, Orders.OrderDate
  FROM Customers, Orders
  WHERE Customers.CustomerID = Orders.CustomerID
</CFQUERY>

<HTML>

<HEAD>
<TITLE>Order Report</TITLE>
</HEAD>

<BODY>

<H1>Order Report</H1>

<CFTABLE QUERY="Report" COLHEADERS HTMLTABLE BORDER>
  <CFCOL HEADER="CustomerID" TEXT="#CustomerID#">
  <CFCOL HEADER="Company" TEXT="#Company#">
  <CFCOL HEADER="OrderID" TEXT="#OrderID#">
  <CFCOL HEADER="Date" TEXT="#DateFormat(OrderDate)#">
</CFTABLE>

</BODY>

</HTML>
```

The WHERE keyword is clearly being used in a new way here. Rather than merely specifying selection criteria as you've seen previously, it is used here to "bind" the Customers and Order tables together. Translated into plain English, this statement might read "Using the CustomerID as a guide, show me the company name for each row in the Customers table, along with the corresponding dates for each order from the Order table." Figure 17.10 shows the results of joining these tables to build an Orders Report.

That WHERE clause is critical to understand. Developers know that the conceptual relationship between the two tables "hinges" on the fact that the rows of the Order table where the CustomerID column is 1 "match up" with the row in the Customers table where CustomerID is 1, and so on. The WHERE clause "explains" this fact to your ODBC driver.

FIG. 17.10

Here you see the results of your first join.

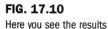

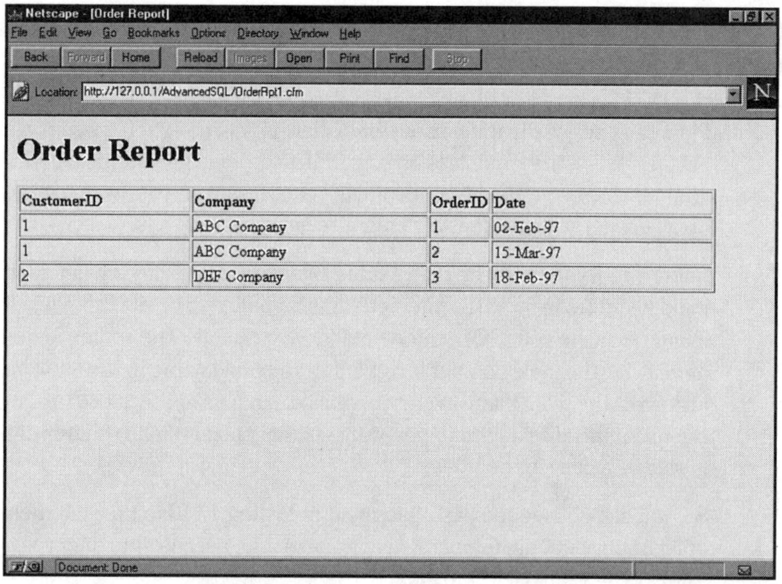

Order Report

CustomerID	Company	OrderID	Date
1	ABC Company	1	02-Feb-97
1	ABC Company	2	15-Mar-97
2	DEF Company	3	18-Feb-97

> **CAUTION**
>
> If you accidentally leave out the WHERE clause, you'll get back a ton of rows. Because there is nothing "binding" the two tables together, SQL has no choice but to return every combination of rows—so you end up with a result set that's as large as the number of rows in the Customers table times the number of rows in the Order table.

I recommend specifying the table name for every column. However, it is only *required* when the column name exists in more than one table. So you may simply refer to Company instead of Customers.Company if you wish. But you cannot omit the table name when referring to the CustomerID column, because a column by that name exists in both tables.

The columns in the join don't have to be named the same. If for some reason the relevant column in the Order table was called Customer_Number instead of CustomerID, you could just use WHERE Customers.CustomerID = Orders.Customer_Number.

However, the datatypes of the columns *do* have to be the same. An error would occur, for instance, if you tried to create a join using Customers.CustomerID = Orders.CustomerID if for some foolish reason you had defined the CustomerID column of the Orders table to be a text-type column. Since the column on the left side of the = is not of the same datatype as the column on the right side, an error would occur and the join would fail.

> **TIP**
>
> If you absolutely need to join columns of different datatypes, you may be able to use the CONVERT Scalar Function (see Table 17.1) on one of the columns as an emergency workaround.

I just can't stress the importance of Listing 17.13 enough. If there is a single listing in this chapter that you shouldn't skim past, this is it. Joins are a critical concept to get your head around. Once you "get it" conceptually, you're well on your way to creating sophisticated relational database applications.

Improving Readability by Using Table Aliases   SQL allows you to use *table aliases* when using multiple tables in an SQL statement. It is a good idea to use them when joining tables together, mainly to make your SQL statements more readable. The syntax is quite simple—just make up an alias for the table and put it right after the table name in the FROM part. Then use that alias instead of the table name everywhere else, such as in the SELECT part and the WHERE part. You can make the alias anything you want—simply using the first letter of the table name is suggested as a convention.

So, you can change the SQL statement in Listing 17.13 to the statement in Listing 17.14. No other changes to the template need to be made, because the query is still delivering the exact same result set to Cold Fusion.

Listing 17.14   Adding *c* and *o* as Table Aliases

```
SELECT
    c.CustomerID, c.Company,
    o.OrderID, o.OrderDate
  FROM Customers c, Order o
  WHERE c.CustomerID = o.CustomerID
```

Joining Three or More Tables   So far so good. Now, what if you wanted to see which books were included with each order? That will involve using the SELECT statement with three tables. The syntax for your first three-table join should come as no great surprise. You'll just add the OrderItems table to the SQL statement in Listing 17.14 and join it to the Order table in the WHERE part. Listing 17.15 shows the new SQL statement that includes the OrderItems table.

Listing 17.15   ORDERRPT2.CFM—A Three-Table Join

```
<CFQUERY NAME="Report" DATASOURCE="A2Z">
  SELECT
    c.CustomerID, c.Company,
    o.OrderID, o.OrderDate,
    oi.OrderLine, oi.BookID
  FROM Customers c, Orders o, OrderItems oi
  WHERE c.CustomerID = o.CustomerID
    AND oi.OrderID = o.OrderID
</CFQUERY>

<HTML>
```

```
<HEAD>
<TITLE>Order Report</TITLE>
</HEAD>

<BODY>

<H1>Order Report</H1>

<CFTABLE QUERY="Report" COLHEADERS HTMLTABLE BORDER>
  <CFCOL HEADER="CustomerID" WIDTH="" ALIGN="" TEXT="#CustomerID#">
  <CFCOL HEADER="Company" WIDTH="" ALIGN="" TEXT="#Company#">
  <CFCOL HEADER="OrderID" WIDTH="" ALIGN="" TEXT="#OrderID#">
  <CFCOL HEADER="Date" WIDTH="" ALIGN="" TEXT="#DateFormat(OrderDate)#">
  <CFCOL HEADER="Line" WIDTH="" ALIGN="" TEXT="#OrderLine#">
  <CFCOL HEADER="BookID" WIDTH="" ALIGN="" TEXT="#BookID#">
</CFTABLE>

</BODY>

</HTML>
```

Part

IV

Ch

17

Note that because both table joins have to be specified in the same WHERE clause, you use the AND keyword between them. This is consistent with specifying multiple criteria in simpler queries (such as Listing 8.7 in Chapter 8. SQL is designed to allow you to think of a table join as just another piece of filtering criteria.

N O T E A four-table join is about as far as you would want to go under most circumstances. Queries that involve more than four tables are certainly possible, but you may start to notice that performance will degrade, especially with file-based databases such as Access tables. ▪

Joining Tables with *INNER JOIN ON* So far, you've done all of your joining using the WHERE part of your queries to describe the relationship between your tables. SQL offers an alternate syntax that could be used to create any of the joins that you've done so far. Instead of specifying the join in the WHERE part of the query, the join is specified in the FROM part of the query with the INNER JOIN and ON keywords.

As you are listing the table names in the FROM part of the query, the words INNER JOIN are placed between the table names. Then the ON keyword is used to indicate the column names to be used in the join. Some developers find the resulting statements to be more readable, because the syntax seems to describe the relationship in something closer to plain English. Listing 17.16 demonstrates the INNER JOIN syntax.

Listing 17.16   Joining Tables with *INNER JOIN* Instead of *WHERE*

```
SELECT
    c.CustomerID, c.Company,
    o.OrderID, o.OrderDate
  FROM Customers c INNER JOIN Orders o
      ON c.CustomerID = o.CustomerID
```

The statements in Listing 17.14 and 17.16 are synonymous. Both tell your database driver to do the same thing, so use the syntax you prefer. You'll probably find that you have a personal preference—I happen to find the WHERE syntax more intuitive. Whatever your preference, it's important to at least be aware that both syntaxes exist, since you are likely to encounter both as a developer.

N O T E   To use three or more tables using the INNER JOIN syntax, you "nest" the join statements using parentheses. The structure would be:

```
SELECT * FROM (table1 INNER JOIN table2
ON table1.columnA = table2.columnA)
INNER JOIN table3 ON table1.columnB = table3.columnB ■
```

Joining to Display All Records from the Master Table   So far, you've used the word "join" as a fairly general term. There are actually two main types of joins that you'll need to use as a Cold Fusion developer:

- An *Inner Join* is the "default" type of join. Inner joins are used when you are interested in values that exist in both tables in a relationship. Only when rows in both tables "sync up" does the query return anything. All of the joins you have explored so far have been inner joins.

- An *Outer Join* is used when you are interested in all values from one of the tables, even when there are no corresponding values in the other table. For instance, you might want to create an "Book Order Report" that shows how many times each book has been ordered—even those books that have not gotten any orders at all.

Say you wanted to display a little "report" that showed how many copies of each book had been ordered. Using the Count aggregate function and a join, you come up with the code in Listing 17.17.

On the CD

Listing 17.17   BOOKRPT1—The Inner Join Version of Your Book Order Report

```
<CFQUERY NAME="Report" DATASOURCE="A2Z">
  SELECT  i.BookID, i.Title, SUM(oi.Quantity) AS CopiesOrdered
  FROM Inventory i INNER JOIN OrderItems oi
                ON i.BookID = oi.BookID
  GROUP BY i.BookID, i.Title
</CFQUERY>

<HTML>

<HEAD>
<TITLE>Book Order Report</TITLE>
</HEAD>

<BODY>

<H1>Book Order Report</H1>

<CFTABLE QUERY="Report" COLHEADERS HTMLTABLE BORDER>
```

```
    <CFCOL HEADER="BookID" TEXT="#BookID#">
    <CFCOL HEADER="Title" TEXT="#Title#">
    <CFCOL HEADER="Orders" TEXT="#NumberFormat(CopiesOrdered)#">
  </CFTABLE>

  </BODY>

  </HTML>
```

Figure 17.11 shows the results of Listing 17.17.

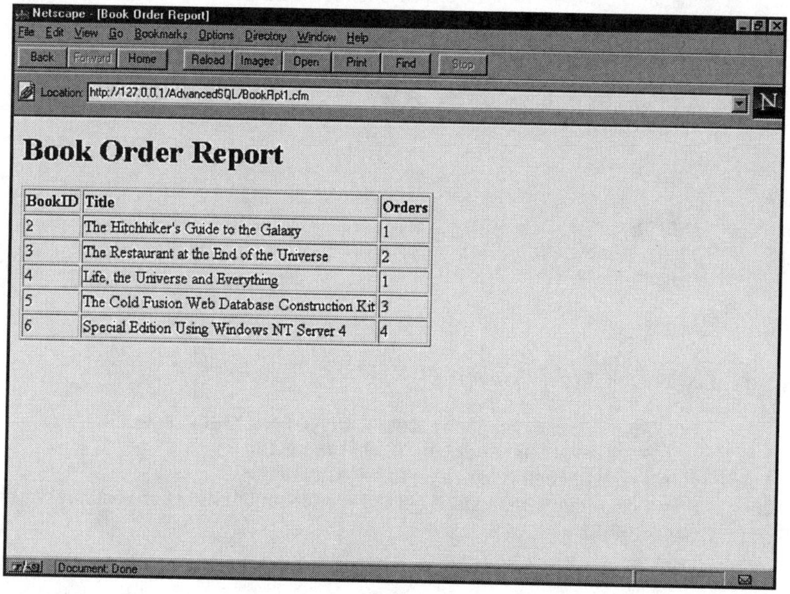

FIG. 17.11

Because you're using an inner join in your query, books that have not been ordered at all don't appear in the results.

The browser display shown in Figure 17.11 looks fine, depending on what the user expects from the application. Notice that *Moby Dick* does not appear in the display at all. Technically speaking, there is nothing wrong. SQL has done exactly what it was asked to do. But a user of your application would probably expect *Moby Dick* to be included in the display, with 0 shown for the number of copies ordered. *Moby Dick's* absence in the list may cause the user to make incorrect assumptions about books that have never been ordered (namely, that they don't exist).

Fortunately, SQL provides a way to deal with this situation, through the use of an outer join. Unlike the simple "inner" joins that you've used so far—where all the tables involved carry the same conceptual weight—writing your SQL statements with outer join syntax tells your database engine that certain tables are more "important" than others, and thus should be represented in the results "no matter what." Specifically, here you want to see all of the appropriate records from one of the tables (the "outer" table), even if there are no matching records from the second table.

Listing 17.18 revises the query from Listing 17.17, using outer join syntax. As you can see, not too much has changed. The word INNER has been changed to OUTER, the word LEFT was added to indicate that the table to the left of the word JOIN is to be considered the *outer* table—in other words, that Inventory is the table that should have all rows returned no matter what. In general, you will usually want the LEFT to "point to" the "one" table in a one-to-many relationship.

On the CD

Listing 17.18   BOOKRPT2.CFM—Changing the Book Order Report to Use Outer Join Syntax

```
<CFQUERY NAME="Report" DATASOURCE="A2Z">
  SELECT  i.BookID, i.Title, SUM(oi.Quantity) AS CopiesOrdered
  FROM Inventory i LEFT OUTER JOIN OrderItems oi
                 ON i.BookID = oi.BookID
  GROUP BY i.BookID, i.Title
</CFQUERY>

<HTML>

<HEAD>
<TITLE>Book Order Report</TITLE>
</HEAD>

<BODY>

<H1>Book Order Report</H1>

<CFTABLE QUERY="Report" COLHEADERS HTMLTABLE BORDER>
  <CFCOL HEADER="BookID" TEXT="#BookID#">
  <CFCOL HEADER="Title" TEXT="#Title#">
  <CFCOL HEADER="Orders" TEXT="#NumberFormat(CopiesOrdered)#">
</CFTABLE>

</BODY>

</HTML>
```

Now the report works the way a user would expect—all books are listed. A book that has gotten orders shows the number of copies that have been ordered. But a book that has not gotten any orders—like Moby Dick—still appears on the list. Figure 17.12 shows the new results.

N O T E If you are using Cold Fusion Studio, the Query Builder makes it a snap to change a join to an outer join. Simply right-click the small square on the line that represents the join, and choose the Select All Rows From option for the appropriate table from the pop-up menu. ■

Depending on the database you are using, there may be other syntax that you can use to specify an outer join. For instance, Microsoft SQLServer 6.5 allows you to use *= or =* instead of LEFT OUTER JOIN or RIGHT OUTER JOIN, respectively.

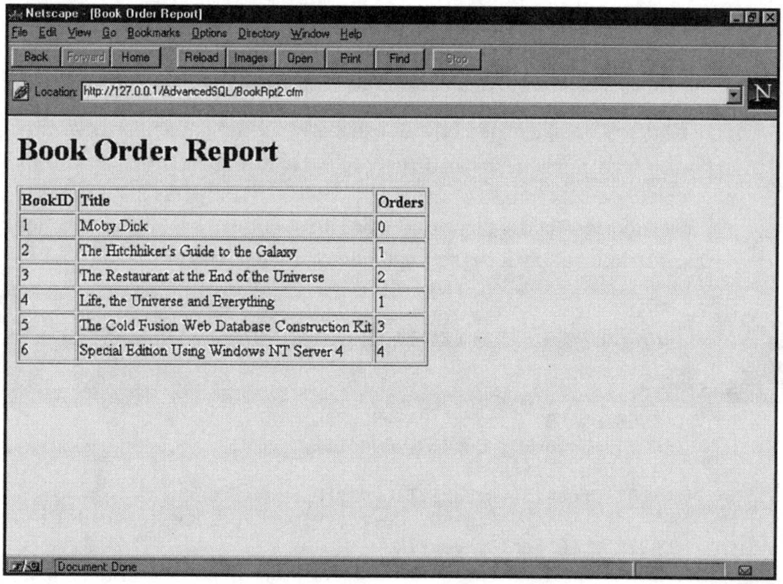

FIG. 17.12

The outer join version of your report shows all master records, even if there are no detail records.

Book Order Report

BookID	Title	Orders
1	Moby Dick	0
2	The Hitchhiker's Guide to the Galaxy	1
3	The Restaurant at the End of the Universe	2
4	Life, the Universe and Everything	1
5	The Cold Fusion Web Database Construction Kit	3
6	Special Edition Using Windows NT Server 4	4

In fact, you'll find that Cold Fusion Studio uses a slight variant on the "pure" OUTER JOIN syntax previously outlined. Actually, Studio is using the ODBC standard's oj command, which is designed to "get around" the fact that some databases want you to construct outer joins slightly differently.

Consult your database documentation for discussions of such alternate syntax, but make yourself aware of any changes that may take place when upgrades are released.

Gaining Extra Flexibility with Subqueries

SQL allows you to "nest" complete SQL statements within other SQL statements for various purposes. These "nested" queries are called *Subqueries*. Subqueries provide great flexibility and really allow the language to get into those "hard to reach" places. Subqueries can be introduced into a SQL statement in two basic ways:

- In the WHERE part of your SQL statement, to correlate data in different tables. Either IN or EXISTS is used to indicate the subquery's role.

- In the SELECT part of your SQL statement, to create an extra "computed" column.

In either case, the subquery itself is put inside parentheses, and can contain just about any valid SELECT statement. The subquery can use dot notation to refer to tables outside of the parentheses, but not vice-versa (the main statement cannot "reach in" and refer to tables inside the parentheses, but the subquery can "reach out" and refer to tables outside the parentheses).

You can insert a subquery into a larger SQL statement to cause the whole unit to find only certain records. Generally, you do this when the logic to select the records is fairly complex, or involves other tables. You include the subquery using the = sign, or the IN or EXISTS keywords.

Part
IV

Ch
17

Including a Subquery with the = Sign The simplest way to include a subquery in your SQL statements is with the = sign. Suppose you wanted to create an account summary page for individual customers, that shows the orders they've placed and so on.

In Chapter 8 you learned how to use WHERE to find particular rows in your tables. For instance, you could use WHERE OrderID = 3 to find all the rows for order number 3. But what if your template doesn't know the OrderID;, instead, it only has a CustomerID to go on? Well, you can put a subquery in the place of the 3. The subquery's job will be to "look up" the relevant OrderID and supply it to the main query. Take a look at Listing 17.19.

On the CD

Listing 17.19 CUSTRPT1.CFM—Customer Report Page that Uses a Subquery

```
<CFQUERY NAME="Report" DATASOURCE="A2Z">
  SELECT OrderID, BookID, Quantity
  FROM OrderItems
  WHERE OrderID = (SELECT OrderID FROM Orders
                   WHERE CustomerID = #URL.CustomerID#)
  ORDER BY OrderID, BookID
</CFQUERY>

<HTML>

<HEAD>
<TITLE>Orders By Customer</TITLE>
</HEAD>

<BODY>

<H1>Customer No. <CFOUTPUT>#URL.CustomerID#</CFOUTPUT></H1>

<CFTABLE QUERY="Report" COLHEADERS HTMLTABLE BORDER>
  <CFCOL HEADER="OrderID" TEXT="#OrderID#">
  <CFCOL HEADER="BookID" TEXT="#BookID#">
  <CFCOL HEADER="Quantity" TEXT="#Quantity#">
</CFTABLE>

</BODY>

</HTML>
```

If you pull the CustRpt1.cfm page (Listing 17.19) up in your browser, passing it a CustomerID parameter of 2 in the URL, you get the results shown in Figure 17.13.

Okay, the template seems to work correctly. Your database system starts from inside the parentheses and works its way out, so it evaluated subquery first. The subquery used the CustomerID of 2 to find a relevant OrderID number, which turned out to be 3. Your database system then plugged the number 3 into the main query, so the main query behaved just as if WHERE OrderID = 3 had been hard-coded into the template in the first place.

FIG. 17.13

This template uses a subquery to look up the OrderID number.

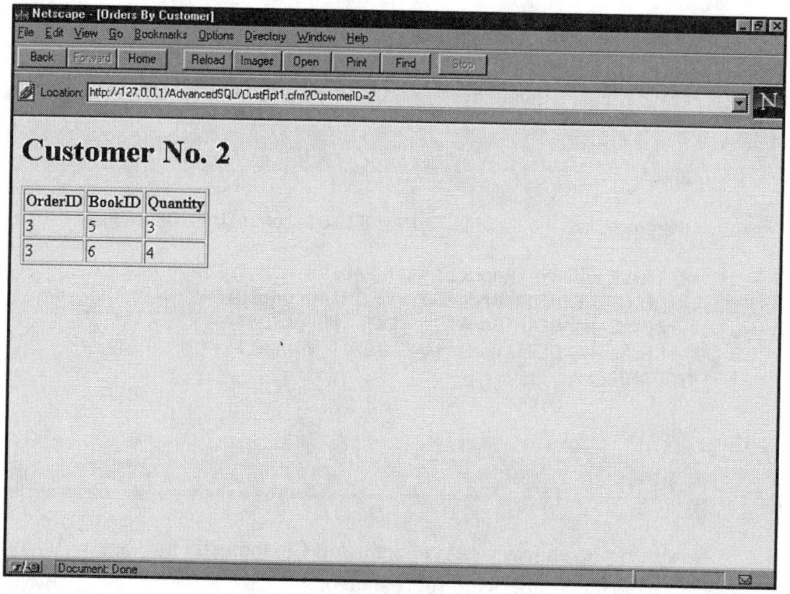

CAUTION

Whenever you use a subquery with the = sign, make sure that only one record will ever be found by the subquery. For instance, more than one OrderID would be found for CustomerID number 1, which would cause an error message to appear. Your code really should use the IN keyword instead, discussed in the following section.

Including a Subquery with the *IN* Keyword   Replace the = sign with the IN keyword to allow subqueries to return more than one value. By using IN instead of =, your database system is expecting any number of values from the subquery, rather than just one. Listing 17.20 introduces IN as the method of including the subquery.

Listing 17.20   CUSTRPT2.CFM—Including the Subquery with *IN* Instead of the = Sign

```
<CFQUERY NAME="Report" DATASOURCE="A2Z">
  SELECT OrderID, BookID, Quantity
  FROM OrderItems
  WHERE OrderID IN (SELECT OrderID FROM Orders
                    WHERE CustomerID = #URL.CustomerID#)
  ORDER BY OrderID, BookID
</CFQUERY>

<HTML>
```

continues

Listing 17.20 Continued

```
<HEAD>
<TITLE>Orders By Customer</TITLE>
</HEAD>

<BODY>

<H1>Customer No. <CFOUTPUT>#URL.CustomerID#</CFOUTPUT></H1>

<CFTABLE QUERY="Report" COLHEADERS HTMLTABLE BORDER>
  <CFCOL HEADER="OrderID" TEXT="#OrderID#">
  <CFCOL HEADER="BookID" TEXT="#BookID#">
  <CFCOL HEADER="Quantity" TEXT="#Quantity#">
</CFTABLE>

</BODY>

</HTML>
```

Now bring up your revised report using CustomerID number 1. As you can see in Figure 17.14, two OrderID numbers are represented.

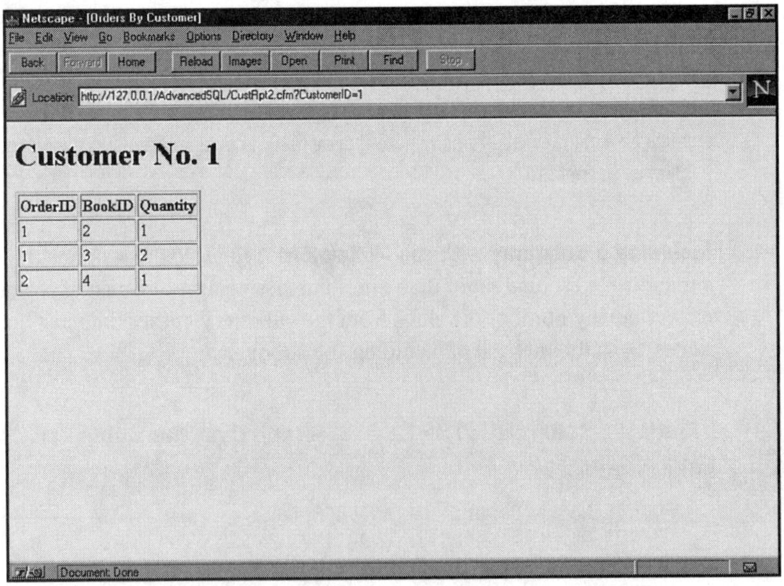

FIG. 17.14

When you introduce a subquery with IN instead of the = sign, it's okay for it to return multiple values.

N O T E You can also include a subquery with EXISTS instead of IN. The EXISTS query causes the database system to consider the main query first. Conceptually, you are asking your database system to move through all rows returned by the main query statement, testing to see if the subquery statement is true for each row as it goes. The following could be used in place of the SQL statement in Listing 17.20:

```
SELECT OrderID, BookID, Quantity
  FROM OrderItems o
  WHERE EXISTS (SELECT * FROM Orders
                WHERE CustomerID = #URL.CustomerID#
                AND OrderID = o.OrderID)
  ORDER BY OrderID, BookID ▪
```

Choosing the Opposite Set of Records with *NOT IN* or *NOT EXISTS*   You may be thinking that subqueries so far just look like a clunky alternative to joins. But using subqueries with IN or EXISTS gets more interesting when you use the NOT operator. The NOT operator does pretty much what you'd think—it causes the records that don't comply with the subquery to be affected.

The query in Listing 17.21 would return the titles of all books that the customer has *not* ordered. Figure 17.15 shows the results.

Part
IV
Ch
17

On the CD

Listing 17.21   CUSTRPT4.CFM—Getting the "Non-Matches" with *NOT IN*

```
<CFQUERY NAME="Report" DATASOURCE="A2Z">
  SELECT BookID, Title
  FROM Inventory o
  WHERE BookID NOT IN (SELECT BookID
                       FROM OrderItems
                       WHERE OrderID IN (SELECT OrderID
                                         FROM Orders
                                         WHERE CustomerID = #URL.CustomerID#) )
  ORDER BY BookID
</CFQUERY>

<HTML>

<HEAD>
<TITLE>Orders By Customer</TITLE>
</HEAD>

<BODY>

<H1>Customer No. <CFOUTPUT>#URL.CustomerID#</CFOUTPUT></H1>

<CFTABLE QUERY="Report" COLHEADERS HTMLTABLE BORDER>
  <CFCOL HEADER="BookID" TEXT="#BookID#">
  <CFCOL HEADER="Title" TEXT="#Title#">
</CFTABLE>

</BODY>

</HTML>
```

Note, also, that you're nesting your subqueries two levels deep here. Your database system starts at the innermost subquery and works its way out. First it performs the SELECT OrderID subquery and passes the results to the SELECT BookID subquery, which passes its results to the main query, which finally passes its results to Cold Fusion.

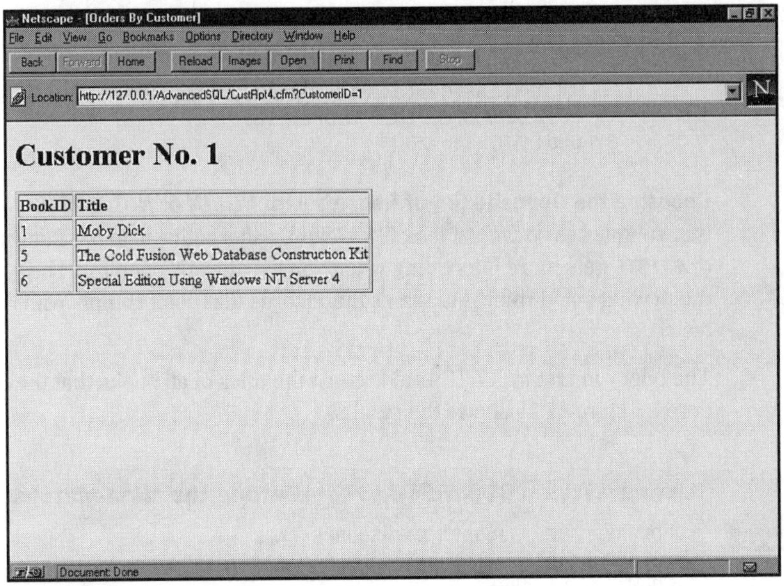

FIG. 17.15

Now you see the opposite list of books the ones the customer has not ordered.

> **TIP**
> You can also use the NOT keyword with EXISTS.

Using a Subquery to Create a New Calculated Value   Up to now, you've only used subqueries in the WHERE part of the main SQL statement. Subqueries can also be used in the SELECT part of the statement to produce a new, calculated value. Just like the aggregate functions you learned about at the beginning of this chapter, the values from subqueries included in the SELECT part of a query appear to Cold Fusion as if they were table columns. The name of the subqueried column is whatever name you make up with the AS keyword (you should recognize this use of AS from your work with aggregate functions as well).

For instance, you could use the syntax in Listing 17.22 to find the total amount of money collected from the sale of each book. Figure 17.16 shows the results.

Listing 17.22   CUSTRPT5.CFM—Using a Subquery in the *SELECT* List to Generate a New, Computed Column

```
<CFQUERY NAME="Report" DATASOURCE="A2Z">
  SELECT OrderID, OrderDate, (SELECT SUM(SalePrice)
                              FROM OrderItems
                              WHERE OrderID = o.OrderID) AS SalePrice_SUM
  FROM Orders o
  WHERE CustomerID = #URL.CustomerID#
</CFQUERY>

<HTML>

<HEAD>
```

```
<TITLE>Orders By Customer</TITLE>
</HEAD>

<BODY>

<H1>Customer No. <CFOUTPUT>#URL.CustomerID#</CFOUTPUT></H1>

<CFTABLE QUERY="Report" COLHEADERS HTMLTABLE BORDER>
  <CFCOL HEADER="OrderID" TEXT="#OrderID#">
  <CFCOL HEADER="Date" TEXT="#DateFormat(OrderDate)#">
  <CFCOL HEADER="Total Of Order" TEXT="#DollarFormat(SalePrice_SUM)#">
</CFTABLE>

</BODY>

</HTML>
```

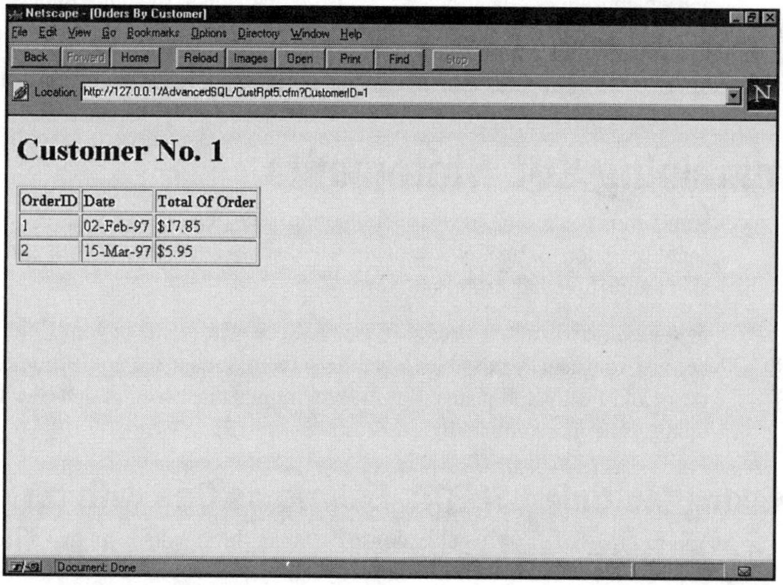

FIG. 17.16

The value computed by the subquery is included as a new "column" for each row from the main query.

Using a Subquery Instead of a Table Join As you can see, it's often possible to write a subquery that returns the same results as a table join. So when should you use which syntax? Unfortunately, there's no easy answer to this question.

In my opinion, using a table join is generally recommended over the equivalent subquery syntax, which is why joins were presented first. Joins will generally provide better performance in the majority of situations—especially as the number of values returned by the subquery increases over time as your database tables come to hold more and more data.

However, there are situations where a subquery will provide equal or better performance, especially if the number of values returned by the inner query is consistently going to be very small.

You may also encounter situations where the table join syntax turns out to be very messy and convoluted, but the equivalent subquery syntax is comparatively intuitive and straightforward.

Usually, simple lookups—like getting one ID number based on another ID number as you did in Listing 17.20—are perhaps better left to subqueries. But when you actually need to get information from more than one table at once, a table join is the way to go.

 TIP Deciding on using a join or a subquery is definitely a judgment call and it may often be best to consider (or try) both alternatives when in doubt. Keep in mind that the difference in performance, if any, may be so slight that either method could be used without any noticeable difference in how your application behaves overall.

In general, a sensible rule of thumb might be to use table joins unless your knowledge of your tables, indexes, and data allow you to construct a subquery that you know will run very quickly, and which returns relatively few rows in comparison to the outer query into which it is placed.

Also, try to think about what you are actually asking SQL to do for you. How hard is that going to be? Does one syntax take advantage of indexes that another does not?

Combining SQL Statements

Sometimes you'll want to write "compound" SQL statements that rely on one another to get something done. The next few pages will discuss using SELECT, INSERT, UPDATE, and DELETE statements together in various ways.

In general, it will not be *necessary* to use these statements in your Cold Fusion applications, because it is usually possible to get the same results using some kind of "looping" constructs in your Cold Fusion templates. But the techniques discussed in these sections can often get things done more efficiently.

Making Multiple *SELECT*s Behave as One with *UNION*

You can use SQL's UNION operator to combine the results from two different queries. Compared to joins and subqueries, UNION is pretty simple, because it doesn't have anything to do relationships between tables. It's simply about combining the results of two different SELECT statements. The SELECTs can be based on the same table, or different tables.

Say you were planning a holiday party, so you wanted to display the names of all employees and customers. You want them in alphabetical order by first name, which means that the employees will be freely intermixed with the customers. Listing 17.23 shows the code used to accomplish this, while Figure 17.17 shows the results.

Listing 17.23   EVERYONE.CFM—Using *UNION* to Combine Two Result Sets

```
<CFQUERY NAME="Report" DATASOURCE="A2Z">
  SELECT FirstName, LastName, Phone
  FROM Customers
```

```
    UNION
    SELECT FirstName, LastName, PhoneExtension
    FROM Employees
    ORDER BY FirstName, LastName
</CFQUERY>

<HTML>

<HEAD>
<TITLE>Invitation List</TITLE>
</HEAD>

<BODY>

<H1>Invitation List</H1>

<CFOUTPUT QUERY="Report">
  #FirstName# #LastName# - #Phone#<BR>
</CFOUTPUT>

</BODY>

</HTML>
```

Part
IV

Ch
17

FIG. 17.17
The ORDER BY sorts
the results of both
SELECT statements as
one unit.

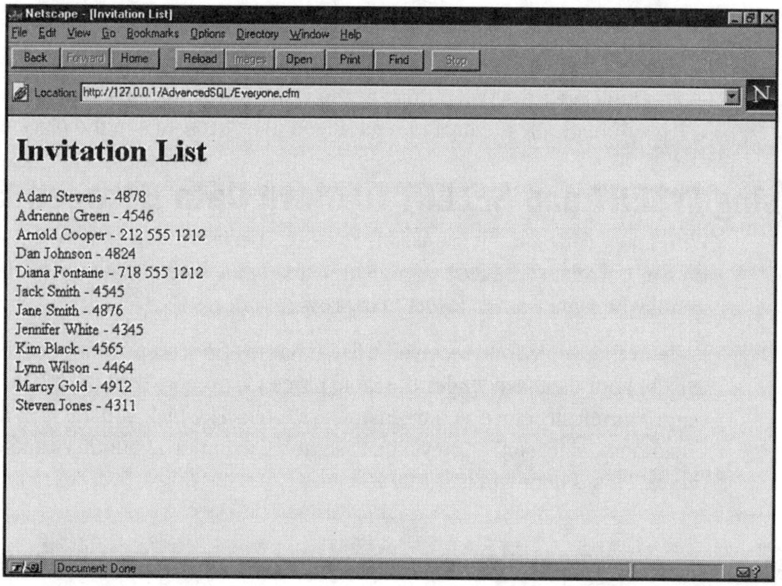

The first SELECT gets the names and phone numbers from the Customers table. The second SELECT gets the name and phone extensions from the Employees table. These two tables are then "stacked" on top of each other conceptually, with the first employee right after the last customer. This new mass of rows is then sorted —according to the ORDER BY clause—and returned to Cold Fusion. The column names FirstName, LastName, and Phone are available for your use in your Cold Fusion code.

N O T E Even though the phone numbers come from columns that have different names, the name from the first SELECT is the one that's available to Cold Fusion. If you were to try to refer to the #PhoneExtension# column in your code, you'd get an error message. ▦

When you are using UNION in your queries, the following rules apply:

- You can use more than one UNION in a SQL statement, so you can use more than two tables together.

- All the SELECT statements have to specify the same number of columns, even though the underlying column names and data don't have to be the same.

- The datatypes—Text, Numeric, Date, and so on—of the columns have to match. However, the text width or numeric precision of the columns may not need to match, depending on the type of database you're using. See your database documentation for details on this rule.

- The column names in the SELECT statements don't have to match. If they don't, the column names from the first SELECT will become the column names that appear in the combined output.

- You can't use the DISTINCT keyword at all.

- BLOB columns—like Memo columns in Access—can't be used.

- There should only be one ORDER BY statement—at the end—and it must only refer to columns names from the first SELECT statement.

- Duplicate rows (rows that are the same from more than one of the SELECTs) will be automatically eliminated, unless you use UNION ALL in the place of UNION.

Using *INSERT* and *SELECT* to Move Data Between Tables

With many databases, it is possible to use a special kind of INSERT statement that gets its data from a "correlated" SELECT statement instead of a VALUES clause. This technique is particularly useful when you want to insert many rows at once.

Pretend that you've just received a list of names from some other source. These new names exist in your database, under the table name CustomersToImport. CustomersToImport has the same column structure as our Customers table. The task at hand is to add the names to the Customers table, so that they'll be assigned CustomerID numbers and be available to our application. This is done in Listing 17.24.

On the CD

Listing 17.24   IMPORT.CFM—Using an *INSERT* with *SELECT*

```
<CFQUERY NAME="Report" DATASOURCE="A2Z">
  INSERT INTO Customers (Company, FirstName, MiddleInit, LastName,
 Address1, Address2, City, State, ZIP, Phone, EMail, CustomerSince)
    SELECT (Company, FirstName, MiddleInit, LastName, Address1, Address2,
 City, State, ZIP, Phone, EMail, #CreateODBCDateTime(Now())#)
    FROM CustomersToImport
</CFQUERY>
```

```
<HTML>

<HEAD>
<TITLE>Import</TITLE>
</HEAD>

<BODY>

<H1>Import</H1>

Import complete.

</BODY>

</HTML>
```

The SELECT part of the statement gets the data, and then "feeds" its results—however many rows that may be—directly into the INSERT part. Note that you don't specify the CustomerID number in either the INSERT or the SELECT parts, because you want your AutoNumber column to kick in and assign the next available CustomerID numbers to these new customers (see Chapter 7 for information about Access's AutoNumber columns).

Also note that the SELECT part can supply constant values as well as table columns—in this example, the CustomerSince column is supplied with the current date, courtesy of Cold Fusion's Now() function.

The INSERT SELECT syntax in Listing 17.24 is a welcome alternative to retrieving all the data with a CFQUERY, and then INSERTing it row-by-row into the new table with a CFLOOP. Because SQL's SELECT statement is so flexible, you can use the INSERT SELECT technique in more complex ways as well. All that's required is that the number of values called for by the INSERT part match the number of columns supplied by the SELECT part, and that the datatypes match up. The SELECT part can contain joins or subqueries, so you can fairly easily create a query where correlated rows from two or more tables are inserted into another table. Listing 9.4 in Chapter 9, "SQL Data Manipulation," provides an example of this.

Using *UPDATE* or *DELETE* with Subqueries

As you learned in Chapter 8 the UPDATE statement can be used to change the values of particular columns in a database table.

SQL allows you to make correlated updates, by including a subquery in the WHERE part of an UPDATE query. Only the rows found by the subquery are updated. The rules for including the subquery in the WHERE clause of an UPDATE statement are the same as for including one in the WHERE clause of a SELECT statement—which means that you can use IN, EXISTS, or the = sign to include the subquery.

Listing 17.25 shows such a UPDATE / subquery combination in action. First, the subquery finds the relevant rows. Then the UPDATE "fires" on those rows, increasing the Pages column by one for each book that has been ordered by Customer number 2. Figure 17.18 shows the results.

On the CD

Listing 17.25 ADJUST.CFM—Using UPDATE with a Subquery

```
<!--- GET THE "BEFORE" INFORMATION --->
<CFQUERY NAME="Before" DATASOURCE="A2Z">
  SELECT * FROM Inventory
</CFQUERY>

<!--- MAKE THE CHANGE --->
<CFQUERY NAME="Report" DATASOURCE="A2Z">
  UPDATE Inventory
  SET Pages = Pages + 1
  WHERE BookID IN (SELECT BookID
                    FROM OrderItems
                    WHERE OrderID IN (SELECT OrderID
                                      FROM Orders
                                      WHERE CustomerID = 2))
</CFQUERY>

<!--- GET THE "AFTER" INFORMATION --->
<CFQUERY NAME="After" DATASOURCE="A2Z">
  SELECT * FROM Inventory
</CFQUERY>

<HTML>

<HEAD>
<TITLE>Inventory Adjustment</TITLE>
</HEAD>

<BODY>

<B>Before</B><BR>

<CFTABLE QUERY="Before" COLHEADERS HTMLTABLE BORDER>
  <CFCOL HEADER="BookID" TEXT="#BookID#">
  <CFCOL HEADER="Title" TEXT="#Title#">
  <CFCOL HEADER="Pages" TEXT="#Pages#">
</CFTABLE>

<BR><B>After</B><BR>

<CFTABLE QUERY="After" COLHEADERS HTMLTABLE BORDER>
  <CFCOL HEADER="BookID" TEXT="#BookID#">
  <CFCOL HEADER="Title" TEXT="#Title#">
  <CFCOL HEADER="Pages" TEXT="#Pages#">
</CFTABLE>

</BODY>

</HTML>
```

Similarly, you can also create a DELETE statement that uses a subquery to choose the rows that get deleted. For instance, by replacing the SQL code in the Report CFQUERY from Listing 17.25 with the SQL in Listing 17.26, you would cause the code to *delete* all the rows that had been ordered by customer number 2.

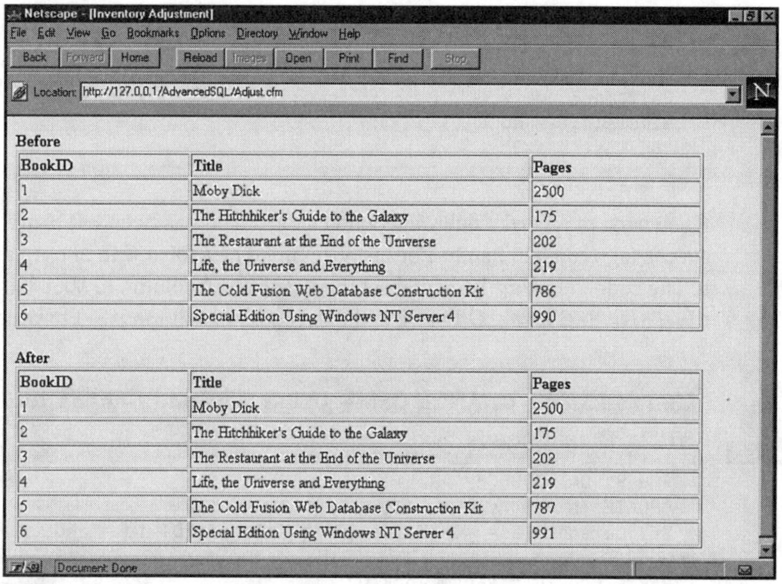

Before

BookID	Title	Pages
1	Moby Dick	2500
2	The Hitchhiker's Guide to the Galaxy	175
3	The Restaurant at the End of the Universe	202
4	Life, the Universe and Everything	219
5	The Cold Fusion Web Database Construction Kit	786
6	Special Edition Using Windows NT Server 4	990

After

BookID	Title	Pages
1	Moby Dick	2500
2	The Hitchhiker's Guide to the Galaxy	175
3	The Restaurant at the End of the Universe	202
4	Life, the Universe and Everything	219
5	The Cold Fusion Web Database Construction Kit	787
6	Special Edition Using Windows NT Server 4	991

FIG. 17.18
Subqueries can be used to "drive" updates.

Listing 17.26 Using *DELETE* with a Subquery

```
DELETE FROM Inventory
  WHERE BookID IN (SELECT BookID
                   FROM OrderItems
                   WHERE OrderID IN (SELECT OrderID
                                     FROM Orders
                                     WHERE CustomerID = 2))
```

Working with *NULL* Values

One of the most confusing concepts in SQL is the idea of a null value. A null value indicates that there is literally *nothing* recorded in the table for that row and column. For instance, consider the `CustomerSince` column of the Customers table. Obviously, if you know this information, you'll record it here. But if you don't, you probably want to leave the column blank, so you'll set it to `NULL`.

To indicate that you want to set a column to a null value, use the keyword `NULL` where you would normally provide the value. So, to update your records, you might use the SQL statement in Listing 17.27. Note that quotes should never be used around the `NULL` keyword, even when dealing with a character-type field. The only time when you'd want to put quotes around the word `NULL` would be if you literally wanted to store the word "NULL" in your database, which is very unlikely.

Listing 17.27 Setting Columns to *NULL*

```
UPDATE Customers SET
  CustomerSince = NULL,
  MiddleInit = NULL
WHERE CustID = 3
```

If you need to record a null value when a form field has been left blank, Cold Fusion's CFIF and CFELSE tags come in handy. For instance, imagine a form with BookID and CategoryID fields on it. The code in Listing 17.28 will set the CategoryID column to NULL if the user leaves the CategoyID field blank. Otherwise, the CategoryID column is set to whatever the user typed in.

On the CD

Listing 17.28 CHANGE.CFM—Using *CFIF* and *CFELSE* to Allow for Setting of *NULLs* Conditionally

```
<CFQUERY DATASOURCE="A2Z">
  UPDATE Inventory
  SET CategoryID = <CFIF Trim(Form.CategoryID) is "">NULL
➥<CFELSE>#Form.CategoryID#</CFIF>
  WHERE BookID = #Form.BookID#
</CFQUERY>

<HTML>

<HEAD>
<TITLE>Record Updated</TITLE>
</HEAD>

<BODY>

<H2>Record Updated.</H2>

</BODY>

</HTML>
```

SQL statements that deal with null values can give unexpected results, because a null value is not equal to anything. Pretend for a moment that there is a row in your Inventory table that has NULL for the CategoryID and NULL for the Title. None of the SQL statements in Listing 17.29 will "find" such a row. You'd probably expect this from the first one, but the rest may surprise you.

Listing 17.29 None of These Will Find the Row that You Updated in Listing 17.30

```
SELECT * FROM Inventory
WHERE CategoryID > 1

SELECT * FROM Inventory
```

```
WHERE CategoryID < 1

SELECT * FROM Inventory
WHERE Title = ""

SELECT * FROM Inventory
WHERE Title <> "Moby Dick"
```

Note that NULL is not less than or greater than any number. It's also not the same thing as an empty string (" "). Perhaps most surprising, it is not even *unequal* to anything, as the last of the four examples illustrates. NULL values are also excluded from the calculations that aggregate functions like Count(*column*) make. In short, NULLs fail any test.

In fact, with database systems that handle nulls absolutely correctly—like Microsoft SQL Server 6.5—even the following SQL statement will not find the record, because a null value by definition must fail any equality test, even against another null value:

```
SELECT * FROM Inventory
WHERE Title = NULL
```

Instead, you need to use the following SQL Statement, which *would* find the record:

```
SELECT * FROM Inventory
WHERE Title IS NULL
```

Therefore, to get all books except *Moby Dick*, you will need to use the tedious and counter-intuitive SQL statement shown here:

```
SELECT * FROM Inventory
WHERE (Title <> 'Bill' OR Title IS NULL)
```

The lesson? If possible, try to avoid null values in your tables, unless you specifically want to represent the fact that a piece of data hasn't been recorded. When in doubt, consider that it often makes sense to allow null values in numeric columns (there is a difference between a CategoryID of 0 and no CategoryID at all), but with text-type columns they almost always lead to trouble (rarely would you encounter a real-world difference between a book that has no title and a book whose title has not been recorded). Keep in mind that when you add a new column to a table, all of the rows in that new column probably hold null values. If you must allow null values, just be careful, especially with character-type columns, and especially when using such a column in a WHERE clause.

The situation is further complicated by the fact that Cold Fusion doesn't have the concept of a null value—only SQL does. Once an SQL statement runs in a Cold Fusion template, if you refer to a column that happens to be null, Cold Fusion will treat it just like an empty string (" "). Which means that the following CFIF code will work, even if the Title column is null in the actual table:

```
<CFIF #Title# is "">
  The value is either null, or just set to an empty string ("").
  We can't tell which from a Cold Fusion template.
</CFIF>
```

Using Views to Simplify and Reuse Your Queries

Many database systems support *views*. A view is a SELECT statement that is given a name and stored as a permanent part of your database, just as your tables are a permanent part of your database. Once a view has been created, it can be thought of as a "virtual table" that can be used in most of the same ways that a normal table can.

The syntax for creating a view is quite simple: just type CREATE VIEW *viewname* AS, followed by virtually any SELECT statement.

TIP

While the name of the view can be anything you want, you may want to follow my lead and use a lowercase v as the first letter, so you can easily distinguish your views from your tables.

Listing 17.30 shows an SQL statement that would create a view of the entire Customers table. *This is not a statement that you would likely want to include in a Cold Fusion template,* because it only needs to be executed once. Instead, you would execute it from your database natively, such as from Microsoft Access itself, or from a tool like Microsoft Query, Cold Fusion Studio, or Microsoft SQL Enterprise Manager.

Listing 17.30   Creating a Simple View

```
CREATE VIEW vInventory AS
SELECT * FROM Inventory
```

Now that the vInventory view has been defined, you can use it in your Cold Fusion application in the same way as the Inventory table. You could do a search-and-replace, changing Inventory to vInventory in all of your templates, and everything should continue to work. In short, Inventory and vInventory have essentially become synonyms. But why would you do such a thing? Well, you probably wouldn't. The example in Listing 17.31 makes a little more sense.

Listing 17.31   Creating a More Practical View

```
CREATE VIEW vCompInventory AS
SELECT * FROM Inventory
WHERE CategoryID = 3
```

Now you can refer to vCompInventory in your Cold Fusion templates and you'll automatically only be "talking about" the books in category number 3 (the computer books). SELECT statements will only return rows about computer books, and INSERT statements will not work if the CategoryID of the new row is not 3. In addition, UPDATE statements will only affect computer books. For instance, you could show that all computer books had sold out with the SQL statement in Listing 17.32, which would only change the NumberInStock column for the computer books, even though there is no WHERE clause.

Listing 17.32 Running an Update Against a View

```
UPDATE vCompInventory
SET NumberInStock = 0
```

By using vCompInventory in your application, you do more than merely save yourself from having to type WHERE CategoryID = 3 over and over again. You have also allowed the whole issue of the CategoryID to become irrelevant as you build your application. In fact, if the database tables you're using are administered by another person, vCompInventory may be all you have to develop with. You may not even know that the Inventory table exists at all. This might make lots of sense if your project was to develop a shopping cart system for computer books only. You could rest easy, knowing that there would be no chance for any other types of books to be revealed just because of a programming oversight on your part.

> **TIP**
> If you're working with Microsoft Access, you will notice that after you use CREATE VIEW, the new view becomes visible in the actual Access program as a Query. The reverse is also true. If you create a Query from within Access, it will be available as a View to Cold Fusion.

This strategy would really pay off later if the business decided to change its categorizing system. For instance, the books handled by the entire application could be changed just by changing the definition of the view. Listing 17.33 shows an SQL statement that would create an alternative vCompInventory view.

Listing 17.33 Changing the Scope of the Application by Editing Only the View

```
CREATE VIEW vCompInventory AS
SELECT * FROM Inventory
WHERE (CategoryID = 3 OR
       Title LIKE '%Active Server Pages%')
```

This changes the scope of the entire Cold Fusion application, without editing a single line of Cold Fusion code. As far as your application is concerned, nothing has changed. However, all of a sudden, books about Active Server Pages would be included, even if they were in category number 2 (Humor) instead of category number 3 (Computers).

By using views to separate your programming tasks from real-world business rules whenever possible, you can save yourself a lot of time and make your code much more abstracted and reusable.

Restricting the View to Certain Columns

You can also create views with more complex SELECT statements. The SQL statement in Listing 17.34 would make only the BookID and Title available in the view. The rating, pricing, and other columns would be inaccessible.

Listing 17.34   View that Accesses Only Certain Columns of the Base Table

```
CREATE VIEW vCompInventory AS
SELECT BookID, Title FROM Inventory
WHERE CategoryID = 3
```

Using More than One Table

Because a view can be based on just about any SELECT statement, you can create views that are based on more than one table by using the various join and subquery techniques you've learned in this chapter.

For instance, the SQL statement in Listing 17.35 would create a view that will allow you to see how many orders a customer has placed without having to bother joining the tables in each query.

Listing 17.35   Creating a View Based on More Than One Table

```
CREATE VIEW vCustomers AS
SELECT CustomerID, Company, (SELECT COUNT(*) FROM Orders
                    WHERE CustomerID = c.CustomerID) AS OrdersPlaced
FROM Customers c
```

Now, SELECT statements issued against the view will automatically contain an OrdersPlaced column that will always reflect the correct number of orders that each customer has made, even though there is no such column in Customers and you are not manually incrementing any kind of counter column anywhere in your application. Listing 17.36 shows the Cold Fusion code that would use the vCustomers view created by Listing 17.35. Figure 17.19 shows the results.

On the CD

Listing 17.36   CUSTRPT6—Putting the *vCustomers* View to Use

```
<CFQUERY NAME="Report" DATASOURCE="A2Z">
  SELECT * FROM vCustomers
</CFQUERY>

<HTML>

<HEAD>
<TITLE>Orders By Customer</TITLE>
</HEAD>

<BODY>

<H1>New York</H1>

<CFTABLE QUERY="Report" COLHEADERS HTMLTABLE BORDER>
  <CFCOL HEADER="CustomerID" TEXT="#CustomerID#">
  <CFCOL HEADER="Company" TEXT="#Company#">
```

```
    <CFCOL HEADER="Orders Made" TEXT="#NumberFormat(OrdersPlaced)#">
</CFTABLE>

</BODY>

</HTML>
```

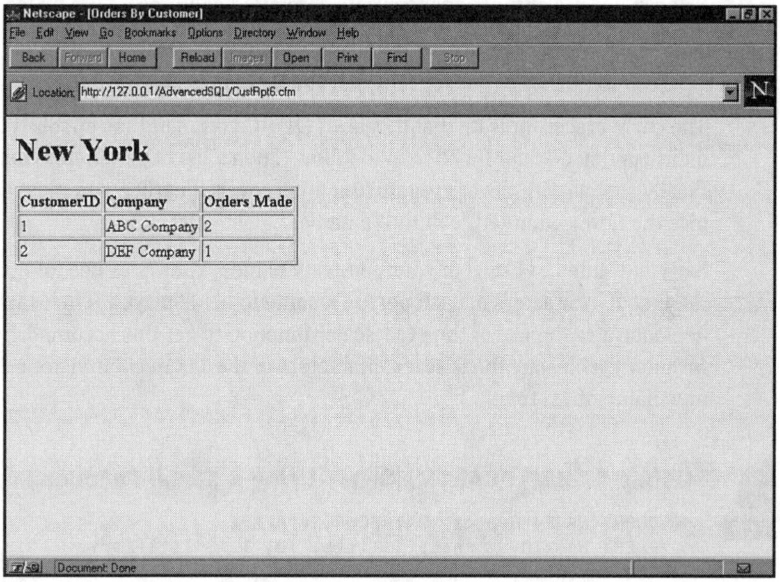

FIG. 17.19
Once a multi-table view is created, using SELECT is a simple task.

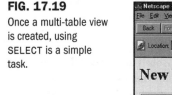

NOTE As you can see, views based on more than one table can be quite useful, but the view will be considered read-only by most database systems. SELECT statements will be allowed, but INSERT and UPDATE statements will generate error messages (which means that CFINSERT and CFUPDATE tags will also fail). ▨

Using Scalar Functions to Manipulate Data Row-By-Row

Occasionally, you may want to create queries that do things like manipulate dates or perform arithmetic on your data. The ODBC standard defines a number of date, time, numeric, and string functions for your use. These are called *scalar functions*. Unfortunately, not all of them are supported by every type of database.

ODBC says that if the database supports a function *natively*, it should be mapped to the appropriate ODBC function to provide some common ground between systems—but nothing's required here. Most databases support only a subset of the complete list. A complete reference on scalar function syntax can be found in Appendix E of the *Microsoft ODBC SDK Programmer's Reference* (visit **http://www.microsoft.com/odbc** to get the reference).

Part
IV

Ch
17

N O T E There are many more scalar functions than those listed in this book. The number of scalar functions supported varies from one driver to another. Consult the documentation of the supplier of your ODBC driver for a complete list of supported functionality. ▪

Using Scalar Functions in the *SELECT* List and the *WHERE* Clause

You can use scalar functions to create computed columns on-the-fly for each row that your query returns. To use these functions in your queries, use the following syntax:

```
{ fn function-name(parameter, parameter ... ) }
```

The curly braces indicate that this is an ODBC command (as opposed to native SQL). The fn indicates that a scalar function is to follow. Then a list of parameters follows, in parentheses. Finally, just as with the aggregate functions covered earlier, you must use the AS keyword to give the new, computed "column" a name.

Say you wanted to list all of your company names. Your boss has told you that she only wants the first 10 characters of each person's name to be displayed. The example in Listing 17.37 demonstrates the use of the LEFT scalar function to get this accomplished. For each row of the Inventory table, just the first ten characters of the Title column are returned—with the column name of TitlePart.

On the CD

Listing 17.37 SCALAR1.CFM—Using a Scalar Function in the *SELECT* List

```
<CFQUERY NAME="Report" DATASOURCE="A2Z">
  SELECT BookID, { fn LEFT(Title, 10) } AS TitlePart
  FROM Inventory
</CFQUERY>

<HTML>

<HEAD>
<TITLE>Scalar Functions</TITLE>
</HEAD>

<BODY>

<H1>SUBSTRING Scalar Function</H1>

<CFTABLE QUERY="Report" COLHEADERS HTMLTABLE BORDER>
  <CFCOL HEADER="BookID" TEXT="#BookID#">
  <CFCOL HEADER="Title" TEXT="#TitlePart#">
</CFTABLE>

</BODY>

</HTML>
```

Other scalar functions would be used in the same way. Figure 17.20 shows the results.

FIG. 17.20
ODBC's scalar functions provide basic text-manipulation capabilities.

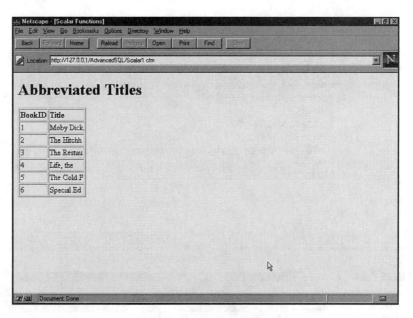

You can also use scalar functions in the WHERE part of your query to select rows based on a calculated condition.

Say you needed to display all the books that were published during the month of November—any November, regardless of the year. Listing 17.38 shows how to accomplish this with the MONTH scalar function. Conceptually, the MONTH function "asks" every row what the month "part" of the value in the PublicationDate column is. Only the rows that "answer" with the number 11 will be returned to Cold Fusion, as shown in Figure 17.21.

On the CD

Listing 17.38   SCALAR2.CFM—Using a Scalar Function in the *WHERE* Part of a Query

```
<CFQUERY NAME="Report" DATASOURCE="A2Z">
  SELECT BookID, Title, PublicationDate
  FROM Inventory
  WHERE { fn MONTH(PublicationDate) } = 11
</CFQUERY>

<HTML>

<HEAD>
<TITLE>Scalar Functions</TITLE>
</HEAD>

<BODY>
```

continues

Listing 17.38 Continued

```
<H1>Published in the month of November</H1>

<TABLE BORDER>
  <TR><TH>BookID</TH><TH>Title</TH><TH>Publication Date</TH></TR>
  <CFOUTPUT QUERY="Report">
    <TR>
      <TD>#BookID#</TD>
      <TD>#Title#</TD>
      <TD>#DateFormat(PublicationDate, 'mmmm, yyyy')#</TD>
    </TR>
  </CFOUTPUT>
</TABLE>

</BODY>

</HTML>
```

FIG. 17.21

Scalar functions can be very useful in the WHERE part of a query.

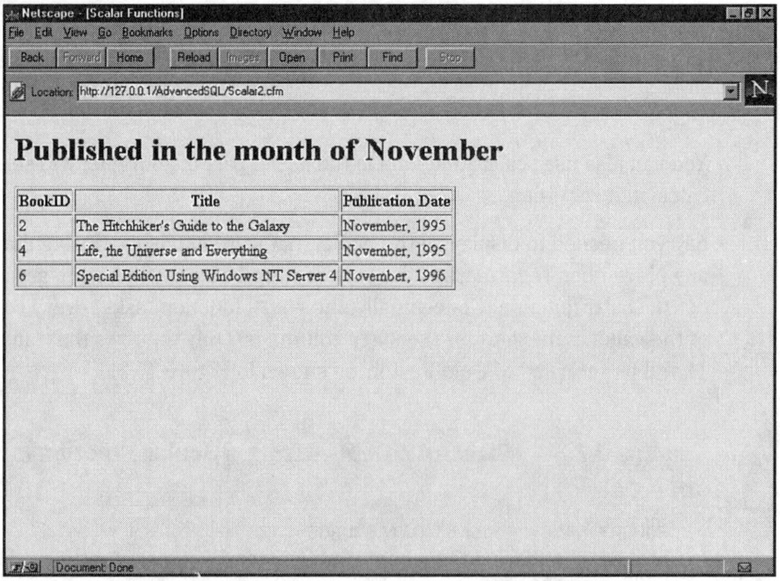

Using Scalar Functions Instead of Cold Fusion Functions

In general, I recommend using Cold Fusion's functions rather than scalar functions in your queries. They're usually easier to use, more versatile, and easier to understand. Also, by using Cold Fusion functions, you won't run into incompatibilities between differing types of databases. And it's just that much less to learn and think about. Who wants to memorize the parameters for both sets of functions?

Sometimes you'll want to use scalar functions, though. To demonstrate when it's a good idea and when it's not, consider the two examples given so far.

My first example used a scalar function in the SELECT list to return a truncated version of the Title column. It would be just as easy—if not easier—to retrieve the Title column with ordinary SELECT syntax. Then Cold Fusion's LEFT function could be used to get the first 10 characters, as shown in Listing 17.39.

Listing 17.39 SCALAR1A.CFM—Getting the Same Results Without Scalar Functions

```
<CFQUERY NAME="Report" DATASOURCE="A2Z">
  SELECT BookID, Title
  FROM Inventory
</CFQUERY>

<HTML>

<HEAD>
<TITLE>Without Scalar Functions</TITLE>
</HEAD>

<BODY>

<H1>Abbreviated Titles</H1>

<CFTABLE QUERY="Report" COLHEADERS HTMLTABLE BORDER>
  <CFCOL HEADER="BookID" TEXT="#BookID#">
  <CFCOL HEADER="Title" TEXT="#Left(Title, 10)#">
</CFTABLE>

</BODY>

</HTML>
```

This "Cold Fusion Function" approach would produce the same exact results in the browser as the "scalar function" approach did (see Figure 17.20). The only difference is *when* the titles are truncated. The scalar function approach does it at the ODBC level—before Cold Fusion ever gets the data. Okay, so if there are tons of rows, the scalar function approach may be slightly more efficient—particularly if the data resides on a different machine than Cold Fusion—because the full text of the titles never have to be retrieved from the datasource. But the real lesson is that you can—and in most cases should—use Cold Fusion functions instead of scalar functions in SELECT lists. As a general practice, they're more flexible and database-independent.

In contrast, my second scalar function example is quite different. The scalar function is in the WHERE part of the query and is doing something that Cold Fusion really can't do so efficiently. Rather than altering the way the rows are returned, it's making decisions about which rows to return—*without sending the "bad rows" back to Cold Fusion.*

To get the same effect without the use of scalar functions, you'd have to SELECT all of the rows, and then test each row one-at-a-time in a CFOUTPUT block, as shown in Listing 17.40.

Listing 17.40   SCALAR2A.CFM—Compare with Listing 17.38

```
<CFQUERY NAME="Report" DATASOURCE="A2Z">
  SELECT BookID, Title, PublicationDate
  FROM Inventory
</CFQUERY>

<HTML>

<HEAD>
<TITLE>Scalar Functions</TITLE>
</HEAD>

<BODY>

<H1>Published in the month of November</H1>

<TABLE BORDER>
  <TR><TH>BookID</TH><TH>Title</TH><TH>Publication Date</TH></TR>
  <CFOUTPUT QUERY="Report">
  <CFIF Month(PublicationDate) is 11>
    <TR>
      <TD>#BookID#</TD>
      <TD>#Title#</TD>
      <TD>#DateFormat(PublicationDate, 'mmmm, yyyy')#</TD>
    </TR>
  </CFIF>
  </CFOUTPUT>
</TABLE>

</BODY>

</HTML>
```

In this second case, the "Cold Fusion Function" approach is less efficient—you're making your application do a lot of extra work. First off, you have to collect every single row in the table—even though you know, as a developer, that only around one-twelfth of the rows are going to be displayed in the end. Then you have Cold Fusion test every row in the table individually to see if it passes the test. It'll work, but it's much less efficient than letting the scalar function do all the work for you in the WHERE clause.

So, in general, scalar functions aren't generally needed in your SELECT lists. However, do consider using them in a WHERE clause if you need to retrieve data based on some kind of calculation that needs to be performed on each row individually.

A Short List of Scalar Functions

Table 17.2, is a summary of scalar functions supported by the Microsoft "Desktop" family of ODBC drivers that shipped with Cold Fusion 3.1 (Access, Paradox, FoxPro, Text, dBASE, Excel). These are not the only scalar functions defined by ODBC—just the ones supported by the desktop drivers. Drivers for other database systems—and drivers from third-party vendors like Visigenic and Intersolv—may provide support for more (or different) functions.

Table 17.2 Scalar Function Quick Reference

Scalar Function	What it Returns	Similar to CF Expression
CONVERT (value, datatype)	Value converted to datatype.	
CONCAT (string1, string)	String1 concatenation with String2.	string1 & string2
LCASE(string)	String converted to lowercase.	LCase(string)
LEFT(string, count)	First count characters of string.	Left(string, count)
LENGTH(string)	Number of characters in string.	Len(string)
LOCATE(substring, string [, start])	Position of substring in string [after start].	Find (substring, string [, start])
LTRIM(string)	String without leading.	LTrim(string)
RIGHT(string, count)	Last count characters of string.	Right(string, count)
RTRIM(string)	String without trailing spaces.	RTrim(string)
SUBSTRING(string, start, count)	Count characters of string after start.	Mid(string, start, count)
UCASE(string)	String converted to uppercase.	UCase(string)
CURDATE()	The current date.	DateFormat(Now())
CURTIME()	The current time.	TimeFormat(Now())
DAYOFMONTH(date)	The day (between 1 and 31).	Day(date)
DAYOFWEEK(date)	The day (between 1 and 7).	DayOfWeek(date)
MONTH(date)	The month (between 1 and 12).	Month(date)
YEAR(date)	The year.	Year(date)
MOD(integer1, integer2)	Remainder of integer1.	integer1 MOD

Datatypes:

SQL_BIGINT	SQL_INTERVAL_YEAR
SQL_INTERVAL_HOUR_TO_MINUTE	SQL_TYPE_TIME
SQL_BINARY	SQL_INTERVAL_YEAR_TO_MONTH
SQL_INTERVAL_HOUR_TO_SECOND	SQL_TYPE_TIMESTAMP
SQL_BIT	SQL_INTERVAL_DAY
SQL_INTERVAL_MINUTE_TO_SECOND	SQL_TINYINT
SQL_CHAR	SQL_INTERVAL_HOUR
SQL_LONGVARBINARY	SQL_VARBINARY
SQL_DECIMAL	SQL_INTERVAL_MINUTE
SQL_LONGVARCHAR	SQL_VARCHAR
SQL_DOUBLE	SQL_INTERVAL_SECOND
SQL_NUMERIC	SQL_WCHAR
SQL_FLOAT	SQL_INTERVAL_DAY_TO_HOUR
SQL_REAL	SQL_WLONGVARCHAR
SQL_INTEGER	SQL_INTERVAL_DAY_TO_MINUTE
SQL_SMALLINT	SQL_WVARCHAR
SQL_INTERVAL_MONTH	SQL_INTERVAL_DAY_TO_SECOND
SQL_TYPE_DATE	

Packaging Chunks of SQL Code into Stored Procedures

Most server-based database systems support *stored procedures*. A stored procedure is a "chunk" of SQL code that's given a name and stored as a part of your database, just as your tables are stored as part of your database. Once the stored procedure has been created, you need merely refer to it by name to run the SQL code.

> **CAUTION**
>
> When you start basing your applications on stored procedures instead of "normal" queries, you introduce a new level of dependency, complexity, and abstraction to your code. So don't fool around with stored procedures until you've gotten pretty comfortable with Cold Fusion and the advanced SQL syntax found elsewhere in this chapter.

SQL stored procedures are similar in many ways to CFML Custom Tags, which are discussed in Chapter 33, "Custom Tags." The following are the similarities:

- Both allow you to store chunks of code for later use.
- Both are compiled the first time they are run to improve performance.

- Both allow *parameters* to be established so that you can pass data into the code you've defined.

- Most importantly, both provide you with a powerful mechanism to "wrap up" complex chunks of code into little packages of functionality that get the job done on their own, thus making your application more modular, reusable, and perhaps easier to maintain.

N O T E Support for stored procedures is a relatively high-end feature, generally supported only by server-based database solutions like Microsoft SQLServer, Sybase, Oracle, InterBase, and so on. File-based databases generally do not support stored procedures. ■

Creating a stored procedure is fairly simple. Just type **CREATE PROCEDURE** *procedurename* **AS**, where *procedurename* is the name that you want to use when executing the stored procedure from your Cold Fusion templates. Then type the SQL statements that you want to store as *procedurename*.

Take a look at the SQL code in Listing 17.41, which creates a very simple stored procedure called ListInventory. *This is not a statement that you would likely want to include in a Cold Fusion template,* since it only needs to be executed once. Instead, you would execute it from your database natively, such as from Microsoft Access itself, or from a tool like Microsoft Query, Cold Fusion Studio, or Microsoft SQL Enterprise Manager.

Part

IV

Ch

17

Listing 17.41   Creating a Simple Stored Procedure

```
CREATE PROCEDURE ListInventory AS
  SELECT BookID, Title, Publisher
  FROM Inventory
```

N O T E The syntax for dealing with stored procedures is not nearly as standardized as the syntax for other SQL operations. It's just not possible to cover stored procedures for every database system out there. Because of its popularity, examples in this chapter use the Microsoft SQLServer syntax for creating stored procedures. While the general concepts will be the same, there may be minor differences in the CREATE PROCEDURE (or equivalent) syntax you can use to create and use stored procedures with your database system. ■

Now the SELECT statement in Listing 17.41 is stored on your database server under the name of ListInventory. Whenever you execute the stored procedure from your Cold Fusion templates, the server will respond by running the SELECT statement and returning the rows back to Cold Fusion, just as if you had placed the SELECT statement itself in a CFQUERY tag.

Using the Stored Procedure in Your Cold Fusion Template

To execute the stored procedure from Listing 17.41 in a Cold Fusion template, use the syntax shown in Listing 17.42. Because different database systems have different syntaxes for executing stored procedure, the ODBC standard includes a CALL command as a "common ground" that should work with any database system that supports stored procedures.

Listing 17.42   Calling the Stored Procedure from a *CFQUERY*

```
<CFQUERY NAME="Report" DATASOURCE="A2Z">
  { CALL ListInventory }
</CFQUERY>

<HTML>

<HEAD>
<TITLE>Books and Publishers</TITLE>
</HEAD>

<BODY>

<H1>Books and Publishers</H1>

<CFTABLE QUERY="Report" COLHEADERS HTMLTABLE BORDER>
  <CFCOL HEADER="BookID" TEXT="#BookID#">
  <CFCOL HEADER="Title" TEXT="#Title#">
  <CFCOL HEADER="Publisher" TEXT="#Publisher#">
</CFTABLE>

</BODY>

</HTML>
```

Here, you use the CALL command to run your ListInventory stored procedure. Notice the use of the curly braces, indicating that you are expecting ODBC to translate the command into the database system's native syntax that executes the stored procedure. In short, the syntax shown in the listing simply tells the database server to run the stored procedure that you created earlier. Once the CFQUERY executes, you can use the data in your Cold Fusion template just as if you were using ListInventory's SELECT statement directly. Figure 17.22 shows the results.

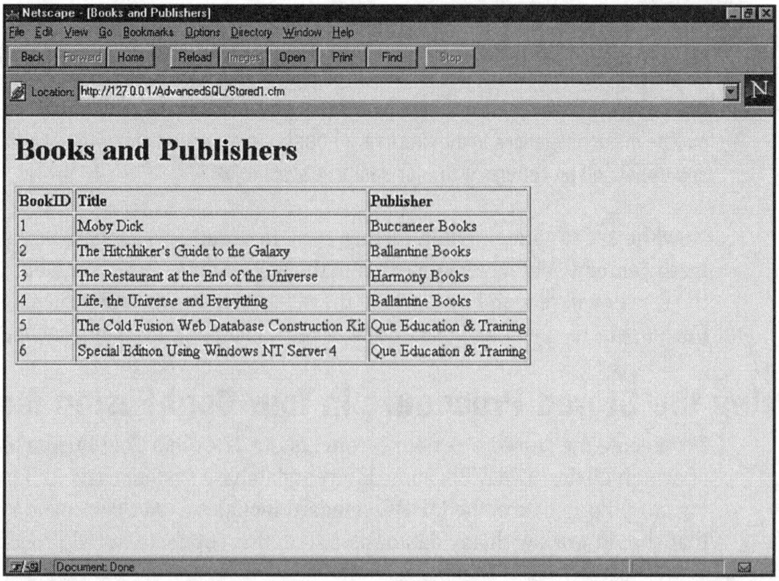

FIG. 17.22

After you execute a stored procedure in a CFQUERY, you can use its output just as you would any SQL statement.

N O T E   The above syntax uses ODBC's CALL command to run the procedure. Whenever you see curly braces in a SQL statement, that indicates that you are using syntax defined by the ODBC standard, rather than using whatever syntax may be native to your database system. So the CALL syntax is the way to call stored procedures in a database-independent way. But you can feel free to use your database system's native syntax for executing a stored procedure if you prefer—for instance, you could use the EXECUTE keyword to run the procedure on a Microsoft SQLServer. See your database server's documentation for details. ▓

There are a few advantages to using stored procedures to encapsulate your SELECT and other SQL statements. They are advantageous in many of the same ways that views are. The following are some of the advantages:

- ▓ You make your SQL code more "modular"—that ListInventory stored procedure can now be dropped into any Cold Fusion statement without modification and without regard for the structure of the database.

- ▓ Stored procedures allow the design of your database to be changed without changing any of your Cold Fusion code. As long as the new version of the stored procedure still outputs whatever columns your Cold Fusion templates need, everything will continue to work just fine.

- ▓ In a corporate or other team environment, stored procedures provide a way for a database developer to provide a Cold Fusion developer with a closely monitored, predetermined set of calls to develop the application with—an "API" of sorts. The Cold Fusion developer may not have any idea what the table structure of the database is. All she cares about is that the stored procedure records or returns whatever information that it's supposed to.

In addition, you can expect stored procedures to run a bit faster than a normal SQL statement, because stored procedures are generally pre-compiled or optimized in some way by your database server (the specifics regarding stored procedures vary among database systems).

Adding Parameters to Stored Procedures

Stored procedures can also take *parameters*, so you can pass data into the procedure for processing. Listing 17.43 creates a ListOrders stored procedure that demonstrates the use of parameters. The first parameter expects an ISBN code to search for, and so uses a varchar datatype (which is the SQLServer equivalent of the Text datatype in Access). The second parameter expects a state to find corresponding orders in.

Listing 17.43   A Stored Procedure with Two Input Parameters

```
CREATE PROCEDURE ListOrders
  @ISBN varchar(13),
  @ShipState varchar(5)
AS
SELECT Inventory.BookID, Orders.OrderDate
```

continues

Part

IV

Ch

17

Listing 17.43   Continued

```
FROM Inventory, Orders, OrderItems
WHERE OrderItems.BookID = Inventory.BookID
AND Orders.OrderID = OrderItems.OrderID
AND Inventory.ISBN = @ISBN
AND Orders.ShipState = @ShipState
```

You could execute the stored procedure from Listing 17.43 in a Cold Fusion template using code like Listing 17.44. Figure 17.23 shows the output of this listing.

On the CD

Listing 17.44   STORED2.CFM—Supplying Parameter Values to a Stored Procedure

```
<CFSET MyOrder = "0789709708">
<CFSET MyState = "NY">

<CFQUERY NAME="Report" DATASOURCE="A2Z">
  { CALL ListOrders('#MyOrder#', '#MyState#')}
</CFQUERY>

<HTML>

<HEAD>
<TITLE>List Orders</TITLE>
</HEAD>

<BODY>

<H1>List Orders</H1>

<CFTABLE QUERY="Report" COLHEADERS HTMLTABLE BORDER>
  <CFCOL HEADER="BookID" TEXT="#BookID#">
  <CFCOL HEADER="Order Date" TEXT="#DateFormat(OrderDate)#">
</CFTABLE>

</BODY>

</HTML>
```

By using more than one SELECT statement, it is possible to create a stored procedure that creates more than one result set. However, Cold Fusion will only be able to "see" the first one. For instance, you could create a stored procedure as shown in Listing 17.45—but you would only be able to refer to #Title# normally. As soon as you tried to use #CustomerID#, you'd get an error message.

Listing 17.45   Rows from the Second *SELECT* Won't be Visible to Cold Fusion

```
CREATE ListEverything AS
SELECT Title FROM Inventory
SELECT CustomerID FROM Customers
```

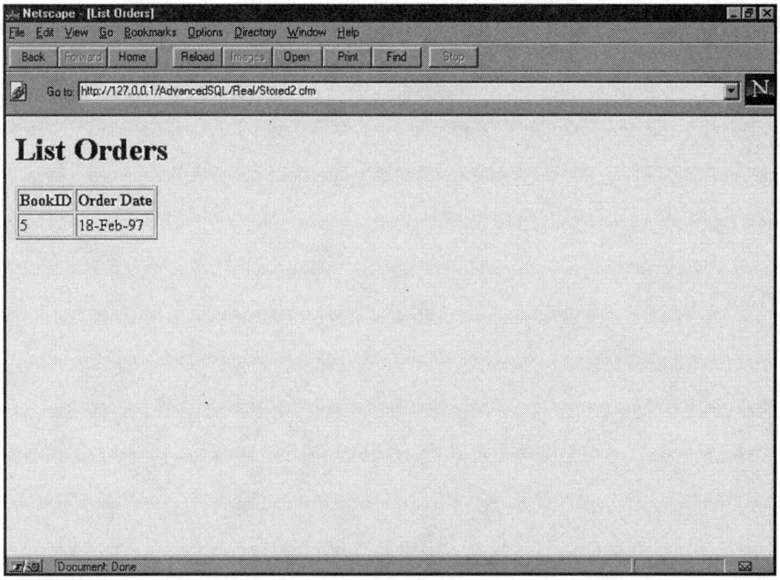

FIG. 17.23

Stored procedures can take parameters to make them respond to specific input.

List Orders

BookID	Order Date
5	18-Feb-97

NOTE With most database systems, a stored procedure can return a *result code, return value,* or *output parameter.* Unfortunately, none of these can be accessed from Cold Fusion 3.1. You should be able to go ahead and use the stored procedure without any problems, but you'll only be able to access information returned as a normal result set (from a SELECT statement in the procedure). ■

Using Stored Procedures for Complex Tasks

With most database systems, stored procedures can be arbitrarily complex. You can freely use as many UPDATE and DELETE statements as you wish.

You can also freely use any of the extended SQL syntax that your database system supports. You may be able to take advantage of advanced program flow keywords—such as IF, WHILE, BEGIN, END, and CASE—within a stored procedure. You may also be able to define and use *table cursors* and *temporary tables* (in general, you will not be able to use table cursors or temporary tables in Cold Fusion templates unless they are in stored procedures). You also may be able to declare and manipulate variables, and even execute external programs.

So consider using stored procedures for complicated tasks that would normally take several separate CFQUERY operations in a Cold Fusion template. Consider them especially for situations where a number of updates and inserts need to be done without displaying information from the various steps to the user. You'll gain performance, because you won't keep moving data back and forth between Cold Fusion and your database server. ●

Part

IV

Ch

17

Advanced Cold Fusion Templates

by Leon Chalnick

Reusing Code

Code reuse has been discussed before, and will be mentioned several more times before the end of this book. Code reuse, and writing code so that it is reusable, is a practice worth learning, understanding, and implementing.

To see why code reuse is so important, look at an example. Figure 18.1 shows a simple search screen. A navigation menu appears on the left of the screen, and a search dialog box is in the main section. After you have entered your search criteria, the results screen shown in Figure 18.2 displays the matching books.

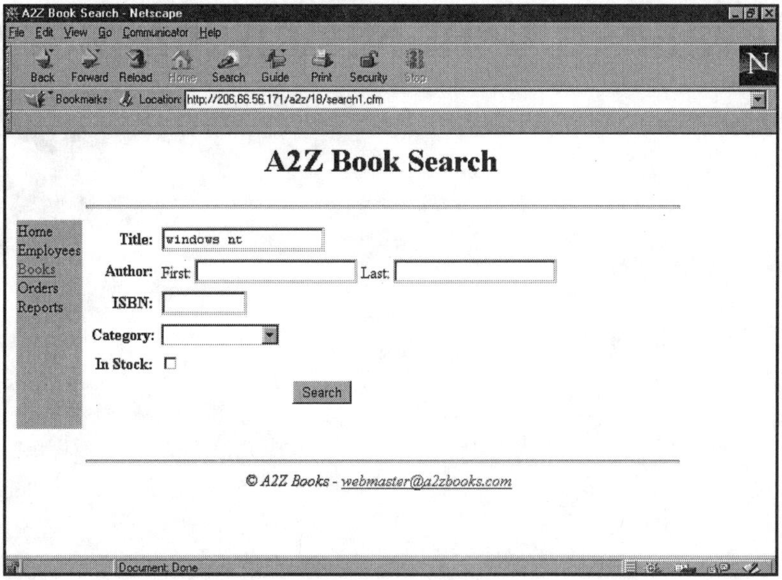

FIG. 18.1

The book search screen displays a navigation menu on the left and a search dialog box in the main section of the screen.

Notice that the results screen displays the exact same navigation bar as the search screen. In fact, the title, header, and copyright information are all identical too.

The code for these two screens is shown in Listing 18.1 and Listing 18.2.

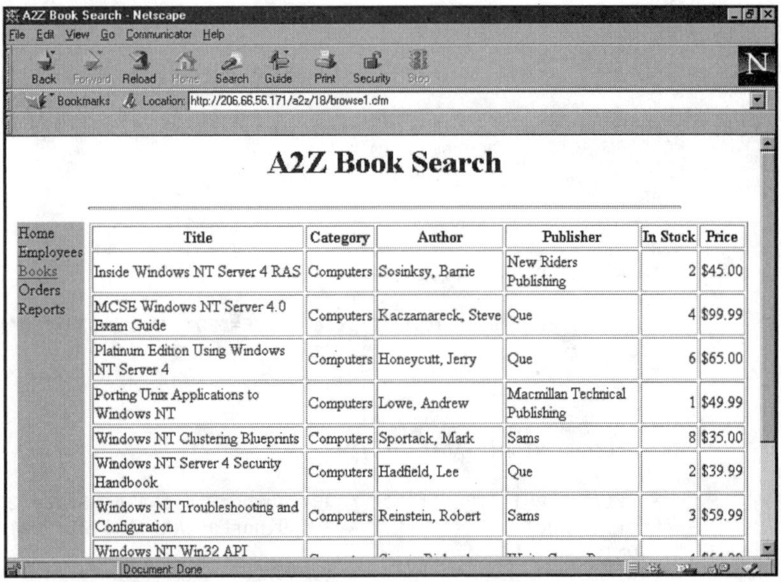

FIG. 18.2

The search results screen displays the same navigation menu as the search screen and the search results.

Part
IV

Ch
18

Listing 18.1 SEARCH1.CFM—Source for SEARCH1.CFM Template

```
<CFQUERY DATASOURCE="A2Z" NAME="categories">
SELECT id, category
FROM category
ORDER BY category
</CFQUERY>

<HTML>

<HEAD>
 <TITLE>A2Z Book Search</TITLE>
</HEAD>

<BODY>

<CENTER>
 <H1>A2Z Book Search</H1>
 <HR WIDTH="80%">
</CENTER>

<TABLE>

<TR VALIGN="TOP">
 <TD NOWRAP BGCOLOR="#C0C0C0">
Home<BR>
  Employees<BR>
  <A HREF="search1.cfm">Books</A><BR>
  Orders<BR>
  Reports<BR>
```

continues

Listing 18.1   Continued

```
</TD>
<TD>

<CFFORM ACTION="browse1.cfm">

<TABLE>

<TR>
 <TH ALIGN="RIGHT">Title:</TH>
 <TD>
  <INPUT TYPE="text" NAME="Title" SIZE="20" MAXLENGTH="30">
 </TD>
</TR>

<TR>
 <TH ALIGN="RIGHT">Author:</TH>
 <TD>
  First: <INPUT TYPE="text" NAME="AuthorFirstName" SIZE="20" MAXLENGTH="20">
  Last: <INPUT TYPE="text" NAME="AuthorLastName" SIZE="20" MAXLENGTH="20">
 </TD>
</TR>

<TR>
 <TH ALIGN="RIGHT">ISBN:</TH>
 <TD>
  <INPUT TYPE="text" NAME="ISBN" SIZE="10" MAXLENGTH="10">
 </TD>
</TR>

<TR>
 <TH ALIGN="RIGHT">Category:</TH>
 <TD>
  <CFSELECT NAME="category_id" QUERY="categories" VALUE="id" DISPLAY=
➥"category" SIZE="1">
  <OPTION VALUE="" SELECTED>
  </CFSELECT>
 </TD>
</TR>

<TR>
 <TH ALIGN="RIGHT">In Stock:</TH>
 <TD>
  <INPUT TYPE="checkbox" NAME="InStock" VALUE="Yes">
 </TD>
</TR>

<TR>
 <TH COLSPAN="2">
  <INPUT TYPE="submit" VALUE="Search">
 </TH>
</TR>

</TABLE>
```

```
  </CFFORM>

  </TD>

 </TR>
 </TABLE>

 <CENTER>
  <P>
  <HR WIDTH="80%">
  <I>&copy; A2Z Books - <A HREF="mailto:webmaster@a2zbooks.com">
➡webmaster@a2zbooks.com</A></I>
 </CENTER>

 </BODY>
 </HTML>
```

On the CD

Listing 18.2   BROWSE1.CFM—Source for BROWSE1.CFM Template

```
<CFPARAM NAME="Title" DEFAULT="">
<CFPARAM NAME="AuthorFirstName" DEFAULT="">
<CFPARAM NAME="AuthorLastName" DEFAULT="">
<CFPARAM NAME="isbn" DEFAULT="">
<CFPARAM NAME="CategoryID" DEFAULT="">
<CFPARAM NAME="InStock" DEFAULT="">

<CFQUERY DATASOURCE="A2Z" NAME="books">
SELECT Title, AuthorFirstName, AuthorLastName,
       NumberInStock, Category, Publisher, Price
FROM Inventory, Category
WHERE Inventory.CategoryID = Category.id

<CFIF Trim(Title) IS NOT "">
 AND Title LIKE '%#Trim(Title)#%'
</CFIF>

<CFIF Trim(AuthorFirstName) IS NOT "">
 AND AuthorFirstName LIKE '#Trim(AuthorFirstName)#%'
</CFIF>

<CFIF Trim(AuthorLastName) IS NOT "">
 AND AuthorLastName LIKE '#Trim(AuthorLastName)#%'
</CFIF>

<CFIF Trim(isbn) IS NOT "">
 AND isbn = '#Trim(isbn)#'
</CFIF>

<CFIF Trim(CategoryID) IS NOT "">
 AND CategoryId = #Trim(CategoryID)#
</CFIF>
```

Part
IV

Ch
18

continues

Listing 18.2   Continued

```
<CFIF Trim(InStock) IS NOT "">
 AND NumberInStock > 0
</CFIF>

ORDER BY title
</CFQUERY>

<HTML>

<HEAD>
 <TITLE>A2Z Book Search</TITLE>
</HEAD>

<BODY>

<CENTER>
 <H1>A2Z Book Search</H1>
 <HR WIDTH="80%">
</CENTER>

<TABLE>

<TR VALIGN="TOP">
 <TD NOWRAP BGCOLOR="#C0C0C0">
Home<BR>
  Employees<BR>
  <A HREF="search1.cfm">Books</A><BR>
Orders<BR>
  Reports<BR>
 </TD>
 <TD>

 <TABLE BORDER="1">

 <TR>
  <TH>Title</TH>
  <TH>Category</TH>
  <TH>Author</TH>
  <TH>Publisher</TH>
  <TH>In Stock</TH>
  <TH>Price</TH>
 </TR>

 <CFOUTPUT QUERY="books">
  <TR>
   <TD>#Trim(Title)#</TD>
   <TD>#Trim(Category)#</TD>
   <TD>#Trim(AuthorLastName)#, #Trim(AuthorFirstName)#</TD>
   <TD>#Trim(Publisher)#</TD>
   <TD ALIGN="RIGHT">#NumberFormat(NumberInStock)#</TD>
   <TD ALIGN="RIGHT">#DollarFormat(Price)#</TD>
  </TR>
 </CFOUTPUT>
```

```
  </TABLE>

  </TD>

 </TR>
 </TABLE>

 <CENTER>
  <P>
  <HR WIDTH="80%">
  <I>&copy; A2Z Books - <A HREF="mailto:webmaster@a2zbooks.com">
➥webmaster@a2zbooks.com</A></I>
 </CENTER>

 </BODY>
 </HTML>
```

Take a look at these two code listings. Everything contained within these templates is code you have seen before. <CFQUERY> is used to retrieve a list of categories in Listing 18.1 and to perform the book search in Listing 18.2. <CFFORM> and <CFSELECT> are used to display the category list in Listing 18.1, and <CFOUTPUT> is used to display the search results in Listing 18.2.

▶ **See** Chapter 11, "Cold Fusion Basics," **p. 193**

▶ **See** Chapter 11, "Cold Fusion Basics," **p. 193**

Now look at the HTML interface code—the code that creates the BODY of the page and displays the title and copyright information and the navigation bar on the left of the screen. The code is *identical* for both listings. (In fact, when creating this example, I just copied and pasted the code from one source file to the other!)

There is nothing wrong with copying chunks of code between files. Web page designers do it all the time within their HTML pages. Actually, HTML developers have no choice but to copy code because HTML itself has no mechanism with which to share common code.

But what happens when you need to make changes to that common code? Perhaps it's something as simple as changing the color of the navigation bar background, or maybe you are fixing a typo or changing the order or color of some text. Whatever the change, no matter how simple or trivial, you must update *every single occurrence* of it manually. Of course, manually updating multiple files exposes you to the risk of introducing new typos and mistakes.

Obviously, this is far from ideal and definitely not scalable or manageable. What you really need is a way to share common code between files, and Cold Fusion allows you to do this using a tag called <CFINCLUDE>.

Using *<CFINCLUDE>*

The <CFINCLUDE> tags is used to include the entire contents of one Cold Fusion template into another. The syntax is simply

```
<CFINCLUDE TEMPLATE="FILE.CFM">
```

This will include the entire contents of FILE.CFM at the location where the `<CFINCLUDE>` tag appears in your code.

To better understand this, modify the earlier example to use common header and footer code. To do this, you create two new templates, HEADER.CFM and FOOTER.CFM. HEADER.CFM, shown in Listing 18.3, contains all the header text to use on both the search page and the results page, including the title and the navigation bar. FOOTER.CFM, shown in Listing 18.4, contains the common footer code, including the copyright information and the end of the navigation bar table.

Listing 18.3   HEADER.CFM—Source for HEADER.CFM Template

```
<HTML>

<HEAD>
 <TITLE>A2Z Book Search</TITLE>
</HEAD>

<BODY>

<CENTER>
 <H1>A2Z Book Search</H1>
 <HR WIDTH="80%">
</CENTER>

<TABLE>

<TR VALIGN="TOP">
<TD NOWRAP BGCOLOR="C0C0C0">
Home<BR>
Employees<BR>
<A HREF="search.cfm">Books</A><BR>
Orders<BR>
Reports<BR>
</TD>
<TD>
```

Listing 18.4   FOOTER.CFM—Source for FOOTER.CFM Template

```
</TD>
</TR>
</TABLE>

<CENTER>
 <P>
 <HR WIDTH="80%">
 <I>&copy; A2Z Books - <A HREF="mailto:webmaster@a2zbooks.com">
➥webmaster@a2zbooks.com</A></I>
</CENTER>

</BODY>
</HTML>
```

Now that the header code and footer code are broken out into their own files, you can modify the search and results pages to include these files directly. Listing 18.5 and Listing 18.6 contain the updated files. You'll see that all header and footer text has been pulled out and replaced with two <CFINCLUDE> calls, one for HEADER.CFM and the other for FOOTER.CFM.

On the CD

Listing 18.5   SEARCH2.CFM—Source for SEARCH2.CFM Template

```
<CFQUERY DATASOURCE="A2Z" NAME="categories">
SELECT id, category
FROM category
ORDER BY category
</CFQUERY>

<CFINCLUDE TEMPLATE="header.cfm">

<CFFORM ACTION="browse2.cfm">

<TABLE>

<TR>
 <TH ALIGN="RIGHT">Title:</TH>
 <TD>
  <INPUT TYPE="text" NAME="Title" SIZE="20" MAXLENGTH="30">
 </TD>
</TR>

<TR>
 <TH ALIGN="RIGHT">Author:</TH>
 <TD>
 First: <INPUT TYPE="text" NAME="AuthorFirstName" SIZE="20" MAXLENGTH="20">
 Last: <INPUT TYPE="text" NAME="AuthorLastName" SIZE="20" MAXLENGTH="20">
 </TD>
</TR>

<TR>
 <TH ALIGN="RIGHT">ISBN:</TH>
 <TD>
  <INPUT TYPE="text" NAME="ISBN" SIZE="10" MAXLENGTH="10">
 </TD>
</TR>

<TR>
 <TH ALIGN="RIGHT">Category:</TH>
 <TD>
  <CFSELECT NAME="category_id" QUERY="categories" VALUE="id" DISPLAY=
➠"category" SIZE="1">
  <OPTION VALUE="" SELECTED>
  </CFSELECT>
 </TD>
</TR>

<TR>
 <TH ALIGN="RIGHT">In Stock:</TH>
```

Part

IV

Ch

18

continues

Listing 18.5 Continued

```
<TD>
 <INPUT TYPE="checkbox" NAME="InStock" VALUE="Yes">
 </TD>
</TR>

<TR>
 <TH COLSPAN="2">
  <INPUT TYPE="submit" VALUE="Search">
 </TH>
</TR>

</TABLE>

</CFFORM>

<CFINCLUDE TEMPLATE="footer.cfm">
```

On the CD

Listing 18.6 BROWSE2.CFM—Source for BROWSE2.CFM Template

```
<CFPARAM NAME="Title" DEFAULT="">
<CFPARAM NAME="AuthorFirstName" DEFAULT="">
<CFPARAM NAME="AuthorLastName" DEFAULT="">
<CFPARAM NAME="isbn" DEFAULT="">
<CFPARAM NAME="CategoryID" DEFAULT="">
<CFPARAM NAME="InStock" DEFAULT="">

<CFQUERY DATASOURCE="A2Z" NAME="books">
SELECT Title, AuthorFirstName, AuthorLastName,
        NumberInStock, Category, Publisher, Price
FROM Inventory, Category
WHERE Inventory.CategoryID = Category.id

<CFIF Trim(Title) IS NOT "">
 AND Title LIKE '%#Trim(Title)#%'
</CFIF>

<CFIF Trim(AuthorFirstName) IS NOT "">
 AND AuthorFirstName LIKE '#Trim(AuthorFirstName)#%'
</CFIF>

<CFIF Trim(AuthorLastName) IS NOT "">
 AND AuthorLastName LIKE '#Trim(AuthorLastName)#%'
</CFIF>

<CFIF Trim(isbn) IS NOT "">
 AND isbn = '#Trim(isbn)#'
</CFIF>

<CFIF Trim(CategoryID) IS NOT "">
 AND CategoryId = #Trim(CategoryID)#
</CFIF>
```

```
<CFIF Trim(InStock) IS NOT "">
 AND NumberInStock > 0
</CFIF>

ORDER BY title
</CFQUERY>

<CFINCLUDE TEMPLATE="header.cfm">

<TABLE BORDER="1">

<TR>
 <TH>Title</TH>
 <TH>Category</TH>
 <TH>Author</TH>
 <TH>Publisher</TH>
 <TH>In Stock</TH>
 <TH>Price</TH>
</TR>

<CFOUTPUT QUERY="books">
 <TR>
  <TD>#Trim(Title)#</TD>
  <TD>#Trim(Category)#</TD>
  <TD>#Trim(AuthorLastName)#, #Trim(AuthorFirstName)#</TD>
  <TD>#Trim(Publisher)#</TD>
  <TD ALIGN="RIGHT">#NumberFormat(NumberInStock)#</TD>
  <TD ALIGN="RIGHT">#DollarFormat(Price)#</TD>
 </TR>
</CFOUTPUT>

</TABLE>

<CFINCLUDE TEMPLATE="footer.cfm">
```

Take a look at the new page in your browser, and you'll see that the end result is exactly the same as when the header and footer code was entered into the files directly.

But although the end result looks the same, under the hood things are very different. Now if you need to change a color or an option, fix a typo, or make any other change to the HEADER.CFM or FOOTER.CFM file, every file that includes these files will be updated automatically. And these changes are dynamic because Cold Fusion includes the header and footer files every time the page is requested.

Writing Code with Reuse in Mind

Now that you've seen how to reuse code using <CFINCLUDE>, here are some guidelines to help you write reusable code:

- When writing code, isolate components that can be shared.
- Try to break out code that is slightly more generic than the main file itself. Code that is template specific is more difficult to reuse.

- Organize your code so that template-specific tasks and more generic tasks are separated from each other. (This is discussed later in the chapter.)
- Menus, toolbars, headers, and footers are prime candidates for breaking out into separate files.

> **TIP**   Many web page designers use CFM files for *all* their HTML pages—not just for pages that use Cold Fusion code—so that they can use `<CFINCLUDE>` to share HTML code between files.

> **N O T E**   When using `<CFINCLUDE>`, remember that the included file shares the scope of the calling file. This means that any variables, queries, form fields, or other data available in the calling file will also be available to the included file. Similarly, any data created in the included file will be visible to the calling file. You must make sure that code in your included file does not mistakenly overwrite variables or data in the calling file. ■

▶ **See** Chapter 33, "Custom Tags," **p. 767**

Organizing Your Code

Most of the code samples and applications so far have been small and therefore quite manageable. But as you start writing bigger and more complex applications, you are going to find that your code becomes more difficult to manage, particularly if you need to revisit code that you have not looked at in a while.

It is therefore important to pay attention to the organization of your code from day one, taking the time to ensure that your code is clean and manageable.

Two of the most important components of code organization are the use of comments and the breaking up of templates into logical sections.

Using Comments and Headers

Programmers don't like writing comments. It's a sad fact, but that's just the way it is. Documenting and commenting code is not glamorous, nor is it as much fun as writing brand new code. Commenting code is also time-consuming, and when time is running out, commenting and documentation are usually the first tasks to be sacrificed.

I have only one comment to make about commenting your code: DO IT! View it as an investment. Whatever time you put into commenting your code up front is time saved when you have to modify or debug the application at a later date.

▶ **See** Chapter 16, "Debugging and Troubleshooting," **p. 325**

For example, look at the code in Listing 18.7. The first thing you'll see is that the page has an entire header block that describes the page contents. This block contains the filename, description, author, date, and usage notes. You can add additional fields to this block if needed, but at least these five fields should be used.

In addition, throughout the code you'll see comments like this:

```
<!--- Retrieve category list for SELECT box --->
```

This makes the code that follows very clear. Anyone—yourself at a later date or another developer—will know right away what the query is and what it is used for.

Listing 18.7   SEARCH3.CFM—Code for SEARCH3.CFM

```
<!---
NAME: SEARCH3.CFM

DESCRIPTION: Search page for book inventory search. Sends
             search request to BROWSE3.CFM.

AUTHOR: Ben Forta

DATE: 12/3/97

NOTES: This file includes HEADER.CFM and FOOTER.CFM, both
       must be present in the current directory or an error
       will be displayed.
--->

<!--- Retrieve category list for SELECT box --->
<CFQUERY DATASOURCE="A2Z" NAME="categories">
SELECT id, category
FROM category
ORDER BY category
</CFQUERY>

<!--- Include header code --->
<CFINCLUDE TEMPLATE="header.cfm">

<!--- This is the search form --->
<CFFORM ACTION="browse3.cfm">

<TABLE>

<TR>
 <TH ALIGN="RIGHT">Title:</TH>
 <TD>
  <INPUT TYPE="text" NAME="Title" SIZE="20" MAXLENGTH="30">
 </TD>
</TR>

<TR>
 <TH ALIGN="RIGHT">Author:</TH>
 <TD>
  First: <INPUT TYPE="text" NAME="AuthorFirstName" SIZE="20" MAXLENGTH="20">
  Last: <INPUT TYPE="text" NAME="AuthorLastName" SIZE="20" MAXLENGTH="20">
 </TD>
</TR>
```

Part

IV

Ch

18

continues

Listing 18.7   Continued

```
<TR>
 <TH ALIGN="RIGHT">ISBN:</TH>
 <TD>
  <INPUT TYPE="text" NAME="ISBN" SIZE="10" MAXLENGTH="10">
 </TD>
</TR>

<TR>
 <TH ALIGN="RIGHT">Category:</TH>
 <TD>
  <CFSELECT NAME="category_id" QUERY="categories" VALUE="id" DISPLAY=
➥"category" SIZE="1">
  <OPTION VALUE="" SELECTED>
  </CFSELECT>
 </TD>
</TR>

<TR>
 <TH ALIGN="RIGHT">In Stock:</TH>
 <TD>
  <INPUT TYPE="checkbox" NAME="InStock" VALUE="Yes">
 </TD>
</TR>

<TR>
 <TH COLSPAN="2">
  <INPUT TYPE="submit" VALUE="Search">
 </TH>
</TR>

</TABLE>

</CFFORM>

<!--- Include footer code --->
<CFINCLUDE TEMPLATE="footer.cfm">
```

Embedded comments obviously increase the size of the physical Cold Fusion files, but the amount of data sent to the end user's browser is not increased at all. Figure 18.3 shows the source code for the updated search screen (the one with the comments in it) as it appears on the browser. As you can see, Cold Fusion stripped out all the comments before the page was sent. This both saves download time and protects your comments from being viewed by your visitors.

N O T E   Make sure that you use <!--- and ---> for your comments (using three dashes, not two). If you use two dashes, your comment is an HTML comment, not a CFML comment. Unlike CFML comments, HTML comments are not stripped out by Cold Fusion and are sent to the user's browser. ▪

FIG. 18.3
Cold Fusion strips
embedded comments
from your code before
the code is sent to the
user's browser.

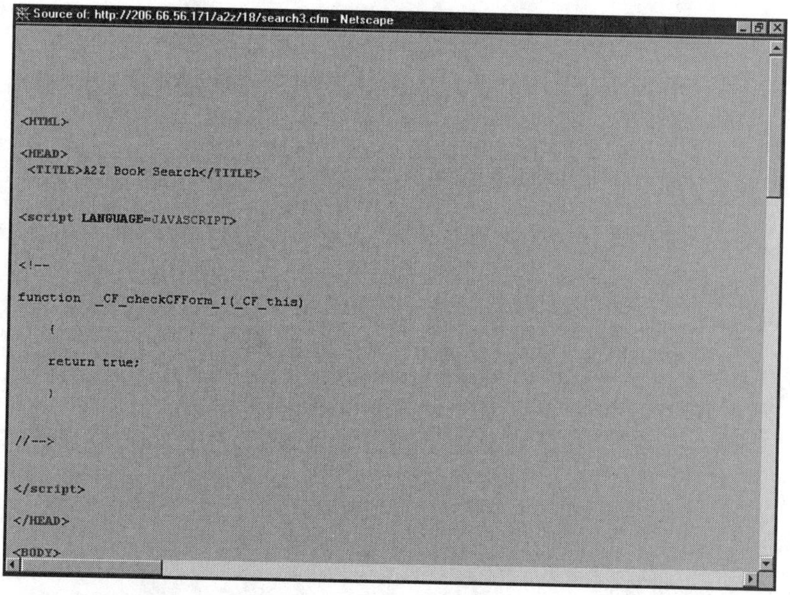

```
Source of: http://206.66.56.171/a2z/18/search3.cfm - Netscape

<HTML>

<HEAD>
 <TITLE>A2Z Book Search</TITLE>

<script LANGUAGE=JAVASCRIPT>

<!--

function _CF_checkCFForm_1(_CF_this)

    {

    return true;

    }

//-->

</script>

</HEAD>

<BODY>
```

TIP Studio users can use the Studio tag snippets feature to save an empty header block that can easily be inserted into your code.

Part
IV

Ch

18

Breaking Templates into Logical Sections

As mentioned earlier, an important part of code organization is breaking your code into logical sections. To illustrate, take a look at an updated version of the results page (it is the same as the example shown earlier, except that this one has comments embedded in it). The code is shown in Listing 18.8.

Listing 18.8   BROWSE3.CFM—Source for BROWSE3.CFM

```
<!---
NAME: BROWSE3.CFM

DESCRIPTION: Perform search for books in the Inventory
             table. All search fields are optional.

AUTHOR: Ben Forta

DATE: 12/3/97

NOTES: This file includes HEADER.CFM and FOOTER.CFM, both
       must be present in the current directory or an error
       will be displayed.
--->
```

continues

Listing 18.8 Continued

```
<!--- Initialize all fields if they do not exist --->
<CFPARAM NAME="Title" DEFAULT="">
<CFPARAM NAME="AuthorFirstName" DEFAULT="">
<CFPARAM NAME="AuthorLastName" DEFAULT="">
<CFPARAM NAME="isbn" DEFAULT="">
<CFPARAM NAME="CategoryID" DEFAULT="">
<CFPARAM NAME="InStock" DEFAULT="">

<!--- Perform actual search, search is on a
        JOIN between Inventory and Category so that
        the category names are retrieved --->
<CFQUERY DATASOURCE="A2Z" NAME="books">
SELECT Title, AuthorFirstName, AuthorLastName,
        NumberInStock, Category, Publisher, Price
FROM Inventory, Category
WHERE Inventory.CategoryID = Category.id

<!--- Filter by title if needed --->
<CFIF Trim(Title) IS NOT "">
 AND Title LIKE '%#Trim(Title)#%'
</CFIF>

<!--- Filter by author first name if needed --->
<CFIF Trim(AuthorFirstName) IS NOT "">
 AND AuthorFirstName LIKE '#Trim(AuthorFirstName)#%'
</CFIF>

<!--- Filter by author last name if needed --->
<CFIF Trim(AuthorLastName) IS NOT "">
 AND AuthorLastName LIKE '#Trim(AuthorLastName)#%'
</CFIF>

<!--- Filter by isbn if needed --->
<CFIF Trim(isbn) IS NOT "">
 AND isbn = '#Trim(isbn)#'
</CFIF>

<!--- Filter by category if needed --->
<CFIF Trim(CategoryID) IS NOT "">
 AND CategoryId = #Trim(CategoryID)#
</CFIF>

<!--- Filter by stock number if needed --->
<CFIF Trim(InStock) IS NOT "">
 AND NumberInStock > 0
</CFIF>

ORDER BY title
</CFQUERY>

<!--- Include header file --->
<CFINCLUDE TEMPLATE="header.cfm">

<!--- Create table for display --->
<TABLE BORDER="1">
```

```
<!--- Table headers --->
<TR>
 <TH>Title</TH>
 <TH>Category</TH>
 <TH>Author</TH>
 <TH>Publisher</TH>
 <TH>In Stock</TH>
 <TH>Price</TH>
</TR>

<!--- Write out the retrieved data --->
<CFOUTPUT QUERY="books">
 <TR>
  <TD>#Trim(Title)#</TD>
  <TD>#Trim(Category)#</TD>
  <TD>#Trim(AuthorLastName)#, #Trim(AuthorFirstName)#</TD>
  <TD>#Trim(Publisher)#</TD>
  <TD ALIGN="RIGHT">#NumberFormat(NumberInStock)#</TD>
  <TD ALIGN="RIGHT">#DollarFormat(Price)#</TD>
 </TR>
</CFOUTPUT>

</TABLE>

<!--- Include footer file --->
<CFINCLUDE TEMPLATE="footer.cfm">
```

The first item in the code is the header block as described earlier.

Next comes variable initialization code using a series of <CFPARAM> tags. This code ensures that the fields that will be used later in the file all exist. If they do not exist (either because the form changed, or the field was not submitted), <CFPARAM> will create them right then and there. Either way, after that block of initialization code has been processed, the variables will exist.

What's the advantage of doing this? These fields are all used in the <CFQUERY> tag, the next item in the file. You could have enclosed each and every <CFIF> statement in another conditional statement to check that the field existed, but that would have made the code more difficult to read. By breaking out the initialization code, the <CFQUERY> is cleaner and does just what it is supposed to do—retrieve data.

The rest of the file follows the same pattern. The <CFQURERY> to retrieve the data could have appeared right in the middle of the HTML output, right before the <CFOUTPUT> tag. So why not do it that way? That would have made the code more difficult to read. But more important, as your files get bigger and more complex you might inadvertently reuse a query name not realizing that it was already used, or you might refer to a query before it was processed, or other similar errors. Keeping the queries isolated from the interface prevents this from happening.

Managing your HTML code also becomes simpler because the HTML code does not have calls to Cold Fusion tags embedded in it, and finding mismatched tags, broken tables, and other common HTML problems becomes much easier.

This kind of organization becomes even more important when you need to verify the contents of a field or abort processing if a field does not exist. You could put all that verification code above any actual processing, keeping your core processing cleaner and more manageable.

The basic rule of thumb here is don't embed initialization and verification code in your core processing. Separate the code into logical blocks, and it'll be easier to maintain and manage.

Although no hard-and-fast rule exists as to how to break up your code, the following layout is a good place to start:

- File description (comments at the top of the page)
- Variable initialization (using <CFPARAM>)
- Verification (often using <CFIF>, <CFABORT>, and <CFLOCATION>)
- All database retrieval (using <CFQUERY>)
- User interface (the HTML itself)

N O T E A nice side effect of breaking up your code this way is that this type of code lends itself very well to code reuse as mentioned earlier. For example, the header and footer text you saw earlier can be broken out into separate files because they are cleanly isolated. We couldn't have done that as easily if Cold Fusion code was embedded right in the middle of the header or footer text. ■

Browsing Next *N* Records

One of the most popular types of interfaces used by web-based applications allows the user to browse the "next *n* records" ("next 10," "next 5," or any other number). This kind of interface is used by the popular online search engines as well as by many sites that allow users to browse through catalogs.

Creating a Browse Next *N* Records Interface

Creating this kind of interface with Cold Fusion is simple as long as you remember one basic rule. As explained in Chapter 2, "Introduction to Cold Fusion," every request made by a web browser must stand on its own two feet. No relationship exists between a request made and any future request. This means that to continue a previous search (display the next five records for example), you must pass back to the server all the information needed to reconstruct the original search.

Even though from the user's perspective, they are continuing an existing search, from your perspective it is a brand new search. The only difference is where to start displaying data from. For the first page of results, you would display records 1 through 5 (assuming that this was a "Next 5" display); for the second page, you would display records 6 through 10, and so on.

Figure 18.4 shows an example of this. A search for "windows nt" was performed, and the first five matching records are displayed. A "Next 5" button at the bottom of the display allows the user to browse though five records at a time. To try this yourself, run the SEARCH4.CFM file.

FIG. 18.4
Cold Fusion can be used to create "next *n* records" style interfaces.

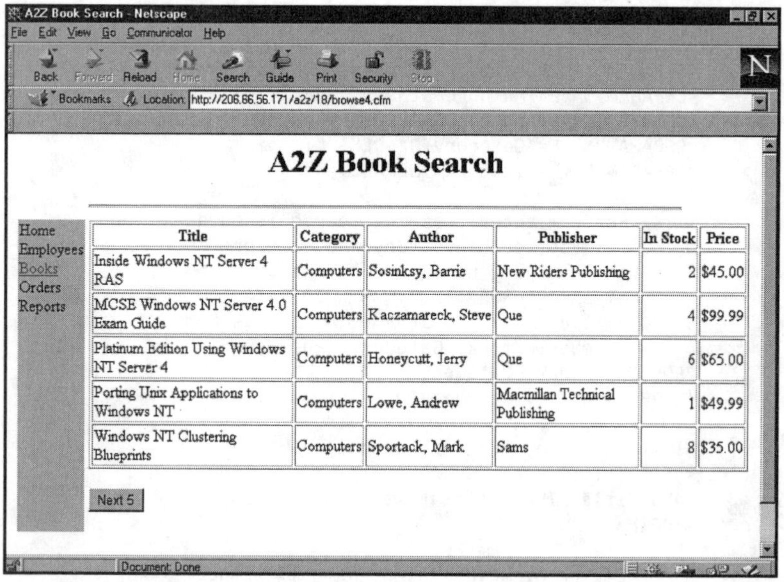

Listing 18.9 contains the updated results page. It is similar to the browser page used earlier, but there are some important differences.

Listing 18.9   BROWSE4.CFM—Code for BROWSE4.CFM File

```
<!---
NAME: BROWSE4.CFM

DESCRIPTION: Perform search for books in the Inventory
             table. All search fields are optional. Results
             are shown 5 records at a time, and a "Next 5"
             button is shown to allow the user to browse
             through the results.

AUTHOR: Ben Forta

DATE: 12/3/97

NOTES: This file includes HEADER.CFM and FOOTER.CFM, both
       must be present in the current directory or an error
       will be displayed.
--->

<!--- Initialize constants --->
<CFSET MaxRows = 5>

<!--- Initialize all fields if they do not exist --->
<CFPARAM NAME="start" DEFAULT="1">
<CFPARAM NAME="Title" DEFAULT="">
```

continues

Part
IV

Ch

18

Listing 18.9   Continued

```
<CFPARAM NAME="AuthorFirstName" DEFAULT="">
<CFPARAM NAME="AuthorLastName" DEFAULT="">
<CFPARAM NAME="isbn" DEFAULT="">
<CFPARAM NAME="CategoryID" DEFAULT="">
<CFPARAM NAME="InStock" DEFAULT="">

<!--- Perform actual search, search is on a
      JOIN between Inventory and Category so that
      the category names are retrieved --->
<CFQUERY DATASOURCE="A2Z" NAME="books">
SELECT Title, AuthorFirstName, AuthorLastName,
       NumberInStock, Category, Publisher, Price
FROM Inventory, Category
WHERE Inventory.CategoryID = Category.id

<!--- Filter by title if needed --->
<CFIF Trim(Title) IS NOT "">
 AND Title LIKE '%#Trim(Title)#%'
</CFIF>

<!--- Filter by author first name if needed --->
<CFIF Trim(AuthorFirstName) IS NOT "">
 AND AuthorFirstName LIKE '#Trim(AuthorFirstName)#%'
</CFIF>

<!--- Filter by author last name if needed --->
<CFIF Trim(AuthorLastName) IS NOT "">
 AND AuthorLastName LIKE '#Trim(AuthorLastName)#%'
</CFIF>

<!--- Filter by isbn if needed --->
<CFIF Trim(isbn) IS NOT "">
 AND isbn = '#Trim(isbn)#'
</CFIF>

<!--- Filter by category if needed --->
<CFIF Trim(CategoryID) IS NOT "">
 AND CategoryId = #Trim(CategoryID)#
</CFIF>

<!--- Filter by stock number if needed --->
<CFIF Trim(InStock) IS NOT "">
 AND NumberInStock > 0
</CFIF>

ORDER BY title
</CFQUERY>

<!--- Include header file --->
<CFINCLUDE TEMPLATE="header.cfm">

<!--- Create table for display --->
<TABLE BORDER="1">
```

```
<!--- Table headers --->
<TR>
 <TH>Title</TH>
 <TH>Category</TH>
 <TH>Author</TH>
 <TH>Publisher</TH>
 <TH>In Stock</TH>
 <TH>Price</TH>
</TR>

<!--- Write out the retrieved data --->
<CFOUTPUT QUERY="books" STARTROW="#start#" MAXROWS="#MaxRows#">
 <TR>
  <TD>#Trim(Title)#</TD>
  <TD>#Trim(Category)#</TD>
  <TD>#Trim(AuthorLastName)#, #Trim(AuthorFirstName)#</TD>
  <TD>#Trim(Publisher)#</TD>
  <TD ALIGN="RIGHT">#NumberFormat(NumberInStock)#</TD>
  <TD ALIGN="RIGHT">#DollarFormat(Price)#</TD>
 </TR>
</CFOUTPUT>

</TABLE>

<!--- What is the next row to start at --->
<CFSET NextStart = Start + MaxRows>

<!--- Next button code --->
<CFOUTPUT>
<FORM ACTION="browse4.cfm" METHOD="POST">
<INPUT TYPE="hidden" NAME="start" VALUE="#NextStart#">
<INPUT TYPE="hidden" NAME="Title" VALUE="#Title#">
<INPUT TYPE="hidden" NAME="AuthorFirstName" VALUE="#AuthorFirstName#">
<INPUT TYPE="hidden" NAME="AuthorLastName" VALUE="#AuthorLastName#">
<INPUT TYPE="hidden" NAME="ISBN" VALUE="#isbn#">
<INPUT TYPE="hidden" NAME="CategoryID" VALUE="#CategoryID#">
<INPUT TYPE="hidden" NAME="InStock" VALUE="#InStock#">
<INPUT TYPE="submit" VALUE="Next #MaxRows#">
</FORM>
</CFOUTPUT>

<!--- Include footer file --->
<CFINCLUDE TEMPLATE="footer.cfm">
```

First, you added a block for constants and then a variable called MaxRows. This value is the maximum number of records to display at once. Set the value to 5; to display 10 records at a time, just change this value to 10.

> **N O T E** Experienced programmers should note that Cold Fusion has no real concept of constants, in that these values are not read-only and can be overwritten. The term "constant" is used here more as a descriptive notice than anything else. ■

Next, you added a new variable to the initialization list—the variable Start. This variable contains the record number of the first record to display. If a Start value is provided, it is used later in this file. If no Start value is provided, a value of 1 (the first record) is used.

The <CFQUERY> tag did not change at all here. The process of displaying a subset of the retrieved data happens at the <CFOUTPUT> level, not at the <CFQUERY> level. <CFQUERY> still retrieves *all* the data that matches your search, regardless of what you actually intend to display.

The filtering occurs in the <CFOUTPUT> tag, which was changed to look like:

```
<CFOUTPUT QUERY="books" STARTROW="#start#" MAXROWS="#MaxRows#">
```

You added two attributes to this tag, the STARTROW attribute tells <CFOUTPUT> from where to start displaying the data. This variable passed to it is the variable initialized earlier. The MAXROWS attribute is the maximum number of rows to display. The value is the constant set above, but you could have just entered MAXROWS="5" as well.

Now that <CFOUTPUT> knows what data you want to display, it handles the filtering itself. If the STARTROW is 1 (first page) and the MAXROWS is 5, <CFOUTPUT> just displays the first five records (or as many records as there are if less than five).

Now create the "Next 5" button. As explained earlier, the next request must be self contained, meaning that it must contain all the information needed to reconstruct the search. To do this, add the following code to the bottom of the file

```
<!--- What is the next row to start at --->
<CFSET NextStart = Start + MaxRows>

<!--- Next button code --->
<CFOUTPUT>
<FORM ACTION="browse4.cfm" METHOD="POST">
<INPUT TYPE="hidden" NAME="start" VALUE="#NextStart#">
<INPUT TYPE="hidden" NAME="Title" VALUE="#Title#">
<INPUT TYPE="hidden" NAME="AuthorFirstName" VALUE="#AuthorFirstName#">
<INPUT TYPE="hidden" NAME="AuthorLastName" VALUE="#AuthorLastName#">
<INPUT TYPE="hidden" NAME="ISBN" VALUE="#isbn#">
<INPUT TYPE="hidden" NAME="CategoryID" VALUE="#CategoryID#">
<INPUT TYPE="hidden" NAME="InStock" VALUE="#InStock#">
<INPUT TYPE="submit" VALUE="Next #MaxRows#">
</FORM>
</CFOUTPUT>
```

First, you created a new variable called NextStart. NextStart is set to the sum of the current start value, plus the MaxRows value. That way, whatever the start value is, NextStart will always be correct. You can also see now why we used a constant for the MaxRows value and didn't hard-code it to 5. By using a constant, you could safely reuse that value. If you changed MaxRows from 5 to 10, the calculation to determine the NextStart value would still be correct.

Next comes a form. The form has a Submit button and a whole set of hidden fields. The Submit button text uses the same MaxRows variable, again ensuring that if you change the value, and then the button text will change accordingly. The hidden form fields embed all the original search fields into this new form. That way when the form is submitted, all the original form field values are submitted too, allowing you to recreate the search. You also embed the NextStart as the value for the Start field. When this form is submitted, a Start value will be passed that contains the correct start position.

Using Previous and Next Buttons

The one final task to complete the application is to support a "Previous 5" button. This will allow a user to browse back and forth through the results, as shown in Figure 18.5.

FIG. 18.5

Previous and Next buttons allow users to browse through search results.

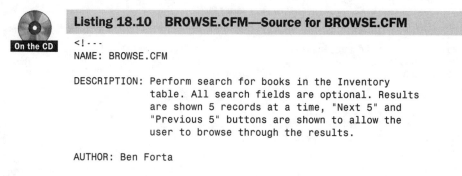

Creating a "Previous 5" button is exactly the same as creating a "Next 5" button, except that instead of adding MaxRows to the current start position, you need to subtract MaxRows. The code for this updated file is shown in Listing 18.10.

On the CD

Listing 18.10   BROWSE.CFM—Source for BROWSE.CFM

```
<!---
NAME: BROWSE.CFM

DESCRIPTION: Perform search for books in the Inventory
             table. All search fields are optional. Results
             are shown 5 records at a time, "Next 5" and
             "Previous 5" buttons are shown to allow the
             user to browse through the results.

AUTHOR: Ben Forta

DATE: 12/3/97
```

continues

Listing 18.10   Continued

```
NOTES: This file includes HEADER.CFM and FOOTER.CFM, both
       must be present in the current directory or an error
       will be displayed.
--->

<!--- Initialize constants --->
<CFSET MaxRows = 5>

<!--- Initialize all fields if they do not exist --->
<CFPARAM NAME="start" DEFAULT="1">
<CFPARAM NAME="Title" DEFAULT="">
<CFPARAM NAME="AuthorFirstName" DEFAULT="">
<CFPARAM NAME="AuthorLastName" DEFAULT="">
<CFPARAM NAME="isbn" DEFAULT="">
<CFPARAM NAME="CategoryID" DEFAULT="">
<CFPARAM NAME="InStock" DEFAULT="">

<!--- Perform actual search, search is on a
       JOIN between Inventory and Category so that
       the category names are retrieved --->
<CFQUERY DATASOURCE="A2Z" NAME="books">
SELECT Title, AuthorFirstName, AuthorLastName,
       NumberInStock, Category, Publisher, Price
FROM Inventory, Category
WHERE Inventory.CategoryID = Category.id

<!--- Filter by title if needed --->
<CFIF Trim(Title) IS NOT "">
 AND Title LIKE '%#Trim(Title)#%'
</CFIF>

<!--- Filter by author first name if needed --->
<CFIF Trim(AuthorFirstName) IS NOT "">
 AND AuthorFirstName LIKE '#Trim(AuthorFirstName)#%'
</CFIF>

<!--- Filter by author last name if needed --->
<CFIF Trim(AuthorLastName) IS NOT "">
 AND AuthorLastName LIKE '#Trim(AuthorLastName)#%'
</CFIF>

<!--- Filter by isbn if needed --->
<CFIF Trim(isbn) IS NOT "">
 AND isbn = '#Trim(isbn)#'
</CFIF>

<!--- Filter by category if needed --->
<CFIF Trim(CategoryID) IS NOT "">
 AND CategoryId = #Trim(CategoryID)#
</CFIF>

<!--- Filter by stock number if needed --->
<CFIF Trim(InStock) IS NOT "">
 AND NumberInStock > 0
</CFIF>
```

```
ORDER BY title
</CFQUERY>

<!--- Include header file --->
<CFINCLUDE TEMPLATE="header.cfm">

<!--- Create table for display --->
<TABLE BORDER="1">

<!--- Table headers --->
<TR>
 <TH>Title</TH>
 <TH>Category</TH>
 <TH>Author</TH>
 <TH>Publisher</TH>
 <TH>In Stock</TH>
 <TH>Price</TH>
</TR>

<!--- Write out the retrieved data --->
<CFOUTPUT QUERY="books" STARTROW="#start#" MAXROWS="#MaxRows#">
 <TR>
  <TD>#Trim(Title)#</TD>
  <TD>#Trim(Category)#</TD>
  <TD>#Trim(AuthorLastName)#, #Trim(AuthorFirstName)#</TD>
  <TD>#Trim(Publisher)#</TD>
  <TD ALIGN="RIGHT">#NumberFormat(NumberInStock)#</TD>
  <TD ALIGN="RIGHT">#DollarFormat(Price)#</TD>
 </TR>
</CFOUTPUT>

<TR>

<!--- What are the previous and next row to start positions --->
<CFSET PrevStart = Start - MaxRows>
<CFSET NextStart = Start + MaxRows>

<!--- Previous button code --->
<TD COLSPAN="3" ALIGN="LEFT">
<CFIF PrevStart GTE 1>
 <CFOUTPUT>
 <FORM ACTION="browse.cfm" METHOD="POST">
 <INPUT TYPE="hidden" NAME="start" VALUE="#PrevStart#">
 <INPUT TYPE="hidden" NAME="Title" VALUE="#Title#">
 <INPUT TYPE="hidden" NAME="AuthorFirstName" VALUE="#AuthorFirstName#">
 <INPUT TYPE="hidden" NAME="AuthorLastName" VALUE="#AuthorLastName#">
 <INPUT TYPE="hidden" NAME="ISBN" VALUE="#isbn#">
 <INPUT TYPE="hidden" NAME="CategoryID" VALUE="#CategoryID#">
 <INPUT TYPE="hidden" NAME="InStock" VALUE="#InStock#">
 <INPUT TYPE="submit" VALUE="Previous #MaxRows#">
 </FORM>
 </CFOUTPUT>
</CFIF>
```

Part
IV

Ch
18

continues

Listing 18.10 Continued

```
<TD COLSPAN="3" ALIGN="RIGHT">
<!--- Next button code --->
<CFIF NextStart LTE Books.RecordCount>
 <CFOUTPUT>
 <FORM ACTION="browse.cfm" METHOD="POST">
 <INPUT TYPE="hidden" NAME="start" VALUE="#NextStart#">
 <INPUT TYPE="hidden" NAME="Title" VALUE="#Title#">
 <INPUT TYPE="hidden" NAME="AuthorFirstName" VALUE="#AuthorFirstName#">
 <INPUT TYPE="hidden" NAME="AuthorLastName" VALUE="#AuthorLastName#">
 <INPUT TYPE="hidden" NAME="ISBN" VALUE="#isbn#">
 <INPUT TYPE="hidden" NAME="CategoryID" VALUE="#CategoryID#">
 <INPUT TYPE="hidden" NAME="InStock" VALUE="#InStock#">
 <INPUT TYPE="submit" VALUE="Next #MaxRows#">
 </FORM>
 </CFOUTPUT>
</CFIF>
</TD>

</TR>

</TABLE>

<!--- Include footer file --->
<CFINCLUDE TEMPLATE="footer.cfm">
```

This time, you create variables for both the previous and next start positions:

```
<!--- What are the previous and next row to start positions --->
<CFSET PrevStart = Start - MaxRows>
<CFSET NextStart = Start + MaxRows>
```

Because both calculations use MaxRows rather than a hard-coded value, you need just change the MaxRows once, and the rest of your code will change automatically.

Embed two forms this time, one for the "Previous 5" and one for the "Next 5" button. Each one has the entire set of search fields embedded in it as well as the appropriate start position. In addition, you also put a `<CFIF>` statement around each of the forms to prevent the buttons from displaying an invalid selection. The code `<CFIF PrevStart GTE 1>` ensures that the previous button is displayed only if there are any previous records (thus the "Previous 5" button will never be displayed on the first results page). The code `<CFIF NextStart LTE Books.RecordCount>` ensures that the next start position is not greater than the number of records retrieved (thus the "Next 5" button will never be displayed on the last results page).

NOTE

You used forms here for the Previous and Next buttons. You could just as easily use text or images and embed the fields as URL parameters. If you do decide to use URL parameters, make sure that you use the `URLEncodedFormat()` function to convert any passed text into URL safe text. ■

Enhancing Forms with *CFFORM*

by Michael Dinowitz

Working with *CFFORM*

This chapter covers two concepts. The major concept, which encompasses the entire chapter, is that although forms are good, they can be better. Cold Fusion goes beyond the standard HTML form capabilities by incorporating easy-to-use controls that allow data validation, enhanced population from queries, and even totally new form types with Java. This brings us to the second concept of the chapter.

If you are morally opposed to Java, prepare to have your views challenged. Cold Fusion has incorporated several small, stable, and useful Java applets into its core system with easy to program controls for them. You should find these tags not only easy to use, but also a major enhancement to some ways of viewing data. All the standard Java fear should go out the window after you see these new tags in action. You don't have to worry about programming Java, learning applet syntax, or even looking at class files. This is Java without fear. On the other hand, those who feel that Java is a religion may be a bit disappointed. Cold Fusion uses Java as a tool to enhance a web page and allow better display of information. The Java here is used in a controlled way that will allow non-Java programmers and even non-programmers to take advantage of its power.

Almost all the tags in this chapter also use JavaScript for data validation and value control. This is JavaScript that's already written for you and that does not have to be touched at all. You'll probably never even look at it. You can actually go and see the JavaScript used by looking at a file named cfform.js in the C:\CFusion\Scripts\ directory (some systems may vary on CFusion directory placement).

Using *CFFORM*

Before you get into the CFFORM subtags, you have to discuss the tag that controls them all—the CFFORM tag itself. To avoid confusion, I will refer to the various tags that go inside the CFFORM block as *subtags*. Every tag discussed in this chapter (with the exception of CFGRIDUPDATE) must be placed within a CFFORM block. CFFORM is a small replacement for the standard HTML form tag that allows you to include the CFFORM subtags onto a page. When a page is actually run, the CFFORM tag creates a standard HTML form element containing links to the JavaScript code mentioned earlier as well as to the Java tags mentioned later. On the whole, there's really very little difference between the CFFORM tag and the HTML form tag. First, you'll read about the tag itself and then you'll go back to CFFORM in general. Table 19.1 shows the various attributes of the CFFORM tag.

Table 19.1 CFFORM Attributes

Name	Status	Description
NAME	Optional	A name for the form you are creating.
ACTION	Required	The name of the Cold Fusion page that will be executed when the form is submitted for processing. This is the exact same thing as the standard HTML form action.
ENABLECAB	Optional	Values are YES or NO with a default of NO. This element provides downloadable Microsoft cabinet (*.cab) files containing the Java classes used for CFFORM that include Java. If ENABLECAB is YES, the users will be asked whether they want to download the CAB file. Note that these CAB files are digitally signed using VeriSign digital IDs to ensure file security. Downloading the Java class CAB files will dramatically reduce the time required to load pages with CFFORM controls that incorporate a Java applet. The ENABLECAB attribute is supported only for MS Internet Explorer clients that have Authenticode 2.0 installed. At this time, there is no Netscape version of this technology.
METHOD	Required	This is the standard HTML method attribute that specifies how the form is sent. The standard options are Get and Post, with Get being the usual default.
TARGET	Optional	This is the standard HTML target syntax. This is used to specify what frame the form should be posted to.
ENCTYPE	Optional	This is the standard HTML form encoding declaration. Currently, the options are application/x-www-form-urlencoded for standard forms and multipart/form-data for forms using file uploading. The default is application/x-www-form-urlencoded.
ONSUBMIT	Optional	JavaScript function to execute after other input validation returns. Use this attribute to execute JavaScript for preprocessing data before the form is submitted.

Part

IV

Ch

19

As you can see, most of the CFFORM attributes are the same as the standard HTML form attributes. In truth, the CFFORM tag will even accept attributes not specified in Table 19.1. Any HTML form attribute that exists now or in the future can be added, and it will be passed directly to the page.

Because CFFORM itself does nothing other than hold Cold Fusion and HTML form subtags, I'm not going to give any specific examples. On the other hand, every CFFORM tag example will have a CFFORM tag around it. This will emphasize the nature of the tag; it holds form elements.

Types of *CFFORM* Subtags

Now that you understand the basic framework of the CFFORM tag, you can examine the subtags. To do so, I'm going to divide the tags into classes.

The first class will comprise CFSELECT and the various types of CFINPUT tags. These tags are processed on the server side and give an output of standard HTML. These server side tags are basically there to enhance both the population and validation of what can be seen as standard tags.

The remainder tags are all processed on the client side using small, standardized Java applets. These client side tags are further divided into classes based on functionality:

- The first class can be referred to as *simple tags*. They are called simple because they have a single tag to do all their work. The tags of this class are currently limited to CFTEXTINPUT and CFSLIDER.

- The second class is referred to as the *container tags*. This class is currently made up of the CFTREE and the CFGRID tags as well as their subelements. These are called containers because they can contain subtags to allow greater control over their functionality.

- The third class is the *container class*. They have no function on their own and can only be used inside the appropriate container. These tags are CFGRIDROW, CFGRIDCOLUMN, and CFTREEITEM.

- The CFAPPLET tag is a special case that falls outside the standard definition of classes. This tag is used to include a foreign Java applet into Cold Fusion. You'll learn more about this tag later. Just be aware that few of the standard CFFORM tag rules apply to CFAPPLET.

The only other exception is the CFGRIDUPDATE tag. This is actually not a CFFORM tag but only works in conjunction with the CFGRID tag. As such it will be discussed here, but none of the CFFORM rules apply to CFGRIDUPDATE.

Other *CFFORM*-Related Issues

Before discussing the individual tags, a few other CFFORM related issues should be examined.

Speed and *CFFORM*s   The CFFORM tag by itself adds only a tiny amount of extra code to the HTML page and takes almost no time to process. The speed problem comes in when you start to use the Java elements. These can take a few moments to download and start running on a system. To combat this, Cold Fusion uses a technique created by Microsoft for use with its browser. By setting the EnableCab attribute to Yes, any Java form element on a page can be installed on a Microsoft web browser. This does require Authenticode security on the client side, but most Microsoft browsers already have it installed. The end result is that instead of downloading a new copy of the applet every time you want to use it on a page, the version installed on the client is called. Clients have the option to disregard this if they want, so there will be few complaints.

Images and *CFFORM* Tags   Many of the CFFORM tags allow the inclusion of images in various manners. Because the CFFORM tags are Java, these images must be in a special directory in relation to the Java class files (see Figure 19.1). The standard location is in your Web server's \CFIDE\Classes\images\ directory. Any images that you may want to include in a CFFORM tag must be either in this directory or a subdirectory of this location. Both .gif and .jpg files can be used, and the size of the file is relatively unlimited. Remember that the graphic has to be downloaded with the Java applet for a CFFORM tag, so don't try to use a 5 MB file. Cold Fusion ships with a number of default images that are mainly used for CFTREE and CFGRID. Figure 19.1 shows these standard images by name.

FIG. 19.1

Standard images shipped with Cold Fusion.

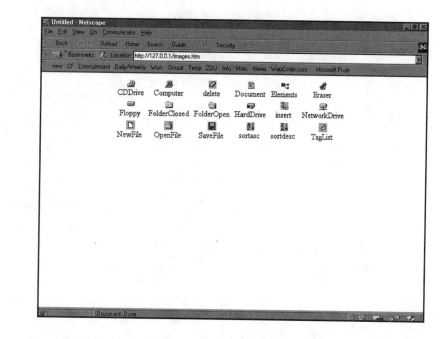

These images are all square .gif files with a byte size of less than 1KB and a graphic size of either 18×18 or 16×16. These graphics were included so that you can easily show disks, folders, drives, and so on. Because the main reason for the CFFORM tags is to enhance the data display to a user, the inclusion of these graphics just makes it better. It should be noted that some tags use an alias for some of these images. The exact name of the alias will be included in the attributes for the tags in question.

Colors and *CFFORM* Tags   Many CFFORM elements allow different colors to be used in many places. These colors can either be placed in a standard hexadecimal format or as predefined color names. If the hexadecimal format is used, the value must either use two pound (#) signs before it or none at all. If you are using the predefined colors, you are limited to Black, Magenta, Cyan, Orange, Darkgrey, Pink, Grey, White, Lightgrey, and Yellow. Note that these colors should be written as single words.

Common Attributes for Client-Side Tags All client side tags have many of the same attributes in common. These attributes have been divided up into tables that describe their general functions.

Table 19.2 contains the standard attributes supported by all the CFFORM Java tags. These range from the required Name attribute through error validation calls on to formatting codes. These are supported by all the standard CFFORM tags. Of all these attributes, the ones that will seem most familiar are the formatting codes. Many of these attributes mirror the HTML of the same type.

Table 19.2 Common Attributes for *CFFORM* Java Tags

Name	Status	Description
NAME	Required	A name for the CFFORM element. This has the same effect as any name element in a standard form tag. Every CFFORM tag must have a name element associated with it. Two CFFORM tags with the same name will result in the later element being sent. The receiving template will see the result as Form.Name.
NOTSUPPORTED	Optional	The text you want to display if the page containing a Java applet-based CFFORM control is opened by a browser that does not support Java or has Java support disabled. This must be in standard HTML. For example: `NOTSUPPORTED="<B> Browser must support Java to view Cold Fusion Java Applets</B>"` By default, if no message is specified, the following message appears: `<B>Browser must support Java to  view Cold Fusion Java Applets!</B>`
ONVALIDATE	Optional	The name of a valid JavaScript function used to validate user input. The form object, input object, and input object value are passed to the specified routine, which should return true if validation succeeds and false otherwise. The use of this element overrides the VALIDATE attribute when it exists.
ONERROR	Optional	The name of a valid JavaScript function you want to execute in the event of a failed validation. This only applies if ONVALIDATE is used.
ALIGN	Optional	Alignment value for the CFFORM element. Valid entries are: top, middle, left, right, bottom, baseline, texttop, absbottom, absmiddle. This is the same as standard HTML alignment format.

Name	Status	Description
BOLD	Optional	Enter YES for boldface text, NO for regular text. This has the same effect as the <B></B> in HTML. The default is NO.
FONT	Optional	Font name for text. The available fonts are limited to those built into the Java language.
FONTSIZE	Optional	Font size for text.
HEIGHT	Optional	Height value in pixels of the control. This is the same as standard HTML height formatting.
HSPACE	Optional	Horizontal spacing of the control. This is the same as standard HTML hspace formatting.
ITALIC	Optional	Enter YES for italicized text, NO for normal text. This has the same effect as the <I></I> in HTML. Default is NO.
VSPACE	Optional	Vertical spacing of the control. This is the same as standard HTML vspace formatting.
WIDTH	Optional	Width value in pixels of the control. This is the same as standard HTML width formatting.

CFFORMs and Cold Fusion Studio   In general, Cold Fusion Studio makes the creation of CFFORMs rather easy. You can just select the tag you want, fill in the attributes, and it's ready to roll. There are a few limitations though. The first can stop any CFFORM-containing page in its tracks. As mentioned earlier, hexadecimal colors have to be prefixed either with two pound (#) signs or with none. The CFFORM wizards always give you the hexadecimal color with a single pound sign. This means that you have to go over all the code to either add or remove a sign to avoid an error. The other killer problem is a little over-enthusiasm when the tag wizards were being written up. Tags were written for CFINPUT with the types of submit, hidden, file, button, and image. Not only are these not part of the CFINPUT tag, use of these options will cause an error on the processing of the Cold Fusion page. The only other limitation of the Studio tag wizards is that they do not give options for the NOTSUPPORTED, ONVALIDATE, and ONERROR attributes. If you want these attributes, you have to add them by hand or depend on the tag completion helper. Because of the number of tags and other considerations, I won't show all the tag wizards in action.

Using *CFSELECT*

CFSELECT was created just to help out Cold Fusion programmers. In the old days, when someone wanted to populate an HTML form select with a query, she had to write some rather long code. For those who used Cold Fusion a lot, this was easy, but for new people, it was just something that had to be learned. CFSELECT took away the need for that chunk of code and wrapped it in a simple interface. Compare the two pieces of code that had to be used. Both will use the query

```
<CFQUERY NAME="GetData" DATASOURCE="CF 3.0 Examples">
        SELECT Employee_ID, FirstName + ' ' + LastName AS FullName FROM
➡Employees
</CFQUERY>
```

The old way was to do the following:

```
<Form ACTION="Test.cfm"
      METHOD="POST">
<SELECT NAME="Employees"
              Size="1">
<CFOUTPUT QUERY="GetData">
        <OPTION VALUE="#Employee_ID#" <CFIF #Employee_ID# is "12">
➡TED</CFIF>>#FullName#
</CFOUTPUT>
</SELECT>
</form>
The new way, using the CFSELECT tag:
<CFFORM ACTION="Test.cfm"
        METHOD="POST">
<CFSELECT NAME="Employees"
        SIZE="1"
        QUERY="GetData"
        VALUE="Employee_ID"
        DISPLAY="FullName"
        SELECTED="12">
</CFSELECT>
</CFFORM>
```

Now the CFSELECT method is a bit tighter, probably faster to write, and a bit nicer to look at. The results are exactly the same, but you have a slight difference in power. The old method allows you much finer control over the outputted variables. What happens if you want to select more than one Employee_ID? CFSELECT doesn't allow that, but it's rather easy to add an OR statement to the old method. The entire point of what I'm saying is that you should look at the job in question and use the method that best suits it.

The result of a CFSELECT method is the same as a standard HTML form element.

```
Form.Select_name=select_value
```

Table 19.3 shows the attributes for this tag.

Table 19.3 *CFSELECT* Attributes

Name	Status	Description
NAME	Required	A name for the form you are creating.
SIZE	Required	Size of the drop-down list box in number of entries.
REQUIRED	Optional	Yes or No. If Yes, a list element must be selected when the form is submitted. Default is No.

Name	Status	Description
MESSAGE	Optional	Message that appears if REQUIRED="Yes" and no selection is made.
ONERROR	Optional	The name of a valid JavaScript function you want to execute in the event of a failed validation.
MULTIPLE	Optional	Yes or No. Yes permits selection of multiple elements in the drop-down list box. The default is No.
QUERY	Optional	Name of the query to be used to populate the drop-down list box.
SELECTED	Optional	Enter a value matching at least one entry in VALUE to preselect the entry in the drop-down list box.
VALUE	Optional	The query column value for the list element. Used with the QUERY attribute.
DISPLAY	Optional	The query column displayed. Defaults to the Value of VALUE. Used with the QUERY attribute.

Using *CFINPUT*

As you've seen, the CFSELECT tag helped with the population of query results. The CFINPUT tag exists to help more with data validation than with straight population. As mentioned earlier, this data validation is done by JavaScript. In a moment, you'll look at this tag and compare it to both the standard HTML input tag and to the client side Java CFTEXTINPUT tag. First, look at the variables for the tag. Table 19.4 shows the attributes for CFINPUT.

Table 19.4 *CFINPUT* Attributes

Name	Status	Description
TYPE	Optional	Valid entries are
		Text(default) Creates a text entry box control.
		Radio Creates a radio button control.
		Checkbox Creates a check box control.
		Password Creates a password entry control.
		All other CFINPUT types are invalid.
NAME	Required	A name for the form input element.
VALUE	Optional	An initial value for the form input element.
REQUIRED	Optional	Enter Yes or No. Default is No.

Part
IV

Ch
19

continues

Table 19.4 Continued

Name	Status	Description
RANGE	Optional	Enter a minimum value; maximum value range separated by a comma. Valid only for numeric data.
VALIDATE	Optional	Valid entries are: date Verifies U.S. date entry in the form mm/dd/yyyy. eurodate Verifies valid European date entry in the form dd/mm/yyyy. time Verifies a time entry in the form hh:mm:ss. float Verifies a floating point entry. integer Verifies an integer entry. telephone Verifies a telephone entry. Telephone data must be entered as ###-###-####. The hyphen separator (-) can be replaced with a blank. The area code and exchange must begin with a digit between 1 and 9. zipcode (U.S. formats only) Number can be a 5-digit or 9-digit zip in the form #####-####. The hyphen separator (-) can be replaced with a blank. creditcard Blanks and dashes are stripped, and the number is verified using the mod10 algorithm. social_security_number Number must be entered as ###-##-####. The hyphen separator (-) can be replaced with a blank.
ONVALIDATE	Optional	The name of a valid JavaScript function used to validate user input. The form object, input object, and input object value are passed to the specified routine, which should return True if validation succeeds and False otherwise. When used, the VALIDATE attribute is ignored.
MESSAGE	Optional	Message text to appear if validation fails.
ONERROR	Optional	The name of a valid JavaScript function you want to execute in the event of a failed validation.
SIZE	Optional	The size of the input control. Ignored if TYPE is Radio or Checkbox.
MAXLENGTH	Optional	The maximum length of text entered when TYPE is Text.
CHECKED	Optional	Places checkmark when TYPE is check box; preselects radio buttons when TYPE is Radio.

To get the best idea of the CFINPUT tag, I'm going to hold off the description until the next section, which is on CFTEXTINPUT. This is the Java version of the input tag and by comparing the methods, you can see which is best in what circumstances.

Using *CFTEXTINPUT*

The CFTEXTINPUT tag is a close relative to the HTML INPUT=text tag. To really show what the CFTEXTINPUT tag is, you should compare it to the other methods of inputting text.

Figure 19.2 shows the three different forms of text input supported by Cold Fusion. You'll notice that they are almost exactly the same except that the Java version (third) is smaller and slightly nicer looking. Why this is so will be discussed later.

FIG. 19.2

The three text input methods.

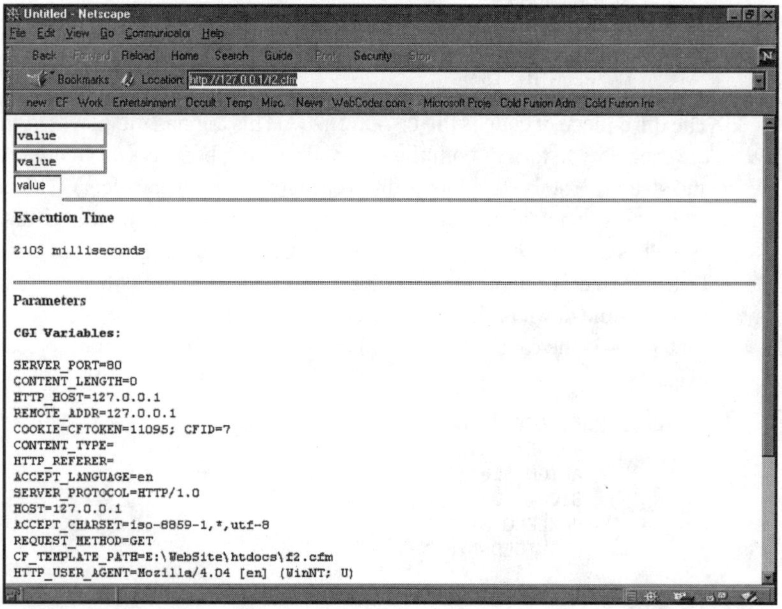

The three displays are built on three different pieces of code that do the same basic thing. The first is the basic form input code. Notice that the actual code is two tags rather than one because the second is needed to specify that the value is required. The advantage to this is that no Java or JavaScript is involved, and you can specify the message returned when validation or required status fails. The disadvantage is that there is a very small range of data validation, and the validation does not take place until the form result page loads:

```
<INPUT TYPE="Text"
       NAME="Name"
       VALUE="Value"
       SIZE="10"
       MAXLENGTH="15">
```

```
<INPUT TYPE="Hidden"
       NAME="Name_Required"
       VALUE="You must enter a name/value">
```

The second piece is a CFINPUT tag for the same thing. Although this is a Cold Fusion tag, the results will be in standard HTML. The advantages to this are a wide range of data validation and the data validation taking place before the form is sent. This is done with client side JavaScript error checking. This, of course, is also one of the disadvantages. If someone either has JavaScript turned off or does not support JavaScript, then there is no data validation. In addition, this tag has to be within a CFFORM tag rather than a standard FORM tag. Although there is almost no speed difference between the two, it has to be noted.

```
<CFINPUT TYPE="Text"
         NAME="Name"
         VALUE="Value"
         ALIGN="Left"
         REQUIRED="Yes"
         SIZE="10"
         MAXLENGTH="15">
```

The third piece of code is the CFTEXTINPUT. This tag has the power of the CFINPUT, but includes the capability to format both the text and the text box. As you've noticed earlier, the basic font and structure of the text box is different (some would say nicer). This is the primary advantage of this tag—being able to alter its display. This tag shares the disadvantages of the CFINPUT tag as well as any disadvantages relating to it being a Java applet. This means that people who have Java turned off or do not support it are in a small amount of trouble. The fact that it takes more time to come down is also a factor. One advantage to this tag—to combat part of its Java disadvantages—is the capability (which is shared by all the Java tags) to specify a non-Java alternative.

```
<CFTEXTINPUT NAME="Name"
             VALUE="Value"
             ALIGN="Left"
             SIZE="10"
             MAXLENGTH="15"
             REQUIRED="Yes">
```

Now the question is, when would you use each of these tags? Is the CFINPUT any better than the standard tag, and is the Java version any better than the others? The answer is both yes and no. The major power of the CFFORM tags in this case is the data validation capabilities. If you just want to make sure that a value is present, then the hidden/required version is good. The CFFORM tags on the other hand allow more forms of data validation. In addition, the Java version allows you to control the font, size, and colors of the text and box. The tag to use in a given situation really depends on what you need. Don't go crazy with the Java version just because it's there. As I've said, Java is a tool, not a way of life.

Now look at the attributes for the CFTEXTINPUT Java control. In addition to the standard tag elements mentioned in the previous sections, CFTEXTINPUT has a few that are specific to its use (see Table 19.5).

Table 19.5 *CFTEXTINPUT* Attributes

Name	Status	Description
VALUE	Optional	Default value for the tag. There is no limit on the size of this value, but the display is limited to the size element below.
REQUIRED	Optional	Yes or No. If Yes, the user must enter or change text.
RANGE	Optional	When using numeric data in the CFTEXTINPUT, this allows a minimum, maximum range to be set. Only useful for numeric data.
VALIDATE	Optional	Defines what sort of validation the data in the CFFORM element will be passed through. Valid entries are:
		Date Verifies U.S. date entry in the form mm/dd/yy.
		Eurodate Verifies valid European date entry in the form dd/mm/yyyy.
		Time Verifies a time entry in the form hh:mm:ss.
		Float Verifies a floating-point entry.
		Integer Verifies an integer entry.
		Telephone Verifies a telephone entry. Telephone data must be entered as ###-###-####. The hyphen separator (-) can be replaced with a blank. The area code and exchange must begin with a digit between 1 and 9.
		Zipcode (U.S. formats only) Number can be a 5-digit or 9-digit zip in the form #####-####. The hyphen separator (-) can be replaced with a blank.
		Creditcard Blanks and dashes are stripped, and the number is verified using the mod10 algorithm.
		social_security_number Number must be entered as ###-##-####. The hyphen separator (-) can be replaced with a blank.
		If the ONVALIDATE element is used, this element is ignored.
MESSAGE	Optional	Message text to appear if validation fails. This only applies if the VALIDATE element is used.
SIZE	Optional	Number of characters displayed before horizontal scrollbar appears. This does not seem to work because a tag is limited to a single line. Both this attribute and the width attribute seem to be able to control the actual size of the tag.
BGCOLOR	Optional	Background color of the control. Uses the standard color definitions for CFFORM.

Part

IV

Ch

19

continues

Table 19.5   Continued

Name	Status	Description
TEXTCOLOR	Optional	Text colors for the control. Uses the standard color definitions for CFFORM.
MAXLENGTH	Optional	The maximum length of text entered.

Listing 19.1 shows two different CFTEXTINPUT boxes. The first is the minimum script needed, whereas the second shows some of the features.

Listing 19.1   Two Different *CFTEXTINPUT* Boxes

```
<CFFORM ACTION="TEST.CFM"
        METHOD="POST"
        NAME="TEST">

<CFTEXTINPUT NAME="TEST1"
            VALUE="STANDARD, MINIMAL TAG">
<BR>
<CFTEXTINPUT NAME="TEST2"
            VALUE="TAG WITH A DIFFERENT BACKGROUND AND TEXT
➥COLOR WITH A NON-SUPPORTED FONT IN ITALIC."
            WIDTH="750"
            FONT="ALEFBET"
            FONTSIZE="20"
            BGCOLOR="##000000"
            TEXTCOLOR="##000FFF"
            ITALIC="YES">
</CFFORM>
```

The Form values returned from a page with a CFTEXTINPUT are straightforward. They take the same form as a standard form value. The preceding examples would result in:

```
TEST1= STANDARD, MINIMAL TAG
test2= Tag with a different background and text
➥color with a non-supported font in italic.
```

CFTEXTINPUT gets a rather raw deal when it comes to Cold Fusion Studio. The button for this tag is not on the tag choicer, and there's no easy way to put it there. On the other hand, the tag is there and will pop up if you have tag completion helper on or try to edit it after it's written.

Using *CFSLIDER*

The CFSLIDER tag is more fun than it is of any extreme value. It places a sliding bar control on a page that allows you to select a numeric value by just moving a knob. The only analogy in HTML would be a form select box with numbers in it. The slider control can be defined with a number of settings for range, default values, colors, formatting, and other features. Table 19.6 shows the attributes for this tag.

Table 19.6 *CFSLIDER* **Attributes**

Name	Status	Description
LABEL	Optional	A label that appears with the slider control, for example:
		LABEL="Volume %value%"
		You can use %value% to reference the slider value. If % is omitted, the slider value appears immediately following the label. Remember to set the refreshlabel attribute to yes when using %value%.
REFRESHLABEL	Optional	Yes or No. If Yes, the label is not refreshed when the slider is moved. Default is Yes.
IMG	Optional	Filename of the image to be used in the slider groove. This image must be in the standard CFFORM image directory or below it.
IMGSTYLE	Optional	Style of the image to appear in the slider groove. Valid entries are Centered, Tiled, and Scaled. Default is Scaled.
RANGE	Optional	Determines the values of the left and right slider range. The slider value appears as the slider is moved. Separate values by a comma, for example:
		RANGE="1,100"
		Default is 0,100. Valid only for numeric data.
SCALE	Optional	An unsigned integer. SCALE defines the slider scale within the value of RANGE. For example, if RANGE=0,1000 and SCALE=100, the incremental values for the slider would be 0, 100, 200, 300, and so on.
VALUE	Optional	Determines the default slider setting. Must be within the values specified in RANGE. Defaults to the minimum value specified in RANGE.
ONVALIDATE	Optional	The name of a valid JavaScript function used to validate user input, in this case, a change to the default slider value.
MESSAGE	Optional	Message text to appear if validation fails.
ONERROR	Optional	The name of a valid JavaScript function you want to execute in the event of a failed validation.
GROOVECOLOR	Optional	Color value of the slider groove. The slider groove is the area in which the slider box moves. Uses the standard color definitions for CFFORM.

Part
IV

Ch
19

continues

Table 19.6 Continued

Name	Status	Description
BGCOLOR	Optional	Background color of slider label. Uses the standard color definitions for CFFORM.
TEXTCOLOR	Optional	Slider label text color. Uses the standard color definitions for CFFORM.

Listing 19.2 shows three different CFSLIDER tags (see Figure 19.3).

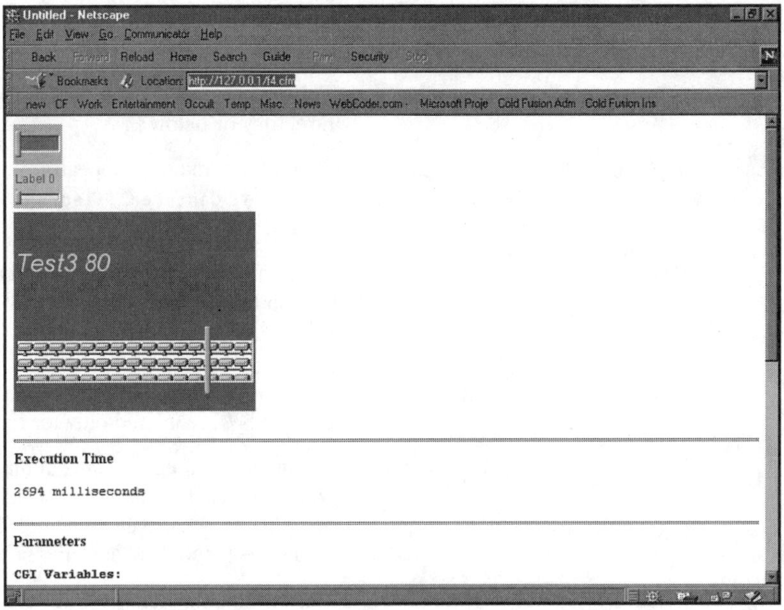

FIG. 19.3
Three *CFSLIDER*
examples.

The first is the minimum code needed to make this tag work. As you can see, it's grey, dull, and tells us nothing. The second example has a bit more in terms of display and usability. Here, we have some nice colors and an updating label. The third example takes us another step by adding in size, fonts, and a picture in the groove. Notice that when a picture is specified for the groove, the color specified for the area is ignored.

Listing 19.2 Three Different *CFSLIDER* Tags

```
<CFFORM ACTION="TEST.CFM"
        METHOD="POST"
        NAME="TEST">
<CFSLIDER NAME="TEST1">
<BR>
<CFSLIDER NAME="TEST2"
```

```
                LABEL="LABEL %VALUE%"
                BGCOLOR="##00FF00"
                TEXTCOLOR="##FF0000"
                GROOVECOLOR="##FFFF00"
                REFRESHLABEL="YES">
  <BR>
  <CFSLIDER NAME="TEST3"
                VALUE="50"
                LABEL="TEST3 %VALUE%"
                RANGE="1,100"
                IMG="NETWORKDRIVE.GIF"
                IMGSTYLE="TILED"
                SCALE="10"
                HEIGHT="200"
                WIDTH="250"
                REFRESHLABEL="YES">
  </CFFORM>
```

The values returned from a page with a CFSLIDER follow the same format as the standard HTML form tags (and CFTEXTINPUT for that matter). The preceding examples would result in:

```
test1= standard, minimal tag
test2= Tag with a different background and text
➥color with a non-supported font in italic.
```

Using *CFTREE* and *CFTREEITEM*

The CFTREE tag creates one of the most powerful and useful controls in Cold Fusion—a branched tree control for the display of data. The CFTREE tag is actually composed of two tags: the CFTREE tag itself (which is like a container for the data) and the CFTREEITEM (which describes how the data will be formatted).

To truly describe the CFTREE tag, you have to build one and see it in action. Table 19.7 contains the attributes needed to build the CFTREE shell.

Part
IV

Ch
19

Table 19.7 Attributes to Build *CFTREE* Shell

Name	Status	Description
REQUIRED	Optional	Yes or No. User must select an item in the tree control. Default is No.
DELIMITER	Optional	The character used to separate elements in the form variable PATH. The default is \.
COMPLETEPATH	Optional	Yes passes the root level of the *treename.path* form variable when the CFTREE is submitted. If omitted or No, the root level of this form variable is not included.

continues

Table 19.7   Continued

Name	Status	Description
APPENDKEY	Optional	Optional. Yes or No. When used with HREF. Yes passes the CFTREEITEMKEY variable along with the value of the selected tree item in the URL to the application page specified in the CFFORM ACTION attribute. The default is Yes.
HIGHLIGHTHREF	Optional	Yes highlights links associated with a CFTREEITEM with an URL attribute value. No disables highlight. The default is Yes.
BORDER	Optional	Places a border around the tree. Default is Yes.
HSCROLL	Optional	Permits horizontal scrolling. Default is Yes.
VSCROLL	Optional	Permits vertical scrolling. Default is Yes.
MESSAGE	Optional	Message text to appear if validation fails.

After you build the CFTREE container, you have to put the data in. This is done using the CFTREEITEM tag.

All data inside a CFTREE must be contained within a CFTREEITEM tag. This can range from data retrieved from queries (DataBase, LDAP, POP, and so on) to data created by hand. After you've examined the attributes (see Table 19.8), you'll build a few examples so that you can get a better idea of what's going on.

Table 19.8   *CFTREEITEM* Attributes

Name	Status	Description
VALUE	Required	Value passed when the CFFORM is submitted. When populating a CFTREE with data from a CFQUERY, columns are specified in a comma-separated list: VALUE="dept_id,emp_id"
DISPLAY	Optional	Optional. The label for the tree item. Default is VALUE. When populating a CFTREE with data from a CFQUERY, display names are specified in a comma-separated list: DISPLAY="dept_name,emp_name"
PARENT	Optional	Value for tree item parent.
IMG	Optional	Image name or filename for the tree item. When populating a CFTREE with data from a CFQUERY, images or filenames for each level of the tree are specified in a comma-separated list.

Name	Status	Description
		The default image name is `Folder`. A number of images are supplied and can be specified using only the image name (no file extension):
		folder
		floppy
		fixed
		cd
		document
		element
		Use commas to separate image names corresponding to Tree level, for example:
		`IMG="folder,document"`
		`IMG=",document`
		To specify your own custom image, specify the path and file extension: `IMG="../images/ page1.gif"`
IMGOPEN	Optional	Icon displayed with open tree item. You can specify the icon filename using a relative path. As with IMG, you can use an image supplied with Cold Fusion.
HREF	Optional	URL to associate with the tree item or a query column for a tree that is populated from a query. If HREF is a query column, then the HREF value is the value populated by the query. If HREF is not recognized as a query column, it is assumed that the HREF text is an actual HTML HREF.
		When populating a CFTREE with data from a CFQUERY, HREFs can be specified in a comma-separated list:
		`HREF="http://dept_server,http://emp_server"`
TARGET	Optional	Target attribute for HREF URL. When populating a CFTREE with data from a CFQUERY, targets are specified in a comma-separated list:
		`TARGET="FRAME_BODY,_blank"`
QUERY	Optional	Query name used to generate data for the tree item.
QUERYASROOT	Optional	Yes or No. Defines specified query as the root level. As in Example 1, this option prevents having to create an additional parent CFTREEITEM.
EXPAND	Optional	Yes or No. Yes expands tree to show tree item children. No keeps tree item collapsed. Default is Yes.

Part

IV

Ch

19

Now build a minimal CFTREE (see Figure 19.4). The data from this tree will come from a query (see Listing 19.3).

FIG. 19.4

A minimal *CFTREE* example.

Listing 19.3 Building a Minimal *CFTREE*

```
<CFQUERY NAME="ENGINEERING" DATASOURCE="CF 3.0 EXAMPLES">
SELECT FIRSTNAME + ' ' + LASTNAME AS NAME
        FROM EMPLOYEES
</CFQUERY>

<CFFORM ACTION="TEST.CFM"
        METHOD="POST"
        ENABLECAB="NO"
        NAME="TEST">
<CFTREE NAME="TREE1">
<CFTREEITEM VALUE="NAME"
            IMG="FOLDER,DOCUMENT"
            QUERY="ENGINEERING">
</CFTREE>
```

As you can see both from the code and the figure, the results are not exactly useful or pretty. To really play with this, you should add in pieces such as images, altered sizes, and other attributes (see Figure 19.5 and Listing 19.4).

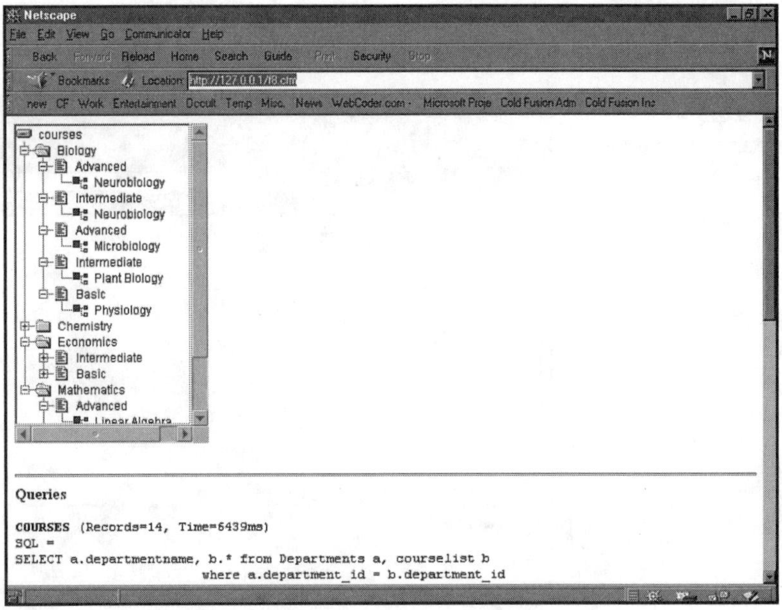

FIG. 19.5

A sample multirow query.

Listing 19.4   Multirow Query Example

```
<CFQUERY NAME="COURSES" DATASOURCE="CF 3.0 EXAMPLES">
        SELECT A.DEPARTMENTNAME, B.* FROM DEPARTMENTS A, COURSELIST B
            WHERE A.DEPARTMENT_ID = B.DEPARTMENT_ID
            ORDER BY B.DEPARTMENT_ID
</CFQUERY>
<CFFORM ACTION="TEST.CFM"
        METHOD="POST"
        ENABLECAB="NO"
        NAME="TEST">
<CFTREE NAME="TREE1"
        BORDER="YES"
        HSCROLL="YES"
        VSCROLL="YES"
        REQUIRED="YES"
        APPENDKEY="YES"
        HIGHLIGHTHREF="YES">
<CFTREEITEM VALUE="DEPARTMENTNAME,COURSELEVEL, COURSENAME"
            IMG="FLOPPY, FOLDER, DOCUMENT, ELEMENT"
            QUERY="COURSES"
            QUERYASROOT="YES"
            EXPAND="YES">
</CFTREE>
```

Part

IV

Ch

19

As you can see, this example shows much of the CFTREE tag in action. You have a multirowed query being outputted in a nice, easy to view manner. This is exactly what CFTREE was designed for.

The final CFTREE example will be creating a tree from scratch with no query (see Listing 19.5 and Figure 19.6). This will also show hyperlinks embedded inside a CFTREEITEM.

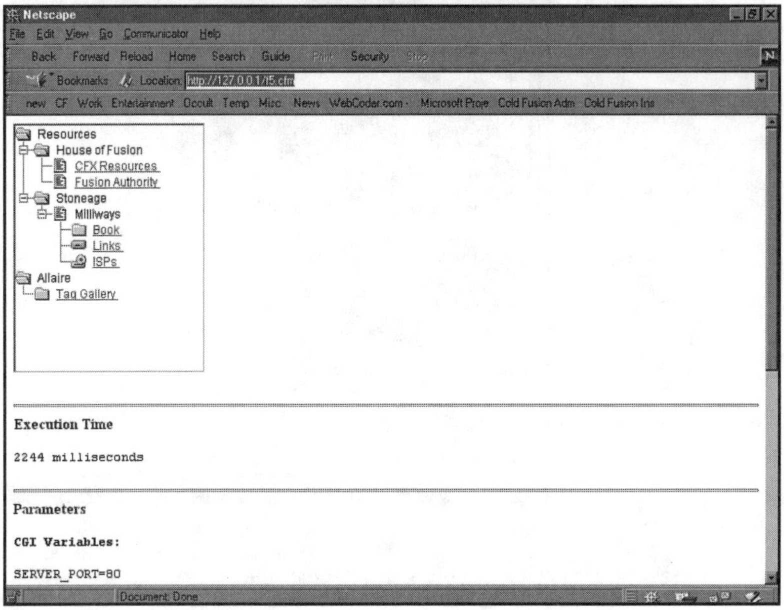

FIG. 19.6

An example of creating a tree from scratch.

Listing 19.5   Creating a Tree from Scratch

```
<CFFORM ACTION="TEST.CFM"
        METHOD="POST"
        NAME="TEST">
<CFTREE NAME="TEST3"
        HIGHLIGHTHREF="YES"
        HEIGHT="250"
        WIDTH="200"
        HSCROLL="NO"
        VSCROLL="NO">
<CFTREEITEM VALUE="RESOURCES" EXPAND="YES">
<CFTREEITEM VALUE="HOUSE OF FUSION"
              PARENT="RESOURCES"
              EXPAND="NO">
<CFTREEITEM VALUE="CFX RESOURCES"
              PARENT="HOUSE OF FUSION"
              IMG="DOCUMENT"
              HREF="HTTP://WWW.HOUSEOFFUSION.COM">
<CFTREEITEM VALUE="FUSION AUTHORITY"
              PARENT="HOUSE OF FUSION"
              IMG="DOCUMENT"
            HREF="HTTP://WWW.HOUSEOFFUSION.COM/CF_COURSE/CF_INST_FRAME.HTML">
<CFTREEITEM VALUE="STONEAGE" PARENT="RESOURCES">
<CFTREEITEM VALUE="MILLIWAYS"
              PARENT="STONEAGE"
              IMG="DOCUMENT">
```

```
<CFTREEITEM VALUE="BOOK"
            PARENT="MILLIWAYS"
            IMG="FOLDER"
            HREF="HTTP://MILLIWAYS.STONEAGE.COM/CF/BOOK.HTML">
<CFTREEITEM VALUE="LINKS"
            PARENT="MILLIWAYS"
            IMG="FLOPPY"
            HREF="HTTP://MILLIWAYS.STONEAGE.COM/CF/LINKS.CFM">
<CFTREEITEM VALUE="ISPS"
            PARENT="MILLIWAYS"
            IMG="CD"
            HREF="HTTP://MILLIWAYS.STONEAGE.COM/CF/ISP/INDEX.CFM">
<CFTREEITEM VALUE="ALLAIRE">
<CFTREEITEM VALUE="TAG GALLERY"
            PARENT="ALLAIRE"
            EXPAND="YES"
            HREF="HTTP://WWW.ALLAIRE.COM/TAGGALLERY">
</CFTREE>
</CFFORM>
```

Data is sent from a CFTREE tag in a slightly different form than you've seen before. Rather than one form value being sent, there are two. The first value is the element you chose. In the example illustrated in Listing 19.5, if you clicked on milliways, your first form result would be just that. The second result would actually be the path that you took to get there—Resources/ Stoneage/Milliways. The values can be retrieved by using the following syntax.

```
form.test3.node = Milliways
form.test3.path = Resources/Stoneage/Milliways
```

As mentioned in the attributes section, the delimiter attribute allows you to change the delimiters in the path results. Although the default is a backslash(/), almost any character can be used. In addition, if the completepath attribute is set to Yes, the full root will be appended to the beginning of the path.

Using *CFGRID*

Although CFGRID was originally a spreadsheet style grid for outputting data, it has grown into more. The current version allows for the adding of new data rows, deleting of rows, sorting of columns, and instant updating of all data in the grid. This tag gives a nice, clean way of displaying spreadsheet type data on a web page.

As with the other CFFORM tags, you really have to build some example applications to see what this tag looks like and what it does.

CFGRID has more than 30 attributes that you can use to customize its appearance and behavior. Any attributes set in the CFGRID tag affect the entire grid. You can also specify options for specific rows or columns by passing attributes to CFGRIDCOLUMN and CFGRIDROW. Options passed to CFGRIDCOLUMN and CFGRIDROW override any options set at the CFGRID level.

Table 19.9 shows the attributes supported by CFGRID.

Part

IV

Ch

19

Table 19.9 *CFGRID* **Attributes**

Name	Status	Description
APPENDKEY	Optional	Controls whether the URL CFGRIDKEY variable should be set containing the selected cell's value; default is Yes.
BGCOLOR	Optional	Background color of the control. Valid entries are: black, magenta, cyan, orange, darkgrey, pink, grey, white, lightgrey, and yellow.
		A hex value can also be entered in the form: BGCOLOR="##xxxxxx" where x is 0-9 or A-F. Use either two pound signs or no pound signs.
COLHEADERALIGN	Optional	Alignment of column header text, valid entries are: left, right, center. Default is center.
COLHEADERBOLD	Optional	Yes to use boldface text in column header; No for regular text. Default is No.
COLHEADERFONT	Optional	Column header font name.
COLHEADERFONTSIZE	Optional	Column header font size.
COLHEADERITALIC	Optional	Yes to use italic text in column header; No for regular text. Default is No.
COLHEADERS	Optional	Yes to display column headers, No to hide column headers. Default is Yes.
GRIDDATAALIGN	Optional	Alignment of cell text; valid entries are: left, right, center. Default is left.
HIGHLIGHTHREF	Optional	Controls whether URLs in cells are highlighted and underlined. Default is Yes.
HREF	Optional	URL (or template) to go to upon cell selection.
MAXROWS	Optional	Maximum number of query rows to display, same as CFOUTPUT MAXROWS.
QUERY	Optional	The name of the query to be displayed in the grid.
ROWHEADER	Optional	Yes to display row headers; No to hide row headers. Default is Yes.
ROWHEADERALIGN	Optional	Alignment of row header text; valid entries are: left, right, center. Default is left.
ROWHEADERBOLD	Optional	Yes to use boldface text in row header; No for regular text. Default is No.
ROWHEADERFONT	Optional	Row header font name.

Name	Status	Description
ROWHEADERFONTSIZE	Optional	Row header font size.
ROWHEADERITALIC	Optional	Yes to use italic text in row header; No for regular text. Default is No.
ROWHEADERWIDTH	Optional	The width, in pixels, of the row header. Defaults to whatever would be the best fit.
SELECTCOLOR	Optional	Background color for selected cells. See BGCOLOR for valid options.
SELECTMODE	Optional	Controls selection mode. Valid entries are: SINGLE (selection of a single cell); ROW (selection of an entire row when a cell is selected); COLUMN (selection of an entire column when a cell is selected); BROWSE (no selection, just browsing is permitted). Default is BROWSE.
TARGET	Optional	Target window for URL; same as HTML TARGET attribute.

To see how CFGRID could be used, see Figure 19.7 and Listing 19.6.

FIG. 19.7

An example of a minimal grid.

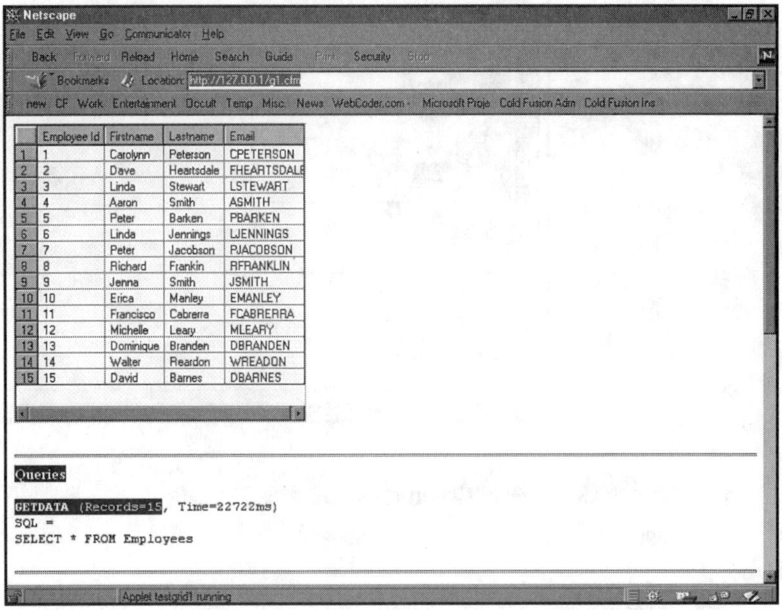

Listing 19.6   Minimal Grid Example

```
<CFQUERY NAME="GETDATA" DATASOURCE="A2Z">
      SELECT * FROM EMPLOYEES
</CFQUERY>
<CFFORM NAME="TEST1" ACTION="TEST.CFM" METHOD="POST">
<CFGRID NAME="TESTGRID1" QUERY="GETDATA">
</CFGRID>
</CFFORM>
```

This example used the minimum code necessary for a grid. No CFGRIDCOLUMN tag is needed because the database fields were used as the default column names. The disadvantage to this is that all the columns returned from the query must be used.

The next example (see Figure 19.8 and Listing 19.7) accomplishes the exact same thing, but this time the grid columns are explicitly provided.

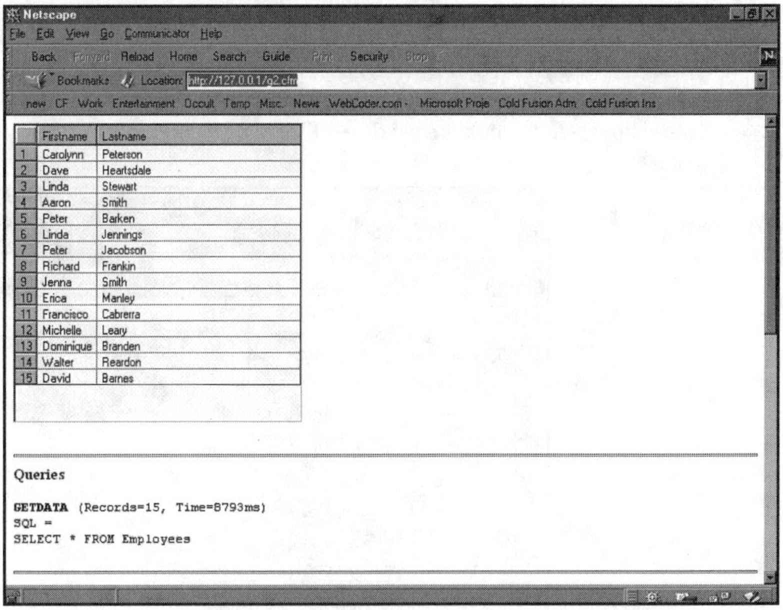

FIG. 19.8

An example with grid columns explicitly provided.

Listing 19.7   Grid Columns Explicitly Provided

```
<CFQUERY NAME="GETDATA" DATASOURCE="A2Z">
      SELECT * FROM EMPLOYEES
</CFQUERY>
<CFFORM NAME="TEST1" ACTION="TEST.CFM" METHOD="POST">
<CFGRID NAME="TESTGRID1" QUERY="GETDATA">
<CFGRIDCOLUMN NAME="FIRSTNAME">
<CFGRIDCOLUMN NAME="LASTNAME">
</CFGRID>
</CFFORM>
```

As you can see, this has allowed us to limit the data displayed.

The control of colors, size, fonts, and other attributes can all be set using CFGRID attributes. The next code sample (see Listing 19.8 and Figure 19.9) is the same grid again, but this time the font and color are specified.

FIG. 19.9

An example of a grid enhanced with display features.

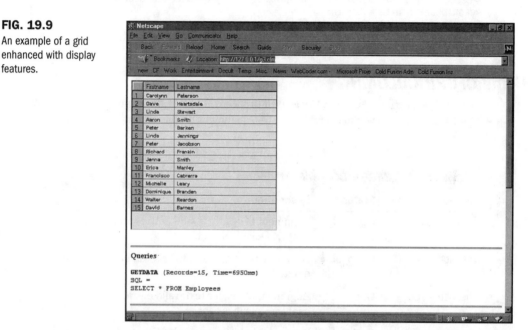

Part

IV

Ch

19

Listing 19.8   Grid Enhanced with Display Features

```
<CFQUERY NAME="getdata" DATASOURCE="CF 3.0 Examples">
       SELECT * FROM Employees
</CFQUERY>
<CFFORM NAME="test1" ACTION="test.cfm" METHOD="POST">
<CFGRID NAME="testgrid1" QUERY="getdata" FONT="Verdana" FONTSIZE="10"
➥BGCOLOR="yellow" BOLD="Yes">
<CFGRIDCOLUMN NAME="Firstname">
<CFGRIDCOLUMN NAME="Lastname">
</CFGRID>
</CFFORM>
```

The cells in a CFGRID can optionally be links to other URLs. To do this, you must allow selection to occur within the grid. The CFGRID SELECTMODE attribute instructs CFGRID to allow or disallow selection. The URL itself is passed to the CFGRID HREF attribute. The URL may be a fully quali-fied URL (starting with http) or just Cold Fusion template. When a user clicks on a cell, the specified URL is called, and the selected cell's value is passed as an URL parameter called CFGRIDKEY. The next example sets SELECTMODE to single (to allow the selection of a single cell) and provides the name of a Cold Fusion template to be called when any state is selected.

```
<CFQUERY NAME="getdata" DATASOURCE="CF 3.0 Examples">
        SELECT * FROM Employees
</CFQUERY>
<CFFORM NAME="test1" ACTION="test.cfm" METHOD="POST">
<CFGRID NAME="testgrid1" QUERY="getdata" FONT="Verdana" FONTSIZE="10"
➥BGCOLOR="yellow" BOLD="Yes" SELECTMODE="Single" HREF="process.cfm">
<CFGRIDCOLUMN NAME="Firstname">
<CFGRIDCOLUMN NAME="Lastname">
</CFGRID>
</CFFORM>
```

Using *CFGRIDCOLUMN*

As mentioned earlier, CFGRIDCOLUMN is used to specify the individual columns within a CFGRID. CFGRIDCOLUMN allows you to override grid-wide settings with the column-specific attributes listed in Table 19.10.

Table 19.10   *CFGRIDCOLUMN* Attributes

Name	Status	Description
DATAALIGN	Optional	Alignment of cell text; valid entries are: left, right, center. Default is left.
HEADER	Optional	Header text; NAME attribute text will be used if this is omitted.
HEADERALIGN	Optional	Alignment of header text; valid entries are: left, right, center. Default is center.
HEADERBOLD	Optional	Yes to use boldface text in header; No for regular text. Default is No.
HEADERFONT	Optional	Header font name.
HEADERFONTSIZE	Optional	Header font size.
HEADERITALIC	Optional	Yes to use italic text in header; No for regular text. Default is No.
HREF	Optional	URL (or template) to go to upon cell selection.
TARGET	Optional	Target window for URL; same as HTML TARGET attribute.

Using *CFGRIDROW*

Up to this point, you've been dealing with grids built with a query. As with the CFTREE tag, you have the option to build a grid from scratch. This is where the CFGRIDROW tag comes in. A separate CFGRIDROW tag must be provided for each row of data to be added to the grid. CFGRIDROW takes a single attribute (see Table 19.11).

Table 19.11 *CFGRIDROW* **Attribute**

Name	Status	Description
DATA	Required	Comma-delimited list of values for each cell in this row; must have a value for each cell. If a value has a comma in it, that value must be escaped with two commas.

In the following example (see Listing 19.9 and Figure 19.10), you've created a grid with data written directly into the code.

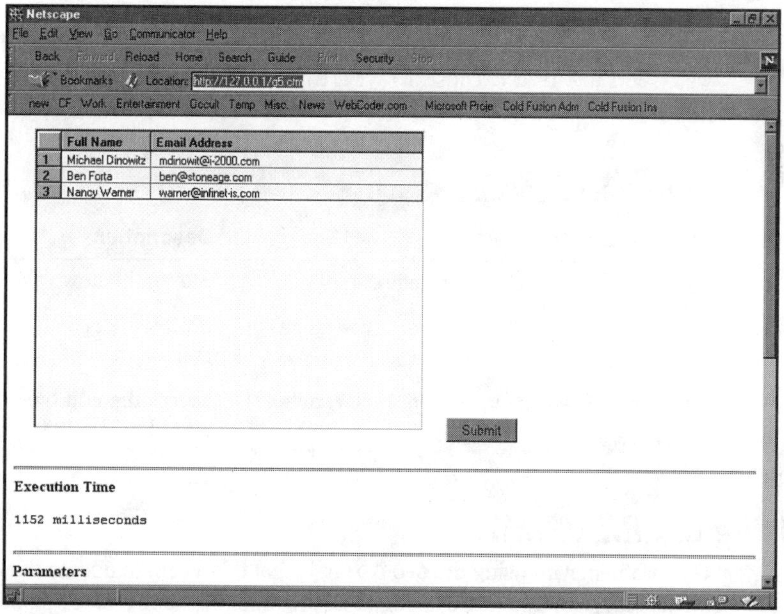

FIG. 19.10

An example of a grid without a query.

Part

IV

Ch

19

Listing 19.9   A Grid Without a Query

```
<CFFORM NAME="GridForm" ACTION="catchme.cfm" >
        <CFGRID NAME="grid_one"
           HEIGHT=300
           WIDTH=400
           HSPACE=20
           VSPACE="6"
           SELECTCOLOR="magenta"
           SELECTMODE="row"
           ROWHEADERS="Yes"
           BOLD="no"
           COLHEADERITALIC="No"
           COLHEADERBOLD="Yes"
           ROWHEADERITALIC="No"
```

continues

Listing 19.9 Continued

```
        ROWHEADERBOLD="Yes">
        <CFGRIDCOLUMN NAME="full_name" HEADER="Full Name">
        <CFGRIDCOLUMN NAME="email_address" HEADER="Email Address">
        <CFGRIDROW DATA="Michael Dinowitz, mdinowit@i-2000.com">
        <CFGRIDROW DATA="Ben Forta, ben@stoneage.com">
        <CFGRIDROW DATA="Nancy Warner, warner@infinet-is.com">
    </CFGRID>
    <INPUT TYPE="Submit" VALUE=" Submit "> <BR>
</CFFORM>
```

Like CFTREE, the CFGRID tag sends back more than one form element to a result page. Not only does the CFGRID send back multiple elements, these elements are one-dimensional arrays as well (see Table 19.12). These arrays are referenced like any other Cold Fusion arrays. The primary use of this data is for record adding and updating using the CFGRIDUPDATE tag.

Table 19.12 *CFGRID* Results

Form Attribute	Description
gridname.colname [row_index]	Stores the new value of an edited grid cell
Gridname.Original.colname [row_index]	Stores the original value of the edited grid cell
Gridname.RowStatus.Action [row_index]	Stores the edit type made against the edited grid cell

Using *CFGRIDUPDATE*

One problem with using the CFGRID tag is that it is a pain to update. New data is added, rows are deleted, and things are changed all the time. To make it easier to add all this data to a database, the CFGRIDUPDATE tag was added in. As mentioned previously, this is not really a CFFORM tag but is included here because it needs a CFGRID tag to operate. This tag takes the current values of the grid, compares them to the original values, and then goes to work. First all the rows that have been deleted are removed, the new rows are inserted, and then the updating happens. Table 19.13 shows the attributes for this tag.

Table 19.13 *CFGRIDUPDATE* Attributes

Name	Status	Description
GRID	Required	The name of the CFGRID form element that is the source for the update action.
DATASOURCE	Required	The name of the ODBC data source for the update action.
TABLENAME	Required	The name of the table you want to update.

Name	Status	Description
USERNAME	Optional	If specified, USERNAME overrides the username value specified in the ODBC setup.
PASSWORD	Optional	If specified, PASSWORD overrides the password value specified in the ODBC setup.
TABLEOWNER	Optional	For data sources that support table ownership (such as SQL Server, Oracle, and Sybase SQL Anywhere), use this field to specify the owner of the table.
TABLEQUALIFIER	Optional	For data sources that support table qualifiers, use this field to specify the qualifier for the table. The purpose of table qualifiers varies across drivers. For SQL Server and Oracle, the qualifier refers to the name of the database that contains the table. For the Intersolv dBase driver, the qualifier refers to the directory where the DBF files are located.
KEYONLY	Optional	Yes or No. Yes specifies that in the update action, the WHERE criteria is confined to just the key values. No specifies that in addition to the key values, the original values of any changed fields are included in the WHERE criteria. Default is Yes.

Using the following example grid, you can do all the changes you want and then submit it to a page containing the CFGRIDUPDATE code for it to go directly into the database.

```
PAGE 1:
<CFQUERY NAME="GETDATA" DATASOURCE="A2Z">
        SELECT * FROM EMPLOYEES
</CFQUERY>
<CFFORM NAME="TEST1" ACTION="TEST.CFM" METHOD="POST">
<CFGRID NAME="TESTGRID1" QUERY="GETDATA">
</CFGRID>
</CFFORM>
PAGE 2:
<CFGRIDUPDATE GRID="TESTGRID1"
        DATASOURCE="A2Z"
        TABLENAME="EMPLOYEES"
        KEYONLY="No">
```

Using *CFAPPLET*

One of the newest and least used or understood features of Cold Fusion 3.1 is the CFAPPLET tag. This tag allows you to extend the power of CFFORM by adding in new Java elements that you can create. This goes beyond a simple Java applet in that you can have the results of the Java applet sent through like a form element. In addition, much of the code you would normally write for a Java applet is handled by Cold Fusion using default values you set during registration.

Assume that you have a Java calculator applet that you want to add to a form. You want the end user to be able to do a calculation, select a few other things on the form, and send the whole thing to be processed. The first step would be to write or acquire the applet.

N O T E You must know the METHOD used by the applet to return data to the screen. Currently CFAPPLET only supports a single return METHOD. ▩

After you have your applet, you have to register it. Go to the Cold Fusion Administrator and select the Applets button. This will show you a list of all registered applets and allow you to add new ones.

As you can see, the Calculator applet is already registered (see Figure 19.11). To register a new applet, type in the applet name and click the Register button (see Figure 19.12).

FIG. 19.11

The applet registration, part 1.

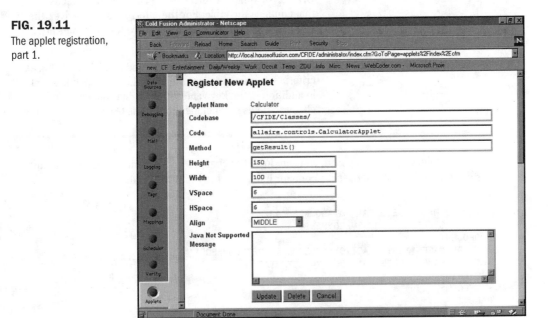

The first thing to do is set the Codebase and Code arguments for the applet. This is basically the location and name of the applet. This must appear exact as it will be used to point to the exact location of the applet. The method is the part of the Java code that will return a value to the screen. You have to specify which method is supplying the information you want to capture and pass. The alignment settings (Height, Width, VSpace, HSpace, Align) here are the defaults and can be changed later when the applet is used on a page. The Java unsupported message allows you to set a message or do an operation when the end user has a browser that doesn't support Java. The final pieces are the default parameters needed for the operation of the methods within the applet. Like above, these are default parameters and can be changed on actual usage.

FIG. 19.12

The applet registration, part 2.

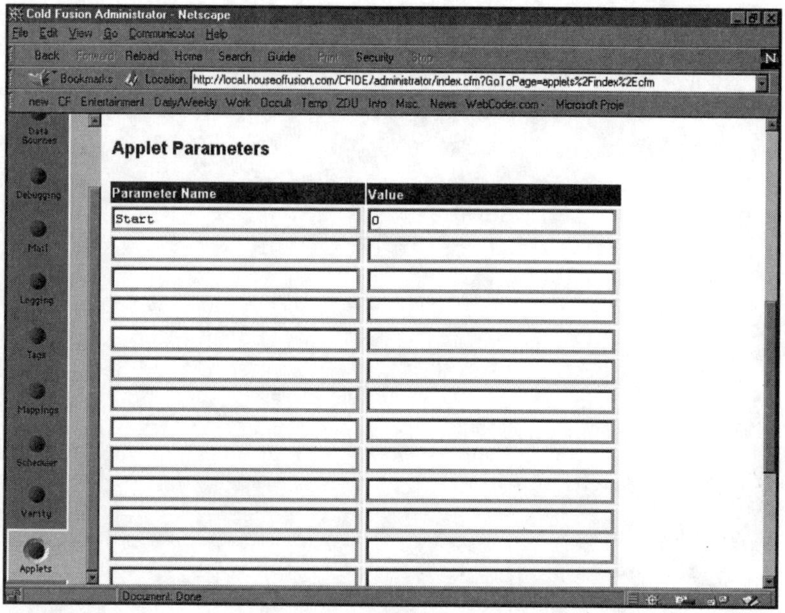

Now that you've registered the applet, use it. The standard syntax for your calculator is

```
<CFFORM NAME="CalculatorForm" ACTION="CalculatorResult.cfm">
<CFApplet APPLETSOURCE="Calculator" NAME="Calculator">
</CFFORM>
```

This is the minimum needed to use a registered applet. CFAPPLETs do not share most of the standard tag elements with the other CFFORM tags. The only ones that are equivalent are the NAME and alignment codes (Height, Width, VSpace, HSpace, Align). All others are specific to CFAPPLET (see Table 19.14).

Part
IV

Ch
19

Table 19.14   *CFAPPLET* Attributes

Name	Status	Description
APPLETSOURCE	Required	The name of the registered applet.
Param	Optional	The valid name of a registered parameter for the applet. Specify a parameter only if you want to override parameter values already defined for the applet using the Cold Fusion Administrator. You can set as many parameters as there are available to the applet.

The results of the CFAPPLET tag can be retrieved on the form action page in the same method as standard HTML forms. That means that the example used will have a result of

```
Calculator=value
```

CHAPTER 20

Interacting with Email

by Leon Chalnick and Ashley King

Interacting with Email

What is the single Internet application that people use more often than any other? Email. Although the NCSA's Mosaic World Wide Web browser was probably the killer application that led to the Internet's current level of popularity, it is email that people use most often. The ability to send and receive potentially critical information almost instantaneously, to and from almost anywhere on the planet, is a compelling reason to use the Internet. Email has had a profound impact on virtually all aspects of how we do business and stay in touch with each other.

Although the web is probably the most compelling reason that people connect to the Internet, its usefulness is significantly enhanced by the integration of email. Of course, the usefulness of your web applications is enhanced by the incorporation of email. The following are some examples of how email can be used with a web application to enhance its usefulness:

- A simple order-entry application sends an order confirmation by email.
- A complex database application sends an email to the developer when a user encounters a runtime error.
- A billing application sends invoices to customers through email.
- An office supply manufacturer uses email to send multimedia catalogs to a group of distributors throughout the world. Different versions of the catalog are sent to different distributors, based on information listed in the manufacturer's database.
- A web-based mailing list archive gives new customers access to older technical support information.

There are lots of excellent examples of integrating email with web applications. In many of the other chapters, you've seen how Cold Fusion makes it easy to manage databases on the web. As you'll see in this chapter, it is also quite simple to integrate email into your web/database applications.

Generating SMTP Mail

Simple Mail Transport Protocol (SMTP) is the standard method of sending and receiving email over the Internet. Post Office Protocol (POP) is the standard method of retrieving mail from an email server. SMTP involves the use of client and server software. When you want to get your mail, you use your client software to log into a POP server and download the mail. When you send mail, you post your message to your SMTP server, which sends it to the intended destination.

If you haven't configured Cold Fusion to use a particular SMTP server, you can still send email by explicitly referring to the optional SERVER attribute in your CFMAIL tag (see Table 20.1). This approach is a bit cumbersome and may create a maintenance problem if used frequently. It's really much simpler to use the Cold Fusion Administrator to set up your SMTP server (see Figure 20.1). If you don't take one of these approaches, your CFMAIL commands will fail.

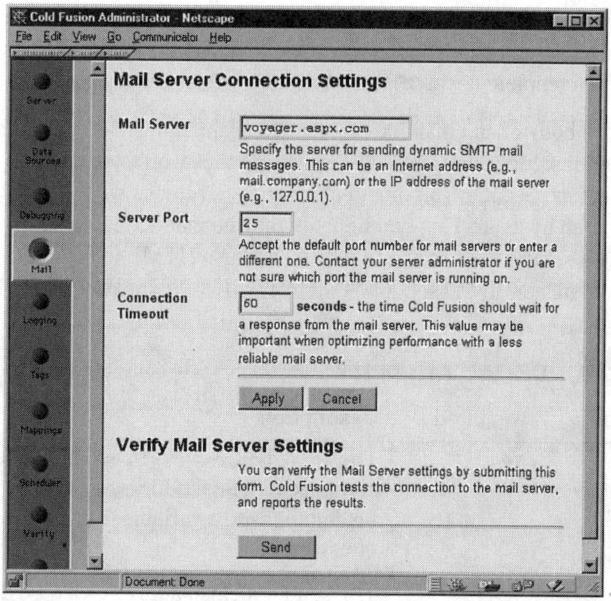

FIG. 20.1
Specify a valid SMTP mail server before using CFMAIL in your applications.

Cold Fusion can be used to generate SMTP mail by using the CFMAIL tag. In its most common application, the body of the email resides in a template and is sent to an address specified in the CFMAIL tag. For example, Listing 20.1 contains code that a simple order-entry application could use to send the customer an email order confirmation. The code that generates the email is in the same template as the HTML code used to generate a "thank you" page.

On the CD

Listing 20.1 LISTRESULTS.CFM—A Cold Fusion Template with a Simple Email Message

```
<CFMAIL
FROM="orders@A2Z.com"
TO="#URL.Email#"
SUBJECT="Order Confirmation"
>
This letter confirms your recent order from our Web site. Your order
has been placed in our system and will be processed as quickly as
possible. Thanks again for your order.
</CFMAIL>

<HTML>
<HEAD>
<TITLE>Thank You for Your Order</TITLE>
</HEAD>
<BODY>
<H1>Thank You!</H1>
Thanks for your recent order. It will be processed as quickly as possible.
Feel free to continue reviewing our site. If there's anything we can
do to make our site more useful, please
<A HREF="mailto:Webmaster@a2zbooks.com">drop us a line</A>.
</BODY>
</HTML>
```

Part
IV

Ch
20

As you can see in listresults.cfm, shown in Listing 20.1, the email address is defined at runtime from an URL parameter. Virtually every parameter in the CFMAIL tag can be specified with a variable. The complete list of CFMAIL attributes is shown in Table 20.1.

Note that the body of an email message is just plain, unformatted text, not HTML. There are two implications. First, using HTML formatting tags won't work in this text; they will appear in the email as text. Second, you must enter carriage returns where they are needed, because the text won't wrap by itself. This functionality may be inadequate in some cases. When this is the case, you can set the TYPE attribute to HTML and use HTML to format the output. This is discussed in detail later in the section "Using HTML to Make Your Email Look Better."

Table 21.1 *CFMAIL* **Attributes**

Attribute	Required	Description
TO	Yes	The email address(es) to which messages are sent. Use commas to delimit addresses if more than one is used. Can be defined with a variable. Can also be defined as a field in a query result.
FROM	Yes	The sender's email address. Can be defined as a variable.
CC	No	Email addresses of people to be copied. Use commas to delimit more than one address. Can be defined with a variable or query output, like TO.
SUBJECT	No	The subject of the message.
TYPE	No	Defines optional data type for the content of the message. Currently, the only valid value is HTML.
MIMEATTACH	No	Defines the path and name of the file to be attached to the email.
QUERY	No	Specifies the name of CFQUERY used in this message. The query can be used to create a list of people to send the message to or to create the content of the message.
MAXROWS	No	Used with the QUERY attribute, this specifies the maximum number of people to whom you want to send the message.
GROUP	No	Used with the QUERY attribute, this specifies the query result column to be used to group sets of related rows.
SERVER	No	Specifies the address of an alternative SMTP server. This is needed only if you want to specify the use of a server other than the server specified in the Cold Fusion Administrator.

Attribute	Required	Description
PORT	No	Specifies an alternative port number. By default, SMTP mail uses TCP/IP port 25, and this is what is used in the Cold Fusion Administrator by default. This is needed only if you want to specify the use of a port other than the port specified in the Cold Fusion Administrator.
TIMEOUT	No	If a connection cannot be made to the SMTP server specified in the Cold Fusion Administrator, this value is the number of seconds that Cold Fusion will wait before timing out the connection. By default, this is specified in the Cold Fusion Administrator as 180 seconds. Use this attribute only if you want to use a value other than the value defined in the Cold Fusion Administrator.

The SERVER, PORT, and TIMEOUT attributes duplicate parameters that are defined by using the Cold Fusion Administrator. You need to use these parameters only if you want to override the values already specified in the Cold Fusion Administrator.

Including Query Results in Email

Listing 20.1 demonstrated how simple it is to include automatically generated email in a Cold Fusion application. It sent a simple confirmation to a customer that had just placed an order, but did not include any information about the order itself. The email message would probably be more helpful if it contained a bit more information about the order.

Suppose that you wanted to actually send a list of the items in the order. You'll want to retrieve the line items in the order from the OrderItems table (using the A2Z.dbm database, which contains the sample data for this application), and this will require the OrderId. When you have this information, you can specify the query in CFMAIL's QUERY attribute. Of course the CFQUERY tag itself must be placed ahead of the CFMAIL tag in this template, as shown in Listing 20.2. To use sendlist.cfm, you must add URL parameters for OrderId and email, such as http://localhost/cfdocs/sendlist.cfm?email=ashley@aspx.com&OrderID=3.

On the CD

Listing 20.2   SENDLIST.CFM—Including the Results of a Query in an Email Message

```
<CFQUERY
DATASOURCE="A2Z"
NAME="GetOrder"
>
SELECT DISTINCTROW OrderItems.*
FROM OrderItems
WHERE OrderID = #URL.OrderId#
</CFQUERY>
```

continues

Listing 20.2 Continued

```
<!-- Error processing code goes here -->

<CFIF GetOrder.RecordCount is 0>

        <HEAD>
        <TITLE>Error</TITLE>
        </HEAD>

        <BODY>

        There were no matching orders.

        </BODY>

        <CFABORT>

</CFIF>

<CFMAIL
QUERY="GetOrder"
FROM="orders@A2Z.com"
TO="#URL.Email#"
SUBJECT="Order Confirmation"
>
This letter confirms your recent order for the items listed below.

## Book                    Qty  Unit Price Extd Price
- - - - - - - - - - - - - - - - - - - - -
<CFOUTPUT>
#RJustify(OrderLine, 2)# #Ljustify(BookID,20)# #Rjustify(Quantity,2)
➥# #RJustify(NumberFormat(UnitPrice, '
➥$(_____._)'),10)# #RJustify(NumberFormat
➥(SalePrice, '$(_____._)'),10)#
</CFOUTPUT>
Please let us know if there are any changes that need to be made.
Thanks again for your order.
</CFMAIL>

<!-- HTML to build 'thank you' doc goes here -->
<HEAD>
<TITLE>Thank you!</TITLE>
</HEAD>
<BODY>
<H2>Thank you!</H2><P>
A confirmation has been sent to you via email.
<P>
</BODY>
</HTML>
```

You can see in Listing 20.2 that the query GetOrder was referred to in the CFMAIL tag. This allowed you to include the query result in the CFOUTPUT section in the email body.

Because the body of the message is just text, you can use Cold Fusion 2.0 string and number formatting functions to get the output of the query to line up with the "header" defined just above the CFOUTPUT section. You know exactly how wide each column is in the header, so the formatting functions (Rjustify() and Ljustify()) can be used to ensure that the output values are formatted to the same width. This works fine as long as the user who receives the email uses fixed-pitch fonts (for example, Courier) to display the email. If he or she uses proportionally spaced fonts (such as Times Roman), this method of formatting won't work too well.

There may be situations in which you want to group the items that appear in the output. In the sample application, for example, it might be nice to group the books ordered by their categories. In other words, all computer books would be grouped together, all math books would be grouped together, and so on.

This is easily accomplished, but requires a slightly more complex query, as shown in Listing 20.3. To use groupoutput.cfm, you must add URL parameters for OrderID and email, such as http://localhost/cfdocs/groupoutput.cfm?email=ashley@aspx.com&OrderID=3.

On the CD

Listing 20.3   GROUPOUTPUT.CFM—Including the Results of a Query in an Email Message

```
<CFQUERY
DATASOURCE="A2Z"
NAME="GetOrder"
>
SELECT DISTINCTROW Category.Category, OrderItems.*
FROM Category INNER JOIN (Inventory INNER JOIN OrderItems ON
    _Inventory.BookID = OrderItems.BookID)
ON Category.ID = Inventory.CategoryID
WHERE OrderItems.OrderID=#URL.OrderID#
ORDER BY Category.Category
</CFQUERY>

<!-- Error processing code goes here -->
<CFMAIL
QUERY="GetOrder"
GROUP="Category"
FROM="orders@A2Z.com"
TO="#URL.Email##
SUBJECT="Order Confirmation"
>
This letter confirms your recent order for the items listed below.

<CFOUTPUT GROUP="Category">
#Category#
<CFOUTPUT>
##  Book                Qty  Unit Price Extd Price
--------------------
#RJustify(OrderLine, 2)# #Ljustify(BookID,20)# #Rjustify(Quantity,2)
➥# #RJustify(NumberFormat(UnitPrice, '$
```

Part
IV

Ch
20

continues

Listing 20.3   Continued

```
➥(_____.__)'),10)# #RJustify(NumberFormat
➥(SalePrice, '$(_____.__)'),10)#
</CFOUTPUT>
</CFOUTPUT>
Please let us know if there are any changes that need to be made.
Thanks again for your order.
</CFMAIL>

<!-- HTML to build 'thank you' doc goes here -->
```

The grouping requirement doesn't really make the Cold Fusion coding much more complex. You merely add the GROUP attribute to the CFMAIL tag and add an additional pair of CFOUTPUT tags for the inner group (refer to Listing 20.3). The complexity comes from the nature of how data is stored in a relational database. The various categories into which books can be classified are stored in the Category table. They are identified by numbers. The category identification number, used to key rows in the Category table, is an attribute of the book—in the Inventory table—and is not found in the OrderItems table.

To get a book's category identification number, you must join the OrderItems records with the Inventory records in the BookID field. To get the actual name of the category—it's the category name that you're grouping on—you must join the Inventory records to the Category records by CagetoryID. Thus, two inner joins are required.

▶ **See** "Joining Tables with *INNER JOIN ON*," **p. 365**

Sending Email to a List of People

If you've been plugged into the Internet for at least one day, you've probably received at least one or two thousand junk email letters. You know, these messages all say essentially the same thing: "How would you like to help us grow our account balance while simultaneously shrinking yours?" Anyway, the point is you weren't the only one to receive this delightfully entertaining, unsolicited message. You can usually tell because the friendly, helpful person who sent it was nice enough to include all the other 3,000 recipients in the "To" list.

You'll be glad to know that by using Cold Fusion, it's easy to return the favor. Suppose that each time you receive one of these wonderful little unsolicited emails, you decide to keep track of the person who sent you the message in a little database. Now suppose that you want to write them all a nice "thank you" letter. Okay, the seed has been planted. Now, let's look at a more appropriate example of how to send email to a list of people stored in a table.

You may recall that A2Z Books' marketing department is looking for a way to notify customers when books they may be interested in have arrived. The A2Z Books sample application includes a customer survey in which customers can identify book categories in which they are interested. Customers can request to be notified when new books in their favorite categories arrive. (You see, the folks at A2Z are sensitive to what happens when Internet-based marketing campaigns run out of control.)

Every so often, someone from the marketing department uses a web page to produce a listing of all new inventory arrivals. From the new-arrivals list, the user can select books that he or she wants to let customers know about. If the user selects a book that is classified in the education category, for example, the process will email all customers who indicated that they want to be notified whenever educational books arrive.

Listing 20.4 contains the form that the A2Z marketing department uses to get the process started. It enables users to answer questions such as "Which books arrived within 14 days of September 16, 1996?" The defaults are set up so that it will list all the books that arrived within the last week. This form invokes the template show_arrivals.cfm (see Listing 20.5), which produces the list of books that recently arrived. Finally, Listing 20.6 contains the send_notifications.cfm template—the code that actually sends the emails.

On the CD

Listing 20.4   SPECIFY_ARRIVALS.HTML—Producing a List of New Book Arrivals

```
<HTML>
<HEAD>
<TITLE>Specify Customer Notifications</TITLE>
</HEAD>
<BODY>
<H2>Specify Customer Notifications</H2>
This form allows you to identify books that we have received within the
specified number of days prior to the specified date. It will generate
a list of books.
<P>
<FORM ACTION="show_arrivals.cfm" METHOD="post">
<INPUT TYPE="hidden" NAME="FromDate_date"
➥VALUE="You must enter a valid 'from _date'">
<INPUT TYPE="hidden" NAME="FromDate_required" VALUE="You must enter a valid
➥ _'from date'">
<INPUT TYPE="hidden" NAME="Days_range" VALUE="MIN=0 MAX=99">
<INPUT TYPE="hidden" NAME="Days_required" VALUE="You must enter a valid 'from
➥ _date'">

<CFOUTPUT>
List all books that arrived up to <INPUT TYPE="text" NAME="Days" VALUE="7"
➥ SIZE="3" MAXLENGTH="3">
day(s) prior to <INPUT TYPE="text" NAME="FromDate"
_VALUE="#DateFormat(Now(),'mm-dd-yyyy')#" SIZE="12">.
</CFOUTPUT>
<BR>
<BR><INPUT TYPE="submit" VALUE="Produce recent arrivals list">
</FORM>
</BODY>
</HTML>
```

Part
IV

Ch
20

Note that the date validation being done in Listing 20.4 results in an ODBC date object being passed to show_arrivals.cfm in Listing 20.5. Data validation is described in detail in Chapter 14, "Form Data Validation." This example requires a bit of date math:

n days are subtracted from the user-specified date, where n is a user-specified number.

The first line of code easily does the trick. The DateAdd() function enables you to add *n* time increments to a date. In this case, the increment is a day (specified by a d) and *n* is the negative value of the number entered by the user in the Form.Days variable. CFSET saves the result of the expression in the variable Date. Date is then used in the SQL statement that follows.

N O T E   When you're doing SQL queries in which you're using parameterized date values, the dates must be in canonical form (for example, { d 'YYYY-MM-DD' }). Cold Fusion 2.0 produces dates this way if you use a date validation on the INPUT object to create the date. If you don't do the date validation, the INPUT tag will simply produce a string value, and this will not be interpreted properly in your SQL. ■

CAUTION

In Listing 20.5, note that you must also use the PreserveSingleQuotes() function to use a parameterized date value. The problem is that Cold Fusion automatically "escapes" the single quotes generated when the INPUT object casts a string into a canonical date.

On the CD

Listing 20.5   SHOW_ARRIVALS.CFM—Producing a List of New Books

```
<!-- Produce set of books that arrived within x days of specified date -->
<CFSET #Date# = #DateAdd("d",-Days,Form.FromDate)#>
<CFQUERY
NAME="GetArrivals"
DATASOURCE="A2Z"
>
SELECT DISTINCTROW Inventory.BookID, Inventory.ArrivalDate,
    _Category.Category, Inventory.Title
FROM Category INNER JOIN Inventory ON Category.ID = Inventory.CategoryID
WHERE Inventory.ArrivalDate>=#PreserveSingleQuotes(Date)#
ORDER BY Category.Category, Inventory.ArrivalDate
</CFQUERY>

<!-- Let user know none found and abort further processing -->
<CFIF GetArrivals.Recordcount is 0>
<HTML>
<HEAD>
<TITLE>No Arrivals</TITLE>
</HEAD>
<BODY>
<H1>No Arrivals</H1>
There were no arrivals in this date range. Go back and expand the range.
</BODY>
</HTML>
<CFABORT>
</CFIF>

<HTML>
<HEAD>
<TITLE>Recent Arrivals</TITLE>
</HEAD>
```

```
<BODY>
<H2>Recent Arrivals</H2>

<!-- Display output in tabular format -->
<TABLE BORDER=1 CELLPADDING=4>
<TR>
<TH ALIGN="left">Category</TH>
Arrival Date</TH>
Title</TH>
</TR>

<CFOUTPUT
QUERY="GetArrivals"
GROUP="Category"
>
<TR>
<TD>#Category#</TD>
<TD>#DateFormat(ArrivalDate)#</TD>
<TD>
<A HREF/A2Z/send_notifications.cfm&BookID=#BookID#">#Title#</A>
</TD>
</TR>
</CFOUTPUT>
</TABLE>
</BODY>
</HTML>
```

On the CD

Listing 20.6   SEND_NOTIFICATIONS.CFM—Sending and Counting Notification Request Emails

```
<!--
Identify book and all customers that requested notification upon
arrival of books in this book's category.
-->
<CFQUERY
NAME="MakeBookList"
DATASOURCE="A2Z"
>
SELECT DISTINCTROW Inventory.BookID, Inventory.ISBN, Inventory.Title,
Inventory.Publisher, Inventory.AuthorFirstName,
Inventory.AuthorLastName, Inventory.Description,
Category.Category, Customers.FirstName, Customers.EMail
        FROM CustomerSurvey INNER JOIN Customers ON CustomerSurvey.
➡CustomerID = _Customers.CustomerID,
Inventory INNER JOIN Category ON Inventory.CategoryID = Category.ID
WHERE ( (Inventory.BookID=#URL.BookID#) AND
(Inventory.CategoryID=CustomerSurvey.Category1 OR
Inventory.CategoryID=CustomerSurvey.Category2 OR
Inventory.CategoryID=CustomerSurvey.Category3 OR
Inventory.CategoryID=CustomerSurvey.Category4
)
)
```

Part
IV

Ch
20

continues

Listing 20.6   Continued

```
ORDER BY Customers.LastName, Category.Category
</CFQUERY>

<!-- If no customer's requested notification, tell user and abort process -->
<CFIF MakeBookList.Recordcount is 0>
<HTML>
<HEAD>
<TITLE>No Notification Requests</TITLE>
</HEAD>
<BODY>
<H1>No Notification Requests</H1>
There were no customers that requested notification upon arrival
of books in the same category as the selected book. Use the
Back button to return to the Recent Arrivals page.
</BODY>
</HTML>
<CFABORT>
</CFIF>

<!-- Send e-mails to all customers in list -->
<CFMAIL
QUERY="MakeBookList"
SUBJECT="Arrival of '#Title#'"
TO="#EMail#"
FROM="sales@A2ZBooks.com"
>
Dear #FirstName#:

Based on your request to be notified when certain categories of
books come in, we're writing to let you know about a book which
we recently received. You can purchase this book by visiting
our Web site or by dropping by our store.

Category: #Category#
Title: #Title#
Author: #AuthorFirstName# #AuthorLastName#
Description: #Description#

</CFMAIL>

<!-- Tell A2Z user how many e-mails were sent -->
<HTML>
<HEAD>
<TITLE>Notifications Sent</TITLE>
</HEAD>
<BODY>
<H2>E-mail sent</H2>
<CFOUTPUT QUERY="MakeBookList">
#MakeBookList.RecordCount# customers were notified about
➥the arrival of _#Title#.
</CFOUTPUT>
Use the Back button to return to the Recent Arrivals page.
</BODY>
</HTML>
```

Figure 20.2 shows the listing of books that recently arrived.

FIG. 20.2

The show_arrivals .cfm template produces this listing of all books that have recently arrived.

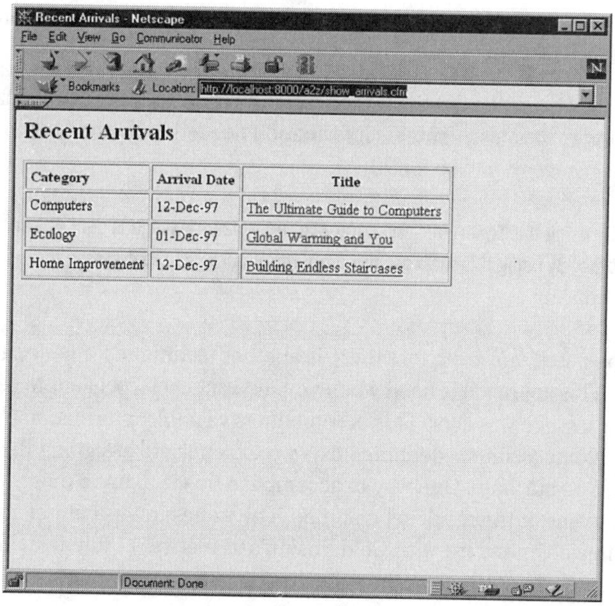

Figure 20.3 shows what the email message looks like when the user receives it in Netscape mail.

FIG. 20.3

This email message notifies A2Z customers that books they may be interested in have arrived.

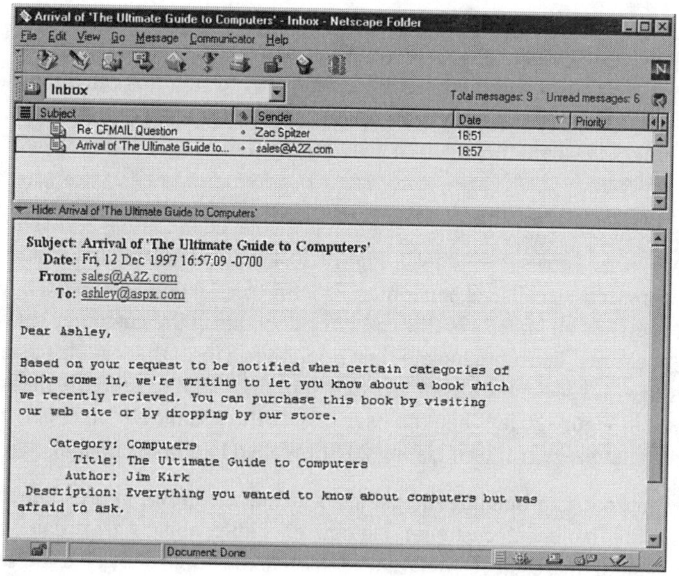

So, the send_notifications.cfm template (see Listing 20.6) does most of the work you're interested in here. In most cases, when you want to send mail to a list of people, you'll wind up using a similar approach: use a query to identify the recipients, and then refer to the query in the TO attributes of CFMAIL tag.

In the previous example, the query generates a result set with one record for each customer. The resulting record also contains information needed in the body of the email (that is, the book's title, category, and so forth).

NOTE By using this "query-driven" approach, an email message is sent to each recipient one at a time. By using this method, the problem of each recipient seeing the entire recipient list can be avoided. ■

It should be noted, however, that there is another technique for generating emails to multiple recipients. This approach is used when you do want each recipient to see all the other people to whom the message was sent. This is sometimes valuable information. This second technique involves building a comma-delimited list of recipients and assigning the value of the list to the CFMAIL tag's TO attribute. One way to accomplish this is to use a query to produce a list of email addresses in one of the result set columns. The values in this column can be easily converted into a comma-delimited list with Cold Fusion's ValueList() function. You then set the value of the CFMAIL tag's TO attribute to the value list, as in the following:

```
<CFMAIL
TO="#ValueList(Query.ColumnName)#"
FROM="sales@A2Zbooks.com"
SUBJECT="Fan mail from some flounder"
>
_
</CFMAIL>
```

This is pretty cool, but there is still another way to skin this cat. Suppose that folks in the A2Z marketing department want to be able to scroll through a customer list, picking and choosing customers to whom they want to send an email message. The next set of listings shows how this is done.

The template create_customer_list.cfm is displayed in Listing 20.7. The resulting document is shown in the browser window in Figure 20.4. This template allows users to select an inventory category. It then calls get_customer_list.cfm (see Listing 20.8), which identifies any customers that specified an interest in this category of books in the customer survey. The get_customer_list.cfm template then generates a form that enables users to create an email message and select the customers to whom they want to send the message. This form is displayed in Figure 20.5. When the user selects the submit button in get_customer_list.cfm, email_customers.cfm (see Listing 20.9) is called to do the emailing.

This approach for building the list takes advantage of two interesting checkbox object behaviors. Note that in get_customer_list.cfm, checkbox objects are created for each customer that winds up in the result set, and that each checkbox object is given the same name: CustList. So, "neat checkbox trick number one" is that when a group of related checkboxes are all given the same name, you can tell whether any of them was checked with Cold Fusion's ParameterExists() function. If none of the checkboxes are selected, ParameterExists(CheckBoxFieldName) returns No.

FIG. 20.4

The resulting document is shown in the browser window.

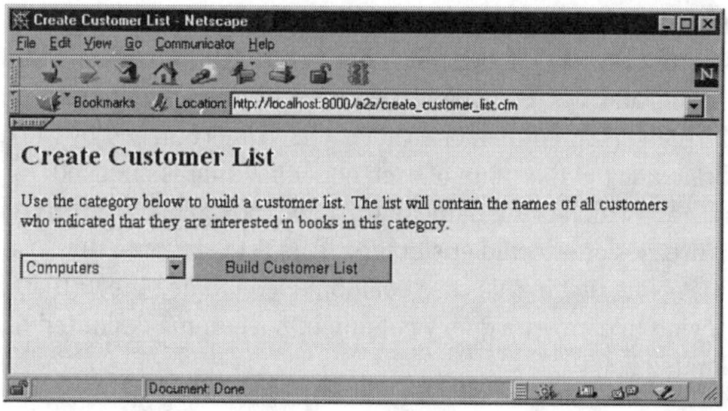

The page in Figure 20.4, produced by the create_customer_list.cfm template in Listing 20.7, enables the user to produce a list of customers that have expressed an interest in books in the selected category.

Listing 20.7   CREATE_CUSTOMER_LIST.CFM—Building a Customer List Based on a Specific Category

```
<!-- Must first get names of all categories -->
<CFQUERY
NAME="GetCategories"
DATASOURCE="A2Z"
>
SELECT Category from Category
</CFQUERY>

<!--
Present form allowing user to select a category and build customer
list.
-->
<HTML>
<HEAD>
<TITLE>Create Customer List</TITLE>
</HEAD>
<BODY>

<H2>Create Customer List</H2>
Use the category below to build a customer list. The list will contain
the names of all customers who indicated that they are interested in
books in this category.
<P>

<FORM ACTION="/A2Z/get_customer_list.cfm" _METHOD="post">
<SELECT NAME="Category">
<CFOUTPUT QUERY="GetCategories">
<OPTION>#Category#
</CFOUTPUT>
</SELECT>
<INPUT TYPE="submit" VALUE="Build Customer List">
</FORM>
</BODY>
</HTML>
```

Part
IV

Ch

20

Look again at get_customer_list.cfm and at Figure 20.5. You'll note that although each checkbox is given the same name, each one has a different value; in this example, it's the customer's email address. So what is "neat checkbox trick number 2"? A group of checkboxes that have the same name return one value. The value returned by the checkbox group is a comma-delimited list of the value of each checkbox that is checked. In your case, the object named CustList (which is the name of the checkbox group) returns a comma-delimited list of the email addresses of selected customers. This list is fed into the TO attribute of the CFMAIL tag in Listing 20.9. Note that in this case you don't need to use the ValueList() function, because you're not trying to convert a query column into a comma-delimited list; you already have a comma-delimited list.

On the CD

Listing 20.8 GET_CUSTOMER_LIST.CFM—Template to Build a Customer List

```
<!-- Must first get ID of category user selected from list -->
<CFQUERY
NAME="GetCategory"
DATASOURCE="A2Z"
MAXROWS=1
>
SELECT ID from Category
WHERE Category = '#Form.Category#'
</CFQUERY>

<!--
Get names, e-mail addr of all customers that expressed any interest
in the selected category (from the customer survey)
-->
<CFQUERY
NAME="GetCustomers"
DATASOURCE="A2Z"
>
SELECT DISTINCTROW Customers.FirstName, Customers.LastName, Customers.EMail
FROM Customers INNER JOIN CustomerSurvey ON
➥ Customers.CustomerID = CustomerSurvey.CustomerID
WHERE CustomerSurvey.Category1=#GetCategory.ID# OR
CustomerSurvey.Category2=#GetCategory.ID# OR
CustomerSurvey.Category3=#GetCategory.ID# OR
CustomerSurvey.Category4=#GetCategory.ID#
</CFQUERY>
<CFIF GetCustomers.Recordcount is 0>
<HTML>
<HEAD>
<TITLE>No Customers Found</TITLE>
</HEAD>
<BODY>
<H2>No Customers Found</H2>
There were no customers interested in <CFOUTPUT>#Form.Category#</CFOUTPUT>.
Use the Back button to go back and make a different selection.
</BODY>
</HTML>
<CFABORT>
```

```
</CFIF>

<HTML>
<HEAD>
<CFOUTPUT>
<TITLE>Customers Who Selected #Form.Category#</TITLE>
</CFOUTPUT>
</HEAD>
<BODY>

<CFOUTPUT>
<H2>Customers Interested in #Form.Category#</H2>

This form allows you to create a custom e-mail message to customers
that have indicated that they're interested in #Form.Category# books.
</CFOUTPUT>

<P>Use the following form to send selected customers a custom
e-mail message.

<FORM ACTION="email_customers.cfm" METHOD="post">
<INPUT TYPE="hidden" NAME="Subject_required" VALUE="You must enter a
➥message subject">
<INPUT TYPE="hidden" NAME="Message_required" VALUE="You must enter a message">
<TABLE>
<TR>
<TD ALIGN="right">Subject:</TD>
<TD><INPUT TYPE="text" NAME="Subject" SIZE="40" MAXLENGTH="100"></TD>
</TR>
<TR>
<TD ALIGN="right" VALIGN="top">Text:</TD>
<TD><TEXTAREA NAME="Message" ROWS="4" COLS="50"></TEXTAREA></TD>
</TR>
<TR>
<TD ALIGN="right">Attachment:</TD>
<TD><INPUT TYPE="text" NAME="Attachment" SIZE="40" MAXLENGTH="120"></TD>
</TR>
</TABLE>

<H2>Select Customers to Receive E-Mail</H2>
<TABLE>
<CFOUTPUT QUERY="GetCustomers">
<TR>
<TD><INPUT TYPE="checkbox" NAME="CustList" VALUE="#EMail#" CHECKED></TD>
<TD>#FirstName# #LastName#</TD>
</TR>
</CFOUTPUT>
</TABLE>
<INPUT TYPE="submit" VALUE="Send the E-Mail">
</FORM>
</BODY>
</HTML>
```

FIG. 20.5

The form used to create an email list.

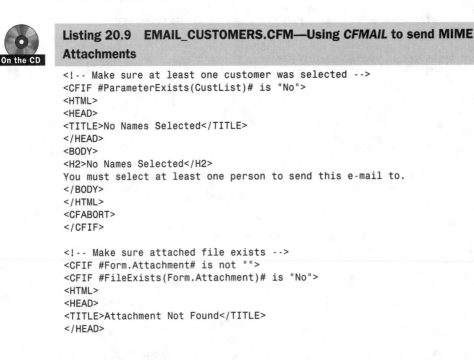

The page in Figure 20.5, produced by the get_customer_list.cfm template in Listing 20.8, is where the user creates an email message and selects individual users to whom the letter will be sent. In Listing 20.9, MIME attachments are sent using CFMAIL. You learn more about MIME attachments later in this chapter.

On the CD

Listing 20.9   EMAIL_CUSTOMERS.CFM—Using *CFMAIL* to send MIME Attachments

```
<!-- Make sure at least one customer was selected -->
<CFIF #ParameterExists(CustList)# is "No">
<HTML>
<HEAD>
<TITLE>No Names Selected</TITLE>
</HEAD>
<BODY>
<H2>No Names Selected</H2>
You must select at least one person to send this e-mail to.
</BODY>
</HTML>
<CFABORT>
</CFIF>

<!-- Make sure attached file exists -->
<CFIF #Form.Attachment# is not "">
<CFIF #FileExists(Form.Attachment)# is "No">
<HTML>
<HEAD>
<TITLE>Attachment Not Found</TITLE>
</HEAD>
```

```
<BODY>
<H2>Attachment Not Found</H2>
The file you specified as an attachment,
<CFOUTPUT>
<STRONG>#Form.Attachment#</STRONG>,
</CFOUTPUT>
could not be found.
<P>You can only attach valid files to your e-mail. Use the
Back button to go back and enter a valid file name or
erase the Attachment name.
</BODY>
</HTML>
<CFABORT>
</CFIF>

<!-- Send the e-mail, using the comma delimted list and attachment -->
<CFMAIL
TO=#CustList#
FROM="sales@A2ZBooks.com"
SUBJECT="#Form.Subject#"
MIMEATTACH="#Form.Attachment#"
>
#Form.Message#
</CFMAIL>
<CFELSE>
<!-- Send the e-mail, using the comma delimted list and NO attachment -->
<CFMAIL
TO=#CustList#
FROM="sales@A2ZBooks.com"
SUBJECT="#Form.Subject#"
>
#Form.Message#
</CFMAIL>
</CFIF>

<HTML>
<HEAD>
<TITLE>EMail Sent</TITLE>
</HEAD>
<BODY>

<H2>EMail Sent</H2>
<CFOUTPUT>
<CFIF #ListLen(CustList)# is 1>
<CFSET #Customer# = "customer">
<CFELSE>
<CFSET #Customer# = "customers">
</CFIF>
The e-mail message was sent to #ListLen(CustList)# #Customer#.

<p>#CustList#

</CFOUTPUT>

</BODY>
</HTML>
```

Using HTML to Make Your Email Look Better

If you have experimented with CFMAIL, you've probably recognized one of its shortcomings: the body of the message is unformatted text. In other words, it works sort of like an HTML PRE tag—what you see is what you get. When you're hard-coding the content of the message, you have control over the formatting and can at least put in carriage returns where needed. But when the body of the message includes text that you cannot explicitly control, things can get ugly.

Suppose, as in the previous example, that you're providing users with a form in which they can create the body of the message themselves. If a user creates a long paragraph without any carriage returns, the message body extends off the right side of the screen.

That CFMAIL messages are just plain text creates other problems too. In the A2Z Books online order system, the customer is sent an email message confirming his or her order. This confirmation contains all the line items that were ordered. Presenting these items in a nice, formatted tabular structure is difficult when using plain text. (An example was provided earlier, however, in the section "Including Query Results in Email.") In fact, unless the recipient has his email reader set up to display messages in a fixed-pitch font, creating this tabular display is virtually impossible.

There is another solution: set the CFMAIL TYPE attribute to "HTML". This allows you to use HTML formatting tags in your email message body. So, in your example, you can use HTML tables to format the order.

Here's an example: A2Z Books is mailing a special notice to all customers who indicated (in the customer survey) that they are interested in science. A2Z Books needs to identify all these customers and then send them a special notice.

N O T E It is important to note that the recipient's email client must be capable of displaying HTML. For example, the Netscape email client can display HTML documents. If the recipient is using an email client that doesn't know how to interpret and format HTML code, the message will appear as plain text—HTML codes and all. Be careful when you use this approach. ■

Figure 20.6 and Listing 20.10 display the CFML code and the resulting HTML-formatted letter.

Listing 20.10   HTML-EMAIL.CFM—Producing an HTML-Formatted Email Message

```
<!-- First get category ID of the 'Science' category -->
<CFQUERY
NAME="GetCategory"
DATASOURCE="A2Z"
>
SELECT DISTINCTROW Category.ID
FROM Category
WHERE Category = 'Science'
</CFQUERY>
```

```
<!--- error processing here --->

<!--- Now get customers who indicated they like science books in survey -->
<CFQUERY
NAME="GetScienceCustomers"
DATASOURCE="A2Z"
>
SELECT DISTINCTROW Customers.FirstName, Customers.LastName,
Customers.Email
FROM Customers INNER JOIN CustomerSurvey ON Customers.CustomerID
➡= CustomerSurvey.CustomerID
WHERE CustomerSurvey.Category1=#GetCategory.ID# OR
CustomerSurvey.Category2=#GetCategory.ID# OR
CustomerSurvey.Category3=#GetCategory.ID# OR
CustomerSurvey.Category4=#GetCategory.ID#
</CFQUERY>

<!--- error processing here --->
<CFIF GetScienceCustomers.RecordCount is 0>

<h2>An error has occurred</h2>
<p>
There were no matching records.

</CFIF>

<CFMAIL
QUERY="GetScienceCustomers"
SUBJECT="Steven Sagan To Appear at A2Z Books!"
TO="#EMail#"
FROM="sales@A2ZBooks.com"
TYPE="HTML"
>
<H2>Renowned Scientist Steven Sagan To Appear for Signing
at A2Z Books!</H2>
Howdy, #FirstName#. We're writing to let you know about
Steven Sagan's upcomming book signing at A2Z Books. Please
find the detail below.
<P>
<TABLE BORDER=1 CELLPADDING=5>
<TR>
<TD ALIGN="right"><STRONG><EM>Who:</EM></STRONG></TD>
<TD ALIGN="left">
All of our <EM>science</EM> club members are being sent
this special invitation.
</TD>
</TR>
<TR>
<TD ALIGN="right"><STRONG><EM>What:</EM></STRONG></TD>
<TD ALIGN="left">
The renowned science fiction writer, Steven Sagan,
will be appearing to sign copies of his latest book,
&quot;Was, Not Is&quot;.
</TD>
</TR>
```

Part
IV

Ch
20

continues

Listing 20.10 Continued

```
<TR>
<TD ALIGN="right"><STRONG><EM>Where:</EM></STRONG></TD>
<TD ALIGN="left">
A2Z Books<BR>
3456 Coolidge Road<BR>
Oak Park, MI 48027<BR>
(313) 55-55
</TD>
</TR>
<TR>
<TD ALIGN="right"><STRONG><EM>When:</EM></STRONG></TD>
<TD ALIGN="left">Saturday, Febrary 30, 197, 10:30 AM EST</TD>
</TR>
</TABLE>
<P>Be there or be...cubed!
</CFMAIL>
```

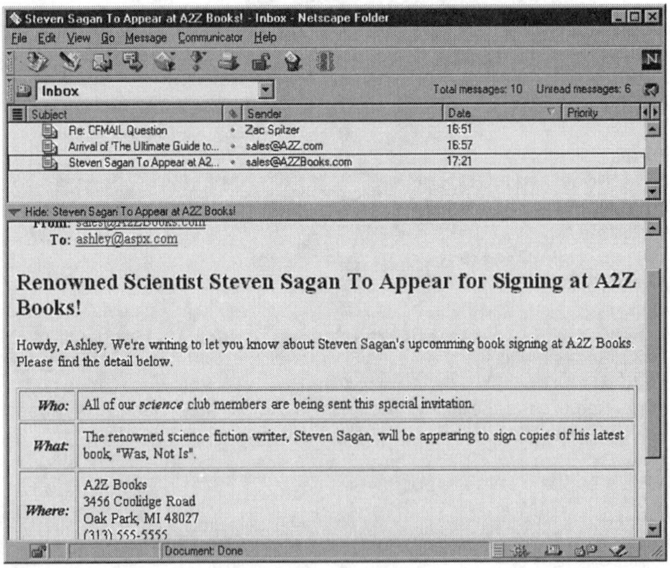

FIG. 20.6

This email was produced by using HTML formatting.

Sending Attachments with Your Email

With Cold Fusion versions 2.0 and later, you can attach documents to your email messages. This powerful new feature makes creating new types of applications extremely simple. Here are some examples:

■ A software developer uses email to send software patches to its registered users on an ongoing basis.

- A sales organization sends its geographically dispersed sales force updates to the customer database via email.

- Our favorite bookstore notifies customers when books they may be interested in arrive from the publisher. A picture of the book cover is attached as a PCX file.

As you may recall from the example in the section "Using HTML to Make Your Email Look Better," the A2Z Bookstore's marketing department has this nifty little function in its system that allows it to identify groups of customers and then send them custom email messages. You may have noticed in Listing 20.9 and Figure 20.5 that this function also enables the user to attach documents. Look for the field named Attachments in the listing.

Take a look at Listing 20.9, specifically the chunk of code that starts

```
<!- Make sure attached file exists ->
<CFIF #Form.Attachment# is not "">
<CFIF #FileExists(Form.Attachment)# is "No">
```

This code chunk first tests to see whether the user entered a filename for the attachment. If the user did, you need to make sure the file actually exists. If the file doesn't exist, Cold Fusion won't tell you that it doesn't. So, when you're attaching a file to your email, unless you're absolutely certain that the file attachment exists, you'll probably want to use the FileExists() function to verify that the file does indeed exist before you send the email.

It's also worth noting that if you're allowing the user to specify the MIME attachment file and they don't specify one, you must use a CFMAIL tag that does not include the MIMEATTACH attribute. The following chunk of code, also from Listing 20.9, is used to create the CFMAIL tag without the MIMEATTACH attribute.

```
<CFELSE>
<!- Send the email, using the comma delimted list and NO attachment ->
<CFMAIL
TO=#CustList#
FROM="sales@A2ZBooks.com"
SUBJECT="#Form.Subject#"
>
```

Your Cold Fusion applications can also retrieve mail from a POP server and display the results like a simple mail client, or use the results in the form of a query. By using CFPOP, you can enhance many common web applications, as well as create new and useful tools:

- A web-based email client on a corporate intranet makes email retrieval easy for users and saves administrators money on software and support.

- A software company creates a mailing list with an archive to make technical support questions and answers available both on the web and by email.

- An Internet service provider emails a customer-satisfaction questionnaire to its customers and automatically tabulates the results received.

Using *CFPOP*

CFPOP encapsulates all the complexity of using the POP protocol into a simple Cold Fusion tag. CFPOP takes an ACTION attribute to specify the operation to be performed. CFPOP supports three ACTION types:

- GETHEADERONLY instructs CFPOP to retrieve all the header information for any messages in the mailbox. Header information includes the sender address, the date and time that the mail was sent, and the message subject. In fact, the only information not in the header is the actual text of the message itself.

- GETALL is used to retrieve header information, as well as the message text, also known as the message body. GETALL is used only when the message body is needed, because retrieving the header information with the message body could take quite a bit longer than just retrieving the header information.

- DELETE can be used to delete one or more messages from a mailbox. Mail is not automatically deleted when it is read (with GETHEADERONLY or GETALL); to delete mail, a specific DELETE operation must be performed.

The following code snippet demonstrates how to retrieve POP mail headers:

```
<!--- Get mail headers --->
<CFPOP
 SERVER="mail.domain.com"
 USERNAME="bob"
 PASSWORD="gr8nHpnGy"
 ACTION="GETHEADERONLY"
 NAME="messages"
>
```

The messages retrieved are stored in a query result set, just like the results returned by CFQUERY. In this example, they are stored in a result set named "messages". CFOUTPUT can be used to process the retrieved list. The following code snippet outputs the sender and the subject of each message retrieved in the previous code example:

```
<!--- List retrieved messages --->
<UL>
<CFOUTPUT QUERY="messages">
 <LI>From: #from# - Subject: #subject#
</CFOUTPUT>
```

The query result set retrieved by CFPOP contains the following columns:

- DATE contains the date and time that the message was sent (this is the contents of the SMTP message date header, and it might not be formatted suitably for use with the Cold Fusion date functions).

- FROM contains the name of the message sender.

- ATTACHMENTS contains a tab-delimited list of attachments, if there are any. This column is available only if the ACTION was GETALL and if the ATTACHMENTPATH attribute was specified.

- ATTACHMENTFILES contains a tab-delimited list of the temporary files created on the server. This column is available only if the ACTION was GETALL and if the ATTACHMENTPATH attribute was specified.

- TO contains the email address to which the message was sent.

- CC contains a comma-delimited list of names and email addresses to whom the message was carbon-copied.

- REPLYTO contains the email address to which any replies should be sent.

- SUBJECT contains the message subject.

- MESSAGENUMBER is a number that uniquely identifies a retrieved message and is used to drill down into or delete a specific message. The ID is a relative ID, not an actual ID. This means that IDs should be used immediately after being obtained, not stored for later use.

- BODY contains the actual message text. This column is available only if the ACTION was GETALL and not if the ACTION was GETHEADERONLY.

In addition to these basic attributes, CFPOP also supports attributes that you may use within your applications. The complete list of additional attributes follows:

- ACTION specifies the operation to be performed. Valid values are GETHEADERONLY, GETALL, and DELETE. If this attribute is omitted, the default value of GETHEADERONLY is used. It is a good idea to always specify the ACTION explicitly.

- ATTACHMENTPATH specifies the fully qualified name of the directory in which to save any email attachments. Attachments are retrieved only if the ACTION is GETALL.

- MAXROWS specifies the maximum number of messages to retrieve. If no value is provided, all messages will be retrieved.

- MESSAGENUMBER is an optional attribute that specifies one or more message numbers on which to perform an operation. It is required, however, if ACTION is DELETE. Multiple message numbers are specified as a Cold Fusion list (a comma-delimited list).

- NAME contains the name of the query to be created if the ACTION is GETALL or GETHEADERONLY, in which case it is a required attribute.

- PASSWORD must contain the POP password if the account has one.

- PORT specifies the POP server's port and defaults to 110 if not specified. Use this attribute only if your mail administrator tells you to.

- SERVER is the host name or IP address of the POP server. This attribute is required, and unlike the Cold Fusion SMTP tag, there is no way to set a systemwide default value.

- STARTROW specifies the position of the first message to be retrieved. It defaults to 1 if no value is specified.

- TIMEOUT specifies the mail server timeout value (in seconds) and defaults to 60 seconds.

- USERNAME is the POP login name and should always be specified. If it is omitted, an anonymous login will be used.

Part
IV

Ch
20

Creating a Complete Mail Client

To better understand how CFPOP may be used, let's create a complete mail client by using Cold Fusion's mail tags. The functions supported will be

- Allowing a user to log in to a mailbox on any POP mail server
- Displaying a list of waiting messages
- Allowing the user to drill down to view message details
- The ability to delete unwanted mail
- A reply function to reply to received mail (this feature uses both CFOP and CFMAIL)

The email client is made up of seven templates:

- LOGIN.CFM (Listing 20.11) is the user login screen.
- MAIL.CFM (Listing 20.12) creates the frames for the mail interface.
- HEADERS.CFM (Listing 20.13) displays the list of available mail messages.
- MESSAGE.CFM (Listing 20.14) displays message details, including the body text.
- DELETE.CFM (Listing 20.15) deletes a message.
- REPLY.CFM (Listing 20.16) is the reply form.
- SENDREPLY.CFM (Listing 20.17) sends the reply.

Creating LOGIN.CFM

This first template, LOGIN.CFM, prompts the user for a POP server name, login name, and password. The user may also specify an email address that will be used when replying to mail. The POP server name and username are the only required fields in this form. The data collected in this form is submitted to MAIL.CFM for processing.

On the CD

Listing 20.11 LOGIN.CFM—User Login Screen

```
<HTML>

<HEAD>
<TITLE>E-Mail Login</TITLE>
</HEAD>

<BODY BGCOLOR="FFFFFF">

<CENTER>

<H1>CF Mail Client</H1>

<FORM ACTION="mail.cfm" METHOD="POST">

<INPUT TYPE="hidden" NAME="pop_server_required" VALUE="MAIL SERVER must be
➥specified!">
<INPUT TYPE="hidden" NAME="pop_username_required" VALUE="LOGIN must be
➥specified!">
```

```
<TABLE BGCOLOR="000000">
 <TR>
  <TH ALIGN="RIGHT" BGCOLOR="C0C0C0">Mail Server:</TH>
  <TD BGCOLOR="FFFFFF"><INPUT TYPE="text" NAME="pop_server"></TD>
 </TR>
 <TR>
  <TH ALIGN="RIGHT" BGCOLOR="C0C0C0">Login:</TH>
  <TD BGCOLOR="FFFFFF"><INPUT TYPE="text" NAME="pop_username"></TD>
 </TR>
 <TR>
  <TH ALIGN="RIGHT" BGCOLOR="C0C0C0">Password:</TH>
  <TD BGCOLOR="FFFFFF"><INPUT TYPE="password" NAME="pop_password"></TD>
 </TR>
 <TR>
  <TH ALIGN="RIGHT" BGCOLOR="C0C0C0">E-Mail Address:</TH>
  <TD BGCOLOR="FFFFFF"><INPUT TYPE="text" NAME="email_address"></TD>
 </TR>
 <TR>
  <TH BGCOLOR="C0C0C0" COLSPAN=2><INPUT TYPE="SUBMIT" VALUE="Login"></TR>
 </TR>
</TABLE>
</FORM>

</CENTER>

</BODY>

</HTML>
```

Creating MAIL.CFM

This mail client uses a split screen window, created using two frames. The left frame contains
the list of messages, and the right frame displays a message when one is selected from the list.
Template MAIL.CFM contains the HTML code to create the frames. The right window is populated with BLANK.CFM, an empty template. The left frame contains template HEADERS.CFM
that retrieves the email messages. The POP login and server information must be passed down
to the HEADERS.CFM template, and because the fields contain invalid URL characters, the
values are all encoded with the URLEncodedFormat() function.

Part
IV

Ch
20

Listing 20.12   MAIL.CFM—Creating Frames for the Mail Interface

```
<CFOUTPUT>

<HTML>

<HEAD>
<TITLE>E-Mail for #Trim(pop_username)#</TITLE>
</HEAD>
```

continues

Listing 20.12 Continued

```
<FRAMESET COLS="50%,50%">
 <FRAME NAME="header" SRC="headers.cfm?pop_server=
➥#URLEncodedFormat(pop_server)#&pop_username=#URLEncodedFormat
➥(pop_username)#&pop_password=#URLEncodedFormat(pop_password)
➥#&email_address=#URLEncodedFormat(email_address)#" SCROLLING="AUTO">
 <FRAME NAME="message" SRC="blank.cfm" SCROLLING="AUTO">
</FRAMESET>

</HTML>

</CFOUTPUT>
```

Creating HEADERS.CFM

The HEADERS.CFM template retrieves the message headers and displays them in a table. Because the messages are returned in a standard Cold Fusion query, the query variables RecordCount and CurrentRow are available for use. Listing 20.13 uses RecordCount to display the number of messages retrieved. The template starts with a CFPOP tag with an ACTION of GETHEADERONLY. Because the message body is not needed in this template, time can be saved by using GETHEADERONLY instead of GETALL. The template also contains two buttons at the top of the page. The REFRESH button calls the same HEADERS.CFM template again and is used to refresh the list of messages. The LOGOUT function returns the user back to the login screen.

The list of messages itself is displayed in an HTML table, and the message number field can be clicked to drill down to see the message details displayed in the right window.

Listing 20.13 HEADERS.CFM—Displaying the List of Available Mail Messages

```
<!--- Get mail headers --->
<CFPOP
 SERVER="#pop_server#"
 USERNAME="#pop_username#"
 PASSWORD="#pop_password#"
 ACTION="GETHEADERONLY"
 NAME="messages"
>

<BODY BGCOLOR="FFFFFF">

<P ALIGN="RIGHT">

<!--- Table for REFRESH and LOGOUT buttons --->
<TABLE>
 <TR>
  <TD>
   <!--- REFRESH button --->
   <FORM ACTION="headers.cfm" METHOD="POST">
   <CFOUTPUT>
```

```
        <INPUT TYPE="hidden" NAME="pop_server" VALUE="#pop_server#">
        <INPUT TYPE="hidden" NAME="pop_username" VALUE="#pop_username#">
        <INPUT TYPE="hidden" NAME="pop_password" VALUE="#pop_password#">
        <INPUT TYPE="hidden" NAME="email_address" VALUE="#email_address#">
        </CFOUTPUT>
        <INPUT TYPE="submit" VALUE="Refresh">
        </FORM>
       </TD>
       <TD>
        <!--- LOGOUT button --->
        <FORM ACTION="login.cfm" METHOD="POST" TARGET="_parent">
        <INPUT TYPE="submit" VALUE="Logout">
        </FORM>
       </TD>
      </TR>
     </TABLE>

     </P>

     <CENTER>

     <!--- How many messages retrieved? --->
     <CFOUTPUT>#messages.RecordCount# messages</CFOUTPUT>

     <TABLE BGCOLOR="000000" WIDTH="100%">
      <TR>
       <TH></TH>
       <TH BGCOLOR="C0C0C0">Date</TH>
       <TH BGCOLOR="C0C0C0">From</TH>
       <TH BGCOLOR="C0C0C0">Subject</TH>
      </TR>

     <!--- Display list of messages, first column links to drill down to message
     itself --->
     <CFOUTPUT QUERY="messages">
      <TR>
       <TD BGCOLOR="FFFFFF"><A HREF="message.cfm?pop_server=#URLEncodedFormat
     ➥(pop_server)#&pop_username=#URLEncodedFormat(pop_username)
     ➥#&pop_password=#URLEncodedFormat(pop_password)#&email_address=
     ➥#URLEncodedFormat(email_address)#&messagenumber=#messagenumber#"
     TARGET="message">#messagenumber#</A></TD>
       <TD BGCOLOR="FFFFFF">#date#</TD>
       <TD BGCOLOR="FFFFFF">#from#</TD>
       <TD BGCOLOR="FFFFFF">#subject#</TD>
      </TR>
     </CFOUTPUT>

     </TABLE>

     </CENTER>

     </BODY>
     </HTML>
```

Part
IV

Ch
20

Creating MESSAGE.CFM

The MESSAGE.CFM template displays the message details. The CFPOP tag has an ACTION of GETALL because the message body is needed. If you want only a single message (the one the user selected), the message number is passed to the CFPOP MESSAGENUMBER attribute. The NAME attribute again specifies the name of the query to be created; in this example, it is named "message". This template also has two buttons at the top of the page: the REPLY button allows the user to reply to a message, and the DELETE button deletes the current message from the mail server. Each of these buttons is a FORM submit button; the POP server and account information and the message number are passed as hidden fields. The message body itself is displayed by using the Cold Fusion ParagraphFormat() function so that paragraph breaks are honored.

On the CD

> **Listing 20.14   MESSAGE.CFM—Displaying Message Details**

```
<!--- Get message --->
<CFPOP
 SERVER="#pop_server#"
 USERNAME="#pop_username#"
 PASSWORD="#pop_password#"
 ACTION="GETALL"
 MESSAGENUMBER="#messagenumber#"
 NAME="message"
>

<BODY BGCOLOR="FFFFFF">

<P ALIGN="RIGHT">

<!--- Table for REPLY and DELETE button --->
<TABLE>
 <TR>
  <TD>
   <!--- REPLY button --->
   <FORM ACTION="reply.cfm" METHOD="POST">
   <CFOUTPUT>
   <INPUT TYPE="hidden" NAME="pop_server" VALUE="#pop_server#">
   <INPUT TYPE="hidden" NAME="pop_username" VALUE="#pop_username#">
   <INPUT TYPE="hidden" NAME="pop_password" VALUE="#pop_password#">
   <INPUT TYPE="hidden" NAME="email_address" VALUE="#email_address#">
   <INPUT TYPE="hidden" NAME="messagenumber" VALUE="#messagenumber#">
   </CFOUTPUT>
   <INPUT TYPE="submit" VALUE="Reply">
   </FORM>
  </TD>
  <TD>
   <!--- DELETE button --->
   <FORM ACTION="delete.cfm" METHOD="POST" TARGET="_parent">
   <CFOUTPUT>
   <INPUT TYPE="hidden" NAME="pop_server" VALUE="#pop_server#">
   <INPUT TYPE="hidden" NAME="pop_username" VALUE="#pop_username#">
   <INPUT TYPE="hidden" NAME="pop_password" VALUE="#pop_password#">
```

```
   <INPUT TYPE="hidden" NAME="email_address" VALUE="#email_address#">
   <INPUT TYPE="hidden" NAME="messagenumber" VALUE="#messagenumber#">
   </CFOUTPUT>
   <INPUT TYPE="submit" VALUE="Delete">
   </FORM>
  </TD>
 </TR>
</TABLE>

</P>

<CFOUTPUT QUERY="message">

<TABLE BGCOLOR="000000">

 <!--- Display message header info --->
 <TR>
  <TH BGCOLOR="C0C0C0" ALIGN="RIGHT">Date:</TH>
  <TD BGCOLOR="FFFFFF">#date#</TD>
 </TR>
 <TR>
  <TH BGCOLOR="C0C0C0" ALIGN="RIGHT">From:</TH>
  <TD BGCOLOR="FFFFFF">#from#</TD>
 </TR>
 <TR>
  <TH BGCOLOR="C0C0C0" ALIGN="RIGHT">Subject:</TH>
  <TD BGCOLOR="FFFFFF">#subject#</TD>
 </TR>
 <TR>
  <TH BGCOLOR="C0C0C0" ALIGN="RIGHT">To:</TH>
  <TD BGCOLOR="FFFFFF">#to#</TD>
 </TR>
 <TR>
  <TH BGCOLOR="C0C0C0" ALIGN="RIGHT">CC:</TH>
  <TD BGCOLOR="FFFFFF">#cc#</TD>
 </TR>

 <!--- Display message body --->
 <TR>
  <TD COLSPAN="2" BGCOLOR="FFFFFF">#ParagraphFormat(body)#</TD>
 </TR>

</TABLE>

</CFOUTPUT>

</BODY>
</HTML>
```

Creating DELETE.CFM

DELETE.CFM deletes a message from the mail server. It calls CFPOP with an ACTION of DELETE and specifies the message number of the message to be deleted. Then the MAIL.CFM template (the template that defines the frames) is called so that both the left and right windows get updated.

Part

IV

Ch

20

Listing 20.15 DELETE.CFM—Deleting a Message

```
<!--- Delete a message --->
<CFPOP
 SERVER="#pop_server#"
 USERNAME="#pop_username#"
 PASSWORD="#pop_password#"
 ACTION="DELETE"
 MESSAGENUMBER="#messagenumber#"
>

<!--- And redisplay entire frame so that headers is updated --->
<CFLOCATION
URL="mail.cfm?pop_server=#URLEncodedFormat(pop_server)#&pop_username=
➥#URLEncodedFormat(pop_username)#&pop_password=#URLEncodedFormat
➥(pop_password)#&email_address=#URLEncodedFormat(email_address)#">
```

Creating REPLY.CFM

REPLY.CFM displays a reply form that can be used to reply to email. First, the message is retrieved with a CFPOP call. Then a form is displayed with the to name (the REPLYTO field) and the subject filled in, and a TEXTAREA box in which to type a reply. The original message is also displayed so that it appears in the reply (beneath a dashed line). When the user clicks the SEND button, the form is submitted to the SENDREPLY.CFM template.

Listing 20.16 REPLY.CFM—The Reply Form

```
<!--- Get message to reply to --->
<CFPOP
 SERVER="#pop_server#"
 USERNAME="#pop_username#"
 PASSWORD="#pop_password#"
 ACTION="GETALL"
 MESSAGENUMBER="#messagenumber#"
 NAME="message"
>

<BODY BGCOLOR="FFFFFF">

<CFOUTPUT QUERY="message">

<!--- Reply form --->
<FORM ACTION="sendreply.cfm" METHOD="POST">

<INPUT TYPE="hidden" NAME="pop_server" VALUE="#pop_server#">
<INPUT TYPE="hidden" NAME="pop_username" VALUE="#pop_username#">
<INPUT TYPE="hidden" NAME="pop_password" VALUE="#pop_password#">
<INPUT TYPE="hidden" NAME="email_address" VALUE="#email_address#">
<INPUT TYPE="hidden" NAME="messagenumber" VALUE="#messagenumber#">
<INPUT TYPE="hidden" NAME="mail_from" VALUE="#email_address#">
```

```
<TABLE BGCOLOR="000000">
 <TR>
  <TH ALIGN="RIGHT" BGCOLOR="C0C0C0">To:</TH>
  <TD BGCOLOR="FFFFFF"><INPUT TYPE="text" NAME="mail_to" VALUE="#Trim
➥(replyto)#"></TD>
 </TR>
 <TR>
  <TH ALIGN="RIGHT" BGCOLOR="C0C0C0">Subject:</TH>
  <TD BGCOLOR="FFFFFF"><INPUT TYPE="text" NAME="mail_subject" VALUE=
➥"Re: #Trim(subject)#"></TD>
 </TR>
 <TR>
  <TD COLSPAN=2 BGCOLOR="FFFFFF">
  <TEXTAREA NAME="mail_body" WRAP="VIRTUAL">

#RepeatString("=", 40)#
#from# wrote:
#body#
  </TEXTAREA>
  </TD>
 </TR>
 <TR>
  <TH COLSPAN=2 BGCOLOR="C0C0C0"><INPUT TYPE="submit" VALUE="Send"></TH>
</TABLE>

</FORM>

</CFOUTPUT>

</BODY>
</HTML>
```

Creating SENDREPLY.CFM

Listing 20.17, SENDREPLY.CFM, sends the message by using the Cold Fusion CFMAIL tag (the SMTP interface) and then redisplays the message (see Figure 20.7).

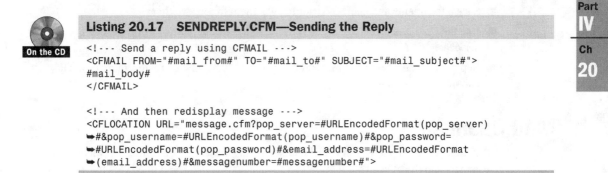

Listing 20.17   SENDREPLY.CFM—Sending the Reply

```
<!--- Send a reply using CFMAIL --->
<CFMAIL FROM="#mail_from#" TO="#mail_to#" SUBJECT="#mail_subject#">
#mail_body#
</CFMAIL>

<!--- And then redisplay message --->
<CFLOCATION URL="message.cfm?pop_server=#URLEncodedFormat(pop_server)
➥#&pop_username=#URLEncodedFormat(pop_username)#&pop_password=
➥#URLEncodedFormat(pop_password)#&email_address=#URLEncodedFormat
➥(email_address)#&messagenumber=#messagenumber#">
```

FIG. 20.7
The web-based email
client.

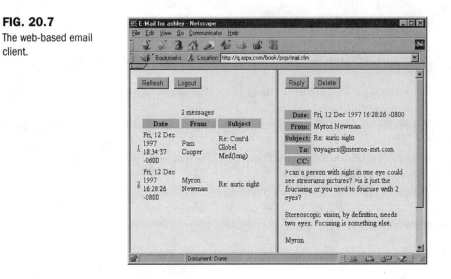

Enhancing the Mail Client

This very basic, albeit functional, email client is a good base on which to write your own email
client. Some suggested enhancements to this application are

- Allow the sending of new mail (not just replies) and sending attachments (using CFFILE
  ACTION="UPLOAD").
- Allow mail forwarding.
- Use cookies or client variables to store the POP server and account information so that
  the user does not have to enter it each time.
- Use cookies or client variables to store the date and time that mail was last retrieved, so
  that on the next visit users can see only new mail.
- Allow mail filtering (by sender, subject, date) and searching (subject and body).
- Save attachments and allow the user to click them to retrieve them.
- Use the Cold Fusion CFLDAP tag to retrieve address book entries from a directory
  service.
- Replace all forms (login, reply, send mail) with CFFORM tags to create a more powerful
  and intuitive user interface.

Mail Daemons

CFPOP is well suited for use within mail daemons. A *daemon* is a program that sits waiting for
some activity and then performs set processes when activity occurs. A good example of this is
a list server daemon. *List servers* are email-based discussion groups that users subscribe to or
unsubscribe from.

To subscribe to a list, a user sends email to a specific email address with a subject such as SUBSCRIBE (the subject could be anything, but SUBSCRIBE has become the accepted keyword). When the daemon encounters a SUBSCRIBE message, it adds the user's email address to a database and sends a confirmation message back to the user. From that point on, any mail sent to the list of users will also be sent to the newly subscribed user, who is now part of that list.

To unsubscribe from a list, a user sends a mail message with a subject of UNSUBSCRIBE. When the daemon encounters this message, it removes the email address from the database and sends back a confirmation message.

The code example in Listing 20.18 is not a complete list server interface, but it demonstrates the basic components required to create your own list server. The template first retrieves a list of messages in the mailbox. Because the message body is not needed, the ACTION is set to GETHEADERONLY. When the mail is retrieved, a CFLOOP is used to loop through the query. A good reason to use CFLOOP and not CFOUTPUT is that CFOUTPUT does not allow some CF tags to be executed within it (such as CFMAIL or CFQUERY). CFLOOP does not have these limitations and can therefore be safely used as long as you place CFOUTPUT tags around your output sections within the loop. The CFLOOP itself contains a CFIF statement that checks the message subject and performs some code. Replace the ellipsis (...) with your own code as appropriate.

Listing 20.18   Basic Elements of a List Server

```
<!--- Get mail headers --->
<CFPOP
 SERVER="mail.domain.com"
 USERNAME="listserv"
 PASSWORD="g8g7ty"
 ACTION="GETHEADERONLY"
 NAME="messages"
>

<!--- Loop through messages --->
<CFLOOP QUERY="messages">

 <CFIF #subject# IS "SUBSCRIBE">

  <!--- User wants to subscribe --->

  ...

 <CFELSEIF #subject# IS "UNSUBSCRIBE">

  <!--- User wants to unsubscribe --->

  ...

 <CFELSE>
```

continues

Part

IV

Ch

20

Listing 20.18   Continued

```
   <!--- Not sure what users wants, send HELP information --->

   ...

   </CFIF>

</CFLOOP>
```

Working with Attachments

Email is not used just to transmit text messages. With MIME, email has become a popular way to send and receive files of all types.

To retrieve attached files with CFPOP, you must do the following:

1. Retrieve messages with CFPOP by using an ACTION value of GETALL and specifying the location (drive and directory) in which to story temporary copies of the attached files. This path is passed to the ATTACHMENTPATH attribute.

2. Examine the ATTACHMENTS field for a list of attachments. The tab-delimited list can be used with the Cold Fusion list function (and CFLOOP) if the tab character is specified as the delimiter (ASCII character with a value of 9).

3. The attached files are stored in the path specified in the ATTACHMENTPATH attribute. The files are not stored by using their actual filenames, because the file may have originated on an operating system that had different file-naming conventions. The physical filenames are stored in the ATTACHMENTFILES column, in a tab-delimited list. This list will always have the same number of elements as the ATTACHMENTS list, and the first attachment listed in ATTACHMENTS will be named with the value in the first element in the ATTACHMENTFILES list.

4. Cold Fusion does not automatically delete the temporary files. It is your responsibility to do so (if you don't, they'll just sit there taking up space). The files can be deleted with the CFFILE tag (using ACTION="DELETE").

If you are going to allow users to retrieve the attached files as web pages (using an URL that points to the file directly), you must make sure that the path specified in the ATTACHMENTPATH attribute is within a web server path (beneath the web server root or in any other mapped drive). The Windows temporary directory (which is generally a good place in which to store temporary files) is therefore not a good choice for this. ●

CHAPTER 21

Online Commerce

by Ashley King

In this chapter

Leveraging the Internet with Cold Fusion

The vast growth of the Internet has been fueled by commerce. As we've all heard in the commercials, businesses large and small have benefited from use of the Internet. Small companies and individuals now market products and services to new markets worldwide, and large companies are saving in sales and delivery costs by setting up shop on the Internet.

Cold Fusion facilitates the construction of highly interactive, easily managed sites for commerce. Merchants have the choice of using many different payment systems, simplifying the purchasing process for customers. "Shopping cart" systems allow customers to easily browse a product selection, marking products for purchase and even retaining these selections between visits. Merchants can track purchases and use this data to recommend other items to customers, increasing the bottom line. In this chapter, you construct a shopping cart system and show how this system can integrate with several different payment systems.

Understanding the Mechanics of Internet Commerce

The first element in Internet commerce is marketing. This is way beyond the scope of this book, but if you build it they'll come only if they know it's there. When you create an Internet site, the goal is to make it easy and fun for potential customers to find what they want, and then make it as painless as possible for them to purchase it.

The purchase must be supported after the sale, and further offers and updates should be given to customers to encourage their return. This process can be broken down into five steps: navigating, selecting, purchasing, delivering, and supporting.

Navigating

If a customer is going to purchase something from your site, he or she first must be able to find it. Navigation includes several elements. First, the customer must know what is in the store in general terms. Second, the products on the site must be organized in a logical manner. Third, and very important, a means should be provided to search for products based on dynamic criteria. In the nonvirtual world, sales agents help customers find their way through a store and assist in the purchase. Your site must make it easy for customers to find what they need quickly and easily.

A good way to put this concept in context is to visualize the organization of your products in terms of a traditional store. As you walk in, there may be several "special" items on display, encouraging impulse purchases. As you venture into the store, departments are usually clearly defined and organized logically. If things are hard to find, they don't sell and customers go elsewhere.

Selecting

When you find the items you are looking for (and many that you weren't looking for but decide to buy anyway), you place the item in a basket so you can continue shopping. Allowing customers to "queue" items for purchase encourages greater sales. After all, stores wouldn't sell much if you could buy only what you could carry to the checkout. This is also an important feature for commerce sites on the Internet. If your site sells more than a few products, a shopping cart is a must.

Purchasing

Purchases require several elements. First, information about the customer must be obtained. Second, a payment method that is mutually feasible for both customer and merchant must be chosen. Third, the merchant must process payment information from the customer. Finally, the customers receive confirmation of their purchases. Gathering data from customers is a step that is different for almost each merchant, but usually name, address, and email are collected, at minimum. Check, credit card, or billing information for the chosen payment method is also collected from the customer for processing.

Of great concern to both developers and consumers is security and encryption of data between the customer and the merchant. This can be accomplished by using the SSL or SHTTP capabilities of your web server to establish a secure connection between the customer and the merchant. Cold Fusion uses these capabilities transparently, using your web server's security features. For some web servers, such as WebSite from O'Reilly and Associates, you may simply direct the user to an URL using port 443, such as **http://www.myserver.com:443/order. cfm**. Other servers use **https://** to precede a secure URL. The documentation for your web server can provide more information on using encryption capabilities in your application.

Processing and confirmation steps depend entirely on the method of payment chosen. Later in the chapter, you explore several popular methods of payment processing and how to use them in your application. Most payment processing systems provide automatic and immediate payment processing, a far cry from the early days of Internet commerce.

Delivering the Product

Delivering the product is different for almost every merchant. For paid access sites, delivery might simply include access to a protected area of the site. For software purchases, a file may be made available for a user to download. Other sites need to fulfill purchases by mail or other form of delivery. Each method of delivery can be supported using Cold Fusion. For protected access sites, a customer could be given a username and password using CFMAIL or by displaying a secure web page. Files can be made available using CFCONTENT or retrieved using CFFTP for software delivery.

Support After the Sale

Support after the sale not only keeps customers happy but also encourages future sales. Some items may not necessarily need support, but newsletters or customized offers can be sent to let the customer know about new specials or other items of interest. For items that need more complex support, a threaded conferencing area could allow customers to post problems and receive quick responses from support staff and other users. Let's see how these elements come together in an example application, the QuickStore custom tag.

Part

IV

Ch

21

Building the QuickStore Application

This example brings together the elements necessary in a basic Internet store. Because many webmasters would like to integrate a store into an existing web site, let's create a custom tag that can be placed into any page. The custom tag will use client and session management, so these must be enabled in the application.cfm file for your application. See Chapter 24, "Session Variables and Cookies," for tips on enabling client and session management. The tag will also use a database to store products, categories, customer information, and sales data. This data can be used for delivery, support, and marketing. When viewing Listings 21.1 through 21.6, remember that they are sequential sections of the same file, QuickStore.cfm. When the QuickStore.cfm template is called from another Cold Fusion template, as shown in Listing 24.7, you will have a complete online shopping cart system. The following sections walk you through the application.

Initializing QuickStore

The initialization process for the QuickStore tag, shown in Listing 21.1, sets up default values for the administration password, whether the URLToken will be appended to internal URLs, the datasource to use, and what type of payment processing will be used. Because each payment processing system has its own parameters, no default values are specified. Client variables are used to identify customers, and session variables are used to store the contents of the shopping basket and the state of the application, or what it is to do next.

On the CD

Listing 21.1   QUICKSTORE.CFM—Initialization in the QuickStore.cfm Template

```
<!--- QuickStore custom tag --->
<!--- Set defaults --->
<CFPARAM NAME="attributes.dsn" DEFAULT="QuickStore">
<CFPARAM NAME="attributes.password" DEFAULT="password">
<CFPARAM NAME="attributes.addToken" DEFAULT="no">
<CFPARAM NAME="attributes.cc" DEFAULT="yes">
<CFPARAM NAME="attributes.processor" DEFAULT="ivcerify">
<CFSET THISPAGE = GETFILEFROMPATH(GETTEMPLATEPATH())>
<CFIF NOT ISDEFINED("session.basket")>
   <CFSET SESSION.BASKET = QUERYNEW("ProductID, Quantity, saleDate")>
</CFIF>
<CFIF ISDEFINED("url.do")>
   <CFSET SESSION.DO = URL.DO>
<CFELSE>
   <CFSET SESSION.DO = "index">
</CFIF>
<CFIF ATTRIBUTES.ADDTOKEN>
   <CFSET VARIABLES.QUERYSTRING = "?#client.URLToken#&">
<CFELSE>
   <CFSET VARIABLES.QUERYSTRING = "?">
</CFIF>
<!--- Do what we need to do --->
<CFIF SESSION.DO IS "action">
   <!--- Handle events --->
   <CFIF ACTION IS "Add Category">
```

```
            <CFQUERY DATASOURCE="#attributes.dsn#">
               INSERT INTO Categories ('Name', 'Description')
            VALUES('#form.name#', '#Form.description#')
            </CFQUERY>

       <CFSET SESSION.DO = "admin">

       <CFQUERY NAME="application.ItemsShort" DATASOURCE="#attributes.dsn#">

            SELECT      Products.ProductID, Products.ProductName, Categories.Name,
       Categories.Description, Categories.CategoryID
            FROM        Products, Categories
            WHERE       Products.CategoryID = Categories.CategoryID
            ORDER BY    Categories.Name, Products.ProductName

            </CFQUERY>

       <CFELSEIF ACTION IS "Delete Category">
            <CFQUERY DATASOURCE="#attributes.dsn#">
               DELETE * FROM Categories
               WHERE CategoryID = #Form.CategoryID#
            </CFQUERY>

            <CFQUERY NAME="application.ItemsShort" DATASOURCE="#attributes.dsn#">

            SELECT      Products.ProductID, Products.ProductName, Categories.Name,
       Categories.Description, Categories.CategoryID
            FROM        Products, Categories
            WHERE       Products.CategoryID = Categories.CategoryID
            ORDER BY    Categories.Name; Products.ProductName

            </CFQUERY>

            <CFSET SESSION.DO = "admin">
         <CFELSEIF ACTION IS "Add Product">
            <CFQUERY DATASOURCE="#attributes.dsn#">
               INSERT INTO Products ('ProductName', 'CategoryID',
       'DescriptionShort', 'DescriptionLong', 'Keywords', 'UnitPrice',
       'ImageSmall', 'ImageLarge')
               VALUES('#form.Productname#', #form.categoryID#,
       '#form.descriptionShort#', '#form.descriptionLong#',
       '#form.keywords#', #form.unitPrice#, '#form.imageSmall#',
       '#form.imageLarge#')
            </CFQUERY>
            <CFQUERY NAME="application.ItemsShort" DATASOURCE="#attributes.dsn#">

            SELECT      Products.ProductID, Products.ProductName, Categories.Name,
       Categories.Description, Categories.CategoryID
            FROM        Products, Categories
            WHERE       Products.CategoryID = Categories.CategoryID
            ORDER BY    Categories.Name, Products.ProductName

            </CFQUERY>

            <CFSET SESSION.DO = "admin">
```

Part
IV

Ch
21

continues

Listing 21.1 Continued

```
<CFELSEIF ACTION IS "Edit Product">

   <CFSET SESSION.EDIT = "yes">
   <CFSET SESSION.DO = "admin">

<CFELSEIF ACTION IS "Update Product">

   <CFIF FORM.EDITACTION IS "Update">

      <CFQUERY DATASOURCE="#attributes.dsn#">

         UPDATE Products
         SET ProductName = '#form.Productname#',
         CategoryID = #form.categoryID#,
         DescriptionShort = '#form.descriptionShort#',
         DescriptionLong = '#form.descriptionLong#',
         Keywords = '#form.keywords#',
         UnitPrice = #form.unitPrice#,
         ImageSmall = '#form.imageSmall#',
         ImageLarge = '#form.imageLarge#'
         WHERE ProductID = #form.productID#

      </CFQUERY>

   <CFELSE>

      <CFQUERY DATASOURCE="#attributes.dsn#">

         DELETE * FROM Products
         WHERE ProductID = #form.productID#

      </CFQUERY>

   </CFIF>
   <CFQUERY NAME="application.ItemsShort" DATASOURCE="#attributes.dsn#">

      SELECT    Products.ProductID, Products.ProductName, Categories.Name,
➥Categories.Description, Categories.CategoryID
      FROM        Products, Categories
      WHERE     Products.CategoryID = Categories.CategoryID
      ORDER BY  Categories.Name, Products.ProductName

   </CFQUERY>

   <CFSET SESSION.DO = "admin">
   <CFSET SESSION.EDIT = "no">

<CFELSEIF ACTION IS "Add to basket">

   <CFSET TEMPVALUE = QUERYADDROW(SESSION.BASKET)>
   <CFSET TEMPVALUE = QUERYSETCELL(SESSION.BASKET, "saleDate", "#Now()#")>
```

```
            <CFSET TEMPVALUE = QUERYSETCELL(SESSION.BASKET, "ProductID",
            FORM.PRODUCTID)>
            <CFSET TEMPVALUE = QUERYSETCELL(SESSION.BASKET, "Quantity",
            FORM.QUANTITY)>

            <CFSET SESSION.DO = "basket">
        <CFELSEIF ACTION IS "Purchase Products">
            <CFQUERY DATASOURCE="#attributes.dsn#">
                INSERT INTO Customers ('CFID', 'FirstName', 'LastName', 'Address',
        'City', 'State', 'PostalCode', 'Country', 'Email')
                VALUES(#client.cfid#, '#form.FirstName#', '#form.LastName#',
        '#form.Address#', '#form.city#', '#form.state#', '#form.PostalCode#',
        '#form.Country#','#form.email#')
            </CFQUERY>

            <CFLOOP QUERY="session.basket">
                <CFQUERY DATASOURCE="#attributes.dsn#">

                    INSERT INTO Sales ('CustomerID', 'ProductID', 'Quantity',
        'SaleDate')
                    VALUES(#client.cfid#, '#session.basket.ProductID#',
        '#session.basket.Quantity#', #session.basket.saleDate#)

                </CFQUERY>
            </CFLOOP>
            <CFSET SESSION.DO = "process">

        </CFIF>

    </CFIF>

    <CFIF NOT ISDEFINED("application.itemsShort")>
        <CFQUERY NAME="application.ItemsShort" DATASOURCE="#attributes.dsn#">

        SELECT      Products.ProductID, Products.ProductName, Categories.Name,
    ➥Categories.Description, Categories.CategoryID
        FROM        Products, Categories
        WHERE       Products.CategoryID = Categories.CategoryID
        ORDER BY    Categories.Name, Products.ProductName

        </CFQUERY>
    </CFIF>
```

Administering QuickStore

The administration area of the application, shown in Listing 21.2, is accessed by appending the URL parameter admin=yes to the starting URL. When the admin page is accessed, the merchant is asked for the administration password. When the correct password is entered, the administration forms are displayed. Merchants add, delete, and edit products. In the product entry dialog, images are entered using relative paths. For instance, if the store template is in the /store/ directory and the images are in the /store/images directory, the image pencil.gif would be entered as images/pencil.gif. The administration page is shown in Figure 21.1.

Part
IV

Ch
21

Listing 21.2   QUICKSTORE.CFM—The Administration Section

```
<CFIF SESSION.DO IS "admin">
    <!--- Administration page --->
      <CFPARAM NAME="session.edit" DEFAULT="no">
    <CFIF ISDEFINED("form.pass")>
        <CFIF FORM.PASS IS ATTRIBUTES.PASSWORD>
            <CFSET SESSION.AUTHENTICATED = "yes">
        </CFIF>
    </CFIF>
    <CFIF NOT ISDEFINED("session.authenticated")>
        <TABLE CELLSPACING="0" CELLPADDING="2" BORDER="1">
        <TR>
            <TD><B>Administration</B>
            </TD>
        </TR>
        <TR>
            <TD>
              <TABLE BORDER=0>
              <TR><TD COLSPAN=2>
              <B>Enter your password:</B><P>
              </TD></TR>
              <CFOUTPUT>
              <FORM METHOD="post" ACTION="#thisPage##queryString#do=admin">
              </CFOUTPUT>
              <TR><TD>
              <INPUT TYPE="hidden" NAME="pass_required"
➥VALUE="You must enter a password">
              <INPUT TYPE="Password" NAME="Pass">
              </TD>
              <TD>
              <INPUT TYPE="Submit" VALUE="Enter">
              </TD></TR>
              </FORM>
              </TABLE>
            </TD>
        </TR>
        </TABLE>
    <CFELSE>
        <CFQUERY NAME="categories" DATASOURCE="#attributes.dsn#">
            SELECT * FROM Categories
            ORDER BY Name ASC
        </CFQUERY>
        <TABLE CELLSPACING="0" CELLPADDING="2" BORDER="1">
        <TR>
            <TD><B>Administration</B>
            </TD>
        </TR>
        <CFIF CATEGORIES.RECORDCOUNT IS NOT 0>
            <!--- Delete category dialog --->
            <TR>
                <TD>
                  <TABLE BORDER=0>
                  <TR><TD COLSPAN=2>
                  <B>Delete a category:</B><P>
                  </TD></TR>
                  <CFOUTPUT>
```

```
              <FORM METHOD="post" ACTION="#thisPage##queryString#do=action">
              </CFOUTPUT>
              <TR><TD>
              <B>Category:</B> <SELECT NAME="CategoryID">
              <CFOUTPUT QUERY="Categories">
              <OPTION VALUE="#CategoryID#">#Name#
              </CFOUTPUT>
              </SELECT>
              </TD>
              <TD>
              <INPUT TYPE="Submit" NAME="action" VALUE="Delete Category">
              </TD></TR>
              </FORM>
              </TABLE>
           </TD>
        </TR>
      </CFIF>
      <!--- Add category dialog --->
      <TR>
          <TD>
            <TABLE BORDER=0>
            <TR><TD COLSPAN=2>
            <B>Add a category:</B><P>
            </TD></TR>
            <CFOUTPUT>
            <FORM METHOD="post" ACTION="#thisPage##queryString#do=action">
            </CFOUTPUT>
            <TR><TD>
            <INPUT TYPE="hidden" NAME="name_required" VALUE="You must enter
➥a category">
            <B>Category:</B> <INPUT TYPE="text" NAME="name">
            </TD><TD>
            <INPUT TYPE="hidden" NAME="description_required" VALUE="You must
➥enter a description">
            <B>Description:</B> <INPUT TYPE="text" NAME="Description">
            </TD></TR>
            <TR>
            <TD COLSPAN=2>
            <INPUT TYPE="Submit" NAME="action" VALUE="Add Category">
            </TD></TR>
            </FORM>
            </TABLE>
          </TD>
      </TR>
      <CFQUERY NAME="products" DATASOURCE="#attributes.dsn#">
         SELECT * FROM Products
         ORDER BY ProductName ASC
      </CFQUERY>
      <CFIF CATEGORIES.RECORDCOUNT IS NOT 0
       AND PRODUCTS.RECORDCOUNT IS NOT 0>
          <!--- Edit product dialog --->
          <TR>
              <TD>
                <TABLE BORDER=0>
                <TR><TD COLSPAN=2>
```

Part

IV

Ch

21

continues

Listing 21.2   Continued

```
                <B>Edit a product:</B><P>
                </TD></TR>
                <CFOUTPUT>
                <FORM METHOD="post" ACTION="#thisPage##queryString#do=action">
                </CFOUTPUT>
                <TR><TD>
                <B>Product:</B> <SELECT NAME="ProductID">
                <CFOUTPUT QUERY="Products">
                <OPTION VALUE="#ProductID#">#ProductName#
                </CFOUTPUT>
                </SELECT>
                </TD>
                <TD>
                <INPUT TYPE="Submit" NAME="action" VALUE="Edit Product">
                </TD></TR>
                </FORM>
                </TABLE>
            </TD>
        </TR>
    </CFIF>
    <CFIF CATEGORIES.RECORDCOUNT IS NOT 0>
        <CFIF NOT SESSION.EDIT>
            <!--- Add a product --->
            <TR>
                <TD>
                  <TABLE BORDER=0>
                  <TR><TD COLSPAN=2>
                  <B>Add a product:</B><P>
                  </TD></TR>
                  <CFOUTPUT>
                  <FORM ACTION="#thisPage##queryString#do=action"
METHOD="POST">
                  </CFOUTPUT>
                  <TR><TD COLSPAN=2>
                  <B>Category:</B> <SELECT NAME="CategoryID">
                  <CFOUTPUT QUERY="Categories">
                  <OPTION VALUE="#CategoryID#">#Name#
                  </CFOUTPUT>
                  </SELECT>
                  </TD></TR>
                  <TR><TD>
                  <TR><TD>
                  <INPUT TYPE="hidden" NAME="Productname_required" VALUE="You
➥must enter a name">
                  <B>Name:</B> <INPUT TYPE="text" NAME="ProductName">
                  </TD><TD>
                  <INPUT TYPE="hidden" NAME="descriptionShort_required"
➥VALUE="You must enter a short description">
                  <B>Short Description:</B> <INPUT TYPE=
➥"text"    NAME="DescriptionShort">
                  </TD></TR>
                  <TR><TD>
                  <INPUT TYPE="hidden" NAME="UnitPrice_required" VALUE="You
➥must enter a unit price">
```

```
                            <B>Unit price:</B> $<INPUT TYPE="text" NAME="UnitPrice">
                            </TD><TD>
                            <INPUT TYPE="hidden" NAME="keywords_required" VALUE="You
➥must enter keywords">
                            <B>Keywords:</B> <INPUT TYPE="text" NAME="Keywords">
                            </TD></TR>
                            <TR>
                            <TD COLSPAN=2>
                            <INPUT TYPE="hidden" NAME="descriptionLong_required"
➥VALUE="You must enter a long description">
                            <B>Long Description:</B><BR>
                            <TEXTAREA NAME="DescriptionLong" COLS="60"
➥ROWS="6"     WRAP="VIRTUAL"></TEXTAREA>
                            </TD></TR>
                            <TR><TD>
                            <INPUT TYPE="hidden" NAME="ImageSmall_required" VALUE="You
➥must enter a path to your image (small)">
                            <B>Image Thumbnail path:</B><BR>
➥  <INPUT TYPE="text"     NAME="ImageSmall">
                            </TD><TD>
                            <INPUT TYPE="hidden" NAME="ImageLarge_required" VALUE="You
➥must enter a path to your image (large)">
                            <B>Image Path:</B><BR> <INPUT TYPE="text" NAME="ImageLarge">
                            </TD></TR>
                            <TD COLSPAN=2>
                            <INPUT TYPE="Submit" NAME="action" VALUE="Add Product">
                            </TD></TR>
                            </FORM>
                            </TABLE>
                        </TD>
                    </TR>
                <CFELSE>
                <!--- Edit a product --->
                    <CFQUERY NAME="ItemsLong" DATASOURCE="#attributes.dsn#">
                        SELECT    Products.ProductID, Products.ProductName,
➥Products.DescriptionLong, Products.DescriptionShort,
➥Products.CategoryID, Products.UnitPrice, Products.ImageLarge,
➥Products.ImageSmall, Products.Keywords, Categories.Name,
➥Categories.CategoryID
                        FROM        Products, Categories
                        WHERE       Products.CategoryID = Categories.CategoryID
                                    AND (Products.ProductID = #form.ProductID#)
                    </CFQUERY>
                    <TR>
                        <TD>
                        <TABLE BORDER=0>
                        <TR><TD COLSPAN=2>
                        <B>Edit product:</B><P>
                        </TD></TR>
                        <CFOUTPUT>
                        <FORM ACTION="#thisPage##queryString#do=action"
➥METHOD="POST">
                        </CFOUTPUT>
                        <TR><TD COLSPAN=2>
                        <B>Category:</B> <SELECT NAME="CategoryID">
```

continues

Part
IV

Ch

21

Listing 21.2   Continued

```
                <CFOUTPUT>
                <OPTION VALUE="#ItemsLong.CategoryID#">#ItemsLong.Name#
                </CFOUTPUT>
                <CFOUTPUT QUERY="Categories">
                <OPTION VALUE="#CategoryID#">#Name#
                </CFOUTPUT>
                </SELECT>
                </TD></TR>
                <TR><TD>
                <CFOUTPUT QUERY="ItemsLong">
                <INPUT TYPE="Hidden" NAME="ProductID"
➥VALUE="#ItemsLong.ProductID#">
                <INPUT TYPE="hidden" NAME="Productname_required" VALUE="You
➥must enter a name">
                <B>Name:</B> <INPUT TYPE="Text" NAME="ProductName"
➥VALUE="#Productname#">
                </TD><TD>
                <INPUT TYPE="hidden" NAME="descriptionShort_required"
➥VALUE="You must enter a short description">
                <B>Short Description:</B> <INPUT TYPE="Text"
➥NAME="DescriptionShort" VALUE="#DescriptionShort#">
                </TD></TR>
                <TR><TD>
                <INPUT TYPE="hidden" NAME="UnitPrice_required" VALUE="You
➥must enter a unit price">
                <B>Unit price:</B> <INPUT TYPE="Text" NAME="UnitPrice"
➥VALUE="#DecimalFormat(UnitPrice)#">
                </TD><TD>.
                <INPUT TYPE="hidden" NAME="keywords_required" VALUE="You
➥must enter keywords">
                <B>Keywords:</B> <INPUT TYPE="Text" NAME="Keywords"
➥VALUE="#Keywords#">
                </TD></TR>
                <TR>
                <TD COLSPAN=2>
                <INPUT TYPE="hidden" NAME="descriptionLong_required"
➥VALUE="You must enter a long description">
                <B>Long Description:</B><BR>
                <TEXTAREA NAME="DescriptionLong" COLS="60" ROWS="6"
➥WRAP="VIRTUAL">#DescriptionLong#</TEXTAREA>
                </TD></TR>
                <TR><TD>
                <INPUT TYPE="hidden" NAME="ImageSmall_required" VALUE="You
➥must enter a path to your image (small)">
                <B>Image Thumbnail path:</B><BR> <INPUT TYPE="Text"
➥NAME="ImageSmall" VALUE="#ImageSmall#">
                </TD><TD>
                <INPUT TYPE="hidden" NAME="ImageLarge_required" VALUE="You
➥must enter a path to your image (large)">
                <B>Image Path:</B><BR> <INPUT TYPE="Text"
➥NAME="ImageLarge" VALUE="#ImageLarge#">
```

```
            </TD></TR>
            <TD COLSPAN=2>
            <SELECT NAME="EditAction">
            <OPTION>Update
               <OPTION>Delete
            </SELECT>
            <INPUT TYPE="Submit" NAME="action" VALUE="Update Product">
            </CFOUTPUT>
            </TD></TR>
            </FORM>
            </TABLE>
         </TD>
      </TR>
   </CFIF>
  </CFIF>
  </TABLE>
</CFIF>
```

FIG. 21.1

The Administration page.

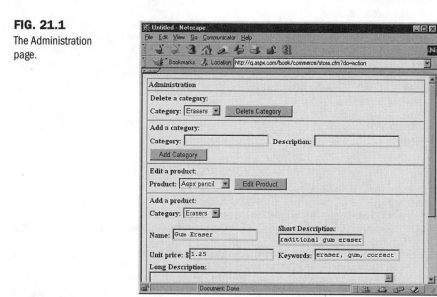

Navigating QuickStore

The navigation interface, shown in Listing 21.3, allows either drill-down navigation by category or a keyword search of products. On the second level, shown in Figure 21.2, products are listed alphabetically with thumbnail images and short descriptions of each. On the third level, the customer sees product detail, including a full description, the unit price, a large image, and a purchase dialog. Customers move up from this level by clicking the category link or return to the top level by clicking the Home link. This is accomplished by using simple queries of the database to retrieve the categories and items. Notice that the main category query is cached using application scope variables to cut down on database accesses.

Listing 21.3   QUICKSTORE.CFM—The Navigation Section

```
<CFELSEIF SESSION.DO IS "index">
   <!--- Main page --->

   <TABLE CELLSPACING="0" CELLPADDING="2" BORDER="1">
   <TR>
      <CFOUTPUT>
      <FORM ACTION="#thisPage##queryString#do=search" METHOD="POST">
      </CFOUTPUT>
       <TD><B>Search</B><INPUT TYPE="Text" NAME="SearchTerms">
       <INPUT TYPE="Submit" NAME="" VALUE="Search">
       </TD>
       </FORM>
   </TR>
   <TR>
       <TD>
         <TABLE BORDER=0>
         <TR><TD COLSPAN=2>
         <B>Categories</B><P>
         </TD></TR>
         <CFOUTPUT QUERY="application.ItemsShort" GROUP="Name">
         <TR>
         <TD><B><A    HREF="#thisPage##queryString#CategoryID=
➥#CategoryID#&do=list">#Name#</A></B></TD>
         <TD>#Description#</TD>
         </TR>
         </CFOUTPUT>
         </TABLE>
       </TD>
   </TR>
   </TABLE>
<CFELSEIF SESSION.DO IS "search">
   <!--- Search results --->
   <CFQUERY NAME="ItemsLong" DATASOURCE="#attributes.dsn#">
      SELECT    ProductID, ProductName, DescriptionShort, ImageSmall
      FROM       Products
      WHERE     (ProductName like '%#form.searchTerms#%'
                OR Keywords like '%#form.searchTerms#%'
                OR DescriptionShort like '%#form.searchTerms#%')
      ORDER BY  ProductName
   </CFQUERY>
   <TABLE CELLSPACING="0" CELLPADDING="2" BORDER="1">
   <TR>
       <TD><B>Search Results</B>
       </TD>
   </TR>
   <TR>
       <TD>
         <TABLE BORDER=0>
         <TR><TD COLSPAN=2>
         <B>Products</B><P>
         </TD></TR>
         <CFOUTPUT QUERY="ItemsLong">
         <TR>
         <TD VALIGN="top"><B><A HREF="#thisPage##queryString#ProductID=
```

```
➥#ProductID#&do=detail">#ProductName#</A></B></TD>
        <TD VALIGN="top"><IMG SRC="#ImageSmall#"
➥BORDER=0 ALIGN="right">#DescriptionShort#</TD>
        </TR>
        </CFOUTPUT>
        </TABLE>
     </TD>
  </TR>
  <TR>
      <TD><CFOUTPUT QUERY="ItemsLong" MAXROWS=1><B>[<A HREF=
➥"#thisPage##queryString#">Home</A>]</B></CFOUTPUT>
     </TD>
  </TR>
  </TABLE>
<CFELSEIF SESSION.DO IS "list">
  <!--- Product listing --->
  <CFQUERY NAME="ItemsLong" DATASOURCE="#attributes.dsn#">
     SELECT     Products.ProductID, Products.ProductName,
➥Products.DescriptionShort, Products.ImageSmall,
➥Categories.CategoryID, Categories.Name
     FROM       Products, Categories
     WHERE      Products.CategoryID = Categories.CategoryID AND
               (Categories.CategoryID = #URL.categoryID#)
     ORDER BY   Products.ProductName
  </CFQUERY>
  <TABLE CELLSPACING="0" CELLPADDING="2" BORDER="1">
  <TR>
      <TD><CFOUTPUT QUERY="ItemsLong" MAXROWS=1><B>#name#</B></CFOUTPUT>
     </TD>
  </TR>
  <TR>
     <TD>
        <TABLE BORDER=0>
        <TR><TD COLSPAN=2>
        <B>Products</B><P>
        </TD></TR>
        <CFOUTPUT QUERY="ItemsLong">
        <TR>
        <TD VALIGN="top"><B><A      HREF="#thisPage##queryString#ProductID=
➥#ProductID#&do=detail">#ProductName#
➥</A></B></TD>
        <TD VALIGN="top"><IMG SRC="#ImageSmall#"
➥BORDER=0 ALIGN="right">#DescriptionShort#</TD>
        </TR>
        </CFOUTPUT>
        </TABLE>
     </TD>
  </TR>
  <TR>
      <TD><CFOUTPUT QUERY="ItemsLong" MAXROWS=1><B>[<A HREF=
➥"#thisPage##queryString#">Home</A>] [<A HREF=
➥"#thisPage##queryString#do=basket">View basket</A>]</B></CFOUTPUT>
     </TD>
  </TR>
  </TABLE>
```

continues

Listing 21.3   Continued

```
<CFELSEIF SESSION.DO IS "detail">
   <!--- Product detail --->
   <CFQUERY NAME="ItemsLong" DATASOURCE="#attributes.dsn#">
      SELECT    Products.ProductID, Products.ProductName,
➥Products.DescriptionLong, Products.CategoryID, Products.UnitPrice,
➥Products.ImageLarge, Categories.Name, Categories.CategoryID
      FROM        Products, Categories
      WHERE       Products.CategoryID = Categories.CategoryID
                  AND (Products.ProductID = #URL.ProductID#)
   </CFQUERY>
   <TABLE CELLSPACING="0" CELLPADDING="2" BORDER="1">
   <TR>
      <TD><CFOUTPUT QUERY="ItemsLong" MAXROWS=1><B>#ProductName#</B>
➥</CFOUTPUT>
      </TD>
   </TR>
   <TR>
      <TD>
         <TABLE BORDER=0>
         <TR><TD COLSPAN=2>
         <B>Detail</B><P>
         </TD></TR>
         <CFOUTPUT QUERY="ItemsLong">
         <TR>
         <TD VALIGN="top"><B>#DollarFormat(UnitPrice)#</B></TD>
         <TD VALIGN="top"><IMG SRC="#ImageLarge#" BORDER=0 ALIGN="right">
➥#DescriptionLong#</TD>
         </TR>
         <FORM ACTION="#thisPage##queryString#do=action" METHOD="POST">
         <TR><TD COLSPAN=2>
         <INPUT TYPE="Hidden" NAME="Quantity_integerinteger" VALUE="You must
➥enter a quantity as a numeric value.">
         <B>Quantity</B>
         <INPUT TYPE="Text" NAME="Quantity" VALUE="1" SIZE="2" MAXLENGTH="3">
         <INPUT TYPE="Hidden" NAME="ProductID" VALUE="#ProductID#">
         <INPUT TYPE="Submit" NAME="action" VALUE="Add to basket">
         </TD></TR>
         </FORM>
         </CFOUTPUT>
         </TABLE>
      </TD>
   </TR>
   <TR>
      <TD><CFOUTPUT QUERY="ItemsLong" MAXROWS=1><B>[<A HREF=
➥"#thisPage##queryString#do=list&CategoryID=#CategoryID#">#Name#
➥</A>] [<AHREF="#thisPage##queryString#">Home</A>] [<A HREF=
➥"#thisPage##queryString#do=basket">View basket</A>]</B></CFOUTPUT>
      </TD>
   </TR>
   </TABLE>
```

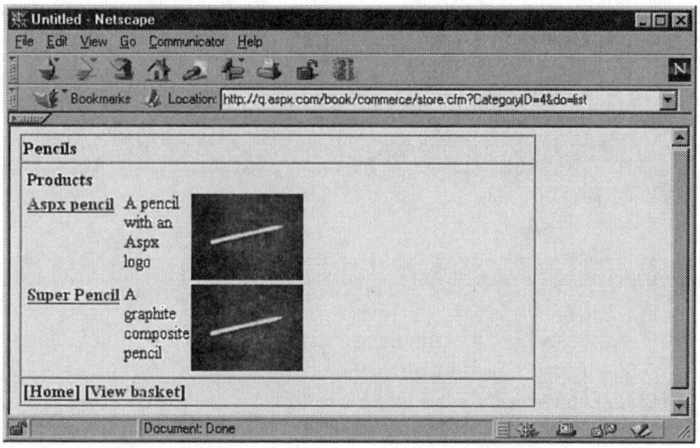

FIG. 21.2
The category menu.

Selecting a QuickStore Item

From the product detail page shown in Listing 21.4, customers select items by entering a quantity and clicking the Add to basket button, as shown in Figure 21.3. This returns a listing of the current products in the customer's shopping bag and a current total, as shown in Figure 21.4. The customer then continues to shop or moves on to the purchase step from this page. The shopping cart is stored in session variables and will time out after a customer leaves your site. To keep the shopping cart persistent, the items can be stored in a database table that references the cfid of the customer, as available in the `client.cfid` variable. See Chapter 24 for more information on client variables.

Listing 21.4   QUICKSTORE.CFM—The Selection Section

```
<CFELSEIF SESSION.DO IS "basket">
   <!--- The shopping basket --->
   <TABLE CELLSPACING="0" CELLPADDING="2" BORDER="1">
   <TR>
      <TD><CFOUTPUT><B>Shopping Basket</B></CFOUTPUT>
      </TD>
   </TR>
   <TR>
      <TD>
        <TABLE BORDER=0>
        <TR><TD COLSPAN=2>
        <B>Items</B><P>
        </TD></TR>
        <CFSET SESSION.TOTAL = 0>
        <CFLOOP QUERY="session.basket">
        <CFQUERY NAME="Item" DATASOURCE="#attributes.dsn#">
           SELECT * FROM Products
           WHERE ProductID = #session.basket.productID#
        </CFQUERY>
        <TR>
        <CFOUTPUT QUERY="Item">
```

continues

Part

IV

Ch

21

Listing 21.4   Continued

```
        <TD VALIGN="top"><B><A HREF="#thisPage##queryString
➡#ProductID=#ProductID#&do=detail">#ProductName#</A></B></TD>
        <TD VALIGN="top">#DollarFormat(UnitPrice)#</TD>
        <CFSET SESSION.TOTAL = EVALUATE(SESSION.TOTAL + UNITPRICE)>
        </CFOUTPUT>
        </TR>
        </CFLOOP>
        <TR>
        <CFOUTPUT>
        <TD VALIGN="top"><B>Total:</B></TD>
        <TD VALIGN="top">#DollarFormat(session.total)#</TD>
        </CFOUTPUT>
        </TR>
        </TABLE>
      </TD>
    </TR>
    <TR>
      <TD><CFOUTPUT><B>[<A HREF="#thisPage##queryString#">Home</A>] [<A
➡HREF="#thisPage##queryString#do=form">Check out</A>]</B></CFOUTPUT>
      </TD>
    </TR>
      </TABLE>
```

FIG. 21.3
The product detail.

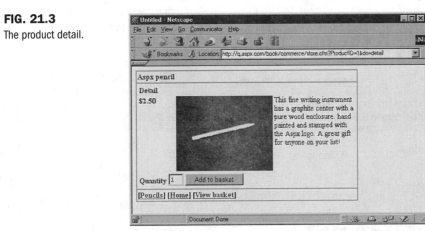

Purchasing a QuickStore Item

The purchase form, shown in Listing 21.5, requires the customer to enter basic personal and payment information. Figure 21.5 shows the layout of this form. Upon submission, the application inserts this information into the database along with the contents of the customer's shopping basket. Other information can be added to this form, including additional shipping information and survey information.

FIG. 21.4

The shopping basket.

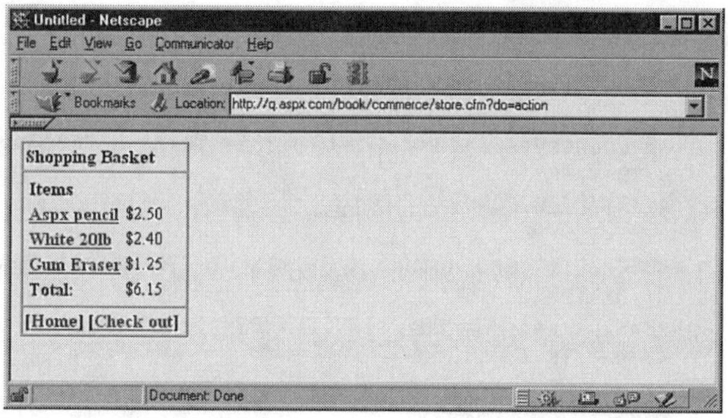

Listing 21.5 QUICKSTORE.CFM—The Purchase Form

```
<CFELSEIF SESSION.DO IS "form">
    <!--- Customer Information form --->
    <TABLE CELLSPACING="0" CELLPADDING="2" BORDER="1">
            <TR><TD COLSPAN=2>
            <B>Please enter your information:</B><P>
            </TD></TR>
            <CFOUTPUT>
            <FORM ACTION="#thisPage##queryString#do=action" METHOD="POST">
            </CFOUTPUT>
            <TR><TD>
            <INPUT TYPE="hidden" NAME="FirstName_required" VALUE="You
➥must enter a name">
            <B>First Name:</B> <INPUT TYPE="text" NAME="FirstName">
            </TD><TD>
            <INPUT TYPE="hidden" NAME="LastName_required" VALUE="You
➥must enter a name">
            <B>Last Name:</B> <INPUT TYPE="text" NAME="LastName">
            </TD></TR>
            <TR><TD COLSPAN=2>
            <INPUT TYPE="hidden" NAME="Address_required" VALUE="You
➥must enter an address">
            <B>Address:</B> <INPUT TYPE="text" NAME="Address">
            </TD></TR>
            <TR><TD>
            <INPUT TYPE="hidden" NAME="City_required" VALUE="You must enter
➥a city">
            <B>City:</B> <INPUT TYPE="text" NAME="City">
            </TD><TD>
            <INPUT TYPE="hidden" NAME="State_required" VALUE="You must enter
➥a state or province">
            <B>State:</B><BR> <INPUT TYPE="text" NAME="State">
            </TD></TR>
            <TR><TD>
            <INPUT TYPE="hidden" NAME="PostalCode_required" VALUE="You must
➥enter a postal code">
            <B>Postal code:</B> <INPUT TYPE="text" NAME="PostalCode">
            </TD><TD>
```

continues

Part

IV

Ch

21

Listing 21.5   Continued

```
                <INPUT TYPE="hidden" NAME="Country_required" VALUE="You must
➥enter a country">
                <B>Country:</B><BR> <INPUT TYPE="text" NAME="Country">
                </TD></TR>
        <CFIF ATTRIBUTES.CC>
                <TR><TD>
                <B>Credit card number:</B> <INPUT TYPE="text" NAME="CCNum">
                </TD><TD>
                <B>Expires:</B><BR> <INPUT TYPE="text" NAME="ExpDate">
                </TD></TR>
        </CFIF>
                <TR><TD COLSPAN=2>
                <INPUT TYPE="hidden" NAME="Email_required" VALUE="You must
➥enter an email address">
                <B>Email:</B> <INPUT TYPE="text" NAME="Email">
                </TD></TR>
                <TR><TD COLSPAN=2>
                <INPUT TYPE="Submit" NAME="action" VALUE="Purchase Products">
                </TD></TR>
                </FORM>
    </TABLE>
```

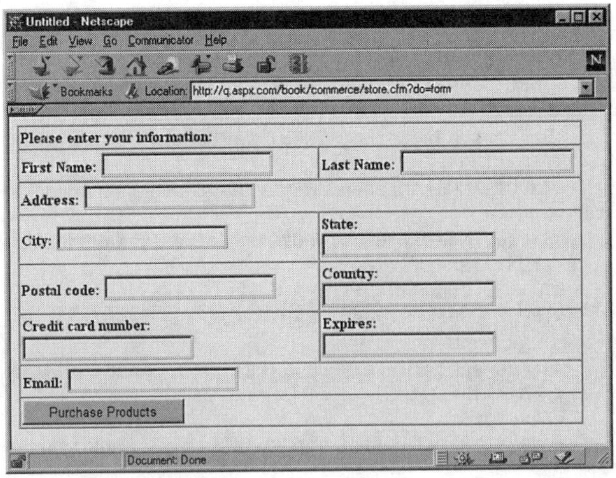

FIGURE 21.5

The customer information form.

Processing Payments

The payment processing section of QuickStore is shown in Listing 21.6. This is where the application hands off to the selected processing system. The application includes Cybercash and ICVerify, which you'll look at later. Each requires separate attributes to be passed to the template. When processing is complete, each tag sets variables so that the success of the transaction can be determined and recorded.

Security can be enhanced at this point by redirecting the user to an SSL or SHTTP version of this page. Data will then be encrypted between the user and your web site.

On the CD

Listing 21.6 QUICKSTORE.CFM—The QuickStore.cfm Template

```
<CFELSEIF SESSION.DO IS "process">
    <!--- Process the order --->
    <CFIF ATTRIBUTES.PROCESSOR IS "icverify">
        <CFX_ICV NAME="process_card"
            IC_SHAREDIR="#attributes.ic_sharedir#"
            TRANS_TYPE="C1"
            ACCOUNT="#form.ccnum#"
            EXPIRES_MO="#left(form.expdate, 2)#"
            EXPIRES_YR="#right(form.expdate, 2)#"
            AMOUNT="#session.total#" >
        <CFOUTPUT QUERY="VALIDATE_CC">
        <CFIF #VALIDATED# IS "Y">
            #VALIDATED# - Credit card was authorized.
            #AUTH_NO#
        <CFELSE>
            <CFIF #VALIDATED# IS NOT "IC_TIMEOUT">
                #AUTH_NO# - Credit card was NOT authorized.
            <CFELSE>
                #AUTH_NO#
                A Timeout occurred waiting to process this order.
                Credit card was NOT authorized.
            </CFIF>
        </CFIF>
        </CFOUTPUT>
        <!--- Add post processing here such as mailing receipts, etc. --->
    <CFELSEIF ATTRIBUTES.PROCESSOR IS "cybercash">
        <CFX_CYBERCASH
            SERVER="#attributes.server#"
            MERCHANTPASSWORD="#attributes.merchantpassword#"
            TRANSTYPE="mauthonly"
            ORDERID="#client.cftoken#"
            AMOUNT="#session.total#"
            CCNUMBER="#form.ccnum#"
            CCEXP="#form.expdate#"
            CCNAME="#form.firstname# #form.lastname#"
            CCADDRESS="#form.address#"
            CCCITY="#form.city#"
            CCSTATE="#form.state#"
            CCZIP="#form.postalcode#"
            CCCOUNTRY="#form.country#"
        >
        <!--- Add post processing here such as mailing receipts, etc.
        Note that Cold Fusion variables MStatus,
        MAuthNumber, and MErrMsg are available for
        processing at this point in the template --->
    </CFIF>
</CFIF>
```

Now that the QuickStore tag is complete, you can add it to any existing Cold Fusion template. Listing 21.7 shows how to call QuickStore from an existing template. Because QuickStore uses the URL of the page calling it, it can be used without modification to your existing application structure.

On the CD

> **Listing 21.7 index.CFM—Calling QuickStore from an Existing Application**

```
<!DOCTYPE HTML PUBLIC "-//W3C//DTD HTML 3.2 Final//EN">
<HTML>
<HEAD>
    <TITLE>A Basic Store</TITLE>
</HEAD>
<BODY>
<CF_QUICKSTORE>
</BODY>
</HTML>
```

Using Payment Processing Systems

Payment processing systems provide the critical link between web applications and the financial world. There are many commercial payment processing systems available to use with your commerce site, and most allow customers to use credit cards as a payment method. Of utmost concern to the majority of potential customers is security. You can help the customer feel safe purchasing on your site by incorporating encrypted pages into your application using SSL or SHTTP and by providing customers with means to contact you if they have concerns.

For you, ease-of-use and reliability are also requirements in a payment processing system. Let's take a look at a few established payment processing systems that are in widespread use on the Internet today: Cybercash, ICVerify, Redi-Check, and Open Market. Table 21.1 shows a comparison of these payment processing systems.

Table 21.1 Payment Processing Systems

Vendor and Product	Accepted Types	Comments
Cybercash	Credit cards, micro payments, checks	Requires the Cash Register software to be installed on your server. Payments are processed over the Internet securely. For more information, visit **http://www.cybercash.com**.
ICVerify	Credit cards	Requires ICVerify software to be installed on your server. Payments are processed via modem connection to a processing network. Information on ICVerify software is available at **http://www.ieverify.com**. The CFX tag for integration with Cold Fusion is available at **http://www.programmersweb.com**.
Redi-Check	Credit cards, checks	Payments are processed via secure HTTP connection. No software is required on your server. For more information, visit **http://www.redicheck.com**.

Vendor and Product	Accepted Types	Comments
Open Market	Credit cards, debit cards, SET, purchase orders	Requires Transact server. Distributed architecture enables centralization of processing enterprisewide. For more information on the Open Market commerce system, visit **http://www/openmarket.com**. The Open Market Fuel Pack is available at **http://www. allaire.com**.

Using Cybercash

Cybercash offers credit card processing, check processing, and micropayment processing. Micropayments involve smaller payments, ranging from around $.25 to $10.00 (US). Cybercash also allows customers using Cybercash wallets to pay without entering a credit card number on your site. Cybercash requires that the Cash Register software be installed on your server. The Cybercash CFX tag communicates with Cash Register, which processes the transaction using a secure connection to the Cybercash network. Cash Register returns success codes for your application to evaluate. An example of the use of the CFX_Cybercash tag is included in the QuickStore application in Listing 21.8. The CFX_Cybercash tag is part of a Cold Fusion fuel pack available from Allaire.

Using ICVerify

ICVerify gives you the most control over payment processing. The entire system resides on your server, which means you are also responsible for monitoring and maintaining the payment system, in addition to your web servers and other concerns. The advantage of this is lower processing fees per transaction, depending on your merchant account. When the ICVerify server receives a processing request, it dials the appropriate processing network, using your modem, and completes the transaction in real time. Settlements, chargebacks, and other transactions can also be done, and all records are stored on your server. ICVerify can reuse connections for heavy-use sites, connecting to the processing network once for several transactions at a time. The CFX_ICV custom tag is a third-party tool developed to integrate the functions of ICVerify into the Cold Fusion language. An example of the use of this tag is included in the QuickStore application in Listing 21.8.

Using Redi-Check

Redi-Check processes both credit cards and checks using secure HTTP connections, making it very simple to integrate in any web commerce site. When a transaction is initiated, the customer is redirected to the Redi-Check secure server for processing, then returned to the URL of your choice for confirmation. Payments can be mailed to you or deposited directly in your account. Redi-Check requires no additional software and can be set up very quickly. An example of a Redi-Check-enabled site is shown in Listing 21.8.

Part
IV

Ch
21

On the CD

Listing 21.8   REDI_CHECK.CFM—Payment Processing Using Redi-Check

```
        <FORM METHOD="POST" ACTION="https://secure.redi-check.com/cgi-bin/
rc3/ord.cgi">
        <INPUT TYPE="hidden" NAME="vendor_id" VALUE="XXXXXX">
        <INPUT TYPE="hidden" NAME="home_page" VALUE="http://www.aspx.com">
        <INPUT TYPE="hidden" NAME="ret_addr" VALUE=
"http://www.aspx.com/store/thanks.cfm">
        <INPUT TYPE="hidden" NAME="email_text" VALUE="Thank you for
purchasing MrPost! Your key and instructions will follow by email.">
        <CFOUTPUT>
        <INPUT TYPE="hidden" NAME="passback" VALUE="Identifier">
        <INPUT TYPE="hidden" NAME="Identifier" VALUE="#variables.
identifier#">
        <INPUT TYPE="hidden" NAME="passback" VALUE="Total">
        <INPUT TYPE="hidden" NAME="Total" VALUE="#DollarFormat(form.Total)#">
        <INPUT TYPE="hidden" NAME="first_name" VALUE="#form.first_name#">
        <INPUT TYPE="hidden" NAME="last_name" VALUE="#form.Last_name#">
        <INPUT TYPE="hidden" NAME="address" VALUE="#form.address#">
        <INPUT TYPE="hidden" NAME="city" VALUE="#form.city#">
        <INPUT TYPE="hidden" NAME="state" VALUE="#form.state#">
        <INPUT TYPE="hidden" NAME="zip" VALUE="#Form.zip#">
        <INPUT TYPE="hidden" NAME="country" VALUE="#form.country#">
        <INPUT TYPE="hidden" NAME="phone" VALUE="#Form.Phone#">
        <INPUT TYPE="hidden" NAME="email" VALUE="#form.email#">
        <INPUT TYPE="hidden" NAME="1-desc" VALUE="Aspx Products" SIZE=8>
        <INPUT TYPE="hidden" NAME="1-cost" SIZE=8 VALUE=
"#DecimalFormat(form.thisTotal)#"></CFOUTPUT>
        <INPUT TYPE="hidden" NAME="1-qty" VALUE="1">
        <TABLE BORDER=1 CELLSPACING=0 CELLPADDING=0>
        <TR>
     <TD VALIGN=TOP COLSPAN=2  BGCOLOR=MAROON><A HREF=
"http://www.redi-check.com"><B>Redi-Check Payment</B></A>
     </TD>
     </TR>
        <TR>
     <TD COLSPAN=2 BGCOLOR=PURPLE><FONT SIZE="-1">For your convenience, we use
Redi-Check's real-time secure transaction gateway. <IMG SRC="http://
www.redi-check.com/images/securekey.gif" BORDER=0> <A HREF="https://
secure.redi-check.com/support/security.html">Security information
</A></FONT><P>
     </TD>
     </TR>
        <TR>
     <TD VALIGN=TOP COLSPAN=2  BGCOLOR=MAROON><B>Checking Account
Information</B>
     </TD>
     </TR>
        <TR>
     <TD COLSPAN=2 BGCOLOR=PURPLE>
<I><FONT SIZE="-1">At the bottom of your check is a series of numbers,
separated by symbols.  It is not necessary to enter symbols or spaces
in the fields provided below.</FONT><BR>
     </TD>
     </TR>
```

```
        <TR>
        <TD VALIGN=TOP BGCOLOR=PURPLE>
        <B> Enter the series of <I>nine</I> numbers <I>between</I>
➥this symbol </B>
        </TD>
        <TD VALIGN=TOP BGCOLOR=PURPLE>
        <IMG SRC="http://www.redi-check.com/images/1.gif">
➥<INPUT NAME="aba" SIZE=9 MAXLENGTH=9>
➥<IMG SRC="http://www.redi-check.com/images/1.gif"><BR>
        </TD>
        </TR>
        <TR>
        <TD VALIGN=TOP BGCOLOR=PURPLE>
        <B>Enter the series of numbers  found <I>before</I> this symbol </B>
        </TD>
        <TD VALIGN=TOP BGCOLOR=PURPLE>
        <IMG SRC="http://www.redi-check.com/images/2.gif"><INPUT NAME="account"
➥SIZE=20 MAXLENGTH=25><IMG SRC="http://www.redi-check.com/images/2.gif">
        </TD>
        </TR>
        <TR>
        <TD COLSPAN=2 BGCOLOR=PURPLE><FONT SIZE=-1>Note: Some banks use a
➥non-standard format in this series of numbers.  If your account number
➥includes this symbol <IMG SRC="http://www.redi-check
➥.com/images/3.gif">,
➥simply disregard the symbols and enter this section of numbers.
</FONT></TD>
        </TR>
            </TABLE>
```

Using Open Market

Open Market is a commerce platform with many options and components, the most important of which are Transact and SecureLink. The Open Market system creates digital offers (DOs) that customers can add to a shopping cart. When the customer is ready to purchase, the transaction is handled by the Transact server. Digital offers can be created and modified using the set of CFX tools in the Open Market Fuel Pack, available from Allaire. The Open Market platform is aware of all elements of the merchant site, from digital offers to fulfillment, providing a highly integrated commerce solution.

Using the Open Market Fuel Pack

The Open market Fuel Pack consists of six CFX tags. These tags make the creation and manipulation of predigital offers (PDOs) much simpler and integrate conversion into digital offers. The tag names are CFX_CREATEPDO, CFX_GETPDO, CFX_SETPDO, CFX_READPDO, CFX_WRITEPDO, and CFX_PDO2DO. For a more detailed discussion of the mechanics of the Open Market platform, specifications of the Transact and SecureLink systems are available at the Open Market web site at **http://www.openmarket.com**. This discussion assumes familiarity with the Open Market components.

Part

IV

Ch

21

Using *CFX_CREATEPDO* The CFX_CREATEPDO tag creates a PDO. This is the starting point for creating a digital offer. The attributes for this tag are listed in Table 21.2.

Table 21.1 *CFX_CREATEPDO*

Attribute	Description
OfferName	The variable that will hold the PDO. This is required.
Attribute	Any of the available attributes for a PDO. All required attributes of a PDO must be included to create a PDO: Name, Type, UniqueID, OfferURL, and Price.

Using *CFX_GETPDO* The CFX_GETPDO tag queries any of the attributes of a PDO created using CFX_CREATEPDO. These attributes can then be changed using CFX_SETPDO. The attributes for this tag are listed in Table 21.3.

Table 21.3 *CFX_GETPDO*

Attribute	Description
OfferValue	The variable that contains the PDO. This is required.
Attribute	Any of the available attributes for a PDO. This is also required.
Variable	The variable that will contain the value of the above attribute. This is required.

Using *CFX_SETPDO* The CFX_SETPDO tag dynamically sets any attribute in a PDO. The current value of an attribute can be queried by CFX_GETPDO and then set using dynamic data from a database or other source. The attributes for this tag are listed in Table 21.4.

Table 21.4 *CFX_SETPDO*

Attribute	Description
OfferName	The variable that contains the PDO. This is required.
OfferValue	A variable that contains a PDO. If this does not match the value in OfferName, a copy of the PDO will be made. This is required.
Attribute	Any of the available attributes for a PDO. This is required.
Variable	The value the attribute will be set to.
Validate	Determines whether the offer will be validated. Optional, defaults to yes.

Using *CFX_READPDO* PDOs contained in files are read using CFX_READPDO. The files are created using CFX_WRITEPDO and are derived from existing PDOs. The attributes for this tag are listed in Table 21.5.

Table 21.5   CFX_READPDO

Attribute	Description
OfferName	The name of the variable that contains the PDO. This is required.
File	The filename to read the PDO from. This is required.
Validate	Determines whether the offer will be validated. Optional, defaults to yes.

Using CFX_WRITEPDO   CFX_WRITEPDO saves an existing PDO to a file. The file can then be read using CFX_READPDO. The attributes for this tag are listed in Table 21.6.

Table 21.6   CFX_WRITEPDO

Attribute	Description
OfferValue	The variable that contains the PDO. This is required.
File	The name of the file that the PDO will be saved to. This is required.

Using CFX_PDO2DO   CFX_PDO2DO converts an existing PDO into a digital offer URL. The attributes for this tag are listed in Table 21.7.

Table 21.7   CFX_PDO2DO

Attribute	Description
OfferValue	The variable that contains the PDO. This is required.
URLVariable	The variable in which the DO will be stored. This is required.
ContentURL	The URL of the content server. This is required.
TransactionURL	The URL of the transaction server. This is required.
FulfillmentURL	The URL of the fulfillment server. This is required.
SubscriptionURL	The URL of the subscription server. This is required.
StoreID	The store identification. This is required.
KeyFile	The filename for the store encryption file.
Encoding	Can be none, z, or radix. Defaults to z.

Part
IV

Ch
21

CHAPTER 22

Transaction Processing

by Steven D. Drucker

In this chapter

Programming for Multiuser Access

As you have discovered, implementing concurrent read-only access to data is relatively easy using Cold Fusion. Unfortunately, designing input forms and save routines for a scenario where more than one person may edit the same record at the same time is not nearly as intuitive.

Concurrency Control

You should consider if database inserts, updates, and deletes will be executed concurrently when designing a data-entry interface. It may be necessary for you to control the sequence of these transactions in order to maintain the consistency of the database. The example most often cited when describing concurrency issues relates to automatic teller bank transactions.

Imagine a scenario where you and a partner maintain joint savings and checking accounts. The savings account contains a starting balance of $1,000 and the checking account maintains $500 in funds for a combined total of $1,500. In order to make your monthly payment on the new Pentium Pro you secretly purchased, a transfer of $500 is required from your savings account into your checking account. Meanwhile, your more responsible partner, seeking to allocate funds for retirement savings, wishes to transfer $250 from checking into savings. These two transactions are represented in Table 22.1 and Figure 22.1.

Table 22.1 Representing Bank Transfer of Funds	
Pentium Pro Payment	**Retirement Allocation**
query(savings)	query(savings)
savings=savings–500	savings=savings+250
update(savings)	update(savings)
query(checking)	query(checking)
checking=checking+500	checking=checking–250
update(checking)	update(checking)

In an amazing coincidence, you both submit these transactions from different ATMs to the central banking computer at exactly the same instant. If the two transactions are executed serially, as depicted in Figure 22.1, the final result would leave the checking account with a balance of $750 and the savings account with a balance of $750. This is the result you would expect to occur.

Suppose, however, that components of the two transactions overlapped during processing, following the schedule depicted in Figure 22.2. The left column depicts the transfer of funds for the Pentium while the right steps through the retirement transfer. The figures on the right represent the values stored in the accounting database after program execution at each time index. In this scenario, the combined transfer of funds has actually netted you an extra $500. Transactions that may interfere with one another are called *interleaved* transactions. Those that produce the same effect, regardless of whether they are run concurrently or serially, are termed *serializable*.

FIG. 22.1

Treating each transaction as a whole unit yields the same results regardless of ordering.

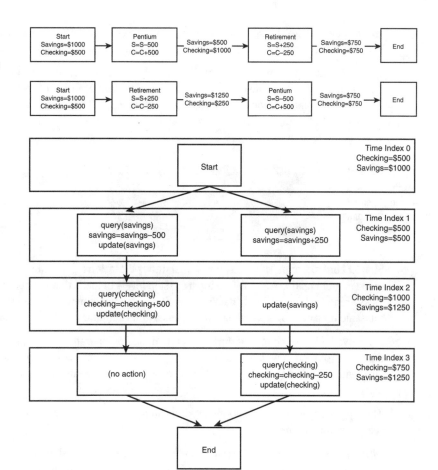

FIG. 22.2

When transactions overlap, data integrity can be compromised.

Locking

One method traditionally used in combating the data consistency problems is to limit access to the affected data object to a single transaction at a time. This was shown in the prior example. It is achieved with a process called *locking*. When a transaction has been granted a lock on an object, that object may only be modified by components of that single transaction. Requests from other transactions will be deferred until the transaction holding the lock releases it.

Locking Scope   Most relational database systems contain locking protocols that dynamically execute whenever a transaction is performed. Row-level locking ensures data consistency within a table record should two (or more) change requests occur simultaneously, referencing elements in the same table row. In desktop application development, this is useful in scenarios where information is being entered directly into a table with changes being constantly refreshed to other users' screens. This is generally the case when using the xBase browse window or the Access dynaset-type record set. In scenarios where copies of data are stored in memory variables for an indeterminate amount of time and the data may be edited (such as a web-based application that uses forms), this Relational Database Management System (RDBMS) locking is insufficient. Timestamping, discussed later in this chapter, should be employed in these cases.

Some applications, such as Microsoft Excel, employ file- or table-level locking. A change request initiates a lock on the entire file or table and prevents editing of any data within the object by other users until the lock is released (see Figure 22.3). The Cold Fusion tag <CFTRANSACTION> implements locking based on the default scheme of the particular ODBC driver being employed.

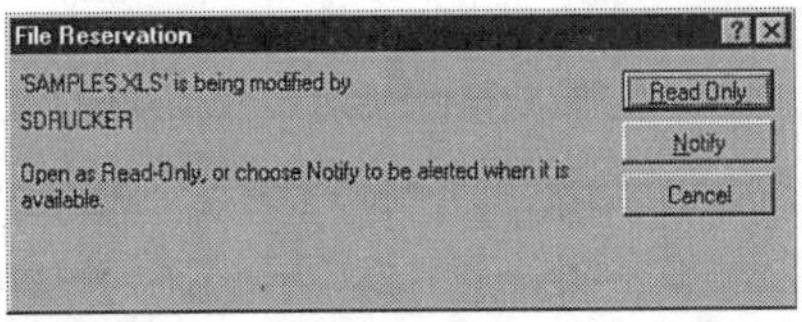

FIG. 22.3
Microsoft Excel uses file-locking to ensure the consistency of a spreadsheet.

Shared Locks, Exclusive Locks, and Consistency Violations

In addition to the physical scope of locking, there are different permission levels of locks that may be granted. Shared locks are issued for read-only data such as SQL select statements. Shared locks may be held on the same data item by several different transactions simultaneously.

Exclusive locks are employed during data modification operations such as insert, update, and delete. A transaction with an exclusive lock has both read and write access to the data item. Only one transaction may have an exclusive lock on a data element at any time. Furthermore, an element that is exclusively locked cannot have a concurrent shared lock.

The types of consistency violations locking can avoid are termed dirty reads, nonrepeatable reads, and phantoms.

Dirty Reads

The term *dirty read* applies to values read from a database that are rendered inconsistent due to a change to the data from a concurrently executing transaction. In the context of the funds transferal example presented earlier in the chapter, consider a scenario where a transaction obtains the value from the data table and subtracts $500. Transaction B, executing concurrently, reads the partially committed value for the savings account. Subsequently, transaction A is rolled back, leaving an inconsistent account balance for transaction B to work with (see Figure 22.4).

Nonrepeatable Reads

Nonrepeatable reads occur when a transaction reads a database row, that row is updated or deleted by a concurrently executing transaction, and the first transaction then reads the row again, retrieving a different value.

Consider the database relation depicted in Figure 22.5. Table 1 has a one-to-many relationship with Table 2. A nonrepeatable read violation could occur under the following circumstances: Transaction A reads the key field value "50" from Table 1 and proceeds to write records to Table 2 based on this value. Meanwhile, transaction B updates the key field value in Table 1 to "100". Transaction A continues, using "100" to write subsequent records to Table 2, unaware that all the records it previously wrote using the value "50" need to be updated for the database to remain consistent.

FIG. 22.4
Dirty reads.

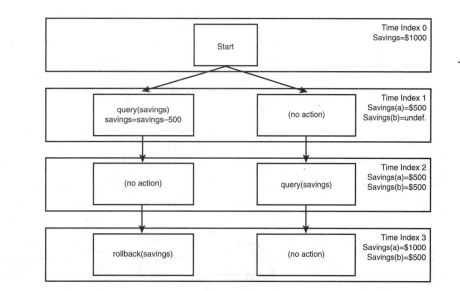

Part
IV

Ch
22

Phantoms   *Phantoms* are the converse of nonrepeatable reads. Transaction A executes a query that retrieves a result set. Transaction B inserts a row that would have been a member of the transaction A result set had it been inserted into the table prior to transaction A. Transaction A continues processing based on an out-of-date result set.

FIG. 22.5
A database containing one-to-many relations based on a key field value may be susceptible to a nonrepeatable read integrity violation.

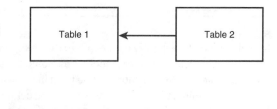

Deadlocks   *Deadlocks* occur when two transactions have locks on separate objects, and each transaction requires a lock on the other's locked object to complete. Some DBMS systems, such as Microsoft SQL Server, will automatically intervene, aborting one of the transactions to break the deadlock. In Figure 22.6, the ordering of instructions within the two transactions causes them to compete for locks on resources, resulting in deadlock. At time index 2, transaction A requests a lock held by transaction B. At time index 3, transaction B requires a lock held by transaction A. You can help avoid this situation by keeping transactions as short as possible, optimizing your database to reduce transaction times, and accessing data tables in the same order in all transactions.

Transactions, Commitments, and Rollbacks

Continuing with the ATM banking example, imagine a scenario where you access a cash machine and request a disbursement of the extra $500 the bank erroneously credited to your account as a result of the previously depicted funds transferal debacle. The central banking computer promptly subtracts $500 from your checking account balance and sends a request to the ATM for it to distribute the funds. Just as your ill-gotten gain is about to flow from the machine, a power outage occurs and you never take possession of the cash. When the lights come back on, you check your account and, to your dismay, your checking account balance has decreased $500 without a cash disbursement.

FIG. 22.6

Deadlocks occur when two transactions require the locking of resources that the other one already has locked.

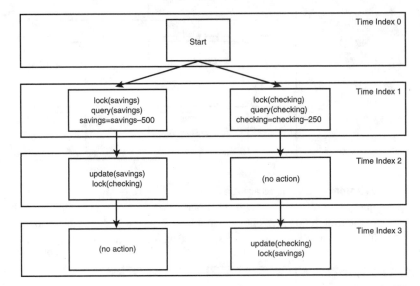

Of course, events like those described here hardly ever occur in the "real world." The individual actions of crediting the account and disbursement of funds would be grouped together as a transaction. Consider that it's normal for a database to be in an inconsistent state while processing individual instructions within a transaction. Individual instructions that have executed within a transaction are said to have been partially committed. They are upgraded to committed status once the transaction has completed successfully. Since the disbursement process aborted, the entire account transaction would be rolled back to the state it was in prior to your eventful trip to the ATM.

Transaction processing rollbacks protect against three types of errors that may lead to database corruption.

- System crash—Despite claims by Microsoft that Windows NT is a robust operating system, hostile applications can sometimes bring it to its knees. Of course, no operating system can protect against a user pressing a reset button, spilling coffee on a keyboard, or other spontaneous hardware failure.

- Program/Logical errors—The transaction cannot finish because bad input was entered in form fields; for example, required fields are missing or a data insert was contingent upon a preexisting foreign key or other dependency.

■ System errors—A data table is locked for exclusive use. For example, Cold Fusion reaches its set limit on the number of simultaneous requests it can handle or your web server similarly gets bogged down with requests resulting in timeouts.

Implementing Transaction Processing Using Cold Fusion

Cold Fusion supports the aggregation of queries into a single transaction through the implementation of the <CFTRANSACTION> tag. Cold Fusion statements contained within a <CFTRANSACTION> block are treated as a single logical unit. Changes to data requested by these queries are not committed to the database until all actions within the transaction block have executed successfully. If an error occurs in any instruction within a <CFTRANSACTION>, all changes made by previous queries within the transaction block are rolled back.

Listing 22.1 illustrates the use of CFTRANSACTION to guarantee that the transfer of $500 from a savings account to a checking account, described in Table 22.1, does not leave the database in an inconsistent state should an error occur in either query.

Listing 22.1   Using *<CFTRANSACTION>* to Group Queries into Logical Units

```
<CFTRANSACTION>

<CFQUERY NAME="decrementSavings" DATASOURCE="Bank">
                    ➥UPDATE Accounts
SET Balance = Balance - #dollaramount#
WHERE AcctID = #Acctid# and accttype="Savings"
</CFQUERY>

<CFQUERY NAME="incrementChecking" DATASOURCE="Bank">
                    ➥UPDATE Accounts
SET Balance = Balance + #dollaramount#
WHERE AcctID = #Acctid# and accttype="Checking"
</CFQUERY>

</CFTRANSACTION>
```

If the savings and checking accounts originally had balances of $1,000 and $500, respectively, the successful execution of the transaction would result in a savings account balance of $0 and a checking account balance of $1,500. If either query fails at any point during execution, the account balances would be reset to their prior values.

Not every ODBC driver supports transactions. When you attempt to start a transaction, Cold Fusion queries the driver for its transaction capabilities and returns an error if the driver indicates that it is unable to implement the request. A list of ODBC drivers and their transaction support capabilities is detailed in Table 22.2.

N O T E <CFTRANSACTION> automatically attempts to place a lock on the first table referenced within the transaction. Subsequent references to other tables within the same transaction block result in an error being generated. ■

Table 22.2 ODBC Drivers Supporting Transaction Processing

Driver	Support?	Isolation Levels
MS SQL Server	Yes	READ_COMMITTED, READ_UNCOMMITTED, SERIALIZABLE
MS Access	Yes	READ_COMMITTED, SERIALIZABLE
Oracle 7	Yes	REPEATABLE_READ, VERSIONING
MS FoxPro 2.x	No	
MS FoxPro 3.x	Yes	READ_COMMITTED, SERIALIZABLE
Borland Paradox	No	
MS Excel	No	

Using Cold Fusion to Lock Data

In addition to handling commits and rollbacks, <CFTRANSACTION> ensures serializability among concurrent transactions by locking database tables.

The optional ISOLATION attribute provides additional control over how the database engine performs locking during the transaction. The valid values for the ISOLATION attribute are READ_UNCOMMITTED, READ_COMMITTED, REPEATABLE_READ, SERIALIZABLE, and VERSIONING (see Table 22.3).

Table 22.3 *<CFTRANSACTION>* Isolation Levels

Isolation Level	Description
READ_COMMITTED	Dirty reads are not permitted, and shared locks will be used when reading data; however, these locks may be released prior to the end of the transaction, possibly resulting in phantoms and nonrepeatable reads. (This is the default level for MS SQL Server.)
READ_UNCOMMITTED	Anything goes. Shared and exclusive locks are not used by the transaction, and locks on data by other concurrently executing transactions are ignored. This may lead to dirty reads, nonrepeatable reads, and phantom values.

Isolation Level	Description
REPEATABLE_READ	Varies depending on platform. On SQL Server, dirty reads, phantom values, and nonrepeatable reads are all disallowed. May permit dirty reads and nonrepeatable reads on other platforms.
SERIALIZABLE	Does not permit any of the serializability violations discussed. Locking is fully implemented, which may result in lower overall throughput because concurrency may be reduced. On SQL Server, REPEATABLE_READ and SERIALIZABLE are interchangeable.
VERSIONING	Transactions are serializable, but this level offers higher concurrency than SERIALIZABLE because a non-locking method, such as time-stamping, is employed.

CAUTION

Not all ODBC drivers support transactions, nor do they necessarily support all values for the <CFTRANSACTION> ISOLATION attribute. Check Table 22.2 for compatibility before implementing these functions.

Using <CFTRANSACTION> to Retrieve a Newly Inserted Identity Field Value

The easiest method for generating a primary key for a data table is to use an Autonumber field. Whenever a new record is inserted into a table, the Autonumber field is assigned a unique value equal to the maximum value ever contained within that column plus one. Because this primary key often doubles as a foreign key value for other related tables, it is often important to capture this value. One of the most useful applications for <CFTRANSACTION> is in determining the value of the Autonumber field of the record last inserted into a table. The code fragment in Listing 22.2, pulled from Chapter 21, "Advanced Forms Techniques," demonstrates this technique.

Listing 22.2 Retrieving the Value of an *Autonumber/Identity* Field

```
<CFTRANSACTION>
<CFQUERY NAME="createneworder" DATASOURCE="a2zdata" >
INSERT INTO orders (customerid,shipto,shipcompany,shipaddress1,
shipaddress2,shipcity,shipstate,_shipzip)
values (#customerid#,'#getcustomer.firstname#
#getcustomer.lastname#','#getcustomer.company#','#getcustomer.address1#',
_'#getcustomer.address2#','#getcustomer.city#','#getcustomer.state#',
_'#getcustomer.zip#')
</CFQUERY>
<CFQUERY NAME="getid" DATASOURCE="a2zdata">
SELECT max(orderid) as neworderid FROM orders
</CFQUERY>
<CFSET #orderid# = #getid.neworderid#>
</CFTRANSACTION>
```

When executed, `<CFTRANSACTION>` performs a table lock on the Orders table. Inserts into the Orders table from other concurrently executing queries are temporarily blocked. The query `createneworder` inserts a new record into the Orders table and an autonumber value is generated for the field `orderid`. By definition, `orderid` for this new record must contain the largest value in the column, so query `getid` is employed to retrieve its value. Since concurrent table inserts are barred during the execution of these queries, serializability is ensured.

N O T E Whereas this method for retrieving autonumber values works with any ODBC driver supporting transactions, a much simpler method exists under Microsoft SQL Server. If you create an `INSERT` trigger for the target data table containing the code select * from inserted, and insert data into the table using `<CFQUERY>` versus `<CFINSERT>`, the identity value will be automatically returned as part of the query result set. ■

Configuring Your Database to Ensure Data Integrity

Despite the existence of several facilities to convert interleaved transactions to serializable transactions, you can guarantee that no accidental data corruptions occur by building referential integrity rules into your database. If an invalid operation is attempted, the DBMS will automatically detect the problem and roll back the transaction.

Building Referential Integrity into Your Database

Referential integrity is a set of rules that ensures that the relationships between records in related tables are valid. In order to discuss referential integrity, you should be familiar with the terms defined in Table 22.4.

Table 22.4 Referential Integrity Terms

Term	Definition
Primary (parent) table	Frequently the "one" in a one-to-many relation. In Figure 22.7, the Orders table is the primary table in its relationship with OrderItems.
Related (child) table	The "many" in a one-to-many relationship. In Figure 22.7, the OrderItems table is related to the Orders table.
Primary key	Usually the field upon which the relationship is based, set in the primary table.
Foreign key	The value in the secondary table upon which the relationship is based. The foreign key value in a secondary table must match a primary key value in the primary table.

With referential integrity being enforced, any attempt to issue inserts, updates, or deletes that would violate the relationships is rejected by the DBMS and generates an ODBC error in Cold Fusion. In order for referential integrity to be defined, the following conditions must be met:

- The related fields must be of the same data type.
- Both tables must be contained in the same database.
- The field in the primary table must be a unique value (usually Autonumber or Identity fields are used in this capacity).

When integrity constraints are being observed, you may not perform the following operations:

- You cannot delete records in a primary table if matching records exist in a related table. In the A2Z database, you could not delete an Orders record if corresponding entries exist in the OrderItems table.
- Conversely, you cannot insert records into the related table if a corresponding entry does not exist in the primary table. In the A2Z database, you may not create records in the OrderItems table if no corresponding entry exists in the Orders table. You may, however, insert records into the related table if the foreign key contains a NULL value. Updating the NULL value, however, may generate an error if the value is not a valid foreign key.
- You cannot change the primary key value of the primary table if matching records exist in the secondary table. For instance, changing the orderid field in the Orders table without referential integrity enforced could leave orphaned records in the OrderItems table.

The benefits of defining referential integrity extend beyond maintaining database integrity. For instance, some database systems permit cascade updates and deletes. In a one-to-many relation, for instance, deleting a record in the primary table causes all related records in the secondary table to be deleted as well. Similarly, modifying a primary key value in a table with cascade updates enforced automatically updates all related records in the secondary table. Also, several tools exist that will represent the relationships between tables graphically (see Figure 22.7), helping you to better understand the dynamics of your database.

FIG. 22.7
Formalizing the relationships between tables can help you maintain data integrity.

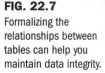

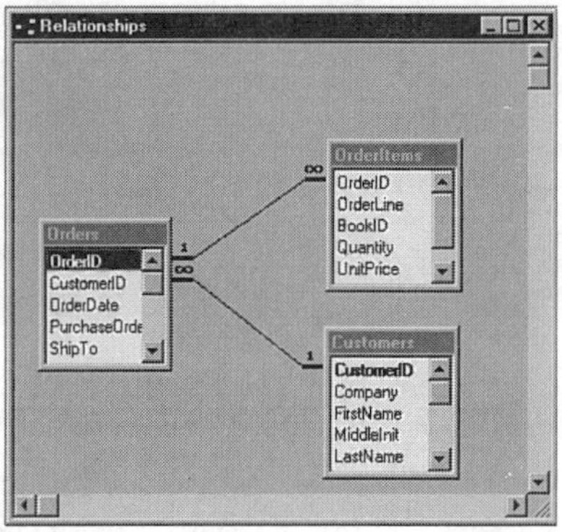

The MS Access Relationships Facility   Access will graphically represent the relationships between tables if you choose Tools, Relationships.

Creating a formalized relationship between tables is simple. Just click and drag the primary key field from the primary table and drop it into the related table. A simple dialog box pops up to guide you through subsequent options (see Figure 22.8).

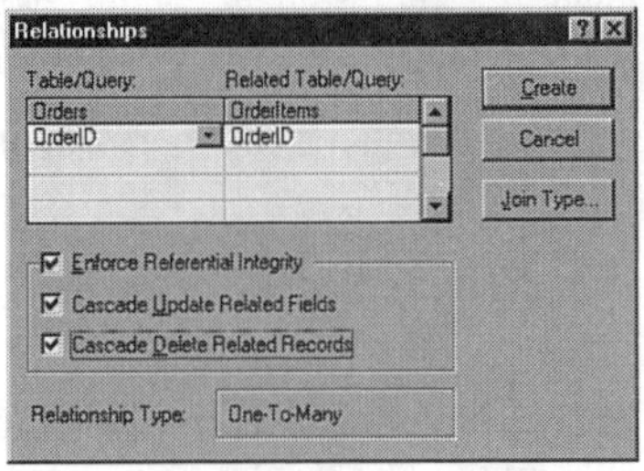

FIG. 22.8
Microsoft Access provides a handy tool for creating relationships between tables.

MS SQL Server   Creating relationships in Microsoft SQL Server is not nearly as intuitive as in Access. In fact, you may consider designing the database in Access first and then using the Access Upsizing Wizard to transfer the definition to SQL Server; you can also use a third-party tool.

The establishment of foreign keys can be achieved by right-clicking the table name, clicking the advanced features button within the Manage Tables dialog box, and selecting the Foreign Key tab as depicted in Figure 22.9. If you enjoy pain, frustration, and tedium, you can opt to write **transact-sql** to define the relationships between tables, as depicted in the code fragment from Listing 22.3.

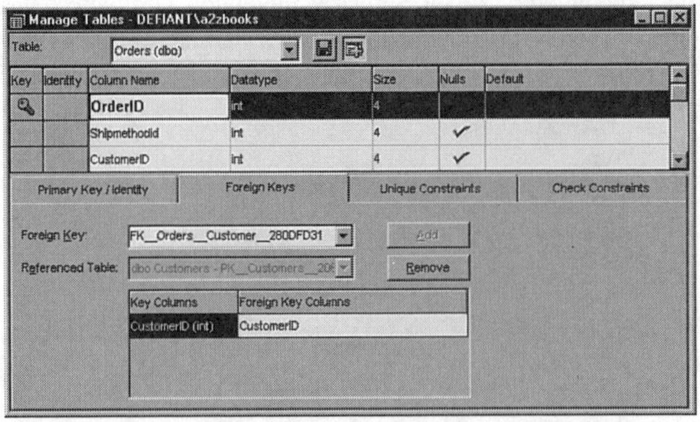

FIG. 22.9
MS SQL Server can serve as a powerful back-end, but its interface for creating relations between tables is not very intuitive.

Listing 22.3   A2Z.SQL—The SQL Server's Generate Scripts Option Translates a Database Schema into transact-sql

```
/****** Object:  Table dbo.Orders   Script Date: 9/27/96 1:18:40 PM ******/
CREATE TABLE dbo.Orders (
OrderID int NOT NULL ,
Shipmethodid int NULL ,
```

```
CustomerID int NULL ,
OrderDate datetime NULL ,
PurchaseOrder char (30) NULL ,
ShipTo char (50) NULL ,
ShipCompany char (40) NULL ,
ShipAddress1 char (50) NULL ,
ShipAddress2 char (50) NULL ,
ShipCity char (40) NULL ,
ShipState char (5) NULL ,
ShipZip char (10) NULL ,
ShippingCharge money NULL ,
Taxable bit NOT NULL ,
OrderOpen smallint NULL ,
CONSTRAINT PK_Orders_39037F09 PRIMARY KEY  NONCLUSTERED
(
OrderID
),
CONSTRAINT FK_Orders_Customer_57880629 FOREIGN KEY
(
CustomerID
) REFERENCES dbo.Customers (
CustomerID
),
CONSTRAINT FK_Orders_Shipmeth_5693E1F0 FOREIGN KEY
(
Shipmethodid
) REFERENCES dbo.ShippingMethod (
Shipmethodid
)
)
GO
```

Third-Party Tools   Several third-party tools, such as Logic Work's ERwin/ERX depicted in Figure 22.10, allow you to graphically define the relationships between tables. ERwin's palette of relationship connectors, as well as its ability to translate a database schema into the specific format of practically every DBMS available (see Figure 22.11), make it a powerful ally of the database application developer. Rendering the unfriendly SQL Server interface moot is enough to justify the purchase price.

Error Recovery Using Transaction Logs

Most client/server systems maintain transaction logs so they can easily restore the database to a prior state. Transaction logs are databases that store the results from each transaction, allowing for point-in-time recovery. Logs should be sized between 10–50% of a database's allocated data space, depending on the frequency of transactions and the period of time you want to elapse before dumping the log. Transaction logs should also be physically located on a different drive from your SQL database so that concurrent writes of data and log information may occur.

> **CAUTION**
>
> Transaction logs, when filled to capacity, result in further transactions being rejected by the SQL Server. Make sure you dump your transaction log periodically to avoid this.

FIG. 22.10

Third-party tools such as Logic Work's ERwin/ERX allow you to graphically define the relationships between tables.

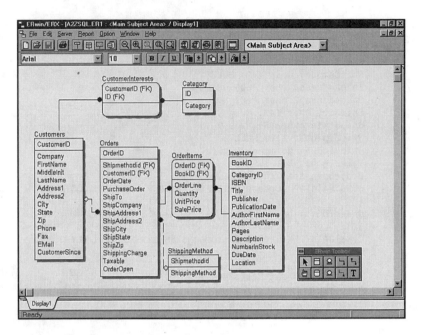

FIG. 22.11

ERwin converts a graphical specification into different database formats with ease.

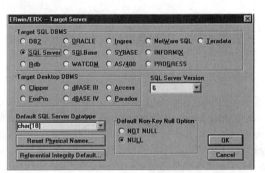

Multiuser Implementation Strategies

Due to the nature of the HTML interface, the best method for insuring serializability between transactions and data consistency is to employ timestamps. Figure 22.12 shows how frames can be used to simulate the concurrent editing of an employee record.

Without a system in place to insure serializability between the concurrent editing, the changes made to the record in the top frame would be overwritten by the data in the middle frame (assuming the user in the top frame submitted changes first), resulting in data loss.

Using a Timestamp to Arbitrate Updates

One method for insuring serializability using Cold Fusion involves using a timestamp. This additional field, implemented in Listing 22.4, may contain either a datetime value representing the last instance the record was saved or an integer counter whose value is incremented every time the record is updated. Figure 22.13 illustrates how you can use frames to simulate the concurrent editing of an employee's record by two users. Information is read into the forms at nearly the same instant, and both forms initially contain all the same values.

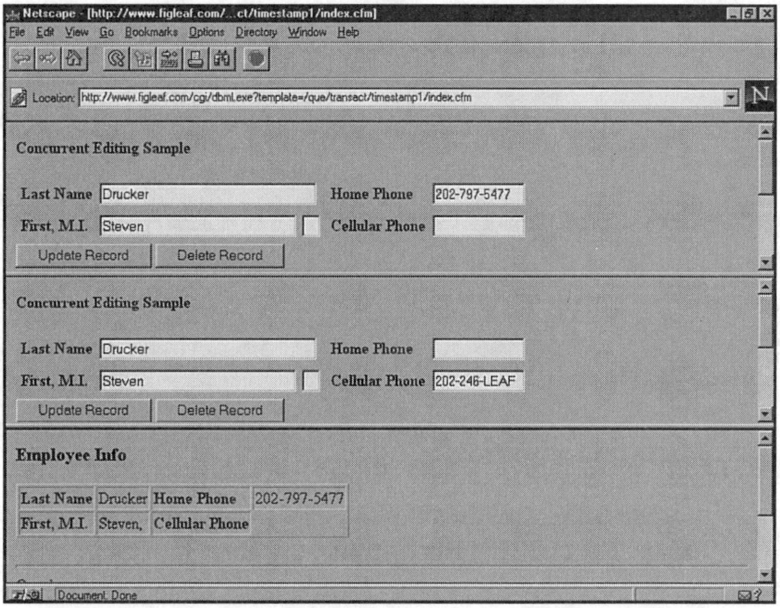

FIG. 22.12

Using frames, you can simulate the concurrent editing of an employee record.

Listing 22.4   EDITEMPLOYEE.CFM—The Timestamp Methodology Requires the Addition of a Special *Timestamp* Field

```
<CFQUERY NAME="getemployee" DATASOURCE="a2zdata">
SELECT * FROM employees where employeeid=2
</CFQUERY>
<HTML>
<BODY BGCOLOR=#C0C0C0>
<H4>Concurrent Editing Sample
</H4>
<FORM ACTION="saveemployee.cfm" METHOD="POST">
<CFINCLUDE TEMPLATE="employeefields.cfm">
<CFOUTPUT>
<INPUT TYPE="HIDDEN" NAME="timestamp" VALUE="#getemployee.timestamp#">
</CFOUTPUT>
</FORM>
</BODY>
</HTML>
```

Once a timestamp field has been implemented, verifying that you are working with the most up-to-date data set involves comparing the form's timestamp value with the one stored in the data table. If the values are not identical, you can ask the user what action should be performed. Listing 22.5 demonstrates one implementation of this methodology.

continues

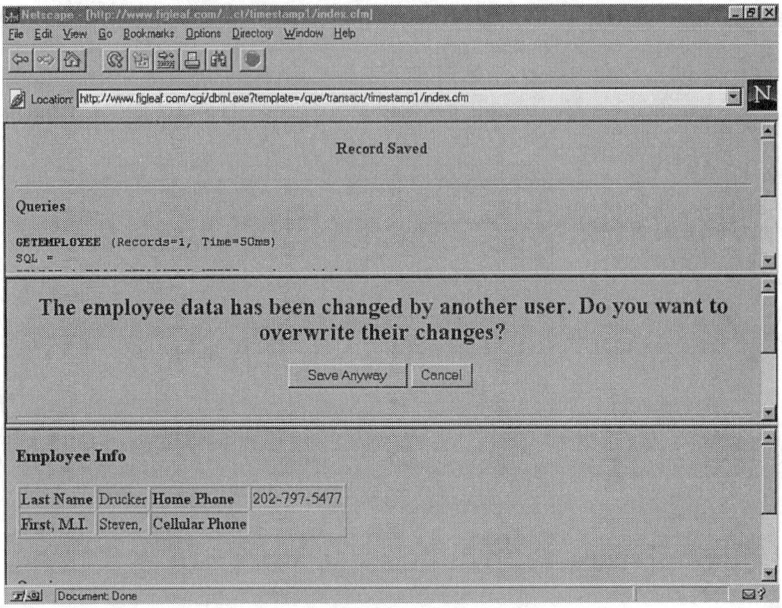

FIG. 22.13

Using a timestamp value, you can inform the user that an update has taken place without his knowledge.

Listing 22.5 SAVEEMPLOYEE.CFM—Using Cold Fusion and a *Timestamp* Field, You Can Arbitrate Between Concurrent Editing

```
<!-------------------------------------------

Saveemployee.cfm - multiuser code for saving/updating employee info
Parameters: override - flag determining whether changes by another
user shall be overwritten
action    - update or delete record button value
--------------------------------------------->

<CFPARAM NAME="override" DEFAULT="">
<CFPARAM NAME="ACTION" DEFAULT="Update">

<CFIF #ACTION# contains "Update">
<CFQUERY NAME="getemployee" DATASOURCE="a2zdata">
SELECT * FROM EMPLOYEES WHERE employeeid=#form.employeeid#
</CFQUERY>

<CFIF #getemployee.recordcount# is 1> <!---record still exists --->
<CFIF (#getemployee.timestamp# is #form.timestamp#) or (#override#
contains "Save")>
<CFTRANSACTION> <!---Update record, increment timestamp --->
<CFUPDATE DATASOURCE="a2zdata" TABLENAME="employees"
FORMFIELDS="lastname,firstname,timestamp,phonecellular,phonehome">
<CFQUERY NAME="settimestamp" DATASOURCE="a2zdata">
UPDATE Employees
SET Employees.[timestamp] = "timestamp"+1
WHERE (("employeeid"=#form.employeeid#))
</CFQUERY>
</CFTRANSACTION>
<CFSET #result# = 1>
```

```
<CFELSE>
<CFSET #result# = 0>
</CFIF>
<CFELSE>
<CFIF #override# contains "Save"> <!---record had been deleted, rein
                    ➥_state record --->
<CFINSERT DATASOURCE="a2zdata" TABLENAME="employees"
FORMFIELDS="employeeid,lastname,firstname,
➥ timestamp,phonecellular,phonehome">
<CFSET #result# = 1>
<CFELSE>
<CFSET #result# = 0>
</CFIF>
</CFIF>
<CFELSE>
<CFQUERY NAME="deleterec" DATASOURCE="a2zdata">
DELETE FROM employees where employeeid=#employeeid#
</CFQUERY>
<CFSET #result# = 3>
</CFIF>


<HTML>
<BODY BGCOLOR=#C0C0C0 OnLoad="top.result.location.href='displayemp.cfm'">
<CFIF #override# is not "Cancel">
<CFIF #result# is 1>
<CENTER><STRONG>Record Saved</STRONG></CENTER>
</CFIF>
<CFIF #result# is 3>
<CENTER><STRONG>Record Deleted</STRONG></CENTER>
</CFIF>
<CFIF #result# is 0> <!---timestamps do not match or record was deleted--->
<FORM ACTION="saveemployee.cfm" METHOD="POST">
<CFOUTPUT>
<INPUT TYPE="hidden" NAME="employeeid"    VALUE=#form.employeeid#>
<INPUT TYPE="hidden" NAME="lastname"      VALUE="#form.lastname#">
<INPUT TYPE="hidden" NAME="phonehome"     VALUE="#form.phonehome#">
<INPUT TYPE="hidden" NAME="firstname"     VALUE="#form.firstname#">
<INPUT TYPE="hidden" NAME="middleinit"    VALUE="#form.middleinit#">
<INPUT TYPE="hidden" NAME="phonecellular" VALUE="#form.phonecellular#">
<INPUT TYPE="hidden" NAME="timestamp" VALUE=#form.timestamp#>
</CFOUTPUT>
<CENTER>
<CFIF #getemployee.recordcount# is 1>
<H2>The employee data has been changed by another user.  Do you want _to
overwrite their changes?</H2>
<CFELSE>
<H2>The employee record has been deleted by another user.  Do you _want to
recreate the record?</H2>
</CFIF>
<INPUT TYPE="submit" NAME="override" value="Save Anyway">
<INPUT TYPE="submit" NAME="override" value="Cancel">
</CENTER>
</FORM>
</CFIF>
<CFELSE>
<CENTER><H3>Save Aborted</H3></CENTER>
</CFIF>
</HTML>
```

Using a Timestamp, Data Dictionary, and Cold Fusion to Reconcile Data Conflicts

The prior example used timestamps to notify the user of a potential conflict among parallel transactions. The user was presented with two choices: blindly overwrite data in a table or roll back his own transaction, which also results in data loss. Although this solution works for resolving conflicts, the user is left with an unenviable choice. Using Cold Fusion, you can develop an interface to enable the user to resolve data conflicts interactively.

Integral to this solution is the use of a data dictionary. Data dictionaries contain information about the database, optionally including a description of every field. The specification for the table Data Dictionary is presented in Table 22.5.

Table 22.5 A Data Dictionary Contains Information About All the Fields in the Database

Field	Description
fieldname	The name of the field in the data table.
tablename	The name of the table in which the field exists.
description	A text description of the field's relevance.

The generalized method presented in Listing 22.6 compares values entered in form fields with values residing in the data table if timestamp values are not equal. The data dictionary is then cross referenced in order to build an interface that allows the user to resolve data consistency through the selection of radio buttons (see Figure 22.14).

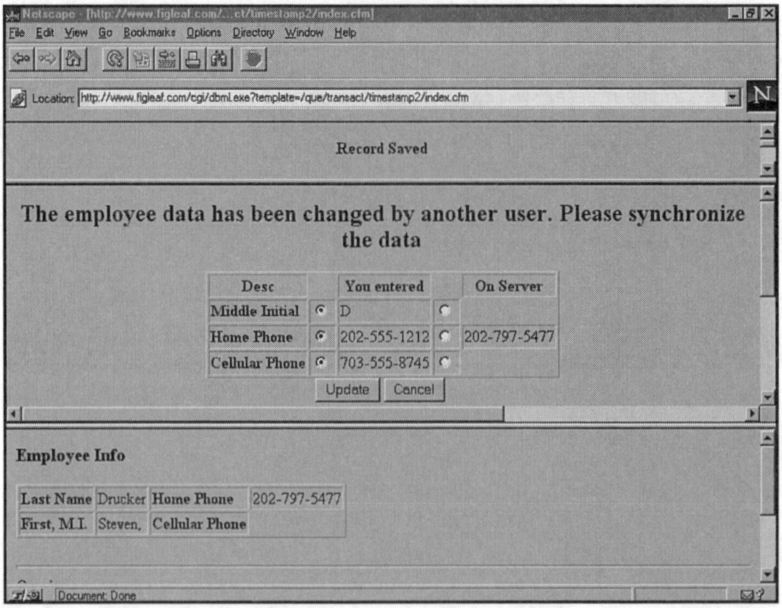

FIG. 22.14

Interactively reconciling changes to a data table.

Listing 22.6 SAVEEMPLOYEE.CFM—Using the New Cold Fusion 2.0 Features, You Can Create a Generalized Method for Resolving Data Conflicts

```
<!-----------------------------------------------
***This version allows the user to reconcile differences in the data***
Saveemployee.cfm - multiuser code for saving/updating employee info
Parameters: override - flag determining whether changes by another
user shall be overwritten
action   - update or delete record button value
------------------------------------------------->

<CFPARAM NAME="override" DEFAULT="">
<CFPARAM NAME="ACTION" DEFAULT="Update">

<CFIF #ACTION# contains "Update">

<!---see what's already in data table --->
<CFQUERY NAME="getemployee" DATASOURCE="a2zdata">
SELECT * FROM EMPLOYEES WHERE employeeid=#form.employeeid#
</CFQUERY>

<CFIF #getemployee.recordcount# is 1> <!---record still exists --->
<CFIF (#getemployee.timestamp# is #form.timestamp#) or
➥(#override#_contains "Save")>
<CFTRANSACTION> <!---Update record, increment timestamp --->
<CFUPDATE DATASOURCE="a2zdata" TABLENAME="employees"
FORMFIELDS="lastname,firstname,middleinit,
➥timestamp,phonecellular,phonehome">
<CFQUERY NAME="settimestamp" DATASOURCE="a2zdata">
UPDATE Employees
SET Employees.[timestamp] = "timestamp"+1
WHERE (("employeeid"=#form.employeeid#))
</CFQUERY>
</CFTRANSACTION>
<CFSET #result# = 1>
<CFELSE>
<CFSET #result# = 0>
</CFIF>
<CFELSE>
<CFIF #override# contains "Save"> <!---record had
➥been deleted, rein _ state record --->
<CFINSERT DATASOURCE="a2zdata" TABLENAME="employees"
FORMFIELDS="employeeid,lastname,firstname,middleinit,
➥timestamp,phonecellular,phonehome"
<CFSET #result# = 1>
<CFELSE>
<CFSET #result# = 0>
</CFIF>
</CFIF>
<CFELSE>
<!---Delete Record --->
<CFQUERY NAME="deleterec" DATASOURCE="a2zdata">
DELETE FROM employees where employeeid=#employeeid#
</CFQUERY>
<CFSET #result# = 3>
</CFIF>


<!---Query the data dictionary for data field descriptions --->
<CFIF #result# is 0>
```

continues

Listing 22.6 Continued

```
<CFQUERY NAME="synchronize" DATASOURCE="a2zdata">
SELECT *
FROM DataDictionary
WHERE INSTR(1,'#form.fieldnames#',DataDictionary.fieldname) > 0
</CFQUERY>
</CFIF>


<HTML>
<!---use Javascript to show user what's currently in the data table --->
<BODY BGCOLOR=#C0C0C0 OnLoad="top.result.location.href='displayemp.cfm'">


<CFIF #override# is not "Cancel">
<CFIF #result# is 1>
<CENTER><STRONG>Record Saved</STRONG></CENTER>
</CFIF>
<CFIF #result# is 3>
<CENTER><STRONG>Record Deleted</STRONG></CENTER>
</CFIF>
<CFIF #result# is 0> <!---timestamps do not match or record was deleted --->
<CENTER>
<CFIF #getemployee.recordcount# is 1>
<H2>The employee data has been changed by another user. Please _synchronize the
➥data</H2>

<FORM ACTION="saveemployee.cfm" METHOD="POST">
<TABLE BORDER=1>
Desc</TH></TH>You entered</TH></TH>On Server</TH>
<CFOUTPUT QUERY="synchronize">
<CFSET #formdata# = "form.#synchronize.fieldname#">
<CFSET #fielddata# = "getemployee.#synchronize.fieldname#">
<CFIF #evaluate(formdata)# is not #evaluate(fielddata)#>
<TR>
<TD><STRONG>#synchronize.description#</STRONG></TD>
<TD><INPUT TYPE="radio" NAME="#fieldname#" VALUE="#evaluate(formdata)#"
 CHECKED>
<TD>#evaluate(formdata)#</TD>
<TD><INPUT TYPE="radio" NAME="#fieldname#" VALUE="#evaluate(fielddata)#">
<TD>#evaluate(fielddata)#</TD>
</TR>
<CFELSE>
<INPUT TYPE="hidden" NAME="#synchronize.fieldname#" VALUE="#evaluate
(fielddata)#">
</CFIF>
</CFOUTPUT>
</TABLE>
<CFOUTPUT>
<INPUT TYPE="hidden" NAME="timestamp" VALUE=#getemployee.timestamp#>
<INPUT TYPE="hidden" NAME="employeeid" VALUE=#getemployee.employeeid#>
</CFOUTPUT>
<INPUT TYPE="submit" NAME="override" value="Update">
<INPUT TYPE="submit" NAME="override" value="Cancel">
</FORM>
</CFIF>
</CENTER>
</CFIF>
<CFELSE>
<CENTER><H3>Save Aborted</H3></CENTER>
</CFIF>
</HTML>
```

Web Application Framework

by Ben Forta

Introducing the Web Application Framework

The Cold Fusion Web Application Framework is a collection of essential tools that can ease your development effort as well as help create a more reliable and robust application. Although these tools are not dependent on one another, they are designed to work together and compliment each other.

The Web Application Framework is made up of several functions.

- The application template, APPLICATION.CFM, is a special Cold Fusion application-level template that is processed every time any other template is requested.

- Persistent client variables, session variables, and application variables enable you to save variables associated with specific client's connections, even between sessions.

- Custom error handling is a mechanism by which you can override the standard Cold Fusion error messages, allowing you to create more polished and complete applications.

Using the Application Template

Every time Cold Fusion processes a template, it looks for a special template file called APPLICATION.CFM. If Cold Fusion finds this template, known as the *application template*, it processes it *before* the requested template is processed.

The application template can contain any Cold Fusion tags or functions. It can perform database queries, set variables, or perform any other processing required. You can even include a conditional call to <CFABORT> to halt processing of the requested template under specific conditions.

Listing 23.1 contains a sample application template. This template does just two things. First, it sets the application name and enables the use of client and session variables. Secondly, it sets constant values that may be used throughout the application. The variable ODBC_DataSource, for example, contains the name of a data source to be used throughout the application. This variable could be used in place of hard-coded, data-source names in <CFQUERY> tags.

Listing 23.1 Sample Application Template

```
<!--- Name application --->
<CFAPPLICATION NAME="A2Z_Internal" CLIENTMANAGEMENT="ON">

<!--- Set application constants --->
<CFSET ODBC_DataSource = "A2Z">
<CFSET BG_Color = "FFFFFF">
<CFSET Font_Face = "Arial">
```

▶ **See** Appendix A, "Cold Fusion Tag Reference," **p. 849**
▶ **See** "Using the *CFQUERY* Tag," **p. 202**

> **TIP**
> The application template is the perfect place for establishing application-wide settings—installing custom error messages, implementing application level security, setting application wide defaults, and setting variable defaults.

Locating the Application Template

Whenever a template is requested, Cold Fusion looks for an application template in the current directory—the directory that the requested template itself is in. If no application template is found, Cold Fusion looks in the requested template's parent directory, and then gradually up the directory tree, one directory at a time. As soon as the first file named APPLICATION.CFM is found, it is used as the application template file.

To understand how application templates are located, look at a sample directory tree. Figure 23.1 shows a web server directory tree. The root directory \A2Z\SCRIPTS contains a file named APPLICATION.CFM, so when requests are made for any of the templates in that directory, or in any directory beneath it, that file \A2Z\SCRIPTS\APPLICATION.CFM will be processed as well.

Part
IV

Ch
23

FIG. 23.1
An application template file in the document root directory is used as the default application template for all directories.

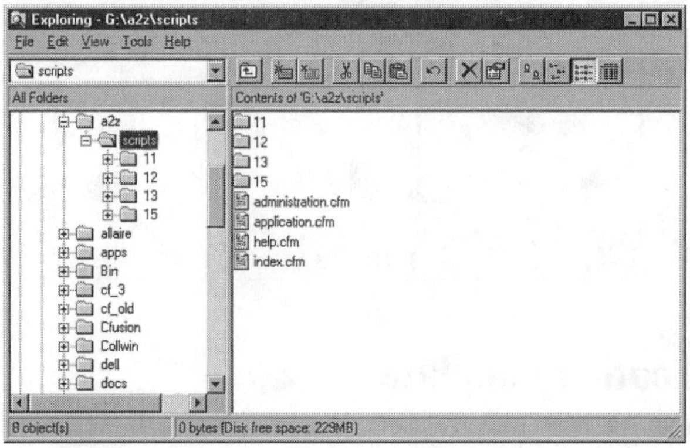

Directory \A2Z\SCRIPTS\13 does not contain an application template files, as seen in Figure 23.2. If a template in that directory is requested, Cold Fusion will try to locate an application template in the parent directory, \A2Z\SCRIPTS. As the parent directory contains an application template file, that file will be processed.

Directory \A2Z\SCRIPTS\15 contains its own application template file, as seen in Figure 23.3. Therefore, if a template in that directory was requested, that local application template file would be processed, and not the one in the parent directory.

> **NOTE** Only one application template file is ever processed. If your document root contains an application template file, and you create another application template file in a sub-directory, that second application template file will be processed *instead* of the first one when a template is requested from that sub-directory. If you need to process both templates, you'll need to include the first one from within the second. ■

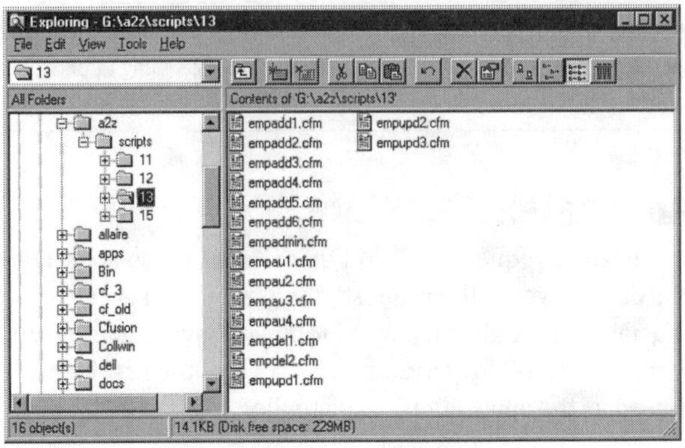

FIG. 23.2

If there is no application template in a directory, a template in a parent directory will be used instead.

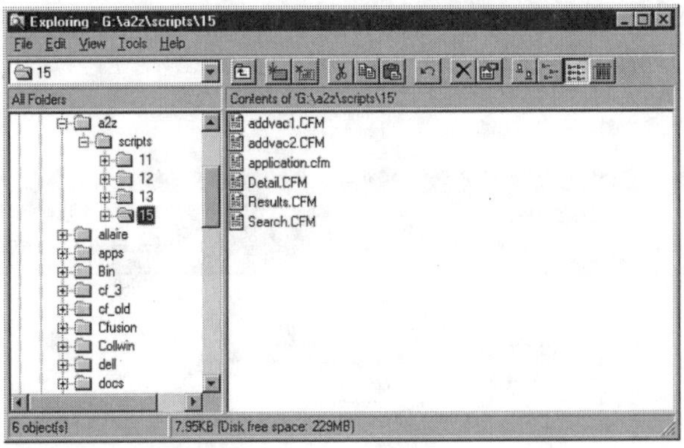

FIG. 23.3

To override the default application template in a specific directory (and any directories beneath it), just provide a different APPLICATION. CFM file in that directory.

Securing Application Templates

Cold Fusion application templates are an ideal place to implement application-level security. Because the application template is processed prior to any other templates, any security checking implemented in it will apply to all templates.

One form of security commonly implemented in intranets is domain-based security. As intranets are usually internal corporate networks, and the IP addresses of hosts on most networks are within one or more known domains, you may restrict access based on the IP address of the requesting host being within one of those known domains.

In the example shown in Listing 23.2, the application template checks to see if the first three sets of numbers in the remote address (the client IP address) are not the first part of a known domain address. If the test returns TRUE, meaning the client is not within the known domain, then an error message is displayed, and processing is halted with a <CFABORT> tag.

Listing 23.2   Sample Security Application Template

```
<!--- Check that host IP address is in allowed domain --->
<CFIF Left(CGI.REMOTE_ADDR, 11) IS NOT "208.193.16.">

  <!--- Unknown host, display "unauthorized" screen --->
  <HTML>
  <HEAD>
  <TITLE>Unauthorized host detected!</TITLE>
  </HEAD>
  <BODY>
  <H1>Unauthorized host detected!</H1>
  </BODY>
  </HTML>

  <!--- And abort processing --->
  <CFABORT>

</CFIF>
```

The application template can also be used to allow users to log in to applications. The template can perform the following steps.

1. Check to see if this client has logged in yet.
2. If user logged in already, allow processing of requested template.
3. If user is not logged in, but a login form has been submitted, then attempt the log in.
4. If not logged in yet, and login form fields are not present, then display the login form.

This kind of security mechanism usually involves creating ODBC tables that list the valid user accounts and passwords. Once you have verified that a user-supplied name and password matches a table row, you'll have to set a flag or variable indicating the successful login. You can do this using fields in your database table, or you can use *persistent client variables*, which are discussed next.

> **N O T E**   Cold Fusion only processes one application template file per request. If your template
> includes other templates that are in other directories (using the <CFINCLUDE> tag),
> application templates in those other directories will not be processed. ∎

Addressing the Web's Statelessness

As explained in Chapter 2, "Introduction to Cold Fusion," web clients do not maintain open connections with web servers while interacting with web-based applications. Rather, every client request stands on its own two feet, with no knowledge of any prior interaction. It is the web's lack of persistence between sessions that is referred to as its *statelessness*. This limitation means that variables or flags set during one processed request are not available during the next processed request.

To get around this problem, web application developers use a variety of techniques to maintain variables and values between sessions. Some of the popular techniques are:

- URL parameters can be used to pass values back and forth between the server and the client with each request. This technique is used by Internet search engines, for example, which embed a field indicating what results have been displayed so that Next and Previous buttons can work correctly.

- Form fields can be used to embed values in hidden fields, for example, in multi-part forms.

- HTTP cookies are variables that are stored on the client browser, and these are submitted along with future requests so that prior set values are known to the server.

▶ **See** Chapter 18, "Advanced Cold Fusion Templates," **p. 401**

All of these techniques have their own advantages and drawbacks. The biggest drawback with all of them is that they are time consuming to implement, and require lots of manual manipulation.

Cold Fusion provides application developers with several different types of variables that address this problem. While each variable type is different, and each has its own purpose, the common goal is providing a mechanism to store information that persists across requests or sessions. The basic variable types are the following:

- Client variables are variables associated with a particular client. They are stored on the server in the system registry. They allow you to maintain state as a user moves from page to page in an application.

- Server variables are associated with the current web server and are available until the Cold Fusion server is shut down. This server scope allows you to define variables that all your Cold Fusion application pages can reference.

- Session variables are tied to an individual client and persist for as long as that Client ID maintains a session. Session variables, like current client variables, require a client name to work, and are only available to that Client ID.

- Application variables are tied to an individual application as defined in the CFAPPLICATION NAME attribute, typically used in the APPLICATION.CFM file. Application variables only work if an application name has been defined.

Session and application variables are enabled or disabled in the Cold Fusion Administrator's Server tab. Client variables must be enabled within your templates using the <CFAPPLICATION> tag. If you decide to use client variables, the APPLICATION.CFM file is the ideal place to enable this feature.

▶ **See** Chapter 24, "Session Variables and Cookies," **p. 557**

Customizing Error Messages

Cold Fusion displays error message screens in two scenarios.

- An error has occurred that prevents Cold Fusion from continuing template processing. This type of error includes Cold Fusion syntax errors, SQL syntax errors, ODBC errors, or NT system errors.
- A form was submitted and the passed values failed the specified validation tests.

When either of these errors occur, a default Cold Fusion error message is displayed to the user. While the default message provides an exact description of what went wrong, that is not always a good thing. You might not want your visitors knowing that you passed an incorrect parameter to a Cold Fusion function, that you misspelled a variable name, or that you constructed an invalid SQL statement. You also might not want your visitors knowing any of the details about the underlying databases used by your application.

For these reasons, and so that you may create more polished-looking applications, Cold Fusion allows you to overwrite the standard error messages with messages of your own.

Creating Custom Error Message Templates

To create your own error messages you must do the following.

1. Create an error message template file. This is the template that will be displayed if an error occurs.
2. Provide Cold Fusion with the name of the error message template file to use. This is done using the <CFERROR> tag.

<CFERROR> requires that you specify the name of the error message template file to use, and the type of error for which to use it. Cold Fusion allows you to specify an error message template for each of the two error types listed above. To provide a template that will be used for all request errors, that is, errors that forced Cold Fusion to halt template processing, specify TYPE="REQUEST". Specify TYPE="VALIDATION" to provide the name of a template that will be used for form validation errors.

> **TIP**
> The application template, discussed earlier in this chapter, is the ideal place to specify Cold Fusion error message templates.

Error message templates may not include references to any Cold Fusion tags, functions, or variables. This is because if a really serious error occurred, for example, one that compromised the integrity of the operating system, further processing could generate additional errors.

The only variables that can be used in error message templates are special ERROR variables. The complete list of variables, and the type of template in which they can be used, is in Table 23.1.

Table 23.1 Cold Fusion Error Message Variables

Type	Field	Description
REQUEST	#ERROR.RemoteAddress#	IP address of the client
REQUEST	#ERROR.Browser#	The browser the client was running, with version and platform information if provided by the browser
REQUEST	#ERROR.DateTime#	The date and time that the error occurred
REQUEST	#ERROR.Diagnostics#	Detailed diagnostic error message returned by Cold Fusion
REQUEST	#ERROR.HTTPReferer#	URL of the page from which the template was accessed
REQUEST	#ERROR.MailTo#	Administrator's Email address, can be used to send notification of the error
REQUEST	#ERROR.QueryString#	The URL's query string
REQUEST	#ERROR.Template#	Template being processed when the error occurred
VALIDATION	#ERROR.InvalidFields#	List of the invalid form fields
VALIDATION	#ERROR.ValidationFooter#	Text for footer of error message
VALIDATION	#ERROR.ValidationHeader#	Text for header of error message

N O T E Cold Fusion tags can not be used within an error message template, and this includes the <CFOUTPUT> tag. To allow you to use the ERROR variables, Cold Fusion treats the entire error message template as if it were enclosed within <CFOUTPUT> tags. ▪

Demonstrating Custom Error Message Templates

To demonstrate how custom error messages can be used, look at an example. The code in Listing 23.3 has a typo in it, there is a T missing from </CFOUTPUT>.

Listing 23.3 Sample Template with an Error in It

```
Your current color settings are:
<UL>
<CFLOOP INDEX="var" LIST="#GetClientVariablesList()#">
<CFOUTPUT>
<LI>#var# = #Evaluate(var)#
</CFOUPUT>
</CFLOOP>
</UL>
```

What happens when this code gets executed? The standard Cold Fusion error message, shown in Figure 23.4, is displayed. This error message contains information that is valuable to you, but downright confusing (and even unprofessional) to your visitors.

Figure 23.5 shows a custom error message displayed for the exact same error condition, but one that is both more friendly and more meaningful to your visitors.

FIG. 23.4

The standard Cold Fusion error message provide visitors with too much information, and create an unpolished appearance.

Part
IV
Ch
23

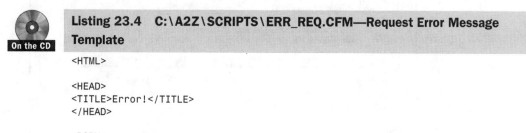

As mentioned earlier, to generate this error message two things had to happen. The error message template had to be created, and Cold Fusion had to be instructed to use this error message template for request errors.

The code that generated the error message shown in Figure 23.5 appears in Listing 23.4. As you can see it is a standard HTML file except for the use of the ERROR variables.

Listing 23.4   C:\A2Z\SCRIPTS\ERR_REQ.CFM—Request Error Message Template

On the CD

```
<HTML>

<HEAD>
<TITLE>Error!</TITLE>
</HEAD>

<BODY>

<CENTER>
```

continues

Listing 23.4 Continued

```
<TABLE BORDER=5>
 <TR>
  <TH>
   An error has occurred that prevents us from completing your request.
  </TH>
 </TR>
 <TR>
  <TD>
   We have logged the following information that will help us identify and
➥correct the problem:
   <UL>
    <LI>Error occurred at <B>#ERROR.Datetime#</B>
    <LI>Your IP address is <B>#ERROR.RemoteAddress#</B>
    <LI>Your browser is <B>#ERROR.Browser#</B>
    <LI>You were trying to process <B>#ERROR.Template#?#ERROR.
➥QueryString#</B>
   </UL>
   If you can provide us with any additional information that would help
➥us fix this problem, please send E-Mail to:
➥<A HREF="mailto:#ERROR.MailTo#">#ERROR.MailTo#</A>.
  </TD>
 </TR>
</TABLE>

</CENTER>

</BODY>

</HTML>
```

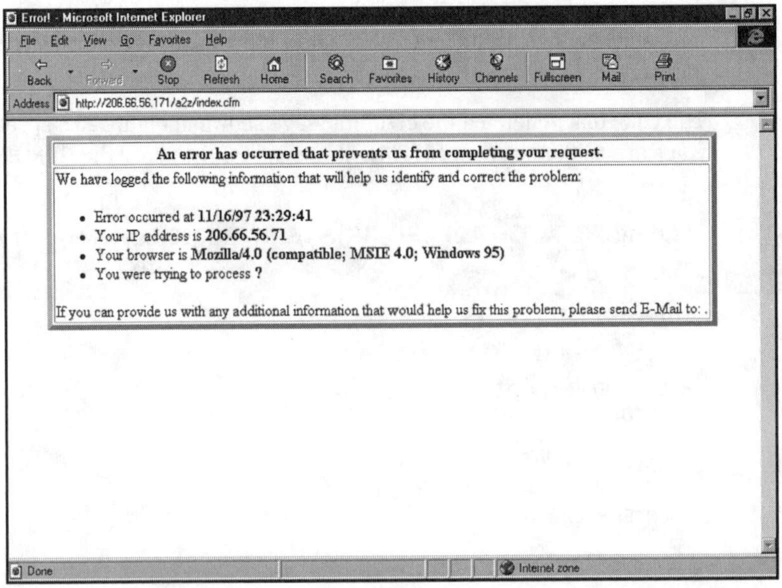

FIG. 23.5

Using the <CFERROR> tag, your application can provide its own error messages.

To instruct Cold Fusion to use this error code for request errors, the following code (from C:\A2Z\SCRIPTS\APPLICATION.CFM) has to be executed:

```
<CFERROR TYPE="REQUEST" TEMPLATE="err_req.cfm" MAILTO="webmaster@a2z.com">
```

▶ **See** Chapter 16, "Debugging and Troubleshooting," **p. 325**

Part
IV

Ch
23

CHAPTER 24

Session Variables and Cookies

by Ashley King

In this chapter

Using Client-State Management Techniques

The web is a stateless environment. To keep track of visitors and users, cookies were developed. Cold Fusion has taken this concept a step further with client and session management. In conjunction with application and server variables, an efficient means of keeping track of users and their information is achieved.

There are four basic ways to keep track of a client browser using Cold Fusion, as shown in Table 24.1. The most obvious is by keeping track of the IP address of a user. The drawbacks of this are that many Internet users browse the web via a proxy server. A proxy server actually receives the files from your server, and re-sends this information to the client browser. This means that a virtually unlimited number of users can share a few or even one IP address. Also, many Internet users have dial-up accounts that change IP addresses each time they log on to their ISP. All in all, IP tracking isn't an effective client management scheme.

Another way to keep track of a user is to send a cookie to the user's browser. A cookie is a variable stored on the user's hard drive by the client browser. A cookie generally can only be viewed or manipulated by the server that sent it. Cookies also have drawbacks. First of all, not all browsers are compatible with cookies, and even if they are, many users turn them off because of security concerns. Also, to store a useful set of data on a client browser, more than one cookie may be required. You must also build cookie management in your application.

A third way to keep track of users is to append data in an URL or pass it with a form. Drawbacks of this method include lengthy URLs for complex data sets and users sharing URLs, thus mixing users sessions. To make client-state management easier, Cold Fusion features built in client and session management that works with or without cookies.

Table 24.1 Client Management Techniques

Scheme	Components	Pros/Cons
IP Tracking	`CGI.REMOTE_ADDR`	Can track client browsers by IP address. Ineffective with clients using proxy servers or dynamic IPs.
Cookies	`<CFCOOKIE>`, cookie variable scope	Data is stored on client browser and can easily be retrieved for use by applications. Some browsers do not support cookies, and many users disable them. Cookies can also be lost.
URL data	URL variable scope, `URLEncodedFormat()`	Does not require cookies, user data can be stored in bookmarks. Not secure. Users can share data by sharing links. Cannot be used to distinguish sessions.

Scheme	Components	Pros/Cons
Cold Fusion client	`<CFAPPLICATION>`, scope client management scope, session	Can be used with or without cookies, large capacity for data storage, sessions are distinguished, secure. CFID must be stored in database to match user records to client data.

Using Cold Fusion Client and Session Management

Cold Fusion client and session management keeps track of client browser activity transparently and is compatible with virtually any browser. In addition to tracking client and session state, Cold Fusion allows you to store information in the context of a particular client or session. Information can also be stored in context with an application, making it available to all users of an application.

Using Client and Session Management

Client and session management enable web applications to maintain a virtual state for each client. This is essential for commerce applications such as shopping carts, document publishing, application security, collaboration applications, and virtually all other highly interactive applications. They are also useful in optimizing web applications by allowing a database to be queried once with the results stored in RAM for application or client use. Data can also be passed from client to client using the application scope, allowing efficient user interaction.

Client and session management also enables you to develop applications without creating a separate management scheme for browsers that do not accept cookies. Data that would normally be passed using URL parameters, or stored on the client browser using cookies, can be hidden from users and eavesdroppers by storing it securely on the Cold Fusion server. Cookies and other management schemes can be used in conjunction with Cold Fusion client and session management, allowing the greatest freedom in application development.

Using Variable Scopes and Application.cfm

Several variable scopes are available to Cold Fusion developers. The ones you're concerned with here are application, client, session, and cookie. These help you develop applications that track users and make data available to both the user and the application. The application.cfm file in an application defines the status of an application, client and session scope variables, and how long they are active. To demonstrate how these scopes interact, you'll construct a virtual pet application that uses only application, session and client variables to pass data between users. This chapter requires an understanding of how variables work and how to create applications in Cold Fusion. The main and most important tag in the application.cfm file is the `<CFAPPLICATION>` tag. This tag defines the name of the application, whether or not Cold Fusion client and session management are active, and how long application and session data will be active on the Cold Fusion server. See Table 24.2 for examples of the usage of `<CFAPPLICATION>`. These values are restricted by global settings in the Cold Fusion administrator, where maximum and default values can be set server-wide.

Part
IV

Ch
24

Table 24.2 <CFAPPLICATION> Parameters

Parameter	Required/Optional	Description
NAME	Required	To enable application scope variables. The name of the application.
CLIENTMANAGEMENT	Optional	Enable Cold Fusion client management.
SESSIONMANAGEMENT	Optional	Enable Cold Fusion session variables.
APPLICATIONTIMEOUT	Optional	The time span for the persistence of application scope variables. Default is specified in the Cold Fusion administrator. Uses CreateTimeSpan().
SESSIONTIMEOUT	Optional	The time span for the persistence of session scope variables. Uses CreateTimeSpan().

For the example application, the application.cfm in Listing 24.1 must enable client and session management, set some default values, and test to see if the client browser accepts cookies. If the client browser does not accept cookies, the CFID and CFTOKEN will be appended to all links in the application using the reserved client variable client.URLToken.

Listing 24.1 application.cfm—Initialization of the Application

```
<!--- My CF_Pet - A Cold Fusion virtual pet --->
<!--- Define the application parameters --->
<CFAPPLICATION NAME="MyPet"
               CLIENTMANAGEMENT="Yes"
               SESSIONMANAGEMENT="Yes"
               SESSIONTIMEOUT=" #CreateTimeSpan(0,0,30,0)#"
               APPLICATIONTIMEOUT=" #CreateTimeSpan(1,0,0,0)#">
<!--- Initialize application variables --->
<CFPARAM NAME="application.lastMessage" DEFAULT="Hello!">
<CFPARAM NAME="application.lastUser" DEFAULT="Nobody">
<!--- Check to see if this is the first time the application has been
accessed by a particular client. If so, set values. --->
<CFIF NOT ISDEFINED("session.rollCount")>
   <CFSET SESSION.ROLLCOUNT = 1>
   <CFSET APPLICATION.LASTUSER = IIF(ISDEFINED("application.currentUser")
➥, "application.currentUser", DE("Nobody"))>
   <CFSET APPLICATION.CURRENTUSER = IIF(ISDEFINED("client.clientName"),
➥"client.clientName", DE("guest from #CGI.REMOTE_ADDR#"))>
   <!--- Try to set a cookie for testing later --->
   <CFCOOKIE NAME="isOn" VALUE="testing">
   <CFSET APPLICATION.ADDTOKEN = "cfid=#client.cfid#&cftoken=#client.
➥cftoken#">
<CFELSE>
   <!--- Check to see if cookies are on. If no, make a query string
variable with the CFID and CFTOKEN. --->
```

```
    <CFSET APPLICATION.ADDTOKEN = IIF(NOT ISDEFINED("cookie.isOn"),
DE("cfid=#client.cfid#&cftoken=#client.cftoken#"), DE("")))>

</CFIF>
```

Using Application Scope   Now that the application is defined, application scope variables can be used. All variable types can be used in the application scope including arrays and queries. In application.cfm, application scope variables are used to show users who visited before them, and also to pass the session key to all links in the application if the client browser does not accept cookies. These values are both used in index.cfm, shown in Listing 24.2. These values can also be read from any template in the application. Notice that index.cfm automatically appends the session key to its links. This is because a cookie may not be set and retrieved from within the same template. The cookie test will not be complete by the time the links in index.cfm are constructed. The completed welcome page is shown in Figure 24.1.

Part

IV

Ch

24

On the CD

Listing 24.2   index.cfm—The Welcome Page

```
<!--- The welcome page --->
<HTML>
<HEAD>
<TITLE>My CF_Pet </TITLE>
</HEAD>
<BODY BGCOLOR="white" TEXT="black" LINK="blue" VLINK="green" ALINK="yellow">
<TABLE ALIGN="center" BGCOLOR="#0000cc" WIDTH="100%" CELLSPACING="0"
➥CELLPADDING="0" BORDER="1">
<TR>
    <TD WIDTH="100%" VALIGN="top">
    <FONT SIZE="+3" COLOR="Yellow"><B><I>My CF_Pet</I></B></FONT>
    </TD>
</TR>
</TABLE>
<P>
<TABLE ALIGN="center" BGCOLOR="#ffffcc" WIDTH="100%" CELLSPACING="0"
➥CELLPADDING="0" BORDER="1">
<TR>
    <TD WIDTH="100%" VALIGN="top">
<CFOUTPUT>
<B>Welcome to the home of the CF_Pet, a web-based virtual pet!  You can
raise your pet from infancy and test your virtual parenting skills!  The
last user to visit, #application.lastUser#, says "#application.lastMessage#".
</B>
</CFOUTPUT>
<P>
<!--- Show separate messages for users and guests --->
<CFIF ISDEFINED("client.status")>
    <CFOUTPUT>
    Welcome back, #client.clientName#! You last visited on #dateFormat(client.
➥lastVisit, "ddd, mmmm dd, yyyy")# at #timeFormat(client.lastVisit,
➥"h:mm tt")#.  Your pet, #client.petName# is ready for your visit.
```

continues

Listing 24.2 Continued

```
    <P>

    <B>[<A HREF="main.cfm?#application.addToken#">Visit #client.petName#
➡</A>]</B>
    <B>[<A HREF="register.cfm?#application.addToken#">Edit your Preferences
➡</A>]</B>
    <B>[<A HREF="action.cfm?endLife=yes&#application.addToken#">
➡Euthanize your pet</A>]</B>
    </CFOUTPUT>
<CFELSE>
    <CFOUTPUT>
    To login and create your pet, <B><A HREF="register.cfm?#application.
➡addToken#">start here!</A></B>
    </CFOUTPUT>
</CFIF>
    </TD>
</TR>
</TABLE>
</BODY>
</HTML>
```

FIG. 24.1

The user is greeted with a welcome page.

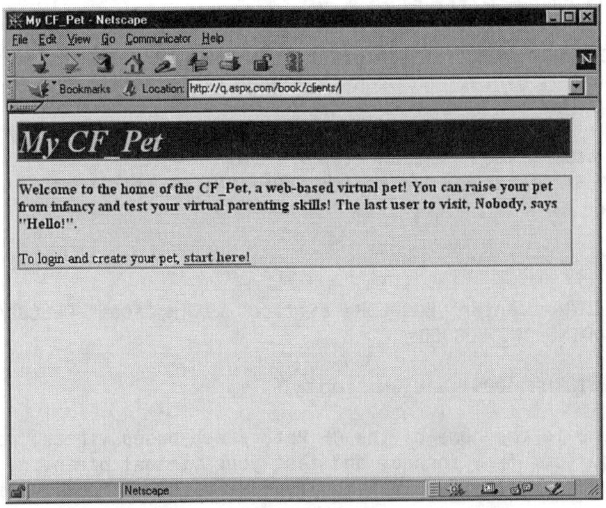

Using Client Scope Now, users must be able to register and create a pet. When a client accesses any page in your application with client management enabled, a CFID and CFTOKEN are automatically generated. If the client browser accepts cookies, these values are stored as cookies on the client browser. If these cookies are not accepted, it is up to your application to pass these values between templates to maintain client state. Only the CFID and CFTOKEN must be passed. Cold Fusion will make all other client and session scope variables available to your application automatically based on these two values. In the CF_Pet application, more information than just a session key is needed to make the application useable. Listing 24.3 shows register.cfm where user attributes such as name and email address are collected, as well as the pet's attributes. When this form is submitted, action.cfm, shown in Listing 24.4, adds this data to the client data already stored by Cold Fusion.

On the CD

Listing 24.3 register.cfm—The Form for the Creation and Modification of the Pet

```
<!--- Form for creating or modifying a pet --->
<HTML>
<HEAD>
<TITLE>My CF_Pet - Registration </TITLE>
</HEAD>
<BODY BGCOLOR="white" TEXT="black" LINK="blue" VLINK="green" ALINK="yellow">
<TABLE ALIGN="center" BGCOLOR="#0000cc" WIDTH="100%" CELLSPACING="0"
➥CELLPADDING="0" BORDER="1">
<TR>
    <TD WIDTH="100%" VALIGN="top">
    <FONT SIZE="+3" COLOR="Yellow"><B><I>My CF_Pet</I></B></FONT>
    </TD>
</TR>
</TABLE>
<P>
<TABLE BGCOLOR="#ffffcc" WIDTH="100%" CELLSPACING="0" CELLPADDING="0"
➥BORDER="1">
<TR>
    <TD WIDTH="100%" VALIGN="top">
<CFIF ISDEFINED("client.status")>
    <B>To modify your preferences, fill out the form below!</B>
<CFELSE>
    <B>To create a new CF_Pet, fill out the form below!</B>
</CFIF>
<P>
<CFOUTPUT>
<FORM METHOD="post" ACTION="action.cfm?#application.addToken#">
<INPUT TYPE="hidden" NAME="clientName_required" VALUE="Please enter
➥your name.">
<INPUT TYPE="hidden" NAME="petName_required" VALUE="Please enter a name for
➥your pet.">
<INPUT TYPE="hidden" NAME="email_required" VALUE="Please enter your email
➥address.">
<TABLE CELLSPACING="2" CELLPADDING="2">
<TR>
    <TD><B>Your Name:</B></TD>
    <TD><INPUT TYPE="Text" NAME="clientName" SIZE="20" <CFIF
ISDEFINED("client.status")>value="#client.clientName#"</CFIF>></TD>
</TR>
<TR>
    <TD><B>Your Pet's Name:</B></TD>
    <TD><INPUT TYPE="Text" NAME="petName" SIZE="20" <CFIF
ISDEFINED("client.status")>value="#client.petName#"</CFIF>></TD>
</TR>
<TR>
```

Part
IV

Ch
24

continues

Listing 24.3 Continued

```
    <TD><B>Your Email Address:</B></TD>
    <TD><INPUT TYPE="Text" NAME="email" SIZE="20"   <CFIF
ISDEFINED("client.status")>value="#client.email#"</CFIF>></TD>
</TR>
<TR>
    <TD><B>Your Pet's Color</B></TD>
    <TD><SELECT NAME="petColor">
    <CFIF ISDEFINED("client.status")><OPTION SELECTED>#client.petColor#</CFIF>
    <OPTION>Yellow
    <OPTION>Brown
    <OPTION>Blue
    </SELECT></TD>
</TR>
<TR>
    <TD><B>Put My Pet In:</B></TD>
    <TD><SELECT NAME="windows">
    <CFIF ISDEFINED("client.status")><OPTION SELECTED>#client.windows#</CFIF>
    <OPTION VALUE="window">A separate window
    <OPTION VALUE="page">The same page
    </SELECT></TD>
</TR>
</TABLE>
<INPUT TYPE="Submit" VALUE="Make My Pet!">
</FORM>
</CFOUTPUT>
    </TD>
</TR>
</TABLE>
</BODY>
</HTML>
```

Client variables are a good place to store user preferences, since they persist between client visits. Since client variables are stored in the registry, you should be careful not to store too much data in client variables, especially in high-traffic applications. A good way to store preference data is to use the CFID client variable to reference preference data stored in a database. The database can then be queried, and the query can be stored as a session variable, eliminating the need for another database access in the user session.

The register.cfm template, shown in Figure 24.2, is also used for modifying preferences, so you check for the existence of the client variable client.status, which is not created until the form is submitted. Once a user has created a pet, this form will be used for modification only.

On the CD

Listing 24.4 action.cfm—Template for Handling Form Submissions

```
<!--- action.cfm - Let the owner take care of the pet. --->
<CFIF ISDEFINED("form.feed")>
    <CFSET CLIENT.PETFED = INCREMENTVALUE(CLIENT.PETFED)>

<CFELSEIF ISDEFINED("form.clean")>
    <CFSET CLIENT.PETCLEANED = INCREMENTVALUE(CLIENT.PETCLEANED)>
```

```
<CFELSEIF ISDEFINED("url.endLife")>
  <CFLOOP INDEX="listElement" LIST="#getClientVariablesList()#">
    <CFSET ISSUCCESS = DELETECLIENTVARIABLE("#listElement#")>
  </CFLOOP>

  <CFLOCATION URL="index.cfm" ADDTOKEN="yes">
<CFELSE>
  <!--- Create a new pet. --->
  <!--- Grab all of the values from the form and add them to the
client varibles scope --->
  <CFLOOP INDEX="listElement" LIST="#form.fieldnames#">
    <CFSET "client.#listElement#" = EVALUATE("form.#listElement#")>
  </CFLOOP>
  <!--- If this is an update, skip the preliminaries --->
  <CFIF NOT ISDEFINED("client.status")>
    <CFSET CLIENT.STATUS="active">
    <CFSET CLIENT.PETBORN = "#Now()#">
    <CFSET CLIENT.PETFED = "1">
    <CFSET CLIENT.PETCLEANED = "1">
    <CFSET SESSION.EMOTION_VALUE = 100>
    <CFSET SESSION.HEALTH_VALUE = 100>
  </CFIF>
  <!--- Go to the main page --->
  <CFLOCATION URL="main.cfm" ADDTOKEN="yes">
</CFIF>
<CFLOCATION URL="#cgi.http_referer#" ADDTOKEN="yes">
```

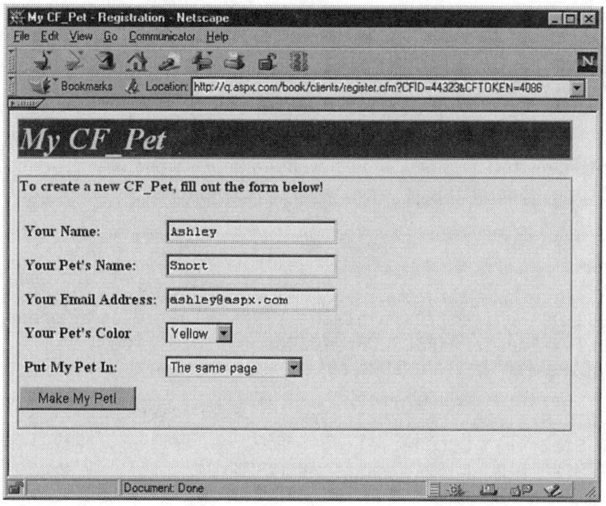

FIG. 24.2

The registration page.

Now, all client variables necessary to maintain the pet have been created. Remember that client scope variables cannot be used to store complex data types such as queries and arrays. Table 24.3 shows the additional reserved variables automatically created and maintained by Cold Fusion in the client scope.

Table 24.3   Reserved Client Variables

Name	Description
CFID	The unique client ID. Part of the session key.
CFTOKEN	A unique ID that forms part of the session key.
LastVisit	Records the date and time of the last visit for a client.
URLToken	The CFID and CFTOKEN together, used to append to an URL.
HitCount	The number of times a client has visited the site.
TimeCreated	The date and time of the creation of the CFID.

When adding variables in this scope, remember that client variables are stored in the registry. Again, this is not a good place to store large amounts of data for each client. In the pet application, store simple values that are manipulated and used elsewhere in the application. These variables are used in main.cfm, shown in Listing 24.5, to determine how the pet is to be displayed in the custom tag checkUp.cfm. Determining how to compute the current state of the pet is shown in Listing 24.6.

On the CD

Listing 24.5   main.cfm—The Virtual Pet Management Area

```
<!--- The main window. --->
<HTML>
<HEAD>
<TITLE>My CF_Pet - <CFOUTPUT>#client.petName#</CFOUTPUT>'s kennel</TITLE>
<!--- window open script --->
<SCRIPT LANGUAGE="JavaScript">
<!---
    function openWin( windowURL, windowName, windowFeatures ) {
        return window.open( windowURL, windowName, windowFeatures ) ;
    }
// --->
</SCRIPT>
</HEAD>
<BODY BGCOLOR="white" TEXT="black" LINK="blue" VLINK="green" ALINK="yellow">
<TABLE ALIGN="center" BGCOLOR="#0000cc" WIDTH="100%"
➥CELLSPACING="0" CELLPADDING="0" BORDER="1">
<TR>
    <TD WIDTH="100%" VALIGN="top">
    <FONT SIZE="+3" COLOR="Yellow"><B><I>My CF_Pet</I></B>  </FONT>
    <FONT SIZE="+2" COLOR="White"><CFOUTPUT>
➥#client.petName#</CFOUTPUT>'s kennel</FONT>
    </TD>
</TR>
</TABLE>
<P>
<TABLE ALIGN="center" BGCOLOR="#ffffcc" WIDTH="100%"
➥CELLSPACING="0" CELLPADDING="0" BORDER="1">
<TR>
    <TD WIDTH="100%" VALIGN="top">
```

```
<CFOUTPUT>
<B>Welcome to CF_Kennels, #client.clientName#!  We do our best to take care
of the needs of your pet, but your pet needs your attention and care.
You must feed your pet at least 3 times a day, and clean up after your
pet as neccesary.  And the more you visit your pet, the happier it gets. </B>
<P>
    <B>[<A HREF="register.cfm?#application.addToken#">
➥Edit your Preferences</A>]</B>
    <B>[<A HREF="action.cfm?endLife=yes&#application.addToken#">
➥Euthanize your pet</A>]</B>
</CFOUTPUT>
<!--- Check preferences and display contents accordingly --->
<CFIF CLIENT.WINDOWS IS "window">
    <CFOUTPUT>
    <B>[<A HREF="JavaScript: newWindow = openWin( 'kennel.cfm?show=
➥pet&#application.addToken#', 'kennel', 'width=250,height=300,
➥toolbar=0,location=0,directories=0,status=
➥0,menuBar=0,scrollBars=1,resizable=1' ); newWindow.focus()">
Open your kennel</A>]</B>
    </CFOUTPUT>
<CFELSE>

    <CFINCLUDE TEMPLATE="pet.cfm">
</CFIF>
    </TD>
</TR>
</TABLE>
</BODY>
</HTML>
```

In action.cfm, the application provides for the complete deletion of the pet and associated client variables. The function GetClientVariablesList() returns a comma-delimited list of all non-read-only client variables. You can use this in conjunction with DeleteClientVariable() and <CFLOOP> to delete all the variables created in the application. If the variable does not exist, DeleteClientVariable() will return No; otherwise, it will return Yes when successful.

Notice also in Listing 24.6 that you're using JavaScript in a new way. Instead of using it for validation, you're using it here to open a new browser window, sized to fit your virtual kennel. This JavaScript was generated by the Cold Fusion Studio Open Window Wizard. For more information on using the Cold Fusion Studio Wizards see Chapter 10, "Introduction to Cold Fusion Studio."

Using Session Scope Now that the user has created a pet and is ready to care for it, the basic values stored in the client scope need to be converted into useable statistics and displayed in an appropriate manner. To do this, create session scope variables for the data you need to use for this session only. Session scope variables can only be defined in the context of a session key, so it is important to make sure any session variables are defined and used only within the same application and only with both client and session management enabled in application.cfm.

Part
IV

Ch
24

In the CF_Pet application, you've encapsulated the conversions in a custom tag, checkUp.cfm. This custom tag, shown in Listing 24.6, reads the current values in the client scope, runs calculations for the pet's health and happiness, and stores these temporary values in the session scope. This is an efficient way to pass data between templates and custom tags because no database queries, form fields, or URL parameters are needed. All of the data is stored in RAM for quick retrieval.

On the CD

Listing 24.6   checkUp.cfm—This Template Is to Calculate How Well the Pet Is Doing

```
<!--- checkUp custom tag.  This template calculates the well-being of the
pet. --->
<!--- First, figure out if the pet has been visited. Figure it should take
about 20 hits per visit to constitute "quality time". --->
<CFSET SESSION.VISITVALUE = EVALUATE("#iif(dateDiff("D", client.petBorn,
➥now()) GT 0, DE("((#CLIENT.HITCOUNT# / 20) / #DATEDIFF("d", CLIENT.
➥PETBORN, NOW())#)"), DE("((#CLIENT.HITCOUNT# / 20) / 1)"))# * 100")>
<CFSET SESSION.VISITVALUE = IIF(SESSION.VISITVALUE LTE 100, DE("#session.
➥visitValue#"), DE("100"))>
<!--- Next, figure out if the pet has received three square meals a day. --->
<CFIF CLIENT.PETFED GT EVALUATE("(#dateDiff("D", client.petBorn, now())
➥# * 3)")>
   <CFSET CLIENT.PETFED = IIF(DATEDIFF("d", CLIENT.PETBORN, NOW()) GT 0,
➥DE("#evaluate("((#DATEDIFF("d", CLIENT.PETBORN,
➥NOW())# * 3) + 1)")#"), DE("4"))>
</CFIF>
<CFSET SESSION.HUNGER = EVALUATE("#iif(dateDiff("D", client.petBorn, now())
➥GT 0, DE("(#CLIENT.PETFED# / (#DATEDIFF("d", CLIENT.PETBORN, NOW
➥())# * 3))"), DE("(#CLIENT.PETFED# / 3)"))# * 100")>
<CFSET SESSION.HUNGER = IIF(SESSION.HUNGER LTE 100, DE("#session.hunger#"),
➥DE("100"))>
<!--- Now, figure out how many times the pooper - scooper has been used.
And remember, not all pets make the same amount of mess. The more it is fed,
the more the mess. --->
<CFSET SESSION.CLEANED = EVALUATE("#iif(dateDiff("D", client.petBorn,
➥now()) GT 0, DE("(#CLIENT.PETCLEANED# / (#DATEDIFF("d", CLIENT.
➥PETBORN, NOW())# * ((#RANDOMIZE(DAY(NOW()))# * 2) +
➥(#CLIENT.PETFED# / (#DATEDIFF("d", CLIENT.PETBORN, NOW())# * 3)))))"),
➥DE("(#CLIENT.PETCLEANED# / ((#RANDOMIZE(DAY(NOW()))# * 2) +
➥(#CLIENT.PETFED# / 3)))"))# * 100")>
<CFSET SESSION.CLEANED = IIF(SESSION.CLEANED LTE 100,
➥DE("#session.cleaned#"), DE("100"))>
<!--- Use the above to figure out how healthy and happy it is. Combine
these for an overall value.  There's no substitute for time well spent.--->
<CFSET SESSION.EMOTION_VALUE = EVALUATE("(((#session.visitValue# * 2) +
➥#session.hunger# + #session.cleaned#) / 4)")>
<CFSET SESSION.HEALTH_VALUE = EVALUATE("((#session.hunger# + #session.
➥cleaned#) / 2)")>
<CFSET VARIABLES.EMOTIONALSTATE = EVALUATE("(((#session.Health_value# * 2)
➥+ #session.Emotion_value#) / 3)")>
<!--- Give the emotion a name --->
<CFIF VARIABLES.EMOTIONALSTATE GT 66
 AND VARIABLES.EMOTIONALSTATE LTE 100>
```

```
   <CFSET SESSION.EMOTION = "Happy">
<CFELSEIF VARIABLES.EMOTIONALSTATE GT 33
 AND VARIABLES.EMOTIONALSTATE LTE 66>

   <CFSET SESSION.EMOTION = "Sad">

 <CFELSE>

   <CFSET SESSION.EMOTION = "Dead">
 </CFIF>
```

Notice how the variable scopes interact in Listing 24.6. You pass data from more persistent scopes such as client and application, to less persistent scopes such as the session scope. You use the variables scope to store temporary values that are not used elsewhere in the application. When using the scopes in an application, it is important to qualify your variables by adding the scope to their name, such as application.myVar instead of myVar. Not only does this speed up the execution of your template, it also helps keep confusion to a minimum.

Server, application, client, and session scope variables are available to multiple templates, so you must make sure that your variable names do not clash. Errors of this type can be hard to debug. Keep track of your variables, and all will turn out well.

Now that the pet has been evaluated by its health professional, this data can be displayed in a graphical manner. One way to do this is to create a *sprite* àla the old Commodore 64 graphics engine. A sprite in this context is simply an 8-pixel×8-pixel grid used to represent an image. Cold Fusion arrays can be stored in application, server and session scopes, so you'll use the session scope to create and store a graphic array as shown in Listing 24.7, makeSprite.cfm.

Listing 24.7   makeSprite.cfm—Template to Generate a Sprite and Store It as an Array

```
<!--- makeSprite.cfm CF_MyPet.MakeSprite custom tag
      Constructs a sprite (like the old time Commodore 64 sprites)
using an array.

--->
<!--- How is the pet feeling?  If it has no feelings, give it some. --->
<CFPARAM NAME="Session.Emotion" DEFAULT="happy">
<!--- Give the pet data on how to make faces --->
<CFSET HAPPY = "66,102,126,219,255,189,66,60">
<CFSET SAD = "66,102,126,219,255,231,90,60">
<CFSET DEAD = "66,102,126,153,255,255,66,60">
<!--- Set array based on emotion --->
<CFSET SESSION.SPRITE = ARRAYNEW(2)>
<CFLOOP INDEX="currentValue" LIST="#evaluate(""variables.#Session.
➥Emotion#"")#">
   <CFPARAM NAME="loopStep" DEFAULT="1">
   <!--- Convert value to binary --->
   <CFSET CURRENTBYTE = FORMATBASEN(CURRENTVALUE, 2)>
   <CFLOOP INDEX="currentBit" FROM="8" TO="1" STEP="-1">
```

Part
IV

Ch
24

continues

Listing 24.7   Continued

```
        <CFIF CURRENTBIT GT LEN(CURRENTBYTE)>
            <CFSET SESSION.SPRITE[LOOPSTEP][CURRENTBIT] = "0">

        <CFELSE>

            <CFSET SESSION.SPRITE[LOOPSTEP][CURRENTBIT] = MID(REVERSE
➥(CURRENTBYTE), CURRENTBIT, 1)>

        </CFIF>
    </CFLOOP>

    <CFSET LOOPSTEP = INCREMENTVALUE(LOOPSTEP)>

</CFLOOP>
```

Now you can use HTML tables to display this sprite on the client browser. Using session scope variables to pass the sprite from custom tag to custom tag allows the tags to optionally be called from separate templates. As long as the current client session does not time out, this sprite is available to any template in the application. The custom tag drawSprite.cfm, shown in Listing 24.8, takes the information stored in the session array variable and converts it to a table display.

Listing 24.8   drawSprite.cfm—Retrieving the Sprite and Drawing on the Client Browser

```
<!--- drawSprite.cfm CF_MyPet.drawSprite
   Draws the face of the pet
--->
<!--- Check to see if makeSprite ran.  If not, kill process --->
<CFIF NOT ISDEFINED("session.sprite")>
   CF_MyPet.makeSprite has not run!
   <CFEXIT>
</CFIF>
<!--- Build table --->
<TABLE BORDER="0" CELLSPACING="0" CELLPADDING="0" ALIGN="CENTER"
➥VALIGN="TOP" BGCOLOR="white">
<!--- Read data from the array --->
<CFLOOP INDEX="currentByte" FROM="1" TO="8">
   <!--- Read bits and make table --->
   <TR>
   <CFLOOP INDEX="currentBit" FROM="1" TO="8">
      <!--- Check to see if bit is on --->
      <CFIF #SESSION.SPRITE[CURRENTBYTE][CURRENTBIT]# IS "1">
         <CFOUTPUT>
         <TD ALIGN="CENTER" VALIGN="TOP" BGCOLOR="#client.petColor#">
➥<FONT SIZE="1"> </FONT></TD>
         <TD ALIGN="CENTER" VALIGN="TOP" BGCOLOR="#client.petColor#">
➥<FONT SIZE="1"> </FONT></TD>
         <TD ALIGN="CENTER" VALIGN="TOP" BGCOLOR="#client.petColor#">
➥<FONT SIZE="1"> </FONT></TD>
         </CFOUTPUT>
```

```
        <CFELSE>
            <TD ALIGN="CENTER" VALIGN="TOP" BGCOLOR="black">
➥<FONT SIZE="1"> </FONT></TD>
            <TD ALIGN="CENTER" VALIGN="TOP" BGCOLOR="black">
➥<FONT SIZE="1"> </FONT></TD>
            <TD ALIGN="CENTER" VALIGN="TOP" BGCOLOR="black">
➥<FONT SIZE="1"> </FONT></TD>
        </CFIF>
    </CFLOOP>
    </TR>
</CFLOOP>
</TABLE>
```

The custom tags to check the pet's health and make and draw the sprite are called from the pet.cfm template, shown in Listing 24.9. A table is constructed to contain the display of the pet and allow it to be portable to any section of the application.

Listing 24.9   pet.cfm—Displaying the Pet

```
<!--- Show the pet --->
    <CF_CHECKUP>
    <CF_MAKESPRITE>
    <TABLE ALIGN="center" CELLSPACING="0" CELLPADDING="0" BORDER=1>
    <TR>
        <TD WIDTH="100%" BGCOLOR="navy"><B><CFOUTPUT><FONT SIZE="+1"
COLOR="White">#client.petName#</FONT></CFOUTPUT></B></TD>
    </TR>
    <TR>
        <TD WIDTH="100%" ALIGN="center" BGCOLOR="#ffffcc">
        <CF_DRAWSPRITE>
        </TD>
    </TR>
    <TR>
        <TD WIDTH="100%">
        <B>Happiness:</B><CFOUTPUT>#round(session.Emotion_value)#</CFOUTPUT><BR>
        <CF_MAKEBAR BARVALUE="#session.Emotion_value#" BARSIZE="1" BARCOLOR=
➥"##9966cc" SCALE="2">

        </TD>
    </TR>
    <TR>
        <TD WIDTH="100%">
        <B>Health:</B><CFOUTPUT>#round(session.Health_value)#</CFOUTPUT><BR>
        <CF_MAKEBAR BARVALUE="#session.Health_value#" BARSIZE="1" BARCOLOR=
➥"##9966cc" SCALE="2">
        </TD>
    </TR>
    <TR>
        <TD WIDTH="100%">
        <TABLE BORDER=0 ALIGN="center">
        <CFOUTPUT>
        <FORM ACTION="action.cfm?#application.addToken#" METHOD="POST">
```

continues

Listing 24.9   Continued

```
    </CFOUTPUT>
    <TR><TD>
    <INPUT TYPE="Submit" NAME="Feed" VALUE="Feed">
    </TD><TD>
    <INPUT TYPE="Submit" NAME="Clean" VALUE="Clean">
    </TD>
    </FORM>
    <CFIF CLIENT.WINDOWS IS "window">

        <FORM>
        <TD>
            <INPUT TYPE="button" ONCLICK="self.close()" VALUE="Close">
        </TD>
        </FORM>
    </CFIF>
    </TR>
    </TABLE>
    </TD>
</TR>
<TR>
    <TD WIDTH="100%">
    <TABLE BORDER=0 ALIGN="center">
    <TR>
    <CFIF SESSION.HUNGER LT 100>
    <TD>
        <CFOUTPUT><FONT SIZE="-1">I'm hungry!</FONT></CFOUTPUT>
    </TD>
    </CFIF>
    <CFIF SESSION.CLEANED LT 100>
    <TD>
        <CFOUTPUT><FONT SIZE="-1">I'm dirty!</FONT></CFOUTPUT>
    </TD>
    </CFIF>
    </TR>
    </TABLE>
    </TD>
</TR>
 </TABLE>
```

In Listing 24.10, the pet.cfm template, additional data is displayed to help the user take care of the pet. Two bar graphs are displayed, along with notices if the pet is hungry or needs to be cleaned. The bar graph is displayed using a simple custom tag that uses tables.

On the CD

Listing 24.10   makeBar.cfm—Generating Bar Graphs Without the Use of Images

```
<!--- makeBar.cfm --->
<!--- Draw a bar graph.  Parameters:
   scale: Display scale of the bar.  Value is x in 1:x
```

```
        color: A hex value including hash
        size:  The size of the bar.  Values 1 - 3    --->
  <TABLE BORDER="0" CELLSPACING="0" CELLPADDING="0">
  <TR>
     <CFLOOP INDEX="loopCount" FROM="1" TO="#evaluate(""100 / #attributes.
  ➥scale#"")#">
        <CFOUTPUT>
        <CFIF LOOPCOUNT LTE #EVALUATE("#attributes.barValue# / #attributes.
  ➥scale#")#>
           <TD BGCOLOR="#attributes.barColor#"><FONT
  ➥SIZE="#attributes.barSize#"> </FONT></TD>
        <CFELSE>
           <TD BGCOLOR="black"><FONT SIZE="#attributes.barSize#"> 
  ➥</FONT></TD>
        </CFIF>
        </CFOUTPUT>
     </CFLOOP>
  </TR>
  </TABLE>
```

Finally, CF_Pet allows users to keep their pet in a separate window. The template kennel.cfm, shown in Listing 24.11, creates the pet display in the window and includes the pet.cfm template. Figure 24.3 shows the pet in its virtual habitat.

On the CD

Listing 24.11   kennel.cfm—The Pet Kennel Window Template

```
<!--- For separate window users.  Show the kennel or the chat window --->
<!DOCTYPE HTML PUBLIC "-//W3C//DTD HTML 3.2 Final//EN">
<HTML>
<HEAD>
</HEAD>
<CFPARAM NAME="show" DEFAULT="pet">
<BODY BGCOLOR="White" TEXT="Black" LINK="Blue" VLINK="Green" ALINK="Yellow">
<CFIF SHOW IS "pet">
   <CFHTMLHEAD TEXT="<TITLE>#Client.petName#'s Kennel</TITLE>">
   <CFINCLUDE TEMPLATE="pet.cfm">
</CFIF>
</BODY>
</HTML>
```

Using Cookies

Cookies can be created, read, and manipulated on the client browser independently of Cold Fusion client and session management. The <CFCOOKIE> tag creates and deletes cookies on the client browser. Values set using <CFCOOKIE> can be read and set using the cookie variable scope. Table 24.4 describes the parameters available for the <CFCOOKIE> tag.

FIG. 24.3

The pet in its virtual environment.

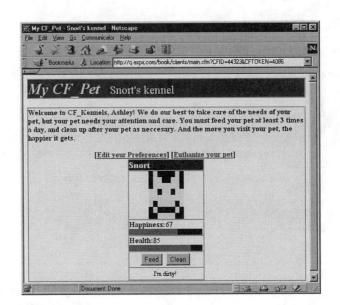

Table 24.4   *<CFCOOKIE>* Parameters

Name	Value	Description
NAME	String	Required. The name of the variable.
VALUE	Any	Required. The value of the variable.
EXPIRES	Date, Number of Days	Optional. Describes when the cookie is NOW, or NEVER scheduled to expire.
SECURE	None	Optional. Requires the cookie to be sent securely using SSL. Cookie will not be sent if client browser does not support SSL.
DOMAIN	Domain name	Required only if PATH is used. The domain for which the cookies are valid. Separate multiple domains with a ; character.
PATH	Web path	Optional. Subset of the URL to which the cookie applies. Separate multiple paths with a ; character.

Setting a Cookie

Cookies are set using the <CFCOOKIE> tag by specifying a name, value, and expiration date for the cookie. The expiration date can be absolute, such as 12/6/2006, or it can be relative, such as "1." Relative values are represented in days, so if your cookie is set as EXPIRES="7", your cookie will expire in one week. You can also specify that the cookie never expires by adding EXPIRES="NEVER". This will in effect cause your cookie to reside permanently on the client browser.

Reading a Cookie

When reading a cookie, it is a good idea to check for the existence of the cookie first using IsDefined(). To read the value of the cookie, simply reference the fully qualified variable. If the name of your cookie is ITEMS, and you would like to see if it is zero, you would use the same syntax as for any other variable, as in Listing 24.12, cookie.cfm.

On the CD

Listing 24.12   cookie.cfm—Checking to See If a Browser Accepts Cookies

```
<!--- Check for the existence of the cookie --->
<cfif IsDefined("cookie.items")>
   <cfif cookie.items is 0>
      There are no items in your basket.
   </cfif>
</cfif>
```

Part

IV

Ch

24

Deleting Cookies

Removing cookies is similar to setting a cookie, but instead of specifying an expiration date in the future, add EXPIRES="NOW". This will immediately delete the cookie from the client browser. ●

CHAPTER 25

File Manipulation

by David E. Crawford

In this chapter

Manipulating Files

File manipulation in Cold Fusion 3.1 is provided through the CFFILE tag. This feature of Cold Fusion takes advantage of features introduced in web browsers, such as Netscape Navigator 2.0, which permit file upload using the HTTP protocol. The method by which files are uploaded to the server using HTTP is documented in the Internet Request for Comment RFC 1867, which can be found at **http://www.cis.ohio-state.edu/htbin/rfc/rfc1867.html**. These features are browser-specific, therefore you should use them carefully in order to provide the maximum capability to your users, while also providing the maximum level of flexibility.

In addition to the ability to upload files, CFFILE also permits local file access through CFML templates. Files can be moved, copied, or deleted by using different action attributes for the CFFILE tag. Additionally, CFFILE provides mechanisms for reading and writing ASCII files with Cold Fusion. Taking advantage of the CFFILE tag provides you with the ability to produce complex applications with file manipulation using a single interface, without having to deal with the additional complexities of protocols such as FTP or NFS. The templates, in which the CFFILE tag are used, can be protected using native server security when the templates are stored in directories below the document root defined for the HTTP server.

N O T E RFC 1867 is the formal documentation of the HTTP file upload process. It specifies the concepts relating to file uploads using MIME file extensions. ■

> **CAUTION**
>
> The file upload mechanism is browser-specific. Netscape Navigator 2.0 and later supports this feature. Microsoft Internet Explorer 4.0 supports this feature natively, while Internet Explorer 3.02 provides file upload support through the addition of an ActiveX control. Other browsers, such as Lynx and Mosaic, may not support this feature. Use of the file upload mechanism should be implemented with this in mind.

The file upload plug-in for Microsoft Internet Explorer 3.02 on Windows 95/NT is on the World Wide Web at **http://www.microsoft.com/msdownload/ieplatform/iewin95/iewin95.asp**.

ON THE WEB

For more information about HTTP File uploads and Microsoft Internet Explorer, check out Microsoft's web page at **http://www.microsoft.com/ie/**.

Understanding the *CFFILE* Tag and Its Attributes

The CFFILE tag utilizes standard HTTP protocols to permit file uploads using a POST operation. The files are transmitted from the client to the server using a multi-part form field definition. The general syntax for the CFFILE tag is in Listing 25.1, with specific values for the ACTION parameter and the other attributes shown in Table 25.1.

Listing 25.1 Syntax for the *CFFILE* Tag

```
<CFFILE ACTION=action ATTRIBUTE=attribute
➥ATTRIBUTE=attribute ATTRIBUTE=attribute>
```

The attributes of the CFFILE tag can be set to multiple values that permit the behavior of the tag to be modified to fit your needs. Each of the attributes can be set dynamically using variables created using the CFSET tag, or the values of query or form fields. When using form fields, extreme care should be taken to ensure that security restrictions are in place to prevent malicious action as a result of dynamic file action. Table 25.1 indicates the attributes and the valid values permitted. Table 25.2 shows the various possible values for the NameConflict attribute, and the corresponding Cold Fusion actions that will occur based on those values.

Table 25.1 *CFFILE* Tag ACTION Attributes

ACTION	Attributes	Comments
APPEND	OUTPUT FILE	Writes the contents of the string specified in OUTPUT to the end of the file specified in FILE.
COPY	SOURCE DESTINATION	Copies file from location specified in SOURCE to location specified in DESTINATION.
DELETE	FILE	Deletes file specified in FILE attribute.
MOVE	SOURCE DESTINATION	Moves file from location specified in SOURCE to location specified in DESTINATION.
READ	FILE VARIABLE	Reads the contents of the file specified in FILE into the variable specified in VARIABLE. The VARIABLE is created if it does not exist.
RENAME	SOURCE DESTINATION	Renames file specified in SOURCE to the filename specified in DESTINATION.
UPLOAD	ACCEPT DESTINATION FILEFIELD NAMECONFLICT	Used to upload files to the server using the filename found in FILEFIELD from the form and resolves filename conflicts using the value of the NAMECONFLICT attribute.
WRITE	OUTPUT FILE	Writes the contents of the string specified as OUTPUT to the file specified in FILE. The file is overwritten if it exists.

Part IV

Ch 25

Table 25.2 Explanation of NAMECONFLICT Attribute

Value	Meaning
ERROR	Generates an error if the file specified already exists.
SKIP	Allows the problem file to be skipped. The file cannot be saved.
OVERWRITE	The file will be overwritten with a new file.
MAKEUNIQUE	Automatically generates a unique filename for the uploaded file.

Once a file is uploaded, or any other file manipulation operation is completed, information about the file is available in reference attributes of the file object. Similar to the URL, FORM, and CGI objects, the FILE object maintains status information about the most recent file operation completed or attempted. Attributes in the FILE object are referenced in the same manner as other variables (for example, #FILE.ContentType#). Table 25.3 identifies the attributes maintained and their meanings.

Table 25.3 File *Object* Attributes

Attribute	Explanation
AttemptedServerFile	Did Cold Fusion attempt to save the file? (Yes/No)
ClientDirectory	Client-side directory where the file was located.
ClientFile	Client-side filename (with extension).
ClientFileExt	Client-side filename extension without the period.
ClientFileName	Client-side filename (without extension).
ContentSubType	MIME content sub-type of file.
ContentType	MIME content type of file.
DateLastAccessed	Returns the date and time the uploaded file was last accessed.
FileExisted	Did a file with same name exist in the specified destination prior to upload, copy, or move? (Yes/No)
FileSize	Size of the uploaded file.
FileWasAppended	Was the file appended to an existing file by Cold Fusion? (Yes/No)
FileWasOverwritten	Was an existing file overwritten by Cold Fusion? (Yes/No)
FileWasRenamed	Was the uploaded file renamed to avoid a conflict? (Yes/No)
FileWasSaved	Was the file saved by Cold Fusion? (Yes/No)
OldFileSize	Size of the file that was overwritten during an upload operation. ServerDirectory Directory on server where file was saved.
ServerFile	Filename of the saved file.

Attribute	Explanation
ServerFileExt	Extension of the uploaded file without the period.
ServerFileName	Filename without extension of the uploaded file.
TimeCreated	Returns the time the uploaded file was created.
TimeLastModified	Returns the date and time of the last modification to the uploaded file.

Uploading Files Using the *CFFILE* Tag

The syntax of the CFFILE tag can be used with selected attributes in order to facilitate the uploading of files to the server. Prior to writing the HTML/CFML necessary to process a file upload, you must carefully examine a number of issues. First and foremost is security. The directory where the files will be uploaded must be secure from outside view, and the templates used to perform the file operations must be protected from unauthorized access. Because the threat of computer viruses is increasing, you must take precautions to protect your system from malicious users. The second issue to examine is the reason you are providing file operations to the users. Is it necessary? Can it be accomplished using other means?

Once you decide on CFFILE you can move on to the next step, which is preparing the user interface. This requires the development of an HTML form, either through writing static HTML, or by creating an HTML form using dynamic code generated using CFML. In either case, the structure of the form is basically the same. Listing 25.2 shows the HTML code necessary to create a form that prompts the user for a file to be uploaded to the server. The result of Listing 25.2 is shown in Figure 25.1. Listing 25.3 shows the form after a file has been selected for uploading.

Part

IV

Ch

25

On the CD

Listing 25.2   UPLOADFORM.HTML—HTML Form for File Upload Using the *CFFILE* Tag

```
<!-- This document was created with Cold Fusion Studio -->
<!DOCTYPE HTML PUBLIC "-//W3C//DTD HTML 3.2 Final//EN">

<HTML>
<HEAD>
<TITLE>CF 3.1 CFFILE Upload Demonstration - Example 1</TITLE>
</HEAD>
<BODY BGCOLOR=="#000000">
<CENTER>CF 3.1 CFFILE Upload Demonstration - Example 1</CENTER>
<HR>
<FORM ACTION="uploadfile.cfm" ENCTYPE="multipart/form-data" METHOD=POST>
File to upload: <INPUT NAME="FileName" SIZE=50 TYPE=FILE><BR>
<INPUT TYPE=SUBMIT VALUE="Upload the File">
</FORM>
</BODY>
</HTML>
```

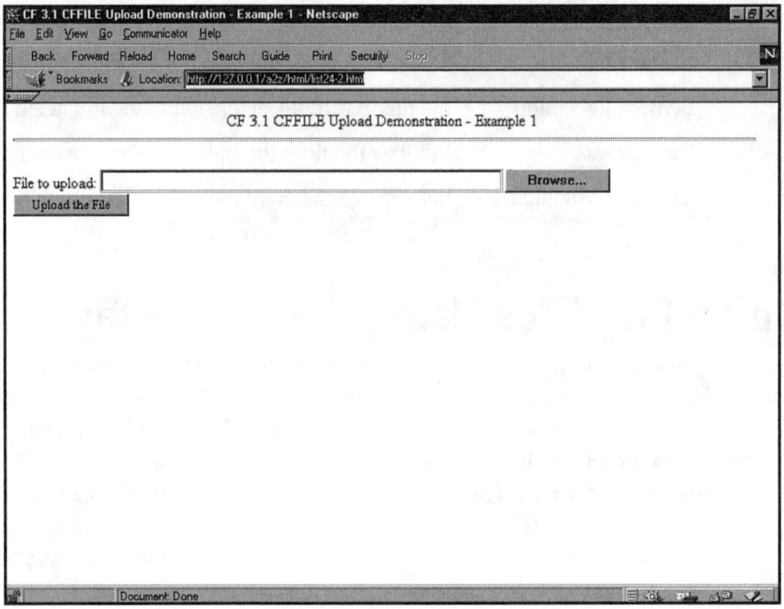

FIG. 25.1

Sample HTML form for file upload.

The primary difference between this form and a "standard" HTML form is the specification of the ENCTYPE value—"multipart/form-data"—which is necessary to process the uploaded file. A second difference is the addition of a new INPUT type called FILE, which tells the browser to process file selection using the standard user interface functionality of the underlying operating system. The ACTION attribute of the FORM tag identifies which Cold Fusion template will be used to process the file. The METHOD attribute is set to POST, which is required by Cold Fusion. Figure 25.2 shows the operating system file selection dialog box.

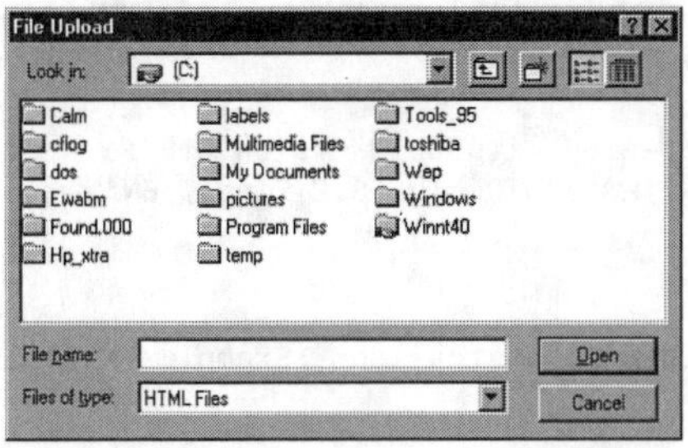

FIG. 25.2

Sample file selection dialog box.

The dialog box shown in Figure 25.2 is specific to the operating system that a browser is running on and will change from one operating system to another. Figure 25.3 shows the HTML form with the text box filled with the selected filename.

FIG. 25.3

Sample HTML form for file upload with selected filename.

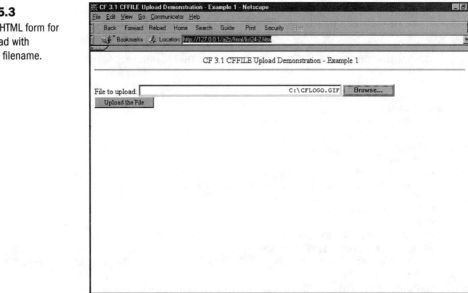

When this form is submitted, the ACTION attribute of the FORM tag causes the selected file to be uploaded. Listing 25.3 shows the CFML code required to process the uploaded file.

Listing 25.3 UPLOADFILE.CFM—CFML Code Required to Process an Uploaded File

```
<!--- This document was created with Cold Fusion Studio --->
<HTML>
<HEAD>
<TITLE>CF 3.1 CFFILE Tag File Upload Demonstration
➥Results - Example 1</TITLE>
</HEAD>
<BODY BGCOLOR="#FFFFFF"="white">
<CFFILE
DESTINATION="H:\website\uploads\"
ACTION="UPLOAD"
NAMECONFLICT="OVERWRITE"
FILEFIELD="FileName">
<CFOUTPUT>
<CENTER>
CF 3.1 CFFILE Tag File Upload Demonstration Results - Example 1<P>
File Upload was Successful! Information about the file is detailed below
</CENTER>
<HR>
<TABLE>
<CAPTION><B>File Information</B></CAPTION>
<TR>
```

continues

Part
IV

Ch
25

Listing 25.3 Continued

```
<TH VALIGN=top ALIGN=LEFT>File Name:</TH>
➥<TD>#File.ServerDirectory#\#FILE.ServerFile#</TD>
<TH VALIGN=top ALIGN=LEFT>Content Type:</TH><TD>#File.ContentType#</TD>
</TR>
<TR>
<TH VALIGN=top ALIGN=LEFT>Content SubType:</TH>
➥<TD>#File.ContentSubType#</TD>
<TH VALIGN=top ALIGN=LEFT>Client Path:</TH>
➥<TD>#File.ClientDirectory#</TD>
</TR>
<TR>
<TH VALIGN=top ALIGN=LEFT>Client File:</TH><TD>#File.ClientFile#</TD>
<TH VALIGN=top ALIGN=LEFT>Client FileName:</TH>
➥<TD>#File.ClientFileName#</TD>
</TR>
<TR>
<TH VALIGN=top ALIGN=LEFT>Client FileExt:</TH>
➥<TD>#File.ClientFileExt#</TD>
<TH VALIGN=top ALIGN=LEFT>Server Path:</TH><TD>#File.ServerDirectory#</TD>
</TR>
<TR>
<TH VALIGN=top ALIGN=LEFT>Server File:</TH><TD>#File.ServerFile#</TD>
<TH VALIGN=top ALIGN=LEFT>Server FileName:</TH>
➥<TD>#File.ServerFileName#</TD>
</TR>
<TR>
<TH VALIGN=top ALIGN=LEFT>Server FileExt:</TH>
➥<TD>#File.ServerFileExt#</TD>
<TH VALIGN=top ALIGN=LEFT>Attempted ServerFile:</TH>
➥<TD>#File.AttemptedServerFile#</TD>
</TR>
<TR>
<TH VALIGN=top ALIGN=LEFT>File Existed?</TH><TD>#File.FileExisted#</TD>
<TH VALIGN=top ALIGN=LEFT>File Was Saved?</TH><TD>#File.FileWasSaved#</TD>
</TR>
<TR>
<TH VALIGN=top ALIGN=LEFT>File Was Overwritten?</TH>
➥<TD>#File.FileWasOverWritten#</TD>
<TH VALIGN=top ALIGN=LEFT>File Was Appended?</TH>
➥<TD>#File.FileWasAppended#</TD>
</TR>
<TR>
<TH VALIGN=top ALIGN=LEFT>File Was Renamed?</TH>
➥<TD>#File.FileWasRenamed#</TD>
<TH VALIGN=top ALIGN=LEFT>File Size:</TH><TD>#File.Filesize#</TD></TH>
</TR>
<TR>
<TH VALIGN=top ALIGN=LEFT>Old File Size:</TH><TD>#File.OldFileSize#</TD>
<TH VALIGN=top align=LEFT>Date Last Accessed:</TH>
➥<TD>#DateFormat(File.DateLastAccessed,'DD MMM YY')#</TD>
</TR>
<TR>
```

```
<TH VALIGN=top align=LEFT>Date/Time Created:</TH>
➥<TD>#DateFormat(File.TimeCreated,'DD MMM YY')# #Timeformat(File.
➥TimeCreated,'HH:MM:SS')#</TD>
<TH VALIGN=top align=LEFT>Date/Time Modified:</TH>
➥<TD>#DateFormat(File.TimeLastModified,'DD MMM YY')
➥# #Timeformat(File.TimeLastModified,'HH:MM:SS')#</TD>
</TR>
</TABLE>
</CFOUTPUT>
</BODY>
</HTML>
```

The CFML template shown in Listing 25.3 processes the uploaded file, stores it in the directory indicated in the DESTINATION attribute of the CFFILE tag, and then prints out the contents of the attributes in the FILE object. Some of the FILE object attributes might not have values, depending on the attributes passed to the CFFILE tag. Figure 25.4 shows the output resulting from the file upload.

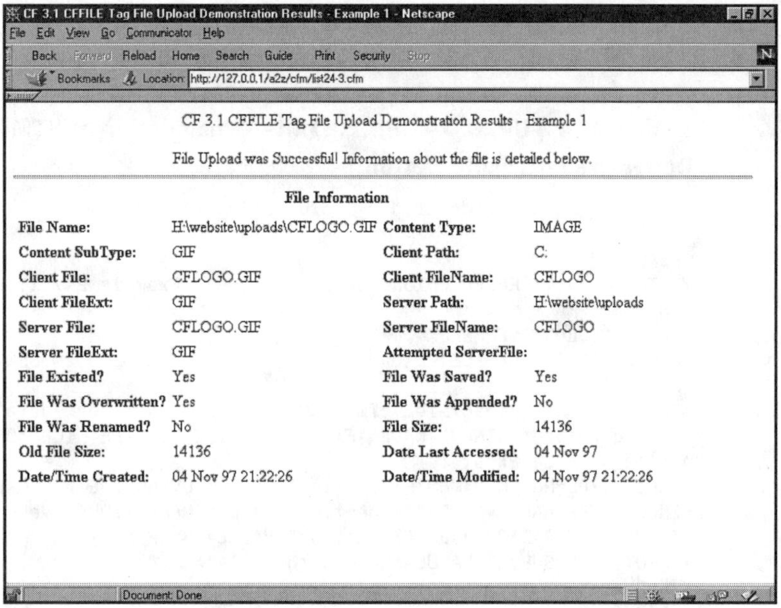

FIG. 25.4

Sample CFML output of uploaded file information.

CF 3.1 CFFILE Tag File Upload Demonstration Results - Example 1

File Upload was Successfull. Information about the file is detailed below.

File Information

File Name:	H:\website\uploads\CFLOGO.GIF	Content Type:	IMAGE
Content SubType:	GIF	Client Path:	C:
Client File:	CFLOGO.GIF	Client FileName:	CFLOGO
Client FileExt:	GIF	Server Path:	H:\website\uploads
Server File:	CFLOGO.GIF	Server FileName:	CFLOGO
Server FileExt:	GIF	Attempted ServerFile:	
File Existed?	Yes	File Was Saved?	Yes
File Was Overwritten?	Yes	File Was Appended?	No
File Was Renamed?	No	File Size:	14136
Old File Size:	14136	Date Last Accessed:	04 Nov 97
Date/Time Created:	04 Nov 97 21:22:26	Date/Time Modified:	04 Nov 97 21:22:26

Now take a look at the use of the CFFILE tag in Listing 25.3. Four of the attributes for the CFFILE tag were used:

```
<CFFILE
ACTION="UPLOAD"
DESTINATION="H:\website\uploads\"
NAMECONFLICT="OVERWRITE"
FILEFIELD="FileName">
```

Part
IV

Ch
25

The ACTION attribute is set to "UPLOAD". The DESTINATION attribute is set to the value "H:\website\uploads\", which is a directory created on a server specifically for storing uploaded files. The directory you choose can be anywhere on the server, provided the appropriate file access privileges (read, write, delete, and so on) are set. The NAMECONFLICT attribute is set to "OVERWRITE", indicating that Cold Fusion should overwrite the file if it finds a file with the same name in the destination directory. The last attribute set is the FILEFIELD attribute. Its value is "FileName", indicating the name of the field on the form from which the multipart/form-data containing the file data will be passed. The remaining code in the example uses attributes from the FORM object to show details about the selected file.

CAUTION

The trailing slash (\) in the destination directory name is required.

Listing 25.4 shows an example that builds on the HTML/CFML code you just wrote. to demonstrate the utilization of variables to set the various attributes of the CFFILE tag. The HTML form is modified by adding a radio button group that is used to set the NAMECONFLICT attribute in the CFFILE tag.

On the CD

Listing 25.4   UPLOADFORM2.HTML—Modification of HTML to Demonstrate Data-Driven Attribute Setting

```
<!-- This document created by Cold Fusion Studio -->
<HTML>
<HEAD>
<TITLE>CF 3.1 CFFILE Upload Demonstration - Example 2</TITLE>
</HEAD>
<BODY BGCOLOR="#FFFFFF"="">
<CENTER>CF 3.1 CFFILE Upload Demonstration - Example 2</CENTER>
<HR>
<FORM ACTION="uploadfile2.cfm" ENCTYPE="multipart/form-data" METHOD=POST>
File to upload: <INPUT NAME="FileName" SIZE=50 TYPE=FILE><BR>
Action if File Exists:
<INPUT TYPE=RADIO NAME="FileAction" VALUE="OVERWRITE" CHECKED>Overwrite
<INPUT TYPE=RADIO NAME="FileAction" VALUE="MAKEUNIQUE">Make Unique
<INPUT TYPE=RADIO NAME="FileAction" VALUE="SKIP">Skip
<INPUT TYPE=SUBMIT VALUE="Upload the File">
</FORM>
</BODY>
</HTML>
```

The radio group was added with the name of FileAction, which will be used in the template to identify the appropriate action to take if a duplicate file is detected. Figure 25.5 shows what the modified form looks like in the browser.

The CFML from Listing 25.3 has to be modified to specify the action to take when data is being passed to the template and a duplicate file exists. Listing 25.5 shows the modifications required.

FIG. 25.5
Modified file upload
form with radio buttons.

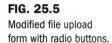

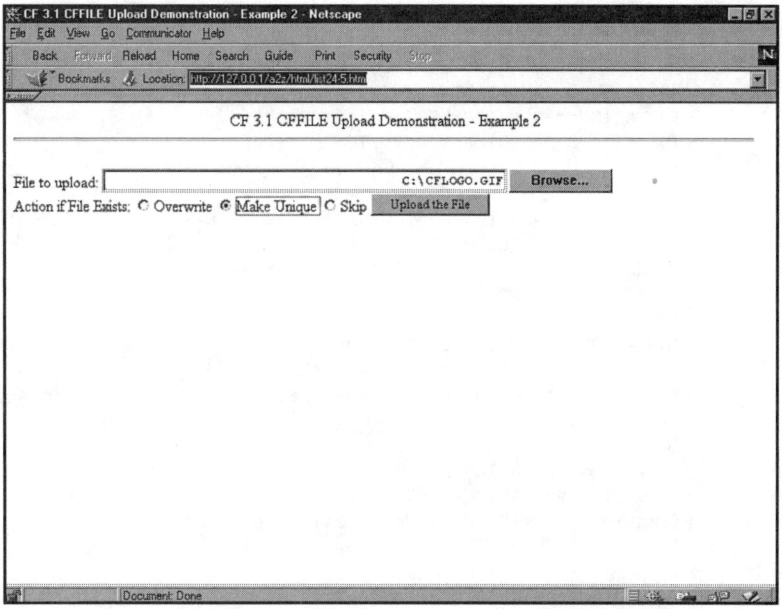

Listing 25.5   UPLOADFILE2.CFM—Modified CFML Code with Data-Driven Attribute Setting

```
<!--- This document was created with Cold Fusion Studio --->
<HTML>
<HEAD>
<TITLE>CF 3.1 CFFILE Tag File Upload Demonstration
➥Results - Example 2</TITLE>
</HEAD>
<BODY BGCOLOR="#FFFFFF">
<CFFILE
DESTINATION="H:\website\uploads\"
ACTION="UPLOAD"
NAMECONFLICT="#FORM.FILEACTION#"
FILEFIELD="FileName">
<CFOUTPUT>
<CENTER>
CF 3.1 CFFILE Tag File Upload Demonstration Results - Example 2<P>
File Upload was Successful! Information about the file is detailed below.
</CENTER>
<HR>
<TABLE>
<CAPTION><B>File Information</B></CAPTION>
<TR>
<TH VALIGN=top ALIGN=LEFT>File
Name:</TH><TD>#File.ServerDirectory#\#FILE.ServerFile#</TD>
<TH VALIGN=top ALIGN=LEFT>Content Type:</TH><TD>#File.ContentType#</TD>
</TR>
<TR>
```

continues

Part
IV
Ch
25

Listing 25.5   Continued

```
<TH VALIGN=top ALIGN=LEFT>Content SubType:</TH>
<TD>#File.ContentSubType#</TD>
<TH VALIGN=top ALIGN=LEFT>Client Path:</TH>
<TD>#File.ClientDirectory#</TD>
</TR>
<TR>
<TH VALIGN=top ALIGN=LEFT>Client File:</TH><TD>#File.ClientFile#</TD>
<TH VALIGN=top ALIGN=LEFT>Client
FileName:</TH><TD>#File.ClientFileName#</TD>
</TR>
<TR>
<TH VALIGN=top ALIGN=LEFT>Client
FileExt:</TH><TD>#File.ClientFileExt#</TD>
<TH VALIGN=top ALIGN=LEFT>Server Path:</TH><TD>#File.ServerDirectory#</TD>
</TR>
<TR>
<TH VALIGN=top ALIGN=LEFT>Server File:</TH><TD>#File.ServerFile#</TD>
<TH VALIGN=top ALIGN=LEFT>Server
FileName:</TH><TD>#File.ServerFileName#</TD>
</TR>
<TR>
<TH VALIGN=top ALIGN=LEFT>Server
FileExt:</TH><TD>#File.ServerFileExt#</TD>
<TH VALIGN=top ALIGN=LEFT>Attempted
ServerFile:</TH><TD>#File.AttemptedServerFile#</TD>
</TR>
<TR>
<TH VALIGN=top ALIGN=LEFT>File Existed?</TH><TD>#File.FileExisted#</TD>
<TH VALIGN=top ALIGN=LEFT>File Was Saved?</TH><TD>#File.FileWasSaved#</TD>
</TR>
<TR>
<TH VALIGN=top ALIGN=LEFT>File Was
Overwritten?</TH><TD>#File.FileWasOverWritten#</TD>
<TH VALIGN=top ALIGN=LEFT>File Was
Appended?</TH><TD>#File.FileWasAppended#</TD>
</TR>
<TR>
<TH VALIGN=top ALIGN=LEFT>File Was
Renamed?</TH><TD>#File.FileWasRenamed#</TD>
<TH VALIGN=top ALIGN=LEFT>File Size:</TH><TD>#File.Filesize#</TD></TH>
</TR>
<TR>
<TH VALIGN=top ALIGN=LEFT>Old File Size:</TH><TD>#File.OldFileSize#</TD>
<TH VALIGN=top align=LEFT>Date Last
Accessed:</TH><TD>#DateFormat(File.DateLastAccessed,'DD MMM YY')#</TD>
</TR>
<TR>
<TH VALIGN=top align=LEFT>Date/Time
Created:</TH><TD>#DateFormat(File.TimeCreated,'DD MMM YY')#
#Timeformat(File.TimeCreated,'HH:MM:SS')#</TD>
<TH VALIGN=top align=LEFT>Date/Time
Modified:</TH><TD>#DateFormat(File.TimeLastModified,'DD MMM YY')#
```

```
#Timeformat(File.TimeLastModified,'HH:MM:SS')#</TD>
</TR>
</TABLE>
</CFOUTPUT>
</BODY>
</HTML>
```

Note that in the example shown in Figure 25.5, the radio button marked "Make Unique" was checked. This caused the CFML to dynamically change its behavior. Because in the first example you uploaded `"cflogo.gif"` to the server, the result of submitting the same file again (with the make unique parameter) is that the server is forced to create a unique name for the file when it is uploaded again. Figure 25.6 shows the results, with the new file name "ACF16.GIF" and the fact that the `FILE.FileWasRenamed` variable was set to "Yes."

FIG. 25.6
Sample output with user-specified NAMECONFLICT attribute.

Part
IV

Ch
25

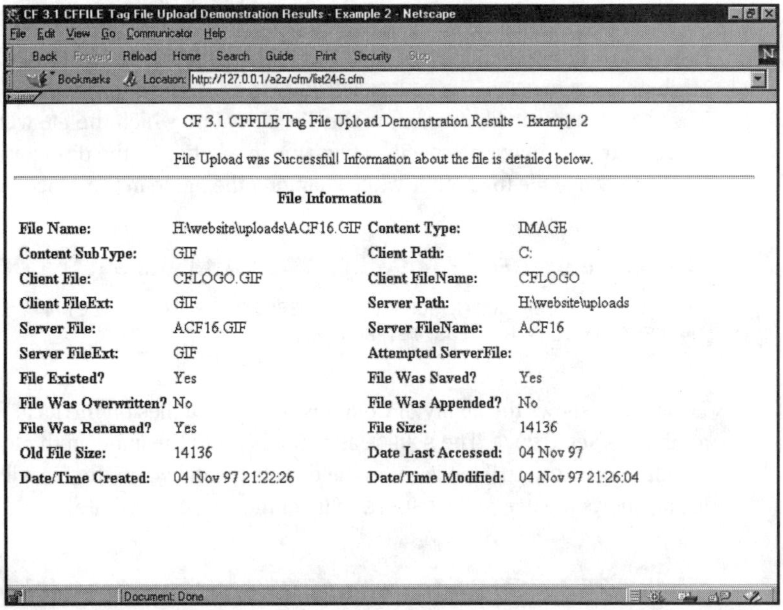

The `CFFILE` tag in this example used data passed from the form in the `FileAction` field to set the value of the `NAMECONFLICT` attribute. The field was referenced in the `CFFILE` tag as follows:

`NAMECONFLICT="#FORM.FILEACTION#"`

Any of the other attributes can also be set using `CFSET` variables, `FORM` attributes, or `URL` attributes. Note, however, that setting the `SOURCE` or `DESTINATION` attributes based on user input can have far reaching consequences. For security reasons, users should not be permitted to specify `SOURCE` or `DESTINATION` attributes using `TEXT` input fields. The `SOURCE` and `DESTINATION` attributes should only be set using template-based code, which is conditionally executed, to provide maximum security.

Accessing the Local File System with *CFFILE*

The CFFILE tag provides the ability to perform local file operations such as COPY, MOVE, and DELETE. Local in this example means local to the HTTP server, not local to the client. These actions have the potential for causing severe damage to the file system, therefore security considerations should be evaluated carefully before developing Cold Fusion templates which provide the ability to COPY, MOVE, or DELETE files.

N O T E Security measures can vary by operating system and from one web server to another. Consult documentation specific to the configuration of your web server for detailed information about security issues. ▓

To provide local file access, the CFFILE tag is used with the ACTION attribute set to COPY, MOVE, or DELETE. In the case of the DELETE action value, the DESTINATION attribute is not required. In all other cases the DESTINATION attribute is required.

Listing 25.6 shows the ability of Cold Fusion to copy files on the local file system. The ACTION attribute is set to COPY. The SOURCE attribute is set to the name of the file that is to be copied. The DESTINATION attribute is set to the directory into which the file will be copied. The DESTINATION attribute may also specify a filename in addition to the directory name, which allows you to copy one file to another while changing the name in the process.

Listing 25.6   *CFFILE* Tag with *ACTION* Attribute Set to *COPY*

```
<CFFILE ACTION="COPY" SOURCE="H:\WEBSITE\UPLOADS\FILE1.TXT"
➡ DESTINATION="H:\WEBSITE\PROCESS\">
```

Listing 25.7 shows the ability of Cold Fusion to move files on the local file system. The ACTION attribute is set to MOVE. The SOURCE attribute is set to the name of the file that is to be moved. The DESTINATION attribute is set to the directory into which the file will be moved. The next listing shows the use of the DELETE value of the ACTION attribute.

Listing 25.7   *CFFILE* Tag with *ACTION* Attribute Set to *MOVE*

```
<CFFILE ACTION="MOVE" SOURCE="H:\WEBSITE\UPLOADS\FILE2.TXT"
➡DESTINATION="H:\WEBSITE\PROCESS\">
```

In Listing 25.8, the ACTION attribute is set to DELETE. The FILE attribute is set to the name of the file you are going to delete. The DESTINATION attribute is not used when the ACTION attribute is set to DELETE.

Listing 25.8   *CFFILE* Tag with *ACTION* Attribute Set to *DELETE*

```
<CFFILE ACTION="DELETE" FILE="H:\WEBSITE\UPLOADS\FILE3.TXT">
```

CAUTION

Use the DELETE action carefully. Access to templates that delete files should be carefully restricted.

Now that you have seen the CFFILE tag used in simple examples, you can move on to modify the example application to add file upload capabilities. You will accomplish this by creating three CFML templates for the purposes of uploading an employee photo to the server, and updating the employee record to reflect the location of the photo. The first template will provide a list of employees from which to pick. The second template will prompt you for the name of the file containing the photo. The third template will actually accept the file and update the employee record. You will start by creating the template to provide the employee list, which is shown in Listing 25.9.

Listing 25.9   EMPLOYEE_PHOTO1.CFM—Employee Listing Template

```
<CFQUERY DATASOURCE="A2Z" NAME="Employees">
SELECT FirstName, LastName, EmployeeId FROM Employees
     ORDER BY LastName, FirstName
</CFQUERY>

<HTML>

<HEAD>
<TITLE>Maintain Employee Photos</TITLE>
</HEAD>

<BODY BGCOLOR="#FFFFFF">

<H1>Maintain Employee Photos</H1>
<HR>
<H3>Click on Employee Name to Add Employee Photo</H3>
<TABLE BORDER>
<TR>
<TH>Name</TH>
<TH>ID</TH>
</TR>
<CFOUTPUT QUERY="Employees">
<TR>
<TD><A HREF="employee_photo2.cfm?EmployeeId=#EmployeeId#">
➥#LastName#, #FirstName#</A></TD>
<TD>#NumberFormat(EmployeeId,'0000')#</TD>
</TR>
</CFOUTPUT>
</TABLE>
</BODY>
</HTML>
```

Figure 25.7 shows what the screen looks like using the template created in Listing 25.9. This template selects a list of employees from the Employees table, and presents a table to select an employee for photo processing.

Part
IV
Ch
25

FIG. 25.7
Employee photo
maintenance list.

FIG. 25.7
Employee photo
maintenance list.

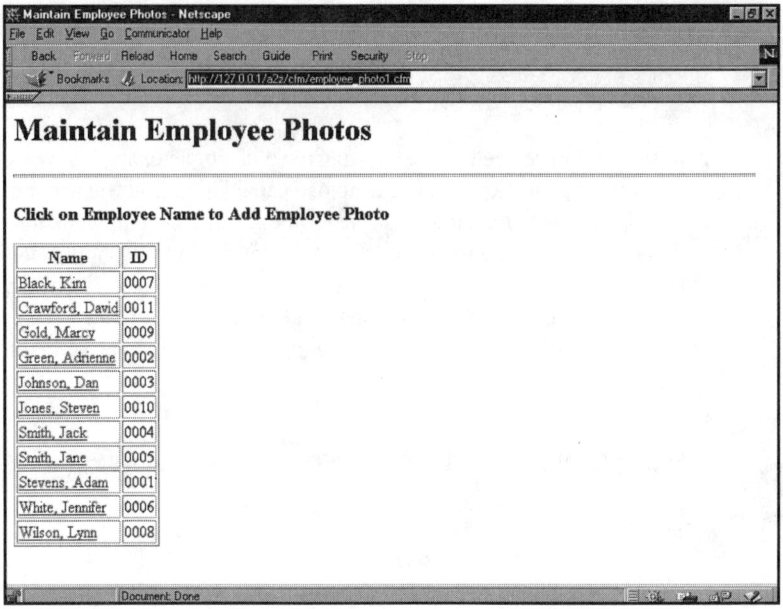

For each employee in the Employees table, a link is created to another template where the photo information can be added or updated. Listing 25.10 shows the CFML code used to create the form necessary to upload the file to the server.

Listing 25.10   EMPLOYEE_PHOTO2.CFM—Employee Photo Maintenance Form

```
<CFQUERY NAME="Employee" DATASOURCE="A2Z">
SELECT LastName,FirstName,EmployeeId from Employees where
EmployeeId=#URL.EmployeeId#
</CFQUERY>

<HTML>
<TITLE>Employee Photo Maintenance Form</TITLE>
<BODY BGCOLOR="#FFFFFF">
<CENTER>Employee Photo Maintenance Form</CENTER>
<HR>
<FORM ACTION="employee_photo3.cfm"
ENCTYPE="multipart/form-data"
METHOD=POST>
<CFOUTPUT>
<INPUT TYPE="hidden" NAME="EmployeeId" VALUE=#Employee.EmployeeId#>
<B>
Employee ID: #NumberFormat(Employee.EmployeeId,'0000')#<BR>
Name: #Employee.LastName#, #Employee.FirstName#<BR>
</B>
</CFOUTPUT>
<BR>
```

```
Photo File to upload: <INPUT NAME="PhotoFile" SIZE=50 TYPE=FILE><BR>
<INPUT TYPE=SUBMIT VALUE="Upload the Photo">
</FORM>
</BODY>
</HTML>
```

This template is a simple modification of the first file upload template that you wrote. Figure 25.8 shows what this template would look like. The value of the employee number is retrieved from the URL.EmployeeId variable and used to retrieve the employee's name from the Employees table.

The employee name and employee number is displayed with leading zeros using the NumberFormat function. A file selection box is also displayed. The button labeled "Upload the Photo" will cause the browser to upload the file to the server where it will be processed by the template in Listing 25.11.

FIG. 25.8

Employee photo upload form.

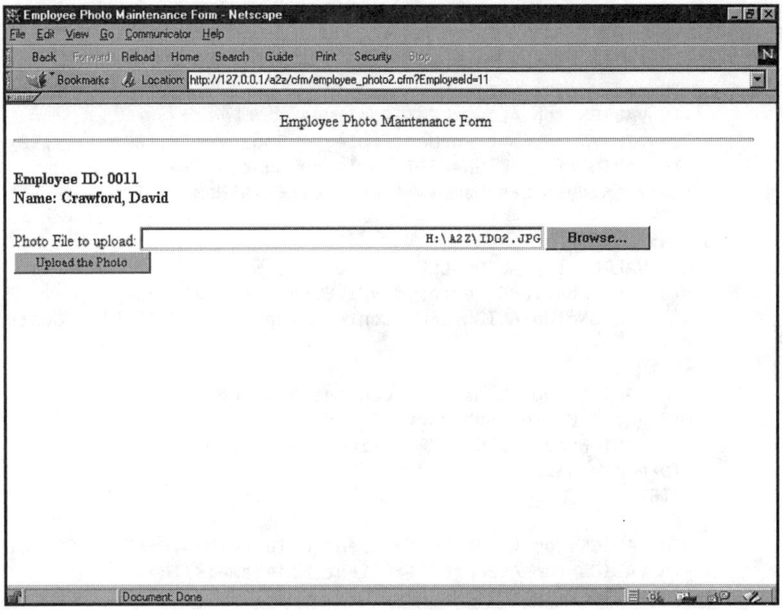

Part
IV

Ch
25

Listing 25.11 \A2Z\CFM\EMPLOYEE_PHOTO3.CFM—Employee Photo Upload Process Template

```
<CFQUERY NAME="Employee" DATASOURCE="A2Z">
SELECT LastName,FirstName,EmployeeId from Employees
➥where EmployeeId=#Form.EmployeeId#
</CFQUERY>
```

continues

Listing 25.11 Continued

```
<HTML>
<TITLE>A2Z Employee Photo Upload Results</TITLE>
<BODY BGCOLOR="#FFFFFF">
<CFFILE
DESTINATION="H:\a2z\employee\photos\"
ACTION="UPLOAD"
NAMECONFLICT="OVERWRITE"
FILEFIELD="PhotoFile"
ACCEPT="image/gif,image/jpeg">
<CFQUERY NAME="UPDATE_EMP" DATASOURCE="A2Z">
UPDATE Employees
SET Photo = '#FILE.ServerDirectory#\#FILE.ServerFile#'
WHERE EmployeeId=#FORM.EmployeeId#
</CFQUERY>
<CFOUTPUT>
Employee Photo File Upload was Successful!
Information about the file is detailed below.
<HR>
<TABLE>
<CAPTION><B>Photo Information</B></CAPTION>
<TR>
<TH VALIGN=top ALIGN=LEFT>Employee
Id:</TH><TD>#NumberFormat(Employee.EmployeeId,'0000')#</TD>
<TH VALIGN=top ALIGN=LEFT>Employee Name:</TH>
<TD>#Employee.LastName#, #Employee.FirstName#</TD>
</TR>
<TR>
<TH VALIGN=top ALIGN=LEFT>Photo File Name:</TH>
<TD>#File.ServerDirectory#\#FILE.ServerFile#</TD>
<TH VALIGN=top ALIGN=LEFT>Content Type:</TH><TD>#File.ContentType#</TD>
</TR>
<TR>
<TH VALIGN=top ALIGN=LEFT>Content SubType:</TH>
<TD>#File.ContentSubType#</TD>
<TH VALIGN=top ALIGN=LEFT>Client Path:</TH>
<TD>#File.ClientDirectory#</TD>
</TR>
<TR>
<TH VALIGN=top ALIGN=LEFT>Client File:</TH><TD>#File.ClientFile#</TD>
<TH VALIGN=top ALIGN=LEFT>Client FileName:</TH>
<TD>#File.ClientFileName#</TD>
</TR>
<TR>
<TH VALIGN=top ALIGN=LEFT>Client FileExt:</TH>
<TD>#File.ClientFileExt#</TD>
<TH VALIGN=top ALIGN=LEFT>Server Path:</TH><TD>#File.ServerDirectory#</TD>
</TR>
<TR>
<TH VALIGN=top ALIGN=LEFT>Server File:</TH><TD>#File.ServerFile#</TD>
<TH VALIGN=top ALIGN=LEFT>Server FileName:</TH>
<TD>#File.ServerFileName#</TD>
</TR>
```

```
<TR>
<TH VALIGN=top ALIGN=LEFT>Server FileExt:</TH>
<TD>#File.ServerFileExt#</TD>
<TH VALIGN=top ALIGN=LEFT>Attempted ServerFile:</TH>
<TD>#File.AttemptedServerFile#</TD>
</TR>
<TR>
<TH VALIGN=top ALIGN=LEFT>File Existed?</TH><TD>#File.FileExisted#</TD>
<TH VALIGN=top ALIGN=LEFT>File Was Saved?</TH><TD>#File.FileWasSaved#</TD>
</TR>
<TR>
<TH VALIGN=top ALIGN=LEFT>File Was Overwritten?</TH>
<TD>#File.FileWasOverWritten#</TD>
<TH VALIGN=top ALIGN=LEFT>File Was Appended?</TH>
<TD>#File.FileWasAppended#</TD>
</TR>
<TR>
<TH VALIGN=top ALIGN=LEFT>File Was Renamed?</TH>
<TD>#File.FileWasRenamed#</TD>
<TH VALIGN=top ALIGN=LEFT>File Size:</TH><TD>#File.Filesize#</TD></TH>
</TR>
<TR>
<TH VALIGN=top ALIGN=LEFT>Old File Size:</TH><TD>#File.OldFileSize#</TD>
<TH VALIGN=top align=LEFT>Date Last Accessed:</TH>
<TD>#DateFormat(File.DateLastAccessed,'DD MMM YY')#</TD>
</TR>
<TR>
<TH VALIGN=top align=LEFT>Date/Time Created:</TH>
<TD>#DateFormat(File.TimeCreated,'DD MMM YY')#
#Timeformat(File.TimeCreated,'HH:MM:SS')#</TD>
<TH VALIGN=top align=LEFT>Date/Time Modified:</TH>
<TD>#DateFormat(File.TimeLastModified,'DD MMM YY')#
#Timeformat(File.TimeLastModified,'HH:MM:SS')#</TD>
</TR>
</TABLE>
</CFOUTPUT>
</BODY>
</HTML>
```

Figure 25.9 shows the screen results. The template you just completed processes the uploaded file and stores it in the specified directory. It also updates the employee record to indicate that an employee photo is on file. The ACCEPT attribute of the CFFILE tag is set to only allow GIF and JPEG images to be uploaded to the server.

Make sure that your Employee table has a field called photo, which is a character string at least 65 characters long.

Employee Photo File Upload was Successful! Information about the file is detailed below.

Photo Information

Employee Id:	0011	Employee Name:	Crawford, David
Photo File Name:	H:\a2z\employee\photos\ID02.JPG	Content Type:	IMAGE
Content SubType:	JPEG	Client Path:	H:\A2Z
Client File:	ID02.JPG	Client FileName:	ID02
Client FileExt:	JPG	Server Path:	H:\a2z\employee\photos
Server File:	ID02.JPG	Server FileName:	ID02
Server FileExt:	JPG	Attempted ServerFile:	
File Existed?	Yes	File Was Saved?	Yes
File Was Overwritten?	Yes	File Was Appended?	No
File Was Renamed?	No	File Size:	10358
Old File Size:	10358	Date Last Accessed:	13 Oct 97
Date/Time Created:	12 Oct 97 18:52:19	Date/Time Modified:	13 Oct 97 20:06:08

Reading and Writing Files with *CFFILE*

You have now demonstrated the capabilities of CFFILE to upload a file to the server, as well as to manipulate files on the local file system by moving, copying, deleting, or renaming them. The last piece of the puzzle is to demonstrate the capability of CFFILE to read and write ASCII files using the CFFILE tag. This capability, combined with other constructs available in Cold Fusion—such as the ability to loop over the results of a query and the ability to evaluate expressions, provides a powerful tool to developers. The next simple example will highlight the ability to read and write files.

In order to demonstrate the capability to read and write files, you will write a template that will query the Employees table and write out an ASCII file containing the following items:

- The name of the employee
- The employee ID
- The name of the file where the employee's photo is maintained, if it is present

The template will then read the file into a variable and display it in the browser window. Listing 25.12 shows the code necessary to accomplish these tasks.

On the CD

Listing 25.12 READWRITE.CFM—Read and Write an ASCII File Using *CFFILE*

```
<!-- This document was created with Cold Fusion Studio -->
<!DOCTYPE HTML PUBLIC "-//W3C//DTD HTML 3.2 Final//EN">
<CFQUERY NAME="EMPLOYEE" DATASOURCE="A2Z">
select LastName,FirstName,EmployeeId,photo from Employees
```

```
</CFQUERY>
<!--- Setup variables to be used in writing the file --->
<!--- Variable to hold output string --->
<CFSET TXTOUTPUT = "">
<!--- File Name to write string into --->
<CFSET OUTFILE = "h:\a2z\employee\photolist.txt">

<CFIF #FileExists(OUTFILE)# is "Yes">
    <CFFILE ACTION="DELETE" FILE="#OUTFILE#">
</CFIF>
<CFLOOP QUERY="EMPLOYEE">
    <CFSET TXTOUTPUT = '"#LASTNAME#","#FIRSTNAME#","
➥#NumberFormat(EMPLOYEEID,'0000')#","#PHOTO#"'>
    <CFIF #FileExists(OUTFILE)# is "No">
        <CFFILE ACTION="WRITE" FILE="#OUTFILE#" OUTPUT="#TXTOUTPUT#">
    <CFELSE>
        <CFFILE ACTION="APPEND" FILE="#OUTFILE#" OUTPUT="#TXTOUTPUT#">
    </CFIF>
</CFLOOP>
<CFFILE ACTION="READ" FILE="#OUTFILE#" VARIABLE="TXTINPUT">

<HTML>
<HEAD>
        <TITLE>CF 3.1 CFFILE Read/Write Demonstration</TITLE>
</HEAD>

<BODY BGCOLOR="#FFFFFF">
<CFOUTPUT>
The contents of the query where written into
➥the file located at #OUTFILE#.<P>
The contents of the file are shown below:
<HR>
<PRE>
#TXTINPUT#
</PRE>
</CFOUTPUT>
</BODY>
</HTML>
```

Figure 25.10 shows the output from the template you just created. The code in the template created a comma-delimited ASCII file containing the LastName, FirstName, EmployeeId, and photo fields from the Employees table.

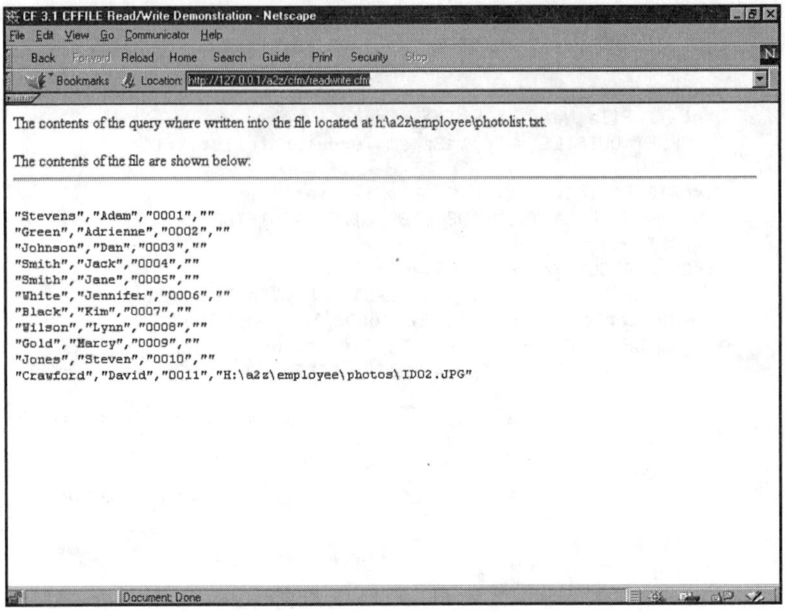

FIG. 25.10
Output from the read/ write demonstration template.

Take a closer look at this template to see what makes it tick. The first part of the template runs a simple query, which selects a number of fields from the Employees table. The following lines are responsible for the query:

```
<CFQUERY NAME="EMPLOYEE" DATASOURCE="A2Z">
select LastName,FirstName,EmployeeId,photo from Employees
</CFQUERY>
```

The next few lines of code set up a number of variables that will be used to pass values to the CFFILE tag. In the following code, the comments indicate what the variables are to be used for:

```
<!--- Setup variables to be used in writing the file --->
<!--- Variable to hold output string --->
<CFSET TXTOUTPUT = "">
<!--- File Name to write string into --->
<CFSET OUTFILE = "h:\a2z\employee\photolist.txt">
```

After setting up the variables you use the FileExists function to determine if the output file you want to create exists on the disk. If it does, you use the CFFILE tag with the DELETE action to remove it before proceeding, as shown in the following:

```
<CFIF #FileExists(OUTFILE)# is "Yes">
        <CFFILE ACTION="DELETE" FILE="#OUTFILE#">
</CFIF>
```

The next few lines of code perform the meat of the work in this template. Using the CFLOOP tag to process each record in the result set from your query, a text variable is set with the values of the fields, separated by commas and enclosed in quotation marks. This following code results in a comma-delimited file when you are all done.

```
<CFLOOP QUERY="EMPLOYEE">
    <CFSET TXTOUTPUT = '"#LASTNAME#","#FIRSTNAME#","
➥#NumberFormat(EMPLOYEEID,'0000')#","#PHOTO#"'>
    <CFIF #FileExists(OUTFILE)# is "No">
        <CFFILE ACTION="WRITE" FILE="#OUTFILE#" OUTPUT="#TXTOUTPUT#">
    <CFELSE>
        <CFFILE ACTION="APPEND" FILE="#OUTFILE#" OUTPUT="#TXTOUTPUT#">
    </CFIF>
</CFLOOP>
```

The CFFILE tag is executed within the loop, and its behavior is changed depending on the existence of the output file specified in the variable #OUTFILE#. If it does not exist (which is true for the first iteration of the loop), the ACTION attribute of the CFFILE tag is set to "WRITE", which will create the file and write the contents of the #TXTOUTPUT# variable into the file. On the remaining iterations through the loop, because the file exists, the ACTION attribute is set to "AP-PEND" which results in the value of the #TXTOUTPUT# variable being written to the end of the file.

The last few lines of the template are used to read the contents of the file you created into a variable and then display the contents in the browser window. This is accomplished by setting the ACTION attribute of the CFFILE tag to "READ" and specifying the name of the variable where the file contents will be stored, as done in the following:

```
<CFFILE ACTION="READ" FILE="#OUTFILE#" VARIABLE="TXTINPUT">

<HTML>
<HEAD>
        <TITLE>CF 3.1 CFFILE Read/Write Demonstration</TITLE>
</HEAD>

<BODY BGCOLOR="#FFFFFF">
<CFOUTPUT>
The contents of the query where written
into the file located at #OUTFILE#.<P>
The contents of the file are shown below:
<HR>
<PRE>
#TXTINPUT#
</PRE>
</CFOUTPUT>
</BODY>
</HTML
```

Full-Text Searching with Verity

by Nate Weiss

Getting to Know Verity

By now, you're convinced that Cold Fusion is the greatest package on the planet for publishing database data to the web. But you haven't really covered how to put together that most popular of web-based applications: the search engine. The success of Yahoo!, Excite, and the like have made the concept of a web-based search tool nearly as ubiquitous on the Internet as the word "ubiquitous" itself. For an increasing number of sites, an intelligent search tool is a must-have. This chapter will show how to integrate the Verity Search97 engine into your Cold Fusion applications.

Verity's Search97 technology—which is included and integrated with Cold Fusion 3.1—is a high-performance search engine that is built specifically for searching text. It excels at finding words in large chunks of "unstructured" text, such as the documents that human beings tend to write. As a developer, you tell it what to search—and what to search for—and it faithfully tries to find it.

Verity can search a variety of files in a variety of languages, and it does all the fancy stuff you'd expect from a sophisticated search engine, such as handling ANDs, ORs, wildcards, and so on. If you've ever used the search interface provided by LEXIS/NEXIS, you can expect the same kind of functionality from your own applications that use Verity.

Conceptually, the Verity layer you'll be learning about in this chapter is a lot like the ODBC/SQL layer that you've learned so much about elsewhere in this book. The main difference is that where ODBC and SQL excel at accessing neat rows and columns of information in structured database tables, Verity excels at accessing "messy" chunks of text, strewn about in various folders on your hard drives.

Most of the inner workings of the Verity engine are thoughtfully hidden from Cold Fusion developers. All you need to be concerned with is creating collections of documents with the Cold Fusion Administrator and including the CFINDEX and CFSEARCH tags in our Cold Fusion templates.

N O T E   When I use the word "Verity" in this chapter, I am really referring to Cold Fusion's integration with a piece of technology called Search97, which is made by a company called Verity. Just as people tend to say "Netscape" when they are really referring to the program called Navigator which is made by Netscape Communications Corp., Cold Fusion developers tend to just say "Verity" when they are talking about putting together full-text search applications. ■

You may not have realized it yet, but you probably already have a Verity-based application running on your server. Unless you chose *not* to install the documentation files when you installed Cold Fusion, full online documentation was installed for you in the CFDOCS folder, directly off your webserver's root directory. As you can see in Figure 26.11, the documentation has a handy search tool. The search tool uses the same Verity functionality that you'll learn about in this chapter.

FIG. 26.1

The search tool for the Cold Fusion online documentation uses Verity to carry out its searches.

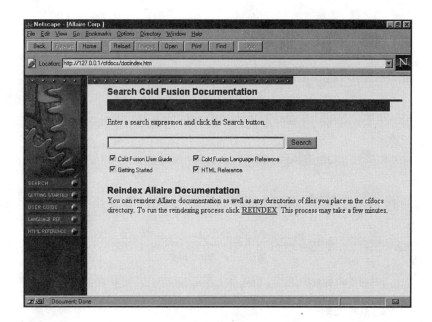

 TIP Check out your Cold Fusion documentation's search tool anytime at (localhost is the name or IP address of your computer):

http://localhost/CFDOCS/docindex.htm

Searching for Different Types of Files with Verity

Cold Fusion's Verity functionality supports a wide variety of file types, including "native" files such as documents produced with many of the Microsoft Office applications. This provides great flexibility when it comes to making files searchable via a web browser.

For instance, in an intranet situation, employees can continue to use the word-processing and spreadsheet applications they use everyday. All they have to do is save the documents in a folder tree that is indexed by a Verity collection. With literally a few lines of code, you can turn those documents into a fully searchable company library. Table 26.1 shows the different types of files that Verity can index and search.

NOTE Support for searching binary file formats (word processor, spreadsheet, and other "native" types of files) is new for Cold Fusion 3.1. Version 3.0 supported only plain-text files (which included HTML files). ■

Part
IV
Ch
26

Table 26.1 File Types that Verity Can Index and Search		
Category	**File Type**	**Limited to Versions**
Word Processing	Lotus AMI Pro	2.x, 3.0, 3.1
	WordPerfect	DOS: 5.0, 5.1, 6.0x, 6.1, 7.0
		Windows: 5.1, 5.2, 6.0x, 6.1, 7.0
		Macintosh: 2.0, 2.1, 3.0–3.5
	Microsoft Word	Windows: 2.0, 6.0, 95 (7.0), 97
		DOS: 4.x, 5.x 6.x
		Macintosh: 4.0, 5.0, 6.0
	WordPad	
	Write for Windows	
Spreadsheets	1-2-3	DOS, Windows: 2.0, 3.0, 4.0, 5.0
		OS/2: Release 2
	Microsoft Excel	Windows: 3.0, 4.0, 5.0, 95 (7.0), 97
		Macintosh: 3.0, 4.0
Text-Based Files	HTML	
	Plain Text	
	Rich Text Format (RTF)	1.x, 2.0
	ASCII and ANSI Text	
	Acrobat PDF files	
Other	Microsoft PowerPoint	Windows: 95 (7.0), 97

N O T E I use the term "document files" whenever I'm talking about files that are being indexed with Verity. As you can see, Verity can handle 1-2-3 spreadsheets, PowerPoint presentations, and so on. When I say "document files," I really mean any word processor, spreadsheet, or other file type listed in Table 26.1. ■

T I P Different file types can be freely mixed and matched in a Verity collection. Don't worry about keeping the HTML and Word files in separate folders or collections. Store them wherever you want.

Integrating Cold Fusion with Other Search Engines

Including Verity functionality is a terrific way to add search capability to your application, making it behave somewhat like a mini-Yahoo! or mini-AltaVista. However, it has nothing to do with actually "integrating" with Yahoo!, AltaVista, or any other commercial search engines. If you want to "integrate" with one of these search engines, you certainly can include standard HREF links from your application to a commercial search engine—but doing so really has nothing to do with the Verity functionality explained in this chapter.

You could also place a search form on one of your pages that has an appropriate URL (within the commercial search engine's domain) as the form's ACTION parameter. Many of the commercial search engines have instructions about how to set this up—such as what to name the form <INPUT> tags, for instance. See their sites for details.

Finally, you could use the <CFHTTP> tag to place a search request to a commercial search engine and display the results on your page with the #CFHTTP.FileContent# variable. See Chapter 30, "Interfacing with HTTP and FTP Using *CFHTTP* and *CFFTP*," for more details about using this extremely flexible tag.

Creating a Search Tool for Your Documents

Say that A2Z's Human Resources department wants to make the company's personnel policies available online so that employees can see what they are allowed to do (and not do) at any time.

The documents are saved as various Word, plain text, and Excel files. Collect all the documents together into a folder on your webserver's local drive. Now explore what will be necessary to make these documents searchable and retrievable from a web browser using Cold Fusion's Verity functionality as the "back end." It's really pretty simple.

N O T E   If you want to follow along with the examples in this section exactly, make a copy of the folder named HR from this chapter's directory on the CD-ROM. Place the folder directly off your webserver's document root, or you can use any random folder of your own documents that you like. Just make sure that the folder is accessible to your webserver. ▇

Part
IV

Ch
26

Creating a New Collection for the Documents

Verity's search functionality centers around a concept of a collection. A Verity *collection* is, quite simply, a mass of documents you want Verity to keep track of and make searchable.

Once Verity has been told which documents belong to a collection, it can index the documents and compile *meta-data* about them for its own use. This allows it to answer questions about your documents quickly, without actually parsing through them line-by-line at run-time. So, conceptually, the key to Verity's strength is its ability to invest a certain amount of time up front to indexing and compiling information about your documents. You get the payoff on that investment when your users are running their searches, because Verity has already "studied" the documents and can therefore return information about them very quickly.

Again, you may find it useful to think of Verity collections as being the full-text search equivalent of ODBC datasources. Just as you need to set up an ODBC datasource before you can use CFQUERY to retrieve data with SQL, you need to set up a collection before you can get started with Verity. And just as with setting up a new ODBC datasource, the place you go to set up a new collection is the Cold Fusion Administrator.

Creating a New Verity Collection

To set up a new collection, go to the Cold Fusion Administrator and click the Verity tab, as shown in Figure 26.2.

You'll probably notice right away that a document collection named CFDocumentation is already created and visible. This is the collection that represents the Cold Fusion documentation, which, as I explained earlier, uses the Verity engine for its little search interface.

FIG. 26.2

All collections on your server are shown on the Verity page of the Cold Fusion Administrator.

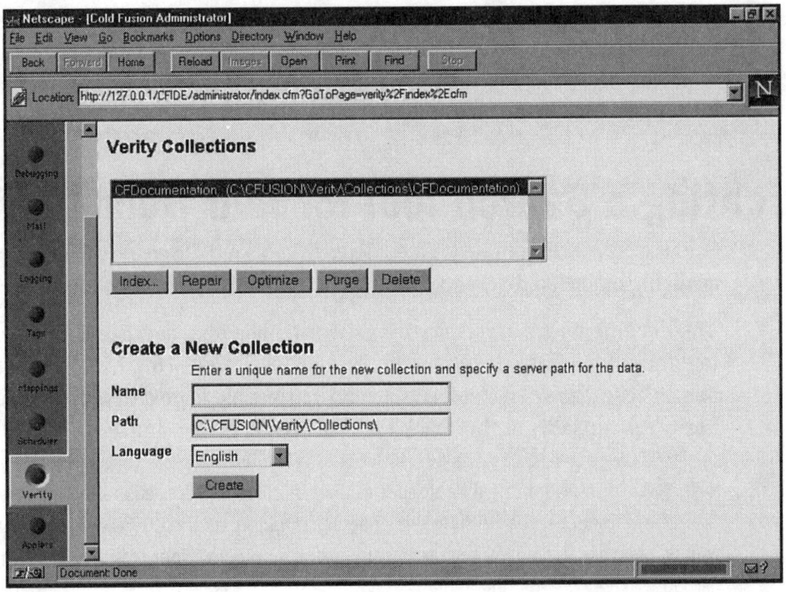

Now you'll create the Verity collection that your Human Resources documents will belong to. Under the Create a New Collection heading, type **HRDocs** for the Name of the new collection.

You can change the Path if you want the collection to be stored in a different location than the default, but you might as well use the default unless you have a specific reason not to (such as drive space or file-permissions issues).

When you're done filling in the blanks, click the Create button (see Figure 26.3). After a moment, your new collection will appear in the list at the top of the page, right along with the predefined CFDocumentation collection.

N O T E The path you fill in when creating a new collection is simply where the Verity's internal data about your documents will be kept. You don't have to point to the path to where the actual documents are at this point. ■

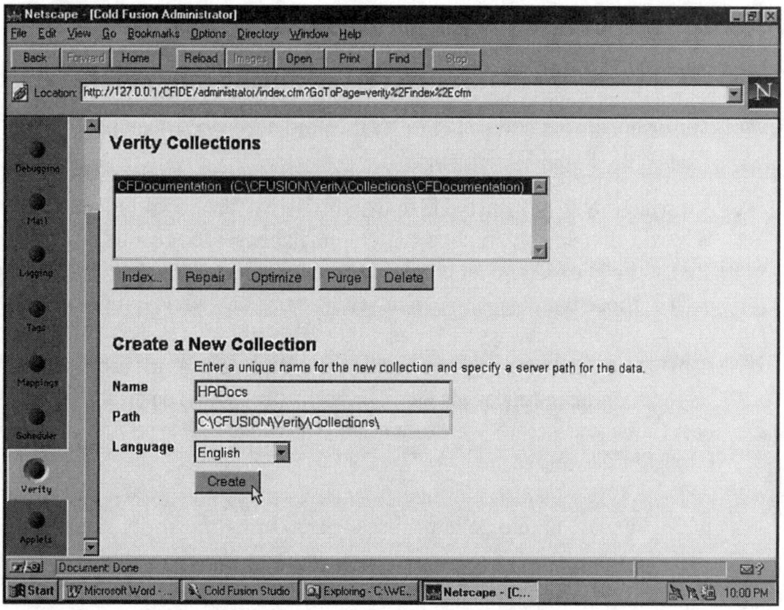

FIG. 26.3

Simply type the name for the new collection and then click Create.

Specifying a Language

If you have the optional Cold Fusion International Search Pack, you can specify a language other than English when you are creating a new collection. The language should match the language that the documents are written in. By knowing what language the documents are written in, Verity can pull off a few neat tricks, such as understanding the role of accented characters. It also uses knowledge of the language to pull off variations on the same word *stem*, or root.

Support for languages other than English is new for Cold Fusion 3.1. You must choose the language when you are first creating the collection. Simply select the language from the drop-down list in the Administrator before you click the Create button (see Figure 26.2). Cold Fusion 3.1's Verity functionality supports the following languages: English, German, French, Danish, Dutch, Finnish, Italian, Norwegian, Portuguese, Spanish, and Swedish.

N O T E You must have purchased the Cold Fusion International Search Pack from Allaire to use languages other than English. If you attempt to do so without the Search Pack installed, you will get a `Verity error -2` message when you click Create. ▧

Try not to mix documents written in different languages in the same collection. If you have documents in several different languages, make separate collections for them.

Part
IV

Ch
26

Creating a Working Search Interface

Now that you've created the HRDocs collection, you can start putting together the Cold Fusion templates to make your documents searchable. You'll see that the code you use to do this is similar in concept and structure to the employee search application you worked through in Chapter 12, "Cold Fusion Forms."

A terrific way to get started is to use the Verity Wizard included in Cold Fusion Studio. The Wizard will help you create a search tool page, search results page, and a detail page. So take a look at the Wizard and let it create some basic templates for you. Then you'll walk through each of those templates, to see how they work and what you can add to them.

N O T E If you're not using Cold Fusion Studio, don't worry. All the code that the Wizard generates is included here as you work through the steps, and is on the CD-ROM that comes with this book for your convenience. The Wizard makes it quick and easy to set up basic Verity templates, but it is by no means required. ▪

In Cold Fusion Studio, follow these steps to bring the Verity Wizard up on your screen:

1. From the File menu, choose New. The New Document window appears.
2. Click the CFML tab in the New Document window.
3. Double-click Verity Wizard from the list of Wizards.

T I P You can also start the Verity Wizard—or any other Wizard—by right-clicking anywhere in the editor and choosing File, then New from the pop-up menu.

As you can see in Figure 26.4, the first step of the Verity Wizard wants you to choose a title for the application and where the Cold Fusion templates should be stored. To complete the first step, do the following:

1. Type **Personnel Policy Documents** for the title. The Wizard will put this title at the top of each of the Cold Fusion (.cfm) templates that it generates.
2. Select the directory that the Cold Fusion (.cfm) templates should be generated in. The folder must already exist, and should be located somewhere within your webserver's document root (so people will be able to access the .cfm files with their web browsers). My webserver's document root is c:\WEBSHARE\WWWROOT, so I've created a folder named c:\WEBSHARE\WWWROOT\HRSearch and selected the path on the server to that folder.

When you're done with the first step, click the Next button to get to Step 2. As you can see in Figure 26.5, this second step asks you about the Verity collection that the generated Cold Fusion templates should refer to. Do the following to complete this second step:

1. For the collection name, enter **HRDocs**, which is the name of the collection that we created in the Cold Fusion Administrator.

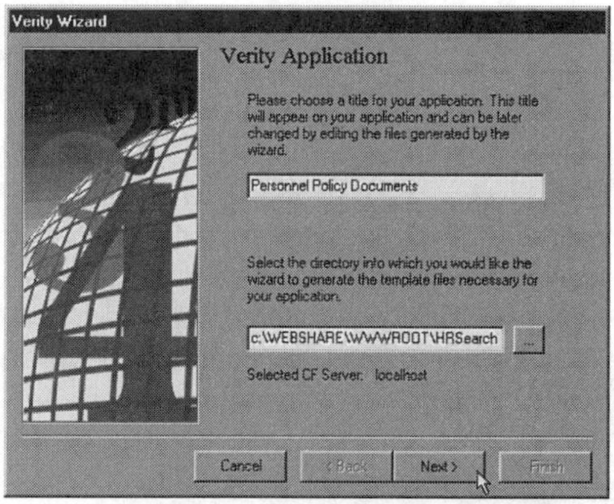

FIG. 26.4

The first step of the Verity Wizard wants an application title and location for the generated .cfm files.

2. Leave the language selected at English, unless you chose a different language when creating the HRDocs collection. The language you choose here should always match the language that you created the collection with in the Cold Fusion Administrator.

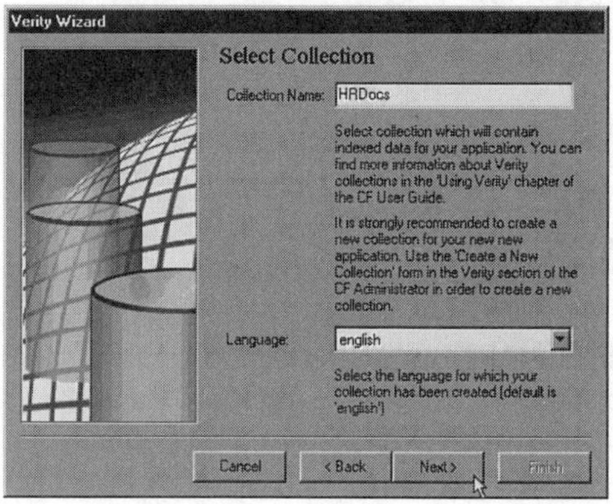

FIG. 26.5

The second step of the Wizard asks about the Verity collection to be used by the generated .cfm files.

When you're done with the second step, click the Next button to get to the third step. As you can see in Figure 26.6, this step is asking you about the document files you actually want Verity to index and make searchable. Do the following to complete this third step:

1. For the Directory Path, select the folder that contains the actual documents you want to make searchable. On my server, the documents are in a folder called Docs, which is in a folder called HR, directly off my web server's root directory. So I've entered c:\WEBSHARE\WWWROOT\HR\Docs\ here.

2. The Recursively Index Subdirectories checkbox indicates whether Verity is to look inside any subdirectories of the Directory Path you just entered. My c:\WEBSHARE\WWWROOT\HR\Docs folder includes a Days Off subfolder that has documents in it that I want searched, so I've left this checkbox checked.

3. For File Extensions, type a list of file extensions that Verity should index. Separate the extensions with commas. I want Verity to make all of the HTML, Word, Excel, and plain text files available for searching, so I've entered .htm, .html, .txt, .doc, .xls in this field. I do not, however, want any files with the .cfm extension to be indexed, so I haven't included .cfm in the list.

4. For Return URL, type the URL version of the document path that you entered above. In other words, what would a user need to type before a filename in order to pull a file from the folder up in his web browser? I have entered http://localhost/HR/Docs here, because that is what someone would need to enter to get to my webserver's c:\WEBSHARE\WWWROOT\HR\Docs\ with his browser.

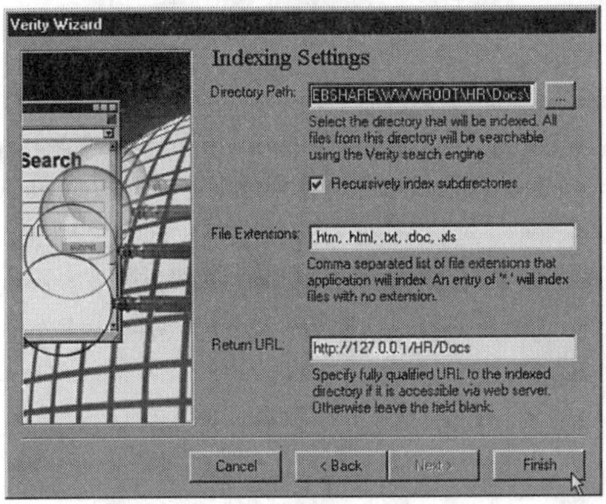

FIG. 26.6

The third step of the Verity Wizard asks about the actual document files.

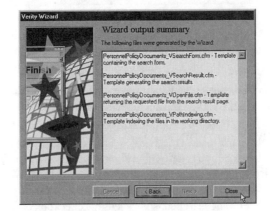

When you are done with the third step, click the Finish button. The Wizard will generate and save four files to the c:\WEBSHARE\WWWROOT\HRSearch folder (or whatever directory you specified in the first step of the Wizard). As you can see in Figure 26.7, the Wizard will then display the four files that it generated in the Wizard Output Summary.

FIG. 26.7

The Verity Wizard generates four .cfm files in all.

Finally, click the Close button to close the Wizard. Cold Fusion Studio will automatically bring up the four files in the editor for your convenience.

Take a look at the search interface the Verity Wizard put together. Bring up the search form in your web browser. The URL will depend on what you entered in step one of the Wizard—on my system, it's called PersonnelPolicyDocuments_VSearchForm.cfm (the PersonnelPolicyDocuments part came from the application title I supplied in step one of the Wizard). Make sure to bring it up in your browser with an HTTP URL (starting with "http://"), rather than as a "local" file (starting with "c:/" or some other drive letter). Figure 26.8 shows what the search form looks like.

FIG. 26.8

The search form includes a link to index the actual documents.

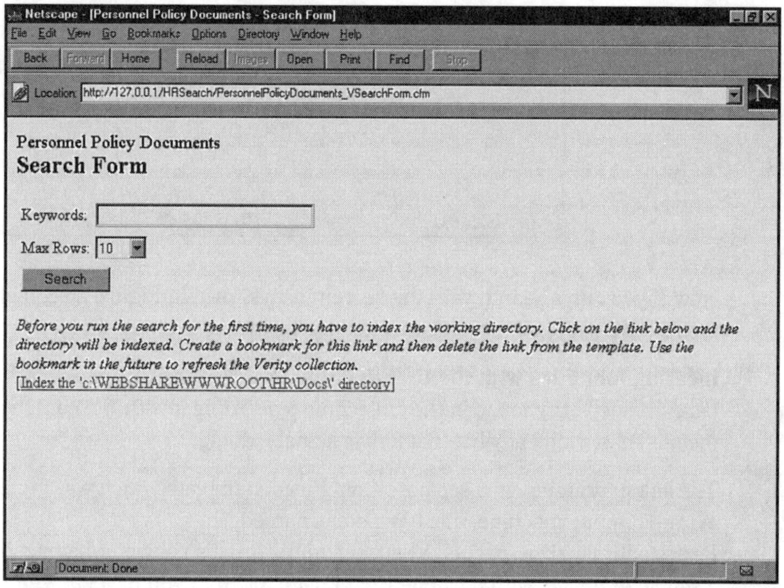

Well, it looks pretty much the way you'd expect a search tool to look. There's a text INPUT field to type keywords into, and a Submit button to start the search.

However, if you were to try to run a search right now, no documents would be found, regardless of what you were searching for. That's because the Verity collection you created in the Cold Fusion Administrator has not been indexed yet. In other words, the collection has been set up, but it's still *empty*.

At the bottom of the search page (shown in Figure 26.8), the Verity Wizard has provided a link that will index the collection. Go ahead and click that link now. Your server's hard drive will whirl around for a bit as Verity indexes the actual documents and saves its internal data about the documents to disk. When the indexing is complete, an Indexing Finished message will appear, as shown in Figure 26.9.

Part

IV

Ch

26

FIG. 26.9

The PersonnelPolicy Documents_VPath Indexing.cfm file indexes the collection, "populating" it with actual documents.

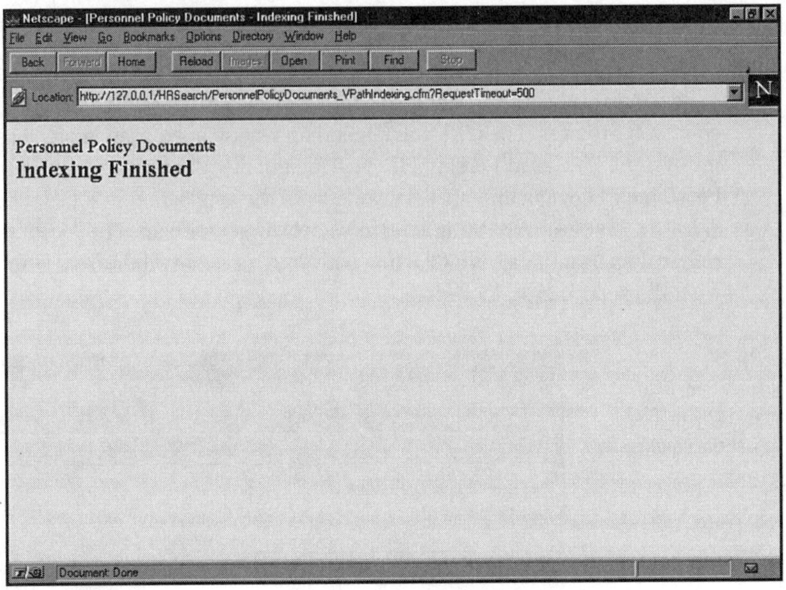

Now, if you run a search with the search form shown in Figure 26.8, it should work. The documents have successfully been indexed by Verity and are searchable.

Indexing Your Files with the *CFINDEX* Tag   You've seen that clicking that link on the search page causes Verity to index the collection, *populating* it with the contents of your actual documents. Take a look at what that link is actually doing.

The link is bringing up a separate Cold Fusion template which was generated by the Verity Wizard. On my machine, this template is named PersonnelPolicyDocuments_VPathIndexing.cfm. It's shown in Listing 26.1 and is actually quite a simple template, with only one Cold Fusion tag that you haven't seen before—<CFINDEX>.

The <CFINDEX> tag is what "cues" Verity to "wake up" and index (or re-index, after the first time) the files in the folder you specify. This is the second step in the overall process of making a Verity application come alive (the first step was creating the collection in the Cold Fusion Administrator, and the third is actually searching the collection with the <CFSEARCH> tag, which is covered shortly).

T I P   Remember, there's nothing special about the code that the Verity Wizard generates. You can use this code—or any code that uses CFINDEX in a similar way—to get the job done, whether you use Cold Fusion Studio and its Verity Wizard or not.

Listing 26.1   PERSONNELPOLICYDOCUMENTS_VPATHINDEXING.CFM— Indexing a Collection

```
<CFSET IndexCollection = "HRDocs">
<CFSET IndexDirectory = "c:\WEBSHARE\WWWROOT\HR\Docs\">
<CFSET IndexRecurse = "YES">
<CFSET IndexExtensions = ".htm, .html, .txt, .doc, .xls">
<CFSET IndexLanguage = "english">

<CFINDEX
    COLLECTION="#IndexCollection#"
    ACTION="REFRESH"
    TYPE="PATH"
    KEY="#IndexDirectory#\"
    EXTENSIONS="#IndexExtensions#"
    RECURSE="#IndexRecurse#"
    LANGUAGE="#IndexLanguage#"
    URLPATH="http://localhost/HR/Docs"
>

<HTML><HEAD>
    <TITLE>Personnel Policy Documents - Indexing Finished</TITLE>
</HEAD><BODY bgcolor="ffffff">

<FONT size="+1">Personnel Policy Documents</FONT> <BR>
<FONT size="+2"><B>Indexing Finished</B></FONT>
```

This template simply sets a few constants at the top of the template with some CFSET tags. It then plugs the values of those constants into the CFINDEX tag. The Verity Wizard has used the CFSET tags at the top—rather than "hard-coding" the values in the parameters of the CFINDEX tag itself—so it'll be easy for you to change the values later on.

Because the CFINDEX tag is what tells Verity to index your actual documents, the various parameters of the CFINDEX tag simply give Verity the particulars about what you want it to do. Take a look at each of the parameters:

- The COLLECTION parameter simply tells Verity which collection to use. In Listing 26.1, the value passed to the COLLECTION parameter is HRDocs, which is the value that I supplied to the Wizard.

- The ACTION parameter tells Verity that you're interested in "refreshing" any data currently in the collection with new information. There are other possible values for ACTION other than REFRESH, which are discussed in "Maintaining Collections" at the end of this chapter.

- The TYPE parameter tells Verity that you're interested in adding documents from a directory path on your webserver. You'll learn about another possible value for TYPE later, when using Verity to index database data rather than document files is covered.

- The KEY parameter tells Verity from which directory path to add documents. This must evaluate to a complete physical file system path to the actual documents you want to index.

- The EXTENSIONS parameter tells Verity which documents in the specified folder should be indexed. This is useful if you only want certain types of documents to become searchable.

- The RECURSE parameter tells Verity whether you want it to index files that are sitting in subfolders of the folder you specified with the KEY parameter. Possible values are YES and NO—usually you will specify YES for this parameter.

- The LANGUAGE parameter tells Verity what language the documents are written in. For the possible values, see "Specifying a Language," earlier in this chapter.

- The URLPATH parameter tells Verity to maintain URLs for each document, as it does its indexing, by appending the filename to the value you supply with this parameter. If RECURSE="YES" and the file is in a subfolder, the folder name will be appended as well. In other words, as long as the value you supply here is the "URL version" of the value you supplied for KEY, Verity will be automatically record the correct URL for each file as it does its indexing. You'll see this in action later, when you use the #URL# column returned by the CFSEARCH tag.

That's about all there is to indexing document files. Now all you have to do is make sure that the code in Listing 26.1 runs whenever somebody saves new documents to the c:\WEBSHARE\WWWROOT\HR\Docs folder.

You may now delete the link to the PersonnelPolicyDocuments_VSearchForm.cfm template as the message at the bottom of the search page suggests (see Figure 26.8 and Listing 26.2), or you may leave it there so that your users can re-index the documents on their own whenever they wish.

The Search Form Page   Next, take a look at the search form that the Verity Wizard created for you. The name of the file depends on what application title you supplied in the first step of the Wizard; on my machine, the file is called PersonnelPolicyDocuments_VSearchForm.cfm (see Listing 26.2).

This search form is very similar to the search forms you worked through in Chapter 12. Refer back to that chapter if you need to refresh your memory about the INPUT and SELECT tags that appear in Listing 26.2.

**Listing 26.2   PERSONNELPOLICYDOCUMENTS_VSEARCHFORM.CFM—
The Search Form Page that the Wizard Created**

```
<!--- template settings --->
<CFSET SearchDirectory = "c:\WEBSHARE\WWWROOT\HR\Docs\">

<HTML><HEAD>
    <TITLE>Personnel Policy Documents - Search Form</TITLE>
</HEAD><BODY bgcolor="ffffff">

<FONT size="+1">Personnel Policy Documents</FONT> <BR>
<FONT size="+2"><B>Search Form</B></FONT>
```

```
<!--- search form definition --->
<FORM action="PersonnelPolicyDocuments_VSearchResult.cfm" method="post">
      <INPUT type="hidden" name="StartRow" value="1">
      <TABLE>
            <TR>
             <TD>Keywords:</TD>
             <TD><INPUT type="text" name="Criteria" size="30"></TD>
            </TR>
            <TR>
             <TD>Max Rows:</TD>
             <TD><SELECT name="MaxRows"> <OPTION> 10 <OPTION> 25
➥<OPTION> 100 </SELECT></TD>
            </TR>
            <TR>
             <TD colspan=2><INPUT type="submit" value="   Search   "></TD>
            </TR>
      </TABLE>
</FORM>

<P>
<I>
Before you run the search for the first time, you have to index the
working directory. Click on the link below and the directory will be
indexed. Create a bookmark for this link and then delete the link from
the template. Use the bookmark in the future to refresh the Verity
collection.</I>
<BR>
[<A href="PersonnelPolicyDocuments_VPathIndexing.cfm?RequestTimeout=500">
➥Index the 'c:\WEBSHARE\WWWROOT\HR\Docs\' directory</A>]

</BODY></HTML>
```

As you can see in Figure 26.8, your search form template contains a form that collects two pieces of information from the user. Most importantly, it collects the keywords that the user wants to search for (the INPUT named Criteria). It also collects the maximum number of "hits" to display per page of search results (the SELECT named MaxRows).

The Search Results Page The Verity Wizard's search form submits these two pieces of information to the PersonnelPolicyDocuments_VSearchResult.cfm template, which contains the code that actually runs the Verity search and displays the results of the search to the user.

Take a look at that template now. As you can see in Listing 26.3, it contains only one Cold Fusion tag that you're not familiar with yet—the <CFSEARCH> tag.

On the CD

**Listing 26.3   PERSONNELPOLICYDOCUMENTS_VSEARCHRESULT.CFM—
The Search Results Page that the Wizard Created**

```
<!--- template settings --->
<CFSET SearchDirectory = "c:\WEBSHARE\WWWROOT\HR\Docs\">
<CFSET SearchCollection = "HRDocs">
<CFSET UseURLPath = "YES">
```

continues

Listing 26.3   Continued

```
<!--- retrieve requested files --->
<CFSEARCH
      name = "GetResults"
      collection = "#SearchCollection#"
      criteria = "#Form.Criteria#"
      maxRows = "#Evaluate(Form.MaxRows + 1)#"
      startRow = "#Form.StartRow#"
>

<HTML><HEAD>
    <TITLE>Personnel Policy Documents - Search Results</TITLE>
</HEAD><BODY bgcolor="ffffff">

<FONT size="+1">Personnel Policy Documents</FONT> <BR>
<FONT size="+2"><B>Search Results</B></FONT>

<P>
<!--- no files found for specified criteria? --->
<CFIF GetResults.RecordCount is 0>
      <B>No files found for specified criteria</B>
<!--- ... else at least one file found --->
<CFELSE>
      <TABLE cellspacing=0 cellpadding=2>
      <!-- table header -->
      <TR bgcolor="cccccc">
            <TD><B>No</B></TD>
            <TD><B>Score</B></TD>
            <TD><B>File</B></TD>
            <TD><B>Title</B></TD>
      </TR>
      <CFOUTPUT query="GetResults" maxRows="#Form.MaxRows#">
      <TR bgcolor="#IIf(CurrentRow Mod 2, DE('ffffff'), DE('ffffcf'))#">
            <!--- current row information --->
            <TD>#Evaluate(Form.StartRow + CurrentRow - 1)#</TD>
            <!--- score --->
            <TD>#Score# </TD>
            <!--- file name with the link returning the file --->
            <TD>
                  <CFIF UseURLPath>      <!--- URL parameter from cfsearch
➡contains URL path info --->
                        <CFSET href = Replace(URL, " ", "%20", "ALL")>
                CFELSE>                  <!--- ... else use OpenFile to return
➡the file --->
                        <CFSET href = "MyApplication_VOpenFile.
➡cfm?serverFilePath=#URLEncodedFormat(Key)#">
            </CFIF>
                  <A href="#href#">#GetFileFromPath(Key)#</A>
            </TD>
            <!--- title for HTML files --->
            <TD>#Title# </TD>
      </TR>
      </CFOUTPUT>
      </TABLE>
```

```
        <!--- CFSEARCH tried to retrieve one more file than the number
specified in the Form.MaxRows parameter. If number of retrieved files is
greater than MaxRows we know that there is at least one file left. The
following form contains only one button which reloads this template with
the new StartRow parameter. --->
        <CFIF GetResults.RecordCount gt Form.MaxRows>
            <FORM action="PersonnelPolicyDocuments_VSearchResult.cfm"
➥method="post">
            <CFOUTPUT>
                <INPUT type="hidden" name="Criteria" value=
➥"#Replace(Form.Criteria, """", "'", "ALL")#">
                <INPUT type="hidden" name="MaxRows" value="#Form.MaxRows#">
                <INPUT type="hidden" name="StartRow" value="#Evaluate(Form
➥.StartRow + ➥Form.MaxRows)#">
                    <INPUT type="submit" value="    More ...    ">
            </CFOUTPUT>
            </FORM>
        </CFIF>
</CFIF>

</BODY></HTML>
```

Clearly, the focus of this template is the CFSEARCH tag near the top. The CFSEARCH tag tells Verity to actually run a search—that is, take the search criteria that the user supplies and try to find documents that match.

Do you remember that Verity searches are a lot like ODBC/SQL queries? Well, with that similarity in mind, it's worth noting that the CFSEARCH tag acts a lot like the CFQUERY tag when you're dealing with database tables.

Take a look at the specific parameters you're supplying to the CFSEARCH tag in Listing 26.3. As you do so, keep in mind that most of these parameters look a lot like the kind of parameters that you'd supply to a CFQUERY tag.

N O T E   The MAXROWS and STARTROW parameters listed below are used in the templates the Wizard generated to create a Next 10 Records feature—where the user can move through pages of search results—just like you see on commercial search engines. I'm not going to explain the Next 10 Records functionality in this chapter, because it's not directly related to Verity. Refer to Chapter 18, "Advanced Cold Fusion Templates," for an explanation of how to use MAXROWS and STARTROW to put together Next 10 Records solutions. ▇

The following are the parameters for CFSEARCH, as used in Listing 26.3:

- The NAME parameter gives the search a name. Whatever results are found by Verity will be available, for your use as a developer, as a "query" that has the name you supply here. You'll be able to use the search results in CFOUTPUT tags and in any of the other ways you normally use query results.

- The COLLECTION parameter tells Verity in which collection to search for documents. In this case, I'm directing it to the HRDocs collection that I created and indexed in this chapter.

- The CRITERIA parameter is probably the most important parameter here. This is what you're actually asking Verity to look for. Here, you're simply passing whatever the user types in the search form to this parameter.

- The MAXROWS parameter tells Verity to return only a certain number of rows. This is just like using the MAXROWS parameter with the CFQUERY tag. Here, you're taking whatever the user indicated in the MaxRows SELECT on the search form and adding one to it.

- The STARTROW parameter tells Verity to return only the search results from a certain row in the search results on down. Here, you're taking the value specified by the hidden field named StartRow on the search form, so this value is always 1 for now. In other words, you're telling Verity to start returning the search results starting with the very first row.

N O T E   CFSEARCH also takes another parameter, TYPE. You can use TYPE="SIMPLE" or TYPE="EXPLICIT" in your search templates. TYPE="SIMPLE" places the STEM and MANY operators into effect automatically (see Appendix C, "Verity Search Language Reference," for information on the STEM and MANY operators). Unless you specify EXPLICIT, SIMPLE is used by default. I recommend that you do not use EXPLICIT unless you have a specific reason to do so. ■

After the CFSEARCH is executed, the rest of Listing 26.3 is concerned with displaying the results to the user. It's fairly straightforward. The main thing to keep in mind is that now that the CFSEARCH has found its results, you're going to treat it just as if it were a CFQUERY named GetResults.

First, there is a CFIF tag that does the now-familiar check to make sure that the built-in RecordCount variable is not zero (which would mean that Verity didn't find any results). See Chapter 12 for more information on the RecordCount variable.

Provided that there are results to display, your code moves into the large CFELSE block that encompasses the remainder of the template. TABLE, TR, and TD tags are used to establish an HTML table in which to display the results, with headers at the top of the table. Look back at Chapter 11, "Cold Fusion Basics," for more examples of building tables row-by-row with query results.

Most of the important stuff happens in the large CFOUTPUT block that follows. The QUERY="GetResults" parameter in the CFOUTPUT tag causes this code to be executed once for each row in the search results, where each row represents a document found. Unlike a result set returned by a CFQUERY—where you've specified what columns your result set will contain by naming the columns in the SELECT part of your SQL statement—result sets returned by Verity searches always contain the same, predefined column names, which are shown in Table 26.2.

Table 26.2   Columns Returned by Verity Searches

Column	Contains
Key	The document's filename.
Title	The title of the document, if Verity is able to determine what the title is. For example, if the file is an HTML document, Verity will obtain the title from the TITLE tags in the document's HEAD section. Verity may not provide a title for other types of documents.
Score	The "relevancy score" for the document, which is meant to indicate how closely the document matched up with the search criteria. The score will always be a value somewhere from 0 to 1, where a score of 1 indicates a perfect match.
URL	The URL that can be used to obtain the file from your webserver. This is based on the information you supplied to the CFINDEX tag with its URLPATH parameter. If you did not specify a URLPATH parameter when indexing the collection, this column will not be available.
CurrentRow	This works just like the CurrentRow column that is returned by a CFQUERY. In a CFOUTPUT block that uses the search results in its QUERY parameter, CurrentRow will be 1 for the first document returned by the CFSEARCH, 2 for the second document, and so on. See Chapter 19, "Enhancing Forms with *CFFORM*." for more discussion on CurrentRow.

As you can see, the code in Listing 26.3 uses these columns to display the score, title, and filename for each document. It also uses the URL column in the HREF attribute of an HTML anchor tag to provide a "link" to the document.

In addition, two predefined variables are available to you after a search runs. Table 26.3 explains these variables.

Part
IV

Ch
26

Table 26.3   Properties Available After a *CFSEARCH* Tag Executes

Property	Indicates
RecordCount	Just as with CFQUERY, the number of "matches" that Verity found. In this example, you access this variable using #GetResults.RecordCount# in your code.
RecordsSearched	The number of records that Verity searched. In other words, the number of records in the collection(s).

You saw `RecordCount` in action in Listing 26.3. `RecordsSearched` can be used in much the same way, if you want to let the user know how many documents were searched to find her "hits." For example, code similar to the following

```
<CFOUTPUT>
#GetResults.RecordCount#
out of
#GetResults.RecordsSearched#
documents found.
</CFOUTPUT>
```

would display something like "*10 out of 4363 documents found.*"

Running a Search Your search tool should already be operational. Pull the search form up in your browser and type **employee** in the blank. When you click Search, you should get a list of relevant documents from your Human Resources department, as shown in Figure 26.10.

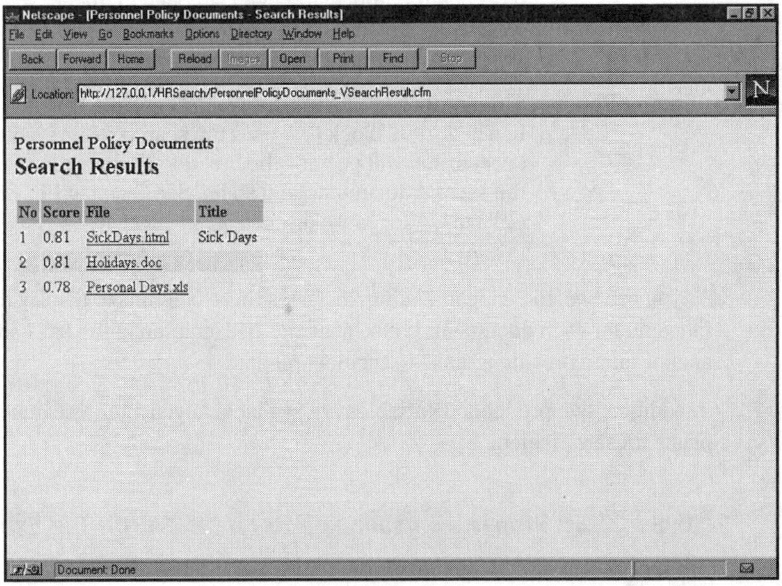

FIG. 26.10

Your Search Results page shows a relevancy score, filename, and title (when available) for each document found.

NOTE If you look at Listing 26.3, you'll see there's a reference to a file called PersonnelPolicyDocuments_VOpenFile.cfm. That code is in the template to provide access to documents that do not reside in the webserver's document root, and only goes into effect if the URL path is left blank when the collection is indexed. This OpenFile template uses the `CFCONTENT` tag to get its job done. See Chapter 28, "MIME Types," and the "Coffee Valley Document Library" example application that installs with Cold Fusion 3.1 for more information on using the `CFCONTENT` tag. ■

Refining Your Search   Often, just typing a few keywords isn't enough to find the documents you want. Verity provides a wealth of search operators to help you get the job done. By including special words such as AND, OR, and NOT in your search criteria, or by using various wildcards, your users can tweak their searches so they find exactly what they're looking for.

As you're reading through this section, note how Verity search criteria end up looking a lot like SQL statements. It's nice that there's some common ground between the two. But it's also important to keep in mind that Verity's search language is not exactly the same thing as SQL.

Using AND, OR, and NOT   If you want to refine your search a little, you can use special search operators in your search criteria to get more specific. Only the most common search operators will be discussed at this point. There are many others available for your use. Refer to Appendix C for all the details on each of the search operators in Verity's search language.

Table 26.4 briefly describes the effect of using AND, OR, and NOT in your search criteria. These operators are very much like the AND, OR, and NOT Boolean operators that were discussed in Chapter 8, "Introduction to SQL."

Table 26.4   Basic Search Operators

Operator	Effect	Example
AND	Searches for documents that have both words in it.	Verity AND Allaire
OR	Searches for documents that has either word in it.	Verity OR Allaire
NOT	Eliminates documents where the word is found.	Verity NOT Allaire

TIP

A comma can be used instead of OR in search criteria. So a search for **Verity, Allaire** is the same as a search for **Verity OR Allaire.**

Part
IV

Ch
26

Using Parentheses and Quote Marks   Search criteria can start to look pretty ambiguous once there are more than two search words present. For instance, if you typed in **Verity AND Allaire OR Cold Fusion**, what would that mean exactly? Documents that definitely contained "Verity" but that only needed to contain "Verity" or "Cold Fusion"? Or documents that contained "Cold Fusion" in addition to documents that contained both "Verity" and "Allaire"?

Use parentheses and quotation marks to indicate this type of criteria, where the "order of evaluation" needs to be specified. They make your intentions clear to Verity, and are fairly easy to explain to users. Table 26.5 summarizes the use of parentheses and quotation marks.

Table 26.5 Examples: Quotation Marks and Parentheses

Character	Purpose	Examples
(Parentheses)	Determines how ANDs and ORs are treated. Words within parentheses are considered as a unit, and are considered first.	Allaire OR (Cold AND Fusion) Fusion AND (Cold NOT Hot)
"Quotation Marks"	Quoted words or phrases are searched for literally. Useful when you want to search for the actual words "and" or "or."	"Simple AND Explicit" Allaire AND "not installed"

Using Wildcards   Verity provides a few wildcards that you can use in your searches, so you can find documents based on incomplete search words or phrases. The wildcards should look pretty familiar to you if you've used the LIKE operator with SQL queries, as discussed in Chapter 8. Table 26.6 summarizes the use of wildcard operators.

Table 26.6 The Two Most Common Wildcards

Wildcard	Purpose
*	Like the % wildcard in SQL, * stands in for any number of characters (including zero). So a search for *Fu** would find *Fusion*, *Fugazi*, and *Fuchsia*.
?	Just as in SQL, ? stands in for any single character. More precise—and thus generally less helpful—than the * wildcard. A search for *?ar?et* would find both *carpet* and *target*, but not *Learjet*.

These aren't the only wildcards available for your use. See the WILDCARD operator in the section entitled "Understanding Evidence Operators" in Appendix C.

Taking Case-Sensitivity into Account   By default, a Verity search automatically becomes case-sensitive whenever the characters provided as the CRITERIA parameter are of mixed case. So a search for "employee"—or a search for "EMPLOYEE"—will find *employee*, *Employee*, and *EMPLOYEE*, but a search for "Employee" will only find *Employee*, not *employee* or *EMPLOYEE*. You may want to make this fact clear to your users by providing a message like "type in all uppercase or all lowercase unless you want the search to be case-sensitive" on your search forms.

To have your application always ignore case no matter what the user types, just use Cold Fusion's LCase function to convert the user's search words to lowercase when you supply them to CFSEARCH. For instance, by replacing the CFSEARCH in Listing 26.3 with the code in Listing 26.4, you guarantee that the search criteria passed to Verity is not of mixed case—so you know the search will be case-insensitive.

Listing 26.4   Using *LCase* to Defeat Case-Sensitivity Even If User's Keywords Are of Mixed Case

```
<!--- retrieve requested files --->
<CFSEARCH
      name = "GetResults"
      collection = "#SearchCollection#"
      criteria = "#LCase(Form.Criteria)#"
      maxRows = "#Evaluate(Form.MaxRows + 1)#"
      startRow = "#Form.StartRow#"
>
```

Indexing Your Files Interactively

You've explored how to use the CFINDEX tag to index your collections. Actually, Cold Fusion provides two different ways to index a Verity collection:

- *Programmatically*, with the CFINDEX tag (see Listing 26.11)
- *Interactively*, with the Cold Fusion Administrator

The *programmatic* method that you've explored already is best suited for the following situations:

- When the documents are always changing
- When it's critical that new documents become searchable right away
- When it's important that your application is as self-tuning as possible, for instance if you are working as an outside consultant
- More complicated applications

However, you also have the option of indexing your documents interactively, using the Index button in the Cold Fusion Administrator. This method is handy for the following situations:

- When the documents change infrequently, or not on a fixed or predictable schedule
- When the documents "live outside" of your Cold Fusion application, such as a folder full of Word files that employees may save and edit without your application knowing about it
- Testing and development
- Less complicated, in-house applications

Take a look at the interactive approach. To do this, go to the Verity page of the Cold Fusion Administrator, highlight your collection, and then click on the Index button. As you can see, all you have to do is fill in a few form fields and then click the Update button. After a few moments—or minutes, depending on the number of files you're indexing—you'll see a message in the Administrator that the operation is complete, as shown in Figure 26.11.

FIG. 26.11

Indexing your files interactively is as simple as filling in a few blanks.

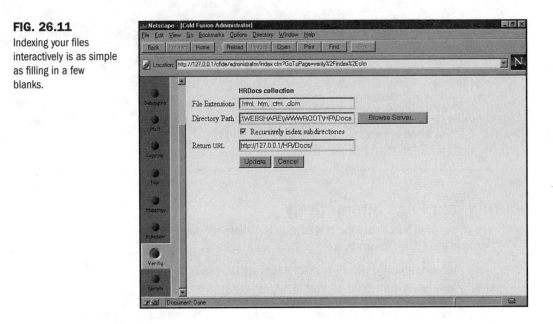

To index files, you must supply four pieces of information:

- File extensions
- Directory path
- Recursively index subdirectories
- Return URL

The file extensions field corresponds to the EXTENSIONS parameter of the CFINDEX tag. Just provide a simple list of file extensions—including the periods—that indicates which documents you want to index.

The directory path field corresponds to the KEY parameter of the CFINDEX tag. Just indicate which directory on your webserver—or local network—that Verity should index. This value must be given as an absolute filesystem path, not an URL, which means that it cannot start with http://.

The recursively Index Subdirectories checkbox corresponds to the RECURSE parameter of the CFINDEX tag. Check this box if you want Verity to search all folders within the directory you specify.

The return URL field corresponds to the URLPATH parameter of the CFINDEX tag. Enter the URL equivalent of the Directory Path that you entered. In other words, what would you put before the filename if you wanted to open a file in this directory in a web browser? This value should start with http:// or https://.

A collection indexed using this method will work the same way as a collection indexed using the `CFINDEX` tag in a Cold Fusion template. It's really just a matter of whether you want to create a template that uses the `CFINDEX` tag or not.

Indexing Data

Okay, so you've seen how easy it is to use Cold Fusion's Verity functionality to index all sorts of files on your system. Now using Verity to index information in your database tables will be covered. Cold Fusion makes it possible to make a Verity index of your database data just as if it were a bunch of document files.

In this section, you'll see how Verity allows you to very neatly get around the limitations that make SQL less-than-perfect for true text-based searching. By the time you're through, you'll have a good understanding of when it makes sense to unleash Verity's rich search capabilities on your database data, and when you're best off leaving things to SQL instead.

N O T E The examples in this section use the populated A2Z.mdb file located in this chapter's folder on the CD-ROM. I've populated the tables with some actual book and order data with which to work. ■

Doing It Without Verity

You don't *need* to use Verity to make your database searchable. But it can make it much easier for you to implement a search interface, and easier for your users to find what they want. Take a look at what you'd need to do to search your data using the tools you already know—`CFQUERY` and SQL.

Say you wanted to set up a little search tool to allow your users to search the Inventory table of the A2Z example database. You just want the user to be able to type a word or two into a form field and then click Search to get the matching books.

The code in Listing 26.5 creates a simple search form. This will remind you a lot of the search forms that were explained in Chapter 12. The form is displayed in a browser as shown in Figure 26.12.

Part IV Ch 26

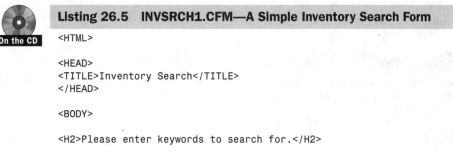

Listing 26.5 INVSRCH1.CFM—A Simple Inventory Search Form

```
<HTML>

<HEAD>
<TITLE>Inventory Search</TITLE>
</HEAD>

<BODY>

<H2>Please enter keywords to search for.</H2>
```

continues

Listing 26.5   Continued

```
<FORM ACTION="invsrch2.cfm" METHOD="POST">

Keywords: <INPUT TYPE="text" NAME="Criteria"><BR>
<P>
<INPUT TYPE="submit" VALUE="Search">

</FORM>

</BODY>

</HTML>
```

FIG. 26.12
Our "Inventory Search" tool collects one or more keywords from the user.

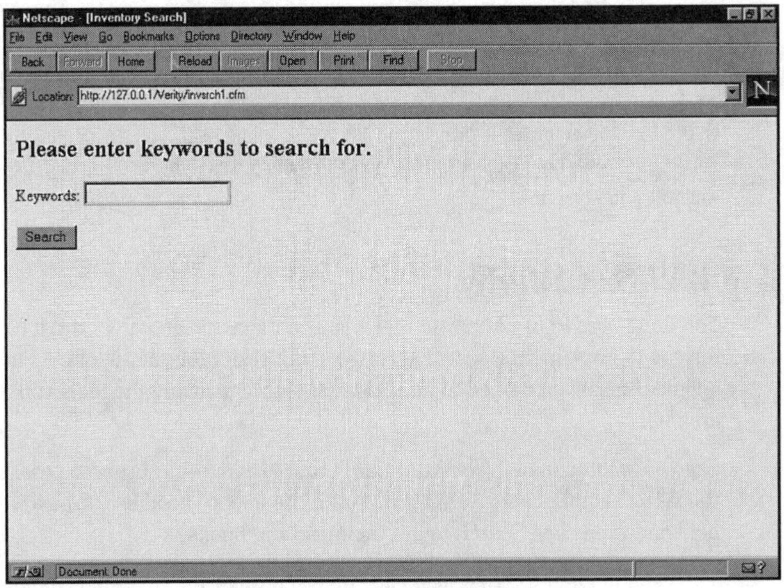

Again borrowing heavily from Chapter 12 you come up with the code in Listing 26.6 for searching and displaying the results from the Inventory table. Note that the LIKE keyword is used along with the % wildcard to search any part of the Description. Refer to Chapter 12 if you need to jog your memory on the use of the LIKE keyword.

On the CD

Listing 26.6   INVSRCH2.CFM—Code for Searching the Inventory Table

```
<CFQUERY NAME="GetResults" DATASOURCE="A2Z">
  SELECT BookID, Title
  FROM Inventory
  WHERE (Description LIKE '%#Form.Criteria#%')
</CFQUERY>
```

```
<HTML>

<HEAD>
<TITLE>Search Results</TITLE>
</HEAD>

<BODY>

<H2><CFOUTPUT>#GetResults.RecordCount# books found for "#Form.Criteria#".</
➥CFOUTPUT></H2>

<UL>
<CFOUTPUT QUERY="GetResults">
  <LI>#Title#
</CFOUTPUT>
</UL>

</BODY>

</HTML>
```

This code would work fine, as long as your application only required simple searching. If the user entered *guide* for the search criteria, SQL's LIKE operator would faithfully find all the books that had the word "guide" somewhere in the description, as shown in Figure 26.13.

FIG. 26.13

Your Verity-free code works fine for simple, one-word searches.

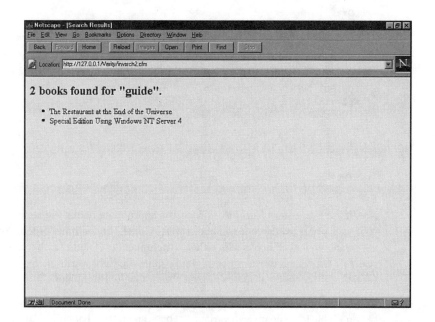

Part

IV

Ch

26

But what if the user entered something like *Hitchhiker Guide*? No records would be found, because there are no records with those exact words in it (only *Hitchhiker's Guide*, with an apostrophe *s*). That's a limitation that your users probably won't find acceptable.

So maybe you need to modify your CFQUERY a little, to account for multiple-word searches. Listing 26.8 contains a revised query that should take multiple words into account. Each individual word is treated separately, because the CFLOOP adds an additional AND condition to the query for each word in the user's input. Only books that contain all of the words entered in the blank will be found. See Chapter 18 for a detailed discussion of the CFLOOP tag.

Listing 26.7 INVSRCH2A.CFM—Getting SQL to Account for Multiple Words

```
<CFQUERY NAME="GetResults" DATASOURCE="A2Z">
  SELECT BookID, Title
  FROM Inventory
  WHERE (0=0
  <CFLOOP LIST="#Form.Criteria#" INDEX="ThisWord" DELIMITERS=" ">
    AND (Description LIKE '%#ThisWord#%')
  </CFLOOP>)
</CFQUERY>


<HTML>

<HEAD>
<TITLE>Search Results</TITLE>
</HEAD>

<BODY>

<H2><CFOUTPUT>#GetResults.RecordCount# books found for "#Form.Criteria#".</
➥CFOUTPUT></H2>

<UL>
<CFOUTPUT QUERY="GetResults">
  <LI>#Title#
</CFOUTPUT>
</UL>

</BODY>

</HTML>
```

Now if the user enters *Hitchhiker Guide*, the appropriate books will be found. But now, what if your user wants to search for all books with "Guide," but without "Hitchhiker"? Or what if the user wants to find all books with either "Hitchhiker" *or* "Guide," rather than "Hitchhiker" *and* "Guide"? Or, what if the user doesn't know quite the right words, so types in "Hitchhikers Guide" or "Hitchhiker's Guides"? What about "Guide, Hitchhiker's"?

This is the kind of intelligence users have come to expect from a search engine. It is theoretically possible to come up with various CFLOOPs and CFIFs that build SQL code to cover all of the above scenarios, but that many WHEREs, LIKEs, ANDs, and ORs would be a real pain to code, debug, and maintain. Plus, performance will degrade as the number of books grows. Indexing the text columns won't improve performance, because the LIKE operator cannot take advantage of indexes when a wildcard operator precedes the search string. There's just got to be a better way.

Indexing Your Table Data: Verity to the Rescue

Cold Fusion's Verity functionality provides a well-performing, easy-to-implement solution that addresses all of these concerns. You create a *custom* Verity collection filled with "documents" that aren't really documents at all. Each "document" is actually just a record from your database tables.

It works like this. You write a CFQUERY that retrieves the data you want to make searchable. You pass this data to a CFINDEX tag, which indexes the data as if it were documents. Additionally, you tell Verity which column from the query should be considered as a document "filename," which column should be considered as a document "title," and which column(s) should be considered as a document's "body." Figure 26.14 illustrates the idea.

FIG. 26.14

Database data becomes searchable, just like regular documents.

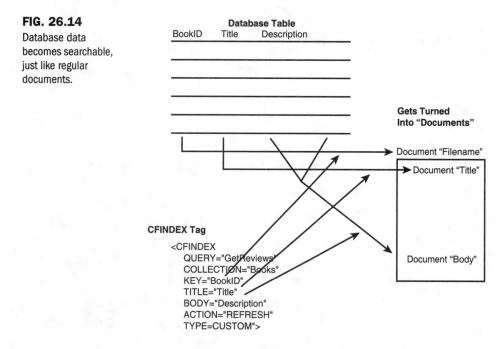

Assume you've just used the Cold Fusion Administrator to create a new Verity collection called Books, as discussed earlier in this chapter. Now, you'll populate this new collection with data from the Inventory database table.

Take a look at the code in Listing 26.8. You'll notice that the CFINDEX tag looks a lot like Listing 26.1, where you indexed your document files. The central differences here are the fact that you're setting TYPE to CUSTOM instead of PATH, and that you're referring to column names from a CFQUERY.

On the CD

Listing 26.8   INDEXDATA.CFM—Code to Index a Collection with Database Data

```
<CFQUERY NAME="GetResults" DATASOURCE="A2Z">
  SELECT BookID, Title, Description
  FROM Inventory
</CFQUERY>

<CFINDEX ACTION="REFRESH"
         COLLECTION="Books"
         KEY="BookID"
         TYPE="CUSTOM"
         TITLE="Title"
         QUERY="GetResults"
         BODY="Description">


<HTML>

<HEAD>
<TITLE>Indexing Complete</TITLE>
</HEAD>

<BODY>

<H2>Indexing Complete</H2>

</BODY>

</HTML>
```

Okay, the CFQUERY part is very simple—just get the basic information about the books. (Obviously, if you only wanted certain books to be indexed, a WHERE clause could be added to the CFQUERY's SQL statement.) Next comes a CFINDEX tag that looks a lot like the CFINDEX tag you used earlier to index your normal document files.

This time around, though, you specify a few new parameters that are necessary when indexing a database table instead of normal documents.

ACTION="REFRESH"	As before, tells Verity that you're supplying new data.
TYPE="CUSTOM"	Says that you're dealing with table data, rather than document files.
QUERY="GetResults"	Specifies from which CFQUERY to get the data.
KEY, TITLE, BODY	Specify which query columns should be treated like which parts of a "document."

That's really about all there is to it! Once the IndexData.cfm template is executed, you should be able to search the Books collection in much the same way as you searched the HRDocs collection back in Listing 26.3.

The code in Listing 26.9 will search through the newly indexed Books collection, based on whatever criteria the user types in the search form. Except for the introduction of the CFSEARCH tag, this code is virtually unchanged from Listing 26.6, which means that the results will be displayed to the user as shown in Figure 26.13.

N O T E You're still using the Inventory Search form from Listing 26.5—just be sure to change the ACTION parameter of the FORM tag to "InvSrch3.cfm". ▨

Listing 26.9 Searching and Displaying Records that Originally Came from a Database

```
<CFSEARCH COLLECTION="Books"
          NAME="GetResults"
          CRITERIA="#Form.Criteria#">

<HTML>

<HEAD>
<TITLE>Search Results</TITLE>
</HEAD>

<BODY>

<H2><CFOUTPUT>#GetResults.RecordCount# books found for
➥"#Form.Criteria#".</CFOUTPUT></H2>

<UL>
<CFOUTPUT QUERY="GetResults">
  <LI>#Title#
</CFOUTPUT>
</UL>

</BODY>

</HTML>
```

Part
IV

Ch
26

As you can see, it was pretty easy to expose your database data to Verity. You really didn't have to do much work at all. Of course, the user will notice a tremendous difference: All of Verity's AND, OR, NOT, wildcarding, and other searching niceties are all of a sudden very much available to her.

Displaying a Summary for Each Record   In addition to the score and title, Verity also provides a summary for each record in the search results. The summary will be the first 3 sentences— or the first 500 characters—of the information you specified for the BODY back when you in- dexed the collection with the CFINDEX tag. The summary is helpful for the user to "eyeball" which documents she is interested in.

To display the summary to the user, simply refer to it in your Cold Fusion templates in the same way you refer to the KEY, SCORE, or TITLE. Listing 26.10 adds the summary to your Search Results page. Figure 26.15 shows what the search results will look like to the user.

On the CD

Listing 26.10 INVSRCH4.CFM—Code to Include a Summary for Each Document

```
<CFSEARCH COLLECTION="Books"
          NAME="GetResults"
          CRITERIA="#Form.Criteria#">

<HTML>

<HEAD>
<TITLE>Search Results</TITLE>
</HEAD>

<BODY>

<H2><CFOUTPUT>#GetResults.RecordCount# books found for
➥"#Form.Criteria#".</CFOUTPUT></H2>

<DL>
<CFOUTPUT QUERY="GetResults">
  <DT><I>#NumberFormat(Round(Score * 100))#%</I>
      <B>#Title#</B>
  <DD><FONT SIZE="-1">#Summary#</FONT>
</CFOUTPUT>
</DL>

</BODY>

</HTML>
```

FIG. 26.15

Displaying the document summary is a slick, professional-looking touch.

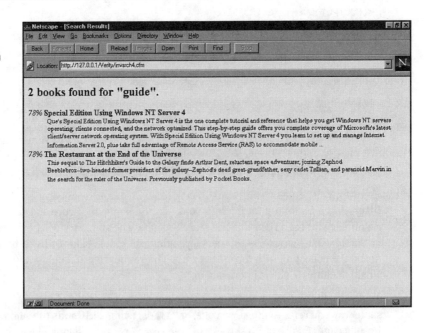

Don't expect Verity summaries to always show the parts of the document that contain the search keywords. That's not how Verity summarization works. The summary is selected for each record by Verity at the time that the collection is indexed, and will always be the same for any given record, regardless of whatever the search criteria were that found it. So the summary does not necessarily contain the keywords that were used as the search criteria.

Indexing Multiple Query Columns as the *BODY* In Listing 26.8, you indexed the Books collection with the results from a query. In that listing, you declared that the Description column from the Inventory table should be considered the body of each book record (by setting the BODY parameter of the CFINDEX tag to "Description").

By default, when your application runs a Verity search, only the BODY part of each record is actually searched for matching words. The information in the TITLE part of the record is not searched.

There are two ways to get the title to be searchable. One way is to specify the title in the CRI-TERIA parameter, using "Relational Operators."

But an easier way is to go back to your CFINDEX tag, and simply supply the information that you're giving to the TITLE parameter to the BODY parameter as well. The BODY parameter can take a comma-separated list of column names (like "Description, Title"), rather than only one column name (like "Description"). So for each record in your database, the searchable part of the record would be comprised of the Description of the book, followed by the Title of the book.

There's no need to stop there. You can put a bunch of column names in the BODY parameter, as shown in Listing 26.11. For each row returned by the query, Cold Fusion concatenates the Description, Publisher, AuthorFirstName, AuthorLastName, and Title columns together and presents it to Verity as the BODY of each "document." The result is all that textual information about the title, publisher, author, and so on is now part of your collection and is instantly searchable. You don't have to change a thing about the code in any of your search templates.

Part
IV

Ch

26

On the CD

Listing 26.11 INDEXDATA2.CFM—Supplying More Than One Column to the *BODY* Parameter

```
<CFQUERY NAME="GetResults" DATASOURCE="A2Z">
  SELECT BookID, Title, Description,
         Publisher, AuthorFirstName, AuthorLastName
  FROM Inventory
</CFQUERY>

<CFINDEX ACTION="UPDATE"
         COLLECTION="Books"
         KEY="BookID"
         TYPE="CUSTOM"
         TITLE="Title"
```

continues

Listing 26.11   Continued

```
            QUERY="GetResults"
            BODY="Description, Publisher, AuthorFirstName, AuthorLastName">

<HTML>

<HEAD>
<TITLE>Indexing Complete</TITLE>
</HEAD>

<BODY>

<H2>Indexing Complete</H2>

</BODY>

</HTML>
```

It's important to note that when you supply several columns to the BODY like this, Verity is not maintaining the information in separate columns or fields or anything. The structure of the underlying table is not preserved. All the information is "mushed" together into one big search-able mass. So don't expect to be able to refer to a #Publisher# variable, for instance, in the same way that you can refer to the #Title# and #Score# variables after a CFSEARCH is executed.

That may or may not feel like a limitation, depending on the nature of the applications that you're building. In a way, it's just the flip side of Verity's concentrating on text in a natural-language kind of way, rather than being obsessed with columns in the way that SQL is.

However, Cold Fusion and Verity do allow you to store a limited amount of information in a database-like way, using something called custom fields.

Indexing Additional Columns with Custom Fields   Cold Fusion allows you to index up to two additional Verity fields when you're indexing database data. The fields are called CUSTOM1 and CUSTOM2, and are treated very much like the Title field you've already worked with. These custom fields come in really handy when you have precise, code-style data you want to keep associated with each record.

In Listing 26.12, you adjust the code from Listing 26.8 to fill the CUSTOM1 field with your ISBN column, and the CUSTOM2 field with your CategoryID column. Conceptually, it's as if Verity is making two little "notes" on each "document" that it makes from the rows of your query. The CUSTOM1 "note" is the ISBN number, and the CUSTOM2 "note" is the CategoryID.

On the CD

Listing 26.12   INDEXDATA3.CFM—Adding Custom Fields to a Collection

```
<CFQUERY NAME="GetResults" DATASOURCE="A2Z">
  SELECT BookID, Title, Description, ISBN, CategoryID
  FROM Inventory
</CFQUERY>
```

```
<CFINDEX ACTION="UPDATE"
         COLLECTION="Books"
         KEY="BookID"
         TYPE="CUSTOM"
         TITLE="Title"
         QUERY="GetResults"
         BODY="Description"
         CUSTOM1="ISBN"
         CUSTOM2="CategoryID">

<HTML>

<HEAD>
<TITLE>Indexing Complete</TITLE>
</HEAD>

<BODY>

<H2>Indexing Complete</H2>

</BODY>

</HTML>
```

Now that Verity knows the CategoryID and ISBN for each record in the collection, it's easy to create a more sophisticated search tool that allows the user to choose Categories or ISBN numbers along with their search words, like Listing 26.13. Figure 26.16 shows what the search form looks like.

On the CD

Listing 26.13   INVSRCH1A—Search Form with User Interface for Custom Search Criteria

```
<HTML>

<HEAD>
<TITLE>Inventory Search</TITLE>
</HEAD>

<BODY>

<H2>Please enter keywords to search for.</H2>

<FORM ACTION="invsrch5.cfm" METHOD="POST">

Keywords: <INPUT TYPE="text" NAME="Criteria"><BR>

Category: <INPUT TYPE="Radio" NAME="CategoryID" VALUE="1">Literature
          <INPUT TYPE="Radio" NAME="CategoryID" VALUE="2">Humor
          <INPUT TYPE="Radio" NAME="CategoryID" VALUE="3">Computers
<P>
Or ISBN:  <INPUT TYPE="text" NAME="ISBN"><BR>
```

continues

Listing 26.13   Continued

```
<INPUT TYPE="submit" VALUE="Search">

</FORM>

</BODY>

</HTML>
```

FIG. 26.16

Custom Fields provide a
simple way to handle
search forms like this
one.

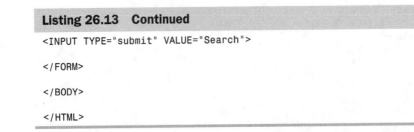

Now you just need to teach the receiving template how to deal with the user's entries for the
CategoryID and ISBN form fields. To specify the additional criteria, you'll make use of Verity's
MATCHES operator, which you're using here for the first time.

The MATCHES operator searches specific document fields—rather than the body—and finds only
exact matches. Document fields that you can use MATCHES with include CF_CUSTOM1,
CF_CUSTOM2, CF_TITLE, and CF_KEY, all of which correspond to the values you supply to the
CFINDEX tag when you indexed the data.

N O T E   Depending on the situation, you could use the Verity operators CONTAINS, STARTS, ENDS,
or SUBSTRING in the place of MATCHES in the this code. Also, you could use numeric
operators such as =, <, and > with the CF_CUSTOM2 field. See "Understanding Relational Operators" in
Appendix C for more information. ■

Listing 26.14 demonstrates the use of the MATCHES search operator. At the top of the template, you
use some CFIF, CFELSE, and CFELSEIF tags to decide what you're going to ask Verity to look for.

If the user specifies an ISBN number, you're not concerned with anything else, so you'll ignore the other form fields if the ISBN is not blank. If the ISBN is blank, however, there are still two possibilities: the category could be specified, keywords could be specified, or both.

So depending on which fields the user may have left blank, the TheCriteria variable will have slightly different values. Then the TheCriteria variable is supplied to the CFSEARCH tag in its CRITERIA parameter.

Listing 26.14   INVSRCH5.CFM—Using the *MATCHES* Operator to Search Custom Fields

```
<!--- DECIDE WHAT CRITERIA WE'LL PASS TO VERITY --->
<CFIF Form.ISBN is not "">
  <!--- IF AN ISBN NUMBER IS GIVEN, USE IT AND IGNORE OTHER INPUT --->
  <CFSET TheCriteria = "CF_CUSTOM1 <MATCHES> #Form.ISBN#">

<CFELSE>
  <CFIF (ParameterExists(Form.CategoryID) is "Yes")
➥AND (Form.Criteria is "")>
    <!--- ONLY A CATEGORY IS SPECIFIED --->
    <CFSET TheCriteria = "(CF_CUSTOM2 <MATCHES> #Form.CategoryID#) ">

  <CFELSEIF (ParameterExists(Form.CategoryID) is "No")
➥AND (Form.Criteria is not "")>
    <!--- ONLY KEYWORDS ARE SPECIFIED --->
    <CFSET TheCriteria = "#Form.Criteria#">

  <CFELSE>
    <!--- CATEGORY AND KEYWORDS ARE SPECIFIED --->
    <CFSET TheCriteria = "(CF_CUSTOM2 <MATCHES> #Form.CategoryID#)
➥AND (#Form.Criteria#)">

  </CFIF>
</CFIF>

<CFSEARCH COLLECTION="Books"
          NAME="GetResults"
          CRITERIA="#TheCriteria#">

<HTML>

<HEAD>
<TITLE>Search Results</TITLE>
</HEAD>

<BODY>

<H2><CFOUTPUT>#GetResults.RecordCount# books found.</CFOUTPUT></H2>

<P ALIGN="RIGHT"><CFOUTPUT>Actual Criteria Used:
➥#HTMLEditFormat(TheCriteria)#</CFOUTPUT></P>
```

continues

Part
IV

Ch

26

Listing 26.14   Continued

```
<DL>
<CFOUTPUT QUERY="GetResults">
  <DT><I>#NumberFormat(Round(Score * 100))#%</I>
        <B>#Title#</B>
  <DD><FONT SIZE="-1"><I>ISBN #Custom1#.</I> #Summary#</FONT>
</CFOUTPUT>
</DL>

</BODY>

</HTML>
```

As you can see in Figure 26.17, this code presents the ISBN number to the user by using the #Custom1# variable in the CFOUTPUT block, along with the summary, score, and other information. Also note that this code displays the criteria that is actually being passed to Verity at the top of the page, so you can fool around with the template a bit if you want and see the effect your CFIF logic is having.

FIG. 26.17
Custom fields let you display related information about each record found.

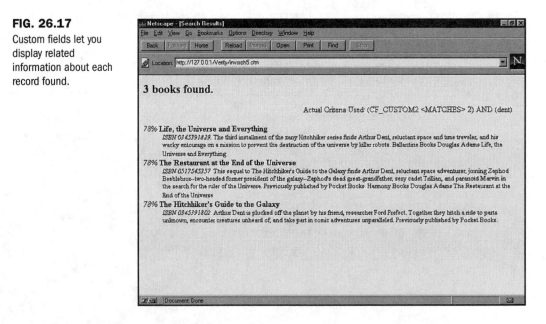

Combining Verity Searches with SQL Queries On-The-Fly

The Custom Fields that you just learned about give you a lot of flexibility. In most cases, you'll be able to search and display records straight from your Verity collection(s), without "bothering" the underlying database tables.

Still, you may encounter situations where you want to get information from Verity *and* your database tables, presenting the information together to the user. Using Cold Fusion's ValueList function along with SQL's IN operator, this kind of thing is quite easy to pull off.

Say you wanted to run a Verity search on the Books collection, but you wanted to be able to show the number of copies in stock for each book. You consider the idea of feeding the NumberInStock column to CUSTOM1 or CUSTOM2, but you decide that the number of copies in stock is such a volatile, ever-changing piece of information that you always want to display the "live" value directly from the database table.

You'll run a CFSEARCH just as you already have, but you won't display anything from it. Instead, you'll just use Verity's results as criteria for a normal SQL query. Verity will supply you with the "key value" for each "document" that it finds, which you know happens to be the BookID from your Inventory table. You'll supply those BookIDs to a normal CFQUERY.

Listing 26.15 shows how to use CFSEARCH results to "drive" a CFQUERY in this manner. Figure 26.18 shows the results.

On the CD

Listing 26.15 INVSRCH6.CFM—Using Verity Results as Criteria for a Normal SQL Query

```
<!--- RUN THE VERITY SEARCH --->
<CFSEARCH COLLECTION="Books"
          NAME="VeritySearch"
          CRITERIA="#Form.Criteria#">

<!--- GET THE RECORDS THAT VERITY FOUND --->
<CFQUERY NAME="GetResults" DATASOURCE="A2Z">
  SELECT BookID, Title, NumberInStock FROM Inventory
  WHERE BookID IN (#ValueList(VeritySearch.KEY)#)
  ORDER BY Title
</CFQUERY>

<HTML>

<HEAD>
<TITLE>Search Results</TITLE>
</HEAD>

<BODY>

<H2><CFOUTPUT>#GetResults.RecordCount# books found for
➥"#Form.Criteria#".</CFOUTPUT></H2>

<CFTABLE QUERY="GetResults" COLHEADERS HTMLTABLE BORDER>
  <CFCOL HEADER="BookID" TEXT="#BookID#">
  <CFCOL HEADER="Title" TEXT="#Title#">
  <CFCOL HEADER="In stock" TEXT="#NumberInStock#">
</CFTABLE>

</BODY>

</HTML>
```

Part
IV

Ch
26

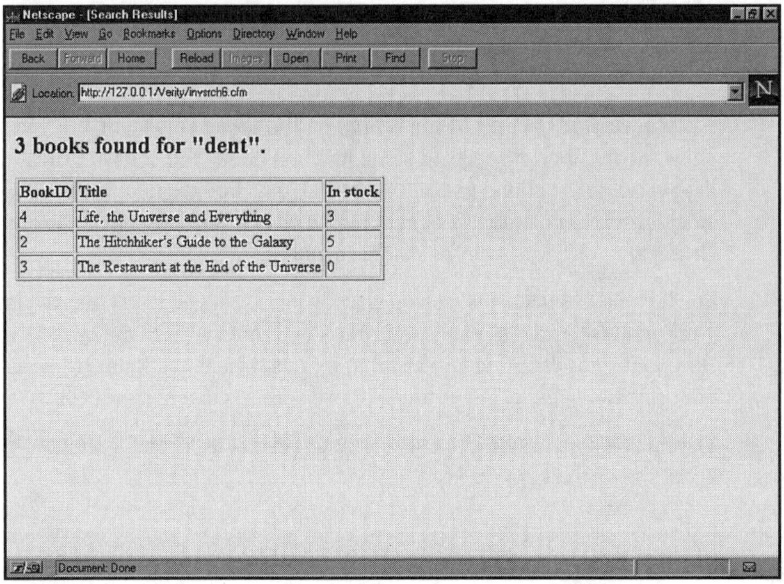

FIG. 26.18

CFSEARCH and CFQUERY can work well together, through SQL's IN keyword and Cold Fusion's ValueList function.

The browser window titled "Netscape - [Search Results]" shows:

3 books found for "dent".

BookID	Title	In stock
4	Life, the Universe and Everything	3
2	The Hitchhiker's Guide to the Galaxy	5
3	The Restaurant at the End of the Universe	0

T I P When you use this strategy, the search results will no longer be sorted by relevance. Instead, they'll be sorted according to the ORDER BY part of your SQL statement. This can be a good or a bad thing, depending on your situation. Keep it in mind.

Understanding Verity and Your Table's Key Values

When you're indexing table data, it's important to understand that Verity doesn't think of the concept of a "key" in the same way that your database tables do. Specifically, Verity does not assume or enforce any rules about uniqueness of values that you feed to it with the CFINDEX's KEY parameter. This means that Verity can and will index two separate "documents" that have the same key value. This can lead to problems, especially if the data you're indexing is derived from two tables that have a master-detail relationship to one another.

For instance, say you wanted to include the names of the people who placed orders for each of the books into the Verity collection as well. As you learned in Chapter 17, "Advanced SQL," it's fairly simple to create a join query that retrieves this information from your database tables.

The problem is, there can be any number of orders placed for each book, which means that if a book has been ordered by 7 different customers, there will be seven rows for that book in the result set. This poses a problem. Verity will dutifully index each of these rows as a separate "document," without understanding that the 7 rows all represent the same book. This means that a search that matches up with the text of the book will find all 7 records and display them to the user. This can make your application look buggy.

Cold Fusion provides no built-in way out of this. CFINDEX doesn't have a GROUP parameter like CFOUTPUT does. And you can't use GROUP when you're displaying the records, because the 7 rows aren't guaranteed to be in consecutive rows when Verity finds them. You either need to avoid this kind of situation altogether, or figure out some way of processing the data between the CFQUERY and the CFINDEX.

Here's one approach. The code in Listing 26.16 takes the query results and manually creates a second query, line-by-line. The new query has the same structure as the original, except that it is guaranteed to have only one row for each book. If the original query had more than one row for a particular BookID (because of multiple orders), the customer names from all the rows are turned into a comma-separated list when they are put into the new query. The result is a query that can be used to index a Verity collection without problems.

On the CD

Listing 26.16 INDEXDATA4.CFM—Solving the Problem by Creating a New, "Uniqued" Query

```
<CFQUERY NAME="GetResults" DATASOURCE="A2Z">
  SELECT i.BookID, i.Title, i.Description, c.Company
  FROM Inventory i, OrderItems oi, Orders o, Customers c
  WHERE i.BookID = oi.BookID
      AND oi.OrderID = o.OrderID
      AND o.CustomerID = c.CustomerID
  ORDER BY i.BookID
</CFQUERY>

<!--- Create new query with same column names --->
<CFSET MyQuery = QueryNew(GetResults.ColumnList)>
<CFOUTPUT QUERY="GetResults" GROUP="BookID">
  <!--- Make a comma-separated list of all papers for this BookID --->
  <CFSET CompanyList = "">
  <CFOUTPUT><CFSET CompanyList = ListAppend(CompanyList, GetResults.
➥Company)></CFOUTPUT>
  <!--- Make new row in MyQuery, with other data just copied from
➥GetResults --->
  <CFSET Temp = QueryAddRow(MyQuery)>
  <CFSET Temp = QuerySetCell(MyQuery,"BookID",GetResults.BookID)>
  <CFSET Temp = QuerySetCell(MyQuery,"Title",GetResults.Title)>
  <CFSET Temp = QuerySetCell(MyQuery,"Description",GetResults.Description)>
  <CFSET Temp = QuerySetCell(MyQuery,"Company",CompanyList)>
</CFOUTPUT>

<CFINDEX ACTION="UPDATE"
        COLLECTION="Books"
        KEY="BookID"
        TYPE="CUSTOM"
        TITLE="Title"
        QUERY="MyQuery"
        BODY="Description, Company">

<HTML>

<HEAD>
<TITLE>Indexing Complete</TITLE>
</HEAD>
```

Part
IV

Ch
26

continues

Listing 26.16   Continued

```
<BODY>

<H2>Indexing Complete</H2>

</BODY>

</HTML>
```

Once this code is run, if the user typed a company name in a search form, the CFSEARCH would find books that the specified company has actually ordered.

Searching on More than One Collection

To specify more than one Verity collection in a CFSEARCH tag, just specify all of the collection names for the COLLECTION parameter, separated by commas. All of the collections will be searched for matching documents.

> **N O T E**   If you have Allaire Forums 2.02 installed on your system, this is how the Search Message
> Titles and Search Titles and Text options work on the Search page. The titles and text are
> separate collections. ■

So, if you wanted to allow your users to choose from several collections, you could add code like Listing 26.17 to your search form.

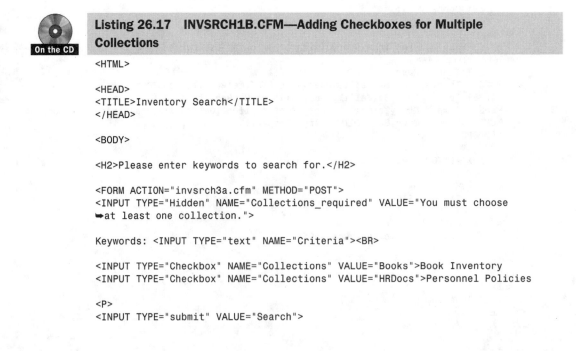

Listing 26.17   INVSRCH1B.CFM—Adding Checkboxes for Multiple Collections

```
<HTML>

<HEAD>
<TITLE>Inventory Search</TITLE>
</HEAD>

<BODY>

<H2>Please enter keywords to search for.</H2>

<FORM ACTION="invsrch3a.cfm" METHOD="POST">
<INPUT TYPE="Hidden" NAME="Collections_required" VALUE="You must choose
➥at least one collection.">

Keywords: <INPUT TYPE="text" NAME="Criteria"><BR>

<INPUT TYPE="Checkbox" NAME="Collections" VALUE="Books">Book Inventory
<INPUT TYPE="Checkbox" NAME="Collections" VALUE="HRDocs">Personnel Policies

<P>
<INPUT TYPE="submit" VALUE="Search">
```

```
</FORM>

</BODY>

</HTML>
```

Because of the convenient way checkboxes are handled by Cold Fusion, the value of the Form.Collections variable will be set to "Books,HRDocs" if the user checks both boxes. So you'd just pass the variable directly to the COLLECTION parameter of the receiving template's CFSEARCH tag.

TIP Note that you can freely mix normal document collections with database-table collections within a single CFSEARCH operation.

Displaying Records in a Different Order   The search results returned by a CFSEARCH tag are ranked in "order of relevance." The closest matches—the ones with the highest score—are first, and the weakest matches are last.

Verity provides a few ways to tweak the way the score is computed (see "Understanding Score Operators" in Appendix C), which gives you a little bit of control over how the documents are ordered. But what if you wanted to display the search results in, say, alphabetical order by title?

There is no built-in function to handle this in Cold Fusion 3.1. At the time of this writing, there is no CFX_QuerySort or similar tag available either. In lieu of these options, Listing 26.18 provides a CFML custom tag that you can use to order your Verity results. Actually, you can use it to sort the output of any Cold Fusion tag that presents its data as a "query," like CFPOP, CFLDAP, and the like.

Part
IV

Ch
26

On the CD

Listing 26.18   QUERYSORT.CFM—A Custom Tag to Sort Query (and Thus Verity) Results

```
<!--- Example of use

<CF_QuerySort
  QUERY="MyQuery"
  SORTCOLUMN="MyColumn"
  SORTORDER="Desc"                <- optional, defaults to Asc
  SORTTYPE="Numeric"              <- optional, defaults to Textnocase
  SORTEDQUERY="MySortedQuery">    <- optional, defaults to "Sorted"

 --->

<!--- SUSPEND OUTPUT --->
<CFSETTING CFOUTPUTONLY="YES">

<!--- REQUIRED PARAMETERS --->
<CFPARAM NAME="Attributes.QUERY">
```

continues

Listing 26.18   Continued

```
<CFPARAM NAME="Attributes.SortColumn">
<!--- OPTIONAL PARAMETERS --->
<CFPARAM NAME="Attributes.SortType" DEFAULT="Textnocase">
<CFPARAM NAME="Attributes.SortOrder" DEFAULT="Asc">
<CFPARAM NAME="Attributes.SortedQuery" DEFAULT="Sorted">

<!--- ESTABLISH LOCAL VERSIONS OF QUERIES --->
<CFSET MyArray = ArrayNew(1)>
<CFSET MyQuery = Evaluate("Caller.#Attributes.Query#")>
<CFSET NewQuery = QueryNew(MyQuery.ColumnList)>
<CFIF MyQuery.RecordCount greater than 999999><CFABORT SHOWERROR="Only
➥Queries with less than one million rows can be sorted.
➥Your Query has #MyQuery.RecordCount# rows."></CFIF>

<!--- ADD ROWNUMBER TO END OF EACH ROW'S VALUE --->
<CFOUTPUT QUERY="MyQuery">
  <CFSET MyArray[CurrentRow] = Evaluate("MyQuery.#Attributes.SortColumn#")
➥& NumberFormat(CurrentRow, "000009")>
  <CFSET Temp = QueryAddRow(NewQuery)>
</CFOUTPUT>

<!--- SORT ARRAY --->
<CFSET Temp = ArraySort(MyArray, Attributes.SortType, Attributes.SortOrder)>

<!--- POPULATE NEW QUERY, ROW BY ROW, WITH APPROPRIATE ROW OF OLD QUERY --->
<CFLOOP FROM=1 TO=#MyQuery.RecordCount# INDEX="This">
  <CFSET Row = Val(Right(MyArray[This], 6))>
  <CFLOOP LIST="#MyQuery.ColumnList#" INDEX="Col">
    <CFSET Temp = QuerySetCell(NewQuery, Col, Evaluate("MyQuery.#Col#
➥[Row]"), This)>
  </CFLOOP>
</CFLOOP>

<!--- PASS SORTED QUERY BACK TO CALLING TEMPLATE --->
<CFSET "Caller.#Attributes.SortedQuery#" = NewQuery>

<!--- RESTORE OUTPUT --->
<CFSETTING CFOUTPUTONLY="NO">
```

If you save the QuerySort.cfm file to your server's CustomTags directory, it should be quite easy to use it to sort your Verity results, as shown in Listing 26.19.

Listing 26.19   SORTED.CFM—Sorting Verity Results by Title

```
<CFSEARCH COLLECTION="Books"
          NAME="GetResults"
          CRITERIA="#Form.Criteria#">

<CF_QUERYSORT QUERY="GetResults"
              SORTEDQUERY="GetResults"
              SORTCOLUMN="Title">
```

```
<HTML>

<HEAD>
<TITLE>Search Results</TITLE>
</HEAD>

<BODY>

<H2><CFOUTPUT>#GetResults.RecordCount# books found for
➥"#Form.Criteria#".</CFOUTPUT></H2>

<UL>
<CFOUTPUT QUERY="GetResults">
  <LI>#Title#
</CFOUTPUT>
</UL>

</BODY>

</HTML>
```

Maintaining Collections

In some rare situations, you may be able to simply create a Verity collection, index it, and forget about it. So if the documents or data that make up the collection never change, you're in luck—you get to skip this whole section of the chapter.

But it's probably pretty likely that you'll have to refresh that data at some point in the future. Even when you don't have to refresh it, you may want to get it to run faster.

Re-Populating Your Verity Collection

Whenever the original documents change from what they were when you indexed them, your collection will be a little bit "out of sync" with reality. The search results will be based on Verity's knowledge of the documents back when you did your indexing. If a document—or database record—has since been edited so that it no longer has certain words in it, it may be found "in error" if someone types in a search for those words. And if the document is deleted altogether, Verity will still find it in its own records, which means that your application might show a "bad link" that leads nowhere.

In a totally perfect world, Verity would dynamically "watch" your document folders and data tables, and reflect any changes, additions, or deletions in your collections immediately. Unfortunately, the world isn't totally perfect, and this stuff doesn't happen automatically for you. The good news is that it's no major chore, either.

If You Index Your Collections Interactively If you recall, there are two ways of indexing a Verity collection: *interactively* with the Cold Fusion Administrator and *programmatically* with the CFINDEX tag. If you did it interactively, there's not much I need to tell you. Just go back to the Verity page in the Administrator and hit the Purge button for your collection. Then hit the

Index button and do the same thing you did the first time. This should bring your collection up to date.

> **TIP**
>
> You would do the same basic thing if the location of the documents had changed.

If You Index Your Collections Programmatically If you indexed the collection using CFINDEX—and you used ACTION="REFRESH" in the CFINDEX tag, as shown in Listing 26.1 and Listing 26.8—you should be able to bring your collection up-to-date simply by running it again.

> **TIP**
>
> You might want to consider scheduling this "Refresh" template to be executed automatically at the end of each week, during off-peak hours. For more information on Cold Fusion's built-in template scheduler, see Chapter 32, "Event Scheduling."

Instead of ACTION="REFRESH", you can use ACTION="UPDATE" in your CFINDEX tag. This updates information on documents already indexed, but without deleting information on documents that no longer exist. You can also use ACTION="PURGE" to completely remove all data from the collection. So the ACTION="REFRESH" previously recommended is really the same thing as a PURGE followed by an UPDATE.

Deleting/Repopulating Specific Records If your application is aware of the moment that a document or table record is deleted or edited, you may want to update the Verity collection right then, so your collection stays in sync with the actual information. But clearly it's not necessary to repopulate the entire collection just because one record has changed. Cold Fusion and Verity address this by allowing you to delete items from a collection by the key value.

For instance, after an edit has been made to the Inventory database table, you could use the code shown in Listing 26.20 to remove the record from the collection and put the new data in its place. This should run much faster than a complete repopulation. This listing assumes that a form has just been submitted that passes the BookID as a hidden field, and contains some other fields that are meant to allow them to update certain columns in the Inventory table (the description, perhaps) for a particular book.

On the CD

Listing 26.20   DELADD.CFM—Deleting and then Re-Adding a Specific Record to a Collection

```
<!--- Perform the update to the database table --->
<CFUPDATE DATASOURCE="A2Z" TABLENAME="Inventory">

<!--- Retrieve updated data back from the database --->
<CFQUERY NAME="GetBook" DATASOURCE="A2Z">
  SELECT BookID, Title, Description
  FROM Inventory
  WHERE BookID = #Form.BookID#
</CFQUERY>
```

```
<!--- Delete the old record from the Verity collection --->
<CFINDEX ACTION="DELETE"
  COLLECTION="Books"
  KEY="#Form.BookID#">

<!--- Get updated version back into the Verity collection --->
<CFINDEX ACTION="UPDATE"
  COLLECTION="Books"
  TYPE="CUSTOM"
  QUERY="GetBook"
  KEY="BookID"
  TITLE="Title"
  BODY="Description">

<HTML>

<HEAD>
<TITLE>Update Complete</TITLE>
</HEAD>

<BODY>

<H2>Update Complete</H2>

</BODY>

</HTML>
```

Optimizing Your Verity Collection

After a Verity collection gets "hit" many times, performance may start to degrade. Depending on your application, this may never become a problem. But if you notice your Verity searches becoming slower over time, you might want to try optimizing your collection. Optimizing your collection is similar conceptually to running Disk Defragmenter on a Windows 95 machine.

Just highlight the collection in the Cold Fusion Administrator and click Optimize. Verity will whirl around for a minute or two as the collection is optimized. If you notice an improvement in performance, you may want to consider indexing the collection on a regular basis. You can do this on your own with the Administrator, or you can use a CFINDEX tag in a short template that does the optimizing for you, as shown in Listing 26.21.

On the CD

**Listing 26.21   OPTIMIZE.CFM—Optimizing a Collection with the
CFINDEX Tag**

```
<CFINDEX ACTION="OPTIMIZE"
         COLLECTION="Books">

<HTML>
```

continues

Part
IV
Ch
26

Listing 26.21 Continued

```
<HEAD>
<TITLE>Optimizing Complete</TITLE>
</HEAD>

<BODY>

<H2>Optimizing Complete</H2>

</BODY>

</HTML>
```

N O T E If for some reason your Verity collection becomes damaged, you can try using the Repair button on the Verity page of the Cold Fusion Administrator. This is similar conceptually to repairing an Access database.

If repairing the collection doesn't help, then you'll need to delete the collection, re-create it, and re-index it. Hopefully, you won't run into this problem. ■

Understanding Verity's Search Syntax

So far, you've explored a number of ways to index information and make it searchable on the web. You've also covered using AND, OR, and wildcards to make your search criteria work harder for you.

It doesn't stop at AND and OR. Verity practically provides a fairly rich set of operators that you can use in your search criteria. In general, don't expect that your users will be using these operators along with their keywords when they are running a search. Most people aren't going to go beyond ANDs and ORs. But you may, in certain circumstances, want to use some of these operators "behind the scenes." Table 26.7 lists all of the operators available by category. Refer to Appendix C for explanations of each of the operators listed in Table 26.7.

Table 26.7 Verity Operator Quick Reference

Category	Operator	Purpose	Description
Concept Operators	AND	To find *documents* where:	All words/conditions are found
	OR		Any one word/ condition is found
Evidence Operators	STEM	To find *words* that:	Are derived from the search words
	WORD		Match the search words

Category	Operator	Purpose	Description
	WILDCARD		Match search words with *, ?, and so on
Proximity Operators	NEAR	To find *words* that are:	Close together
	NEAR/N		Within *N* words of each other
	PARAGRAPH		In same paragraph
	PHRASE		In same phrase
	SENTENCE		In same sentence
Relational Operators	CONTAINS	To find *words* that are:	Within a specific field
	MATCHES		The text of an entire field
	STARTS		At the start of a specific field
	ENDS		At the end of a specific field
	SUBSTRING		Within a specific field as fragments
	=, <, >, <=, >=		(For numeric and date values only)
Search Modifiers	CASE	To change Verity's behavior so that:	The search is case-sensitive
	MANY		Documents are ranked by relevance matching
	NOT		Documents should not be found
	ORDER		Words must appear in documents in order
Score Operators	YESNO	To *rank* documents found:	Equally (no ranking)
	COMPLEMENT		In reverse order
	PRODUCT		By pushing multiple hits up faster
	SUM		By pushing multiple hits up much faster

Part

IV

Ch

26

CHAPTER 27

Directory Services

by Ben Forta

In this chapter

Understanding Directory Services

Directories are lists of objects, usually lists of users. Anyone who has ever logged into a network, or accessed email, has used a Directory Service. The Directory Service is the directory of users, login names, passwords, and other information used to validate user account and logins.

In the past, network operating systems and applications maintained their own directories. Network administrators have grown accustomed to having to add new users to multiple databases, perhaps one for the network, another for an email account, another for remote access, and yet others for specific applications. Obviously, managing these directories is both difficult and time consuming. Administrators must make sure to make changes to all directories, just as users changing passwords must make sure to make the change in multiple locations to ensure that the passwords are kept in synch.

But this is all changing. Network administrators are now establishing corporate directories. These directories can store all sorts of information, including:

- User names and login information
- Passwords
- Locations and addresses
- Phone numbers and extensions
- Group affiliation
- Security and access information
- Binary data, such as pictures of employees
- Encryption keys
- … and much more

These new directories are accessible by multiple applications and, in an ideal environment, by all applications on a network. The centralized directory helps ensure that data is always accurate, current, and easily managed.

The directories themselves, and the tools used to manage them, are referred to as "Directory Services." Examples of Directory Services include:

- Banyan StreetTalk
- Microsoft Active Directory (part of NT5)
- Microsoft Exchange (MAPI)
- Novell NDS (Novell Directory Services)
- X.500 compliant directories

These directories are more than simple address books, although they can be that too. Directory Services are complete databases of users, objects, resources, security equivalencies, rights, and the tools with which to manage this information. Directory Services are usually extremely security conscious, and have built-in access controls and restrictions enabling the administrator to specify who has access to what information, and what they can do to it.

Understanding LDAP

A Directory Service is only useful if applications can take advantage of it. And while every one of the Directory Service products previously listed are powerful and useable solutions, interfacing with them has never been a trivial task.

For application developers to support these Directory Services, they'd have to write code specifically for each product, using each product's API. Supporting multiple API's is time consuming, and usually requires that the developer have a very good understanding of the Directory Service, so as to be able to write code at as low a level as is required.

To solve this problem, and so to facilitate simple and consistent Directory Service interaction, LDAP, the Lightweight Directory Access Protocol, was developed at the University of Michigan at Ann Arbor. LDAP is a slimmed-down version of DAP, the Directory Access Protocol of the international X.500 standard for directories.

LDAP has broad industry support. The list of vendors that have committed themselves to LDAP includes AT&T, Banyan, HP, IBM, Lotus, Microsoft, Netscape, and Novell. In addition, many of the public Internet directories, such as BigFoot, Four11, Switchboard, and WhoWhere?, have created LDAP interfaces for public use.

LDAP is a client-server directory access protocol that enables LDAP-compliant clients to communicate with LDAP-compliant servers. All of the Directory Service products previously listed are LDAP-compliant (or have add-ons or gateways that provide LDAP support). Users can simply point their address books to any directory, whether it's on a local machine, on their corporate address book, or a public Internet directory.

LDAP hides the differences between Directory Services from the client application. All the client needs to know is the address (DNS name or IP address) of the LDAP server so that LDAP requests can be submitted to it. The same LDAP client software can talk to *any* LDAP compliant server, and no special drivers are needed on the client side. The LDAP software of the server itself handles the translation between the native databases and LDAP.

To help understand this concept, think of LDAP as being to Directory Services as ODBC is to databases. LDAP allows clients to talk to a single interface, and thereby access many different Directory Service products. The big difference between LDAP and ODBC, however, is that ODBC requires that the client install different database drivers and know the type of database being accessed. LDAP places this requirement on the server; the client needs no knowledge of the underlying Directory Service.

▶ **See** Chapter 2, "Introduction to Cold Fusion," **p. 15**

▶ **See** Chapter 8, "Introduction to SQL," **p. 129**

LDAP is most frequently used to search Directory Services. But the LDAP protocol also provides the means to manage directories as well. Using LDAP, a single client application could be used to search, add to, update, and delete from a directory.

Many new applications are being turned into LDAP clients. Netscape Communicator 4, Microsoft Exchange 5, and Microsoft Internet Mail are examples of applications that can talk to

LDAP servers to access Directory Service information. Figure 27.1 shows the LDAP-driven user search feature in the Netscape Navigator 4.0 Address Book.

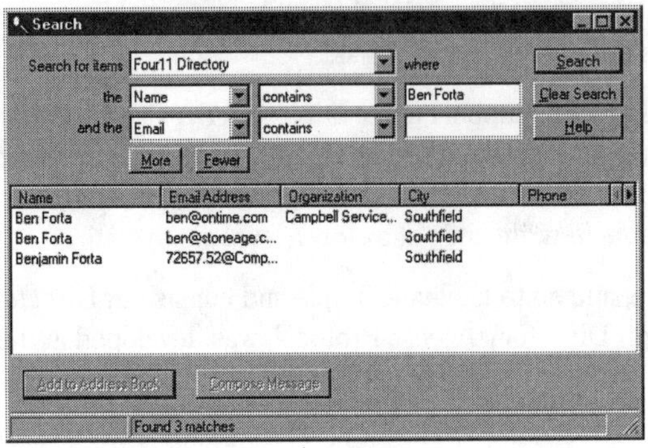

FIG. 27.1
The Netscape Messenger Address Book uses LDAP to allow users to search public user directories.

Keep in mind, however, that LDAP is a relatively new standard, and one that is still evolving. Not all LDAP servers and clients are created equally, and the ultimate goal of complete Directory Service independence has yet to be attained. In the short term, you will probably need to familiarize yourself with the exact level of support provided by a specific LDAP server, paying close attention to the supported attributes (columns).

N O T E Version 3 of LDAP is on the horizon. That version provides some of the key missing components that have prevented LDAP client from being totally server-independent. Cold Fusion will support LDAP version 3 in the future. ▣

Understanding <*CFLDAP*>

As mentioned earlier, ideally Directory Services need to be accessible by all network applications, and Cold Fusion applications are no exception. Cold Fusion developers often find themselves having to implement security systems, check passwords, determine email addresses, and more. And if a Directory Service is already in place, then all this information already exists. All the Cold Fusion developer needs is a mechanism with which to access this data.

And this is where <CFLDAP> fits in. <CFLDAP> is the Cold Fusion LDAP client tag. Yes, you read that right. <CFLDAP> encapsulates the entire LDAP client protocol and supporting code in a single, simple to use, Cold Fusion tag.

<CFLDAP> allows several different operations, specified using the ACTION attribute.

- QUERY is used to browse or search a directory.
- ADD is used to add records to a directory.
- MODIFY & MODIFYDN are both used to update entries.
- DELETE is used to remove data from a directory.

When used to retrieve data, <CFLDAP> returns data in the standard Cold Fusion query format, into a query named as specified in the NAME attribute. This allows you to use standard query manipulation—including CFOUTPUT, CFTABLE, CFLOOP, CFMAIL, CFSELECT, CFGRID, and CFTREE—to display or process the data.

▶ **See** Chapter 11, "Cold Fusion Basics," **p. 193**

▶ **See** Chapter 19, "Enhancing Forms with *CFFORM*," **p. 427**

Retrieving Data with *<CFLDAP>*

The best way to learn how to use <CFLDAP> is to see examples of it used. The first example uses <CFLDAP> to retrieve a list of employees whose last names are Smith (or begin with Smith).

The NAME attribute specifies the name of the query result set to be created, just like the NAME attribute in CFQUERY. The SERVER attribute specifies the DNS name of the LDAP server where the request is to be sent. As this is a query operation, the ACTION attribute is set to type QUERY. (Because ACTION="QUERY" is the default operation, this attribute could actually have been omitted). The ATTRIBUTES attribute specifies which LDAP attributes are to be returned. An LDAP attribute is kind of like a column in a database table. Whenever you query an LDAP server you must specify which columns, or attributes, you want returned to you. This example requests the cn (common name, or full name) attribute, and the email (email address) attribute. The attributes are specified as a comma delimited list, and a column will be created in the query for each attribute in the list. The SORT attribute specifies the sort order, and this example specifies that the data be sorted by common name (cn) in ascending (ASC) order. The final attribute is the required START attribute, which specifies the actual search text.

The query results returned by <CFLDAP> are used to populate a HTML unordered list that displays the list of names, and allows the user to click a name to send email to that employee.

```
<!--- Retrieve all employees named Smith --->
<CFLDAP
 NAME="Employees"
 SERVER="ldap.company.com"
 ACTION="QUERY"
 ATTRIBUTES="cn,email"
 SORT="cn ASC"
 START="cn=Smith"
>
<!--- Display list and create URL for mailto --->
<UL>
<CFOUTPUT QUERY= "">
<LI><A HREF=mailto:#email#>#cn#</A>
</CFOUTPUT>
</UL>
```

As this example demonstrates, Cold Fusion makes interacting with a LDAP server simple and convenient.

Using <CFLDAP>

Now that you have seen what <CFLDAP> can do, take a look at the complete set of tag attributes shown in Table 27.1.

Table 27.1   <CFLDAP>

Attributes	Description
ACTION	Required—As previously described, must be either ADD, DELETE, MODIFY, MODIFYDN, or QUERY.
ATTRIBUTES	Required (if ACTION="QUERY", ACTION="ADD", or ACTION="MODIFY") comma-delimited list of columns to be returned or updated. If ACTION="QUERY", the query result set will contain a column for each entry in this list.
DN	Required (if ACTION="ADD", ACTION="DELETE", ACTION="MODIFY", or ACTION="MODIFYDN") "distinguished name" of the entry to be changed. The "distinguished name" is the LDAP equivalent of a database table's primary key. A "distinguished name" uniquely identifies an entry in a directory.
FILTER	Optional filter to be used when querying data. May contain one or more conditions in a comma-delimited list in the format of attribute=filter, attribute=filter. If no FILTER is specified, then all entries will be returned.
MAXROWS	Optional maximum number of rows to be returned by CFLDAP. Note that many LDAP servers impose their own maximum that cannot be overridden. Similar to the <CFQUERY> MAXROWS attribute.
NAME	Required (only if ACTION="QUERY") name of the query result set to be created by CFLDAP. The query will contain the columns specified in the ATTRIBUTES attribute.
PASSWORD	Optional password to be used if a USERNAME is provided.
PORT	Optional port number that the LDAP server responds to. Defaults to 389 if not specified. (This attribute will rarely be needed.)
SCOPE	Optional search scope used when ACTION="QUERY". There are three possible values: ONELEVEL searches all entries one level beneath the entry specified in the Start attribute (this is the default value), BASE searches only the entry specified in the Start attribute, SUBTREE searches the entry specified in the Start attribute, as well all entries at all levels beneath it.
SERVER	Required DNS name or IP address of the LDAP server to which the request is to be sent.

Attributes	Description
SORT	Optional attribute to sort query results by. If specified, the attribute must be one of those listed in the ATTRIBUTES attribute. The column may be followed by the keyword ASC to sort ascending, or DESC to sort descending. If neither ASC nor DESC are specified, then the column will be sorted in ascending order.
START	Required (only if ACTION="QUERY") search conditions. Can contain one or more attributes in a comma-delimited list in the format of attribute=value, attribute=value.
TIMEOUT	Optional operation timeout value. Will default to 60 seconds if not specified. (60 seconds is more than enough time for most operations on most LDAP servers.)
USERNAME	Optional user name to be used to login to the LDAP server. If no name is specified, than an anonymous login will be used. LDAP servers are often configured to allow different levels of access (for both requesting data, and changing data) based on login. Note that some LDAP servers deny anonymous login attempts; ask your network administrator for login details. All public Internet LDAP servers allow basic data retrieval via anonymous login.

Accessing Public LDAP Servers

As mentioned earlier, many of the public Internet directories have LDAP interfaces that you can freely access. Table 27.2 lists some of the more popular directories that support LDAP, their homepages, and their LDAP server names.

Table 27.2   Public LDAP Servers

Service	Homepage	LDAP Server
Bigfoot	http://www.bigfoot.com	ldap.bigfoot.com
Four11	http://www.four11.com	ldap.four11.com
InfoSpace	http://www.infospace.com	ldap.infospace.com
Switchboard	http://www.switchboard.com	ldap.switchboard.com
WhoWhere?	http://www.whowhere.com	ldap.whowhere.com

Part
IV

Ch
27

To access any of these directories via <CFLDAP>, all you need is the name of that LDAP server. All of these services allow querying via anonymous login, so no login name and password is required.

Creating an LDAP Client

To demonstrate working with LDAP, take a look at a sample application. The A2Z Contact Lookup is designed to be used by customer service or support personnel allowing them to try to locate names on any of five public user directories.

Figure 27.2 shows the search screen. The interface allows you to enter a name (or part thereof), and select a server from the list of available LDAP servers. Figure 27.3 shows the formatted returned results.

FIG. 27.2

Many of the major online user directories support public LDAP lookups.

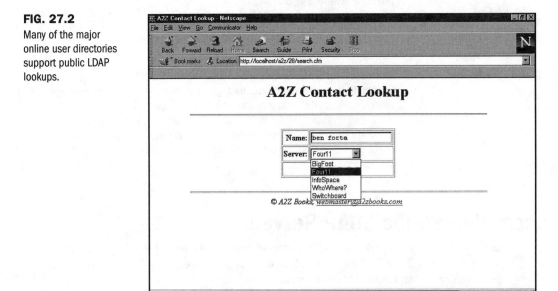

The application is made up of five files.

HEADER.CFM is the header file shared by both the search and results screens.

FOOTER.CFM is the footer file shared by both the search and results screens.

SERVERS.CFM contains the list of available servers.

SEARCH.CFM is the search screen, with a drop-down list of servers dynamically driven by the server list in SERVERS.CFM.

RESULTS.CFM performs the actual LDAP lookup and displays the results.

▶ **See** Chapter 18, "Advanced Cold Fusion Templates," **p. 401**

Creating the Services List

The list of servers is stored in SERVERS.CFM, shown in Listing 27.1.

FIG. 27.3
The attributes
(information) returned
by each LDAP server
might differ from one
server to the next.

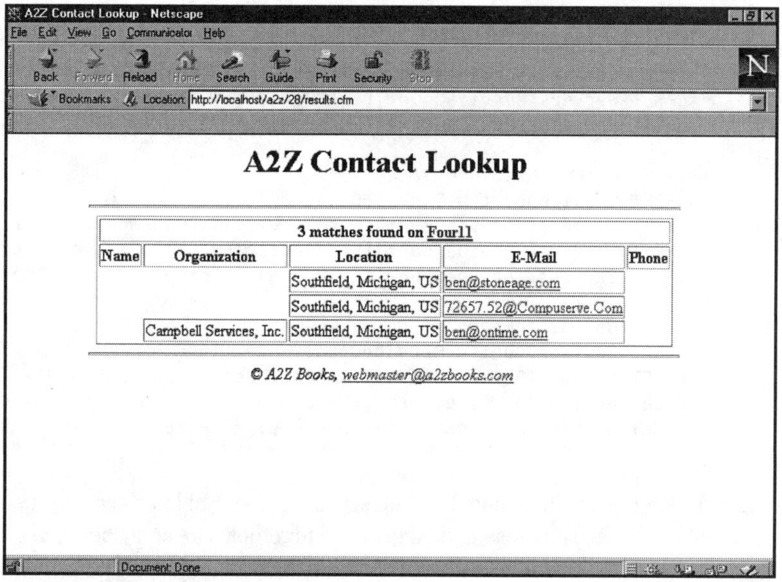

On the CD

Listing 27.1   C:\A2Z\SCRIPTS\28\SERVERS.CFM—Source for SERVERS.CFM File

```
<!--- Array columns --->
<CFSET LDAPService = 1>
<CFSET LDAPServer = 2>
<CFSET LDAPHome = 3>

<!--- Two dimensional array to hold servers --->
<CFSET Servers = ArrayNew(2)>

<!--- Number of services available --->
<CFSET ServiceCount = 0>

<!--- Add BigFoot to array --->
<CFSET ServiceCount = ServiceCount + 1>
<CFSET Servers[ServiceCount][LDAPService] = "BigFoot">
<CFSET Servers[ServiceCount][LDAPServer] = "ldap.bigfoot.com">
<CFSET Servers[ServiceCount][LDAPHome] = "http://www.bigfoot.com">

<!--- Add Four11 to array --->
<CFSET ServiceCount = ServiceCount + 1>
<CFSET Servers[ServiceCount][LDAPService] = "Four11">
<CFSET Servers[ServiceCount][LDAPServer] = "ldap.four11.com">
<CFSET Servers[ServiceCount][LDAPHome] = "http://www.four11.com">

<!--- Add InfoSpace to array --->
<CFSET ServiceCount = ServiceCount + 1>
```

Part

IV

Ch

27

continues

Listing 27.1 Continued

```
<CFSET Servers[ServiceCount][LDAPService] = "InfoSpace">
<CFSET Servers[ServiceCount][LDAPServer] = "ldap.infospace.com">
<CFSET Servers[ServiceCount][LDAPHome] = "http://www.infospace.com">

<!--- Add WhoWhere? to array --->
<CFSET ServiceCount = ServiceCount + 1>
<CFSET Servers[ServiceCount][LDAPService] = "WhoWhere?">
<CFSET Servers[ServiceCount][LDAPServer] = "ldap.whowhere.com">
<CFSET Servers[ServiceCount][LDAPHome] = "http://www.whowhere.com">

<!--- Add Switchboard to array --->
<CFSET ServiceCount = ServiceCount + 1>
<CFSET Servers[ServiceCount][LDAPService] = "Switchboard">
<CFSET Servers[ServiceCount][LDAPServer] = "ldap.switchboard.com">
<CFSET Servers[ServiceCount][LDAPHome] = "http://www.switchboard.com">
```

As you can see in Listing 27.1, the servers are stored in an array, a special type of variable that allows you to store sets of data grouped together. The array being used here is a two dimensional array, kind of like a two dimensional grid, created with the code

```
<CFSET Servers = ArrayNew(2)>
```

This creates an array called Servers with two dimensions (you can think of a two dimensional array as having rows and columns, making up the two dimensions).

As servers are added to the array, rows are automatically added. The code `<CFSET Servers[ServiceCount][LDAPService] = "Four11">` sets the first column (LDAPServer is set to 1) of the first row (ServiceCount equals one for the first row) to Four 11.

While this might seem overly complex, what you are in fact doing is creating something that looks like a Cold Fusion query, but is more flexible and dynamic. Once the SERVERS.CFM has been processed, a fully populated array will exist ready for use in both the search and results templates.

▶ **See** "Array Manipulation Functions," **p. 957**

Creating the Search Screen

The code for the search screen itself, shown in Listing 27.2, is much like any of the forms you have created until now. `<CFINCLUDE>` tags are used to include the common headers and footers, and the SERVERS.CFM file.

Listing 27.2   C:\A2Z\SCRIPTS\28\SEARCH.CFM—Code for SEARCH.CFM File

```
<!--- Include LDAP server list --->
<CFINCLUDE TEMPLATE="servers.cfm">

<!--- Include page header --->
<CFINCLUDE TEMPLATE="header.cfm">
```

```
<CENTER>

<!--- Search form --->
<FORM ACTION="results.cfm" METHOD="POST">

<TABLE BORDER>

<TR>
 <!--- Name to search for --->
 <TH ALIGN="RIGHT">Name:</TH>
 <TD><INPUT TYPE="text" NAME="name"></TD>
</TR>
<TR>
 <!--- Server to search --->
 <TH ALIGN="RIGHT">Server:</TH>
 <TD>
  <!--- Dynamically build server list from server array --->
  <SELECT NAME="server">
   <CFLOOP INDEX="service" FROM="1" TO="#ArrayLen(Servers)#">
    <CFOUTPUT><OPTION VALUE="#service#">#Servers[service][LDAPService]
➥#</CFOUTPUT>
   </CFLOOP>
  </SELECT>
 </TD>
</TR>
<TR>
 <TH COLSPAN=2><INPUT TYPE="submit" VALUE="Search"></TH>
</TR>

</TABLE>

</FORM>

</CENTER>

<!--- Include page footer --->
<CFINCLUDE TEMPLATE="footer.cfm">
```

The SELECT box for the server selection is populated using a <CFLOOP>, using this code:

```
<CFLOOP INDEX="service" FROM="1" TO="#ArrayLen(Servers)#">
```

This creates a loop that loops through from 1 to the length of the array, in this case it is 5. Each time the loop loops, a variable called "service" will contain the current service number. It'll be 1 the first time, then 2, and so on.

The SELECT box OPTION tags are populated using this code:

```
<OPTION VALUE="#service#">#Servers[service][LDAPService]#
```

The #service# variable will be replaced by the current service number (the loop counter). The displayed text will be the service name. For the first item in the list, the code #Servers[service][LDAPService]# becomes #Servers[1][1]# referring to first column of the first row which as the value "BigFoot".

The end result is the screen shown previously in Figure 27.2.

Part
IV

Ch
27

Creating the Results Screen

Now look at the results screen, the code for which is in Listing 27.3.

Listing 27.3   C:\A2Z\SCRIPTS\28\RESULTS.CFM—Code for RESULTS.CFM File

```
<!--- Include LDAP server list --->
<CFINCLUDE TEMPLATE="servers.cfm">

<!--- Perform LDAP lookup using passed server info --->
<CFLDAP
 SERVER="#Servers[server][LDAPServer]#"
 ACTION="QUERY"
 NAME="results"
 START="cn=#name#,c=US"
 FILTER="(cn=#name#)"
 ATTRIBUTES="cn,o,l,st,c,mail,telephonenumber"
 SORT="cn ASC"
>

<!--- Include page header --->
<CFINCLUDE TEMPLATE="header.cfm">

<!--- Display results --->
<CENTER>

<TABLE BORDER>
 <TR>
  <TH COLSPAN=5><CFOUTPUT>#results.RecordCount# matches found on <A
HREF="#Servers[server][LDAPHome]#">#Servers[server][LDAPService]#</A>
➥</CFOUTPUT></TH>
 </TR>
 <TR>
  <TH>Name</TH>
  <TH>Organization</TH>
  <TH>Location</TH>
  <TH>E-Mail</TH>
  <TH>Phone</TH>
 </TR>
<CFOUTPUT QUERY="results">
 <TR>
  <TD>#Trim(cn)#</TD>
  <TD>#Trim(o)#</TD>
  <TD>#Trim(l)#, #Trim(st)#, #Trim#</TD>
  <TD><A HREF="mailto:#Trim(mail)#">#Trim(mail)#</A></TD>
  <TD>#Trim(telephonenumber)#</TD>
 </TR>
</CFOUTPUT>
</TABLE>

</CENTER>
```

```
<!--- Include page footer --->
<CFINCLUDE TEMPLATE="footer.cfm">
```

Once again, this file uses <CFINCLUDE> to include the header, footer, and services files.

Then comes the LDAP call itself:

```
<!--- Perform LDAP lookup using passed server info --->
<CFLDAP
 SERVER="#Servers[server][LDAPServer]#"
 ACTION="QUERY"
 NAME="results"
 START="cn=#name#,c=US"
 FILTER="(cn=#name#)"
 ATTRIBUTES="cn,o,l,st,c,mail,telephonenumber"
 SORT="cn ASC"
>
```

The SERVER attribute is passed the name of the LDAP server as extracted from the servers array. The variable "server" contains the "row number" of the server that was selected in the SEARCH.CFM file.

As you want to perform a search, the ACTION is set to "QUERY" and the NAME attribute is used to provide the name of the query to be created.

The START and FILTER attributes specify the search to perform, using the "name" field submitted from the SEARCH.CFM screen.

ATTRIBUTES lists the columns that you want returned. The query that will be created by <CFLDAP> (the query named in the QUERY attribute) will have a column for each attribute listed here. Not all columns will have data, many will be empty.

The SORT attribute specifies the sort order for the data. The value "cn ASC" specifies that the data should be sorted by common name (full name) in ascending order.

The rest of the code should be very familiar by now. A <CFOUTPUT> block is used to display the results, and the output screen will look something like the one shown previously in Figure 27.3.

Adding, Modifying, and Deleting LDAP Entries

While LDAP is mostly used to retrieve data from Directory Services, it also provides the mechanisms to perform entry administration too. Adding, modifying, and deleting entries is fully supported by <CFLDAP>.

Directory service entry manipulation is almost never allowed via an anonymous login. You will need a login name and password to perform these functions. In addition, many directories are set up so that different levels of access are granted to different login names. Your network administrator should be able to provide you with login information if it is required.

When directly manipulating directory service entries, the "unique id" of that entry must be known. In LDAP terms this is known as the dn attribute, or the "distinguished name." This is usually a comma-delimited list of attributes (containing at minimum the country, organization, and name) that together uniquely identity a specific entry. It is good practice to use LDAP to retrieve the dn attribute of the entry to be changed or deleted so that that same value may be passed for the MODIFY or DELETE operation.

When adding or modifying entries, the ATTRIBUTES attribute must be used to specify the list of attributes be set or altered, and their values.

N O T E   University of Michigan at Ann Arbor is the birthplace of LDAP, and is home to some of the most comprehensive information about the protocol at **http://www.umich.edu/ ~rsug/ldap**. ▧

CHAPTER 28

MIME Types

by Steven D. Drucker and Ben Forta

In this chapter

Generating Non-HTML Documents

Now that you are familiar with using Cold Fusion to output the contents of web pages, you can investigate methods for generating non-HTML documents.

Your browser communicates with Web servers through a protocol called HTTP (Hyper text Transfer Protocol). HTTP stipulates that before a web server sends a file to your browser it must first transmit a character string, called a Content Type, indicating what kind of document you are about to receive. The browser then uses this information to correctly interpret the downloading information. In the vast majority of cases, your browser receives the Content Type text/html indicating that it is about to receive a text file containing HTML tags. However, you may want to transfer information in other formats, such as a Microsoft Excel-compatible spreadsheet, a Microsoft Word-compatible report, or a PostScript document.

You will be investigating methods of using Cold Fusion to dynamically create these types of documents, as well as learning how to configure your browser to properly view them.

Defining MIME

Back in the early days of the Internet, the contents of electronic mail were limited to ASCII text only. As the numbers of different computer systems connected to the Internet grew, and the popularity of using electronic mail increased, a new standard was defined to allow for the cross-platform exchange of messages between these otherwise incompatible systems. This standard, named Multipurpose Internet Mail Extensions (MIME), includes support for non-textual information such as graphics, executable files, audio, and video. It also supports *multipart* messages which may combine several body parts (attachments), possibly of different types of data, into a single message.

MIME is an open, extensible protocol. The following example is an actual electronic mail message with attachments sent during the authoring of this book.

```
Return-Path: <ben@stoneage.com>
Received: from stoneage1.stoneage.com ([208.193.16.1]) by www.figleaf.com
(post.office MTA v1.9.3 ID# 0-13931) with ESMTP id AAA177
for <sdrucker@figleaf.com>; Tue, 6 Aug 1996 13:54:59 -0400
Received: from milliways.stoneage.com ([208.193.16.20])
by stoneage1.stoneage.com (post.office MTA v1.9.1 ID# 0-12155)
with ESMTP id AAA287; Tue, 6 Aug 1996 14:28:29 -0400
From: ben@stoneage.com (Ben Forta)
To: "Steve Drucker" <sdrucker@figleaf.com>
Subject: Sample chapters and database
Date: Tue, 6 Aug 1996 13:28:47 -0400
X-MSMail-Priority: High
X-Priority: 1
X-Mailer: Microsoft Internet Mail 4.70.1132
MIME-Version: 1.0
Content-Type: multipart/mixed;
➥boundary="----=_NextPart_000_01BB839B.32CBB0C0"
Content-Transfer-Encoding: 7bit
Message-ID: <19960806182825064.AAA287@milliways.stoneage.com>
```

```
This is a multi-part message in MIME format.

------=_NextPart_000_01BB839B.32CBB0C0
Content-Type: text/plain; charset=ISO-8859-1
Content-Transfer-Encoding: 7bit

Hi,
Please find attached copies of two book chapters. These are unedited early
drafts, but they should give you an idea of the sample app and what it
includes.

Thanks.

-- Ben

-----------------------------------------------------------------
Ben Forta - Stoneage Corporation
E-Mail: ben@stoneage.com
Home page: http://www.stoneage.com
------=_NextPart_000_01BB839B.32CBB0C0
Content-Type: application/octet-stream; name="09708_6.doc"
Content-Transfer-Encoding: base64
Content-Description: 09708_6.doc (Microsoft Word Document)
Content-Disposition: attachment; filename="09708_6.doc"
```

```
0M8R4KGxGuEAAAAAAAAAAAAAAAAAAAAAAPgADAP7/CQAGAAAAAAAAAAAAAAABAAAAOgAAAAAAAAA
EAAAOwAAAAEAAAD+////AAAAADkAAAD////////////////////////////////////////////
////////////////////////////////////////////////////////////////////////
```

```
------=_NextPart_000_01BB839B.32CBB0C0
```

This message contains two parts, a text message describing the attached Microsoft Word document and the first few coded lines of the Microsoft Word document itself. Take special note of the Content Type headings. The first instance in the message informs the mail client that it has received a multipart message and defines a sequence of characters to use as a boundary to separate the text part of the message from the binary-encoded attachment. Later instances of Content Type describe the encoding of each individual section. Cold Fusion supports sending multipart email through its MIMEATTACH option in the <CFMAIL> tag. You will now use the Cold Fusion <CFCONTENT> tag to dynamically set the Content Type header to generate and transfer non-HTML data to your Web browser.

The formal specification for MIME is available via the World Wide Web at **http://www.oac.uci.edu/indiv/ehood/MIME/MIME.html**.

MIME Content Types

The MIME Content Type header field is used to describe the incoming data stream to the browser so that the data can be acted on in an appropriate manner. The header field is defined as [general type of data]/[specific format of data]. Thus, a browser receiving the line

```
Content-Type: text/html
```

Part

IV

Ch

28

is notified that it is about to receive ASCII text formatted using the HTML specification so that it may render the document accordingly. Similarly, a Content Type of `application/msword` informs your browser that it is about to receive an application-dependent file in Microsoft Word format; your browser may, in turn, launch the Microsoft Word application to properly view the file.

There are currently seven pre-defined MIME categories. They are listed in Table 28.1.

Table 28.1   MIME Categories

Category	Description
Text	Textual information that, without further enhancement or decoding, would be readable by the user. No special software is required to display the data, although the specified character set must be supported by the client software. HTML documents belong in this category.
Image	Graphical data that requires output on either a monitor or printer to be understood. Scanned photos in GIF format are part of this class.
Video	A set of moving images. The video may contain interlaced audio. Video files may require the use of additional hardware and software for proper viewing. Digitized movie trailers in Apple QuickTime format belong to this type.
Audio	A file requiring a sound card and speakers to be heard. ABC News broadcasts its reports over the Internet in RealAudio format.
Application	Other types of data, usually requiring the use of a specific software application to be properly decoded. Examples include a Microsoft Excel spreadsheet, compressed files in .ZIP format, Adobe PDF files, and executable program files.
Multipart	Used almost exclusively for electronic mail applications, multipart data indicates that a single file is comprised of several independent body types or attachments, each with its own Content Type. An electronic mail message with an Excel spreadsheet attachment would be coded as a multipart data type.
Message	An electronic mail message as an attachment to another electronic mail message.

Each MIME category contains several subtypes, listed in Table 28.2. Entries in the form `x-subtype` indicate an experimental or local type. Later in this chapter you will create your own, private MIME type `text/x-csv-excel` in order to generate and properly format a Microsoft Excel-compatible spreadsheet.

Table 28.2   Commonly Used MIME Content Types and Subtypes on the WWW

MIME Type	MIME Subtype	Application
Text	html	The most common MIME type on the Web, your standard HTML file.
	plain	Unformatted text.
Image	gif	A graphic encoded in Graphic Interchange Format, readable by most Web browsers.
	jpeg	A graphic compressed using JPEG lossy compression, readable by most Web browsers.
	tiff	A graphic encoded in Tagged Image File Format, usually requires an external viewer.
Application	postscript	An output document in postscript format.
	octet-stream	An executable program.
	pdf	A document in Adobe Portable Document Format. Requires a PDF viewer such as Adobe Acrobat or the Adobe Acrobat Amber plug-in.
	msword	A document in Microsoft Word format. Requires additional software.
	zip	PKZIP archive compressed file. Requires WinZip or PKUNZIP utility to decode.
Audio	basic	A digitized sound sample (.au format), supported by most browsers.
	x-pn-realaudio	A sound sample, compressed into RealAudio streamed format. Requires special software for both the client browser and Web server.video
	msvideo	Microsoft video file in .AVI format.
	quicktime	Video file compressed using Apple QuickTime format.

Configuring Your Browser

You can customize how your browser will respond when encountering a MIME document. These actions are limited to displaying the document within the browser, saving the document to disk, launching an external program to view the data, or asking the user to decide what action is to be performed. Every web browser contains a database of MIME Content Types and file extensions. File extensions are necessary because some web protocols, such as FTP, do not send Content Type headers. You will now define your own experimental Content Type in two of the most popular web browsers.

Netscape Navigator

You can access the Netscape Navigator 3.0 database of MIME types by selecting Options, General Preferences from the Netscape menu bar and then clicking the Helpers tab. A table

Part
IV

Ch
28

containing MIME types, file extensions, and actions should appear, similar to the one depicted in Figure 28.1.

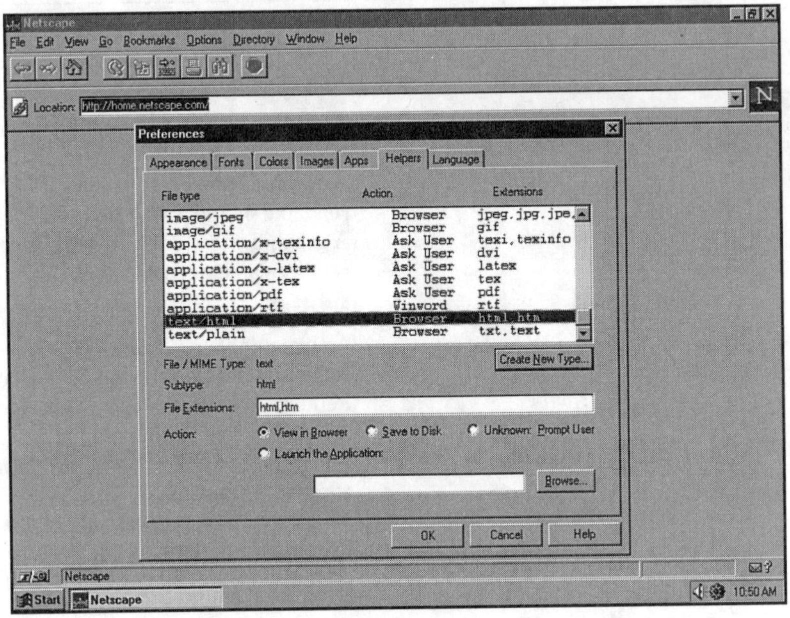

FIG. 28.1

The Helpers tab in Netscape Navigator 3.0 General Preferences allows you to customize your browser's MIME settings.

To add your experimental MIME type, click the Create New Type button in the Netscape Preferences window and type in the MIME type and MIME subtype, as shown in Figure 28.2.

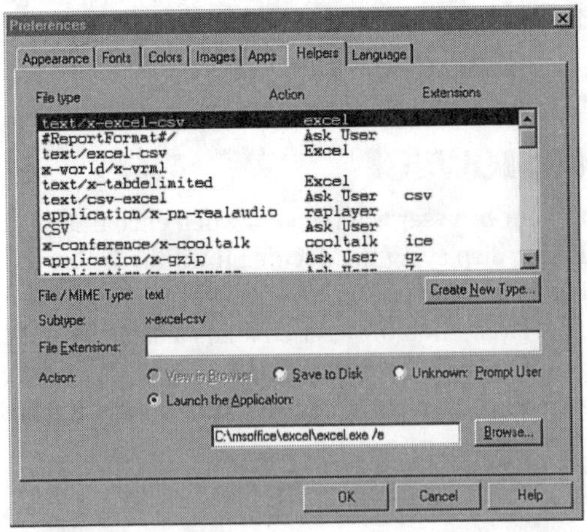

FIG. 28.2

Netscape Navigator 3.0 lets you easily add your own custom MIME type.

In order to complete the process, you must fill in the file extension for your new MIME type and choose an action to be performed when your Cold Fusion-generated file is received by the browser. If you have Microsoft Excel, select the Launch the Application radio button, click the Browse button, and select Excel using the file dialog box. Your completed MIME definition should resemble Figure 28.3.

TIP If you do not have Excel, you may download the free Microsoft Excel Viewer from **www.microsoft.com**.

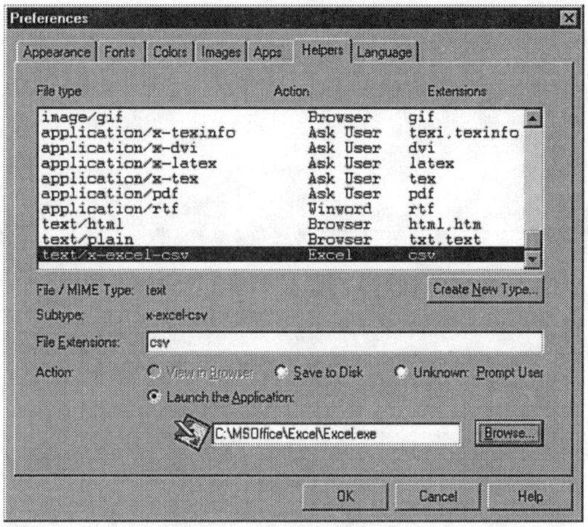

FIG. 28.3
Associate a file type extension with your MIME type and tell Netscape to launch the appropriate viewer when it is encountered.

Microsoft Internet-Enabled Applications

All Microsoft Internet-enabled products (Internet Explorer) reference a database of MIME types that is stored in the Windows 95/NT Registry. Unlike Netscape Navigator 3.0, which launches Microsoft viewers outside of the Navigator window, Microsoft Internet Explorer (MSIE) 3.0 integrates other Microsoft applications within an MSIE 3.0 frame or window. If you are creating an intranet application which outputs MIME to a Microsoft Office application, you may want to consider using Internet Explorer as your primary browser.

You can modify MIME actions for Microsoft applications through either the Windows 95/NT 4.0 Explorer or by editing the registry directly.

Modifying MIME Types Using Windows 95/NT Explorer   You can access the Microsoft database of MIME types by selecting View, Options from the Windows Explorer menu bar, and then clicking the File Types tab. A dialog box, similar to the one depicted in Figure 28.4, should appear on screen.

To add your experimental MIME type, scroll down the list of file types and select the option Microsoft Excel Comma Separated.... Fill in the form as shown in Figure 28.5.

Part
IV

Ch
28

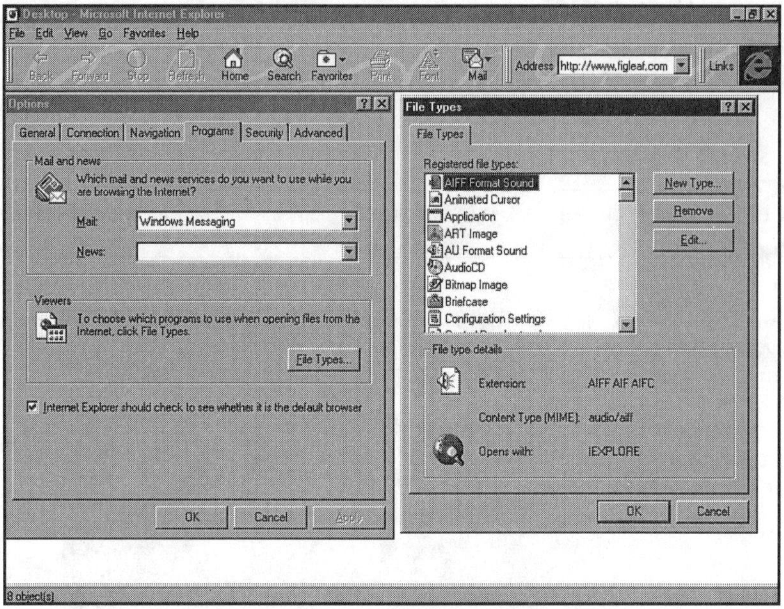

FIG. 28.4

The Options feature in the Windows 95/NT 4.0 Explorer allows you to customize MIME for all Microsoft Internet-enabled applications, including Internet Explorer.

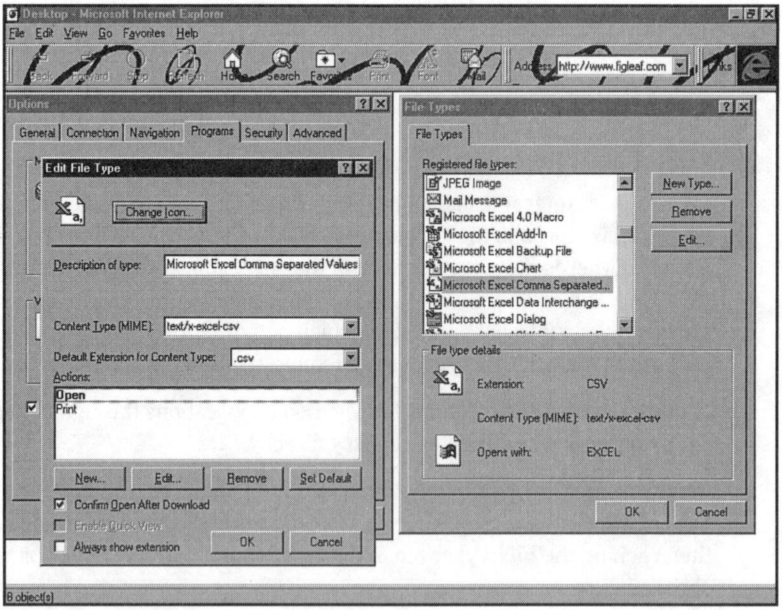

FIG. 28.5

You can associate a MIME Content Type with any Microsoft application file type.

Modifying MIME Types by Using the Windows 95/NT Registry   You can also configure MSIE, as well as any other Microsoft Internet clients for custom MIME types by editing the Windows

95/NT 4.0 registry. You can start the Registry Editor, shown in Figure 28.6, by executing the file regedit32.exe (Windows 95/NT 3.51) or regedit.exe (Windows NT 4.0).

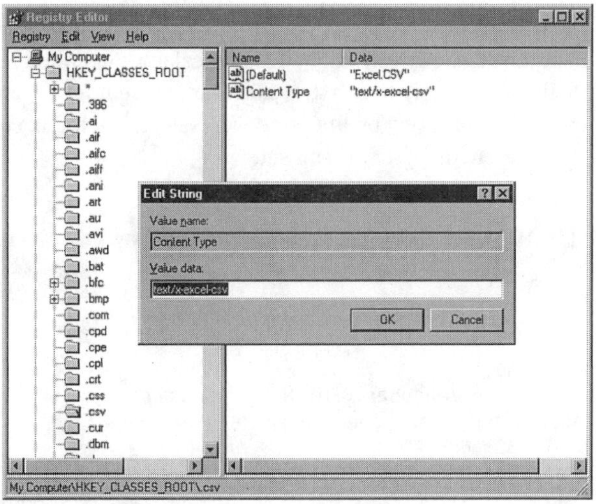

FIG. 28.6
The Windows 95/NT 4.0 Registry Editor allows you to link MIME types to file extensions.

File extensions are stored under the HKEY_CLASSES_ROOT key. Scroll down the list until you find the .csv file extension. Left click the .csv file folder. Settings for the .csv file type appear. If a Content Type does not exist for this subkey, you can add it by right-clicking the .csv file folder and selecting New, String Value and filling in the form as depicted in Figure 28.6.

Returning MIME Content Types with Cold Fusion *<CFCONTENT>*

The *<CFCONTENT>* tag has two attributes. The mandatory TYPE attribute specifies which MIME Content Type is being returned by the current template. The optional FILE attribute dynamically inserts a file from the web server into the output stream.

The following example demonstrates the use of *<CFCONTENT>* to output the image of an employee where the path to the image (i.e. C:\images\steve.jpeg) is stored in the field employees.photo.

```
<CFQUERY NAME="GetEmployeeImageFile" DATASOURCE="A2Z">
SELECT photo FROM employees
WHERE employees.employeeid=#URL.employeeid#
</CFQUERY>
<CFCONTENT TYPE="image/jpeg" FILE="#GetEmployeeImageFile.photo#">
```

Part
IV

Ch
28

Using Cold Fusion to Generate a Report in Multiple Formats

The HTML file format is wonderful as a cross-platform language for displaying text and graphics from within a web browser. However, most desktop applications, such as Microsoft Word and Microsoft Excel, do not currently support this format, making it difficult for a user to export and edit web-generated reports without resorting to cut-and-paste operations and retyping. Fortunately, Cold Fusion through the `<CFCONTENT>` tag, allows you to output data in formats desktop applications can natively understand.

In Listing 28.1 and Listing 28.2, you will build an interface, illustrated in Figure 28.7, that allows a user at your fictional company to save the exact same inventory report in three different file formats. The three examples rely on the same SQL select statement, contained in the file invquery.cfm, to generate the query result set.

On the CD

Listing 28.1   ADMIN.CFM—Using a Frames-Based "Systems Administration" Interface

```
<TITLE>A2Z Books - System Administration</TITLE>

<FRAMESET ROWS="55,*">
<FRAME SRC="../common/menubar.CFM" NAME="menubar"
➥noresize scrolling=no marginheight=3 marginwidth=3>
<FRAMESET COLS="35%,65%">
<FRAME SRC="options.CFM" MARGINWIDTH=0>
<FRAME SRC="../common/instructions.CFM" NAME="display" MARGINWIDTH=0>
</FRAMESET>
</FRAMESET>
<NOFRAMES>
<CFINCLUDE TEMPLATE="../common/noframes.CFM">
</NOFRAMES>

</HTML>
```

FIG. 28.7

A frames-based interface allows the user to more easily distinguish the formatting differences between the file types.

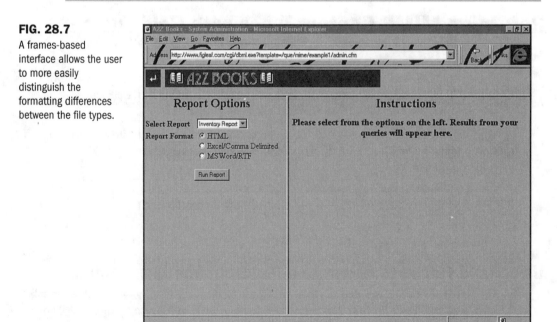

On the CD

Listing 28.2   OPTIONS.CFM—Enabling Users to Select a File Format and MIME Type to Generate a Report

```
<CFINCLUDE TEMPLATE="../common/header.CFM">
<CENTER><H2>Report Options</H2>

<FORM ACTION="/cgi/cf.exe/report.csv?template=
➥/a2z/mime/example1/runreport.CFM"
target="display" METHOD="POST">
<TABLE BORDER=0>
<TR>
     <TD>
     <STRONG>Select Report</STRONG>
     </TD>
     <TD>
     <SELECT NAME="ReportType">
     <OPTION VALUE=1>Inventory Report
     </SELECT>
     </TD>
</TR>
<TR>
     <TD VALIGN="TOP">
     <STRONG>Report Format</STRONG>
     </TD>
     <TD>
     <INPUT TYPE="RADIO" NAME="ReportFormat" VALUE="text/html" CHECKED>
HTML<BR>
     <INPUT TYPE="RADIO" NAME="ReportFormat" VALUE="text/x-excel-csv">
Excel/Comma Delimited<BR>
     <INPUT TYPE="RADIO" NAME="ReportFormat" VALUE="application/rtf">
MSWord/RTF<BR>
     </TD>
</TR>
</TABLE>
<BR>
<INPUT TYPE="SUBMIT" VALUE="Run Report">
</FORM>
</CENTER>
</BODY>
</HTML>
```

Using Cold Fusion to Set Default File Names   Many viewer applications examine the first few characters of the data file they are loading and try to make a decision about how to best represent the data onscreen. Certain file formats, such as RTF, contain coding that is functionally similar to the MIME Content Type, indicating to the viewer application how the incoming data should be interpreted. Other formats, such as comma-delimited text, do not contain such coding and thus may not be displayed properly. A secondary technique data viewers use is to represent data based on filename extension. Thus a comma separated format file named report.txt may not produce the desired results in Microsoft Excel; however, the same file, renamed report.csv, with the .csv file extension properly associated in Windows 95 Explorer, will be loaded properly. You can force Cold Fusion to assign a default filename and extension to a downloading file by using the method illustrated in Listing 28.3.

Part
IV

Ch
28

Listing 28.3   RUNREPORT.CFM—Placing a Default Filename Within the Call to Cold Fusion to Transfer Reports to the Browser with Appropriate Filename Extensions

```
<CFIF #reportformat# contains "html">
    <CFLOCATION URL="/cgi/cf.exe/report.html?template=/a2z/mime/example1/
htmlreport.CFM">
</CFIF>

<CFIF #reportformat# contains "excel">
    <CFLOCATION URL="/cgi/cf.exe/report.csv?template=/a2z/mime/example1
➥/csvreport.CFM">
</CFIF>

<CFIF #reportformat# contains "rtf">
    <CFLOCATION URL="/cgi/cf.exe/report.rtf?template=/a2z/mime/example1
➥/rtfreport.CFM">
</CFIF>
```

Using Cold Fusion and <CFCONTENT> to Output HTML   Cold Fusion uses text/html as its default Content Type. Therefore, when generating a report in HTML format, issuing a <CFCONTENT> statement is unnecessary. Listing 28.4 demonstrates a method for outputting a list of inventory by using HTML tables to maintain a columnar format and CF to group books by category. The results are depicted in Figure 28.8.

Listing 28.4   HTMLREPORT.CFM—Generating HTML Output

```
<CFINCLUDE TEMPLATE="invquery.CFM">
<CFINCLUDE TEMPLATE="../common/header.CFM">
<H2>Available Inventory</H2>
<UL>
<CFOUTPUT QUERY="getinventory" GROUP="category">
<LI><H3>#getinventory.category#<H3></LI>
<TABLE BORDER=1>
    <TH><H5>Book ID</H5></TH>
    <TH><H5>ISBN</H5></TH>
    <TH><H5>Title</H5></TH>
    <TH><H5>Publisher</H5></TH>
    <TH><H5>Location</H5></TH>
<CFOUTPUT>
        <TR>
        <TD>#Bookid#</TD>
        <TD>#ISBN#</TD>
        <TD>#Title#</TD>
        <TD>#Publisher#</TD>
        <TD>#Location#</TD>
        </TR>
    </CFOUTPUT>
</TABLE>
</CFOUTPUT>
</UL>
</BODY>
</HTML>
```

FIG. 28.8
By using Cold Fusion and HTML, you can generate a read-only "preview" of the data to be exported.

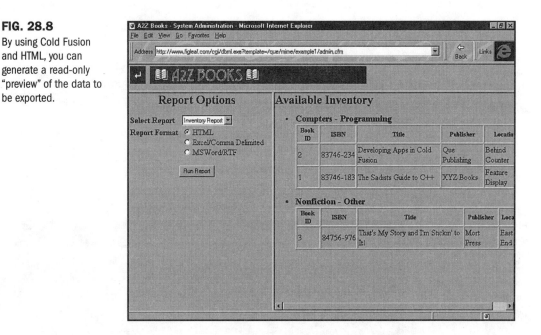

Using Cold Fusion and *<CFCONTENT>* to Output Comma-Separated Values (CSV)   Comma-separated value files (CSVs) are used principally for the exporting and importing of data into a spreadsheet or database table. This format uses the comma character (,) as a separator to delineate column data, and a carriage return/line feed to indicate the presence of a new row. In Listing 28.5, line 3 outputs the report title `Available Inventory`. Line 4 sets up column headings, and your CFOUTPUT query dynamically generates columns of inventory information on lines 5 and 6. The .CSV result, loaded into Microsoft Excel, is shown in Figure 28.9.

> **N O T E**   Cold Fusion strips all text output which occurs in a template before the occurrence of the
> <CFCONTENT> tag. ▪

There are several issues to keep in mind when attempting to output a non-HTML file type. All text following the <CFCONTENT> tag will be output as plain ASCII. Therefore, HTML tags, such as <H1>..</H1> and <STRONG>..</STRONG>, will not have the desired effect on the output file. Remember, you're no longer generating code for a web browser to interpret. Your only concern must be how the helper application will interpret the data in the output file. Also, any tabs or carriage returns inserted after the <CFCONTENT> tag will be inserted into your result set. For example, the following code snippets are not functionally equivalent:

```
<CFOUTPUT QUERY="getinventory">#Category#,#Bookid#,#ISBN#,#Title#,#Publisher#
</CFOUTPUT>

<CFOUTPUT QUERY="getinventory">
#Category#,#Bookid#,#ISBN#,#Title#,#Publisher#
</CFOUTPUT>
```

Part
IV

Ch
28

In the prior example, the second code listing would insert an extra carriage and line feed into your generated file.

On the CD

Listing 28.5 CSVREPORT.CFM—Output in CSV Format Requiring a <CFCONTENT> Tag and Careful Placement of the <CFOUTPUT> Statement

```
<CFINCLUDE TEMPLATE="invquery.CFM">
<CFCONTENT TYPE="text/x-excel-csv">Available Inventory
Category,Book ID,ISBN,Title,Publisher,Location
<CFOUTPUT QUERY="getinventory">
#Category#,#Bookid#,#ISBN#,#Title#,#Publisher#,#Location#
</CFOUTPUT>
```

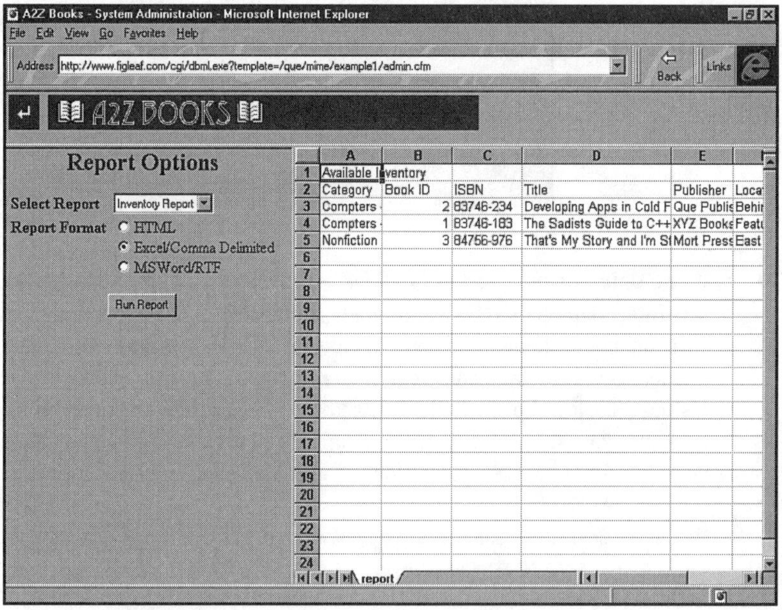

FIG. 28.9

Microsoft applications, such as Excel, can be configured to execute from within an Internet Explorer frame when viewing MIME documents.

Using Cold Fusion and <CFCONTENT> to Output Rich Text Format   Rich Text Format (RTF), the native format for Windows Help Files, is supported by nearly all Windows word processors. Rich Text constructs are similar in format to HTML—a series of tags denote style settings and formats. In the following example, you first prototype a document in Microsoft Word, inserting a graphic and defining a specifications table, and then save the document in Rich Text Format. By analyzing the resulting file, and through a process of trial and error, you can determine the appropriate placement of <CFOUTPUT> tags within the file. To make the following program listing more concise, you place the top of the document, containing a bitmap, into a separate file and used <CFINCLUDE> to import it at execution time. Listing 28.6 demonstrates an implementation of this methodology, while Figure 28.10 depicts the resulting file, loaded into Microsoft Word.

On the CD

Listing 28.6   RTFREPORT.CFM—Inventory Report—Output in the HTML-Like Rich Text Format

```
<CFINCLUDE TEMPLATE="invquery.CFM">
<CFCONTENT TYPE="application/rtf"><CFINCLUDE TEMPLATE="rtfhdr.rtf">
<CFOUTPUT QUERY="getinventory" GROUP="category">
{\b\fs24 #category#
\par }\trowd \trgaph108\trleft-108 \clbrdrt\brdrs\brdrw30\brdrcf1
\clbrdrb\brdrs\brdrw15\brdrcf1 \clcfpat1\clcbpat8\clshdng6000
\cellx1663\clbrdrt\brdrs\brdrw30\brdrcf1 \clbrdrb\brdrs\brdrw15\brdrcf1
\clcfpat1\clcbpat8\clshdng6000 \cellx3434\clbrdrt
\brdrs\brdrw30\brdrcf1 \clbrdrb\brdrs\brdrw15\brdrcf1
\clcfpat1\clcbpat8\clshdng6000 \cellx5205\clbrdrt\brdrs\brdrw30\brdrcf1
\clbrdrb\brdrs\brdrw15\brdrcf1 \clcfpat1\clcbpat8\clshdng6000
\cellx6976\clbrdrt\brdrs\brdrw30\brdrcf1 \clbrdrb
\brdrs\brdrw15\brdrcf1 \clcfpat1\clcbpat8\clshdng6000 \cellx8747
\pard \widctlpar\intbl
{\b\fs24\cf8 Book\cell }
{\fs24\cf8 ISBN\cell Title\cell Publisher\cell Location\cell }\pard
\widctlpar\intbl {\fs48\cf8 \row }\trowd \trgaph108\trleft-108
\clcfpat1\clcbpat8\clshdng3000
\cellx1663\cellx3434\cellx5205\cellx6976\cellx8747 \pard
<CFOUTPUT>
\widctlpar\intbl
{\b\fs24 #title# \cell }
{\fs24 #isbn#\cell #title#\cell #publisher#\cell #location#\cell }\pard
➥\widctlpar\intbl {\fs48 \row }\trowd \trgaph108\trleft-108 \clbrdrb
\brdrs\brdrw30\brdrcf1 \clcfpat1\clcbpat8\clshdng3000
➥\cellx1663\clbrdrb\brdrs\brdrw30\brdrcf1 \cellx3434
➥\clbrdrb\brdrs\brdrw30
➥\brdrcf1 \cellx5205\clbrdrb\brdrs\brdrw30\brdrcf1 \cellx6976
➥\clbrdrb\brdrs\brdrw30\brdrcf1 \cellx8747
\pard \widctlpar\intbl\pard
</CFOUTPUT>
}
</CFOUTPUT>
```

Example Using Cold Fusion to Format a WebSite Server Access Log

Cold Fusion allows you to take virtually any file format with column definitions and use MIME to reformat the information for a helper application. The O'Reilly WebSite web server does not currently include a web-based administration interface. Through some clever manipulation of Cold Fusion, you can build an interface to make the web site access log file available from a web browser.

The WebSite Windows-format access log is natively formatted as a tab-delimited file. In the following example you will save the log to a Microsoft Access memo field, and then use <CFCONTENT> to provide a web-based method to view it.

Part
IV

Ch

28

FIG. 28.10

Rich Text Format, while more difficult to understand than HTML, enables you to generate complex reports which are editable in any Windows word processor.

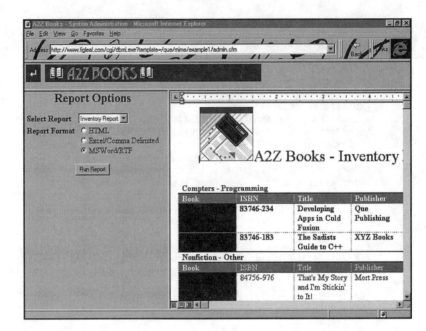

Setting Up the Example   The data requirements for this example are summarized in Table 28.3.

Table 28.3   The Data Table Specification for Saving Your Web Site Access Log

Field Name	Data Type	Description
log_id	autonumber	Primary key, unique identifier
log_date	date/time	Time and date the log is saved
log_contents	memo	Where you store the tab-delimited web site log

Once again you use the same frames-based interface, detailed in Listing 28.7, depicted in Figure 28.11, and first introduced in the prior example.

On the CD

Listing 28.7   ADMIN.CFM—Frames-Based Interfaces Used with Internet Explorer 3.0

```
<TITLE>A2Z Books - System Administration</TITLE>

<FRAMESET ROWS="55,*">
<FRAME SRC="../common/menubar.CFM" NAME="menubar"
➥noresize scrolling=no marginheight=3 marginwidth=3>
```

```
<FRAMESET COLS="35%,65%">
<FRAME SRC="options.CFM" MARGINWIDTH=0>
<FRAME SRC="../common/instructions.CFM" NAME="display" MARGINWIDTH=0>
</FRAMESET>
</FRAMESET>
<NOFRAMES>
<CFINCLUDE TEMPLATE="../common/noframes.CFM">
</NOFRAMES>

</HTML>
```

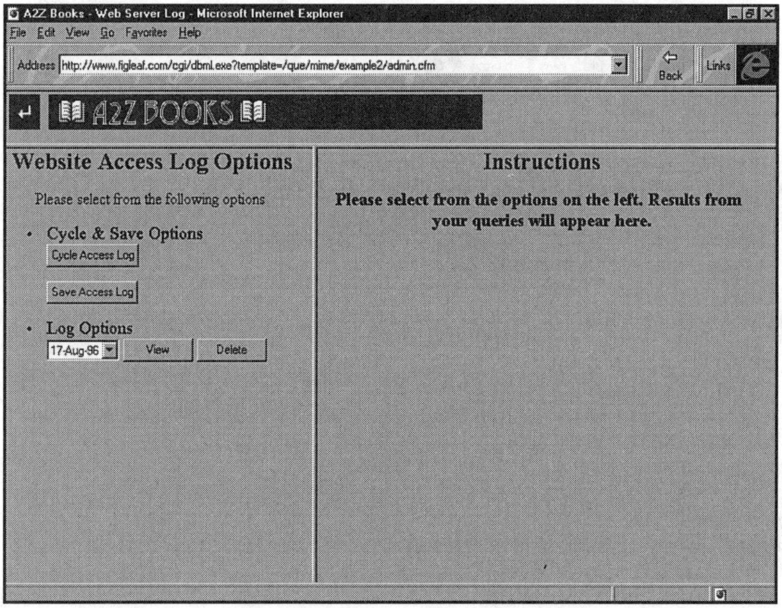

FIG. 28.11
By using Cold Fusion you can save a web site access log into a database for later viewing.

Cycling the O'Reilly WebSite Access Log   The WebSite web server constantly saves access information to a file named access.log. The web site keeps a constant file lock on this file, thereby making it inaccessible to Cold Fusion, but provides support for a special URL (/~cycle.acc) which, when accessed, causes the server process to cycle the log. The current log is renamed access.001 and the web site creates a new access.log file. Listing 28.8 demonstrates the method for initiating the cycle process.

Listing 28.8   OPTIONS.CFM—Initiating a Web Site's Cycling of its Access Log

```
<CFQUERY NAME="getlogs" DATASOURCE="a2zdata">
    SELECT * FROM websitelog order by log_id
</CFQUERY>
```

continues

Part
IV

Ch

28

Listing 28.8   Continued

```
<CFINCLUDE TEMPLATE="../common/header.cfm">
<CENTER>
<H2>Website Access Log Options</H2>
Please select from the following options
</CENTER>


<LI><FONT SIZE="+1">Cycle & Save Options</FONT><BR>
<FORM ACTION="/~cycle-acc" METHOD="POST" TARGET="display">
<INPUT TYPE="SUBMIT" VALUE="Cycle Access Log"><BR>
</FORM>
<FORM ACTION="savelog.cfm"
METHOD="POST" TARGET="display">
<INPUT TYPE="SUBMIT" VALUE="Save Access Log">
</FORM>


<LI><FONT SIZE="+1">Log Options</FONT><BR>
<CFIF #getlogs.recordcount# is not 0>
<FORM ACTION="viewform.cfm"
        TARGET="display" METHOD="POST">
    <SELECT NAME="Logid">
        <CFOUTPUT QUERY="getlogs">
            <OPTION VALUE=#log_id#>#dateformat(log_date)#
        </CFOUTPUT>
    </SELECT>

<INPUT TYPE="SUBMIT" NAME="LogAction" VALUE="View">
<INPUT TYPE="SUBMIT" NAME="LogAction" VALUE="Delete">
<BR>
</FORM>
<CFELSE>
Sorry, no logs are available for display.
</CFIF>
</UL>

</BODY>
</HTML>
```

Saving the Access Log into a Database Table   Your algorithm requires the webmaster to make the directory containing web-site access logs available as a CF template directory. Once the access.001 file has been created, you can use the <CFINCLUDE> tag to import the file into an HTML form text area and ask the user to save the information into an Access memo file. Once the information has been saved into Access, you use <CFFILE> to delete the now-redundant access.001 file and update your log selection form. Listing 28.9 demonstrates the technique for reading in the log to a form text area, while Listing 28.10 details the save and delete processes.

On the CD

Listing 28.9 SAVELOG.CFM—Importing the Access Log into a Form Using <CFINCLUDE>

```
<CFINCLUDE TEMPLATE="../common/header.cfm">

<FORM ACTION="writelog.cfm" METHOD="POST">

<CENTER>
<H2>Website Log Contents</H2>

<TEXTAREA NAME="log_contents" ROWS=5 COLS=60>
<CFINCLUDE TEMPLATE="/website/access.001">
</TEXTAREA>

<BR><BR>
<INPUT TYPE="SUBMIT" NAME="action" VALUE="Save Log">
<INPUT TYPE="SUBMIT" NAME="action" VALUE="Discard Log">
</CENTER>
</FORM>

</BODY>
</HTML>
```

On the CD

Listing 28.10 WRITELOG.CFM—Saving and Deleting an Access Log

```
<CFIF #action# contains "Save">
<CFINSERT
DATASOURCE="a2zdata"
TABLENAME="websitelog"
FORMFIELDS="log_contents"
>
<CFFILE ACTION="DELETE" FILE="E:\website\logs\access.001" >
<CFELSE>
<CFFILE ACTION="DELETE" FILE="E:\website\logs\access.001" >
</CFIF>

<CFINCLUDE TEMPLATE="../common/header.cfm">

<SCRIPT>
function refreshoptions() {
top.options.location.href="options.cfm"}
</SCRIPT>

<CFIF #action# contains "Save">
    <BODY ONLOAD="refreshoptions()">
    <CENTER>
    <BR>
    <H2>Your log file has been saved</H2>
    </CENTER>
```

continues

Part

IV

Ch

28

Listing 28.10 Continued

```
<CFELSE>
    <CENTER>
    <H2>Your log file has been discarded</H2>
    </CENTER>
</CFIF>

</BODY>
</HTML>
```

Displaying the Access Log as a MIME Type   Once you have the web site log contained within the Access table, displaying it using <CFCONTENT> becomes a trivial exercise. Note in Listing 28.11 that you have once again defined an experimental MIME type named text/x-tabdelimited. For the example to generate the results shown in Figure 28.12, your browser needs to be configured to recognize this Content Type.

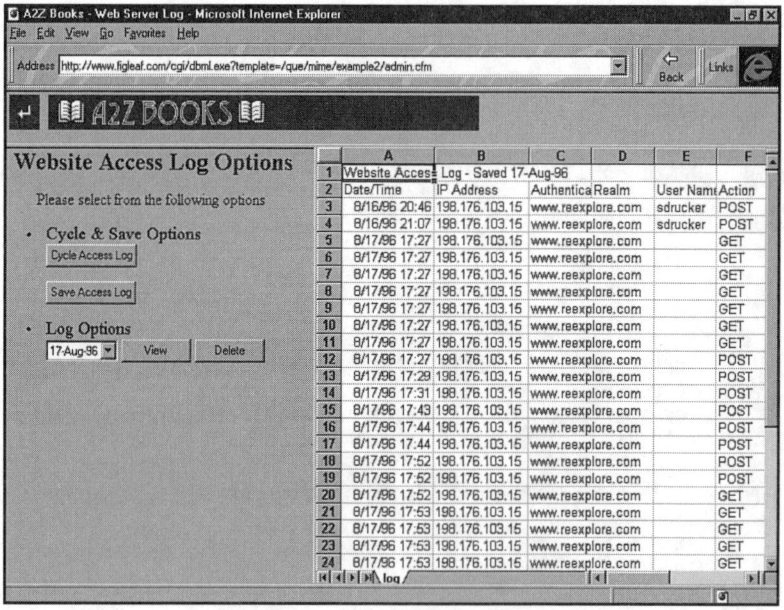

FIG. 28.12

The final result: a nicely formatted web site access log displayed within Microsoft Excel.

N O T E   The spaces in between the headers are actually tab characters. In this example, tab characters are required for Excel to correctly parse the table. ▪

On the CD

Listing 28.11   VIEWFORM.CFM—Using *<CFCONTENT>* to Add Column Headers and Display the Access Log as an Excel File

```
<CFQUERY NAME="getlog" DATASOURCE="a2zdata">
    SELECT * FROM websitelog where log_id=#logid#
</CFQUERY>

<CFIF #getlog.recordcount# is 1>

<CFIF #logaction# contains "View">

<CFCONTENT TYPE="text/x-tabdelimited">Website Access Log - Saved
<CFOUTPUT>#dateformat(getlog.log_date)#</CFOUTPUT>
Date/Time      IP Address           Authentication Server        Realm
➥            User Name           Action            Bytes Transferred
➥ w/header            Bytes Transferred w/o header
<CFOUTPUT QUERY="getlog">#log_contents#</CFOUTPUT>
<CFELSE>
    <CFINCLUDE TEMPLATE="../common/header.cfm">
    <CENTER>
    <BR>
    <H2>Delete Log</H2>
    <CFOUTPUT>
    <STRONG>
    Please confirm: Delete access log saved on
➥#dateformat(getlog.log_date)#
at #timeformat(getlog.log_date)#?<BR>
    </STRONG>
    <FORM ACTION="delete.cfm?log_id=#logid#"
METHOD="POST">
    <INPUT TYPE="SUBMIT" NAME="action" VALUE="Delete">
    <INPUT TYPE="SUBMIT" NAME="action" VALUE="Cancel">
    </FORM>
    </CFOUTPUT>
    </BODY>
    </HTML>
</CFIF>

<CFELSE>
    <CFINCLUDE TEMPLATE="../common/header.cfm">
    <CENTER>
    <BR>
    <H2>Sorry, this log has been deleted!</H2>
    </BODY>
    </HTML>
</CFIF>
```

Part

IV

Ch

28

Configuring Your Web Server's MIME Types and When NOT to Use *<CFCONTENT>*

Despite the shameless evangelizing of <CFCONTENT> in this chapter, there are instances when it is more efficient not to use Cold Fusion as a mechanism for transmitting MIME. As part of the HTTP specification, all web servers insert a MIME Content Type header into every document served. Web servers handle MIME mappings in a method similar to browsers—they rely on file name extensions as a method for determining which Content Type header to use. Also, like browsers, every web server keeps an extensible database relating file extensions to Content Types.

In instances when you want to transmit a static, pre-existing document, such as an Adobe PDF file, you can use either of the following two methodologies:

Method 1—Using Cold Fusion to transmit a static pdf file named pdffile.pdf requires a separate .CFM file containing the following code:

```
<CFCONTENT TYPE="application/pdf" FILENAME="E:\pdf\pdffile.pdf">
```

Method 2—Using your built-in web server functionality does not require a separate .CFM file. A simple HTML anchor reference does the job.

```
<A HREF="/pdf/pdffile.pdf">Click here to download the PDF file</A>
```

 TIP You may want to invoke method 1 if you have security concerns about making your file available via a publicly accessible URL.

In most cases, Method 2 is clearly a better choice. It requires less overhead and is easier to maintain.

In the following sections, you will learn how to define custom Content Type mappings for your web server.

N O T E For every Content Type mapping defined on your web server, there should exist an identical mapping on the clients' browsers. Remember to inform your users when any content mapping change takes place so that they can update their browsers. ■

Configuring O'Reilly WebSite

The O'Reilly WebSite software provides a Windows interface for editing MIME Content Types. To add a new Content Type, you must follow these steps:

1. Run Server Admin and click the Mapping tab. Clicking the Content Types radio button displays the list of predefined Content Type mappings.
2. Place the cursor in the File Extension (class) field and type in the your new file extension (**.xls**).

3. Press Tab to move the cursor to the MIME Content Type field and type in your new Content Type (**application/x-excel**).

4. Press Tab to select the Add button. Press Enter to save the new MIME type.

5. Click the Apply button to update the server.

Configuring Microsoft Internet Information Server

The Microsoft Internet Information Server (IIS) stores its MIME type information in the Windows NT Registry, depicted in Figure 28.13. To add a new Content Type, you must follow these steps:

1. Open the server's Registry by running REGEDIT.EXE.

2. Using your mouse, open the following path:

   HHEY_LOCAL_MACHINE

   SYSTEM

   CURRENTCONTROLSET

   SERVICES

   INETINFO

   PARAMETERS

   MIMEMAP

3. MIME Content Type mappings are listed in the Registry Editor's right window. You can add a new Content Type by selecting Edit from the pull-down menu and then clicking on New, String Value.

FIG. 28.13

The Microsoft Internet Information Server stores MIME types as Registry keys.

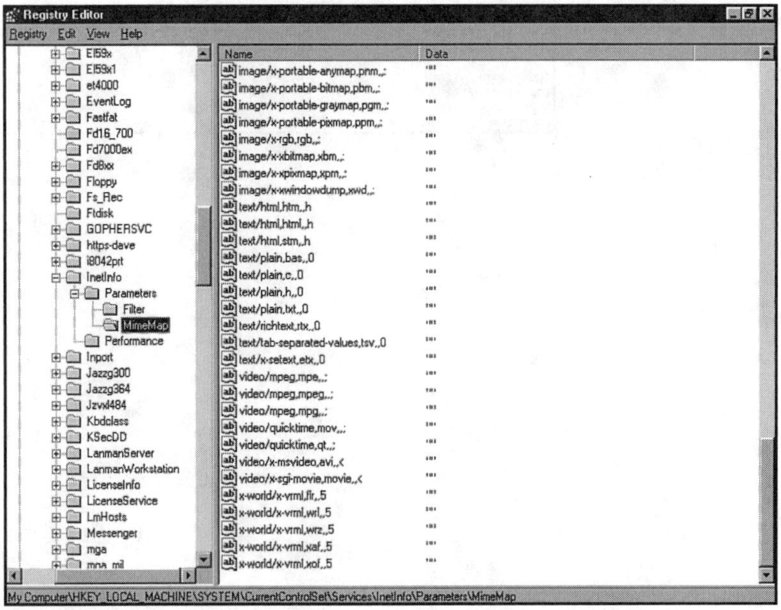

Configuring Netscape Enterprise Server

The Netscape Enterprise Server stores its MIME database as an ASCII text file as depicted in Figure 28.14. To add a new Content Type, you must observe the following steps:

1. Run notepad.exe.

2. Using Notepad, open the following file:

   \Netscape\Server\https-*myserver*\config\mime.types

   where *myserver* is the name you assigned to your Netscape Server installation.

3. Insert the new MIME type as depicted in Figure 28.14.

FIG. 28.14

Netscape Enterprise
Server keeps a
database of MIME types
in a text file.

```
mime.types - Notepad                                                    _ □ ×
File  Edit  Search  Help
#--Netscape Communications Corporation MIME Information
# Do not delete the above line. It is used to identify the file type.

type=application/octet-stream  exts=bin
type=application/oda           exts=oda
type=application/pdf           exts=pdf
type=application/postscript    exts=ai,eps,ps
type=application/rtf           exts=rtf
type=application/x-mif         exts=mif
type=application/x-csh         exts=csh
type=application/x-dvi         exts=dvi
type=application/x-hdf         exts=hdf
type=application/x-latex       exts=latex
type=application/x-netcdf      exts=nc,cdf
type=application/x-sh          exts=sh
type=application/x-tcl         exts=tcl
type=application/x-tex         exts=tex
type=application/x-texinfo     exts=texinfo,texi
type=application/x-troff       exts=t,tr,roff
type=application/x-troff-man   exts=man
type=application/x-troff-me    exts=me
type=application/x-troff-ms    exts=ms
type=application/x-wais-source exts=src
type=application/zip           exts=zip
type=application/x-gtar        exts=gtar
type=application/x-shar        exts=shar
type=application/x-tar         exts=tar
type=application/mac-binhex40  exts=hqx

type=audio/basic               exts=au,snd
type=audio/x-aiff              exts=aif,aiff,aifc
type=audio/x-wav               exts=wav

type=image/gif                 exts=gif
type=image/ief                 exts=ief
type=image/jpeg                exts=jpeg,jpg,jpe
type=image/tiff                exts=tiff,tif
```

Graphing

by David Watts

Fusing Your Data with Java and Cold Fusion

You've probably seen plenty of web pages that use Java to provide multimedia elements. If you're like most business-oriented developers, you might have been impressed with the visual effects and the handling of graphics, but haven't found a place for Java to provide useful content to your pages. The makers of Cold Fusion liked the way Java could display graphics, so they developed a connection between Java and Cold Fusion to easily display dynamically created charts and graphs retrieved by Cold Fusion. In this section, you will read a little background information about Java and learn about the connection between Java and Cold Fusion.

The Basics of Java

What exactly is Java? An outside observer might have a little trouble answering this question because of all the hype surrounding Java. Java is just a programming language and a set of specifications for a runtime environment. Java applications are written in a language similar to C++, compile into a non-machine-specific bytecode format, and execute within a runtime environment known as a virtual machine.

Simply put, you can develop Java applications that run on any platform that supports a Java runtime environment. You don't have to worry about platform-specific issues, APIs, or screen layouts. Your Java applications operate the same on any of these platforms, and you don't have to create different compiles, maintain separate sources, or any of the other problems normally associated with multi-platform development.

The makers of Java originally intended it only as a language for small, embedded processors, but some features of Java make it a programming language for the web. Java's runtime environment allows for security settings that prevent untrusted code from seriously harming the system, and provides verification of Java bytecodes before execution to ensure the safety of that code. This runtime environment is small and can easily be included as part of a browser. Netscape Navigator 2 and later and Microsoft Internet Explorer 3 and later contain a Java runtime, and the latest releases of Windows NT, Windows 95 from Microsoft, and IBM's OS/2 will most likely contain a Java runtime. Other browsers and operating systems will probably follow.

Most important, Java provides a mechanism for developing applications that can be executed from a web page. These applications are called applets. Applets work in concert with the browser and the Java runtime to display within a web page or even within a separate frame on the desktop. Applets communicate only with the server from which they are called, and can send and retrieve data between the desktop and the server.

This is, of course, a very brief and incomplete explanation of Java. If you want to know more, pick up one of the many available books about Java, such as Que's *Special Edition Using Java*.

Using Java Applets on Your Web Pages

Java applets can add graphics and effects to your Web pages as well as display meaningful data from your databases. Several methods can be used to accomplish this. Each method varies in complexity and results. The easiest way is to simply include existing applets within your pages and generate dynamic parameters for them by using Cold Fusion. This doesn't require that you know anything about DCF or Java development because you only need to include an applet within your pages. To do this, you need the applet and its list of parameters.

Here's a simple example, using one of the demonstration applets that comes with the Java Development Kit from Sun Microsystems, the original developers of Java.

The first step is to place the applet (consisting of one or more Java class files) somewhere within your visible document tree. In this example, the file Chart.class is in the /java/ directory of www.a2z.com.

You want to call the applet from within a web page by using the APPLET tag. Listing 29.1 shows the example HTML file with the APPLET tag and a list of parameters within it.

TIP You can place HTML text and graphics within an APPLET tag that will appear only if viewed with a browser that isn't Java-enabled.

On the CD

Listing 29.1   BARGRAPH.HTML—HTML File Containing an *APPLET* Container Tag with Parameter Tags Within It

```
<HTML>
<HEAD>
<TITLE>Bar Chart</TITLE>
</HEAD>

<BODY>
<HR>
<APPLET CODE="Chart.class" WIDTH=251 HEIGHT=125>
<PARAM NAME=c1 VALUE="10">
<PARAM NAME=c2 VALUE="20">
<PARAM NAME=c3 VALUE="5">
<PARAM NAME=c4 VALUE="30">
<PARAM NAME=c1_label VALUE="Q1">
<PARAM NAME=c2_label VALUE="Q2">
<PARAM NAME=c3_label VALUE="Q3">
<PARAM NAME=c4_label VALUE="Q4">
<PARAM NAME=c1_color VALUE="blue">
<PARAM NAME=c2_color VALUE="green">
<PARAM NAME=c3_color VALUE="magenta">
<PARAM NAME=c4_color VALUE="yellow">
<PARAM NAME=c1_style VALUE="striped">
<PARAM NAME=c2_style VALUE="solid">
<PARAM NAME=c3_style VALUE="striped">
<PARAM NAME=c4_style VALUE="solid">
<PARAM NAME=title VALUE="Performance">
<PARAM NAME=columns VALUE="4">
<PARAM NAME=orientation VALUE="horizontal">
<PARAM NAME=scale value="5">
</APPLET>
<HR>

</BODY>
</HTML>
```

CAUTION

Java is a case-sensitive language, so be sure to specify exactly the name and parameters of the applet. You must also make sure that all the class files used by a specific applet are in their correct locations and are properly referenced in your APPLET CODE and CODEBASE values. In addition, the name of the class you are calling must match case with the name of the class file. For example, the class file barchart.class, as installed by Cold Fusion, must be referenced in your APPLET CODE value as BarChart.class; otherwise you will receive a java.lang.ClassFormatError error message.

Figure 29.1 shows the HTML file and its applet displayed within the browser.

FIG. 29.1

The barchart from Listing 29.1 displayed in Netscape.

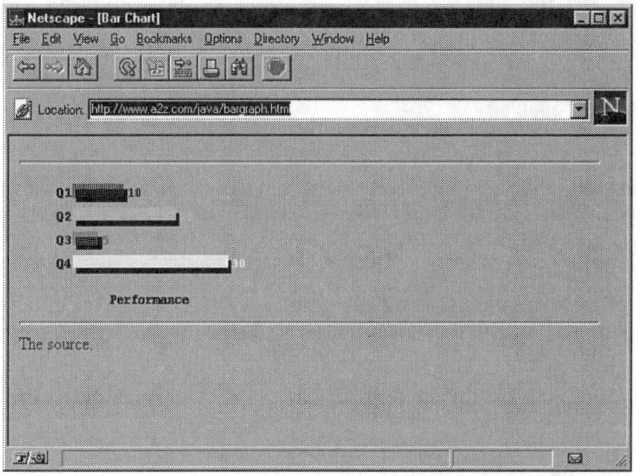

With a little modification, you can adapt this applet to display data retrieved by Cold Fusion. Figure 29.2 shows a template that performs a query of the book inventory and then generates a bar chart. The code shown in Listing 29.2 generates parameters for the applet by using Cold Fusion.

On the CD

Listing 29.2   BARGRAPH.CFM—Using Query Output to Generate Parameters for a Chart Applet

```
<CFQUERY NAME="BookGraphInfo" DATASOURCE="A2Z">
SELECT Title, NumberInStock FROM Inventory
</CFQUERY>

<HTML>

<HEAD>
<TITLE>A2Z Simple Bar Graph of Inventory</TITLE>
</HEAD>

<BODY>
```

```
<APPLET CODE="Chart.class" width=500 height=125>

<PARAM NAME=title VALUE="Inventory">
<PARAM NAME=orientation VALUE="horizontal">
<PARAM NAME=scale VALUE="5">

<CFSET #LoopCount# = 1>
<CFSET #Color# = "red">

<CFOUTPUT QUERY="BookGraphInfo">
<PARAM NAME=c#LoopCount# VALUE="#BookGraphInfo.NumberInStock#">
<PARAM NAME=c#LoopCount#_label VALUE="#BookGraphInfo.Title#">
<PARAM NAME=c#LoopCount#_color VALUE="#Color#">
<CFSET #LoopCount# = #LoopCount# + 1>
<CFIF #Color# IS "red">
<CFSET #Color# = "green">
<CFELSEIF #Color# IS "green">
<CFSET #Color# = "blue">
<CFELSEIF #Color# IS "blue">
<CFSET #Color# = "yellow">
<CFELSEIF #Color# IS "yellow">
<CFSET #Color# = "red">
</CFIF>
</CFOUTPUT>

<CFSET #LoopCount# = #LoopCount# - 1>
<CFOUTPUT><PARAM NAME=columns VALUE="#LoopCount#"></CFOUTPUT>

</APPLET>

</BODY>

</HTML>
```

FIG. 29.2

The bar graph generated by parameters set by using Cold Fusion.

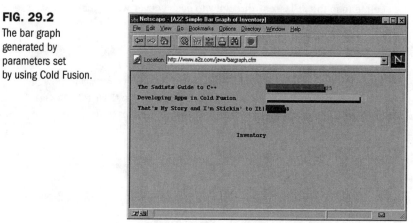

Using DCF as a Bridge Between Java and Cold Fusion

As you've seen, you can easily use an existing Java applet to display data from Cold Fusion queries. It is a little difficult to configure and is just a static display. The next step is to use the Cold Fusion Graphlets provided in the Cold Fusion package by Allaire. By using the DCF interface, these applets display static data and can refresh this data repeatedly after a user-specified interval. In addition, you can easily write your APPLET tags because Graphlets accept lists of parameters that can be easily generated and arranged within your tags by using the ValueList formatting function.

The DCF interface is a set of Java classes provided with Cold Fusion that contain methods to retrieve formatted data from URLs. You don't have to know anything about DCF or Java programming to use the graphlets, and you'll learn more about DCF itself in the next section.

Using the Allaire DCF Graphlets

Allaire has made it easy for you to use the DCF. Seven DCF graphlets and the DCF classes install onto your server when you install Cold Fusion. You only need to start using the graphlets in your Web pages. This section covers the steps you need to perform to use graphlets.

Configuring Your Server

The Cold Fusion installation creates a directory with a subdirectory in the root of your web server's document tree, /Classes/CFGraphs/, that contains another subdirectory, /Allaire/, as well as seven Java class files. Six of these files are your graphlets. Within the /Allaire/ subdirectory are the Java class files that make up the Database Component Framework.

Once you install Cold Fusion, the Java files are ready to run. If your server is multihoming, however, you will need to map the /Classes/ directory to each server with which you want to use graphlets.

> **CAUTION**
>
> If you move your graphlets to a different location, make sure that you maintain the exact subdirectory structure found within the CFGraphs directory. The Allaire subdirectory contains the Allaire DCF package. Packages in Java are groups of related classes, and the directory structure matches the class hierarchy within the package.

Using Graphlets

All APPLET tags share some characteristics. The first line of a typical APPLET tag looks like this:

```
<APPLET CODE="BarChart.class" CODEBASE="/Classes/CFGraphs/"
➥ WIDTH=250 HEIGHT=100>
```

This line contains four parameters that must be specified. CODE is the name of the specific Java applet and is case-sensitive. CODEBASE is the directory in which the applet is located and is also case-sensitive. Notice that, in this instance, the directory is the default installation directory. WIDTH and HEIGHT are measured in pixels and specify the size of the applet within the page. The last line is the closing tag, </APPLET>. You place parameter tags between these two APPLET tags.

Some of the parameters you can set, whereas some parameters you must set (like the ones used for the initial loading of data). The parameters that must be set will be covered first.

CAUTION

Remember that parameter names are case-sensitive. ChartData.Columns is different from CHARTDATA.COLUMNS. The Graphlet will try, in the absence of the expected parameters, to match uppercase and lowercase variants, but don't expect it to work as well as if you had correctly specified the parameters.

Using Data List Parameters   Data parameters for graphlets are named ChartData. *ParameterName* and take comma-delimited lists for their values.

The first data parameter, ChartData.Columns, sets the number and names of other data parameters. The following line shows this parameter set to list two other parameters, Items and Values.

```
<PARAM NAME="ChartData.Columns" VALUE="Items,Values">
```

You can then include those parameters that you've named. The following lines show parameters for ChartData.Items and ChartData.Values that contain the months in the year and the number of days in each month:

```
<PARAM NAME="ChartData.Items"
VALUE="Jan,Feb,Mar,Apr,May,Jun,Jul,Aug,Sep,Oct,Nov,Dec">
<PARAM NAME="ChartData.Values"
VALUE="31,28,31,30,31,30,31,31,30,31,30,31">
```

You can also specify colors for each item within your graph by using the ChartData.Colors parameter:

```
<PARAM NAME="ChartData.Colors"
VALUE="red,green,blue,yellow,red,green,blue,yellow,red,green,blue,yellow">
```

This parameter takes any of these colors:

- Red
- Blue
- Green
- Yellow
- Magenta
- Cyan

- Orange
- Pink
- Dark gray

If you don't specify this parameter, the applets display your graph items in these colors in the order listed above, one for each item in the graph, until the last color is reached. If your graph has more than nine items, additional items will be displayed as dark gray. If you use this parameter and have more items in your graph than you have colors specified, they will also be displayed as dark gray.

If you include the ChartData.Colors parameter, don't forget to include it in your ChartData.Columns.

```
<PARAM NAME="ChartData.Columns" VALUE="Items,Values,Colors">
```

Using Dynamic Data Population of Parameters You've seen how to use graphlets with static data. Now you'll see how Cold Fusion can dynamically generate comma-delimited lists by using the ValueList function to fill the data parameters.

Listing 29.3 shows part of a Cold Fusion template that queries the A2Z Books database for a book's ISBN and the number of copies in stock, and then generates value lists for the ChartData.Items and ChartData.Values parameters.

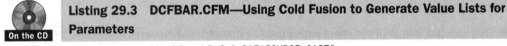

Listing 29.3 DCFBAR.CFM—Using Cold Fusion to Generate Value Lists for Parameters

On the CD

```
<CFQUERY NAME="BookGraphInfo" DATASOURCE="A2Z">
SELECT ISBN, NumberInStock FROM Inventory
</CFQUERY>

<APPLET CODE="BarChart.class" CODEBASE="/Classes/CFGraphs/"
➥WIDTH=500 height=250>

<CFOUTPUT>
<PARAM NAME="ChartData.Columns" VALUE="Items,Values">
<PARAM NAME="ChartData.Items" VALUE="#ValueList(BookGraphInfo.ISBN)#">
<PARAM NAME="ChartData.Values" VALUE=
➥"#ValueList(BookGraphInfo.NumberInStock)#">
</CFOUTPUT>

</APPLET>
```

Using Data Refresh Parameters You can do anything you did with the graphlets with any applet that accepts parameters (see Listing 29.1), but one difference makes graphlets better.

The essential difference between graphlets and regular Java applets is that graphlets can call a Cold Fusion template and refresh its data display with two parameters: RefreshTime and RefreshDataFromURL. The RefreshTime parameter is the time, in seconds, that the graphlet should wait before it retrieves data. By default, this value is zero and does not refresh the data.

The RefreshDataFromURL parameter specifies a fully qualified Cold Fusion template URL from which the graphlet gets its data. The following example refreshes data every minute from a template named currentstock.cfm.

```
<PARAM NAME="RefreshTime" VALUE="60">
<PARAM NAME="RefreshDataFromURL"
VALUE="http://www.a2z.com/a2z/java/currentstock.cfm">
```

The template used to refresh data should contain only the CFQUERY to retrieve the data, labels for the output columns, and the output columns themselves.

```
<CFQUERY NAME="CurrentStock" DATASOURCE="A2Z">
SELECT ISBN, NumberInStock FROM Inventory
</CFQUERY>

Columns:Items,Values
<CFOUTPUT QUERY="CurrentStock">
#ISBN#,#NumberInStock#
</CFOUTPUT>
```

The RefreshTime parameter from the original APPLET tag is added to the URL request made by the applet, so you can use it in this template.

Using Optional Parameters   All the graphlets accept the optional parameters listed in Table 29.1. In addition, different graphlets have additional optional parameters as listed next.

Table 29.1   Optional Parameters for All Graphlets

Parameter	Description	Default Value
Title	Chart title	Chart
TitleFontName	Font for the chart title	Times Roman
TitleFontHeight	Font size for the chart title	12
DrawBorders	Outlines around bars or slices by using the font color	No
ShowDateTime	Date and time display below chart title	Yes
BackgroundColor	Hexadecimal color value for background	C0C0C0
FontColor	Hexadecimal color value for font and borders	000000
GridLineColor	Hexadecimal color value for grid lines and axes descriptions	808080

The TitleFontName refers to fonts available to Java rather than native system font types such as TrueType or Adobe Type Manager fonts. These fonts depend on the implementation of the Java virtual machine, so some fonts are available on some systems but not others. The three most commonly found are TimesRoman (without a space between the two words), Helvetica, and Courier.

N O T E   The ShowDateTime parameter is fixed format, so you can't customize the display of the date and time. ■

CAUTION

If you provide a color value by using one of the color string names commonly used by Java, the graphlet will fail to load, producing a java.lang.NumberFormatException error.

Differentiating Graphlet Types

All of the previous information applies to all types of graphlets; this section deals with the differences between their optional parameters. The graphlets can be divided into two categories. The first, which includes bar charts and pie charts, are suited to displaying simple data that can be represented within a two-dimensional array structure of items and values, like a spreadsheet. The second, which includes area, line, multibar, and 3D multibar charts, allows you to add a third dimension of groups to items and values.

Using Bar Chart and Pie Charts   Bar charts and pie charts display two-dimensional data arrays in bars of different lengths or as slices of a circular pie. The optional parameters accepted by these applets are listed in Table 29.2.

Table 29.2   Optional Parameters

Parameter	Description	Default Value	Used By
ShowLegend	Display a legend for the chart	Yes	Pie Chart
Orientation	Horizontal or vertical bar orientation	Vertical	Bar Chart
Shadow	Number of pixels used to display shadow effect	4	Bar Chart

Using Area, Line, Multibar, and 3D Multibar Charts   These four charts display multidimensional data arrays that can be used to display data in more than the two dimensions used by the pie and bar charts. The optional parameters used by these applets are listed in Table 29.3.

Table 29.3   Optional Parameters

Parameter	Description	Default Value	Used By
Cumulative	Cumulate the data	No	Area Chart, Line Chart
DotSize	Size of the dots in pixels	2	Line Chart
Rotation Chart	Angle rotation from 0 to 90 degrees	10	3D Multibar
Elevation Chart	Angle of elevation from 0 to 90 degrees	30	3D Multibar
Distance Chart	Viewing distance in graph widths	3	3D Multibar

Refreshing Graphlet

Now that you've seen what makes up a graphlet, you'll build an example HTML page—using frames—that displays a dynamically updating graphlet. Because no one else will be updating your sample database, you'll update it yourself from the lower frame. Figure 29.3 shows what it looks like when first shown.

FIG. 29.3
The first display of the chart uses data specified as applet parameters.

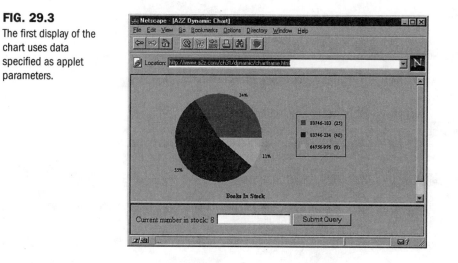

Listing 29.4 shows the HTML frame that contains the document with the applet and the document used to modify the database.

On the CD

Listing 29.4   DYNAMICCHART.HTML—A Simple Frame Document Containing the Applet Document

```
<HTML>

<HEAD>
<TITLE>A2Z Dynamic Chart</TITLE>
</HEAD>

<FRAMESET ROWS="80%,20%">
<FRAME NAME="chart" SRC="chart.cfm">
<FRAME NAME="controls" SRC="controls.cfm">
</FRAMESET>

</HTML>
```

The actual document that invokes the applet is in Listing 29.5. Notice that it contains the RefreshDataFromURL—which must contain a fully qualified URL—and RefreshTime.

On the CD

Listing 29.5   CHART.CFM—The Contents of the Chart Applet Document

```
<CFQUERY NAME="GetBookInfo" DATASOURCE="A2Z">
SELECT ISBN, NumberInStock FROM Inventory
</CFQUERY>

<HTML>

<HEAD>
<TITLE>Chart Applet</TITLE>
</HEAD>

<BODY>

<APPLET CODE="PieChart.class"
CODEBASE="/Classes/CFGraphs/" WIDTH="450" HEIGHT="250">

<!-- Required data parameters used to start the Graphlet -->

<CFOUTPUT>
<PARAM NAME="ChartData.Columns" VALUE="Items,Values">
<PARAM NAME="ChartData.Items" VALUE="#ValueList(GetBookInfo.ISBN)#">
<PARAM NAME="ChartData.Values" VALUE=
➥"#ValueList(GetBookInfo.NumberInStock)#">
</CFOUTPUT>

<!-- Optional display parameters -->

<PARAM NAME="Title" VALUE="Books In Stock">

<!-- Refresh parameters -->

<PARAM NAME="RefreshTime" VALUE="2">
<PARAM NAME="RefreshDataFromURL" VALUE=
➥"http://www.a2z.com/ch28/dynamic/refresh.cfm">
```

```
<!-- Display something to non-Java-capable browsers -->

<H1>Your browser does not support Java!</H1>
Download a new one from Netscape or Microsoft!<BR>

</APPLET>

</BODY>

</HTML>
```

You'll use a template to select the record for the book with the least number of copies in stock, and then permit the user to change this value in a form (see Listing 29.6).

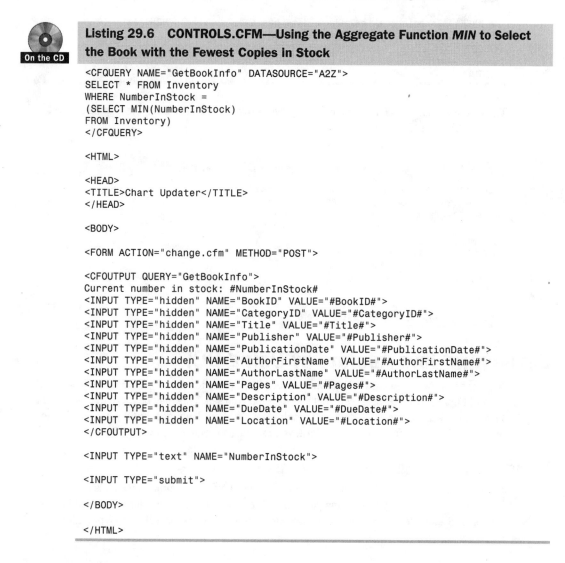

Listing 29.6   CONTROLS.CFM—Using the Aggregate Function *MIN* to Select the Book with the Fewest Copies in Stock

```
<CFQUERY NAME="GetBookInfo" DATASOURCE="A2Z">
SELECT * FROM Inventory
WHERE NumberInStock =
(SELECT MIN(NumberInStock)
FROM Inventory)
</CFQUERY>

<HTML>

<HEAD>
<TITLE>Chart Updater</TITLE>
</HEAD>

<BODY>

<FORM ACTION="change.cfm" METHOD="POST">

<CFOUTPUT QUERY="GetBookInfo">
Current number in stock: #NumberInStock#
<INPUT TYPE="hidden" NAME="BookID" VALUE="#BookID#">
<INPUT TYPE="hidden" NAME="CategoryID" VALUE="#CategoryID#">
<INPUT TYPE="hidden" NAME="Title" VALUE="#Title#">
<INPUT TYPE="hidden" NAME="Publisher" VALUE="#Publisher#">
<INPUT TYPE="hidden" NAME="PublicationDate" VALUE="#PublicationDate#">
<INPUT TYPE="hidden" NAME="AuthorFirstName" VALUE="#AuthorFirstName#">
<INPUT TYPE="hidden" NAME="AuthorLastName" VALUE="#AuthorLastName#">
<INPUT TYPE="hidden" NAME="Pages" VALUE="#Pages#">
<INPUT TYPE="hidden" NAME="Description" VALUE="#Description#">
<INPUT TYPE="hidden" NAME="DueDate" VALUE="#DueDate#">
<INPUT TYPE="hidden" NAME="Location" VALUE="#Location#">
</CFOUTPUT>

<INPUT TYPE="text" NAME="NumberInStock">

<INPUT TYPE="submit">

</BODY>

</HTML>
```

After this form has been submitted, it launches the CFUPDATE tag in change.cfm (see Listing 29.7).

On the CD

Listing 29.7 CHANGE.CFM—Updating the Inventory Table

```
<CFUPDATE DATASOURCE="A2Z" TABLENAME="Inventory">
<HTML>

<HEAD>
<TITLE>Chart Updater</TITLE>
</HEAD>

<BODY>

<A HREF="controls.cfm"><H2>Chart data has been updated!</H2></A>

</BODY>

</HTML>
```

The Graphlet that is executing refresh.cfm every two seconds retrieves the new data. See Listing 29.8 for refresh.cfm.

On the CD

Listing 29.8 REFRESH.CFM—Retrieving Data Updates

```
<CFQUERY NAME="GetBookInfo" DATASOURCE="A2Z">
SELECT ISBN, NumberInStock FROM Inventory
</CFQUERY>

Columns: Items,Values
<CFOUTPUT QUERY="GetBookInfo">
#ISBN#,#NumberInStock#
</CFOUTPUT>
```

Figure 29.4 shows the result of the update.

Developing Java Applets by Using DCF

You've seen how to use the DCF graphlets that Allaire provides. But the DCF can also be used to Cold Fusion-enable Java applets that you develop yourself. This may be more than you want to get into, because Java is a relatively complex development language; but if you're willing to invest the time and effort in learning Java, you can easily create your own DCF applets.

Using the Java Language

It is beyond the scope of this book to introduce you to Java programming, which is comparable in syntax and complexity to C++. Instead, a little bit of Java knowledge will be assumed in this section and a simple description of the Database Component Framework will be provided.

FIG. 29.4

The updated graph.

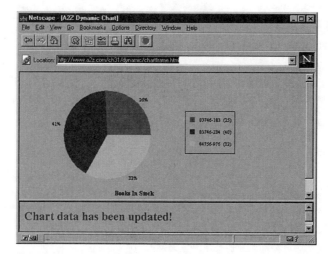

What you will need to use this section is a Java development environment and a little background knowledge of Java. You can use the freeware Java Development Kit from Sun, available for download from **http://www.javasoft.com**. Or, you can use one of the many Java development environments available now, such as Symantec Café, Sun's Java Workshop, or Microsoft Visual J++.

Once you have this installed, you will also have to include the Allaire DCF classes within your classpath. The classpath is the path that the Java development environment uses to find classes included in the classes you compile. The DCF classes themselves are installed in the /Classes/ CFGraphs/Allaire/ directory within your web server's document tree. You can either include this directory in your classpath, or you can copy the Allaire directory to your existing Java library root directory. Check your Java development environment's documentation for more details on setting the classpath.

Building a Simple DCF Applet

For this example, you will build a very simple applet, possibly the simplest DCF applet you can make. Your applet will not perform any complex graphing, like the Allaire DCF Graphlets, but instead will display two fields, ISBN and NumberInStock, from your Inventory database. The ISBN number will be listed in a choice box, which is the Java name for a drop-down box. When the user selects an entry from this choice box, the matching NumberInStock value will be displayed to the right by using a label control.

Most of Listing 29.9 is typical applet code to handle starting, stopping, and refreshing details. The part you want to read carefully is the retrieveData method, which uses the DCF classes to retrieve data from the template that calls the applet and from a refresh template, if one exists.

Listing 29.9 DCFDEMO.JAVA—Java Code for a Simple DCF Applet

```java
// Import the java classes for this applet
import java.awt.*;
import java.applet.Applet;
import java.awt.Graphics;
import java.awt.Color;
import java.awt.Font;
import java.awt.FontMetrics;
import java.io.*;
import java.lang.*;
import java.net.URL;

// Import the DCF classes
import allaire.dcf.recordset.*;
import allaire.util.*;

public class DCFDemo extends Applet implements Runnable {

// This thread is used to run the applet
Thread        runner;

// These variables are for use with the DCF.
// The Recordset and Query instances come
// from the DCF classes of the same name.
// The refreshTime and debugInfoEnabled
// are used to set DCF-specific parameters.
Recordset    formData;
Query        query;
int          refreshTime = 0;
boolean      debugInfoEnabled = true;

// These variables are used for the data
// retrieved using the DCF.
String[]     ISBN;
String[]     numberInStock;
int          columns;

// These variables are used to display the data
Label labelISBN;
Label labelInStock;
Choice choiceISBN;
Label displayNumberInStock;

// standard construction start, stop, run for applet
// running as thread
public void start() {
if (runner == null) {
runner = new Thread(this);
runner.start();
}
}

public void stop() {
if (runner != null) {
runner.stop();
```

```
runner = null;
}
}

public void run() {
while (true) {
if ( refreshTime == 0 ) {
// stop thread if no refresh required
stop();
return;
}
pause(refreshTime * 1000);
// refresh data and repaint applet
this.retrieveData();
repaint();
}
}
private void pause(int time) {
try { Thread.sleep(time); }
catch (InterruptedException e) {
if ( debugInfoEnabled ) Debug.write(e.getMessage());
}
}

// The init method creates the screen layout,
// and calls the data retrieval method.
public synchronized void init() {

super.init();

setLayout(new FlowLayout());
resize(300,200);
labelISBN = new Label("ISBN:");
add(labelISBN);
labelISBN.reshape(10,10,50,20);
choiceISBN = new Choice();
add(choiceISBN);
labelInStock = new Label("Number In Stock:");
add(labelInStock);
displayNumberInStock = new Label();
add(displayNumberInStock);

// This section retrieves the refresh time and URL, if any.
// If they exist, the applet will append the refresh time to
// the query URL when it is called, so that you can read that
// in your refresh query template if you want.
String rs;
rs = getParameter("RefreshTime");
if (rs == null) {
refreshTime = 0;
} else {
refreshTime = Integer.parseInt(rs);
rs = getParameter("RefreshDataFromURL");
if (rs == null) {
// if no URL selected - do not refresh
```

continues

Listing 29.9 Continued

```
refreshTime = 0;
} else {
// query definition
query = new Query(rs);
// add refreshTime parameter to the URL
query.addParam( "RefreshTime", String.valueOf(refreshTime) );
}
}

this.retrieveData();

}

// Here is the most important method in this applet.
// This method retrieves data from a Cold Fusion query
// using instances of the DCF Query and Recordset classes.
private void retrieveData() {

try {

// This decision tree either retrieves data from the
// initial applet parameters, or retrieves it from a
// refresh template.
if ( formData == null ) {
formData = new AppletParamRecordset(this);
} else {
query.execute();
formData = query.getRecordset();
}

columns = formData.getRowCount();

ISBN = new String[columns];
numberInStock = new String[columns];

// This for loop retrieves the data from the comma-delimited
// lists in the template, and adds ISBN numbers to the choice
// box.
for (int i = 0; i < columns; i++) {
ISBN[i] = formData.getData(i + 1, "ISBN");
numberInStock[i] = formData.getData(i + 1, "NumberInStock");
choiceISBN.addItem(ISBN[i]);
}

displayNumberInStock.setText(numberInStock[0]);

} catch (Exception e) {
if (debugInfoEnabled) Debug.write(e.getMessage());
}
}

// This event method is triggered by selecting an entry from the
// choice box.
```

```java
public void selectedChoiceISBN() {
int selectedISBNIndex = choiceISBN.getSelectedIndex();
displayNumberInStock.setText(numberInStock[selectedISBNIndex]);
}

public boolean handleEvent(Event event) {
if (event.id == Event.ACTION_EVENT && event.target == choiceISBN) {
selectedChoiceISBN();
return true;
}

return super.handleEvent(event);
}

}
```

First, examine the `init` method, which is used to prepare the applet for display. In the case of a DCF applet, this also means retrieving parameters and initial data sets. The simple applet is retrieving only two regular parameters, and it uses the standard `getParameter` method to do so. These parameters are `RefreshTime` and `RefreshDataFromURL`. If these parameters exist, they will be used for the query execution in the `retrieveData` method every time that method is called from the `run` method.

The part deserving most of your attention, the `retrieveData` method, is doing all the interesting stuff. The entire method is wrapped in a `try...catch` exception catcher, in case there is any problem retrieving data. Within the `try` portion, the first step is to determine whether the applet has previously read any data in—because this method is called every time the applet repaints—and then either read the initial data or execute the refresh query.

```java
if (formData == null) {
formData = new AppletParamRecordset(this);
} else {
query.execute();
formData = query.getRecordset();
}
```

The next step is to find out how many columns of data there are, and then create string arrays with enough space to hold all the columns.

```java
columns = formData.getRowCount();

ISBN = new String[columns];
numberInStock = new String[columns];
```

Finally, in this method you retrieve the data from the recordset into the array variables, and then fill the choice box. The last line shown here initializes the display label with the value for the first ISBN number:

```java
for (int i = 0; i < columns; i++) {
ISBN[i] = formData.getData(i + 1, "ISBN");
numberInStock[i] = formData.getData(i + 1, "NumberInStock");
choiceISBN.addItem(ISBN[i]);
}

displayNumberInStock.setText(numberInStock[0]);
```

Listing 29.10 shows the template you'll use to call this applet. It uses a query to get the initial data for the applet.

On the CD

Listing 29.10   DCFDEMO.CFM—Calling and Initializing the Applet

```
<CFQUERY NAME="DCFDemo" DATASOURCE="A2Z Books">
SELECT ISBN, NumberInStock FROM Inventory
</CFQUERY>

<HTML>

<HEAD>

<TITLE>DCF Demo</TITLE>

</HEAD>

<BODY>

<APPLET CODE="DCFDemo.class" CODEBASE="/Classes/CFGraphs/" WIDTH="300"

HEIGHT="300">
<PARAM NAME="columns" value="ISBN,NumberInStock">
<CFOUTPUT QUERY="DCFDemo">
<PARAM NAME="ISBN" VALUE="#ValueList(DCFDemo.ISBN)#">
<PARAM NAME="NumberInStock" VALUE="#ValueList(DCFDemo.NumberInStock)#">
</CFOUTPUT>
<PARAM NAME="RefreshTime" VALUE="0">
<PARAM NAME="RefreshDataFromURL"
VALUE="http://www.a2z.com/ch31/DCFDemo/refresh.cfm">
</APPLET>

</BODY>

</HTML>
```

The refresh template contains the same query as the previous template, but outputs just the data as explained in the graphlet section.

This has been a very simple introduction to DCF programming. If you're interested in learning more, a good idea would be to DCF-enable some of the sample applets that come with the Java Development Kit. Listing 29.11 shows a DCF-enabled version of the Chart applet from the JDK.

On the CD

Listing 29.11   DCFCHART.JAVA—A Sample DCF-Enabled Chart Applet

```
import java.awt.Graphics;
import java.awt.Color;
import java.awt.Font;
import java.awt.FontMetrics;
import java.io.*;
import java.lang.*;
```

```java
import java.net.URL;

import allaire.dcf.recordset.*;
import allaire.util.*;

public class DCFChart extends java.applet.Applet implements Runnable {
//*** the Runnable interface - applet can run as separate thread

static final int      VERTICAL = 0;
static final int       HORIZONTAL = 1;

static final int      SOLID = 0;
static final int      STRIPED = 1;

int              orientation;
String          title;
Font          titleFont;
FontMetrics          titleFontMetrics;
int              titleHeight = 15;
int              columns;
int              values[];
Object          colors[];
    Object          labels[];
int              styles[];
int              scale = 10;
int              maxLabelWidth = 0;
int              barWidth;
int              barSpacing = 10;
int              max = 0;

// DCF declarations for recordset and query
Recordset      chartData;
Query          query;

int          refreshTime;
boolean      debugInfoEnabled;

Thread      runner;


public synchronized void init() {

    // The return string variable used to get parameters
    String rs;

// Get the title parameter
    titleFont = new java.awt.Font("Courier", Font.BOLD, 12);
    titleFontMetrics = getFontMetrics(titleFont);
    title = getParameter("title");
    if (title == null) {
        title = "Chart";
    }

// Get the scale parameter
rs = getParameter("scale");
```

continues

Listing 29.11   Continued

```
        if (rs == null) {
            scale = 10;
        } else {
            scale = Integer.parseInt(rs);
        }

// Get the orientation parameter
        rs = getParameter("orientation");
        if (rs == null) {
            orientation = VERTICAL;
        } else if (rs.toLowerCase().equals("vertical")) {
            orientation = VERTICAL;
        } else if (rs.toLowerCase().equals("horizontal")) {
            orientation = HORIZONTAL;
        } else {
            orientation = VERTICAL;
        }

// Get the data refresh parameters
rs = getParameter("RefreshTime");
if (rs == null) {
refreshTime = 0;
} else {
refreshTime = Integer.parseInt(rs);
rs = getParameter("RefreshDataFromURL");
if (rs == null) {
// if no URL selected - do not refresh
refreshTime = 0;
} else {
// query definition
query = new Query(rs);
// add refreshTime parameter to the URL
query.addParam( "RefreshTime", String.valueOf(refreshTime) );
}
}

        // should the debug info window be enabled?
        rs = getParameter("DebugInfoEnabled");
        if (rs == null) {
            debugInfoEnabled = false;
        } else if ( rs.toLowerCase().equals("yes") ) {
            debugInfoEnabled = true;
        } else {
debugInfoEnabled = false;
        }

// retrieve graph data from params
this.getData();

    }

// getData method retrieves data from applet params
// or from refresh template
private void getData() {
```

```
int      i;
String   rs;
int      value;

try {

if ( chartData == null ) {
// initial data come from the applet params ...
chartData = new AppletParamRecordset(this, "ChartData");
} else {
// ... otherwise get data from refresh template
query.execute();
chartData = query.getRecordset();
}

// show info in the status bar
if ( refreshTime == 0 ) {
getAppletContext().showStatus("Done");
} else {
getAppletContext().showStatus("...");
}

columns = chartData.getRowCount();

// set dimension for the arrays
values = new int[columns];
colors = new Color[columns];
labels = new String[columns];
styles = new int[columns];

// scroll thru records
for ( i = 0; i < columns; i++) {

        // retrieve style type or set default if not defined
if ( !chartData.columnExists("Styles") ) {
        styles[i] = (chartData.getData ( i + 1, "Labels").
➥toLowerCase().equals("striped"))
                        ? STRIPED : SOLID ;
        } else {
            styles[i] = SOLID;
        }

// retrieve label
labels[i] = chartData.getData ( i + 1, "Labels" );
            maxLabelWidth = Math.max(
                titleFontMetrics.stringWidth( chartData.getData
➥( i+1, "Labels" ) ),
                    maxLabelWidth);

// retrieve value
            try {
                value = Integer.parseInt
➥( chartData.getData ( i+1, "Values" ));
} catch (Exception e) {
```

continues

Listing 29.11   Continued

```
value = 0;
}
values[i] = value;
max = Math.max( max, value);

// retrieve color
if ( !chartData.columnExists("Colors") ) {
colors[i] = Color.black;
} else {
rs = chartData.getData ( i + 1, "Colors" );
if ( rs.equals ( "red" )) {
                       colors[i] = Color.red;
} else if (rs.equals ( "green" )) {
                       colors[i] = Color.green;
} else if (rs.equals("blue")) {
                       colors[i] = Color.blue;
} else if (rs.equals("pink")) {
                       colors[i] = Color.pink;
} else if (rs.equals("orange")) {
                       colors[i] = Color.orange;
} else if (rs.equals("magenta")) {
                       colors[i] = Color.magenta;
} else if (rs.equals("cyan")) {
                       colors[i] = Color.cyan;
} else if (rs.equals("white")) {
                       colors[i] = Color.white;
} else if (rs.equals("yellow")) {
                       colors[i] = Color.yellow;
} else if (rs.equals("gray")) {
                       colors[i] = Color.gray;
} else if (rs.equals("darkGray")) {
                       colors[i] = Color.darkGray;
} else {
                       colors[i] = Color.black;
}
}
}

} catch (Exception e) {

if ( debugInfoEnabled ) Debug.write(e.getMessage());

}

switch (orientation) {
        case VERTICAL:
        default:
          barWidth = maxLabelWidth;
          resize(Math.max(columns * (barWidth + barSpacing),
                  titleFontMetrics.stringWidth(title)) +
              titleFont.getSize() + 5,
              (max * scale) + (2 * titleFont.getSize()) + 5 + titleFont.
```

```
➥getSize());
        break;
    case HORIZONTAL:
        barWidth = titleFont.getSize();
        resize(Math.max((max * scale) +
➥titleFontMetrics.stringWidth("" + max),
                titleFontMetrics.stringWidth(title)) + maxLabelWidth + 5,
            (columns * (barWidth + barSpacing)) + titleFont.getSize() + 10);
        break;
    }

}

// standard construction start, stop, run for applet
// running as thread
public void start() {
if (runner == null) {
runner = new Thread(this);
runner.start();
}
}

public void stop() {
if (runner != null) {
runner.stop();
runner = null;
}
}

public void run() {
while (true) {
if ( refreshTime == 0 ) {
// stop thread if no refresh required
stop();
return;
}
pause(refreshTime * 1000);
// refresh data and repaint graph
this.getData();
repaint();
}
}

private void pause(int time) {
try { Thread.sleep(time); }
catch (InterruptedException e) {
if ( debugInfoEnabled ) Debug.write(e.getMessage());
}
}


public synchronized void paint(Graphics g) {
    int i, j;
    int cx, cy;
    char l[] = new char[1];
```

continues

Listing 29.11 Continued

```
            // draw the title centered at the bottom of the bar graph
            g.setColor(Color.black);
            i = titleFontMetrics.stringWidth(title);
            g.setFont(titleFont);
            g.drawString(title, Math.max((size().width - i)/2, 0),
                    size().height - titleFontMetrics.getDescent());
        for (i=0; i < columns; i++) {
            switch (orientation) {
              case VERTICAL:
              default:
              // set the next X coordinate to account for the label
              // being wider than the bar size().width.
              cx = (Math.max((barWidth + barSpacing),maxLabelWidth) * i) +
                  barSpacing;

              // center the bar chart
              cx += Math.max((size().width - (columns *
                            (barWidth + (2 * barSpacing))))/2,0);

              // set the next Y coordinate to account for the size().height
              // of the bar as well as the title and labels painted
              // at the bottom of the chart.
              cy = size().height - (values[i] * scale) - 1 - (2 * titleFont.
➥getSize());

              // draw the label
              g.setColor(Color.black);
              g.drawString((String)labels[i], cx,
                        size().height - titleFont.
➥getSize() - titleFontMetrics.getDescent());

              // draw the shadow bar
              if (colors[i] == Color.black) {
                  g.setColor(Color.gray);
              }
              g.fillRect(cx + 5, cy - 3, barWidth,  (values[i] * scale));
              // draw the bar with the specified color
              g.setColor((Color)(colors[i]));
              switch (styles[i]) {
                case SOLID:
                default:
                  g.fillRect(cx, cy, barWidth, (values[i] * scale));
                  break;
                case STRIPED:
                  {
                    int steps = (values[i] * scale) / 2;
                    int ys;

                    for (j=0; j < steps; j++) {
                        ys = cy + (2 * j);
                        g.drawLine(cx, ys, cx + barWidth, ys);
                    }
                  }
                  break;
```

```
}
g.drawString("" + values[i],
        cx,
        cy - titleFontMetrics.getDescent());
break;
 case HORIZONTAL:
// set the Y coordinate
cy = ((barWidth + barSpacing) * i) + barSpacing;

// set the X coordinate to be the size().width of the widest
// label
cx = maxLabelWidth + 1;

cx += Math.max((size().width - (maxLabelWidth + 1 +
                titleFontMetrics.stringWidth("" +
                                max) +
                (max * scale))) / 2, 0);
// draw the labels and the shadow
g.setColor(Color.black);
g.drawString((String)labels[i], cx - maxLabelWidth - 1,
        cy + titleFontMetrics.getAscent());
if (colors[i] == Color.black) {
    g.setColor(Color.gray);
}
g.fillRect(cx + 3,
        cy + 5,
        (values[i] * scale),
        barWidth);

// draw the bar in the current color
g.setColor((Color)(colors[i]));
switch (styles[i]) {
  case SOLID:
  default:
    g.fillRect(cx,
            cy,
            (values[i] * scale),
            barWidth);
    break;
  case STRIPED:
    {
     int steps = (values[i] * scale) / 2;
     int ys;

     for (j=0; j < steps; j++) {
         ys = cx + (2 * j);
         g.drawLine(ys, cy, ys, cy + barWidth);
     }
    }
    break;
}
g.drawString("" + values[i],
        cx + (values[i] * scale) + 3,
        cy + titleFontMetrics.getAscent());
```

continues

Listing 29.11 Continued

```
        break;
      }
    }
  }
}
```

Describing DCF Classes

You'll need to know the details of the DCF classes, including their variables, constructors, and methods, if you want to use all the features of the DCF.

Using the *allaire.dcf.recordset* Class The public class Query extends java.lang.Object. This class executes Cold Fusion templates on remote servers. The templates typically contain one or more SQL queries, which are returned in text format and then parsed into Recordset objects for use by the client object. The constructor for this class is

```
public Query(String strTemplateURL)
```

which creates a new query object that's linked to a template on a remote server. Constructing a Query object does not cause the query to be executed (this is accomplished by using the execute() method). The strTemplateURL parameter is the fully qualified URL of the template to be used by the query.

The addParam method,

```
public void addParam(String strName, String strValue)
```

adds a named parameter to the query, which will be URL-encoded and appended to the URL submitted to the remote server.

The resetParams method,

```
public void resetParams()
```

resets the parameter list to empty. This erases all parameters previously added by using the addParam() method.

The execute method,

```
public void execute() throws Exception
```

executes the template on the remote server by using the specified parameters. All Recordsets returned by the template will be parsed by using the getRecordset class methods.

The getRecordset method,

```
public Recordset getRecordset() throws Exception
```

or

```
public Recordset getRecordset(String strName) throws Exception
```

gets the Recordset, or one of a group of named Recordsets, fetched by the query from the remote template.

The getRecordsets method,

```
public Dictionary getRecordsets()
```

returns all Recordsets from the query.

Using the *allaire.dcf.recordset* Class   The public class Recordset extends
java.lang.Object. This class represents comma-delimited data from templates as a set of
rows and columns. Recordsets can be created from applet parameters or executed queries.

The constructor for this class is

```
public Recordset()
```

which creates a new empty Recordset. Usually, you will have already created a recordset by
using the Query or AppletParamRecordset classes.

The getRowCount method,

```
public int getRowCount()
```

returns the number of rows in the recordset.

The getColumnNames method,

```
public Vector getColumnNames()
```

returns the column names in the recordset.

The columnExists method,

```
public boolean columnExists(String strColumnName)
```

checks whether the column named in the parameter exists in the recordset.

The getData method,

```
public String getData(int iRow, String strColumnName) throws Exception
```

returns the data value from the intersection of the row value and the column name.

The getColumnData method,

```
public Vector getColumnData(String strColumnName) throws Exception
```

returns all the data from the named column.

Using the *allaire.dcf.recordset* Class   The public class AppletParamRecordset extends
Recordset. This class is used to instantiate a Recordset from applet parameters.

This class can be constructed in two ways:

```
public AppletParamRecordset(Applet applet) throws Exception
```

or

```
public AppletParamRecordset(Applet applet, String strName) throws Exception
```

The second allows you to specify multiple named recordsets within your template, and refer to
them by using separate AppletParamRecordset instances.

N O T E   The methods for this class are all inherited from the Recordset class. There are no
methods specific to this class. ◼

Using the DCF to Update Data

The DCF is designed primarily to allow you to display data from within a Java applet. It doesn't
fare so well when updating. You can write an applet to update data by calling a template with an
update CFQUERY in it rather than a select query, but you will be limited in what you can update.
This is because the DCF methods don't support the HTTP POST method, only GET. So, you can
send as much data to an update query as you can fit on an URL by using the Query.addParam
method previously listed. ●

CHAPTER 30

Interfacing with HTTP and FTP Using *CFHTTP* and *CFFTP*

by David E. Crawford

In this chapter

Using the *CFHTTP* Tag

CFHTTP provides mechanisms to retrieve pages from remote web servers for display locally, to execute either GET or POST operations, to retrieve information from or upload information to a remote server, and to post a wide variety of different variables to the server.

HTTP, the Hypertext Transfer Protocol, is the method by which communications between web clients (browsers) and servers are managed. Normally, HTTP processes HTML (Hypertext Markup Language) files, but it can support binary, audio and video, graphics, and other disparate file types using the MIME (Multipurpose Internet Mail Extensions) standard. For further information on the use of MIME with Cold Fusion, see Chapter 28, "MIME Types."

CFHTTP implements two of the most commonly used HTTP operations (GET and POST) to control Cold Fusion's interface with the HTTP servers. The syntax of the CFHTTP tag is simple, yet it offers several different options for creating output, resolving embedded links, and even the capability to build Cold Fusion queries from delimited text files.

The syntax for the CFHTTP tag is

```
<CFHTTP URL="hostname"
    USERNAME="username"
    PASSWORD="password"
    NAME="queryname"
    COLUMNS="query_columns"
    PATH="path"
    FILE="filename"
    METHOD="get_or_post"
    DELIMITER="character"
    TEXTQUALIFIER="character"
    RESOLVEURL="Yes/No"
    PROXYSERVER="hostname">
</CFHTTP>
```

N O T E POST operations using CFHTTP should be terminated with </CFHTTP>. GET operations do not require termination. ■

The CFHTTP tag's behavior can be changed depending on the value of the attributes supplied to it during execution. Table 30.1 explains the attributes and their functions.

Table 30.1 Attributes of the *CFHTTP* Tag

Attribute	Description
URL	Required. Full URL of the host name or IP address of the server on which the specified file resides.
METHOD	Required. GET or POST. Use GET to retrieve a binary or text file or to build a query using the contents of a text file. Use POST to send information to a CGI program or server page for processing. POST operations require use of one or more CFHTTPPARAM tags.

Attribute	Description
USERNAME	Optional. Submitted when a server requires a username for access.
PASSWORD	Optional. Submitted when a server requires a password for access.
NAME	Optional. Name to assign to a query object when a query is to be constructed from a text file.
COLUMNS	Optional. Column names for a query. If no column names are specified, defaults to the columns listed in the first row of the text file.
PATH	Optional. Path to the directory (local) in which a file is to be stored. If a path is not specified in a GET or POST operation, the results are created in the CFHTTP.FileContent variable for output.
FILE	Required in a POST operation if PATH is specified. The filename in which the results of the specified operation will be stored. Path to the file is specified in the PATH attribute.
DELIMITER	Required for creating a query. Valid characters are a tab or a comma. Default is a comma (,).
TEXTQUALIFIER	Required for creating a query. Indicates the start and finish of a column. Must be escaped when embedded in a column. If the qualifier is a quotation mark, it should be escaped as "". If there is no text qualifier in the file, specify a blank space as " ". Default is the quotation mark (").
RESOLVEURL	Optional. YES or NO. For GET and POST operations. When set to YES, any link referenced in the remote page will have its internal URL fully resolved and returned to the CFHTTP.FileContent variable so that the links remain intact. The following HTML tags, which may contain links, will be resolved: IMG SRC, A HREF, FORM ACTION, APPLET CODE, SCRIPT SRC, EMBED SRC, EMBED PLUGINSPACE, BODY BACKGROUND, FRAME SRC, BGSOUND SRC, OBJECT DATA, OBJECT CLASSID, OBJECT CODEBASE, OBJECT USEMAP.
PROXYSERVER	Optional. Host name or IP address of a proxy server, if required.

Part
IV

Ch
30

Using the *CFHTTPPARAM* Tag

The use of the CFHTTPPARAM tag is required when using CFHTTP for a POST operation.

The syntax for the CFHTTPPARAM tag is

```
<CFHTTPPARAM NAME="name"
   TYPE="transaction type"
   VALUE="value"
   FILE="filename" >
```

The attributes of the CFHTTPPARAM tag are shown in Table 30.2.

Table 30.2   Attributes of the *CFHTTPPARAM* Tag

Attribute	Description
NAME	Required. A variable name for data being passed.
TYPE	Required. The transaction type. Valid entries are URL, FormField, Cookie, CGI, and File.
VALUE	Optional for TYPE="*File*". Specifies the URL, FormField, Cookie, File, or CGI variable being passed to the server.
FILE	Required for TYPE="*File*". Fully qualified local filename to be uploaded to server. Example: c:\temp\amazon.lst.

Now that you have looked at the various attributes and syntax descriptions for the CFHTTP and CFHTTPPARAM tags, you will now write some examples to demonstrate the various facets of the CFHTTP tag in operation.

Putting the *CFHTTP* Tag to Use

Using CFHTTP with the GET method is a relatively simple one-way transaction. The web client, whether it is a browser or a Cold Fusion application, makes an HTTP request to an HTTP server and the server returns the requested document. The POST operation is two way, in which the web client sends specific information to the server or CGI application, and processed data is returned.

Using the *GET* Method

The first example you'll create will demonstrate a simple GET operation. Listing 30.1 shows the CFML code necessary to use the CFHTTP tag in a GET operation. This example will fetch the index page from **www.excite.com** (a large search engine site) and then display the results.

On the CD

**Listing 30.1   CFHTTP_1.CFM—Retrieving the Index Page from
www.excite.com by Using the *CFHTTP* Tag**

```
<CFHTTP METHOD="GET" URL="http://www.excite.com" RESOLVEURL="YES">

<CFOUTPUT>
#CFHTTP.FileContent#
</CFOUTPUT>
```

Figure 30.1 shows the output of your example, with the index page from **www.excite.com** fully displayed, including all of its graphics and links.

FIG. 30.1

Output of the index page from **www.excite.com**, rendered using the CFHTTP tag.

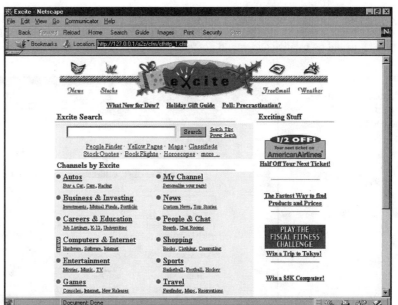

In this example, you left out the FILE and PATH attributes, which forced the result of the CFHTTP tag to be stored in the CFHTTP.FileContent variable. You set the RESOLVEURL attribute to YES, indicating that you wanted the internal links in the page to be turned into absolute versus relative links. Otherwise when the template was run, any relative link would have pointed to the local HTTP server instead.

The next example will demonstrate using CFHTTP with the GET method to save the results to a file. You will modify your previous example to specify the PATH and FILE attributes. Instead of outputting the CFHTTP.FileContent variable, you will use the CFFILE tag to read the contents of the download file into a variable and then display the results. The listing of the modified template is shown in Listing 30.2.

Listing 30.2   CFHTTP_2.CFM—Using the *CFHTTP* Tag with the *GET* Method to Download a File

```
<CFHTTP METHOD="GET" URL="http://www.excite.com" FILE="exciteindex.html"
PATH="c:\temp\" RESOLVEURL="YES">

<CFFILE ACTION="READ" VARIABLE="HTTPFILE" FILE="C:\temp\exciteindex.html">
<CFOUTPUT>
#HTTPFILE#
</CFOUTPUT>
```

Figure 30.2 shows the output from your second example. Note that images that were based on relative URLs from the index are not displayed. This is because the RESOLVEURL attribute is ignored when the PATH and FILE attributes are specified. Also, even though the majority of the hypertext links are displayed, if the HTML source of the page were displayed, all of the URLs would be relative and would not work on the local server.

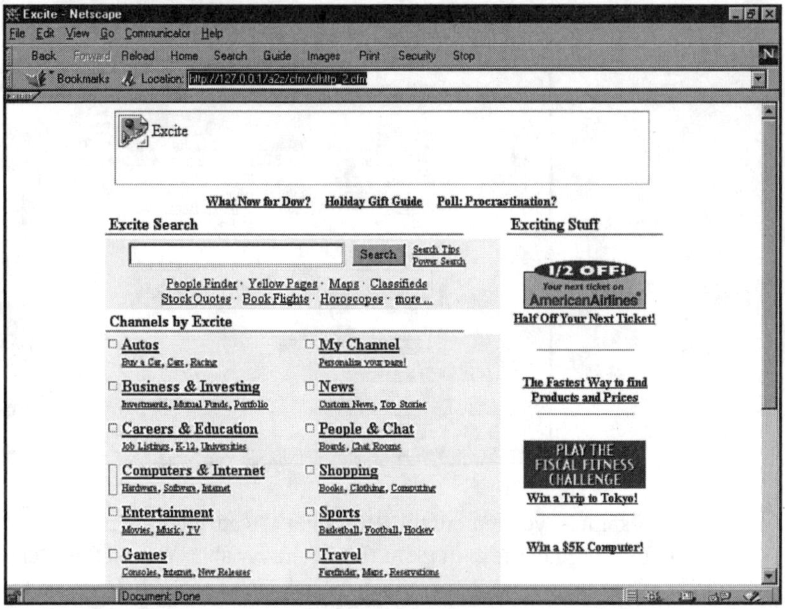

FIG. 30.2

Output of the CFHTTP tag using the GET method to save results to a local file.

The preceding examples have used the GET method to display the output of a CFHTTP tag. You will now build a template that will download a binary file from a remote web server using CFHTTP and the GET method. An additional variable showing the MimeType (see Chapter 28 for more information on MIME) of the downloaded file will be shown. Listing 30.3 shows the modified example. As an example, you will download the employee photo you uploaded back in Chapter 25.

On the CD

Listing 30.3   CFHTTP_3.CFM—Using the *CFHTTP* Tag with the *GET* Method to Download a Binary File

```
<CFHTTP METHOD="GET" URL="http://127.0.0.1/a2z/employee/photos/id02.jpg"
        FILE="id02.jpg" PATH="c:\temp\" RESOLVEURL="YES">

<CFOUTPUT>
MimeType of Downloaded File=#CFHTTP.MimeType#
</CFOUTPUT>
```

Make sure to change the URL in the preceding example to match your installation, if it is different from the example.

On the CD

The image file used as an example employee photo (ID02.JPG), which is just a small bitmapped image, is on the CD-ROM that accompanies this book.

This example is a simple modification of the second example, introducing the CFHTTP.MimeType variable, which is displayed after the file is downloaded. In this example the MimeType of the file is image/jpeg, since it is a JPEG file. Figure 30.3 shows the results of this example.

FIG. 30.3
Output from the CFHTTP tag after downloading a binary file using the GET method.

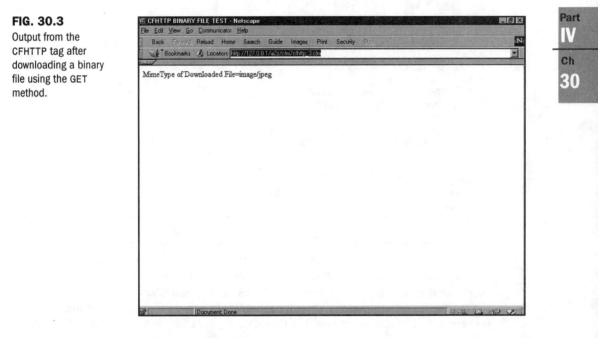

Building a Query from a Text File

The last example, using the GET method, will be to read a text file and create a query object from it. Back in Chapter 25, you created a comma-delimited file that contained the names, IDs, and photo files for the employees in the A2Z Employee table. Using that file, you will create a query and manipulate it using standard CF techniques. The source for this example is shown in Listing 30.4.

On the CD

Listing 30.4   CFHTTP_4.CFM—Using the *CFHTTP* Tag to Build a Query Using a Text File

```
<HTML>
<HEAD>
<TITLE>CFHTTP QUERY TEST</TITLE>
</HEAD>
<BODY>
<CFHTTP METHOD="GET" URL="http://127.0.0.1/a2z/employee/photolist.txt"
```

continues

Listing 30.4   Continued

```
➥NAME="EMPLOYEES"
         DELIMITER="," TEXTQUALIFIER="""""
➥COLUMNS="LASTNAME,FIRSTNAME,ID,PHOTOFILE">
<TABLE BORDER>
<TR>
<TH ALIGN="LEFT">Last Name</TH>
<TH ALIGN="LEFT">First Name</TH>
<TH ALIGN="LEFT">Employee ID</TH>
<TH ALIGN="LEFT">Photo File</TH>
</TR>
<CFOUTPUT QUERY="EMPLOYEES">
<TR>
<TD ALIGN="LEFT">#lastname#</TD>
<TD ALIGN="LEFT">#firstname#</TD>
<TD ALIGN="LEFT">#id#</TD>
<TD ALIGN="LEFT"><CFIF #photofile# is ""> 
➥<CFELSE>#photofile#</CFIF></TD>
</TR>
</CFOUTPUT>
</TABLE>
</BODY>
</HTML>
```

Here you added a number of attributes to the CFHTTP tag, to permit it to read an ASCII file and create a query object. The NAME attribute was set to EMPLOYEES indicating that you wanted the query object to be named EMPLOYEES. Since you knew the structure of the file, you specified the DELIMITER to be , (comma), and the TEXTQUALIFER to be " " (quotation marks). In this particular case, the file did not have a row of column headers in it, so you specified the column names you wanted in the COLUMNS attribute. You then used normal Cold Fusion techniques (CFOUTPUT) to display the data in the query using an HTML table. Figure 30.4 shows the output from this example.

To summarize, text files are processed by the CFHTTP tag using the following guidelines:

- The NAME attribute specifies the name of the query object that is created by Cold Fusion.

- A delimiter is specified with the DELIMITER attribute. If the delimiter is contained within a field in the file, it must be quoted using the character specified in the TEXTQUALIFIER attribute.

- The first row of the text file is interpreted as the column headers by default. This can be overridden using the COLUMNS attribute.

- When Cold Fusion encounters duplicate column names, it adds an underscore (_) character to the duplicate column name to make it unique.

Using the *POST* Method

In contrast to the GET method, which is essentially one-way, the POST method, when used with CFHTTP, provides a two-way transactional environment. To demonstrate this, you will develop a number of examples that will evolve from simple to complex.

FIG. 30.4

Output from the query created using the CFHTTP tag.

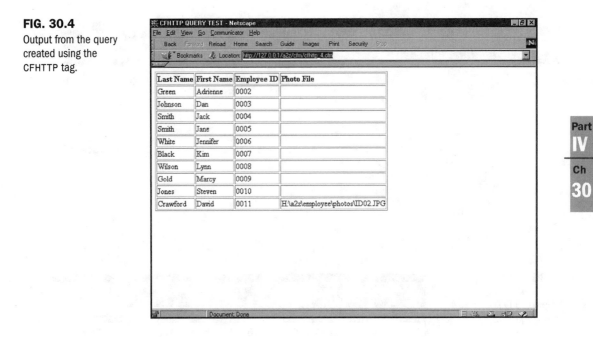

The first example will demonstrate the capability to transmit multiple variable types to a remote web server or CGI application. Using a Cold Fusion template, you will transmit the data to another CF template using the CFHTTP tag and then display the generated output. The code is shown in Listing 30.5.

Listing 30.5 CFHTTP_5.CFM—*CFHTTP* with the *POST* Method

```
<CFHTTP METHOD="POST" URL="http://127.0.0.1/a2z/cfm/cfhttp_6.cfm">
<CFHTTPPARAM NAME="form_test" TYPE="FormField"
➥VALUE="This is a form variable.">
<CFHTTPPARAM NAME="url_test" TYPE="URL" VALUE="This is a URL variable.">
<CFHTTPPARAM NAME="cgi_test" TYPE="CGI" VALUE="This is a CGI variable.">
<CFHTTPPARAM NAME="cookie_test" TYPE="Cookie" VALUE="This is a cookie.">
</CFHTTP>

<CFOUTPUT>
#CFHTTP.FileContent#
</CFOUTPUT>
```

The code in Listing 30.5 simply posts some information to the template in Listing 30.6. The results are then displayed using a simple CFOUTPUT tag. Figure 30.5 shows the results.

Part
IV

Ch
30

Listing 30.6 CFHTTP_6.CFM—Template That Processes the *CFHTTP POST* Method Variables

```
<HTML>
<HEAD>
<TITLE>CFHTTP Post Test</TITLE>
</HEAD>
<BODY>
<CFOUTPUT>
The following variables where POSTED here via the CFHTTP_5.CFM template.<P>
Form_Test: #Form.form_test#<BR>
URL_Test: #URL.url_test#<BR>
CGI_Test: #CGI.cgi_test#<BR>
Cookie_Test: #COOKIE.cookie_test#<BR>
</CFOUTPUT>
</BODY>
</HTML>
```

FIG. 30.5

Output from the CFHTTP tag using the POST method.

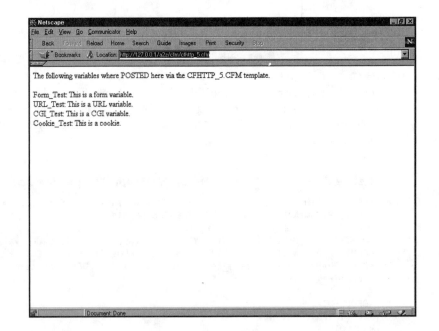

This example showed four of the five variable types that the CFHTTPPARAM tag supports. It did not show the FILE type, since that requires additional processing. In order to demonstrate the FILE variable in a POST operation, modify the previous example to upload a file to the server, using a template that you created back in Chapter 25. The code for this example is shown in Listing 30.7.

On the CD

Listing 30.7 CFHTTP_7.CFM—Using the *POST* Method to Upload a File

```
<CFHTTP METHOD="POST" URL="http://127.0.0.1/a2z/cfm/list25-3.cfm">
<CFHTTPPARAM NAME="filename" TYPE="FILE" FILE="c:\temp\cflogo.gif">
</CFHTTP>
<CFOUTPUT>
#CFHTTP.FileContent#
</CFOUTPUT>
```


Note that instead of specifying the `VALUE` attribute, you specified the `FILE` attribute, which contained the name of the file to be uploaded. The file was passed to the template in Listing 25.3, which was created in Chapter 25. The output from the upload operation was then displayed using the `CFHTTP.FileContent` variable. Figure 30.6 shows the output from this demonstration.

FIG. 30.6
Output from `CFHTTP` tag using `POST` method to upload a file.

CF 3.1 CFFILE Tag File Upload Demonstration Results - Example 1 - Netscape
File Edit View Go Communicator Help
Back Forward Reload Home Search Guide Images Print Security Stop
Bookmarks Location: http://127.0.0.1/a2z/cfm/cfhttp_7.cfm
CF 3.1 CFFILE Tag File Upload Demonstration Results - Example 1
File Upload was Successful! Information about the file is detailed below.
File Information
File Name: H:\website\uploads\CFLOGO.GIF
Content Type:
Content SubType:
Client Path: C:\TEMP
Client File: CFLOGO.GIF
Client FileName: CFLOGO
Client FileExt: GIF
Server Path: H:\website\uploads
Server File: CFLOGO.GIF
Server FileName: CFLOGO
Server FileExt: GIF
Attempted ServerFile:
File Existed? Yes
File Was Saved? Yes
File Was Overwritten? Yes
File Was Appended? No
File Was Renamed? No
File Size: 14136
Old File Size: 14136
Date Last Accessed: 07 Dec 97
Date/Time Created: 07 Dec 97 16:29:46
Date/Time Modified: 07 Dec 97 16:29:48
Document: Done

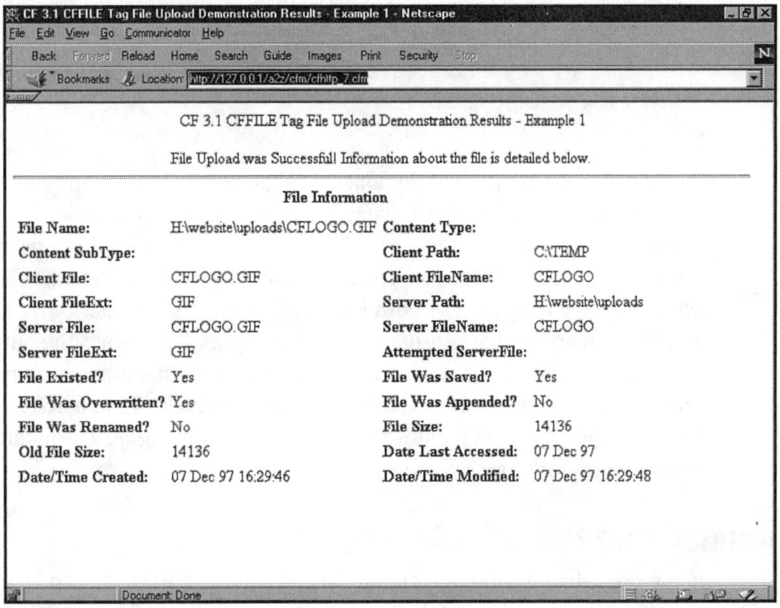

Pulling It All Together

The last example of the `CFHTTP` tag you will develop will show the use of the `POST` operation to pass information from your local server to a book search engine at **www.amazon.com** and then display the results. This requires a little more work, since first you have to identify the fields that the search engine requires and then code your template accordingly. The code in Listing 30.8 shows the fields that need to be passed to the search engine. For demonstration purposes, you will simplify the process and only search on an author's name, which in this case will be Ben Forta, the lead author of this book.

Listing 30.8 CFHTTP_8.CFM—Passing Information to the *www.amazon.com* Book Search Engine Using *CFHTTP*

```
<CFHTTP METHOD="POST" URL="http://www.amazon.com/exec/obidos/ats-query/
➥6994-1392532-213589" RESOLVEURL="YES">
<CFHTTPPARAM NAME="author-mode" TYPE="formfield" value="full">
<CFHTTPPARAM NAME="author" TYPE="formfield" value="FORTA, BEN">
</CFHTTP>
<CFOUTPUT>
#CFHTTP.FileContent#
</CFOUTPUT>
```

> **CAUTION**
>
> The use of the CFHTTP tag to extract HTML from remote web servers should be used with caution from an intellectual property perspective. The copyright laws with regard to the Internet are not yet clear, and use of another individual's or corporations content without their permission may open you to liability under copyright or trademark law. Exercise good judgment when posting to, or downloading from, a remote web server that is not under your exclusive control.

The code is very simple, yet demonstrates the power of the CFHTTP tag. By researching the form fields necessary to drive a search engine, a powerful function can be added to your Cold Fusion templates. Only two form fields are required to drive this particular engine. The author-mode field tells the search engine how to search for the data contained in the author field. The full **www.amazon.com** book search engine provides other functionality, but for this example, a more simple approach was need. Figure 30.7 shows the output from this example. Note that several images are not displayed properly. This is because in this example, a client-side map is used, which is not resolved by the URL resolution mechanism of the CFHTTP tag. However, the important point is that a remote search engine was manipulated using a Cold Fusion template running on a local server.

Summarizing the *CFHTTP* Tag

In the preceding examples, you have seen how the CFHTTP tag can be used to interact with remote web servers and CGI applications. From the simplest request to download a file, to remotely operating a search engine, the CFHTTP tag comes with plenty of power. The ability to create queries using text files opens the doors to many different methods of receiving data and processing it using Cold Fusion. A new data source becomes available to the developer that can accept a delimited file of orders from a customer for processing, as just one example. File uploads, downloads, and interaction with CGI applications such as search engines or other Cold Fusion templates provide Cold Fusion developers with more tools to draw on as they approach application design.

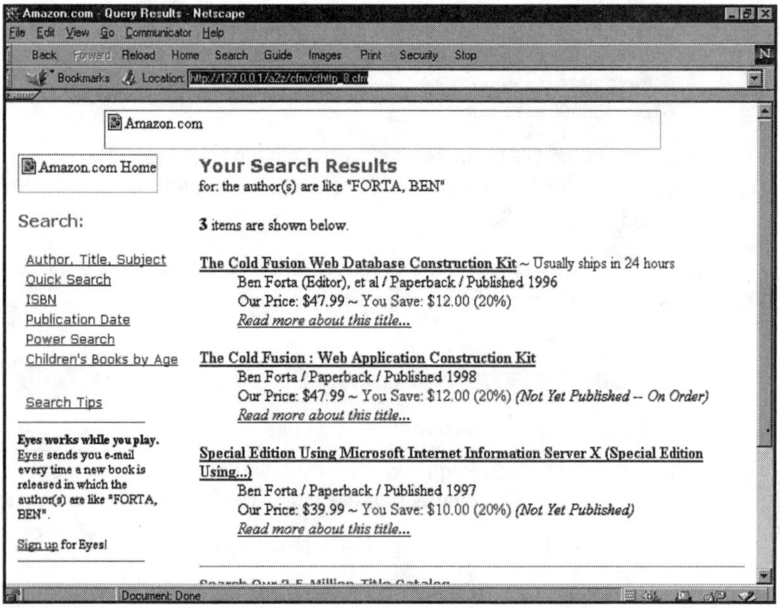

FIG. 30.7
Output from the
www.amazon.com
book search engine,
with data provided by
the CFHTTP tag.

Using the *CFFTP* Tag

Another method provided by Cold Fusion to interact with remote servers is the CFFTP tag. The CFFTP tag operates using the File Transfer Protocol (FTP), which is an Internet standard for transferring files from one computer to another. Both ASCII and binary transfers are supported by the FTP protocol, so it is a common method for distributing software across the Internet.

> **CAUTION**
> CFFTP is not supported in Cold Fusion for Solaris 3.1.

CFFTP permits the Cold Fusion developer to implement FTP operations. In its default configuration, the CFFTP tag caches connections for reuse within the same template.

Operations using the CFFTP tag are divided into two areas:

■ Establishing or closing a connection

■ File and directory operations

The syntax for the CFFTP tag is

```
<CFFTP ACTION="action"
   USERNAME="username"
   PASSWORD="password"
   SERVER="server"
   TIMEOUT="timeout in seconds"
```

```
PORT="port"
CONNECTION="name"
AGENTNAME="name"
RETRYCOUNT="number"
STOPONERROR="Yes/No">
```

This form of the CFFTP tag is used to establish or close a FTP connection. If you are using a previously cached connection, the USERNAME, PASSWORD, and SERVER attributes do not have to be specified.

The attributes that control the behavior of the CFFTP tag during the establishment or closure of a session are shown in Table 30.3.

Table 30.3 *CFFTP* Tag Attributes

Attribute	Description
ACTION	Required. Determines the FTP operation to perform. To open an FTP connection use Open. To close an FTP connection use Close.
USERNAME	Required. Username to pass to the FTP server.
PASSWORD	Required. Password to log on the user specified in USERNAME.
SERVER	Required. The FTP server to connect to, such as **ftp.allaire.com**.
TIMEOUT	Optional. Value in seconds for the timeout of all operations, including individual data request operations. Defaults to 30 seconds.
PORT	Optional. The remote TCP/IP port to connect to. The default is 21 for FTP.
CONNECTION	Optional. Name of the FTP connection. Used to cache the FTP connection information or to reuse a previously opened connection.
AGENTNAME	Optional. Application or entity conducting transfer.
RETRYCOUNT	Optional. Number of retries until failure is reported. Default is one (1).
STOPONERROR	Optional. Yes or No. When Yes, halts all processing and displays an appropriate error. Default is Yes. When No, three variables are created and populated: CFFTP.Succeeded—Yes or No CFFTP.ErrorCode—Error number (see table of FTP error codes below) CFFTP.ErrorText—Message text explaining error type

Establishing a Connection

Listing 30.9 shows a simple template that establishes an FTP connection.

On the CD

Listing 30.9   CFFTP_1.CFM—Establishing an FTP Connection

```
<CFFTP ACTION="Open" USERNAME="anonymous" PASSWORD="info@a2zbooks.com"
➥SERVER="ftp.allaire.com" NAME="ALLAIRE" STOPONERROR="No">

<CFOUTPUT>
Opening the connection.<BR>
FTP Operation Successful: #CFFTP.SUCCEEDED#<BR>
FTP Error Code: #CFFTP.ErrorCode#<BR>
FTP Error Text: #CFFTP.ErrorText#<BR>
</CFOUTPUT>

<CFFTP ACTION="Close" NAME="ALLAIRE" STOPONERROR="No">
<CFOUTPUT>
Closing the Connection.<BR>
FTP Operation Successful: #CFFTP.SUCCEEDED#<BR>
FTP Error Code: #CFFTP.ErrorCode#<BR>
FTP Error Text: #CFFTP.ErrorText#<BR>
</CFOUTPUT>
```

Part
IV

Ch
30

CAUTION

The CFFTP tag is a COM object (see Chapter 34, "Interfacing with COM and DCOM Objects") that only runs on Windows NT 4.0, or Windows 95 with the DCOM update. Before using the CFFTP tag on your site, be sure that your server is capable of using COM objects.

This simple example opens an FTP connection to Allaire's FTP server, checks the status, and then closes the connection. Figure 30.8 shows the results from this code.

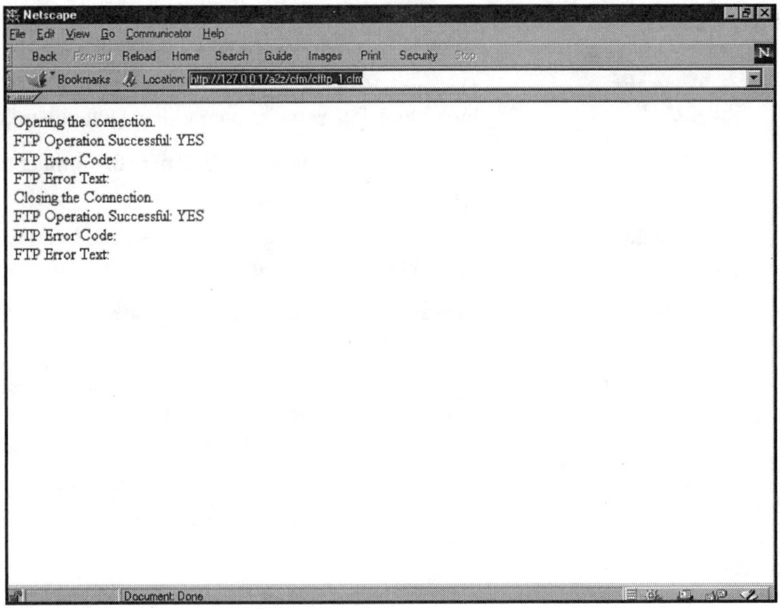

FIG. 30.8

Output after opening and closing an FTP connection to Allaire's FTP server.

```
Opening the connection.
FTP Operation Successful: YES
FTP Error Code:
FTP Error Text:
Closing the Connection.
FTP Operation Successful: YES
FTP Error Code:
FTP Error Text:
```

Note that the USERNAME and PASSWORD attributes are required by the CFFTP tag. In many cases you will be using anonymous FTP, so you would set the USERNAME attribute to anonymous and the PASSWORD attribute to be the full email address of the user that is making the connection. In the case of a Cold Fusion template application, the system administrator's email address would be sufficient.

Using File and Directory Operations with *CFFTP*

Once an FTP connection is established, you can perform various file and directory operations to send files to the server or receive files and directory listings from the server.

The attributes of the CFFTP tag vary slightly from the attributes required to open or close a connection. The attributes for file and directory operations are shown in the Table 30.4.

Table 30.4   *CFFTP* File and Directory Operations Attributes

Attribute	Description
ACTION	Required if connection is not already cached using the CONNECTION attribute. Determines the FTP operation to perform. This can be one of the following: ChangeDir, CreateDir, ListDir, GetFile, PutFile, Rename, Remove, GetCurrentDir, GetCurrentURL, ExistsDir, ExistsFile, or Exists.
USERNAME	Required if the connection is not already cached. See table of attributes for establishing an FTP connection.
PASSWORD	Required if the connection is not already cached. See table of attributes for establishing an FTP connection.
SERVER	Required if the connection is not already cached. See table of attributes for establishing an FTP connection.
TIMEOUT	Optional. Value in seconds for the timeout of all operations, including individual data request operations. Defaults to 30 seconds.
PORT	Optional. The remote TCP/IP port to connect to. The default is 21 for FTP.
CONNECTION	Optional. Name of the FTP connection. Used to cache the FTP connection information or to reuse a previously opened connection.
NAME	Required for ACTION="*ListDir*". Specifies query object in which results will be stored.
ASCIIEXTENSIONLIST	Optional. Semicolon-delimited list of file extensions that will force ASCII transfer mode when TRANSERMODE="Autodetect". The default list is txt, htm, html, cfm, cfml, shtm, shtml, css, asp, and asa.
TRANSFERMODE	Optional. The FTP transfer mode. Valid entries are ASCII, Binary, and Autodetect. Default is Autodetect.

Attribute	Description
AGENTNAME	Optional. Application or entity conducting transfer.
FAILIFEXISTS	Optional. Yes or No. Defaults to Yes. Specifies whether a GetFile operation will fail if a local file of the same name exists.
DIRECTORY	Required for ACTION=ChangeDir, CreateDir, ListDir, and ExistsDir. Specifies directory on which operation will be performed.
LOCALFILE	Required for ACTION=GetFile and PutFile. Specifies file on local file system.
REMOTEFILE	Required for ACTION=GetFile, PutFile, and ExistsFile. Specifies the filename on the FTP server.
ATTRIBUTES	Optional. Defaults to Normal. A comma-delimited list of attributes. Specifies the file attributes for the local file in a GetFile operation. This can be any combination of the following: ReadOnly, Hidden, System, Archive, Directory, Compressed, Temporary, and Normal. The file attributes will vary according to the operating system environment.
ITEM	Required for ACTION=Exists and Remove. Specifies the file, object, or directory for these actions.
EXISTING	Required for ACTION=Rename. Specifies the current name of the file or directory on the remote server.
NEW	Required for ACTION=Rename. Specifies the new name of the file or directory on the remote server.
RETRYCOUNT	Optional. Number of retries until failure is reported. Default is one (1).
STOPONERROR	Optional. Yes or No. When Yes, halts all processing and displays an appropriate error. Default is Yes. When No, three variables are created and populated: CFFTP.Succeeded—Yes or No. CFFTP.ErrorCode—Error number (see Table 30.7 for a list of FTP error codes). CFFTP.ErrorText—Message text explaining error type.

Caching Connections

An established, FTP connections can be reused to perform additional FTP operations. This is done by setting the CONNECTION attribute when the FTP connection is established. Subsequent calls to the CFFTP tag in the same template use the same CONNECTION name. This forces CFFTP to automatically reuse the connection information, which results in faster connections and improves file transfer performance.

N O T E Using a cached connection, the USERNAME, PASSWORD, and SERVER attributes do not have to be respecified. ■

When using frames, developers need to make sure that only a single frame refers to a particular cached connection. FTP connections are only cached in the current template. To cache connections across multiple pages, a session variable needs to be used for the CONNECTION attribute.

Before establishing a session variable, you need to ensure that you have enabled session variables. See the CFAPPLICATION tag reference for further information.

To establish a session variable for the CONNECTION, specify the CONNECTION value to be session.*variablename* where *variablename* is the name of the connection you want to establish.

 N O T E Making changes to cached connections such as changing the RETRYCOUNT or TIMEOUT may require the connection to be re-established. ■

The attributes required for CFFTP actions when a cached connection is used are shown in Table 30.5. If a cached connection is not used, the USERNAME, PASSWORD, and SERVER attributes must be set.

Table 30.5   *CFFTP*—Required Attributes Shown by Action

Action	Attribute	Action	Attribute
Open	none	Rename	EXISTING, NEW
Close	none	Remove	SERVER, ITEM
ChangeDir	DIRECTORY	GetCurrentDir	none
CreateDir	DIRECTORY	GetCurrentURL	none
ListDir	NAME, DIRECTORY	ExistsDir	DIRECTORY
		ExistsFile	REMOTEFILE
GetFile	LOCALFILE REMOTEFILE	Exists	ITEM
PutFile	LOCALFILE REMOTEFILE		

Creating an Example

Building on the first example, you will now do some directory operations using the CFFTP tag while connected to Allaire's FTP site. You will retrieve a file listing and display the results. You will turn on automatic error checking by setting the STOPONERROR attribute to YES. Connection caching will be used so that you can maintain a connection to the server. The code is shown in Listing 30.10.

On the CD

Listing 30.10 CFFTP_2.CFM—File and Directory Operations Using the *CFFTP* Tag

```
<CFFTP ACTION="Open" USERNAME="anonymous" PASSWORD="info@a2zbooks.com"
SERVER="ftp.allaire.com" CONNECTION="ALLAIRE" STOPONERROR="Yes">

<CFFTP CONNECTION="ALLAIRE" ACTION="GetCurrentDir" STOPONERROR="Yes">

<CFOUTPUT>
FTP Directory Listing of #CFFTP.returnvalue#.<P>
</CFOUTPUT>

<CFFTP CONNECTION="ALLAIRE" ACTION="ListDir" DIRECTORY="/Evaluations"
➥ NAME="DirList" STOPONERROR="Yes">
<HR>
<TABLE BORDER>
<TR>
<TH>Name</TH>
<TH>Path</TH>
<TH>URL</TH>
<TH>Length</TH>
<TH>LastModified</TH>
<TH>Is Directory</TH>
</TR>
<TR>
<CFOUTPUT QUERY="DirList">
<TD>#name#</TD>
<TD>#path#</TD>
<TD>#url#</TD>
<TD>#length#</TD>
<TD>#DateFormat(lastmodified)#</TD>
<TD>#isdirectory#</TD>
</TR>
</CFOUTPUT>
</TABLE>

<CFFTP ACTION="Close" CONNECTION="ALLAIRE" STOPONERROR="Yes">
```

In this example, you establish a connection to the Allaire FTP server (**ftp.allaire.com**). You then execute a directory list of the Evaluations directory, which is stored in the query named DirList. The results are then output, using CFOUPUT, into an HTML table. Note the new variable #CFFTP.returnvalue#, which is used to display the current directory. Figure 30.9 shows the output from this example.

The CFFTP tag may return a number of different variables, depending on the setting of its attributes. These are CFFTP.ReturnValue—the three variables described in the STOPONERROR attribute, and a query object if the ACTION="ListDir". In the previous example, you used the value of the CFFTP.ReturnValue to output the current directory, and the query object DirList to display the directory listing. The various values of the CFFTP.ReturnValue variable are shown in Table 30.6.

FIG. 30.9

The CFFTP directory listing.

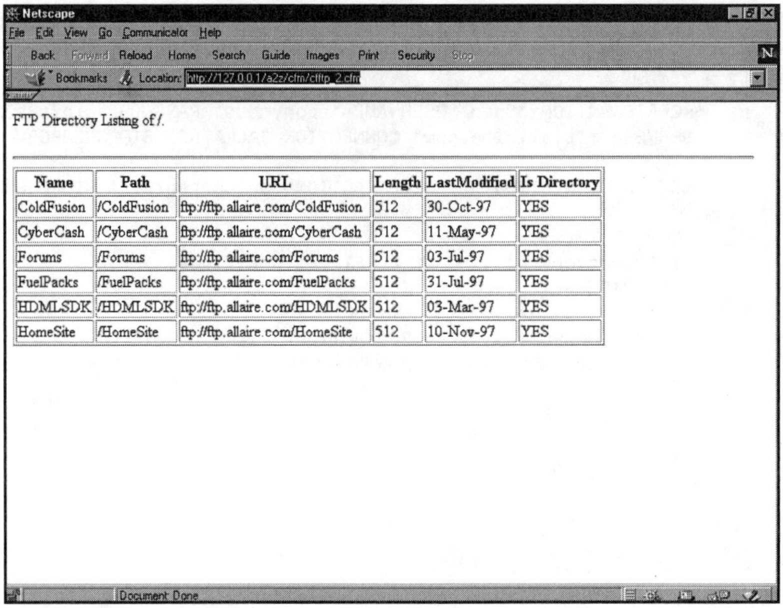

Table 30.6 Values of the *CFFTP.ReturnValue* Variable

CFFTP Action	Value of *CFFTP.ReturnValue*
GetCurrentDir	String value containing name of the current directory
GetCurrentURL	String value containing the current URL
ExistsDir	Yes or No
ExistsFile	Yes or No
Exists	Yes or No

The variables set when the STOPONERROR attribute is set to NO may contain error codes. Table 30.7 shows the error codes that may be returned and the text explanation of the numeric codes.

Table 30.7 *CFFTP* Error Codes

Error Code	Description
0	Operation succeeded
1	System error (operating system or FTP protocol error)

Error Code	Description
2	An Internet session could not be established
3	FTP session could not be opened
4	File transfer mode not recognized
5	Search connection could not be established
6	Invoked operation valid only during a search
7	Invalid timeout value
8	Invalid port number
9	Not enough memory to allocate system resources
10	Cannot read contents of local file
11	Cannot write to local file
12	Cannot open remote file for reading
13	Cannot read remote file
14	Cannot open local file for writing
15	Cannot write to remote file
16	Unknown error
17	Reserved
18	File already exists
19	Reserved
20	Reserved
21	Invalid retry count specified

As was shown in the second CFFTP example (CFFTP_2.CFM), a query object is created when the ACTION attribute is set to "ListDir". The NAME attribute is then set to the name of the query object that is to be created. Once created, the query object contains columns that can be referenced using the following form:

`queryname.columnname[row]`

queryname is the value specified in the NAME attribute, and *columnname* is one of the columns defined in the query object, as shown in Table 30.8. *row* is an integer representing the specific row in the query object returned by the ListDir operation. Information about each file found in the specified directory is stored in a separate row in the query.

Table 30.8   *CFFTP* Query Object Definition

Column	Description
Name	Name of the file or directory
Path	File path (without drive designation)
URL	Complete URL of the file or directory
Length	Number indicating size of the file
LastModified	Date/time value indicating when file or directory was last modified
Attributes	String indicating attributes of file or directory
IsDirectory	Boolean value indicating if element is a directory

To finish up your look at the CFFTP tag, you will create a template that will download a specific file from the server. Listing 30.11 shows the code necessary to download a file. In this example you will specify a particular file using a cached connection. Set the STOPONERROR attribute to be NO so that you can get more detailed error information. You will also force the TRANSFERMODE to be BINARY.

Listing 30.11   CFFTP_3.CFM—Code to Download a Binary File Using *CFFTP*

```
<CFFTP ACTION="Open" USERNAME="anonymous" PASSWORD="info@a2zbooks.com"
SERVER="ftp.allaire.com" CONNECTION="ALLAIRE" STOPONERROR="Yes">


<CFFTP CONNECTION="ALLAIRE" ACTION="GetFile" LOCALFILE="c:\temp\graphlets.zip"
       REMOTEFILE="/Evaluations/FuelPacks/graphlets.zip" STOPONERROR="No"
       TRANSFERMODE="BINARY" FAILIFEXISTS="No">

<CFOUTPUT>
FTP Operation Return Value: #CFFTP.ReturnValue#<BR>
FTP Operation Successful: #CFFTP.Succeeded#<BR>
FTP Operation Error Code: #CFFTP.ErrorCode#<BR>
FTP Operation Error Message: #CFFTP.ErrorText#<BR>
</CFOUTPUT>

<CFFTP ACTION="Close" CONNECTION="ALLAIRE" STOPONERROR="Yes">
```

Figure 30.10 shows the output from this example.

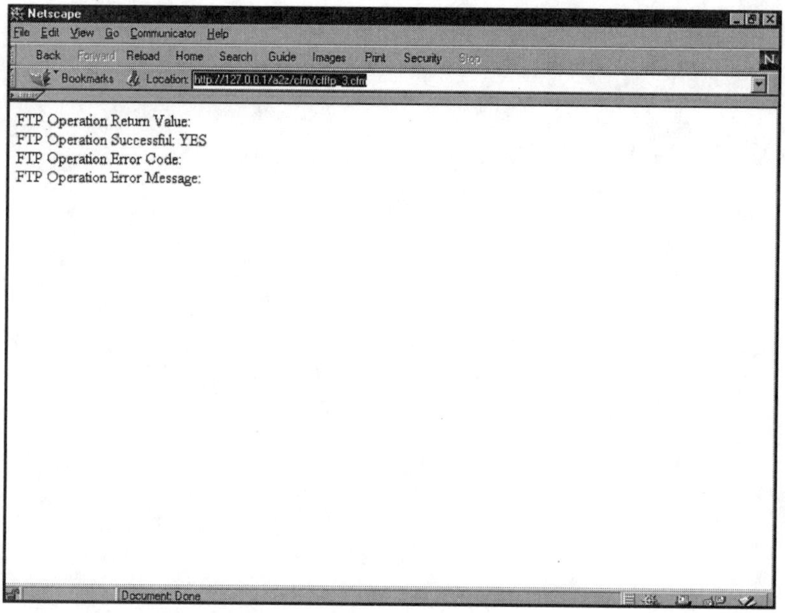

FIG. 30.10

Output from binary file
download using CFFTP.

FTP Operation Return Value:
FTP Operation Successful: YES
FTP Operation Error Code:
FTP Operation Error Message:

Part
IV

Ch
30

Version Control

by Ashley King

In this chapter

Using Version Control

Developing a Cold Fusion application requires many different versions of files to be integrated into the completed project. In development, a file may need to be changed several times, and keeping track of what was changed and by whom can become complicated. Version control systems provide a solution to this common problem by organizing projects in a single place and tracking changes made to any files within the project.

As you develop applications, you may develop your own version control system. Many developers save copies of a project into several different folders, while others rename older files in case they need to fall back to a previous version of code. Versions 2.0 source control software is included with the Cold Fusion Studio development environment and makes keeping track of your project intuitive and easy.

In developing an application or web site, you may have tried experimental code in some of your files, only to find yourself reverting to a previous version. Even worse, you may have spent hours on a file only to find it has been corrupted by some malevolent system gremlin. Version control keeps previous versions of your files in a safe place along with critical information about what has been changed, when it was changed, and by whom. Without a version control system, it may be difficult to figure out which file is the correct file to use, especially in a large project or a project that involves multiple developers.

Version control systems also help to organize a project, keeping all related files in one place. Images, templates, notes, and specifications can all be kept together, along with previous versions of all files in a project and a record of all changes. Security is also enhanced by version control systems, as all files can be protected by a password and all accesses can be recorded.

Version control systems also allow developers in disparate locations to work together in a coordinated manner. Tasks in the development of an application can be assigned, and developers can only access files pertinent to their tasks. Project managers can more easily track the progress of development, and better manage resources and time.

Understanding Version Control

An understanding of version control terminology will help you to more quickly grasp how version control systems work. Definitions for frequently used terms are listed in Table 31.1.

Table 31.1   Version Control Terms

Term	Definition
Administrator	The project manager. By default, the creator of the project. Manages all settings, team members, and milestones.
Audit log	Contains audit entries detailing every action taken during the development of a project. These entries form the audit trail, which is used to track project modifications.

Term	Definition
Build	The act of gathering, linking, and assembling all necessary files to create an application. Also designating the completion of a step in the development of a project. When a build is specified, a set of non-permanent files is created and labeled with the name of the build.
Check out	The modification process begins with a team member checking out a file. This action creates a working copy of the file and logs an entry in the audit log. A lock is also placed on the file.
Check in	Similar to saving a file, checking in occurs when a team member relinquishes control of a file. When a file is checked in, the new version of the file is stored in the vault, along with information about the file in the database. The lock is also broken.
Database	The database in which information about the project, sub projects, team members, project files, and version information is stored.
Label	When a milestone or build is designated, a title or description is assigned to all files in the current version.
Lock	A file that is checked out cannot be modified by another team member and is considered locked until the lock is broken by an administrator or the file is checked in. Locks can be designated read-only so that other team members can view the file as necessary.
Milestone	An event in project development that represents a major step towards completion. Designation of a milestone creates a set of permanent versions of files with the label of the milestone. Milestones can be alpha, beta, or final releases of products or any other significant step in progress.
Non-permanent version	A version of a file that is not part of a set of permanent version files and can be automatically deleted when the maximum number of non-permanent versions is reached or when the file is purged.
Permanent version	When a version of a project file is designated a permanent version—this file cannot be purged or removed automatically when the maximum number of non-permanent versions is reached. The project file must be locked to be deleted or designated non-permanent.
Project	A set of related files that comprise an application and its documentation, images, and other files. Also includes all sub-projects linked to it.
Project file	A file that is part of a project or sub project and is referenced in the database.
Purge	The deletion of non–permanent versions of a file. The last checked-in version and any permanent versions cannot be purged. A file must be locked to be purged.

continues

Table 31.1   Continued

Term	Definition
Subproject	A subset of files within a project that are related.
Team	All developers involved in the creation of an application.
Vault	Directory where all versions of all project files are stored. The vault can be compressed for efficient use of disk space and increased performance.
Working directory	Directory in which current versions of all checked out files are stored. Can be determined by the team member or mandated by the administrator.

Your application or web site is organized into a project—and usually sub-projects. The overall application is the project, while sub projects contain components of the larger project. Images, documentation, and subdirectories are all good candidates for subprojects. The developers working on a project and its subprojects are called the team and a project administrator manages the team.

The project administrator decides how a project is structured and how it progresses. The project administrator also manages access to project files, designates milestones, and oversees and audits the project. Information about project files, version history, team members, and milestones is stored in the project database. The vault is stored with the project database and contains all files that are a part of the project.

When a team member requires access to a project file, it is noted in the audit log. The audit log tracks all actions taken by team members. Once noted, the file is checked out and a copy is stored in a working directory. Checking out a file places a lock on it so no other members can modify the file until it is checked in or the lock is broken. Only an administrator or the team member who created the lock can break a lock placed on a file by another team member. When the modifications are completed, the project file is checked in, and any working copies can be deleted. The previous versions of the file are stored along with the latest version and auditing data, including when and by whom the file is modified.

When a project milestone is reached, the administrator can designate this milestone and label the file versions with relevant information. A build or permanent version can be designated also, and non-permanent versions can be retained or purged.

Now that you have an understanding of version control, see these concepts in action as you create a project using Versions 2.0.

Using Versions 2.0

The version control interface in Cold Fusion Studio makes working with version control software fast and painless. Using this interface eliminates many of the steps required to create a project, and makes checking files in and out virtually transparent to team members. To fully understand how the Cold Fusion Studio version control interface works, and to better manage your projects, it is good to know some of the basics of using the Versions 2.0 software.

Planning Your Project

The first step in version control is deciding what your needs are. To properly create a project, you must first answer a few basic questions:

Is this a single project, or does this project require the use of sub projects?

Most Cold Fusion applications and web sites use sub-directories that accomplish certain functions, such as an images or administration directory. Documentation, notes, and project specifications are also involved with most. These are all perfect candidates for subprojects. If you are developing a small project with no images, notes, or other related material, subprojects may not be useful to you.

How many people are in my team, and how is my team structured?

If more than one person is working on a project, the tasks of each person should be analyzed. Decide what portions of the project each person requires access to.

Where will the files be stored?

A network-accessible directory must be chosen to store both the project database and the project vault. Choose a directory where the working copies of the project and sub-projects will reside, or if each team member will choose a directory on their own machine. Decide if compression is to be used with your project.

Are security and auditing required?

It is a good idea to use security and auditing by default. Enabling security requires all team members to enter a password before gaining access to a project. This also limits the actions non–administrators can perform. Only a project administrator can create a sub-project, delete files, modify project properties, change version information for a file, open locks, and designate permanent versions, milestones, builds, and non–permanent versions. Restricting these actions can save much frustration in the long run.

Auditing records all actions taken by any team member on any file, project or subproject. This is useful in tracking work completed, and who is working on what items. It can also help you track down bugs and keep track of changes. Auditing is a must in developing any project.

Creating a Project in Versions 2.0

To create a new project in Versions 2.0, complete the following steps:

1. Create a working directory. Create a directory on your C: drive named Projects.
2. Create a subdirectory in C:\Projects called myproject.
3. Copy some Cold Fusion templates into this directory, such as the example application from Chapter 25. This set of files will become the new project.

4. From the Start menu, choose Programs, Versions 2.0. Click the Versions icon to start the Versions 2.0 software.

5. In Versions, create a new project from the Project menu by selecting New.

6. The New Project dialog box will appear, shown in Figure 31.1. Fill in the options in the dialog box.

You will be prompted for a name for your new project. Project names must not contain forward slashes (/), back slashes (\) or exclamation marks (!) and can be up to 228 characters long. Enter **My New Project.**

FIG. 31.1

Creating a new project in Versions 2.0.

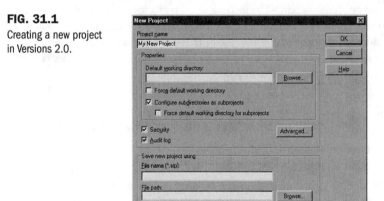

Choose a Default Working Directory by typing in the path you chose above for your working directory, or by selecting a path using the Browse button.

If you wish to require all team members to use this directory as their default, check the Force Default Working Directory box. This option applies to the team members' individual workstations. For instance, if you choose c:\Projects\myproject as the working directory, each team member will use c:\Projects\myproject on his or her workstation as the working directory, not on the machine where the project is created. Leaving this box unchecked allows team members to choose the working directory of their choice. For this project, you'll allow team members to choose their own working directory, so leave this box unchecked.

Your test project may contain subprojects in the future, so check the Configure Subdirectories As Subprojects box to cause Versions to create new subprojects for any subdirectories of your working directory.

The Force Default Working Directory For Subprojects box, when checked, will force team members to use subproject directories within the default working directory. This box is only active if Configure Subdirectories As Subprojects is checked. Check this box to keep a consistent directory structure for your project for all team members.

The Security checkbox, when checked, forces all team members to use a password when accessing the project. Checking this box also limits the actions team members can perform, and delegates these actions to the authority of the administrator. Check this box to make your project secure. Checking the Audit Log box causes Versions to log all actions taken on a project by team members. Check both boxes (Security and Audit Log) to create an audit trail for your project.

The Save New Project Using section defines the File Name (myproject.stp) and File Path for the database of your new project. All Versions 2.0 project database files must have the filename extension .stp. Choose the path under which the database and project vault will be stored. The database can't reside in the same directory as the project itself, so choose **C:\Projects**. The project database must be in a location that is network assessable to all team members for this project.

Additional project options can be configured by clicking the Advanced Project Settings button. The Advanced Project Settings dialog box will appear, as shown in Figure 31.2. This dialog box is organized into four tabs: Defaults, Commands, Exclude, and Description.

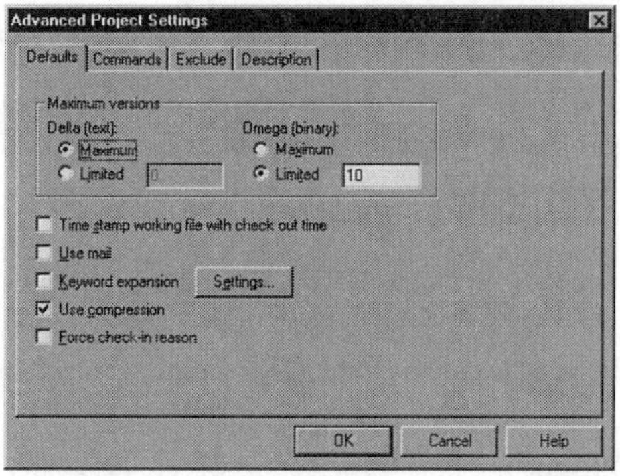

FIG. 31.2

Advanced project options in Versions 2.0.

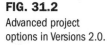

The Defaults tab sets project defaults for files. Maximum versions allows you to set the maximum number of previous versions that are retained for Delta (text, HTML, non-encrypted Cold Fusion Templates) and Omega (Encrypted Cold Fusion templates, executables and other binary files) files. Setting the limit to Maximum will retain up to 32,767 previous versions of any file, depending on disk space. For this project, click the Time Stamp Working File With Check Out Time to create an easy way to tell the last time of modification. Click OK in this dialog box, and OK in the New Project dialog box.

Versions will now ask you for a user profile. Enter a username, your full name, and a password. Click OK. Your project is now created!

Using Cold Fusion Studio Source Control Integration

Now that you know the specifics of creating a project in Versions 2.0, use Cold Fusion Studio's source control integration to create and manage a project. Cold Fusion Studio's source control integration simplifies project management by giving you one set of controls that can be used with any source-code control (SCC) compliant software. SCC-compliant software packages include Versions 2.0, Microsoft Visual Source Safe, and Intersolv PVCS.

Cold Fusion Studio source control commands allow you to do the following tasks with any SCC compliant software.

- Create a new project
- Add new files
- Remove files
- Check in files
- Check out files
- Get the latest version of a file and copy it, leaving the file checked in
- Open the source control software

With these basic commands, most day-to-day tasks can be completed without exiting the Cold Fusion Studio environment so you can spend more time in development and less time in project management.

Creating a Project in Cold Fusion Studio

Source control in Cold Fusion Studio is project-based, so source control can only be used while working with an existing project. For more information using Cold Fusion Studio, see Chapter 10, "Introduction to Cold Fusion Studio."

First you need to create a Cold Fusion Studio project. Complete the following steps:

1. In Cold Fusion Studio, click the Projects tab in the Resource dialog box.
2. Right-click inside the gray projects panel. Click Create Project and the Project Wizard dialog will appear.
3. Create a project from existing files by selecting Create A Project From An Existing Directory Structure, then click Next.
4. You are now prompted for a project name. Enter **My New Project**, and select a directory with an existing application, as shown in Figure 31.3. Choose Web Documents Only and check Include Sub-folders.
5. Click Next, then Finish. Your project is now created in Cold Fusion Studio.

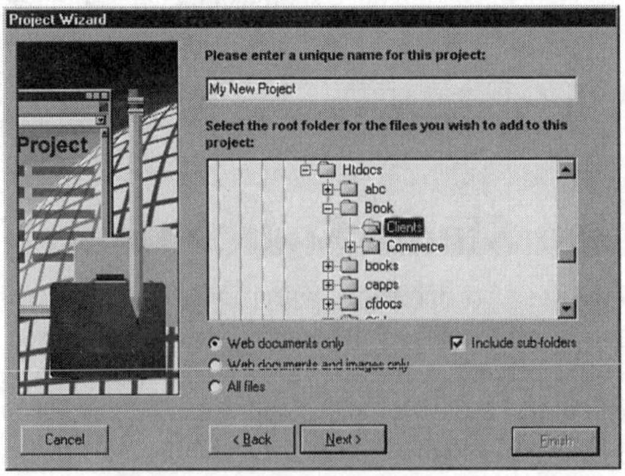

FIG. 31.3

Creating a project in Cold Fusion Studio.

Now that you have a project, add this project to source control.

1. Right click My New Project in the Projects pane.

2. Choose Add Project To Source Control from the context menu. Cold Fusion Studio will now ask you to specify a project for Source Code Control. At this point, it is important to remember that source control projects are actually managed by your source control software, and are not the same as Cold Fusion Studio projects. You can use an existing source control project or a new source control project can be created now. For now, use the project you created earlier in the chapter.

3. Click Open and the Select A Versions Project File For dialog box appears, as shown in Figure 31.4. Navigate to the C:\Projects directory and select myproject.stp.

4. Click Open to reveal the Log On dialog box. Enter the password you chose earlier in the chapter, click OK, and the Cold Fusion Studio project is now added to your source control project.

Part
IV

Ch
31

FIG. 31.4

Adding a project to an existing source control project.

Cold Fusion Studio's source control integration can also create a new source control project, saving you the step of creating it beforehand. First, create a new Cold Fusion Studio project as you did before. Once the project has been created, right click the name of the project and select Add Project To Source Control. When you are asked to specify the project for Source Code Control, click New. Does the dialog box in Figure 31.5 look familiar? You now see the New Project dialog box from Versions 2.0 (or your SCC-compliant application). Now, you can create a new project using the techniques you learned earlier in the chapter. You didn't even have to open your source control application.

Adding Files to Source Control

Now that you've created projects in both Cold Fusion Studio and your source control application, files in the project can be added to source control. To add files to source control, complete the following steps.

1. Select the file or files in your project that you wish to add.

2. Right click your selection, choose Source Control, and then Add To Source Control.

3. The Add Files dialog box appears with a list of all the files selected (see Figure 31.6). Make sure the box to the left of each file is checked. If you would like to use the files immediately, select Check Out Immediately.

4. Click OK and the files are now added to source control.

FIG. 31.5

New Project dialog box.

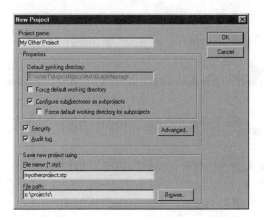

FIG. 31.6

Adding a project to a new source control project.

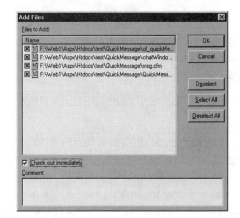

Managing Files in Source Control

The files in your project are now under source control management, and your source control application is now tracking the files of your project in the background. This means you no longer can immediately open a file to edit, because all files under source control must either be checked out or copied first. You can easily tell at a glance which files in your project are checked out by noting whether or not there is a small green check next to the file name, as shown in Figure 31.7. If it is present, this means the file is checked out by you and is available for editing. Double-clicking this file will immediately open it.

If a file is not checked out, there are two ways to check a file out from the file list.

The first method is to double click the file name as you would when opening it. You are now prompted to choose how you would like to open the file, as shown in Figure 31.8. Choosing Open It As Read-Only will open a read-only copy of the version of the selected file as stored in your working directory. This version may not be the most current version if other team members are involved in this project. Selecting Get The Latest Copy

From Source Control And Open It As Read-Only makes a copy of the most recent version of the file. Both of these selections do not allow you to modify the file, so the best choice would probably be to select Check It Out Of Source Control (see Figure 31.8). This gives you exclusive access to the file.

Another method of checking out a file is to right-click the file you wish to check out, select Source Control from the context menu, then choose Check Out. If another user has not checked the file out, it is checked out immediately.

FIG. 31.7
Determining if a file is checked out.

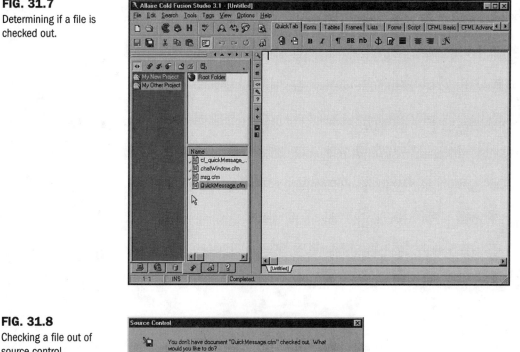

FIG. 31.8
Checking a file out of source control.

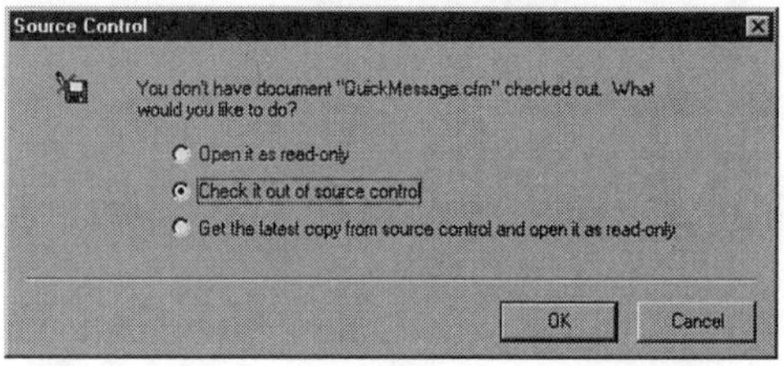

It is a very good idea to check the file back in once it has been modified. This updates the version history for the file, adds entries to the audit log, and makes the file available to other team members. To check in a file, first save any changes you have made as you normally would. Now, right-click the file you wish to check in, select Source Control from the context menu, and choose Check In. You'll now see the Check In Files dialog box pictured in Figure 31.9. Make sure the box next to the file you are checking in is checked, then click OK.

FIG. 31.9

Checking a file in to source control.

Event Scheduling

by Michael Dinowitz

Scheduling Template Execution

One of the most awaited features of Cold Fusion is the ability to schedule template execution. Ever since the first release of the product, people have been finding ways to set a template to run at specific times. With the release of Cold Fusion 3.1, this feature has not only been given to programmers, but several features have been added to it making it exceptionally well received. The ability to use the administrator for clean control of scheduled tasks, the additional ability to program tasks from a template as well as from the administrator, and the ability to have static pages generated from any task makes this feature the pride of the 3.1 release.

N O T E   CFSCHEDULE is only supported by the server version of Cold Fusion. ■

Understanding Scheduled Tasks

The CFSCHEDULE tag allows a programmer to cause the execution of a page to take place anytime from now to a specific point in the future. You can set a template to be run once at a specific time, continually with a set interval, with a specific time limit, or with any combination of these features.

Events are currently limited to calls to a web page by CFHTTP. While this may seem like a limitation, there's almost no limit to what can actually be done with this. Despite how it may look, this does not mean that you are limited to pages on your own site. One of the best features of this tag is that it will allow you to call ANY web page from anywhere and even save it to a physical file on your server. Combine this with the ability to use any of Cold Fusion's abilities in the called template and the sky's the limit.

Creating a Scheduled Task

As mentioned, there are two ways to create, run, and delete scheduled tasks. The first is to use the programmed interface provided by the Cold Fusion administrator. The major advantage to this is that it also gives you a list of all scheduled tasks. Of course the disadvantage is that anyone who wants to set a scheduled task has to have access to the administrator. Luckily, you have an additional way to create scheduled tasks. This is to code a task directly into a page that must be saved and executed to be recognized by the CFSCHEDULE service. This allows for a more customized interface and access for all, but does not include the list of tasks that already exist. Any task set this way need only be set once to be recognized by the scheduler. Additional executions of a task scheduling tag will simply replace the previous tasks.

There is actually a third way of setting a scheduled event, but it's not one I'd ever suggest anyone use. This is to go directly into the system registry and add, alter, or delete tasks directly. While I don't suggest doing this for tasks, there is a reason for going into the registry.

When a scheduled event is set, it is not recognized by the system until a certain interval is passed. This interval, shown in the middle of Figure 32.1, determines how often the scheduling service checks the list of scheduled task list for a new entry. When the service refreshes, the new (or modified) task is added to the list of tasks to do and these are checked every minute for execution.

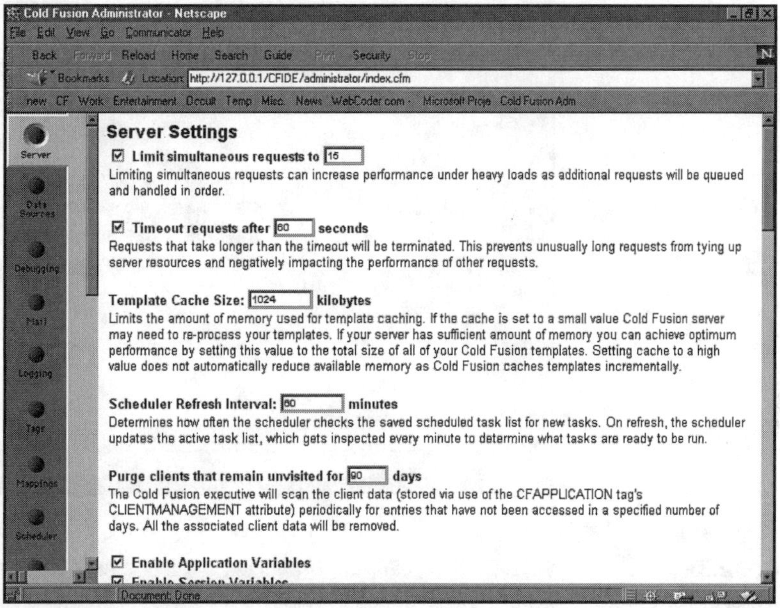

FIG. 32.1
Administrator page
showing schedule
refresh interval.

The registry entry for this value is slightly different. This interval is set in the key called CheckInterval in the HKEY_LOCAL_MACHINE\SOFTWARE\Allaire\ColdFusion\ CurrentVersion\Schedule path. This entry has a default value of 3600, which is the amount of seconds in an hour. Even though Cold Fusion deals with intervals in a minute format, the entry in the registry is in a second format. You can alter this interval to any number, but I would not suggest changing it as a normal practice. One trick is to set your scheduled event, set the refresh interval to 1 minute, wait the time for it to be read, and then reset it to 60 minutes. You do not want to keep it at a low number due to overhead. Stopping and restarting the Cold Fusion service also resets the refresh counter, but is a bit more drastic than is necessary.

Using the Administrator to Create Tasks

The scheduler section of the administrator starts out with a rundown of all the scheduled tasks that exist, what operation they are performing (limited to HTTP Requests at the moment), when they will start and end, and the interval between each execution (see Figure 32.2). This information allows you to keep a good handle on your timed tasks and edit them when necessary.

To create a task, all you have to do is enter a name for it, select an operation, and press the Add New Task button (see Figure 32.3).

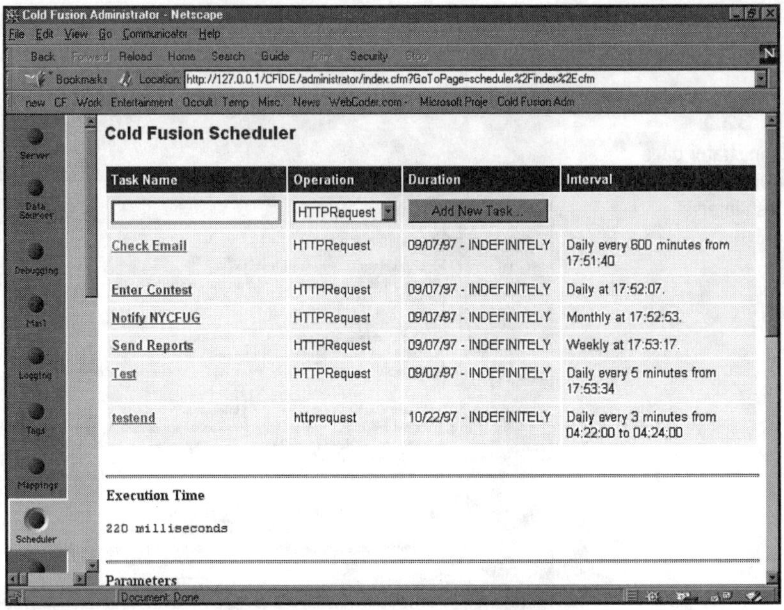

FIG. 32.2

Administrator list of all scheduled tasks.

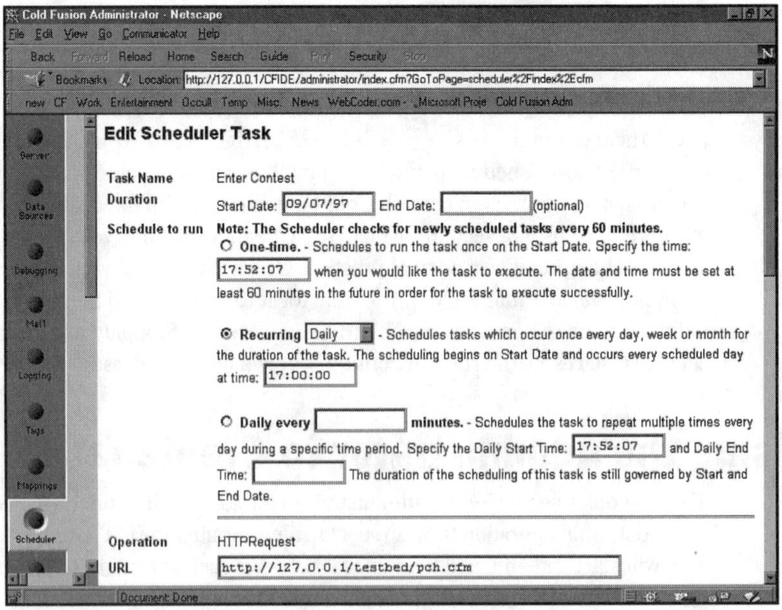

FIG. 32.3

Administrator screen showing specific task.

The resulting page is where you do all of your work in creating a new scheduled task. The start date and time defaults to the current date and time and usually isn't changed unless you want an action that starts at a future date. The end date is used to set a limit on how long your operation will run. Operations can be set for either a single use at a specific time, a reoccurring time every day, week, or month, and a reoccurring time in a single day.

An operation set for a one-time run will be executed once and never again. The execution does not erase the record of this operation, but it cannot be used again unless the time is reset. Actually, if no end date is set, this will result in an operation that will run once a year. Operations set to daily, weekly, or monthly will simply run once in the desired time period until the end date is reached, or forever if none is set. Daily events are a bit different than the other events. If an event is set with no end time, it'll simply run every X number of minutes until the end date, or forever if none is set. This is useful for continuously changing data like stock indexes, but should have some boundaries. Stock indexes, for example are only updated between the hours of 9:00 a.m. and 5:00 p.m. (or so) and doing a call for them outside those times is wasteful. In this case, you can set a start time and end time for this operation equal to the times in question. This will cause the template to be called every day starting at 9:00 a.m. and stopping at 5:00 p.m.

> **TIP**
>
> Remember that every scheduled event that is executed is the same as any other HTTP request by a user. The more that happens, the more of a hit on your site. Try to set your scheduled executions to use the least amount of time and resources. Tight code is essential for big sites.

Now that you've set the time, you have to deal with the operation that will be performed (see Figure 32.4). The only required piece here is the URL. Every timed event has to have an URL that will be executed. All the other fields are just extras to enhance the HTTP process or control the creation of static pages. Remember that the URL can reside almost anywhere and is not limited to local files.

Part
IV

Ch
32

FIG. 32.4
Additional schedule
information.

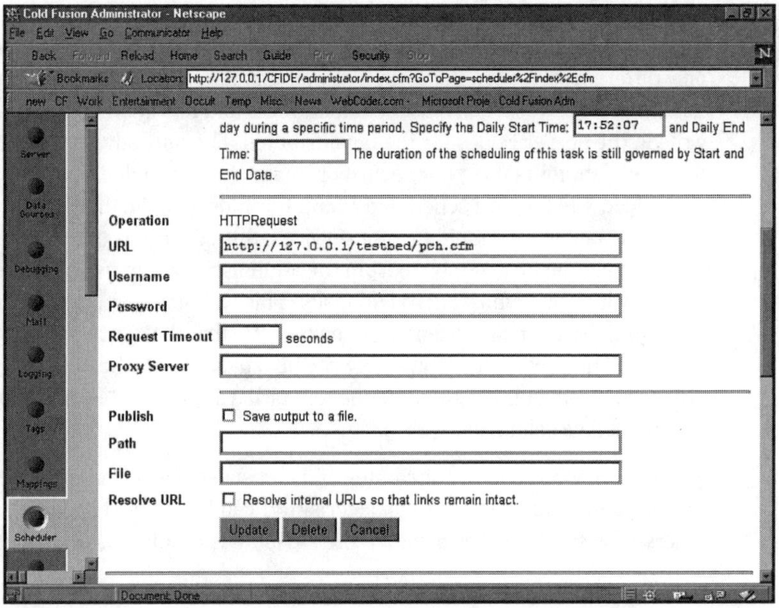

The username and password fields are used when the requested page is behind web server-based security. These values are sent along, allowing the page to be executed in a secure environment. The request timeout field allows you to set the length (in seconds) that the HTTP request will run before returning an error. This is the same as the RequestTimeOut URL variable.

The Publish checkbox toggles the creation of static pages. Static pages are created from the results of the HTTP request. If publish is checked, the path and file boxes must also be filled in. These two boxes allow you to set the directory path and file name of the resultant static page. The result of any page executed by the scheduler is then written to a file using these values. Included is the ability to resolve any URLs that are being saved. This is important when saving information from others sites as it keeps the links pointing to their proper locations.

Using the Administrator to Edit Tasks

The Administrator also allows you to edit a task by simply selecting it from the first screen and changing any values you want. This makes the one-time executions using the Now option make more sense. Once a task is selected, any value associated with it can be altered. Once the changes are done, pressing Update loads the task into the registry. You should note that this has the same effect as a new task in all ways; the old one is gone and the new one has to be recognized by the scheduling service. Deletion of tasks are handled the same way, but with a single button for removal.

Programming Control Tasks with the *CFSCHEDULE* Tag

The Administrator control is simply a form-based interface for using the CFSCHEDULE tag. The only difference between the Administrator and using the CFSCHEDULE tag is that the administrator can access a record of all scheduled events and has in error checking to make sure you write in the proper values for the tag attributes. The only advantage of the CFSCHEDULE tag over the administrator is that your security is maintained. You don't have to allow someone administrator access to create a scheduled event. For most people, this will not mean anything, but for ISPs that want to offer Cold Fusion services, this security is essential. For this reason, I suggest copying the form template from the administrator and using that as a front end when dealing with users who want to add tasks. This will be helpful to them, maintains the security of your administration pages, and also makes sure that the CFSCHEDULE tag is always formatted properly. This means you'll have to write up a page to test the data before running the CFSCHEDULE tag, but that shouldn't be too hard. Chapter 14, "Form Data Validation," has information on data validation.

Table 32.1 shows all of the attributes of the CFSCHEDULE tag, as well as provides a brief description of each. Status items with an asterisk (*) can be optional in some cases and required in others. The specific cases in which the attribute is required is always noted.

Table 32.1 *CFSCHEDULE* Tag Attributes

Name	Status	Description
ACTION	Required	Valid entries are Delete, Update, or Run. Update creates a new task if one does not exist. If a task already exists, Update will overwrite the current task of the same name. Run executes a task "now." Delete removes the task from the list of current tasks.
TASK	Required	The name of the task to delete, update, or run.
OPERATION	Required*	Required when creating tasks with ACTION="UPDATE". The type of operation the scheduler should perform when executing this task. For now, Cold Fusion only supports OPERATION="HTTPRequest" used for calling remote and local pages for execution.
STARTDATE	Required*	Required when creating tasks with ACTION="Update". The date when scheduling of the task should start.
STARTTIME	Required*	Required when creating tasks with ACTION="Update". The time when scheduling of the task should start. This should be a complete time value either in military standard (13:00:00 = 1:00:00 pm) or with the a.m./p.m. appended to it.
URL	Required*	Required when creating tasks with ACTION="Update". This is the URL to be executed by the scheduler.
INTERVAL	Required*	Required when creating tasks with ACTION="UPDATE". Interval at which task should be scheduled. Can be set in minutes or as DAILY, WEEKLY, MONTHLY, and EXECUTE. The default interval is one hour and the minimum interval is one minute. The EXECUTE interval seems to set to daily while an interval of NOW sets the operation to execute immediately.
PUBLISH	Optional	YES or NO. Specifies whether the result should be saved to a file.
FILE	Optional*	Required with PUBLISH="YES". A valid filename for the published file.
PATH	Optional*	Required with PUBLISH="YES". The path location for the published file.
ENDDATE	Optional	The date when the scheduled task should end.

Part

IV

Ch

32

Table 32.1	Continued	
Name	**Status**	**Description**
ENDTIME	Optional	The time when the scheduled task should end. This value should be in a valid time format.
REQUESTTIMEOUT	Optional	Customizes the REQUESTTIMEOUT for the task operation. Can be used to extend the standard timeout for time-intensive operations.
USERNAME	Optional	Username if URL is protected.
PASSWORD	Optional	Password if URL is protected.
PROXYSERVER	Optional	Host name or IP address of a proxy server.
RESOLVEURL	Optional	YES or NO. Specifies whether to resolve links in the result page to absolute references.

Setting *CFSCHEDULE* Attributes

The first things you have to define in a CFSCHEDULE tag are the TASK name of the scheduled event and the ACTION you want to perform. At present there are three actions to select from:

UPDATE   Used to create a scheduled event. This writes an event to the registry that will be run either by the timer or by the RUN action.

RUN   Used to execute a previously scheduled event now (useful for static page creation).

DELETE   Used to remove a scheduled event.

At this point, you would set the OPERATION and URL. The problem is that the only operation you can do now is HTTP Request. This is far from a limitation. With some creative code in the template being called, almost anything can be done. I expect that either this will be removed and HTTP request will be the only action allowed or others will be added in and HTTP request will be made default. Neither case really effects anything you'll be doing. When creating or updating a task, an URL must be supplied as an attribute. If not, the tag will fail to run and have to be fixed. There seems to be no difference between having an 'http://' before the URL or not, but it doesn't hurt for clean and descriptive code.

Now, the only thing needed for a working CFSCHEDULE is some time code. This is basically the same as what was described in the administration page, but you get to write it all down rather than setting it in a form.

At this point, you have a fully working schedule. Everything else is either and extra that enhances the scheduled task or static page generation code.

One fast and easy way to write up the CFSCHEDULE code is to use the CFSCHEDULE button (see Figure 32.5) in either HomeSite or Cold Fusion Studio.

FIG. 32.5
The CFSCHEDULE
button.

Selecting this button will give you a full editor for the tag with access to all of its attributes. In many ways it is like the administration page, just without the layout or data verification.

This tag generator (see Figure 32.6) does almost everything needed to write the tag. There are a few bugs in it that will probably be fixed by the time you read this, but if not, you should be aware. The major one is that the requesttimeout setting writes an attribute called limmittime. This has no use to the tag, but will not stop it from operating.

FIG. 32.6
The CFSCHEDULE tag
generator.

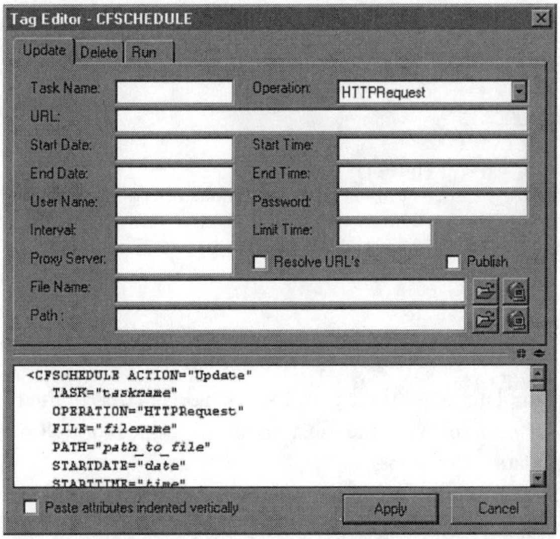

Tag Editor - CFSCHEDULE

| Update | Delete | Run |

Task Name:
Operation: HTTPRequest
URL:
Start Date: Start Time:
End Date: End Time:
User Name: Password:
Interval: Limit Time:
Proxy Server: ☐ Resolve URL's   ☐ Publish
File Name:
Path:

```
<CFSCHEDULE ACTION="Update"
    TASK="taskname"
    OPERATION="HTTPRequest"
    FILE="filename"
    PATH="path_to_file"
    STARTDATE="date"
    STARTTIME="time"
```

☐ Paste attributes indented vertically   Apply   Cancel

Part
IV

Ch
32

A pitfall to watch out for is the interval setting. This can either be a word or a number, as mentioned in the administration section. The major problem is, the number is not in minutes, but in seconds. This means that any number you want to set here should be multiplied by 60 in order to be near what you want. This is all due to the evolution of the scheduling engine and what values it can support. Hopefully this will also be addressed in some way in the future.

Dynamically Creating Static Pages

One of the great uses of CFSCHEDULE is to combine it with Server or Application scope variables. This allows you to take some of the information that you may be calling or generating on every page and call it only once at a specific interval.

For example, I have a site that has a live stock feed for every page. Every time someone calls a page, a CFHTTP is called to get the live information from another server. This is nice, but a lot of overhead—especially if a lot of people are on at once. The solution is to call the same information from a scheduled page every minute, store the results as APPLICATION variables and give the users the stored information. The reduction in overhead, network traffic, and pages being called makes the site a little faster—something to really think about.

N O T E The timers for the GetIndex.cfm template, UPDATE_GETINDEX.CFM, are the schedules and templates for a small stock index application. ▪

Listing 32.1 is the schedule for the GetIndex1.cfm template. It's set to run every day between the hours of 9:00 a.m. and 5:00 p.m., once a minute.

Listing 32.1 Schedule for GetIndex1

```
<cfschedule
        action="UPDATE"
        task="GetIndex1"
        operation="HTTPRequest"
        url="http://127.0.0.1/stocks/GetIndex1.cfm"
        startdate="01/01/97"
        starttime="9:00:00"
        endtime="17:00:00"
        interval="60"
        limittime="120">
```

Listing 32.2 is a template to get the current stock index and save the results to application variables. This is used to provide the most up-to-date values to multiple people without having each run the template.

On the CD

Listing 33.2 GETINDEX1.CFM—A Scheduled Template for Getting Stock Indexes

```
<!--- Try to get the stock index from the first site. --->
<CF_RPC_StockIndex Server="PCQuote">
<!--- If it fails, try the next one. If this fails, the default values
➥will be used --->
<CFIF #live# is "NO">
        <CF_RPC_StockIndex Server="Bloomberg">
</CFIF>
<!--- Set application values to the stock indexes returned --->
<CFSET #application.djia#=#Dow#>
<CFSET #application.djia2#=#dow2#>
<CFSET #application.sp#=#spx#>
<CFSET #application.sp2#=#spx2#>
<CFSET #application.nq#=#comp#>
<CFSET #application.nq2#=#comp2#>
```

While the GetIndex1.cfm template simply loaded the indexes into application variables, you want this to be a tight setup. That means that the GetIndex1.cfm will stop executing at 5:00 p.m. You now need a way for the last values to be preserved till 9:00 the next day. That's where the publishing comes in. You call GetIndex2.cfm, which writes the values to a file in a format you can use. GetIndex3.cfm is a static file containing some CFSET commands to load the stock index data (defaulted to 0.00 for display) into the application variables. You add some code to the application.cfm to see if the attributes have timed out or not. If they have, the GetIndex3.cfm will run, loading them back into memory. Setups like this are needed in case the machine goes down, the application values time out, or something else happens. The key to a good dynamic site is making sure that you always have some data being returned. Nothing looks as bad as a missing data error.

Listing 32.3 is the scheduled event for the GetIndex2.cfm template. This will run once a day at 5:00 p.m. and write the results to a file with the name and location listed in the tag.

Listing 33.3 Schedule for GetIndex2

```
<cfschedule action="UPDATE"
            task="GetIndex2"
            operation="HTTPRequest"
            url="http://127.0.0.1/stocks/GetIndex2.cfm"
            startdate="01/01/97"
            starttime="17:00:00"
            interval="Daily"
            limittime="240"
publish="Yes"
            file="GetIndex3.cfm"
            path="E:\WebSite\htdocs\stock">
```

Listing 32.4 is the GetIndex2.cfm template which is called by the previous schedule and writes a static page to the webserver. This static page is called GetIndex3.cfm and will contain in it the last stock index values for the day.

Listing 33.4 GETINDEX2.CFM—A Scheduled Template for Writing the Stock Indexes to a File

```
<!--- Try to get the stock index from the first site. --->
<CF_RPC_StockIndex Server="PCQuote">
<!--- If it fails, try the next one.
➥If this fails, the default values will be used --->
<CFIF #live# is "NO">
        <CF_RPC_StockIndex Server="Bloomberg">
</CFIF>
<!--- Set application values to the stock indexes returned --->
<CFOUTPUT>
&lt;CFSET ##application.djia##="#Dow#"&gt;
&lt;CFSET ##application.djia2##="#dow2#"&gt;
```

continues

Part
IV

Ch
32

Listing 32.4   Continued

```
&lt;CFSET ##application.sp##="#spx#"&gt;
&lt;CFSET ##application.sp2##="#spx2#"&gt;
&lt;CFSET ##application.nq##="#comp#"&gt;
&lt;CFSET ##application.nq2##="#comp2#"&gt;
</CFOUTPUT>
```

Listing 32.5 is a static page that simply contains the last stock indexes for the day and when it is called, it will write these values to application variables.

Listing 33.5   GETINDEX3.CFM—Static Page Generated from GetIndex2.cfm

```
<CFSET #application.djia#="0.00">
<CFSET #application.djia2#="0.00">
<CFSET #application.sp#="0.00">
<CFSET #application.sp2#="0.00">
<CFSET #application.nq#="0.00">
<CFSET #application.nq2#="0.00">
```

Logging Scheduled Events

The execution of all scheduled files are recorded in the schedule.log file located in the \cfusion\log\ directory. The log is a comma-delimited list of information, each surrounded by quotes (see Listing 32.6).

Listing 33.6   SCHEDULE.LOG—Sample Line from Schedule Log

```
"Information","TID=237","10/05/97","17:53:24","Scheduled action
➥Enter Contest, template http://127.0.0.1/testbed/pch.cfm
➥completed successfully."
```

The first simply says information. This may hold more in the future, but for now seems to be a placeholder. The second value is simply the thread ID of the process, which has value only to Allaire personnel for debugging. The third and forth values are for the date and time of the execution of the event. The fifth value contains the name of the event run, the URL that was called, and the success status of the operation. The schedule log simply records the fact that a template was run by a scheduled event. The event is also recorded in other log files as appropriate to the event.

Custom Tags

by Ben Forta

Understanding Custom Tags

CFML, the Cold Fusion Markup Language, is a tag-based language, similar to HTML itself. The tag orientation has enabled Cold Fusion creators to provide sophisticated functionality (database integration, POP and SMTP support, and LDAP integration, for example) without having to expose developers to any of the low-level details. But these tags were an integral part of Cold Fusion, and developers had no way of enhancing the language with their own tags.

This changed with the release of Cold Fusion version 2. Allaire published an API that would allow C and C++ programmers to write add-on tags as DLLs which could be called directly from within Cold Fusion templates. With Cold Fusion version 3, Allaire has taken this openness even further by adding support for COM and DCOM objects, and by allowing Custom Tags to be written in CFML.

Table 33.1 lists the various forms of language extensions supported by Cold Fusion 3 or later.

Table 33.1   Extending the Cold Fusion Language

Interface	Description
CFAPI	The Cold Fusion API (also called CFX); tags are written in C or C++; see Chapter 35, "CFAPI, The Cold Fusion API," for more information.
COM Objects	Written in C, C++, Java, Visual Basic, Delphi, and other languages; supported via the CFOBJECT tag; see Chapter 34, "Interfacing with COM and DCOM objects," for more information.
Custom Tags	Written in CFML; explained in this chapter.

Unlike CFAPI and the COM DCOM interface, Custom Tags are written in CFML, the same language you are already using to write your Cold Fusion applications. If you can write a Cold Fusion template, you already know most of what you need to be able to write custom tags.

All of the Custom Tags introduced in this chapter can be found on the accompanying CD-ROM, along with a collection of other Custom Tags that you may find useful.

Defining Custom Tags

A Cold Fusion Custom Tag is a Cold Fusion template, just like any other template in your Cold Fusion application. The template is written in CFML just like any other template. It may make ODBC calls via <CFQUERY>, set variables with <CFSET>, access local files using <CFFILE>, and even call other tags. In fact, Custom Tags can do *anything* that regular Cold Fusion templates can do, because Custom Tags are Cold Fusion templates themselves.

What makes Custom Tags different, however, is how they interact with the rest of your application.

To understand this, look at a simple example. Suppose you had a standard format for displaying the current date and time on your page. You could use the CFML Now() function to return the current date and time, and then use DateFormat() and TimeFormat() to display the information as desired. The code might be as simple as

```
<CFOUTPUT>#DateFormat(Now())# #TimeFormat(Now())#</CFOUTPUT>
```

Rather than copying this code into every template, you could encapsulate it into a tag called CF_DateTime (or any other name you wanted), and just call <CF_DateTime> wherever you wanted to display the data and time information.

This way, if you wanted to change the formatting, you could just change the code in the Custom Tag knowing that the new format will be displayed correctly wherever the tag is used.

Of course, you could accomplish the same thing with a <CFINCLUDE> statement, and for code as simple as this, that would be a very workable solution. But for more complex tags, tags that take attributes as parameters or tags that return values, Custom Tags are a far more elegant solution. In fact, there are two very important differences between Custom Tags and included templates.

- Templates included with <CFINCLUDE> are actually included right into the calling template at the location of the <CFINCLUDE> statement. Any variables or queries defined above the <CFINCLUDE> are visible to the included code. Similarly, any variables set within the included template are visible to any code in the calling template that comes after the <CFINCLUDE> statement. Custom Tags, on the other hand, have their own scope, and are treated as entirely separate templates. Any variables set in the calling template are not visible within the Custom tag, and vice-versa.

- There is no way to pass parameters to an included template. To pass values you must set them as local variables, and then refer to the variables explicitly within the included template. Custom Tags are true tags. That is, they can take attributes just like any other HTML or CFML tag. This makes it possible to formalize the interface between a Custom Tag and any calling code, which in turn enables you to *black box* (or encapsulate) code.

N O T E Only read-write variables are hidden from the Custom Tag's scope. This is to prevent them from being overwritten accidentally. Read-only variables, like CGI variables, form fields, and URL parameters, are visible within Custom Tags because they cannot be overwritten anyway. ■

Using Custom Tags

Before you are actually introduce any tags, and to appropriately whet your appetite, here is a list of some of the things you might want to use Custom Tags for.

- Creating standard menus and toolbars.
- Writing agents that communicate with other HTTP or FTP servers.
- Black boxing code, hiding complex sets of functionality from novice or inexperienced developers. You could instruct them to call a tag, and give them any necessary attributes if appropriate, without requiring them to know what is happening under the hood.

Part
IV

Ch
33

- Wrapping Java and ActiveX controls into easy-to-use tag interfaces.
- Securing code or processes from prying eyes or careless misuse.

In fact, the reasons to use Custom Tags almost always fall into one of the following three categories.

- Hiding complex functionality behind a simple interface.
- Facilitating code reuse.
- Securing code so that it may be executed but not modified (or even seen).

Any code that falls into one or more of these categories is a candidate for turning into a Custom Tag.

TIP If you are looking for Custom Tags, the best place to start is the Allaire Tag Gallery at **http://www.allaire.com/taggallery**. The Tag Gallery is an online Custom Tag exchange containing hundreds of freeware, shareware, and commercial Custom Tags for you to download. The Tag Gallery is also a great place to publish any Custom Tags you write that you'd like to share with the rest of the Cold Fusion development community.

Locating Custom Tags

As noted previously, a Custom Tag is simply a Cold Fusion template. So what makes it a Custom Tag? The answer is simply, "Where it is located."

Go back to the example used before. If you were to include the code <CF_DateTime> in your template, Cold Fusion would attempt to locate a tag named CF_DateTime. The actual file name for this tag would be DATETIME.CFM (the CF_ is what tells Cold Fusion that this is a Custom Tag, the rest of the tag name is the tag file name).

Cold Fusion would first try to find a file named DATETIME.CFM in the current directory—the same directory as the calling template. If the file did not exist there, Cold Fusion would look in a directory named CustomTags beneath the Cold Fusion directory (usually C:\CFUSION), or any directory beneath it. As soon as the first file name DATETIME.CFM was found, Cold Fusion would execute it.

> **CAUTION**
>
> Make sure to uniquely name each Custom Tag you write. If you have more than one file with the same name, Cold Fusion will execute the first one it locates, and that might not be the one you expect.

This means that you can write *global* tags and *local* tags. Global tags are visible to all templates in all applications. Local tags are visible only to templates in the same directory.

 TIP Global Custom Tags are stored in the Cold Fusion CustomTags directory, or any directory beneath it. It is a good idea not to store all your tags in this directory, but rather to create subdirectories beneath it, and group tags in some logical structure. This will make managing your tags much easier.

Creating a Simple Example

To understand custom tags, look at a simple example. The code shown in Listing 33.1 is the complete code for a custom tag called CF_DateTime. Save this code as DATETIME.CFM in the directory called CustomTags beneath the Cold Fusion directory on your web server (this is usually C:\CFUSION\CustomTags), or in any directory beneath that.

On the CD

Listing 33.1 DATETIME.CFM—Code for CF_DateTime Tag

```
<!--- Display date and time --->
<CFOUTPUT>
#DateFormat(Now())# #TimeFormat(Now())#
</CFOUTPUT>
```

To test the tag, create a CFM file in any directory beneath your web server root, and add the code <CF_DateTime> to it. Then point to that CFM file with your browser. You should see a display similar to the one shown in Figure 33.1.

FIG. 33.1

Custom Tags can be used to encapsulate user interface elements.

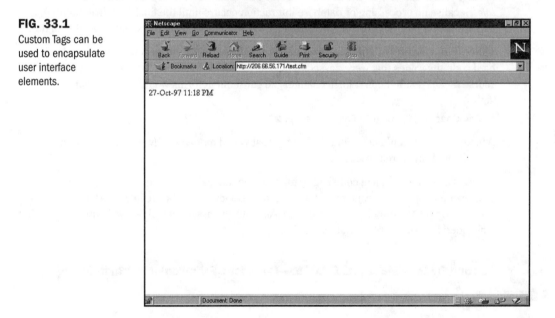

Part
IV
Ch
33

Now look at the code in Listing 33.1 again. It contains the same simple CFML that you looked at earlier. In fact, there is nothing special about it at all. What is special is the fact that the file was stored in the CustomTags directory structure.

And that's all there is to writing Custom Tags.

Creating the CF_EmbedFields Example

The <CF_DateTime> example is extremely simple but not entirely useful. So look at another example. As HTML forms are extremely limiting, HTML authors often create multi-part forms. These are simply HTML forms whose values are passed to another form. That second form passes the values it receives to a third form, and so on, until an operation is completed. As each part of the multi-part form is processed individually (each part is a separate page or template), the form can be changed or customized on-the-fly based on prior field submissions.

A popular way to pass values that are submitted by one form to another form is to embed the passed values as hidden form fields within the second form. The Cold Fusion syntax for this would look something like

```
<CFOUTPUT><INPUT TYPE="hidden" NAME="dob" VALUE="#dob#"></CFOUTPUT>
```

Hidden HTML form fields are submitted along with all other form fields when the user clicks the submit button, but they are not displayed on the screen, nor can they be edited or changed.

Passing values between forms as hidden fields also means that the application is *back button safe*. Because no processing or database interaction occurs until the final form is submitted, the user can safely use the browser's back and forward buttons (as users expect to be able to do).

The only complexity with passing form fields as hidden fields is that each form is required to hard code the values that were passed to it so as to be able to embed them correctly. This of course means that if the first form changes, all subsequent forms would have to change accordingly.

▶ **See** Chapter 12, "Cold Fusion Forms," **p. 225**

A better solution would be a Cold Fusion tag that would *automatically* embed any submitted form fields if any were present.

Listing 33.2 is the complete code listing for a custom tag called CF_EmbedFields. To use it in your own multi-part forms, just add the code <CF_EmbedFields> between your <FORM> and </FORM> (or <CFFORM> and </CFFORM>) tags. Any and all passed form fields will automatically be embedded into your form as hidden fields.

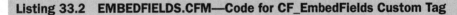

Listing 33.2   EMBEDFIELDS.CFM—Code for CF_EmbedFields Custom Tag

On the CD

```
<!---
NAME:
CF_EmbedFields

DESCRIPTION:
Cold Fusion custom tag to embed all submitted form fields as hidden
fields in another form. Designed to be used within multi part forms.
To use just call this module between the <FORM> and </FORM> tags.

ATTRIBUTES:
None.
```

```
NOTES:
Tag processes the comma delimited list of field names available as
FORM.fieldnames (this variable is automatically available if any
form fields were submitted). Each field is checked to see that
it has not already been processed (if there were multiple fields
with the same name then they'd appear multiple times in the
FORM.fieldnames list), and then it is written out as a hidden
FORM field (INPUT TYPE="hidden").

USAGE:
To use, just include <CF_EmbedFields> anywhere between the <FORM>
and </FORM> tags (or <CFFORM> and </CFFORM>). Any passed form
fields will automatically be embedded. If no form fields are
present then nothing is embedded, and processing continues.

AUTHOR:
Ben Forta (ben@forta.com) 7/15/97
--->

<!--- Check that fieldnames exists --->
<CFIF IsDefined("FORM.fieldnames")>

 <!--- Create empty list of processed variables --->
 <CFSET fieldnames_processed = "">

 <!--- Loop through fieldnames --->
 <CFLOOP INDEX="form_element" LIST="#FORM.fieldnames#">

  <!--- Try to find current element in list --->
  <CFIF ListFind(fieldnames_processed, form_element) IS 0>

   <!--- Make fully qualified copy of it (to prevent accessing the wrong
➥field type) --->
   <CFSET form_element_qualified = "FORM." & form_element>

   <!--- Output it as a hidden field --->
   <CFOUTPUT>
   <INPUT TYPE="hidden" NAME="#form_element#"
➥VALUE="#Evaluate(form_element_qualified)#">
   </CFOUTPUT>

   <!--- And add it to the processed list --->
   <CFSET fieldnames_processed = ListAppend(fieldnames_processed, form
➥element)>

  </CFIF>

 </CFLOOP>

</CFIF>
```

Now look at the code in Listing 33.2.

Custom Tags should always be as crash-proof as possible. You should never make assumptions about what users will or will not pass to you, and what environment you are running under.

Part

IV

Ch

33

This is why the entire code portion of the <CF_EmbedFields> tag is enclosed in a <CFIF> statement that tests for the existence of FORM.fieldnames. This field will only be present if the calling template received any form fields, and so testing for its existence, and only executing the actual processing code if it does indeed exist, ensures that errors will not be generated if the tag is misused.

The actual processing code uses a <CFLOOP> to loop through FORM.fieldnames, which is a comma-delimited list of all submitted form fields. Each field is then written out as a hidden form field only if it has not already been written (FORM.fieldnames can contain multiple occurrences of the same field name if more than one field had the same name).

The CFML Evaluate() function is used to dynamically determine the value of the form field being processed within each loop iteration.

Commenting Custom Tags   The code in Listing 33.2 starts off with detailed comments describing the tag and what it does, in fact, the comments take up more room than the tag code itself.

This is not a bad thing at all. Actually, it is a habit you should get into immediately. Custom Tags are often written and put away, and not looked at again for quite a while. The next time you need to modify the tag, you'll greatly appreciate the comments. This is even more true if you write tags for others to use. If your code contains all the documentation needed to use the tag, you'll find yourself having to provide less user support and hand-holding.

There is no fixed format for commenting tags, but as a rule your comments should include a description, usage notes, author information (so users can contact you if needed), and usage examples if appropriate.

Testing *CF_EmbedFields*   To test <CF_EmbedFields>, create any form with any form controls in it, and set the form ACTION attribute to another template containing a form. Add the code <CF_EmbedFields> anywhere between the <FORM> and </FORM> tags on the second template.

When you submit the first form, all the submitted form fields will be embedded into the second form. To verify this, use your browser to view the source of the second form.

Passing Data To and From Custom Tags

The examples you have looked at so far have all worked with local data (<CF_DateTime>), or data that was visible to them (<CF_EmbedFields>). To really harness the power of Custom Tags, you need to be able to pass values to them and retrieve data from them.

As mentioned earlier, the code in a Custom Tag is hidden from the calling template, and vice-versa. The visibility of data is known as its *scope*, and Custom Tags and the templates that call them each have their own scopes.

This means that you cannot simply set a variable using <CFSET> or <CFPARAM>, and expect to use it within your Custom Tag. If you want data exposed to your Custom Tag, you must specifically expose it. And just like HTML and CFML tags, the way data is exposed to Custom Tags is via tag *attributes*.

Working with Attributes

Many tags take attributes. The HTML <BODY> tag takes many *optional* attributes that let you specify things like text color and background file. Other tags have *required* attributes, for example, the DATASOURCE attribute in the CFML <CFQUERY> tag.

Some attributes are single words without values, other attributes are passed in pairs of ATTRIBUTE=VALUE, with each attribute separated by a white-space character (space, tab, newline character). This following <BODY> tag is being passed 3 attributes.

```
<BODY BGCOLOR="white" ALINK="blue" VLINK="blue" LINK="blue">
```

Attributes may be passed in any order, so the previous code accomplishes the exact same thing as this next example.

```
<BODY ALINK="blue" LINK="blue" VLINK="blue" BGCOLOR="white">
```

Attributes are case-insensitive, so BGCOLOR="white" is the same as bgcolor="white". In addition, the values passed to attributes may or may not be enclosed within double quotes. The only time quotes are required is if the value has spaces in it, in which case the quotes tell the browser that the entire text (including the spaces, and text after them) is part of the value.

T I P It is generally good practice to enclose all attribute values within double quotes. There is no downside to doing this, and if you do end up with spaces in a value at a later date, your code won't break.

Referring to Passed Attributes Within a Custom Tag

To refer to a passed attribute within a Custom Tag, you must use the ATTRIBUTES type specifier. So, to refer to a passed attribute called NAME you'd refer to ATTRIBUTES.NAME. If you omit the specifier, Cold Fusion will assume that you are referring to a local variable (or some other visible variable), and, if it does not exist, an error will be thrown.

To see how passed attributes are used, update your <CF_DateTime> tag. The new and improved version (call this one <CF_DispDateTime> to distinguish them) will allow the caller to specify whether or not to display the individual date and the time elements. For example, the following call would display just the time.

```
<CF_DispDateTime SHOWDATE="No" SHOWTIME="Yes">
```

The code for this new Custom Tag is shown in Listing 33.3. The tag accepts two optional parameters, SHOWDATE (value of YES to show the date, or NO to not), and SHOWTIME (same possible values). You may pass both, either, or none of these attributes. Modify the test CFM page you wrote earlier so that it calls <CF_DispDateTime> instead of <CF_DateTime>, and experiment with the different attribute combinations.

Part
IV

Ch
33

Listing 33.3   DISPDATETIME.CFM—Code for CF_DispDateTime Custom Tag

```
<!--- Initialize values --->
<CFSET display_date = "Yes">
<CFSET display_time = "Yes">

<!--- Should date be displayed? --->
<CFIF IsDefined("ATTRIBUTES.showdate")>
 <CFSET display_date = ATTRIBUTES.showdate>
</CFIF>

<!--- Should time be displayed? --->
<CFIF IsDefined("ATTRIBUTES.showtime")>
 <CFSET display_time = ATTRIBUTES.showtime>
</CFIF>

<!--- Display date and time as requested --->
<CFOUTPUT>
<CFIF display_date>#DateFormat(Now())#</CFIF>
<CFIF display_time>#TimeFormat(Now())#</CFIF>
</CFOUTPUT>
```

Now take a closer look at Listing 33.3. The code starts off by initializing two local variables display_date and display_time, both of which are set to default values of Yes.

Next, the code checks to see if ATTRIBUTES.showdate or ATTRIBUTES.showtime were passed by using the IsDefined() function. If any of them are present, then the display_date and display_time variables are updated with the passed values. So the following code would cause display_date to retain its Yes value, while display_time would be updated with a No value.

```
<CF_DispDateTime SHOWDATE="No">
```

Finally, the tag displays the actual date and time elements if they were requested.

Figure 33.2 is an example of what the prior call might display.

Using Optional and Required Attributes

Custom Tags have no built-in mechanism to automatically flag attributes as required. If your Custom Tag requires that certain attributes be present, it is your responsibility to verify that they exist, and you must also handle any error reporting or processing as desired. This next example demonstrates one technique you can use to accomplish this.

CF_MailForm is a very useful tag, it simply sends the contents of any submitted form to a specified email address. There are basically two functions in this tag, the form field processing and the mail generation. The form field processing is very similar to the <CF_EmbedFields> example you looked at earlier. The mail generation is accomplished using the standard Cold Fusion <CFMAIL> tag.

The code for <CF_MailForm> is shown in Listing 33.4. Once again, the tag starts off with detailed comments, usage notes, and code examples.

FIG. 33.2

Custom Tags may take one or more attributes that may change the tags behavior.

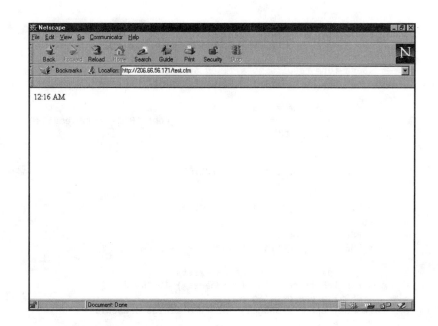

On the CD

Listing 33.4   MAILFORM.CFM—Code for CF_MailForm Custom Tag

```
<!---
DESCRIPTION:
Cold Fusion custom tag to automatically E-Mail the contents of
any form to a specified E-Mail address.

ATTRIBUTES:
FROM    - (required) Sender's E-Mail address.
SUBJECT - (optional) Message subject, defaults to
          "Form submission" if not specified.
TO      - (required) Recipient's E-Mail address.

NOTES:
Tag processes the comma delimited list of field names available
as FORM.fieldnames. Each field is checked to see that it has not
already been processed (if there were multiple fields with the
same name then they'd appear multiple times in the FORM.fieldnames
list). The finished list of fields are then sent via E-Mail to
the specified recipient. The message is formatted with each field
on its own line, in "FIELD: value" format. The message is also
automatically date and time stamped.

USAGE:
To use, just enter <CF_MailForm> on any form action page, making
sure you specify TO and FROM addresses. An optional SUBJECT may be
specified too if desired.
```

Part

IV

Ch

33

continues

Listing 33.4   Continued

```
EXAMPLES:
 Send form results to a fixed address:
  <CF_MailForm TO="webmaster@forta.com" FROM="#FORM.email#">

 Specifying the message subject:
  <CF_MailForm TO="webmaster@forta.com" FROM="#FORM.email#" SUBJECT=
➥"#FORM.subject#">

AUTHOR:
Ben Forta (ben@forta.com) 9/25/97
--->

<!--- Initialize variables --->
<CFSET proceed = "Yes">
<CFSET error_message = "">
<CFSET CRLF = Chr(13) & Chr(10)>

<!--- Check that fieldnames exists --->
<CFIF IsDefined("FORM.fieldnames") IS "No">
 <CFSET proceed = "No">
 <CFSET error_message = "No form fields present!">
</CFIF>

<!--- Check that TO and FROM were specified --->
<CFIF proceed>
 <CFIF (IsDefined("ATTRIBUTES.to") IS "No") OR (IsDefined("ATTRIBUTES.from")
➥IS "No")>
  <CFSET proceed = "No">
  <CFSET error_message = "TO and FROM attributes are required!">
 </CFIF>
</CFIF>

<!--- Check that TO and FROM are not empty --->
<CFIF proceed>
 <CFIF (Trim(ATTRIBUTES.to) IS "") OR (Trim(ATTRIBUTES.from) IS "")>
  <CFSET proceed = "No">
  <CFSET error_message = "TO and FROM may not be left blank!">
 </CFIF>
</CFIF>

<!--- If okay to go, process it --->
<CFIF proceed>

 <!--- Create variable for message body --->
 <CFSET message_body = "">

 <!--- Create empty list of processed variables --->
 <CFSET fieldnames_processed = "">

 <!--- Loop through fieldnames --->
 <CFLOOP INDEX="form_element" LIST="#FORM.fieldnames#">

  <!--- Try to find current element in list --->
  <CFIF ListFind(fieldnames_processed, form_element) IS 0>
```

```
    <!--- Make fully qualified copy of it (to prevent accessing the wrong
➥field type) --->
    <CFSET form_element_qualified = "FORM." & form_element>

    <!--- Append it to message body --->
    <CFSET message_body = message_body & form_element & ": "
➥& Evaluate(form_element_qualified) & CRLF>

    <!--- And add it to the processed list --->
    <CFSET fieldnames_processed = ListAppend(fieldnames_processed, form_
➥element)>

  </CFIF>

 </CFLOOP> <!--- End of loop through fields --->

 <!--- Build subject --->
 <CFIF IsDefined("ATTRIBUTES.subject")>
  <CFSET subject = ATTRIBUTES.subject>
 <CFELSE>
  <CFSET subject = "Form submission">
 </CFIF>

 <!--- Send mail message --->
 <CFMAIL FROM="#ATTRIBUTES.from#" TO="#ATTRIBUTES.to#" SUBJECT="#subject#">
 The following is the contents of a form submitted on
➥#DateFormat(Now())# at #TimeFormat(Now())#:

#message_body#
</CFMAIL>

<CFELSE>

 <!--- Error occurred --->
 <CFOUTPUT><H1>#error_message#</H1></CFOUTPUT>
 <CFABORT>

</CFIF>
```

Take a close look at Listing 33.4. It starts off by initializing a set of variables, one of which is called proceed which is initialized to Yes. The proceed variable is used here as a flag indicating that it is safe to proceed with the actual processing, and every operation in this Custom Tag first checks to see if it is safe to proceed by calling <CFIF proceed>.

If any operation fails, proceed is set to No. This prevents any other operations from being executed. In addition, a variable named error_message is set with a description of the failure which can be displayed later on.

<CF_MailForm> has two required attributes, FROM and TO. The Custom Tag first checks to see that both are defined (that is, if they were passed to the tag). If either is not present, then the proceed flag it set to No. If, however, both are present, the tag checks to ensure that they are not empty, and, once again, if this test fails, the proceed tag is set to No.

Part

IV

Ch

33

Once all the testing has been complete, the actual processing occurs. The Custom Tag loops through FORM.fieldnames to extract each field and its value, and appends it to an ever-growing text field named message_body. By the time all the form fields have been processed, message_body contains the entire form contents as they are to be mailed. The last step is to actually send the mail using <CFMAIL>.

The following is generally a good layout to follow when writing Custom Tags

- Display comments and a description.
- Initialize variables and set any default values.
- Check for the existence of required attributes or the lack thereof.
- Perform the actual tag processing.

N O T E   Using <CFABORT> in a Custom Tag aborts *all* processing, even calling template processing. Cold Fusion 3.1 introduced a new tag called <CFEXIT> that can be used to exit a Custom Tag (essentially aborting Custom Tag processing) while continuing to process the calling template. ■

Using Caller Variables

Custom Tags often need to return data back to the calling template, and while tags can receive parameters in the form of attributes, they have no way to return data.

To work around this limitation, Cold Fusion allows Custom Tags to explicitly access the scope of the calling template. By preceding a variable name with the CALLER specifier, Custom Tags can both read and write to variables within the calling templates scope. So to refer to a variable named *company* in the calling template, code in the Custom Tag would refer to CALLER.*company*.

The CALLER specifier is *required* to access the calling templates scope. If it is not specified, Cold Fusion will assume you are referring to a local variable.

To demonstrate the use of the CALLER specifier, take a look at another Custom Tag. CF_CapFirst, shown in Listing 33.5, takes a string of text in a required attribute named text, and converts the text so that each word is capitalized.

On the CD

Listing 33.5   CAPFIRST.CFM—Code for CF_CapFirst Custom Tag

```
<!---
DESCRIPTION:
Cold Fusion custom tag to capitalize the first letter of each
word in a string, and lower case the rest.

ATTRIBUTES:
TEXT - (required) the text to be converted.

NOTES:
Tag processes the passed string (passed to TEXT attribute)
as a space-delimited list, this allows the loop to process
one word at a time. The code within the loop gradually builds
```

a new string by appending one word at a time, and capitalizing
the first letter of each word.

```
LIMITATIONS:
The tag only treats a space as a delimiter.
Multiple spaces in a string will be converted to a single space.
--->

<!--- Check TEXT attribute was passed --->
<CFIF IsDefined("ATTRIBUTES.text")>

 <!--- Create empty string to store converted text --->
 <CFSET converted_text = "">

 <!--- Loop through words, one word at a time --->
 <CFLOOP INDEX="word" LIST="#ATTRIBUTES.text#" DELIMITERS=" ">

  <!--- Append converted first character to converted string --->
  <CFSET converted_text = converted_text & " " & UCase(Left(word, 1))>

  <!--- If the word to be converted is more than 1 char long,
        append rest of word --->
  <CFIF Len(word) GT 1>
   <CFSET converted_text = converted_text & LCase(Right(word, Len(word)-1))>
  </CFIF>

 </CFLOOP>

 <!--- And write converted string to caller template as "text" --->
 <CFSET CALLER.text = converted_text>

<CFELSE>

 <!--- If TEXT not passed, display an error message, and halt processing --->
 <H1>Error!</H1>TEXT attribute not specified!
 <CFABORT>

</CFIF>
```

By now most of the code here should be familiar. The tag first checks to see that the text attribute was passed, and then loops through the text using CFLOOP to extract one word at a time. Using the UCase() and LCase() functions, each word is converted so that only the first letter is capitalized. Once the processing is complete, the following code is executed.

```
<CFSET CALLER.text = converted_text>
```

This creates (or overwrites) a variable in the calling templates scope called text and saves the converted text into it.

Putting It All Together

To wrap up this discussion, look at one last example. <CF_SpiderSubmit> is a very powerful Custom Tag, one that demonstrates many techniques you'll find useful when writing tags of your own.

Part IV

Ch

33

<CF_SpiderSubmit> submits URLs to Internet search engines and spiders. You pass it the URL to submit, and it contacts each of the supported search engines and submits an add URL request. This is accomplished using the <CFHTTP> tag that lets you make HTTP requests from within your Cold Fusion templates.

The code for <CF_SpiderSubmit>, shown in Listing 33.6, is extensively commented, as it is designed to be updated by users if needed.

On the CD

Listing 33.6   SPIDERSUBMIT.CFM—Code for CF_SpiderSubmit Custom Tag

```
<!---
NAME:
CF_SpiderSubmit

DESCRIPTION:
Cold Fusion custom tag to submit URL's to Internet search
engines and spiders.

ATTRIBUTES:
EMAIL    - (required) E-Mail address of the person responsible for
           search engine submissions, many search engines will refuse
           entries without a valid E-Mail address. Typically this
           is set to the webmaster address.
ENGINES  - (optional) Comma delimited list of the engines to submit
           the URL to; if omitted, then URL will be sent to ALL
           listed engines. Valid engines are:
            * ALTAVISTA
            * EXCITE
            * HOTBOT
            * INFOSEEK
            * LYCOS
            * WEBCRAWLER
NAME     - (optional) Name of the query to be returned containing
           the submission status information. If specified, then
           a query will be returned with the following columns:
            * NAME    - The search engine or spider name
            * SUCCESS - YES if submission was successful,
                            NO if not
            * RESULTS - The complete HTML results page as
                            returned from the search engine
URL      - (required) The URL to submit, must be a fully qualified
           URL beginning with HTTP.

NOTES:
This tag submits URL's to Internet search engines and spiders,
and optionally returns a query containing status information for
each submission. URL submissions can be time consuming, particularly
if submitting to multiple engines. Make sure you specify a
RequestTimeout high enough so that the process does not time out
prematurely. For more information on the RequestTimeout parameter
see the Cold Fusion documentation.

USAGE:
To use just call <CF_SpiderSubmit URL="url" EMAIL="email"> from
within yourCold Fusion template, obviously replacing "url" with
```

the URL to be submitted,and email with a valid E-Mail address.
All other attributes are optional.

```
EXAMPLES:
 Submit URL to all engines:
  <CF_SpiderSubmit
   EMAIL="webmaster@allaire.com"
   URL="http://www.allaire.com">

 Submit dynamic URL to a single engine:
  <CF_SpiderSubmit
   EMAIL="#email#"
   URL="#url#"
   ENGINES="ALTAVISTA">

 Checking submission status:
  <CF_SpiderSubmit
   EMAIL="webmaster@allaire.com"
   URL="http://www.allaire.com"
   NAME="submissions">
  <CFOUTPUT QUERY="submissions">
  #name# - #success#<BR>
  </CFOUTPUT>

AUTHOR:
Ben Forta (ben@forta.com) 9/23/97
--->

<!---
=====================================================================
This first section lists all the search engines and spiders
supported by this tag. To add a spider, add a record to the
"engines" query, copying a block of code from those below.
NAME should be set to a UNIQUE name that identifies the search
engine, URL is the URL where requests should be sent, and SUCCESS
is a string of text that can be used to identify a completed
submission. When specifying the URL, enter the text *URL* where
the URL should go, and #EMAIL# where the E-Mail address should go,
and the tag will replace those tokens with the actual values prior
to submission.
=====================================================================
--->

<!--- Create query to contain search engine info  --->
<CFSET engines = QueryNew("name, url, success")>

<!--- AltaVista --->
<CFSET LastRow = QueryAddRow(engines)>
<CFSET temp = QuerySetCell(engines, "name", "ALTAVISTA")>
<CFSET temp = QuerySetCell(engines, "url", "http://add-url.altavista.
➥digital.com/cgi-bin/newurl?ad=1&q=*URL*")>
<CFSET temp = QuerySetCell(engines, "success", "This URL has been recorded
➥by our robot")>
```

Part

IV

Ch

33

continues

Listing 33.6 Continued

```
<!--- Excite --->
<CFSET LastRow = QueryAddRow(engines)>
<CFSET temp = QuerySetCell(engines, "name", "EXCITE")>
<CFSET temp = QuerySetCell(engines, "url",
➥"http://www.excite.com/cgi/add_url.cgi?url=*URL*&email=*EMAIL*")>
<CFSET temp = QuerySetCell(engines, "success", "Thank you")>

<!--- HotBot --->
<CFSET LastRow = QueryAddRow(engines)>
<CFSET temp = QuerySetCell(engines, "name", "HOTBOT")>
<CFSET temp = QuerySetCell(engines, "url",
➥"http://www.hotbot.com/addurl.html?newurl=*URL*&email=*EMAIL*")>
<CFSET temp = QuerySetCell(engines, "success", "Got it")>

<!--- Infoseek --->
<CFSET LastRow = QueryAddRow(engines)>
<CFSET temp = QuerySetCell(engines, "name", "INFOSEEK")>
<CFSET temp = QuerySetCell(engines, "url",
➥"http://www.infoseek.com/AddURL/addurl?url=*URL*&pg=URL.html&ud5=
➥Add%2FUpdate+URL")>
<CFSET temp = QuerySetCell(engines, "success", "has been submitted")>

<!--- Lycos --->
<CFSET LastRow = QueryAddRow(engines)>
<CFSET temp = QuerySetCell(engines, "name", "LYCOS")>
<CFSET temp = QuerySetCell(engines, "url", "http://www.lycos.com/cgi-bin/
spider_now.pl?query=*URL*&email=*EMAIL*")>
<CFSET temp = QuerySetCell(engines, "success", "We successfully spidered
➥your page")>

<!--- WebCrawler --->
<CFSET LastRow = QueryAddRow(engines)>
<CFSET temp = QuerySetCell(engines, "name", "WEBCRAWLER")>
<CFSET temp = QuerySetCell(engines, "url", "http://info.webcrawler.com/cgi-bin/
addURL.cgi?action=add&url=*URL*")>
<CFSET temp = QuerySetCell(engines, "success", "has been scheduled for
➥indexing")>

<!---
=================================================================
This next section initializes variables, and checks that required
attributes are present.
=================================================================
--->

<!--- Initialize variables --->
<CFSET proceed = "Yes">
<CFSET error_message = "">
<CFSET feedback = "">

<!--- Check required attributes present --->
<CFIF (IsDefined("ATTRIBUTES.url") IS "No") OR (IsDefined("ATTRIBUTES.
➥email") IS "No")>
```

```
 <CFSET error_message = "ERROR! URL and EMAIL attributes are required!">
 <CFSET proceed = "No">
</CFIF>

<!--- Check required attributes not empty --->
<CFIF (Trim(ATTRIBUTES.url) IS "") OR (Trim(ATTRIBUTES.email) IS "")>
 <CFSET error_message = "ERROR! URL and EMAIL attributes may not be empty!">
 <CFSET proceed = "No">
</CFIF>

<!--- Get list of search engines to submit to --->
<CFSET engine_list = ""> <!--- Initialize variables --->
<CFIF IsDefined("ATTRIBUTES.engines")> <!--- If specified, use instead
of default --->
 <CFSET engine_list = ATTRIBUTES.engines>
</CFIF>
<CFIF Trim(engine_list) IS ""> <!--- Verify didn't get set to "" --->
 <CFSET engine_list = ValueList(engines.name)> <!--- Default to all --->
</CFIF>

<!--- Check that feedback query is not empty if specified --->
<CFIF IsDefined("ATTRIBUTES.name")>
 <CFIF Trim(ATTRIBUTES.name) IS "">
  <CFSET error_message = "ERROR! NAME must not be empty if specified!">
  <CFSET proceed = "No">
 <CFELSE>
  <!--- Feedback required, set feedback variable to query name --->
  <CFSET feedback = "CALLER." & ATTRIBUTES.name>
 </CFIF>
</CFIF>


<!---
=================================================================
If okay to proceed, this next section performs the actual
submissions, and provides any user feedback.
=================================================================
--->

<!--- Okay to proceed? --->
<CFIF proceed IS "Yes">

 <!--- If providing feedback, create feedback query --->
 <CFIF feedback IS NOT "">
  <CFSET "#feedback#" = QueryNew("name, success, results")>
 </CFIF>

 <!--- Loop through engines --->
 <CFLOOP QUERY="engines">

  <!--- Is this one on the list? --->
  <CFIF ListFind(engine_list, engines.name)>
```

continues

Part
IV

Ch
33

Listing 33.6   Continued

```
    <!--- Build URL to submit, replace tokens with actual values --->
    <CFSET submit_url = #ReplaceList(engines.url, "*URL*,*EMAIL*",
"#URLEncodedFormat(ATTRIBUTES.url)#,#ATTRIBUTES.email#")#>

    <!--- Submit it --->
    <CFHTTP METHOD="GET" RESOLVEURL="Yes" URL="#submit_url#">
    </CFHTTP>

    <!--- Provide feedback if required --->
    <CFIF feedback IS NOT "">

     <!--- Add a row --->
     <CFSET LastRow = QueryAddRow(Evaluate(feedback))>

     <!--- Set name column --->
     <CFSET temp = QuerySetCell(Evaluate(feedback), "name", "#engines.name#")>

     <!--- Set SUCCESS column to either YES or NO --->
     <CFSET temp = QuerySetCell(Evaluate(feedback), "success",
➥"#IIf(Find(engines.success, CFHTTP.FileContent)
➥IS 0, DE("No"), DE("Yes"))#")>

     <!--- Save results from CFHTTP call --->
     <CFSET temp = QuerySetCell(Evaluate(feedback), "results", "#CFHTTP.
➥FileContent#")>

    </CFIF>

  </CFIF>

 </CFLOOP>

<CFELSE>

 <!--- Failed, display error and abort --->
 <CFOUTPUT><H1>#error_message#</H1></CFOUTPUT>
 <CFABORT>

</CFIF>
```

`<CF_SpiderSubmit>` starts off by manually creating a query in which to store the properties of the supported spiders and search engines. This is the same type of query that is returned by the `<CFQUERY>` tag, except that it is created using calls to `QueryNew()` (to create the query), `QueryAddRow()` (to add rows to the query), and `QuerySetCell()` (to set query cell values).

▶ **See** Chapter 11, "Cold Fusion Basics," **p. 193**

The advantage in using a query here instead of just setting variables (or even an array) is that Cold Fusion queries are easy to work with, and important tags, like `<CFLOOP>`, support them automatically. Simulating query results in this fashion allows you to break your code into clean distinct parts, and lets you use standard tags and procedures just as if you were deriving data from a database lookup. In addition, because the list is stored as a query, adding another spider to the list is simply a matter of modifying one section of the code, and everything else falls into place automatically.

The next section initializes variables, and verifies that the required attributes were passed.

Next comes the actual submission. The tag loops through the list of engines (or the passed list if only a subset are wanted), and submits the request to each one of them using the <CFHTTP> tag.

▶ **See** Chapter 30, "Interfacing with HTTP and FTP Using *CFHTTP* and *CFFTP*," **p. 719**

In addition, if the user requested feedback, another query is built, this time in the calling templates scope. This query is again constructed using the previously mentioned query manipulation functions, and it allows the caller to check the status of each submission to each spider or search engine.

Unlike in the <CF_CapFirst> example, the data returned to the caller template (in this example the query) is not hard coded to a specific name, rather, the user passes the desired query name, and the Custom Tag creates it. This is consistent with how CFML tags like <CFQUERY> and <CFPOP> work, and is a safer and more scalable interface.

Securing Your Tags

By now you should be convinced that Cold Fusion's Custom Tags are powerful, scalable, and very useable. You are probably already coming up with ideas for tags of your own. But before you run off, there's one last topic to cover; securing your tags.

Cold Fusion Custom Tags are written in CFML, and CFML is readable code. If you give someone a copy of your Custom Tag, they can both read the code and make changes to it.

So how do you protect your code, both from prying eyes, and from careless users?

Using CFCRYPT

Cold Fusion comes with a utility called CFCRYPT that lets you *encrypt* your Cold Fusion templates. Encrypted templates have the same CFM extension as regular templates, but their contents are not readable by anything other than Cold Fusion itself.

CFCRYPT is in your Cold Fusion executable directory (usually C:\CFUSION\BIN). To use it, simply execute CFCRYPT and pass the name of the file to encrypt and an optional file to be created. If you omit the destination file, the file you specify will be overwritten with an encrypted version.

CAUTION

There is no way to *decrypt* encrypted templates. Make sure you always keep a copy of your unencrypted templates for future use.

Part
IV

Ch
33

CFCRYPT can also be used to encrypt entire directory structures. To encrypt the contents of a directory and all subdirectories, use the /r parameter.

 T I P   Execute CFCRYPT.EXE without any parameters to display the usage instructions.

Distributed Processing

Another form of code security is distributed processing. What this means is that you break up the code into two (or more) parts. One part makes processing requests, the other part fulfills the requests and returns the results to the first part.

For example, suppose you published a Custom Tag that returned confidential sales figures. You'd want the users of the Custom Tag to have access to the results returned by the tag, but not to the underlying logic that interacts with your databases.

To safely accomplish this, you could create two Custom Tags, one that actually interacts with your databases, and one that submits HTTP requests (using <CFHTTP>) to the former. You'd only distribute the second tag, and when users executed it, it would submit a request to your own tag, which in turn would process the request, and return the results.

▶ **See** Chapter 30, **p. 719**

CHAPTER 34

Interfacing with COM and DCOM Objects

by Michael Dinowitz

In this chapter

Understanding the *CFOBJECT* Tag

The CFOBJECT tag is basically a remote call to an external program extension called a COM object. The call itself initializes the object and makes it accessible to the Cold Fusion page that's calling it:

```
<CFOBJECT Action="Connect" Name="NTAccess" Class="NTUser.Group">
```

What this says is that you're connecting to an object on your machine with an identity of ntuser.groups. This object allows you to play around with the groups a person belongs to in the Windows NT user database. The object has been initialized with a name of ntaccess. In previous chapters you've learned about the scope of variables; this is now the scope of any variable going to and coming from the object.

CFOBJECT allows you to use almost any COM object that happens to be on your machine, another machine on the network, and in a special case even objects on machines on other networks. At the moment CFOBJECT only supports COM, but in time CORBA and JavaBeans will be added in (according to studio). From what I can find from Allaire and Microsoft, COM is currently only supported by Windows NT 4.0 and Windows 95. A UNIX port is being worked on, and will probably be public by the time you read this. To use COM with Windows 95 you have to download DCOM for Windows Version 1.1 from **http://www.microsoft.com/msdn**.

What You Need to Use an Object

To use an object, you need to know the program ID or filename of the object, the methods and properties available for it, and the arguments and return types of the object's methods. In most cases all this information will be provided to you in the documentation of the object. If it's not, you'll have to hunt it down yourself using the OLEView utility (see "Understanding the OLEView Program," later in this chapter).

Now that you have the Program ID of the object, you have to say how you want to connect to it. Basically there are two ways you connect, which also fits the two types of objects there are. The standard connect method is Create which takes a COM object that's usually a .dll file and instantiates it, which means the CFOBJECT tag tells it to wake up to be used. The other connection type is the Connect method, which links to an object (usually an EXE file) that is already running on the server. All you need now is a scope name and you're ready to use the object.

Of course there are a few other attributes and options for the tag. These are listed in Table 34.1.

Table 34.1   *CFOBJECT* Attributes

Name	Status	Description
ACTION	Required	Create or Connect. Use Create to instantiate a COM object (typically a DLL) prior to invoking methods or properties. Use Connect to connect to a COM object (typically an EXE) that is already running on the server specified in SERVER.

Name	Status	Description
CLASS	Required	Enter the component ProgID for the object you want to invoke.
NAME	Optional	Enter a name for the object. This is the scope for all operations with the object later in the template.
TYPE	Optional	This specifies the type of object connecting to. This is not supported by CFOBJECT at this moment but may be put in soon. Values can be COM, CORBA, and JavaBeans. COM is the default.
SERVER	Required*	Required when CONTEXT="Remote". Enter a valid server name using UNC (Universal Naming Convention) or DNS (Domain Name Server) conventions, in one of the following forms: SERVER="\\lanserver" SERVER="lanserver" SERVER="http://www.servername.com" SERVER="www.servername.com" SERVER="127.0.0.1"

Using an Object

Now that Table 34.1 showed how to connect to an object, you have to actually use it. This is done by making use of the CFSET tag. Using this tag, you set a variable to the return value of some operation of the object. Use the CFOBJECT, defined above, in Listing 34.1, which connects to the object called ntaccess.groups and allows you to view and manipulate user and group information on an NT server. This example returns the full name of a user (#username#) on a server named HOME. The object used can be found at this link: **http://www.zaks.demon.co.uk/code/**.

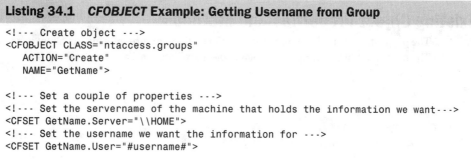

Part

IV

Ch

34

Listing 34.1   CFOBJECT Example: Getting Username from Group

```
<!--- Create object --->
<CFOBJECT CLASS="ntaccess.groups"
    ACTION="Create"
    NAME="GetName">

<!--- Set a couple of properties --->
<!--- Set the servername of the machine that holds the information we want--->
<CFSET GetName.Server="\\HOME">
<!--- Set the username we want the information for --->
<CFSET GetName.User="#username#">
```

continues

Listing 34.1   Continued

```
<!--- Call a method with a property --->
<CFSET GetName.User = GetName.StripDomain(GetName.User)>
<CFSET NAME = GetName.GetUsersFullName()>

<!--- Output result --->
<CFOUTPUT>
    #name#
</CFOUTPUT>
```

Once you connect to the object, you have to set some of the properties for the object.

Setting Object Properties

A property is basically a variable setting within the object itself. You can read from it and write to it. Setting properties is basically passing information into the object to be used later. A property value is saved for the life of the template on which it is called. Properties can be used alone as variables or combined with methods, which are the actual workers of the COM object. A method is basically a function that does some operation. Methods can use pre-set properties as arguments or can have arguments added into their operation. When an argument is used in a method, it must be contained within double quotes. The following method call calls a method called geterrorinfo and passes it 3 attributes:

```
<cfset temp = ftp.geterrorinfo("ErrorCode", "WinErrorCode", "ErrorText")>
```

The first property set was the server. While in these examples the object scope was set on the left side, normally it can be set on either. One note with this specific program is that the getname.user property holds both the username and the domain he's attached to. For this reason, the first method used is stripdomain. This method takes a username that has already been set and removes the domain information from it. This has to be done because the second method, GetUsersFullName, needs just the username. You'll notice that this method doesn't send any arguments. This is because it uses the current username set as a property. All methods have to have open and close parentheses at the end even if no arguments are being passed. Now you're thinking this all looks rather easy; well, it is. Now look at what properties and methods actually exist for this object.

Existing Object Properties and Methods

The properties of an object often return information or store information about a component. The properties of the ntaccess.groups object are listed in Table 34.2.

Table 34.2   Properties for *ntaccess.groups* Object

Property	Description
User	The user name to be queried, either "DOMAIN\USERNAME" or "USERNAME". If calling a domain controller, it appears that the domain name part must be removed, the function StripDomain exists to do this.
Server	This holds the server name (in the "\\servername" format), or can be left blank to reference the local machine.
Global	This specifies whether local groups or global groups are queried, global groups are only available using domain controllers, and should be set to TRUE for global groups.

Methods (also called functions) perform actions and have return values you can use. They are always set with a place for arguments, even if no arguments are present. Some of the methods used by the ntaccess.groups object are listed in Table 34.3.

Table 34.3   Methods for *ntaccess.groups* Object

Method	Description
GetGroups	This queries the specified server and fetches the relevant list of groups. 0 is returned for success, other numbers indicate failure.
CheckGroups ("GroupName")	This searches the previously retrieved list of groups for the specified group, this is not case sensitive, and returns true if the specified group is found.
StripDomain ("domain\username")	This takes a string and removes the domain part. The string is returned.
GetUsersFullName	This returns the user's full name as set in the user manager, the server and user properties must be set first.

Examine a method in a bit more detail. Assume you're using the OLEViewer to look at the method of an object (more on the OLEViewer later). The Execute method for this object has 3 arguments:

```
Recordset* Execute(
[in] BSTR CommandText,
[out, optional] VARIANT* RecordsAffected,
[in, optional, defaultvalue(-1)] long Options);
```

Part

IV

Ch

34

The first is expecting a variable in and is required. The second is expecting to return the number of records affected to a variable name you select. This variable name must be in quotes. According to the information on the method, this is optional. The final attribute, which is also optional, is an attribute that can be set with an option and has a default value of -1.

Example 1:

```
<CFSET INSQL="select country from countries where country LIKE 'b%'" >
<CFSET RecordCount=0>
<CFSET #rsGrid#=dataConn.Execute(INSQL,"RecordCount",1) >
```

Example 2:

```
<CFSET #rsGrid#=dataConn.ExecuteINSQL,"RecordCount") >
```

Example 3:

```
<CFSET #rsGrid#=dataConn.Execute(INSQL) >
```

Example 4:

```
<CFSET #rsGrid#=dataConn.Execute("select country
➥from countries where country LIKE 'b%'") >
```

Notice that Example 1 is the most comprehensive. It takes into account all of the arguments of the method, sets a default value on the variable being returned, and sets the query as a variable for neatness and ease of alteration.

Threading Problems

While COM is a very nice technique, it is still a growing technology. This means that in some cases, a module will not work as normally expected. If Cold Fusion seems to hang after executing a template that contains a CFOBJECT tag then you may have a threading problem. This may be because the object does not have a threading model, and potentially has not been made thread-safe. This may be due to older versions of Delphi or Visual Basic being used. To work around these, you should change the threading model to "Free" by using the OLEView program.

Changing the Threading Model

To change the threading model to "Free," run the OLEView program and find the object as follows:

1. Select the object and click the Implementation tab in the right window.

2. For the entry marked Inproc Server check the Threading Model.

3. If it is set to None, you must change it to Apartment.

Threading will be explored in more detail later, when you build an *object* from scratch (see "Creating COM Objects," later in this chapter).

Looping Over a COM Collection

Besides the standard character, integer, and string data types, CFOBJECT support arrays both as input arguments and return values. Returned arrays are referred to as collections. A collection is referred to as a group rather than individually. This means that a single variable can contain multiple pieces of returned data. You can normally access the first piece of data from the collection, but not the others. To solve this problem, the CFLOOP tag has been modified to add a collection attribute to it. This setting allows you to go over each element in a collection returned from an object.

In Listing 34.2, ITEM is assigned a variable called file2, so that with each cycle in the CFLOOP, each item in the collection is referenced. In the CFOUTPUT section, the name property of the file2 item is referenced for display.

The example employs a COM object to output a list of files. In this example, FFUNC is a collection of file2 objects.

Listing 34.2   Item Assigned a Variable Called *File2*

```
<CFOBJECT CLASS=FileFunctions.files
    NAME=FFunc
    ACTION=Create>

<CFSET FFunc.Path = "c:\">
<CFSET FFunc.Mask = "*.*" >
<CFSET FFunc.attributes = 16 >
<CFSET x=FFunc.GetFileList()>

<CFLOOP COLLECTION=#FFUNC# ITEM=file2>
    <CFOUTPUT>
        #file2.name# <BR>
    </CFOUTPUT>
</CFLOOP>
```

N O T E   The CFOBJECT tag can be disabled from the Cold Fusion Administrator for security reasons. It can also be disabled from the registry by setting the value EnableCFOBJECT to 0 in the Software/Allaire/Coldfusion/Currentversion/Server sub-key of the HKEY_LOCAL_MACHINE hive. Personally, I wouldn't suggest touching the Registry unless you know what you're doing and you've got a very recent backup. ■

Part
IV

Ch
34

With the release of Cold Fusion Studio, the inclusion of tags such as CFOBJECT has gotten a lot easier. A CFOBJECT button has been added to the Advanced Cold Fusion Tags section of the control bar. By pressing this button, you will get a small wizard that will prompt you for the values you want for your object (see Figure 34.1). This is simply the CFOBJECT tag itself, not the setting of variables or a view of the objects that exist. That's covered next. One work of warning, though. The TYPE setting is not implemented in the current version of CFOBJECT. Currently only COM is supported. The type setting makes it look like CORBA and JavaBeans are supported as well. You'll have to wait for 4.0 to see if this is true.

FIG. 34.1
The CFOBJECT tag
wizard.

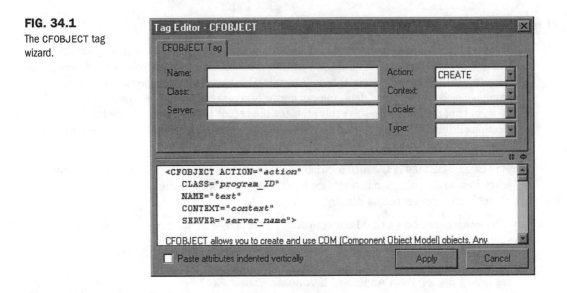

Understanding the OLEView Program

The OLEView program is probably the single most important tool you will use when dealing with COM objects. To use a COM object, you must know its Program ID, methods, and properties. This information will usually come in the documentation bundled with a distributed object. When this information is not given, it must still be found. That's where the OLEView program comes in.

The OLEView program retrieves all OLE objects and controls from the Registry, then presents the information in an easy-to-use format that can be viewed. Figure 34.2 shows the components sorted into groups for easy viewing.

By selecting the category and then component you want to use, you can see the Program ID (see Figure 34.3), in this case ColdFusion.CFFtp.3. This also gives you access to options for the operation of the object. Treading will be discussed later, one of the options that can be controlled at this point.

The selected object can now be expanded to show all of the interfaces supported (see Figure 34.4). In most cases, the interface on top has the information needed. By right clicking the object, an option will come up to view it. This will access the TypeInfo view, which contains the methods and properties of the object. Some objects will not have any access to the TypeInfo area. This is determined when an object is built and the language used.

FIG. 34.2
Objects are retrieved
and sorted into
categories.

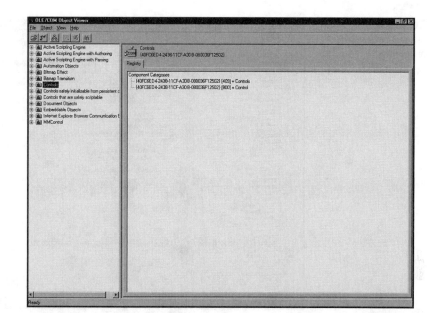

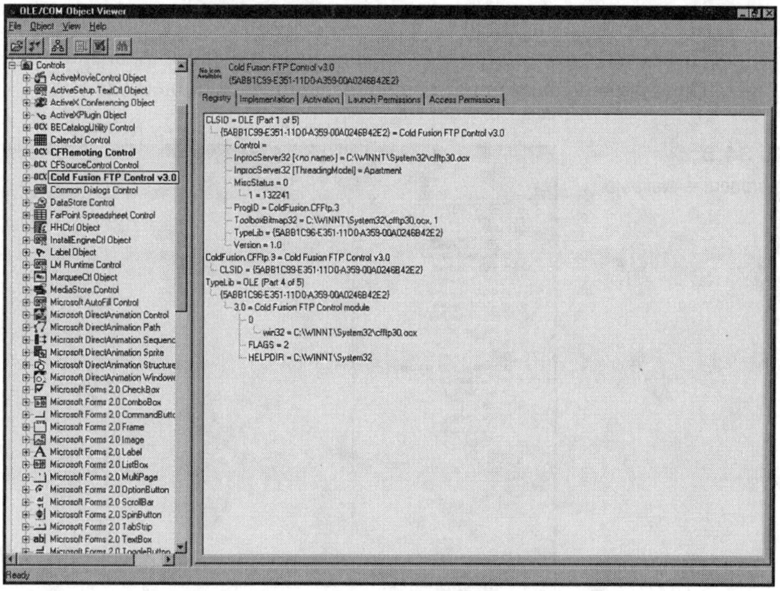

FIG. 34.3
Selecting a component
will show its ID.

Part
IV

Ch
34

FIG. 34.4

All interfaces supported for an object.

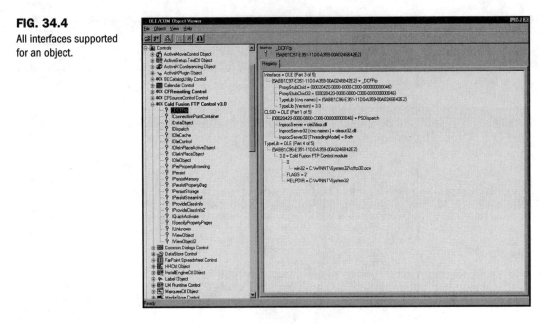

The properties of an object are information that can be read from or written to the object.

These can be seen as storage variables that hold information in the object (see Figure 34.5). These become more important when combined with methods.

FIG. 34.5

The properties available.

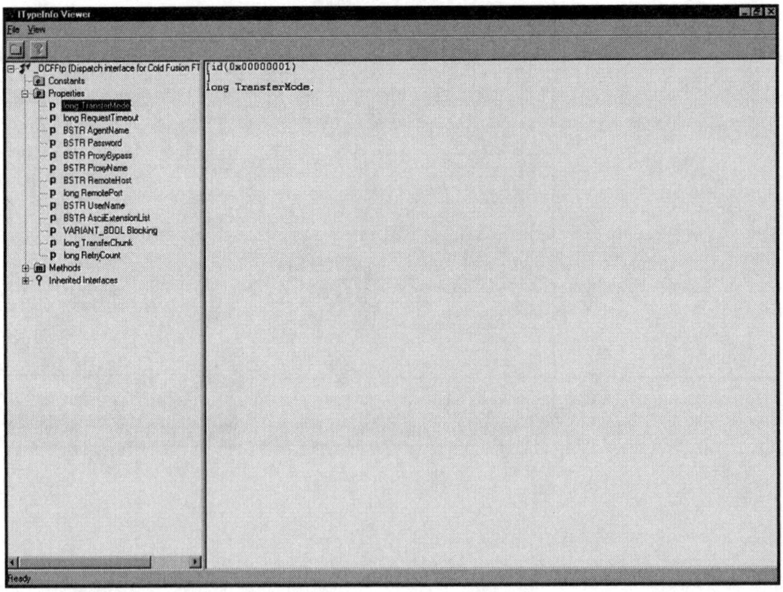

Methods are functions that are used to execute an operation. These operations are the core of the COM object. A method passes information to this core code and, in many cases, returns a result (see Figure 34.6).

This program is now a standard item included with the distribution of Visual C++ 5. The latest version can always be downloaded from the Microsoft site at **http://www.microsoft.com/oledev/olecom/oleview.htm**. The current version hasn't changed in the last year, though.

FIG. 34.6
The methods available.

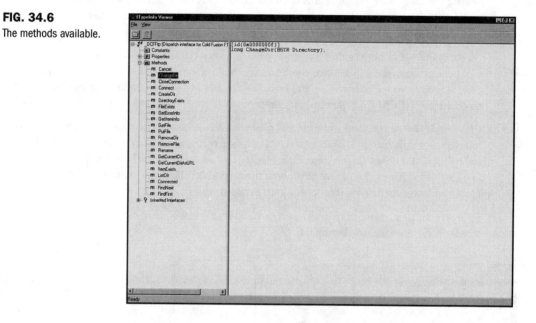

Once you've acquired the object you want to use, you may need to register it with Windows NT in order for Cold Fusion (or anything else) to find it. Some objects may be deployed with their own setup programs that register objects automatically, while others may require the use of the Windows NT regsvr32 utility. You can invoke regsvr32.exe either from a command prompt (a.k.a. a DOS box) or using the NT Run command, in the following form:

```
regsvr32 c:\path\filename.dll
```

This is the standard registration for VC++ and VB COM objects. Java-based objects have to be placed in the Java path. Other objects written in other languages may have different registration needs. These should be in the documentation that comes with the object.

Understanding COM

This is the point in the chapter where everyone will roll their eyes and move on. Everyone wants to use COM, but few really care what it is. I'll try to be short and to the point on this so as not to cause my readers to die of boredom.

COM is the Component Object Model set forth as a software specification from Microsoft. It is an evolving software technique that includes such things as Active Server/Active X components, Active Data Objects (ADO), OCX, Normandy server components, Windows NT BackOffice server components, and third-party controls. One of the biggest problems with COM is that the name keeps changing. That makes it hard to know what you're really dealing with.

COM objects, as used by Cold Fusion, are dynamically linked (late binding) components. Late binding means that the component is not linked into Cold Fusion until it's actually needed. This means that if you want to change a component on a live site, you just have to make sure no one is using it and it's free to be swapped out.

Objects can be distributed either as dynamic link libraries (DLLs) or as executables (EXEs). COM components are fully language independent and can be written using almost any procedural language from modern VC++ and Java down to Ada and Pascal. Almost any language can be modified to use COM components. Later in the chapter you'll write up a simple object in VC++.

COM works by taking chunks of code and giving specific access to them through interfaces. An interface is an abstraction layer between two software components. On one side is the service calling the COM object (in this case, Cold Fusion) and on the other is the object itself. The calling service doesn't have to know anything about the object it's calling, only what interface is supported and what methods and properties are exposed.

To represent an interface graphically, you use a floating box with plug-in jacks extending to one side for each interface (see Figure 34.7).

FIG. 34.7
Graphical representation
of a COM object.

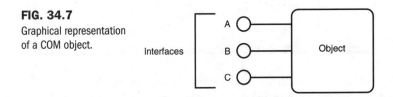

The COM objects used by Cold Fusion must be server-side, non-visual objects rather than ones with a user interface. If one with a user interface is used, the interface will pop up on the web server each time it is called. This can use up the machine's memory, pulling the site to a halt.

COM components can be transparently relocated on a network. A component on a different machine on a network is treated the same as a component on the local system. Components can also be referenced on machines outside of the local network by using DCOM.

DCOM (Distributed Component Object Model) is an extension of COM that was created to allow transparent access to components residing on other machines. This is greater than the standard COM ability to be used by any machine on a network. DCOM can be accessed across the Internet. This is a big push for Microsoft when dealing with big businesses that have Wide Area Networks (WANs). The CFOBJECT tag deals with this just by setting the location and then treating it like any other COM object. One thing to note is that DCOM is also known as COM+.

Creating COM Objects

For your example on a COM framework, you'll be using Microsoft Visual C++, version 5.0. This release has a built-in wizard to help in the generation of the structure of a COM object. Because COM is both an extension of an old idea for Microsoft (OLE) and the core of a new one (ASP), most of the Microsoft visual languages (Visual Basic, Visual C++, Visual Java) have COM wizards built into them. The wizard exists to make the writing of an object quick and easy. Older methods of object writing took a long time with lots of code. This is still needed when using languages without a COM wizard.

Once you start up your Visual C++, select File and choose the New File selector (Ctrl+N also works). Because this is a COM object, you're going to chose the ATL COM AppWizard and then enter a project name (see Figure 34.8). You really don't have to worry about a location as it's generated based on the name you give. The only reason the option is given is if you want the files stored somewhere else.

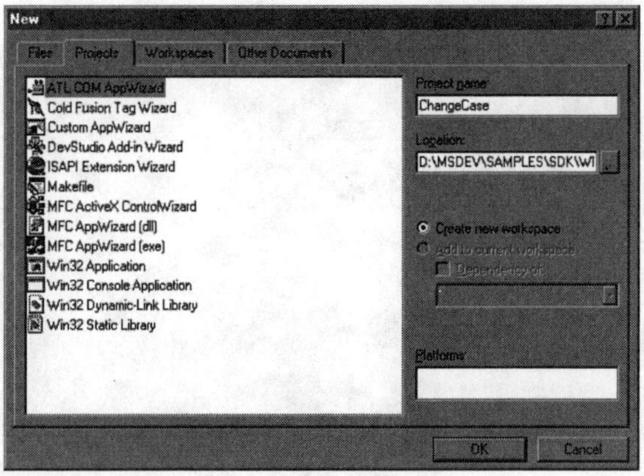

FIG. 34.8
Start building COM object with the ATL COM AppWizard.

You're only going to write up a small object, so all you want is a .dll file (see Figure 34.9). It is rare that you'll ever write any form of COM executable or service, so these should not be worried about. The merging of proxy and stub code is really used when you're writing an executable object. It cuts down on size by lumping all the files into a single package. As you're not dealing with executables, ignore that. The support MFC (Microsoft Foundation Classes) will allow you to program using MFC. The good thing is that MFC has a lot of nice and easy commands that can enhance your code. The bad thing is that you will have to distribute the MFC runtime DLL with any code you write using it. If you don't need MFC, don't check this box. At this point you're finished with the basics and can choose Finish. Once you do so, the program will generate all of the basic code you will need for your object.

Part
IV

Ch
34

FIG. 34.9

Setting server types.

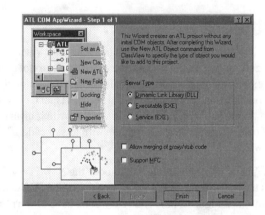

You now have a skeleton to hold the real pieces of the object (see Figure 34.10). To add these pieces, you'll have to go to the Insert menu and select New ATL Object.

FIG. 34.10

All of the basic skeleton code is generated.

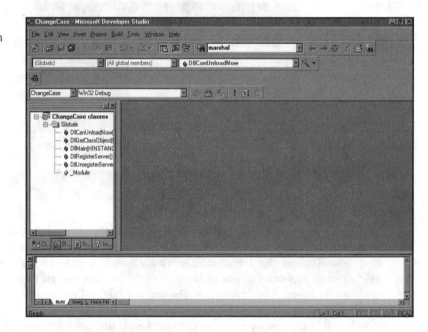

Remember that you're just writing up a basic, non-graphical object. This means that you are really limited at this point about what you can choose. Select the Object category and select the Simple Object icon (see Figure 34.11). This and the code that goes behind it are really all you need for the generation of your object.

FIG. 34.11
Selecting the object type.

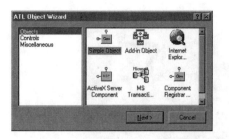

Here you can control all of the naming conventions of your object (see Figure 34.12). A simple, yet descriptive name is usually best. Once you write in a short name, it will be copied over to all of the fields with slight variations. Usually you wouldn't touch any of these except for the prog ID. This is how the CFOBJECT tag communicates with the object, and many developers like to alter it with easier-to-read variables. I've got a massive object running on a server by me that does thousands of stock operations, yet has a prog ID of tal. To finish this part of the process you have to go to the Attributes tab.

FIG. 34.12
Adding the object information.

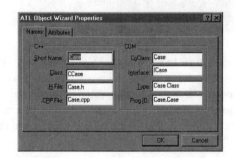

Remember that threading issue mentioned earlier? Well, this is where it comes from, in some cases. Without going deeply into threading, just assume that Both is the option you want. This allows multiple users to use the object and makes sure the object can be used with both older and newer COM applications.

The next point is the interface method used. You want your object to be late binding, while early binding is the default. For this choose Duel, so you can use what you need. Aggregation is used when one object is actually a front end to another object. On the whole, I doubt you'll ever do that, but just in case you should know that this is where you set it. For now, set it to No (see Figure 34.13). As for the final options, you're not going to deal with them at all and they can be ignored.

You now have your object. It's totally legal and will compile okay at this point. The only thing it is missing is something to do and a way to communicate with the outside. To give an object something to do, you need to create a method (see Figure 34.14).

Part
IV

Ch
34

FIG. 34.13

Setting object attributes.

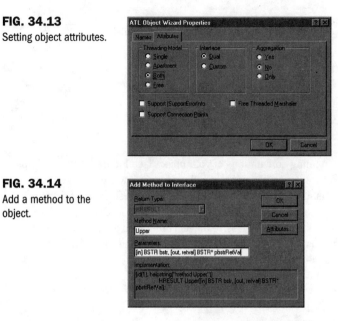

FIG. 34.14

Add a method to the object.

This is the point where you really have to know some VC++ (or whatever language you're using). You must give the method a name, which will be used to call it. The parameters of the method are set as what is expected in and what is expected out (if anything). In this case, you're setting a single parameter in what will be a string value. The return value will be of the same value. You can also set attributes for the method if you want, but in this case it has no effect.

While you're not using any properties with this example, they can be set using the same basic instructions as the method. Properties consist of a few simple settings (see Figure 34.15)—a type, which is the value it expects to store; a name to access the property with; and a location for parameters, if you want to add any custom information to the property. Finally there is a section to define the access status of the property. While it doesn't actually use these words, the idea of read-only, write-only, and full access is here.

Now that the method is defined, all you have to do is set some code to go with it and you're done. The following example is a modified sample given out by Microsoft for teaching COM. The first method takes in a string and changes it to uppercase.

```
CComBSTR bstrTemp(bstr);
wcsupr(bstrTemp);
*pbstrRetVal = bstrTemp.Detach();
return S_OK;
```

FIG. 34.15

Add a property to the object.

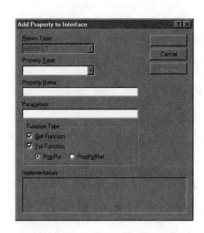

The second method does the same thing, except returns lowercase.

```
CComBSTR bstrTemp(bstr);
wcslwr(bstrTemp);
*pbstrRetVal = bstrTemp.Detach();
return S_OK;
```

As you can see, a COM object is relatively easy to write. ●

CFAPI, The Cold Fusion API

by Steven D. Drucker

Getting Started with the CFAPI

Before you start experimenting with the CFAPI, you must purchase, install, and properly configure Microsoft Visual C++. In addition, you should have some familiarity with object-oriented paradigms such as those found in JavaScript, and be acquainted with C, Java, or JavaScript syntax.

Installing and Configuring Microsoft Visual C++

Before you begin working with the CFAPI, you must purchase and install Microsoft Visual C++ 4.0. Visual C++ is a component of Microsoft's Developer Studio and includes a full C++ compiler, linker, debugger, Crystal Reports report writer, full online documentation for the MFC (Microsoft Foundation Class) libraries, and several other useful utilities. Installing Microsoft Visual C++ is straightforward. Simply insert the Microsoft Visual C++ CD-ROM into your CD-ROM drive, double-click the setup.exe program, and select Install Visual C++ 4.0. Installation requires a minimum of 17MB of hard disk space with the typical installation requiring 84MB. After installation, the program group Microsoft Visual C++ 4.0 is visible. Clicking the Microsoft Developer Studio icon starts the Visual C++ programming environment (see Figure 35.1).

Microsoft Developer Studio is an interface encapsulating the Microsoft Visual C++ compiler, Microsoft Test, Microsoft Fortran Powerstation, the Microsoft Developer Library, and the Books Online help system. Throughout this chapter, the terms Developer Studio and Visual C++ are used interchangeably.

TIP   The Microsoft Visual C++ CD-ROM contains a very brief, animated tutorial of the Developer Studio interface. You can access this by selecting the What's so cool about Visual C++? option on the Visual C++ Master Setup screen and then selecting Online Documentation.

Configuring the Include Directory List   The first step you should perform after installing Visual C++ is to add the path of the Cold Fusion file cfx.h into the Includes directory list. This file should be located in your /cfusion/cfapi/include directory. Configure the list by performing the following steps:

1. Select Tools, Options from the Developer Studio menu bar.
2. Click the Directories tab in the Options dialog box. Your screen should look similar to the one presented in Figure 35.2.
3. Select Include Files from the pull-down menu labeled Show Directories.
4. Double-click the first empty line in the directories listing.
5. Type in the path to your **cfx.h** file and click OK.

Verify the Existence of the Cold Fusion Tag Wizard   The final step in ensuring that Developer Studio is properly configured, is to ascertain if the Cold Fusion Tag Wizard was properly installed. From the Developer Studio menu bar, select New. Next, double-click the Project Workspace entry in the New Dialog box. Scroll through the list of New Project Workspace types until you find one called Cold Fusion Tag Wizard.

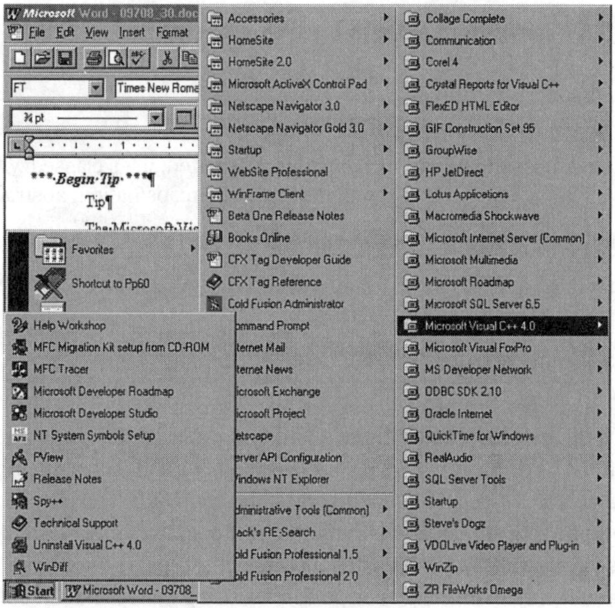

FIG. 35.1

Microsoft Visual C++ is a component of Microsoft Developer Studio. Throughout this chapter the two names are used synonymously.

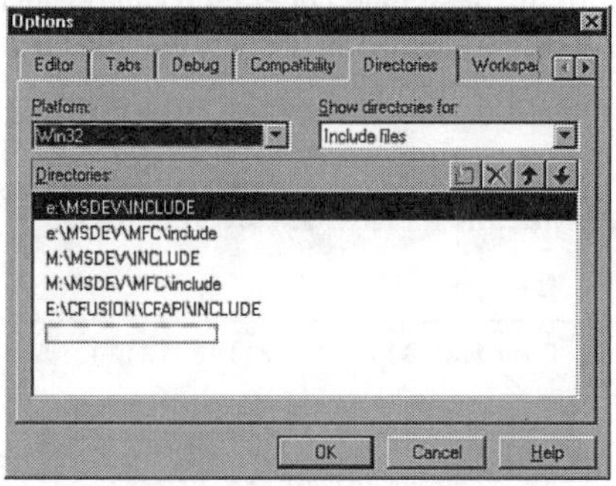

FIG. 35.2

Manually add the path of the Cold Fusion cfx.h file into the Include files directory list.

If an entry does not exist for the Cold Fusion Tag Wizard, close Microsoft Developer Studio, reinstall Cold Fusion, and run through this procedure again. The Cold Fusion installation program should recognize that you have VC++ installed on your system and automatically install the Cold Fusion Tag Wizard.

The Object-Oriented Paradigm

Visual C++ contains a number of object constructs similar to JavaScript. You will find, however, that C++ is not as "developer friendly" when it comes to dealing with variable types and case sensitivity. Table 35.1 illustrates some of the differences between these two languages.

Table 35.1   JavaScript versus C++ Comparison

JavaScript	C++
Loosely Typed	Strongly Typed
Object-based, uses methods	Fully object-oriented, uses classes with inheritance, polymorphism, encapsulation, abstraction, and modularity
Interpreted	Compiled
Code embedded in HTML	Source code compiled into a 32-bit dynamic linked library (.DLL)
Executed at runtime by client	Executed at runtime by server

Strongly Typed Variable Declarations   Unlike JavaScript, C++ implements strong typing. Variables must be declared as a type or class member and, subsequently, may only contain values of that type. Once instantiated, a variable may not be redeclared as a different type within the same scope. Function parameters and operators in C++ are usually type-specific; you cannot pass in a variable or value of an incompatible type. In JavaScript, for instance, the + operator would either sum values or perform a string concatenation operation, depending on the types of variables involved. Performing the same operations in C++, however, requires the explicit conversion of types before the designated operation can be performed. Table 35.2 illustrates the differences and relative difficulty levels between performing a string concatenation operation in JavaScript versus C++.

Table 35.2   String Concatenation in JavaScript versus C++

JavaScript	C++
`var s1="The value is:"`	`CString s1("The value is:"), s3`
`var s2=5`	`int s2=5`
`s1+=s2`	`s3.GetBuffer(80);s1+=s3.Format("%d",s2)`

Fully Object-Oriented   C++ supports the concepts of abstraction, encapsulation, inheritance, modularity, and polymorphism. You do not need to understand these concepts to understand the simple examples presented in this chapter. If you decide to use the CFAPI to develop more complicated, "real world" solutions involving MFC or other API sets, however, understanding the following concepts will give you insight into object-oriented programming and set you on the path to become a true Cold Fusion master.

Abstraction   Abstraction defines characteristics of an object that make it unique, without requiring the user to understand how the object is implemented. For instance, the Cold Fusion lists loosely qualify as an abstraction of comma-delimited string sets. You do not need to know how memory allocates for the set or how the strings concatenate. You do not necessarily need to know that each element is separated by a delimiter. To make use of a list, the only thing you need is a definition of functions which operate on the object.

Encapsulation   While abstraction seeks to hide the "nitty-gritty" details about how an object implements, encapsulation seeks to group functions which operate on the object into a class. The Cold Fusion list functions `listlen()`, `listfirst()`, and `listlast()` could be considered to be encapsulated into a class of routines that deals only with operating on a list object. Following the principle of abstraction, you do not need to be concerned about how these functions accomplish their tasks—just knowing what operation they perform and how to syntactically invoke them is enough.

Inheritance   Inheritance helps you leverage your existing code by enabling you to create a new class of functions containing routines from a pre-existing class. The VC++ box contains the slogan "make reuse a reality." Consider a scenario where you want to build a class of functions to deal with matrix operations. The matrix rows are implemented as Cold Fusion lists. Using inheritance, you could import all the lower-level list functions and then manipulate them to create a higher-level matrix transformation function instead of having to rebuild the class from scratch. You are, in effect, building a class hierarchy where your matrix class incorporates the functions into the list class.

Polymorphism   Polymorphism is an attribute of object-oriented programming whereby each class in a class hierarchy may contain functions which share the same function, even though that function implements its task in a class-specific manner. For instance, the matrix class may contain a member function `getdata()` which retrieves a data element at a specific coordinate from a matrix. Similarly, the class containing the lower-level list functions may also contain a member function `getdata()` which retrieves a data element from a specified location in a list.

Modularity   The concept of modularity resulted from the development of increasingly complex applications. A module is, in essence, a collection of classes that provide some higher-level behavior. If you were developing a huge application containing hundreds of classes, you might consider combining the CFAPI classes into a single module.

A Compiled Language   Unlike JavaScript, you must recompile C++ source code whenever changes are made. During the compilation process, the source code translates into a binary format that only the operating system can understand. While compiled languages execute faster than interpreted ones, facilities for dynamically evaluating expressions provided by interpreted languages such as the JavaScript `eval()` method and its CFML counterpart, `evaluate()`, do not exist.

A Server-Side Process   CFX tags execute on your web server as an extension of the Cold Fusion service. This makes them an excellent vehicle for deploying custom data validation functions, performing Windows NT OS functions (such as using NT security to manage Cold Fusion user authentication), or linking with other server processes and vendor's APIs. Despite the fact that you're using Visual C++, discount the visual aspects of the development environment because they mostly apply to interface design and you'll be exclusively developing programs that interact only with other server-based processes.

Part

IV

Ch

35

Building Your First CFX Tag

Using the CFAPI is really very simple. Cold Fusion comes packaged with a Cold Fusion Tag Wizard that automatically sets up a valid project and a working tag to customize. The following section guides you step-by-step to load Developer Studio, to use the tag wizard to generate your first tag, and to deploy it within a Cold Fusion template. If you do not understand all the code, don't panic. This section is merely intended to give you an overall grasp of the CFX development process.

Getting Started

The first step in creating a tag is to set up a project directory. Next, by using Microsoft Developer Studio and the Cold Fusion Tag Wizard, you can create and register your first DLL file.

Create a Root Directory for Your Custom Tags　The first step in creating a CFX tag is to create a directory on your hard disk to hold your C++ projects and source code. Using the File Manager or MS Explorer, create the directory \cftag\.

Start MS Developer Studio and Create a New Project　Once you decide where to store your projects, launch Microsoft Visual C++ (MS Developer Studio). When VC++ finishes loading, select File, New from the VC++ menu bar to display the dialog box shown in Figure 35.3.

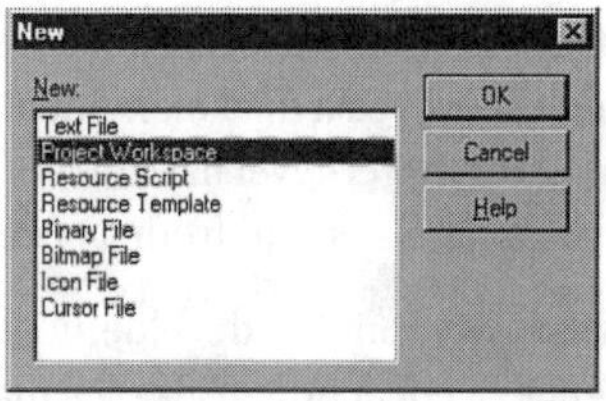

FIG. 35.3
Creating a new project workspace.

Select Project Workspace from the New dialog box and click OK. The New Project Workspace dialog box will pop up. Scroll down the list of project types until you see one called Cold Fusion Tag Wizard. Select it, fill out the form shown in Figure 35.4, and click OK.

N O T E　All CFX tags must be named with a prefix of CFX_, for example, CFX_mytag. ▓

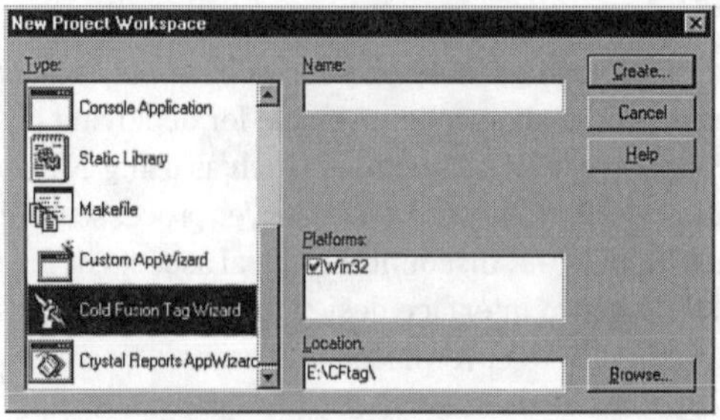

FIG. 35.4
Cold Fusion comes packaged with a CFX tag wizard.

The Cold Fusion application wizard now appears. Fill it out as shown in Figure 35.5. This wizard automatically builds a simple, working CFX tag for you to customize and registers it with the Cold Fusion Administrator.

Once you press OK, MS Developer Studio summarizes the actions it will execute in the New Project Information dialog box, shown in Figure 35.6. Click OK to create your new project files. Load the Cold Fusion Administrator to confirm that your new tag was properly registered, as shown in Figure 35.7.

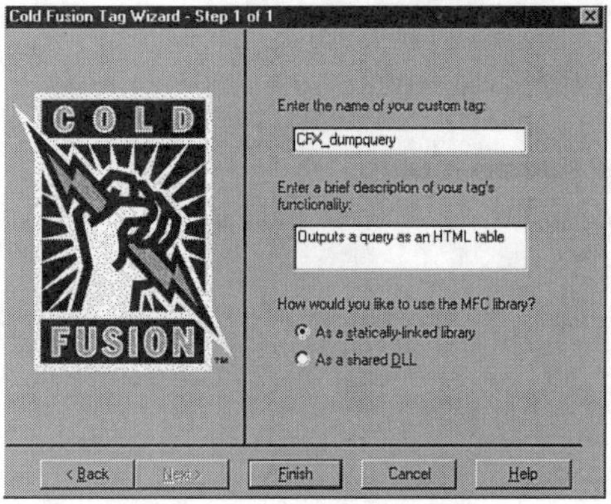

FIG. 35.5
The Cold Fusion tag wizard.

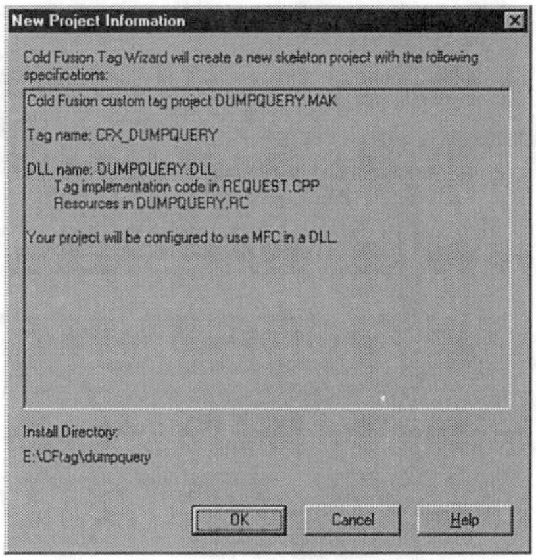

FIG. 35.6
The New Project Information dialog box.

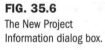

The MS Developer Studio Interface

Once you complete the Cold Fusion Tag Wizard to set up your project, you're ready to start programming using the CFAPI. The Developer Studio interface, shown in Figure 35.8, is optimized for your coding enjoyment. The window containing a list of CFAPI classes, shown in Figure 35.9, is called the Project Workspace dialog box. As its name indicates, this is where you manage all aspects of your project. At the bottom of the dialog box are four tabs so you can switch between different project views. These are ClassView (the default), ResourceView, FileView, and InfoView. You can view and edit any project class with the ClassView, shown in Figure 35.9. This is the view you will probably use most of the time. The ResourceView lists interface and other visual objects your projects use. This tab is irrelevant due to the nature of the programs you will be developing here. The FileView lists all the files in your project in alphabetical order and, like the ClassView, lets you edit them. The InfoView displays the Visual C++ and MFC Books Online help topics.

FIG. 35.7

Your new tag is automatically registered with the Cold Fusion Administrator.

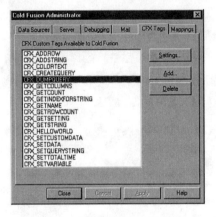

FIG. 35.8

The MS Developer Studio interface.

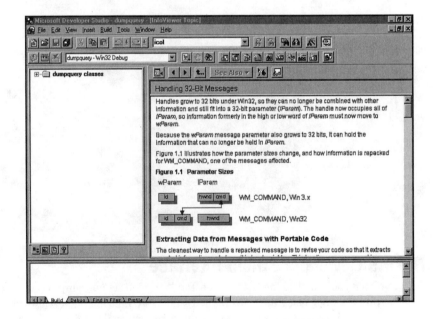

T I P An animated introduction to the Developer Studio interface is included on the Visual C++ installation CD-ROM.

You can open the source code to your CFX tag by switching to the ResourceView tab and selecting Dumpquery Classes—Globals and double-clicking the entry ProcessTagRequest(). The code in Listing 35.1 should appear in the editing window.

FIG. 35.9
The ClassView enables you to view and edit any aspects of your project.

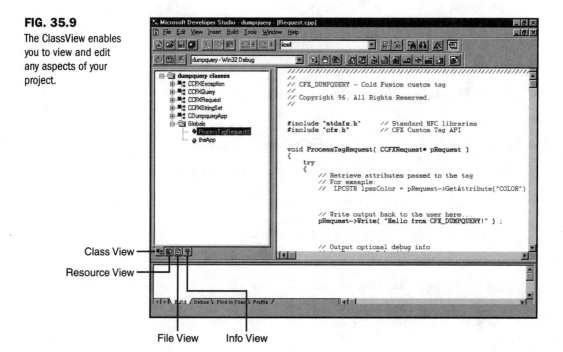

Class View
Resource View

File View   Info View

The CFX Framework

The function ProcessTagRequest() is the default starting point of execution for tags created with the Cold Fusion Tag Wizard. The parameter (automatically passed to it by Cold Fusion) is a tag request object, represented by the class CCFXRequest. Member functions of this class enable you to access every aspect of the request and to perform functions, such as writing HTML output to a user (CCFXRequest::Write) and access information in a query result set (CCFXRequest::GetQuery()). The try and catch blocks make up the foundation of an error trapping framework, insuring that a rogue CFX tag will not crash your Cold Fusion service. The default behavior of the newly created CFX tag, detailed in Listing 35.1, is to output the string Hello from CFX_mytag to the user accessing the .CFM file which invokes it.

Part
IV

Ch
35

Listing 35.1   HELLOWORLD\REQUEST.CPP—The Cold Fusion Tag Wizard Creates a Template from Which You Build Custom Tags

```cpp
///////////////////////////////////////////////////////////////////
//
// CFX_HELLOWORLD - Cold Fusion custom tag
//
// Copyright 96. All Rights Reserved.
//


#include "stdafx.h"          // Standard MFC libraries
#include "cfx.h"             // CFX Custom Tag API


void ProcessTagRequest( CCFXRequest* pRequest )
{
try
{
// Retrieve attributes passed to the tag
// For example:
//      LPCSTR lpszColor = pRequest->GetAttribute("COLOR") ;



// Write output back to the user here...
pRequest->Write( "Hello from CFX_HELLOWORLD!" ) ;



// Output optional debug info
if ( pRequest->Debug() )
{
pRequest->WriteDebug( "Debug info..." ) ;
}
}

// Catch Cold Fusion exceptions & re-raise them
catch( CCFXException* e )
{
pRequest->ReThrowException( e ) ;
}

// Catch ALL other exceptions and throw them as
// Cold Fusion exceptions (DO NOT REMOVE! --
// this prevents the server from crashing in
// case of an unexpected exception)
catch( ... )
{
pRequest->ThrowException(
"Error occurred in tag CFX_HELLOWORLD",
"Unexpected error occurred while processing tag." ) ;
}
}
```

Outputting a Query in Table Format

Your first tag is going to be just a bit more ambitious than the ubiquitous (and uninteresting) "Hello World" example. Listing 35.2 contains the source code necessary to automatically output a query in HTML <TABLE> format. You may either type the listing into your editor or cut and paste it from the file included on the CD-ROM. All the function calls within the listing belong to classes of the CFAPI.

On the CD

Listing 35.2   DUMPQUERY\REQUEST.CPP—Writing CFAPI Custom Tags Gives You Ultimate Control over Query Output

```cpp
///////////////////////////////////////////////////////////////////////
//
// CFX_DUMPQUERY - Cold Fusion custom tag
//
// This tag outputs a query in HTML format
//
// Example Use:
//
// <CFQUERY NAME="myquery" DATASOURCE="mydatasource">
//          SELECT * from mytable
// </CFQUERY>
// <HTML>
// <BODY>
// <CFX_DUMPQUERY QUERY="myquery">
// </BODY>
// </HTML>
//
///////////////////////////////////////////////////////////////////////

#include "stdafx.h"          // Standard MFC libraries
#include "cfx.h"             // CFX Custom Tag API


void ProcessTagRequest( CCFXRequest* pRequest )
{
try
{

// retrieve the query name passed to the tag
CCFXQuery* pQuery = pRequest->GetQuery();

if ( pQuery == NULL) {
pRequest->ThrowException(
"Missing QUERY parameter",
"You must pass a QUERY parameter for"
"this function to work properly.");
}

// check row count
if (pQuery->GetRowCount() > 0){
```

continues

Part

IV

Ch

35

Listing 35.2   Continued

```
// get column information
CCFXStringSet* pColumns = pQuery->GetColumns();
int nNumColumns = pColumns->GetCount();

// Write out table column headings
pRequest->Write("<TABLE WIDTH=100% BORDER=1>\n");
for (int i=1; i<=nNumColumns; i++) {
pRequest->Write("");
pRequest->Write( pColumns->GetString(i));
pRequest->Write("</TH>\n");
}

// Write out data elements
for (i=1; i<=pQuery->GetRowCount(); i++) {
pRequest->Write("<TR>\n");
for (int j=1; j<=nNumColumns; j++) {
pRequest->Write("<TD>\n");
pRequest->Write(pQuery->GetData(i,j));
pRequest->Write("</TD>\n");
}
pRequest->Write("</TR>\n");
}
pRequest->Write("</TABLE>");
} // rowcount == 0


// Output optional debug info
if ( pRequest->Debug() )
{
pRequest->WriteDebug( "Debug info..." ) ;
}
}

// Catch Cold Fusion exceptions & re-raise them
catch( CCFXException* e )
{
pRequest->ReThrowException( e ) ;
}

// Catch ALL other exceptions and throw them as
// Cold Fusion exceptions (DO NOT REMOVE! --
// this prevents the server from crashing in
// case of an unexpected exception)
catch( ... )
{
pRequest->ThrowException(
"Error occurred in tag CFX_DUMPQUERY",
"Unexpected error occurred while processing tag." ) ;
}
}
```

Compiling and Debugging the CFX

To compile a project into a .DLL file, select the Build dumpquery.dll from the Build menu in Developer Studio or press the F7 key. As the compilation process executes, status, warning, and error messages appear in the lower status window, and are depicted in Figure 35.10.

If an error is detected during the build processes, you can jump to its location in your source code by double-clicking the error/warning message in the status window. For runtime debugging or stepping through the DLL as it executes, you must configure VC++ debug options, depicted in Figure 35.11 by performing the following steps:

1. From the Developer Studio menu bar, select Build, Settings.
2. Select the Debug tab.
3. Set Executable for debug session to the full path of the Cold Fusion executable (CFML.EXE).
4. Set the Program arguments setting to DEBUG.

FIG. 35.10

As the compilation processes executes, status messages output to the lower message window.

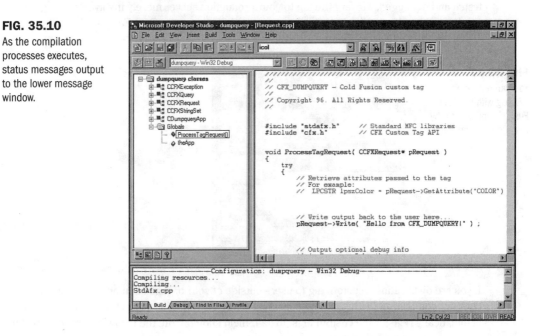

Transferring the CFX Tag to Your Production Server

Before you transfer your tag to your production server, you may want to recompile the tag without storing the debug information within it. To accomplish this, simply use the pull-down menu bar on the Developer Studio button bar to change it from reading as "dumpquery-Win 32 debug" to "dumpquery-Win 32 release" and rebuild the .DLL by pressing F7.

Part
IV

Ch

35

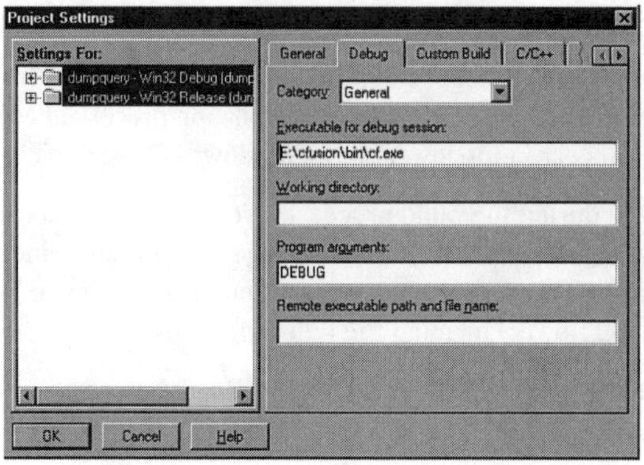

FIG. 35.11

Configuring the VC++ debug options.

Project Settings

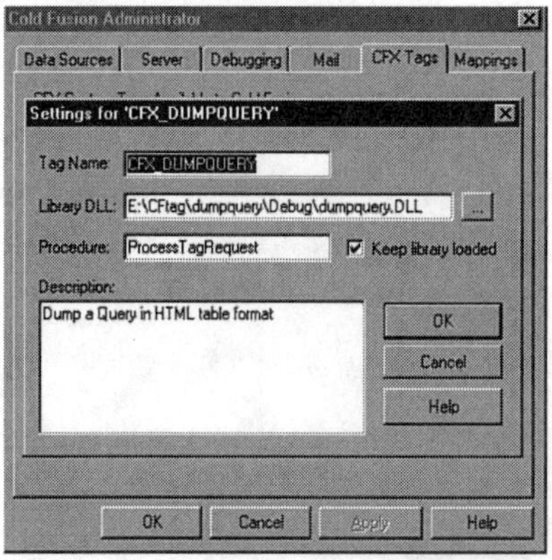

FIG. 35.12

You can register your CFX tag with the Cold Fusion Administrator by filling out a short form.

Cold Fusion Administrator

As mentioned previously, the Visual C++ Custom Tag Wizard automatically registers custom tags with the Cold Fusion Administrator on your development machine so that they can be tested and debugged. Moving the tag to your production server merely involves copying the resultant .DLL file to a directory on the server and filling out the Cold Fusion Administrator CFX Tags tab as depicted in Figure 35.12.

If you are distributing a custom tag to users outside of your organization or for resale, you may consider configuring the InstallShield product (bundled with Microsoft Developer Studio) to automatically register the custom tags. InstallShield should write the following entries directly into the Windows NT Registry:

Hive	HKEY_LOCAL_MACHINE
Key	SOFTWARE\Allaire\ColdFusion\CurrentVersion \CustomTags\<YourTagsName>
Values	LibraryPath—Full path to the DLL that implements the custom tag.
ProcedureName	Name of the procedure to call for processing tag requests (usually ProcessTagRequest).
Description	Description of tag's functionality for browsing by end users.

Deploying the Custom Tag in a CFM Template

Once your custom CFX compiles and registers with the Cold Fusion Administrator, you may deploy it in your templates just like any other native Cold Fusion tag. Listing 35.3 uses the CFX tag you just built to output the results of the getemployees query to the user.

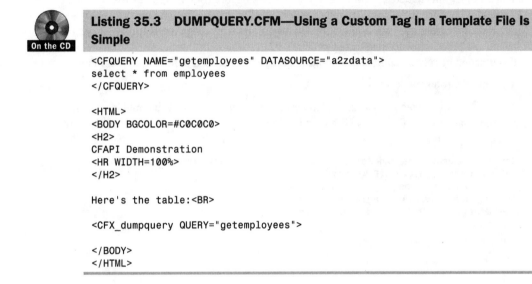

Listing 35.3 DUMPQUERY.CFM—Using a Custom Tag in a Template File Is Simple

```
<CFQUERY NAME="getemployees" DATASOURCE="a2zdata">
select * from employees
</CFQUERY>

<HTML>
<BODY BGCOLOR=#C0C0C0>
<H2>
CFAPI Demonstration
<HR WIDTH=100%>
</H2>

Here's the table:<BR>

<CFX_dumpquery QUERY="getemployees">

</BODY>
</HTML>
```

The CFAPI Classes

The CFAPI includes a set of four classes encompassing 27 functions. The classes and their descriptions are listed in Table 35.3. You may recognize the class names from the Developer Studio ClassView dialog box. Part of the process that the CFX tag wizard performs is to automatically import these classes into your project.

Table 35.3 CFAPI Classes

Class Name	Description
CCFXQuery	Contains query manipulation functions, including the adding of rows, editing of data elements, and retrieving query properties such as a query's name and record count.
CCFXRequest	Represents a request made to a CFX. It includes functions for writing output to the user, creating and manipulating Cold Fusion variables, creating queries, and initiating an error process.
CCFXStringSet	Class that contains functions for Cold Fusion list manipulation. Lists (comma-delimited strings) must be initially created using the CCFXRequest::CreateStringSet function.
CCFXException	Class that represents an error thrown during processing of a CFX function.

Each class contains a set of functions that operate only on objects instantiated as members of that class. A pointer to a new member of CCFXQuery can thus be created by using the following syntax:

```
CCFXQuery* myquery;
```

When myquery instantiates, it contains a default value of NULL. Before you can use functions within the CCFXQuery class on this object, you must allocate a block of memory to hold the actual data that myquery will point to. Alternatively, you may assign a value to myquery that points to a preexisting CCFXQuery object. The CFAPI function CCFXRequest::GetQuery() fulfills this function by returning the location of the query object passed to the tag by Cold Fusion.

```
myquery = GetQuery();
```

Now, armed with a pointer to a valid member of the CCFXQuery class, you could invoke any of the functions listed in Table 35.4. The next few lines of code demonstrate some calling conventions:

```
int newrowid=myquery->AddRow();                  /* Adds new row to query */
int numrows=myquery->GetRowCount();        /*
➡Retrieves # of rows in query result set */
CString queryname=(CString) myquery->
➡GetName();   /* Retrieves name of query */
```

N O T E   A return type of void indicates that the function returns no value. ▪

Table 35.4 *CCFXQuery* **Class Members**

Return Type	Name	Description
int	AddRow()	Adds a new row to a query. Returns the index of the row added to the query results.
CCFXStringSet *	GetColumns()	Returns a list of the queries column names as a CF List.
LPCSTR	GetData	Returns a data element from (int row,int col) a query at location row,col.
LPCSTR	GetName()	Returns the name of a query.
int	GetRowCount()	Returns the number of rows in the query.
void	SetData	Sets a data element within a (int row,int col) query (LPCSTR dat).
void	SetQueryString	Sets the query string to be (LPCSTR query) displayed in debug mode.
void	SetTotalTime	Sets the number of (DWORD dwms) milliseconds required to process the query to be displayed in debug output.

Use the CCFXRequest functions listed in Table 35.5 to operate on the CCFXRequest object auto-matically passed to your CFX tag ProcessTagRequest() function by the Cold Fusion process. No further instantiations of CCFXRequest objects are required to begin using these functions. The following code snippet demonstrates the initial instantiation of CCFXRequest pointer pRequest and the subsequent application of methods CCFXRequest::GetQuery() and CCFXRequest::ThrowException().

```
void ProcessTagRequest( CCFXRequest* pRequest )
{
try
{

// retrieve the query name passed to the tag
CCFXQuery* pQuery = pRequest->GetQuery();

if ( pQuery == NULL) {
pRequest->ThrowException(
"Missing QUERY parameter",
"You must pass a QUERY parameter for"
"this function to work properly.");
}
```

Table 35.5 *CCFXRequest* Functions

Return Type	Name	Description
CCFXQuery*	AddQuery	Adds a query to the calling (LPCSTR qname, template. CCFXStringSet* pCols).
BOOL	AttributeExists	Returns true or false based on (LPCSTR lpszName) whether the attribute lpszName was passed to the CFX tag.
CCFXStringSet*	CreateStringSet()	Creates a new instance of a list (string set).
BOOL	Debug()	Checks to see whether the tag contains the debug attribute.
LPCSTR	GetAttribute	Returns the value of the (LPCSTR lpszname) passed attribute.
CCFXStringSet	GetAttributeList()	Returns a list of all attribute names passed to a CFX tag as a list object (comma-delimited string).
void	GetCustomData()	Retrieves tag specific data for the request (see SetCustomData()).
CCFXQuery*	GetQuery()	Returns the query specified as the QUERY attribute passed to the tag.

continues

Part

IV

Ch

35

Table 35.5   Continued

Return Type	Name	Description
LPCSTR	GetSetting	Returns the value of a custom (LPCSTR SettingName) tag setting, stored in a Registry key.
void	ReThrowExeception	Re-initiates an error trap [CCFXException* (error occurred during exception) processing].
void	SetCustomData()	Attaches a data element to a (LPVOID lpvData) request. This data element can then be referenced using GetCustomData().
void	SetVariable	Sets a variable in the calling (LPCSTR lpszName, template. Analogous to LPCSTR lpszVal) <CFSET>.
void	ThrowException	Throws an exception and ends (LPCSTR lpszError, processing of the request. LPC lpszDiag).
void	Write	Outputs text to the user's (LPCSTR lpszOutput) browser.
void	WriteDebug	Outputs text to the user's browser (LPCSTR lpszOutput) if the DEBUG attribute is passed to the tag.

CCFXStringSet class functions are analogous to Cold Fusion list functions. Before you can use the methods listed in Table 35.6, you must instantiate a CCFXStringSet by using the CCFXRequest::CreateStringSet() function.

Table 35.6   *CCFXStringSet* Classes

Return Type	Syntax	Function
int	AddString	Adds a string to the end of (LPCSTR stringval) the list and returns its index
int	GetCount()	Returns the number of elements in the list
LPCSTR	GetString(int index)	Returns the string value located at index
int	GetIndexForString	Finds the string stringval in (LPCSTR stringval) the list and returns its location index

CCFXQuery

The CCFXQuery class contains functions that enable you to manipulate query result sets.

CCFXQuery: AddRow　　AddRow adds a new row to a query result set and returns the index of the row appended. No parameters are required.

Queries may either be passed to a tag using the QUERY attribute or created using the CCFXRequest::AddQuery function.

Listing 35.4 demonstrates a technique for adding a row to a query result set containing the fields Lastname and Firstname.

On the CD

> **Listing 35.4　ADDROW\REQUEST.CPP—Adding a Row to a Cold Fusion Query Result Set Is Easy**

```
// retrieve the query name passed to the tag
CCFXQuery* pQuery = pRequest->GetQuery();

if ( pQuery == NULL) {
pRequest->ThrowException(
"Missing QUERY parameter",
"You must pass a QUERY parameter for"
"this function to work properly.");
}

// check to make sure the lastname,firstname columns
// exist and get their locations

CCFXStringSet* pColumns = pquery->GetColumns;
int lnamelocation = pColumns->GetIndexForString("LASTNAME");
if (lnamelocation == CFX_STRING_NOT_FOUND ) {
pRequest->ThrowException(
"Missing Column: LASTNAME");
}

int fnamelocation = pColumns->GetIndexForString("FIRSTNAME");
if (fnamelocation == CFX_STRING_NOT_FOUND ) {
pRequest->ThrowException(
"Missing Column: FIRSTNAME");
}

// add the row

int newrowindex=pQuery->AddRow();
pQuery->SetData(lnamelocation,newrowindex,"Drucker");
        pQuery->SetData(fnamelocation,newrowindex,"Steven");
```

CCFXQuery::GetColumns　　The GetColumns() function returns the list of column names contained in a query result set.

No parameters are required.

Part
IV

Ch
35

The column names are returned as an object of class CCFXStringSet and may be accessed by any of the functions contained in Table 35.5. Any memory allocated for storing the string set is automatically freed by Cold Fusion after the CFX tag finishes processing.

Listing 35.5 demonstrates a technique to output the list of columns in a query result set in comma delimited format.

On the CD

Listing 35.5   GETCOLUMNS\REQUEST.CPP—The *getcolumns()* Function Retrieves the List of Column Names as a *CCFXStringSet* Object from a *QueryResult* Set

```
// get a pointer to the query passed to the tag
CCFXQuery* pQuery = pRequest->GetQuery();

if ( pQuery == NULL) {
pRequest->ThrowException(
"Missing QUERY parameter",
"You must pass a QUERY parameter for"
"this function to work properly.");
}

// get the column names
CCFXStringSet* pColumns = pquery->GetColumns;
int numcolumns = pColumns->GetCount();

// output the column list in comma delimited format
for (int i=1; i<=numcolumns; i++){
pRequest->Write (pColumns->GetString(i)) ;
if (i<numcolumns) {
pRequest->Write(",");
}
          }
```

CCFXQuery::GetData   Getdata(int *iRow*, int *iColumn*) returns a data element from the specified row and column of a query result set.

Parameter *iRow* is the row index of the item you wish to retrieve. Parameter *iColumn* corresponds to the column of the item you wish to retrieve. Both are integer values. The starting value for row and column location indices is 1.

CCFXQuery::GetRowCount returns the number of rows in a query result set. Retrieving the number of columns in a set is a two-step process. First, you must retrieve the list of the query's column names into a string set variable by using the CCFXQuery::GetColumns function. The number of columns can then be ascertained by calling the CCFXStringSet::GetCount function on the resulting string set.

Listing 35.6 uses the GetData function to output a query result set in HTML table format.

Listing 35.6 GETDATA\REQUEST.CPP—Using the *GetData* Function, You Can Create Your Own Customized *<CFOUTPUT>* Tag

```
// retrieve the query passed to the tag
CCFXQuery* pQuery = pRequest->GetQuery();

if ( pQuery == NULL) {
pRequest->ThrowException(
"Missing QUERY parameter",
"You must pass a QUERY parameter for"
"this function to work properly.");
}

// check row count
if (pQuery->GetRowCount() > 0){

// get column information
CCFXStringSet* pColumns = pQuery->GetColumns();
int nNumColumns = pColumns->GetCount();

// Write out table column headings
pRequest->Write("<TABLE WIDTH=100% BORDER=1>\n");
for (int i=1; i<=nNumColumns; i++) {
pRequest->Write("");
pRequest->Write( pColumns->GetString(i));
pRequest->Write("</TH>\n");
}

// Write out data elements
for (i=1; i<=pQuery->GetRowCount(); i++) {
pRequest->Write("<TR>\n");
for (int j=1; j<=nNumColumns; j++) {
pRequest->Write("<TD>\n");
pRequest->Write(pQuery->GetData(i,j));
pRequest->Write("</TD>\n");
}
pRequest->Write("</TR>\n");
}
pRequest->Write("</TABLE>");
            } // rowcount == 0
```

CCFXQuery::GetName   The GetName() function returns the name of the query passed to the tag. The query's name is returned as a read-only 32-bit string pointer (LPCSTR). Only one query may be passed to a CFX tag through the QUERY attribute.

No parameters are required.

Listing 35.7 retrieves the name of the query and writes it to the user's browser while demonstrating string concatenation using the MFC class CString.

Listing 35.7   GETNAME\REQUEST.CPP—The *GetName()* Function Returns the Name of the Query Passed to the CFX Tag

```cpp
try
{
// retrieve the query passed to the tag
CCFXQuery* pQuery = pRequest->GetQuery();

if ( pQuery == NULL) {
pRequest->ThrowException(
"Missing QUERY parameter",
"You must pass a QUERY parameter for"
"this function to work properly.");
}

CString outstr( "The name of the query passed to this CFX tag is: " );
pRequest->Write(outstr + CString(pQuery->GetName()));

// Output optional debug info
if ( pRequest->Debug() )
{
pRequest->WriteDebug( "Debug info..." ) ;
}
    }
```

CCFXQuery::GetRowCount   The GetRowCount() function is analogous to the CFML attribute query.recordcount. They both return the number of rows in the query result set as an integer value.

No parameters are required.

In Listing 35.8, GetRowCount() is used in conjunction with CCFXQuery::GetData to sum a column of values and output the result.

Listing 35.8   GETROWCOUNT\REQUEST.CPP—Use the *GetRowCount* Function to Set the Range for Scanning a Query Result Set

```cpp
double ltotal = 0;

// retrieve the query passed to the tag
CCFXQuery* pQuery = pRequest->GetQuery();

if ( pQuery == NULL) {
pRequest->ThrowException(
"Missing QUERY parameter",
"You must pass a QUERY parameter for"
"this function to work properly.");
}

// verify that the column exists & get its location
CCFXStringSet* pColumns = pQuery->GetColumns();
int totcolumn = pColumns->GetIndexForString("TOTAL");
```

```
if (totcolumn == CFX_STRING_NOT_FOUND ) {
pRequest->ThrowException(
"Missing Column: TOTAL",
"Your query must contain a column named TOTAL");
}

// read through the column values and sum their values
// note: GetData() returns all query values as strings
// therefore you must use the strtod() function to convert
// from string to decimal.

for (int i=1; i<=pQuery->GetRowCount(); i++) {
ltotal=ltotal + atof(pQuery->GetData(i,totcolumn));
}

// Now that you have to total in decimal (double) format,
// you've got to convert it back to a string for output.
// sprintf() allows you to format a string just like you would
// format output

char outstr[256];
sprintf( outstr, "%9.2f", ltotal);

// output the total to the user

        pRequest->Write(outstr);
```

CCFXQuery::SetData   The SetData(int *iRow*, int *iColumn*, LPCSTR *lpszData*) function sets a data element in a query result set at location(*iRow*,*iColumn*) as *lpszData*.

Parameter *iRow* is the row index of the item you wish to set. Parameter *iColumn* corresponds to the column of the item you wish to set. Both are integer values. The origin of a query result matrix is located at coordinates 1,1.

Before attempting to set a data element, you should verify the location exists in the result table. Use CCFXQuery::GetRowCount to return the maximum row coordinate in the matrix. Similarly, using CCFXQuery::GetColumns() in conjunction with CCFXStringSet::GetCount returns the maximum column coordinate to accomplish this task.

If you are appending new rows, your call to SetData must be preceded by a call to CCFXQuery::AddRow(). AddRow() appends a blank row to the result set and returns the row coordinate you will then pass to SetData(). (See Listing 35.9.)

On the CD

Listing 35.9   SETDATA\REQUEST.CPP—The *CCFXQuery::SetData* Function Gives You the Capability to Build any Query Result Set

```
int dispyear, dispmonth, daysinmonth;
int irow=0;
CTime ctdatetime;
CString str;
```

Part
IV

Ch
35

continues

Listing 35.9   Continued

```
str.GetBuffer(3);

// define days of week
CCFXStringSet* daysofweek=pRequest->CreateStringSet();
daysofweek->AddString("Sunday");
daysofweek->AddString("Monday");
daysofweek->AddString("Tuesday");
daysofweek->AddString("Wednesday");
daysofweek->AddString("Thursday");
daysofweek->AddString("Friday");
daysofweek->AddString("Saturday");

// create query
CCFXQuery* calquery=pRequest->AddQuery("Calendar",daysofweek);

// initialization
if (pRequest->AttributeExists("MONTH")
➥&& pRequest-_>AttributeExists("YEAR")) {
dispmonth=atoi(pRequest->GetAttribute("MONTH"));
dispyear=atoi(pRequest->GetAttribute("YEAR"));
if (dispmonth < 1 ¦¦ dispmonth > 12) {
pRequest->ThrowException(
"Invalid Value: MONTH attribute",
"The MONTH attribute must be a number between 1 and _12");
}
if (dispyear < 1900 ¦¦ dispyear > 2100) {
pRequest->ThrowException(
"Invalid Value: YEAR attribute",
"The YEAR attribute must be in the range 1900-2100");
}
}
else {

CTime currenttime = CTime::GetCurrentTime();
dispyear=currenttime.GetYear();
dispmonth=currenttime.GetMonth();

}

// figure out # of days in month
switch( dispmonth ) {
case 2:
daysinmonth=28;
case 4:
daysinmonth=30;
case 6:
daysinmonth=30;
case 9:
daysinmonth=30;
case 11:
daysinmonth=30;
default :
daysinmonth=31;
}
```

```
// add first row to query
irow=calquery->AddRow();

for (int i=1;i<=daysinmonth; i++) {
ctdatetime = CTime(dispyear,dispmonth,i,0,0,0);
if (ctdatetime.GetDayOfWeek()==1) {
irow=calquery->AddRow();
}
str.Format("%d",i);
calquery->SetData(ctdatetime.GetDayOfWeek(),irow,str);
        }
```

CCFXQuery::SetQueryString   The SetQueryString(LPCSTR *lpszQuery*) function sets the query string to be displayed for the tag when the Show Debug Info for Queries box is checked in the Cold Fusion Administrator (depicted in Figure 35.9).

Parameter *lpszQuery* is the text string you want to display in the debug output for the tag.

In listing 35.10, the list of attributes and values passed to the CFX tag are output in debug mode where the SQL query would appear.

On the CD

> **Listing 35.10   SETQUERYSTRING\REQUEST.CPP—You Can Dynamically Modify the Debug Output for Your CFX Tag to Include the Attributes Passed to It**

```
CString Outputstr("Attributes:");

// retrieve the query passed to the tag
CCFXQuery* pQuery = pRequest->GetQuery();

if ( pQuery == NULL) {
pRequest->ThrowException(
"Missing QUERY parameter",
"You must pass a QUERY parameter for"
"this function to work properly.");
}

// get the list of attributes passed to the tag
CCFXStringSet* tagAttributes=pRequest->GetAttributeList();

// extract the attributes and place in a string object
for (int i=1; i<= tagAttributes->GetCount(); i++) {
Outputstr+=(CString)tagAttributes->GetString(i);
Outputstr+="=";
Outputstr+=(CString)pRequest->GetAttribute(tagAttributes-_>GetString(i));
if (i<tagAttributes->GetCount()) {
Outputstr+=",";
}
}

// Set the Query String
        pQuery->SetQueryString(Outputstr);
```

CCFXQuery::SetTotalTime The SetTotalTime(DWORD *dwMilliseconds*) function enables you to set the debug output variable flag for the amount of time the system spent processing the CFX tag.

The parameter *dwMilliseconds* is an integer specifying the number of milliseconds spent processing the tag. It can be calculated by using the function GetTickCount() that returns the number of milliseconds that elapsed because Windows was started. To protect against possible numeric overflow, the variable used to contain the elapsed time should be of type DWORD, a 32-bit unsigned integer with a maximum value of 4,294,967,295.

Listing 35.11 demonstrates a methodology to calculate elapsed time.

On the CD

Listing 35.11 SETTOTALTIME\REQUEST.CPP—Using the
***CCFXQuery::SetTotalTime()* Function and the *GetTickCount()* Function,**
You Can Track the Length of Time Your Tag Took to Execute

```
DWORD dwResult;

// get the current time
DWORD starttime = GetTickCount();

// do some processing...

// retrieve the query passed to the tag
CCFXQuery* pQuery = pRequest->GetQuery();

if ( pQuery == NULL) {
pRequest->ThrowException(
"Missing QUERY parameter",
"You must pass a QUERY parameter for"
"this function to work properly.");
}

pRequest->Write("Time for a donut!  Why you ask?
➥It's always a _>fine time for a donut!");

// subtract the currenttime from the start time
dwResult=GetTickCount() - starttime;

// set the elapsed time for debug output
        pQuery->SetTotalTime(dwResult);
```

CCFXStringSet

CCFXStringSet is an abstract class representing a comma delimited string set, analogous to a Cold Fusion list. Elements in the set are referenced by numeric index with the head of the list bearing an index of 1. Member functions bear a striking similarity to Cold Fusion list functions. CCFXStringSet objects are integral in creating new queries, retrieving column names from a passed query, and retrieving the list of attributes passed to a tag. To instantiate a new CCFXStringSet object, you must use CCFXRequest::CreateStringSet.

CCFXStringSet::AddString()   The CCFXStringSet::AddString(LPCSTR *lpszString*) function adds a new element to the end of a string set, returning its location in the list as an integer.

The parameter *lpszString* is the string value to be added to the list.

Listing 35.12 demonstrates the creation of a CCFXStringSet in order to facilitate the creation of a new query.

Listing 35.12   ADDSTRINGREQUEST.CPP—Use of the *AddString* Function Is Necessary in Order to Create a New Query

```
// define days of week
CCFXStringSet* daysofweek=pRequest->CreateStringSet();
daysofweek->AddString("Sunday");
daysofweek->AddString("Monday");
daysofweek->AddString("Tuesday");
daysofweek->AddString("Wednesday");
daysofweek->AddString("Thursday");
daysofweek->AddString("Friday");
daysofweek->AddString("Saturday");

// create query
        CCFXQuery* calquery=
➥pRequest->AddQuery("Calendar",daysofweek);
```

CCFXStringSet::GetCount()   The CCFXStringSet::GetCount() function retrieves the number of entries in the string set as an integer value.

No parameters are required.

Listing 35.13 demonstrates using the GetCount() function to retrieve a list of query column headings and print them out as HTML table headings.

Listing 35.13   GETCOUNT\REQUEST.CPP—You Can Use the *GetColumns()* Function to Iterate Through a List of Strings

```
// retrieve the query passed to the tag
CCFXQuery* pQuery = pRequest->GetQuery();

if ( pQuery == NULL) {
pRequest->ThrowException(
"Missing QUERY parameter",
"You must pass a QUERY parameter for"
"this function to work properly.");
}

// get column information
CCFXStringSet* pColumns = pQuery->GetColumns();
int nNumColumns = pColumns->GetCount();
```

Part
IV

Ch
35

continues

Listing 35.13 Continued

```
// Write out table column headings
for (int i=1; i<=nNumColumns; i++) {
pRequest->Write("");
pRequest->Write( pColumns->GetString(i));
pRequest->Write("</TH>\n");
        }
```

CCFXStringSet::GetString()   The CCFXStringSet::GetString(int *iindex*) function retrieves an individual string from a stringset.

Parameter *iindex* is an integer value corresponding to the location of the string in the string set you wish to retrieve.

Listing 35.14 demonstrates using the GetString() function to output a query's column headings as HTML table headers.

Listing 35.14 GETCOUNT/REQUEST.CPP—Using the *GetString()* Function, You Can Retrieve the Individual Strings that Form a String Set

```
// retrieve the query passed to the tag
CCFXQuery* pQuery = pRequest->GetQuery();

if ( pQuery == NULL) {
pRequest->ThrowException(
"Missing QUERY parameter",
"You must pass a QUERY parameter for"
"this function to work properly.");
}

// get column information
CCFXStringSet* pColumns = pQuery->GetColumns();
int nNumColumns = pColumns->GetCount();

// Write out table column headings
for (int i=1; i<=nNumColumns; i++) {
pRequest->Write("");
pRequest->Write( pColumns->GetString(i));
pRequest->Write("</TH>\n");
        }
```

CCFXStringSet::GetIndexForString()   The function CCFXStringSet::
GetIndexForString(LPCSTR *lpszString*) searches for the string lpszString within a string set and, if found, returns its location as an integer value.

The parameter *lpszString* is the character string you are searching for. If lpszString is not found in the string set, GetIndexForString() returns the constant CFX_STRING_NOT_FOUND.

Listing 35.15 utilizes the GetIndexForString function to locate the position of a passed-in column name and sums all the values within that column.

Listing 35.15 GETINDEXFORSTRING\REQUEST.CPP—You Can Use the
***GetIndexForString()* Function to Verify that a Particular Attribute Was Passed**
to Your CFX Tag

```
double ltotal=0;

// retrieve the query passed to the tag
CCFXQuery* pQuery = pRequest->GetQuery();

if ( pQuery == NULL) {
pRequest->ThrowException(
"Missing QUERY parameter",
"You must pass a QUERY parameter for"
"this function to work properly.");
}


if (pRequest->AttributeExists("FIELDNAME")==FALSE)
{
pRequest->ThrowException("Attribute FIELDNAME not found.",
"The FIELDNAME attribute is required by this tag");
}

// get id of column to sum
CCFXStringSet *pColumns = pQuery->GetColumns();
int icol=pColumns->GetIndexForString(pRequest-_>GetAttribute("FIELDNAME"));

if (icol==CFX_STRING_NOT_FOUND) {
CString Errmsg="Column " + (CString) (pRequest-_>GetAttribute("FIELDNAME"));
Errmsg+=" not found in query";
pRequest->ThrowException(Errmsg,"The query must contain a _column
➥with the same name as the passed attribute FIELDNAME");
}
// sum up column
for (int i=1; i<=pQuery->GetRowCount();i++) {
ltotal+=atof(pQuery->GetData(i,icol));
}

// Convert total to a string
char outstr[256];
sprintf( outstr, "%9.2f", ltotal);

// output the total to the user
        pRequest->Write(outstr);
```

CCFXRequest

Functions in the CCFXRequest class give you the capability to output HTML, create queries and
stringsets, create and manipulate <CFSET> variables, access the contents of attributes passed to
a tag, and throw exceptions. There is also a facility to attach a data element to a request so that
it may be read wherever a valid pointer to the request exists.

CCFXRequest::AddQuery   The CCFXRequest::AddQuery(LPCSTR *lpszName*, CCFXStringSet *pColumns*) function creates a new query that is accessible by the Cold Fusion template invoking the tag. Once the query is created, its data may be accessed within the .CFM file through standard CFML techniques.

Parameter *lpszName* is a string containing the name you wish to assign to the new query. The name must be unique within the scope of the calling template. Parameter *pColumns* is a CCFXStringSet defining the column names of the query.

Listing 35.16 demonstrates using AddQuery() to create a query named Calendar, containing columns named the days of the week.

Listing 35.16   \SETDATA\REQUEST.CPP—Using the CFAPI, You Can Create our Own Handcrafted Query Result Set

```
// define days of week
CCFXStringSet* daysofweek=pRequest->CreateStringSet();
daysofweek->AddString("Sunday");
daysofweek->AddString("Monday");
daysofweek->AddString("Tuesday");
daysofweek->AddString("Wednesday");
daysofweek->AddString("Thursday");
daysofweek->AddString("Friday");
daysofweek->AddString("Saturday");

// create query
        CCFXQuery* calquery=p
➥Request->AddQuery("Calendar",daysofweek);
```

CCFXRequest::AttributeExists   Use the CCFXRequest::AttributeExists(LPCSTR *lpszName*) function to perform a case insensitive search to verify whether or not an attribute was passed to your CFX tag. If the attribute is present, the Boolean value TRUE is returned, otherwise the function returns FALSE.

Parameter *lpszName* is a string containing the name of the parameter you wish to verify.

Listing 35.17 demonstrates the use of this function by verifying that the attribute Fieldname was passed to the tag. If it was not passed, an exception is raised.

Listing 35.17   GETINDEXFORSTRING\REQUEST.CPP—Use the AttributeExists() Function to Verify if an Attribute Was Passed to a CFX Tag

```
if (pRequest->AttributeExists("FIELDNAME")==FALSE)
{
pRequest->ThrowException("Attribute FIELDNAME not found.",
"The FIELDNAME attribute is required by this tag");
        }
```

CCFXRequest::CreateStringSet   Use `CCFXRequest::CreateStringSet` to instantiate a new string set. `CCFXRequest` objects are similar in structure to Cold Fusion lists. Structurally, they are a list of comma delimited strings. Functionally, they play an important role in creating new queries, retrieving the names of a query's columns, and deriving a list of attributes passed to your CFX tag.

No parameters are required. `CreateStringSet` allocates memory and returns a pointer to a new string set object. The memory allocated for the string set is automatically freed once the CFX tag finishes executing. (See Listing 35.18.)

On the CD

Listing 35.18 \SETDATA\REQUEST.CPP—Use *CreateStringSet* to Instantiate a Comma-Delimited List of Values

```
// define days of week
CCFXStringSet* daysofweek=pRequest->CreateStringSet();
daysofweek->AddString("Sunday");
daysofweek->AddString("Monday");
daysofweek->AddString("Tuesday");
daysofweek->AddString("Wednesday");
daysofweek->AddString("Thursday");
daysofweek->AddString("Friday");
daysofweek->AddString("Saturday");

// create query
        CCFXQuery* calquery=pRequest->AddQuery("Calendar",
➥daysofweek);
```

CCFXRequest::Debug   Use the `CCFXRequest::Debug()` function to determine whether the DEBUG attribute has been passed to your CFX tag.

No parameters are required. `Debug()` returns the Boolean value TRUE if the DEBUG attribute is present. Otherwise it returns FALSE.

Listing 35.19 checks to see if the DEBUG has been passed to a CFX tag.

On the CD

Listing 35.19 DEBUG\REQUEST.CPP—You Can Use the *DEBUG* Function to Determine Whether or Not Your Tag Should Output Debugging Information

```
if (pRequest->Debug()) {
pRequest->WriteDebug("This tag created
➥by Steven D. Drucker @ Fig Leaf Software");
pRequest->WriteDebug("Copyright 1996, all rights reserved.");
pRequest->WriteDebug("E-mail info@figleaf.com for more information");
}
```

CCFXRequest::GetAttribute   The `CCFXRequest::GetAttribute(LPCSTR lpszName)` function returns the value of attribute *lpszName* as a string.

Part
IV

Ch
35

Parameter *lpszName* is the case insensitive name of the attribute you want to retrieve. If the attribute was not passed to the tag, the function returns the empty string.

Listing 35.20 utilizes GetAttribute() to retrieve the values of two attributes, MONTH and YEAR. The values are subsequently converted to integers using the atoi() function and verified for accuracy.

Listing 35.20   SETDATA\REQUEST.CPP—Use the *GetAttribute()* Function to Retrieve the Value of an Attribute Passed to a Tag

```
dispmonth=atoi(pRequest->GetAttribute("MONTH"));
dispyear=atoi(pRequest->GetAttribute("YEAR"));
if (dispmonth < 1 ¦¦ dispmonth > 12) {
pRequest->ThrowException(
"Invalid Value: MONTH attribute",
"The MONTH attribute must be a number between 1 and _12");
}
if (dispyear < 1900 ¦¦ dispyear > 2100) {
pRequest->ThrowException(
"Invalid Value: YEAR attribute",
"The YEAR attribute must be in the range 1900-2100");
                    }
```

CCFXRequest::GetAttributeList   The function CCFXRequest::GetAttributeList() returns a list of all the attributes passed to a custom tag as a CCFXStringSet.

No parameters are required.

Listing 35.21 demonstrates using the GetAttributeList() function to retrieve a list of attributes and then output the attributes and their values in the debug stream.

Listing 35.21   SETQUERYSTRING\REQUEST.CPP—The *GetAttributeList()* Function Returns the List of All Attributes Passed to a Tag as a *CCFXStringSet*

```
// get the list of attributes passed to the tag
CCFXStringSet* tagAttributes=pRequest->GetAttributeList();
// extract the attributes and place in a string object
for (int i=1; i<= tagAttributes->GetCount(); i++) {
Outputstr+=(CString)tagAttributes->GetString(i);
Outputstr+="=";
Outputstr+=(CString)pRequest->GetAttribute(tagAttributes-_>GetString(i));
if (i<tagAttributes->GetCount()) {
Outputstr+=",";
}
}

// Set the Query String
        pQuery->SetQueryString(Outputstr);
```

CCFXRequest::GetCustomData   The CFAPI enables you to simplify passing parameters between your C classes and functions through the use of `GetCustomData` and `SetCustomData`. Using these two functions, you can define a single data object containing multiple fields and attach it directly to the `CCFXRequest`. The `CCCFXRequest::GetCustomData()` function retrieves the data structure you attached to a request. Conversely, the `CCFXRequest::SetCustomData` function attaches a data structure to a request.

No parameters are required. `GetCustomData` returns a generic pointer to a data object (`LPVOID`).

For more information, see `CCFXRequest::SetCustomData` under this heading.

CCFXRequest::GetQuery   The `CCFXRequest::GetQuery` enables you to access a query data set. The function returns a pointer to a `CCFXQuery` object. Queries are passed to your CFX tag in a .CFM template by using the `QUERY` attribute.

No parameters are required. If no query was passed to the CFX tag, `GetQuery` returns `NULL`.

Listing 35.23 demonstrates using `GetQuery` to create a pointer to a valid `CCFXQuery` object. If no query attribute was passed to the tag, an exception is raised, ending processing of the tag.

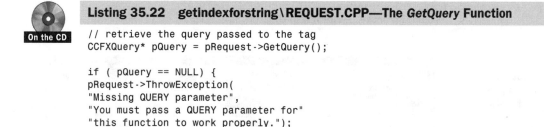

Listing 35.22   getindexforstring\REQUEST.CPP—The *GetQuery* Function

```
// retrieve the query passed to the tag
CCFXQuery* pQuery = pRequest->GetQuery();

if ( pQuery == NULL) {
pRequest->ThrowException(
"Missing QUERY parameter",
"You must pass a QUERY parameter for"
"this function to work properly.");
            }
```

Once the `GetQuery` function successfully executes, you may use functions in the `CCFXQuery` class to access data in the query.

CCFXRequest::GetSetting   The `CCFXRequest::GetSetting(LPCSTR lpszSettingName)` function enables you to retrieve the value of any tag setting stored within the `CustomTags` section of the Cold Fusion Registry key.

The parameter *lpszSettingName* is a string containing the name of the setting you wish to retrieve. It is case insensitive. If the specified custom tag setting exists, `GetSetting` returns its value as a string. If it does not exist, an empty string is returned.

Listing 35.24 demonstrates using the `GetSetting` function to retrieve and display the values of settings for the `GetSetting` CFX tag 9 (see Figure 35.13).

Listing 35.23   GETSETTING\REQUEST.CPP—*GetSetting* Allows You to Retrieve Registry Settings for Your CFX Tag

```
        CString CacheLibrary=pRequest->GetSetting("CACHELIBRARY");
CString Description=pRequest->GetSetting("DESCRIPTION");
        CString LibraryPath=pRequest->GetSetting("LIBRARYPATH");
CString ProcedureName=pRequest->GetSetting("PROCEDURENAME");

// output back to user

pRequest->Write("Cache Library:");
pRequest->Write(CacheLibrary);
pRequest->Write("<BR>\n");

pRequest->Write("Description:");
pRequest->Write(Description);
pRequest->Write("<BR>\n");

pRequest->Write("Library Path:");
pRequest->Write(LibraryPath);
pRequest->Write("<BR>\n");

pRequest->Write("Procedure Name:");
pRequest->Write(ProcedureName);
        pRequest->Write("<BR>\n");
```

FIG. 35.13

The GetSetting function allows you to retrieve the values of tag-specific entries stored in the Windows NT Registry.

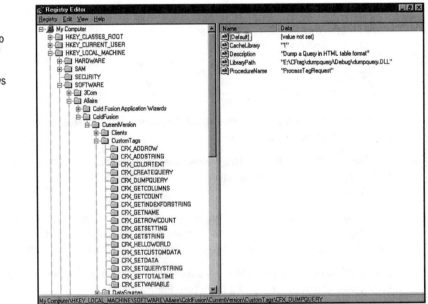

CCFXRequest::ReThrowException CCFXRequest::ReThrowException(CCFXException* e) ensures that C++ exceptions thrown by your code do not adversely affect the Cold Fusion process. By structuring your code using try and catch blocks in a manner similar to Listing 35.25, you can trap all exceptions that occur, end processing of the tag gracefully, and display an error message to the user.

On the CD

Listing 35.24   REQUEST.CPP—Code Structuring to Trap C++ Runtime Errors in Your Tag

```
try
{
// perform some procesing
}

// Catch Cold Fusion exceptions & re-raise them
catch( CCFXException* e )
{
pRequest->ReThrowException( e ) ;
}

// Catch ALL other exceptions and throw them as
// Cold Fusion exceptions (DO NOT REMOVE! --
// this prevents the server from crashing in
// case of an unexpected exception)
catch( ... )
{
pRequest->ThrowException(
"Error occurred in tag",
"Unexpected error occurred while processing tag." ) ;
    }
```

CCFXRequest::SetCustomData   The SetCustomData(LPVOID *lpvdata*) function enables you to attach a pointer to a data structure to be passed along with the request to functions you define within your CFX tag.

Parameter *lpvdata* is a pointer to your data structure. The function returns no value.

Listing 35.26 demonstrates using SetCustomData to pass along information to a subroutine that, in turn, outputs the data to the user.

On the CD

Listing 35.25   SETCUSTOMDATA\REQUEST.CPP—*SetCustomData* Helps You Pass Information Between Functions

```
#include "stdafx.h"          // Standard MFC libraries
#include "cfx.h"             // CFX Custom Tag API

struct MYSTRUCTURE {         // Declare the data structure
char lastname[50];
```

continues

Part
IV

Ch
35

Listing 35.25 Continued

```
char firstname[50];
int age;
};


void MyFunc(CCFXRequest* pRequest) {

try
{
MYSTRUCTURE* PersonData =
(MYSTRUCTURE*)pRequest->GetCustomData();

pRequest->Write(PersonData->lastname);
pRequest->Write(",");
pRequest->Write(PersonData->firstname);

}

// Catch Cold Fusion exceptions & re-raise them
catch( CCFXException* e )
{
pRequest->ReThrowException( e ) ;
}

// Catch ALL other exceptions and throw them as
// Cold Fusion exceptions (DO NOT REMOVE! --
// this prevents the server from crashing in
// case of an unexpected exception)
catch( ... )
{
pRequest->ThrowException(
"Error occurred in tag CFX_SETCUSTOMDATA",
"Unexpected error occurred while processing tag." ) ;
}
}


void ProcessTagRequest( CCFXRequest* pRequest )
{
try
{

MYSTRUCTURE employeedata;

strcpy (employeedata.lastname,"Drucker");
strcpy (employeedata.firstname,"Steve");
employeedata.age=27;


pRequest->SetCustomData((LPVOID) &employeedata );


MyFunc(pRequest);
```

```
// Output optional debug info
if ( pRequest->Debug() )
{
pRequest->WriteDebug( "Debug info..." ) ;
}
}

// Catch Cold Fusion exceptions & re-raise them
catch( CCFXException* e )
{
pRequest->ReThrowException( e ) ;
}

// Catch ALL other exceptions and throw them as
// Cold Fusion exceptions (DO NOT REMOVE! --
// this prevents the server from crashing in
// case of an unexpected exception)
catch( ... )
{
pRequest->ThrowException(
"Error occurred in tag CFX_SETCUSTOMDATA",
"Unexpected error occurred while processing tag." ) ;
}
}
```

CCFXRequest::SetVariable   The function CCFXRequest::SetVariable(LPCSTR *lpszName*, LPCSTR *lpszValue*) sets a variable in the calling template. It is functionally equivalent to issuing a <CFSET> in your template.

Parameter *lpszName* is a string containing the name of the form variable you wish to create. *LpszValue* is a string representing the initialization value of the variable. If the variable already exists on the form, its value is replaced with *lpszvalue*.

Listing 35.26 demonstrates using the SetVariable function to return the current time and date as the form variable TimeIn.

On the CD

Listing 35.26   SETVARIABLE\REQUEST.CPP—Use the *SetVariable* Function to Return Values to the Calling Template

```
// Get the current time
CTime currenttime;
currenttime = CTime::GetCurrentTime();

// format the current time as a string
CString setstr =currenttime.Format( "%A, %B %d, %Y" );

// create the form variable TimeIn
        pRequest->SetVariable("TimeIn",setstr);
```

Part
IV

Ch
35

CCFXRequest::ThrowException The CCFXRequest::ThrowException(LPCSTR *lpszError*, LPCSTR *lpszDiagnostics*) function throws an exception, outputting the string parameters *lpszError* and *lpszDiagnostics* to the user. Further processing of the request is canceled once a ThrowException function is encountered.

Parameter *lpszError* is a string containing a short, identifying error message. Use the *lpszDiagnostics* parameter to output additional diagnostic information.

Listing 35.28 executes the ThrowException function as a result of the user failing to pass a query to your CFX tag. Figure 35.14 demonstrates the subsequent error message that the user receives.

On the CD

Listing 35.27 THROWEXCEPTIO\REQUEST.CPP—Use the *ThrowException* Function to Trap Errors in Your CFX Tags

```
// retrieve the query passed to the tag
CCFXQuery* pQuery = pRequest->GetQuery();

if ( pQuery == NULL) {
pRequest->ThrowException(
"Missing QUERY parameter",
"You must pass a QUERY parameter for"
"this function to work properly.");
        }
```

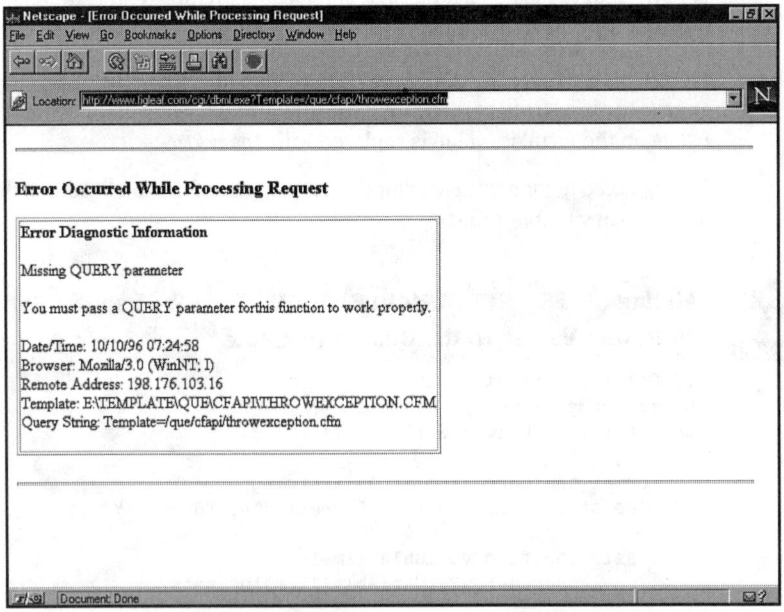

FIG. 35.14

The ThrowException function traps errors and outputs your own custom error message.

Netscape - [Error Occurred While Processing Request]

File Edit View Go Bookmarks Options Directory Window Help

Location: http://www.figleaf.com/cgi/dbml.exe?Template=/que/cfapi/throwexception.cfm

Error Occurred While Processing Request

Error Diagnostic Information

Missing QUERY parameter

You must pass a QUERY parameter for this function to work properly.

Date/Time: 10/10/96 07:24:58
Browser: Mozilla/3.0 (WinNT; I)
Remote Address: 198.176.103.16
Template: E:\TEMPLATE\QUE\CFAPI\THROWEXCEPTION.CFM
Query String: Template=/que/cfapi/throwexception.cfm

Document: Done

CCFXRequest::Write Use the `CCFXRequest::Write(LPCSTR lpszOutput)` function to output text to the user.

Parameter `lpszOutput` is a string containing the text you wish to output. The function returns no value.

Use the C function `sprintf()` or the MFC function `CString::Format()` function to convert numeric values to strings. (See Listing 35.28.)

On the CD

Listing 35.28   REQUEST.CPP—You Can Send Custom Output to the User by Invoking the *CCFXRequest::Write* Function

```
double myval=22.44;

CString str;      // Instantiate the string object
str.GetBuffer(1024);

str.Format("%d", myval);     // convert the number to a string

pRequest->Write(str);             // output the string to the user
```

CCFXRequest::WriteDebug Use the `CCFXRequest::WriteDebug(LPCSTR lpszOutput)` function to output data into the debug stream buffer. Debug information displays to the user only if the DEBUG attribute passes to the tag.

Parameter `lpszOutput` is the character string you wish to output in the debug stream. The function returns no values. (See Listing 35.29.)

On the CD

Listing 35.29   DEBUG\REQUEST.CPP—The *WriteDebug()* Function Allows You to Output Debugging Information About the Tag Whenever the *DEBUG* Attribute Is Present

```
if (pRequest->Debug()) {
pRequest->WriteDebug("This tag created by Steven D. Drucker @ Fig Leaf
➥ Software");
pRequest->WriteDebug("Copyright 1996, all rights reserved.");
pRequest->WriteDebug("E-mail info@figleaf.com for more information");
}
```

CCFXException

`CCFXException` is an abstract class devoted to error trapping in your CFX tags. There are no member functions. Error trapping is accomplished by using the `CCFXRequest::ThrowException` and `CCFXRequest::ReThrowException` functions. It is important that your functions be structured to handle exceptions or else an inadvertent programming error could cause your Cold Fusion process to halt. See `CCFXRequest::ReThrowException`, earlier in this chapter, for more information about this topic. ●

Appendixes

Cold Fusion Tag Reference

by Ben Forta

The Cold Fusion tags are the CFML extensions to HTML. These tags are the instructions to Cold Fusion to perform database queries, process results, perform transaction processing, send email, and much more.

The tags are presented here in alphabetical order, and are cross-referenced to any related tags wherever appropriate.

<CFABORT>

Description: The <CFABORT> tag is used to immediately halt processing of a Cold Fusion template. <CFABORT> attributes are listed in Table A.1. By default, Cold Fusion aborts processing without displaying an error message. The SHOWERROR attribute allows you to specify an error message to be displayed.

Syntax: <CFABORT SHOWERROR="*Error text*">

Table A.1   *<CFABORT>* Attributes

Attribute	Description	Notes
SHOWERROR	Error message	This attribute is optional.

Example: The following example aborts template processing if the user is not in a specific range of valid IP addresses.

```
<CFIF Left(CGI.REMOTE_ADDR, 11) NEQ "208.193.16.">
 <H1>Unauthorized host detected! Access denied!</H1>
 <CFABORT SHOWERROR="You are not authorized to use this function!">
</CFIF>
```

TIP

<CFABORT> can be used to safely terminate the processing of a template if an error condition occurs. For example, if your template was expecting a URL parameter to be passed, you could use the ParameterExists or IsDefined functions to verify its existence, and terminate the template with an appropriate error message if it did not in fact exist.

See also: <CFEXIT>

<CFAPPLET>

Description: <CFAPPLET> is used to embed user-supplied Java applets into CFFORM forms. Table A.2 gives a complete list of attributes supported by <CFAPPLET>. In addition, you may pass your own attributes, as long as they have been registered along with the applet itself.

Before you can use an applet with <CFAPPLET>, it must be registered with the Cold Fusion Administrator.

<CFAPPLET> must be used within <CFORM> and </CFORM> tags.

Syntax: `<CFAPPLET ALIGN="`*`Alignment`*`" APPLETSOURCE="`*`Registered Name`*`" HEIGHT="`*`Height`*`"` `HSPACE="`*`Horizontal Spacing`*`" NAME="`*`Field Name`*`" NOTSUPPORTED="`*`Text for non-Java`* *`browsers`*`" VSPACE="`*`Vertical Spacing`*`" WIDTH="`*`Width`*`">`

Table A.2 *<CFAPPLET>* Attributes

Attribute	Description	Notes
ALIGN	Applet alignment	Valid values are left, right, bottom, top, texttop, middle, absmiddle, baseline, and absbottom. This attribute is optional.
APPLETSOURCE	Name of the registered applet	This attribute is required.
HEIGHT	Height in pixels	This attribute is optional.
HSPACE	Horizontal spacing in pixels	This attribute is optional.
NAME	Form field name	This attribute is required.
NOTSUPPORTED	Text to display on browsers that do not support Java.	This attribute is optional.
VSPACE	Vertical spacing in pixels	This attribute is optional.
WIDTH	Width in pixels	This attribute is optional.

Example: The following example embeds a Java spin-control applet into a `<CFFORM>` form, passing the required attributes and two applet-specific attributes.

```
<CFFORM ACTION="process.cfm">
<CFAPPLET APPLETSOURCE="spin" NAME="quantity" MIN="1" MAX="10">
</CFFORM>
```

▶ **See** Chapter 4, "Administering Cold Fusion," **p. 55**

▶ **See** Chapter 19, "Enhancing Forms with *CFFORM*," **p. 427**

N O T E Controls embedded with `<CFAPPLET>` will only be accessible by users with Java-enabled browsers. ■

See also: `<CFFORM>`, `<CFGRID>`, `<CFSLIDER>`, `<CFTEXTINPUT>`, and `<CFTREE>`

<CFAPPLICATION>

Description: `<CFAPPLICATION>` is used to name an application—or part thereof— and to restrict the scope of any client, session, and application variables. By default, these variables are visible to all templates. `<CFAPPLICATION>` allows you to name part of an application so that variables created in other templates are not visible to it, and variables created within it are not visible to other parts of the application. <CFAPPLICATION> attributes are shown in Table A.3.

Syntax: <CFAPPLICATION APPLICATIONTIMEOUT ="*Timeout*" CLIENTMANAGEMENT ="*Yes or No*" NAME="*Application Name*" SESSIONMANAGEMENT ="*Yes or No*" SESSIONTIMEOUT ="*Timeout*">

Table A.3   *<CFAPPLICATION>* Attributes

Attribute	Description	Notes
APPLICATIONTIMEOUT	Timeout interval for application variables	Application variable timeout, defaults to the value in Cold Fusion Administrator.
CLIENTMANAGEMENT	Enable or disable client variables	This optional attribute defaults to "No."
NAME	Name of application	This attribute is required if you are using application variables.
SESSIONMANAGEMENT	Enable or disable session variables	This optional attribute defaults to "No."
SESSIONTIMEOUT	Timeout interval for session variables	Session variable timeout. Defaults to the value in Cold Fusion Administrator.

Example: The following example names part of an application Administration and enables session variables.

<CFAPPLICATION NAME="Administration" SESSIONMANAGEMENT="Yes">

T I P

The <CFAPPLICATION> tag is best used in the APPLICATION.CFM template, as explained in Chapter 23, "Web Application Framework."

▶**See** Chapter 4, **p. 55**

▶**See** Chapter 24, "Session Variables and Cookies," **p. 557**

See also: <CFSET>

<CFCONTENT>

Description: The <CFCONTENT> tag allows you to send non-HTML documents to a client's browser. <CFCONTENT> lets you specify the MIME type of the file, and an optional file name to transmit. The complete list of supported attributes is explained in Table A.4.

Syntax: <CFCONTENT TYPE="*MIME Type*" FILE="*File Name*" DELETEFILE>

Table A.4 *<CFCONTENT>* Attributes

Attribute	Description	Notes
TYPE	Content MIME type	This attribute is required.
FILE	Name of file to be sent to user	This is an optional attribute that specifies the fully qualified path of a file to be transmitted to the user's browser.
DELETEFILE	Delete the file once sent	Useful if serving dynamically created graphics. This attribute is optional.

Example: The following example sends data-driven VRML to the user.

```
<CFCONTENT TYPE="x-world/x-vrml">
<CFOUTPUT QUERY="world">
#world#
</CFOUTPUT>
```

This next example sends a Microsoft Word document.

```
<CFCONTENT TYPE="application/msword" FILE="C:\MyDocs\Proposal.DOC">
```

This final example sends a dynamically created map to the user, and then deletes it upon completion of the transmission,

```
<CFCONTENT TYPE="image/gif" FILE="C:\Images\Maps\Temp123.gif" DELETEFILE>
```

▶ **See** Chapter 28, "MIME Types," **p. 665**

<CFCOOKIE>

Description: <CFCOOKIE> allows you to set *cookies,* or persistent client-side variables, on the client browser. Cookies allow you to set variables on a client's browser, which are then returned every time a page is requested by a browser. Cookies may be sent securely if required. Table A.5 lists <CFCOOKIE> attributes.

To access a returned cookie, specify its name preceded by the COOKIE designator, as in #COOKIE.USER_ID#.

As not all browsers support cookies, you must *never* make assumptions about the existence of the cookie. Always use the ParameterExists function to check for the existence of the cookie before referencing it.

Syntax: <CFCOOKIE NAME="*Cookie Name*" VALUE="*Value*" EXPIRES="*Expiration*" SECURE DOMAIN="*Domain Name*" PATH="*Path*">

Table A.5   _<CFCOOKIE>_ Attributes

Attribute	Description	Notes
DOMAIN	The domain for which the cookies are valid	Required only if PATH is used. Separate multiple domains with a ; character.
EXPIRES	Cookie expiration date	The cookie expiration date may be specified as a definite date (as in ë10/1/97'), relative days (as in ë100'), NOW, or NEVER. This attribute is optional.
NAME	Name of cookie	This attribute is required.
PATH	Subset of the URL to which the cookie applies	This attribute is optional. Separate multiple paths with a ; character.
SECURE	Specify that cookie must be sent securely	This attribute is optional. If it is specified and the browser does not support SSL, the cookie is not sent.
VALUE	Cookie value	This attribute is required.

Example: The following example sends a cookie containing a user ID, and sets the expiration date to 60 days from now.

```
<CFCOOKIE NAME="USER_ID" VALUE="100" EXPIRES="60">
```

The next example sets a secure cookie that never expires (until manually deleted).

```
<CFCOOKIE NAME="access" VALUE="admin" SECURE EXPIRES="never">
```

N O T E   If you use the SECURE attribute to specify that the cookie *must* be sent securely, it will only be sent if the browser supports SSL. If the cookie cannot be sent securely, then it will not be sent at all. ▓

N O T E   Cookies are domain-specific, meaning they can be set so just the server that set them can retrieve them. ▓

T I P   Setting a cookie expiration date of NOW effectively deletes the cookie from the client's browser.

▶**See** Chapter 24, **p. 557**

See also: ParameterExists

<CFDIRECTORY>

Description: <CFDIRECTORY> is used for all directory manipulation, including obtaining directory lists and creating or deleting directories.

<CFDIRECTORY> is a flexible and powerful tag, and has many attributes, some of which are mutually exclusive. The values passed to the ACTION attribute dictate what other attributes may or may not be used. The possible ACTION values are listed in Table A.6. If no ACTION is specified, then LIST is assumed. Table A.8 contains the list of columns returned if ACTION="LIST".

Syntax: <CFDIRECTORY ACTION="*Action Type*" DIRECTORY="*Directory Name*" FILTER="*Search Filter*" MODE="*Unix Permissions Mode*" NAME="*Query Name*" NEWDIRECTORY="*New Directory Name*" SORT="*Sort Order*">

Table A.6   *<CFDIRECTORY>* Attributes

Attribute	Description	Notes
ACTION	Tag action (see Table A.7)	This attribute is optional, and will default to LIST if omitted.
DIRECTORY	Directory name	This attribute is required.
FILTER	Filter spec	This attribute is optional and is only valid if ACTION="LIST". Filter may contain wildcard characters.
MODE	Permissions mode	This optional attribute is only valid if ACTION="CREATE". It is only used by the Solaris version of Cold Fusion, and is ignored by the Windows versions.
NAME	Query name	Required if ACTION="LIST". Query to hold retrieved directory listing.
NEWDIRECTORY	New directory rename	Required if ACTION="RENAME"; ignored by all other actions.
SORT	Sort order	Optional, comma-delimited list of columns to sort by. Each may use ASC for ascending or DESC for descending. Default is ascending.

Table A.7   *<CFDIRECTORY>* Actions

Action	Description
CREATE	Creates a new directory
DELETE	Deletes a directory
LIST	Obtains a list of directory contents
RENAME	Renames a directory

Table A.8 **<CFDIRECTORY> LIST Columns**

Action	Description
ATTRIBUTES	File attributes
DATELASTMODIFIED	Last modified date
MODE	Permissions mode (Solaris only)
NAME	File or directory name
SIZE	Size in bytes
TYPE	Type, F for file or D for directory

Example: This first example creates a new directory.

```
<CFDIRECTORY ACTION="CREATE" DIRECTORY="C:\STUFF">
```

This next example retrieves a directory list, sorted by file name.

```
<CFDIRECTORY ACTION="LIST" DIRECTORY="C:\STUFF" NAME="Stuff" SORT="Name">
```

▶ **See** Chapter 25, "File Manipulation," **p. 577**

See also: <CFFILE>

<CFERROR>

Description: <CFERROR> allows you to override the standard Cold Fusion error messages, and replace them with templates that you specify. <CFERROR> requires that you specify the type of error message to be overridden, and the template containing the error message to be displayed. The <CFERROR> attributes are shown in Table A.9.

There are two different types of error messages in Cold Fusion: REQUEST errors occur while processing a template, and VALIDATION errors occur when FORM field validation errors occur. In each scenario, a special set of Cold Fusion fields is available to you for inclusion in your error message template. The complete list of fields is shown in Table A.10.

Syntax: <CFERROR TYPE="*Error Type*" TEMPLATE="*Error Message Template*" MAILTO="*Administrator's Email Address*">

Table A.9 **<CFERROR> Attributes**

Attribute	Description	Notes
MAILTO	The administrator's email address	The email address of the administrator to be notified of any error messages. This value is available with the error message template as #ERROR.MailTo#.
TEMPLATE	Error message template	Name of the template containing the error message to display. This attribute is required.

Attribute	Description	Notes
TYPE	Type of error message	Possible values are REQUEST or VALIDATION. If this attribute is omitted, the default value of REQUEST will be used.

Table A.10 Cold Fusion Error Message Variables

Type	Field	Description
REQUEST	#ERROR.RemoteAddress#	IP address of the client.
REQUEST	#ERROR.Browser#	The browser the client was running, with version and platform information if provided by the browser.
REQUEST	#ERROR.DateTime#	The date and time that the error occurred (can be passed to any of the date/time manipulation functions as needed).
REQUEST	#ERROR.Diagnostics#	Detailed diagnostic error message returned by Cold Fusion.
REQUEST	#ERROR.HTTPReferer#	URL of the page from which the template was accessed.
REQUEST	#ERROR.MailTo#	Administrator's email address. Can be used to send notification of the error.
REQUEST	#ERROR.QueryString#	The URL's query string.
REQUEST	#ERROR.Template#	Template being processed when the error occurred.
VALIDATION	#ERROR.InvalidFields#	List of the invalid form fields.
VALIDATION	#ERROR.ValidationFooter#	Text for footer of error message.
VALIDATION	#ERROR.ValidationHeader#	Text for header of error message.

Example: The following example establishes an error message template for REQUEST errors. Listing A.1 contains the source code for the error message template which returns a detailed error message to the administrator by email.

```
<CFERROR TYPE="REQUEST" TEMPLATE="ERROR_REQUEST.CFM" MAILTO="admin@a2zbooks.com">
```

Listing A.1 Sample Request Error Template

```
<HTML>

<HEAD>
<TITLE>Application Error!</TITLE>
</HEAD>
```

continues

Listing A.1 Continued

```
<BODY>
<H1>Application Error!</H1>
A critical error has occurred, please try your request later.

</BODY>

</HTML>
```

> **TIP** The <CFERROR> tag is best used in the APPLICATION.CFM template, as explained in Chapter 23, "Web Application Framework."

<CFEXIT>

Description: <CFEXIT> is used to abort the processing of a Custom Tag without aborting processing of the calling template. <CFEXIT> may only be used within Custom Tags. Unlike <CFABORT>, which will terminate caller template processing, <CFEXIT> stops processing the Custom Tag and returns control to the caller.

Syntax: <CFEXIT>

Example: The following example checks to see if any form fields exist, and stops processing if there are none.

```
<CFIF IsDefined("FORM.formfields") IS "No">
 <CFEXIT>
</CFIF>
```

▶ **See** Chapter 33, "Custom Tags," **p. 767**

See also: <CFABORT>

<CFFILE>

Description: <CFFILE> is used to perform various types of file management, including uploading files from a browser, moving, renaming, copying, and deleting files, as well as reading and writing of text files.

<CFFILE> is a flexible and powerful tag and has many attributes (see Table A.11), many of which are mutually exclusive. The values passed to the ACTION attribute dictate what other attributes may or may not be used. The possible ACTION values are listed in Table A.12.

<CFFILE> creates a FILE object after every <CFFILE> operation. You may use the variables in this object as you would any other Cold Fusion variables, allowing you to check the results of an operation. However, only one FILE object exists, and as soon as you execute a new <CFFILE> tag, the prior FILE object is overwritten with the new one. The fields available to you in the FILE object are listed in Table A.14.

Syntax: <CFFILE ACCEPT="*Filter*" ACTION="*Action Type*" DESTINATION="*Destination Directory or File Name*" FILE="*File Name*" FILEFIELD="*Field Containing File Name*" NAMECONFLICT="*Conflict Option*" OUTPUT="*Text To Output*" SOURCE="*Source File Name*" VARIABLE="*Variable Name*">

Table A.11 <CFFILE> Attributes

Attribute	Description	Notes
ACCEPT	File type filter	This optional attribute is used to restrict the types of files that may be uploaded, and may only be used if ACTION is UPLOAD. The filter is specified as a MIME type (e.g. image/* to allow all image types, but nothing else), and multiple MIME types may be specified separated by commas.
ACTION	Desired action	This attribute is required. For possible values see Table A.12.
DESTINATION	Destination file location	This attribute may only be used if ACTION is one the following: APPEND, COPY, MOVE, RENAME, UPLOAD. Destination may be a file name, or a fully qualified file path.
FILE	Name of local file to access	This attribute may only be used if ACTION is APPEND, DELETE, READ, or WRITE, in which case it is required.
FILEFIELD	Name of the form field containing the file	This attribute may only be used if ACTION is UPLOAD, in which case it is required.
NAMECONFLICT	What to do in case of name conflicts	This optional attribute may be used if ACTION is UPLOAD. It specifies the action to be performed if a name conflict arises. Possible values are listed in Table A.13. If this attribute is omitted, the default value of ERROR will be used.
OUTPUT	Text to output to file	This attribute may only be used if ACTION is WRITE.
SOURCE	Source file name	Name of the source file to be written to, copied, or moved. May be used only if ACTION is COPY, MOVE, or RENAME.
VARIABLE	Variable to store contents of read file	This attribute may only be used if ACTION is READ, in which case it is required.

Table A.12 *<CFFILE>* Actions

Action	Description
APPEND	Append one text file to the end of another
COPY	Copy a file
DELETE	Deletes a specified file
MOVE	Moves a specified file from one directory to another, or from one filename to another
READ	Read the contents of a text file
RENAME	Does the same thing as MOVE, see MOVE
UPLOAD	Receive an uploaded file
WRITE	Writes specified text to the end of a text file

Table A.13 File Upload Name Conflict Options

Option	Description
ERROR	The file will not be saved, and Cold Fusion will immediately terminate template processing.
SKIP	Neither saves the file, nor generates an error message.
OVERWRITE	Overwrite the existing file.
MAKEUNIQUE	Generates a unique file name and saves the file with that new name. To find out what the new name was generated, inspect the #FILE.ServerFile# field.

Table A.14 *<CFFILE>* *FILE* Object Fields

Field	Description
#FILE.AttemptedServerFile#	The original attempted file name. Will be the same as #FILE.ServerFile# unless the name had to be changed to make it unique.
#FILE.ClientDirectory#	The client directory from where the file was uploaded, as reported by the client browser.
#FILE.ClientFile#	The original file name as reported by the client browser.
#FILE.ClientFileExt#	The original file extension, as reported by the client browser.
#FILE.ClientFileName#	The original file name as reported by the client browser, but without the file extension.

Field	Description
`#FILE.ContentSubType#`	The MIME sub-type of an uploaded file.
`#FILE.ContentType#`	The primary MIME type of an uploaded file.
`#FILE.FileExisted#`	`Yes` if file already existed, `No` if not.
`#FILE.FileWasOverwritten#`	`Yes` if file was overwritten, `No` if not.
`#FILE.FileWasRenamed#`	`Yes` if file was renamed, `No` if not.
`#FILE.FileWasSaved#`	`Yes` is file was save, `No` if not.
`#FILE.ServerDirectory#`	The server directory in which the uploaded file was saved.
`#FILE.ServerFile#`	The name of the file as saved on the server (takes into account updated file name if it was modified to make it unique).

Example: The first example receives any uploaded files, and generates an error message if the specified file name already exists.

```
<CFFILE ACTION="Upload" FILEFIELD="UploadFile" DESTINATION=
➥"C:\UPLOADS\FILE.TXT">
```

The next example restricts the upload to Microsoft Word documents, and changes the file name to something unique if it already exists.

```
<CFFILE
 ACTION="Upload"
 FILEFIELD="UploadFile"
 DESTINATION="C:\UPLOADS\FILE.TXT"
 ACCEPT="application/msword"
 NAMECONFLICT="MAKEUNIQUE"
>
```

This example appends a log entry to a text file.

```
<CFFILE
 ACTION="APPEND"
 FILE="C:\LOGS\DAILY.LOG"
 OUTPUT="#CGI.REMOTE_ADDR#, #Now()#"
>
```

The following example reads a file called C:\LOGS\DAILY\LOG into a variable called `LOG`, and then displays the results.

```
<CFFILE
 ACTION="READ"
 FILE="C:\LOGS\DAILY.LOG"
 VARIABLE="LOG"
>
<CFOUTPUT>
<B>Log file:</B><P>#LOG#
</CFOUTPUT>
```

The next example deletes the C:\LOGS\DAILY.LOG file.

```
<CFFILE
 ACTION="DELETE"
 FILE="C:\LOGS\DAILY.LOG"
>
```

▶ **See** Chapter 25, **p. 577**

See also: <CFDIRECTORY>

<CFFORM> </CFFORM>

Description: <CFFORM> and </CFFORM> are replacements for the standard HTML <FORM> and </FORM> tags. <CFFORM> itself adds no real value to your forms, but <CFFORM> does allow you to embed other tags (<CFGRID>, <CFINPUT>, <CFSELECT>, <CFTEXTINPUT>, <CFTREE>, or any Java applets of your own using <CFAPPLET>). The code generated by <CFFORM> is standard FORM HTML code.

Syntax: <CFFORM ACTION="*Action Page*" >

Table A.15   *<CFFORM>* Attributes

Attribute	Description	Notes
ACTION	Form action page	This attribute is required.
ENABLECAB	Header value	This optional attribute allows the downloading Java classes in Microsoft cabinet files. If YES, on opening the page, users are asked if they want to download the CAB file.
NAME	Form name	This attribute is optional. If used you must ensure that the form name is unique.
ONSUBMIT	JavaScript OnSubmit	Optional name of function JavaScript function to be executed prior to form submission.

N O T E   <CFFORM> automatically embeds METHOD="POST" into your form for you. ■

See also: <CFAPPLET>, <CFGRID>, <CFINPUT>, <CFSELECT>, <CFSLIDER>, <CFTEXTINPUT>, <CFTREE>

<CFFTP>

Description: <CFFTP> is the Cold Fusion interface to the file transfer protocol. Using <CFFTP> you may interact with remote file systems, retrieve directory lists, and get and put files. <CFFTP> is a very powerful and complex tag, Table A.16 lists its attributes, and Table A.17 lists the possible actions. When calls to <CFFTP> are completed, a series of variables are set so you can determine the success or failure of the operation, these variables are listed in Table A.18. If an error occurs, an error code is set, Table A.19 lists the complete set of error codes, and what they mean. <CFFTP> can be used to retrieve remote directory lists. Lists are returned in Cold Fusion query format, and Table A.20 lists the query columns.

<CFFTP> is designed to be used two ways, either for single operations, or to batch operations together. To use the batch mode (called cached mode) you must specify a unique name in the CONNECTION attribute that you can use in future <CFFTP> calls.

Syntax: `<CFFTP ACTION="Action" AGENTNAME="Name" ASCIIEXTENSIONLIST="List" ATTRIBUTES="Attributes" CONNECTION="Connection Name" DIRECTORY="Directory" EXISTING="Name" FAILIFEXISTS="Yes¦No" ITEM="Name" LOCALFILE="Name" NAME="Query Name" NEW="Name" PASSWORD="Password" PORT="Port" REMOTEFILE="Name" RETRYCOUNT="Count" SERVER="Server Address" STOPONERROR="Yes¦No" TIMEOUT="Seconds" TRANSFERMODE="Mode" USERNAME="User Name">`

Table A.16   <CFFTP> Attributes

Attribute	Description	Notes
ACTION	Action	Required attribute. See Table A.17.
AGENTNAME	Agent name	Optional attribute. Application name.
ASCIIEXTENSIONLIST	ASCII extensions	Optional attribute. Semicolon-delimited list of extensions to be treated as ASCII extensions if using TRANSFERMODE of AutoDetect. Default is txt;htm;html;cfm;cfml;shtm;shtml;css;asp;asa.
ATTRIBUTES	Attributes list	Comma-delimited list of attributes. Specifies the file attributes for the local file. Possible values are: READONLY, HIDDEN, SYSTEM, ARCHIVE, DIRECTORY, COMPRESSED, TEMPORARY, and NORMAL.
CONNECTION	Connection name	Optional attribute. Used to cache connections to be able to perform batches of operations.
DIRECTORY	Directory name	Required if ACTION is CHANGEDIR, CREATEDIR, LISTDIR, or EXISTSDIR. Specifies the directory on which to perform the operation.

continues

Table A.16   Continued

Attribute	Description	Notes
EXISTING	Existing item name	Required if ACTION is RENAME.
FAILIFEXISTS	Fail if exists	Optional attribute. If Yes, puts will fail if the file already exists, default is Yes.
ITEM	Item name	Required if ACTION is EXISTS or REMOVE.
LOCALFILE	Local file name	Required if ACTION is GETFILE or PUTFILE, local file name.
NAME	Query name	Query name, required if ACTION is GETLIST (see Table A.20 for column list).
NEW	New item name	Required if ACTION is RENAME.
PASSWORD	Login password	Required attribute.
PORT	Server port	Optional attribute. Defaults to 21.
REMOTEFILE	Remote file name	Required if ACTION is EXISTSFILE, GETFILE, or PUTFILE, local file name.
RETRYCOUNT	Retries	Optional retry count. Defaults to 1.
SERVER	Server name	Required attribute. DNS or IP address of FTP server.
STOPONERROR	Error handling	Optional attribute. Defaults to Yes.
TIMEOUT	Timeout value	Optional attribute. Timeout value in seconds.
TRANSFERMODE	Transfer mode	Optional attribute. Values can be ASCII, binary, or AutoDetect. Default is AutoDetect.
USERNAME	Login user name	Required attribute.

Table A.17   <CFFTP> Actions

Action	Description
CHANGEDIR	Change directory
CLOSE	Close a cached connection
CREATEDIR	Create a directory
EXISTS	Checks to see if an object exists
EXISTSDIR	Checks if a directory exists
EXISTSFILE	Checks to see if a file exists

GETCURRENTDIR	Get current directory
GETCURRENTURL	Get current URL
GETFILE	Retrieve a file
LISTDIR	Retrieve directory list
OPEN	Opens a cached connection
PUTFILE	Send a file
REMOVE	Delete a file
RENAME	Rename a file

Table A.18 *<CFFTP>* Status Variables

Variable	Description
#CFFTP.ErrorCode#	Error codes (see Table A.19 for error code list)
#CFFTP.ErrorText#	Error text
#CFFTP.Succeeded#	Success, Yes or No

Table A.19 *<CFFTP>* Error Codes

Code	Description
0	Operation succeeded
1	System error (OS or FTP protocol error)
2	An Internet session could not be established
3	FTP session could not be opened
4	File transfer mode not recognized
5	Search connection could not be established
6	Invoked operation valid only during a search
7	Invalid timeout value
8	Invalid port number
9	Not enough memory to allocate system resources
10	Cannot read contents of local file
11	Cannot write to local file
12	Cannot open remote file for reading

continues

Table A.19 Continued

Code	Description
13	Cannot read remote file
14	Cannot open local file for writing
15	Cannot write to remote file
16	Unknown error
18	File already exists
21	Invalid retry count specified

Table A.20 *<CFFTP>* Query Columns

Column	Description
ATTRIBUTES	Comma delimited list of attributes
ISDIRECTORY	Yes if directory, No if file
LASTMODIFIED	Date and time last modified
LENGTH	File length
NAME	Object name
PATH	Full path to object
URL	Full URL to object

Examples:

The following example opens a connection and reads a directory list into a query named dir.

```
<CFFTP CONNECTION="FTP" USERNAME="#username#" PASSWORD="#password#"
➥ SERVER="ftp.a2zbooks.com" ACTION="Open">
<CFFTP CONNECTION="FTP" ACTION="LISTDIR" DIRECTORY="/*." NAME="dir">
<CFFTP CONNECTION="FTP" ACTION="CLOSE">
```

▶ **See** Chapter 30, "Interfacing with HTTP and FTP Using *CFHTTP* and *CFFTP*," **p. 719**

See also: <CFHTTP>

<CFGRID> <CFGRIDCOLUMN> <CFGRIDROW> </CFGRID>

Description: <CFGRID> embeds a Java grid control into your HTML forms. Grids are similar to spreadsheet style interfaces, and <CFGRID> grids can be used to browse, select, and even edit data. Grids may be populated by a query, or by specifying each row using the <CFGRIDROW> tag. <CFGRIDCOLUMN> may be used to configure the individual columns with a grid.

<CFGRID> must be used between <CFFORM> and </CFFORM> tags. <CFGRID> attributes are listed in Table A.21, <CFGRIDCOLUMN> attributes are listed in Table A.22, and <CFGRIDROW> attributes are listed in Table A.23.

Syntax: <CFGRID ALIGN="*Alignment*" APPENDKEY="*Yes¦No*" BGCOLOR="*Color*" BOLD="*Yes¦No*" COLHEADERALIGN="*Alignment*" COLHEADERBOLD="*Yes¦No*" COLHEADERFONT="*Font Face*" COLHEADERFONTSIZE="*Font Size*" COLHEADERITALICS="*Yes¦No*" COLHEADERS="*Yes¦No*" DELETE="*Yes¦No*" DELETEBUTTON="*Button Text*" FONT="*Font Face*" FONTSIZE="*Font Size*" GRIDDATAALIGN="*Alignment*" GRIDLINES="*Yes¦No*" GRIDKEY="*Key*" HEIGHT="*Control Height*" HIGHLIGHTHREF="*Yes¦No*" HREF="*URL*" HREFKEY="*Key*" HSPACE="*Horizontal Spacing*" INSERT="*Yes¦No*" INSERTBUTTON="*Button Text*" ITALIC="*Yes¦No*" NAME="*Field Name*" NOTSUPPORTED="*Non Java Browser Code*" ONERROR="*Error Function*" ONVALIDATE="*Validation Function*" PICTUREBAR="*Yes¦No*" QUERY="*Query NAME*" ROWHEADER="*Yes¦No*" ROWHEADERALIGN="*Alignment*" ROWHEADERBOLD="*Yes¦No*" ROWHEADERFONT="*Font Face*" ROWHEADERFONTSIZE="*Font Size*" ROWHEADERITALICS="*Yes¦No*" ROWHEIGHT="*Height*" ROWHEADERWIDTH="*Width*" SELECTCOLOR="*Color*" SELECTMODE="*Mode*" SORT="*Yes¦No*" SORTASCENDINGBUTTON="*Button Text*" SORTDESCENDINGBUTTON="*Button Text*" TARGET="*Target Window*" VSPACE="*Vertical Spacing*" WIDTH="*Control Width*">

<CFGRIDCOLUMN BOLD="*Yes¦No*" DATAALIGN="*Alignment*" DISPLAY="*Yes¦No*" FONT="*Font Face*" FONTSIZE="*Font Size*" HEADER="*Header Text*" HEADERALIGN="*Alignment*" HEADERBOLD="*Yes¦No*" HEADERFONT="*Font Face*" HEADERFONTSIZE="*Font Size*" HEADERITALIC="*Yes¦No*" HREF="*URL*" HREFKEY="*Key*" ITALIC="*Yes¦No*" NAME="*Column Name*" NUMBERFORMAT="*Format Mask*" SELECT="*Yes¦No*" TARGET="*Target Window*" TYPE="*Type*" WIDTH="*Column Width*">

<CFGRIDROW DATA="*Data*">

Table A.21 *<CFGRID>* Attributes

Attribute	Description	Notes
ALIGN	Control alignment	Optional attribute. Possible values are Top, Left, Bottom, Baseline, TextTop, AbsBottom, Middle, AbsMiddle, Right.
APPENDKEY	Append item key to URL	Optional attribute. If Yes, a variable named GRIDKEY is appended to the URL containing the item selected, defaults to Yes.
BGCOLOR	Background color	Optional attribute. Possible values are black, cyan, darkgray, gray, lightgray, magenta, orange, pink, white, yellow, or any color specified in RGB form.

continues

Table A.21   Continued

Attribute	Description	Notes
BOLD	Bold face text	Optional attribute. Must be Yes or No is specified, defaults to No.
COLHEADERALIGN	Column header alignment	Optional attribute. May be left, center, right. Default is left.
COLHEADERBOLD	Column header in bold	Optional. If Yes, the column header is displayed in a bold font, default is No.
COLHEADERFONT	Column header font	Optional font to use for column header.
COLHEADERFONTSIZE	Column header font	Optional font size size to use for column header.
COLHEADERITALIC	Column header in italics	Optional. If Yes, the row column is displayed in an italic font, fault is No.
COLHEADERS	Display column headers	Optional attribute. Column headers are displayed if Yes, default is Yes
DELETE	Allow delete	Optional. If Yes allows records to be deleted from the grid. Default is No.
DELETEBUTTON	Delete button text	Optional text to use for the delete button. Default is Delete.
FONT	Font face	Optional font face to use.
FONTSIZE	Font Size	Optional font size.
GRIDDATAALIGN	Data alignment	Data alignment. May be left, right, or center, and can be overridden at the column level.
GRIDLINES	Display grid lines	Optional grid lines displayed, if Yes. Default is Yes.
HEIGHT	Control height	Optional height in pixels.
HIGHLIGHTHREF	Highlight links	Optional attribute. If Yes, the links will be highlighted and underlined. Defaults to Yes.
HREF	URL	Optional URL to go to upon item selection. If populated buy a query, this may be a query column.
HREFKEY	Primary key column	Optional name of column to be used as the primary key.
HSPACE	Control horizontal spacing	Optional horizontal spacing in pixels.

Attribute	Description	Notes
INSERT	Allow insert	Optional. If Yes, allows records to be added to the grid. Default is No.
INSERTBUTTON	Insert button text	Optional text to use for the insert button. Default is Insert.
ITALIC	Italic face text	Optional attribute. Must be specified Yes or No, defaults to No.
NAME	Unique control name	This attribute is required.
NOTSUPPORTED	Text to be used for non-Java browsers	Optional text (or HTML code) to be displayed on non-Java capable browsers.
ONERROR	JavaScript error function	Optional override to your own JavaScript error message function.
ONVALIDATE	JavaScript validation function	Optional override to your own JavaScript validation function
PICTUREBAR	Display picture bar with icons	Optional attribute. If Yes, a button bar with icons is displayed for insert, delete, and sort. Default is No.
QUERY	Query to populate grid	Optional name of query to be used to populate the grid.
ROWHEADER	Display row header	Optional attribute displays header if Yes. Default is Yes.
ROWHEADERALIGN	Row header alignment	Optional attribute. May be left, center, right. Default is left.
ROWHEADERBOLD	Row header in bold	Optional. If Yes, the row header is displayed in a bold font. Default is No.
ROWHEADERFONT	Row header font	Optional font to use for row header.
ROWHEADERFONTSIZE	Row header font size	Optional font size to use for row header.
ROWHEADERITALIC	Row header in italics	Optional. If Yes, the row header is displayed in an italic font. Default is No.
ROWHEADERWIDTH	Row header width	Optional row header width in pixels.
ROWHEIGHT	Row height	Optional height of row in pixels.
SELECTCOLOR	Selection color	Optional attribute. Possible values are black, cyan, darkgray, gray, lightgray, magenta, orange, pink, white, yellow, or any color specified in RGB form.

continues

Table A.21 Continued

Attribute	Description	Notes
SELECTMODE	Selection mode	Optional attribute. May be EDIT, SINGLE, ROW, COLUMN, or BROWSE. Default is BROWSE.
SORT	Allow sorting	Optional. If Yes allows grid data to be sorted. Default is No.
SORTASCENDINGBUTTON	Sort ascending	Optional text to use button text for the sort ascending button. The default is A -> Z.
SORTDESCENDINGBUTTON	Sort descending	Optional text to use button text for the sort descending button.
TARGET	Link target window	Optional name of target window for HREF URL.
VSPACE	Control vertical spacing	Optional vertical spacing in pixels
WIDTH	Control width	Optional width in pixels.

Table A.22 <CFGRIDCOLUMN> Attributes

Attribute	Description	Notes
BOLD	Bold face text	Optional attribute. Must be Yes or No is specified. Defaults to No.
DATAALIGN	Data alignment	Optional attribute. May be left, center, right. Default is left.
DISPLAY	Display column	Optional attribute. If No, the column is hidden. Default is Yes.
FONT	Font face	Optional font face to use.
FONTSIZE	Font Size	Optional font size.
HEADER	Header text	Optional header text. Defaults to column name.
HEADERALIGN	Header alignment	Optional attribute. May be left, center, right. Default is left.
HEADERBOLD	Header in bold	Optional. If Yes, the header is displayed in a bold font. Default is No.
HEADERFONT	Header font	Optional font to use for header.
HEADERFONTSIZE	Header font size	Optional font size to use for header.

Attribute	Description	Notes
HEADERITALIC	Header in italics	Optional. If Yes, the header is displayed in an italic font. Default is No.
HREF	URL	URL for selection in this column. May be absolute or relative.
HREFKEY	Primary key	Optional primary key to use for this column.
ITALIC	Italic face text	Optional attribute. Must be Yes or No is specified. Defaults to No.
NAME	Column name	Required attribute. If using a query to populate the grid, this must be a valid column name.
NUMBERFORMAT	Number formatting	Optional attribute. Uses NumberFormat() function masks, see that function for mask details.
SELECT	Allow selection	Optional attribute. If No, selection or editing is not allowed in this column.
TARGET	Target window	Optional target window for HREF.
TYPE	Data type	Optional attribute. May be image or numeric. If image, an appropriate graphic will be displayed for the cell value.
WIDTH	Column width	Optional column width in pixels.

Table A.23　*<CFGRIDROW>* Attributes

Attribute	Description	Notes
DATA	Row data	Comma-delimited list of data to be displayed, one item for each row in the grid.

Examples: The first example displays the results of a query in a simple browse only grid.

```
<CFFORM ACTION="process.cfm">
<CFGRID NAME="Users" QUERY="Users">
</CFGRID>
</CFFORM>
```

The next example specifies the columns to be displayed, and allows editing, but prevents the primary key from being edited.

```
<CFFORM ACTION="process.cfm">
<CFGRID NAME="Users" QUERY="Users" MODE="EDIT">
```

```
<CFGRIDCOLUMN NAME="ID" DISPLAY="No">
<CFGRIDCOLUMN NAME="LastName">
<CFGRIDCOLUMN NAME="FirstName">
</CFGRID>
</CFFORM>
```

▶ **See** Chapter 19, "Enhancing Forms with CFFORM," **p. 427**

N O T E   The <CFGRID> control will only be accessible by users with Java-enabled browsers. ■

See also: <CFFORM>, <CFGRIDUPDATE>, <CFINPUT>, <CFSELECT>, <CFSLIDER>, <CFTEXTINPUT>, <CFTREE>

<CFGRIDUPDATE>

Description: <CFGRIDUPDATE> provides the action back end to support <CFGRID> in edit mode. <CFGRIDUPDATE> performs all inserts, deletes, and updates in one simple operation. <CFGRIDUPDATE> may only be used in an action page to which a form containing a <CFGRID> control was submitted. <CFGRIDUPDATE> attributes are listed in Table A.24.

Syntax: <CFGRIDUPDATE DATASOURCE="*ODBC Data Source Name*" GRID="*Grid Name*" KEYONLY="*Yes¦No*" PASSWORD="*Password*" TABLENAME="*Table Name*" TABLEOWNER="*Table Owner Name*" TABLEQUALIFIER="*Table Qualifier*" USERNAME="*User Name*">

Table A.24   *<CFGRIDUPDATE>* Attributes

Attribute	Description	Notes
DATASOURCE	ODBD data source	This attribute is required.
GRID	Grid name	This attribute is required. The name of the grid in the submitted form with which to update the table.
KEYONLY	WHERE clause construction	If Yes, the WHERE clause generated by <CFGRID> contains just the primary key. Default is Yes.
PASSWORD	ODBC login password	Optional ODBC login password.
TABLENAME	Table name	This attribute is required.
TABLEOWNER	Table owner	Optional ODBC table owner.
TABLEQUALIFIER	Table qualifier	Optional ODBC table qualifier.
USERNAME	ODBC user name	Optional ODBC user name.

Examples: The following example updates a table with the data in a editable grid.

```
<CFGRIDUPDATE DATASOURCE="A2Z" TABLE="Employees" GRID="Emp">
```

▶ **See** Chapter 19, "Enhancing Forms with CFFORM," **p. 427**

See also: <CFFORM>, <CFGRID>

<CFHEADER>

Description: <CFHEADER> allows you to control the contents of specific HTTP headers.

Syntax: <CFHEADER NAME="Header Name" VALUE="Value">

Table A.25   *<CFHEADER>* Attributes

Attribute	Description	Notes
NAME	HTTP header to be set	This attribute is required.
VALUE	Header value	This attribute is required.

Example: The following example sets the expiration header to Now() in order to prevent in from being cached.

```
<CFHEADER NAME="Expires" VALUE="#Now()#">
```

N O T E There is usually little need to use <CFHEADER> because Cold Fusion sets the HTTP headers automatically to optimum values. ■

<CFHTMLHEAD>

Description: <CFHTMLHEAD> writes text into the header section of your web page, programmatically under CF control. You may call <CFHTMLHEAD> anywhere in your page, not just at the top (as you must do with straight HTML).

Syntax: <CFHTMLHEAD TEXT="*Text*">

Table A.26   *<CFHTMLHEAD>* Attributes

Attribute	Description	Notes
TEXT	Header text	This attribute is required.

Example: The example writes a <TITLE> tag into the head section.

```
<CFHTMLHEAD TEXT="<TITLE>A2Z Home Page</TITLE>">
```

<CFHTTP> <CFHTTPPARAM> </CFHTTP>

Description: <CFHTTP> allows you to process HTTP GET and POST requests within your Cold Fusion code. If using the POST method, parameters may be passed using the <CFHTTPPARAM> tag. <CFHTTPPARAM> may only be used between <CFHTTP> and </CFHTTP> tags.

<CFHTTP> attributes are listed in Table A.27, <CFHTTPPARAM> attributes are listed in Table A.28. <CFHTTP> sets special variables upon completion that you may inspect, these are listed in Table A.29.

Syntax: `<CFHTTP COLUMNS="`*`Column Names`*`" DELIMITER="`*`Delimiter Character`*`" FILE="`*`File Name`*`" METHOD="`*`Get¦Post`*`" NAME="`*`Query Name`*`" PASSWORD="`*`Password`*`" PATH="`*`Directory`*`" PROXYSERVER="`*`Host Name`*`" RESOLVEURL="`*`Yes¦No`*`" TEXTQUALIFIER="`*`Text Qualifier`*`" URL="`*`Host Name`*`" USERNAME="`*`User Name`*`">`

`<CFHTTPPARAM FILE="`*`File Name`*`" NAME="`*`Field Name`*`" TYPE="`*`Type`*`" VALUE="`*`Value`*`">`

Table A.27   *<CFHTTP>* Attributes

Attribute	Description	Notes
COLUMNS	Query columns	Optional attribute. Query columns for retrieved data.
DELIMITER	Column delimiter	Required if NAME is used. Default delimiter is a comma.
FILE	File name	Required only if PATH is used, file to save.
METHOD	Submission method	This attribute is required. It must be either GET or POST. Use POST to use <CFHTTPPARAM>.
NAME	Query name	Optional attribute. Name of query to be constructed with HTTP results.
PASSWORD	User password	Optional attribute. User password if required by server.
PATH	File path	Optional attribute. Path to save file if method is POST.
PROXYSERVER	Server name	Optional name of proxy server to use.
RESOLVEURL	Resolve URL	Optional attribute. Defaults to No. If Yes, will fully resolve embedded URLs.
TEXTQUALIFIER	Text qualifier	Required if NAME is used. Delimiter indicating start and end of column.
URL	Host URL	This attribute is required. Must be DNS name or IP address of a valid host.
USERNAME	User name	Optional attribute. User name if required by server.

Table A.28   *<CFHTTPPARAM>* Attributes

Attribute	Description	Notes
FILE	File name	Required if TYPE is File.
NAME	Field name	This attribute is required.

Attribute	Description	Notes
TYPE	Field type	This attribute is required. Must be URL, FORMFIELD, COOKIE, CGI, or FILE.
VALUE	Field value	This attribute is optional unless TYPE is File.

Table A.29   <CFHTTP> Returned Variables

Field	Description
#FILE.FileContent#	Content returned by HTTP request
#FILE.MimeType#	MIME type of returned data

Examples: This example retrieves the A2Z home page.

```
<CFHTTP URL="www.a2zbooks.com/" METHOD="GET">
```

> **T I P**
>
> <CFHTTP> is especially useful in creating intelligent "agents." See Chapter 33, "Custom Tags," for an example of this.

See also: <CFFTP>

<CFIF> <CFELSEIF> <CFELSE> </CFIF>

Description: The <CFIF> set of tags are what allow you to create conditional CFML code. <CFIF>, and its supporting tags <CFELSEIF> <CFELSE> and </CFIF>, will likely be the tags you use most in your applications.

Every <CFIF> tag must have a matching </CFIF> tag. The <CFELSEIF> and <CFELSE> tags are entirely optional. You may use as many <CFELSEIF> tags as needed in a <CFIF> statement, but only one <CFELSE>. <CFELSE> must always be the last compare performed if it is used.

<CFIF> uses operators to compare values. The full list of operators, and their abbreviated forms, appear in Table A.30. Conditions can also be combined to perform more complex comparisons, the Boolean operators are listed in Table A.31.

You may compare *any* values, including static text and numbers, Cold Fusion fields, database column values, and function results.

Syntax: <CFIF *Condition*><CFELSEIF *Condition*><CFELSE></CFIF>

Table A.30   Cold Fusion Conditional Operators

Operator	Alternate	Description
IS	EQUAL, EQ	Checks that the right value is equal to the left value.
IS NOT	NOT EQUAL, NEQ	Checks that the right value is not equal to the left value.
CONTAINS	none	Checks that the right value is contained within the left value.
DOES NOT CONTAIN	none	Checks that the right value is not contained within the left value.
GREATER THAN	GT	Checks that the left value is greater than the right value.
LESS THAN	LT	Checks that the left value is less than the right value.
GREATER THAN OR EQUAL	GTE	Checks that the left value is greater than or equal to the right value.
LESS THAN OR EQUAL	LTE	Checks that the left value is less than or equal to the right value.

The Boolean operators available to you are shown in Table A.31.

Table A.31   Cold Fusion Boolean Operators

Operator	Description
AND	Conjunction, returns TRUE only if both expressions are true.
OR	Disjunction, returns TRUE if either expression is true.
NOT	Negation.

The first example checks to see if a field named LastName exists.

```
<CFIF ParameterExists(LastName)>
```

The following example checks to see if both the FirstName and LastName fields exist.

```
<CFIF (ParameterExists(FirstName)) AND (ParameterExists(LastName))>
```

To check for either a first name or a last name, you could do the following:

```
<CFIF (ParameterExists(FirstName)) OR (ParameterExists(LastName))>
```

Often you will want to verify that a field is not empty, and that it does not contain blank spaces. The following example demonstrates how this can be accomplished.

```
<CFIF Trim(LastName) IS NOT "">
```

To check if a value is within a range of values, you can use the CONTAINS operator:

```
<CFIF "KY,MI,MN,OH,WI" CONTAINS State>
```

or:

```
<CFIF TaxableStates CONTAINS State>
```

More complex expressions can be created by combining conditions within parentheses. For example, the following condition checks to see if a payment is by check or credit card, and, if payment is by credit card, it then checks to ensure that there is an approval code.

```
<CFIF (PaymentType IS "Check") OR ((PaymentType IS "Credit")
➡ApprovalCode IS NOT ""))>
```

The following example is a complete conditional statement that uses <CFELSEIF> to perform additional comparisons, and <CFELSE> to specify a default for values that pass none of the compares.

```
<CFIF State IS "MI">
 Code for Michigan only goes here
<CFELSEIF State IS "IN">
 Code for Indiana only goes here
<CFELSEIF (State IS "OH") OR (State IS "KY")>
 Code for Ohio or Kentucky goes here
<CFELSE>
 Code for all other states goes here
</CFIF>
```

▶ **See** "Using *CFIF* to Create Conditional Code," **p. 294**

<CFINCLUDE>

Description: <CFINCLUDE> includes the contents of another template into the one being processed. Tag attributes are explained in Table A.32.

Syntax: <CFINCLUDE TEMPLATE="*Template File Name*">

Table A.32   *<CFINCLUDE>* Attributes

Attribute	Description	Notes
TEMPLATE	Name of template to include	This attribute is required. Only relative paths are supported.

Example: The following example includes the footer file in the current directory if it exists, and a default footer if not.

```
<CFIF FileExists("FOOTER.CFM")>
 <CFINCLUDE TEMPLATE="FOOTER.CFM">
<CFELSE>
 <CFINCLUDE TEMPLATE="/DEFAULT/FOOTER.CFM">
</CFIF>
```

TIP

<CFINCLUDE> can help you reuse templates. By using <CFINCLUDE>, you may break out common components (like page headers and footers) so you can share them among multiple templates.

▶**See** Chapter 18, "Advanced Cold Fusion Templates," **p. 401**

See also: <CFLOCATION>

<CFINDEX>

Description: <CFINDEX> is used to populate Verity collections with index data. Before a collection can be populated it must be created with the Cold Fusion Administrator. <CFINDEX> can be used to index physical files (in which case the file name is returned in searches) or query results (in which case the primary key is returned in searches).

<CFINDEX> attributes are listed in Table A.33.

Syntax: <CFINDEX ACTION="*Action*" BODY="*Text*" COLLECTION="*Collection Name*" CUSTOM1="*Data*" CUSTOM2="*Data*" EXTENSIONS="*File Extensions*" EXTERNAL="*Yes¦No*" KEY="*Key*" QUERY="*Query Name*" RECURSE="*Yes¦No*" TITLE="*Text*" TYPE="*Type*" URLPATH="*Path*">

Table A.33   <CFINDEX> Attributes

Attribute	Description	Notes
ACTION	Action	Required attribute (see Table A.34).
BODY	Body to index	Required if TYPE is Custom. If indexing files, this must be the path to the file to be indexed. If indexing a query, this must be the column to be indexed.
COLLECTION	Collection name	Required. Name of the collection to be indexed. If using external collections, this must be a fully qualified path to the collection.
CUSTOM1	Custom data	Optional attribute for storing data during indexing.
CUSTOM2	Custom data	Optional attribute for storing data during indexing.
EXTENSIONS	File extensions	Optional list of extensions of files to be indexed. List must be comma-delimited. Used only if TYPE is PATH.
EXTERNAL	External collection	Optional attribute. Must be Yes if indexing an external collection.

Attribute	Description	Notes
KEY	Unique key	Optional attribute. Used to indicate what makes each record unique. If TYPE is file, this should be the document file name. If TYPE is path, this should be a full path to the document. If TYPE is custom, this should be any unique identifier.
QUERY	Query name	Optional attribute.
RECURSE	Recurse directories	Optional attribute. If Yes, all sub-directories are indexed too.
TITLE	Document title	Required if TYPE is Custom.
TYPE	Index type	Optional attribute. Must be FILE PATH or CUSTOM.
URLPATH	URL path	Optional attribute. Specifies the URL path for files when TYPE = File or TYPE = Path.

Table A.34 <CFINDEX> Actions

Action	Description
DELETE	Deletes a key from a collection
OPTIMIZE	Optimizes a collection
PURGE	Clears all data from a collection
REFRESH	Clears all data from a collection and repopulates it
UPDATE	Updates a collection and adds a key if it does not exist

Examples: This examples indexes all HTM and HTML files in all directories beneath the web server document root.

```
<CFINDEX COLLECTION="Docs" TYPE="Path" KEY="c:\inetpub\wwwroot"
➥ URLPATH="http://127.0.0.1/" EXTENSIONS=".htm, .html" RECURSE="Yes">
```

▶ **See** Chapter 26, "Full-Text Searching with Verity," **p. 601**

See also: <CFSEARCH>

<CFINPUT>

Description: <CFINPUT> is an enhancement to the standard HTML <INPUT> tag. <CFINPUT> allows you to automatically embed JavaScript client-side validation code in your HTML forms. <CFINPUT> must be used between <CFFORM> and </CFORM> tags. <CFINPUT> is not a Java control. The <CFINPUT> attributes are listed in Table A.35.

App

A

Syntax: <CFINPUT CHECKED MAXLENGTH="*Length*" MESSAGE="*Message Text*" NAME="*Field Name*" ONERROR="*JavaScipt Error Function*" ONVALIDATE="*JavaScript Validation Function*" RANGE="*Range Values*" REQUIRED="*Yes¦No*" SIZE="*Field Size*" TYPE="*Type*" VALIDATE="*Validation Type*" VALUE="*Initial Value*">

Table A.35   *<CFINPUT>* Attributes

Attribute	Description	Notes
CHECKED	Checked state	Optional. Only valid if type is RADIO or CHECKBOX. If present, radio button or checkbox is pre-checked.
MAXLENGTH	Maximum number of characters	Optional attribute.
MESSAGE	Validation failure message	Optional message to display upon validation failure.
NAME	Unique control name	This attribute is required.
ONERROR	JavaScript error function	Optional override to your own JavaScript error message function.
ONVALIDATE	JavaScript validation function	Optional override to your own JavaScript validation function.
RANGE	Range minimum and maximum	Optional range for numeric values only. Must be specified as two numbers separated by a comma.
REQUIRED	Field is required	Optional required flag. Must be Yes or No is specified, defaults to No.
SIZE	Field size	Optional number of characters to display before needing horizontal scrolling.
TYPE	Input type	Must be TEXT, RADIO, CHECKBOX, or PASSWORD.
VALIDATE	Field validation	Optional field validation. If specified, must be any of the validation types listed in Table A.36.
VALUE	Initial value	Optional initial field value.

Table A.36   *<CFINPUT>* Validation Types

Type	Description
Creditcard	Correctly formatted credit card number verified using mod10.
Date	Date in MM/DD/YY format.

Type	Description
Eurodate	European date in DD/MM/YY format.
Float	Number with decimal point.
Integer	Number with no decimal point.
Social_Security_Number	Social Security number formatted as 999-99-9999 (using hyphens or spaces as separators).
Telephone	Phone number in 999-999-9999 format (using hyphens or spaces as separators). Area code and exchange must not begin with 0 or 1.
Time	Time in hh:mm or hh:mm:ss format
Zipcode	U.S. Zipcode, either 99999 or 99999-9999 format.

Examples: The following example creates a simple text file that is flagged as required.

```
<CFFORM ACTION="process.cfm">
<CFINPUT TYPE="text" NAME="name" REQUIRED="Yes" MESSAGE="NAME is required!">
</CFFORM>
```

The next example creates a field that will only accept a valid telephone number.

```
<CFFORM ACTION="process.cfm">
<CFINPUT TYPE="text" NAME="phone" VALIDATE="telephone"
➥MESSAGE="You entered an invalid phone number!">
</CFFORM>
```

> **N O T E** <CFINPUT> does not support input fields of type HIDDEN.
>
> ▶ **See** Chapter 14, "Form Data Validation," **p. 297** ■

See also: <CFFORM>, <CFGRID>, <CFSELECT>, <CFSLIDER>, <CFTEXTINPUT>, <CFTREE>

<CFINSERT>

Description: <CFINSERT> adds a single row to a database table. <CFINSERT> requires that the database and table names be provided. All other attributes are optional. The full list of <CFINSERT> attributes is explained in Table A.37.

Syntax: <CFINSERT DATASOURCE="*ODBC Data Source*" TABLENAME="*Table Name*"
USERNAME="*User Name*" PASSWORD="Password" FORMFIELDS="*List of Fields to Insert*">

Table A.37	*<CFINCLUDE>* Attributes	
Attribute	**Description**	**Notes**
DATASOURCE	Name of ODBC data source	The specified data source must already exist. This attribute is required.

continues

Table A.37 Continued

Attribute	Description	Notes
FORMFIELDS	List of fields to insert	This optional attribute specifies which fields are to be inserted, if they are present. Any fields present that are not in the list will not be inserted.
PASSWORD	ODBC data source password	This optional attribute is used to override the ODBC login password specified in the Cold Fusion Administrator.
TABLENAME	Name of table to insert data into	Some ODBC data sources require fully qualified table names. This attribute is required.
USERNAME	ODBC data source login name.	This optional attribute is used to override the ODBC login name specified in the Cold Fusion Administrator.

N O T E For <CFINSERT> to work correctly, your form field names *must* match the column names in the destination table. ■

T I P If your form contains fields that are not part of the table into which you are inserting data, use the FORMFIELDS attribute to instruct Cold Fusion to ignore those fields.

T I P For more control over the insertion of rows into a database table, you may use the <CFQUERY> tag specifying INSERT as the SQL statement.

Example: The following example inserts a new row into the Employees table in the A2Z data source.

```
<CFINSERT DATASOURCE="A2Z" TABLENAME="Employees">
```

The next example inserts a new row into the same table, but will only insert values into the three specified fields *if* they exist.

```
<CFINSERT DATASOURCE="A2Z" TABLENAME="Employees"
➥FORMFIELD="LastName,FirstName,PhoneExtension">
```

▶ **See** Chapter 13, "Using Forms to Add or Change Data," **p. 261**

See also: <CFQUERY>, <CFUPDATE>

<CFLDAP>

Description: <CFLDAP> is used for all interaction with LDAP servers. <CFLDAP> can be used to search an LDAP server, as well as to add, change, or delete data. Table A.38 lists the attributes for <CFLDAP>.

Syntax: `<CFLDAP ACTION="`*Action*`" ATTRIBUTES="`*Attributes List*`" DN="`*Name*`"`
`FILTER="`*Filter*`" MAXROWS="`*Number*`" NAME="`*Query Name*`" PASSWORD="`*Password*`" PORT="`*Port*
Number`" SCOPE="`*Scope*`" SERVER="`*Server Address*`" SORT="`*Sort Order*`" START="`*Start*
Position`" STARTROW="`*Number*`" TIMEOUT="`*Timeout*`" USERNAME="`*Name*`">`

Table A.38   *<CFLDAP>* Attributes

Attribute	Description	Notes
ACTION	Action	Required attribute. See Table A.39 for possible values.
ATTRIBUTES	Desired attributes	Required if ACTION is QUERY. Comma-delimited list of desired attributes. Query specified in NAME attribute will contain these columns.
DN	Distinguished name	Required if ACTION is ADD, MODIFY, MODIFYDN, or delete.
FILTER	Search filter	Optional search filter used if ACTION is QUERY.
MAXROWS	Maximum rows to retrieve	Optional attribute.
NAME	Query name	Name of query for returned data. Required if ACTION is QUERY.
PASSWORD	User password	Optional user password. Might be required for update operations.
PORT	Port number	Optional port number. Defaults to 389 if not specified.
SCOPE	Search scope	Optional search scope if ACTION is QUERY. Valid values are ONELEVEL, BASE, and SUBTREE. Default is ONELEVEL.
SERVER	Server name	Required DNS name or IP address of LDAP server.
SORT	Sort order	Optional attribute used if ACTION is QUERY. Specifies the sort order as a comma-delimited list. May use ASC for ascending, and DESC for descending. Default is ASC.
START	Start name	Required if ACTION is QUERY. Distinguished name at which to start search.
STARTROW	Start row	Optional start row. Defaults to 1.
TIMEOUT	Timeout value	Optional timeout value.
USERNAME	User login name	Optional user login name. Might be required for update operations.

Table A.39   *<CFLDAP>* Actions

Action	Description
ADD	Adds an entry to an LDAP server
DELETE	Deletes an entry from an LDAP server
MODIFY	Updates an entry on an LDAP server
MODIFYDN	Updates the distinguished name of an entry on an LDAP server
QUERY	Performs a query against an LDAP server

Example: The following example retrieves a list of names from a public directory.

```
<CFLDAP NAME="seach" SERVER="ldap.four11.com" ACTION="Query" ATTRIBUTES="cn"
➥SCOPE="Subtree" SORT="cn Asc" FILTER="(sn=*)" START="#search#, c=US">
```

▶ **See** Chapter 27, "Directory Services," **p. 651**

<CFLOCATION>

Description: `<CFLOCATION>` is used to redirect a browser to a different URL. Tag attributes are explained in Table A.40.

Syntax: `<CFLOCATION URL="URL">`

Table A.40   *<CFLOCATION>* Attributes

Attribute	Description	Notes
ADDTOKEN	Optional attribute	If Yes, and client variables are being used, the CFID and CFTOKEN values will automatically be appended to the URL.
URL	URL (or relative URL) to redirect to	This attribute is required.

Example: The following example redirects a user to the Allaire home page.

```
<CFLOCATION URL="http://www.allaire.com">
```

The next example redirects a user to a Cold Fusion file in the same directory.

```
<CFLOCATION URL="thanks.cfm">
```

N O T E   Unlike `<CFINCLUDE>`, any text or CFML after the `<CFLOCATION>` tag will be ignored by Cold Fusion.

See also: `<CFINCLUDE>`

<CFLOOP> <CFBREAK> </CFLOOP>

Description: <CFLOOP> allows you to create loops within your code. Loops are blocks of code that are executed repeatedly until a specific condition is met. <CFBREAK> allows you to unconditionally terminate a loop. Cold Fusion support four kinds of loops.

- **For loops** loop a specific number of times.
- **While loops** loop until a set condition returns FALSE.
- **Query loops** loop through the results of a <CFQUERY>, once for each row returned.
- **List loops** loop through the elements of a specified list.

Table A.41 lists the <CFLOOP> attributes.

Syntax: For loop: <CFLOOP INDEX="*Index*" FROM="*Loop Start*" TO="*Loop End*" STEP="*Step Value*">

While loop: <CFLOOP CONDITION="*Expression*">

Query loop: <CFLOOP QUERY="*Query Name*" STARTROW="*Start Row Value*" ENDROW="*End Row Value*">

List loop: <CFLOOP INDEX="*Index*" LIST="*List*" DELIMITERS="*Delimiters*">

N O T E The syntax and use of <CFLOOP> varies based on the type of loop being executed. ■

Table A.41 *<CFLOOP>* Attributes

Attribute	Description	Notes
CONDITION	While loop condition	This attribute is required for while loops, and must be a valid condition.
DELIMITERS	List loop delimiters	This is an optional list loop attribute. If it is omitted, the default delimiter of a comma will be used.
ENDROW	Query loop end position	This is an optional query loop attribute. If it is omitted, all rows will be processed.
FROM	For loop start position	This attribute is required for for loops, and must be a numeric value.
INDEX	Current element	This attribute is required for for loops and list loops, and contains the name of the variable that will contain the current element.
LIST	List loop list	This attribute is required for list loops, and can be a Cold Fusion list field, or a static string.

continues

Table A.41 Continued

Attribute	Description	Notes
QUERY	Query loop query	This attribute is required for query loops, and must be the name of a previously executed <CFQUERY>.
STARTROW	Query loop start position	Thus is an optional query loop attribute. If it is omitted, the loop will start at the first row.
STEP	"or loop step value	This is an optional for loop attribute. If it is omitted then the default value of 1 will be used.
TO	For loop end position	This attribute is required for for loops, and must be a numeric value.

Example: The following is a for loop used in a FORM to populate a select field with the years 1901 to 2000 (the alternative would have been to enter 100 OPTION values manually).

```
<SELECT NAME="year">
 <CFLOOP INDEX="YearValue" FROM="1901" TO="2000">
 <OPTION><CFOUTPUT>#YearValue#</CFOUTPUT>
</SELECT>
```

The following example does the exact same thing, but presents the list in reverse order, this is done by specifying a STEP value of -1.

```
<SELECT NAME="year">
 <CFLOOP INDEX="YearValue" FROM="2000" TO="1901" STEP="-1">
  <OPTION><CFOUTPUT>#YearValue#</CFOUTPUT>
 </CFLOOP>
</SELECT>
```

The next example loops until any random number between 1 and 10, excluding 5, is generated.

```
<CFSET RandomNumber = 0>
<CFLOOP CONDITION= "(#RandomNumber# GT 0) AND (#RandomNumber# NEQ 5)">
 <CFSET RandomNumber = RandRange(1, 10)>
</CFLOOP>
```

The following example creates a query loop to process an existing <CFQUERY> named Orders, but only processed rows 100 through 150.

```
<CFLOOP QUERY="Orders" STARTROW="100" ENDROW="150">
 <CFOUTPUT>
  #OrderNum# - #DateFormat(OrderDate)# - #DollarFormat(Total)#<BR>
 </CFOUTPUT>
</CFLOOP>
```

The next example loops through a user-supplied list of titles, displaying them one at a time.

```
<CFLOOP INDEX="Title" LIST="#FORM.Titles#">
 <CFOUTPUT>
  Title: #Title#<BR>
 </CFOUTPUT>
</CFLOOP>
```

The following example uses `<CFBREAK>` to terminate a loop when a specific row is reached, in this case, an order number greater than `10000`.

```
<CFLOOP QUERY="Orders" >
 <CFIF OrderNum GT 10000>
  <CFBREAK>
 </CFIF>
 <CFOUTPUT>
  #OrderNum# - #DateFormat(OrderDate)# - #DollarFormat(Total)#<BR>
 </CFOUTPUT>
</CFLOOP>
```

T I P Using `<CFLOOP>` to process queries is substantially slower than using `<CFOUTPUT>`. Whenever possible, use `<CFOUTPUT>` to loop through query results.

N O T E The `<CFLOOP>` tag may be nested, and there is no limit placed on the number of nested loops allowed. ■

<CFMAIL> </CFMAIL>

Description: `<CFMAIL>` is used to generate SMTP mail from within Cold Fusion templates. `<CFMAIL>` can be used to output query results, just like `<CFOUTPUT>`, or on its own. The `<CFMAIL>` tag itself is used to setup the mail message, all text between the `<CFMAIL>` and `</CFMAIL>` tags is sent as the message body. `<CFMAIL>` requires that you specify a sender address, recipient address, and subject. All other attributes are optional. The complete list of attributes is explained in Table A.42.

Syntax: `<CFMAIL CC="Carbon Copy Addresses" FROM="Sender Address" GROUP="Group Name" MAXROWS="Maximum Mail Messages" PORT="SMTP TCP/IP Port" QUERY="Query Name" SERVER="SMTP Server Address" SUBJECT="Subject" TIMEOUT="SMTP Connection Timeout" TO="Recipient Address" TYPE="Message Type">`

`Message`

`</CFMAIL>`

Table A.42 *<CFMAIL>* Attributes

Attribute	Description	Notes
CC	Carbon copy addresses	Optional. One or more carbon copy addresses separated by commas.
FROM	Sender's address	Required sender's email address.
GROUP	Query column to group on	Optional attribute that specifies column to group on. See `<CFOUTPUT>` for more information on grouping data.

continues

Table A.42   Continued

Attribute	Description	Notes
MAXROWS	Maximum message to send	Optional attribute specifying the maximum number of email messages to generate.
PORT	TCP/IP SMTP port	Optional TCP/IP SMTP port. Will override the default value of 25 if specified.
QUERY	<CFQUERY> to draw data from	Email can be generated based on the results of a <CFQUERY>. To do this, specify the name of the <CFQUERY> here. This is an optional attribute.
SERVER	SMTP mail server	Optional SMTP mail server name. Will override the default setting if specified.
SUBJECT	Message subject	Required message subject.
TIMEOUT	Connection timeout interval	Optional SMTP connection timeout interval. Will override the default setting if specified.
TO	Recipient's address	Required recipient's email address.
TYPE	Message type	Optional message type. Currently the only supported type is HTML indicating that there is HTML code embedded in the message.

Example: The following is a simple email message based on a form submission. It uses form fields in both the attributes and the message body itself.

```
<CFMAIL
 FROM="#FORM.EMail#"
 TO="sales@a2zbooks.com"
 SUBJECT="Customer inquiry"
>
The following customer inquiry was posted to our web site:
Name: #FORM.name#
E-Mail: #FORM.EMail#

Message:
#FORM.Message#

</CFMAIL>
```

The next example send an email message based on <CFQUERY> results, the message is sent once for each row retrieved.

```
<CFMAIL
 QUERY="MailingList"
 FROM="sales@a2zbooks.com"
 TO="#EMailAddress#"
 SUBJECT="Monthly Online Newsletter"
```

```
>
Dear #FirstName#,

This E-Mail message is to remind you that our new monthly
➥online newsletter is now on our web site.

You can access it at http://www.a2zbooks.com/newsletter/

Thanks for you continued interest in our product line.

A2Z Books Sales

</CFMAIL>
```

> **TIP**
>
> Unlike web browsers, email programs do not ignore white space. If you embed carriage returns between the <CFMAIL> and </CFMAIL> tags, carriage returns will be displayed in the email message.

NOTE To use <CFMAIL>, the Cold Fusion SMTP interface must be set up and working. If email is not being sent correctly, use the Cold Fusion Administrator to verify that Cold Fusion can connect to your SMTP mail server. ■

NOTE In normal operation the PORT, SERVER, and TIMEOUT attributes will never be used. These are primarily used for debugging and troubleshooting email problems. ■

NOTE Email errors are logged to the \CFUSION\MAIL\LOG directory. Messages that cannot be delivered are stored in the \CFUSION\MAIL\UNDELIVR directory.

▶ **See** Chapter 20, "Interacting with Email," **p. 461** ■

See also: <CFPOP>

<CFMODULE>

Description: <CFMODULE> is used to call a Custom Tag explicitly stating it's full or relative path. Table A.3636 lists the <CFMODULE> attributes. Your own tag attributes may be added to this list too.

Syntax: <CFMODULE NAME="*Path*" TEMPLATE="*Path*" ...>

Table A.43   *<CFMODULE>* Attributes

Attribute	Description	Notes
NAME	Fixed path to tag file	Either TEMPLATE or NAME must be used, but not both at once. Use for directory delimiters.
TEMPLATE	Relative path to tag file	Either TEMPLATE or NAME must be used, but not both at once.

Examples: The following example calls a custom tag named ShowMenu in the parent directory.

```
<CFMODULE TEMPLATE="../showmenu.cfm">
```

▶ **See** Chapter 33, "Custom Tags," **p. 767**

 TIP   As a rule, you are almost always better off *not* using <CFMODULE>, but rather invoking Custom Tags by using the CF_convention as seen in Chapter 33.

<CFOBJECT>

Description: <CFOBJECT> allows you to use COM and DCOM objects within your Cold Fusion applications. To use an object you need to know its ID or file name, as well as its methods and properties. <CFOBJECT> attributes are listed in Table A.44.

To use an object with <CFOBJECT>, that object must be already installed on the server.

Syntax: *<CFOBJECT ACTION="Action" CLASS="Class ID" CONTEXT="Context" NAME="Name" SERVER="Server Name">*

Table A.44   *<CFOBJECT>* Attributes

Attribute	Description	Notes
ACTION	Action	Required attribute. Must be either CREATE to instantiate an object, or CONNECT to connect to a running object.
CLASS	Component ProgID	This attribute is required.
CONTEXT	Operation context	Optional attribute. Must be InProc, Local, or Remote. Uses registry setting is not specified.
NAME	Object name	This attribute is required.
SERVER	Valid server name	Server name as UNC, DNS, or IP address. Required only if CONTEXT = remote.

Example: The following example instantiates an object named NT.Exec, and invokes a method.

```
<CFOBJECT CLASS="NT.Exec" ACTION="CREATE" NAME="Exec">
<CFSET Exec.Command = "DIR C:\">
<CFSET temp = Exec.Run()>
```

▶ **See** Chapter 34, "Interfacing with COM and DCOM Objects," **p. 789**

N O T E   Use of <CFOBJECT> can be disabled in the Cold Fusion Administrator program. ■

<CFOUTPUT> </CFOUTPUT>

Description: <CFOUTPUT> is used to output the results of a <CFQUERY>, or any time text includes variables that are to be expanded. If <CFQUERY> is used to process the results of a <CFQUERY> tag, any code between <CFOUTPUT> and </CFOUTPUT> is repeated once for every row. <CFOUTPUT> can be used with the GROUP attribute to specify a data group. Data that is grouped together is displayed so that only the first occurrence of each value is output. Table A.45 lists the <CFOUTPUT> attributes. If you are using <CFOUTPUT> to display query results, then two additional variables are available to you, as listed in Table A.45.

Syntax: <CFOUTPUT QUERY="*Query Name*" MAXROWS="*Maximum Rows*" STARTROW="*Start Row*" GROUP="*Group Column*">

Code

</CFOUTPUT>

Table A.45   *<CFOUTPUT>* Attributes

Attribute	Description	Notes
GROUP	Column to group on	This optional attribute allows you to define output groups.
MAXROWS	Maximum rows to display	This optional attribute specifies the maximum number of rows to display. If omitted, all rows are displayed.
QUERY	Query name	This optional query name is used to refer to the query results within <CFOUTPUT> text.
STARTROW	First row to display	This optional attribute specifies the output start row.

Table A.46   *<CFOUTPUT>* Fields

Field	Description
#CurrentRow#	The number of the current row, starting at 1, and incremented each time a row is displayed.
#RecordCount#	The total number of records to be output.

Example: Any time you use variables or fields within your template, you must enclose them within <CFOUTPUT> tags as shown in the following example, or else the field name will be sent as is and not expanded.

```
<CFOUTPUT>
 Hi #name#, thanks for dropping by again.<P>
 You have now visited us #NumberFormat(visits)# times since your
➡first visit on #DateFormat(first_visit)#.
</CFOUTPUT>
```

The next example uses <CFOUTPUT> to display the results of a query in an unordered list.

```
<UL>
<CFOUTPUT QUERY="Employees">
 <LI>#LastName#, #FirstName# - Ext: #PhoneExtension#
</CFOUTPUT>
</UL>
```

To group output results you can use the GROUP attribute as shown in the following example which lists employees within departments.

```
<UL>
 <CFOUTPUT QUERY="Employees" GROUP="Department">
  <LI><B>#Department#</B>
   <UL>
    <CFOUTPUT>
     <LI>#LastName#, #FirstName# - Ext: #PhoneExtension#
    </CFOUTPUT>
   </UL>
 </CFOUTPUT>
</UL>
```

N O T E   There is no limit to the number of nested groups that you may use in a <CFOUTPUT>. However, every column used in a GROUP must be part of the SQL statement ORDER BY clause. ▪

T I P   The STARTROW and MAXROWS attribute can be used to implement a display next *n* of *n* type display. You should note however, that even though only a subset of the retrieved data is displayed, it has *all* been retrieved by the <CFQUERY> statement. So, while the page might be transmitted to the browser quicker, because it contains less text, the SQL operation itself takes no less time.

▶**See** Chapter 11, "Cold Fusion Basics," **p. 193**

See also: <CFLOOP>, <CFMAIL>, <CFQUERY>, <CFTABLE>

<CFPARAM>

Description: <CFPARAM> lets you specify default values for parameters and parameters that are required. <CFPARAM> requires that a variable name be passed to it. If a VALUE is passed as well, that value will be used as the default value if the variable is not specified. If VALUE is not specified, <CFPARAM> will require that the named variable be passed, and will generate an error message if it is not. Table A.47 lists the attributes for the <CFPARAM> tag.

Syntax: <CFPARAM NAME="*Parameter Name*" VALUE="*Value*">

Table A.47   *<CFPARAM>* Attributes

Attribute	Description	Notes
NAME	Name of variable	Name should be fully qualified with variable type. This attribute is required.

Attribute	Description	Notes
VALUE	Default variable value	This attribute is optional. If specified, the value will be used as the default value whenever this variable is used.

Example: The following example specifies a default value for a field that is to be used in a <CFQUERY> tag, making it unnecessary to write conditional code to build a dynamic SQL statement.

```
<CFPARAM NAME="Minimum" VALUE="10">
<CFQUERY NAME="OverDue" DATASOURCE= "A2Z">
 SELECT * FROM Inventory WHERE NumberInStock < #Minimum#
</CFQUERY>
```

The next example makes the Minimum field required, so if the template was requested and that field was not specified, an error would be generated.

```
<CFPARAM NAME="Minimum" >
<CFQUERY NAME="OverDue" DATASOURCE= "A2Z">
 SELECT * FROM Inventory WHERE NumberInStock < #Minimum#
</CFQUERY>
```

See also: <CFSET>

<CFPOP>

Description: <CFPOP> is used to retrieve and manipulate mail in a POP3 mail box. To access a POP mailbox you must know three things: the POP server name, the POP login name, and the account password. <CFPOP> has three modes of operation. It can be used to retrieve just mail headers, entire message bodies, and to delete messages. POP messages are not automatically deleted when they are read, and must be deleted explicitly with a DELETE operation. Table A.48 lists the <CFPOP> attributes, Table A.49 lists the <CFPOP> actions, and Table A.50 lists the columns returned when retrieving mail or mail headers.

Syntax: <CFPOP ACTION="*Action*" ATTACHMENTSPATH="*Path*" MAXROWS="*Number*" MESSAGENUMBER="*Messages*" NAME="*Query Name*" PASSWORD="*Password*" PORT="*Port Number*" SERVER="*Mail Server*" STARTROW="*Number*" TIMEOUT="*Timeout*" USERNAME="*User Name*">

Table A.48   *<CFPOP>* Attributes

Attribute	Description	Notes
ACTION	Action (see Table A.49)	Optional. Defaults to GETHEADERONLY.
ATTACHMENTSPATH	Attachment path	Optional path to store mail attachments.
MAXROWS	Maximum messages to retrieve	Optional attribute. Ignored ID MESSAGENUMBER is used.

continues

Table A.48   Continued

Attribute	Description	Notes
MESSAGENUMBER	Message number	Optional message number (or comma-delimited list of message numbers). Required if ACTION is DELETE. Specifies the messages to be deleted or retrieved.
NAME	Query name	Required if ACTION is GETALL or GETHEADERONLY, name of query to be returned. Query columns are listed in Table A.50.
PASSWORD	Password	Optional POP account password (most POP servers will require this).
PORT	Mail server port	Optional attribute, defaults to port 110.
SERVER	Mail server	Required. DNS name or IP address of the POP mail server.
STARTROW	Start row	Optional start row. Defaults to 1, ignored if MESSAGENUMBER is used.
TIMEOUT	Timeout value	Optional timeout value.
USERNAME	Login name	Optional POP login name (most POP servers will require this).

Table A.49   *<CFPOP>* Actions

Action	Description
DELETE	Deletes messages from a POP mailbox
GETALL	Gets message headers and body
GETHEADERONLY	Gets just message headers

Table A.50   *<CFPOP>* Query Columns

Column	Description
ATTACHMENTFILES	List of saved attachments, only present if ACTION is GETALL and an ATTACHMENT path was specified.
ATTACHMENTS	List of original attachment names, only present if ACTION is GETALL and an ATTACHMENT path was specified.
CC	List of any carbon copy recipients.

Column	Description
DATE	Message date.
FROM	Sender name.
HEADER	Mail header.
MESSAGENUMBER	Message number for use in calls with future calls.
REPLYTO	Email address to reply to.
SUBJECT	Message subject.
TO	Recipient list.

Examples: The following example retrieves a list of waiting mail in a POP mailbox, and then displays the message list in an HTML list.

```
<CFPOP SERVER="mail.a2zbooks.com" USERNAME=#username# PASSWORD=#pwd#
➥ACTION="GETHEADERONLY" NAME="msg">
<UL>
<CFOUTPUT QUERY="msg">
<LI>From: #from# - Subject: #subject#
</CFOUTPUT>
</UL>
```

N O T E   <CFPOP> is used to retrieve mail only. To send mail use the <CFMAIL> tag.

▶ **See** Chapter 20, "Interacting with Email," **p. 461** ∎

See also: <CFMAIL>

<CFQUERY> </CFQUERY>

Description: <CFQUERY> is the tag you'll use to submit SQL statements to an ODBC driver. SQL statements are not limited to SELECT statements, but can also be INSERT, UPDATE, and DELETE statements, as well as calls to stored procedures. <CFQUERY> returns results in a named set if you specify a query name in the NAME attribute. The <CFQUERY> attributes setup the query, and any text between the <CFQUERY> and </CFQUERY> tags become the SQL statement that is sent to the ODBC driver. Cold Fusion conditional code may be used between the <CFQUERY> and </CFQUERY> tags, allowing you to create dynamic SQL statements. The complete set of <CFQUERY> attributes is listed in Table A.51.

Syntax: <CFQUERY NAME="*Parameter Name*" DATASOURCE="*ODBC Data Source*"
USERNAME="*User Name*" PASSWORD="*Password*">

SQL statement

</CFQUERY>

Table A.51 *<CFQUERY>* **Attributes**

Attribute	Description	Notes
DATASOURCE	ODBC data source	This optional attribute is used to override the ODBC data source specified when the report was created.
NAME	Query name	This optional query name is used to refer to the query results in <CFOUTPUT>, <CFMAIL>, or <CFTABLE> tags.
PASSWORD	ODBC data source password	This optional attribute is used to override the ODBC login password specified in the Cold Fusion Administrator.
USERNAME	ODBC data source login name	This optional attribute is used to override the ODBC login name specified in the Cold Fusion Administrator.

The following example is a simple data retrieval query.

```
<CFQUERY
 DATASOURCE="A2Z"
 NAME="Employees"
>
 SELECT FirstName, LastName, PhoneExtension FROM Employees
</CFQUERY>
```

The next example demonstrates how dynamic SQL statements can be constructed using the Cold Fusion conditional tags.

```
<
 CFQUERY
 DATASOURCE="A2Z"
 NAME="Employees"
>
 SELECT FirstName, LastName, PhoneExtension, EmployeeID
      FROM Employees
      WHERE EmployeeID = EmployeeID

<CFIF #FirstName# IS NOT "">
 AND FirstName LIKE '#FirstName#%'
</CFIF>

<CFIF #LastName# IS NOT "">
 AND LastName LIKE '#LastName#%'
</CFIF>

<CFIF #PhoneExtension# IS NOT "">
 AND PhoneExtension LIKE '#PhoneExtension#%'
</CFIF>

ORDER BY LastName, FirstName

</CFQUERY>
```

<CFQUERY> can be used to execute *any* SQL statements, and the following example demonstrates how <CFQUERY> can be used to delete rows from a table.

```
<CFQUERY
 DATASOURCE="A2Z"
>
DELETE FROM Employees WHERE EmployeeID = #EmployeeID#"
</CFQUERY>
```

▶ **See** Chapter 11, "Cold Fusion Basics," **p. 193**

▶ **See** Chapter 12, "Cold Fusion Forms," **p. 225**

▶ **See** Chapter 13, "Using Forms to Add or Change Data," **p. 261**

See also: <CFOUTPUT>, <CFMAIL>, <CFTABLE>

<CFREPORT> </CFREPORT>

Description: <CFREPORT> is the Cold Fusion interface to reports created with the Crystal Reports Professional report writer. <CFREPORT> only requires a single attribute, the name of the report to be processed. The full list of supported attributes is explained in Table A.52.

Syntax: <CFREPORT REPORT="*Report File*" ORDERBY="*Sort Order*" DATASOURCE="*ODBC Data Source*" USERNAME="*User Name*" PASSWORD="*Password*" @FORMULANAME="*Formula*">

Optional filter conditions

</CFREPORT>

Table A.52   *<CFREPORT>* Attributes

Attribute	Description	Notes
DATASOURCE	ODBC data source	This optional attribute is used to override the ODBC data source specified when the report was created.
ORDERBY	Report sort order	This optional attribute overrides the default sort order specified when the report was created.
PASSWORD	ODBC data source password	This optional attribute is used to override the ODBC login password specified in the Cold Fusion Administrator.
REPORT	Name of RPT file to process	This attribute is required.
USERNAME	ODBC data source login name	This optional attribute is used to override the ODBC login name specified in the Cold Fusion Administrator.
@FORMULANAME	Crystal Reports formula override	This optional parameter allows you to override Crystal Reports formulas with passed formula text. Formula names *must* begin with a @ character.

Example: The following example processes a report created with Crystal Reports Professional, and passes it an optional filter condition.

```
<CFREPORT REPORT="\a2z\scripts\emplist.rpt">
 {Departments.Department} = "Sales"
</CFREPORT>
```

The next example processes a report and specifies parameters to override the ODBC data source, user login name and password, and a formula named title derived from a HTML form.

```
<CFREPORT REPORT="\a2z\scripts\emplist.rpt" DATASOURCE="A2ZInternal"
➥ USERNAME="HR" PASSWORD="anarchy" @Title="#FORM.title#">
 {Departments.Department} = "Sales"
</CFREPORT>
```

▶ **See** Chapter 15, "The Report Writer," **p. 315**

<CFSCHEDULE>

Description: <CFSCHEDULE> allows you to run a specified page at scheduled intervals with the option to write out static HTML pages. This allows you to offer users access to pages that publish data, such as reports, without forcing users to wait while a database transaction is performed in order to populate the data on the page. Cold Fusion scheduled events must be registered using the Cold Fusion Administrator before they can be executed. Information supplied by the user includes the scheduled Cold Fusion page to execute, the time and frequency for executing the page, and if the output from the task should be published. If the output is to be published, a path and file is specified.

<CFSCHEDULE> attributes are listed in Table A.53.

Syntax: <CFSCHEDULE ACTION="*Action*" ENDDATE="*Date*" ENDTIME="*Time*" FILE="*File Name*" INTERVAL="*Interval*" LIMITIME="*Seconds*" OPERATION="*HTTPRequest*" PASSWORD="*Password*" PATH="*Path*" PROXYSERVER="*Server Name*" PUBLISH="*Yes¦No*" RESOLVEURL="*Yes¦No*" STARTDATE="*Date*" STARTTIME="*Time*" TASK="*Task Name*" URL="*URL*" USERNAME="*User Name*">

Table A.53   *<CFSCHEDULE>* Attributes

Attribute	Description	Notes
ACTION	Action (see Table A.54)	Required attribute.
ENDDATE	Event end date	Optional attribute. Date the scheduled task should end.
ENDTIME	Event end time	Optional attribute. Time the scheduled task should end. Enter value in seconds.
FILE	File to create	Required if PUBLISH is Yes.
INTERVAL	Execution interval	Required if ACTION is UPDATE, may be specified as number of seconds, or as daily, weekly, monthly, or execute.

LIMITTIME	Maximum execution time	Optional attribute. Maximum number of seconds allowed for execution.
OPERATION	Operation	Required if ACTION is UPDATE, currently only HTTPRequest is supported.
PASSWORD	Password	Optional password for protected URLs.
PATH	Path to save published files	Required if PUBLISH is Yes.
PROXYSERVER	Proxy server name	Optional name of proxy server.
PUBLISH	Publish static files	Optional attribute. Yes if the scheduled task should publish files. Default is No.
RESOLVEURL	Resolve URLs	Optional attribute. If Yes, resolve URLs to fully qualified URLs. Default is No.
STARTDATE	Event start date	Optional attribute. Date the scheduled task should start.
STARTTIME	Event start time	Optional attribute. Time the scheduled task should start. Enter value in seconds.
TASK	Task name	Required attribute. The registered task name.
URL	URL	Required if ACTION is UPDATE, the URL to be executed.
USERNAME	User name	Optional user name for protected URLs.

Table A.54   <CFSCHEDULE> Actions

Action	Description
DELETE	Delete a task
UPDATE	Update a task
RUN	Execute a task

Example: The following example executes a task and allows it to run for 30 minutes.

```
<CFSCHEDULE TASK="SalesReports" ACTION="RUN" LIMITTIME="1800">
```

▶ **See** Chapter 32, "Event Scheduling," **p. 755**

N O T E   Execution of <CFSCHEDULE> can be disabled in the Cold Fusion Administrator. ▪

<CFSEARCH>

Description: <CFSEARCH> is used to perform searches against Verity collections (in much the same way as <CFQUERY> is used to perform searches against ODBC data sources). To use <CFSEARCH>, you must specify the collection to be searched and the name of the query to be returned. You may search more than one collection at once, and you may also perform searches against Verity collections created with applications other than Cold Fusion. Table A.55 lists the <CFSEARCH> attributes.

Syntax: <CFSEARCH COLLECTION="*Collection Name*" CRITERIA="*Search Criteria*" CUSTOM1="*Data*" CUSTOM2="*Data*" EXTERNAL="*Yes¦No*" MAXROWS="*Number*" NAME="*Name*" STARTROW="*Number*" TYPE="*Type*">

Table A.55   *<CFSEARCH>* Attributes

Attribute	Description	Notes
COLLECTION	Collection name	Required attribute. The name of the collection or collections to be searched. Multiple collections must be separated by commas. For external collections, specify the full path to the collection.
CRITERIA	Search criteria	Optional attribute. Search criteria as shown in Appendix C.
CUSTOM1	Custom data storage	Optional attribute. Used to store custom data during an indexing operation.
CUSTOM2	Custom data storage	Optional attribute. Used to store custom data during an indexing operation.
EXTERNAL	External collection	Optional attribute. Must be Yes if using an external collection. Default is No.
MAXROWS	Maximum rows to retrieve	Optional attribute. Defaults to all.
NAME	Value column	Optional attribute. Column to be used for OPTION VALUE attribute.
STARTROW	Start row	Optional attribute. Default is first row.
TYPE	Search type	Optional attribute. May be SIMPLE or EXPLICIT.

Examples: The following example performs a search with a user supplied search criteria.

<CFSEARCH NAME="search" COLLECTION="site" TYPE="SIMPLE" CRITERIA="#search#">

▶ **See** Chapter 26, "Full-Text Searching with Verity," **p. 601**

▶ **See** Appendix C, "Verity Search Language Reference," **p. 975**

See also: <CFINDEX>

<CFSELECT> </CFSELECT>

Description: `<CFSELECT>` is used to simplify the process of creating data driven `SELECT` controls. `<CFSELECT>` is not a Java control. `<CFSELECT>` requires that you pass it the name of a query to use to populate the drop-down list box. `<CFSELECT>` attributes are listed in Table A.56.

You may add your own options to the `SELECT` list by adding `<OPTION>` tags between the `<CFSELECT>` and `</CFSELECT>` tags.

Syntax: `<CFSELECT DISPLAY="Column Name" MESSAGE="Message Text" MULTIPLE="Yes¦No" NAME="Field Name" ONERROR="JavaScript Error Function" QUERY="Query Name" REQUIRED="Yes¦No" SELECTED="Value" SIZE="Size" VALUE="Column Name"></CFSELECT>`

Table A.56   *<CFSELECT>* Attributes

Attribute	Description	Notes
DISPLAY	Column to display	Optional query. Column to use as the displayed text.
MESSAGE	Validation failure message	Optional message to display upon validation failure.
MULTIPLE	Allow multiple selection	Optional attribute. Defaults to No.
NAME	Unique field name	This attribute is required.
ONERROR	JavaScript error function	Optional override to your own JavaScript error message function.
QUERY	Query name	Required attribute. Query to be used to populate the SELECT box.
REQUIRED	Field is required	Optional required flag. Must be Yes or No is specified, defaults to No.
SELECTED	Selected value	Value of the OPTION to be pre-selected.
SIZE	List size	Required attribute. Number of options to display without scrolling.
VALUE	Value column	Optional attribute, Column to be used for OPTION VALUE attribute.

Example: The following example creates a simple data-driven `SELECT` control.

```
<CFFORM ACTION="process.cfm">
<CFSELECT QUERY="Users" VALUE="id" DISPLAY="Name" SIZE="1">
</CFSELECT>
</CFFORM>
```

See also: `<CFFORM>`, `<CFGRID>`, `<CFINPUT>`, `<CFSLIDER>`, `<CFTEXTINPUT>`, `<CFTREE>`

<CFSET>

Description: <CFSET> is used to assign values to variables. <CFSET> can be used to set both client variables (type CLIENT), and standard variables (type VARIABLES). Unlike almost all other Cold Fusion tags, <CFSET> takes no attributes, just the name of the variable being assigned, and its value.

Syntax: <CFSET "*Variable*" = "*Value*">

Example: The following example creates a local variable containing a constant value.

```
<CFSET MaxDisplay = 25>
```

The following creates a client variable called #BGColor# which will contain a user-specified value, and explicitly states the variable type.

```
<CFSET CLIENT.BGColor = FORM.Color>
```

The next example stored tomorrow's date in a variable called Tomorrow.

```
<CFSET Tomorrow = Now() + 1>
```

<CFSET> can also be used to concatenate fields.

```
<CFSET VARIABLES.FullName = FORM.FirstName FORM.LastName>
```

Values of different data types may be concatenated too.

```
<CFSET Sentence = FORM.FirstName FORM.LastName & "is"
➡& FORM.age & "years old">
```

T I P   If you ever find yourself performing a calculation, or combining strings, more than once in a specific template, you're better off doing it once and assigning the results to a variable with <CFSET> than using that variable instead.

See also: <CFAPPLICATION>, <CFCOOKIE>, <CFPARAM>

<CFSETTING>

Description: <CFSETTING> is used to control various aspects of page processing, such as controlling the output of HTML code in your pages. One benefit of this option is managing white space that can occur in output pages that are served by Cold Fusion. <CFSETTING> attributes are listed in Table A.57.

When using <CFSETTING> to disable an option, make sure you have a matching enable option later in the file.

Syntax: <CFSETTING ENABLECFOUTPUTONLY="*Yes¦No*">

Table A.57   <CFSETTING> Attributes

Attribute	Description	Notes
ENABLECFOUTPUTONLY	Only output text within a <CFOUTPUT>	This attribute is required. It must be block Yes or No.

Examples:

The following demonstrates how `<CFSETTING>` can be used to control generated white space.

```
This text will be displayed
<CFSETTING ENABLECFOUTPUTONLY="Yes">
This text will not be displayed as it is not in a CFOUTOUT block
<CFOUTPUT>This will be displayed</CFOUTOUT>
<CFSETTING ENABLECFOUTPUTONLY="No">
This text will be displayed even though it is not in a CFOUTPUT block
```

<CFSLIDER>

Description: `<CFSLIDER>` embeds a Java slider control into your HTML forms. Slider controls are typically used to select one of a range of numbers. `<CFSLIDER>` must be used in between `<CFFORM>` and `</CFFORM>` tags. Table A.58 lists the entire set of `<CFSLIDER>` attributes.

Syntax: `<CFSLIDER ALIGN="Alignment" BGCOLOR="Background Color" BOLD="Yes¦No" FONT="Font Face" FONTSIZE="Font Size" GROOVECOLOR="Groove Color" HEIGHT="Control Height" HSPACE="Horizontal Spacing" IMG="Groove Image" IMGSTYLE="Groove Image Style" ITALIC="Yes¦No" LABEL="Slider Label" MESSAGE="Error Message" NAME="Field Name" NOTSUPPORTED="Non Java Browser Code" ONERROR="Error Function" ONVALIDATE="Validation Function" RANGE="Numeric Range" REFRESHLABEL="Yes¦No" SCALE="Increment Value" TEXTCOLOR="Text Color" VALUE="Initial Value" VSPACE="Vertical Spacing" WIDTH="Control Width">`

Table A.58 *<CSLIDER>* **Attributes**

Attribute	Description	Notes
ALIGN	Control alignment	Optional attribute. Possible values are Top, Left, Bottom, Baseline, TextTop, AbsBottom, Middle, AbsMiddle, Right.
BGCOLOR	Background color	Optional attribute. Possible values are black, cyan, darkgray, gray, lightgray, magenta, orange, pink, white, yellow, or any color specified in RGB form.
BOLD	Bold face text	Optional attribute. Must be Yes or No is specified, defaults to No.
FONT	Font face	Optional font face to use.
FONTSIZE	Font Size	Optional font size.
GROOVECOLOR	Groove color	Optional attribute. Possible values are black, cyan, darkgray, gray, lightgray, magenta, orange, pink, white, yellow, or any color specified in RGB form.

continues

Table A.58	Continued	
Attribute	**Description**	**Notes**
HEIGHT	Control height	Optional height in pixels.
HSPACE	Control horizontal spacing	Optional horizontal spacing in pixels.
IMG	Groove image	Optional file name of image to be used for the slider groove.
IMGSTYLE	Grove image style	Optional attribute. May be Centered, Tiled, Scaled. Default is Scaled.
ITALIC	Italic face text	Optional attribute. Must be Yes or No is specified, defaults to No.
LABEL	Slider label	Optional attribute. May contain the variable %value%, in which case the current value will be displayed as the slider is moved.
MESSAGE	Validation failure message	Optional message to display upon validation failure.
NAME	Unique control name	This attribute is required.
NOTSUPPORTED	Text to be used for non Java browsers	Optional text (or HTML code) to be displayed on nonJava-capable browsers.
ONERROR	JavaScript error function	Optional override to your own JavaScript error message function.
ONVALIDATE	JavaScript validation function	Optional override to your own JavaScript validation function.
RANGE	Range minimum and maximum	Optional range for numeric values only, must be specified as two numbers separated by a comma, defaults to 0,100.
REFRESHLABEL	Refresh label as slider is moved	Optional attribute. Default is Yes. If you are not using a variable label, this attribute should be set to No to prevent unnecessary refreshing.
SCALE	Increment scale	Optional increment. Defaults to 1.
TEXTCOLOR	Text color	Optional attribute. Possible values are black, cyan, darkgray, gray, lightgray, magenta, orange, pink, white, yellow, or any color specified in RGB form.
VALUE	Initial value	Optional initial field value. If range is used, this value must be within the specified range.
VSPACE	Control vertical spacing	Optional vertical spacing in pixels.
WIDTH	Control width	Optional width in pixels.

Example: The following example displays a Java Slider control, specifying the height, width, font, and color, and label.

```
<CFFORM ACTION="process.cfm">
<CFSLIDER NAME="volume" HEIGHT="100" WIDTH="200" FONT="Verdana"
➡BGCOLOR="Black" TEXTCOLOR="White" GROOVECOLOR="White" LABEL="Volume %value%">
</CFFORM>
```

▶ **See** Chapter 19, "Enhancing Forms with *CFFORM,*" **p. 427**

N O T E The <CFSLIDER> control will only be accessible by users with Java-enabled browsers. ■

See also: <CFFORM>, <CFGRID>, <CFINPUT>, <CFSELECT>, <CFTEXTINPUT>, <CFTREE>

<CFTABLE> <CFCOL> </CFTABLE>

Description: <CFTABLE> allows you to easily create a table for displaying data. <CFTABLE> can create HTML tables (by generating the <TABLE> tag), or preformatted text tables that will display on all browsers. Using <CFTABLE> involves two tags: <CFTABLE> defines the table itself, and one or more <CFCOL> tags define the table columns. The <CFTABLE> attributes are listed in Table A.59, and the <CFCOL> attributes are listed in Table A.60.

Syntax: <CFTABLE QUERY="*Query Name*" MAXROWS="*Maximum Rows*" COLSPACING="*Column Spacing*" COLHEADERS HEADERLINES ="*Header Lines*" HTMLTABLE>

<CFCOL HEADER="*Header Text*" WIDTH ="*Width*" ALIGN ="*Alignment*" TEXT="*Body Text*">

</CFTABLE>

Table A.59   *<CFTABLE>* Attributes

Attribute	Description	Notes
COLHEADERS	Displays column headers	If this optional attribute is present, column headers will be displayed.
COLSPACING	Spaces between columns	This optional attribute overrides the default column spacing of 2 if present.
HEADERLINES	Number of header lines	The default number of header lines is 2: one for the header, and a blank row between the header and the body. You may increase this number if needed.
HTMLTABLE	Creates an HTML table	If this attribute is present, an HTML table will be created. If not, a preformatted text table will be created.
MAXROWS	Maximum number of table rows	This optional attribute is used to specify the maximum number of rows to be displayed in the table.
QUERY	<CFQUERY> name	The name of the query from which to derive the table body text.

Table A.60   *<CFCOL>* Attributes

Attribute	Description	Notes
ALIGN	Column alignment	Valid values are LEFT, CENTER, or RIGHT.
HEADER	Column header text	
TEXT	Column text	The text attribute is the body of what is displayed in each column. Hypertext jumps may be included, as may any table fields. Expressions may not be included in the TEXT attribute.
WIDTH	Column width	Optional column width. Defaults to 20 if not specified. Any text that will not fit into the cell will be truncated.

Example: The following example creates an HTML table with two columns labeled Name, and Extension.

```
<CFTABLE QUERY="Employees" COLHEADERS HTMLTABLE>
 <CFCOL HEADER="Name" ALIGN=LEFT TEXT ="#LastName#, #FirstName#">
<CFCOL HEADER="Extension" ALIGN=LEFT TEXT ="#PhoneExtension#">
</CFTABLE>
```

TIP

The <CFTABLE> tag is an easy and efficient way to create tables for displaying query results. For greater control over table output, including cell spanning, text, and background colors, borders, background images, and nested tables, you should create HTML tables manually.

▶**See** "Displaying Results in Tables," **p. 212**

See also: <CFOUTPUT>, <CFQUERY>

<CFTEXTINPUT>

Description: <CFTEXTINPUT> embeds a highly configurable Java text input control into your HTML forms. <CFTEXTINPUT> must be used in between <CFFORM> and </CFFORM> tags. Unlike the standard HTML INPUT, <CFTEXTINPUT> lets you configure the exact height and width of the edit control, as well as color, font, size, and spacing. <CFTEXTINPUT> can also automatically generate field JavaScript validation code. Table A.61 lists the entire set of <CFTEXTINPUT> attributes.

Syntax: <CFTEXTINPUT ALIGN="*Alignment*" BGCOLOR="*Background Color*" BOLD="*Yes¦No*" FONT="*Font Face*" FONTSIZE="*Font Size*" HEIGHT="*Control Height*" HSPACE="*Horizontal Spacing*" ITALIC="*Yes¦No*" MAXLENGTH="*Maximum Length*" MESSAGE="*Error Message*" NAME="*Field Name*" NOTSUPPORTED="*Non-Java Browser Code*" ONERROR="*Error Function*" ONVALIDATE="*Validation Function*" RANGE="*Numeric Range*" REQUIRED="*Yes¦No*" SIZE="*Field Size*" TEXTCOLOR="*Text Color*" VALIDATE="*Validation Type*" VALUE="*Initial Value*" VSPACE="*Vertical Spacing*" WIDTH="*Control Width*">

Table A.61 *<CFTEXTINPUT>* Attributes

Attribute	Description	Notes
ALIGN	Control alignment	Optional attribute. Possible values are Top, Left, Bottom, Baseline, TextTop, AbsBottom, Middle, AbsMiddle, and Right.
BGCOLOR	Background color	Optional attribute. Possible values are black, cyan, darkgray, gray, lightgray, magenta, orange, pink, white, yellow, or any color specified in RGB form.
BOLD	Bold face text	Optional attribute. Yes or No must be specified. Defaults to No.
FONT	Font face	Optional font face to use.
FONTSIZE	Font Size	Optional font size.
HEIGHT	Control height	Optional height in pixels.
HSPACE	Control horizontal spacing	Optional horizontal spacing in pixels.
ITALIC	Italic face text	Optional attribute. Yes or No must be specified. Defaults to No.
MAXLENGTH	Maximum number of characters	Optional attribute.
MESSAGE	Validation failure message	Optional message to display upon validation failure.
NAME	Unique control name	This attribute is required.
NOTSUPPORTED	Text to be used for non-Java browsers	Optional text (or HTML code) to be displayed on nonJava-capable browsers.
ONERROR	JavaScript error function	Optional override to your own JavaScript error message function.
ONVALIDATE	JavaScript validation function	Optional override to your own JavaScript validation function.
RANGE	Range minimum and maximum	Optional range for numeric values only, must be specified as two numbers separated by a comma.
REQUIRED	Field is required	Optional required flag. Yes or No must be specified. Defaults to No.
SIZE	Field size	Optional number of characters to display before needing horizontal scrolling.

continues

Table A.61   Continued

Attribute	Description	Notes
TEXTCOLOR	Text color	Optional attribute. Possible values are `black`, `cyan`, `darkgray`, `gray`, `lightgray`, `magenta`, `orange`, `pink`, `white`, `yellow`, or any color specified in RGB form.
VALIDATE	Field validation	Optional field validation. If specified, must be any of the validation types listed in Table A.62.
VALUE	Initial value	Optional initial field value.
VSPACE	Control vertical spacing	Optional vertical spacing in pixels.
WIDTH	Control width	Optional width in pixels.

Table A.62   <CFTEXTINPUT> Validation Types

Type	Description
Creditcard	Correctly formatted credit card number verified using mod10.
Date	Date in MM/DD/YY format.
Eurodate	European date in DD/MM/YY format.
Float	Number with decimal point.
Integer	Number with no decimal point.
Social_Security_Number	Social security number formatted as 999-99-9999 (using hyphens or spaces as separators).
Telephone	Phone number in 999-999-9999 format (using hyphens or spaces as separators). Area code and exchange must not begin with 0 or 1.
Time	Time in hh:mm or hh:mm:ss format.
Zipcode	U.S. Zipcode, either 99999 or 99999-9999 format.

Example: The following example displays a simple Java text edit control, specifying the height, width, font, and color.

```
<CFFORM ACTION="process.cfm">
<CFTEXTINPUT NAME="name" HEIGHT="100" WIDTH="200" FONT="Verdana"
➥BGCOLOR="Black" TEXTCOLOR="White">
</CFFORM>
```

▶ **See** Chapter 19, "Enhancing Forms with *CFFORM*," **p. 427**

N O T E The <CFTEXTINPUT> control will only be accessible by users with Java-enabled browsers. ■

See also: <CFFORM>, <CFGRID>, <CFINPUT>, <CFSELECT>, <CFSLIDER>, <CFTREE>

<CFTRANSACTION> </CFTRANSACTION>

Description: <CFTRANSACTION> is used to implement transaction and rollback processing. Any <CFQUERY> tags placed between <CFTRANSACTION> and </CFTRANSACTION> tags will be automatically rolled back if an error occurs. The <CFTRANSACTION> attributes are list in Table A.63.

Syntax: <CFTRANSACTION ISOLATION="*Lock Type*">

Queries

</CFTRANSACTION>

Table A.63 *<CFTRANSACTION>* **Attributes**

Attribute	Description	Notes
ISOLATION	Type of ODBC lock	Optional lock type. Possible values are READ_UNCOMMITTED, READ_COMMITTED, REPEATABLE_READ, SERIALIZABLE, and VERSIONING.

Example: The following example shows how <CFTRANSACTION> would be used to ensure that an operation dependent on two queries would not leave the databases in an inconstant state if one operation failed.

```
<CFTRANSACTION>
 <CFQUERY
  DATASOURCE="Accounts"
 >
  UPDATE Accounts SET Total = Total - #Withdrawal#
➥WHERE AccountNum = #AccountNum#
 </CFQUERY>
 <CFQUERY
  DATASOURCE="Accounts"
 >
 UPDATE Accounts SET Total = Total + #Withdrawal#
➥WHERE AccountNum = #AccountNum#
 </CFQUERY>
</CFTRANSACTION>
```

N O T E Not all lock types are supported by all ODBC drivers. Consult your database documentation *before* using the ISOLATION attribute. ■

▶ **See** Chapter 22, "Transaction Processing," **p. 525**

<CFTREE> <CFTREEITEM> </CFTREE>

Description: <CFTREE> embeds a Java tree control into your HTML forms. The tree control is similar to the explorer window in Windows 95 and Windows NT. The tree is made up of root entries and branches that may be expanded or closed. Branches may be nested too. Each branch has a graphic that is displayed next to it, and you can select from any of the supplied graphics, or use any of your own.

<CFTREE> trees are constructed using two tags: <CFTREE> creates the tree control, and <CFTREEITEM> adds the entries into the tree. Trees may be populated one branch at a time or using query results. <CFTREEITEM> must be used between <CFTREE> and </CFTREE> tags. <CFTREE> attributes are listed in Table A.64, <CFTREEITEM> attributes are listed in Table A.65.

Syntax: <CFTREE ALIGN="*Alignment*" APPENDKEY="*Yes¦No*" BOLD="*Yes¦No*" BORDER="*Yes¦No¦*" CFTREEITEMKEY="*Key*" COMPLETEPATH="*Yes¦No*" DELIMITER="*Delimiter Character*" FONT="*Font Face*" FONTSIZE="*Font Size*" HEIGHT="*Control Height*" HIGHLIGHTHREF="*Yes¦No*" HSPACE="*Horizontal Spacing*" HSCROLL="*Yes¦No*" ITALIC="*Yes¦No*" MESSAGE="*Error Message*" NAME="*Field Name*" NOTSUPPORTED="*Non-Java Browser Code*" ONERROR="*Error Function*" ONVALIDATE="*Validation Function*" REQUIRED="*Yes¦No*" VSCROLL="*Yes¦No*" VSPACE="*Vertical Spacing*" WIDTH="*Control Width*">

<CFTREEITEM DISPLAY="*Display Text*" EXPAND="*Yes¦No*" HREF="*URL*" IMG="*Images*" IMGOPEN="*Images*" QUERY="*Query Name*" QUERYASROOT="*Yes¦No*" TARGET="*Target Name*" PARENT="*Parent Branch*" VALUE="*Values*">

Table A.64   *<CFTREE>* Attributes

Attribute	Description	Notes
ALIGN	Control alignment	Optional attribute. Possible values are Top, Left, Bottom, Baseline, TextTop, AbsBottom, Middle, AbsMiddle, and Right.
APPENDKEY	Append item key to URL	Optional attribute. If Yes, a variable named.
CFTREEITEMKEY		Is appended to the URL containing the item selected, defaults to Yes.
BOLD	Bold face text	Optional attribute. Yes or No must be specified. Defaults to No.
BORDER	Display border around control	Optional attribute. Defaults to Yes.
COMPLETEPATH	Pass complete path to selected item	Optional attribute. If Yes, the full tree path to the selected item is returned. Defaults to No.
DELIMITER	Path delimiter	Optional attribute. Defaults to \.

Attribute	Description	Notes
FONT	Font face	Optional font face to use.
FONTSIZE	Font Size	Optional font size.
HEIGHT	Control height	Optional height in pixels.
HIGHLIGHTHREF	Highlight links	Optional attribute. If Yes, links will be high-lighted and underlined. Defaults to Yes.
HSPACE	Control horizontal	Optional spacing horizontal spacing in pixels.
HSCROLL	Display horizontal scroll bar	Optional attribute. Default is Yes.
ITALIC	Italic face text	Optional attribute. Must be Yes or No is specified, defaults to No.
MESSAGE	Validation failure message	Optional message to display upon validation failure.
NAME	Unique control name	This attribute is required.
NOTSUPPORTED	Text to be used for non-Java browsers	Optional text (or HTML code) to be displayed on non-Java-capable browsers.
ONERROR	JavaScript error function	Optional override to your own JavaScript error message function.
ONVALIDATE	JavaScript validation function	Optional override to your own JavaScript validation function.
REQUIRED	Selection is required	Optional attribute. Must be Yes or No, defaults to No.
VSPACE	Control vertical spacing	Optional vertical spacing in pixels.
VSCROLL	Display vertical scroll bar	Optional attribute. Default is Yes.
WIDTH	Control width	Optional width in pixels.

Table A.65   *<CFTREEITEM>* Attributes

Attribute	Description	Notes
DISPLAY	Display text	Optional attribute. Defaults to value if not specified. If populating with a query result set this value should be a comma-delimited list of values, one for each tree item.
EXPAND	Open expanded	Optional attribute. If Yes, branch is initially expanded. Defaults to No.

continues

Table A.65   Continued

Attribute	Description	Notes
HREF	Item URL	Optional attribute. URL to go to when an item is selected. If populating with a query result set, this value can be a comma-delimited list of URLs, one for each tree item, or it can be a column name in which case it is populated dynamically.
IMG	Image	Optional attribute. Image to be displayed. If populating with a query result set, this value should be a comma-delimited list of images, one for each tree level. Images can be folder, floppy, fixed, CD, document, element, or any image file of your own.
IMGOPEN	Open image	Optional attribute. Image to be displayed when branch is open. If populating with a query result set, this value should be a comma-delimited list of images, one for each tree level. Images may be folder, floppy, fixed, cd, document, element, or any image file of your own. If omitted, the IMG image will be used if populating with a query result set. This value should be a comma-delimited list of images, one for each tree item.
QUERY	Query name	Optional query name to be used to populate the list.
QUERYASROOT	Use query name as root	Optional attribute. If Yes, query name itself is the tree root branch. Defaults to No.
TARGET	Link target window	Optional attribute. The page to open the link in. If populating with a query result set, this value can be a comma-delimited list of targets, one for each tree item.
PARENT	Branch parent	Optional attribute. Name of parent to which to attach this branch.
VALUE	Value to be returned	Required attribute. If populating with a query result set, this value should be a comma-delimited list of values, one for each tree item.

Examples: The following first example creates a simple Java tree control with three branches.

```
<CFFORM ACTION="process.cfm">
<CFTREE NAME="states">
<CFTREEITEM VALUE="US">
```

```
<CFTREEITEM VALUE="CA" DISPLAY="California" PARENT="US">
<CFTREEITEM VALUE="MI" DISPLAY="Michigan" PARENT="US">
<CFTREEITEM VALUE="NY" DISPLAY="New York" PARENT="US">
</CFTREE>
</CFFORM>
```

The next example populates a tree with a query called Users.

```
<CFFORM ACTION="process.cfm">
<CFTREE NAME="peopletree" HSPACE="20" HSCROLL="no" VSCROLL="Yes" DELIMITER="?"
BORDER="Yes">
<CFTREEITEM VALUE="cn" QUERYASROOT="Yes" QUERY="Users" IMG="folder,document">
</CFTREE>
</CFFORM>
```

▶ **See** Chapter 19, "Enhancing Forms with *CFFORM*," **p. 427**

N O T E The <CFTREE> control will only be accessible by users with Java-enabled browsers. ▓

N O T E For examples of how <CFTREE> can be used to browser directories, take a look at the Cold Fusion Administrator. ▓

See also: <CFFORM>, <CFGRID>, <CFINPUT>, <CFSELECT>, <CFSLIDER>, <CFTEXTINPUT>

<CFUPDATE>

Description: <CFUPDATE> updates a single row to a database table. <CFUPDATE> requires that the database and table names be provided. All other attributes are optional. The full list of <CFUPDATE> attributes is explained in Table A.66.

Syntax: <CFUPDATE DATASOURCE="*ODBC Data Source*" TABLENAME="*Table Name*"
USERNAME="*User Name*" PASSWORD="*Password*" FORMFIELDS="*List of Fields to Update*">

Table A.66   *<CFUPDATE>* Attributes

Attribute	Description	Notes
DATASOURCE	Name of ODBC data source	The specified data source must already exist. This attribute is required.
FORMFIELDS	List of fields to insert	This optional attribute specifies which fields are to be updated if they are present. Any fields present that are not in the list will not be inserted.
PASSWORD	ODBC data source password	This optional attribute is used to override the ODBC login password specified in the Cold Fusion Administrator.

continues

Table A.66   Continued

Attribute	Description	Notes
TABLENAME	Name of table to insert data into	Some ODBC data source require fully qualified table names. This attribute is required.
USERNAME	ODBC data source login name	This optional attribute is used to override the ODBC login name specified in the Cold Fusion Administrator.

N O T E   For <CFUPDATE> to work correctly, your form field names *must* match the column names in the destination table, and the primary key value of the row to be updated *must* be specified. ■

 If your form contains fields that are not part of the table you are updating, use the FORMFIELDS attribute to instruct Cold Fusion to ignore those fields.

 For more control over the updating of rows into a database table, you may use the <CFQUERY> tag specifying UPDATE as the SQL statement.

Example: The following example updates a row in the Employees table in the A2Z data source.

```
<
CFUPDATE
DATASOURCE="A2Z"
TABLENAME="Employees"
>
```

The next example updates a row in the same table, but will only update values into the three specified fields *if* they exist.

```
<
CFUPDATE
DATASOURCE="A2Z"
TABLENAME="Employees"
FORMFIELD="LastName,FirstName,PhoneExtension"
>
```

▶ **See** Chapter 13, "Using Forms to Add or Change Data," p. 261

See also: <CFINSERT>, <CFQUERY>

Cold Fusion Function Reference

by Ben Forta

In this chapter

Using Cold Fusion Functions

Cold Fusion provides a complete set of data manipulation and formatting functions. When using functions, here are some things to remember:

- Function names are case-insensitive, so NOW() is the same as now() which is the same as Now().
- When functions are used in body text rather than within a Cold Fusion tag, they *must* be enclosed within <CFOUTPUT> tags.
- Functions may be nested.

To make this function reference easier to use, the functions have been grouped into logical sets. As there are some functions that overlap these groupings, each function has a *See also:* list of related functions. The function groupings are as follows:

- **String Manipulation Functions** are a complete set of text parsing, comparison, and conversion functions.
- **Date and Time Functions** can be used to create, parse, compare, and manipulate date and time values.
- **Data Formatting Functions** allow you to display data in a variety of formats.
- **Mathematical Functions** can be used to perform calculations, conversions, and generate random numbers.
- **International Functions** provide localization support for dates, times, and other data types.
- **List Manipulation Functions** are used to control lists of values.
- **Array Manipulation Functions** are used to create and manage two- and three-dimensional arrays.
- **Query Manipulation Functions** are used to create and manage Cold Fusion queries.
- **System Functions** give you access to system directories, temporary files, and path manipulation functions.
- **Client Variable Manipulation Functions** enable you to control client variables.
- **Expression Evaluation Functions** enable you to create and evaluate expressions on-the-fly.
- **Bit and Set Manipulation Functions** can be used to perform bit-level operations.
- **Miscellaneous Functions** are an assortment of functions you can use to check for the existence of parameters, format URLs, and manipulate lists to be passed to SQL statements.

String Manipulation Functions

The Cold Fusion string manipulation functions may be used to perform operations on character data. Strings may be hard coded constants, table column values, or Cold Fusion fields. As with all Cold Fusion functions, these string manipulation functions may be nested.

Asc

Description: Asc returns the ASCII value of the leftmost character of a string.

Syntax: Asc(*character*)

Example: The following example returns 72, the ASCII value of the character H.

```
#Asc("Hello")#
```

TIP The Asc function only processes the leftmost character in a string. To return the ASCII characters of an entire string, you'll have to loop through the string and process each character individually.

See also: Chr, Val

Chr

Description: Chr converts an ASCII value into a printable character.

Syntax: Chr(*number*)

Example: The following example returns the letter H whose ASCII value is 72.

```
#Chr(72)#
```

See also: Asc, Val

CJustify

Description: CJustify centers a string within a field of a specified length. It does this by padding spaces before and after the specified text. CJustify takes two parameters: the string to process, and the desired string length.

Syntax: CJustify(*string, length*)

Example: The following example center justifies the word Hello so that it is centered within a 20 character-wide field.

```
#CJustify("Hello", 20)#
```

See also: LJustify, LTrim, RJustify, RTrim, Trim

Compare, CompareNoCase

Description: The Compare and CompareNoCase functions both compare two string values. Compare performs a case-sensitive comparison, CompareNoCase performs a case-insensitive function. Both of these functions return a negative number if the first string is less than the second string, a positive number if the first string is greater than the second string, and 0 if the strings are the same.

Syntax: Compare(*String1, String2*)

CompareNoCase(*String1, String2*)

Example: The following example returns a negative value, because the first string is less than the second string.

```
#Compare("Ben", "Bill")#
```

The next example uses the case-insensitive comparison function, and returns 0 because, aside from case, the strings are the same.

```
#CompareNoCase("Michigan", "MICHIGAN")#
```

N O T E The two comparison functions treat white space as characters to be compared. Therefore, if you compare two strings that are identical except for extra spaces at the end of one of them, the compare will *not* return 0. ▓

Find, FindNoCase, REFind

Description: Cold Fusion provides three functions to search for a specific text within another string. Find performs a case-sensitive search, FindNoCase performs a case-insensitive search, and REFind performs a search using regular expressions. The parameters for all these three functions are the same. The first parameter is the string (or regular expression) to search for, the second parameter is the target string, or string to be searched. An optional third parameter may be provided to specify the position in the target string at which to start the search. All of these functions return the starting position of the first occurrence of the search string within the specified target string. If the search string is not found then 0 is returned.

Syntax: Find(*SearchString*, *TargetString* [, *StartPosition*])

FindNoCase(*SearchString*, *TargetString* [, *StartPosition*])

REFind(*RegularExpression*, *TargetString* [, *StartPosition*])

Example: The first example returns 18, the start position of the word America.

```
#Find("America", "United States of America")#
```

The next example returns 0, because Find performs a case-sensitive search.

```
#Find("AMERICA", "United States of America")#
```

The FindNoCase function performs a case-insensitive search, as the following example shows.

```
#FindNoCase("AMERICA", "United States of America")#
```

The next example searched for the word of in the string "The Flag of the United States of America", and specifies that the search should start from position 15. This example will return 31, the position of the second of. Had the optional start position parameter been omitted, the return value would have been 10, the position of the first of.

```
#Find("of", "The Flag of the United States of America", 15)#
```

See also: FindOneOf, GetToken, Left, Mid, Right

FindOneOf

Description: FindOneOf returns the position of the first target string character that matches any of the characters in a specified set. FindOneOf takes three parameters. The first parameter is a string containing the set of characters for which to search. The second parameter is the target string, or string to be searched, and the third parameter is an optional starting position from which to start the search. This function returns the starting position of the first occurrence of any of the characters in the search set within the specified target string. If no matching characters are found, 0 is returned.

Syntax: FindOneOf(*SearchSet*, *TargetString*, [, *StartPosition*])

App
B

Example: The following example returns the position of the first vowel with a Cold Fusion field called LastName.

```
The first vowel in your last name is at position #FindOneOf("aeiou", LastName)#
```

> **TIP** The FindOneOf function is case-sensitive, and there is no case-insensitive equivalent function. To perform a case-insensitive FindOneOf search you must first convert both the search and target strings to either uppercase or uppercase (using the UCase or LCase functions).

See also: Find, FindNoCase

GetToken

Description: Tokens are delimited sets of data within a string. The GetToken function allows you to extract a specific token from a string by specifying the token number, or index. GetToken takes three parameters. The first parameter is the string to search. The second parameter is the index of the token to extract, so 3 will extract the third token and 5 will extract the fifth. The third parameter is an optional set of delimiters that GetToken will use to determine where each token starts and finishes. If the delimiters parameter is not provided, the default of spaces, tabs, and new line characters, will be used. The default delimiters effectively allow this function to be used to extract specific words for a string. GetToken returns the token in the specified position, or any empty string if *Index* is greater than the number of token present.

Syntax: GetToken(*String*, *Index* [, *Delimiters*])

Example: The following example uses a hyphen as a delimiter to extract just the area code from a phone number.

```
#GetToken("800-555-1212", 1, "-")#
```

> **TIP** When working with strings that contain lists of data, use the Cold Fusion list functions instead of GetToken.

InputBaseN

Description: InputBaseN converts a string into a number using the base specified by radix. Valid radix values are 2 through 36.

Syntax: InputBaseN(*String*, *Radix*)

Example: The following example converts the string containing the binary number 10100010 into its base 10 equivalent of 162.

`#InputBaseN("10100010", 2)#`

 The code InputBaseN(String, 10) is functionally equivalent to the code Val(String). If you are converting a number that is base 10, the Val function is simpler to use.

See also: FormatBaseN, Val

Insert

Description: Insert is used to insert text into a string. Insert takes three parameters. The first parameter, SourceString, is the string you want to insert. The second parameter, TargetString, is the string into which you are going to insert the SourceString. The third parameter, Position, is a numeric value that specifies the location in the TargetString at which to insert the SourceString. Insert returns the modified string.

Syntax: Insert(*SourceString*, *TargetString*, *Position*)

Example: The following example inserts a field called area code in front of a phone number.

`#Insert(area_code, phone, 0)#`

 To insert a string at the very beginning of another, use the Insert function specifying a position of 0.

See also: RemoveChars, SpanExcluding, SpanIncluding

LCase

Description: LCase converts a string to uppercase. LCase takes a single parameter, the string to be converted, and returns the converted string.

Syntax: LCase(*String*)

Example: The following example converts a user-supplied string to uppercase.

`#LCase(*string_field*)#`

See also: UCase

Left

Description: Left returns the specified leftmost characters from the beginning of a string. Left takes two parameters: the string from which to extract the characters, and the number of characters to extract.

Syntax: Left(*String, Count*)

Example: The following example returns the first 3 characters of a phone number column.

```
#Left(phone_number, 3)#
```

See also: Find, Mid, RemoveChars, Right

Len

Description: Len returns the length of a specified string. Len takes a single parameter, the string whose length you want to determine.

Syntax: Len(*String*)

Example: The following example returns the length of a user-supplied *address* field after it has been trimmed.

```
#Len(Trim(address))#
```

LJustify

Description: LJustify left-aligns a string within a field of a specified length. It does this by padding spaces after the specified text. LJustify takes two parameters: the string to process, and the desired string length. The syntax of the LJustify function is.

Syntax: LJustify(*String, Length*)

Example: The following example left-justifies the string First Name: so that it is left-aligned within a 25 character-wide field.

```
#LJustify("First Name:", 25)#
```

See also: CJustify, LTrim, RJustify, RTrim, Trim

LTrim

Description: LTrim trims white space (spaces, tabs, and new line characters) from the beginning of a string.

LTrim takes a single parameter, the string to be trimmed.

Syntax: LTrim(*String*)

Example: The following example trims spaces from the beginning of a table notes field.

```
#LTrim(notes)#
```

See also: CJustify, LJustify, RJustify, RTrim, Trim, StripCR

Mid

Description: Mid returns a string of characters from any location in a string. Mid takes three parameters. The first parameter is the string from which to extract the characters, the second is the desired characters' starting position, and the third is the number of characters required.

Syntax: Mid(*String, StartPosition, Count*)

Example: The following example extracts 8 characters from the middle of a table column, starting at position 3.

```
#Mid(order_number, 3, 8)#
```

See also: Find, Left, RemoveChars, Right

RemoveChars

Description: RemoveChars returns a string with specified characters removed from it. This function is the exact opposite of the Mid function. RemoveChars takes three parameters: the first is the string from which to remove the characters, the second is the starting position of the characters to be removed, and the third is the number of characters to be removed.

Syntax: RemoveChars(*String, StartPosition, Length*)

Example: The following example returns a field with characters 10 through 15 removed.

```
#RemoveChars(product_code, 10, 5)#
```

See also: Left, Mid, Right

RepeatString

Description: RepeatString returns a string that is made up of a specified string multiple times. RepeatString takes two parameters; the first is the string to repeat, and the second is the number of occurrences.

Syntax: RepeatString(*String, Count*)

Example: The following example creates a horizontal line made up of equal signs.

```
#RepeatString("=", 80)#
```

Replace, REReplace

Description: Replace and REReplace both allow you to replace text within strings with alternative text. Replace does a simple text comparison to locate the text to be replaced. REReplace performs the same operation but uses regular expressions.

Both functions take four parameters. The first parameter is the string to be processed, the second parameter is the text to be replaced, and the third parameter is the text to replace it with. The fourth parameter is optional, and specifies the scope of the replacements. Possible scope values are ONE to replace the first occurrence only, ALL to replace all occurrences, and RECURSIVE to replace all occurrences recursively.

Syntax: Replace(*String, WhatString, WithString* [, *Scope*])

REReplace(*String, WhatString, WithString* [, *Scope*])

Example: The following example replaces all occurrences of the text US in an address field with the text USA.

```
#Replace(address, "US", "USA", "ALL")#
```

The next example replaces the area code (313) with the area code (810). Because no scope is specified, only the first occurrence of (313) will be replaced.

```
#Replace(phone, "(313)", "(810)")#
```

 The Replace and REReplace functions are case-sensitive, and there is no case-insensitive equivalent functions. To perform a case-insensitive replacement you must first convert both the search and target strings to either uppercase or lowercase (using the UCase or LCase functions).

See also: ReplaceList

ReplaceList

Description: ReplaceList replaces all occurrences of elements in one string with corresponding elements in another. Both sets of elements must be specified as comma-delimited values, and there must be an equal number of values in each set. ReplaceList takes three parameters. The first is the string to be processed, the second is the set of values to be replaced, and the third is the set of values to replace them with.

Syntax: ReplaceList(*String, FindWhatList, ReplaceWithList*)

Example: The following example replaces all occurrences of several state names with their appropriate abbreviations.

```
#ReplaceList(address, "CA, IN, MI", "California, Indiana, Michigan")#
```

 The ReplaceList function is case-sensitive, and there is no case-insensitive equivalent function. To perform case-insensitive replacements you must first convert both the search and target strings to either uppercase or lowercase (using the UCase or LCase functions).

N O T E Unlike other replacement functions, the ReplaceList function takes no scope parameter. ReplaceList replaces *all* occurrences of matching elements.

See also: Replace

Reverse

Description: Reverse reverses the characters in a string. Reverse takes a single parameter, the string to be reversed.

Syntax: Reverse(*String*)

Example: The following example reverses the contents of a user supplied field.

```
#Reverse(sequence_id)#
```

Right

Description: Right returns the specified rightmost characters from the end of a string. Right takes two parameters: the string from which to extract the characters, and the number of characters to extract.

Syntax: Right(*String*, *Count*)

Example: The following example returns the last 7 characters of a phone number column.

```
#Right(phone_number, 7)#
```

 Right does not trim trailing spaces before extracting the specific characters. To ignore white space when using Right, you should nest the RTrim within Right, as in #Right(RTrim(*String*), Count)# .

See also: Find, Left, Mid, RemoveChars

RJustify

Description: RJustify right-aligns a string within a field of a specified length. It does this by padding spaces before the specified text. RJustify takes two parameters: the string to process, and the desired string length. The syntax of the RJustify function is.

Syntax: RJustify(*string*, *length*)

Example: The following example right-justifies the contents of a field named Zip so that it is right-aligned within a 10 character-wide field.

```
#RJustify(Zip, 10)#
```

See also: CJustify, LJustify, LTrim, RTrim, Trim

RTrim

Description: RTrim trims white space (spaces, tabs, and new line characters) from the end of a string. RTrim takes a single parameter, the string to be trimmed.

Syntax: RTrim(*String*)

Example: The following example trims spaces from the end of a user-supplied field.

```
#RTrim(first_name)#
```

See also: CJustify, LJustify, LTrim, RJustify, Trim, StripCR

SpanExcluding

Description: SpanExcluding extracts characters from the beginning of a string until a character that is part of a specified set is reached. SpanExcluding takes two parameters: the string to process, and a comma-delimited set of values to compare against.

Syntax: SpanExcluding(*String*, *Set*)

Example: The following example extracts the first word of a sentence by specifying a space as the character to compare against.

```
#SpanExcluding(sentence, " ")#
```

 The SpanExcluding function is case-sensitive, and there is no case-insensitive equivalent function. To perform a case-insensitive extraction you must first convert both the search and target strings to either uppercase or lowercase (using the UCase or LCase functions).

See also: SpanIncluding

SpanIncluding

Description: SpanIncluding extracts characters from the beginning of a string only as long as they match characters in a specified set. SpanIncluding takes two parameters: the string to process, and a comma-delimited set of values to compare against.

Syntax: SpanIncluding(*String*, *Set*)

Example: The following example extracts the house number from a street address by specifying a set of values that are digits only.

```
#SpanIncluding(address, "1,2,3,4,5,6,7,8,9,0")#
```

 The SpanIncluding function is case-sensitive, and there is no case-insensitive equivalent function. To perform a case-insensitive extraction you must first convert both the search and target strings to either uppercase or lowercase (using the UCase or LCase functions).

See also: SpanExcluding

StripCR

Description: StripCR removes all carriage return characters from a string. StripCR takes a single parameter, the string to process.

Syntax: StripCR(*String*)

Example: The following example removes carriage returns for a field to be displayed in a preformatted text block.

```
<PRE>#StripCR(comments)#</PRE>
```

 TIP   The StripCR function is particularly useful when displaying a string within HTML preformatted text tags (<PRE> and </PRE>) where carriage returns are not ignored.

See also: CJustify, LJustify, LTrim, RJustify, RTrim, Trim

Trim

Description: Trim trims white space (spaces, tabs, and new line characters) from both the beginning and the end of a string. Trim takes a single parameter, the string to be trimmed.

Syntax: Trim(*String*)

Example: The following example trims spaces from both the beginning and the end of a user-supplied field.

```
#Trim(notes)#
```

See also: CJustify, LJustify, LTrim, RJustify, RTrim, StripCR

UCase

Description: UCase converts a string to uppercase. UCase takes a single parameter, the string to be converted, and returns the converted string.

Syntax: UCase(*String*)

Example: The following example converts the contents of a table column called State to uppercase.

```
#UCase(State)#
```

See also: LCase

Val

Description: Val converts the beginning of a string to a number. Val takes a single parameter, the string to process. Conversion is only possible if the string beings with numeric characters. If conversion is impossible, 0 is returned.

Syntax: Val(*String*)

Example: The following example extracts the Hour portion from a time field. Only the hour portion is converted because the : character is not a digit.

```
Hour: #Val(time)#
```

T I P Val converts characters to numbers using a base of 10 only. To convert the string to numbers with a base other than 10, use the InputBaseN function.

See also: Asc, Chr, InputBaseN, IsNumeric

Date and Time Functions

The Cold Fusion Date and Time functions allow you to perform date and time manipulation on table columns and user-supplied fields.

Many of these functions work with *date/time objects*. A date/time object is a Cold Fusion internal representation of a complete date and time, with accuracy to the second. These objects are designed to facilitate the passing of date/time information between different Cold Fusion functions, and are not designed to be displayed as is. If you need to display a date/time object, you'll need to use one of the date/time formatting functions.

N O T E Cold Fusion date/time objects are not the same as ODBC data/time fields. Use the CreateODBCDateTime function to convert Cold Fusion date/time objects to the ODBC format.

Many Cold Fusion date and time functions take date and time values as parameters. These parameters must be valid and within a set range, or a Cold Fusion syntax error will be generated. The range of values allowed for each date and time field are listed in Table B.1.

Table B.1 Valid Cold Fusion Date and Time Values

Field	Min	Max
Year	0	9999
Month	1	12
Day	1	31
Hour	0	23
Minute	0	59
Second	0	59

N O T E Year values of less than 100 are treated as 20th century values, and 1900 will be added automatically to them.

Several of the Cold Fusion date and time functions allow you to work with parts of the complete date/time object, for example, to add days or weeks to a date, or to find out how many weeks apart two dates are. These functions require that you pass a date/time part specifier which is passed as a string (it must have quotes around them). The complete list of specifiers is explained in Table B.2.

Table B.2   Cold Fusion Date Time Specifiers

Specifier	Description
D	Day
H	Hour
M	Month
N	Minute
Q	Quarter
S	Second
W	Weekday (day of week)
WW	Week
Y	Day of year
YYYY	Year

CreateDate

Description: The CreateDate function returns a Cold Fusion date/time object that can be used with other date manipulation or formatting functions. CreateDate takes three parameters: the date's year, month, and day.

Syntax: CreateDate(*Year, Month, Day*)

Example: The following example creates a date/time object based on three user-supplied fields.

#CreateDate(*birth_year, birth_month, birth_day*)#

N O T E   As the CreateDate function takes no time values as parameters, the time portion of the created date/time object is set to all zeros. ■

See also: CreateDateTime, CreateODBCDate, CreateTime

CreateDateTime

Description: The CreateDateTime function returns a Cold Fusion date/time object that can be used with other date and time manipulation or formatting functions. CreateDateTime takes six parameters: the date's year, month, and day, and the time's hour, minute, and second.

Syntax: CreateDateTime(*Year, Month, Day, Hour, Minute, Second*)

Example: The following example creates a date/time object for midnight on New Year's Day 1997.

```
#CreateDateTime(1997, 1, 1, 0, 0, 0)#
```

See also: CreateDate, CreateODBCDateTime, CreateTime, ParseDateTime

CreateODBCDate

Description: The CreateODBCDate function returns an ODBC date/time field that can safely be used in SQL statements. CreateODBCDate takes a single parameter, a Cold Fusion date/time object.

Syntax: CreateODBCDate(*Date*)

Example: The following example creates an ODBC date/time field for the current day (retrieved with the Now() function).

```
#CreateODBCDate(Now())#
```

> **N O T E** CreateODBCDate always creates an ODBC date/time field that has the time values set to zeros, even if the passed date/time object had valid time values. ■

TIP CreateODBCDate takes a date/time object as a parameter. If you want to pass individual date values as parameters, use the CreateDate as the function parameter, and pass it the values.

See also: CreateDate, CreateODBCDateTime, CreateODBCTime

CreateODBCDateTime

Description: The CreateODBCDateTime function returns an ODBC date/time field that can safely be used in SQL statements. CreateODBCDateTime takes a single parameter, a Cold Fusion date/time object.

Syntax: CreateODBCDate(*Date*)

Example: The following example creates an ODBC date/time field for the current day (retrieved with the Now() function).

```
#CreateODBCDateTime(Now())#
```

TIP CreateODBCDateTime takes a date/time object as a parameter. If you want to pass individual date and time values as parameters, use the CreateDateTime as the function parameter, and pass it the values.

See also: CreateDate, CreateODBCDate, CreateODBCTime

CreateODBCTime

Description: The CreateODBCTime function returns an ODBC date/time field that can safely be used in SQL statements. CreateODBCTime takes a single parameter, a Cold Fusion date/time object.

Syntax: CreateODBCTime(*Date*)

Example: The following example creates an ODBC date/time field for the current day (retrieved with the Now function).

```
#CreateODBCTime(Now())#
```

 N O T E   CreateODBCTime always creates an ODBC date/time field that has the date values set to zeros, even if the passed date/time object had valid date values. ▪

T I P   CreateODBCTime takes a date/time object as a parameter. If you want to pass individual time values as parameters, use the CreateTime as the function parameter, and pass it the values.

See also: CreateODBCDate, CreateODBCDateTime, CreateTime

CreateTime

Description: The CreateTime function returns a Cold Fusion date/time object that can be used with other time manipulation or formatting functions. CreateTime takes three parameters: the time's hour, minute, and second.

Syntax: CreateTime(*Hour, Minute, Second*)

Example: The following example creates a date/time object based on three Cold Fusion fields.

```
#CreateTime(hh, mm, ss)#
```

 N O T E   As the CreateTime function takes no date values as parameters, the date portion of the created date/time object is set to all zeros. ▪

See also: CreateDate, CreateDateTime, CreateODBCTime

CreateTimeSpan

Description: CreateTimeSpan creates a date/time object that can be used to rapidly perform date- and time-based calculations. CreateTimeSpan takes four parameters: days, hours, minutes, and seconds. Any of these values may be set to 0 if not needed.

Syntax: CreateTimeSpan(*Days, Hours, Minutes, Seconds*)

Example: The following example creates a date/time object with a time exactly 6 hours from now.

```
<CFSET #detonation# = #Now()# + #CreateTimeSpan(0, 6, 0, 0)#>
```

The `CreateTimeSpan` function is designed to speed up the process of performing date- and time-based calculations. Creating a date/time object with 30 days, using standard addition operators to add this to an existing date/time object, is quicker than using the `DateAdd` function.

See also: `DateAdd`

DateAdd

Description: `DateAdd` is used to add or subtract values to a date/time object, for example, to add a week or subtract a year. `DateAdd` takes three parameters: the first is the date specifier (see Table B.2), the second is the number of units to add or subtract, and the third is the date/time object to be processed. `DateAdd` returns a modified date/time object.

Syntax: `DateAdd( Specifier, Units, Date)`

Example: The following example return tomorrow's date (it adds 1 day to today's date).

```
#DateAdd('D', 1, Now())#
```

The next example returns a date exactly 10 weeks less than the date in a table column.

```
#DateAdd('WW', -10, Now())#
```

To subtract values from a date/time object, use the `DateAdd` function and pass a negative number of units. For example, `-5` subtracts 5 units of whatever specifier was passed.

DateCompare

Description: `DateCompare` allows you to compare two dates to see if they are the same or if one is greater than the other. `DateCompare` takes two parameters: the dates to compare, which may be specified as date/time objects, or string representations of dates. `DateCompare` returns `-1` if the first date is less than the second date, `0` if they are the same, and `1` if the first date is greater than the second date.

Syntax: `DateCompare(Date1, Date2)`

Example: The following example verifies that a user-supplied order ship date is valid (not already passed).

```
<CFIF DateCompare(ship_date, Now()) IS -1>
 We can't ship orders yesterday!
</CFIF>
```

See also: `DateDiff`, `DatePart`

DateDiff

Description: `DateDiff` returns the number of units of a passed specifier by which one date is greater than a second date. Unlike `DateCompare`, which returns which date is greater, `DateDiff` will tell you how many days, weeks, or months, it is greater by. DateDiff takes three parameters: the first is the date specifier (see Table B.2), and the second and third are the dates to compare.

Syntax: DateDiff(*Specifier, Date1, Date2*)

Example: The following example returns how many weeks are left in this century by specifying today's date (using the Now() function) and the first date of the next century (using the CreateDate function) as the two dates to compare.

```
There are #DateDiff("WW", Now(), CreateDate(2000, 1, 1))# weeks left in this
century!
```

N O T E   If the first date passed to DateDiff is greater than the second date, then a negative value will be returned. Otherwise, a positive value will be returned. ▪

See also: DateCompare, DatePart

DatePart

Description: DatePart returns the specified part of a passed date. DatePart takes two parameters; the first is the date specifier (see Table B.2), and the second is the date/time object to process.

Syntax: DatePart(*Specifier, Date*)

Example: The following example returns the day of week that a user was born on (and converts it to a string date using the DayOfWeekAsString function).

```
You were born on a #DayOfWeekAsString(DatePart('W', dob))#
```

See also: DateCompare, DateDiff, Day, DayOfWeek, DayOfYear, Hour, Minute, Month, Quarter, Second, Week, Year

Day

Description: Day returns a date/time object's day of month as a numeric value, with possible values of 1 to 31. Day takes a single parameter, the date/time object to be processed.

Syntax: Day(*Date*)

Example: The following example returns today's day of month.

```
Today is day #Day(Now())# of this month
```

See also: DayOfWeek, DayOfYear, Hour, Minute, Month, Quarter, Second, Week, Year

DayOfWeek

Description: DayOfWeek returns a date/time object's day of week as a numeric value, with possible values of 1 to 7. DayOfWeek takes a single parameter, the date/time object to be processed.

Syntax: DayOfWeek(*Date*)

Example: The following example returns today's day of week.

```
Today is day #DayOfWeek(Now())# of this week
```

See also: Day, DayOfYear, Hour, Minute, Month, Quarter, Second, Week, Year

DayOfWeekAsString

Description: DayOfWeekAsString returns the English weekday name for a passed day of week number. DayOfWeekAsString takes a single parameter, the day of week to process, with a value of 1 to 7.

Syntax: DayOfWeekAsString(*DayNumber*)

Example: The following example returns today's day of week as a string.

```
Today is day #DayOfWeekAsString(DayOfWeek(Now()))# of this week
```

See also: DayOfWeek, MonthAsString

DayOfYear

Description: DayOfYear returns a date/time object's day of year as a numeric value, taking into account leap years. DayOfYear takes a single parameter, the date/time object to be processed.

Syntax: DayOfYear(*Date*)

Example: The following example returns today's day of year.

```
Today is day #DayOfYear(Now())# of year #Year(Now())#
```

See also: Day, DayOfWeek, Hour, Minute, Month, Quarter, Second, Week, Year

DaysInMonth

Description: DaysInMonth returns the number of days in a specified month, taking into account leap years. DaysInMonth takes a single parameter, the date/time object to evaluate.

Syntax: DaysInMonth(*Date*)

Example: The following example returns the number of days in the current month.

```
This month has #DaysInMonth(Now())# days
```

 TIP DaysInMonth takes a date/time object as a parameter, and there is no equivalent function that takes a year and month as its parameters. Fortunately this can easily be accomplished by combining the DaysInMonth and CreateDate functions. For example, to determine how many days are in February 2000, you can create a statement that looks like: #DaysInMonth(CreateDate(2000, 2, 1))#.

See also: DaysInYear, FirstDayOfMonth

DaysInYear

Description: DaysInYear returns the number of days in a specified year, taking into account leap years. DaysInYear takes a single parameter, the date/time object to evaluate.

Syntax: DaysInYear(*Date*)

Example: The following example returns the number of days in the current year.

```
This year, #Year(Now())#, has #DaysInYear(Now())# days
```

TIP   DaysInYear takes a date/time object as a parameter, and there is no equivalent function that takes just a year as its parameter. Fortunately this can easily be accomplished by combining the DaysInYear and CreateDate functions. For example, to determine how many days are in the year 2000, you can create a statement that looks like: #DaysInYear(CreateDate(2000, 1, 1))#.

See also: DaysInMonth, FirstDayOfMonth

FirstDayOfMonth

Description: FirstDayOfMonth returns the day of the year on which the specified month starts. FirstDayOfMonth takes a single parameter, the date/time object to evaluate.

Syntax: FirstDayOfMonth(*Date*)

Example: The following example returns the day in year when the current month starts.

```
#FirstDayOfMonth(Now())#
```

TIP   FirstDayOfMonth takes a date/time object as a parameter, and there is no equivalent function that takes just a month and year as its parameters. Fortunately this can easily be accomplished by combining the FirstDayOfMonth and CreateDate functions. For example, to determine the day of year that March 1999 start on, you can create a statement that looks like: #FirstDayOfMonth(CreateDate(1999, 3, 1))#.

See also: DaysInMonth, DaysInYear

Hour

Description: Hour returns a date/time object's hour as a numeric value with possible values of 0 to 23. Hour takes a single parameter, the date/time object to be processed.

Syntax: Hour(*Date*)

Example: The following example returns the current hour of day.

```
This is hour #Hour(Now())# of the day
```

See also: Day, DayOfWeek, DayOfYear, Minute, Month, Quarter, Second, Week, Year

IsDate

Description: IsDate checks to see if a string contains a valid date, and returns TRUE if it does, and FALSE if it does not. IsDate takes a single parameter, the string to be evaluated.

Syntax: IsDate(*String*)

Example: The following example checks to see if a user-supplied date string contains a valid date.

```
<CFIF IsDate(ship_date) IS "No">
 You entered an invalid date!
</CFIF>
```

N O T E IsDate checks U.S. style dates only. Use the LSIsDate function for international date support.

See also: IsLeapYear, LSIsDate, ParseDateTime

IsLeapYear

Description: IsLeapYear checks to see if a specified year is a leap year. IsLeapYear takes a single parameter, the year to check, and returns TRUE if it is a leap year, and FALSE if it is not.

Syntax: IsLeapYear(*Year*)

Example: The following example checks to see if this year is a leap year.

```
<CFIF IsLeapYear(Year(Now()))>
 #Year(Now())# is a leap year
<CFELSE>
#Year(Now())# is a not leap year
</CFIF>
```

 T I P IsLeapYear takes a year as a parameter, not a date/time object. To check if a date stored in a date/time object is a leap year, use the Year function to extract the year, and pass that as the parameter to IsLeapYear.

See also: IsDate

IsNumericDate

Description: IsNumericDate checks to see that a value passed as a date in the Cold Fusion internal date format is in fact a legitimate date. IsNumericDate takes a single parameter, the date to be checked. This date is a floating point value with precision until the year 9999. IsNumericDate returns TRUE if the passed date value is valid, and FALSE if it is not.

Syntax: IsNumericDate(*Real*)

Example: The following example checks to see if a local variable contains a valid date.

```
<CFIF IsNumericDate(var.target_date) IS "Yes">
```

See also: IsDate

App

B

Minute

Description: Minute returns a date/time object's hour as a numeric value with possible values of 0-59. Minute takes a single parameter, the date/time object to be processed.

Syntax: Minute(*Date*)

Example: The following example returns the current time's minutes.

```
#Minute(Now())# minutes have elapsed since #Hour(Now())# o'clock
```

See also: Day, DayOfWeek, DayOfYear, Hour, Month, Quarter, Second, Week, Year

Month

Description: Month returns a date/time object's month as a numeric value with possible values of 1 to 12. Month takes a single parameter, the date/time object to be processed.

Syntax: Month(*Date*)

Example: The following example returns current month.

```
It is month #Month(Now())# of year #Year(Now())#
```

See also: Day, DayOfWeek, DayOfYear, Hour, Month, Quarter, Second, Week, Year

MonthAsString

Description: MonthAsString returns the English month name for a passed month number. MonthAsString takes a single parameter, the number of the month to process, with a value of 1 to 12.

Syntax: MonthAsString(*MonthNumber*)

Example: The following example returns the English name of the current month.

```
It is #MonthAsString(Now())#
```

See also: DayOfWeek, Month

Now

Description: Now returns a date/time object containing the current date and time precise to the second. Now takes no parameters.

Syntax: Now()

Example: The following example returns the current date and time formatted for correct display.

```
It is now #DateFormat(Now())# #TimeFormat(Now())#
```

N O T E The Now function returns the system date and time of the computer running the Cold Fusion service, not of the system running the web browser. ▪

ParseDateTime

Description: ParseDateTime converts a date in string form into a Cold Fusion date/time object. ParseDateTime takes a single parameter, the string to be converted.

Syntax: ParseDateTime(*String*)

Example: The following example converts a user-supplied string containing a date into a Cold Fusion date/time object.

```
<CFSET ship_date = ParseDateTime(FORM.ship_date)>
```

N O T E ParseDateTime supports U.S. style dates and times only. Use the LSParseDateTime function for international date and time support.

See also: CreateDateTime, LSParseDateTime

Quarter

Description: Quarter returns a date/time object's quarter as a numeric value, with possible values of 1 to 4. Quarter takes a single parameter, the date/time object to be processed.

Syntax: Quarter(*Date*)

Example: The following example returns the current quarter.

```
We are in quarter #Quarter(Now())# of year #Year(Now())#
```

See also: Day, DayOfWeek, DayOfYear, Hour, Minute, Month, Second, Week, Year

Second

Description: Second returns a date/time object's hour as a numeric value, with possible values of 0 to 59. Second takes a single parameter, the date/time object to be processed.

Syntax: Second(*Date*)

Example: The following example returns the current minute's seconds.

```
We are now #Second(Now())# seconds into the current minute
```

See also: Day, DayOfWeek, DayOfYear, Hour, Minute, Month, Quarter, Week, Year

Week

Description: Week returns a date/time object's week in year as a numeric value, with possible values of 1 to 52. Week takes a single parameter, the date/time object to be processed.

Syntax: Week(*Date*)

Example: The following example returns the current week in year.

```
This is week #Week(Now())# of year #Year(Now())#
```

See also: Day, DayOfWeek, DayOfYear, Hour, Minute, Month, Quarter, Second, Year

Year

Description: Year returns a date/time object's year as a numeric value, with possible values of 100 to 9999. Year takes a single parameter, the date/time object to be processed.

Syntax: Year(*Date*)

Example: The following example returns the current year value.

```
It is year #Year(Now())#
```

See also: Day, DayOfWeek, DayOfYear, Hour, Minute, Month, Quarter, Second, Week

Data Formatting Functions

Powerful data manipulation functions and database interaction capabilities are pretty useless unless there are ways to display data in a clean readable format. Cold Fusion data addresses this need by providing an array of highly capable formatting functions.

Many of these functions take optional format masks as parameters, thereby giving you an even greater level of control over the final output.

DateFormat

Description: DateFormat displays the date portion of a date/time object in a readable format. DateFormat takes two parameters. The first is the date/time object to be displayed, and the second is an optional mask value allowing you to control exactly how the data is formatted. If no mask is specified, the default mask of DD-MMM-YY is used. The complete set of date masks is listed in Table B.3.

Syntax: DateFormat(*Date* [, *mask*])

Table B.3 *DateFormat* **Mask Characters**

Mask	Description
D	Day of month in numeric form, with no leading zero for single digit days
DD	Day of month in numeric form, with a leading zero for single digit days
DDD	Day of week as a three letter abbreviation (for example, Sun for Sunday)
DDDD	Day of week as its full English name
M	Month in numeric form, with no leading zero for single digit months
MM	Month in numeric form, with a leading zero for single digit months
MMM	Month as a three letter abbreviation (for example, Jan for January)
MMMM	Month as its full English name
Y	Year as last two digits of year, with no leading zero for years less than 10
YY	Year as last two digits of year, with a leading zero for years less than 10
YYYY	Year as full four digits

Example: The following example displays today's date with the default formatting options.

```
Today is: #DateFormat(Now())#
```

The next example displays the same date, but uses the full names of both the day of week and the month.

```
It is #DateFormat(Now(), "DDDD, MMMM DD, YYYY")#
```

The final example displays today's date in the European format (day/month/year).

```
It is #DateFormat(Now(), "DD/MM/YY")#
```

 N O T E Unlike the TimeFormat function mask specifiers, the DateFormat function mask specifiers are case-insensitive. ■

 N O T E DateFormat supports U.S. style dates only. Use the LSDateFormat function for international date support. ■

See also: LSDateFormat, TimeFormat

DecimalFormat

Description: DecimalFormat is a simplified number formatting function that outputs numbers with two decimal places, commas to separate the thousands, and a minus sign for negative values. DecimalFormat takes a single parameter, the number to display.

Syntax: DecimalFormat(*Number*)

Example: The following example displays a table column in the decimal format.

```
Quantity: #DecimalFormat(quantity)#
```

T I P For more precise numeric display, use the NumberFormat function instead.

See also: NumberFormat

DollarFormat

Description: DollarFormat is a simplified U.S. currency formatting function that outputs numbers with a dollar sign at the front, two decimal places, commas to separate the thousands, and a minus sign for negative values. DollarFormat takes a single parameter, the number to display.

Syntax: DollarFormat(*Number*)

Example: The following example displays the results of an equation (quantity multiplied by item cost) in the dollar format.

```
Total cost: #DollarFormat(quantity*item_cost)#
```

T I P   For more precise currency display, use the `NumberFormat` function instead.

N O T E   `DollarFormat` supports U.S. dollars only. Use the `LSCurrencyFormat` function for international currency support. ▓

See also: `LSCurrencyFormat, NumberFormat`

FormatBaseN

Description: `FormatBaseN` converts a number to a string using the base specified. Valid `radix` values are 2 through 36.

Syntax: `FormatBaseN(Number, Radix)`

Example: The following example converts a user supplied number into hexadecimal notation.

`#FormatBaseN(Number, 16)#`

To convert a number to it's binary format, you can do the following:

`#FormatBaseN(Number, 2)#`

See also: `InputBaseN`

HTMLCodeFormat

Description: `HTMLCodeFormat` displays text with HTML codes with a preformatted HTML block (using the `<PRE>` and `</PRE>` tags). `HTMLCodeFormat` takes a single parameter, the text to be processed.

Syntax: `HTMLCodeFormat(Text)`

Example: The following example uses preformatted text to display the code used to generate a dynamic web page.

`#HTMLEditFormat(page)#`

T I P   `HTMLCodeFormat` is very useful for displaying data into `FORM TEXTAREA` fields.

See also: `HTMLCodeFormat, ParagraphFormat`

HTMLEditFormat

Description: `HTMLEditFormat` converts supplied text into a *safe* format, with any HTML control characters converted to their appropriate entity codes. `HTMLEditFormat` takes a single parameter, the text to convert.

Syntax: `HTMLEditFormat(Text)`

Example: The following example displays the HTML code that is used to render a dynamic web page inside a bordered box.

```
<TABLE BORDER>
 <TR>
  <TD>#HTMLEditFormat(page)#</TD>
 </TR>
</TABLE>
```

T I P Use HTMLEditFormat to display HTML code and tags within your page.

App

B

See also: HTMLCodeFormat, ParagraphFormat

NumberFormat

Description: NumberFormat allows you to display numeric values in a readable format. NumberFormat takes two parameters: the number to be displayed, and an optional mask value. If the mask is not specified, then the default mask of ,99999999999999 will be used. The complete set of number masks is listed in Table B.4.

Syntax: NumberFormat(*Number* [, *mask*])

Table B.4 *NumberFormat Mask* Characters

Mask	Description
_	Optional digit placeholder.
9	Optional digit placeholder (same as _ but shows decimal place more clearly).
.	Location of decimal point.
0	Force padding with zeros.
( )	Display parentheses around the number if it is less than 0.
+	Display a plus sign in front of positive numbers, and a minus sign in front of negative numbers.
-	Display a minus sign in front of negative numbers, leave a space in front of positive numbers.
,	Separates thousands with commas.
C	Center justify number within mask width.
L	Left justify number within mask width.
$	Place a dollar sign in front of the number.
^	Specify the exact location for separating left and right formatting.

Example: To demonstrate how the number masks can be used, Table B.5 lists examples of different masks being used to format the numbers 1453.876 and -1453.876.

Table B.5   Number Formatting Examples

Mask	Result	Notes
NumberFormat(1453.876, "9999")	1454	Because no decimal point was specified in the mask, the number is rounded to the nearest integer value.
NumberFormat(-1453.876, "9999")	-1454	
NumberFormat(1453.876, "9999.99")	1453.88	Even though a decimal point is provided, the number of decimal places specified is less than is needed, and so the decimal portion must be rounded to the nearest integer value.
NumberFormat(1453.876, "(9999.99)")	1453.88	Because the number is a positive number, the parentheses are ignored.
NumberFormat(-1453.876, "(9999.99)")	(1453.88)	Because the number is a negative number, parentheses are displayed around the number.
NumberFormat(1453.876, "-9999.99")	1453.88	Because the number is a positive number, the minus is ignored.
NumberFormat(-1453.876, "-9999.99")	-1453.88	Because the number is a negative number, the minus is displayed.
NumberFormat(1453.876, "+9999.99")	+1453.88	Because the number is a positive number, a plus sign is displayed.
NumberFormat(-1453.876, "+9999.99")	-1453.88	Because the number is a negative number, a minus is displayed.
NumberFormat(1453.876, "$9999.99")	$1453.88	
NumberFormat(1453.876, "C99999^9999")	1453.876	Because position six of the mask is a carat character, the decimal point will be positioned there even though there are less six digits before the decimal point. This allows you to align columns of numbers at the decimal point.

N O T E Use the `LSNumberFormat` function for international number support. ▪

See also: `DecimalFormat`, `DollarFormat`, `LSNumberFormat`

TimeFormat

Description: `TimeFormat` displays the time portion of a date/time object in a readable format. `TimeFormat` takes two parameters. The first is the date/time object to be displayed, and the second is an optional mask value allowing you to control exactly how the data is formatted. If no mask is specified, the default mask of `hh:mm tt` is used. The complete set of date masks is listed in Table B.6.

Syntax: `TimeFormat(Date [, mask ])`

Table B.6 *TimeFormat* **Mask Characters**

Mask	Description
h	Hours in 12-hour clock format, with no leading zero for single digit hours
hh	Hours in 12-hour clock format, with a leading zero for single digit hours
H	Hours in 24-hour clock format, with no leading zero for single digit hours
HH	Hours in 24-hour clock format, with a leading zero for single digit hours
m	Minutes, with no leading zero for single digit minutes
mm	Minutes, with a leading zero for single digit minutes
s	Seconds, with no leading zero for single digit seconds
ss	Seconds, with a leading zero for single digit seconds
t	Single character meridian specifier, either A or "
tt	Two character meridian specifier, either AM or PM

Example: The following example displays the current time with the default formatting options.

```
The time is: #TimeFormat(Now())#
```

The next example displays the current time with seconds in 24-hour clock.

```
The time is: #TimeFormat(Now(), "HH:mm:ss")#
```

N O T E Unlike the `DateFormat` function mask specifiers, the `TimeFormat` function mask specifiers are case-sensitive. ▪

N O T E `TimeFormat` supports U.S. style times only. Use the `LSTimeFormat` function for international time support. ▪

See also: DateFormat, LSTimeFormat

ParagraphFormat

Description: ParagraphFormat converts text with embedded carriage returns for correct HTML display. HTML ignores carriage returns in text. For these to be displayed correctly they must be converted to HTML paragraph markers (the <P> tag). ParagraphFormat takes a single parameter, the text to be processed.

Syntax: ParagraphFormat(*Text*)

Example: The following example displays a converted text files inside a FORM TEXTAREA field.

```
<TEXTAREA NAME="comments>#ParagraphFormat(comments)#</TEXTAREA>
```

TIP   ParagraphFormat is very useful for displaying data into FORM TEXTAREA fields.

See also: HTMLCodeFormat, HTMLEditFormat

YesNoFormat

Description: YesNoFormat converts TRUE and FALSE values to Yes and No. YesNoFormat takes a single parameter, the number, string, or expression to evaluate. When evaluating numbers, YesNoFormat treats 0 as FALSE, and any non-zero value as TRUE.

Syntax: YesNoFormat(*Value*)

Example: The following example converts a table Boolean value to a Yes or No string.

```
Member: #YesNoFormat(member)#
```

See also: IsBoolean

Mathematical Functions

To assist you in performing calculations, Cold Fusion comes with a complete suite of mathematical and random number generation functions, and arithmetic expressions. As with all Cold Fusion functions, these mathematical functions may be nested.

Some of the mathematical functions take one or more numeric values as parameters. You may pass real values, integer values, as well as Cold Fusion fields, to these functions.

Table B.7 lists the complete set of Cold Fusion mathematical functions. Table B.8 lists the supported arithmetic expressions.

Table B.7   Cold Fusion Mathematical Functions

Function	Parameters	Returns
Abs	(number)	Absolute value of the passed number.
Atn	(number)	Arc tangent of passed number.
Ceiling	(number)	The closest integer greater than the passed number.
Cos	(number)	Cosine of the passed number.
DecrementValue	(number)	Number decremented by 1.
Exp	(number)	E to the power of the passed number.
Fix	(number)	If the passed number is greater or equal to 0, Fix returns closest integer smaller than the passed number. If not, it returns the closest integer greater than the passed number.
IncrementValue	(number)	Number incremented by 1.
Int	(number)	The closest integer smaller than the passed number.
Log	(number)	Natural logarithm of the passed number.
Log10	(number)	Base-10 log of the passed number.
Max	(number1, number2)	The greater of the two passed numbers.
Min	(number1, number2)	The smaller of the two passed numbers.
Pi		Value of pi as 3.14159265359.
Rand		A random number between 0 and 1.
Randomize	(number)	Seed the random number generator with the passed number.
RandRange	(number1, number2)	A random integer value between the two passed numbers.
Round	(number)	The integer closest (either greater or smaller) to the passed number.
Sgn	(number)	Sign, either -1, 0, or 1, depending on whether the passed number is negative, zero, or positive.
Sin	(number)	Sine of the passed number.
Sqr	(number)	Square root of the passed number.
Tan	(number)	Tangent of the passed number.

App

B

Table B.8 Cold Fusion Arithmetic Expressions

Expression	Description
+	Addition
-	Subtraction
*	Multiplication
/	Division
MOD	Modular (finds remainder)
\	Integer division (both values must be integers)
^	Power

Example: This first example returns the natural logarithm of the number 10.

```
#Log(10)#
```

The next example returns the value of pi rounded to the nearest integer value, 3.

```
#Round(Pi())#
```

The following example uses the `Min()` and `Max()` functions to determine the greater and smaller of two Cold Fusion fields.

```
Of the two numbers #Num1# and #Num2#, Max(#Num1#, #Num2#) is the greater,
and Min(#Num1#, #Num2#) is the smaller
```

To generate random numbers, you can use the Rand and RandRange functions. The following example will generate a random number between 1 and 1000.

```
#RandRange(1, 1000)#
```

This next example creates a variable that contains a total cost of several items.

```
<CFSET #total# = quantity * item_price>
```

N O T E   If the `Rand()` or `RandRange()` functions are used prior to issuing a `Randomize()` statement, then the random number generator will be seeded with a random value. ■

International Functions

Cold Fusion fully supports the display, formatting, and manipulation of international dates, times, numbers, and currencies. In order to use Cold Fusion's international support, you must specify the *locale* to used. A locale is an encapsulation of the set of attributes that govern the display and formatting of international date, time, number, and currency values. The complete list of supported locales is shown in Table B.9.

Table B.9   Cold Fusion Locales

Locale

Dutch (Belgian)

Dutch (Standard)

English (Australian)

English (Canadian)

English (New Zealand)

English (UK)

English (US)

French (Belgian)

French (Canadian)

French (Standard)

French (Swiss)

German (Austrian)

German (Standard)

German (Swiss)

Italian (Standard)

Italian (Swiss)

Norwegian (Bokmal)

Norwegian (Nynorsk)

Portuguese (Brazilian)

Portuguese (Standard)

Spanish (Mexican)

Spanish (Modern)

Spanish (Standard)

Swedish

To set the locale you must use the SetLocale function. You can retrieve the name of the locale currently in use using the GetLocale function.

To utilize Cold Fusion's international support, you must use the LS functions listed below. These functions behave much like the standard date, time, and formatting functions, but they honor the "current locale" setting.

N O T E   The Cold Fusion server variable `Server.ColdFusion.SupportedLocales` contains a comma-delimited list of the supported locales. ■

GetLocale

Description: `GetLocale` returns the name of the locale currently in use.

Syntax: `GetLocale()`

Example: The following example saves the current locale to a local variable.

```
<CFSET current_locale = GetLocale()>
```

See also: `SetLocale`

LSCurrencyFormat

Description: `LSCurrencyFormat` displays currency information formatted for the current locale. `LSCurrencyFormat` takes two parameters: the number to display, and an optional format type. If type is specified, its value must be `none`, `local`, or `international`. Type defaults to `none`.

Syntax: `LSCurrencyFormat(Number [, Type])`

Example: The following example displays the results of an equation (quantity multiplied by item cost) in formatting appropriate for the French locale.

```
<CFSET previous_locale = SetLocale("French(Standard)")>
Total cost: #LSCurrencyFormat(quantity*item_cost)#
```

T I P   For more precise currency display, use the `NumberFormat` function instead.

N O T E   For U.S. currency formatting you may use the simpler `DollarFormat` function. ■

See also: `DollarFormat`, `NumberFormat`

LSDateFormat

Description: `LSDateFormat` displays the date portion of a date/time object in a readable format. `LSDateFormat` is the locale specific version of the `DateFormat` function. Like `DateFormat`, `LSDateFormat` takes two parameters; the first is the date/time object to be displayed, and the second is an optional mask value allowing you to control exactly how the data is formatted. If no mask is specified, a format suitable for the current locale is used. The complete set of date masks is listed previously in Table B.3 in the description of the `DateFormat` function.

Syntax: `LSDateFormat(Date [, mask ])`

Example: The following example displays today's date with the default formatting options for the current locale.

```
Today is: #LSDateFormat(Now())#
```

The next example displays the same date, but uses the current locale's full names of both the day of week and the month.

```
It is #LSDateFormat(Now(), "DDDD, MMMM DD, YYYY")#
```

N O T E For U.S. dates, you may use the simpler DateFormat function. ■

App B

See also: DateFormat, LSNumberFormat, LSTimeFormat

LSIsCurrency

Description: LSIsCurrency checks to see if a string contains a valid currency for the current locale, and returns TRUE if it does, and FALSE if it does not. LSIsCurrency takes a single parameter, the string to be evaluated.

Syntax: LSIsCurrency(*String*)

Example: The following example checks to see if a user supplied date string contains a valid German currency value.

```
<CFSET previous_locale = SetLocale("German (Standard)")>
<CFIF LSIsCurrency(total) IS "No">
 You entered an invalid currency amount!
</CFIF>
```

See also: IsNumber, LSIsNumeric

LSIsDate

Description: LSIsDate checks to see if a string contains a valid date for the current locale, and returns TRUE if it does, and FALSE if it does not. LSIsDate takes a single parameter, the string to be evaluated.

Syntax: LSIsDate(String)

Example: The following example checks to see if a user supplied date string contains a valid German date.

```
<CFSET previous_locale = SetLocale("German (Standard)")>
<CFIF LSIsDate(ship_date) IS "No">
 You entered an invalid date!
</CFIF>
```

N O T E To check U.S., dates you may use the IsDate function. ■

See also: IsDate, IsLeapYear, LSParseDateTime, ParseDateTime

LSIsNumeric

Description: LSIsNumeric checks to see if a specified value is numeric. LSIsNumeric is the locale-specific version of the IsNumeric function. LSIsNumeric takes a single parameter, the value to be evaluated.

Syntax: LSIsNumeric(*Value*)

Example: The following example checks to ensure that a user entered a valid locale specific age (numeric characters only).

```
<CFIF LSIsNumeric(age) IS "No">
 You entered an invalid age!
</CFIF>
```

N O T E You may use the simpler IsNumeric function for U.S. number support. ■

See also: InputBaseN, IsNumeric, Val

LSNumberFormat

Description: LSNumberFormat allows you to display numeric values in a locale-specific readable format. LSNumberFormat is the local specific version of the NumberFormat function. LSNumberFormat takes two parameters: the number to be displayed, and an optional mask value. If the mask is not specified, then the default mask of ",99999999999999" will be used. The complete set of number masks is listed in Table B.4, in the description of the NumberFormat function.

Syntax: LSNumberFormat(*Number* [, *mask*])

N O T E To display numbers in the any of the U.S. formats, you may use the NumberFormat function. ■

Example: The following displays a submitted form field in the default format for the current locale.

```
#LSNumberFormat(FORM.quantity)#
```

See also: DecimalFormat, DollarFormat, LSCurrencyFormat, LSParseNumber, NumberFormat

LSParseCurrency

Description: LSParseCurrency converts a locale-specific number in string form into a valid number. LSParseCurrency takes two parameters: the string to be converted, and an optional type. If type is specified, its value must be none, local, or international. Type defaults to all types if not provided.

Syntax: LSParseCurrency(*String* [, *Type*])

Example: The following example converts a user supplied currency string into a number.

```
<CFSET sale_price = LSParseCurrency(FORM.sale_price)>
```

See also: LSCurrencyFormat, LSParseNumber

LSParseDateTime

Description: LSParseDateTime converts a locale specific date in string form into a Cold Fusion date/time object. LSParseDateTime is the locale specific version of the ParseDateTime function. LSParseDateTime takes a single parameter, the string to be converted.

Syntax: LSParseDateTime(*String*)

Example: The following example converts a user supplied string containing a date into a Cold Fusion date/time object.

```
<CFSET ship_date = LSParseDateTime(FORM.ship_date)>
```

N O T E   For U.S. dates and times, you may use the simpler ParseDateTime function. ■

CAUTION

Unlike the ParseDateTime function, the LSParseDateTime function does not support POP date time fields. Passing a POP date/time field to LSParseDateTime will generate an error.

See also: CreateDateTime, ParseDateTime

LSParseNumber

Description: LSParseNumber converts a locale-specific number in string form into a valid number. LSParseNumber takes a single parameter, the string to be converted.

Syntax: LSParseNumber(*String*)

Example: The following example converts a user supplied numeric string into a number.

```
<CFSET quantity = LSParseNumber(FORM.quantity)>
```

See also: LSCurrencyFormat, LSParseCurrency, Val

LSTimeFormat

Description: LSTimeFormat displays the time portion of a date/time object in a local-specific readable format. LSTimeFormat is the locale-specific version of the TimeFormat function. LSTimeFormat takes two parameters. The first is the date/time object to be displayed, and the second is an optional mask value allowing you to control exactly how the data is formatted. If no mask is specified, a mask appropriate for the current locale is used. The complete set of time masks is listed in Table B.6 in the description of the TimeFormat function.

App

B

Syntax: `LSTimeFormat(Date [, mask ])`

Example: The following example displays the current time with the default formatting options for the current locale.

```
The time is: #LSTimeFormat(Now())#
```

> **NOTE**   For U.S. times you may use the simpler `TimeFormat` function. ■

See also: `LSDateFormat`, `LSNumberFormat`, `TimeFormat`

SetLocale

Description: `SetLocale` sets the name of the locale to be used by any subsequent calls to the LS functions. `SetLocale` also returns the name of the currently active locale so that it may be saved if needed.

Syntax: `SetLocale(locale)`

Example: The following example sets the locale to UK English, and saves the current locale to a local variable.

```
<CFSET previous_locale = SetLocale("English (UK)")>
```

See also: `GetLocale`

List Manipulation Functions

Cold Fusion lists are an efficient way to manage groups of information. Lists are made up of elements, values separated by delimiting characters. The default delimiter is a comma, but you can change it to any character or string if so required. Lists are actually simple two dimensional arrays. For more complex or multi-dimensional lists, you should use arrays instead.

This list format is very well suited for Cold Fusion applications because it is both the format that HTML forms uses to submit fields with multiple values, and the format used by SQL to specify lists is SQL statements.

When using the list manipulation functions, remember the following:

- List manipulation functions that add to, delete from, or change a list, do *not* alter the original list passed to them. Rather, they return an altered list to you for manipulation. If you do need to update the passed list itself, you must use <CFSET> to replace the list with the newly modified list.

- All list functions accept as an optional last parameter a string with delimiters to be used in the processing of the list. If this parameter is omitted, the comma default delimiter is used.

> **NOTE**   All of the Cold Fusion list manipulation functions have names that begin with the word `list`, making them easy to spot in your code. ■

> **T I P** Lists may be used in conjunction with the <CFLOOP> tag for processing.

ListAppend

Description: ListAppend adds an element to a list and returns the new list with the appended element. ListAppend takes two parameters; the first is the current list, and the second is the element to be appended.

Syntax: ListAppend(*List*, *Element*)

Example: The following example appends "John" to an existing list of users, and replaces the old list with the new one.

```
<CFSET Users = ListAppend(Users, "John")>
```

See also: ListInsertAt, ListPrepend, ListSetAt

ListChangeDelims

Description: ListChangeDelims returns a passed list reformatted to use a different delimiter. ListChangeDelims takes two parameters. The first is the list to be reformatted, and the second is the new delimiter character.

Syntax: ListChangeDelims(*List*, *Delimiter*)

Example: The following example creates a new list containing the same elements as the original list, but separated by plus signs.

```
<CFSET URLUsers = ListChangeDelims(Users, "+")>
```

> **T I P** The default list delimiter, a comma, is the delimiter used by SQL lists. If you are going to be passing Cold Fusion lists to SQL statements, you should use the default delimiter.

ListContains, ListContainsNoCase

Description: The ListContains and ListContainsNoCase functions search through a list to find the first element that contains the specified search text. If the search text is found, the position of the element containing the text is returned. If no match is found, 0 is returned. ListContains performs a case-sensitive search, ListContainsNoCase performs a case-insensitive search. Both functions take two parameters. The first parameter is the list to be searched, and the second parameter is the value to search for.

Syntax: ListContains(*List*, *Value*)

ListContainsNoCase(*List*, *Value*)

Example: The following example returns the position of the first element to contain the text cash (regardless of case).

```
Element #ListContainsNoCase(Payments, "cash")# contains the word "cash".
```

App
B

> **N O T E**   ListContains and ListContainsNoCase find substrings within elements that match
> the specified search text. To perform a search for a matching element, use the ListFind
> and ListFindNoCase functions instead. ■

See also: ListFind, ListFindNoCase

ListDeleteAt

Description: ListDeleteAt deletes a specified element from a list. ListDeleteAt takes two parameters. The first is the list to be processed, and the second is the position of the element to be deleted. ListDeleteAt returns a modified list, with the specified element deleted. The specified element position must exist, if you specify an element that is beyond the range of the list, an error message will be generated.

Syntax: ListDeleteAt(*List, Position*)

Example: The following example delete the second element in a list, but first verifies that it in fact exists.

```
<CFIF ListLen(Users) GTE 2>
 <CFSET Users = ListDeleteAt(Users, 2)>
</CFIF>
```

See also: ListRest

ListFind, ListFindNoCase

Description: The ListFind and ListFindNoCase functions search through a list to find the first element that matches the specified search text. If a matching element is found, the position of that element is returned. If no match is found, 0 is returned. ListFind performs a case-sensitive search, ListFindNoCase performs a case-insensitive search. Both functions take two parameters: the first is the list to be searched, and the second is the element text to search for.

Syntax: ListFind(*List, Value*)

ListFindNoCase(*List, Value*)

Example: The following example returns the position of the first element whose value is MI.

```
MI is element #ListFind(States, "MI")#
```

> **N O T E**   ListFind and ListFindNoCase only find elements that exactly match the specified
> search text. To perform a search for substrings within elements, use the ListContains
> and ListContainsNoCase functions instead. ■

See also: ListContains, ListContainsNoCase

ListFirst

Description: ListFirst returns the first element in a list. ListFirst takes a single parameter, the list to be processed.

Syntax: ListFirst(*List*)

Example: The following example returns the first selection from a field of book titles submitted by a user.

```
The first title you selected is #ListFirst(titles)#
```

See also: ListGetAt, ListLast, ListRest

ListGetAt

Description: ListGetAt returns the list element at a specified position. ListGetAt takes two parameters; the first is the list to process, and the second is the position of the desired element. The value passed as the position parameter must not be greater than the length of the list, or a Cold Fusion error message will be generated.

Syntax: ListGetAt(*List, Position*)

Example: The following example returns the name of the fourth selection from a field of book titles submitted by a user.

```
The fourth title you selected is #ListGetAt(titles, 4)#
```

See also: ListFirst, ListLast, ListRest

ListInsertAt

Description: ListInsertAt inserts a specified element into a list, shifting all elements after it one position to the right. ListInsertAt takes three parameters. The first parameter is the list to be processed, the second is the desired position for the new element, and the third is the value of the new element. The position parameter must be no greater than the number of elements in the list, if a greater value is provided than a Cold Fusion error message will be generated.

Syntax: ListInsertAt(*List, Position, Value*)

Example: The following example inserts John into the third position of an existing list of users, and replaces the old list with the new one.

```
<CFSET Users = ListInsertAt(Users, 3, "John")>
```

See also: ListAppend, ListPrepend, ListSetAt

ListLast

Description: ListLast returns the first element in a list. ListLast takes a single parameter, the list to be processed.

Syntax: ListLast(*List*)

Example: The following example returns the last selection from a field of book titles submitted by a user.

```
The last title you selected is #ListLast(titles)#
```

See also: ListFirst, ListGetAt, ListRest

ListLen

Description: ListLen returns the number of elements present in a list. ListLen takes a single parameter, the list to be processed.

Syntax: ListLen(*List*)

Example: The following example returns the number of books selected by a user.

```
You selected #ListLen(titles)# titles
```

ListPrepend

Description: ListPrepend inserts an element at the beginning of a list, pushing any other elements to the right. ListPrepend returns the new list with the prepended element. ListPrepend takes two parameters; the first is the current list, and the second is the element to be prepended.

Syntax: ListPrepend(*List*, *Element*)

Example: The following example prepends John to an existing list of users, and replaces the old list with the new one.

```
<CFSET Users = ListPrepend(Users, "John")>
```

See also: ListAppend, ListInsertAt, ListSetAt

ListRest

Description: ListRest returns a list containing all the elements after the first element. If the list contains only one element, an empty list (an empty string) will be returned. ListRest takes a single parameter, the list to be processed.

Syntax: ListRest(*List*)

Example: The following example replaces a list with the list minus the first element.

```
<CFSET Users = ListRest(Users)>
```

See also: ListDeleteAt

ListSetAt

Description: ListSetAt replaces the value of a specific element in a list with a new value. ListSetAt takes three parameters. The first parameter is the list to be process, the second is the position of the element to be replaced, and the third is the new value. The value passed to the position parameter must be no greater than the number of elements in the list, or a Cold Fusion error message will be generated.

Syntax: `ListSetAt(List, Position, Value)`

Example: The following searches for an element with the value of `Ben`, and replaces it with the value `Benjamin`.

```
<CFIF ListFindNoCase(Users, "Ben") GT 0>
 <CFSET Users = ListSetAt(Users, ListFindNoCase(Users, "Ben"), "Benjamin")>
</CFIF>
```

See also: `ListAppend`, `ListInsertAt`, `ListPrepend`

Array Manipulation Functions

App
B

Arrays are special variables that are made up of collections of data. Array elements are accessed via their index into the array, for example, to access the third element of a simple array you would refer to `array[3]`.

Cold Fusion supports arrays with one to three dimensions. A single dimensional array is very similar to a list. A two-dimensional array is kind of like a grid (in fact, under the hood, Cold Fusion queries are essentially two-dimensional arrays). Three-dimensional arrays are more like cubes.

Arrays are created using the `ArrayNew` function. To create an array you must specify the number of dimensions needed, between one and three. You do need to specify how many elements will be stored in the array, and Cold Fusion automatically expands the array as needed.

> **N O T E** Array elements may be added in any order. If you add an element 10 to an array that has only 5 elements, Cold Fusion will automatically create elements 6 to 9 for you. ■

ArrayAppend

Description: `ArrayAppend` adds an element to the end of an array. `ArrayAppend` takes two parameters; the array to append the element to, and the data to be stored in that element. `ArrayAppend` returns `TRUE` if the operation was successful.

Syntax: `ArrayAppend(Array, Value)`

Example: The following example appends an element containing the word `January` to an array.

```
#ArrayAppend(Month, "January")#
```

This next example appends an element to a three-dimensional array, setting the value of element `[10][1]`.

```
#ArrayAppend(Users[10][1], "January")#
```

> **N O T E** You may set the values of explicit array elements using the `<CFSET>` tag. ■

See also: `ArrayInsertAt`, `ArrayPrepend`

ArrayAvg

Description: ArrayAvg returns the average numeric value in an array. ArrayAvg takes a single parameter, the array to be checked.

Syntax: ArrayAvg(*Array*)

Example: The following example reports the average cost of items in an array.

The average cost of each item in the list is #DollarFormat(ArrayAvg(items))#

N O T E   ArrayAvg only works with arrays containing numeric data. Do not use this function with arrays that contain text data. ▪

See also: ArrayMin, ArrayMax, ArraySum

ArrayClear

Description: ArrayClear deletes all data from an array. ArrayClear takes a single parameter, the array to be deleted. ArrayClear returns TRUE if the operation was successful.

Syntax: ArrayClear(*Array*)

Example: The following example empties an existing array.

<CFSET result = ArrayClear(Items)>

N O T E   ArrayClear does not delete the actual array, rather, it removes all the contents from it. The array itself remains and may be reused. ▪

See also: ArrayDeleteAt, ArrayIsEmpty

ArrayDeleteAt

Description: ArrayDeleteAt deletes an element from an array at a specified position, pulling all remaining elements back one place. ArrayDeleteAt takes two parameters: the array to delete the element from, and the position of the element to delete. ArrayDeleteAt returns TRUE if the operation was successful.

Syntax: ArrayDeleteAt(*Array, Position*)

Example: The following example deletes the ninth element from an array.

#ArrayDeleteAt(Items, 9)#

See also: ArrayClear, ArrayInsertAt

ArrayInsertAt

Description: ArrayInsertAt inserts an element into an array at a specified position, pushing all existing elements over one place. ArrayInsertAt takes three parameters: the array to insert the element into, the position to insert the element at, and the data to be stored in that element. `ArrayInsertAt` returns TRUE if the operation was successful.

Syntax: `ArrayInsertAt(Array, Position, Value)`

Example: The following example inserts an element containing the word `Alaska` into the second position of an existing two dimensional array, and then sets the abbreviation `AK` into the matching second dimension.

```
<CFSET result = ArrayInsertAt(States[1], 2, "Alaska")>
<CFSET States[2][2] = "AK">
```

See also: `ArrayAppend, ArrayDeleteAt, ArrayPrepend`

App
B

ArrayIsEmpty

Description: `ArrayIsEmpty` checks to see if an array has data or not. `ArrayIsEmpty` takes a single parameter, the array to be checked. `ArrayIsEmpty` returns TRUE if the array is empty, and FALSE if it is not.

Syntax: `ArrayIsEmpty(Array)`

Example: The following example reports whether or not an array is empty.

```
<CFOUTPUT>Array empty: #YesNoFormat(ArrayIsEmpty(Users))#</CFOUTPUT>
```

See also: `ArrayClear, ArrayLen, IsArray`

ArrayLen

Description: `ArrayLen` returns the length of a specified array. `ArrayLen` takes a single parameter, the array to be checked.

Syntax: `ArrayLen(Array)`

Example: The following example reports the size of an array.

```
The items array has #ArrayLen(items)# elements
```

See also: `ArrayIsEmpty, ArrayResize`

ArrayMax

Description: `ArrayMax` returns the largest numeric value in an array. `ArrayMax` takes a single parameter, the array to be checked.

Syntax: `ArrayMax(Array)`

Example: The following example reports the cost of the most expensive item in an array.

```
The most expensive item in the list costs #DollarFormat(ArrayMax(items))#.
```

N O T E ArrayMax only works with arrays containing numeric data. Do not use this function with arrays that contain text data.

See also: `ArrayAvg, ArrayMin, ArraySum`

ArrayMin

Description: ArrayMin returns the smallest numeric value in an array. ArrayMin takes a single parameter, the array to be checked.

Syntax: ArrayMin(*Array*)

Example: The following example reports the cost of the least expensive item in an array.

```
The least expensive item in the list costs #DollarFormat(ArrayMin(items))#.
```

N O T E   ArrayMin only works with arrays containing numeric data. Do not use this function with arrays that contain text data. ■

See also: ArrayAvg, ArrayMax, ArraySum

ArrayNew

Description: ArrayNew is used to create an array. ArrayNew takes a single parameter, the number of dimensions needed. Valid dimensions are one through three. ArrayNew returns the array itself.

Syntax: ArrayNew(*Dimensions*)

Example: The following example creates a single dimensional array.

```
<CFSET Users = ArrayNew(1)>
```

N O T E   Once an array is created, Cold Fusion automatically expands it as needed. To manually resize an array, use the ArrayResize function. ■

See also: IsArray, ListToArray

ArrayPrepend

Description: ArrayPrepend adds an element to the beginning of an array. ArrayPrepend takes two parameters: the array to insert the element into, and the data to be stored in that element. ArrayPrepend returns TRUE if the operation was successful.

Syntax: ArrayPrepend(*Array, Value*)

Example: The following example inserts an element containing the word Alabama into the beginning of an array.

```
#ArrayPrepend(States, "Alabama")#
```

N O T E   You may set the values of explicit array elements using the <CFSET> tag. ■

See also: ArrayAppend, ArrayInsertAt

ArrayResize

Description: ArrayResize is used to change the size of an array, padding it with empty elements if needed. ArrayResize takes two parameters: the array to be resized, and the size to resize it to. ArrayResize returns TRUE if the operation was successful.

Syntax: ArrayResize(*Array, Size*)

Example: The following example creates an array and immediately resizes it to hold 100 elements.

```
<CFSET Users = ArrayNew(1)>
<CFSET result = ArrayResize(Users, 100)>
```

 TIP Dynamically expanding arrays is a slow operation. You can dramatically optimize Cold Fusion's array processing by resizing the array to the anticipated size right after creating it with ArrayNew.

See also: ArrayLen, ArraySet

ArraySet

Description: ArraySet initializes one or more elements in an array with a specified value. ArraySet takes four parameters: the array itself, the element starting and ending positions, and the value to use. ArraySet returns TRUE if the operation is successful.

Syntax: ArraySet(*Array, Start, End, Value*)

Example: The following example sets elements one through one hundred with the value 0.

```
#ArraySet(OrderItems, 1, 100, 0)#
```

See also: ArrayResize, ArraySort, ArraySwap

ArraySort

Description: ArraySort is used to sort the data in an array. ArraySort takes three parameters: the array to be sorted, the sort type, and an optional sort order. If the sort order is omitted than the default order of ascending is used. ArraySort supports three sort types, as listed in Table B.10.

Table B.10   *ArraySort* Sort Types

Type	Description
Numeric	Sorts numerically
Text	Sorts text alphabetically, uppercase before lowercase
TextNoCase	Sorts text alphabetically; case is ignored

Syntax: ArraySort(*Array, Type* [, *Order*])

Example: The following example sorts an array alphabetically using a case-insensitive sort (also known as a dictionary sort).

```
#ArraySort(Users, "textnocase")#
```

NOTE ArraySort sorts the actual passed array, not a copy of it. ■

See also: ArraySet, ArraySwap

ArraySum

Description: ArraySum returns the sum of all values in an array. ArraySum takes a single parameter, the array to be checked.

Syntax: ArraySum(*Array*)

Example: The following example reports the total cost of all items in an array.

```
The total cost of all item in the list is #DollarFormat(ArraySum(items))#.
```

NOTE ArraySum only works with arrays containing numeric data. Do not use this function with arrays that contain text data. ■

See also: ArrayAvg, ArrayMin, ArrayMax

ArraySwap

Description: ArraySwap is used to swap the values in two array elements. ArraySwap takes three parameters: the array itself, and the positions of the two elements to be swapped. ArraySwap returns TRUE if the operation is successful.

Syntax: ArraySwap(*Array*, *Position1*, *Position2*)

Example: The following example swaps elements 10 and 11 in an array.

```
#ArraySwap(Users, 10, 11)#
```

See also: ArraySet, ArraySort

ArrayToList

Description: ArrayToList converts a single dimensional Cold Fusion array into a list. ArrayToList takes two parameters: the array to be converted, and an optional list delimiter. If no delimiter is specified, the default comma delimiter is used. ArrayToList creates a new list.

Syntax: ArrayToList (*Array* [, *Delimiter*])

Example: The following example converts an array of users into a list.

```
<CFSET UserList = ArrayToList(UserArray)>
```

See also: ListToArray

IsArray

Description: IsArray checks to see if a variable is a valid Cold Fusion array, and to check that an array has a specific number of dimensions. IsArray takes two parameters: the variable to be checked, and an optional number of dimensions to check for. IsArray returns TRUE if the variable is an array, and FALSE if it is not.

Syntax: IsArray (*Array* [, *Dimension*])

Example: The following example checks to see if a variable named Users is an array.

```
#IsArray(Users)#
```

This next example checks to see if Users is a three-dimensional array.

```
#IsArray(Users, 3)#
```

See also: ArrayIsEmpty

ListToArray

Description: ListToArray converts a Cold Fusion list to an single dimensional array. ListToArray takes two parameters: the list to be converted, and an optional list delimiter. If no delimiter is specified, then the default comma delimiter is used. ListToArray creates a new array.

Syntax: ListToArray(*List* [, *Delimiter*])

Example: The following example converts a list of users into an array.

```
<CFSET UserArray = ListToArray(UserList)>
```

See also: ArrayToList

Query Manipulation Functions

Cold Fusion uses "queries" to return sets of data. Most queries are created with the <CFQUERY> tag, but other tags (such as <CFPOP> and <CFLDAP>) return data in queries too. Cold Fusion also allows you to programmatically create your own queries using the QueryNew function, and set query values using QuerySetCell.

N O T E Cold Fusion queries are essentially arrays with named columns. You may, therefore, use any of the array functions with queries. ■

IsQuery

Description: IsQuery checks to see if a variable is a valid Cold Fusion query. IsQuery takes a single parameter, the variable to be checked. IsQuery returns TRUE if the variable is a query, and FALSE if it is not.

Syntax: IsQuery (*Query*)

Example: The following example checks to see if a variable named Users is a query.

```
<CFIF IsQuery(Users)>
```

 TIP IsQuery is particularly useful within Custom Tags that expect queries as parameters. IsQuery can be used to check that a valid value was passed before any processing occurs.

QueryAddRow

Description: QueryAddRow is used to add a row to an existing Cold Fusion query. QueryAddRow takes two parameters: the query to add a row to, and an optional number of rows to add. If the number of rows is omitted, the default number of one will be used.

Syntax: QueryAddRow(*Query* [, *Number*])

Example: The following example creates a new query called Users, and adds ten rows to it.

```
<CFSET Users = QueryNew("FirstName, LastName")>
<CFSET temp = QueryAddRow(Users, 10)>
```

See also: QueryNew, QuerySetCell

QueryNew

Description: QueryNew is used to create a new Cold Fusion query. QueryNew takes a single parameter, a comma-delimited list of columns for the new query. QueryNew returns the newly created query.

Syntax: QueryNew(*Columns*)

Example: The following example creates a new query called Users, and adds ten rows to it.

```
<CFSET Users = QueryNew("FirstName, LastName")>
<CFSET temp = QueryAddRow(Users, 10)>
```

See also: QueryAddRow, QuerySetCell

QuerySetCell

Description: QuerySetCell is used to set the values of specific cells in a table. QuerySetCell takes four parameters: the query name, the column name, the value, and an optional row number. If the row number is omitted, the cell in the last query row will be set.

Syntax: QuerySetCell(*Query*, *Column*, *Value* [, *Row*])

Example: The following sets the FirstName column in the third row to the value Ben.

```
<CFSET temp = QuerySetCell(Users, "FirstName", "Ben", 3)>
```

N O T E Query cells can also be set using the <CFSET> tag treating the query as a two dimensional array.

See also: QueryAddRow, QueryNew

System Functions

The Cold Fusion system functions allow you to perform manipulation of file paths, create temporary files, and verify file existence.

ExpandPath

Description: ExpandPath converts a path relative to the web server document root into a fully qualified path. ExpandPath takes a single parameter, the path to be converted.

Syntax: ExpandPath(*Path*)

Example: The following example returns the full path of the server's default document.

```
#ExpandPath("index.cfm")#
```

See also: GetTemplatePath

FileExists

Description: FileExists checks for the existence of a specified file, and returns either TRUE or FALSE. FileExists takes a single parameter, the name of the file to check for. The file name cannot be a relative path, but must be specified as a fully qualified path.

Syntax: FileExists(*File*)

Example: The following example checks for the existence of an image file before using it in an IMG tag.

```
<CFIF FileExists("C:\root\images\logo.gif")>
 <IMG SRC="/images/logo.gif">
</CFIF>
```

TIP So as not to have to hard code the file name passed to the FileExists function, use the ExpandPath function to convert the a relative path to an actual file name.

GetDirectoryFromPath

Description: GetDirectoryFromPath extracts the drive and directory (with a trailing backslash) from a fully specified path. GetDirectoryFromPath takes a single parameter, the path to be evaluated.

Syntax: GetDirectoryFromPath(*Path*)

Example: The following example returns the directory portion of a current template's full file path.

```
#GetDirectoryFromPath(GetTemplatePath())#
```

See also: GetFileFromPath

GetFileFromPath

Description: GetFileFromPath extracts the file name from a fully specified path. GetFileFromPath takes a single parameter, the path to be evaluated.

Syntax: GetFileFromPath(Path)

Example: The following example returns the file name portion of a temporary file.

```
#GetFileFromPath(GetTempFile(GetTempDirectory(), "CF"))#
```

See also: GetDirectoryFromPath

GetTempDirectory

Description: GetTempDirectory returns the full path of the Windows temporary directory with a trailing backslash. GetTempDirectory takes no parameters.

Syntax: GetTempDirectory()

Example: The following example returns the name of a temporary file beginning with the letters CF in the Windows temporary directory.

```
#GetTempFile(GetTempDirectory(), "CF")#
```

See also: GetTempFile

GetTempFile

Description: GetTempFile returns the full path to a temporary file for use by your application. The returned file name is guaranteed to be unique. GetTempFile takes two parameters. The first parameter is the directory where you'd like the temporary file created, and the second is a file name prefix of up to three characters. You may not omit the prefix, but you may pass an empty string ("").

Syntax: GetTempFile(Directory, Prefix)

Example: The following example returns the name of a temporary file beginning with the letters CF in the Windows temporary directory.

```
#GetTempFile(GetTempDirectory(), "CF")#
```

 TIP To create a temporary file in the Windows temporary directory, pass the GetTempDirectory function as the directory parameter.

See also: GetTempDirectory

GetTemplatePath

Description: GetTemplatePath returns the fully qualified path of the base template being processed. GetTemplatePath takes no parameters.

Syntax: GetTemplatePath()

Example: The following example returns the full path of the base template being processed.

```
Processing: #GetTemplatePath()#
```

N O T E GetTemplatePath returns the path of the base template being processed. If you are using GetTemplatePath in a template that is being included in a second template, the path of that second template will be returned. ∎

Client Variable Manipulation Functions

Client variables allow you to store client information so that it is available between sessions. Client variables may be accessed just like any other Cold Fusion variables, and so standard variable access tools, like <CFSET> can be used to set variables. In addition, these functions provide special variable manipulation capabilities.

▶ **See** Chapter 23, "Web Application Framework," **p. 545**

DeleteClientVariable

Description: DeleteClientVariable deletes the client variable whose name is passed as a parameter. Unlike other Cold Fusion variables, client variables persist over time and must be deleted with this function. DeleteClientVariable takes a single parameter, the name of the variable to delete. DeleteClientVariable returns TRUE if the variable was delete, and FALSE if it was not.

Syntax: DeleteClientVariable(*Variable*)

Example: The following example delete a variable named login_name and sets a local variable with the function return value.

```
<CFSET DeleteSuccessful = DeleteClientVariable("login_name")>
```

GetClientVariablesList

Description: GetClientVariablesList returns a comma-delimited list of the read-write client variables available to the template. The standard read-only system client variables, listed in Table B.11, are not returned. GetClientVariablesList takes no parameters.

Syntax: GetClientVariablesList()

Table B.11 Read-only Client Variables

Variable	Description
CFID	Unique ID assigned to this client
CFToken	Unique security token which is used to verify the authenticity of a CFID value
URLToken	Text to append to URLs, contains both CFID and CFToken. (Appended automatically to <CFLOCATION> URLs)

Example: The following example retrieves the entire list of read-write client variables.

```
#ListLen(GetClientVariablesList())# read-write client variables
➥are currently active.
```

 T I P   The list of variables returned by the GetClientVariablesList function is comma-delimited, which makes it very suitable for processing with the Cold Fusion list functions.

Expression Evaluation Functions

Cold Fusion allows you to perform dynamic expression evaluation. This is an advanced technique that allows you to build and evaluate expression on-the-fly.

Dynamic expression evaluations are performed on string expressions. A string expression is just that, a string that contains an expression. The string "1+2" contains an expression that, when evaluated, will return 3. String expressions can be as simple or as complex as needed.

Additional information on Cold Fusion expressions is available later in this chapter, in the section entitled "Bit and Set Manipulation Functions."

DE

Description: DE stands for Delay Evaluation. This function is designed to be used with the IIF and Evaluate functions. It takes a string as a parameter, and returns the same string enclosed within quotes, and with all double quotes escaped. This allows you to pass a string to IIf and Evalaute without them being evaluated.

Syntax: DE(*String*)

Example: The following example uses DE to ensure that the string A is evaluated, instead of the variable A.

```
#Evaluate(DE("A"))#
```

Evaluate

Description: Evaluate is used to evaluate string expressions. Evaluate takes one or more string expressions as parameters, and evaluates them from left to right.

Syntax: Evaluate(String1, ...)

Example: The following example evaluates the variable A.

```
#Evalutate("A")#
```

IIf

Description: IIf evaluates a Boolean condition, and evaluates one of two expressions depending on the results of that evaluation. If the Boolean condition returns TRUE, then the first expression is evaluated, if the condition returns FALSE, then the second expression is evaluated.

Syntax: `IIF(Boolean condition, Expression if TRUE, Expression if FALSE)`

Example: The following example checks to see if `#cnt#` has a value of 1, and evaluates `A` if it does and `B` if it does not.

`#IIf("#cnt# IS 1", "A", "B")#`

SetVariable

Description: `SetVariable` sets a specified variable to a passed value.

Syntax: `SetVariable(Variable, Value)`

Example: The following example set variable `#cnt#` to the value returned by the passed expression.

`#SetVariable(#cnt#, "A")#`

Bit and Set Manipulation Functions

Cold Fusion provides a complete set of bit manipulation functions for use by advanced developers only. These functions allow you to manipulate the individual bits within a 32-bit integer.

The complete set of bit manipulation functions is listed in Table B.12. The descriptions for each function are given in the C/C++ syntax.

N O T E Any `start`, `length`, or `position` parameters, passed to the bit manipulation functions, must be in the range of 0 to 31. ■

Table B.12   Cold Fusion Bit and Set Manipulation Functions

Function	Description
`BitAnd(x, y)`	*x* and *y*
`BitMaskClear(x, start, length)`	*x* with length bits starting from start cleared
`BitMaskRead(x, start, length)`	the value of the length bits starting from start
`BitMaskSet(x, mask, start, length)`	*x* with mask occupying the `length` bits starting from `start`
`BitNot(x)`	~*x*
`BitOr(x, y)`	*x* ¦ *y*
`BitSHLN(x, n)`	*x* << *n*
`BitSHRN(x, n)`	*x* >> *n*
`BitXor(x, y)`	*x*^*y*

Miscellaneous Functions

These miscellaneous functions are some of the most important ones, and are ones you'll likely find yourself using repeatedly.

IsBoolean

Description: IsBoolean checks to see whether a value can be converted to a Boolean value, or not. Boolean values have two states only, ON or OFF (or TRUE and FALSE). IsBoolean takes a single parameter, the number, string, or expression to evaluate. When evaluating numbers, IsBoolean treats 0 as FALSE, and any non-zero value as TRUE.

Syntax: IsBoolean(*Value*)

Example: The following example checks to see if a value can be safely converted into a Boolean value before passing it to a formatting function.

```
<CFIF IsBoolean(status) IS "Yes">
 #YesNoFormat(status)#
</CFIF>
```

See also: YesNoFormat

IsDefined

Description: IsDefined checks to see if a specified variable exist. IsDefined returns TRUE if the specified variable exists, and FALSE if it does not. IsDefined takes a single parameter, the variable to check for. This parameter may be passed as a fully qualified variable, with a preceding variable type designator. The variable name *must* be enclosed in quotes, or else Cold Fusion will check to see if the contents of the variable exists rather than the variable itself.

Syntax: IsDefined(*Parameter*)

Example: The following example checks to see if a variable of any type named USER_ID exists.

```
<CFIF IsDefined("USER_ID")>
```

The next example checks to see if a CGI variable, named USER_ID exists, and ignores variables of other types.

```
<CFIF IsDefined("CGI.USER_ID") >
```

N O T E IsDefined it a little more complicated to use than ParameterExists, but it does allow you to dynamically evaluate and redirect expressions. ■

See also: Evaluate, IsSimpleValue, ParameterExists

IsNumeric

Description: IsNumeric checks to see if a specified value is numeric. IsNumeric takes a single parameter, the value to be evaluated.

Syntax: IsNumeric(Value)

Example: The following example checks to ensure that a user entered a valid age (numeric characters only).

```
<CFIF IsNumeric(age) IS "No">
 You entered an invalid age!
</CFIF>
```

N O T E   For international number support, use the LSIsNumeric function. ■

See also: InputBaseN, LSIsNumeric, Val

IsSimpleValue

Description: IsSimpleValue checks to see if a value is a string, number, true/false value, or date/time value. IsSimpleValue takes a single parameter, the value to be checked. IsSimpleValue returns TRUE if the value is a simple value, and FALSE if it is not.

Syntax: IsSimpleValue(*Value*)

Example: The following example checks to see that a description field is a simple value.

```
<CFIF IsSimpleValue(Description)>
```

See also: Evaluate, IsDefined, ParameterExists

ParameterExists

Description: ParameterExists checks to see if a specified variable exists. ParameterExists returns TRUE if the specified variable exists, and FALSE if it does not. ParameterExists takes a single parameter, the variable to check for. This parameter may be passed as a fully qualified variable, with a preceding variable type designator. Do not enclose the variable name in quotes.

Syntax: ParameterExists(*Parameter*)

Example: The following example checks to see if a variable of any type named USER_ID exists.

```
<CFIF ParameterExists(USER_ID) IS "Yes">
```

The next example checks to see if a CGI variable named USER_ID exists, and ignores variables of other types.

```
<CFIF ParameterExists(CGI.USER_ID) IS "Yes">
```

N O T E   One of the most important uses of the ParameterExists function is creating dynamic SQL statements using the <CFSQL> tag. ■

See also: Evaluate, IsDefined, IsSimpleValue

PreserveSingleQuotes

Description: `PreserveSingleQuotes` is used to instruct Cold Fusion to not *escape* single-quotes contained in values derived from dynamic parameters. `PreserveSingleQuotes` takes a single parameter, the string to be preserved.

Syntax: `PreserveSingleQuotes(String)`

Example: The following example uses `PreserveSingleQuotes` to ensure that a dynamic parameter in a SQL statement is included correctly.

```
SELECT * FROM Customers
WHERE CustomerName IN (#PreserveSingleQuotes(CustNames)#)
```

QuotedValueList, ValueList

Description: `QuotedValueList` and `ValueList` are used to drive one query with the results of another. Both functions take a single parameter—the name of a query column—and returns a list of all the values in that column. `QuotedValueList` returns a list of values that are each enclosed within quotation marks and separated by commas. `ValueList` returns the list separated by commas, but not enclosed in quotation marks.

Syntax: `QuotedValueList(Column)`

`ValueList(Column)`

Example: The following example to ensure that a dynamic parameter in a SQL statement is included correctly.

```
SELECT * FROM Customers
WHERE CustomerName IN (#PreserveSingleQuotes(CustNames)#)
```

> **N O T E** The `QuotedValueList` and `ValueList` functions are typically only used when constructing dynamic SQL statements. ▪

 The values returned by `QuotedValueList` and `ValueList` are both in the standard Cold Fusion list format, and can therefore be manipulated by the list functions.

TIP As a general rule, unless you need to manipulate the values in the list, you should always try to combine both the queries into a single SQL statement. The time it will take to process one combined SQL statement will be far less than the time to process two simpler statements.

URLEncodedValue

Description: `URLEncodedValue` encodes a string in a format that may be safely used within URLs. URLs may not contain spaces, and other non-alphanumeric characters. The `URLEncodedValue` function replaces spaces with a plus sign, and non-alphanumeric characters with equivalent hexadecimal escape sequences. `URLEncodedValue` takes a single parameter, the string to be encoded, and returns the encoded string.

Syntax: URLEncodedValue(*String*)

 N O T E Cold Fusion will automatically decode all URL parameters that are passed to a template. ■

Example: The following example creates an URL with a name parameter that may safely include any characters.

```
<A HREF="details.cfm?name=#URLEncodedFormat(name)#">Details</A>
```

Verity Search Language Reference

by Nate Weiss

In this chapter

This appendix describes each of the search operators that can be passed to Verity in the CRITE-RIA parameter of a CFSEARCH tag. Refer to Chapter 26, "Full-Text Searching with Verity," for details on incorporating Verity into your Cold Fusion applications.

This is not meant to be an exhaustive reference. You should consult your Cold Fusion documentation for the precise definition and syntax for each operator. Verity's web site is also a good resource for information regarding the syntax and impact of the search operators discussed in this appendix. There are many "FAQ" (frequently asked questions) and examples of search syntax in action. Just keep in mind that Verity's Search97 product is not a Cold Fusion-only thing. You will find references to Search97 features which are not exposed to you as a Cold Fusion developer. Verity's web site can be found at **http://www.verity.com/**.

Using Angle Brackets Around Operators

With the exception of AND, OR, and NOT, you must use angle brackets around all Verity operators. This tells Verity that you're interested in actually using the NEAR operator, for example, rather than just trying to search for the word "near" in your document. The following line is not searching for the word near:

```
CRITERIA="Sick <NEAR> Days"
```

Again, AND, OR, and NOT do not need the angle brackets—the idea is they will be used very often, and people infrequently need to search for the actual words "and" or "or" or "not" in their documents. So the following two lines are equivalent:

```
CRITERIA="Sick AND Days"
CRITERIA="Sick <AND> Days"
```

Operators Are Not Case-Sensitive

Verity search operators are not case-sensitive, even when the search itself may be case-sensitive. So these two statements are also equivalent:

```
CRITERIA="Sick <NEAR> Days"
CRITERIA="Sick <near> Days"
```

Using Prefix Instead of Infix Notation

All Verity operators—except for the Evidence Operators: STEM, WILDCARD, and WORD—can be specified using something called Prefix Notation.

For instance, suppose that you have several search words on which you want to use the NEAR operator. Instead of sticking <NEAR> between each word, you can just specify NEAR once and then put the list of words in parentheses. So the following two lines are equivalent:

```
CRITERIA="sick <NEAR> days <NEAR> illness"
CRITERIA="<NEAR>(sick,days,illness)"
```

Searching for Special Characters As Literals

Special characters—most obviously, the < and > characters—have special meaning for Verity. If you want to actually search for these characters, you need to use a \ (backslash) to "escape" each special character. For example, if you wanted to search for documents that contained <TABLE>, you would need to do it like this:

```
CRITERIA="\<TABLE\>"
```

Understanding Concept Operators

Verity's Concept Operators are used when you are specifying more than one search word or search element. The Concept Operator tells Verity whether you mean that all of the words/elements must be present in the document for it to count as a match, or if any one word/element makes the document count as a match. The Concept Operators include:

- AND
- OR
- ACCRUE

App

C

The AND operator indicates that all of the search words/elements must be present in a document for the document to count as a match. Some examples are

```
CRITERIA="sick AND days AND illness"
CRITERIA="sick <AND> days <AND> illness"
CRITERIA="AND (sick,days,illness)"
```

 Remember that unlike other Operators, AND does not need angle brackets around it.

The OR operator indicates that a document counts as a match as soon as any of the search words/elements are present in the document. Some examples are

```
CRITERIA="sick OR days OR illness"
CRITERIA="sick <OR> days <OR> illness"
CRITERIA="OR (sick,days,illness)"
```

 Remember that unlike other Operators, OR does not need angle brackets around it.

Understanding Evidence Operators

Verity's Evidence Operators control whether Verity "steps in" and searches for words that are slightly different from the search words you actually specify.

Remember that, unlike other operators, Evidence Operators cannot be used with Prefix Notation. Instead, they must be specified with Infix Notation—that is, they must be inserted between each word of a set. See the example for STEM, below.

The Evidence Operators include:

- STEM
- WILDCARD
- WORD

The STEM operator tells Verity to "expand" the search to include grammatical variations of the search words you specify. In other words, Verity takes each word and finds its root, then searches for all the common variations of that root. So if the search was for "permitting," Verity would take it upon itself to also search for "permit" and "permitted." Some examples are

```
CRITERIA="<STEM> permitting"
CRITERIA="AND (<STEM> permitting, <STEM> smoke)"
```

The WILDCARD operator tells Verity that the search words contain wildcards that should be considered while the search is occurring. Note that two of the wildcard characters—the ? (question mark) and the * (astirisk)—are automatically assumed to be wildcard characters, even if you don't specify the WILDCARD operator. But the other wildcard characters will only behave as wildcards if the WILDCARD operator is used. The following statements are examples:

```
CRITERIA="smok*"
CRITERIA="smok?"
CRITERIA="<WILDCARD>smok*"
CRITERIA="<WILDCARD>'smok{ed,ing}'"
```

Table C.1 summarizes the possible operators for a wildcard value.

Table C.1 Verity Wildcards

Wildcard	Purpose
*	Like the % wildcard in SQL, * stands in for any number of characters (including zero).
	So a search for Fu* would find *Fusion, Fugazi*, and *Fuchsia*.
?	Just as in SQL, ? stands in for any single character. More precise—and thus generally less helpful—than the * wildcard. A search for ?ar?et would find both *carpet* and *target*, but not *Learjet*.
{ }	Allows you to specify a number of possible word fragments, separated by commas. So a search for {gr,frag,deodor}rant would find documents that contained *grant, fragrant*, or *deodorant*.
[ ]	Like { }, except stands in for only one characters at a time. So a search for f[eao]ster would find documents that contained *fester, faster*, or *Foster*.
-	Allows you to place a range of characters within square brackets. So searching for A[C-H]50993 is the same as searching for A[CDEFGH]50993.

If you use any wildcard other than ? or *, you must use either single or double quotation marks around the actual wildcard pattern. I recommend that you use single quotes around the wildcard pattern, since the criteria parameter as a whole should be within double quotes.

The WORD operator tells Verity to perform a simple word search, without any wildcarding or stemming. Including a WORD Operator is a good way to suppress Verity's default use of the STEM operator, or if you didn't want the ? in a search for Hello? to be treated as a wildcard character. Some examples of this are

```
CRITERIA="<WORD>smoke"
CRITERIA="<WROD>Hello?"
```

Understanding Proximity Operators

Verity's Proximity Operators are used to specify how close together search words must be to each other within a document in order for that document to count as a match. For example, if you were looking for rules about where smoking is permitted, you might only want documents that have the words "smoking" and "permitted" sitting pretty close to one another within the actual text. A document that has the word "smoking" at the beginning and the word "permitted" way at the end would probably not interest you. The Proximity Operators include:

- NEAR
- NEAR/N
- PARAGRAPH
- SENTENCE

The NEAR operator specifies that you are most interested in documents where the search words are closest to one another. All documents where the words are within 1000 words of each other are considered "found," but the closer together the words, the higher the document's score, which means it will be up at the top of the list. An example of this is

```
CRITERIA="smoking <NEAR> permitted"
```

The NEAR/N operator is just like NEAR, except that you get to specify how close together the words have to be to qualify as a match. Documents are still ranked based on the closeness of the words. So in reality, NEAR is just shorthand for NEAR/1000. Some examples of the NEAR/N operator are as follows:

```
CRITERIA="smoking <NEAR/3> permitted"
CRITERIA="<NEAR/3>(smoking,permitted)"
```

The PARAGRAPH and SENTENCE operators specify that the words need to be in the same paragraph or sentence, respectively. Sometimes using these are better than NEAR or NEAR/N, because you know that the words are related in some way having to do with their actual linguistic context, rather than their physical proximity to one another. Some examples are as follows:

```
CRITERIA="smoking <paragraph> permitted"
CRITERIA="<SENTENCE> (smoking,permitted)"
```

Understanding Relational Operators

Verity's Relational Operators allow you to search for words within specific document fields, such as the title of the document or a Custom Field. Searches that use these operators are not ranked by relevance. The Relational Operators include:

- CONTAINS
- MATCHES
- STARTS
- ENDS
- SUBSTRING
- =, <, >, <=, and >=

Table C.2 summarizes the document fields available for use with Relational Operators.

Table C.2 Document Fields Available for Use with Relational Operators

Field	Explanation
CF_TITLE	The filename of the document if the collection is based on normal documents, or whatever table column you specified for TITLE if the collection is based on database data.
CF_CUSTOM1	Whatever table column you specified for CUSTOM1, if any, if your collection is based on database data.
CF_CUSTOM2	Whatever table column you specified for CUSTOM2, if any, if your collection is based on database data.
CF_KEY	The filename of the document if the collection is based on normal documents, or whatever table column you specified for KEY if the collection is based on database data. You'd use Relational Operators with this field if the user already knows the unique ID for the record that you wanted, like a "knowledge base" article number.
CF_URL	The URL path to the document, as defined when you indexed the collection.

The CONTAINS operator finds documents where a specific field contains the exact word(s) you specify, like using the WORD Operator on a specific field. If you specify more than one word, the words must appear in the correct order for the document to be considered a match. The following are some examples:

```
CRITERIA="CF_TITLE <CONTAINS> smoking"
CRITERIA="CF_TITLE <CONTAINS>'smoking,policy'"
```

The MATCHES operator finds documents where the entirety of a specific field is exactly what you specify. The field is looked at as a whole, not as individual words. So a search for "Smoking Policy" in the CF_TITLE field would only match documents where the title was literally

"Smoking Policy," verbatim. This feature is probably most useful with Custom Fields, if the Custom Field holds nothing more than some kind of rating, category code, and so on. Here are some examples:

```
CRITERIA="CF_TITLE <MATCHES>'Smoking Policy'"
CRITERIA="CF_CUSTOM1 <MATCHES> Policies"
```

The STARTS operator finds documents where a specific field starts with the characters you specify, such as:

```
CRITERIA="CF_TITLE <STARTS> smok"
```

The ENDS operator finds documents where a specific field ends with the characters you specify, such as:

```
CRITERIA="CF_TITLE <ENDS> olicy"
```

The SUBSTRING operator finds documents where a specific field contains any portion of what you specify. Unlike CONTAINS (above), this will match incomplete words. Here is an example:

```
CRITERIA="CF_TITLE <SUBSTRING> smok"
```

The =, <, >, <=, and >= operators perform arithmetic comparisons on numeric and date values stored in specific fields. These are probably only useful with Custom Fields, if the table columns you specified for the Custom Fields held only numeric or date values. Note that these operators don't need angle brackets around them. The following are some examples:

```
CRITERIA="CF_CUSTOM1 = 5"
CRITERIA="CF_CUSTOM2 >= 1990"
```

Understanding Search Modifiers

Verity's Search Modifiers cause the search engine to behave slightly differently than it would otherwise. The Search Modifiers include:

- CASE
- MANY
- NOT
- ORDER

The CASE modifier forces Verity to perform a case-sensitive search, even if the search words are all lowercase or all uppercase. Here are some examples:

```
CRITERIA="<CASE>smoking"
CRITERIA="AND(<CASE>smoking,<CASE>policy)"
```

Verity will often run case-sensitive searches even if the CASE operator is not used.

The MANY operator ranks documents based on the density of search words or search elements found in a document. It is automatically in effect whenever the search type is SIMPLE and cannot be used with the Concept Operators: AND, OR, and ACCRUE. The following are some examples:

```
CRITERIA="<MANY>(smoking,policy)"
CRITERIA="<MANY> smoking"
```

The NOT modifier causes Verity to eliminate documents that are found by the search word(s), such as:

```
CRITERIA="NOT smoking"
CRITERIA="smoking NOT policy"
CRITERIA="NOT(smoking,days)"
CRITERIA="<NOT>(smoking,days)"
```

Note that if you want to find documents that contained "not smoking", you will need to indicate this to Verity by using quotes, such as:

```
CRITERIA="'not smoking'"
CRITERIA="AND('not',smoking)"
CRITERIA="AND(""not"",smoking)"
```

When used with a PARAGRAPH, SENTENCE, or NEAR/N operator, the ORDER modifier indicates that your search words must be found in the document—in the order that you specified them—for the document to be considered a match. The following is an example:

```
CRITERIA="<ORDER><PARAGRAPH>(smoking,policy)"
```

Understanding Score Operators

Every time Verity finds a document, it assigns the document a "score" that represents how closely the document matches the search criteria. The score is always somewhere from 0 to 1, where 1 is a "perfect match" and 0 is a "perfectly miserable" match. In most cases, Verity orders the search results in score order, with the highest scores at the top.

Score Operators tell Verity to compute this score differently than it would normally. To a certain extent, this allows you to control the order of the documents in the result set. The Score Operators include:

- YESNO
- COMPLEMENT
- PRODUCT
- SUM

The YESNO operator forces the Score for any match to be 1, no matter what. In other words, all documents that are relevant at all are equally relevant. The records will not appear in any particular order—even though Verity is trying to rank the search results by relevance—because sorting by a bunch of 1s doesn't really do anything. Here is an example:

```
CRITERIA="YESNO(policy)"
```

The COMPLEMENT operator is kind of strange. With this operator, the Score is subtracted from 1 before it's returned to you. A closely matching document that would ordinarily get a score of .97 would now get a score of only .03. So if Verity is ranking records by relevance, using COMPLEMENT will make the search results appear in "reverse order" (best matches last instead of first). Unfortunately, this also means that a score of 0 now has a score of 1, which means that all documents that didn't match at all will be returned—and returned first.

So, if for some bizarre reason you only wanted documents that were completely unrelated to smoking—ranked by irrelevance—you could use:

```
CRITERIA="<COMPLEMENT>smoking"
```

The PRODUCT operator causes Verity to calculate the score for the document by *multiplying* the scores for each search word found. The net effect is that relevant documents appear to be even more relevant, and less relevant documents are even less relevant. This operator may cause fewer documents to be found. The following is an example:

```
CRITERIA="<PRODUCT>smoking"
```

The SUM operator causes Verity to calculate the score for the document by *adding* the scores for each search word found, up to a maximum document score of 1. The net effect is that more documents appear to get "perfect" scores. Here is an example:

```
CRITERIA="<SUM>smoking"
```

App

C

Index

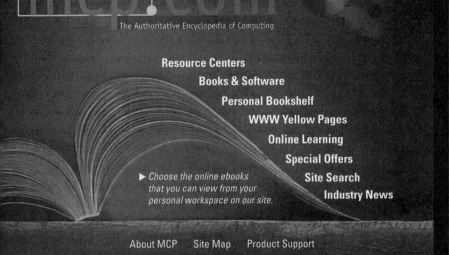

MACMILLAN COMPUTER PUBLISHING USA
A VIACOM COMPANY

Technical

Support

If you need assistance with the information
provided by Macmillan Computer Publishing,
please access the information available on our
web site at **http://www.mcp.com/feedback.** Our
most Frequently Asked Questions are answered
there. If you do not find the answers to your
questions on our web site, you may contact
Macmillan User Services at **(317) 581-3833** or
email us at **support@mcp.com.**

Licensing Agreement

By opening the software package, you are agreeing to be bound by the following agreement:

Some of the software included with this product might be copyrighted, in which case all rights are reserved by the respective copyright holder. You are licensed to use software copyrighted by the Publisher and its licensors on a single computer. You may copy and/or modify the software as needed to facilitate your use of it on a single computer. Making copies of the software for any other purpose is a violation of the United States copyright laws.

This software is sold as is, without warranty of any kind, either expressed or implied, including but not limited to the implied warranties of merchantability and fitness for a particular purpose. Neither the publisher nor its dealers or distributors assumes any liability for any alleged or actual damages arising from the use of this program. (Some states do not allow for the exclusion of implied warranties, so the exclusion might not apply to you.)